General Management On Ethical Decision-Making and Moral Development

Integrating Ethics and Moral Development into Management Decision-Making Processes in Crucial Topics

GENERAL MANAGEMENT

First Edition

Dr. Lamin Tombekai Kamara

RoseDog Books
PITTSBURGH, PENNSYLVANIA 15238

RoseDog Books
585 Alpha Drive, Suite 103
Pittsburgh, PA 15238
Visit our website at *www.rosedogbookstore.com*

ISBN: 979-8-89211-386-1
eISBN: 979-8-89211-883-5

Dedication

To my wife

Mrs. Catherine K. Kamara

Love is patient, love is kind.
It doesn't envy.
It doesn't boast, it's not proud.
It isn't nice... It's not rude, it's not self-seeking.
It's not easily angered, and it keeps no record of wrongs.
Love does not delight in evil but rejoices with the truth.
It always protects, always trusts, always hopes, and always perseveres.
1 Corinthians 13:4-7

Table of Contents

PART I – Ethical Decision-Making

Part II – Responsible Leadership

PART III – Risk Management

PART IV - The Role of Emotional Intelligence in Effective Decision-Making by Managers

Preface

Ethical decision-making is a fundamental aspect of our lives, shaping the choices we make and the values we uphold. Every day, we are faced with countless dilemmas that require us to consider the impact of our actions on ourselves, others, and the world around us. And yet, despite the importance of ethical decision-making, many individuals and organizations struggle to navigate the complexities of this process.

This book, "Ethical Decision-Making: A Guide to Responsible Choices," aims to provide a comprehensive understanding of the principles, theories, and frameworks that underpin ethical decision-making. It is written by Dr. Lamin Tombekai Kamara, an esteemed expert in the field of ethics, drawing on his decades of experience working as a philosopher, educator, and consultant.

In this book, Dr. Kamara not only explores various approaches to ethical decision-making but also delves into the influence of culture, ethics in leadership, and the relationship between ethics and technology. The goal is to empower individuals, regardless of their educational background or professional field, to become more aware and effective ethical decision-makers.

Chapter I: Foundations of Ethical Decision-Making

The first part of this book sets the stage by examining the foundational elements of ethical decision-making. Dr. Kamara begins by defining ethics and exploring its relevance in contemporary society. He introduces the concept of ethical relativism and discusses the limitations and potential pitfalls associated with this viewpoint. The importance of ethical leadership and the role it plays in shaping ethical decision-making is also given due consideration.

Furthermore, Part I explores various theories and frameworks that can guide ethical decision-making processes. From consequentialism and deontology to virtue ethics and care ethics, Dr. Kamara offers a comprehensive analysis of each approach, highlighting their strengths and weaknesses. In doing so, readers gain a nuanced understanding of the philosophies that underpin ethical decision-making and are better equipped to evaluate their values and decision-making processes.

Chapter II: Cultural Influence on Ethical Decision-Making

In Chapter II, Dr. Kamara delves into the importance of cultural context in ethical decision-making. He recognizes that ethics are not inherently universal but rather shaped by cultural norms, values, and beliefs. By exploring cultural diversity and its impact on ethical perspectives, readers are encouraged to view ethics through various lenses and consider how cultural differences can shape ethical dilemmas and decision-making processes in both personal and professional settings.

The chapters in this section offer insights from different cultural perspectives, examining the nuances and tensions that arise when navigating ethical dilemmas within multicultural environments. Through case studies and real-life examples, readers gain a deeper appreciation for the complexity of ethical decision-making in an increasingly interconnected world.

Chapter III: Ethics in Leadership

Chapter III focuses on the crucial role of ethical leadership in fostering responsible decision-making. Dr. Kamara explores the qualities that define an ethical leader, emphasizing the importance of integrity, transparency, and accountability. He examines the ethical dilemmas that leaders often face and provides practical guidelines for navigating them effectively.

Furthermore, this section delves into the role of organizational culture in shaping ethical decision-making within a leadership context. The reader gains an understanding of how ethical leadership can positively influence organizational culture, fostering an environment that prioritizes values, collaboration, and ethical conduct.

Chapter IV: Ethics in the Technological Age

The final section of this book considers the ethical implications of technological advancements. Dr. Kamara recognizes that rapid technological progress has raised new ethical quandaries, requiring individuals and organizations to critically examine the impact of their actions on privacy, security, and technological integrity.

Chapter IV, readers explore emerging ethical concerns such as artificial intelligence, big data, and the influence of social media. Dr. Kamara provides a framework for evaluating the ethical dimensions of technological decision-making, emphasizing the need for responsible innovation and the consideration of long-term consequences.

“Ethical Decision-Making: A Guide to Responsible Choices” serves as a roadmap for anyone seeking to navigate the intricacies of ethical decision-making. Dr. Kamara’s expertise, coupled with his engaging writing style and practical approach, ensures readers develop the necessary tools and insights to make informed, responsible choices in both personal and professional realms.

By exploring the foundational principles of ethics, cultural influences, leadership, and the ethical implications of technology, this book equips readers with a comprehensive understanding of the complexities that underpin ethical decision-making. Through case studies, thought-provoking questions, and practical examples, readers are challenged to reflect on their values, biases, and decision-making processes, encouraging personal growth and fostering a commitment to ethical conduct.

Ultimately, “Ethical Decision-Making: A Guide to Responsible Choices” strives to inspire individuals to become ethical leaders who actively engage in conversations surrounding ethics and integrate ethical considerations into their decision-making processes. Through responsible choices, we can contribute to a more just and ethical world.

The Author's Take

Managing and avoiding biases and prejudices in the workplace

Managing biases and prejudices as a leader is crucial for creating an inclusive and fair work environment. Here are some steps you can take to address and manage your own biases:

1. Self-awareness: Recognize that everyone has biases, including yourself. Be open to acknowledging and understanding your biases and how they may impact your decision-making.

2. Education and learning: Educate yourself about different cultures, backgrounds, and perspectives. Engage in diversity and inclusion training, read books, attend workshops, and actively seek out diverse voices and experiences.

3. Reflect and challenge your assumptions: Regularly reflect on your thoughts, beliefs, and assumptions. Ask yourself why you hold certain biases and explore alternative viewpoints. Challenge your thinking and seek to understand others' perspectives.

4. Build diverse relationships: Actively seek out relationships with people from different backgrounds and perspectives. Engaging in open and honest conversations with diverse individuals can help challenge your biases and broaden your understanding.

5. Encourage diverse perspectives: Create an inclusive environment where all team members feel comfortable sharing their perspectives. Encourage open dialogue, actively listen to others, and consider diverse viewpoints when making decisions.

6. Check your decision-making process: Be mindful of how your biases may influence your decision-making. Take a step back and evaluate if your judgments are fair and objective. Consider involving others in the decision-making process to gain different perspectives.

7. Establish inclusive policies and practices: Implement policies and practices that promote diversity and inclusion within your organization. This can include diverse hiring practices, mentoring programs, and creating a safe space for employees to report bias incidents.

8. Hold yourself accountable: Regularly evaluate your progress in managing biases and prejudices. Hold yourself accountable for any biases that may emerge and take steps to address them promptly.

Remember, managing biases is an ongoing process. It requires continuous self-reflection, learning, and commitment to creating an inclusive environment.

PART I

On Ethical Decision-Making and Moral Development

Chapter One

The General Foundations of Ethical Decision-making

The foundations of ethical decision-making lie in considering the principles of honesty, fairness, and respect for others. Ethical decision-making involves evaluating the potential impact of our actions on others and society. It requires considering moral values, legal obligations, and the long-term consequences of our choices.

Ethical Decision-Making: A Guide to Responsible Choices

In today's complex and interconnected world, ethical decision-making holds immense significance. It serves as a critical framework for individuals and organizations to identify the right course of action when faced with challenging dilemmas. At its core, ethical decision-making involves evaluating choices based on moral principles, values, and beliefs. It requires considering the potential consequences and impact on various stakeholders, including oneself, others, and society. This essay will delve into the process of ethical decision-making, explore its various frameworks and models, and examine real-world examples to shed light on the complexities involved.

Understanding Ethical Decision-Making:

Ethical decision-making entails a systematic process that individuals or groups undertake to arrive at responsible choices. It starts with recognizing the existence of an ethical dilemma, a situation in which there are conflicting interests or values. Once an ethical dilemma is identified, the decision-maker must gather all relevant information, considering the facts, emotions, and potential consequences associated with different options. It is crucial to ensure that biases, personal interests, and external influences do not cloud judgment during this stage.

Frameworks and Models:

1. Utilitarianism: This consequentialist approach suggests that ethical decisions should aim to maximize overall happiness or utility for the greatest number of people. It requires weighing the positive and negative consequences of each alternative action, ultimately choosing the option that produces the most favorable outcome for the majority.

2. Deontological ethics: Deontological ethics, often associated with philosopher Immanuel Kant, focuses on the inherent morality of a chosen action, rather than its consequences. According to this approach, ethical decisions should be guided by a set of universal rules and principles, such as honesty, fairness, and respect for human dignity.

3. Virtue ethics: This ethical framework emphasizes cultivating virtues and moral character as the foundation of ethical decision-making. Drawing from ancient Greek philosophy, virtue ethics suggests that individuals should analyze their actions based on desirable character traits, such as honesty, compassion, or integrity.

4. Ethical egoism: Contrary to ethical frameworks that prioritize the welfare of others, ethical egoism asserts that individuals should focus solely on pursuing their self-interests. According to this perspective, acting ethically aligns with maximizing one's long-term welfare.

5. Feminist ethics: This framework acknowledges the unique experiences and perspectives of women and highlights the importance of care, empathy, and relationships in ethical decision-making. It challenges traditional ethical models, which often reflect a male-dominated perspective.

The Ethical Decision-Making Process:

While ethical frameworks provide a theoretical foundation, the decision-making process itself relies on a set of steps to guide individuals toward responsible choices. These steps may vary in their application, but generally include the following:

1. Identify the ethical dilemma: Recognize the conflicting values, interests, or rights involved in the decision.

Identifying ethical dilemmas is essential for individuals and organizations to navigate complex situations and make morally sound decisions. Ethical dilemmas occur when individuals are faced with two or more conflicting choices, each of which has a moral or ethical consequence. These dilemmas often arise when there is a clash between personal values, societal norms, legal obligations, or professional standards. To help identify ethical dilemmas, here are some examples:

a. Privacy vs. Public Safety: In the age of digital technology and surveillance, there is a constant struggle between protecting individual privacy and ensuring public safety. For instance, law enforcement agencies face a dilemma when deciding whether to use invasive surveillance techniques to prevent potential threats against public safety, while potentially violating individuals' privacy rights.

b. Whistleblowing: Employees may encounter ethical dilemmas when they witness illegal activities or unethical behavior within their organizations. Deciding whether to blow the whistle and risk personal and professional consequences or to remain silent and perpetuate the wrongdoing, is a challenging ethical dilemma.

c. End-of-Life Decisions: Healthcare professionals often face ethical dilemmas when dealing with end-of-life decisions, such as whether to continue life-sustaining treatments for terminally ill patients who have expressed a desire to die with dignity. Deciding between prolonging life and respecting the patient's autonomy poses a complex ethical dilemma.

d. Environmental Conservation vs. Economic Growth: Businesses and governments frequently encounter ethical dilemmas concerning the prioritization of environmental conservation or economic growth. An example is when a company considers whether to implement sustainable practices that may increase production costs but contribute to long-term environmental sustainability.

e. Conflict of Interest: Professionals, such as doctors, lawyers, and financial advisors, may face ethical dilemmas when there is a potential conflict between their interests and the best interests of their clients. For instance, a financial advisor who recommends investment products that benefit them more than their clients could be entangled in an ethical dilemma.

f. Workplace Discrimination: Organizations encounter ethical dilemmas related to discrimination, such as hiring or promoting employees based on their gender, race, or other protected characteristics rather than merit and qualifications. Deciding whether to prioritize diversity and fairness or succumb to biases poses a challenging ethical dilemma.

g. Animal Testing: The practice of animal testing for scientific research often raises ethical dilemmas. Researchers must weigh the potential benefits of medical advancements against the ethical concerns of subjecting animals to harm and cruelty.

h. Intellectual Property Rights: Ethical dilemmas arise in situations where individuals or organizations infringe on intellectual property rights. Copying software, illegally downloading music, and plagiarizing others' work are examples that raise ethical questions about respecting and protecting creative output.

i. Genetic Testing and Privacy: With advances in genetic testing, individuals face ethical dilemmas regarding the disclosure of personal genetic information. Deciding whether to reveal genetic predispositions to diseases to family members carries ethical implications for privacy, autonomy, and potential discrimination.

j. Corporate Social Responsibility: Organizations may face ethical dilemmas when deciding how to allocate resources for corporate social responsibility initiatives. Selecting between investments in community development, environmental sustainability, or employee welfare creates ethical dilemmas related to determining the most impactful and morally justifiable choice.

In conclusion, ethical dilemmas are prevalent in various aspects of society, ranging from personal choices to organizational decisions. Recognizing and analyzing these dilemmas is crucial to finding appropriate ethical solutions that balance conflicting values and responsibilities. By understanding the examples provided above and continually assessing the ethical consequences of different actions, individuals and organizations can navigate through moral complexities and make better-informed decisions.

2. Gather information: Seek all relevant facts, data, and opinions related to the situation at hand.

Gathering accurate and relevant business information is crucial for making informed decisions and achieving success in today's competitive landscape. To gather reliable information and seek relevant facts, consider the following strategies:

a. Define your information needs: Begin by clearly articulating your information needs and objectives. Identify the specific questions you want to answer or the areas you need more information about. This will help guide your information-gathering efforts and ensure you focus on collecting the right data.

b. Conduct thorough research: Utilize various research methods to gather business information. This can include online research using search engines, databases, industry reports, and academic journals. Additionally, consider utilizing primary research methods like surveys, interviews, and focus groups to gather firsthand information from customers, employees, suppliers, or industry experts.

c. Identify credible sources: When conducting research, make sure to gather information from credible and reliable sources. Look for reputable industry publications, government websites, academic institutions, and established research organizations. Be cautious of biased or unverified sources that may provide inaccurate or misleading information.

d. Use data analytics: Leverage data analytics tools and techniques to extract meaningful insights from large volumes of data. Analyzing data can help identify trends, patterns, and correlations, providing a solid foundation for decision-making. Tools like data visualization software can also help present complex information in a more easily digestible format.

e. Seek expert advice: Consult with industry experts, mentors, or advisors who possess deep knowledge and experience in your field. Their insights and perspectives can provide valuable information and help validate your findings. Networking events, conferences, and professional associations are great avenues to connect with experts in your industry.

f. Monitor competitors and market trends: Stay updated on industry news, competitor activities, and market trends. Monitoring your competitors can provide valuable insights into their strategies, strengths, and weaknesses. Additionally, keeping tabs on market trends can help identify emerging opportunities and potential disruptions that may impact your business.

g. Maintain a feedback loop: Establish mechanisms for collecting feedback from customers, employees, and other stakeholders. Their perspectives and input can provide valuable insights that may not be captured through traditional research methods. Regularly engaging with stakeholders and encouraging open communication can help foster a culture of transparency and continuous improvement.

In summary, gathering business information and seeking relevant facts involves defining your information needs, conducting thorough research, utilizing credible sources, leveraging data analytics, seeking expert advice, monitoring competitors and market trends, and maintaining a feedback loop. By employing these strategies, you can ensure the information you gather is reliable, accurate, and actionable, enabling you to make informed business decisions that drive success.

3. Identify stakeholders: Determine who may be affected by the decision and consider their interests.

Identifying stakeholders in business is a critical step in understanding and effectively managing relationships with individuals or groups that have a vested interest in the success or outcomes of the organization. Stakeholders can include employees, customers, investors, suppliers, government agencies, local communities, and even competitors. Recognizing and understanding the diverse array of stakeholders helps businesses address their needs, manage expectations, and build mutually beneficial relationships. Here are some strategies to identify stakeholders in the business context:

a. Internal stakeholders: Start by identifying individuals or groups within the organization who have a direct stake in its operations, goals, and outcomes. This includes employees at all levels, managers, executives, and board members. Internal stakeholders may hold various roles, possess different interests, and have unique perspectives on the organization's functioning and success.

b. Customers: Customers are crucial stakeholders for any business. They are the individuals or organizations who purchase or use a company's products or services. Identifying different types of customers, such as individuals, businesses, or institutions, and understanding their specific needs, preferences, and expectations is vital for customer satisfaction and retention.

c. Suppliers: Suppliers provide the necessary inputs, resources, or services that enable a business to operate and deliver its products or services. It is important to identify key suppliers and understand their role in the value chain. Developing strong relationships with suppliers can enhance operational efficiency, quality control, and supply chain management.

d. Investors and Shareholders: Investors and shareholders have a financial stake in the business. These stakeholders may include individual shareholders, institutional investors, venture capitalists, or private equity firms. Identifying and communicating with investors is essential for maintaining transparency, fulfilling reporting requirements, and addressing their expectations for returns on investment.

e. Regulators and Government Agencies: Depending on the industry and location, businesses are subject to regulations and oversight by government agencies. Identifying relevant regulatory bodies and understanding their expectations, compliance requirements, and potential impacts on the business is crucial. Building positive relationships with regulatory stakeholders can help mitigate risks and facilitate smooth operations.

f. Competitors: Although competitors may seem counterintuitive as stakeholders, they play a significant role in shaping the business landscape and industry dynamics. Being aware of competitors and their strategies helps businesses anticipate market trends, benchmark performance, and identify potential areas for collaboration or differentiation.

g. Local Communities and NGOs: Businesses have an impact on the communities in which they operate. Identifying local communities and understanding their social, cultural, and environmental concerns is essential for sustainable and responsible business practices. Engaging with local communities and relevant non-governmental organizations (NGOs) helps build positive relationships and contribute to social and environmental initiatives.

h. Industry Associations and Trade Organizations: Industry associations and trade organizations bring together businesses in specific industries or sectors. Identifying and participating in relevant associations can provide opportunities for networking, knowledge sharing, advocacy, and staying updated on industry trends. These stakeholders can also represent common interests and contribute to shaping industry standards and best practices.

i. Media and Press: Recognizing the media as stakeholders is important for managing the organization's public image, reputation, and communication strategies. Identifying key media outlets, journalists, and influential bloggers in the industry allows businesses to proactively engage with the press and communicate their key messages effectively.

j. Interest Groups and Activists: Some businesses may attract the attention of interest groups or activists due to their operations, products, or impact on specific causes. These stakeholders may have strong opinions, engage in advocacy, or take actions that could influence a business's reputation or operations. Identifying these interest groups and activists helps businesses anticipate potential challenges, address concerns, and engage in constructive dialogue.

In conclusion, identifying stakeholders in business is a multifaceted process that involves recognizing individuals or groups with a vested interest in the organization. By systematically considering internal stakeholders, customers, suppliers, investors, regulators, competitors, local communities, industry associations, media, and interest groups, businesses can gain a comprehensive understanding of their stakeholder landscape. This knowledge allows them to tailor strategies, manage relationships, and align organizational goals and actions to meet the expectations and needs of various stakeholders, ensuring sustainable and responsible business practices.

4. Explore possible alternatives: Generate various options that address the ethical dilemma.

Generating various options that address ethical dilemmas is a critical step in ethical decision-making. When individuals or organizations are faced with complex moral challenges, it is essential to explore and evaluate multiple alternatives to identify the most ethically sound course of action. The following comprehensive guide offers strategies and techniques to generate a range of options for addressing ethical dilemmas.

a. Analyze the Ethical Dilemma: Begin by thoroughly understanding the ethical dilemma at hand. This involves identifying conflicting moral values, principles, or obligations, and recognizing the potential consequences of various actions. Analyzing the specific ethical dimensions of the situation provides a foundation for generating options that comprehensively address the dilemma.

b. Seek Diverse Perspectives: Engage with various stakeholders and seek their perspectives on the ethical dilemma. This can include employees, customers, community members, and subject matter experts. Different viewpoints can shed light on alternative ways of addressing the dilemma that may not have been initially apparent.

c. Brainstorming: Encourage a creative and open-minded brainstorming session to generate a wide range of options. Create a collaborative environment where individuals involved in the decision-making process can freely contribute ideas without fear of judgment or criticism. Ensure that all ideas, regardless of their initial feasibility or practicality, are captured.

d. Challenge Assumptions and Biases: Scrutinize and challenge any assumptions or biases that may influence the generation of options. Encourage individuals to question long-held beliefs, preconceived notions, and personal biases that may limit the range of potential solutions. This helps foster a more inclusive and innovative approach to generating options.

e. Employ Ethical Theories and Principles: Utilize ethical theories and principles as a framework to generate options that align with moral principles. Ethical theories such as consequentialism, deontology, virtue ethics, and ethics of care provide different perspectives on how to address ethical dilemmas. Consider how various principles, such as fairness, justice, integrity, and empathy, can guide the creation of ethically viable options.

f. Evaluate Legal and Professional Standards: Review applicable laws, regulations, and professional codes of ethics that govern the specific industry or field. Ensure that generated options are not in violation of legal requirements or professional standards. Considering these guidelines helps narrow down options to those that are legal and ethical.

g. Conduct Research and Benchmarking: Research existing practices, case studies, and best practices in addressing similar ethical dilemmas. Benchmarking against industry standards and successful examples provides insights into potential solutions and inspires innovative options that have proven effective elsewhere.

h. Consider Long-Term Implications: Prioritize options that consider the long-term implications of the decision. Assess how each option impacts stakeholders, sustainability, reputation, and the organization's overall ethical standing. Generate options that promote long-term value creation and ethical integrity.

i. Implement Ethical Decision-Making Models: Embrace established ethical decision-making models to guide the generation of options. Models such as the Ethical Decision-Making Framework, the Potter Box, or the Four-Component Model provide step-by-step processes that help generate a range of options and assess their ethical implications.

j. Quantify Ethical Considerations: Explore ways to quantify and measure ethical considerations, such as social impact, environmental impact, or the well-being of stakeholders. Tools like cost-benefit analysis, social return on investment, or triple-bottom-line analysis can provide a structured approach for comparing and evaluating different ethical options.

k. Consider Creative Approaches: Explore unconventional or innovative approaches to address ethical dilemmas. Think outside the box, challenge conventional wisdom, and consider alternative ways of solving the problem. Generating unique options can lead to breakthrough solutions that effectively address the ethical dimensions of the dilemma.

l. Prioritize Collaboration: Foster open communication and collaboration among individuals involved in the decision-making process. Encourage active dialogue, invite diverse perspectives, and facilitate group discussions that promote the generation of collective options. Collaboration allows for the synthesis of different ideas, leading to more comprehensive and insightful ethical solutions.

m. Redefine the Problem: Shift the focus from the problem itself to the underlying values, needs, and interests involved. Reframing the ethical dilemma can open up new possibilities and generate options that address the root causes rather than the symptoms. This helps generate creative and transformative solutions.

n. Evaluate and Refine Options: Assess each generated option against ethical principles, legal requirements, organizational values, and stakeholder interests. Eliminate options that are unethical or impractical. Refine and consolidate the remaining options into a manageable set that can be further evaluated.

o. Engage in Ethical Deliberation: Engage in ethical deliberation and structured discussion to evaluate the remaining options. Gather input and feedback from stakeholders, seek expert opinions, and invite different viewpoints. Deliberation helps weigh the ethical implications, trade-offs, and consequences of each option to facilitate the selection of the most ethical and viable path forward.

p. Conduct Scenario Analysis: Consider potential scenarios and their implications for each generated option. Assess how each option would respond to different factors, such as changing market conditions, stakeholder expectations, or technological developments. Scenario analysis provides insights into the resilience and adaptability of each option, enabling more informed decision-making.

q. Reflect on Organizational Values: Reflect on the organization's mission, values, and ethical commitments. Evaluate how each option aligns with these core principles and contributes to the organization's overall ethical integrity. Prioritize options that are congruent with the organization's values and purpose.

r. Consider Ethical Leadership: Recognize the crucial role of ethical leadership in generating options that address ethical dilemmas effectively. Leaders should model ethical behavior, promote a culture of integrity, and create an environment that encourages the generation of ethical options. Ethical leadership inspires and guides the decision-making process towards the most ethical outcomes.

In conclusion, generating a range of options to address ethical dilemmas requires a systematic approach that encompasses analysis, diversity of perspectives, brainstorming, challenging assumptions, and employing ethical theories and principles. By incorporating research, legal and professional standards, long-term implications, ethical decision-making models, creative approaches, collaboration, and scenario analysis, individuals and organizations can navigate ethical challenges and identify the most ethically sound solutions. Furthermore, reflecting on organizational values and demonstrating ethical leadership enhances the ethical decision-making process, promoting integrity and long-term ethical success.

5. Evaluate the alternatives: Weigh the potential consequences, both positive and negative, of each alternative.

Evaluating the alternatives is a crucial step in decision-making, as it allows individuals or organizations to assess the various options generated to address a problem or dilemma. By carefully evaluating each alternative, the decision-maker can determine which course of action is most appropriate, ethical, and aligned with their goals and values. Below are strategies and factors to consider when evaluating alternatives during the decision-making process.

a. Identify Evaluation Criteria: Start by defining the criteria against which each alternative will be evaluated. These criteria should reflect the goals, values, and priorities of the decision-maker or organization. Common evaluation criteria include feasibility, effectiveness, ethical considerations, potential risks, cost-effectiveness, and impacts on stakeholders.

b. Weight the Criteria: Assign weights to each evaluation criterion to reflect its relative importance. Some criteria may be more critical than others, and assigning weights helps prioritize them in the evaluation process. For example, if ethical considerations are of utmost importance, assign a higher weight to this criterion.

c. Gather Relevant Information: Collect the necessary information and data related to each alternative. This may include research, conducting experiments, consulting experts, or analyzing past performance data. The information should cover all aspects relevant to the decision, such as costs, benefits, risks, feasibility, and any legal or regulatory requirements.

d. Analyze the Pros and Cons: Evaluate the advantages and disadvantages of each alternative. Create a list or matrix that compares the strengths and weaknesses of each option based on the identified evaluation criteria. This analysis will provide a clear overview of the potential benefits and drawbacks associated with each alternative.

e. Consider Short-Term and Long-Term Implications: Assess the potential short-term and long-term implications of each alternative. Look beyond immediate consequences and consider the possible effects on stakeholders, resources, reputation, and the organization's overall goals. Evaluating alternatives with a long-term perspective helps avoid short-sighted decisions and promotes sustainable outcomes.

f. Assess Risk and Uncertainty: Evaluate the level of risk and uncertainty associated with each alternative. Consider the probability of success, potential obstacles, and the degree of uncertainty in each option. Assessing risk allows decision-makers to make informed choices and consider contingencies for potential challenges.

g. Test or Pilot Alternatives: Whenever feasible, consider testing or piloting each alternative on a smaller scale before implementing it on a broader level. This allows decision-makers to gather real-world data and feedback, assess the practicality and effectiveness of each option, and make adjustments if necessary.

h. Consider Resource Allocation: Evaluate the resources required for each alternative, including financial, human, time, or technological resources. Consider the availability and feasibility of allocating resources to support each option. If an alternative demands excessive resources beyond the organization's capacity, it may not be a viable choice.

i. Evaluate Ethical Implications: Assess how each alternative aligns with ethical considerations and values. Consider the potential impacts on stakeholders, social responsibility, and ethical standards. Evaluate whether the alternatives adhere to ethical principles, compliance requirements, and organizational values. Prioritize alternatives that demonstrate ethical integrity and social responsibility.

j. Consider Trade-Offs: Recognize potential trade-offs and compromises associated with each alternative. It is rare for an alternative to satisfy all criteria perfectly. Identify which criteria might conflict with each other and assess how willing or able the decision-maker is to accept trade-offs. Evaluating trade-offs helps individuals or organizations understand the potential benefits and drawbacks of prioritizing specific criteria over others.

k. Solicit Stakeholder Input: Seek input from relevant stakeholders who may be affected by the decision. Consider their perspectives, concerns, and preferences. Engage stakeholders through surveys, focus groups, or individual consultations to gain valuable insights and ensure that their voices are considered in the evaluation process.

l. Consider Implementation and Scalability: Evaluate each alternative's implementation requirements and scalability potential. Assess whether the option can be effectively executed, whether it aligns with existing processes, and whether it can be adapted or expanded in the future. This evaluation helps avoid choosing alternatives that might be difficult to implement or maintain in the long run.

m. Consider Decision-Making Models: Employ decision-making models to assist in evaluating alternatives. Models such as cost-benefit analysis, multi-criteria decision analysis, decision trees, or SWOT analysis can provide structured frameworks for comprehensively evaluating the pros and cons of each option. These models help minimize biases and ensure a systematic evaluation of alternatives.

n. Seek Feedback and Expert Opinions: Seek feedback and opinions from trusted advisors, experts, or individuals with relevant experience. Expert opinions can provide valuable insights and guidance in evaluating the alternatives. Engage in constructive discussions and consider the credibility and expertise of those providing feedback to inform the decision-making process.

o. Develop Scenarios and Contingency Plans: Consider the potential outcomes and scenarios associated with each alternative. Develop contingency plans that outline actionable steps to address potential challenges or unexpected developments. Anticipating different scenarios helps decision-makers prepare for potential risks, uncertainties, and unforeseen consequences of implementing each option.

p. Consider Timing and Deadlines: Evaluate whether certain alternatives must be implemented within specific time constraints or deadlines. Assess the feasibility of meeting these time constraints and whether the alternatives align with the overall timeline and strategic objectives. Timing considerations can impact the viability and success of each option.

q. Evaluate Organizational Capacity: Assess the organization's capacity to execute each alternative effectively. Consider factors such as existing capabilities, competencies, and available resources. Evaluating organizational capacity helps determine whether the organization can support the chosen alternative successfully.

r. Conduct a Final Evaluation and Selection: Consolidate the evaluation results and weigh the pros, cons, and other relevant factors. Compare each alternative objectively against the identified evaluation criteria and assigned weights. Based on this comprehensive evaluation, select the alternative that best aligns with the pre-determined goals, values, constraints, and priorities.

In conclusion, evaluating alternatives in the decision-making process involves systematically assessing the pros, cons, risks, and trade-offs associated with each option. Employing established evaluation criteria, gathering relevant information, considering short-term and long-term implications, assessing risks, and evaluating ethical considerations are crucial steps. Additionally, feedback from stakeholders and experts, as well as the use of decision-making models, can enhance the evaluation process. By carefully assessing and comparing each alternative, decision-makers can make informed choices that align with their objectives and values.

6. Consider ethical frameworks: Apply ethical frameworks or models to analyze the alternatives and their alignment with moral principles.

Ethical analysis of alternatives involves evaluating how each option aligns with moral principles and ethical frameworks. This process provides a structured approach to assess the ethical implications and consequences of each alternative to make informed decisions that uphold moral integrity. In this guide, we will explore various ethical frameworks and principles that can be employed to analyze alternatives and ensure their alignment with moral principles.

a. Utilitarianism: Utilitarianism is an ethical framework that focuses on maximizing overall happiness and minimizing harm for the greatest number of people. When evaluating alternatives through a utilitarian lens, the primary consideration is the net positive or negative impact on well-being. The option that produces the greatest overall benefit and minimizes harm is considered ethically preferable.

b. Deontology: Deontology emphasizes adherence to moral duties, principles, and obligations when analyzing alternatives. This framework looks beyond the potential outcomes and focuses on whether the alternative aligns with moral rules or duties. Deontological analysis involves assessing the ethicality of each option based on principles such as respect for autonomy, fairness, honesty, and justice.

c. Virtue Ethics: Virtue ethics prioritizes the development of moral character and emphasizes the importance of virtues such as honesty, compassion, courage, and integrity. When analyzing alternatives through a virtue ethics framework, the focus is on whether each option promotes virtuous behavior and character development. Ethical evaluation involves considering how each alternative aligns with the cultivation of virtues and contributes to the overall moral development of individuals or organizations involved.

d. Ethics of Care: The ethics of care framework emphasizes the significance of nurturing and maintaining caring relationships. When analyzing alternatives through this lens, the focus is on the impact on individuals and the quality of relationships. Ethical evaluation involves considering how each alternative demonstrates care, empathy, and compassion towards stakeholders and promotes the well-being of those affected by the decision.

e. Rights-based Approaches: Rights-based approaches to ethics emphasize the protection of individual rights and dignity. When evaluating alternatives from this perspective, the focus is on whether each option respects and upholds fundamental rights, such as the right to life, liberty, privacy, or freedom of speech. Analyzing alternatives through a rights-based approach involves ensuring that the chosen option does not infringe upon the rights of individuals or groups.

f. Sustainability and Environmental Ethics: Evaluating alternatives through the lens of sustainability and environmental ethics involves considering the impact on the environment and future generations. This framework requires assessments of how each option aligns with the principles of environmental responsibility, conservation, and intergenerational equity. Ethical evaluation includes determining whether the alternative promotes environmental stewardship, minimizes ecological harm, and contributes to sustainable practices.

g. Cultural Relativism: Cultural relativism recognizes that ethical standards may vary across cultures and societies. When analyzing alternatives through this framework, the focus is on understanding and respecting cultural norms and values. Ethical evaluation involves considering whether each option aligns with the moral expectations and accepted standards within a specific cultural context.

h. Principlism: Principlism combines elements of different ethical principles to analyze alternatives. This approach involves identifying key ethical principles relevant to the decision at hand, such as autonomy, beneficence, non-maleficence, and justice. Ethical evaluation using Principlism includes weighing the considerations and potential conflicts among these principles about each alternative.

i. Rawlsian Theory of Justice: The Rawlsian theory of justice emphasizes fairness and equity in distributing societal resources and opportunities. When applying this framework, the focus is on whether each alternative promotes the principles of fairness, equal opportunity, and justice for all. Ethical evaluation involves assessing whether the chosen option benefits the least advantaged members of society and reduces inequalities.

j. Golden Rule: The Golden Rule, found in various religions and ethical frameworks, emphasizes treating others as you would like to be treated. When evaluating alternatives through this framework, the focus is on whether each option respects the dignity and well-being of others. Ethical evaluation includes assessing whether the chosen option upholds the principle of treating others ethically and fosters empathy, respect, and fairness.

When analyzing alternatives in alignment with moral principles, it is essential to consider the following steps:

k. Define the moral principles: Identify the relevant moral principles or ethical frameworks that should guide the evaluation process. Consider the specific values, duties, responsibilities, and obligations that apply to the decision or situation.

l. Review the alternatives: Identify and clarify the available alternatives to be evaluated. Ensure that all potential options are considered, taking into account the generated alternatives through the decision-making process.

m. Evaluate ethical implications: Assess how each alternative aligns with the identified moral principles. Consider the potential impacts on stakeholders, the community, the environment, and any relevant legal or professional standards. Examine whether the alternative promotes ethical integrity, upholds moral duties, and respects the rights and dignity of individuals or groups.

n. Identify ethical considerations and conflicts: Identify any ethical considerations or conflicts that arise when comparing the alternatives. Determine whether any alternative violates a moral principle or creates tension between different ethical frameworks. Consider how these ethical conflicts might be resolved or mitigated.

o. Weigh the ethical dimensions: Weigh the importance and significance of each ethical dimension or principle in evaluating the alternatives. Consider the relative weight assigned to different moral principles and their impact on the overall ethical analysis.

p. Consider contextual factors: Take into account the situational or contextual factors that may affect the ethical analysis. Consider the specific circumstances, constraints, cultural norms, and stakeholder expectations that influence the evaluation of each alternative.

q. Assess the practicality and feasibility: Evaluate the practicality and feasibility of implementing each alternative from an ethical standpoint. Consider whether the chosen option can be realistically executed and maintained while upholding moral principles and ethical standards.

r. Consult stakeholders and experts: Seek input and feedback from relevant stakeholders and subject matter experts throughout the evaluation process. Engage in dialogue and consider multiple perspectives to ensure a comprehensive analysis of the ethical implications of each alternative.

s. Reflect on the overall ethical outcome: Reflect on the overall ethical outcome of each alternative. Consider the net ethical benefits, potential harm, and trade-offs involved. Assess the alignment of each option with the broader moral principles, values, and organizational or personal ethical commitments.

t. Make an informed decision: Based on the ethical analysis, make an informed decision that upholds moral principles and aligns with the identified ethical frameworks. Select the alternative that best satisfies the ethical considerations, respects the rights and dignity of stakeholders, and promotes the well-being of individuals and communities affected by the decision.

In conclusion, ethical analysis of alternatives involves a systematic evaluation of how each option aligns with moral principles and ethical frameworks. By considering various ethical frameworks such as utilitarianism, deontology, virtue ethics, ethics of care, rights-based approaches, sustainability, cultural relativism, Principlism, Rawlsian theory of justice, and the Golden Rule, decision-makers can ensure a comprehensive and balanced ethical evaluation. By following the steps of defining moral principles, reviewing alternatives, evaluating ethical implications, identifying ethical considerations and conflicts, weighing ethical dimensions, considering contextual factors, assessing practicality and feasibility, consulting stakeholders and experts, reflecting on the overall ethical outcome, and making an informed decision, individuals and organizations can navigate complex decisions while upholding moral integrity.

7. Decide: Opt for the alternative that best aligns with ethics and values.

Aligning alternatives with ethics and values is essential for making ethical decisions that reflect an individual's or organization's moral compass. When evaluating alternatives, it is crucial to consider how each option aligns with ethical principles, values, and the desired outcomes. In this guide, we will explore how to identify alternatives that best align with ethics and values.

a. Clarify Ethics and Values: Before evaluating alternatives, it is important to clarify the ethics and values that guide decision-making. By clearly defining the ethical principles and core values that are essential to the decision-maker or organization, it becomes easier to evaluate alternatives that are in alignment.

b. Identify Key Ethical Principles: Determine the relevant ethical principles that should guide the evaluation process. These may include principles such as integrity, honesty, respect for autonomy, fairness, justice, empathy, or environmental responsibility. Identify the most significant ethical principles that should inform the analysis of alternatives.

c. Prioritize Core Values: Identify the core values that are most important to the decision-maker or organization. These values might include integrity, accountability, sustainability, customer satisfaction, social responsibility, or innovation. By prioritizing core values, decision-makers can assess alternatives that uphold these values.

d. Evaluate Consistency: Examine how each alternative aligns with the ethical principles and values identified. Assess whether the options are consistent with the desired ethical standards, whether they uphold moral virtues, and whether they reflect the organization's mission and vision. Evaluate the extent to which each alternative promotes ethical behavior and integrity.

e. Assess the Impact on Stakeholders: Consider how each alternative affects stakeholders. Evaluate whether the options have positive or negative implications for employees, customers, suppliers, shareholders, communities, or the environment. Prioritize alternatives that consider the well-being and interests of all stakeholders involved.

f. Consider Ethical Implications: Examine the ethical implications and consequences of each alternative. Assess whether the options are likely to result in positive outcomes, promote social justice, or enhance environmental sustainability. Ensure that the alternatives do not cause harm, violate rights, or compromise ethical principles.

g. Evaluate Transparency and Accountability: Evaluate whether each alternative promotes transparency, accountability, and responsible decision-making. Consider whether the options prioritize open communication, ethical behavior, and adherence to laws and regulations. Review whether the alternatives encourage responsible actions and ethical decision-making processes.

h. Align with Legal and Regulatory Requirements: Ensure that each alternative aligns with legal and regulatory requirements. Evaluate whether the options comply with all applicable laws, regulations, and industry standards. Discard alternatives that are illegal or in violation of ethical or legal obligations.

i. Promote Fairness and Justice: Assess whether each alternative prioritizes fairness and justice. Evaluate whether the options treat all individuals and groups involved equitably and with respect. Consider whether the alternatives promote diversity, equality, and inclusivity. Prioritize alternatives that distribute benefits and burdens fairly.

j. Consider Long-Term Consequences: Assess the long-term consequences of each alternative. Consider the impact on future generations, the environment, and the sustainability of resources. Evaluate whether the options promote long-term value creation, and ethical behavior, and contribute to the organization's overall reputation and success.

k. Emphasize Ethical Leadership: Consider whether each alternative aligns with ethical leadership principles. Evaluate whether the options demonstrate ethical leadership behaviors such as setting a moral example, promoting accountability, and fostering an ethical culture. Prioritize alternatives that reflect and reinforce ethical leadership principles.

l. Evaluate fit with Organizational Culture: Assess the fit of each alternative with the organization's culture and values. Consider whether the options are compatible with the organization's mission, vision, and overarching goals. Ensure that the alternatives align with the existing culture and maintain consistency with the organization's values and identity.

m. Assess Resource Allocation: Evaluate whether each alternative effectively utilizes available resources. Consider whether the options optimize the allocation of financial, human, and technological resources. Prioritize alternatives that maximize value creation and minimize waste while upholding ethical principles.

n. Involve Stakeholders: Seek input and feedback from relevant stakeholders. Engage in dialogue and consider multiple perspectives to ensure that the alternatives are consistent with the values and expectations of stakeholders. Involve stakeholders to build trust, enhance decision-making, and incorporate diverse viewpoints.

o. Consider Ethical Decision-Making Models: Utilize ethical decision-making models to evaluate the alignment of alternatives with ethics and values. Models such as the Ethical Decision-Making Framework, the Potter Box, or the Four-Component Model provide step-by-step processes for assessing ethical considerations and ensuring alignment with ethical principles and values.

p. Reflect on Ethical Scenarios and Case Studies: Reflect on ethical scenarios and case studies to gain insights into similar situations and evaluate how alternatives align with ethics and values. Consider real-world examples and best practices to inform the decision-making process and guide the evaluation of alternatives.

q. Conduct Ethical Risk Analysis: Assess the ethical risks associated with each alternative. Identify potential ethical pitfalls, conflicts of interest, or unintended consequences that may arise. Evaluate the likelihood and severity of ethical risks and prioritize alternatives that minimize these risks.

r. Seek External Expertise: When needed, consult with external experts or professionals who specialize in ethics and values. Seek guidance from individuals with expertise in the specific field or industry to evaluate alternatives from an ethical perspective.

In conclusion, evaluating alternatives in alignment with ethics and values requires a thoughtful and systematic approach. By clarifying ethical principles and core values, evaluating consistency, assessing the impact on stakeholders, considering ethical implications, and taking into account legal requirements, fairness, and long-term consequences, decision-makers can identify alternatives that align with ethics and values. Additionally, by emphasizing ethical leadership, assessing fit with organizational culture, involving stakeholders, utilizing ethical decision-making models, reflecting on ethical scenarios, conducting ethical risk analysis, and seeking external expertise, decision-makers can ensure a comprehensive evaluation and select alternatives that uphold ethical standards and promote moral integrity.

8. Take action: Implement the chosen course of action and evaluate its effectiveness.

Implementing and evaluating the effectiveness of an action is a critical step in the decision-making process. Taking action involves putting the chosen alternative into practice while evaluating effectiveness allows for continuous improvement and ensures that the desired outcomes are achieved. In this guide, we will explore the steps involved in implementing and evaluating the effectiveness of an action.

a. Develop an Action Plan: Start by developing a detailed action plan that outlines the specific steps, tasks, and timelines required to implement the chosen alternative. The action plan should clearly define responsibilities, allocate resources, and establish milestones for tracking progress.

b. Communicate the Plan: Communicate the action plan to all relevant stakeholders. Ensure that everyone involved understands their roles and responsibilities, as well as the objectives and expected outcomes of the action. Effective communication is essential to gain buy-in, support, and cooperation throughout the implementation process.

c. Allocate Resources: Allocate the necessary resources, including financial, human, technological, and physical resources, to support the implementation of the action plan. Ensure that resources are available when needed to facilitate smooth execution. Regularly assess resource allocation to address any potential gaps or constraints.

d. Monitor Progress: Implement a monitoring system to track progress and ensure that the action plan is being executed according to the established timeline and milestones. Regularly review and update the progress against the plan, identifying any deviations and taking corrective action if necessary.

e. Address Barriers and Challenges: Identify and address any barriers or challenges that arise during the implementation process. Anticipate potential obstacles and develop contingency plans to mitigate risks. Monitor the progress closely, and proactively address any issues that may hinder the effective implementation of the action plan.

f. Document and Review: Document all activities, decisions, and modifications made during the implementation process. Maintain clear records of progress, challenges, and solutions for future reference. Regularly review and update the documentation to ensure accuracy and facilitate continuous improvement.

g. Collect Data and Measure Results: Collect relevant data to assess the effectiveness of the action. This may involve quantitative data, such as performance metrics or financial indicators, as well as qualitative data, such as feedback and observations. Define key performance indicators (KPIs) or other measures of success that align with the objectives of the action.

h. Analyze and Interpret Data: Analyze the collected data to evaluate the effectiveness of the action. Compare the actual results against the expected outcomes to identify any discrepancies. Use statistical or analytical tools to interpret the data and gain insights into the strengths and weaknesses of the implemented action.

i. Evaluate Impact and Outcomes: Review the impact and outcomes of the action about the desired objectives. Assess whether the action has achieved the intended results, addressed the initial problem or challenge, and aligned with the identified goals. Consider both short-term and long-term effects to ensure a comprehensive evaluation.

j. Seek Feedback: Seek feedback from relevant stakeholders, including those directly impacted by the action and those involved in its implementation. Solicit input through surveys, interviews, focus groups, or other feedback mechanisms. Assess the extent to which stakeholders perceive the action as effective and identify areas for improvement.

k. Analyze Lessons Learned: Analyze the lessons learned during the implementation process. Reflect on what worked well and what could be improved in future actions. Identify best practices and areas that require adjustments or modifications. Incorporate these insights into the evaluation process to inform future decision-making and action plans.

l. Adjust and Refine: Based on the evaluation of effectiveness and the lessons learned, make necessary adjustments to the action plan or implementation strategy. Refine the approach to enhance performance, address shortcomings, and optimize outcomes. Continuously iterate and improve the action plan based on the evaluation results.

m. Review Ethical Considerations: Assess the action's alignment with ethical considerations and values. Evaluate whether the implementation process adhered to ethical principles respected the rights and dignity of stakeholders, and promoted fairness, transparency, and accountability. Consider any ethical issues that emerged during implementation and address them appropriately.

n. Engage in Continuous Improvement: Embrace a mindset of continuous improvement throughout the implementation and evaluation process. Encourage ongoing learning, adaptation, and innovation. Seek opportunities to enhance the effectiveness of actions and ensure alignment with changing circumstances or emerging priorities.

o. Communicate Results and Lessons Learned: Share the evaluation results, lessons learned, and improvements made with relevant stakeholders. Communicate the impact of the action and the steps taken to address challenges or shortcomings. Foster a culture of transparency and accountability by sharing both successes and areas for improvement.

p. Update Action Plans and Strategies: Update action plans, strategies, and decision-making processes based on the evaluation feedback. Incorporate the insights gained from the evaluation into future planning and decision-making to improve the effectiveness of actions going forward.

q. Engage in Continuous Evaluation: Implement an ongoing evaluation process to regularly assess the effectiveness of actions. Embed evaluation mechanisms into organizational practices, ensuring that evaluations are conducted at appropriate intervals to track progress and identify opportunities for improvement.

r. Embrace a Learning Culture: Foster a culture of learning, adaptability, and continuous improvement within the organization. Encourage open dialogue and collaboration to share knowledge and insights gained from the implementation and evaluation process. Emphasize the importance of learning from both successes and failures.

By following these steps, decision-makers can effectively implement actions and evaluate their effectiveness. This approach allows for continuous improvement, ensuring that actions align with objectives, values, and ethical considerations. By monitoring progress, collecting data, seeking feedback, and making necessary adjustments, decision-makers can make informed decisions, enhance performance, and achieve desired outcomes.

9. Reflect and learn: Critically evaluate the outcome and learn from the decision-making process to improve future ethical judgments.

Real-World Examples:

To grasp the complexities and challenges of ethical decision-making, examining real-world examples is essential.

a. The Example of Enron: The infamous Enron scandal serves as a reminder of the significance of ethical decision-making within organizations. Enron's leaders made unethical choices, manipulating financial records to mislead investors, employees, and regulators. The consequences were devastating, leading to bankruptcy and harming numerous stakeholders. This example highlights the importance of integrity, accountability, and transparency in decision-making processes.

b. The Trolley Problem: A classic ethical conundrum, the trolley problem poses a moral dilemma where a runaway trolley is heading towards a group of people tied to the tracks. The decision-maker is faced with the choice of either allowing the trolley to proceed, causing multiple deaths, or diverting it onto another track where a single person will be killed instead. This ethical dilemma prompts individuals to consider the ethical frameworks and weigh the value of multiple lives versus individual sanctity.

Ethical decision-making is a critical skill that individuals and organizations must cultivate to navigate the complexities of modern life. It requires a comprehensive understanding of ethical frameworks, a systematic decision-making process, and a commitment to accountability and moral responsibility. By adhering to these principles, individuals and organizations can strive for ethical excellence, ensuring that their choices align with the highest standards of integrity, fairness, and compassion.

What is Ethical Decision-making?

Ethical decision-making is the process of evaluating and choosing actions that align with ethical principles and values. It involves considering the potential consequences and impacts of different options on various stakeholders and society. Ethical decision-making requires individuals to consider fairness, honesty, integrity, and respect for the rights and well-being of others. It often involves weighing conflicting interests and making choices that prioritize ethical considerations over personal or organizational gain. Ethical decision-making frameworks, such as utilitarianism, deontology, and virtue ethics, provide guiding principles and moral criteria to help individuals navigate complex ethical dilemmas. Utilitarianism is an ethical framework that focuses on maximizing overall happiness or utility. It was first proposed by philosophers like Jeremy Bentham and John Stuart Mill in the 18th and 19th centuries. According to utilitarianism, the morality of an action is determined by its consequences.

In utilitarianism, the goal is to choose the action that brings about the greatest net benefit or happiness for the greatest number of people. Utility is often measured in terms of pleasure or well-being and is considered a desirable outcome.

Utilitarianism considers the consequences of actions and weighs the potential benefits and harms they may bring. It emphasizes the idea of impartiality and treating everyone's happiness as equally valuable. This implies that the interests and well-being of all individuals, not just one's own or a particular group, should be considered in decision-making.

Utilitarianism also recognizes that not all pleasure or happiness is of equal value. Higher-quality happiness or well-being is considered more valuable than lower-quality ones. This entails promoting long-term, sustainable happiness and considering potential unintended consequences.

However, utilitarianism has faced criticisms as well. Some argue that it may overlook the rights or dignity of individuals in pursuit of the greater good. Others question whether happiness or well-being can be objectively measured or compared across different individuals or situations.

Despite these debates, utilitarianism remains a significant ethical framework that offers a consequentialist approach to decision-making, emphasizing the overall happiness or utility produced by different actions.

Ethical frameworks and theories provide a systematic approach to understanding and evaluating ethical issues and making ethical decisions. They offer guiding principles and moral criteria that can help individuals and organizations navigate complex ethical dilemmas. Here are brief explanations of some commonly known ethical frameworks and theories:

1. Utilitarianism is an ethical framework that focuses on maximizing overall happiness or utility. It was first proposed by philosophers like Jeremy Bentham and John Stuart Mill in the 18th and 19th centuries. According to utilitarianism, the morality of an action is determined by its consequences, whereas the goal is to choose the action that brings about the greatest net benefit or happiness for the greatest number of people. Utility is often measured in terms of pleasure or well-being and is considered a desirable outcome.

Utilitarianism considers the consequences of actions and weighs the potential benefits and harms they may bring. It emphasizes the idea of impartiality and treating everyone's happiness as equally valuable. This implies that the interests and well-being of all individuals, not just one's own or a particular group, should be considered in decision-making.

Utilitarianism also recognizes that not all pleasure or happiness is of equal value. Higher-quality happiness or well-being is considered more valuable than lower-quality ones. This entails promoting long-term, sustainable happiness and considering potential unintended consequences.

However, utilitarianism has faced criticisms as well. Some argue that it may overlook the rights or dignity of individuals in pursuit of the greater good. Others question whether happiness or well-being can be objectively measured or compared across different individuals or situations.

Despite these debates, utilitarianism remains a significant ethical framework that offers a consequentialist approach to decision-making, emphasizing the overall happiness or utility produced by different actions.

2. Deontology: Deontological ethics emphasizes the importance of adherence to moral duties and principles. It asserts that certain actions are inherently right or wrong, regardless of their consequences. The theory emphasizes concepts like moral rights, duties, and obligations. Its ethical framework focuses on the inherent morality of an

action rather than its consequences. It is a non-consequentialist approach that was popularized by philosopher Immanuel Kant in the late 18th century. Deontologists believe that certain moral duties and principles are binding, guiding individuals to act ethically regardless of the outcome.

At the core of deontology is the concept of duty. According to Kant, morality is grounded in the "categorical imperative," which asserts that individuals have a moral obligation to act in a way that could be universally applied without contradiction. In other words, an action is considered ethical if it can be willed as a universal law that all rational beings should follow. For example, telling the truth is considered a duty because it can be universally applied and does not involve any contradiction.

Deontologists argue that ethical decisions should be made based on a set of universal rules and principles. These principles are meant to be objective and do not depend on individual desires or subjective preferences. For instance, the principle of respect for human dignity necessitates treating every individual as an end in themselves, not merely to an end.

Deontological ethics also emphasizes the importance of autonomy and individual rights. It posits that individuals have intrinsic value and should be treated as rational beings capable of making their own moral choices. This perspective opposes treating individuals as mere instruments for achieving certain ends.

However, deontology does present some challenges. One of the criticisms is that it can be rigid and inflexible, as it does not consider the consequences of actions. Critics argue that there may be situations where lying or breaking a rule could lead to a better outcome. Additionally, deontology can be difficult to apply in real-world contexts where conflicting duties may arise.

In essence, deontology is an ethical framework that prioritizes moral duties, principles, and the inherent morality of actions. It shifts the focus from consequences and emphasizes the importance of universal rules and obligations. While it presents challenges and criticisms, deontology provides a structured approach to ethical decision-making that appeals to those who believe in the existence of universal moral truths.

3. Virtue Ethics: Virtue ethics emphasizes the development of moral character and virtues. It focuses on being a good person rather than focusing solely on individual actions. Virtue ethics asks the question, "What kind of person should I be?" rather than "What action should I take?"

Virtue ethics is an ethical framework that emphasizes the importance of character traits and virtues in guiding ethical decision-making. Unlike consequentialist or deontological ethics, virtue ethics is concerned with the development of moral character rather than focusing solely on actions or consequences.

Virtue ethics dates to ancient Greek philosophy, with thinkers like Aristotle being central to its development. According to virtue ethics, ethical actions are the result of individuals cultivating virtuous character traits through habituation and moral education.

Instead of asking what one should do in each situation, virtue ethics asks, "What kind of person should I be?" Virtue theorists argue that by building virtuous traits such as honesty, compassion, integrity, courage, and generosity, individuals are more likely to make ethical choices consistently.

Unlike other ethical frameworks that rely on rules or principles, virtue ethics is more flexible and context dependent. The focus is on the overall moral character of an individual rather than following rigid guidelines. Virtue ethicists argue that virtues are built through habit and practice, and they provide a foundation for individuals to act ethically in various situations.

Virtue ethics also considers the importance of personal relationships and social connections. It recognizes that one's character is reflected in how one interacts with others and how one contributes to the well-being of their community or society.

Critics of virtue ethics argue that it lacks clear guidance for decision-making and can be subjective. Since virtues may differ across cultures and individuals, determining which character traits are virtuous can be challenging. Additionally, in situations of moral conflict, virtue ethics may not provide a clear answer on how to prioritize competing virtues or resolve dilemmas.

However, virtue ethics provides a valuable perspective on ethical decision-making, focusing on the development of moral character and the importance of personal virtues. It emphasizes the role of individual intention and moral development in leading a good and ethical life.4. Rights-Based Ethics: Rights-based ethics is centered around the idea that individuals possess certain fundamental rights that must be respected and protected. It emphasizes the importance of treating others with dignity and recognizing their inherent rights to autonomy, freedom, and well-being.

4. Ethical Relativism: Ethical relativism states that ethical principles and judgments are subjective and vary from person to person or from society to society. It suggests that what is morally acceptable or right can differ depending on cultural, social, or personal perspectives.

Ethical relativism is an ethical theory that asserts that ethical principles and judgments are subjective and vary across individuals, cultures, societies, and historical periods. According to ethical relativism, there are no objective or universal moral standards that apply to everyone, as moral values and beliefs are solely a product of one's cultural or personal upbringing. This theory posits that what is considered morally right or wrong is relative to the specific culture or society in which it is being evaluated. Different cultures may hold contrasting moral views on issues such as honesty, sexuality, or punishment. For instance, while a particular culture may consider homosexuality to be immoral, another culture might accept it as a normal variation of human behavior. Ethical relativism argues that neither of these views is objectively right or wrong, as they are contingent upon the cultural context.

Cultural relativism, a specific form of ethical relativism, suggests that cultural norms and practices serve as the ultimate basis for determining what is moral within a given society. It maintains that judgments about right and wrong are relative to the culture in question and should not be externally imposed or judged by individuals from outside that culture.

One of the key arguments supporting ethical relativism is that it promotes tolerance and respect for cultural diversity. By recognizing and accepting different moral viewpoints, ethical relativism advocates for a non-judgmental attitude toward cultural practices and beliefs. It acknowledges that there is no absolute or superior culture and that different societies may have valid reasons for holding their ethical beliefs.

However, ethical relativism also faces significant criticisms. One key objection is that it leads to moral skepticism, where it becomes impossible to critically evaluate or judge the actions of other individuals or cultures. If morality is entirely subjective, there is no basis for discussing or questioning the ethical practices of any society or individual. This lack of moral universality can undermine efforts to promote human rights, justice, and equality across cultures.

Another criticism of ethical relativism is its susceptibility to the "might makes right" argument. According to this view, any action or practice, no matter how morally objectionable, could be justified within a particular culture simply because it is widely accepted or endorsed by those in power. Ethical relativism does not provide a solid framework to challenge or question oppressive or unjust cultural practices.

Furthermore, ethical relativism can also lead to cultural imperialism. Since ethical relativism suggests that all moral principles are subjective and relative, it implies that there is no basis for promoting human rights or criticizing cultural practices that may violate fundamental principles of justice and equality. This position undermines our ability to address issues such as genocide, slavery, or gender inequality.

While ethical relativism may have its merits in recognizing and respecting cultural diversity, its limitations, and potential negative consequences cannot be ignored. A more nuanced approach would involve recognizing the importance of cultural context, while also acknowledging a set of universal ethical principles that can be used as a basis for dialogue, critique, and the pursuit of ethical progress. This approach allows for respectful engagement with different cultures while promoting fundamental values such as human rights, justice, and the well-being of all individuals. Utilitarianism, as an ethical framework, focuses on maximizing overall happiness or utility for the greatest number of people. While utilitarianism is often seen as a valuable approach to decision-making, it is important to consider its potential benefits and harms:

Potential Benefits of Utilitarianism

1. Promotion of General Well-being: Utilitarianism prioritizes the well-being and happiness of individuals and seeks to maximize overall utility. This may lead to actions and policies that promote the welfare of the majority, potentially improving the quality of life for many people.

2. Consideration of Consequences: Utilitarianism emphasizes considering the potential consequences of actions, considering both short-term and long-term impacts. This can lead to more thoughtful decision-making and a focus on long-term sustainability and societal welfare.

3. Impartiality and Equality: Utilitarianism aims to treat all individuals equally and considers the interests and well-being of all stakeholders. It emphasizes fairness and impartiality, ensuring that decisions are not biased towards specific individuals or groups.

4. Ethical Calculations: Utilitarianism encourages a systematic analysis of ethical dilemmas, evaluating the potential benefits and harm that various options may bring. This can provide a structured approach to decision-making and facilitate a comprehensive assessment of the ethical implications of choices.

Potential Harms of Utilitarianism

1. Sacrificing Minority Interests: In some situations, utilitarianism may prioritize the overall happiness of the majority over the well-being of minority groups. This can result in the marginalization or neglect of the interests and needs of vulnerable or underrepresented populations.

2. Difficulty in Quantifying Happiness: Measuring and comparing happiness or utility across individuals can be challenging. Assigning numerical values to subjective experiences may raise questions about the accuracy and fairness of utilitarian calculations.

3. Ignoring Individual Rights and Freedoms: Critics argue that utilitarianism may overlook the importance of individual rights and freedoms in pursuit of overall utility. Protecting individual autonomy, privacy, and rights to self-determination may be undervalued in a utilitarian framework.

4. Potential for Exploitation: Utilitarianism may be susceptible to justifying unethical actions if they are deemed to bring about the greatest overall utility. This can raise concerns about the potential for exploitation or the violation of certain ethical principles in the name of maximizing happiness.

It is essential to consider these potential benefits and harms when applying utilitarianism as an ethical framework. Utilitarianism should be accompanied by ethical reflection, critical evaluation, and a strong commitment to fairness and justice to address these concerns.

1. Ethical frameworks and theories

Examining Different Approaches to Moral Decision-Making

Ethics encompasses a vast field of study that attempts to provide guidance and principles for individuals to make morally justifiable decisions. Understanding different ethical frameworks and theories can assist individuals and societies in navigating complex dilemmas and establishing a moral compass. This essay explores various ethical frameworks, including consequentialism, deontology, virtue ethics, and care ethics. It analyzes their key principles, applications, strengths, and limitations, ultimately providing insights into their contributions to moral decision-making.

Consequentialism

Consequentialism, also known as teleological ethics, asserts that the morality of an action is determined by its consequences. This approach focuses on achieving the greatest amount of overall good or utility.

Consequentialism is a moral theory that states an action's morality is primarily determined by its outcome or consequence. This ethical framework focuses on the consequences of an action rather than the intentions behind it. According to consequentialism, an action is considered morally right if its consequences bring about more overall happiness or utility than any other alternative action. In this essay, we will explore consequentialism in detail, discussing its key features, criticisms, and various subdivisions like utilitarianism and ethical egoism.

Key Features of Consequentialism

Consequentialism can be identified by several key features that differentiate it from other ethical theories.

First, consequentialism emphasizes the importance of outcomes. According to this theory, the morality of an action is assessed by its consequences, rather than the action itself or the underlying motive. For example, if an action leads to more happiness or utility for most people, it is considered morally right, regardless of the original intention.

Second, consequentialism is committed to the idea of impartiality. It states that an individual must consider the overall consequences of an action, considering the welfare and happiness of all affected parties, rather than just their interest. This emphasis on impartiality calls for the consideration of the greater good, even if it may require personal sacrifice.

Third, consequentialism focuses on the long-term consequences of an action. It looks beyond immediate outcomes, considering the wider and lasting effects on future generations. This emphasis on long-term outcomes distinguishes consequentialism from other ethical theories that may only focus on immediate consequences or individual intentions.

Subdivisions of Consequentialism

Consequentialism encompasses several subdivisions, each with its unique principles and variations. Two of the most prominent subdivisions are utilitarianism and ethical egoism.

Utilitarianism

Utilitarianism is a consequentialist theory that places the greatest importance on maximizing overall happiness or utility. Developed by Jeremy Bentham and John Stuart Mill, utilitarianism posits that the morally right action is the one that maximizes happiness and minimizes suffering for the greatest number of people. This theory upholds the idea of the "greatest happiness principle" and advocates for the overall well-being of all sentient beings.

Utilitarianism is often associated with the concept of hedonic calculus, which is used to measure and compare the pleasure and pain resulting from different actions. By quantifying pleasure and pain, utilitarianism attempts to objectively determine the moral value of an action. Critics argue that this quantification oversimplifies complex human experiences and ignores the subjective nature of happiness and well-being.

Ethical Egoism

Ethical egoism is another subdivision of consequentialism that focuses on self-interest and personal welfare. This theory asserts that an action is morally right if it promotes one's self-interest or maximizes personal utility. Ethical egoism draws a distinction between selfishness (which only considers one's interests) and self-interest (which considers others' welfare as long as it benefits oneself).

Ethical egoism allows individuals to prioritize their well-being and aims to maximize personal happiness. Critics argue that ethical egoism lacks impartiality and fails to consider the well-being of others, leading to a society that is focused solely on self-interest, potentially resulting in harm and inequality.

Critiques of Consequentialism

While consequentialism offers a compelling ethical framework, it is not without its criticisms. These critiques challenge various aspects of consequentialism, including its emphasis on outcomes, impartiality, and the quantification of happiness.

One common criticism of consequentialism is that it may justify actions that are typically considered morally wrong. For example, consequentialism could justify lying or torturing a single individual if it ultimately results in more overall happiness or utility for the majority. Critics argue that this disregard for certain moral principles undermines consequentialism's ability to provide consistent moral guidance.

Another criticism of consequentialism is its emphasis on impartiality. Critics argue that the demand for impartiality is unrealistic and potentially unfair. They claim that individuals naturally prioritize their interests and the interests of their loved ones over strangers, making impartiality an unrealistic moral expectation.

Furthermore, some critics question the feasibility of quantifying happiness and utility. They argue that emotions, well-being, and utility are complex and subjective experiences that cannot be easily measured or compared. Attempting to assign objective values to subjective experiences oversimplifies the complexities of human nature and diminishes the true value of moral decision-making.

Alternative Ethical Theories

In response to the criticisms and challenges faced by consequentialism, alternative ethical theories have emerged that offer different perspectives on moral decision-making. Some notable alternatives include deontology, virtue ethics, and contractually.

Deontology

Deontology is an ethical theory that focuses on the inherent morality of actions rather than their consequences. Unlike consequentialism, deontology gives higher importance to duties, obligations, and moral rules. Immanuel Kant is one of the most famous proponents of deontology, arguing that individuals have certain moral duties that should guide their actions, regardless of the outcome.

Deontological ethics promotes the idea of acting out of a sense of duty rather than prioritizing the consequences of an action. Critics argue that deontological ethics can lead to rigid moral rules that may not always align with common sense or practicality. However, proponents argue that deontology is valuable in providing moral clarity and upholding certain absolute ethical principles.

Virtue Ethics

Virtue ethics is an ethical theory that emphasizes the character and virtues of an individual rather than focusing solely on their actions or consequences. This approach believes that moral actions flow from virtuous character traits and aims to nurture and promote these virtues in individuals.

Virtue ethics focuses on developing virtues such as honesty, compassion, justice, and courage. Critics argue that virtue ethics lacks clear guidelines for making moral decisions and can be subjective, depending on an individual's interpretation of what constitutes a virtue. However, proponents argue that virtue ethics provides a more holistic and comprehensive approach to ethics, emphasizing the cultivation of moral character.

Contractualism

Contractualism is an ethical theory that revolves around social contracts and agreements among individuals. It argues that moral principles can be derived from hypothetical agreements that individuals would willingly consider based on rational self-interest.

Contractualism promotes the idea that moral rules are based on mutually acceptable agreements that promote the overall well-being of society. Critics argue that contractualism is overly hypothetical and relies on subjective interpretations of what individuals would agree upon. However, proponents argue that contractualism provides a framework for moral decision-making that respects individual autonomy and societal consensus.

Consequentialism is a moral theory that assesses the morality of an action based on its consequences, rather than intentions or inherent principles. It considers the overall utility or happiness that an action brings and seeks to maximize these outcomes. Utilitarianism and ethical egoism are prominent subdivisions of consequentialism that further develop these ideas.

While consequentialism offers a comprehensive ethical framework, it is not without its criticisms. Detractors argue that consequentialism may justify actions that are traditionally considered morally wrong and question the feasibility of quantifying happiness and utility. As a result, alternative ethical theories like deontology, virtue ethics, and contractualism have emerged, offering different perspectives on moral decision-making.

In conclusion, consequentialism provides an important perspective on ethics, emphasizing the importance of outcomes and the overall well-being of society. However, it also faces significant challenges and criticisms, necessitating the exploration and development of alternative ethical theories.

Utilitarianism, a prominent consequentialist theory, popularized by philosophers such as Jeremy Bentham and John Stuart Mill, posits that actions are morally right if they maximize pleasure or happiness for the greatest number of people.

Utilitarianism heavily relies on the calculation of costs and benefits when evaluating ethical decisions. Though this framework offers a quantitative measure for assessing morality, it has been criticized for its potential to disregard individual rights and the inherent value of certain actions. Nonetheless, consequentialism's focus on promoting the greater good remains central to many modern debates surrounding topics like resource allocation, public policy, and global issues.

Summarizing Deontology

Deontological ethics is based on the belief that some actions are inherently right or wrong, regardless of the consequences they produce. Immanuel Kant's moral philosophy offers a significant deontological perspective, emphasizing the importance of moral duties and obligations. According to Kant, moral principles should be grounded in reason, and actions should be guided by universalizable maxims or categorical imperatives.

Deontology places a strong emphasis on the intention behind an action, rather than its consequences. By prioritizing principles and the inherent worth of individuals, deontologists argue for the protection of human rights and the preservation of moral integrity. However, critics argue that strict adherence to deontological principles may lead to moral rigidity or conflicts, especially when faced with complex real-world scenarios. Balancing conflicting duties and making difficult ethical judgments can challenge the practicality of deontology in moral decision-making.

Summarizing Virtue Ethics

Virtue ethics emphasizes the development of moral character and virtues. Unlike consequentialism and deontology, which focus primarily on actions, virtue ethics encourage individuals to cultivate moral virtues like honesty, compassion, or courage within themselves. Rooted in the works of ancient Greek philosophers such as Aristotle, virtue ethics highlights the importance of living a virtuous life rather than merely following ethical rules or seeking optimal outcomes.

In virtue ethics, moral actions are a natural consequence of cultivating good character, and ethical decisions are guided by personal values, integrity, and virtues. Critics argue that virtue ethics lacks clear guidelines for making moral decisions, relying more on personal judgment. However, its emphasis on characters and virtues resonates with the broader idea of long-term moral development and achieving the flourishing of humanity.

Care Ethics:

Care ethics, a relatively newer addition to ethical frameworks, focuses on the importance of relationships and interconnectedness in ethical decision-making. Care ethicists argue that moral judgments should be based on empathy, compassion, and the responsibility to care for others. Feminist scholars, such as Carol Gilligan, have heavily influenced this framework by emphasizing the historically overlooked significance of caring and nurturing relationships.

Care ethics challenges traditional ethical theories by asserting that context and relationships matter significantly when making moral judgments. While care ethics is often seen as nurturing and inclusive, it also faces criticism for its potential to be biased or overly emotional. Nevertheless, this framework's attention to the importance of care acknowledges the relational aspects of human lives and expands the ethical sphere to encompass a wider range of considerations.

Ethical frameworks and theories offer distinct approaches to morally justifiable decision-making. Consequentialism focuses on maximizing overall good, deontology emphasizes universalizable moral principles, virtue ethics highlights the importance of character development, and care ethics underscores the significance of relationships and care. Each framework has its strengths and limitations, and their applications can vary depending on the context and dilemma at hand.

Understanding these ethical frameworks equips individuals and societies with a broader perspective on moral decision-making, allowing for thoughtful analysis and critical evaluation. By recognizing the fundamental principles and underlying assumptions of each framework, individuals can navigate complex ethical dilemmas more effectively and contribute to the betterment of society. It is through these ethical frameworks and theories that we strive to uphold moral values, foster social progress, and establish a more just and compassionate world.

2. Moral reasoning and moral development

Understanding the Process of Ethical Decision-Making

Moral reasoning and moral development play crucial roles in shaping how individuals make ethical decisions. These concepts involve the cognitive processes and psychological development that individuals go through to determine right from wrong and act accordingly. This essay explores the theories of moral reasoning, including Lawrence Kohlberg's stages of moral development and Carol Gilligan's gender-based approach. It analyzes the factors influencing moral development, the progression of moral reasoning, and the implications for ethical decision-making.

Moral Reasoning

Moral reasoning refers to the cognitive process individuals use to evaluate ethical dilemmas and arrive at moral judgments. It involves analyzing the situation, considering relevant moral principles, and deciding upon a course of action. Various theories attempt to explain the stages through which moral reasoning evolves.

Lawrence Kohlberg's Stages of Moral Development

Lawrence Kohlberg's theory of Moral Development is one of the most influential theories in the field of psychology, particularly around moral psychology. Kohlberg proposed that moral reasoning develops in predictable stages, with individuals progressing from lower to higher levels of moral development.

Based on research conducted by Kohlberg, he identified six stages of moral development, which are further divided into three levels – pre-conventional, conventional, and post-conventional. The conventional level is characterized by a focus on self-interest and obedience, whereas the conventional level centers around societal norms and expectations. The post-conventional level goes beyond these societal norms and focuses on universal ethical principles and individual conscience.

At the pre-conventional level, individuals are motivated by self-interest and personal gain. In Stage 1, obedience and punishment orientation, individuals obey rules to avoid punishment. In Stage 2, instrumental and relativist orientation, individuals recognize that there is a difference between doing something wrong and getting caught, and they make decisions based on what will benefit them personally.

At the conventional level, individuals begin to internalize societal norms and values. In Stage 3, interpersonal and conformity orientation, individuals make moral judgments based on maintaining relationships and fulfilling others' expectations. In Stage 4, authority and social-order orientation, individuals focus on maintaining social order and obeying laws and authority figures.

Finally, at the post-conventional level, individuals develop their own set of universal ethical principles. In Stage 5, social contract orientation, individuals recognize that laws and rules are created by people and can be changed if they are unfair. They adhere to these rules to maintain the social contract. In Stage 6, universal ethical principles orientation, individuals have their own set of deeply held moral principles, which they apply to all situations regardless of societal norms or laws.

Kohlberg's theory of Moral Development has had a significant impact on understanding moral reasoning and behavior. It has been widely used in research, education, and even in legal and justice systems. The theory suggests that individuals hierarchically progress through the stages, with each stage building upon the previous one. However, it is important to note that not everyone reaches the highest level of moral development, as progression can be influenced by various factors such as culture, education, and personal experiences.

Critics of Kohlberg's theory argue that it is biased toward Western, individualistic cultures and does not consider cultural and contextual differences in moral reasoning. Additionally, some critics argue that the theory places too much emphasis on abstract reasoning and may overlook the role of emotions and intuition in moral decisions.

Despite these criticisms, Kohlberg's theory remains a valuable framework for understanding moral development. It provides a guide for educators, parents, and policymakers to promote moral growth in individuals. By understanding the stages of moral development, individuals can be encouraged to progress toward higher levels of moral reasoning and behavior, ultimately contributing to a more just and ethical society.

Lawrence Kohlberg, a prominent psychologist, proposed a theory of moral development that consists of six stages, grouped into three levels. The first level is the pre-conventional level, where morality is primarily based on self-interest and obedience to authority. The second level is the conventional level, where individuals adopt societal norms and rules as the basis for their moral decisions. The last level is the post-conventional level, where individuals develop their moral principles and follow them regardless of societal expectations. The theory suggests that moral reasoning evolves throughout an individual's lifespan, progressing from a self-centered perspective to a more principled and universal standpoint. However, it has been criticized for primarily focusing on Western cultures and being biased towards abstract moral reasoning. Despite these limitations, Kohlberg's theory provides a valuable framework for understanding the stages individuals pass through in moral development.

The six stages of Lawrence Kohlberg's Moral Development Theory comprised of the following:

The six stages of Lawrence Kohlberg's theory of Moral Development are as follows:

1. Stage 1: Obedience and punishment orientation - Individuals in this stage make decisions based on avoiding punishment. They focus on self-interest and obey rules to prevent negative consequences.

2. Stage 2: Instrumental and relativist orientation - Individuals in this stage recognize that doing something wrong and getting caught are not necessarily the same. They make decisions based on what will personally benefit them and may consider others' interests only to the extent that they serve their own.

3. Stage 3: Interpersonal and conformity orientation - Individuals in this stage make moral judgments based on maintaining relationships and fulfilling others' expectations. They conform to societal norms and values to be accepted by others.

4. Stage 4: Authority and social-order orientation - Individuals in this stage focus on maintaining social order, obeying laws, and respecting authority figures. They adhere to rules and regulations to avoid chaos and ensure societal stability.

5. Stage 5: Social contract orientation - Individuals in this stage recognize that laws and rules are created by people and can be changed if they are unfair. They adhere to these rules to maintain the social contract and ensure that society functions effectively.

6. Stage 6: Universal ethical principles orientation - Individuals in this highest level of moral development have their own set of deeply held moral principles that guide their decisions. They apply these principles to all situations, regardless of societal norms or laws. These principles are based on the concepts of justice, equality, and universal ethical values.

Carol Gilligan's Gender-Based Approach

Carol Gilligan's work in moral development challenged Kohlberg's theory by highlighting gender differences in moral reasoning. Gilligan argued that men primarily rely on justice-based reasoning, focusing on abstract principles and rights, while women tend to emphasize care and relationships as central to ethical decision-making. Gilligan posited that care ethics, which emphasizes empathy and compassion, is an essential component of moral reasoning that had been overlooked in traditional theories.

Gilligan's gender-based approach challenged the assumption that there is a single, universal path to moral development and provided a fresh perspective on the role of care and relationships in ethical decision-making. It acknowledged the importance of context and relationships in shaping moral reasoning and offered a more inclusive framework that underscores the significance of caring for others.

The Arguments and Challenges of Carrol Gilligan against Lawrence Kohlberg's Theory of Moral Development

Carol Gilligan's gender-based approach to moral development challenges Lawrence Kohlberg's theory by focusing on the differences in moral reasoning between males and females. Gilligan posits that Kohlberg's theory is biased towards male experiences and fails to capture the unique moral perspective of women.

Gilligan argues that women's moral development is characterized by an ethic of care, which emphasizes relationship, empathy, and responsibility toward others. Contrarily, Kohlberg's theory primarily emphasizes an ethic of justice, which is more prevalent in male moral development.

Gilligan conducted her research on women's moral development and identified three stages within her framework:

Stage 1: Orientation to individual survival - In this stage, individuals prioritize their own needs and survival. They are concerned with avoiding harm and meeting their own basic needs before considering others.

Stage 2: Focus on goodness as self-sacrifice - In this stage, individuals prioritize the needs and well-being of others. They define what is morally right based on self-sacrifice and meeting the expectations and needs of others, often neglecting their own needs in the process.

Stage 3: Morality of nonviolence - In this stage, individuals prioritize both their own needs and the needs of others. Instead of sacrificing themselves for others, they seek solutions that promote the well-being of all parties involved, emphasizing care and nonviolence.

Gilligan's gender-based approach challenges Kohlberg's theory by highlighting the importance of relational ethics and care-oriented moral reasoning. It suggests that women's moral development cannot be fully understood or evaluated using the same framework as men.

However, Gilligan's approach has its limitations and challenges. Some critics argue that her research and theory perpetuate gender stereotypes by suggesting that women are inherently more caring and relationship-focused than men. Additionally, her theory is often criticized for essentializing gender, as individuals vary greatly in their moral reasoning and development regardless of gender.

Furthermore, Gilligan's theory has faced criticism for not adequately considering intersectionality - how gender interacts with other social identities, such as race, class, and culture. It is important to recognize that individuals' moral development is influenced by various factors beyond gender alone.

Despite these challenges, Gilligan's gender-based approach has contributed to a broader understanding of moral development and sparked conversations about the importance of care ethics in moral reasoning. Her work has led to further research and scholarship in the field of moral psychology, expanding our understanding of diverse perspectives and experiences in ethical decision-making.

Factors Influencing Moral Development:

Several factors contribute to an individual's moral development, shaping their moral reasoning and ethical decision-making abilities.

Cognitive Development

Jean Piaget's theory of cognitive development suggests that moral reasoning is intimately linked to cognitive development. Piaget posits that as children go through different stages of cognitive development, their moral understanding and reasoning abilities advance. This theory emphasizes the importance of intellectual growth and the acquisition of cognitive skills in shaping moral reasoning.

Jean Piaget's theory on cognitive development is based on the idea that children actively construct their understanding of the world through a series of developmental stages. Piaget believed that children are active learners who actively interact with their environment to acquire knowledge and understanding.

Piaget's theory is founded on the following key principles:

1. Schema: According to Piaget, individuals develop mental structures called schemas, which are organized patterns of thought or knowledge that help in interpreting and understanding the world. Schemas can be flexible and adaptable, allowing individuals to assimilate new information or accommodate existing schemas to fit new information.

2. Assimilation: This process occurs when individuals incorporate new information or experiences into their existing schemas. For example, a child who has a schema for a dog may assimilate a new breed of dog into their existing schema.

3. Accommodation: Accommodation takes place when individuals modify their existing schemas to fit new information or experiences that cannot be assimilated easily. This process involves restructuring and revising the schemas to encompass the new information accurately.

4. Equilibration: Piaget believed that individuals strive for equilibrium, which is the balance between assimilation and accommodation. Equilibration occurs when individuals successfully adapt their schemas to new information and achieve a higher level of cognitive development.

5. Stages of cognitive development: Piaget proposed four major stages of cognitive development, which occur in a fixed, sequential order. These stages are the sensorimotor stage (0-2 years), the preoperational stage (2-7 years), the concrete operational stage (7-11 years), and the formal operational stage (11 years and beyond). Each stage is characterized by specific cognitive abilities and limitations.

Throughout these stages, Piaget noted important cognitive processes and milestones. For example, during the sensorimotor stage, infants develop object permanence, which is the understanding that objects continue to exist even when they are out of sight. In the preoperational stage, children acquire symbolic thinking and engage in pretend play. In the concrete operational stage, children begin to think logically about concrete objects and perform operations like conservation. Finally, in the formal operational stage, individuals develop abstract thinking, hypothetical reasoning, and can engage in advanced problem-solving.

Piaget's theory of cognitive development has had a significant impact on the field of psychology and education. It highlights the active role of learners in constructing their knowledge and understanding, and it has influenced educational practices by emphasizing the importance of hands-on learning and providing developmentally appropriate tasks and materials for children. However, it is important to note that Piaget's theory has also faced criticism, including the criticism that it may underestimate the cognitive abilities of children and overlook individual differences in developmental timing and pace.

Comparing and contrasting Cognitive Development and Moral Development

Moral development and cognitive development are distinct yet interconnected areas of human development. While they involve different aspects of a person's growth, they influence and shape each other in significant ways. Here is a comparison and contrast of moral development and cognitive development:

Comparison:

1. Sequential Stages: Both moral development and cognitive development involve progressing through sequential stages. Lawrence Kohlberg's theory of moral development and Jean Piaget's theory of cognitive development propose that individuals go through distinct stages in a specific order.

2. Influenced by Social Experiences: Both moral development and cognitive development are influenced by social interactions and experiences. Socialization, cultural norms, and societal expectations play a role in shaping an individual's moral reasoning and cognitive abilities.

3. Gradual Progression: Both moral and cognitive development are gradual processes. They do not occur abruptly but unfold over time, with individuals gradually acquiring new skills, knowledge, and abilities.

Contrast:

1. Focus and Domain: Moral development primarily focuses on the development of ethical reasoning and moral decision-making. It pertains to understanding right and wrong, moral values, and how individuals make ethical choices. On the other hand, cognitive development encompasses broader cognitive abilities, including perception, language, memory, problem-solving, and logical reasoning.

2. Theoretical Perspectives: The main theoretical frameworks of moral development and cognitive development differ. Lawrence Kohlberg's theory of moral development emphasizes the sequential stages individuals progress through, while Jean Piaget's theory of cognitive development focuses on the development of cognitive structures and abilities.

3. Nature vs. Nurture: Moral development places more emphasis on factors such as social learning, cultural influences, and role models in shaping an individual's moral reasoning. Cognitive development, in contrast, also recognizes biological maturation and the interplay between genetic and environmental factors in shaping cognitive abilities.

4. Subjectivity vs. Objectivity: Moral development involves subjective aspects, as individuals' moral reasoning can differ based on personal values, cultural backgrounds, and individual perspectives. In contrast, cognitive development tends to focus more on objective measures of cognitive abilities, such as memory capacity or problem-solving strategies.

5. Applications: Moral development theory has been applied in fields such as education, psychology, and ethics, aiming to foster moral growth and ethical behavior. Cognitive development theory has influenced educational practices in designing appropriate learning environments and curricula that match children's cognitive abilities.

Despite these contrasts, it's important to note that moral development and cognitive development are intertwined processes. Cognitive development contributes to individuals' moral reasoning abilities by providing them with the cognitive skills necessary to think about and evaluate ethical dilemmas. Moral development, on the other hand, guides individuals in applying their cognitive abilities to make moral decisions and navigate complex social situations.

Decision-Making under Uncertainty

How Managers Make their Decisions, Investigate Risks, and Handle Uncertainty in a Highly Dynamic and Unpredictable Business Environment

In today's fast-paced and unpredictable business environment, decision-making has become an increasingly complex and challenging task for managers. Uncertainty is a constant factor that managers must contend with, as they face numerous risks that can have significant implications for their organizations. This article dives into the realm of decision-making under uncertainty, exploring how managers make their decisions, investigate risks, and handle uncertainty in highly dynamic business environments.

I. Understanding Decision-Making under Uncertainty:

Decision-making under uncertainty refers to the process of selecting a course of action when the outcome and probabilities associated with various alternatives are uncertain. Managers often lack complete information and face vast amounts of ambiguity, which makes decision-making a multi-faceted task. To navigate this complexity, managers employ various decision-making models and strategies.

Decision-Making Models:

a) The Rational Model: The rational decision-making model assumes that managers act as optimal decision-makers, weighing all possible alternatives and selecting the one that maximizes expected utility. However, in highly uncertain and dynamic environments, the rational model faces limitations due to the unavailability of complete information.

b) The Satisficing Model: Herbert Simon proposed the satisficing model, which acknowledges that managers may not always make optimal decisions but instead aim to find satisfactory solutions given their limited resources and cognitive capabilities. This model allows managers to make faster decisions even in the face of uncertainty.

Decision-Making Strategies:

a) Intuitive Decision-Making: In uncertain situations with limited information, managers often rely on their intuition to make decisions. Intuition is the immediate understanding or knowing something without conscious reasoning. Managers develop intuition through experience, expertise, and pattern recognition, allowing them to quickly make decisions in dynamic environments.

b) Scenario Planning: Scenario planning is a strategy that enables managers to consider and prepare for multiple plausible future scenarios. It involves creating several future scenarios based on different assumptions, analyzing their potential implications, and developing strategies to address each scenario. This approach helps managers identify potential risks and make more informed decisions in uncertain environments.

II. Investigating Risks in Uncertain Business Environments:

Risks abound in highly dynamic and unpredictable business environments. Managers must carefully investigate these risks to understand their nature, potential impact, and likelihood of occurrence. By effectively assessing risks, managers can make informed decisions and devise suitable risk mitigation strategies.

Identifying Risks:

a. Internal Risks: Internal risks stem from within the organization and can include operational inefficiencies, inadequate resource allocation, poor company culture, or weak leadership. Identifying internal risks requires a comprehensive analysis of organizational processes, structures, and procedures.

b. External Risks: External risks arise from factors beyond an organization's control, such as economic fluctuations, political instability, regulatory changes, or natural disasters. Managers must analyze the external environment, including macroeconomic indicators, industry trends, and competitive dynamics, to identify potential risks.

Assessing Risk Impact and Likelihood:

a. Risk Impact: Managers need to assess the potential impact of identified risks on the organization's objectives, resources, and stakeholders. This assessment helps quantify the potential consequences and prioritize risks that require immediate attention or mitigation.

b. Risk Likelihood: Managers must evaluate the likelihood of each identified risk occurring and the probability of its occurrence. This evaluation incorporates historical data, industry research, expert opinions, and statistical models to estimate the likelihood of risks materializing.

Risk Mitigation Strategies:

a. Risk Avoidance: In some cases, managers may decide to avoid risks altogether by preventing situations that could lead to negative outcomes. This could involve diversifying the business, withdrawing from certain markets, or ceasing particular activities.

b. Risk Transfer: Managers can also transfer risks to external entities such as insurance companies or through contractual agreements. By transferring risks, the organization shares potential losses with other parties, reducing the impact on its resources.

c. Risk Reduction: Managers can implement strategies to reduce the likelihood or impact of risks, such as improving operational processes, implementing quality control measures, or investing in technology. These actions help mitigate the potential negative consequences of uncertain events.

III. Handling Uncertainty in Highly Dynamic Business Environments:

Uncertainty is pervasive in highly dynamic business environments, where market conditions, customer preferences, and technological advancements rapidly change. To effectively handle uncertainty, managers need to develop adaptive strategies and foster organizational resilience.

Agile Decision-Making:

Agile decision-making is a management approach that emphasizes quick decision-making cycles, frequent reassessment, and flexible adaptation to changing circumstances. This approach allows managers to respond swiftly to uncertainty by empowering employees, decentralizing decision-making, and encouraging experimentation.

Agile decision-making is a collaborative and interactive approach to making decisions in a fast-paced and uncertain environment. It is commonly used in Agile project management methodologies such as Scrum or Kanban. The main principles behind Agile decision-making are transparency, inspection, and adaptation.

Transparency is about making sure that all relevant information is available to the decision-makers. This includes sharing data, insights, and perspectives from different stakeholders. By having a clear understanding of the situation, decision-makers can make informed choices.

Inspection refers to regularly evaluating the impact of decisions. Agile decision-making encourages short feedback loops, allowing teams to quickly assess the outcomes of their decisions. This helps to identify any issues or opportunities that may arise and adjust the decision-making process accordingly.

Adaptation is the key to Agile decision-making. It recognizes that in a rapidly changing environment, decisions may need to be modified or even completely reversed. Agile teams are encouraged to be flexible and open to adjusting their decisions based on new information or changing circumstances.

Agile decision-making also emphasizes collaboration and involvement of all relevant stakeholders. It encourages cross-functional teams to come together, share their expertise, and collectively make decisions. This helps to foster a sense of ownership and accountability among team members.

In summary, Agile decision-making is a dynamic and inclusive approach that promotes transparency, inspection, and adaptation. It enables teams to make more effective and timely decisions in complex and uncertain situations.

Real-Time Data Analysis:

Keeping up with rapidly changing business environments requires managers to access and analyze real-time data. By leveraging advanced analytics tools and techniques, managers can gain insights into emerging trends, customer preferences, and market dynamics. Real-time data analysis helps managers make more informed decisions and adapt their strategies accordingly.

Real-time data analysis refers to the process of analyzing data as it is generated or received, allowing for immediate insights and actions. It involves collecting, processing, and interpreting data in real-time to make informed decisions or take immediate actions based on the analysis.

Real-time data analysis is particularly valuable in situations where timely information is crucial, such as in financial markets, cybersecurity, logistics, or customer service. It enables organizations to respond quickly to changing conditions, identify patterns or anomalies, and make data-driven decisions promptly.

The process of real-time data analysis typically involves the following steps:

1. Data collection: Real-time data is collected from various sources, such as sensors, social media feeds, transaction records, or website interactions. This data is often streamed or continuously updated.

2. Data processing: The collected data is processed and transformed into a format suitable for analysis. This may involve cleaning and filtering the data, aggregating, or summarizing it, or applying algorithms to extract relevant information.

3. Analysis and visualization: The processed data is analyzed using various techniques, such as statistical analysis, machine learning, or predictive modeling. The results are then visualized in a meaningful way, such as through dashboards or real-time reports, to facilitate understanding and decision-making.

4. Action and feedback: Based on the analysis, organizations can take immediate actions or make real-time adjustments. For example, in e-commerce, real-time data analysis can trigger personalized recommendations or adjust pricing in response to customer behavior. Feedback from these actions can also be incorporated into the analysis loop, allowing for continuous improvement.

Real-time data analysis requires robust infrastructure and technologies that can handle large volumes of data, process it quickly, and deliver insights in real-time. This may involve using technologies such as streaming data platforms, real-time analytics tools, or cloud-based solutions.

Overall, real-time data analysis enables organizations to stay agile, responsive, and proactive in their decision-making by leveraging up-to-date information and insights. It empowers businesses to make faster and more accurate decisions, optimize operations, and deliver better customer experiences.

Continuous Learning and Experimentation:

In highly uncertain environments, managers must foster a culture of continuous learning and experimentation. By promoting an environment where failures are seen as learning opportunities, managers encourage their teams to explore new ideas, test hypotheses, and adapt their approaches based on feedback and data.

Decision-making under uncertainty is a complex and challenging task for managers operating in highly dynamic and unpredictable business environments. By employing various decision-making models and strategies, investigating risks, and handling uncertainty effectively, managers can mitigate the potential negative consequences and position their organizations for success. Embracing adaptive strategies, fostering continuous learning, and leveraging real-time data analysis are essential for thriving in today's uncertain business landscape.

Cultural and Environmental Factors

Cultural values, societal norms, and environmental factors significantly influence an individual's moral development. The moral standards and beliefs taught by families, educational institutions, and religious institutions shape an individual's moral reasoning. Cultural diversity may give rise to different moral perspectives and priorities, while exposure to diverse viewpoints can broaden an individual's ethical understanding.

The Effects of Cultural and Environmental Factors on the Individual

Cultural and environmental factors play a crucial role in shaping the development and behavior of individuals. People are born into a specific culture, and the environmental factors they encounter further influence their beliefs, values, attitudes, and behaviors. In this essay, we will explore the effects of these factors on individuals, analyzing real-world examples to illustrate the diverse ways in which cultural and environmental influences impact human development.

1. Cultural Factors:

Language and Communication:

Language is a critical cultural factor that shapes an individual's communication patterns, cognitive development, and social interactions. For instance, in cultures where honorifics and formal speech are valued, individuals learn to express respect and hierarchy in their communication. Conversely, in cultures with a more egalitarian approach, language may be more informal and democratic.

Norms and Values:

Cultural norms and values define societal expectations, ethical codes, and social rules. These norms guide behavior and moral reasoning. Examples include collectivist cultures, such as many Asian societies, where the emphasis is on interdependence, cooperation, and harmony. In such cultures, decisions are often made considering the impact on the group rather than individual desires.

Gender Roles and Expectations:

Cultural factors strongly influence gender roles and expectations. In many societies, traditional gender roles assign different responsibilities and opportunities to men and women. For instance, in some cultures, women are expected to prioritize family and caregiving, while men are encouraged to pursue careers and assert leadership roles.

Religion and Spirituality:

Religion and spirituality provide a framework for understanding the world, moral values, and shaping individual behavior. Religious beliefs inform ethical decisions and guide what is considered good or bad. For example, the Islamic concept of "halal" determines what is permissible in terms of food, daily activities, and social interactions.

2. Environmental Factors:

Environmental factors that influence the individual include air quality, water quality, noise levels, light exposure, temperature, and access to green spaces. These factors can impact physical and mental health, productivity, and overall well-being. They play a crucial role in shaping an individual's lifestyle, habits, and daily routines.

Socioeconomic Status:

Socioeconomic status (SES) encompasses an individual's income, education, and occupation. It has a significant impact on various aspects of life, including access to resources, quality of education, and healthcare. Examples include children growing up in low-income neighborhoods, which often lack adequate resources and educational opportunities, leading to developmental disadvantages.

Family Background:

Family influences, including parenting styles, attachment relationships, and familial values, significantly shape an individual's development. For instance, children growing up in families with authoritative parenting, characterized by warmth, support, and clear expectations, tend to have positive outcomes in terms of self-esteem, academic achievement, and social competence.

Peer Groups and Social Interactions:

Peers and social interactions influence an individual's values, behaviors, and socialization process. For example, individuals who spend significant time with peers engaging in substance abuse may be more likely to develop addiction issues themselves. Conversely, positive peer groups can promote prosocial behaviors and provide emotional support.

Education and Schooling:

Education and schooling are vital environmental factors that shape cognitive development, knowledge acquisition, and socialization. For instance, individuals growing up in societies with strong educational systems and high literacy rates tend to have better career opportunities and improved life outcomes compared to those without access to quality education.

Examples

Cultural Influence:

Consider the example of Japanese culture, where harmony and maintaining social order, known as "wa," are highly valued. This cultural belief influences decision-making processes, leading to a focus on consensus-building and avoiding open conflicts.

Societal Expectations and Gender Roles

In India, cultural norms and expectations place a significant emphasis on the concept of "arranged marriage." This practice reflects the societal expectation that marriages should be based on compatibility between families rather than personal preferences or love.

Socioeconomic Disparities

In low-income communities in the United States, limited access to quality healthcare and nutritious food creates health disparities. This results in higher rates of chronic diseases, shorter life expectancies, and increased psychological stressors compared to individuals residing in more affluent neighborhoods.

Influence of Education:

In Finland, an emphasis on high-quality education has led to remarkable academic achievement and better educational outcomes for students. This focus on education contributes to a highly literate population, as evidenced by Finland's consistently high rankings in international education assessments.

Cultural and environmental factors are influential in shaping individual development, beliefs, values, and behaviors. The examples provided demonstrate how individuals are impacted by these factors in real-world contexts. It is vital to recognize that individuals are not passive recipients, but rather active agents who navigate and interact with their cultural and environmental surroundings. By understanding these influences, we can foster environments that promote positive growth, shape societal norms, and work towards greater equity and inclusivity.

Education and Moral Instruction

Formal and informal education play a pivotal role in moral development. Through education, individuals are exposed to moral teachings and ethical discussions that help them critically evaluate their values and understand different perspectives. Moral instruction can shape individuals' moral reasoning by providing guidance and fostering reflective thinking.

Education is a powerful tool that plays a crucial role in shaping individuals and society. It goes beyond imparting knowledge and academic skills; education also carries the responsibility of providing moral instruction. Moral instruction within the educational framework helps develop individuals who possess strong ethical values, empathy, and a sense of responsibility towards others. In this essay, we will explore why education and moral instruction are intertwined and examine the impact they have on individuals and society.

Education is often seen as the key to personal and societal development. Through education, individuals acquire knowledge, critical thinking skills, and the ability to analyze and interpret information. This provides them with the tools to navigate through life, make informed decisions, and contribute meaningfully to society. However, education is not limited to cognitive development alone. It should encompass various dimensions, including emotional and social growth. Moral instruction helps in achieving this holistic approach to education.

Moral instruction involves teaching individuals about right and wrong, ethics, values, and virtues. It encompasses imparting a sense of justice, empathy, honesty, integrity, and respect for oneself and others. This instruction is not confined to explicit lessons but permeates the entire educational experience, from the curriculum to the teaching methodologies used. Incorporating moral instruction in education develops individuals who can make ethical choices and apply empathetic reasoning in interactions. It helps them navigate complex moral dilemmas, fosters social cohesion, and cultivates a compassionate and just society.

One of the main reasons why education and moral instruction are intertwined is the role education plays in shaping value systems. Education is not neutral; it carries inherent biases and influences the formation of individual beliefs and values. By integrating moral instruction within education, we can consciously shape these values in a way that aligns with desirable ethical standards. Guiding moral values helps individuals develop a strong moral compass that guides their actions and decisions throughout life. It enables them to distinguish between right and wrong and gives them the courage to stand up for what they believe is just.

Furthermore, education and moral instruction go hand in hand in fostering social cohesion and reducing societal conflicts. Education not only provides individuals with the knowledge and skills to participate in the workforce but also equips them with the ability to engage in public discourse and contribute to democratic processes. Moral instruction helps foster a sense of citizenship, social responsibility, and respect for diversity. By ensuring that individuals are exposed to different cultures, beliefs, and perspectives, education can mitigate prejudice and promote mutual understanding and tolerance.

Moreover, addressing moral instruction in education is essential in addressing societal issues such as crime, violence, and discrimination. Education is a powerful means to empower individuals and societies to address these challenges effectively. By cultivating empathy and teaching conflict resolution skills, education can reduce aggression and promote peaceful coexistence. Moral instruction also helps create a safer environment where individuals can express themselves freely without fear of discrimination or oppression. Education provides a platform to challenge biases and stereotypes, fostering inclusivity and equal opportunities for all.

In addition to shaping individuals' behavior, education and moral instruction also contribute significantly to personal growth and well-being. Education, when combined with moral instruction, can enhance individuals' self-esteem, resilience, and emotional intelligence. It equips them with tools to navigate challenges, manage relationships effectively, and make responsible choices. By promoting self-reflection and introspection, education encourages individuals to develop a sense of purpose and meaning in life. This holistic approach to education ensures that individuals thrive not only academically but also emotionally and socially.

However, incorporating moral instruction into education is not without challenges. One of the key challenges is establishing shared values that reflect societal consensus. Different societies have different cultural, religious, and ethical perspectives. Balancing these diverse values in a way that respects pluralism without compromising fundamental ethical principles can be a complex task. Education systems must strike a delicate balance between promoting shared moral values and ensuring respect for individual beliefs and rights.

Moreover, the responsibility of moral instruction in education does not solely lie with schools and teachers. Parents, families, and communities also play a crucial role in instilling moral values and shaping individuals' character. Education should be seen as a collaborative effort between various stakeholders, with each playing their part in providing consistent moral guidance. This collaboration can help bridge any potential gaps that may arise and create a supportive environment for individuals' moral development.

In conclusion, education and moral instruction are inseparable. Integrating moral instruction within education is crucial to developing individuals who possess strong ethical values, empathy, and a sense of responsibility toward others. Education shapes individuals' value systems, fosters social cohesion, reduces conflicts, and promotes personal growth and well-being. While challenges exist in implementing moral instruction, collaboration between schools, families, and communities can ensure the successful integration of moral education into the educational system. By prioritizing moral instruction within education, we can create a society that upholds ethical standards, respects diversity, and promotes justice and compassion.

Peer Influence and Socialization

Peers and social groups can greatly impact an individual's moral development. Peer interactions, conformity pressures, and social norms influence moral reasoning and ethical decision-making. The desire for acceptance and approval from the peer group may, at times, lead individuals to prioritize social conformity over personal moral principles.

Implications for Ethical Decision-Making

Understanding the process of moral reasoning and moral development has significant implications for ethical decision-making.

Ethical decision-making is a critical aspect of our lives, influencing our personal and professional behavior, relationships, and interactions with others. The implications of ethical decision-making are far-reaching, impacting not only individuals but also organizations, society, and the overall well-being of humanity. In this essay, we will explore the implications of ethical decision-making and how it affects various spheres of life.

At the individual level, ethical decision-making has significant implications for personal growth, self-esteem, and character development. When individuals make ethical choices, they align their actions with their values, beliefs, and principles. This consistency between actions and values fosters a sense of integrity and authenticity, contributing to a strong sense of self. Ethical decision-making also requires individuals to reflect on their choices, consider the potential consequences, and weigh different ethical perspectives. This critical thinking process enhances cognitive and moral development, promoting personal growth and a deeper understanding of oneself and others.

Furthermore, ethical decision-making has profound implications for interpersonal relationships. Trust is a fundamental element in any relationship, and ethical behavior is a crucial factor in building and maintaining trust. When individuals consistently make ethical choices, they establish themselves as reliable and trustworthy individuals. Ethical decision-making also promotes fairness, empathy, and respect for others, fostering positive communication and cooperative interactions. By considering the impact of their decisions on others, individuals can create strong bonds and meaningful connections, leading to healthier and more fulfilling relationships.

Ethical decision-making is equally important within organizations and has significant implications for their culture, reputation, and long-term success. A culture of ethical decision-making within an organization promotes trust, transparency, and a positive work environment. When employees feel valued, respected, and supported in making ethical choices, they are more likely to be engaged and committed to the organization's goals and values. This, in turn, leads to increased productivity, higher employee satisfaction, and improved organizational performance.

Moreover, organizations that prioritize ethical decision-making build a strong reputation in the market. Customers, investors, and other stakeholders are increasingly concerned about the ethical conduct of the organizations they engage with. Ethical decision-making helps organizations establish themselves as trustworthy and responsible entities, attracting customers who value ethical considerations and building long-term relationships. Organizations that consistently make ethical choices also tend to be perceived as reliable and transparent, which can positively impact their brand image and market position.

Ethical decision-making also has implications for society. In a society where individuals and organizations prioritize ethical behavior, the overall well-being and prosperity of the community are enhanced. Ethical decision-making ensures fairness, justice, and equal opportunities for all members of society. It promotes social cohesion, reduces conflicts, and fosters a sense of community and shared values. By considering the broader impact of their decisions on society, individuals and organizations can contribute to a more equitable and sustainable future.

Furthermore, ethical decision-making contributes to the development of ethical leaders in various fields. Ethical leaders inspire others to make ethical choices and create a positive ethical climate within their organizations, communities, and society. They lead by example and uphold values that prioritize fairness, integrity, and the common good. Ethical leadership is crucial in navigating complex moral dilemmas, making difficult decisions, and setting an ethical standard for others to follow.

However, the implications of ethical decision-making are not without challenges. When faced with competing priorities, complexities, and pressures, individuals and organizations may find themselves in ethical dilemmas. Ethical decision-making requires individuals to navigate conflicting interests, evaluate competing ethical theories, and assess potential consequences. It demands moral courage and resilience to stand up for what is right, even in the face of opposition or personal risks.

Moreover, ethical decision-making can be influenced by various factors, such as social norms, cultural differences, and personal biases. Social norms may shape individuals' perceptions of what is ethical or acceptable behavior, potentially leading to unethical choices. Cultural differences can also impact ethical decision-making, as different cultures have diverse values, beliefs, and ethical frameworks. Personal biases, such as confirmation bias or self-interest, can cloud individuals' judgment and hinder their ability to make fully ethical decisions.

To mitigate these challenges and enhance ethical decision-making, individuals and organizations can adopt several strategies. First, fostering a culture of ethical awareness, education, and open dialogue can enhance individuals' ethical decision-making skills. Organizations can provide training programs, ethics committees, and platforms for discussion and reflection. Individuals can engage in continuous self-reflection, seeking feedback from others, and updating their understanding of ethical principles.

Second, incorporating ethical considerations into decision-making processes can help individuals and organizations systematically evaluate the moral dimensions of their choices. Tools such as ethical frameworks, decision-making models, and ethical codes can guide individuals in analyzing the potential consequences, identifying ethical conflicts, and considering alternative actions.

Third, promoting moral leadership and accountability is crucial in encouraging ethical decision-making. Organizations should select and promote leaders who embody ethical values, provide clear guidelines for ethical conduct, and hold individuals accountable for their choices. Ethical leaders should serve as role models, mentor others in ethical decision-making, and create a supportive environment for ethical behavior.

In conclusion, ethical decision-making has profound implications for individuals, relationships, organizations, and society. It contributes to personal growth, builds trust, enhances organizational culture, and fosters a sense of community. Ethical decision-making is crucial for establishing strong relationships, maintaining a positive reputation, and achieving long-term success. While challenges exist, strategies such as ethical awareness, decision-making frameworks, and moral leadership can enhance ethical decision-making and ensure that individuals and organizations contribute positively to the well-being of humanity.

Ethical Consistency and Reflective Thinking

By recognizing the stages of moral development, individuals can strive for ethical consistency and coherence in their decision-making. Engaging in reflective thinking and critically evaluating moral principles can help individuals ensure that their actions align with their ethical values.

Consideration of Context and Relationships:

Gilligan's gender-based approach highlights the importance of considering context and relationships in ethical decision-making. Recognizing the significance of caring, empathy, and interconnectedness encourages individuals to appreciate the impact of their decisions on others and incorporate these factors into their moral reasoning.

Ethical Education and Awareness

Promoting moral development through education and awareness is vital for fostering ethical decision-making. By providing individuals with the necessary knowledge, ethical frameworks, and opportunities for reflection, societies can cultivate individuals who make more informed, principled, and ethical choices.

Moral reasoning and moral development are essential components of ethical decision-making. Through stages of moral development, individuals progress in their ability to understand and evaluate ethical dilemmas. Factors such as cognitive development, cultural and environmental influences, education, and peer interactions shape an individual's moral development. Understanding these factors and the theory of moral reasoning allows individuals to apply ethical principles consistently, consider contextual factors and relationships, and make well-informed decisions. Ultimately, a deeper understanding of moral reasoning and moral development can contribute to fostering a more ethical and compassionate society.

3. Ethical principles and values

A Comprehensive Exploration of Moral Guidelines

Ethical principles and values serve as moral guidelines that shape human behavior and decision-making. They provide a framework for individuals and societies to navigate complex dilemmas, uphold moral integrity, and promote the greater good. This essay explores various ethical principles and values, including autonomy, beneficence, justice, nonmaleficence, and respect for persons. It analyzes their significance, applications, and interrelationships, ultimately highlighting the importance of adhering to these principles to maintain a just and ethical society.

Autonomy

Autonomy refers to an individual's right to make decisions freely and act according to their values and beliefs. Respecting autonomy entails recognizing and honoring the self-determination and independence of individuals. This principle is foundational to medical ethics, where doctors are required to seek informed consent from patients, respecting their right to make choices about their healthcare.

The principle of autonomy acknowledges the importance of individual rights and personal freedom. However, it is not absolute and must be balanced with other ethical principles, especially when conflicts arise. For example, the autonomy of an individual may be limited if it poses harm to others or infringes upon societal well-being. Nevertheless, autonomy remains a significant ethical principle that promotes individual agency and self-determination.

Beneficence

Beneficence refers to the ethical duty to act in the best interest of others and promote their well-being. This principle highlights the importance of doing good and actively seeking opportunities to benefit others. In healthcare, for instance, beneficence requires healthcare professionals to prioritize the welfare of their patients, providing the best possible care and ensuring their overall health and recovery.

While beneficence is a fundamental ethical principle, there may be challenges in determining what actions truly promote the well-being of others. Ethical considerations, such as cultural differences and personal values, may influence how individuals interpret and prioritize the concept of beneficence. Striking a balance between acting in the best interests of others and respecting their autonomy is crucial to actualizing the principle of beneficence.

Justice:

Justice refers to a fair and equitable distribution of resources, opportunities, and benefits within society. It encompasses elements such as fairness, impartiality, and equal treatment. The principle of justice obliges individuals and institutions to uphold fairness, ensure access to basic human rights, and address societal disparities. Inequities related to race, gender, socioeconomic status, and other factors are considered significant ethical concerns.

The concept of justice can be complex, involving various theories, such as distributive justice, which focuses on the fair allocation of resources, and social justice, which aims to address systemic inequalities. Upholding justice often requires examining the broader context and considering how individual actions and societal structures contribute to inequalities. Promoting justice entails striving for a more equitable world, where every individual has equal opportunities and access to essential resources.

Nonmaleficence:

Nonmaleficence, also known as the principle of "not harm," emphasizes the moral obligation to avoid causing harm or inflicting unnecessary suffering. It imposes a duty to prevent harm and minimize risks, aiming to ensure the well-being and safety of others. In healthcare ethics, for instance, healthcare providers are expected to prioritize the avoidance of harm to patients and mitigate any potential risks associated with their actions.

Nonmaleficence is closely related to beneficence, as both principles seek to promote well-being. However, nonmaleficence takes a more cautious approach by emphasizing the avoidance of harm, even when intending to benefit others. Balancing nonmaleficence with beneficence can be challenging, as decisions may involve inherent risks or potential conflicts between these two principles. Striving for the optimal balance ensures that actions are ethically sound and do not cause unnecessary harm.

Respect for Persons

Respect for people is a fundamental ethical principle that recognizes the inherent dignity, autonomy, and worth of all individuals. It involves treating others with dignity, valuing their perspectives, and honoring their autonomy and rights. Respecting persons requires acknowledging and upholding the equal value and intrinsic worth of all human beings, without discrimination or prejudice.

In healthcare, respect for people manifests through practices such as informed consent and confidentiality. In research ethics, it is expressed through the protection of participants' rights and ensuring their voluntary participation. Respecting persons entails actively listening to and acknowledging diverse viewpoints, promoting inclusivity, and fostering an environment that values and upholds human dignity.

Interrelationships among Ethical Principles and Values:

Ethical principles and values are interconnected and mutually reinforced. While each principle has its distinct focus, they often overlap and rely on one another to guide ethical decision-making.

For instance, upholding autonomy often requires respecting individuals' rights and treating them with dignity, which aligns with the principle of respect for persons. In promoting beneficence, respect for individuals' autonomy must also be considered to ensure that actions are in line with their values and wishes. Similarly, justice involves considering the equitable distribution of resources and opportunities, which intertwines with the principle of beneficence to ensure the well-being of others.

Ethical decision-making often requires striking a delicate balance between these principles. In complex situations, some principles may take precedence over others, depending on the context and the values at stake. Ethical dilemmas may arise when these principles seem to conflict, highlighting the importance of thoughtful consideration, ethical reflection, and open dialogue in resolving ethical challenges.

Ethical principles and values provide a moral compass to guide human behavior and decision-making. Autonomy emphasizes individual rights and personal freedom, while beneficence promotes actions that benefit others. Justice focuses on fairness and equal treatment, nonmaleficence seeks to prevent harm, and respect for persons underscores the inherent worth and dignity of all individuals. These principles are interrelated and mutually reinforcing, requiring careful balance and consideration in ethical decision-making.

By embracing and upholding these ethical principles and values, individuals and societies can strive for a more just, compassionate, and ethical world. Thoughtful engagement with these principles helps to establish a moral foundation that guides actions, promotes the well-being of all, and upholds the shared values of humanity.

4. Ethical dilemmas and conflicts

Navigating Complex Moral Challenges

Ethical dilemmas and conflicts are not uncommon in our personal and professional lives. They arise when individuals are faced with choices that involve conflicting ethical principles, values, or obligations. Navigating these complex challenges requires careful reflection, ethical reasoning, and a deep understanding of the underlying ethical principles. This essay explores the nature of ethical dilemmas and conflicts, their causes, and various approaches to resolving them. By examining real-life examples and ethical theories, we can gain insights into making informed and morally justifiable decisions.

Nature of Ethical Dilemmas:

Ethical dilemmas arise when individuals confront situations where multiple courses of action are morally justifiable, but each choice conflicts with different ethical principles or values. These dilemmas often evoke inner turmoil, as individuals grapple with the weighty responsibility of making ethically sound decisions. Ethical dilemmas can occur in various contexts, including healthcare, business, research, and personal relationships.

Ethical conflicts are situations where individuals are forced to choose between competing moral obligations or principles, often leading to tension or disagreement. These conflicts may arise due to divergent cultural norms, personal beliefs, or professional obligations.

Causes of Ethical Dilemmas and Conflicts:

1. Conflicting Ethical Principles: Ethical dilemmas and conflicts often emerge when different ethical principles, such as autonomy, beneficence, and justice, come into conflict. For example, a physician may face a dilemma when a patient's autonomy to refuse a certain treatment conflict with the principle of beneficence to provide the best possible care.

2. Cultural Differences: Cultural diversity can contribute to ethical dilemmas and conflicts when different cultural norms or values clash. What may be perceived as morally acceptable in one culture may be considered unethical in another. Bridging these cultural gaps requires sensitivity and understanding.

3. Organizational Pressures: Workplace environments may impose ethical dilemmas and conflicts when individual values clash with organizational goals or policies. For instance, a salesperson may face pressure to deceive customers to meet sales targets, conflicting with their value of honesty.

4. Conflicting Professional Obligations: Professionals in various fields, such as law, healthcare, and journalism, may face ethical conflicts when their duties to clients, patients, or the public conflict with their personal beliefs or moral compass.

5. Limited Resources: Scarce resources can lead to dilemmas where individuals must decide how to allocate resources fairly. Choices must be made while considering principles like distributive justice and promoting the greatest overall good.

Approaches to Resolving Ethical Dilemmas and Conflicts:

1. Ethical Theories and Frameworks: Utilizing ethical theories and frameworks can guide individuals in resolving ethical dilemmas and conflicts. Consequentialist theories like utilitarianism prioritize outcomes, while deontological theories like Kantian ethics emphasize adherence to moral principles. Virtue ethics focuses on personal character

and virtues, and care ethics emphasizes relationships and compassion. Applying these theories can provide a structured approach to analyzing ethical dilemmas.

2. Ethical Decision-Making Models: Ethical decision-making models, such as the Four-Component Model by James Rest or the Principle-Based Framework proposed by Beauchamp and Childress, offer step-by-step processes for analyzing ethical dilemmas. These models encourage individuals to gather relevant facts, identify ethical issues, consider possible options, and evaluate the implications of each choice based on ethical principles.

3. Reflective Thinking and Moral Reasoning: Engaging in reflective thinking and moral reasoning allows individuals to critically evaluate the ethical dimensions of a dilemma. This involves analyzing the potential consequences, considering ethical principles, consulting others, and reflecting on personal values. Engaging in ethical dialogue or seeking guidance from professionals or mentors can also help in resolving ethical dilemmas.

4. Balancing Ethical Principles: In some cases, resolving ethical dilemmas requires finding a delicate balance between conflicting ethical principles. This necessitates prioritizing certain principles based on their moral importance or considering mitigating factors. Striving for a practical compromise that minimizes harm while maximizing overall benefit can guide decision-making in challenging ethical conflicts.

5. Ethical Committees and Codes: In professional settings, ethical committees and codes of conduct provide structures and guidance for resolving ethical conflicts. These committees can help individuals navigate complex dilemmas by providing a neutral and objective perspective, considering legal and ethical standards, and ensuring the fair adjudication of conflicting interests.

Real-life Examples:

1. The Trolley Problem: One classic ethical dilemma involves a runaway trolley heading towards five people. A bystander can redirect the trolley to a different track, saving the five but diverting it to another track where one person stands. This dilemma raises questions about the ethics of sacrificing one life to save many.

2. Whistleblowing: Employees may face ethical conflicts when they witness wrongdoing within their organization. Whistleblowing raises ethical dilemmas as individuals must weigh their duty to expose unethical behavior against potential retaliation, harm to their careers, or harm to the organization they work for.

3. End-of-Life Decisions: In healthcare, ethical dilemmas often arise around end-of-life decisions. Physicians and families may encounter conflicts between upholding a patient's autonomy and ensuring the patient's best interests when considering withdrawing life-sustaining treatment.

Ethical dilemmas and conflicts are integral to human life and decision-making. These complex challenges arise when individuals are confronted with multiple morally justifiable choices that conflict with different ethical principles or values. By understanding the causes of ethical dilemmas and conflicts, engaging in ethical reasoning, and applying ethical theories and decision-making frameworks, individuals can navigate these challenges more effectively. Striving to strike a balance between conflicting principles, seeking guidance when necessary, and reflecting on personal values are key to making informed and morally justifiable decisions. By approaching ethical dilemmas and conflicts with thoughtfulness and moral integrity, individuals can contribute to a more just and ethical society.

5. Ethical decision-making models

A Comprehensive Guide to Ethical Reasoning and Action

Ethical decision-making is the process by which individuals and organizations evaluate moral dilemmas and choose appropriate courses of action. It involves considering ethical principles, values, and consequences to navigate complex ethical challenges. This essay explores the nature of ethical decision-making, the factors that influence it, and various models and frameworks for making ethical choices. By examining real-life examples and considering the limitations and challenges of ethical decision-making, we can better understand this critical process and its significance in promoting ethical behavior.

Nature of Ethical Decision-Making

Ethical decision-making is a multifaceted process that entails the evaluation of moral dilemmas, the consideration of ethical principles, and the selection of the most morally justifiable course of action. It requires individuals to reflect on their values, engage in moral reasoning, and examine the potential impacts of their choices on various stakeholders. Ethical decision-making extends beyond personal choices and applies to professional and organizational contexts as well.

Factors Influencing Ethical Decision-Making

1. Individual Factors: Personal values, beliefs, and moral development greatly influence ethical decision-making. An individual's character, experiences, cultural background, and cognitive abilities shape their perception of moral dilemmas and the way they approach ethical choices.

2. Ethical Awareness: Recognizing and acknowledging ethical dilemmas is a crucial step in ethical decision-making. Raising awareness about ethical issues, fostering ethical sensitivity, and encouraging ethical reflection enable individuals to identify and address ethical challenges more effectively.

3. Ethical Knowledge: Understanding ethical principles, codes of conduct, and relevant laws and regulations is vital for making informed and morally justifiable decisions. Ethics education and training help individuals develop the necessary knowledge and insights to navigate ethical dilemmas.

4. Organizational Culture: The culture, norms, and values of an organization significantly influence ethical decision-making. An organization that prioritizes integrity, transparency, and ethical conduct fosters an environment where ethical decision-making is valued and supported.

5. Social and Peer Influences: Social factors, such as peer pressure, social expectations, and cultural norms, can impact ethical decision-making. External influences can either assist or hinder individuals in making ethically sound choices.

Models and Frameworks for Ethical Decision-Making

1. The Four-Component Model by James Rest: This model proposes four components - moral sensitivity, moral judgment, moral motivation, and moral character - that contribute to ethical decision-making. It emphasizes the importance of recognizing moral dilemmas, evaluating alternative courses of action, and integrating moral values into decision-making processes.

2. The Principle-Based Framework by Beauchamp and Childress: This framework suggests four principles - autonomy, beneficence, nonmaleficence, and justice - as a basis for ethical decision-making in healthcare. It advocates for systematically applying these principles, considering the specific context and relevant moral considerations.

3. The Ethical Decision-Making Model by Kidder: This model proposes a nine-step approach to ethical decision-making. It encourages individuals to define the problem, gather information, identify ethical issues, propose alternative solutions, evaluate consequences, consider ethical standards, decide, implement the chosen option, and reflect on the outcome.

4. The Front-Page-of-the-Newspaper Test: This approach encourages individuals to consider how their decisions and actions would be viewed by others if they were publicized. This test provokes individuals to consider the potential reputational and ethical consequences of their choices.

Real-life Examples

1. Environmental Dilemma: A company must decide whether to continue using manufacturing processes that harm the environment or invest in eco-friendly alternatives. Ethical decision-making involves evaluating the environmental impact, potential financial implications, and long-term sustainability.

2. Whistleblowing: A whistleblower discovers evidence of unethical or illegal activities within an organization and must decide whether to report it. Ethical decision-making entails considering the potential consequences, including personal and professional risks, and evaluating the moral obligation to uphold ethical standards.

3. Allocation of Scarce Resources: During a crisis, healthcare professionals face the ethical dilemma of deciding who receives limited life-saving resources. Ethical decision-making involves balancing the principles of distributive justice, maximizing overall benefit, and treating individuals fairly in a challenging resource allocation situation.

Limitations and Challenges of Ethical Decision-Making:

1. Ethical Relativism: Ethical decision-making can be challenging due to the existence of different moral perspectives and cultural relativism. Differing ethical views may complicate the process, requiring individuals to engage in ethical dialogue and reach a consensus.

2. Cognitive Biases: Human cognitive biases, such as confirmation bias or self-serving bias, can influence ethical decision-making. These biases may hinder individuals from objectively evaluating alternative solutions and considering diverse perspectives.

3. Time Constraints and Pressure: Ethical decision-making can be compromised when individuals face time constraints, conflicting priorities, or external pressures. These factors may impact the thoroughness and thoughtfulness of the decision-making process.

4. Complex Ethical Dilemmas: Some ethical dilemmas defy easy resolution due to conflicting moral principles, ambiguous consequences, or limited information. In such situations, individuals must make the best possible decision based on the available facts and ethical reasoning.

Ethical decision-making is a complex and vital process that guides individuals and organizations in choosing morally justifiable courses of action. Consideration of personal values, ethical principles, and consequences are essential factors in ethical decision-making. Various models and frameworks guide in analyzing ethical dilemmas, evaluating options, and making informed choices. Although ethical decision-making is subject to individual biases, cultural influences, and situational challenges, fostering ethical awareness, knowledge, and an ethical organizational culture can enhance the integrity and effectiveness of ethical decision-making. By engaging in ethical reasoning, seeking diverse perspectives, and reflecting on the potential impacts of choices, individuals and organizations can navigate complex moral challenges and contribute to a more ethical and just society.

6. Ethical leadership and organizational culture

Fostering Ethical Behavior and Promoting a Culture of Integrity

Ethical leadership and organizational culture play crucial roles in shaping the ethical behavior and moral compass of individuals and organizations. Ethical leadership involves leaders who demonstrate integrity, transparency, and a commitment to ethical values, inspiring others to follow suit. Organizational culture refers to the shared beliefs, values, norms, and practices within an organization. When ethical leadership and a culture of integrity are established, they create an environment that supports ethical decision-making, promotes accountability, and enhances the overall ethical climate of the organization. This essay explores the concept of ethical leadership, the influence of organizational culture on ethical behavior, and strategies for building an ethical organizational culture.

Ethical Leadership

Ethical leadership is a style of leadership that promotes ethical behavior, upholds moral values, and establishes a foundation of integrity within an organization. Ethical leaders serve as role models, demonstrating honesty, fairness, and respect, and inspiring their followers to act ethically. Ethical leadership is characterized by transparency, inclusivity, accountability, and a commitment to the greater good.

Components of Ethical Leadership

1. Moral Purpose: Ethical leaders are guided by a strong sense of moral purpose, aligning their actions and decisions with ethical values and principles. They prioritize the well-being of stakeholders and strive for the greater good.

2. Integrity: Ethical leaders demonstrate consistency between their words and actions, maintaining high ethical standards and inspiring trust and respect among their followers. They lead by example and uphold their personal and professional values.

3. Ethical Decision-Making: Ethical leaders consider the moral implications of their decisions, relying on ethical principles and moral reasoning to guide their choices. They involve others in the decision-making process, promoting transparency and inclusivity.

4. Accountability and Responsibility: Ethical leaders take responsibility for their actions and decisions, being transparent about their intentions and outcomes. They foster a culture of accountability, encouraging others to take ownership of their behavior and acknowledging and learning from mistakes.

5. Empowering and Developing Others: Ethical leaders empower and develop their followers, nurturing their ethical awareness, skills, and decision-making capabilities. They support ethical growth and create opportunities for individuals to contribute to ethical initiatives.

The Influence of Organizational Culture on Ethical Behavior:

Organizational culture plays a vital role in shaping ethical behavior within an organization. It encompasses shared values, norms, beliefs, and practices that guide individuals' behavior and decision-making. When an ethical culture is nurtured, it creates an environment that supports and reinforces ethical behavior, encouraging individuals to act with integrity.

Components of an Ethical Organizational Culture

1. Clear Ethical Values: An ethical organizational culture establishes clear ethical values that reflect the organization's mission, vision, and desired outcomes. These values serve as guides for decision-making and behavior, demonstrating the organization's commitment to integrity.

2. Ethical Norms and Practices: An ethical culture promotes and enforces ethical norms and practices throughout the organization. These norms are manifested through policies, codes of conduct, and ethical training programs, ensuring that ethical behavior is expected and recognized.

3. Accountability and Transparency: An ethical culture involves an environment of accountability and transparency, where individuals are held responsible for their actions and decisions. Transparency encourages open communication, enables the reporting of unethical behavior, and promotes integrity throughout the organization.

4. Ethical Leadership: Ethical leadership is a crucial component of an ethical organizational culture. Leaders who model ethical behavior and promote integrity set the tone for the entire organization. Their actions and decisions align with ethical values, inspiring trust, and ethical conduct among employees.

5. Employee Engagement and Participation: An ethical culture encourages employee engagement and participation in ethical initiatives. Employees are actively involved in decision-making processes, allowing their voices to be heard, contributing to ethical discussions, and promoting a sense of ownership.

Strategies for Building an Ethical Organizational Culture:

1. Selection and Recruitment: Hiring individuals with a strong ethical orientation and values aligning with the organization's ethical culture is vital. Incorporating ethics into the selection and recruitment processes ensures that employees share the organization's ethical vision and are more likely to act with integrity.

2. Ethical Training and Education: Providing employees with ongoing ethical training and education helps develop their awareness of ethical issues, enhances their ethical decision-making skills, and reinforces the organization's ethical values. Ethics training should be integrated into regular training programs and address real-life scenarios.

3. Code of Conduct and Policies: Developing a comprehensive code of conduct and relevant policies enables the organization to communicate its expectations regarding ethical behavior. The code should be easily accessible, regularly reviewed, and periodically reinforced to ensure employee awareness and compliance.

4. Ethical Leadership Development: Providing leadership development programs that emphasize ethical leadership skills and competencies is crucial for cultivating a strong ethical organizational culture. These programs should focus on ethical decision-making, integrity, and the role of leaders in influencing ethical behavior.

5. Encouraging Ethical Communication: Fostering an environment where open and honest communication is valued contributes to an ethical culture. Encouraging the reporting of ethical concerns, providing anonymous channels for reporting, and protecting whistleblowers are essential aspects of promoting ethical communication.

Challenges and Limitations:

Building and sustaining an ethical organizational culture poses several challenges:

1. Resistance to Change: Employees may resist changing existing norms, practices, or the status quo if they perceive the changes as threatening or unfamiliar. Addressing resistance to change requires effective communication, involvement of employees in the change process, and leadership support.

2. Conflicting Priorities: Ethical dilemmas may arise when organizational goals or financial considerations conflict with ethical principles. Leaders must ensure that ethical considerations are prioritized and integrated into decision-making processes.

3. Inconsistent Behavior: Inconsistencies between espoused values and actual behavior may undermine efforts to build an ethical culture. Leaders must model ethical behavior consistently and hold others accountable for their actions to cultivate trust and integrity.

4. Cultural Dynamics: Organizations operating across different cultural contexts must navigate cultural differences

and adapt their ethical approaches to specific cultural norms and values. Striking a balance between global ethical values and local cultural nuances is crucial.

5. Pressure and Time Constraints: Excessive pressure and time constraints may compromise ethical decision-making within organizations. Creating a supportive environment that encourages ethical considerations, providing sufficient resources, and allowing time for ethical deliberation can mitigate these challenges.

Ethical leadership and an ethical organizational culture are critical components in fostering ethical behavior, integrity, and a sense of responsibility within organizations. Ethical leaders serve as role models, embodying values such as integrity, accountability, and transparency. They establish an environment that supports ethical decision-making, employee engagement, and ethical growth. Organizational culture plays a significant role in shaping ethical behavior, providing a framework of shared values, norms, and practices. By promoting values-based decision-making, transparency, and accountability, an ethical culture empowers individuals to act with integrity and contribute to the overall ethical climate of the organization. Overcoming challenges and consistently reinforcing ethical principles are essential for building and sustaining an ethical organizational culture. By prioritizing ethical leadership and nurturing an ethical culture, organizations can create a foundation for ethical behavior, trust, and long-term success.

7. Legal and regulatory aspects of ethical decision-making

Balancing Ethics and Compliance

Ethical decision-making is not solely influenced by moral principles and values; it is also shaped by legal and regulatory considerations. Organizations and individuals must navigate a complex web of laws, regulations, and industry standards to ensure their actions are both ethically and legally sound. This essay explores the legal and regulatory aspects of ethical decision-making, the importance of compliance, and strategies for integrating ethical considerations within legal frameworks.

Importance of Legal and Regulatory Considerations

1. Protection of Individuals and Society: Laws and regulations are established to protect the rights, safety, and well-being of individuals and society. Compliance with legal requirements ensures that ethical decisions prioritize the interests and welfare of all stakeholders.

2. Preserving Trust and Reputation: Acting within legal boundaries is crucial for maintaining a strong reputation. Violations of laws and regulations can damage an organization's reputation, leading to a loss of public trust, financial penalties, and other negative consequences.

3. Ensuring Fairness and Equality: Laws and regulations often aim to promote fairness, equality, and social justice. Complying with legal requirements helps organizations create a level playing field, minimize discrimination, and promote equal opportunities for all.

4. Accountability and Responsibility: Legal standards establish a framework for holding individuals and organizations accountable for their actions. Compliance ensures that ethical decision-makers take responsibility for their choices, promoting transparency and trust in the process.

Integrating Ethics and Compliance

1. Knowledge of Applicable Laws and Regulations: Ethical decision-makers must have a comprehensive understanding of relevant laws, regulations, and industry-specific frameworks. Stay updated with current legal requirements and seek legal advice when necessary to ensure compliance.

2. Ethical Decision-Making Models and Frameworks: Ethical decision-making models, such as those proposed by James Rest or Beauchamp and Childress, incorporate legal considerations into the decision-making process. These frameworks guide individuals in analyzing the ethical dimensions of a situation while also considering legal obligations.

3. Ethical Training and Education: Provide employees with regular ethical training that integrates legal and regulatory aspects. This training helps individuals understand the legal boundaries within which ethical decisions should be made and equips them with the knowledge to navigate ethical dilemmas effectively.

4. Preemptive Legal Review: Before making important decisions, conduct legal reviews to identify potential legal risks and ensure compliance. Involving legal experts in the decision-making process can help identify any legal constraints or implications.

5. Ethics and Compliance Programs: Develop and implement comprehensive ethics and compliance programs. Such programs should include clear policies, codes of conduct, and procedures that address legal and ethical obligations.

6. Establishing Reporting Mechanisms: Implement reporting mechanisms, such as hotlines or helplines, to encourage employees to report potential legal or ethical violations. These mechanisms facilitate the reporting of unethical behavior and allow for a timely response to address and rectify any issues.

Legal and Ethical Conflicts:

Ethical decision-making may at times conflict with legal requirements or regulations. In such situations, it is crucial to navigate these conflicts carefully, aiming to find a balance between legal compliance and ethical considerations. Strategies for addressing legal and ethical conflicts include:

1. Seek Legal Advice: Consult legal professionals when faced with legal and ethical conflicts to understand the legal requirements and the potential consequences of various courses of action.

2. Ethical Dialogue and Reflection: Engage in ethical dialogue within the organization to explore alternative approaches and perspectives. Reflecting on the ethical dimensions of the situation can help identify potential solutions that align with both legal and ethical considerations.

3. Lobby for Ethical Change: Advocacy and lobbying efforts may be necessary to challenge or change laws and regulations that conflict with ethical principles. Engaging with relevant stakeholders, such as policymakers, can help drive positive legal changes that align with ethical values.

4. Establish Ethical Safeguards: Establish internal procedures and safeguards that minimize the likelihood of legal and ethical conflicts arising. Involving legal and ethical experts early in decision-making processes can help ensure legal compliance while fostering ethical behavior.

Legal and regulatory considerations are integral to ethical decision-making. Complying with applicable laws and regulations is essential for protecting individuals and society, safeguarding reputation, and promoting fairness. Combining ethical decision-making models, ethical training, and legal expertise helps integrate ethical and legal considerations. When legal and ethical conflicts arise, organizations and individuals must navigate these challenges carefully, seeking legal advice, engaging in ethical dialogue, and aligning actions with ethical principles. Striking a balance between legal compliance and ethical behavior is crucial for maintaining trust, upholding social responsibility, and promoting a culture of integrity. By integrating ethical and legal considerations, organizations can navigate complex decision-making processes in a manner that is both ethically and legally sound.

Balancing Patient Autonomy, Beneficence, and Justice

Ethical decision-making in healthcare and medical ethics involves navigating complex moral dilemmas, considering the rights and well-being of patients, and balancing ethical principles such as patient autonomy, beneficence, and justice. Healthcare professionals encounter ethical challenges daily, requiring them to assess the best course of action while upholding ethical standards. This essay explores ethical decision-making in healthcare, principles of medical ethics, and real-life examples that illustrate the complexities of ethical decision-making in healthcare settings.

Principles of Medical Ethics

Medical ethics refers to the field of ethics specific to the healthcare profession. Several core principles guide ethical decision-making in healthcare:

1. Respect for Autonomy: Respecting patient autonomy entails acknowledging their right to make informed decisions about their healthcare. This principle emphasizes the importance of obtaining informed consent, promoting patient self-determination, and respecting their values, beliefs, and preferences.

2. Beneficence: The principle of beneficence requires healthcare professionals to act in the best interest of their patients, promoting their well-being and providing the most appropriate care. Beneficence involves minimizing harm, maximizing benefits, and balancing risks and benefits in treatment decisions.

3. Nonmaleficence: Nonmaleficence refers to the duty of healthcare professionals to not harm. This principle involves avoiding intentional harm, preventing harm when possible, and carefully assessing the risks and benefits of treatments or interventions to minimize potential harm.

4. Justice: The principle of justice demands fairness and equity in the distribution of healthcare resources. It requires healthcare professionals to allocate resources, treatments, and services fairly, regardless of factors such as socioeconomic status, ethnicity, or other characteristics.

Real-life Examples of Ethical Decision-Making in Healthcare:

1. End-of-Life Decision-Making: When a patient's condition is terminal, ethical dilemmas may arise concerning their end-of-life care. Healthcare professionals must navigate decisions regarding the withdrawal or continuation of life-sustaining treatments, respecting patient autonomy while considering the principles of beneficence and nonmaleficence.

2. Allocation of Limited Resources: In crises or during a public health emergency, healthcare providers may face the ethical dilemma of allocating scarce resources, such as ventilators or vaccines. Ethical decision-making involves distributing resources fairly and maximizing overall benefits while considering the principles of justice and beneficence.

3. Confidentiality and Privacy: Physicians and healthcare providers are bound by ethical obligations to maintain patient confidentiality and respect their privacy. Ethical decision-making requires balancing the need to protect patient information while ensuring the provision of appropriate care and the fulfillment of legal and professional obligations.

4. Informed Consent: Healthcare professionals must obtain informed consent from patients before providing treatment or interventions. Ethical decision-making involves ensuring patients have the necessary information to make an informed decision, respecting their autonomy, and balancing beneficence in providing necessary care.

Challenges and Limitations

1. Cultural and Religious Diversity: Healthcare professionals must navigate diverse cultural and religious beliefs that may impact treatment decisions. Ethical decision-making requires sensitivity, respect, and understanding of patients' cultural values and beliefs while adhering to ethical principles.

2. Conflict of Interest: The presence of financial, personal, or institutional conflicts of interest can compromise ethical decision-making. Healthcare professionals must identify and address potential conflicts and prioritize patient interests above any conflicting allegiances.

3. Physician-Assisted Death: Ethical dilemmas arise in jurisdictions where physician-assisted death or euthanasia is legally permissible. Healthcare professionals must navigate complex legal and ethical considerations, balancing respect for patient autonomy with the principles of nonmaleficence and justice.

4. Emerging Technologies and Genetic Testing: Advancements in technology and genetic testing present new ethical challenges. Ethical decision-making involves addressing privacy concerns, managing the potential for discrimination, and ensuring informed consent when utilizing emerging technologies and genetic information.

Ethical decision-making in healthcare and medical ethics requires healthcare professionals to navigate complex and often conflicting ethical dilemmas. Balancing the principles of patient autonomy, beneficence, and justice is crucial in ensuring ethical healthcare provision. Real-life examples highlight the challenging nature of ethical decision-making in healthcare settings, demonstrating the need to weigh patient autonomy, respect for rights, and the well-being of individuals and society. Understanding the principles of medical ethics, staying informed about legal and regulatory requirements, and engaging in ongoing ethical training can equip healthcare professionals to make informed, ethically sound decisions that prioritize patient welfare and uphold professional standards. By embracing ethical decision-making, healthcare professionals contribute to a healthcare system that values patient autonomy, promotes justice and beneficence, and fosters trust between patients and providers.

9. Ethical decision-making in business and corporate ethics

The Importance of Ethical Decision-Making in Business and Corporate Ethics

Ethical decision-making is of paramount importance in the realm of business and corporate ethics. As businesses operate within complex socioeconomic and legal frameworks, ethical decision-making ensures that organizations uphold moral standards, maintain trust among stakeholders, and contribute to a just and sustainable society. This essay explores the significance of ethical decision-making in business, its impact on stakeholders, the role of corporate culture, the benefits of ethical behavior, and strategies for promoting ethical decision-making.

1. Upholding Organizational Values and Reputation: Ethical decision-making enables organizations to uphold their stated values, maintain a positive reputation, and engender trust among stakeholders. Consistently making ethical choices reinforces an organization's commitment to its ethical principles and enhances its credibility and goodwill.

2. Stakeholder Trust and Relationships: Ethical decision-making fosters trust and strong relationships with stakeholders, including shareholders, employees, customers, and the broader community. Engaging in ethical behavior signifies an organization's respect for stakeholders, enhancing loyalty, and long-term partnerships.

3. Employee Engagement and Retention: Ethical decision-making creates a culture in which employees feel valued and respected. Employees are more likely to be engaged, committed, and motivated when they perceive that their work aligns with ethical principles. Additionally, ethical organizations are better positioned to attract and retain top talent. Employee engagement and retention are vital aspects of any successful organization.

Engaged and committed employees contribute to higher productivity, improved customer satisfaction, and overall organizational success. On the other hand, high turnover rates and disengaged employees can result in decreased productivity, increased costs, and a negative impact on organizational culture. In this article, we will explore the importance of employee engagement and retention and discuss various strategies and practices that organizations can adopt to foster a positive work environment.

Importance of Employee Engagement:

1. Increased Productivity: Engaged employees are more likely to be motivated, committed, and willing to go the extra mile to achieve organizational goals. When employees are engaged, they demonstrate higher levels of productivity, which positively impacts business outcomes.

2. Improved Customer Satisfaction: Engaged employees provide better customer service as they feel more connected to the organization's mission and values. They are more likely to understand customers' needs and offer personalized solutions, resulting in improved customer satisfaction and loyalty.

3. Higher Employee Morale: Engaged employees feel a sense of purpose and fulfillment in their work, leading to higher levels of job satisfaction and morale. This, in turn, creates a positive work environment and fosters a culture of collaboration and teamwork.

4. Enhanced Innovation and Creativity: Engaged employees are more likely to share ideas and actively participate in problem-solving and decision-making processes. Their increased commitment and enthusiasm contribute to a culture of innovation and creativity within the organization.

Strategies for Employee Engagement:

1. Effective Communication: Open and transparent communication is crucial for employee engagement. Regularly sharing organizational updates, providing feedback and recognition, and encouraging two-way communication channels can help employees feel valued and connected.

Example: Google, renowned for its employee-centric culture, encourages open and transparent communication through various channels like town hall meetings, employee surveys, and manager-employee check-ins. This allows employees to voice their opinions and concerns, leading to increased engagement and a sense of belonging.

2. Opportunities for Growth and Development: Providing opportunities for employees to learn and develop their skills not only enhances their competency but also increases their engagement and commitment. Organizations can offer training programs, mentorship opportunities, and career advancement pathways to empower employees to grow and develop within the organization.

Example: IBM, a multinational technology company, offers various learning programs, such as IBM Skills Academy and IBM Corporate Service Corps, to enhance employees' skills and capabilities. These initiatives not only contribute to the growth and development of employees but also ensure their long-term engagement and retention.

3. Recognition and Rewards: Acknowledging employees' contributions and achievements is essential for fostering a positive work environment and increasing engagement. Recognizing employees' efforts and providing rewards, such as monetary incentives, bonuses, or employee-of-the-month programs, reinforces their value and encourages continued high performance.

Example: The Ritz-Carlton, a luxury hotel chain, has a culture of recognition and appreciation. Through their "WOW Stories" program, employees can share exceptional service experiences, and individuals are recognized and rewarded for their outstanding contributions. This culture of recognition contributes to high employee engagement and retention.

4. Supportive Leadership: Strong and supportive leadership is crucial for fostering employee engagement. Leaders who communicate effectively, provide guidance, and empower employees to make decisions contribute to a positive work environment where employees feel valued and motivated.

Example: The leadership style of Reed Hastings, the CEO of Netflix, is often cited as an example of supportive leadership. Hastings promotes a culture of "freedom and responsibility" where employees are encouraged to take ownership of their work and make independent decisions. This leadership approach fosters employee engagement and innovation within the organization.

Importance of Employee Retention:

1. Cost Savings: High turnover rates can be costly for organizations due to hiring, onboarding, and training new employees. Retaining skilled employees reduces these expenses and ensures the continuity of knowledge and expertise within the organization.

2. Organizational Stability: High employee turnover can disrupt workflow, affect team dynamics, and decrease overall organizational stability. Retaining experienced employees minimizes disruptions, promotes continuity, and allows for the development of long-term relationships with clients and customers.

3. Talent Retention: In competitive industries, attracting and retaining top talent is crucial for organizational success. High employee retention rates signal a positive work environment and can attract high-quality candidates, contributing to the organization's growth and success.

Strategies for Employee Retention:

1. Competitive Compensation and Benefits: Offering competitive compensation packages and attractive benefits is essential for attracting and retaining talented employees. Organizations should conduct market research to ensure their salary and benefits packages are competitive within the industry.

Example: Google offers its employees a comprehensive benefits package, including stock options, medical and dental coverage, parental leave, and wellness programs. These benefits, in addition to competitive compensation, contribute to high employee retention rates.

2. Work-Life Balance: Providing a healthy work-life balance is crucial for employee retention. Organizations can offer flexible work arrangements, telecommuting options, and paid time off policies that prioritize the well-being of employees.

Example: Patagonia, an outdoor clothing company, is renowned for its family-friendly policies and commitment to work-life balance. Patagonia offers on-site childcare, paid parental leave, and flexible work schedules, resulting in high employee retention rates and a positive organizational culture.

3. Employee Development Opportunities: Investing in employee development not only promotes engagement but also contributes to retention. Offering opportunities for growth, such as mentoring programs, leadership training, or educational reimbursements, shows employees that they have a future within the organization.

Example: Apple encourages employee development through its Apple University program, which offers various development opportunities, including courses on leadership, management, and technical skills. This commitment to employee growth contributes to high retention rates and a culture of continuous learning.

4. Positive Organizational Culture: Creating a positive organizational culture built on trust, respect, and inclusivity is crucial for employee retention. Organizations should foster a supportive and inclusive environment where employees feel valued and have a sense of belonging.

Example: Zappos, an online shoe, and clothing retailer, has a distinct organizational culture that emphasizes customer service and employee satisfaction. Zappos offers a unique onboarding process called "The Offer," where they provide new employees with a financial bonus to leave if they feel the company is not the right fit. This commitment to hiring employees who align with the company's values results in high employee retention rates.

Employee engagement and retention are critical factors that contribute to the success and growth of organizations. Engaged employees are more productive, customer-focused, and innovative, leading to better business outcomes. Similarly, retaining skilled employees reduces costs, promotes stability, and allows for the development of a positive organizational culture. By implementing strategies that foster engagement and provide growth opportunities, organizations can create a work environment where employees feel valued, supported, and motivated, resulting in higher retention rates and a thriving organization.

5. Legal Compliance and Risk Management: Ethical decision-making ensures that organizations comply with relevant laws, regulations, and industry standards. By adhering to legal requirements and mitigating risks, businesses protect themselves from legal repercussions and potential damage to their reputation.

6. Social Responsibility and Sustainability: Ethical decision-making promotes social responsibility and contributes to sustainable practices. Organizations that consider the impact of their actions on the environment, society, and future generations demonstrate a commitment to long-term sustainability.

7. Financial Performance and Shareholder Value: Ethical behavior positively impacts financial performance and shareholder value. Ethical organizations tend to foster a positive reputation, attract investors, and mitigate financial risks associated with unethical practices.

8. Ethical Leadership and Corporate Culture: Ethical decision-making starts at the top, with ethical leaders setting an example and establishing a culture of integrity. Ethical leadership and a strong corporate culture align employees' behaviors, choices, and decision-making processes with the organization's ethical values.

9. Consumer Loyalty and Brand Reputation: Ethical decision-making enhances consumer loyalty. Customers are increasingly conscious of ethical business practices and are more likely to support companies that align with their values. Ethical behavior strengthens brand reputation and customer loyalty, leading to a competitive advantage.

10. Stakeholder Alignment: Ethical decision-making fosters alignment between the interests and expectations of different stakeholders. By considering the perspectives of various stakeholders, businesses can make decisions that balance the needs of the organization with broader social and environmental concerns. Stakeholder alignment is a crucial aspect of any successful project, business, or organization. It refers to the process of ensuring that the interests, goals, and expectations of all stakeholders are identified, understood, and managed effectively. When stakeholders are aligned, they are more likely to actively support and contribute to the project, which increases the likelihood of achieving the desired outcomes.

Here, we will explore the importance of stakeholder alignment and provide real-world examples to highlight its significance.

Benefits of Stakeholder Alignment:

1. Increased collaboration: When stakeholders are aligned, they are more willing to collaborate and work together towards achieving common goals. This collaboration ensures that projects progress smoothly and efficiently, leading to better outcomes.

Example: In the construction industry, stakeholder alignment is crucial for successful project completion. Architects, engineers, contractors, subcontractors, and clients need to work collaboratively to ensure that the project meets all specifications and requirements. When all stakeholders are aligned in terms of project expectations, timelines, and quality standards, the construction process becomes more streamlined and efficient, resulting in a successful project.

2. Reduced conflicts and misunderstandings: Stakeholder alignment helps minimize conflicts and misunderstandings that may arise due to differing expectations. When all stakeholders have a shared understanding of the project's objectives, roles, and responsibilities, the likelihood of conflicts is reduced, and effective communication is enhanced.

Example: In the healthcare industry, stakeholder alignment is crucial for ensuring the smooth operation of medical facilities. Doctors, nurses, administrators, and patients must all be aligned in terms of the patient care plan, treatment protocols, and financial considerations. When all stakeholders are on the same page, conflicts and misunderstandings are minimized, allowing for optimal patient care.

3. Improved decision-making: Stakeholder alignment enables better decision-making by ensuring that all relevant perspectives and interests are considered. When stakeholders are aligned, they are more likely to provide valuable insights and support informed decision-making, leading to better project outcomes.

Example: In the technology sector, stakeholder alignment is vital for product development. Developers, designers, marketers, and customers all need to be aligned in terms of product features, usability, and target audience. When stakeholders are aligned, they can provide valuable input and feedback, leading to better decision-making and ultimately a more successful product.

4. Enhanced stakeholder satisfaction: When stakeholders' interests and expectations are met, their satisfaction levels increase. Stakeholder alignment ensures that projects are designed and executed in a manner that addresses their needs and preferences, resulting in improved stakeholder satisfaction.

Example: In the hospitality industry, stakeholder alignment is crucial for ensuring a positive customer experience. Hotel owners, managers, staff, and guests must all be aligned in terms of service quality, cleanliness, amenities, and pricing. When all stakeholders are aligned, customers are more likely to have a satisfactory experience, leading to positive reviews, repeat business, and increased revenue.

Real-world Examples of Stakeholder Alignment:

1. Tesla and Electric Vehicle Stakeholders:

Tesla, an electric vehicle manufacturer, exemplifies stakeholder alignment by considering the interests and expectations of various stakeholders. Tesla's stakeholders include customers, investors, employees, regulatory authorities, and environmental organizations. By aligning with these stakeholders, Tesla has managed to create a unique brand image that focuses on sustainable transportation and renewable energy sources. By actively considering these stakeholders' preferences, Tesla has successfully built a customer base that values eco-friendly and technologically advanced vehicles.

2. Procter & Gamble and Sustainability:

Procter & Gamble (P&G), a consumer goods company, demonstrates stakeholder alignment through its sustainability initiatives. P&G's stakeholders include customers, employees, suppliers, and environmental organizations. In response to increasing concerns about environmental sustainability, P&G has aligned with these stakeholders to develop and implement sustainable practices throughout its supply chain. By incorporating sustainable sourcing, packaging, and manufacturing processes, P&G has gained the support and loyalty of environmentally conscious consumers, investors, and employees.

3. McDonald's and Responsible Sourcing:

McDonald's, a global fast-food chain, showcases stakeholder alignment through its responsible sourcing initiatives. McDonald's stakeholders include customers, employees, franchisees, suppliers, and animal welfare organizations. With increasing consumer demand for ethically sourced food, McDonald's has aligned with these stakeholders by implementing guidelines and auditing programs for its suppliers. By ensuring responsible sourcing of ingredients, McDonald's has successfully addressed concerns related to animal welfare, environmental sustainability, and food safety, gaining the trust and support of its stakeholders.

4. Nike and Social Responsibility:

Nike, a renowned sportswear company, demonstrates stakeholder alignment through its commitment to social responsibility. Nike's stakeholders include customers, employees, suppliers, and human rights organizations. In response to criticism regarding labor practices at its overseas factories, Nike aligned with stakeholders to develop and implement the Nike Code of Conduct, which outlines ethical standards for its suppliers' working conditions. Through stakeholder alignment, Nike has been able to improve working conditions, adhere to labor laws, and contribute positively to local communities, thus strengthening its brand reputation.

Stakeholder alignment plays a significant role in achieving project success and organizational growth. By ensuring that the interests, goals, and expectations of all stakeholders are identified, understood, and effectively managed, projects and businesses can benefit from increased collaboration, reduced conflicts, improved decision-making, and enhanced stakeholder satisfaction. Real-world examples, such as Tesla, Procter & Gamble, McDonald's, and Nike, highlight the importance of stakeholder alignment in various industries and its positive impact on business outcomes.

10. Long-Term Sustainability and Business Continuity: Ethical decision-making contributes to the long-term sustainability and continuity of businesses. By prioritizing ethical values, organizations minimize the risk of legal and reputational damage and build stronger relationships with stakeholders, ensuring their ongoing support and cooperation.

Long-term sustainability and business continuity are crucial aspects of any organization's success. Sustainable practices ensure that businesses operate in a way that is economically, socially, and environmentally responsible. This approach not only benefits the environment and society but also contributes to long-term business viability and resilience. In this article, we will explore the importance of long-term sustainability and business continuity, discuss their interdependencies, and provide strategies for organizations to achieve both.

Importance of Long-term Sustainability:

1. Environmental Protection: Long-term sustainability focuses on minimizing the negative impact on the environment by conserving resources, reducing waste, and lowering emissions. By adopting sustainable practices, organizations can contribute to environmental protection, reducing their carbon footprint and helping mitigate climate change.

2. Social Responsibility: Long-term sustainability encompasses social responsibility, addressing various societal issues such as labor rights, diversity and inclusion, and community engagement. By prioritizing social responsibility, organizations can build stronger relationships with stakeholders, enhance their reputation, and attract socially conscious customers and investors.

3. Cost Savings: Sustainable practices often lead to cost savings in the long run. Energy-efficient operations, waste reduction, and responsible resource management can result in reduced operational costs, improved efficiency, and increased profitability.

4. Future Opportunities: Embracing long-term sustainability prepares organizations for future market trends and regulatory requirements. As consumers and governments increasingly prioritize sustainability, businesses that proactively adopt sustainable practices are better positioned to seize opportunities, gain a competitive edge, and create new revenue streams.

Importance of Business Continuity:

1. Risk Mitigation: Business continuity planning involves identifying and mitigating potential risks and disruptions that could impact organizational operations. By implementing strategies to minimize risks, organizations can safeguard against unexpected events and maintain operational continuity in the face of challenges.

2. Customer Confidence: Maintaining business continuity reassures customers that products and services will be available consistently. This builds trust and confidence, leading to increased customer loyalty and long-term relationships.

3. Employee Engagement and Retention: Business continuity efforts demonstrate organizational commitment to employee well-being and job security. This can foster higher employee engagement and motivation, leading to increased productivity and employee retention.

4. Reputation Management: Organizations that effectively manage business continuity are better equipped to handle crises and maintain their reputation. How a business handles challenges and disruptions can greatly impact its image, customer perception, and stakeholder trust.

Interdependencies of Long-term Sustainability and Business Continuity:

Long-term sustainability and business continuity are closely interconnected. To achieve true sustainability, organizations must have robust business continuity plans in place, as unexpected disruptions can undermine sustainable practices. Conversely, effective business continuity planning incorporates sustainability principles, ensuring that organizational operations are resilient and aligned with long-term environmental and social goals.

1. Risk Assessment: Both long-term sustainability and business continuity planning require organizations to conduct comprehensive risk assessments. Identifying risks related to climate change, resource scarcity, regulatory changes, or supply chain disruptions helps organizations design strategies that mitigate those risks and ensure operational continuity while fostering sustainability.

2. Supply Chain Resilience: Sustainable supply chain management is essential for long-term environmental and social impact mitigation. Organizations need to assess supply chain vulnerabilities, diversify suppliers, and prioritize ethical sourcing. By doing so, they not only contribute to sustainability but also enhance business continuity by reducing dependency on single suppliers and minimizing disruptions.

Supply chain resilience is an organization's ability to anticipate, respond to, and recover from disruptions and risks in the supply chain. It involves robust planning, proactive risk management, and the ability to adapt and recover quickly when faced with challenges. In today's globalized and interconnected business environment, building supply chain resilience has become essential for organizations to ensure continuity of operations, minimize disruptions, and maintain customer satisfaction. In this article, we will explore the importance of supply chain resilience, discuss its key elements, and provide strategies for organizations to enhance their supply chain resilience.

Importance of Supply Chain Resilience:

1. Minimizing Disruptions: Disruptions in the supply chain can arise from various sources, such as natural disasters, geopolitical events, economic downturns, pandemics, or cyber-attacks. These disruptions can cause delays, shortages, increased costs, and reputational damage. By building supply chain resilience, organizations can minimize the impact of such disruptions and ensure continuity of operations.

2. Sustaining Customer Satisfaction: Supply chain disruptions can result in delays in product availability, inferior quality, or poor customer service. These issues can jeopardize customer satisfaction and loyalty, leading to potential revenue loss. A resilient supply chain enables organizations to meet customer demands in a timely and efficient manner, enhancing customer satisfaction and maintaining strong relationships.

3. Managing Risk: Building supply chain resilience involves identifying, assessing, and managing risks throughout the supply chain. Organizations that proactively manage risks are better prepared to mitigate potential disruptions and minimize the associated impacts. This allows for better risk management and protection of the organization's reputation and financial performance.

4. Adapting to Changing Business Environment: The business environment is dynamic, with evolving customer demands, technology advancements, and regulatory changes. A resilient supply chain enables organizations to quickly adapt and respond to these changes, ensuring competitiveness and sustainable growth.

Key Elements of Supply Chain Resilience:

1. Risk Management: Effective risk management is a critical element of supply chain resilience. This involves assessing and prioritizing risks, developing contingency plans, and implementing proactive measures to mitigate potential disruptions. Organizations should conduct comprehensive risk assessments, identify critical vulnerabilities, and develop strategies to manage and mitigate these risks.

2. Redundancy and Flexibility: Building redundancy and flexibility into the supply chain allows organizations to respond to disruptions by utilizing alternative suppliers, production facilities, transportation modes, or inventory locations. This diversification minimizes reliance on a single source and increases the ability to adapt to unexpected changes in the business environment.

3. Collaboration and Transparency: Collaboration and transparency are essential for building supply chain resilience. Organizations should establish strong relationships with key suppliers, customers, and other stakeholders to foster open communication, information sharing, and joint problem-solving. This collaboration allows for better visibility into potential risks and enables timely response and recovery.

4. Technology and Data Analytics: Leveraging technology and data analytics can enhance supply chain visibility, efficiency, and decision-making. Utilizing tools such as real-time tracking, predictive analytics, and supply chain management systems allows organizations to identify potential disruptions, monitor inventory levels, and optimize operations. This data-driven approach enables proactive decision-making and timely response to potential disruptions.

Strategies to Enhance Supply Chain Resilience:

1. Risk Mapping and Assessment: Conduct a comprehensive risk mapping exercise to identify potential risks and vulnerabilities. Assess the impact and likelihood of each risk and prioritize them based on their potential impact on the supply chain. Develop contingency plans and mitigation strategies to address these risks effectively.

2. Supplier Management: Establish strong relationships with key suppliers and conduct regular assessments to evaluate their financial stability, production capacity, and risk management capabilities. Maintain alternative suppliers or dual-sourcing strategies to overcome disruptions in the supply chain. Develop clear communication channels and contingency plans to address any potential issues with suppliers.

3. Demand Forecasting and Inventory Management: Accurate demand forecasting is essential for preventing stockouts or excess inventory. Use collaborative forecasting techniques and advanced analytics to gain visibility into demand patterns. Optimize inventory levels to balance customer satisfaction and cost considerations. Implement just-in-time or vendor-managed inventory systems to minimize excess inventory and maximize responsiveness.

4. Technology Adoption: Leverage technology solutions to enhance supply chain resilience. Implement supply chain management systems and visibility tools to gain real-time insights into operations, track shipments, and identify potential disruptions. Adopt advanced analytics and machine learning capabilities to forecast demand, optimize inventory levels, and identify potential risks.

5. Supply Chain Collaboration: Foster collaboration with key stakeholders, including suppliers, customers, logistics providers, and regulatory authorities. Establish regular communication channels, and share information on demand forecasts, production plans, and potential disruptions. Identify opportunities for joint problem-solving and develop contingency plans together.

6. Scenario Planning and Simulation: Conduct scenario planning exercises to evaluate potential risks and assess the impact on the supply chain. Simulate different scenarios to test the effectiveness of contingency plans and identify areas for improvement. Regularly update these plans based on changing business conditions and collaborate with stakeholders to ensure alignment and readiness.

7. Continuous Improvement and Learning: Establish a culture of continuous improvement and learning within the organization. Conduct post-incident reviews to identify lessons learned from disruptions and incorporate those learnings into future risk management strategies. Encourage employees to share best practices and innovative ideas to enhance supply chain resilience.

Building supply chain resilience is a critical aspect of organizational success in today's dynamic and interconnected business environment. Organizations that prioritize supply chain resilience are better equipped to address disruptions, adapt to changing market conditions, and maintain customer satisfaction. By focusing on risk management, collaboration, technology adoption, and continuous improvement, organizations can enhance their supply chain resilience and ensure the continuity of operations, minimize disruptions, and drive long-term business success.

8. Stakeholder Engagement: Meaningful engagement with stakeholders is crucial for both sustainability and business continuity. Engaging with customers, employees, suppliers, local communities, and government bodies helps incorporate diverse perspectives and gain support for sustainability efforts. Additionally, effective stakeholder communication enhances business resilience, ensuring all relevant parties are informed and involved in continuity planning.

9. Technology and Innovation: Technology and innovation play a vital role in achieving both long-term sustainability and business continuity. Sustainable technologies and practices can drive operational efficiency, reduce waste, and lower costs. Similarly, adopting innovative technologies and digital tools can enhance business continuity by enabling remote work capabilities, data backup systems, and effective crisis communication.

Strategies for Long-term Sustainability and Business Continuity:

1. Develop a Sustainability Strategy: Organizations should create a clear and comprehensive sustainability strategy that outlines long-term objectives, targets, and action plans. This strategy should consider environmental, social, and economic aspects, addressing resource efficiency, waste reduction, employee well-being, social responsibility, and community engagement.

2. Conduct Risk Assessments: Regularly assess risks and vulnerabilities related to sustainability and business continuity. This can include climate change impacts, regulatory changes, supply chain disruptions, natural disasters, cybersecurity threats, and pandemics. Develop strategies and contingency plans to mitigate these risks and ensure operational continuity.

3. Foster a Culture of Sustainability: Embed sustainability principles within the organizational culture. Promote awareness and education on sustainable practices, encourage employee engagement, and empower employees to contribute to sustainability initiatives. Incorporate sustainability into performance metrics, ensuring that sustainable practices are recognized and rewarded.

4. Invest in Resilient Infrastructure and Technology: Allocate resources to enhance operational resilience and efficiency. This can involve upgrading infrastructure, implementing energy-efficient technologies, adopting renewable energy sources, and implementing robust data backup and cybersecurity measures. Investing in these areas not only improves sustainability but also provides the infrastructure needed for business continuity.

5. Collaborate and Engage with Stakeholders: Engage with stakeholders to align sustainability and business continuity objectives. Collaborate with suppliers to ensure responsible sourcing and contingency plans. Engage with customers and local communities to understand their expectations and incorporate their feedback into sustainability efforts and business continuity plans.

6. Continually Monitor and Adapt: Regularly monitor progress towards sustainability goals. Collect and analyze data on resource consumption, waste generation, and emissions to identify opportunities for improvement. Similarly, assess the effectiveness of business continuity strategies through simulations, drills, and post-incident evaluations. Continually adapt strategies based on new information, emerging risks, and changing stakeholder expectations.

Long-term sustainability and business continuity are intertwined imperatives for organizations in the modern world. By adopting sustainable practices, organizations can contribute to environmental protection, social responsibility, and cost savings while positioning themselves for future opportunities. Simultaneously, effective business continuity planning ensures operational resilience, mitigates risks, and safeguards reputation. The interdependencies between long-term sustainability and business continuity require organizations to align strategies, engage stakeholders, invest in resilient infrastructure, and foster a culture of sustainability and preparedness. Organizations that successfully integrate sustainability and business continuity set themselves up for long-term success, resilience, and responsible growth.

Strategies for Promoting Ethical Decision-Making

1. Ethical Leadership: Cultivate ethical leadership at all levels of the organization. Ethical leaders set the tone, model ethical behavior, and guide employees, creating a culture of integrity.

2. Establish Ethical Codes and Policies: Develop and implement ethical codes of conduct and policies that outline expected behaviors and provide guidance for decision-making in various contexts.

3. Ethics Training and Education: Provide regular ethics training and education to all employees. This training should enhance ethical awareness, equip employees with ethical decision-making tools, and address real-life ethical dilemmas.

4. Ethical Decision-Making Models: Utilize ethical decision-making models, such as Rest's Four-Component Model or the Principle-Based Framework, to provide employees with a structured approach to analyzing ethical dilemmas and making informed choices.

5. Open Communication and Transparency: Foster an environment that encourages open communication, where employees can freely voice ethical concerns and seek guidance without fear of retaliation. Promote transparency in decision-making processes and communicate the ethical rationale behind organizational decisions.

6. Ethical Risk Assessment: Conduct regular ethical risk assessments to identify potential ethical challenges and develop strategies to address them. Identify areas where ethical dilemmas are likely to arise and proactively implement measures to mitigate risks.

7. Accountability and Reporting Mechanisms: Establish mechanisms for employees to report unethical behavior confidentially. Ensure that these mechanisms protect whistleblowers and enable timely resolution of reported concerns.

8. Supplier and Partner Selection: Consider ethical factors when selecting suppliers and partners. Collaborate with ethically aligned businesses to ensure that ethical standards extend beyond the organization's internal operations.

9. Regular Ethical Audits: Conduct regular ethical audits to assess the organization's compliance with ethical standards, identify areas of improvement, and reinforce ethical decision-making practices.

10. Continuous Improvement and Learning: Foster a culture of continuous learning and improvement in ethical decision-making. Encourage employees to reflect on past decisions, learn from mistakes, and continually refine ethical practices.

Ethical decision-making is integral to the success, reputation, and sustainability of businesses. By making ethical choices, organizations uphold their values, maintain stakeholder trust, mitigate risks, and contribute to a just and sustainable society. Ethical decision-making promotes a positive corporate culture, enhances employee engagement, and aligns stakeholder interests. Strategies such as ethical leadership, education and training, open communication, and accountability mechanisms support the development of an ethical business environment. By prioritizing ethical decision-making, businesses can position themselves as responsible corporate citizens, drive sustainable growth, and contribute to the betterment of society.

10. Ethical decision-making in technology and artificial intelligence

As technology and artificial intelligence (AI) continue to shape various aspects of our lives, it is crucial to consider the ethical implications associated with their development, implementation, and use. Ethical decision-making in technology and AI involves navigating complex issues such as privacy, bias, transparency, accountability, and the potential impact on society. This essay explores the importance of ethical decision-making in these domains, the need for responsible AI, the role of industry and government, and strategies for promoting ethical practices in technology and AI.

1. Mitigating Bias and Discrimination: Ethical decision-making in technology and AI involves recognizing and addressing bias and discrimination. Algorithms and AI systems can unintentionally perpetuate biased outcomes, such as discriminatory hiring practices or biased facial recognition. Ethical considerations demand the development of algorithms that are fair, unbiased, and inclusive.

2. Protecting Privacy and Data Security: Ethical decision-making in technology ensures the protection of privacy and data security. As technological advancements enable easy collection and analysis of personal data, it is essential to establish robust security measures and respect individuals' privacy rights. Ethical frameworks guide organizations in handling data responsibly and transparently.

3. Ensuring Transparency and Explainability: Ethical decision-making in technology and AI emphasizes the need for transparency and explainability. Users should understand how algorithms and AI systems make decisions and the criteria involved. Transparent practices enable users to hold technology providers accountable and build trust in the technology.

4. Promoting Human-Centered Design: Ethical decision-making in technology prioritizes human needs, values, and well-being. Designing technology and AI systems with a human-centered approach ensures that they augment human abilities, promote inclusivity, and serve the best interests of individuals and society.

5. Minimizing Unintended Consequences: Ethical decision-making requires considering the potential unintended consequences of technology and AI. Measures should be taken to minimize these risks, including unintended job displacement, social inequality, and technological dependence. Ethical frameworks promote proactive assessment and mitigation strategies to address these concerns.

6. Industry Responsibility and Self-Regulation: Ethical decision-making in technology calls upon industry leaders to take responsibility for the ethical use and development of technology and AI. Self-regulation initiatives that establish ethical guidelines, codes of conduct, and industry standards can help ensure responsible practices and build public trust.

7. Government Regulation and Accountability: Ethical decision-making in technology also requires governments to play a role in ensuring accountability and responsible AI practices. Governments can develop regulations and policies that promote transparency, protect individual rights, and hold organizations accountable for unethical uses of technology and AI.

8. Ethical AI Design and Development: Organizations should integrate ethical considerations throughout the entire AI design and development process. Ethical guidelines and impact assessments should be incorporated from the early stages to identify and address potential ethical challenges before deploying AI systems.

9. Continuous Monitoring and Evaluation: Ethical decision-making requires ongoing monitoring and evaluation of technology and AI systems. This entails regular assessments to identify any ethical concerns that may arise during their use. Organizations should commit to addressing these concerns promptly and transparently.

10. Multi-Stakeholder Collaboration: Ethical decision-making in technology necessitates collaboration among multiple stakeholders including industry, government, academia, and civil society. Engaging diverse perspectives and expertise fosters a more comprehensive understanding of ethical challenges and enables the development of holistic solutions.

Ethical decision-making is of utmost importance in technology and AI due to their potential impact on individuals, society, and the broader ethical landscape. By recognizing and addressing issues such as bias, privacy, transparency, and unintended consequences, ethical practices can enhance the trustworthy and responsible development and use of technology and AI. It is the collective responsibility of industry, government, and other stakeholders to promote ethical decision-making, establish regulations when necessary, and foster a culture of ethical practices in the technology sector. Through responsible AI, we can harness the full potential of technology while safeguarding human rights, promoting equality, and ensuring the well-being of individuals and society.

Ethical decision-making in environmental sustainability

11. Ethical decision-making in research and scientific ethics

Protecting Participants, Ensuring Integrity

Ethical decision-making in research and scientific ethics is essential to protect the rights, well-being, and dignity of research participants and maintain the integrity of the scientific process. It involves adhering to a set of ethical principles and guidelines in conducting research, ensuring informed consent, safeguarding participant confidentiality, and promoting responsible research practices. This essay explores the importance of ethical decision-making in research, the role of research ethics committees, key ethical considerations, challenges and dilemmas in research ethics, and strategies for promoting ethical conduct in the scientific community.

The Importance of Ethical Decision-Making in Research:

1. Protection of Research Participants: Ethical decision-making is crucial to protect the rights and well-being of research participants. By following ethical guidelines, researchers minimize the risk of harm, ensure informed consent, and maintain participant confidentiality.

2. Integrity of the Scientific Process: Ethical decision-making maintains the integrity of the scientific process. It ensures that research is conducted with rigor, transparency, and intellectual honesty, fostering public trust in the scientific community.

3. Compliance with Regulatory Requirements: Ethical decision-making ensures compliance with legal and regulatory requirements governing research. Researchers must adhere to laws and regulations that protect participants' rights, such as privacy laws and guidelines regarding the use of human subjects.

4. Responsible Conduct of Research: Ethical decision-making promotes responsible conduct in research, including transparent reporting of methods, data, and results, as well as the avoidance of scientific misconduct such as plagiarism or fabrication. Ethical practices are essential for maintaining scientific integrity and credibility.

The Role of Research Ethics Committees

Research ethics committees, also known as institutional review boards (IRBs), play a critical role in promoting ethical decision-making in research. The functions of research ethics committees include:

1. Reviewing Research Protocols: Ethics committees assess research proposals to ensure they meet ethical standards and protect research participants. They evaluate research design, participant recruitment methods, privacy safeguards, and informed consent procedures.

2. Providing Guidance and Recommendations: Ethics committees guide researchers on ethical considerations, ways to minimize risks, and strengthen the ethical dimensions of their research. They offer recommendations to address any ethical issues identified during the review process.

3. Balancing Ethical Considerations: Ethics committees balance the potential benefits of the research against the potential risks and ethical concerns. They consider the importance of the research question and the potential impact on participants to make informed decisions about research approval.

4. Ongoing Monitoring: Ethics committees frequently monitor ongoing research to ensure compliance with ethical standards. They may conduct periodic audits or reviews of research progress and can suspend or terminate studies if ethical concerns arise.

Key Ethical Considerations in Research:

1. Informed Consent: Obtaining informed consent from research participants is a fundamental ethical requirement. Researchers must provide clear and comprehensive explanations of the research purpose, procedures, potential risks, and benefits to enable participants to make autonomous decisions about participation.

2. Confidentiality and Privacy: Researchers have a responsibility to safeguard participant data and ensure confidentiality. Guidelines should be in place to protect participant privacy, limit access to identifiable information, and maintain data security throughout the research process.

3. Minimizing Harm and Risks: Ethical decision-making involves minimizing harm and risks associated with research participation. Researchers must assess and mitigate potential physical, psychological, social, and economic risks to participants.

4. Avoiding Coercion and Exploitation: Researchers must ensure that participation in research is voluntary and free from coercion or undue influence. They should avoid situations where vulnerable populations may be exploited, ensuring fair recruitment and equitable access to research benefits.

5. Research Integrity and Conflict of Interest: Ethical decision-making requires researchers to conduct their work with integrity and to disclose any conflicts of interest that may influence the research process or results. Transparency and accountability are crucial to maintain scientific integrity.

Challenges and Dilemmas in Research Ethics:

1. Balancing Risk and Benefit: Ethical decision-making involves balancing potential risks to participants against potential benefits to society. Researchers must make judgments about acceptable levels of risk and weigh these against the potential value of research outcomes.

2. Cultural and International Variations: Ethical considerations may vary across cultures and countries due to differences in norms, values, and legal requirements. Researchers must navigate these variations when conducting international or cross-cultural research.

3. Informed Consent with Vulnerable Populations: Obtaining informed consent can be challenging when working with vulnerable populations, such as children, individuals with cognitive impairments, or marginalized communities. Extra precautions must be taken to ensure understanding and protect their rights.

4. Emerging Technologies and Big Data: Ethical decision-making is challenged by emerging technologies, such as artificial intelligence and big data analytics. Researchers must address concerns related to privacy, data protection, and potential biases embedded in these technologies.

Promoting Ethical Conduct in the Scientific Community:

1. Education and Training: Incorporate research ethics training into academic curricula and provide ongoing education to researchers. Foster discussions about ethical considerations, dilemmas, and best practices within the scientific community.

2. Ethical Guidelines and Standards: Develop and disseminate ethical guidelines that outline best practices for research ethics. These guidelines should address specific issues, such as informed consent, data protection, authorship, and conflicts of interest.

3. Cross-Disciplinary Collaboration: Foster collaboration and dialogue among researchers, ethicists, and other relevant stakeholders to promote responsible and ethical research conduct. Engaging in ethical debates can help establish common ethical standards and facilitate learning from diverse perspectives.

4. Peer Review: Establish rigorous peer review processes that include ethical dimensions. Peer reviewers should assess whether studies were conducted ethically, with attention to informed consent, data integrity, study design, and participant protection.

5. Research Ethics Consultation: Provide researchers with access to research ethics consultation services, where they can seek guidance and support in addressing complex ethical challenges that may arise during their research.

Ethical decision-making is vital in research and scientific ethics to protect participants, maintain the integrity of the scientific process, and ensure responsible conduct. Research ethics committees play a crucial role in guiding ethical decision-making and promoting compliance with ethical standards. Key considerations in research ethics include informed consent, confidentiality, minimizing harm, and avoiding exploitation. Challenges may arise in balancing risks and benefits, navigating cultural variations, and addressing emerging technologies. Strategies to promote ethical conduct in research include education and training, the development of ethical guidelines, and fostering cross-disciplinary collaboration. By upholding ethical principles, the scientific community can ensure that research contributes positively to society while respecting the rights and well-being of participants.

12. Ethical decision-making in journalism and media ethics

Navigating the Complexities of Truth, Sensationalism, and Public Interest.

Ethical decision-making in journalism and media ethics is vital to uphold the principles of truth, accuracy, fairness, and transparency in the dissemination of information. Journalists play a crucial role as watchdogs, providing the public with reliable and unbiased news. However, the emergence of digital media, clickbait culture, and the pressure to attract audiences have presented challenges for ethical decision-making. This essay explores the importance of ethical decision-making in journalism, key ethical considerations in media ethics, challenges and dilemmas faced by journalists, and strategies to promote ethical conduct in the media industry.

The Importance of Ethical Decision-Making in Journalism:

1. Preserving Public Trust: Ethical decision-making in journalism is crucial to maintaining public trust in the media. By adhering to ethical guidelines, journalists ensure the accuracy and reliability of news reporting, giving the audience confidence in the information they consume.

2. Safeguarding Democracy: Ethical decision-making in journalism is essential for a functioning democracy. Journalists provide the public with important information about government actions, public policies, and societal issues. Their ethical conduct ensures that citizens are well-informed, enabling them to make informed decisions in democratic processes.

3. Protecting Individuals' Rights: Ethical decision-making in journalism respects individuals' rights to privacy, dignity, and fair representation. Journalists must navigate the delicate balance between freedom of expression and the potential harm caused by invading personal privacy or reporting false or misleading information.

4. Promoting Diversity and Inclusion: Ethical decision-making in journalism promotes diversity and inclusion by ensuring fair representation of diverse voices and viewpoints. Journalists have a responsibility to avoid stereotyping, bias, and discriminatory reporting.

Key Ethical Considerations in Media Ethics:

1. Truth and Accuracy: Ethical decision-making in journalism requires journalists to seek and report the truth. Journalists must strive for accuracy, verify sources, fact-check information, and correct errors promptly to maintain credibility.

2. Fairness and Impartiality: Ethical decision-making necessitates fair and impartial reporting. Journalists should seek multiple perspectives, provide balanced coverage, and avoid favoritism or bias, especially in politically or emotionally charged topics.

3. Privacy and Sensationalism: Respecting individuals' privacy is an ethical imperative in journalism. Journalists should obtain consent when reporting personal information, refrain from harassing or intrusive tactics, and avoid exploiting personal tragedies for sensationalism or clickbait.

4. Conflict of Interest and Independence: Ethical decision-making demands that journalists avoid conflicts of interest that could compromise their independence and objectivity. Journalists should disclose potential conflicts of interest, such as financial or personal relationships, that could influence their reporting.

5. Editorial Independence and Corporate Influence: Journalists must navigate the tension between editorial independence and corporate influence. Ethical decision-making requires journalists to resist undue interference from media owners and advertisers, ensuring the integrity of their reporting.

Challenges and Dilemmas in Journalism and Media Ethics:

1. Digital Media and Misinformation: The rise of social media and the internet presents challenges to journalistic ethics. Journalists must combat the spread of misinformation, distinguish between reliable sources and fake news, and resist the pressure for click-driven reporting.

2. Breaking News and Rush to Publish: Journalists often face the dilemma of reporting breaking news in real-time while maintaining accuracy and verification. Ethical decision-making requires taking the time to verify information before publishing, even in a fast-paced news environment.

3. Sensationalism and Audience Appeal: The pursuit of high audience ratings or web traffic can lead to sensationalism, clickbait, and trivialization of news stories. Journalists must balance the desire for audience engagement with the responsibility to provide substantive and balanced reporting.

4. Conflicts between Public Interest and Privacy: Ethical decision-making often involves balancing the public's right to information against an individual's right to privacy. Journalists must carefully evaluate whether disclosing certain information outweighs the potential harm it may cause to the individuals involved.

Promoting Ethical Conduct in Journalism

1. Training and Education: Incorporate ethics training into journalism education, emphasizing the importance of ethical decision-making. Journalists should be equipped with the skills to navigate ethical challenges and dilemmas, and news organizations should provide ongoing training to their employees.

2. Ethical Guidelines and Standards: Develop and disseminate ethical guidelines that provide clear principles and practical advice on ethical decision-making. These guidelines should address issues such as sourcing, verification, conflicts of interest, privacy, and avoiding sensationalism.

3. Responsible Editing and Fact-Checking: Establish rigorous editorial processes that prioritize fact-checking, source verification, and independent verification of sensitive information. Editors should ensure that journalists adhere to ethical guidelines and uphold high standards of accuracy and fairness.

4. Transparency and Corrections: Ethical decision-making includes transparently correcting inaccuracies and mistakes. News organizations should promptly correct errors, issue public apologies if necessary, and maintain transparency about the corrections made.

5. Independent Ombudsman or Public Editor: Appoint an independent ombudsman or public editor to address ethical concerns raised by the public or within the news organization. This role serves as an accountability mechanism that provides a platform for the public to voice concerns and seek redress.

6. Peer Review and Newsroom Ethics Discussions: Establish peer review processes within news organizations to allow journalists to engage in ethical discussions and receive feedback on their work. Promoting a culture of ethical reflection and accountability can strengthen ethical decision-making in newsrooms.

Ethical decision-making in journalism and media ethics is crucial for preserving public trust, protecting individuals' rights, and promoting democratic processes. Journalists must navigate the complexities of truth, sensationalism, and public interest while upholding principles of accuracy, fairness, and transparency. Key ethical considerations include truth and accuracy, fairness and impartiality, privacy, conflict of interest, and corporate independence. Challenges arise from the digital media landscape, misinformation, sensationalism, and conflicts between public interest and privacy. Promoting ethical conduct in journalism requires education, the development of ethical guidelines, responsible editing, transparency, and accountability mechanisms. By adhering to ethical principles, journalists can fulfill their vital role as guardians of truth and reliable sources of information, contributing to a well-informed society.

13. Ethical decision-making in public policy and governance

Balancing Public Interest, Values, and Responsibility

Ethical decision-making in public policy and governance entails navigating complex issues, making value-based choices, and balancing the interests of diverse stakeholders. Public officials and policymakers encounter ethical dilemmas that require rigorous analysis and consideration of ethical principles, laws, and societal values. This essay explores the importance of ethical decision-making in public policy, ethical principles in governance, key ethical considerations, challenges faced by policymakers, and strategies to promote ethical conduct in public policy and governance.

The Importance of Ethical Decision-Making in Public Policy

1. Public Interest and Welfare: Ethical decision-making in public policy prioritizes the interests and welfare of the public. Policymakers have policies to promote the highest overall well-being and advancement of society.

2. Democratic Governance: Ethical decision-making ensures the functioning of democratic governance by considering the principles of representation, participation, transparency, and accountability. Policymakers must engage with the public, respect their rights and opinions, and make decisions that reflect the will of the people.

3. Social Justice and Equity: Ethical decision-making in public policy upholds principles of social justice and equity. Policymakers should address disparities, protect the rights of marginalized groups, and ensure equal access to opportunities and resources.

4. Interdisciplinary Considerations: Ethical decision-making in public policy necessitates considering diverse perspectives from various disciplines, such as economics, sociology, and ethics. Policymakers must assess the social, economic, and environmental impacts of their decisions and strive for comprehensive and balanced solutions.

Ethical Principles in Governance

1. Transparency and Accountability: Ethical decision-making in governance requires transparency in processes, decision-making, and resource allocation. Policymakers should be accountable to the public, ensuring that decisions are made in an open and accountable manner.

2. Rule of Law: Ethical decision-making promotes adherence to the rule of law. Policymakers must respect and uphold the legal framework, ensuring that policies are enacted and implemented within the limits of the law.

3. Public Participation and Engagement: Ethical decision-making values public participation and engagement. Policymakers should actively seek input from affected stakeholders and engage in inclusive dialogue to ensure that different perspectives are taken into account.

4. Integrity and Avoiding Conflicts of Interest: Ethical decision-making requires policymakers to act with integrity and avoid conflicts of interest. Policymakers must prioritize the public interest over personal or private interests and maintain the highest ethical standards in their decision-making processes.

Key Ethical Considerations in Public Policy

1. Balancing Individual and Collective Interests: Ethical decision-making in public policy requires policymakers to strike a balance between individual rights and collective well-being. Policymakers should consider the potential impact of policies on diverse communities and ensure fairness in the distribution of burdens and benefits.

2. Global Responsibility: Ethical decision-making in public policy extends beyond national borders. Policymakers should consider the global impact of their decisions, addressing international issues such as climate change, human rights, and sustainable development.

3. Ethical Use of Power: Ethical decision-making in public policy acknowledges the power and authority entrusted to policymakers. Policymakers should use this power responsibly, avoiding abuse or manipulation of authority for personal gain.

4. Long-Term Thinking and Sustainability: Ethical decision-making requires policymakers to adopt a long-term perspective and consider the sustainability of policies. Policymakers should balance immediate needs with the needs of future generations, ensuring policy coherence and sustainable development.

Challenges and Dilemmas in Ethical Decision-Making in Public Policy

1. Ethical Complexity: Ethical decision-making in public policy often involves navigating competing values, perspectives, and interests. Policymakers must analyze complex ethical dilemmas, give weight to various considerations, and find principled solutions.

2. Conflict of Interest: Policymakers may face conflicts of interest when personal or private interests clash with the public interest. Policymakers should disclose potential conflicts and work to avoid situations where personal gain compromises the integrity of decision-making.

3. Political Pressures: Ethical decision-making may be influenced by political pressures, lobbying, or partisan interests. Policymakers should be aware of and resist undue political influence, ensuring decisions are grounded in ethical and evidence-based considerations.

Strategies to Promote Ethical Conduct in Public Policy and Governance

1. Ethical Guidelines and Codes of Conduct: Develop and implement clear ethical guidelines and codes of conduct that outline expected behaviors for policymakers. These guidelines should address conflicts of interest, transparency, accountability, and the responsible use of power.

2. Ethical Training and Education: Provide policymakers with ongoing training and education on ethical decision-making. This training should include case studies, ethical dilemmas, and discussions to build their ethical reasoning skills.

3. Independent Oversight and Review: Establish independent oversight mechanisms to monitor and evaluate the ethical conduct of policymakers. This can include ethics committees, ombudsperson offices, or specialized commissions responsible for monitoring compliance with ethical standards.

4. Public Engagement and Consultation: Encourage public participation and engagement in the policy-making process. Seek input from affected stakeholders, conduct public consultations, and provide feedback to ensure transparency, inclusivity, and accountability.

5. Ethical Impact Assessments: Conduct ethical impact assessments to evaluate the potential ethical implications of policies. These assessments should identify potential risks, conflicts, and unintended consequences and inform policymakers in their decision-making.

Ethical decision-making in public policy and governance is essential for promoting the public interest, maintaining democratic governance, and advancing social justice. Policymakers face complex challenges when navigating ethical dilemmas, balancing competing interests, and upholding ethical principles. By adhering to ethical guidelines, promoting transparency, engaging the public, and ensuring accountability, policymakers can make informed decisions that reflect the values and best interests of society. Upholding ethical standards strengthens governance, fosters public trust, and promotes a just and equitable society.

Public policy plays a vital role in democratic states as it shapes the direction, priorities, and governance of a society. It encompasses a range of decisions, actions, and regulations implemented by governments to address social, economic, and political issues. In this article, we will explore the importance and value of public policy in a democratic state, discussing its role in promoting citizen welfare, facilitating social progress, ensuring accountability, and fostering equitable governance.

1. Promoting Citizen Welfare:

One of the primary objectives of public policy in a democratic state is to promote the welfare and well-being of its citizens. Through policies on healthcare, education, social security, and poverty alleviation, governments strive to enhance the quality of life for their citizens, ensuring equal opportunities for all. Public policy initiatives such as universal healthcare, affordable housing programs, and access to quality education are aimed at reducing inequalities and improving the standard of living for the entire population.

2. Facilitating Social Progress:

Public policies play a pivotal role in facilitating social progress and addressing societal challenges. They enable governments to respond to emerging issues, such as climate change, technological advancements, and demographic shifts. By implementing policies that encourage sustainable development, renewable energy, and environmental conservation, governments can mitigate the adverse effects of climate change and promote a more sustainable future.

Similarly, public policies can address the social impact of technological advancements, ensuring equitable access to digital infrastructure, bridging the digital divide, and promoting digital literacy. Additionally, policies on immigration, diversity, and inclusion contribute to social cohesion and integration, fostering a tolerant and multicultural society.

3. Ensuring Accountability:

Public policy is instrumental in ensuring accountability and transparency in government actions. Elected representatives are held accountable by citizens for the decisions they make and the policies they implement. Through public policy, governments are required to act in the best interests of the public and be responsive to citizens' needs and concerns.

Moreover, public policies often include mechanisms for oversight, evaluation, and public participation, strengthening accountability and the democratic process. Citizens can hold their governments accountable for the implementation and outcomes of policies, thereby fostering trust in democratic institutions.

4. Fostering Equitable Governance

In democratic states, public policy serves as a mechanism for fostering equitable governance. Through policies addressing income inequality, discrimination, and social disparities, governments can promote fairness and justice. Policies such as progressive taxation, affirmative action, and anti-discrimination laws aim to reduce disparities and ensure equal opportunities for all citizens, irrespective of their background or socio-economic status.

Public policies also play a role in promoting participatory democracy. By involving citizens in policy-making processes through consultations, public hearings, and referenda, democratic states can ensure that policies are responsive to the needs and aspirations of the people. This participatory approach strengthens citizens' trust in government and enhances the legitimacy of the decisions made.

5. Managing Externalities:

Public policy is crucial in managing externalities, which are the unintended consequences of economic activities on society and the environment. Government regulations, laws, and policies are essential for addressing negative externalities such as pollution, environmental degradation, and public health risks. By implementing regulations and incentives for responsible business practices, governments can ensure that external costs are accounted for and minimize harm to public goods and individuals.

Public policies also play a role in managing positive externalities, such as investments in education, research, and development. By providing subsidies, grants, and incentives, governments encourage private sector investments in socially desirable activities that benefit society.

6. Balancing Interests and Public Goods:

Public policy is indispensable in striking a balance between different interests within society and promoting the greater public good. Governments must navigate conflicting interests and make decisions that consider the needs and aspirations of diverse stakeholders. Public policies act as a mechanism to reconcile these interests, ensuring that decisions are made based on evidence, public input, and fair deliberation. This ensures that policies reflect the collective interest and well-being of citizens rather than catering to the interests of a particular group or sector.

Public policy is an important and valuable aspect within a democratic state, as it allows governments to shape the future of society, address societal challenges, and promote citizen welfare. Through policies, governments can strive for social progress, build a fair and inclusive society, ensure accountability, and manage the externalities of economic activities. It is through public policy that democratic states can govern in the best interests of their citizens, foster equitable governance, and promote the values of democracy. Effective public policymaking involving citizen participation, evidence-based decision-making, and transparency is essential for vibrant and resilient democratic societies.

Accountability is a critical aspect of effective management in any organization. It refers to the responsibility and answerability of individuals and teams for their actions, decisions, and outcomes. Accountability ensures that managers and employees are aware of their responsibilities, perform their duties effectively, and are held responsible for their performance and results. In this article, we will explore the importance of accountability in management, discuss the benefits it brings to organizations, and provide strategies for fostering a culture of accountability.

Importance of Accountability in Management:

1. Performance and Results: Accountability serves as a driver for achieving individual and organizational goals. When managers are accountable for their actions and decisions, they are more likely to focus on delivering high-quality work, meeting targets, and achieving desired outcomes. Accountability fosters a culture of performance, where individuals take ownership of their responsibilities and strive for excellence.

2. Trust and Transparency: Accountability promotes trust and transparency throughout the organization. When managers and employees are accountable for their actions, it enhances trust among team members and stakeholders. Transparent processes, clear expectations, and open communication build a culture where everyone understands their roles and responsibilities, allowing for effective collaboration and problem-solving.

3. Learning and Improvement: Accountability encourages a learning mindset and supports continuous improvement. When managers and employees take responsibility for their actions, they are more likely to reflect on their performance and seek ways to enhance their skills and knowledge. A culture of accountability fosters a supportive environment where individuals learn from their mistakes and share lessons learned, leading to ongoing organizational improvement.

4. Employee Engagement and Morale: Accountability contributes to higher employee engagement and morale. When managers hold themselves and their teams accountable, it demonstrates a commitment to fair treatment and a focus on achieving results. This sense of fairness and recognition for good performance creates a positive work environment where employees feel valued and motivated to excel in their roles.

5. Leadership and Organizational Culture: Accountability starts at the top with leaders setting the example for their teams. When managers are accountable for their actions and decisions, it sets the tone for a culture of accountability throughout the organization. This culture influences employee behavior, decision-making processes, and overall organizational performance. A strong culture of accountability helps align individual and organizational goals, leading to sustainable success.

Strategies for Fostering Accountability:

1. Clear Communication and Expectations: Effective communication is crucial for establishing accountability. Managers should communicate expectations, goals, and performance standards to their teams. This involves setting SMART (specific, measurable, attainable, relevant, and time-bound) goals, providing regular feedback, and ensuring that employees understand how their work contributes to the organization's objectives. Clear communication helps employees align their efforts with organizational priorities and enhances accountability for their performance.

2. Individual and Team Goal Setting: Set clear individual and team goals that are aligned with the organization's strategic objectives. When employees have clear goals, they are more likely to take ownership of their work and be accountable for achieving those goals. Managers should regularly review progress, provide feedback, and support employees in achieving their objectives.

3. Performance Measurement and Evaluation: Establish performance measurement systems and evaluation processes to assess individual and team performance. Regular performance reviews provide an opportunity to discuss achievements, identify areas for improvement, and set future goals. Managers should provide constructive feedback and recognize accomplishments to reinforce accountability and motivate employees.

4. Empowerment and Delegation: Empower employees by delegating authority and decision-making responsibilities. When employees have a sense of autonomy and ownership in their roles, they are more likely to take accountability for their actions and decisions. Managers should provide necessary resources, training, and support to ensure that employees are equipped to make informed and responsible choices.

5. Clear Roles and Responsibilities: Clearly define roles and responsibilities within the organization. Designate decision-making authority and ensure that employees understand their specific duties and expectations. This clarity helps prevent confusion and ensures that everyone knows what is expected of them, promoting accountability, and avoiding duplication or gaps in work.

6. Recognition and Incentives: Recognize and reward employees who demonstrate accountability and achieve desired outcomes. This can be done through verbal praise, public acknowledgment, or formal recognition programs. Incentives such as performance bonuses or promotions encourage employees to take ownership of their responsibilities and strive for excellence.

7. Learning and Development: Provide opportunities for learning and professional development to enhance individual and team skills. Offer training programs, workshops, or mentorship opportunities that support accountability and growth. Continuous learning helps employees stay relevant, adapt to changing circumstances, and take responsibility for their professional development.

8. Consequences for Non-Accountability: It is essential to establish consequences for non-accountability. While accountability is encouraged and rewarded, managers must enforce consequences when employees consistently fail to meet expectations or neglect their responsibilities. This helps maintain the integrity of the accountability framework and ensures that everyone is held to the same standards.

Accountability is a critical element of effective management in any organization. It establishes clear expectations, promotes performance and results, fosters trust and transparency, and enhances employee engagement and morale. By fostering a culture of accountability, organizations can create an environment where individuals take responsibility for their actions and decisions, continuously learn and improve, and contribute to the overall success of the organization. Through clear communication, performance measurement, empowerment, recognition, and consequences for non-accountability, managers can build and sustain a culture of accountability that drives individual and organizational performance.

14. Ethical decision-making in education and academic ethics

Upholding Integrity, Equity, and Excellence

Ethical decision-making in education and academic ethics is crucial for creating a foundation of integrity and excellence in learning environments. Teachers, administrators, and educational leaders face numerous ethical dilemmas that require thoughtful analysis, adherence to ethical principles, and the promotion of equitable practices. This essay explores the importance of ethical decision-making in education, key ethical considerations in academic settings, challenges faced by educators, strategies to promote ethical conduct, and the role of academic ethics in fostering integrity and academic excellence.

The Importance of Ethical Decision-Making in Education:

1. Student Welfare and Development: Ethical decision-making in education prioritizes the well-being and development of students. Educators have a responsibility to create safe, inclusive, and supportive learning environments that nurture students' intellectual, social, emotional, and physical growth.

2. Equity and Access to Education: Ethical decision-making ensures equity and equal access to education. Educators should address disparities, eliminate barriers, and promote inclusive practices that ensure all students, regardless of their background or abilities, have fair and equal opportunities to succeed.

3. Professional Responsibility and Accountability: Ethical decision-making upholds professional responsibility and accountability. Educators should abide by professional standards, codes of ethics, and legal requirements, ensuring that their actions align with the best interests of students and society.

4. Educational Leadership and System Integrity: Ethical decision-making is essential for educational leaders to provide effective leadership and maintain the integrity of the education system. Leaders should inspire trust, promote ethical behavior, and create a culture that values integrity, fairness, and excellence.

Key Ethical Considerations in Education and Academic Ethics:

1. Academic Honesty and Integrity: Ethical decision-making in academic settings centers on promoting academic honesty and integrity. Teachers, administrators, and students should uphold the principles of truth, fairness, and originality while avoiding plagiarism, cheating, and unethical academic practices.

2. Equity and Inclusion: Ethical decision-making in education emphasizes equity and inclusion. Educators should address bias, discrimination, and inequality, ensuring that all students have equal opportunities to learn, thrive, and reach their full potential.

3. Student Privacy and Confidentiality: Ethical decision-making in education respects student privacy and confidentiality. Educators should safeguard sensitive information, maintain the trust of students and families, and adhere to legal and ethical guidelines related to data protection and privacy.

4. Culturally Responsive Pedagogy: Ethical decision-making includes embracing culturally responsive pedagogy. Educators should recognize and honor students' diverse cultural backgrounds, experiences, and identities, fostering an inclusive and respectful learning environment.

Challenges and Dilemmas in Ethical Decision-Making in Education:

1. Balancing Stakeholder Needs: Ethical decision-making in education often involves balancing the needs and expectations of various stakeholders, including students, parents, administrators, and communities. Educators must navigate conflicting interests and make choices that prioritize the best interests of students.

2. Conflicts of Interest: Educators may encounter conflicts of interest when personal, financial, or professional interests clash with their professional responsibilities. Ethical decision-making requires educators to avoid actions that compromise the integrity of the educational process.

3. Educational Inequality: Ethical decision-making in education requires addressing educational inequalities and systemic barriers that hinder equitable access to quality education. Educators must strive to close achievement gaps, dismantle barriers faced by marginalized groups, and promote inclusivity and social justice.

Strategies to Promote Ethical Conduct in Education and Academic Ethics:

1. Ethical Guidelines and Codes of Conduct: Develop and disseminate clear ethical guidelines and codes of conduct that outline expected behavior for educators, administrators, and students. These guidelines should address issues such as academic honesty, respect for diversity, and maintaining student privacy.

2. Professional Development and Training: Provide educators with ongoing professional development and training on ethical decision-making and academic ethics. This training should include case studies, ethics-focused workshops, and discussions to enhance educators' knowledge and ethical reasoning skills.

3. Ethical Leadership: Educational leaders should demonstrate ethical leadership by modeling ethical behavior, fostering a culture of integrity, and providing support and guidance for educators in ethical decision-making.

4. Ethical Committees and Consultation: Establish ethical committees or consultative bodies within educational institutions to provide guidance, assistance, and oversight regarding ethical dilemmas and decisions. These committees can serve as resources for educators and can guide ethical inquiries or disputes.

5. Parent and Community Engagement: Foster partnerships with parents and the wider community to promote ethical conduct in education. Engage parents in discussions about ethics, communicate policies and expectations, and involve the community in decision-making processes, fostering transparency and accountability.

The Role of Academic Ethics in Fostering Integrity and Academic Excellence

1. Promoting Intellectual Growth and Critical Thinking: Academic ethics encourage intellectual growth and the development of critical thinking skills. By adhering to ethical principles such as academic honesty, students are encouraged to engage in authentic learning experiences and develop their intellectual abilities.

2. Ensuring Fair Evaluation and Recognition: Academic ethics ensures fair evaluation and recognition of students' achievements. Educators must approach assessment and grading practices with fairness, avoid bias, and provide constructive feedback to support students' growth and development.

3. Fostering a Culture of Intellectual Curiosity: Academic ethics cultivates a culture of intellectual curiosity, inquiry, and academic rigor. By upholding ethical principles, educators create an environment that values intellectual exploration, academic excellence, and the pursuit of knowledge.

4. Promoting Lifelong Ethical Behavior: Academic ethics plays a crucial role in shaping students' ethical behavior beyond their educational journey. By instilling ethical values and promoting ethical conduct, educators contribute to the formation of responsible citizens who will lead and contribute to society ethically and responsibly.

Ethical decision-making in education and academic ethics is foundational for fostering integrity, equity, and academic excellence. Educators and educational leaders face various ethical dilemmas and challenges, such as balancing stakeholder needs, addressing educational inequalities, and promoting academic honesty. By promoting ethical conduct through the development and implementation of ethical guidelines, continuous professional development, ethical leadership, and engagement with stakeholders, educators can create learning environments that prioritize student welfare, foster equity, and promote intellectual growth. Upholding academic ethics ensures fair evaluation, recognition, and the cultivation of a culture of intellectual curiosity, leading to a lifelong commitment to ethical behavior and academic excellence.

Chapter Two

The Foundations of Ethical Decision-making in Nursing and Medicine

Ethical decision-making is a crucial aspect of human behavior that involves choosing between different possible courses of action based on moral principles and values. The foundations of ethical decision-making are rooted in various philosophical, psychological, cultural, and religious perspectives. These foundations provide a framework for individuals to assess, judge, and make decisions that consider ethical implications. In this section, we will explore the key elements that form the foundations of ethical decision-making and the role they play in shaping moral reasoning in Nursing and Medicine.

Philosophical Foundations

Ethical decision-making has long been a subject of philosophical inquiry. Some of the foundational concepts in philosophical ethics include consequentialism, deontology, and virtue ethics. Consequentialism, as advocated by philosophers like John Stuart Mill, states that the morality of an action is determined by its consequences. On the other hand, deontology, championed by Immanuel Kant, argues that actions should be judged based on whether they adhere to certain moral duties or principles, regardless of the outcomes. Meanwhile, virtue ethics, influenced by Aristotle, emphasizes the cultivation of virtuous character traits as the core of ethical decision-making.

These philosophical perspectives provide individuals with different lenses to consider when making ethical decisions. They highlight the importance of understanding the potential consequences of one's actions, the ethical duties or rules that should guide behavior, and the development of character traits that lead to virtuous conduct. By understanding these philosophical foundations, individuals can gather a comprehensive understanding of the underlying principles that inform ethical decision-making.

Ethical decision-making involves making morally right choices, just, and aligned with ethical principles and values. These decisions are based on a framework that is influenced by philosophical foundations. Philosophy provides the fundamental principles and theories that underpin the understanding and application of ethics. In this article, we will explore the philosophical foundations of ethical decision-making, discussing key ethical theories, moral principles, and their implications for decision-making.

1. Consequentialism:

Consequentialism is an ethical theory that focuses on the consequences or outcomes of an action. According to consequentialism, the morality of an action is determined by its consequences. The most prominent form of consequentialism is utilitarianism, which argues that actions are morally right if they maximize overall happiness or utility for the greatest number of people.

In ethical decision-making, consequentialism requires individuals to consider the potential outcomes and choose the action that produces the greatest overall happiness or utility. This approach emphasizes the importance of balancing competing interests and maximizing societal welfare. However, critics argue that consequentialism can overlook individual rights and justice concerns in the pursuit of maximizing overall utility.

2. Deontology:

Deontology is a moral theory that focuses on duties, rights, and moral obligations. According to deontologists, there are inherent principles that guide ethical decision-making, regardless of the consequences. Actions are deemed morally right or wrong based on whether they align with these universal rules or duties.

Immanuel Kant's categorical imperative is a central tenet of deontological ethics. It states that individuals should act in a way that they would want their actions to be universally followed. Deontological decision-making requires individuals to consider ethical principles and their moral obligations when faced with a choice. This approach emphasizes the importance of individual rights, fairness, and justice. However, deontology can sometimes lead to conflicting duties or absolutist approaches that may not consider the context or consequences of actions.

3. Virtue Ethics:

Virtue ethics focuses on the development of virtuous character traits and moral excellence. It emphasizes the importance of cultivating virtues such as honesty, integrity, compassion, and courage. According to virtue ethics, ethical decision-making is guided by personal character, and moral actions flow naturally from virtuous individuals.

In virtue ethics, the emphasis is not placed solely on following rules or maximizing outcomes but on developing virtuous character traits. Ethical decisions are made by considering how virtuous individuals would act in a given situation. This approach emphasizes the importance of personal integrity, moral development, and moral intuition. Critics argue that virtue ethics may lack clear guidance in complex decision-making situations and can be subjective depending on different cultural or individual interpretations of virtuous behavior.

4. Ethics of Care:

The ethics of care is a moral theory that emphasizes the importance of interpersonal relationships, empathy, and compassion. It centers on the moral obligation to care for and nurture others, especially in contexts of vulnerability or dependency. Ethical decision-making based on the ethics of care involves considering the impact of actions on others and fostering compassionate relationships.

The ethics of care challenges traditional ethical theories by focusing on the relational and emotional aspects of moral decision-making. This approach emphasizes the importance of empathy, trust, and reciprocity in ethical choices. Critics argue that the ethics of care may prioritize caretaker relationships over other ethical considerations, potentially neglecting justice concerns or broader societal implications.

The ethics of care is an important framework in the fields of nursing and medicine as it emphasizes the importance of patient-centered care, empathy, and nurturing relationships. In healthcare, the ethics of care focuses on the holistic well-being of patients, acknowledging their vulnerability, and promoting compassionate and ethical decision-making. In the following paragraphs, we will explore why the ethics of care is crucial in the fields of nursing and medicine, discussing its implications for patient care, healthcare relationships, and the overall ethical climate in healthcare settings.

1. Patient-Centered Care:

The ethics of care places the patient at the center of healthcare practice. It recognizes the individuality, autonomy, and unique needs of each patient, acknowledging that their well-being and interests should be the primary concern. In a patient-centered care model, healthcare providers strive to understand and respond to the physical, emotional, and psychological needs of their patients.

In nursing and medicine, patient-centered care is foundational to ethical practice. It involves active listening, empathetic communication, and shared decision-making. By applying the ethics of care, healthcare professionals develop a deeper understanding of their patients' values, preferences, and concerns, leading to more personalized and effective care.

2. Relationship-Centered Care:

The ethics of care emphasize the importance of building and nurturing relationships in healthcare. Healthcare providers establish trusting and respectful relationships with their patients, recognizing the inherent interdependence and vulnerability in healthcare interactions. These relationships are characterized by empathy, compassion, and mutual respect.

In nursing and medicine, relationship-centered care is instrumental in building trust and therapeutic alliances with patients. Strong relationships enhance communication, enable shared decision-making, and foster collaboration. The ethics of care supports healthcare providers in acknowledging and addressing the unique needs and concerns of each patient, leading to enhanced patient satisfaction, improved health outcomes, and a patient-centered care experience.

3. Ethical Decision-Making:

Ethical decision-making in healthcare often involves complex and morally challenging situations. The ethics of care provides a valuable framework for navigating these dilemmas. It encourages healthcare providers to consider the impact of decisions on patients, families, and the broader healthcare team.

The ethics of care promotes the importance of context, relationship, and empathy when making difficult decisions. Healthcare providers are encouraged to consider the implications of decisions on the well-being and interests of all individuals involved, recognizing, and respecting the inherent vulnerabilities inherent in healthcare relationships. This approach contributes to more ethically sound decisions that consider the multidimensional aspects of patient care.

4. Addressing Health Inequalities:

The ethics of care is particularly significant in addressing health inequalities and promoting social justice. It recognizes that certain patient populations may experience systemic disadvantages and vulnerabilities that affect their access to healthcare and health outcomes. The ethics of care urges healthcare professionals to consider these disparities and work towards reducing them.

In nursing and medicine, healthcare providers who apply the ethics of care are more likely to advocate for equitable access to healthcare services, address social determinants of health, and work towards eliminating healthcare disparities. By implementing a care ethic that prioritizes the needs of marginalized and vulnerable populations, healthcare professionals can contribute to more just and equitable healthcare systems.

5. Ethical Climate in Healthcare Settings:

The ethics of care not only inform individual interactions but also contribute to the ethical climate of healthcare settings. A care-centered approach fosters a culture of compassion, empathy, and collaboration among healthcare providers. It encourages teamwork, respect for diversity, and a commitment to patient well-being.

In nursing and medicine, an ethical climate that is grounded in the ethics of care promotes open communication, shared values, and ethical decision-making. This climate supports healthcare providers in their moral deliberation, provides a foundation for ethical practice, and ultimately enhances the quality of patient care.

6. Professional Well-being:

The ethics of care have implications for the professional well-being of healthcare providers. By recognizing the significance of relationships and empathy in healthcare, the ethics of care helps healthcare professionals find meaning and fulfillment in their work. It encourages a supportive work environment and promotes mutual respect among colleagues.

In nursing and medicine, practicing the ethics of care allows healthcare professionals to address their own emotional needs and the ethical challenges they encounter. By considering the care and support they provide to patients and each other, healthcare professionals can create a culture of well-being, leading to increased job satisfaction and reduced burnout.

The ethics of care is a fundamental framework in the fields of nursing and medicine. Its emphasis on patient-centered care, relationship building, ethical decision-making, and addressing health inequalities contributes to the overall ethical climate of healthcare settings. By applying the ethics of care, healthcare professionals can foster therapeutic relationships, advocate for patient rights, and work towards equitable healthcare access. This approach also supports the professional well-being of healthcare providers by fostering a supportive work environment. By integrating the ethics of care into ethical practice, nursing, and medical professionals can provide compassionate and high-quality care that meets the unique needs of their patients.

Patient rights are essential in healthcare as they protect the autonomy, dignity, and well-being of individuals seeking medical care. These rights encompass a wide range of principles and protections to ensure that patients receive quality care, are fully informed about their treatment, have control over their healthcare decisions, and are treated with respect and dignity. In this article, we will explore patient rights in detail, discussing their importance, key components, legal framework, and implications for healthcare practice.

Importance of Patient Rights:

Patient rights play a crucial role in healthcare, as they promote ethical, equitable, and patient-centered care. These rights are fundamental to upholding the principles of autonomy, dignity, and respect for individuals seeking medical treatment. By protecting the rights of patients, healthcare systems can maintain trust, foster collaborative relationships, promote shared decision-making, and enhance patient satisfaction.

1. Autonomy and Informed Consent:

One of the fundamental rights of patients is autonomy, which refers to their ability to make decisions about their healthcare without coercion or undue influence. Autonomy recognizes that patients have the right to refuse or accept medical treatment, access their medical records, and participate in discussions about their care.

Informed consent is closely linked to autonomy, ensuring that patients have all the necessary information about their diagnosis, treatment options, potential risks, and benefits before making decisions about their care. Informed consent is a legal requirement in many countries and is crucial for respecting the autonomy and decision-making capacity of patients.

2. Privacy and Confidentiality:

Patients have the right to privacy and confidentiality regarding their medical information. Healthcare providers are legally and ethically obliged to maintain strict confidentiality of patients' personal health information. This includes protecting their medical records, conversations, and any other personal healthcare information.

Respecting patient privacy and confidentiality is essential for establishing trust and preserving the autonomy and dignity of patients. Patients must feel confident that their personal health information will be kept private and only shared with authorized individuals for legitimate healthcare purposes.

3. Access to Information:

Patients have the right to access accurate and understandable information about their health conditions, treatment options, and potential outcomes. Healthcare providers should provide information in a way that patients can comprehend, ensuring they can ask questions, seek clarification, and actively participate in their care.

Access to information allows patients to understand their health status, make informed decisions about their treatment, and have realistic expectations about the outcomes. It empowers patients to take an active role in their healthcare journey and encourages shared decision-making between patients and healthcare providers.

4. Quality and Safety of Care:

Patients have the right to receive safe, competent, and high-quality care. This includes the right to receive treatment from qualified healthcare providers, access appropriate diagnostic tests and medications, and receive care in a safe and clean environment.

Healthcare providers should follow evidence-based practices, adhere to clinical guidelines, and continuously strive to improve the quality and safety of care provided. Patients have the right to be treated with dignity and respect, regardless of their race, ethnicity, gender, or any other characteristic.

5. Complaints and Redress:

Patients have the right to voice complaints, express dissatisfaction, and seek resolution in case of any problems or concerns about their care. Healthcare providers should have a mechanism in place to address patient grievances promptly and transparently.

Patient rights include the right to lodge a complaint, receive a timely response, and be informed about the steps taken to resolve the issue. This ensures accountability, encourages quality improvement, and strengthens the overall patient-provider relationship.

Legal Framework of Patient Rights:

Patient rights are protected by legislation and legal frameworks in many countries. These laws vary across jurisdictions but generally aim to uphold the principles of autonomy, informed consent, privacy, and non-discrimination. Some countries have specific legislation that guarantees and protects patient rights, while others rely on general principles of healthcare ethics and practice standards.

For example, in the United States, the Health Insurance Portability and Accountability Act (HIPAA) establishes standards for the privacy and security of patients' health information. The Patient Self-Determination Act ensures that individuals receive information about their right to make healthcare decisions and to document their preferences through advance directives, such as living wills or healthcare proxies.

In other countries, patient rights may be protected through constitutional rights, healthcare acts, or specific patient charters. The exact legal framework for patient rights may differ, but the underlying principles, such as autonomy, privacy, and access to information, are generally consistent.

Implications for Healthcare Practice:

Respecting patient rights has significant implications for healthcare practice. It requires healthcare providers to establish a patient-centered approach that prioritizes the well-being, autonomy, and dignity of patients. Here are some implications of patient rights for healthcare practitioners:

1. Communication and Shared Decision-Making:

Healthcare providers need to communicate effectively with patients, ensuring they understand their health conditions, treatment options, and potential outcomes. This involves using clear and understandable language, actively listening to patients' concerns, and providing them with the necessary information to make informed decisions.

Practicing shared decision-making allows patients and healthcare providers to collaborate in the decision-making process, considering patients' preferences, values, and context. By involving patients in their care plans, healthcare providers respect patient autonomy, enhance patient satisfaction, and improve treatment adherence.

2. Informed Consent and Decision-Making Capacity:

Healthcare providers must obtain informed consent from patients before initiating any medical treatment or procedure. This requires providing information about the nature, purpose, benefits, risks, and alternatives to the proposed treatment.

Healthcare providers should also assess patients' decision-making capacity, particularly when dealing with patients who may have impaired decision-making abilities due to their medical condition or other factors. In such cases, healthcare providers may need to involve substitute decision-makers, such as family members or legal guardians, while still respecting the patients' best interests.

3. Privacy and Confidentiality:

Healthcare providers have a legal and ethical obligation to maintain patient privacy and confidentiality. This includes securing patient records and information, limiting access to authorized personnel, and obtaining patients' consent before sharing their health information with third parties.

Healthcare providers must also educate patients about their rights regarding privacy and confidentiality, assuring them that their personal health information will be kept private and confidential. Respecting patient privacy enhances trust, promotes open communication, and protects patient autonomy.

4. Cultural Sensitivity and Non-Discrimination:

Healthcare providers should be culturally sensitive and respectful of the diverse backgrounds, beliefs, and values of their patients. Treating patients with dignity and respect means recognizing and appreciating their cultural, religious, and social identities.

Healthcare providers should strive to eliminate discrimination, bias, and prejudice in all aspects of care. Respecting patient rights requires providing equitable access to healthcare services, regardless of a patient's race, nationality, gender, sexual orientation, or any other characteristic.

5. Complaints and Redress:

Healthcare providers should establish a robust system that allows patients to voice complaints, express dissatisfaction, and seek resolution. They should respond to patient grievances promptly, transparently, and in a manner that respects the patient's rights and concerns.

By addressing patient complaints effectively, healthcare providers demonstrate accountability, improve the quality of care, and strengthen the patient-provider relationship. Patient feedback and complaints can serve as valuable opportunities for quality improvement and learning.

Patient rights are essential for ensuring ethical, equitable, and patient-centered care. By upholding patient rights, healthcare systems and providers respect patient autonomy, promote shared decision-making, protect patient privacy, and provide high-quality care. Patient rights are protected through legal frameworks in many countries, emphasizing the principles of autonomy, informed consent, privacy, and non-discrimination. In healthcare practice, recognizing and respecting patient rights requires effective communication, shared decision-making, cultural sensitivity, and a commitment to quality improvement. By prioritizing patient rights, healthcare providers can establish trust, enhance patient satisfaction, and deliver compassionate and high-quality care.

6. Rights-Based Ethics:

Rights-based ethics asserts that individuals have inherent rights that should be protected and respected. These rights are often grounded in ideas of human dignity, autonomy, and freedom. Ethical decision-making based on rights-based approaches requires considering the rights of all individuals involved and ensuring that actions do not violate those rights.

Rights-based decision-making approaches prioritize individual rights and liberty. This approach emphasizes protecting vulnerable individuals, ensuring fair treatment, and safeguarding justice. However, different interpretations of rights and conflicting rights can present challenges in determining the appropriate course of action in complex ethical dilemmas.

Implications for Ethical Decision-Making

The philosophical foundations of ethical decision-making provide different perspectives and frameworks for addressing moral challenges. When making ethical decisions, it is essential to consider the following:

1. Reflect on ethical principles and theories: Engage in critical reflection and consider the ethical theories and principles that resonate with personal values and the organizational context. Understanding different philosophical foundations can inform the decision-making process and guide ethical reasoning.

2. Contextualize ethical decision-making: Consider the specific circumstances and context of the decision. Ethical theories and principles provide a framework, but they may need to be adapted to incorporate situational factors and specific stakeholders' needs and values.

3. Seek a balance between ethical considerations: Recognize that ethical decision-making often involves balancing competing ethical considerations. By understanding the principles and values associated with different ethical theories, individuals can navigate the complexities and conflicting obligations inherent in ethical decision-making.

4. Reflect on consequences and impacts: Consider the potential consequences of decisions on various stakeholders, considering long-term impacts, potential risks, and benefits. Consider the wider societal implications of actions and the potential ripple effects that decisions may have.

5. Develop moral judgment and intuition: Enhance moral judgment and intuition through ongoing moral development and reflection. Engage in ethical discussions, seek feedback, and learn from past experiences. Moral intuition can be honed by continually considering ethical principles and theories in decision-making processes.

6. Foster a culture of ethical decision-making: Build an organizational culture that promotes and supports ethical decision-making. Develop clear ethical standards, provide ethical training and guidance, and encourage open dialogue and ethical reflection among employees.

The philosophical foundations of ethical decision-making provide different lenses through which individuals can approach moral dilemmas. Consequentialism emphasizes outcomes and maximizing societal welfare, while deontology focuses on duties and universal ethical principles. Virtue ethics centers on character development, and the ethics of care emphasizes empathy and compassion. Rights-based ethics prioritizes protecting individual rights and freedoms. By understanding and applying these ethical theories and principles, individuals can navigate complex decision-making situations, balancing competing interests and guiding their actions toward morally sound outcomes.

Psychological Foundations

Psychological theories also contribute to the foundations of ethical decision-making. The field of psychology explores human behavior, cognition, and emotion, thereby shedding light on how individuals approach and make ethical decisions. One notable theory, developed by Lawrence Kohlberg, focuses on the moral development stages that individuals go through. According to Kohlberg's theory, people progress from a self-centered perspective to a more socially oriented and principled approach to moral decision-making.

Kohlberg's stages of moral development provide insight into how individuals acquire ethical reasoning skills. They suggest that ethical decision-making is influenced by an individual's cognitive abilities, their capacity for empathy and fairness, and their exposure to diverse social perspectives. Understanding these psychological foundations can help individuals appreciate the complexity of ethical decision-making and how it evolves.

Psychological foundations play a crucial role in decision-making, influencing the processes, biases, and factors that shape our choices. Understanding the psychological aspects of decision-making helps us comprehend how cognitive, emotional, social, and cultural factors affect our decision-making processes. In this article, we will explore the psychological foundations of decision-making, discussing key theories, cognitive biases, emotions, social influences, and how they impact our choices.

1. Rational Choice Theory:

Rational choice theory is a cornerstone of decision-making research. According to this theory, individuals make decisions by maximizing their expected utility or benefits while considering the associated risks and costs. It assumes that decision-makers are rational, possess complete information, and make choices that align with their preferences and values.

Rational choice theory provides a framework for understanding decision-making processes by emphasizing the importance of weighing the pros and cons, evaluating alternatives, and making decisions that maximize personal gain. However, critics argue that true rationality is often limited by cognitive biases, emotions, and incomplete information.

2. Cognitive Biases:

Cognitive biases are systematic patterns of deviation from rationality that influence decision-making. These biases occur due to mental shortcuts, limited information processing capacity, and unconscious biases. Several cognitive biases impact decision-making, including:

- Confirmation bias: Tendency to favor information that confirms one's preexisting beliefs and ignore conflicting evidence.
- Anchoring bias: Relying too heavily on initial information when making judgments or decisions.
- Availability heuristic: Basing judgments on readily available examples that come to mind easily, even if they are not representative.
- Overconfidence bias: Overestimating one's abilities, knowledge, or the accuracy of judgments.
- Framing effect: How information is presented significantly influences decision-making.
- Loss aversion: People tend to strongly prefer avoiding losses over acquiring equivalent gains.
- Status quo bias: Preference for maintaining the current situation due to perceived familiarity or fear of change.

Understanding cognitive biases is crucial to improving decision-making by being aware of these systematic errors and employing strategies to mitigate their effects.

3. Emotions in Decision-Making:

Emotions play a significant role in decision-making by influencing our evaluation of alternatives and the overall decision-making process. Emotions can influence decision-making in several ways:

- Affect-as-information theory: Emotions serve as a heuristic or cue to evaluate the desirability or likelihood of outcomes. Positive emotions tend to produce more positive evaluations, and negative emotions may lead to more cautious decision-making.

- Somatic markers: Emotions can provide physiological signals or "gut feelings" that guide decision-making. These somatic markers help us quickly process information, make intuitive decisions, and evaluate potential risks and rewards.

- Emotional framing: Emotional responses to decision contexts or the way choices are presented can influence our decision-making. Positive emotional framing can enhance our openness to risk, while negative emotions may make us more risk averse.

4. Social Influences:

Decision-making is not solely an individual process but is also influenced by social factors. Social influences can shape our decisions in various ways:

- Social norms: Norms, explicit or implicit rules within a group, shape our behavior and can influence decision-making. Individuals tend to conform to social norms to gain acceptance and avoid disapproval.
- Social comparison: Comparing oneself to others affects decision-making. People may adjust their choices based on others' behavior, opinions, or perceived success.
- Groupthink: In group decision-making, the desire for consensus can lead to the suppression of dissenting opinions or critical thinking, resulting in flawed decision outcomes.

5. Cultural Influences:

Cultural backgrounds and norms significantly impact decision-making processes. Cultural factors that influence decision-making include:

- Individualism vs. collectivism: Individualistic cultures prioritize personal goals and independence, while collectivistic cultures emphasize group goals and interdependence. These cultural differences influence how decisions are made and the importance placed on individual versus societal needs.
- Uncertainty avoidance: Cultures may vary in their tolerance for ambiguity and uncertainty. Some cultures prefer clear rules, procedures, and known outcomes, while others are more comfortable with ambiguity and uncertainty in decision-making.
- Time orientation: Cultural attitudes towards time significantly impact decision-making. Some cultures may prioritize immediate outcomes and short-term gains, while others emphasize patience, long-term planning, and delayed gratification.

Understanding cultural influences is important for decision-making within diverse settings, as it helps recognize and appreciate different perspectives and approaches to decision-making.

The psychological foundations of decision-making provide valuable insights into the processes, biases, emotions, and social and cultural influences that shape our choices. Rational choice theory provides a framework for decision-making based on utility maximization, while cognitive biases highlight the limitations of purely rational decision-making. Emotions influence our evaluations and decision-making, while social and cultural factors affect our choices through social norms, group dynamics, and cultural values. By understanding these psychological foundations, individuals can become more aware of their decision-making processes, identify cognitive biases, and employ strategies to make more informed and effective choices.

Cultural Foundations

Cultural perspectives also play a significant role in the foundations of ethical decision-making. Cultural norms, values, and beliefs shape the ethical frameworks within which individuals operate. Different cultures have diverse moral systems that reflect their traditions, customs, and religious beliefs. For example, Eastern cultures often prioritize collective well-being and harmony, while Western cultures may emphasize individual autonomy and rights.

Cultural foundations influence ethical decision-making by shaping individuals' understanding of right and wrong. They provide a context within which moral judgments are made, and they influence the moral principles individuals consider when making ethical decisions. Recognizing cultural differences is essential in promoting cross-cultural understanding and addressing ethical dilemmas in diverse societies.

The cultural foundations of decision-making are a fundamental aspect of human behavior, influencing the way individuals and groups make choices based on their cultural beliefs, values, and norms. Culture provides a framework that shapes the decision-making process, incorporating elements such as beliefs, language, socialization, and shared knowledge. In this article, we will explore the cultural foundations of decision-making, discussing the impact of cultural dimensions, cultural biases, cross-cultural decision-making, and cultural influences on group decision-making.

1. Cultural Dimensions:

Numerous researchers have identified various dimensions that help analyze and understand different cultures' values, attitudes, and behaviors, and how they affect decision-making. Some of the common cultural dimensions include:

- Individualism vs. Collectivism: Hofstede's cultural dimension distinguishes between cultures that prioritize individual goals over collective goals. Individualistic cultures value personal autonomy, freedom, and self-achievement, while collectivistic cultures emphasize group harmony, loyalty, and cooperation.
- Power Distance: This dimension reflects the degree of acceptance or resistance to hierarchical power structures within a society. High power distance cultures value hierarchies and authority, while low power distance cultures promote equality and participatory decision-making.
- Uncertainty Avoidance: Cultural variation in uncertainty tolerance impacts decision-making. Cultures with high uncertainty avoidance seek stability and prefer clear rules and guidelines, while cultures with low uncertainty avoidance tolerate ambiguity and are more comfortable with risk-taking and uncertainty.
- Masculinity vs. Femininity: This dimension describes the extent to which a culture values assertiveness, achievement, and competition (masculinity) versus collaboration, nurturing, and quality of life (femininity).

Understanding these cultural dimensions helps explain how different cultures approach decision-making, prioritize values, and balance individual versus collective needs.

2. Cultural Biases:

Cultural biases influence decision-making by shaping the way individuals perceive, evaluate, and process information. These biases can manifest in various forms:

- Ethnocentrism: Ethnocentrism refers to the belief that one's own culture is superior to others, leading to biased evaluations of different options or choices. This bias can influence decision-making by favoring the cultural norms and values of one's own culture.
- Stereotyping: Stereotyping involves categorizing individuals based on cultural or ethnic backgrounds, leading to assumptions and bias in decision-making. These stereotypes can influence judgments about competence, trustworthiness, or suitability for roles, impacting decision outcomes.
- Cultural frames: Cultural frames refer to the lenses through which individuals interpret and evaluate information. These frames are influenced by cultural values, beliefs, and norms. Different cultural frames can result in divergent interpretations of information and subsequent decisions.

Being aware of these cultural biases is essential for fostering fair, inclusive, and effective decision-making processes.

3. Cross-Cultural Decision-Making:

Cross-cultural decision-making involves making choices in a multicultural or diverse context. This type of decision-making requires an understanding of cultural differences to ensure fair and effective processes. Factors to consider in cross-cultural decision-making include:

- Cultural intelligence: Cultural intelligence involves the ability to understand and adapt to different cultural perspectives. Developing cultural intelligence helps individuals navigate diverse decision-making contexts and bridge cultural gaps.

- Cultural empathy: Cultural empathy refers to the ability to understand and appreciate different cultural perspectives and experiences. It involves actively listening, valuing diversity, and considering alternative viewpoints in decision-making.

Cross-cultural decision-making requires open-mindedness, flexibility, and the ability to recognize and respect cultural differences while striving for fair and inclusive outcomes.

4. Cultural Influences on Group Decision-Making:

Group decision-making is strongly influenced by cultural factors. Cultural influences can impact group decision-making in the following ways:

- Communication styles: Cultural variations in communication styles, such as directness, the degree of hierarchy, and the importance of harmony, affect how groups discuss options, negotiate, and make decisions. Understanding these differences helps prevent misunderstandings and conflicts that may disrupt the decision-making process.
- Consensus versus authority: Cultures have different preferences for decision-making processes. Some cultures emphasize reaching a consensus through discussion and collaboration, while others rely on hierarchical decision-making where authority figures make choices. Awareness of these cultural tendencies is key to fostering effective group decision-making within diverse teams or organizations.

5. Cultural Diversity and Creativity in Decision-Making:

Cultural diversity influences decision-making processes and outcomes. Research shows that diverse cultural perspectives can promote creativity and innovative solutions. When individuals from diverse cultural backgrounds collaborate, they bring unique knowledge, experiences, and problem-solving approaches to the decision-making process. This cultural diversity can enhance creativity and lead to more comprehensive and effective decisions.

The cultural foundations of decision-making highlight the profound influence that culture has on individuals' and groups' choices. Cultural dimensions, biases, cross-cultural decision-making, and cultural influences on group decision-making all play a significant role in shaping decision-making processes and outcomes. Understanding cultural foundations enriches decision-making by enabling individuals to appreciate and respect different cultural perspectives, mitigate cultural biases, and leverage cultural diversity for creative and effective decision-making. By embracing cultural sensitivity and diversity, individuals and organizations can foster equitable, inclusive, and successful decision-making processes.

Religious Foundations

Religion has also been a significant influence in shaping the foundations of ethical decision-making. Religious teachings provide moral guidelines for believers, outlining the moral obligations and prohibitions they should adhere to. For example, the Ten Commandments in Christianity and the Five Pillars of Islam offer clear ethical guidelines for followers to navigate their decision-making processes.

Religious foundations influence ethical decision-making by providing a definitive source of moral authority. They offer individuals a set of principles and values that guide behavior and decision-making. Religion plays a crucial role in shaping the moral compass of believers, helping them navigate ethical dilemmas in their personal, professional, and societal lives.

The religious foundations of decision-making have a profound impact on individuals and societies, shaping values, beliefs, and ethical frameworks that guide choices and actions. Religion provides a moral compass and a set of principles that influence decision-making processes. Whether directly or indirectly, religious beliefs and practices shape how individuals perceive the world, evaluate alternatives, and make choices based on their faith. In this article, we will explore the religious foundations of decision-making, discussing the role of religious beliefs, moral values, ethical frameworks, and the implications for decision-making in different religious contexts.

1. Religious Beliefs and Value Systems:

Religious beliefs form the foundation of decision-making for individuals who adhere to a particular faith. These beliefs often encompass views on the nature of the divine, the purpose of life, and moral principles that guide ethical behavior. Religious beliefs provide a framework for understanding the world, interpreting experiences, and making choices that align with religious teachings.

For example, in Christianity, the belief that human beings are created in the image of God and possess inherent dignity and worth informs decisions related to human rights, social justice, and the ethical treatment of others. In Islam, the belief in submission to God's will (Islam) directs decision-making processes, seeking to align choices with religious teachings and the pursuit of righteousness.

Religious beliefs can influence decisions related to personal behavior, relationships, consumption, and various aspects of life based on the moral values and ethical guidelines established by religious traditions.

2. Moral and Ethical Frameworks:

Religious traditions provide moral and ethical frameworks that guide decision-making and shape the values and principles individuals follow. These frameworks often include ethical principles and commandments that provide moral guidelines for believers. For instance:

- The Ten Commandments in Judaism and Christianity offer a set of moral imperatives that guide decision-making in areas such as honesty, respect for parents, respect for life, and fidelity in relationships.
- The Five Pillars of Islam provide principles for ethical behavior, including acts of worship, charity, abstaining from prohibited activities, and adhering to moral conduct.

These frameworks define what is considered right or wrong, providing religious believers with a moral compass and guidance for making ethical decisions.

3. Religious Authority:

Religious authority, such as religious leaders, scriptures, or religious texts, can influence decision-making by providing guidance, interpretations, and moral teachings. Individuals may seek the counsel of religious leaders to help them make informed choices. Religious texts, like the Bible, Quran, or Torah, are often considered authoritative and provide teachings and examples that inform decision-making in religious contexts.

Religious authority helps believers navigate complex ethical dilemmas and answer questions related to personal conduct, interpersonal relationships, and societal issues. The guidance and interpretations provided by religious authority figures play a significant role in helping individuals align their decisions with religious teachings.

4. Rituals and Practices:

Religious rituals and practices also shape decision-making processes. Practices such as prayer, meditation, fasting, and pilgrimage contribute to self-reflection, seeking divine guidance, and strengthening faith. These practices can provide individuals with clarity, insight, and a sense of spiritual connection, which may inform their decision-making processes.

For example, in Buddhism, meditation practices aim to develop mindfulness and cultivate a clear mind, which can improve decision-making by reducing cognitive biases and enhancing self-awareness.

5. Religious Community and Communal Decision-Making:

Religious communities play a role in decision-making, particularly in matters that affect the collective. In many religious traditions, communal decision-making involves seeking consensus or taking guidance from religious authorities and community leaders.

Collective decision-making processes involve prayer, consultation, and seeking agreement or consensus among community members. This approach emphasizes the importance of communal values, shared beliefs, and the pursuit of the common good. The communal decision-making process can influence choices related to community affairs, social issues, or ethical concerns.

6. Challenges and Nuances:

While religious foundations provide valuable guidance for decision-making, challenges, and nuances arise due to the diverse interpretations of religious teachings and individual differences within religious communities. Different religious denominations or sects may interpret religious texts differently, leading to varying belief systems or moral guidelines.

Moreover, individuals may hold varying levels of religious commitment, resulting in diverse practices and interpretations of religious teachings. This diversity can lead to differences in decision-making processes and outcomes even within the same religious tradition.

The religious foundations of decision-making significantly impact individuals and societies, guiding choices based on religious beliefs, moral values, ethical frameworks, and religious authority. Religious beliefs and values shape perceptions, values, and moral principles that influence decision-making processes. Religious frameworks provide guidance and principles for ethical behavior and inform choices in various spheres of life. Practices, rituals, religious authority, and communal decision-making further influence the decision-making process. While the religious foundations of decision-making are significant, the nuances within religious communities, diverse interpretations, and individual differences present challenges and complexities. Recognizing these complexities allows for a more comprehensive understanding of how religious beliefs shape decision-making and highlights the importance of respecting diverse perspectives within religious contexts.

Interplay of Foundations

The foundations of ethical decision-making are interconnected and often coexist in individuals' moral reasoning. Philosophical perspectives, psychological theories, cultural influences, and religious beliefs shape an individual's ethical decision-making process simultaneously. These foundations inform one another, influencing individuals' values, principles, and moral priorities.

For instance, an individual's cultural upbringing and religious beliefs can influence their understanding of philosophical concepts such as consequentialism, deontology, and virtue ethics. Likewise, psychological factors, such as empathy and cognitive development, can be influenced by cultural and religious factors, shaping how individuals approach and make ethical decisions.

In conclusion, the foundations of ethical decision-making encompass various philosophical, psychological, cultural, and religious perspectives. These foundations provide individuals with a framework to assess, judge, and make decisions that consider ethical implications. By understanding the diverse elements that shape ethical decision-making, individuals can develop a well-rounded approach to navigating ethical dilemmas. Recognizing the interplay between philosophical, psychological, cultural, and religious foundations is essential in fostering ethical decision-making in personal, professional, and societal contexts.

Chapter Three

Ethics in Leadership

Ethics in leadership is a fundamental aspect of effective and responsible leadership. It entails making decisions and leading others based on moral principles and values that prioritize integrity, fairness, and social responsibility. Ethical leaders not only inspire and guide their teams but also set a positive example for others to follow. They recognize the impact of their actions on individuals and society and strive to promote greater good through their leadership. In this section, we will explore the importance of ethics in leadership and how it shapes organizational culture, decision-making processes, and overall success.

Introduction to Ethics in Leadership

Leadership ethics refers to the moral principles and values that guide the behavior and decision-making of leaders. It entails making ethical choices and taking responsibility for the impact of those choices on individuals, organizations, and society. Leadership ethics play a crucial role in shaping the character and reputation of a leader, determining their ability to inspire trust, and establishing the ethical culture within an organization.

In the first paragraph, it is important to highlight the significance of ethics in leadership. Effective leadership requires a deep understanding of moral principles and a commitment to ethical behavior. Leaders must possess a strong moral compass and actively integrate ethical considerations into their decision-making process.

The second paragraph could delve into the concept of ethical decision-making. Leaders are often faced with complex, challenging situations that demand them to make difficult choices. Ethical decision-making involves gathering relevant information, evaluating various options, and choosing the course of action that aligns with moral principles and values. Leaders who prioritize ethics strive to do what is morally right rather than what is expedient or advantageous.

The third paragraph emphasizes the role of integrity and trust in leadership ethics. Leaders' actions and decisions should reflect consistency between their stated values and their behavior. Demonstrating integrity entails being honest, transparent, and accountable for one's actions. Trust is vital in leadership because it fosters open communication, collaboration, and loyalty among followers. Leaders who act ethically cultivate trust among their team members and inspire them to act with integrity as well.

In the fourth paragraph, it may be beneficial to discuss the ethical responsibilities leaders have towards stakeholders. Leaders have a broad range of responsibilities, including considering the interests of employees, customers, shareholders, and society at large. Ethical leaders prioritize the well-being and fair treatment of all stakeholders and actively seek to create a positive impact through their leadership actions.

Finally, the fifth paragraph can touch upon the importance of promoting an ethical culture within organizations. Leadership ethics not only guide the actions of individual leaders but also set an ethical tone within an organization. Leaders who emphasize ethical behavior and enforce ethical norms create an environment that fosters trust, respect, and fairness. An ethical culture promotes collaboration, innovation, and long-term success, as it aligns the interests of the organization with the interests of all stakeholders.

Overall, leadership ethics involves making moral choices, prioritizing integrity and trust, considering the interests of stakeholders, and promoting an ethical culture. These introductory paragraphs provide an overview of the essential elements of leadership ethics and set the foundation for a deeper exploration of the topic.

The Significance of Ethics in Leadership Positions

Ethics play a significant role in leadership as they guide and shape the behavior and decision-making of leaders. Here are ten paragraphs explaining the significance of ethics in leadership.

1. Ethics serve as a compass for leaders, providing them with a moral framework to navigate their actions and decisions. By adhering to ethical principles, leaders can ensure that their behavior is aligned with what is morally right and just. This helps maintain the trust and respect of their followers, as well as their integrity.

Ethics plays a significant role in guiding leaders in large organizations by serving as a compass that helps them navigate through complex decision-making processes and ensure responsible behavior. Here are some ways ethics can serve as a compass for leaders in large organizations along with examples:

a. Ethical Decision Making: Leaders use ethical principles to make decisions that are fair, just, and in the best interest of all stakeholders. For example, leaders may opt for transparency and accountability by disclosing financial information accurately, even if it negatively impacts shareholders in the short term.

b. Corporate Social Responsibility: Leaders utilize ethics to guide their organizations toward being socially responsible by considering the impact of their decisions on the environment, society, and communities. For instance, a leader may choose to invest in sustainable practices or support community development programs.

c. Fair Treatment and Equality: Leaders adhere to ethical values to ensure fair treatment and equal opportunities for employees. They promote diversity, and inclusivity, and avoid any form of discrimination or prejudice. This could be exemplified by implementing policies to minimize the gender pay gap or prioritizing the hiring of individuals from disadvantaged backgrounds.

d. Integrity and Trustworthiness: Leaders prioritize ethical behavior that fosters trust and credibility with stakeholders. They set the tone at the top by exemplifying honesty, transparency, and keeping their promises. For instance, a leader may maintain confidentiality regarding sensitive information or take responsibility for errors made by the organization.

e. Stakeholder Engagement: Leaders use ethical principles to engage with stakeholders, considering their interests and listening to their concerns. They involve stakeholders in decision-making processes and seek consensus wherever possible. For example, leaders may gather feedback from customers before launching a new product or engaging with local communities while planning expansion projects.

f. Ethical Leadership: Leaders display ethical leadership qualities by empowering employees, providing mentorship, and promoting a culture of integrity. They set high ethical standards and hold themselves and others accountable. For instance, leaders may provide channels for employees to report unethical behavior without fear of retaliation.

g. Compliance and Legal Requirements: Leaders ensure their organizations follow ethical standards and comply with relevant laws and regulations. They establish ethical codes of conduct and implement effective compliance programs. For example, leaders may enforce antitrust and anti-bribery policies to prevent unlawful business practices.

By using ethics as a compass, leaders in large organizations can create a positive organizational culture, make ethical decisions, and build trust among stakeholders, leading to long-term sustainability and success.

2. Ethical leadership sets the tone within an organization and contributes to the development of a positive ethical culture. When leaders consistently act with integrity and hold themselves and others accountable for ethical conduct, it creates a ripple effect throughout the entire organization. Employees are more likely to embrace and model ethical behaviors when they witness their leader's prioritizing ethics.

Ethical leadership sets the tone within an organization and plays a crucial role in developing a positive ethical culture in the following ways:

a. Model Ethical Behavior: Ethical leaders lead by example, demonstrating integrity, transparency, and fairness in their actions and decisions. By embodying ethical behavior, leaders set a standard for others to follow, creating a culture where ethical conduct is valued and expected.

b. Communicate Ethical Expectations: Ethical leaders communicate their expectations regarding ethical behavior to their employees. They establish ethical guidelines, and codes of conduct, and provide training to ensure everyone understands the organization's values and ethical standards. This clarity helps shape the culture and reinforces the importance of ethical decision-making.

c. Foster Trust and Transparency: Ethical leaders build trust among employees by creating an environment of open communication and transparency. They encourage employees to voice their concerns and provide feedback without fear of retribution. This trust enables employees to make ethical decisions and report any unethical behavior they witness.

d. Encourage Ethical Decision-Making: Ethical leaders empower and support employees in making ethical decisions. They provide guidance when faced with complex ethical dilemmas and encourage critical thinking. By emphasizing the ethical implications of decisions, leaders cultivate a culture where employees prioritize ethical considerations in their day-to-day work.

e. Promote Accountability: Ethical leaders hold themselves and others accountable for their actions. They establish mechanisms for reporting unethical behavior and ensure investigations are conducted impartially. By consistently enforcing ethical standards, leaders demonstrate that unethical behavior will not be tolerated, further reinforcing the culture of ethics.

f. Develop Ethical Leaders: Ethical leaders invest in the development of their employees' ethical leadership capabilities. They provide mentoring, coaching, and training opportunities to help shape the next generation of ethical leaders within the organization. This commitment to developing ethical leaders contributes to the sustainability of a positive ethical culture even as the organization grows and evolves.

Overall, ethical leadership is critical in establishing a positive ethical culture within an organization. It sets the tone, communicates expectations, and fosters trust, transparency, ethical decision-making, accountability, and the development of ethical leaders. These factors combined create a culture where ethics are valued, integrated into daily operations, and form an integral part of the organization's identity.

3. Ethical leadership enhances trust and credibility. Trust is the foundation of effective leadership, and ethical behavior is a critical factor in earning and maintaining the trust of followers. Leaders who consistently make ethical choices and prioritize the well-being of their constituents demonstrate their reliability and commitment to doing what is right. This, in turn, fosters trust and credibility, making it easier to inspire and influence others.

Ethical leadership plays a vital role in enhancing trust and credibility within an organization. Here are some key ways ethical leadership accomplishes this:

a. Consistency and Transparency: Ethical leaders consistently demonstrate ethical behavior and uphold the organization's values. They communicate openly and honestly, ensuring transparency in decision-making processes. This consistency builds trust as employees see that the leader's actions align with their words, promoting credibility.

b. Integrity and Honesty: Ethical leaders exhibit a high level of integrity and honesty in their interactions. They behave ethically, even in challenging situations, and do not compromise their principles for personal gain. Employees who observe this unwavering commitment to integrity are more likely to trust and have confidence in their leader's decisions and actions.

c. Accountable and Responsible: Ethical leaders take responsibility for their actions and decisions. They hold themselves accountable and accept the consequences, which fosters trust among employees. By accepting accountability, leaders demonstrate a genuine commitment to ethical behavior, which enhances their credibility.

d. Deliberate and Ethical Decision-Making: Ethical leaders prioritize ethical considerations when making decisions. They consider the potential impact on stakeholders and evaluate alternative courses of action based on ethical standards. Employees who observe their leader's commitment to ethical decision-making are more likely to trust their judgment and credibility.

e. Empathy and Fairness: Ethical leaders demonstrate empathy and fairness in their interactions with individuals and groups. They consider the perspectives and needs of others and treat them equitably. Employees feel valued and respected when their leader exhibits fairness, which contributes to enhanced trust and credibility.

f. Employee Development and Support: Ethical leaders invest in the development of their employees and provide support to help them succeed. They promote personal and professional growth, provide mentorship, and create a supportive environment. This commitment to employee development builds trust and enhances the leader's credibility as employees recognize their genuine care and investment in their success.

g. Ethical Communication: Ethical leaders communicate openly and authentically. They share relevant information and involve employees in decision-making processes when appropriate. By openly communicating and actively listening, leaders promote trust and credibility as employees feel included and informed.

When ethical leaders consistently demonstrate integrity, transparency, accountability, ethical decision-making, fairness, and support for their employees, they enhance trust and credibility within the organization. Employees feel confident in their leader's character, actions, and decision-making, leading to a supportive and ethical work environment. This trust and credibility foster cooperation, collaboration, and a sense of shared purpose that contributes to the organization's overall success.

4. Ethical leaders promote fairness and justice. By considering the interests and needs of all stakeholders, ethical leaders create a culture of fairness and equality within their organizations. They make decisions that are unbiased and impartial, ensuring that everyone is treated with respect and given equal opportunities. This fosters a sense of loyalty and dedication among employees, leading to increased engagement and productivity.

Ethical leaders promote fairness and justice within an organization by ensuring equal treatment, addressing biases, and creating a culture that values diversity and inclusivity. Here are some examples of how ethical leaders promote fairness and justice:

a. Equal Opportunities: Ethical leaders ensure that all employees have equal access to opportunities for growth, advancement, and recognition. They do not discriminate based on factors such as gender, race, age, or other protected characteristics. For example, an ethical leader may implement policies to ensure gender pay equity and provide equal access to training and development programs for employees at all levels.

b. Bias Awareness and Mitigation: Ethical leaders are aware of their own biases and work to mitigate their impact on decision-making processes. They actively seek diverse perspectives and encourage open dialogue to challenge and address biases. For instance, an ethical leader may implement unconscious bias training for managers to enhance awareness and reduce the influence of unconscious biases during hiring or promotion processes.

c. Inclusive Decision-Making: Ethical leaders involve diverse stakeholders in decision-making processes to ensure fairness and justice. They create forums for open discussion and actively seek input from individuals with different backgrounds and perspectives. This inclusivity promotes fair decision-making and reduces the risk of overlooking diverse viewpoints. For example, an ethical leader may establish a diverse task force to review and provide input on policies that could impact marginalized groups.

d. Anti-Discrimination Policies: Ethical leaders create policies and guidelines that prohibit discrimination and harassment within the organization. They establish a zero-tolerance approach to address any instances of unfair treatment or discriminatory behavior. For instance, an ethical leader may implement comprehensive anti-discrimination policies that clearly define prohibited behaviors and establish reporting mechanisms to address any violations promptly.

e. Support for Marginalized Groups: Ethical leaders actively support and advocate for marginalized groups within the organization. They create an environment that embraces diversity and promotes inclusivity. For example, an ethical leader may establish employee resource groups to provide support and visibility for underrepresented employees while actively seeking ways to include their perspectives in decision-making processes.

f. Fair Performance Evaluation and Reward Systems: Ethical leaders ensure that performance evaluation systems are fair, transparent, and based on objective criteria. They actively monitor and address bias in evaluation processes to avoid favoritism or unfair treatment. For instance, an ethical leader may implement calibration sessions where managers review and discuss performance ratings to minimize bias and ensure consistency in evaluations.

g. Ethics Training and Communication: Ethical leaders provide ongoing ethics training and communication to reinforce the importance of fairness and justice. They establish clear guidelines and expectations regarding ethical behavior and guide navigating complex situations. For example, an ethical leader may conduct regular ethics training sessions that focus on promoting fairness, addressing bias, and upholding principles of justice.

By actively promoting fairness and justice, ethical leaders create an environment where individuals are treated equitably and have equal opportunities for growth and success. This fosters a culture of trust, respect, and inclusivity, ultimately benefiting both the employees and the organization.

5. Ethical leadership encourages responsible decision-making. Leaders who prioritize ethics are more likely to thoroughly analyze the potential consequences of their actions on various stakeholders. They consider the long-term effects and strive to make decisions that maximize benefits while minimizing harm. Ethical leaders take responsibility for their choices and are willing to face the consequences of their actions.

Ethical leadership encourages responsible decision-making by prioritizing ethical considerations, promoting accountability, and fostering a culture of responsibility within an organization. Here are some examples of how ethical leadership encourages responsible decision-making:

a. Ethical Considerations: Ethical leaders consider the potential impact of their decisions on stakeholders, including employees, customers, communities, and the environment. They consider ethical principles such as fairness, honesty, and integrity when evaluating options and choosing a course of action. For instance, an ethical leader may consider the environmental impact before approving a project or prioritize the well-being of employees when considering changes to company policies.

b. Stakeholder Engagement: Ethical leaders encourage the involvement of stakeholders in decision-making processes to ensure that their perspectives and concerns are taken into account. They seek input from employees, customers, and other relevant parties to gather diverse viewpoints and make informed decisions. For example, an ethical leader may conduct focus groups or surveys to solicit feedback before implementing significant changes within the organization.

c. Transparency and Communication: Ethical leaders foster an environment of transparency and open communication, ensuring that decision-making processes are clear and understandable to stakeholders. They provide the rationale behind decisions, share relevant information, and encourage dialogue to help stakeholders understand the responsible considerations involved. For instance, an ethical leader may hold town hall meetings or send regular updates to employees to explain the reasoning behind strategic decisions.

d. Accountability and Consequences: Ethical leaders create a culture of accountability within the organization. They hold themselves and others responsible for their decisions and actions. They establish clear expectations and consequences for unethical behavior, ensuring that individuals are held accountable for any negative impact their decisions may have. For example, an ethical leader may establish a whistleblowing policy to encourage employees to report unethical behavior and establish disciplinary measures to address violations.

e. Ethical Decision-Making Frameworks: Ethical leaders provide guidance and tools to support responsible decision-making. They may establish ethical frameworks or decision-making models to help employees evaluate alternatives and consider ethical implications in their decision-making process. These frameworks may include criteria such as legality, fairness, impact on stakeholders, and adherence to organizational values. For instance, an ethical leader may guide employees to use the "triple bottom line" framework, considering the economic, social, and environmental impacts of their decisions.

f. Continuous Learning and Development: Ethical leaders invest in the development of their employees' ethical decision-making abilities. They provide training, mentorship, and resources to equip employees with the necessary skills to make responsible decisions. They encourage critical thinking, ethical reasoning, and guide navigating complex situations. For example, an ethical leader may organize workshops or seminars on ethical decision-making to enhance employees' abilities in this area.

By emphasizing ethical considerations, promoting stakeholder engagement, fostering transparency and communication, establishing accountability, providing decision-making frameworks, and investing in employee development, ethical leaders create an environment that encourages responsible decision-making. This approach helps in mitigating ethical risks, building trust, and ensuring the long-term sustainability and success of the organization.

6. Ethical leadership promotes transparency and accountability. Leaders who act ethically are open and transparent about their decisions and actions. They communicate honestly with their constituents, take responsibility for their mistakes, and hold themselves and others accountable for their behavior. This creates an environment of trust and openness, where issues and concerns can be addressed openly and resolved effectively.

Ethical leadership promotes transparency and accountability by encouraging a culture of openness, honesty, and integrity within an organization. It ensures that leaders set a positive example, hold themselves accountable for their actions, and promote ethical behavior among the team members. Here are a few examples of how ethical leadership promotes transparency and accountability:

a. Clear communication: Ethical leaders believe in open and transparent communication. They provide clear instructions, share information about goals, expectations, and progress, and actively listen to feedback from their team. This transparency in communication promotes accountability as team members are aware of the expectations and can align their actions accordingly.

b. Setting high ethical standards: Ethical leaders set high standards of ethical behavior and hold themselves accountable to those standards. By leading with integrity, they inspire others to follow suit, creating a culture of accountability within the organization. For example, a CEO who not only talks about the importance of ethical conduct but also demonstrates it in their decision-making will promote a sense of accountability among employees.

c. Encouraging reporting mechanisms: Ethical leaders establish robust reporting mechanisms, such as whistleblower channels or anonymous feedback systems, where employees can report unethical activities without fear of retribution. Such mechanisms ensure transparency in addressing misconduct and holding individuals accountable for their actions. For instance, an ethical leader may implement regular audits and encourage employees to report any suspicious activities they come across.

d. Transparent decision-making processes: Ethical leaders involve stakeholders in decision-making processes as much as possible, ensuring transparency in how decisions are made. They consider different perspectives, gather all relevant information, and share the rationale behind their decisions. This transparency promotes accountability as it allows team members to understand the reasoning behind decisions and evaluate their fairness. A leader who conducts team discussions and seeks feedback before making important decisions promotes transparency and accountability.

e. Ethical code of conduct: Ethical leaders develop and enforce a code of conduct that outlines the organization's ethical standards and expectations. This code acts as a guide for employees, ensuring transparency in behavior and promoting accountability. It sets clear boundaries and helps employees understand what is expected of them. For example, a leader who establishes a code of conduct that prohibits conflicts of interest or unethical financial practices promotes transparency and accountability in those areas.

In summary, ethical leadership promotes transparency and accountability by fostering clear communication, setting high ethical standards, creating reporting mechanisms, employing transparent decision-making processes, and enacting an ethical code of conduct. These practices ensure that leaders and employees are accountable for their actions, create trust within the organization, and uphold ethical values.

7. Ethical leaders value diversity and inclusion. They recognize and appreciate the unique perspectives and contributions of individuals from diverse backgrounds. Ethical leadership involves creating an inclusive environment where everyone feels valued and respected, regardless of their race, gender, nationality, or other characteristics. Leaders who prioritize ethics understand that diversity and inclusion are not only moral imperatives but also essential for innovation and growth.

Ethical leaders value diversity and inclusion because they recognize the inherent worth and potential of every individual, regardless of their background, race, gender, age, or other characteristics. They understand that a diverse and inclusive workforce brings numerous benefits to the organization, such as enhanced innovation, increased creativity, improved decision-making, and better performance overall. Here's how and why ethical leaders prioritize diversity and inclusion:

a. Embrace different perspectives: Ethical leaders understand that diverse teams bring a variety of perspectives, experiences, and viewpoints to the table. They value and actively seek out these diverse perspectives because they recognize that it leads to more robust discussions, innovative solutions, and better decision-making. By embracing different perspectives, ethical leaders ensure that all voices are heard and considered, fostering a culture of inclusion.

b. Foster a sense of belonging: Ethical leaders create an environment where everyone feels valued, respected, and included. They promote inclusivity by ensuring equal opportunities for growth and development, providing a safe space for individuals to express themselves, and encouraging collaboration among team members. By fostering a sense of belonging, ethical leaders promote diversity and make employees feel more engaged and motivated to contribute their best.

c. Mitigate bias and discrimination: Ethical leaders actively work to mitigate bias and discrimination within their organization. They implement policies and practices that promote fairness and equality, ensuring that decisions about hiring, promotions, and assignments are based on merit and not influenced by bias. They also educate themselves and others about unconscious biases and work towards creating an inclusive culture that values diversity. By addressing bias and discrimination, ethical leaders create a more inclusive and equitable workplace.

d. Tap into a broader talent pool: Ethical leaders recognize that a diverse workforce attracts and retains top talent from a wider range of backgrounds. They understand that diversity leads to increased creativity and innovation, as people with different experiences and perspectives bring unique ideas and solutions to the table. By valuing diversity, ethical leaders tap into a broader talent pool and create a competitive advantage for their organization.

e. Fulfill societal responsibilities: Ethical leaders recognize that diversity and inclusion are not just organizational imperatives but also societal responsibilities. They understand the importance of creating a workplace that reflects the diversity of the communities they serve. By embracing diversity and inclusion, ethical leaders contribute to building a more equitable and just society.

In summary, ethical leaders value diversity and inclusion because they appreciate the benefits that such an environment brings to individuals and organizations alike. They embrace different perspectives, foster a sense of belonging, mitigate bias and discrimination, tap into a broader talent pool, and fulfill their societal responsibilities. Through their actions, ethical leaders create an inclusive and diverse workplace that not only benefits employees but also enhances the organization's performance and reputation.

8. Ethical leadership promotes ethical decision-making throughout the organization. When leaders consistently act ethically, it sets an example for the entire team. It encourages employees to consider ethical principles when making decisions and empowers them to voice concerns or raise ethical dilemmas. Ethical leadership creates an environment where employees feel comfortable speaking up and can collaborate on finding ethical solutions.

Ethical leadership plays a crucial role in promoting ethical decision-making throughout the organization. Ethical leaders set the tone for an ethical culture by their actions, behaviors, and values, thereby influencing the decision-making processes of their team members. Here's how ethical leadership promotes ethical decision-making:

a. Role modeling: Ethical leaders lead by example and consistently demonstrate ethical behavior and decision-making. They adhere to a strong moral compass, making ethical choices even in challenging situations. This role modeling inspires and influences employees to emulate ethical behavior and consider ethical factors in their decision-making processes.

b. Establishing clear values and standards: Ethical leaders define and communicate the organization's core values and ethical standards. By creating a framework within which decisions are made, ethical leaders provide a guide that employees can reference to ensure their actions align with ethical principles. This clarity helps to promote ethical decision-making as employees understand the organization's expectations.

c. Encouraging open discussion and dissent: Ethical leaders create an environment that encourages open dialogue and the expression of diverse perspectives. They welcome and value constructive criticism, encouraging team members to question and challenge decisions to ensure that ethical considerations are thoroughly explored. This fosters a culture of ethical decision-making by promoting transparency, critical thinking, and a broader understanding of potential ethical dilemmas.

d. Providing ethical guidance and support: Ethical leaders provide guidance and support to employees when faced with ethical challenges or dilemmas. They are available to provide advice, facilitate discussions, and assist in analyzing potential ethical implications of decisions. Providing this support empowers employees to make decisions based on ethical considerations and promotes a culture of ethical decision-making.

e. Establishing accountability mechanisms: Ethical leaders create accountability mechanisms within the organization to ensure that ethical decision-making is upheld. They implement ethical codes of conduct, establish reporting mechanisms for ethical violations or concerns, and hold individuals accountable for their actions. By fostering a culture of accountability, ethical leaders reinforce the importance of ethical decision-making.

f. Offering ethical training and education: Ethical leaders invest in ongoing ethical training and education for employees. They provide resources, workshops, and discussions that help employees understand ethical principles, recognize ethical dilemmas, and develop the skills needed to make ethical decisions. By providing this education, ethical leaders equip employees with the tools and knowledge necessary to navigate ethical challenges effectively.

In summary, ethical leadership promotes ethical decision-making by setting an example through role modeling, establishing clear values and standards, encouraging open discussions, providing guidance and support, establishing accountability mechanisms, and offering ethical training and education. By championing ethics and integrating ethical considerations into all aspects of decision-making, ethical leaders create a culture that values ethical behavior and ensures that ethical decision-making is consistently practiced throughout the organization.

9. Ethical leadership contributes to the reputation and sustainability of an organization. Leaders who make ethical choices and prioritize values build a strong reputation for integrity and reliability. This reputation attracts talented individuals, fosters customer loyalty, and enhances the organization's overall image. Ethical leadership also ensures that the organization operates sustainably, considering environmental and social impacts in its decision-making processes.

Ethical leadership significantly contributes to the reputation and sustainability of an organization. It establishes a strong foundation of trust, integrity, and social responsibility, which enhances the organization's image and ensures its long-term viability. Here are some ways in which ethical leadership contributes to reputation and sustainability:

a. Trust and credibility: Ethical leadership fosters trust among stakeholders, including employees, customers, partners, and the wider community. By consistently exhibiting honesty, transparency, and fairness in their actions, ethical leaders build a reputation for trustworthiness and credibility. This trust strengthens relationships, attracts loyal customers, and fosters long-term partnerships, all of which contribute to the organization's reputation and sustainability.

b. Employee engagement and retention: Ethical leadership creates a positive work environment where employees feel valued, respected, and motivated. Ethical leaders prioritize fairness, treat employees with dignity, and provide opportunities for growth and development. Such practices enhance employee satisfaction, engagement, and loyalty. Engaged employees are more likely to contribute their best, leading to increased productivity, better customer service, and overall organizational success.

c. Attracting and retaining customers: Ethical leadership influences customers' perceptions and choices. Customers are increasingly mindful of the ethical practices of organizations and prefer to associate with those that align with their values. Ethical leaders ensure that the organization upholds ethical standards, respects consumer rights, supports social causes, and prioritizes sustainability. By doing so, they build a positive reputation and attract customers who value ethical conduct, contributing to the organization's long-term sustainability.

d. Reputation management and crisis prevention: Ethical leaders proactively manage the organization's reputation by addressing potential ethical risks and vulnerabilities. They develop robust ethical guidelines, align business practices with legal and ethical requirements, and implement effective risk management strategies. By taking a proactive approach, ethical leaders minimize the risk of ethical misconduct that can damage the organization's reputation and contribute to its long-term sustainability.

e. Social and environmental responsibility: Ethical leaders emphasize corporate social responsibility and environmental sustainability. They integrate these principles into the organization's values, strategy, and operations. By demonstrating commitment to social and environmental issues, ethical leaders contribute to the well-being of communities and the preservation of the environment. This positively impacts the organization's reputation and sustainability, attracting stakeholders who value responsible and sustainable practices.

f. Long-term planning and stakeholder management: Ethical leaders take a long-term perspective in their decision-making, considering the impacts on various stakeholders, including employees, customers, suppliers, and the community. They prioritize ethical considerations along with financial goals, balancing short-term gains with long-term sustainability. By actively managing the relationships with stakeholders and aligning their interests with ethical principles, ethical leaders contribute to a positive reputation and sustainable success.

In summary, ethical leadership is instrumental in building and maintaining the reputation and sustainability of an organization. By fostering trust, engaging employees, attracting customers, managing reputation, promoting social responsibility, and considering the interests of stakeholders, ethical leaders create a resilient and responsible organization. This not only contributes to the organization's long-term viability but also enhances its standing in the eyes of stakeholders, ensuring its continued success.

10. Finally, ethical leadership contributes to a more just and ethical society. Leaders have a significant impact beyond their organizations. By demonstrating ethical behavior and promoting ethical values, leaders can influence the larger society. Ethical leaders advocate for fairness, justice, and the common good, inspiring others to also act in ways that benefit society as a whole.

Ethical leadership plays a vital role in shaping a more just and ethical society. It influences not only the organization it operates within but also extends its impact to broader society. Here are some ways in which ethical leadership contributes to a more just and ethical society:

a. Setting an ethical example: Ethical leaders lead by example, demonstrating ethical behavior, values, and principles. Their actions inspire others and serve as a model for ethical conduct. When ethical leaders consistently make choices based on fairness, integrity, and social responsibility, they influence others to emulate those behaviors, both within and beyond the organization. This ripple effect promotes a culture of ethics and justice in society.

b. Promoting fairness and equality: Ethical leaders actively promote fairness and equality within their organizations and advocate for these values in society. They ensure that policies and practices are unbiased, provide equal opportunities, and address systemic inequalities. By championing fairness and equality, ethical leaders contribute to creating a more just society where everyone can thrive.

c. Advocating for ethical practices: Ethical leaders seek to uphold and advance ethical practices in their industry and society. They work to establish industry standards, lobby for regulations that promote ethical conduct, and collaborate with other organizations and stakeholders to drive ethical behavior. This advocacy helps in fostering a society where ethical practices are the norm rather than the exception.

d. Addressing social issues: Ethical leaders recognize their responsibility to address social issues and contribute to positive change. They use their influence and resources to support social causes, tackle societal problems, and promote a more equitable society. Ethical leaders may actively engage in initiatives such as promoting diversity and inclusion, supporting environmental sustainability, or advocating for social justice. By doing so, they contribute to creating a more just and ethical society.

e. Emphasizing corporate social responsibility: Ethical leaders consider the broader impacts of their organization's actions on society. They prioritize corporate social responsibility and ensure that their organization operates in a manner that positively contributes to society. This may involve taking steps to minimize the environmental footprint, prioritizing community engagement and support, and seeking to create shared value for all stakeholders. By embracing corporate social responsibility, ethical leaders contribute to enhancing the well-being of society.

f. Inspiring ethical leaders of the future: Ethical leaders have a profound impact on the individuals they lead and mentor. By cultivating and nurturing ethical leadership in others, they create a pipeline of future leaders who will continue to shape a more just and ethical society. Through their guidance and mentorship, ethical leaders influence others to lead with integrity, empathy, and a commitment to ethical behavior, creating a ripple effect that extends beyond their actions.

In summary, ethical leadership directly contributes to a more just and ethical society by setting an ethical example, promoting fairness and equality, advocating for ethical practices, addressing social issues, emphasizing corporate social responsibility, and inspiring ethical leaders of the future. By fostering a culture of ethical behavior and working towards broader societal goals, ethical leaders contribute to creating a society that values justice, fairness, and ethical conduct.

In summary, ethics are significant in leadership as they guide leaders' behavior, shape organizational culture, promote trust and credibility, encourage responsible decision-making, transparency, and accountability, value diversity and inclusion, and contribute to an organization's reputation and sustainability. Ethical leadership also impacts society by promoting justice and the common good.

The Concept of Decision-Making

Decision-making is a cognitive process that involves selecting a course of action among various alternatives. It is a fundamental aspect of human behavior and is utilized in personal, professional, and organizational contexts. The concept of decision-making encompasses various factors such as information gathering, analysis, evaluation, and ultimately making a choice. Here are twelve paragraphs explaining the concept of decision-making in detail.

1. Decision-making begins with recognizing the need to decide. This can arise from a problem, opportunity, or a desired outcome. It is essential to define the decision-making task clearly to understand the problem or objective at hand and the desired result.

2. Gathering information is a crucial step in decision-making. This involves collecting relevant data, facts, and opinions related to the decision. Information can be gathered through research, consultation, observation, or analysis of past experiences. The objective is to have a comprehensive understanding of the situation and the factors that may influence the decision.

3. Once the necessary information is gathered, it needs to be analyzed and evaluated. This involves assessing the quality, relevance, reliability, and potential impact of the information. Analyzing information helps identify patterns, trends, and potential outcomes to aid in decision-making.

4. Generating alternatives is the next step in decision-making. Based on the analysis of the information, multiple options or solutions can be identified. The purpose of generating alternatives is to consider different possibilities and approaches that may lead to the desired outcome.

5. Evaluating the alternatives requires weighing the pros and cons of each option. This involves considering the potential benefits, risks, costs, and consequences of each alternative. Decision-makers assess the feasibility and viability of each option to determine its potential effectiveness.

6. Decision-makers need to consider and apply decision-making models or frameworks during this process. Models such as the rational model, bounded rationality model, or the intuitive model provide structured approaches to decision-making. These models help organize information, prioritize factors, and evaluate alternatives systematically.

7. Making the final decision involves selecting the best alternative based on the analysis and evaluation of the available options. The decision-maker must consider personal values, objectives, and priorities to make a choice that aligns with their goals.

8. Implementing the decision is an essential phase that involves putting the chosen alternative into action. This requires planning, organizing resources, and communicating the decision to relevant stakeholders. The implementation phase may also require adjustments, monitoring, and feedback to ensure the decision is effectively executed.

9. After the decision is implemented, the outcomes are observed and evaluated. This involves assessing whether the decision achieved the desired objectives and evaluating its effectiveness. Evaluating the outcomes provides valuable feedback for future decision-making and helps to improve the decision-making process.

10. Decision-making can be influenced by various cognitive biases and heuristics. Cognitive biases are mental shortcuts or patterns of thinking that can lead to irrational or imperfect decision-making. Being aware of these biases, such as confirmation bias or anchoring bias, helps decision-makers mitigate their impact and make more objective choices.

11. Group decision-making is another important aspect to consider. In organizations, decisions are often made collectively, involving multiple individuals with different perspectives and expertise. Group decision-making allows for a broader range of ideas and a more comprehensive evaluation of alternatives. However, it can also be challenging due to conflicts, power dynamics, and the potential for group thinking.

12. Continuous learning and adaptation are crucial in decision-making. The process of decision-making is not fixed but rather iterative and dynamic. Decision-makers should actively seek feedback, reflect on the outcomes, and incorporate lessons learned into future decision-making processes. This ongoing learning helps improve decision-making skills and enhances the quality of decisions over time.

In summary, decision-making is a multi-faceted process that involves recognizing the need for a decision, gathering information, analyzing alternatives, evaluating options, and making a choice. It requires critical thinking, assessing risks and benefits, considering personal values, and implementing the selected alternative. Decision-making is influenced by cognitive biases and can be done individually or in groups. Continuous learning and adaptation play a vital role in refining decision-making skills and improving future decision outcomes.

The Role of Integrity and Trust in Leadership Ethics

Integrity and trust are integral elements in leadership ethics as they serve as the foundation for effective leadership and ethical behavior. Here are fifteen paragraphs explaining in detail the role of integrity and trust in leadership ethics.

1. Integrity is the adherence to moral and ethical principles, consistently acting in alignment with one's values and beliefs. In leadership ethics, integrity is essential as it establishes the character and reputation of a leader. Leaders who demonstrate integrity build trust and credibility among their followers by consistently acting in a manner that is honest, transparent, and ethical.

2. Trust is the belief in the reliability, honesty, and competence of a person or entity. In leadership ethics, trust is crucial as it is the key ingredient that fosters open communication, collaboration, and willingness to follow a leader. Trust is earned by leaders who consistently act with integrity, fulfilling their commitments, and demonstrating fairness and respect towards their followers.

3. Leaders with integrity act as role models for ethical behavior. Their consistent actions and decisions reflect their moral values and serve as an example for others to emulate. When leaders consistently demonstrate ethical behavior, it establishes a standard of conduct within the organization and promotes a culture of integrity.

4. Trust is essential for effective communication and collaboration within a team or organization. When followers trust their leader, they feel comfortable expressing their opinions, concerns, and ideas openly. This open communication fosters a sense of psychological safety and encourages innovative thinking, problem-solving, and creative collaboration.

5. Leaders with integrity are transparent and honest in their communication. They provide clear and accurate information, share their thought processes behind decisions, and admit their mistakes when they occur. This transparency builds trust, as followers feel that their leader is genuine and trustworthy.

6. Trust allows leaders to delegate tasks and empower their followers. When followers trust their leader, they are more willing to take ownership of their work, make decisions, and take risks. This delegation of responsibility not only increases productivity but also develops the skills and capabilities of individuals within the organization.

7. Integrity and trust are essential in creating a positive organizational culture. When leaders consistently act with integrity and uphold ethical standards, it sets the tone for the entire organization. This ethical culture promotes a work environment in which individuals feel respected, valued, and motivated to do their best.

8. Trust facilitates loyalty and commitment among followers. When leaders act with integrity, they inspire loyalty as their followers trust their decisions and believe in their vision. This loyalty leads to increased commitment and dedication to the organization's goals and objectives.

9. Leaders with integrity are consistent in their actions, which builds predictability and reliability. When leaders consistently act ethically, followers can depend on them to make decisions that are fair, just, and aligned with organizational values. This consistency and predictability contribute to a stable work environment and reduce anxiety and uncertainty.

10. Trust is crucial for building strong relationships between leaders and followers. When followers trust their leader, they are more likely to seek guidance, support, and feedback. Trust also allows leaders to provide constructive criticism and developmental opportunities without fear of retaliation, as followers believe in their leader's genuine concern for their growth and development.

11. Integrity and trust are vital for fostering a culture of accountability within an organization. When leaders demonstrate integrity in their actions, they set the expectation that all individuals within the organization should act ethically and take responsibility for their actions. This creates a culture where individuals feel empowered to speak up, take ownership of their work, and hold themselves and others accountable.

12. Trust strengthens the resilience of an organization. In challenging times or during periods of change, trust becomes even more crucial. Leaders with integrity who have built trust among their followers can effectively navigate difficult situations, maintain stability, and inspire confidence in the face of adversity.

13. Integrity and trust contribute to the reputation of an organization. When leaders consistently make ethical decisions and act with integrity, it enhances the organization's reputation and credibility. This reputation attracts talented individuals, fosters strong relationships with stakeholders, and enhances the organization's overall success and prosperity.

14. Leaders with integrity inspire loyalty and reduce turnover in an organization. When followers trust their leader and believe in their ethical standards, they are more likely to remain committed to the organization and less likely to seek opportunities elsewhere. This reduces turnover rates and ensures a stable and dedicated team.

15. Ultimately, integrity and trust are cornerstones of effective leadership ethics. Leaders who prioritize integrity and build trust among their followers inspire loyalty, promote an ethical culture, strengthen relationships, and enhance the success and sustainability of their organizations. By acting with integrity and fostering trust, leaders can create positive change and make a lasting impact on individuals, organizations, and society.

Ethical Responsibilities Leaders Have towards Stakeholders.

Leaders have several ethical responsibilities towards stakeholders. Stakeholders are individuals or groups who have a vested interest in the success of an organization. Here are fifteen paragraphs explaining the ethical responsibilities leaders have towards stakeholders.

1. Leaders have an ethical responsibility to act in the best interests of their stakeholders. This includes considering the needs and concerns of employees, customers, investors, and the broader community.

2. Leaders should prioritize the well-being and safety of their employees. This involves providing a safe and healthy work environment, fair wages, opportunities for growth and development, and ensuring a work-life balance.

3. Leaders have a responsibility to be transparent and honest in their communication with stakeholders. They should provide accurate and timely information about the organization's goals, strategies, and performance, and be forthcoming about any challenges or risks.

4. Ethical leaders value and respect the rights and dignity of their employees. This includes promoting diversity, inclusion, and equal opportunities for all individuals within the organization. Leaders should ensure that discriminatory practices or actions are not tolerated.

5. Leaders have a responsibility to make socially responsible decisions. They should consider the impact of their actions on the environment, local communities, and society. This involves minimizing negative impacts, supporting sustainable practices, and contributing to the social good.

6. Leaders should prioritize ethical behavior in their interactions with customers and clients. This includes providing quality products and services, being honest in marketing and advertising efforts, and respecting customer privacy and confidentiality.

7. Leaders should consider the interests of investors and shareholders. This involves making informed and responsible financial decisions, ensuring transparency in financial reporting, and providing a fair return on investment.

8. Ethical leaders should engage in responsible and fair business practices. This includes adhering to laws and regulations, promoting fair competition, and avoiding unethical practices such as bribery or corruption.

9. Leaders have a responsibility to foster trust and collaboration with their suppliers and business partners. This includes treating suppliers fairly, honoring contracts and agreements, and promoting mutually beneficial relationships.

10. Ethical leaders should be active and engaged members of the community. This involves supporting community initiatives, contributing to charitable causes, and being a responsible corporate citizen.

11. Leaders have a responsibility to manage conflicts of interest ethically. They should avoid situations that could compromise their judgment or create bias in decision-making. Leaders should act in the best interest of stakeholders rather than personal gain.

12. Ethical leaders should promote a culture of ethical conduct within the organization. This involves establishing a code of ethics, providing ethics training, and holding individuals accountable for unethical behavior.

13. Leaders should listen to the concerns and feedback of stakeholders. This involves creating channels for open communication, actively seeking input from stakeholders, and considering their perspectives when making decisions.

14. Ethical leaders should be accountable for their decisions and actions. This includes taking responsibility for mistakes, learning from failures, and being willing to make amends or rectify any harm caused.

15. Leaders have a responsibility to promote long-term sustainability and success. This involves making decisions that consider the organization's long-term goals and interests rather than pursuing short-term gains at the expense of stakeholders.

In summary, leaders have ethical responsibilities towards stakeholders that include acting in their best interests, prioritizing employee well-being, being transparent and honest, promoting diversity and equal opportunities, making socially responsible decisions, engaging in fair business practices, fostering trust and collaboration, being engaged community members, managing conflicts of interest, promoting a culture of ethics, listening to stakeholders, being accountable, and promoting long-term sustainability. By fulfilling these responsibilities, leaders can build trust, foster positive relationships, and ensure the success and ethical reputation of their organizations.

The Importance of Promoting an Ethical Culture within Organizations

Promoting an ethical culture within organizations is crucial for several reasons. Here are fourteen paragraphs explaining the importance of promoting an ethical culture.

1. An ethical culture establishes clear expectations and norms. It defines the values, principles, and standards that guide the behavior and decision-making of individuals within the organization. This clarity helps employees understand what is expected of them and promotes consistency in ethical conduct.

2. An ethical culture fosters trust and credibility. When employees believe that their organization operates with integrity and values ethical behavior, it builds trust. Trust is essential for healthy relationships, effective communication, and collaboration within the organization.

3. Promoting an ethical culture reduces the risk of unethical behavior. Employees who work in an ethical culture are less likely to engage in misconduct, fraud, or other unethical actions. This leads to a decrease in legal issues, reputational damage, and financial losses for the organization.

4. An ethical culture attracts and retains top talent. Individuals are more likely to seek employment with organizations that prioritize values and ethics. Employees are motivated to work for organizations where they feel their values align, and their contributions are valued.

5. An ethical culture enhances employee engagement and satisfaction. When employees feel that their organization is committed to ethical behavior, they are more engaged and satisfied with their work. This leads to higher levels of productivity and a positive work environment.

6. Promoting an ethical culture improves decision-making. Employees in an ethical culture are more likely to consider ethical principles when making decisions. Ethical decision-making involves considering long-term consequences, assessing the impact on stakeholders, and choosing the morally right course of action.

7. An ethical culture encourages open communication and transparency. When organizations prioritize ethics, employees feel more comfortable speaking up, voicing concerns, and reporting unethical behavior. This fosters a culture of openness, accountability, and continuous improvement.

8. Promoting an ethical culture strengthens the organization's reputation. Organizations known for their ethical conduct build trust and credibility with customers, partners, and the wider community. A positive reputation attracts stakeholders and contributes to long-term success.

9. An ethical culture promotes responsible and sustainable practices. Organizations that prioritize ethics consider the broader impact of their decisions on the environment, society, and future generations. This leads to corporate social responsibility initiatives, sustainability practices, and ethical supply chain management.

10. Promoting an ethical culture reduces the risk of legal and regulatory non-compliance. When organizations prioritize ethics, they are more likely to operate within the boundaries of laws and regulations. This minimizes legal risks, penalties, and potential damage to the organization's reputation.

11. An ethical culture supports employee development and growth. In an ethical culture, individuals have opportunities to engage in ethical training, discussions, and decision-making processes. This empowers employees to develop their ethical reasoning skills, expand their knowledge, and become ethical leaders themselves.

12. Promoting an ethical culture increases stakeholder trust and loyalty. Customers, investors, and partners are more likely to engage with organizations known for their ethical conduct. Trust and loyalty from stakeholders lead to long-term relationships, repeat business, and sustainable growth.

13. An ethical culture mitigates the risks associated with unethical behavior in leadership. When organizations prioritize ethics, leaders are held to high ethical standards. This reduces the likelihood of leaders abusing their power, engaging in corruption, or making unethical decisions that harm the organization and its stakeholders.

14. Promoting an ethical culture contributes to the overall well-being and satisfaction of employees. Ethical organizations prioritize the health, safety, and work-life balance of their employees. This leads to a positive work environment, increased job satisfaction, and decreased employee stress levels.

In summary, promoting an ethical culture within organizations is essential for building trust, reducing unethical behavior, attracting top talent, enhancing decision-making, fostering open communication, strengthening reputation, promoting responsible practices, ensuring legal compliance, supporting employee development, increasing stakeholder trust, mitigating risks in leadership, and promoting employee well-being. By actively promoting an ethical culture, organizations can create a positive impact on their employees, stakeholders, and society.

Chapter Four

Sustainable Management Practices

The Importance of Environmental Sustainability and Social Responsibility

Sustainable management practices involve integrating environmental, social, and economic considerations into business operations. This approach aims to minimize negative impacts on the environment, contribute positively to society, and ensure long-term economic viability. By implementing sustainable management practices, organizations can promote responsible and ethical business conduct while driving innovation and long-term success.

Introduction to Sustainable Management

In today's rapidly changing world, the concept of sustainable management has gained significant attention across various sectors. Sustainable management is an approach that focuses on integrating environmental, social, and economic considerations into the decision-making processes and operations of organizations. It aims to ensure the long-term well-being of both the planet and society.

The urgency for sustainable management stems from the realization that businesses and public sector entities have a responsibility to address pressing global challenges such as climate change, resource depletion, pollution, social inequality, and poverty. It recognizes that the pursuit of economic growth should not come at the expense of the environment and society. Instead, it emphasizes the need to achieve a harmonious balance between economic development, environmental preservation, and social equity.

At the heart of sustainable management lies the concept of sustainability. Sustainability refers to meeting the needs of the present without compromising the ability of future generations to meet their own needs. It recognizes the interconnectedness and interdependence of environmental, social, and economic systems, highlighting the need for holistic and integrated solutions to address complex challenges.

The three pillars of sustainability, often referred to as the triple bottom line, provide a framework for understanding the different dimensions of sustainable management. These pillars are:

1. Economic Sustainability: Economic sustainability focuses on the long-term viability and profitability of organizations. It involves creating economic value while considering the impact of business activities on society and the environment. Organizations pursue economic sustainability by adopting strategies that promote responsible financial practices, innovation, competitiveness, and ethical business conduct.

2. Environmental Sustainability: Environmental sustainability recognizes the finite nature of natural resources and the urgent need to protect and preserve the environment. It involves minimizing the use of non-renewable resources, reducing greenhouse gas emissions, conserving energy and water, managing waste effectively, and protecting biodiversity. Organizations strive for environmental sustainability through sustainable practices such as recycling, energy-efficient operations, and the promotion of renewable energy sources.

3. Social Sustainability: Social sustainability focuses on the well-being of individuals and communities. It encompasses aspects such as social justice, human rights, gender equality, labor standards, community engagement, and the overall improvement of quality of life. Organizations address social sustainability by promoting fair labor practices, supporting community development initiatives, ensuring employee health and safety, and fostering diversity and inclusion.

The integration of these three pillars into organizational decision-making processes is at the core of sustainable management. It requires organizations to adopt a proactive and long-term perspective, considering the impact of their actions on all stakeholders including employees, customers, shareholders, communities, and the environment. By embracing sustainable management practices, organizations can create shared value, enhance their reputation, attract customers and investors, drive innovation, and contribute to a resilient and sustainable future.

The importance of sustainable management extends beyond individual organizations; it also has broader implications for society and the planet. Sustainable management has the potential to address complex global challenges and promote more inclusive and equitable development. By fostering responsible business practices, sustainable management can contribute to poverty reduction, stimulate economic growth, enhance social cohesion, and protect the environment. Additionally, sustainable management practices can help organizations anticipate and adapt to future challenges, build resilience, and ensure their long-term competitiveness in an increasingly interconnected and environmentally conscious world.

Sustainable management is not an isolated endeavor, but rather a collaborative effort that requires engagement and cooperation from various stakeholders, including governments, businesses, civil society organizations, academia, and individuals. It calls for partnerships and collective action to drive systemic change and create a sustainable future.

In conclusion, sustainable management is an approach that acknowledges the interconnections between economic, environmental, and social systems. It recognizes the responsibility of organizations to consider the long-term implications of their actions on the planet and society. By embracing sustainable management practices, organizations can contribute to a resilient and sustainable future, while also reaping benefits such as enhanced reputation, improved financial performance, and increased stakeholder satisfaction. Sustainable management is imperative in today's world, and its importance will only continue to grow as we strive for a more sustainable and inclusive society.

The Concept of Sustainable Management

The concept of sustainable management has gained significant prominence in recent years as organizations recognize the need to balance economic growth with environmental protection and social responsibility. Sustainable management involves the integration of sustainability principles into the decision-making processes and operations of businesses and public sector entities. It aims to ensure that present actions do not compromise the ability of future generations to meet their own needs.

At its core, sustainable management encompasses three key pillars: economic, environmental, and social sustainability. Economic sustainability refers to the long-term viability and profitability of organizations while minimizing negative impacts on society and the environment. Environmental sustainability focuses on reducing resource consumption, mitigating pollution, and preserving natural ecosystems. Social sustainability emphasizes the fair and inclusive treatment of employees, stakeholders, and communities, promoting equity, diversity, and respect for human rights.

The principles of sustainable management serve as a guiding framework for organizations to align their strategies and operations with sustainability goals. These principles include:

1. Stewardship: Organizations should act as responsible stewards of the resources they use, ensuring their long-term availability and sustainability. This includes sustainable resource management, minimizing waste generation, and promoting circular economy practices.

2. Integration: Sustainability should be integrated into all aspects of an organization's decision-making processes, strategies, and operations. It should not be treated as an add-on or separate function but rather as a core element of business practices.

3. Transparency and Accountability: Organizations should promote transparency by disclosing their environmental, social, and economic performance to stakeholders. They should be accountable for their actions and strive for continual improvement in sustainability performance through well-defined targets and metrics.

4. Stakeholder Engagement: Engagement with stakeholders is vital to understand their expectations, concerns, and needs. Organizations should actively involve stakeholders in decision-making processes and seek their input to ensure that their actions align with societal goals and values.

5. Long-term Perspective: Sustainable management goes beyond short-term profit maximization. It considers the long-term impacts and consequences of decisions and aims to create value for stakeholders over the long haul.

6. Innovation and Resilience: Organizations need to foster innovation to develop new technologies, processes, and products that enhance sustainability. They should also build resilience to adapt to changing environmental, social, and economic conditions.

Implementing sustainable management in business requires a comprehensive approach that encompasses various aspects of organizational functioning. This includes sustainability planning, where organizations set goals and develop strategies to integrate sustainability into their core operations. It involves conducting assessments to identify environmental and social impacts, setting measurable targets, and establishing indicators to track progress.

Sustainable resource management plays a significant role in reducing environmental impacts. It involves optimizing resource use, minimizing waste generation, and adopting sustainable procurement practices. Such practices can include energy and water conservation, waste reduction, recycling, and responsible sourcing.

Another critical aspect of sustainable management is stakeholder engagement. Organizations should actively involve stakeholders such as employees, customers, suppliers, and communities in decision-making processes to ensure their perspectives are considered. Stakeholder engagement can be achieved through dialogue, participatory decision-making, and a partnership approach.

Corporate social responsibility (CSR) is closely connected with sustainable management. It involves organizations voluntarily taking responsibility for the social and environmental impacts of their activities. By practicing CSR, businesses can contribute to societal well-being beyond profit-making. CSR initiatives may include philanthropy, employee volunteering, environmental conservation projects, and adherence to ethical business practices.

Sustainability reporting is an essential tool for promoting transparency and accountability in sustainable management. Organizations can communicate their sustainability performance and progress to stakeholders through sustainability reports, which adhere to international reporting standards such as the Global Reporting Initiative (GRI) or integrated reporting frameworks.

Despite the numerous benefits and opportunities associated with sustainable management, it also faces several challenges and barriers. These include a lack of awareness and understanding of sustainability issues, short-term financial focus, conflicting interests, and regulatory complexities. Overcoming these challenges requires leadership commitment, cultural change, collaboration, innovation, and education.

In conclusion, sustainable management is a holistic approach that strives to balance economic, environmental, and social aspects of organizational practices. By incorporating sustainability principles into decision-making processes and operations, organizations can contribute to a resilient future, ensuring the well-being of current and future generations. Adopting sustainable management practices benefits organizations by enhancing their reputation, attracting customers, optimizing resource use, and promoting long-term profitability.

Sustainable Management is an important tool for general management

Sustainable management is an important tool for general management because it allows organizations to navigate the complexities of the business landscape while addressing environmental and social challenges. By integrating sustainability principles into general management practices, organizations can enhance their long-term viability, mitigate risks, and seize opportunities. Here are some examples of how sustainable management serves as an essential tool for general management:

1. Risk mitigation: Sustainable management helps organizations identify and mitigate various risks associated with environmental, social, and governance factors. For example, by integrating climate change considerations

into their risk management strategies, companies can proactively address physical risks (such as extreme weather events) and transition risks (such as policy changes and shifting market preferences). By doing so, organizations can safeguard their operations, supply chains, and reputations.

2. Cost savings and efficiency: Sustainability practices can lead to cost savings and operational efficiencies. For instance, optimizing energy and water usage can reduce utility bills. Implementing waste reduction and recycling initiatives can minimize disposal costs. Using sustainable sourcing and supply chain practices can enhance efficiency and minimize disruptions. In this way, sustainable management improves a company's bottom line and resource utilization.

3. Brand reputation and customer loyalty: Embracing sustainable management practices can boost brand reputation and customer loyalty. Consumers are increasingly seeking out socially and environmentally responsible products and services. Organizations that demonstrate a commitment to sustainability tend to attract a growing base of environmentally conscious customers. For example, companies like Patagonia, known for their sustainable practices and environmental advocacy, have gained a dedicated customer base due to their perceived commitment to sustainability.

4. Talent attraction and retention: Sustainable management practices can also attract and retain top talent. Studies indicate that employees, particularly millennials and Gen Z, are increasingly seeking employment opportunities that align with their values and offer a sense of purpose. Companies that prioritize sustainability and social responsibility appeal to potential employees who prioritize these aspects, ultimately enhancing recruitment and retaining a motivated, engaged workforce.

5. Innovation and competitiveness: Sustainable management fosters innovation, driving organizations to develop new products, technologies, and processes that minimize environmental impacts and provide solutions to societal challenges. For instance, the growing demand for renewable energy has compelled businesses in the energy sector to invest in solar, wind, and other sustainable energy sources. Organizations that embrace sustainable management principles are more likely to stay ahead of changing market dynamics and gain a competitive advantage.

6. Regulatory compliance: Sustainable management helps organizations stay compliant with evolving environmental and social regulations. Government bodies and regulatory agencies are increasingly implementing stricter rules regarding emissions, waste management, labor practices, and ethical sourcing. By integrating sustainability into general management practices, organizations can proactively adapt to regulatory changes, reducing the risk of non-compliance and potential legal, financial, and reputational consequences.

7. Stakeholder engagement and partnerships: Sustainable management necessitates effective stakeholder engagement, including dialogue, collaboration, and partnerships. Organizations that engage with customers, suppliers, employees, and local communities can build trust, foster positive relationships, and gain valuable insights. Sustainable management practices facilitate the building of partnerships with stakeholders, allowing for shared goals and co-created solutions to sustainability challenges.

In summary, incorporating sustainable management practices into general management enables organizations to manage risks, drive cost savings and efficiency, enhance reputation and customer loyalty, attract and retain top talent, foster innovation, ensure regulatory compliance, and engage with stakeholders effectively. By leveraging sustainable management as a tool, organizations can navigate the ever-evolving business landscape while contributing to a more sustainable and resilient future.

Why is Environmental Sustainability and Social Responsibility a Key Factor to General Management?

Environmental Sustainability and Social Responsibility

In recent years, there has been increased global awareness regarding the pressing need for environmental sustainability and social responsibility. As the world faces escalating environmental challenges, such as climate change, pollution, and resource depletion, organizations across various sectors are recognizing their role in promoting sustainability and addressing social issues. This paper aims to explore the concepts of environmental sustainability and social responsibility, their significance, and the practical strategies employed by organizations to fulfill their obligations in these areas.

Environmental Sustainability

Environmental sustainability refers to the responsible management and conservation of natural resources to meet the needs of the present generation while ensuring the ability of future generations to meet their own needs. It encompasses measures that minimize environmental degradation, protect biodiversity, reduce greenhouse gas emissions, and foster the sustainable use of natural resources.

One of the key aspects of environmental sustainability is mitigating and adapting to climate change. Organizations should strive to reduce their greenhouse gas emissions through energy efficiency measures, the use of renewable energy sources, and the implementation of sustainable transportation systems. Additionally, strategies such as carbon offsetting and implementing sustainable supply chain practices can help to further reduce the environmental impact of organizations.

Furthermore, organizations can contribute to environmental sustainability through effective resource management. This includes practices such as water conservation, waste reduction, and promoting circular economy principles. By implementing recycling and waste management programs, organizations can minimize the amount of waste sent to landfills and decrease the strain on natural resources. Water conservation measures can include water-efficient technologies, rainwater harvesting, and responsible water use in manufacturing and operations.

Social Responsibility

Social responsibility involves the recognition that organizations should contribute positively to society, beyond their economic performance. Social responsibility encompasses considerations such as ethical behavior, human rights, fair labor practices, community engagement, and philanthropy. It reflects a commitment to the well-being and welfare of employees, customers, suppliers, local communities, and society at large.

Ethical behavior forms the foundation of social responsibility. Organizations should conduct their operations with integrity, adhering to ethical standards and promoting transparency and accountability. This includes ensuring compliance with relevant laws and regulations, as well as treating stakeholders with fairness and respect.

Fair labor practices are another essential element of social responsibility. Organizations should uphold fundamental labor rights, and provide safe and healthy working conditions, and fair wages to employees. Additionally, they should foster diversity and inclusion, promoting equal opportunities for all employees regardless of their gender, race, ethnicity, or other protected characteristics.

Community engagement and philanthropy serve as avenues for organizations to contribute to society. By actively engaging with local communities and addressing their needs, organizations can build positive relationships and generate shared value. Philanthropic initiatives, such as supporting education, health, and community development programs, further demonstrate an organization's commitment to social responsibility.

Integrating Environmental Sustainability and Social Responsibility

The integration of environmental sustainability and social responsibility into organizational practices is critical for long-term success and the creation of shared values. Organizations that successfully integrate these concepts into their strategies and operations can enhance their reputation, attract customers and investors, reduce risks, and foster innovation.

One approach to integrating environmental sustainability and social responsibility into organizational practices is through adopting a sustainability framework, such as the United Nations Sustainable Development Goals (SDGs). The SDGs provide a global framework for addressing the most urgent social and environmental issues. By aligning their efforts with relevant SDGs, organizations can contribute to overarching sustainability objectives while addressing specific challenges relevant to their industry and operations.

Another key aspect of integration is the development and implementation of a sustainability strategy. This involves setting specific goals and targets related to environmental sustainability and social responsibility and integrating them into the organization's overall strategic planning process. By incorporating these goals and targets into performance evaluations and reporting mechanisms, organizations can ensure accountability and monitor progress.

Organizations can also engage their stakeholders in the pursuit of environmental sustainability and social responsibility. This includes regular communication and consultation with employees, customers, suppliers, and local communities. Engaging stakeholders enables organizations to gain valuable insights, identify potential social and environmental risks, and foster relationships built on trust and shared values.

In addition, organizations can collaborate with external partners to enhance their sustainability efforts. This can involve collaborating with NGOs, governments, and other businesses to develop innovative solutions, share best practices, and advocate for policy changes that promote sustainability and social responsibility. Partnerships can greatly enhance the effectiveness and impact of an organization's sustainability initiatives.

Real-world Examples of Environmental Sustainability and Social Responsibility

Many organizations have embraced environmental sustainability and social responsibility, and their efforts serve as exemplary models for others. Some notable examples include:

1. Patagonia: Patagonia, a leading outdoor clothing company, has made environmental sustainability and social responsibility integral to its business model. The company is committed to reducing its ecological footprint, promoting fair labor practices, and advocating for environmental protection. Patagonia invests in renewable energy, implements responsible sourcing practices, and donates a portion of its revenue to environmental organizations.

2. Unilever: Unilever, a multinational consumer goods company, has prioritized sustainability and social responsibility through its Sustainable Living Plan. The plan aims to reduce the company's environmental impact, improve the well-being of one billion people, and source 100% of agricultural raw materials sustainably. Unilever has implemented various initiatives, such as reducing water and energy consumption, promoting gender equality, and supporting smallholder farmers.

3. Tesla: Tesla, an electric vehicle manufacturer, is at the forefront of promoting environmental sustainability. By manufacturing electric vehicles, Tesla aims to reduce reliance on fossil fuels and mitigate climate change. The company also develops renewable energy solutions, such as solar panels and energy storage systems, to promote a transition to a sustainable energy future.

4. Starbucks: Starbucks, a global coffeehouse chain, is known for its commitment to social responsibility and sustainability. The company focuses on ethical sourcing of coffee beans, supporting farmers and their communities, and reducing its environmental impact. Starbucks has set goals to achieve 100% ethically sourced coffee, eliminate plastic straws, and reduce water consumption in its stores.

Environmental sustainability and social responsibility are essential components of responsible and ethical organizational practices. By integrating these concepts into their strategies and operations, organizations can contribute positively to society, mitigate environmental risks, and build long-term resilience. Through practices such as climate change mitigation, resource management, fair labor practices, and community engagement, organizations can drive impactful change and create shared value. The examples of organizations that have successfully embraced environmental sustainability and social responsibility demonstrate the benefits of integrating these concepts into organizational practices. As awareness of global challenges continues to increase, the importance of environmental sustainability and social responsibility for organizations will only grow, creating opportunities for innovation and a sustainable future.

Paradigm of Environmental Sustainability and Social Responsibility

The paradigm of environmental sustainability and social responsibility in general management refers to the integration of sustainable practices and ethical decision-making into the overall management strategies and operations of an organization. This paradigm recognizes the importance of considering the impact of business activities on the environment and society, as well as the long-term viability and reputation of the organization.

Environmental sustainability involves managing resources and processes in a way that minimizes negative environmental impacts, while social responsibility encompasses the ethical obligations and contributions of the organization to the well-being of its stakeholders and society at large.

In general management, the paradigm of environmental sustainability and social responsibility encourages organizations to adopt a proactive approach towards sustainability. This includes setting goals and targets for reducing carbon emissions, conserving resources, and promoting renewable energy sources. It also involves integrating environmental and social considerations into decision-making processes, such as supply chain management and product development.

The paradigm also emphasizes the importance of stakeholder engagement and collaboration. Organizations are encouraged to actively involve stakeholders, including employees, customers, communities, and non-governmental organizations, in the planning and implementation of sustainable practices. This helps ensure that management decisions align with the needs and expectations of various stakeholders and that sustainability initiatives are effective and meaningful.

Furthermore, the paradigm of environmental sustainability and social responsibility recognizes that achieving sustainability requires a holistic and long-term perspective. It involves considering the interdependencies between environmental, social, and economic factors and striving for a balance between them. It also acknowledges that organizations can create shared value by addressing societal needs through their core business activities, contributing to sustainable development and the well-being of communities.

Overall, the paradigm of environmental sustainability and social responsibility in general management is a shift towards a more integrated and responsible approach to business. It recognizes that organizations have a role to play in addressing pressing global challenges, such as climate change and social inequality, and that sustainable and responsible management is not only beneficial for the environment and society but also for the long-term success and competitiveness of the organization.

Businesses and organizations should focus on environmental sustainability for several reasons:

1. Ethical responsibility: As key contributors to environmental degradation, businesses have a moral obligation to minimize their negative impact on the environment. By prioritizing sustainability, organizations demonstrate their commitment to ethical practices and their responsibility towards future generations.

2. Reputation and brand image: Consumers are increasingly demanding sustainable products and services, and they often choose to support companies with strong environmental credentials. By focusing on environmental sustainability, businesses can enhance their reputation, build trust, and attract environmentally conscious customers.

3. Regulatory compliance: Governments are introducing stricter environmental regulations and policies to address climate change, pollution, and resource depletion. Organizations that fail to comply with these regulations may face legal liabilities, fines, and reputational damage. Prioritizing environmental sustainability enables businesses to stay ahead of regulatory requirements.

4. Cost savings and efficiency: Sustainable practices often lead to cost savings and operational efficiencies. For example, energy-efficient technologies can reduce utility expenses, waste reduction initiatives can lower disposal costs, and supply chain optimization can improve resource utilization. By implementing environmentally sustainable measures, organizations can enhance their bottom line.

5. Risk mitigation: Climate change and environmental issues pose significant risks to businesses, such as disruptions in supply chains, resource scarcity, and reputational damage. By prioritizing environmental sustainability, organizations can better prepare for and mitigate these risks, ensuring their long-term resilience and stability.

6. Innovation and market opportunities: Environmental challenges necessitate innovative solutions, creating new market opportunities for businesses. By focusing on sustainability, organizations can develop and market eco-friendly products and services, tapping into a growing consumer demand and staying ahead of competitors.

7. Employee engagement and retention: Employees, particularly millennials and members of Generation Z, prioritize their companies' environmental and social responsibility when deciding where to work. Businesses that demonstrate a commitment to environmental sustainability can attract and retain top talent, leading to a more engaged and motivated workforce.

In summary, businesses and organizations should focus on environmental sustainability because it aligns with ethical responsibility, enhances reputation, ensures regulatory compliance, delivers cost savings, mitigates risks, opens new market opportunities, and fosters employee engagement. By prioritizing environmental sustainability, organizations can create a win-win situation, benefiting both the environment and their long-term success.

What is the importance of Social Responsibility in every Organization?

Organizations should consider social responsibility a must for the following several reasons:

1. Building reputation and trust: Socially responsible organizations gain a positive reputation and are more likely to be trusted by customers, employees, and other stakeholders. This can lead to increased customer loyalty, improved employee morale, and stronger relationships with investors.

Building reputation and trust is the process of creating a positive perception and credibility among individuals, groups, or organizations. It involves consistently delivering on promises, meeting expectations, and establishing a reputation for reliability, integrity, and ethical behavior. Trust is the foundation of any successful relationship, whether it is between individuals, businesses, or institutions.

Building reputation and trust requires several key elements:

a. Consistency: Being consistent in actions, behavior, and communication is crucial. People rely on consistency to form an opinion about someone's character, and a consistent track record builds trust.

b. Honesty and Transparency: Being honest and transparent in all interactions fosters trust. This includes being upfront about limitations, risks, and challenges, as well as admitting mistakes and taking responsibility for them.

c. Reliability: Being reliable means consistently delivering on promises and meeting commitments. This builds confidence in the person or organization and strengthens trust.

d. Listening and Communication: Active listening and effective communication are important aspects of building trust. It involves valuing others' opinions, being open to feedback, and addressing concerns or issues promptly and appropriately.

e. Integrity: Demonstrating integrity means acting ethically and maintaining high standards of behavior. Upholding moral principles and doing what is right even when no one is watching reinforces trust.

f. Building Relationships: Trust is built through personal connections and mutually beneficial relationships. Investing time and effort into developing relationships, understanding others' needs and expectations, and delivering value to them helps establish trust.

g. Consistent Quality: Delivering a high-quality product or service consistently creates trust in the reliability and competence of an individual or organization.

h. Credibility: Being knowledgeable, experienced, and demonstrating competence in a particular domain builds credibility. People are more likely to trust someone who is an expert in their field.

i. Fulfilling Promises: Making promises and fulfilling them builds trust. This includes meeting deadlines, providing accurate information, and delivering what was agreed upon.

j. Accountability: Taking responsibility for one's actions and being accountable for the outcomes helps establish trust. Admitting mistakes, rectifying them, and learning from them contribute to building a positive reputation.

Overall, building reputation and trust is a continuous process that requires consistency, reliability, integrity, and effective communication. It is the foundation for successful relationships, collaborations, and interactions, both in personal and professional settings.

1. Attracting and retaining talent: Today's employees, especially millennials and Gen Z, prioritize working for companies that have a social and environmental impact. By demonstrating social responsibility, organizations can attract and retain top talent, boosting their competitiveness in the job market.

Attracting and retaining talents refers to the process of attracting highly skilled and competent individuals to work for a company or organization, and then ensuring their long-term commitment and engagement to the company.

To attract talent, organizations need to develop effective strategies to promote their brand and create a positive reputation in the job market. This can include showcasing a strong corporate culture, offering competitive compensation and benefits packages, providing opportunities for career growth and development, and having a healthy work-life balance.

Retaining talents, on the other hand, involves creating an environment that motivates employees to stay with the organization for a longer duration. This can be achieved by offering a positive work environment, encouraging open communication and collaboration, recognizing, and rewarding employees' contributions, providing opportunities for learning and advancement, and offering competitive salaries and perks.

Overall, attracting and retaining talents is essential for organizations to have a skilled and motivated workforce, which ultimately leads to increased productivity, innovation, and success in the long run.

2. Mitigating risks: Organizations that ignore their social and environmental impacts face potential legal, financial, and reputational risks. Adopting responsible practices helps mitigate these risks and ensures compliance with laws and regulations.

Mitigating risks refers to the process of reducing or minimizing the potential negative impact of uncertain events or circumstances. It involves identifying potential risks, analyzing their likelihood and potential consequences, and implementing measures to reduce their impact or likelihood of occurrence.

There are several strategies and techniques that organizations can employ to mitigate risks:

a. Risk identification: This involves actively identifying and recognizing potential risks that the organization may face. It can be done through risk assessments, brainstorming sessions, and analysis of historical data.

b. Risk analysis: Once risks are identified, organizations need to assess their potential impact and likelihood. This helps prioritize risks based on their severity and allows organizations to allocate resources accordingly.

c. Risk avoidance: Some risks can be mitigated by avoiding certain activities or situations altogether. This can include not entering high-risk markets or refraining from engaging in activities with a high level of uncertainty.

d. Risk transfer: Organizations can transfer some risks to other parties. This can be done through contracts, insurance policies, or outsourcing certain activities to external vendors.

e. Risk reduction: Organizations can implement measures to reduce the likelihood or impact of identified risks. This includes implementing safety protocols, quality control systems, redundancy plans, or backup systems to minimize the impact of potential disruptions.

f. Risk acceptance: In some cases, organizations may decide to accept certain risks if the cost of mitigating them outweighs the potential consequences. However, this should be a conscious decision made after a thorough analysis of the risks involved.

g. Monitoring and review: Risk mitigation is an ongoing process, and organizations should continuously monitor and review their risk management strategies. This allows them to adapt and adjust as necessary to address new or changing risks.

Overall, mitigating risks is crucial for organizations to protect their assets, maintain business continuity, and minimize financial, operational, and reputational losses. It requires proactive planning, analysis, and implementation of appropriate measures to reduce the impact and likelihood of potential risks.

3. Enhancing customer relationships and sales: Consumers are increasingly making purchasing decisions based on the values and ethics of companies. Social responsibility initiatives, such as sustainable sourcing, fair trade, or charitable partnerships, can differentiate organizations and attract socially conscious customers, leading to increased sales.

Enhancing customer relationships refers to the process of actively developing and nurturing strong connections with customers to build loyalty, trust, and mutual satisfaction. It involves various strategies and practices aimed at understanding and meeting customer needs, delivering exceptional service, and fostering long-term partnerships.

here are some key strategies to enhance customer relationships:

a. Effective communication: Regular and transparent communication is essential for building and maintaining strong customer relationships. Organizations should listen to their customers, respond promptly to their inquiries or concerns, and keep them informed about relevant updates, promotions, or changes.

b. Personalization: Tailoring products, services, and experiences to meet individual customer preferences and needs can greatly enhance customer relationships. This can include personalized offers, recommendations, or customer-specific marketing messages.

c. Customer feedback: Actively seeking and leveraging customer feedback is vital for understanding their expectations and areas for improvement. This can be done through surveys, feedback forms, or social media channels. Organizations should then use this feedback to make necessary adjustments and demonstrate their commitment to customer satisfaction.

d. Exceptional service: Providing exceptional customer service is a powerful way to enhance customer relationships. This includes training and empowering employees to deliver personalized, timely, and efficient service. Resolving issues and addressing complaints promptly and effectively is also crucial for maintaining customer satisfaction.

e. Rewards and loyalty programs: Offering rewards, incentives, or loyalty programs can encourage customers to continue doing business with the organization. This can include discounts, exclusive offers, or a tiered system that provides additional benefits to loyal customers.

f. Relationship-building initiatives: Organizing events, webinars, or workshops specifically designed for customers can facilitate relationship-building. These initiatives provide opportunities for customers to engage with the organization, learn more about its products or services, and network with other customers.

g. Continuous improvement: Organizations should consistently evaluate and improve their processes, products, and services based on customer feedback and evolving needs. Showing a commitment to continuous improvement demonstrates to customers that their satisfaction and feedback are valued.

By implementing these strategies, organizations can foster strong and lasting customer relationships. Building trust, delivering value, and providing exceptional service are key components of enhancing customer relationships, leading to increased customer loyalty, advocacy, and long-term success.

4. Supporting sustainable development: Organizations have a responsibility to contribute positively to society and the environment. By addressing social and environmental challenges, organizations can contribute to sustainable development goals, make a positive impact on their communities, and help create a better future for all.

Supporting sustainable development involves promoting practices and initiatives that meet the needs of the present without compromising the ability of future generations to meet their own needs. It requires adopting a holistic approach that considers the environmental, social, and economic aspects of development. Here are some key ways to support sustainable development:

a. Environmental conservation: Prioritizing environmental conservation is crucial for sustainable development. This can involve reducing waste and promoting recycling, conserving natural resources, adopting renewable energy sources, minimizing pollution, and protecting ecosystems and biodiversity.

b. Social inclusivity: Ensuring social inclusivity is an important aspect of sustainable development. It involves promoting equal opportunities, reducing inequality, and empowering marginalized groups. This can be achieved through measures such as promoting diversity, providing access to education and healthcare, supporting fair labor practices, and promoting human rights.

c. Economic stability: Supporting sustainable development requires fostering a stable and resilient economy. This includes promoting responsible business practices, encouraging innovation and entrepreneurship, investing in sustainable infrastructure, and promoting fair trade and ethical consumerism.

d. Collaboration and partnerships: Collaborating with stakeholders is essential for supporting sustainable development. This can involve partnering with governments, NGOs, local communities, and other organizations to share knowledge, resources, and best practices. By working together, a collective effort can be made to address complex sustainability challenges.

e. Education and awareness: Raising awareness and educating individuals about sustainable development is vital. This can include providing information on the importance of sustainable practices, offering training programs on sustainable technologies and strategies, and promoting sustainable behavior change among individuals and communities.

f. Policy and regulations: Governments play a crucial role in supporting sustainable development through the implementation of policies and regulations. This can include setting targets and frameworks for sustainable development, providing incentives for sustainable practices, and enforcing environmental and social standards.

g. Long-term planning: Supporting sustainable development requires long-term planning and foresight. Decision-makers should consider the long-term implications of any development project, considering its environmental, social, and economic impact. This can involve conducting thorough impact assessments and considering alternatives that minimize negative effects.

h. Corporate social responsibility: Businesses can support sustainable development by adopting responsible and sustainable business practices. This can include integrating sustainability into business strategies, reducing carbon emissions, promoting ethical sourcing, and engaging in social initiatives that benefit communities and the environment.

Supporting sustainable development is a global responsibility that requires collective effort from individuals, organizations, and governments. By embracing sustainability principles and practices, we can ensure a better future for all, protecting the planet, improving quality of life, and promoting equitable economic growth.

5. Strengthening investor confidence: Socially responsible organizations are often seen as less risky and more financially viable in the long term. Investors value companies that prioritize responsible practices, leading to increased investor confidence, potential access to impact investment funds, and favorable financial performance.

Strengthening investor confidence refers to the actions and strategies undertaken to build trust and credibility among investors. It involves creating an environment where investors feel confident in investing their capital and believe that their investments will yield positive returns. Here are some key factors in strengthening investor confidence:

a. Transparency and disclosure: Providing transparent and accurate information to investors is crucial for building trust. Companies should disclose relevant financial and non-financial information promptly, including financial statements, market updates, and any material changes or risks that may affect their investments.

b. Corporate governance: Having strong corporate governance practices is essential for investor confidence. This includes having a clear and accountable board of directors, independent audit committees, and robust internal controls. Investors want assurance that their interests are protected, and that the organization is being managed ethically and responsibly.

c. Regulatory compliance: Adhering to regulatory requirements and demonstrating compliance with relevant laws and regulations is crucial for investor confidence. Companies should maintain proper records, adhere to accounting standards, and conduct regular audits to ensure compliance.

d. Financial performance: Consistently delivering strong financial performance is a key factor in building investor confidence. Investors want to see evidence of a company's ability to generate profits, maintain a healthy cash flow, and effectively manage risks. Companies should strive to meet or exceed financial targets and communicate their financial performance clearly to investors.

f. Effective risk management: Demonstrating robust risk management practices is vital for maintaining investor confidence. Companies should identify and assess potential risks to their business and implement appropriate strategies to mitigate or manage these risks. Good risk management practices provide investors with assurance that their investments are being protected.

g. Investor relations: Establishing effective investor relations is essential for maintaining open and transparent communication with investors. This includes regularly engaging with investors through meetings, conferences, and reporting, as well as promptly addressing investor inquiries and concerns. Strong investor relations can help build long-term relationships and foster trust.

h. Reputation management: Organizations should proactively manage their reputation to strengthen investor confidence. This involves demonstrating ethical behavior, being socially responsible, and actively addressing any negative publicity or issues that may affect investor trust. A positive corporate reputation contributes to investor confidence and attracts new investors.

i. Long-term strategy and growth prospects: Investors are interested in organizations that have a clear strategy for long-term growth and value creation. Companies should communicate their vision and strategic plans effectively to investors, demonstrating how they are positioned to capitalize on market opportunities and deliver sustainable returns.

By focusing on these factors, organizations can bolster investor confidence and attract a broader base of investors. Strengthening investor confidence leads to increased investment inflows, improved liquidity, and a positive market reputation, ultimately contributing to the overall growth and success of the organization.

6. Regaining public trust: In an era of corporate scandals and unethical behavior, organizations that prioritize social responsibility can help restore public trust in the business community. By demonstrating commitment to ethical practices, transparency, and responsible governance, organizations can contribute to rebuilding trust in the corporate world.

Regaining public trust is a process that organizations or individuals undertake when they have faced a loss of credibility or a breakdown in public confidence. It requires transparent and concerted efforts to rebuild trust and restore faith in the organization or individual. Here are some key steps for regaining public trust:

a. Acknowledge and take responsibility: The first step in regaining public trust is acknowledging the issue or wrongdoing that led to the loss of trust. Organizations or individuals must take responsibility for their actions or failures and openly admit their mistakes. This demonstrates accountability and a willingness to address the problem.

b. Transparency and openness: Rebuilding trust requires transparency in communication and decision-making. Organizations or individuals should provide accurate and timely information about their operations, intentions, and any steps taken to rectify the situation. Openness in sharing information helps bridge the gap between the organization and the public.

c. Apologize and make amends: A sincere and meaningful apology is crucial in regaining public trust. Organizations or individuals should apologize for their actions, or any harm caused and express genuine remorse. They should also take steps to make amends, such as compensating affected parties or implementing measures to prevent a recurrence of the issue.

d. Demonstrating change: Rebuilding trust requires tangible actions that demonstrate a commitment to positive change. Organizations or individuals should implement reforms, adopt best practices, and enforce strict ethical standards. This visible demonstration of change reassures the public that lessons have been learned and that efforts are being made to avoid similar mistakes in the future.

e. Engage with the public: Reestablishing a direct and meaningful relationship with the public is essential. Organizations or individuals should actively engage with stakeholders, listen to their concerns, and involve them in decision-making processes. Open channels of communication help rebuild trust and create a sense of inclusivity.

f. Consistency and reliability: Consistency in behavior and actions is crucial to regain public trust. Organizations or individuals must demonstrate reliability by consistently delivering on promises and commitments made. Operating with integrity and a strong sense of ethics helps rebuild credibility.

g. Rebuilding credibility through partnerships: Seeking collaborations and partnerships with credible and trusted organizations can also aid in rebuilding public trust. Aligning with reputable entities can provide an external validation of the organization or individual's commitment to change and ethical behavior.

h. Long-term commitment: Regaining public trust is not a one-time event but a continuous process. Organizations or individuals must show a long-term commitment to upholding ethical standards and maintaining transparency in their operations. Consistently demonstrating integrity and ethical behavior over time will reinforce public trust.

It is important to note that rebuilding public trust takes time and effort. It requires consistent actions, transparent communication, and a genuine desire to change and improve. With a concerted and sincere effort, organizations and individuals can regain public trust and rebuild their reputations.

Overall, embracing social responsibility is not only the right thing to do ethically, but it also brings numerous benefits to organizations, including improved reputation, risk mitigation, competitive advantage, and long-term sustainability.

Chapter Five

Cultural Influence on Ethical Decision-Making And Diversity and Inclusion

---

Cultural influence plays a significant role in shaping diversity and inclusion within a society or organization. Culture encompasses the beliefs, values, customs, and behaviors of a specific group or community, which in turn impact how diversity is embraced, and inclusion is fostered. Cultural influence can either promote or hinder diversity and inclusion efforts, depending on the extent to which it values and respects different perspectives, experiences, and identities. Embracing and celebrating cultural diversity is vital in creating an inclusive environment that values and respects the contributions of all individuals, regardless of their background or heritage.

Cultural Influence on Ethical Decision-Making

And Diversity and Inclusion

Cultural influence plays a significant role in shaping diversity and inclusion. The connections between cultural influence, diversity, and inclusion can be seen in the following ways:

1. Awareness and Understanding: Cultural influence raises awareness about different cultures, traditions, and perspectives. This understanding is necessary for fostering diversity and inclusion as it helps individuals recognize and appreciate the value of different cultures, promoting a more inclusive environment.

2. Representation: Cultural influence promotes diverse representation in various areas such as media, arts, and leadership positions. When different cultures are represented, it sends a message of inclusivity, encouraging individuals from all backgrounds to feel welcomed and embraced.

3. Empathy and Respect: Cultural influence allows people to develop a sense of empathy and respect for others. Learning about different cultures and understanding their customs, beliefs, and practices can lead to a more inclusive and tolerant society.

4. Mitigating Stereotypes and Bias: Cultural influence challenges stereotypes and biases that may exist within a society. By exposing individuals to different cultural perspectives, cultural influence can break down preconceived notions, reducing prejudice and discrimination.

5. Collaboration and Innovation: Diversity resulting from cultural influence brings together individuals with different backgrounds, experiences, and perspectives. This diversity of thought fosters creativity, innovation, and problem-solving, as people approach challenges from various angles, resulting in more effective solutions.

6. Social Cohesion: Cultural influence helps build bridges between different communities, promoting social cohesion. When people feel their cultural identities are respected and valued, it enhances a sense of belonging and strengthens social bonds between diverse groups.

7. Policy and Advocacy: Cultural influence plays a role in shaping policies and practices related to diversity and inclusion. Awareness of different cultures' needs and perspectives helps advocate for inclusive policies that address equality, access, and representation.

Overall, cultural influence acts as a catalyst for promoting diversity and inclusion by fostering awareness, understanding, respect, collaboration, and social cohesion among the members of a society. Examining the Intersection of Values and Norms

Ethical decision-making plays a crucial role in various aspects of human life, including personal conduct, business practices, and societal development. These decisions are influenced by a plethora of factors, among which culture plays a significant role. Culture shapes individuals' values, beliefs, and norms, ultimately impacting their ethical decision-making processes. This article aims to explore the relationship between culture and ethical decision-making, examining how cultural influences shape individuals' moral reasoning and the potential consequences of cultural conflicts on ethical judgments. By understanding the cultural dimensions that impact ethical decision-making, we can foster cross-cultural understanding and develop strategies to promote ethical behavior in diverse settings.

Ethical decision-making is a complex process that involves carefully considering the moral implications of one's actions. While human beings share certain universal ethical principles, ethical frameworks often vary across cultures. Culture, comprising shared values, beliefs, and norms, significantly influences individuals' ethical decision-making processes. This article provides an in-depth analysis of cultural influence on ethical decision-making, discussing various cultural dimensions and their impacts on moral reasoning.

1. Cultural Relativism and Ethical Decision-Making:

Cultural relativism is an anthropological concept suggesting that ethical principles are relative to a particular culture and should be judged within that context. This section explores the implications of cultural relativism on ethical decision-making, examining how cultural diversity challenges the notion of a universal ethical framework.

a. Navigating the Challenges of Cultural Diversity

Cultural relativism is an anthropological concept that suggests ethical principles are relative to a particular culture and should be judged within that context. This article explores the impact of cultural relativism on ethical decision-making, highlighting its benefits, limitations, and the challenges it presents in navigating cultural diversity. By understanding the complexities of cultural relativism, we can critically examine the role of culture in ethical decision-making and develop strategies to foster intercultural understanding and promote ethical behavior across diverse settings.

Ethical decision-making is a complex process that considers the moral implications of one's actions. Cultural relativism challenges the notion of a universal ethical framework, asserting that ethical values and norms vary across cultures and should be understood and evaluated within their cultural context. This article aims to delve into the relationship between cultural relativism and ethical decision-making, addressing the benefits and limitations of this perspective and examining the challenges it presents in a culturally diverse world.

b. Understanding Cultural Relativism:

Cultural relativism posits that ethical judgments should not be absolute but rather should be assessed based on the cultural context in which they occur. This section provides an overview of cultural relativism, discussing its historical origins, key principles, and its relation to cultural diversity and moral relativism.

c. Benefits of Cultural Relativism:

Cultural relativism offers certain benefits in ethical decision-making by encouraging tolerance, respect for diversity, and cultural sensitivity. This section explores the positive aspects of cultural relativism, highlighting how it promotes a nuanced understanding of different cultural perspectives and fosters cross-cultural understanding.

d. Limitations of Cultural Relativism:

While cultural relativism offers valuable insights, it has inherent limitations. This section discusses the criticisms raised against cultural relativism, including the potential for ethnocentrism, the challenge of balancing universality and cultural diversity, and the implications on fundamental human rights.

e. Challenges in Ethical Decision-Making and Cultural Relativism:

Cultural relativism poses challenges in practical ethical decision-making, particularly in a culturally diverse world. This section examines how cultural relativism can create moral dilemmas, cultural clashes, and conflicting judgments when faced with contrasting cultural values and norms.

f. The Role of Universal Ethical Standards:

Amidst the nuances of cultural relativism, the role of universal ethical principles becomes significant in shaping ethical decision-making. This section explores the tension between cultural relativism and universal ethical standards, discussing how cultural values can be balanced with foundational ethical principles.

g. Cultivating Intercultural Understanding:
Navigating cultural diversity requires cultivating intercultural understanding and empathy. This section presents strategies to foster intercultural understanding, such as cross-cultural communication, intercultural education, and engaging in dialogue between cultures.

h. Ethical Decision-Making in a Globalized World:
In an increasingly globalized world, cultural relativism presents challenges when addressing global ethical issues. This section examines how cultural relativism, and its limitations affect ethical decision-making in a globalized context, such as environmental sustainability, human rights, and social justice.

i. Promoting Ethical Behavior Across Cultures:
Promoting ethical behavior across diverse cultures requires an inclusive approach that recognizes both cultural diversity and universality. This section discusses strategies to promote ethical behavior in culturally diverse settings, including cultural competency training, ethical leadership development, and fostering cross-cultural collaboration.

Cultural relativism offers valuable insights into understanding and respecting cultural diversity during the ethical decision-making process. However, it also carries limitations that require careful consideration. By critically examining cultural relativism and its impacts on ethical decision-making, we can develop a nuanced understanding of ethical challenges in culturally diverse contexts and strive to bridge cultural gaps while upholding universal ethical principles. This understanding is crucial for creating harmonious and ethical environments that promote intercultural understanding, tolerance, and a shared commitment to ethical behavior.

2. Individualism vs. Collectivism:

Individualism and collectivism represent two broad cultural orientations that significantly impact ethical decision-making. The section examines the central cultural dimensions of individualism and collectivism and their influence on moral reasoning, emphasizing the tension between the individual's rights and the community's welfare.

a. The Cultural Dimensions and Their Impact on Ethical Decision-Making
Individualism and collectivism are cultural dimensions that significantly influence individuals' values, beliefs, and behaviors. This article explores the concepts of individualism and collectivism, their cultural manifestations, and their implications on ethical decision-making. By examining the dynamics of these cultural orientations, we can better understand the ethical challenges and opportunities that arise within individualistic and collectivistic societies.

Individualism and collectivism represent two distinct cultural orientations that shape individuals' views on self, relationships, and society. They influence various aspects of human behavior, including ethical decision-making. This article aims to delve into the concepts of individualism and collectivism, exploring their cultural manifestations and how they impact ethical decision-making processes.

b. Understanding Individualism and Collectivism:
This section provides a comprehensive overview of individualism and collectivism, exploring their definitions, origins, and cultural manifestations. It examines the contrasting values and beliefs that underpin these cultural orientations and the role they play in shaping individuals' identities and social interactions.

c. Individualism: A Focus on the Self:
Individualistic cultures prioritize personal goals, autonomy, and individual achievements. This section delves into the characteristics of individualistic societies, the emphasis on personal freedom and self-expression, and how these cultural values and beliefs influence ethical decision-making processes.

d. Collectivism: The Primacy of the Group:
Collectivistic cultures prioritize group cohesion, cooperation, and harmony. This section explores the characteristics of collectivistic societies, the importance of in-group relationships and social harmony, and how these cultural values and beliefs impact ethical decision-making processes.

e. Individualism and Ethical Decision-Making:
Individualistic cultures exhibit distinct patterns in ethical decision-making. This section discusses how individualistic values, such as personal autonomy and self-interest, can influence moral reasoning. It also addresses potential ethical challenges that can arise in individualistic societies, such as an emphasis on self-centeredness and the potential for moral relativism.

f. Collectivism and Ethical Decision-Making:
Collectivistic cultures also demonstrate unique patterns in ethical decision-making. This section explores how collectivistic values, such as interdependence and the preservation of group harmony, shape moral reasoning. It examines the potential ethical challenges within collectivistic societies, such as groupthink and the suppression of individual autonomy.

g. Balancing Individualism and Collectivism:
This section highlights the need to strike a balance between individualistic and collectivistic values in ethical decision-making. It explores the potential benefits of integrating individualistic and collectivistic perspectives, such as considering both personal autonomy and collective welfare in ethical judgments.

h. Cultural Conflicts and Ethical Decision-Making:
Cultural conflicts can arise when individuals from different cultural orientations encounter conflicting ethical values and norms. This section examines how cultural conflicts between individualism and collectivism influence ethical decision-making, discussing the potential for misunderstandings, misinterpretations, and clashes of values.

i. Promoting Ethical Decision-Making in Individualistic and Collectivistic Societies:
Promoting ethical decision-making in diverse cultural contexts requires strategies that acknowledge the influence of individualism and collectivism. This section presents approaches to fostering ethical behavior, such as promoting cultural diversity awareness, encouraging dialogue between cultures, and developing culturally sensitive ethical frameworks.

Individualism and collectivism are cultural dimensions that significantly influence ethical decision-making. Understanding these cultural orientations provides valuable insights into the complexities of moral reasoning within different cultural contexts. By recognizing the impact of individualism and collectivism on ethical decision-making, we can foster cross-cultural understanding, promote ethical behavior, and build harmonious societies that value both personal autonomy and collective well-being.

3. Power Distance and Ethical Decision-Making

Power distance refers to the extent to which individuals in a culture accept and expect power inequalities. This section explores how power distance influences ethical decision-making, particularly within hierarchical societies, and the potential for abuse of power in such contexts.

a. The Impact of Hierarchical Cultures
Power distance is a cultural dimension that reflects the extent to which individuals in a society accept and expect power inequalities. This article explores the concept of power distance, its cultural manifestations, and its influence on ethical decision-making. By examining the intersection between power distance and moral

reasoning, we can gain a deeper understanding of the challenges and opportunities that arise in hierarchical cultures.

Power distance is an essential cultural dimension that significantly shapes individuals' attitudes toward authority, hierarchy, and social inequalities. It influences various aspects of human behavior, including ethical decision-making. This article aims to explore the concept of power distance, its cultural implications, and how it impacts the ethical decision-making processes within hierarchical societies.

b. Understanding Power Distance:

This section provides an overview of power distance, discussing its definition, origins, and cultural manifestations. It explores the contrasting attitudes towards authority and hierarchy in high and low-power distance cultures, highlighting their impact on social relationships and decision-making processes.

c. High Power Distance Cultures

High power distance cultures exhibit a strong acceptance of social hierarchies and authority. This section delves into the characteristics of high-power distance societies, the reverence for authority figures, and the influence of power imbalances on ethical decision-making processes.

d. Low Power Distance Cultures

Low power distance cultures manifest a more egalitarian approach, with reduced acceptance of social hierarchies and a greater emphasis on equal relationships. This section explores the characteristics of low power distance societies, the tendency for participative decision-making, and the impact of reduced power differentials on ethical judgments.

e. Power Distance and Cultural Influences on Ethics

Power distance plays a significant role in shaping individuals' ethical decision-making processes in hierarchical societies. This section delves into how power distance influences cultural values and norms, social roles, and perceptions of authority, ultimately impacting moral reasoning and ethical judgments.

f. Challenges and Ethical Dilemmas in High Power Distance Contexts:

High power distance cultures often face ethical challenges due to the concentration of power in a few individuals or groups. This section discusses the potential ethical dilemmas that arise within high power distance contexts, such as abuses of power, corruption, and the potential for unethical behavior to be rationalized or tolerated.

g. Opportunities and Ethical Advantages in Low Power Distance Contexts:

Low power distance cultures have the potential to foster ethical decision-making due to their more egalitarian structures. This section explores the ethical advantages in low power distance contexts, such as increased transparency, accountability, and the potential for greater participation and collaboration in decision-making processes.

h. Power Distance and Leadership:

Leadership styles and practices are deeply influenced by power distance. This section examines the relationship between power distance and ethical leadership, discussing how leaders in hierarchical cultures can adapt their approaches to promote ethical behavior and mitigate the negative effects of power imbalances.

i. Promoting Ethical Decision-Making in Power-Distant Cultures:

Promoting ethical decision-making in hierarchical cultures requires strategies that address power imbalances and enhance ethical awareness. This section discusses approaches such as promoting transparency, accountability, ethics training, fostering ethical leadership, and encouraging open communication to bridge the gap between power distance and ethical behavior.

Power distance is a significant cultural dimension that influences individuals' attitudes toward authority and hierarchy. Its impact on ethical decision-making within hierarchical cultures is substantial and complex. Understanding the dynamics of power distance allows us to critically examine the ethical challenges associated with power imbalances while identifying opportunities for promoting ethical behavior within these cultural contexts. By creating a culture of transparency, accountability, and ethical leadership, we can strive towards more equitable and ethical decision-making processes, regardless of power distance.

4. Uncertainty Avoidance and Ethical Decision-Making:

Uncertainty avoidance represents a cultural dimension that measures a society's tolerance for ambiguity and uncertainty. This section explores how high or low uncertainty avoidance impacts ethical decision-making, discussing the relationship between cultural attitudes toward risk and moral reasoning.

a. Navigating Cultural Attitudes towards Risk and Ambiguity

Uncertainty avoidance is a cultural dimension that reflects a society's tolerance for ambiguity, the unknown, and risk. This article explores the concept of uncertainty avoidance, its cultural manifestations, and its impact on ethical decision-making. By examining the intersection between uncertainty avoidance and moral reasoning, we can gain insights into the challenges and opportunities that arise in culturally diverse settings.

Uncertainty avoidance plays a crucial role in shaping individuals' behaviors and attitudes toward ambiguity and risk. It greatly influences various aspects of human life, including ethical decision-making. This article aims to explore the concept of uncertainty avoidance, its cultural implications, and its impact on ethical decision-making processes in different cultural settings.

b. Understanding Uncertainty Avoidance:

This section provides an overview of uncertainty avoidance, discussing its definition, origins, and cultural manifestations. It explores the contrasting attitudes towards uncertainty and risk in high and low-uncertainty avoidance cultures, highlighting their impact on decision-making processes.

c. High Uncertainty Avoidance Cultures:

High uncertainty avoidance cultures have a low tolerance for ambiguity and prefer structured and predictable situations. This section delves into the characteristics of high uncertainty avoidance societies, the need for rules and formalized procedures, and the influence of risk aversion on ethical decision-making processes.

d. Low Uncertainty Avoidance Cultures:

Low uncertainty avoidance cultures exhibit a higher tolerance for ambiguity, uncertainty, and risk. This section explores the characteristics of low uncertainty avoidance societies, the flexibility in adapting to change, and the impact of risk acceptance on ethical judgments.

e. Cultural Influences on Ethical Decision-Making:

Uncertainty avoidance significantly influences individuals' ethical decision-making processes within cultural contexts. This section delves into how uncertainty avoidance impacts cultural values and norms, risk perception, decision-making styles, and moral reasoning, ultimately shaping ethical judgments.

f. Ethical Challenges in High Uncertainty Avoidance Contexts:

High uncertainty avoidance cultures face specific challenges in ethical decision-making due to their aversion to uncertainty. This section discusses potential ethical dilemmas that arise within high uncertainty avoidance contexts, such as rigid adherence to rules and traditions, resistance to change, and the potential for risk avoidance to hinder ethical progress.

g. Ethical Opportunities in Low Uncertainty Avoidance Contexts:
Low uncertainty avoidance cultures present opportunities for ethical decision-making due to their greater openness to ambiguity and change. This section explores the ethical advantages in low uncertainty avoidance contexts, such as adaptability, innovation, and the potential for risk-taking to foster ethical progress.

h. Ethical Leadership and Uncertainty Avoidance:
Leadership styles and practices are influenced by uncertainty avoidance. This section examines the relationship between uncertainty avoidance and ethical leadership, discussing how leaders in different cultural contexts can adapt their approaches to promote ethical behavior in uncertain and ambiguous situations.

i. Promoting Ethical Decision-Making in Uncertainty-Averse Cultures:
Promoting ethical decision-making in uncertainty-averse cultures requires strategies that address the cultural tendencies toward risk aversion. This section discusses approaches such as fostering ethical awareness, enhancing ethical reasoning skills, promoting ethical role models, and encouraging transparency and open communication to bridge the gap between uncertainty avoidance and ethical behavior.

Uncertainty avoidance is an essential cultural dimension that influences individuals' attitudes toward ambiguity, risk, and decision-making processes. Its impact on ethical decision-making within different cultural contexts is significant and multifaceted. Understanding the dynamics of uncertainty avoidance allows us to navigate challenges and embrace the opportunities of uncertainty in ethical decision-making. By promoting adaptability, ethical leadership, and open communication, we can strive towards more nuanced and effective ethical decision-making processes, regardless of uncertainty avoidance tendencies.

5. Long-Term Orientation vs. Short-Term Orientation:

Long-term orientation emphasizes perseverance, thrift, and a focus on long-term goals, while short-term orientation values immediate gratification and living in the present moment. This section examines how these distinct cultural orientations influence ethical decision-making, as individuals prioritize different time horizons.

A Comparative Analysis

In our constantly evolving world, understanding cultural differences and their impact on various aspects of life has become increasingly important. One of the critical dimensions in analyzing cultural variations is the concept of long-term orientation (LTO) versus short-term orientation (STO). This dimension, developed by Geert Hofstede, examines how societies prioritize values such as immediate gratification versus long-term planning. This essay aims to delve into the characteristics, influences, and implications of long-term orientation and short-term orientation, highlighting their significance in organizational management, societal behavior, and global contexts.

Defining Long-Term Orientation:

Long-term orientation is a cultural value orientation that emphasizes long-range planning, persistence, perseverance, thrift, and tradition. Societies with high LTO place great importance on maintaining and building upon the experiences and wisdom of previous generations. These cultures value prudence, thrift, and savings, considering them vital for future prosperity. They emphasize long-term goals over short-term gains, focus on delayed gratification, and value hard work and perseverance to achieve success.

Influences and Characteristics of Long-Term Orientation:

The roots of long-term orientation can be traced back to Confucian philosophy, which is predominant in East Asian cultures. Confucianism places significant importance on ancestral heritage, harmonious relationships, and the cultivation of virtue. These core beliefs have shaped the values and behaviors of societies like China, Japan, and South Korea, which are known for their long-term orientation.

a. Persistence and Perseverance: Cultures with high long-term orientation emphasize endurance and perseverance as critical virtues. They value hard work and believe success is achieved through consistent effort, despite obstacles and setbacks.

b. Delayed Gratification: Individuals and societies with high LTO are willing to sacrifice immediate pleasures in favor of long-term rewards. They prioritize investment, savings, and preparation for future contingencies over immediate indulgence.

c. Respect for Tradition: Long-term-oriented cultures have deep respect for their traditions, customs, and history. Their emphasis on ancestral heritage affects various aspects of life, including moral values, education, and business practices.

d. Prudence and Thrift: Cultures with high LTO have a strong inclination toward prudent financial practices. They value saving money, avoiding unnecessary debt, and maintaining a strong financial foundation.

e. Mutual Obligation: Long-term-oriented societies emphasize the importance of harmonious relationships and mutual obligation. They believe in fulfilling their roles and responsibilities in family, work, and wider social contexts to uphold social harmony.

Defining Short-Term Orientation:

Short-term orientation is a cultural value orientation that prioritizes immediate gratification, quick results, and individual indulgence. Cultures with high STO seek instant happiness and prioritize present pleasures rather than planning for the long term. They value individual freedom and personal fulfillment, often disregarding traditional norms and practices.

Influences and Characteristics of Short-Term Orientation:

The origins of short-term orientation can be attributed to societies heavily influenced by Taoism, Buddhism, or other philosophical traditions that emphasize embracing the present moment. Western societies, such as the United States and most European nations, are commonly associated with short-term orientation due to their focus on immediate gains and individualism.

a. Immediate Gratification: Cultures with high STO prioritize immediate pleasure and individual satisfaction. They tend to focus on short-term results rather than long-term consequences, often valuing the "here and now" over future planning.

b. Individualism: Societies with high STO emphasize individual freedom, autonomy, and self-expression. They emphasize personal achievement and self-interest, valuing personal success over familial or societal obligations.

c. Risk-Taking: Short-term-oriented cultures often tend to be more open to taking risks, embracing change, and experimenting with new ideas. This risk-taking mindset is influenced by the inclination towards immediate rewards rather than long-term stability.

d. Innovation and Adaptability: Cultures with high STO value innovation and adaptability, focusing on improvisation and problem-solving skills. They are more open to change and readily adopt new practices or technologies.

e. Egalitarianism: Societies with short-term orientation often promote egalitarianism and equality among individuals. They value fairness, equal opportunities, and inclusive practices.

Implications of Long-Term Orientation and Short-Term Orientation:

a. Organizational Management: Cultural dimensions, such as LTO and STO, have significant implications for effective management practices. Organizations operating in long-term-oriented cultures may prioritize stability, have a long-term strategic perspective, and promote teamwork and loyalty. In contrast, those in cultures with high STO may focus on individual achievements, be more flexible to changes, and promote innovation and risk-taking.

b. Economic Development: Long-term-oriented societies tend to have a higher level of economic development as they emphasize savings, investment, and long-term planning. The emphasis on education and cultivating skills for future generations contributes to human capital development. In contrast, short-term-oriented societies may experience rapid economic growth due to their higher risk tolerance, adaptability, and innovation.

c. Global Interactions: Understanding long-term orientation and short-term orientation is crucial in the context of global interactions. Cultural differences affect negotiations, cross-cultural collaborations, and the understanding of behaviors, attitudes, and expectations in international trade, policymaking, and diplomacy.

d. Sustainability and Environmental Concerns: Long-term orientation is closely linked to sustainability as it promotes responsible resource management, conservation, and intergenerational equity. Societies with long-term focus tend to prioritize environmental concerns and take actions to mitigate the impact of their actions on future generations. Short-term-oriented societies, however, may prioritize economic growth over environmental sustainability, leading to negative environmental impacts.

Long-term orientation and short-term orientation are two contrasting cultural dimensions that shape societal behaviors, attitudes, and values. While long-term orientation focuses on perseverance, prudence, and harmonious relationships, short-term orientation prioritizes immediate gratification, individuality, and risk-taking. Understanding these cultural dimensions is crucial for effective cross-cultural communication, management practices, economic development, and sustainable decision-making in our increasingly interconnected world. Recognizing and respecting these differences can facilitate harmonious interactions, fostering global cooperation and cultural diversity.

6. Masculinity vs. Femininity

Masculinity and femininity are cultural dimensions that reflect societal expectations of gender roles. This section discusses how gender roles impact ethical decision-making, highlighting the influence of cultural expectations on moral reasoning and the potential implications for gender equality.

The Concept of Masculinity and Femininity: A Comprehensive Analysis

The concept of masculinity and femininity is deeply ingrained in societies across the world. These gender-related beliefs, attitudes, and behaviors have significant implications for culture, social roles, relationships, and even organizational practices. Developed by Geert Hofstede, the cultural dimension of masculinity versus femininity examines the extent to which societies value assertiveness, achievement, and material success (masculinity) versus nurturing, quality of life, and relationship-building (femininity). This essay aims to provide a detailed exploration of masculinity and femininity, highlighting their characteristics, influences, and implications in various societal contexts.

Defining Masculinity

Masculinity is a cultural value orientation that prioritizes assertiveness, competitiveness, achievement, and material success. Cultures with a high emphasis on masculinity typically value power, status, and individual accomplishments. Men, in particular, are often expected to exhibit stoicism, assertiveness, and toughness in these societies.

Influences and Characteristics of Masculinity

The origins of masculinity can be traced back to the historical division of labor, where men were often responsible for hunting and providing for their families. Socio-cultural factors, including patriarchal systems, military history, and the influence of heroic epics, have also shaped the value of masculinity in societies.

a. Achievement and Ambition: Masculine-oriented cultures place great emphasis on success, ambition, and competition. These societies value personal accomplishment, desire hierarchical structures, and encourage individuals to strive for advancement.

b. Assertiveness and Dominance: Assertiveness and dominance are highly valued characteristics in societies that uphold masculinity. People in these cultures are expected to be decisive, assert their opinions, and actively pursue their goals. Competitiveness is seen as a desirable trait.

c. Material Success: Cultures emphasizing masculinity often associate success with material wealth and possessions. These societies value economic growth, emphasize financial power, and recognize material wealth as a symbol of achievement and social status.

d. Emotional Restraint: Masculine-oriented societies often expect individuals, particularly men, to exhibit emotional control and stoicism. Expressing vulnerability or weakness may be viewed as a sign of inadequacy or a threat to masculinity.

e. Gender Roles and Division of Labor: In these cultures, gender roles are often clearly defined, with men typically assigned instrumental or breadwinning tasks. There tends to be a clear separation of labor responsibilities between men and women, reinforcing traditional gender roles.

Defining Femininity:

Femininity is a cultural value orientation that prioritizes nurturing, quality of life, relationship-building, and cooperation. Societies emphasizing femininity value cooperation, empathy, and the well-being of others. In these cultures, there is often less emphasis on material success and achievement, and more focus on maintaining harmonious relationships.

Influences and Characteristics of Femininity:

The concept of femininity is influenced by factors such as historical gender roles, maternal instincts, collectivist cultures, and the values of care and empathy.

a. Nurturing and Care: Feminine-oriented societies place a high value on nurturing, care, and empathy. These societies emphasize the importance of supporting others, building strong relationships, and creating harmonious social structures.

b. Quality of Life and Well-being: Cultures with high femininity prioritize the quality of life and the well-being of individuals. Happiness, life balance, and enjoying leisure time are valued aspects of life in these societies.

c. Collaboration and Cooperation: Cooperation is a central component of feminine-oriented cultures. These societies emphasize the importance of collaboration, consensus-building, and maintaining harmonious relationships within the community.

d. Emotional Expressiveness: Feminine-oriented cultures tend to encourage and value emotional expressiveness. Both men and women are often permitted to display a wider range of emotions and may be supported in expressing vulnerability, empathy, and care.

e. Gender Equality: Societies emphasizing femininity generally strive for greater gender equality, promoting equal opportunities and rights for both men and women. These cultures aim to challenge traditional gender roles and stereotypes and advocate for greater inclusion and diversity.

Implications of Masculinity and Femininity:

a. Gender Roles and Equality: The cultural dimensions of masculinity and femininity significantly influence societal expectations and gender roles. Societies that emphasize masculinity may maintain traditional gender roles, whereas those valuing femininity may strive for gender equality and challenge gender norms.

b. Leadership and Management: Different cultural orientations affect leadership styles and management practices. Masculine-oriented cultures often associate leadership with assertiveness, dominance, and decisiveness. In contrast, feminine-oriented cultures may prioritize collaborative decision-making, empathy, and relationship-building.

c. Work-Life Balance: Femininity-oriented societies tend to value work-life balance, recognizing the importance of personal well-being and leisure time. These cultures may have policies and practices that support flexibility, family-friendly initiatives, and paid leave.

d. Power Distance: Cultural dimensions of masculinity and femininity also impact power distance, which refers to the acceptance and expectation of hierarchical structures within society. Masculine-oriented societies may have higher power distance, acknowledging and reinforcing authority, whereas feminine-oriented societies may strive for more egalitarian structures.

e. Sexual Identity and Expression: Cultural orientations influence attitudes towards sexual identity and expression. Societies emphasizing masculinity might have more rigid views on sexuality, while femininity-oriented cultures may be more accepting of diverse sexual orientations and expressions.

Masculinity and femininity are core dimensions of culture that shape beliefs, attitudes, and behaviors related to gender roles, power dynamics, and societal expectations. Understanding the characteristics and influences of these orientations provides valuable insights into various societal contexts. While masculinity values assertiveness, competition, and material success, femininity emphasizes nurturing, care, and quality of life. The implications of these dimensions range from leadership styles and gender roles to work-life balance and power dynamics. Acknowledging and respecting these differences can foster discussions on gender equality, promote diverse perspectives, and ultimately create more inclusive societies.

7. Consequences of Cultural Conflicts on Ethical Judgments:

Cultural conflicts can arise when individuals from different cultural backgrounds hold contrasting ethical values and norms. This section explores how such conflicts can affect ethical decision-making, including the potential for ethical relativism, ethnocentrism, and cultural clashes.

Cultural conflicts arise when individuals or groups with differing cultural backgrounds and values encounter situations where their beliefs, norms, and practices clash. These conflicts can heavily impact ethical judgment, as cultural diversity significantly influences moral frameworks. Understanding the consequences of cultural conflicts on ethical judgments is crucial for promoting ethical behavior, resolving conflicts, and fostering cross-cultural understanding. This essay aims to delve into the consequences of cultural conflicts on ethical judgment, exploring how conflicts can challenge, shape, and even alter individuals' ethical decisions and perspectives.

Cultural Differences and Ethical Judgment:

Cultural diversity plays a critical role in shaping individuals' ethical judgments. Ethical principles and standards vary across cultures due to differences in religious beliefs, social norms, historical contexts, and philosophical traditions. While one culture may prioritize individual rights and autonomy, another may emphasize collectivism and social harmony. These cultural differences not only influence personal ethical beliefs but also impact how conflicts between cultures are perceived and approached.

a. Ethical Relativism: Cultural conflicts can lead individuals to adopt ethical relativism, the belief that ethical standards are subjective and vary across cultures. When confronted with conflicting cultural norms, individuals may question the existence of universal ethical principles, opting instead to adhere to the moral values they were raised with. This relativistic standpoint can make it challenging to find common ethical ground and facilitate conflict resolution.

b. Ethnocentrism: Cultural conflicts may also reinforce ethnocentrism, the belief in the superiority of one's own culture over others. When faced with conflicting cultural practices, individuals may interpret them through the lens of their cultural values, leading to biases and judgments. Ethnocentric tendencies can hinder objective moral reasoning and create obstacles to understanding and appreciating diverse perspectives.

c. Moral Disengagement: Cultural conflicts can stimulate moral disengagement, a psychological mechanism that enables individuals to justify unethical behavior. When confronted with cultural clashes, individuals may resort to cognitive distortions and moral justifications to alleviate cognitive dissonance and maintain a positive self-image. This disengagement from ethical standards can result in compromised decision-making and unethical behavior.

d. Cultural Relativism: Cultural conflicts can also foster cultural relativism, the belief that all cultural practices are equally valid and acceptable. While this perspective promotes tolerance and understanding, it can also lead to the uncritical acceptance of unethical or harmful practices. The elevation of cultural relativism above ethical considerations can undermine efforts to protect human rights and promote global ethics.

Consequences of Cultural Conflicts on Ethical Judgment:

a. Moral Dilemmas: Cultural conflicts can present individuals with moral dilemmas, where they must choose between conflicting ethical principles or cultural norms. These conflicts can create internal turmoil, as individuals struggle to reconcile their cultural values with the demands of the situation or the dominant culture. Resolving these dilemmas requires evaluating and prioritizing ethical principles based on individual judgment and rational argumentation.

b. Bias and Stereotyping: Cultural conflicts may reinforce stereotypes and bias, leading individuals to make snap judgments based on cultural generalizations. Conflict situations may heighten prejudices and biases, leading to unfair judgments based on cultural stereotypes rather than individual merits. This can perpetuate discrimination, hinder collaboration, and impede the establishment of equitable and inclusive environments.

c. Miscommunication and Misunderstanding: Cultural conflicts can result in miscommunication and misunderstanding, impeding individuals' abilities to comprehend others' perspectives and intentions. Differences in language, non-verbal cues, and cultural context can lead to misconceptions, leading to further conflict escalation and breakdown of dialogue. Successful resolution of cultural conflicts requires open-mindedness, active listening, and cross-cultural communication skills.

d. Exclusion and Marginalization: Cultural conflicts may lead to the exclusion and marginalization of individuals or groups whose values, practices, or beliefs clash with the dominant culture. This exclusion can negatively impact individuals' sense of belonging and self-esteem, perpetuating social divisions and exacerbating cultural conflicts. Recognizing and valuing cultural diversity can foster inclusivity and contribute to conflict resolution.

e. Ethical Dilemmas in Cross-Cultural Contexts: Cultural conflicts may pose ethical dilemmas in cross-cultural contexts, particularly when individuals are operating in international or multicultural environments. Varying ethical standards and practices can create challenges for individuals navigating complex ethical terrain. Professionals working in such environments must develop cross-cultural competence and engage in ongoing ethical reflection and dialogue to navigate these dilemmas.

Strategies for Addressing Cultural Conflicts and Ethical Judgment:

a. Ethical Reflection and Sensitivity Training: Individuals should engage in ethical reflection, examining their own biases, values, and assumptions. Sensitivity training programs can provide opportunities for individuals to understand and respect diverse cultural perspectives, facilitating ethical decision-making in multicultural contexts.

b. Cross-Cultural Communication and Understanding: Effective cross-cultural communication skills are essential for resolving cultural conflicts and promoting ethical judgment. Building cultural competence enables individuals to bridge potential communication gaps, avoid misunderstandings, and cultivate empathy toward different cultural perspectives.

c. Mediation and Conflict Resolution: Mediation processes can help individuals and groups navigate cultural conflicts by providing a neutral forum for dialogue, promoting understanding, and facilitating compromise. Mediators skilled in cross-cultural communication and conflict resolution techniques can assist in finding common ethical ground.

d. Cultural Awareness and Diversity Programs: Organizations and educational institutions should prioritize cultural awareness and diversity programs. These initiatives can increase understanding of different cultural perspectives, foster respect for cultural diversity, and promote ethical judgment within multicultural contexts.

e. Ethical Leadership and Role Modeling: Ethical leadership plays a crucial role in resolving cultural conflicts and encouraging ethical judgment. Leaders should model inclusive behaviors, demonstrate cultural sensitivity, and create environments that foster open dialogue and the sharing of diverse perspectives.

Cultural conflicts have significant consequences on ethical judgment. These conflicts can lead individuals to adopt ethical relativism, reinforce ethnocentrism, promote moral disengagement, or foster cultural relativism. Understanding the consequences of cultural conflicts is vital for addressing ethical challenges in multicultural environments and promoting ethical decision-making. By actively engaging in cross-cultural communication, ethical reflection, and cultural sensitivity training, individuals can bridge cultural gaps, foster understanding, and navigate cultural conflicts ethically. Organizations, educational institutions, and leaders play a crucial role in promoting cultural awareness, diversity, and inclusivity, ultimately facilitating ethical judgment, and creating harmonious environments for all.

8. Promoting Ethical Decision-Making in Cross-Cultural Contexts:

Fostering ethical decision-making practices in increasingly diverse environments requires strategies that bridge cultural gaps. This section focuses on promoting ethical behaviors across cultures by fostering cross-cultural understanding, ethical leadership development, and creating harmonious multicultural work environments.

Culture plays a crucial role in shaping individuals' ethical decision-making processes. By understanding the cultural dimensions that influence moral reasoning, we can navigate cultural diversity and promote ethical behavior in various contexts. Recognizing the influence of culture on ethical decision-making is essential for developing more inclusive ethical frameworks that respect diverse cultural perspectives while upholding universal ethical principles.

Ethical decision-making is a complex process influenced by various factors, including cultural values, norms, and practices. In cross-cultural contexts, individuals are often faced with ethical dilemmas that require navigating differing cultural perspectives and values. Promoting ethical decision-making in such contexts involves understanding and respecting cultural diversity, developing cross-cultural competence, and fostering an environment that encourages open dialogue and ethical reflection. This essay aims to explore strategies for promoting ethical decision-making in cross-cultural contexts, highlighting the importance of cultural sensitivity, communication, and ethical leadership.

Understanding Cultural Influences on Ethical Decision-Making:

Culture plays a significant role in shaping individuals' ethical frameworks and decision-making processes. Cultural values, norms, and practices influence how individuals perceive and prioritize ethical principles and guide their behaviors. Understanding the cultural influences on ethical decision-making is crucial for promoting ethical behavior in cross-cultural contexts.

a. Cultural Relativism: Cultural relativism is the belief that moral standards are subjective and vary across different cultures. In cross-cultural contexts, individuals may encounter conflicting ethical perspectives, making it important to recognize and understand cultural relativism. Recognizing the diversity of ethical principles and moral judgments allows for more nuanced discussions and promotes tolerance while respecting different cultural perspectives.

b. Ethical Universals: While ethical values may differ across cultures, there are also ethical universals – principles that are recognized across cultures as morally good. These universals, such as honesty, fairness, and respect for human dignity, provide a common ground for ethical decision-making in cross-cultural contexts. Emphasizing these universals can help bridge cultural differences and facilitate dialogue on shared ethical values.

c. Cultural Bias: Cultural biases can influence ethical decision-making by shaping individuals' perceptions and judgments. Individuals may interpret ethical dilemmas through the lens of their cultural values, leading to biased judgments and overlooking alternative perspectives. Recognizing and overcoming these biases is critical for making fair and ethical decisions in cross-cultural contexts.

Strategies for Promoting Ethical Decision-Making in Cross-Cultural Contexts:

a. Develop Cross-Cultural Competence: Cross-cultural competence involves acquiring knowledge, skills, and attitudes that enable individuals to effectively navigate cross-cultural interactions and understand different cultural perspectives. Organizations and individuals should invest in cross-cultural training and education to enhance their ability to make ethical decisions in diverse contexts.

b. Cultural Sensitivity: Cultural sensitivity entails awareness and respect for cultural differences, avoiding judgment or assumptions based on one's cultural background. Cultural sensitivity promotes empathy, open-mindedness, and the ability to understand ethical dilemmas from multiple cultural perspectives. Individuals must strive to become culturally sensitive by actively engaging in learning about different cultures and appreciating their values, norms, and practices.

c. Promote Diversity and Inclusion: Organizations should create an inclusive and diverse environment that encourages the expression of diverse perspectives and values. Promoting diversity and inclusion allows for the integration of multiple cultural perspectives, fostering ethical decision-making through the incorporation of various viewpoints. Organizations should prioritize diversity initiatives, including recruitment practices, mentoring programs, and diversity training.

d. Effective Cross-Cultural Communication: Effective cross-cultural communication is crucial for promoting ethical decision-making in cross-cultural contexts. Open and respectful communication facilitates understanding and helps individuals navigate cultural differences. Strategies for effective cross-cultural communication include active listening, non-judgmental questioning, and a willingness to seek clarification and understanding.

e. Foster Ethical Leadership: Ethical leadership is essential for promoting ethical decision-making in cross-cultural contexts. Leaders should model ethical behavior, display cultural sensitivity, and create an environment that encourages open dialogue and ethical reflection. Ethical leaders prioritize fairness, integrity, and respect for diverse perspectives, setting the tone for ethical decision-making throughout the organization or community.

f. Encourage Ethical Reflection: Ethical reflection involves critically examining one's values, beliefs, and biases and considering their impact on ethical decision-making. Encouraging individuals to engage in ethical reflection promotes self-awareness and enables them to navigate ethical dilemmas in cross-cultural contexts more effectively. Organizations can facilitate ethical reflection through ethics training, mentoring programs, and regular opportunities for ethical discussions.

g. Develop Ethical Frameworks: Cross-cultural contexts benefit from the development of ethical frameworks that consider multiple cultural perspectives. Organizations and individuals can create ethical decision-making models or frameworks that integrate ethical principles from various cultures, promoting a more inclusive approach to ethical judgment. These frameworks should encourage open dialogue and prioritize ethical universals while recognizing cultural differences.

h. Inclusive Decision-Making Processes: Inclusive decision-making processes are essential for promoting ethical decision-making in cross-cultural contexts. Including individuals with diverse cultural backgrounds in decision-making processes allows for the incorporation of different perspectives and prevents the dominance of a single cultural viewpoint. Organizations should strive for participatory decision-making that fosters collaboration, information sharing, and consensus-building.

i. Foster Organizational Ethics: Organizations should establish clear ethical guidelines and policies that address cultural diversity and promote ethical decision-making. Leaders should communicate these ethical standards effectively, ensuring that individuals understand their responsibilities in cross-cultural contexts. Regular ethics training, monitoring, and support systems should be in place to promote ethical behavior and address ethical dilemmas.

j. Collaboration and Partnerships: Collaboration and partnerships between organizations, communities, and cultures can significantly contribute to ethical decision-making in cross-cultural contexts. Joint efforts can improve understanding, build relationships, and foster shared ethical frameworks. Collaborative approaches to decision-making can help reconcile conflicting ethical perspectives and promote ethical behavior.

Promoting ethical decision-making in cross-cultural contexts requires the recognition and appreciation of cultural diversity, the development of cross-cultural competence, and fostering an inclusive environment. Cultural factors influence individuals' ethical judgments and biases, making it essential to understand and overcome these influences. Strategies for promoting ethical decision-making include developing cross-cultural competence, practicing cultural sensitivity, effective cross-cultural communication, fostering ethical leadership, and encouraging ethical reflection. By integrating these strategies, organizations and individuals can navigate cross-cultural ethical challenges, promote understanding, and foster ethical behavior that respects diverse cultural perspectives.

Chapter Six

Cultural Intelligence and Diversity

While diversity and inclusion are becoming increasingly important in today's workplace, there is still room for further exploration of cultural intelligence and its impact on effective management. Uncovering ways to leverage diversity and maximize the benefits of multicultural teams.

Cultural Intelligence and Diversity: Navigating the Globalized World

In an increasingly interconnected and globalized world, cultural intelligence and diversity have emerged as crucial concepts for individuals, organizations, and societies. Cultural intelligence refers to an individual's ability to adapt and interact effectively with people from different cultural backgrounds, while diversity encompasses a wide range of human differences, including but not limited to race, ethnicity, gender, age, religion, and sexual orientation. This essay explores the importance of cultural intelligence and diversity, their benefits, challenges, and strategies for fostering inclusivity in various contexts.

Understanding Cultural Intelligence

In today's globalized world, cultural intelligence has become an increasingly important skill for individuals and organizations. As people interact with diverse cultures, both at home and abroad, it is crucial to understand cultural intelligence to navigate effectively in these multicultural settings. Cultural intelligence refers to the ability to comprehend, adapt, and communicate effectively across different cultural contexts. It involves recognizing cultural differences, being aware of one's own biases, and developing the necessary skills and knowledge to effectively interact with people from various backgrounds. In this essay, we will delve deeper into the concept of cultural intelligence, its components, and its significance in fostering understanding and collaboration among people with different cultural backgrounds.

What is Cultural Intelligence?

Cultural intelligence (CQ) is a relatively new concept that has emerged as a key dimension of intelligence, complementary to IQ and EQ (emotional intelligence). It encompasses several interconnected elements that enable individuals to interact effectively with people from diverse cultures. Christopher Earley and Soon Ang, the pioneers in the field, describe cultural intelligence as "the ability to adapt successfully to a new cultural setting." However, CQ goes beyond adaptation; it also encompasses the ability to understand, appreciate, and effectively engage with diversity.

Components of Cultural Intelligence

Cultural Intelligence is comprised of four main components:

Cognitive CQ: Cognitive CQ refers to the knowledge and understanding of different cultures. It involves learning about the customs, traditions, values, beliefs, and social norms of various groups. This aspect requires individuals to actively seek information about other cultures and develop a broad understanding of cultural diversity.

Emotional CQ: Emotional CQ emphasizes the awareness and management of emotions in intercultural interactions. It involves being open-minded, non-judgmental, and empathetic towards individuals from different cultures. Emotional CQ enables individuals to adapt their behavior to specific social situations and respond appropriately to emotional cues expressed by people from diverse backgrounds.

Physical CQ: Physical CQ refers to the ability to adapt physically to different cultures. It includes nonverbal communication, such as body language, gestures, and facial expressions. Understanding and adjusting to nonverbal cues is crucial for effective cross-cultural communication, as cultural norms may vary significantly in this aspect.

Behavioral CQ: Behavioral CQ involves displaying appropriate behavior in intercultural encounters. It emphasizes adapting one's behavior to fit the cultural context, such as communication style, decision-making, and negotiation practices. Behavioral CQ also encompasses the ability to manage conflict and build rapport with people from diverse backgrounds.

Significance of Cultural Intelligence:

Cultural intelligence plays a pivotal role in several aspects of personal and professional life, including:

Global Business: In today's interconnected world, businesses are operating in diverse markets, and cultural intelligence is crucial for success. It helps in building strong relationships with international clients, understanding local market dynamics, and adapting business strategies to suit different cultural contexts. Cultural intelligence enables businesses to navigate cultural differences, avoid misunderstandings, and improve collaboration and productivity across international teams.

Interpersonal Relationships: Cultural intelligence facilitates effective communication and understanding between individuals from different cultural backgrounds. It promotes empathy, respect, and tolerance, leading to better interpersonal relationships and reduced conflicts. Cultural intelligence allows people to appreciate and celebrate diversity, fostering a sense of inclusivity and belonging.

Conflict Resolution: Cultural intelligence empowers individuals to manage and resolve conflicts arising from cultural differences. By understanding and respecting others' perspectives, negotiating compromises, and recognizing potential misunderstandings, conflicts can be mitigated effectively. Cultural intelligence helps identify common ground and build bridges between conflicting parties.

Tourism and Hospitality: As the tourism industry continues to grow, cultural intelligence is crucial for professionals in the hospitality and tourism sectors. Having an in-depth understanding of different cultures enables professionals to provide personalized and culturally sensitive services to guests from around the world. Cultural intelligence enhances the overall guest experience, leading to customer satisfaction and repeat business.

Education: Cultural intelligence is increasingly recognized as an essential skill in educational institutions. It helps create inclusive learning environments, promotes cross-cultural understanding, and prepares students to thrive in a diverse society. Cultural intelligence helps students appreciate other cultures, develop global perspectives, and become effective global citizens.

Developing Cultural Intelligence:

Cultural intelligence is not an innate trait but can be developed and enhanced through deliberate efforts. Several strategies can help individuals improve their cultural intelligence:

Cultural Immersion: Immersing oneself in different cultures through travel, studying abroad, or engaging in cultural exchange programs helps develop cultural intelligence. Experiencing firsthand the customs, traditions, and social norms of a particular culture improves one's understanding and appreciation of diversity.

Cross-Cultural Training: Participating in cross-cultural training programs equips individuals with the knowledge and skills to interact effectively with diverse populations. These programs provide insights into specific cultures, enhance cultural sensitivity, and teach strategies for effective cross-cultural communication.

Lifelong Learning: Being a lifelong learner, actively seeking knowledge about different cultures, and challenging one's own biases are essential for developing cultural intelligence. Reading books, attending workshops, following multicultural influencers, or taking online courses are ways to continuously expand one's cultural knowledge.

Building Relationships: Actively seeking relationships with people from different cultures fosters understanding and empathy. Building genuine connections, asking questions, and showing curiosity about others' cultures can enhance cultural intelligence through shared experiences and perspectives.

Understanding cultural intelligence is crucial for effectively navigating multicultural settings and fostering understanding across diverse populations. It encompasses cognitive, emotional, physical, and behavioral dimensions, all of which are interconnected and necessary for successful intercultural interactions. Cultural intelligence has significant implications in various aspects of life, such as global business, interpersonal relationships, conflict resolution, tourism, hospitality, and education. By continuously developing and enhancing cultural intelligence, individuals can become more culturally competent, facilitating better collaboration, and building bridges between diverse communities.

Definition and Components of Cultural Intelligence

In today's globalized world, cultural intelligence has become an essential skill for individuals and organizations. With the increasing interconnectedness of cultures, it is crucial to understand and navigate the complexities of diverse cultural contexts. Cultural intelligence (CQ) refers to the ability to understand, adapt, and effectively communicate across different cultural settings. It involves recognizing cultural differences, being aware of one's own biases, and developing the necessary skills and knowledge to interact with people from various cultural backgrounds. In this essay, we will explore the definition and components of cultural intelligence to gain a comprehensive understanding of this vital skill.

The Definition of Cultural Intelligence:

Cultural intelligence, also known as cultural quotient, is a relatively new concept that has gained prominence in the field of intercultural communication and intelligence studies. Cultural intelligence is often referred to as "the capability to function effectively in situations characterized by cultural diversity" (Earley & Ang, 2003). Christopher Earley and Soon Ang, the pioneers in the field, define cultural intelligence as "the ability to adapt successfully to new cultural settings" (2003).

Cultural intelligence differs from other types of intelligence, such as cognitive intelligence (IQ) and emotional intelligence (EQ), as it specifically focuses on intercultural competence. It goes beyond adaptation to encompass understanding, appreciating, and effectively engaging with diversity.

Components of Cultural Intelligence:

Cultural intelligence comprises several interrelated components that work together to provide individuals with the necessary skills and knowledge to navigate various cultural contexts. These components include cognitive CQ, emotional CQ, physical CQ, and behavioral CQ.

Cognitive CQ:

Cognitive CQ refers to the knowledge and understanding of different cultures. It involves learning about the customs, traditions, values, beliefs, and social norms of various groups. Individuals with high cognitive CQ possess a deep understanding of the cultural nuances and differences that exist across societies.

Developing cognitive CQ requires individuals to actively seek information about other cultures through reading, research, or educational programs. It involves acquiring knowledge about the history, language, art, religion, and social structures of different cultures.

Emotional CQ:

Emotional CQ emphasizes the awareness and management of emotions in intercultural interactions. It involves being open-minded, non-judgmental, and empathetic towards individuals from different cultural backgrounds. Emotional CQ enables individuals to adapt their behavior to specific social situations and respond appropriately to emotional cues expressed by people from diverse backgrounds.

Emotional CQ encompasses the ability to recognize and regulate one's emotions, as well as understanding and empathizing with the emotions of others in cross-cultural encounters. Individuals with high emotional CQ are sensitive to the emotional dynamics present in intercultural interactions and can effectively manage potential conflicts or misunderstandings.

Physical CQ:

Physical CQ refers to the ability to adapt physically to different cultures. It includes nonverbal communication, such as body language, gestures, and facial expressions. Understanding and adjusting to nonverbal cues is crucial for effective cross-cultural communication, as cultural norms may vary significantly in this aspect.

Individuals with high physical CQ can interpret and correctly respond to nonverbal cues in different cultural contexts. They understand the cultural meanings attached to different gestures, facial expressions, and body postures and can adjust their physical behavior accordingly.

Behavioral CQ:

Behavioral CQ involves displaying appropriate behavior in intercultural encounters. It emphasizes adapting one's behavior to fit the cultural context, such as communication style, decision-making, and negotiation practices. Behavioral CQ also encompasses the ability to manage conflict and build rapport with people from diverse backgrounds.

Individuals with high behavioral CQ are adept at modifying their behavior to align with cultural expectations. They can engage in effective cross-cultural communication, adapt their leadership style, and navigate complex social and business interactions across different cultural settings.

The Interconnectedness of Cultural Intelligence Components:

While these components can be discussed individually, it is important to recognize that they are interconnected and mutually reinforcing. Each component relies on the others to form a comprehensive understanding of cultural intelligence.

For example, cognitive CQ provides the foundation for emotional CQ by enabling individuals to understand the cultural factors that influence emotions and social interactions. Emotional CQ, in turn, enhances physical CQ by facilitating the recognition and interpretation of nonverbal cues given by individuals from different cultures. Behavioral CQ is influenced by all the other components as it requires individuals to apply their cognitive, emotional, and physical understanding in practical intercultural situations.

The significance of Cultural Intelligence:

Cultural intelligence plays a pivotal role in various aspects of personal and professional life. It has significant implications for individuals, organizations, and societies.

Personal Growth and Adaptability:

Cultural intelligence promotes personal growth by expanding one's worldview and broadening perspectives. It enhances adaptability by enabling individuals to navigate diverse cultural contexts with ease and proficiency. Developing cultural intelligence leads to increased self-awareness, empathy, and curiosity about other cultures, fostering personal growth and lifelong learning.

Global Business and Workplace:

In today's interconnected business world, cultural intelligence is essential for success. It allows individuals and organizations to build strong relationships with international clients, understand local market dynamics, and adapt business strategies to suit different cultural contexts. High levels of cultural intelligence within organizations lead to increased productivity, innovation, and collaboration across global teams.

Intercultural Communication and Relationships:

Cultural intelligence facilitates effective communication and understanding between individuals from different cultural backgrounds. It promotes empathy, respect, and tolerance, leading to better interpersonal relationships and reduced conflicts. Through cultural intelligence, individuals can appreciate and celebrate diversity, fostering a sense of inclusivity and belonging.

Conflict Resolution:

Cultural intelligence empowers individuals to manage and resolve conflicts arising from cultural differences. By understanding and respecting others' perspectives, negotiating compromises, and recognizing potential misunderstandings, conflicts can be mitigated effectively. Cultural intelligence helps identify common ground and build bridges between conflicting parties.

Cultural intelligence is a multifaceted skill that involves cognitive, emotional, physical, and behavioral components. It enables individuals to navigate and adapt effectively in various cultural contexts, fostering understanding, collaboration, and mutual respect. Understanding the components of cultural intelligence is crucial for personal growth, global business success, intercultural communication, and conflict resolution. By actively developing and enhancing cultural intelligence, individuals and organizations can better navigate the complexities and opportunities presented by our diverse world.

Importance of Cultural Intelligence in a Globalized World

In today's increasingly globalized world, the concept of cultural intelligence (CQ) is of paramount importance. With the rapid advancements in technology, the ease of international travel, and the rise of global trade, individuals and organizations across the globe are becoming interconnected like never before. Cultural intelligence, the ability to effectively adapt and function in diverse cultural settings, has emerged as a crucial skillset for success in these new intercultural landscapes.

Cultural intelligence encompasses the knowledge, skills, and attitudes required to interact effectively with people from different cultural backgrounds. It goes beyond being simply aware of different cultures; it involves the ability to comprehend and appreciate the complexities and subtleties of different cultural norms, values, and practices. With globalization breaking down barriers and creating a melting pot of diverse experiences, developing cultural intelligence has become essential for several reasons.

Firstly, cultural intelligence fosters effective communication and understanding. Language barriers, non-verbal cues, and different communication styles can often hinder effective interaction between people from diverse cultural backgrounds. By developing cultural intelligence, individuals can learn to navigate these challenges and build bridges of understanding. They can recognize and adapt their communication styles to be more inclusive, respectful, and effective, promoting collaboration and cooperation.

Secondly, cultural intelligence enhances empathy and empathy fosters deeper relationships. By understanding and appreciating different cultural perspectives, individuals are better able to put themselves in someone else's shoes, see the world through different lenses, and develop a sense of empathy. This empathy allows for stronger connections to be forged, as people genuinely feel understood and appreciated. In a globalized world, where working and collaborating across cultures is becoming increasingly common, empathy enables successful collaborations and partnerships.

Furthermore, cultural intelligence promotes innovation and creativity. Cultural diversity brings a wealth of knowledge, experiences, ideas, and approaches to problem-solving. By embracing this diversity and integrating different perspectives, individuals can tap into a wide range of insights, ultimately leading to more innovative solutions. Cultural intelligence provides the ability to identify, extract, and leverage these diverse perspectives, creating an environment that fosters creativity and innovation.

Moreover, cultural intelligence contributes to effective leadership. In a globalized world, leaders are often required to manage and lead diverse teams spread across different cultural contexts. Leaders with high cultural intelligence are better equipped to understand their team members' needs, motivations, and aspirations, leading to improved team dynamics, higher levels of engagement, and increased productivity. Cultural intelligence also enables leaders to adapt their leadership styles to fit different cultural contexts, maximizing their effectiveness and influence.

Additionally, cultural intelligence is crucial for international business success. As organizations expand globally, they encounter different consumers, clients, suppliers, and stakeholders who come from diverse cultural backgrounds. Cultural intelligence allows businesses to navigate these cultural nuances, thereby ensuring that their products, services, and communication strategies align with the local cultural expectations and preferences. This adaptability enhances customer satisfaction, brand perception, and ultimately, business success in different markets.

Furthermore, cultural intelligence plays a pivotal role in conflict resolution and negotiation. In an increasingly interconnected world, conflicts and misunderstandings are inevitable. Cultural intelligence equips individuals with the tools needed to navigate these conflicts by understanding the underlying cultural factors at play. It helps individuals develop a diplomatic and inclusive approach to conflict resolution, leading to more productive outcomes and the preservation of positive relationships.

Moreover, cultural intelligence is crucial for ethical decision-making. Cultural norms and values vary significantly across cultures, and what may be deemed acceptable in one culture may be considered unethical in another. By developing cultural intelligence, individuals become more aware of these cultural variations, allowing for more informed and ethical decision-making. This is particularly important for multinational corporations that operate in different cultural contexts and must ensure their business practices align with local ethical standards.

Finally, cultural intelligence drives personal growth and fosters a global mindset. As individuals develop their cultural intelligence, they gain a deeper understanding of their own cultural identity and biases. This self-awareness facilitates personal growth and reflection, fostering a more open and inclusive mindset. It encourages individuals to challenge their assumptions, broaden their horizons, and develop a global perspective. Cultural intelligence provides the foundation for lifelong learning and adaptability, enabling individuals to thrive in an ever-changing globalized world.

In conclusion, cultural intelligence is of utmost importance in a globalized world. It enhances effective communication, empathy, innovation, and leadership. It facilitates successful international business ventures, conflict resolution, and ethical decision-making. Furthermore, cultural intelligence promotes personal growth and develops a global mindset. As the world becomes increasingly interconnected, developing cultural intelligence is essential for individuals and organizations to effectively navigate the complexities of diverse cultural landscapes and realize their fullest potential in a globalized society.

Developing Cultural Intelligence: Knowledge, Motivation, and Skills

Cultural intelligence (CQ) refers to the capability of individuals to function effectively in culturally diverse settings. As the world becomes increasingly interconnected, developing CQ has become a vital skill for individuals and organizations. CQ is composed of three key components: knowledge, motivation, and skills.

Firstly, knowledge is an essential aspect of developing cultural intelligence. It involves understanding the cultural values, norms, customs, and history of different groups. This knowledge allows individuals to appreciate and respect diverse perspectives and behaviors. It is important to stay informed about global events, learn about different cultures, and challenge any preconceived notions or stereotypes. By expanding their knowledge, individuals can develop a deeper understanding and empathy for people from diverse backgrounds.

Motivation is another critical component of cultural intelligence. It refers to the willingness and desire to interact with individuals from different cultural backgrounds. Motivation can be nurtured through developing a genuine interest in learning about different cultures, embracing diversity, and fostering curiosity. Being motivated to engage with diverse cultures helps individuals overcome biases, build relationships, and develop a sense of openness. Motivated individuals are more likely to seek out cross-cultural experiences and actively participate in multicultural environments.

Finally, skills are the practical abilities required to effectively interact and adapt in multicultural settings. These skills include communication, empathy, flexibility, and conflict resolution. Effective communication involves being able to express oneself clearly, but also being a good listener, understanding non-verbal cues, and adapting communication styles to different cultural situations. Empathy allows individuals to put themselves in the shoes of others, understand their perspectives, and foster a sense of inclusivity. Flexibility is crucial in adapting to different cultural norms, practices, and even time orientations. Conflict resolution skills are necessary to navigate potential misunderstandings or disagreements that may arise in a multicultural context.

Developing cultural intelligence offers several benefits. Firstly, it enhances personal growth and expands individuals' worldviews, making them more open-minded and adaptable. Secondly, it facilitates effective collaboration in multicultural teams and workplaces, leading to better problem-solving and innovation. In a globally interconnected world, organizations with culturally intelligent employees have a competitive edge in international markets and are better equipped to navigate diverse customer bases. Cultural intelligence also plays a crucial role in building healthy relationships, promoting inclusivity, and minimizing conflicts in diverse societies.

To develop cultural intelligence, individuals can engage in various activities and practices. Reading books, attending cultural events, and traveling are great ways to expand knowledge about different cultures. Seeking out interactions with individuals from diverse backgrounds through socializing, volunteering, or joining multicultural groups can build motivation and develop relationships. Additionally, taking courses or workshops on intercultural communication or conflict resolution can enhance the skills required for effective cross-cultural interactions.

In conclusion, developing cultural intelligence is a valuable skill in today's interconnected world. Knowledge, motivation, and skills are the key components of cultural intelligence. By expanding one's knowledge, nurturing motivation, and developing practical skills, individuals can become culturally intelligent and thrive in diverse environments.

The Benefits of Cultural Intelligence and Diversity

As the world becomes increasingly interconnected, cultural intelligence (CQ) has emerged as a crucial skill set for individuals and organizations. Cultural intelligence refers to the ability to understand, appreciate, and work effectively in culturally diverse settings. It encompasses knowledge, motivation, and skills that enable individuals to navigate and adapt to different cultural contexts. The benefits of developing cultural intelligence extend beyond personal growth and have significant implications for professional success, intercultural collaboration, and global business opportunities.

One of the primary benefits of cultural intelligence is enhanced intercultural effectiveness. Individuals with high cultural intelligence possess a deep understanding of the values, norms, customs, and history of different cultures. This knowledge allows them to appreciate and respect diverse perspectives, behaviors, and communication styles. By developing cultural intelligence, individuals can effectively navigate potential cultural misunderstandings and adapt their behavior to specific cultural contexts. This leads to increased effectiveness in collaborating with individuals from different cultural backgrounds, as well as improved communication and relationship building.

In today's globalized world, cultural intelligence is an asset in the workplace. Organizations that prioritize cultural intelligence create an environment that values diversity and inclusivity. Culturally intelligent employees can contribute positively to team dynamics and problem-solving. They bring a broader range of perspectives and approaches, leading to more creative and innovative solutions. Additionally, cultural intelligence enables individuals to work effectively in multicultural teams, bridging cultural gaps and facilitating collaboration. This improves team cohesiveness, productivity, and overall performance.

Cultural intelligence also plays a significant role in leadership effectiveness. Culturally intelligent leaders possess the ability to lead diverse teams and manage cross-cultural interactions successfully. They can adapt their leadership styles to different cultural contexts, demonstrating empathy and understanding. Culturally intelligent leaders can foster an inclusive and respectful work environment, where individuals feel valued and supported. This contributes to higher employee engagement, retention, and satisfaction. Furthermore, cultural intelligence enables leaders to navigate global business opportunities, establish strong relationships with international partners, and effectively negotiate in diverse cultural contexts.

Organizations that prioritize cultural intelligence gain a competitive edge in the global marketplace. With cultural intelligence, businesses can understand and respond to the needs and preferences of different market segments. This allows for the development of tailored marketing strategies and products that resonate with customers from different cultures. Culturally intelligent organizations are also better equipped to navigate international business negotiations, as they understand cultural nuances and adapt their approach accordingly. By demonstrating cultural competence, organizations can build trust, credibility, and long-term business relationships with international partners and clients.

Another benefit of cultural intelligence is the ability to foster positive cross-cultural relationships. Culturally intelligent individuals are more likely to approach interactions with an open mind and a willingness to learn from others. They possess empathy and respect for different cultural perspectives, which helps build meaningful relationships with individuals from diverse backgrounds. This fosters a sense of inclusivity, mutual understanding, and cooperation. In culturally diverse societies, individuals with high cultural intelligence contribute to social cohesion and harmony by promoting tolerance, acceptance, and appreciation of diverse cultures.

Furthermore, cultural intelligence contributes to personal growth and self-awareness. Developing cultural intelligence requires individuals to challenge their own biases, beliefs, and assumptions. This process of self-reflection and introspection leads to increased self-awareness and a deeper understanding of one's cultural upbringing. Individuals with high cultural intelligence are mindful of their cultural perspectives and biases, allowing them to be more open and accepting of different cultural practices and viewpoints. This personal growth leads to greater flexibility, adaptability, and resilience in the face of different cultural situations.

In conclusion, the benefits of developing cultural intelligence are numerous and far-reaching. It enhances intercultural effectiveness, enabling individuals to understand, appreciate, and effectively navigate diverse cultural contexts. Cultural intelligence positively influences professional success, contributing to improved teamwork, leadership effectiveness, and business opportunities. It also fosters positive cross-cultural relationships and contributes to social cohesion. Additionally, developing cultural intelligence leads to personal growth and self-awareness. In an increasingly interconnected world, cultural intelligence is a vital skill set with wide-ranging benefits for individuals, organizations, and societies.

Enhanced Interpersonal Relationships

Enhanced interpersonal relationships play a vital role in our overall well-being and happiness. When we have meaningful and healthy connections with others, we experience a sense of belonging, support, and fulfillment. These relationships encompass various spheres of our lives, including family, friendships, romantic partnerships, and professional connections. By nurturing and developing our interpersonal relationships, we can experience numerous benefits, ranging from improved mental and physical health to increased personal growth and fulfillment.

One of the primary benefits of enhanced interpersonal relationships is improved mental health. Strong social connections have been consistently linked to lower rates of depression, anxiety, and stress. When we have quality relationships with others, we have a support system in place, which provides emotional validation and encouragement during challenging times. Being able to share our thoughts, feelings, and experiences with trusted individuals helps alleviate mental burdens and promotes emotional well-being. Additionally, interpersonal relationships create a sense of belonging and purpose, which is essential for cultivating a positive mindset and combating loneliness and isolation.

Strong interpersonal relationships also contribute to our physical health and longevity. Research has shown that individuals with robust social networks tend to have lower rates of chronic diseases, such as heart disease, diabetes, and stroke. Having quality connections with others promotes healthy lifestyle choices, as we often engage in physical activities and healthy habits together. Furthermore, social support acts as a buffer against the harmful effects of stress, which can lead to improved immune system function and reduced inflammation in the body. Thus, enhanced interpersonal relationships support not only our emotional well-being but also our physical health.

Another benefit of enhanced interpersonal relationships is personal growth and self-awareness. Through our interactions with others, we gain insights into different perspectives, values, and beliefs. This exposure broadens our horizons and challenges our assumptions, leading to increased self-reflection and personal growth. Interpersonal relationships provide us with opportunities to learn from others, develop empathy, and acquire new skills and knowledge. Moreover, constructive feedback from trusted individuals in our lives helps us identify our strengths and areas for improvement, fostering self-awareness and personal development.

Enhanced interpersonal relationships also contribute to our overall happiness and life satisfaction. It is well-established that individuals with strong social connections tend to report higher levels of subjective well-being. Interpersonal relationships provide us with a sense of belonging and connectedness, which is essential for our psychological and emotional fulfillment. Moreover, engaging in meaningful activities and sharing experiences with others deepens our sense of joy and purpose. When we have people in our lives who genuinely care about our well-being, celebrate our successes, and offer support during challenging times, we experience a greater sense of happiness and fulfillment in life.

Furthermore, enhanced interpersonal relationships support our personal and professional success. Strong connections with others provide us with a network of support and resources that can help us seize opportunities and navigate challenges. Networking and collaboration with others in professional settings can open doors to new career opportunities, mentorship, and professional growth. In addition, interpersonal relationships foster teamwork and cooperation, leading to more effective problem-solving, creativity, and innovation. By developing strong interpersonal skills, such as effective communication, active listening, and empathy, we can build and strengthen our professional relationships, enhancing our chances for success.

Moreover, enhanced interpersonal relationships contribute to a sense of community and social cohesion. When individuals foster healthy connections with each other, it creates a ripple effect that extends beyond the immediate relationship. Positive interactions with others spread, leading to a more supportive and compassionate society. Strong interpersonal relationships cultivate a sense of trust, respect, and mutual understanding, which are essential for building bridges across different social groups. This sense of community fosters social harmony, empathy, and collective well-being.

In conclusion, enhanced interpersonal relationships have numerous benefits that positively impact our well-being and overall quality of life. These relationships contribute to improved mental and physical health, personal growth, and self-awareness. They also support our happiness, life satisfaction, and personal and professional success. Additionally, strong interpersonal connections foster a sense of community and social cohesion. By prioritizing and investing in our interpersonal relationships, we can experience greater fulfillment, support, and a deeper sense of connection with others.

Improved Communication and Collaboration

Improved communication and collaboration are foundational elements for success in all aspects of life, be it personal relationships, professional settings, or community engagement. Effective communication allows for the exchange of ideas, understanding, and problem-solving, while collaboration enables individuals to work together toward a common goal. By enhancing communication and collaboration skills, individuals and organizations can experience a myriad of benefits, including improved relationships, increased productivity, innovation, and overall success.

One of the significant benefits of improved communication and collaboration is the establishment of strong relationships. Effective communication allows individuals to express their thoughts, emotions, and ideas clearly, while also actively listening to and understanding others. It fosters a sense of trust, empathy, and respect, which is essential in building meaningful connections. When individuals communicate openly and honestly, it creates a safe and supportive environment for everyone involved. Trust and mutual understanding form the foundation of successful relationships, whether they are personal or professional. Moreover, effective communication helps resolve conflicts, prevents misunderstandings, and promotes healthy dialogue, leading to stronger and more fulfilling relationships.

Enhanced communication and collaboration also contribute to increased productivity and efficiency. When individuals communicate effectively, they can convey their expectations, goals, and responsibilities. This clarity fosters a shared understanding and ensures that everyone is working towards the same objectives. Additionally, effective communication enables individuals to delegate tasks, coordinate efforts, and constructively provide feedback. It promotes seamless teamwork and prevents unnecessary duplication of work. By improving processes and reducing miscommunication, enhanced communication and collaboration help streamline workflows, save time, and increase productivity.

Furthermore, improved communication and collaboration foster innovation and creativity. When individuals feel comfortable expressing their ideas and perspectives, it creates an environment conducive to brainstorming and exploration of new possibilities. Effective communication allows for the exchange of diverse viewpoints, which often leads to the generation of novel and innovative solutions. Collaboration brings together individuals with different experiences, expertise, and skills, contributing to a more comprehensive and well-rounded approach to problem-solving. By encouraging open dialogue, active listening, and mutual respect, enhanced communication, and collaboration can unlock the potential for creativity and innovation within individuals and teams.

In addition to individual benefits, improved communication and collaboration also contribute to organizational success. Effective communication is essential for the smooth operation of any organization, as it ensures that everyone is aligned with the mission, vision, and goals. It enables individuals at all levels of the organization to understand their roles, responsibilities, and expectations, reducing ambiguity and facilitating decision-making.

Additionally, effective communication facilitates information sharing, enabling individuals to stay informed and make well-informed decisions. This promotes transparency and a sense of ownership, which is crucial for a healthy organizational culture.

Collaboration within organizations encourages teamwork, cooperation, and synergy. It breaks down silos and fosters a sense of collective responsibility, where individuals work towards shared goals rather than individual success. Collaboration involves pooling together diverse perspectives, skills, and expertise, leading to more comprehensive problem-solving and decision-making. By leveraging the strengths and talents of all team members, collaboration encourages creativity and innovation. It also promotes a sense of camaraderie and support among employees, leading to higher job satisfaction, employee engagement, and retention within the organization.

Improved communication and collaboration also have significant benefits in intercultural and global contexts. In today's interconnected world, organizations and individuals regularly interact with people from different cultural, linguistic, and social backgrounds. Effective communication in such diverse settings requires intercultural competence, which involves understanding and adapting to cultural differences in communication styles, norms, and expectations. By developing intercultural communication skills, individuals can bridge cultural gaps, build relationships, and navigate diverse environments with success. Additionally, collaboration in a global context brings together individuals from different countries and cultures, facilitating the exchange of knowledge, skills, and perspectives. Global collaboration promotes cultural exchange, intercultural understanding, and the development of innovative solutions that transcend cultural boundaries.

Improved communication and collaboration also benefit the wider community and society as a whole. Effective communication is crucial for civic engagement, public discourse, and participatory decision-making. It enables individuals to voice their opinions, contribute to public debates, and make informed decisions about issues that affect their communities. Collaboration within communities brings together diverse stakeholders, such as individuals, organizations, and government entities, to work towards common goals, such as sustainable development, social justice, and community well-being. When individuals and organizations collaborate effectively, it facilitates resource sharing, knowledge transfer, and collective problem-solving. This leads to stronger and more resilient communities that can address challenges and seize opportunities collectively.

In conclusion, improved communication and collaboration are essential for success and growth in personal, professional, and community settings. They contribute to the establishment of strong relationships, increased productivity, innovation, and overall success. Effective communication fosters trust, understanding, and a sense of belonging, creating an environment conducive to healthy dialogue and conflict resolution. Collaboration brings together diverse perspectives and skills, enabling comprehensive problem-solving and fostering creativity and innovation. Improved communication and collaboration not only benefit individuals and organizations but also contribute to the well-being and development of communities and society as a whole. By prioritizing and enhancing communication and collaboration skills, individuals and organizations can unlock their full potential and achieve greater success.

Increased Creativity and Innovation

Increased creativity and innovation are invaluable assets in today's rapidly changing and competitive world. They play a vital role in problem-solving, driving growth, and staying ahead of the curve. By fostering a culture of creativity and nurturing innovative thinking, individuals and organizations can reap a multitude of benefits, including generating novel ideas, improving products and services, increasing productivity, and achieving long-term success.

One of the significant benefits of increased creativity and innovation is the generation of novel ideas. Creativity allows individuals to think outside the box, challenge conventional wisdom, and explore new possibilities. It opens doors to different perspectives and approaches, leading to the discovery of unique solutions to problems. When individuals feel empowered to be creative, they can tap into their creativity and generate fresh ideas that have the potential to revolutionize industries, businesses, and societies. Moreover, fostering a culture of creativity encourages continuous learning, curiosity, and a willingness to take risks, all of which are essential ingredients for generating breakthrough ideas.

Enhanced creativity and innovation also facilitate improvements in products, services, and processes. By encouraging individuals to think critically and creatively, organizations can identify areas for improvement and develop innovative solutions. Creativity enables individuals to identify unmet needs, anticipate future trends, and envision products and services that meet those needs. Innovation drives the development of more efficient and effective processes, ultimately leading to improved productivity, reduced costs, and increased customer satisfaction. By continuously innovating, organizations can stay ahead of the competition and differentiate themselves in the market.

Furthermore, increased creativity and innovation contribute to the growth and success of organizations. Creativity is the catalyst for progress and allows organizations to adapt and thrive in a rapidly changing business landscape. In today's dynamic world, organizations need to be agile and embrace new ideas and technologies to stay relevant. By fostering a culture that values and rewards creativity and innovation, organizations can encourage employees to think creatively, take risks, and experiment with new ideas. This promotes a culture of continuous improvement and growth. Organizations that prioritize creativity and innovation are better equipped to seize opportunities, overcome challenges, and adapt to market demands.

In addition to organizational benefits, increased creativity and innovation have positive impacts on the individuals involved. Creative thinking fosters personal growth, as individuals are encouraged to explore their passions, interests, and talents. It allows individuals to express themselves, think critically, and challenge existing ways of doing things. Engaging in creative activities provides a sense of fulfillment and achievement, fostering a positive mindset and improved well-being. Moreover, innovative thinking encourages individuals to continuously learn and seek new knowledge and skills, leading to personal and professional development.

Furthermore, increased creativity and innovation stimulate a culture of continuous learning and adaptation. Creativity encourages individuals to seek out new experiences, think critically, and embrace diverse perspectives. It promotes a growth mindset, where individuals are open to learning from failures and setbacks. By encouraging individuals to take risks and experiment with new ideas, organizations create an environment that fosters continuous learning and adaptation. This helps individuals and organizations to stay agile, embrace change, and thrive in constantly evolving environments.

Another benefit of increased creativity and innovation is the creation of competitive advantages. Organizations that prioritize creativity and innovation gain a unique edge over their competitors. They are better able to anticipate market trends, respond to customer needs, and develop products and services that stand out in the market. By continuously innovating, organizations can develop a portfolio of unique and valuable offerings that attract and retain customers. Moreover, the ability to consistently innovate enables organizations to stay one step ahead of the competition and maintain market leadership.

Increased creativity and innovation also contribute to positive social and environmental impact. Innovative thinking allows individuals and organizations to find solutions to pressing social and environmental challenges. It drives the development of sustainable practices, technologies, and business models that promote environmental stewardship and social responsibility. By encouraging individuals to think creatively and explore alternative approaches, organizations can address issues such as climate change, poverty, and inequality. Increased creativity and innovation empower individuals and organizations to make a positive difference in the world.

Furthermore, increased creativity and innovation foster collaboration and teamwork. Creative thinking encourages individuals to share ideas, collaborate, and build on each other's strengths. Teamwork and collaboration create synergy, where the collective intelligence and expertise of individuals lead to more innovative ideas and solutions. Collaborative environments provide opportunities for individuals from diverse backgrounds and perspectives to come together and contribute their unique insights. By fostering a culture of collaboration and supporting interdisciplinary approaches, organizations can unlock the full potential of their workforce and enhance creativity and innovation.

In conclusion, increased creativity and innovation have numerous benefits for individuals and organizations. They contribute to the generation of novel ideas, improvement of products and services, and overall growth and success. Creativity allows individuals to think critically, challenge existing assumptions, and explore new possibilities. Innovation leads to improved processes, increased productivity, and competitive advantages. Increased creativity and innovation also foster personal growth, continuous learning, and adaptation. Moreover, they have positive social and environmental impacts, driving positive change in society. By prioritizing and nurturing creativity and innovation, individuals and organizations can unlock their full potential, drive growth, and achieve long-term success.

Global Business Success

Global business success is the achievement of growth, profitability, and long-term sustainability in international markets. In today's interconnected world, businesses have access to global opportunities but also face challenges such as cultural differences, diverse markets, and intense competition. To achieve global business success, organizations must navigate these complexities and adapt their strategies to effectively operate in the global marketplace. By developing a global mindset, fostering innovation, building strong relationships, and embracing diversity, businesses can position themselves for success and capitalize on global opportunities.

One of the primary drivers of global business success is the development of a global mindset. A global mindset entails an awareness and understanding of the interconnectedness of the world, as well as the cultural, political, and economic differences that exist across markets. Businesses with a global mindset are open to new ideas, perspectives, and approaches. They embrace diversity and view it as a source of strength and innovation rather than a challenge. A global mindset enables businesses to adapt to different cultural contexts, anticipate market trends, and form meaningful connections with customers and partners around the world.

Another key factor contributing to global business success is innovation. In today's rapidly changing and competitive global landscape, businesses must continuously innovate to stay ahead and meet the evolving needs of customers. Innovation can take various forms, such as developing new products or services, implementing novel business models, or improving operational processes. By fostering a culture of innovation, businesses can encourage employees to think creatively, take risks, and challenge the status quo. Embracing innovation enables businesses to differentiate themselves in the global market, gain a competitive edge, and drive growth.

Building strong relationships is also crucial for global business success. Establishing trust, credibility, and rapport with customers, suppliers, and partners is essential for long-term success in international markets. Businesses need to invest time and effort in building and nurturing relationships, as they serve as the foundation for effective collaboration, knowledge sharing, and mutual growth. Strong relationships enable businesses to navigate cultural nuances, overcome language barriers, and adapt to local preferences. By building relationships built on trust and mutual understanding, businesses can establish a solid presence in global markets and foster long-term success.

Furthermore, embracing diversity and inclusivity is vital for global business success. In today's interconnected world, businesses operate in markets that are increasingly diverse in terms of culture, language, and social norms. By embracing diversity, businesses can tap into the collective wisdom and creativity of a diverse workforce, leading to a broader range of perspectives, ideas, and solutions. Diversity also enables businesses to better understand and connect with diverse customer segments, leading to more effective marketing strategies and customer engagement. Embracing inclusivity creates an environment where individuals feel valued, respected, and motivated to contribute their best. Businesses that foster diversity and inclusivity are better positioned to attract and retain talent from around the world, reflecting the global nature of their operations.

In addition, adapting to local contexts is crucial for global business success. Businesses need to understand and adapt to the unique characteristics and requirements of different markets. This includes factors such as cultural norms, legal and regulatory frameworks, consumer preferences, and purchasing power. Adapting to local contexts involves tailoring products, services, and marketing strategies to meet the specific needs and preferences of customers in different markets. It also requires a deep understanding of the competitive landscape and an ability to differentiate offerings to align with local market demands. Businesses that successfully adapt to local contexts demonstrate their commitment to serving customers effectively and gain a competitive advantage in global markets.

Furthermore, strong leadership is a critical factor in driving global business success. Effective leaders have a global vision and the ability to inspire and align their organizations toward global objectives. They promote a culture of continuous learning, adaptability, and innovation. Strong leaders understand the complexities of the global landscape and are skilled at navigating diverse cultural contexts. They prioritize diversity and inclusivity, foster strong relationships and collaboration, and empower their teams to embrace change and take risks. Effective leadership is crucial for navigating the challenges of global business, seizing opportunities, and driving the long-term success of organizations in international markets.

Moreover, leveraging technology and digital innovation is paramount for global business success. Technology has significantly transformed the way businesses operate and interact with customers and partners on a global scale. It has enabled businesses to reach a broader customer base, expand into new markets, and improve operational efficiencies. Embracing digital innovation allows businesses to optimize their operations, gather actionable insights through data analytics, and enhance customer experiences. Additionally, technology provides platforms for seamless communication and collaboration across borders, enabling businesses to build and maintain global networks. By leveraging technology effectively, businesses can gain a competitive advantage and capitalize on global opportunities.

In conclusion, global business success requires organizations to navigate the complexities of the global marketplace and adapt their strategies to diverse markets. By developing a global mindset, fostering innovation, building strong relationships, embracing diversity, adapting to local contexts, demonstrating strong leadership, and leveraging technology, businesses can position themselves for success in international markets. Achieving global business success involves continuous learning, adaptability, and a willingness to embrace change. Businesses that effectively execute these strategies can unlock growth, profitability, and long-term sustainability in the dynamic and interconnected world of global business.

Social Cohesion and Harmony

Social cohesion and harmony are essential elements for the well-being and progress of societies. They refer to the existence of positive relationships, trust, and cooperation among individuals and groups within a community. When social cohesion and harmony are present, individuals feel a sense of belonging and connection, leading to a peaceful and inclusive society. By promoting social cohesion and harmony, societies can achieve numerous benefits, including reduced conflict, increased resilience, improved health and well-being, and sustainable development.

One of the primary benefits of social cohesion and harmony is the reduction of conflicts and tensions within a society. When individuals feel a strong sense of connection and belonging, they are more likely to resolve conflicts peacefully and work towards mutual understanding and cooperation. Social cohesion and harmony promote open dialogue, active listening, and empathy, allowing differences to be understood and accepted. By fostering a culture of tolerance and respect for diversity, societies can prevent and address conflicts more effectively, leading to greater stability and peace.

Furthermore, social cohesion and harmony contribute to increased resilience in the face of challenges and crises. In times of adversity, societies with strong social cohesion are better equipped to come together, support one another, and find solutions collectively. Individuals and communities that are connected and cohesive can mobilize resources, share information, and assist those in need more effectively. They are also more likely to adapt and recover quickly from crises. Social cohesion and harmony promote a sense of unity and shared responsibility, which strengthens communities and enables them to overcome challenges and build resilience.

In addition to mitigating conflicts and enhancing resilience, social cohesion and harmony have positive impacts on health and well-being. Research has consistently shown a strong link between social cohesion and improved mental and physical health outcomes. When individuals feel socially connected and supported, they experience lower levels of stress, anxiety, and depression. They also have better access to social support networks, leading to improved overall well-being. Furthermore, social cohesion and harmony promote healthy behaviors and lifestyles, as individuals are more likely to take care of themselves and engage in positive social interactions. By prioritizing social cohesion and harmony, societies can contribute to the overall health and well-being of their citizens.

Moreover, social cohesion and harmony are crucial for achieving sustainable development. Inclusive and cohesive societies are better positioned to address social, economic, and environmental challenges and promote equitable development. Social cohesion and harmony promote collaboration and cooperation among diverse stakeholders, including government, civil society, and the private sector. This enables societies to develop policies and strategies that foster social inclusion, reduce inequality, and ensure the well-being of all individuals. Sustainable development requires the active engagement and participation of all members of society, and social cohesion and harmony provide the necessary foundation for collective action towards common goals.

Furthermore, social cohesion and harmony have positive economic impacts. In cohesive societies, trust and cooperation among individuals and groups lead to increased economic productivity and competitiveness. Individuals are more likely to engage in productive activities, collaborate, and innovate, which drives economic growth. Social connections and networks facilitate the exchange of resources, knowledge, and opportunities, leading to improved business and employment outcomes. Additionally, social cohesion and harmony contribute to social stability, which is essential for attracting investments, encouraging entrepreneurship, and fostering a conducive business environment. By promoting social cohesion and harmony, societies can unlock the full economic potential of their communities.

Inclusive and harmonious societies also foster social justice and equality. Social cohesion and harmony promote a sense of fairness and mutual respect, challenging discriminatory practices and addressing inequalities. In cohesive societies, individuals have equal opportunities to participate in social, economic, and political activities. Moreover, social cohesion and harmony enable marginalized groups to have a voice and representation, contributing to the realization of human rights and social justice. By promoting social cohesion and harmony, societies can strive towards equality and justice for all individuals, creating a more inclusive and just society.

Furthermore, social cohesion and harmony contribute to the preservation of cultural diversity and heritage. In cohesive societies, different cultural and ethnic groups coexist harmoniously, respecting and valuing each other's traditions, beliefs, and values. Social cohesion and harmony provide a space for intercultural dialogue and understanding, fostering cultural exchange and appreciation. This enriches the social fabric of the community and promotes a sense of shared cultural heritage. By embracing cultural diversity and promoting social cohesion, societies can benefit from the richness and vibrancy that diverse cultural expressions bring.

Social cohesion and harmony also play a crucial role in promoting active citizenship and democratic participation. In cohesive societies, individuals are more likely to engage in civic activities, participate in decision-making processes, and work towards common goals for the betterment of their communities. Social cohesion and harmony foster a sense of ownership and responsibility, empowering individuals to actively contribute to social change. Moreover, social cohesion and harmony ensure that diverse voices and perspectives are heard and valued, leading to more inclusive and effective decision-making processes. By promoting social cohesion and harmony, societies can strengthen democracy, promote social justice, and foster active citizenship.

In conclusion, social cohesion and harmony are fundamental for the well-being, progress, and sustainability of societies. They promote positive relationships, trust, and cooperation among individuals and groups, leading to reduced conflicts, increased resilience, improved health and well-being, and sustainable development. Social cohesion and harmony contribute to peace and stability, enabling societies to address challenges and crises effectively. They also promote social justice, economic growth, and cultural preservation. By prioritizing social cohesion and harmony, societies can foster inclusive communities that value diversity, promote equity and justice, and empower individuals to actively participate in the democratic processes.

Challenges in Cultural Intelligence and Diversity

Cultural intelligence and diversity pose significant challenges in today's globalized and diverse world. Cultural intelligence refers to an individual's ability to understand, adapt to, and effectively interact with people from different cultural backgrounds. Diversity encompasses various dimensions, including race, ethnicity, gender, sexual orientation, religion, and age. While cultural intelligence and diversity bring numerous benefits, they also present challenges that individuals, organizations, and societies must address. These challenges include stereotypes and biases, communication barriers, resistance to change, and the need for inclusive practices.

One of the primary challenges in cultural intelligence and diversity is the presence of stereotypes and biases. Stereotypes are generalizations and oversimplified beliefs about a particular group based on their cultural, racial, or ethnic background. Biases are preconceived notions and prejudices that individuals hold, often unconsciously, towards people who are different from them. Stereotypes and biases can hinder effective intercultural communication, collaboration, and understanding. They create barriers and perpetuate misunderstandings, leading to friction and conflict. Overcoming stereotypes and biases requires individuals to challenge their assumptions, develop empathy, and seek a genuine understanding of different cultures and perspectives. Organizations and societies need to promote awareness, education, and policies that challenge stereotypes and biases and foster inclusion.

Communication barriers present another significant challenge to cultural intelligence and diversity. Effective communication is critical for building relationships, understanding diverse viewpoints, and resolving conflicts. However, differences in language, communication styles, and nonverbal cues can impede communication and lead to misunderstandings. Moreover, cultural norms and values influence communication patterns, such as directness, indirectness, or the use of gestures and body language. Overcoming communication barriers requires individuals to be open-minded, patient, and adaptable. Developing intercultural communication skills, such as active listening, asking clarifying questions, and seeking feedback, is crucial. Organizations can facilitate effective communication by providing language training and fostering an inclusive environment that values diverse perspectives.

Resistance to change is another challenge in cultural intelligence and diversity. Cultural intelligence requires individuals to be open to new ideas, experiences, and ways of thinking. However, individuals may resist change due to fear, insecurity, or attachment to familiar cultural norms and values. This resistance can hinder the integration of diversity into organizations and communities. Overcoming resistance to change requires creating an environment that encourages continuous learning, growth, and adaptation. Organizations and societies need to promote a culture of inclusivity, where individuals feel safe and supported in exploring and embracing different perspectives. Education and awareness are critical to demonstrate the benefits of diversity and the importance of cultural intelligence.

Furthermore, the need for inclusive practices is a significant challenge in cultural intelligence and diversity. Inclusivity entails creating environments where all individuals feel valued, respected, and included, regardless of their cultural, racial, or ethnic background. However, organizational and societal practices often inadvertently exclude certain groups or perpetuate inequalities. For example, biased recruitment and promotion processes may limit the representation of diverse individuals in leadership positions. Inclusive practices require organizations to promote diversity from top to bottom, including diverse representation in decision-making processes, developing inclusive policies, and providing equal opportunities for all individuals. It also necessitates creating safe spaces for dialogue, fostering intercultural understanding, and addressing systemic barriers that hinder diversity and inclusivity.

Moreover, managing cultural intelligence and diversity can be challenging due to the complexity of human interactions and the evolving nature of culture. Cultural intelligence goes beyond knowledge of cultural norms; it requires individuals to be adaptable, flexible, and willing to continuously learn from new cultural experiences. Similarly, diversity is not a fixed characteristic but an ever-evolving concept that encompasses intersectionality and an understanding of the multitude of identities individuals hold. Managing cultural intelligence and diversity requires individuals and organizations to engage in a lifelong process of self-reflection, learning, and adaptation. It requires humility, open-mindedness, and a commitment to ongoing personal and professional development.

Furthermore, a lack of awareness and understanding of cultural intelligence and diversity is a challenge that needs to be addressed. Many individuals and organizations may be unaware of the impact and importance of cultural intelligence and diversity. This lack of awareness can perpetuate stereotypes, biases, and exclusionary practices. Organizations and societies need to invest in education and training programs that promote cultural intelligence and diversity awareness. This includes workshops, seminars, and cultural exchange programs that expose individuals to diverse perspectives and foster empathy. By increasing awareness and understanding, individuals and organizations can develop the skills and knowledge necessary to navigate cultural intelligence and promote diversity effectively.

In conclusion, cultural intelligence and diversity bring numerous benefits but also present challenges that individuals, organizations, and societies must address. Overcoming stereotypes and biases, communication barriers, resistance to change, and the need for inclusive practices are key challenges. These challenges require individuals to challenge their assumptions, develop intercultural communication skills, embrace change, and foster inclusivity. Organizations and societies play a crucial role in promoting awareness, education, and policies that facilitate cultural intelligence and diversity. By embracing these challenges, societies can harness the full potential of cultural intelligence and diversity to foster growth, innovation, and social harmony.

Stereotypes and Prejudices

Stereotypes and prejudice are pervasive in society and have profound impacts on individuals and communities. Stereotypes refer to generalized beliefs or assumptions about a particular group of people based on their characteristics, such as race, ethnicity, gender, religion, or age. Prejudice, on the other hand, refers to preconceived opinions or attitudes towards individuals or groups based on stereotypes or baseless judgments. Stereotypes and prejudice can lead to discrimination, marginalization, and social inequalities. Understanding and challenging stereotypes and prejudice are crucial in creating a more inclusive, equitable, and just society.

One of the primary impacts of stereotypes and prejudice is the perpetuation of social inequalities. Stereotypes often originate from historical, cultural, and societal biases that favor certain groups while marginalizing others. These biases can reinforce social hierarchies and power imbalances, leading to unequal access to resources, opportunities, and social privileges. For example, racial stereotypes have long been used to justify discriminatory practices such as racial profiling, housing segregation, and hiring biases. Similarly, gender stereotypes can limit women's access to educational and career opportunities and contribute to the gender wage gap. Prejudice based on sexual orientation, religion, or disability can also lead to exclusion and unequal treatment. By perpetuating stereotypes and prejudices, individuals and societies contribute to systemic inequalities and hinder social progress.

Moreover, stereotypes and prejudice can have significant psychological impacts on individuals who are targets of such biases. When individuals are repeatedly exposed to stereotypes and prejudice, they may internalize these negative assumptions, leading to decreased self-esteem, self-worth, and psychological well-being. This can contribute to mental health issues such as depression, anxiety, and low self-confidence. Moreover, the fear of being stereotyped or prejudiced can lead individuals to engage in self-censorship, hiding their true identities or conforming to societal expectations. This can result in a loss of authenticity, personal fulfillment, and overall life satisfaction. Stereotypes and prejudice can also create a hostile and unwelcoming environment, leading to increased stress, isolation, and social exclusion.

Furthermore, stereotypes and prejudice can hinder intergroup relationships and contribute to social divisions. When individuals hold negative stereotypes or prejudiced attitudes toward other groups, it becomes difficult to establish trust, understanding, and cooperation. Stereotypes and prejudice can lead to bias-motivated behaviors, discrimination, and even hate crimes. They foster an "us versus them" mentality, perpetuating social divisions and conflicts based on race, religion, ethnicity, or other characteristics. Stereotypes can also create barriers to effective communication and collaboration, preventing individuals from working together towards common goals. Overcoming stereotypes and prejudice is essential for building inclusive and cohesive societies, where individuals can truly embrace diversity and appreciate the richness that different cultures, perspectives, and experiences bring.

In addition to these social and psychological impacts, stereotypes and prejudice also affect decision-making processes, policies, and institutions. Stereotypes and prejudice can bias individuals' judgment and lead to discriminatory practices in various domains, including education, employment, healthcare, and criminal justice. For example, racial stereotypes can influence how teachers perceive and evaluate the abilities and potential of students from different racial or ethnic backgrounds, leading to achievement gaps. Similarly, gender stereotypes can influence hiring decisions, promotion opportunities, and salary allocations, perpetuating gender inequalities in the workplace. Prejudice and bias can also impact the criminal justice system, leading to disparities in arrests, convictions, and sentencing. Addressing stereotypes and prejudice is necessary for creating fairer and more just institutions that provide equal opportunities and treatment for all individuals.

Moreover, stereotypes and prejudice impede diversity and inclusion efforts in organizations and institutions. Stereotyping individuals based on their background or characteristics can lead to biases in recruitment, promotion, and decision-making processes. These biases can limit the representation and advancement of individuals from marginalized or underrepresented groups. Stereotypes and prejudice can also create hostile work environments where individuals feel excluded or discriminated against. This can result in lower employee morale, decreased productivity, and increased turnover. Organizations that embrace diversity and challenge stereotypes and prejudice are more likely to foster a culture of inclusivity, creativity, and innovation. Diversity promotes different perspectives and experiences, leading to stronger decision-making processes and better outcomes.

Furthermore, stereotypes and prejudice can hinder efforts to address important social issues, such as climate change, poverty, and inequality. Stereotypes can contribute to the perception that certain groups bear more responsibility or are less affected by these issues, leading to apathy or resistance to collective action. Prejudice can shape public opinion and policy decisions, leading to biased or ineffective solutions. Overcoming stereotypes and prejudice is necessary for promoting collective responsibility and collaboration in addressing these pressing challenges. It requires recognizing the interconnectedness of social issues and embracing the contributions and perspectives of all individuals and communities.

Challenging stereotypes and prejudice is a complex and long-term process that requires multiple levels of intervention. Education and awareness play a crucial role in challenging stereotypes and promoting inclusivity. Learning about different cultures, histories, and experiences helps individuals understand the complexity and diversity of human identities. Educational institutions should incorporate multicultural curricula, promote diversity in their faculty and staff, and develop initiatives that encourage empathy, respect, and understanding. Media outlets also play a significant role in shaping perceptions and dismantling stereotypes. Media organizations should strive to present diverse narratives and avoid perpetuating harmful stereotypes or biases. Governments and policymakers should enact legislation that protects against discrimination, promotes inclusivity, and fosters diversity in all aspects of society.

Furthermore, fostering intergroup contact and dialogue is essential in breaking down stereotypes and prejudices. Individuals can challenge their assumptions by actively seeking out opportunities to engage with people from different backgrounds, cultures, and experiences. Platforms for constructive and open conversations, such as community forums, workshops, and cultural exchange programs, can facilitate the building of bridges between different groups and promote understanding and empathy. Building intergroup relationships helps combat stereotypes by allowing individuals to see beyond the generalized assumptions and understand the unique identities, stories, and contributions of others.

In conclusion, stereotypes and prejudice have far-reaching impacts on individuals, communities, institutions, and societies. They perpetuate inequalities, hinder social progress, and create divisions. Stereotypes and prejudice affect individuals' psychological well-being, erode trust, and limit opportunities. They also influence decision-making processes, contribute to biased practices, and impede diversity and inclusion efforts. Overcoming stereotypes and prejudice requires a multifaceted approach involving education, awareness, dialogue, and policy changes. Creating a more inclusive, equitable, and just society necessitates challenging stereotypes and fostering empathy, respect, and understanding for the diverse and complex identities of all individuals.

Communication Barriers

Communication is a fundamental aspect of human interaction, enabling the exchange of ideas, information, and emotions. However, communication barriers can hinder effective communication and lead to misunderstandings, conflicts, and inefficiencies. These barriers can arise from various factors, including language differences, cultural disparities, technological limitations, and personal biases. Understanding and addressing these barriers is essential for building strong relationships, fostering collaboration, and achieving successful communication in personal, professional, and societal contexts.

One of the primary communication barriers is language differences. When individuals do not share a common language, communication becomes challenging. Language barriers can impede understanding, leading to misinterpretations and confusion. Even when individuals have some level of language proficiency, nuances, dialects, and idiomatic expressions can still create barriers to effective communication. Language diversity is increasingly prevalent in global contexts, where individuals from different linguistic backgrounds interact. To overcome language barriers, individuals can use translation services, rely on visual aids and nonverbal communication, or invest in language learning to improve their proficiency. Organizations can also promote the use of clear and concise language, provide language training, and utilize interpreters to facilitate communication across language barriers.

Cultural disparities pose another significant communication barrier. Cultural differences influence communication styles, norms, and values, which can lead to misunderstandings and misinterpretations. High-context cultures, where much of the meaning is conveyed through nonverbal cues or subtle messages, may face challenges when interacting with low-context cultures that rely more on explicit language. Cultural taboos, social norms, and different communication hierarchies can further complicate interactions. To overcome cultural barriers, individuals need to develop cultural sensitivity and awareness. This includes active listening, being open-minded, and seeking to understand cultural differences. Cross-cultural training programs can also be beneficial in promoting intercultural understanding and effective communication.

Technological limitations can also create communication barriers. While advancements in technology have facilitated global communication, they can still present challenges. Connectivity issues, language barriers in digital communication, and the absence of nonverbal cues can hinder effective communication. Misinterpretation of messages can occur in digital communication, as written words may not always convey the intended tone and emotions. To address technological barriers, individuals can use video-conferencing tools to enhance virtual communication, utilize translation technologies, and be mindful of the limitations of the medium. It is essential to choose the appropriate communication platform based on the nature of the message and ensure clarity in written communication.

Personal biases and stereotypes can be significant obstacles to effective communication. Preconceptions, prejudices, and assumptions about individuals or groups can influence how messages are perceived and interpreted. Biases can lead to selective listening, misjudgment, and unfair evaluations. Overcoming personal biases requires self-reflection, empathy, and active efforts to challenge stereotypes and prejudices. Individuals need to approach communication with an open mind, suspend judgment, and engage in genuine dialogue. Organizations can promote diversity and inclusivity, create safe spaces for open discussions, and implement policies and training programs that address biases and promote equitable communication practices.

Emotional barriers can also impede effective communication. Emotional states such as anger, frustration, or stress can interfere with clear and rational communication. Emotions can lead to biases and distort perceptions, resulting in miscommunications. Active listening skills, emotional intelligence, and self-awareness can help overcome emotional barriers. Individuals should practice empathy, regulate their own emotions, and be mindful of their tone and nonverbal cues. Creating a supportive and inclusive environment where individuals feel comfortable expressing their emotions can also contribute to effective communication.

Moreover, hierarchical structures and power imbalances can create communication barriers. In organizations and societies with hierarchical structures, individuals at different levels may feel hesitant to voice their opinions or provide feedback. Power imbalances can result in one-way communication, where information flows from top to bottom without meaningful dialogue. Overcoming these barriers requires fostering a culture of inclusivity and open communication. Organizations can promote transparency, encourage feedback, and create opportunities for employees to express their views regardless of their position in the hierarchy. Active listening, respect, and valuing diverse perspectives are essential to overcome these barriers.

Physical barriers can also hinder communication. Distance, environmental factors, and accessibility limitations can impede face-to-face communication. For example, noisy environments, poor lighting, or physical disabilities can affect the quality of communication. To address physical barriers, individuals can seek suitable environments for communication, ensure proper lighting and sound conditions, and make accommodations for individuals with disabilities. Organizations and institutions should strive to provide accessible spaces and incorporate universal design principles to minimize physical barriers that hinder effective communication.

Miscommunication due to perceptual differences is yet another communication barrier. Individuals have diverse mental models, perspectives, and experiences, which influence how they perceive and interpret messages. Filters such as values, beliefs, and prior knowledge impact information processing and can cause misunderstandings. Miscommunication can be mitigated by active listening, checking for understanding, seeking clarification, and purposeful communication. Employing visual aids, using plain language, and providing examples can also help bridge perceptual gaps.

In conclusion, communication barriers can hinder effective communication, leading to misunderstandings, conflicts, and inefficiencies. Language differences, cultural disparities, technological limitations, personal biases, emotional barriers, hierarchical structures, physical obstacles, and perceptual differences are among the most common barriers. Understanding and addressing these barriers are crucial in personal, professional, and societal contexts. Building language proficiency, fostering cultural sensitivity, embracing technology, promoting inclusivity, overcoming biases, managing emotions, and creating open communication environments are key strategies to overcome these barriers. By actively working towards effective communication, individuals and organizations can enhance understanding, promote collaboration, foster healthy relationships, and enable success in diverse and interconnected environments.

Ethnocentrism and Cultural Bias

Ethnocentrism and cultural bias are two concepts that play a significant role in understanding the dynamics of human interactions and the challenges faced in diverse societies. Ethnocentrism refers to the tendency to view one's cultural group as superior to others, while cultural bias involves the unconscious prejudices and stereotypes that influence our perceptions and judgments about other cultures. These phenomena can create communication barriers, hinder empathy, perpetuate inequality, and limit our ability to appreciate and understand different cultures. It is important to recognize and address these biases to promote inclusivity, foster intercultural understanding, and build more harmonious societies.

Ethnocentrism is a widespread human tendency observed across cultures throughout history. It stems from the innate human need to belong and identify with a particular group. Often, individuals view their own culture, values, customs, and behaviors as the norm and, consequently, judge other cultures based on their standards. Ethnocentrism can manifest in various ways, such as prejudice, stereotypes, discrimination, and even hostility towards other cultures. This mindset can lead to division, conflict, and the perpetuation of inequalities.

Cultural bias, on the other hand, refers to the subconscious prejudices and stereotypes that individuals hold towards cultures different from their own. These biases can shape our perceptions, judgments, and behaviors towards individuals from other cultures, often leading to unfair treatment and misunderstanding. Cultural bias operates at both an individual and societal level and can be deeply ingrained due to socialization processes, media influence, and personal experiences.

The impact of ethnocentrism and cultural bias on communication cannot be overstated. With ethnocentric views, individuals tend to interpret the actions, words, and behaviors of others from different cultures through their cultural lens. This can result in misinterpretations, misunderstandings, and miscommunication, leading to conflicts and barriers in building effective relationships. Cultural bias reinforces these communication barriers by creating stereotypes and assumptions about individuals from other cultures, limiting our ability to genuinely listen, understand, and engage with people from diverse backgrounds.

To overcome ethnocentrism and cultural bias, individuals and societies must acknowledge and confront these biases. The first step is self-awareness, recognizing our biases, and actively challenging them. By being aware of our cultural lens, we can seek to understand others' perspectives and experiences without judgment or prejudice. An open mindset and curiosity about other cultures can help break down barriers and foster genuine intercultural communication.

Education plays a crucial role in addressing ethnocentrism and cultural bias. By integrating cultural studies and promoting diversity and inclusion in the curriculum, educational institutions can help students develop a broader understanding and appreciation for different cultures. Additionally, exposing individuals to diverse experiences, such as travel, intercultural exchanges, and immersion programs, can significantly contribute to reducing ethnocentrism and cultural bias.

Creating platforms and opportunities for intercultural dialogue is also vital for challenging ethnocentrism and cultural bias. By encouraging open discussions, individuals can share their perspectives, experiences, and cultural knowledge, fostering mutual understanding and empathy. Organizations can also promote diversity and inclusion by embracing cultural differences, ensuring equal opportunities, and providing training on cultural competence and intercultural communication.

It is essential to recognize that ethnocentrism and cultural bias are not fixed traits but rather learned behaviors. By actively engaging with individuals from different cultures, challenging our prejudices, and seeking diverse perspectives, we can broaden our understanding and reduce the impact of these biases. Building friendships and relationships with individuals from different cultures can be a powerful means to challenge ethnocentrism and cultural bias as it promotes empathy, respect, and appreciation for diversity.

The media also plays a critical role in shaping and reinforcing cultural biases. Media representations often perpetuate stereotypes and distort perceptions of different cultures. It is important to promote media literacy, encouraging critical analysis of media portrayals and providing platforms for marginalized voices to be heard. By diversifying media representation and providing accurate and balanced portrayals of different cultures, we can reduce cultural bias and foster a more inclusive society.

Additionally, policymakers and institutions need to address systemic biases that perpetuate inequalities and limit opportunities for individuals from certain cultures. This involves implementing policies that promote diversity, fairness, and inclusion in areas such as education, employment, healthcare, and justice systems. By removing barriers and ensuring equal access to resources and opportunities, societies can work towards a more equitable and inclusive future.

In conclusion, ethnocentrism and cultural bias are significant barriers to understanding, empathy, and effective communication in diverse societies. These biases can lead to misinterpretations, and conflicts, and perpetuate inequalities. Recognizing and addressing these biases through education, intercultural dialogue, media representation, and policy changes are essential for fostering inclusivity and promoting intercultural understanding. By actively challenging our own biases, engaging with diverse perspectives, and creating opportunities for genuine intercultural communication, we can build a more harmonious and equitable world.

Resistance to Change

Resistance to change is a common phenomenon that individuals, organizations, and societies often encounter when implementing new ideas, practices, or transformations. It refers to the reluctance or opposition to embrace, accept, or adapt to change. Resistance to change can manifest in various ways, including skepticism, fear, lack of understanding, and attachment to familiar routines or ways of doing things. Understanding the sources of resistance to change, its impacts, and strategies to manage it is crucial for achieving successful change initiatives and fostering growth and innovation in personal, professional, and societal contexts.

There are several sources of resistance to change that individuals and organizations may face. First, individuals may resist change due to the fear of the unknown and uncertainty. Change disrupts routines and brings about new challenges, which can create feelings of anxiety and resistance. Second, resistance to change may stem from the belief that the current way of doing things is effective or satisfactory, leading to complacency and an aversion to change. Third, there may be a lack of trust or confidence in the change initiative or the individuals driving it. If individuals do not trust those leading the change or perceive inconsistencies in the change process, they may resist the proposed changes. Fourth, resistance to change can arise from the perception of personal or professional threats. Individuals may fear that change will result in job loss, reduced status, or require new skills that they may not possess. Finally, resistance to change can be driven by cultural factors and existing norms and values that are deeply entrenched in an organization or society.

Resistance to change can have significant impacts on individuals, organizations, and societies. At an individual level, resistance to change can result in stress, anxiety, and decreased job satisfaction. Individuals may struggle to adapt to new roles, responsibilities, or expectations, leading to decreased motivation and productivity. Organizational impacts include the potential for decreased efficiency, missed opportunities for innovation, and decreased competitiveness. Resistance to change can also contribute to a negative organizational culture, characterized by a lack of trust, cooperation, and collaboration. In societal contexts, resistance to change can hinder progress, social transformation, and the development of more equitable and inclusive societies.

Effective strategies for managing resistance to change include open communication, involvement, and a supportive environment. Communication plays a crucial role in addressing resistance to change. Leaders and change agents need to communicate the benefits and rationale behind the change, addressing concerns and addressing possible challenges. Providing clear and transparent information can help reduce uncertainty and alleviate fear. Additionally, involving individuals and stakeholders in the change process can promote ownership, engagement, and a sense of empowerment. By soliciting input, listening to concerns, and considering alternative viewpoints, organizations can foster a collaborative culture that promotes buy-in and reduces resistance. It is also important to create a supportive environment that encourages learning, experimentation, and growth. Organizations can provide training and resources to support individuals through the change, acknowledging and validating their emotions and experiences. By fostering a culture of learning, adaptability, and resilience, organizations can better manage resistance and facilitate successful change implementation.

Leadership plays a critical role in managing resistance to change. Leaders need to effectively articulate the vision, purpose, and benefits of the change while demonstrating empathy and understanding for individuals' concerns. They should act as change champions, advocating for the change and setting an example through their actions and behavior. Leaders should foster an inclusive and supportive environment that encourages collaboration, learning, and innovation. By addressing resistance directly, leaders can create an atmosphere of trust and openness, allowing individuals to express their concerns and fears. Developing effective change management strategies, such as clear communication plans, training and support, and recognizing and rewarding progress, can also facilitate successful change implementation.

Building a culture of change readiness can help organizations and individuals proactively address resistance to change. This involves developing a mindset and skill set that embraces new ideas, encourages innovation, and values continuous learning and adaptation. Organizations can invest in professional development programs that focus on change management, resilience, and learning agility. By promoting a growth mindset, encouraging experimentation, and recognizing and celebrating innovation, organizations can build a culture that perceives change as an opportunity for growth and improvement rather than a threat. Individuals can also cultivate their change readiness by seeking out new experiences, engaging in continuous learning, and nurturing their adaptability and openness to change.

In conclusion, resistance to change is a common and often understandable reaction to new ideas, practices, or transformations. The fear of the unknown, lack of trust, perceptions of threats, and attachment to familiar routines are some of the sources of resistance to change. The impacts of resistance can be significant, including stress, decreased productivity, negative organizational culture, missed opportunities, and a hindrance to social progress. Strategies for managing resistance include open communication, involvement, and creating a supportive environment. Leadership plays a crucial role in addressing resistance, emphasizing the benefits of change, and fostering a culture of learning and adaptation. By cultivating change readiness and embracing a growth mindset, individuals and organizations can proactively manage resistance and embrace change as an opportunity for growth and innovation.

Unconscious Bias

Unconscious bias is a phenomenon that affects individuals' thoughts, decisions, and behavior in subtle and often unconscious ways. It refers to the biases or prejudices that individuals hold towards certain groups of people, based on characteristics such as race, gender, age, appearance, or other factors. These biases are unintentional and often contrary to an individual's conscious beliefs and values. Unconscious bias is deeply ingrained in our subconscious and can influence our perceptions, attitudes, and actions without our awareness. Understanding and addressing unconscious bias is crucial for fostering diversity, inclusion, and equality in various aspects of life, including education, workplaces, and social interactions.

Several factors contribute to the development of unconscious biases. First, socialization and upbringing play a significant role in shaping our beliefs and attitudes toward others. From an early age, individuals are exposed to societal messages, stereotypes, and cultural norms, which can influence the formation of unconscious biases. Media, family, peers, and education all contribute to the development of our belief systems and biases. Second, cognitive processes and mental shortcuts, known as heuristics, also contribute to unconscious biases. The brain relies on these shortcuts to process information efficiently. However, they can lead to biases by creating stereotypes or generalizations. For example, our brains may automatically associate certain characteristics or behaviors with specific groups due to the cognitive shortcut of categorization. Third, personal experiences also shape our unconscious biases. Negative or positive encounters with individuals from specific groups can lead to biases, as our brains generalize these experiences to all members of that group. These biases are often unconscious and can persist even in the face of contradictory evidence or personal beliefs.

Unconscious biases can have significant negative impacts on individuals and communities. In education, unconscious biases can influence teachers' perceptions and expectations of students, leading to differential treatment based on factors such as race, gender, or socioeconomic status. This can perpetuate inequities and contribute to achievement gaps between different groups of students. In workplaces, unconscious biases can affect hiring decisions, promotions, and work assignments, leading to a lack of diversity, inequality, and reduced opportunities for underrepresented groups. Unconscious biases can also affect interpersonal interactions, leading to microaggressions, exclusion, and a lack of understanding and empathy. Furthermore, unconscious biases can contribute to systemic discrimination and prejudice, perpetuating stereotypes, and exclusion in society.

Addressing unconscious bias requires awareness, education, and intentional efforts. The first step is to recognize and acknowledge that unconscious biases exist and can influence our thoughts and behaviors. This involves understanding that no one is immune to biases, and they are not an indicator of personal moral character. Instead, they are a result of socialization and cognitive processes that can be challenged and changed. Education and training programs on unconscious bias can help individuals become aware of their own biases and their impacts. These programs can provide individuals with tools and strategies to overcome biases and make fair, equitable, and unbiased decisions. By deconstructing stereotypes, challenging assumptions, and promoting empathy and understanding, individuals can work towards mitigating the impacts of unconscious bias.

Organizations play a crucial role in addressing unconscious bias within their structures and practices. They can implement diversity and inclusion initiatives that promote equal opportunities for all employees and challenge biased practices. For example, diverse hiring panels can help reduce unconscious biases in the recruitment process. Implementing blind screening processes, where personal markers such as names and photos are removed, can also help mitigate biases. Organizations can provide unconscious bias training for employees at all levels to increase awareness and create a culture that values diversity and inclusion. Additionally, fostering an inclusive work environment where employees feel safe to voice concerns and challenge bias can help create a culture of accountability and continuous improvement.

In addition to individual and organizational efforts, there are broader societal strategies for addressing unconscious bias. Media representation plays a significant role in shaping attitudes and perceptions towards different groups of people. By promoting accurate and diverse representations, media can challenge stereotypes and contribute to positive social change. Education systems can also play a role in combating unconscious bias by implementing inclusive and diverse curricula that reflect the experiences and contributions of marginalized groups. Society can benefit from promoting cultural exchange, dialogue, and understanding, fostering empathy, and breaking down barriers between different groups.

It is crucial to recognize that addressing unconscious bias is a continuous process that requires ongoing self-reflection and commitment. It is not enough to simply be aware of biases; individuals and society need to actively challenge and confront them. This can be done by seeking out diverse perspectives, engaging in uncomfortable conversations, and examining the impact of biases in decision-making processes. It requires individuals to continually educate themselves, challenge their assumptions, and be open to change.

In conclusion, unconscious bias is a pervasive and often unnoticed phenomenon that affects individuals' thoughts, decisions, and behaviors. It is influenced by socialization, cognitive processes, and personal experiences. Unconscious biases can have significant negative impacts on individuals, organizations, and society. Addressing unconscious bias requires awareness, education, and intentional efforts at individual, organizational, and societal levels. By acknowledging biases, promoting education and awareness, and implementing inclusive practices, individuals and organizations can work towards creating a more equitable and inclusive society that values diversity and fosters equality.

Strategies for Fostering Cultural Intelligence and Diversity

Fostering cultural intelligence and diversity is essential for creating inclusive and thriving environments, whether in personal, professional, or societal contexts. Cultural intelligence refers to the capability to understand, appreciate, and effectively navigate cultural differences, while diversity encompasses the recognition, acceptance, and celebration of the differences among individuals and groups. Embracing cultural intelligence and diversity brings numerous benefits, including enhanced innovation, improved problem-solving, increased creativity, and stronger relationships. To foster cultural intelligence and diversity, individuals and organizations can employ various strategies, such as promoting awareness and education, fostering inclusive practices, encouraging intercultural exchange, and cultivating leadership commitment.

One of the most important strategies for fostering cultural intelligence and diversity is promoting awareness and education. This involves increasing individuals' understanding of different cultures, beliefs, and perspectives. Providing education about cultural differences, stereotypes, biases, and unconscious prejudices helps individuals recognize their assumptions and encourages them to challenge and unlearn deeply ingrained biases. Educational initiatives can include workshops, seminars, and training focused on cultural intelligence, diversity appreciation, and cross-cultural communication. These initiatives should emphasize the importance of developing empathy, fostering intercultural understanding, and recognizing the value and contribution of diverse voices and perspectives.

Fostering inclusive practices is another crucial strategy for promoting cultural intelligence and diversity. Inclusive practices involve creating an environment where all individuals, regardless of their cultural background, feel valued, respected, and have equal access to resources and opportunities. Organizations can review their policies, procedures, and practices to eliminate bias and discrimination. Strategies may include implementing diverse hiring and promotion practices, ensuring equitable resource distribution, and establishing grievance mechanisms. Providing flexibility and accommodation that account for cultural differences can also foster inclusivity. By creating a culture of inclusiveness, organizations foster innovation, creativity, and better decision-making by drawing upon diverse perspectives.

Encouraging intercultural exchange is a powerful strategy for building cultural intelligence and fostering diversity. Organizations and educational institutions can create opportunities for individuals from different cultural backgrounds to interact and learn from one another. This can be achieved through programs such as mentorship initiatives, cross-cultural collaboration projects, or study-abroad programs that facilitate immersion in different cultural environments. Exposure to diverse perspectives, customs, and values enriches individuals' understanding of different cultures and helps build bridges across cultural differences. Embracing intercultural exchange cultivates mutual respect and empathy, supports relationship-building, and contributes to the development of cultural intelligence.

Cultivating leadership commitment is crucial for fostering cultural intelligence and diversity within organizations and communities. Leaders play a significant role in setting the tone and direction for promoting cultural intelligence and diversity. Leaders need to demonstrate their commitment to diversity and inclusion. They can model inclusive behaviors, engage in ongoing learning, and create opportunities for open dialogue and feedback. Leaders should also recognize and reward diverse perspectives and contributions, ensuring that diversity and cultural intelligence are prioritized in decision-making processes. By fostering a culture that values and celebrates diversity, leaders can inspire individuals and motivate them to embrace and promote cultural intelligence and diversity throughout the organization or community.

Promoting mentorship and allyship is another effective strategy for fostering cultural intelligence and diversity. Establishing mentorship programs that connect individuals from different cultural backgrounds allows for mutual learning and support. Mentors can provide guidance, share experiences, and help mentees navigate challenges related to cultural differences. Allyship involves individuals from privileged groups actively advocating for and supporting individuals from marginalized groups. Allies can actively challenge biases and stereotypes, amplify marginalized voices, and work towards creating inclusive spaces. By fostering mentorship and allyship, individuals and organizations create networks of support, encourage learning, and promote the development of cultural intelligence and diversity.

Creating inclusive spaces and platforms for dialogue is crucial for fostering cultural intelligence and diversity. Organizations and communities can establish safe spaces for individuals to share their experiences, perspectives, and concerns. These spaces can take the form of diversity and inclusion committees, employee resource groups, or community forums. These platforms provide opportunities for individuals to dialogue, learn from one another, and collaborate on projects that promote inclusive practices. Inclusive spaces should prioritize active listening, respectful communication, and the recognition of diverse perspectives. By creating an environment that supports open dialogue, organizations and communities foster mutual understanding, respect, and collaboration among individuals from different cultural backgrounds.

Additionally, integrating cultural intelligence and diversity into performance evaluations and feedback processes can further foster their prominence within organizations and communities. Evaluating individuals based on their ability to understand and effectively navigate cultural differences and their contributions to promoting diversity sends a clear signal that cultural intelligence and diversity are valued. By providing feedback that recognizes and rewards individuals for their cultural intelligence and inclusivity, organizations and communities motivate individuals to continue developing these skills and behaviors.

Periodic assessments and evaluations of diversity and inclusion efforts are essential for monitoring progress and identifying areas for improvement. Organizations and communities should analyze data related to diversity, such as representation, recruitment, and retention rates, to identify disparities and implement targeted strategies. Regular evaluation provides insights into the effectiveness of initiatives and identifies potential barriers to fostering cultural intelligence and diversity. Data-driven decision-making allows organizations and communities to develop evidence-based strategies that address challenges, promote inclusiveness, and foster cultural intelligence.

In conclusion, fostering cultural intelligence and diversity requires intentional efforts from individuals and organizations. Strategies to promote cultural intelligence and diversity include promoting awareness and education, fostering inclusive practices, encouraging intercultural exchange, cultivating leadership commitment, promoting mentorship and allyship, creating inclusive spaces for dialogue, integrating diversity into performance evaluations, and regularly evaluating diversity and inclusion efforts. By embracing these strategies and actively promoting cultural intelligence and diversity, individuals and organizations can create inclusive environments that value diverse perspectives, drive innovation, and foster collaboration.

Education and Awareness Programs

Education and awareness programs play a vital role in addressing various social, cultural, and environmental issues in today's world. These programs aim to educate individuals and communities about specific topics, raise awareness, and inspire action toward positive change. From promoting health and well-being to advocating for social justice and environmental sustainability, education and awareness programs are essential for shaping informed and engaged citizens. This article explores the importance of education and awareness programs, their key benefits, and strategies for designing effective initiatives.

Education and awareness programs serve as powerful tools for disseminating knowledge, fostering critical thinking, and promoting social change. They provide individuals with the necessary information and skills to understand complex issues and make informed decisions. By offering access to accurate and reliable information, these programs empower individuals to challenge existing beliefs, question norms, and develop a broader perspective. Education and awareness initiatives also encourage the development of critical thinking skills, enabling individuals to analyze and evaluate information, identify biases, and make well-informed choices.

One of the main benefits of education and awareness programs is their capacity to promote positive behavior change. By effectively informing individuals about the consequences of their actions, these programs can encourage healthier choices and behaviors. For example, programs that focus on promoting healthy eating habits and physical activity can contribute to reducing obesity rates and improving overall well-being. Similarly, awareness campaigns against smoking can help decrease rates of tobacco use and related illnesses. Education and awareness initiatives that address societal issues like gender equality, racial discrimination, and human rights violations can also create significant social change by challenging existing stereotypes and advocating for equality and justice.

Education and awareness programs also foster empathy and understanding towards marginalized groups and individuals. By providing information on diverse cultures, experiences, and perspectives, these initiatives promote tolerance and inclusivity. They dismantle stereotypes and biases, enabling individuals to recognize their prejudices and embrace diversity. By engaging in discussions and activities that encourage empathy, individuals develop a heightened awareness of social issues and the challenges faced by marginalized communities. This increased understanding promotes a more inclusive society where differences are celebrated, and everyone is afforded equal rights and opportunities.

Furthermore, education and awareness programs can shape attitudes and beliefs, particularly in young individuals. Early exposure to educational initiatives that promote principles of respect, kindness, and acceptance can help shape positive values and behaviors. For instance, programs that teach children about environmental sustainability can instill a sense of responsibility towards the planet, leading to environmentally conscious habits that last a lifetime. By engaging children and youth in age-appropriate learning experiences, education and awareness programs lay the foundation for a more informed and socially aware generation.

Effective design and implementation are key to creating impactful education and awareness programs. Here are some strategies to consider:

1. Identify the target audience and objectives: Clearly define the target audience and the specific objectives of the program. This will help tailor the content, style, and delivery method to best meet the needs of the intended audience. Whether it is school-aged children, community members, employees, or specific demographic groups, understanding the audience is crucial for designing effective programs.

2. Utilize multiple formats and platforms: Incorporate a variety of educational tools and platforms to reach a wider audience. This could include workshops, seminars, webinars, online modules, social media campaigns, videos, and interactive activities. By using diverse formats, education and awareness programs can cater to different learning styles and engage individuals across various platforms.

3. Collaborate with experts and stakeholders: Collaborating with experts, community leaders, and stakeholders can increase the credibility and relevance of the program. Involve individuals with specialized knowledge and experiences in the design and delivery of the program, ensuring that the content is accurate, up-to-date, and reflective of diverse perspectives.

4. Tailor the message and approach: Consider the cultural, social, and linguistic backgrounds of the target audience when creating program materials. Aim to use inclusive language and culturally appropriate examples to ensure that the message resonates with all participants. This approach demonstrates respect for diverse backgrounds and enhances the program's effectiveness.

5. Ensure accessibility: Make the education and awareness program accessible to individuals with disabilities or other access limitations. This includes providing materials in alternative formats, ensuring physical spaces are accessible, and providing any necessary support or accommodations. Ensuring accessibility promotes inclusivity and allows individuals from different backgrounds to engage fully in the program.

6. Incorporate interactive and participatory activities: Engage participants by incorporating interactive and participatory activities that encourage active learning. This could include group discussions, role-playing scenarios, case studies, problem-solving exercises, and practical applications of the concepts being taught. Interactive activities help reinforce knowledge and enable participants to apply what they have learned in real-life situations.

7. Evaluate and update the program: Continually assess the effectiveness of the education and awareness program through participant feedback, evaluation surveys, and metrics. This data will provide valuable insights into what is working well and areas that may require improvement. Regular evaluation allows for program updates and enhancements to ensure ongoing relevance and impact.

In conclusion, education and awareness programs are invaluable for addressing social, cultural, and environmental challenges. These programs offer opportunities to educate, inform, and inspire individuals toward positive change. By providing accurate information, promoting critical thinking, and encouraging empathy and inclusivity, education and awareness programs foster informed decision-making, behavior change, and the development of a more socially aware and engaged society. With thoughtful design and careful implementation, these programs have the potential to reshape attitudes, empower individuals, and create lasting social impact.

Cross-Cultural Training and Workshops

Cross-cultural training and workshops have emerged as crucial tools in today's globalized world, where individuals from diverse backgrounds interact daily. In this fast-paced environment, understanding and adapting to different cultures is essential for both personal and professional success. Cross-cultural training programs and workshops provide individuals with the necessary skills and knowledge to effectively navigate and bridge cultural gaps, fostering better communication, teamwork, and cooperation.

Cross-cultural training is designed to raise awareness of cultural differences, facilitate understanding, and develop intercultural competencies. These programs aim to equip individuals with the skills needed to interact and communicate effectively across cultures. By providing participants with insights into diverse cultural norms, traditions, and values, these programs enhance cultural intelligence and promote mutual respect.

One key aspect of cross-cultural training is the development of cultural self-awareness. Understanding one's own cultural biases, assumptions, and values is crucial to appreciating and adapting to different cultural perspectives. Through self-reflection and interactive exercises, participants learn to recognize their cultural lens and proactively respond to cultural differences without judgment or ethnocentrism.

Another important component of cross-cultural training is the acquisition of cultural knowledge. Participants are introduced to various cultural dimensions, such as Hofstede's cultural dimensions theory, which includes concepts such as individualism vs. collectivism, power distance, uncertainty avoidance, masculinity vs. femininity, and long-term vs. short-term orientation. By understanding these dimensions, individuals gain insights into the values, attitudes, and behaviors of different cultures, enabling them to navigate cross-cultural interactions more effectively.

Cross-cultural training workshops often incorporate experiential learning activities to enhance participants' understanding and appreciation of different cultures. These activities may include role-plays, case studies, simulations, and group discussions, aiming to replicate real-world cross-cultural encounters. Through these immersive experiences, individuals learn to adapt their communication styles, negotiation strategies, and problem-solving approaches to different cultural contexts.

Effective cross-cultural training also addresses intercultural communication skills. Communication style varies significantly across cultures, with differences in verbal and nonverbal cues, directness, politeness, and the use of silence. By learning about these differences, individuals can avoid miscommunication, misunderstandings, and unintended offense. Training may also cover topics such as active listening, empathy, and adapting communication styles to different cultural contexts.

Cross-cultural training also emphasizes the importance of cultural sensitivity and cultural adaptation. Cultural sensitivity refers to the ability to recognize, understand, and appreciate the norms, values, and practices of another culture. In contrast, cultural adaptation involves modifying one's behavior and approach to align with cultural expectations. By developing these skills, individuals can build rapport, establish trust, and foster successful relationships with individuals from different cultural backgrounds.

Beyond individual skills, cross-cultural training workshops often aim to improve cultural competence within teams and organizations. In today's globalized business environment, effective teamwork across cultures is essential. Cross-cultural training enhances team productivity and collaboration by promoting inclusivity, understanding, and respect. By recognizing and valuing diverse perspectives, teams can leverage the strengths of different cultures to solve problems, generate innovative ideas, and make sound decisions.

In addition to teamwork, cross-cultural training also focuses on leadership skills within multicultural environments. Leaders and managers who are culturally competent can inspire and motivate their teams, effectively communicate organizational goals across cultures, and adapt their leadership styles to suit diverse cultural contexts. These leaders are better equipped to manage conflict, mitigate risk, and drive organizational success in today's globally interconnected marketplace.

While cross-cultural training and workshops offer numerous benefits, it is important to note that they are not a one-size-fits-all solution. Each organization, industry, or individual may have unique cross-cultural challenges. Therefore, training programs must be tailored to specific needs and contexts. Pre-assessments, follow-up coaching, and feedback mechanisms are effective strategies to ensure the relevance and impact of these programs.

In conclusion, cross-cultural training and workshops have become indispensable tools in today's globalized world. By promoting cultural understanding, communication, and adaptability, these programs equip individuals with the skills and knowledge to navigate the complexities of cross-cultural interactions. Whether in the realm of business, education, or social interactions, cross-cultural training fosters inclusivity, collaboration, and mutual respect, paving the way for a more interconnected and harmonious world.

4.3 Recruitment and Hiring Practices

Recruitment and hiring practices play a critical role in any organization's success. The process of attracting and selecting top talent is essential for building a strong and capable workforce. Effective recruitment and hiring practices not only identify individuals with the right skills and experience but also focus on diversity, cultural fit, and long-term potential. In this article, we will explore the key elements of recruitment and hiring practices and discuss best practices for organizations to adopt.

The recruitment process begins with identifying the organization's needs and defining the roles or positions to be filled. This involves analyzing the organization's strategic objectives, assessing future workforce requirements, and identifying any skills or talent gaps. A clear understanding of these goals and requirements provides the foundation for crafting effective job descriptions and specifications.

Job descriptions and specifications serve as the primary communication tool between the organization and potential candidates. They should clearly outline the responsibilities, qualifications, skills, and experience required for the role. Additionally, the job description should accurately portray the organization's culture, values, and desired behavioral traits. Aligning these aspects with the organization's overall mission and vision attracts candidates who share a similar mindset and are more likely to contribute positively to the organizational culture.

Once the job description is finalized, the recruitment process moves on to sourcing and attracting candidates. Traditional methods such as job postings on career websites, print advertisements, and referrals are still effective. However, organizations are increasingly exploring innovative recruitment channels such as social media, professional networks, and online job platforms to reach a wider pool of potential candidates. Social media platforms like LinkedIn provide opportunities for targeted talent searches, networking, and engaging with passive job seekers.

In addition to using diverse recruitment channels, organizations must also prioritize diversity and inclusion in their hiring practices. Diversity encompasses various dimensions, including gender, race, ethnicity, age, sexual orientation, abilities, and cultural backgrounds. Research has consistently shown that diverse teams contribute to better problem-solving, innovation, and overall organizational performance. To foster diversity, organizations need to ensure that job advertisements, candidate assessments, and interview panels are free from biases and unconscious assumptions.

Candidate assessments play a crucial role in evaluating potential candidates' skills, qualifications, and fit with the organizational culture. These assessments may include resume screening, aptitude tests, cognitive ability tests, personality assessments, and work samples. Conducting structured interviews using a combination of behavioral and situational questions can provide valuable insights into a candidate's ability to handle various real-life scenarios. It is important to ensure that assessments are fair, consistent, and aligned with the specific requirements of the role.

Interviews are a critical component of the hiring process as they provide an opportunity for direct interaction between the organization and the candidate. It is important to design interviews that assess not only technical competencies but also cultural fit and values alignment. Behavioral-based questions that focus on past experiences and specific examples allow candidates to demonstrate their skills, values, and problem-solving abilities. Panel interviews, where multiple interviewers assess the candidate, provide a well-rounded evaluation and help mitigate personal biases.

To enhance the accuracy of the hiring process, organizations may also consider implementing practical exercises or assignment-based evaluations. These exercises can provide candidates with an opportunity to showcase their skills in real-world or simulated scenarios. This method not only gauges a candidate's capabilities in a practical setting but also gives insight into their problem-solving, creativity, and ability to work under pressure.

Reference checks and background screenings are important steps in the hiring process. These verifications ensure that the information provided by candidates is accurate and that they have the necessary qualifications and experience. Checking references helps in validating a candidate's skills, work ethic, and compatibility with co-workers and supervisors. Background screenings, including criminal record checks and employment verification, provide additional assurance to organizations and protect against any potential risks.

Once the candidate evaluation process is complete, organizations need to ensure a transparent and efficient decision-making process. Timely follow-up with candidates, providing feedback, and keeping them informed about the progress of their applications is crucial for maintaining a positive employer brand and candidate experience. Organizations need to treat all candidates with respect and professionalism throughout the entire recruitment process, regardless of the outcome.

In addition to the traditional recruitment and hiring practices, organizations are increasingly adopting innovative approaches such as employer branding and recruitment marketing. Employer branding refers to the organization's reputation as an employer and its ability to attract, engage, and retain top talent. Creating a strong employer brand involves showcasing the organization's values, culture, employee benefits, and development opportunities to differentiate it from competitors. Recruitment marketing uses marketing techniques to promote the organization as an employer of choice, targeting potential candidates who may not be actively job searching.

Finally, organizations should continuously evaluate and refine their recruitment and hiring practices. Regular data analysis can reveal insights into the effectiveness of various recruitment channels, selection methods, and decision-making processes. This data-driven approach allows organizations to identify areas for improvement, implement necessary changes, and optimize their recruitment and hiring practices.

In conclusion, recruitment and hiring practices are vital for organizations to attract, select, and retain top talent. By focusing on clear job descriptions, diverse sourcing, unbiased assessments, effective interviews, and transparent decision-making, organizations can build a strong and capable workforce. Moreover, by prioritizing diversity, ensuring cultural fit, and fostering a positive candidate experience, organizations can enhance their employer brand and attract the best possible candidates. Continuous evaluation and refinement of recruitment strategies enable organizations to continuously improve their ability to identify and hire top talent, contributing to long-term success.

Inclusive Leadership and Management

Inclusive leadership and management have gained significant attention in recent years as organizations recognize the value of diverse perspectives and the importance of fostering an inclusive culture. Inclusive leaders are those who actively and intentionally promote diversity, equity, and inclusion within their teams and organizations. They create an environment where all individuals feel valued, respected, and supported, irrespective of their background or identity. In this article, we will explore the key elements of inclusive leadership and management and discuss best practices for organizations to cultivate inclusive leaders.

At the heart of inclusive leadership is the recognition that diversity brings a multitude of perspectives, ideas, and experiences that can drive innovation and enhance organizational performance. Inclusive leaders understand the value of these diverse perspectives and actively seek out and value input from individuals with different backgrounds, experiences, and viewpoints. They create an environment where everyone feels safe and empowered to contribute their unique insights, fostering a culture of collaboration, creativity, and high performance.

One of the foundational elements of inclusive leadership is self-awareness. Inclusive leaders understand their own biases, assumptions, and privileges, and actively work to challenge and overcome them. They engage in continuous self-reflection and seek feedback from others to understand how their behaviors and decisions may affect individuals from different backgrounds. Through this self-awareness, inclusive leaders can identify and address their blind spots, and make more informed and inclusive decisions.

Inclusive leaders also actively promote diversity and inclusion in their teams and organizations. They are committed to attracting, recruiting, and retaining individuals from diverse backgrounds. This involves creating inclusive hiring practices and ensuring that diverse candidates have equal opportunities to succeed and advance within the organization. Inclusive leaders understand that a diverse workforce is a competitive advantage and actively seek to expand the pool of talented individuals from underrepresented groups.

Once a diverse team is established, inclusive leaders create a culture of inclusion by fostering psychological safety and belonging. They create an environment where all individuals feel free to express their ideas, raise concerns, and challenge the status quo without fear of retribution or discrimination. Inclusive leaders actively listen to their team members, value their perspectives, and empower them to contribute to decision-making and problem-solving processes. They create opportunities for open dialogue and encourage feedback, ensuring that all voices are heard and considered.

Inclusive leaders also champion equity, ensuring that all individuals have access to equal opportunities for growth, development, and advancement. They proactively identify and address barriers that may prevent certain individuals or groups from fully participating or advancing within the organization. This may involve implementing mentoring programs, providing training and development opportunities, and using performance evaluations that are fair and unbiased. By promoting equity, inclusive leaders create a level playing field where everyone has an equal chance to succeed and thrive.

Inclusive leaders also foster cultural competence within their teams and organizations. They invest in their own and their team's understanding of diverse cultures, traditions, and values. This may involve providing cross-cultural training, organizing cultural awareness workshops, or creating opportunities for employees to share their unique cultural backgrounds and experiences. Inclusive leaders recognize that cultural competence is essential in today's globalized world, where individuals from diverse backgrounds regularly interact and collaborate.

Effective inclusive leaders promote collaboration and teamwork. They create an environment where individuals are encouraged to work together, combining their diverse perspectives and skills to achieve shared goals. Inclusive leaders can foster a sense of cohesion and camaraderie within their teams, creating an atmosphere of trust and mutual support. They actively seek to build connections and relationships among team members, recognizing that inclusive teams are more innovative, creative, and successful.

Inclusive leaders also hold themselves and others accountable for promoting diversity, equity, and inclusion. They establish clear expectations around inclusive behaviors and challenge any discriminatory or exclusionary actions or attitudes. Inclusive leaders are not afraid to address bias or discrimination when it occurs, and they strive to create a workplace culture where such behaviors are not tolerated. They lead by example, modeling inclusive behaviors and demonstrating a commitment to diversity and inclusion in their actions and decisions.

To cultivate inclusive leadership within organizations, it is important to provide training and development opportunities for current and future leaders. This may include workshops on unconscious bias, cross-cultural communication, inclusive decision-making, and managing diverse teams. Training programs can help leaders develop the skills and knowledge necessary to lead inclusively and create a culture of diversity and belonging within their teams and organizations.

In conclusion, inclusive leadership and management are critical for organizations that aim to create an inclusive and diverse workforce. Inclusive leaders actively promote diversity, equity, and inclusion, recognizing the value of different perspectives and experiences. They foster an environment of psychological safety and belonging, where individuals can thrive and contribute their unique insights. By championing equity, fostering cultural competence, promoting collaboration, and holding themselves and others accountable, inclusive leaders create a culture where everyone has an equal opportunity to succeed and feel valued. Cultivating inclusive leadership requires self-awareness, training, and a commitment from organizations to embrace and champion diversity and inclusion.

Employee Resource Groups and Affinity Networks

Employee Resource Groups (ERGs) and affinity networks have gained significant popularity in recent years as organizations recognize the value of fostering diverse and inclusive workplaces. ERGs and affinity networks are employee-led groups that bring together individuals with shared characteristics or backgrounds, providing a platform for connection, support, and advocacy. These groups play a crucial role in promoting diversity, equity, and inclusion within organizations. In this article, we will explore the concept of ERGs and affinity networks, discuss their benefits, and outline best practices for organizations to establish and support these groups effectively.

Employee Resource Groups, also known as Employee Resource Networks, are voluntary, employee-led groups that provide support, networking, and advocacy for individuals with shared characteristics or backgrounds. These groups can be based on various dimensions such as gender, race, ethnicity, sexual orientation, age, disability, or other factors. ERGs aim to create a sense of belonging, foster community, and facilitate personal and professional development within the workplace.

Affinity networks, on the other hand, are like ERGs but often focus on a specific professional or personal interest. These networks bring together employees who share a common interest or passion, regardless of a specific demographic characteristic. Affinity networks often revolve around topics such as parenting, military veterans, wellness, women in leadership, or any other area that employees find relevant and meaningful.

Both ERGs and affinity networks play a crucial role in promoting diversity and inclusion within organizations. By providing a platform for connection and support, these groups help individuals with shared characteristics or interests build networks, share experiences, and access resources. ERGs and affinity networks also serve as important voices for addressing challenges, advocating for change, and promoting inclusivity within the organization.

Establishing ERGs and affinity networks within an organization offers numerous benefits. Here are some key advantages of these groups:

1. Representation and Visibility: ERGs and affinity networks provide a visible presence for underrepresented or marginalized groups within the organization. This representation is important for fostering a sense of belonging and ensuring that the needs and perspectives of these groups are recognized and addressed.

2. Community and Support: ERGs and affinity networks offer a sense of community and belonging, creating a safe space for individuals to connect, share experiences, and discuss common challenges. This support is particularly crucial for individuals who may face unique obstacles or discrimination in the workplace.

3. Networking and Professional Development: These groups provide opportunities for networking, mentorship, and professional development. ERGs and affinity networks often organize events, workshops, speaker series, and skill-building sessions that help members enhance their skills, expand their networks, and advance their careers.

4. Employee Engagement and Retention: The existence of ERGs and affinity networks demonstrates the organization's commitment to diversity and inclusion, contributing to higher levels of employee engagement and satisfaction. These groups can help create a supportive work environment that values and celebrates individual differences, leading to increased employee retention.

5. Talent Acquisition and Recruitment: ERGs and affinity networks can play a significant role in attracting top talent. Prospective employees often seek out organizations that prioritize diversity and inclusion. The presence of robust ERGs and affinity networks can demonstrate a commitment to fostering an inclusive workplace culture.

To establish effective ERGs and affinity networks, organizations should consider the following best practices:

1. Leadership Support and Sponsorship: For ERGs and affinity networks to thrive, it is essential to have visible and committed support from senior leaders within the organization. Leaders can serve as advocates, provide resources, and create a supportive climate that encourages participation and engagement.

2. Employee Involvement and Ownership: ERGs and affinity networks should be inclusive and open to all interested employees. These groups must be employee-led, allowing members to take ownership and drive the direction and activities of the group. This involvement empowers employees, builds a sense of ownership, and ensures the group's relevance and sustainability.

3. Clear Goals and Objectives: ERGs and affinity networks should have clearly defined goals and objectives that align with the organization's overall diversity and inclusion strategy. These goals may include fostering a sense of belonging, providing professional development opportunities, or advocating for change within the organization. Clear objectives help guide the activities and initiatives of the group.

4. Resources and Support: Organizations should provide the necessary resources to support ERGs and affinity networks. This may include funding, meeting spaces, access to technology, communication channels, and time allocated during work hours for group meetings and activities. Providing these resources demonstrates the organization's commitment to these groups' success and helps them operate more effectively.

5. Integration with Organizational Initiatives: ERGs and affinity networks should be integrated with the organization's overall diversity and inclusion strategy. These groups should work collaboratively with HR, leadership, and other departments to align their activities and initiatives with organizational goals. Integration ensures that ERGs and affinity networks are not operating in isolation but are part of the broader diversity and inclusion efforts.

6. Measuring Impact and Success: It is important to establish metrics to measure the impact and success of ERGs and affinity networks. Organizations can track participation rates, employee engagement, professional development outcomes, employee feedback, and other relevant data. Regular evaluations and feedback loops enable organizations to measure the effectiveness of these groups, make improvements, and communicate the value of these initiatives to leadership and employees.

7. Collaboration and Partnership: ERGs and affinity networks should collaborate and partner with other groups and departments within the organization. This collaboration can facilitate knowledge-sharing, foster cross-functional relationships, and leverage resources and expertise. By working together, these groups can create a more significant impact and promote an inclusive culture throughout the organization.

In conclusion, Employee Resource Groups (ERGs) and affinity networks play a crucial role in fostering diversity, equity, and inclusion within organizations. These employee-led groups create a sense of community, support, and advocacy for individuals with shared characteristics or interests. ERGs and affinity networks offer numerous benefits, including representation, support, networking, professional development, and enhanced employee engagement and retention. By following best practices, organizations can establish and support these groups effectively, creating an inclusive workplace culture where all individuals feel valued and empowered to contribute their unique perspectives and talents.

Creating Safe Spaces for Open Dialogue

Creating safe spaces for open dialogue is essential for fostering a culture of inclusion, respect, and meaningful communication within organizations. Safe spaces provide individuals with the freedom and comfort to express their thoughts, ideas, and concerns openly, without fear of judgment, backlash, or discrimination. In this article, we will explore the importance of safe spaces, discuss the key elements of creating them, and provide best practices for organizations to establish and maintain safe spaces for open dialogue.

The importance of safe spaces for open dialogue cannot be overstated. These spaces allow individuals to share their perspectives, engage in honest discussions, and contribute to problem-solving and decision-making processes. Safe spaces promote psychological safety, which is crucial for fostering creativity, innovation, and collaboration within teams and organizations. When individuals feel safe expressing themselves authentically, it leads to increased engagement, trust, and a sense of belonging.

Creating safe spaces for open dialogue involves several key elements:

1. Respectful and Non-judgmental Environment: Safe spaces require a culture of respect and non-judgment, where individuals feel valued, and their opinions are treated with dignity. It is crucial to establish ground rules that emphasize respectful communication, active listening, and empathy. In this environment, everyone's perspectives and experiences are acknowledged and validated, creating a foundation for open dialogue.

2. Trust and Confidentiality: Building trust is fundamental to creating safe spaces. Individuals need assurances that their views will be treated confidentially and that they can express themselves without fear of negative consequences. Organizations can establish clear policies and guidelines that emphasize the confidentiality of discussions held within safe spaces. By honoring and respecting confidentiality, individuals feel secure in sharing their thoughts and experiences.

3. Adherence to Inclusivity and Diversity Principles: Safe spaces should be inclusive and respect diverse perspectives, viewpoints, and backgrounds. It is important to establish a commitment to diversity and inclusion within these spaces, ensuring that all individuals have an equal opportunity to participate and contribute. Leadership and facilitators should actively create an environment that welcomes and values different voices and experiences.

4. Facilitation and Ground Rules: Effective facilitation is crucial to creating safe spaces. The role of facilitators is to guide conversations, ensure everyone has an opportunity to contribute and maintain the established ground rules. They should promote active listening, encourage constructive feedback, and manage any conflicts that may arise. Facilitators play a critical role in creating a sense of safety and openness within space.

5. Active Listening and Empathy: To create safe spaces for open dialogue, individuals need to feel heard and understood. Practice active listening, which involves giving full attention to the speaker, seeking clarification, and summarizing the speaker's main points. Empathy is also essential in safe spaces, as it helps individuals understand and appreciate different perspectives, even if they don't necessarily agree.

6. Constructive Feedback and Conflict Resolution: Safe spaces should encourage constructive feedback and provide guidelines for resolving conflicts that may arise during discussions. Organizations can establish processes or techniques for individuals to express dissenting opinions respectfully and engage in healthy debates. Conflict resolution strategies, such as mediation or facilitated discussions, should be available to address any disagreements that may arise.

Organizations can implement best practices to create and maintain safe spaces for open dialogue:

1. Communicate the Purpose: Communicate the purpose and goals of safe spaces to all employees. Explain how these spaces contribute to fostering inclusion, respect, and creativity within the organization. This helps individuals understand the value and importance of participating in these discussions.

2. Training and Education: Provide training and resources to employees on active listening, communication skills, empathy, and inclusive dialogues. This equips individuals with the necessary tools to engage in respectful and constructive conversations. Organizations can also bring in external facilitators or subject-matter experts to provide specialized training on specific topics or sensitive discussions.

3. Rotate Facilitators and Participants: To sustain safe spaces, organizations should consider rotating attendees and facilitators for each discussion. This allows for fresh perspectives and prevents a single individual or group from dominating the conversation. Regularly rotating participants also ensures that various departments, levels, and demographics have an opportunity to contribute and learn from each other.

4. Supportive Leadership: Leadership plays a crucial role in creating and promoting safe spaces. Leaders should lead by example and actively participate in dialogues. Their support and involvement send a message to employees that these discussions are valued and can lead to positive change within the organization.

5. Regular Evaluation and Feedback: Continuous assessment of safe spaces is important to ensure their effectiveness and impact. Organizations should solicit feedback from participants to understand their experiences and gather suggestions for improvement. Regular evaluations help identify potential improvements to the facilitation process, ground rules, and communication around safe spaces.

6. Maintain Accountability and Follow-Up: Organizations should take appropriate action on any issues raised during safe space discussions. This includes addressing concerns, resolving conflicts, and implementing solutions to problems identified. Consistent action and follow-up demonstrate that employees' contributions are valued and taken seriously.

7. Provide Resources and Support: Organizations should offer resources and support to individuals who experience discomfort or challenges during discussions within safe spaces. This could include access to counseling, employee assistance programs, or additional training resources. Supportive measures promote well-being, enhance engagement, and reinforce the commitment to creating safe spaces.

Creating safe spaces for open dialogue requires ongoing effort and attention. Organizations must maintain momentum and foster a culture that encourages open communication and respect for diverse perspectives. By establishing a foundation of trust, empathy, inclusivity, and respect, organizations can create an environment where all individuals feel safe and empowered to contribute their unique insights, ultimately leading to stronger collaboration, innovation, and organizational success.

Cultural Intelligence and Diversity in Organizations

In today's globalized world, understanding and managing cultural diversity has become a critical aspect of organizational success. With the increased interconnectedness of societies and the rise of multinational corporations, organizations are increasingly dealing with employees and customers from diverse cultural backgrounds. Cultural intelligence (CQ) is a concept that has gained significant attention in recent years as it enables individuals and organizations to effectively navigate and capitalize on the opportunities presented by cultural diversity. This article will explore the concept of cultural intelligence, its relevance in organizations, and its impact on overall organizational performance.

Understanding Cultural Intelligence:

Cultural intelligence, also known as cultural quotient, is the ability to understand, appreciate, and adapt to cultural differences. It encompasses a set of skills and knowledge that enable individuals to function effectively in culturally diverse environments. CQ consists of four dimensions: cognitive, emotional, physical, and metacognitive. The cognitive dimension refers to knowledge about cultures, norms, and traditions, while the emotional dimension involves being aware of and expressing empathy toward diverse cultural perspectives. The physical dimension pertains to the ability to adjust one's behavior to fit diverse cultural contexts, and the metacognitive dimension involves being mindful of one's cultural assumptions and biases.

Importance of Cultural Intelligence in Organizations:

1. Global Workforce: Organizations that operate in multiple countries have a diverse workforce comprising individuals from different cultural backgrounds. Cultural intelligence allows employees to understand and appreciate each other's perspectives, fostering collaboration, innovation, and creativity.

2. Effective Communication: Cultural intelligence helps in overcoming language and cultural barriers, enabling effective communication within organizations. It facilitates better understanding and interpretation of messages, preventing miscommunication and conflicts that often arise due to cultural differences.

3. Multicultural Markets: With the increasing globalization of markets, organizations need to understand and cater to the needs and preferences of culturally diverse customers. Cultural intelligence helps in identifying cultural variations, enabling organizations to develop appropriate products, services, and marketing strategies.

4. Talent Acquisition and Retention: Organizations that value diversity and promote cultural intelligence attract and retain talented individuals from diverse backgrounds. Cultural intelligence creates an inclusive and welcoming environment, fostering employee engagement, productivity, and satisfaction.

Implementing Cultural Intelligence in Organizations:

1. Leadership Support: Leaders play a vital role in fostering a culture of cultural intelligence. They should champion diversity initiatives, set an example by demonstrating cultural intelligence, and integrate diversity and inclusion into core organizational values and practices.

2. Training and Development: Organizations should provide cultural intelligence training programs to employees at all levels. These programs may include workshops, simulations, and interactive sessions to enhance cultural sensitivity, empathy, and adaptability.

3. Global Mindset: Organizations should encourage employees to develop a global mindset by promoting international experiences, cross-cultural training, and job rotations. This helps individuals develop a broader perspective and enhances their ability to adapt to different cultural contexts.

4. Inclusive Policies and Practices: Organizations should have inclusive policies to support diversity and cultural intelligence. This includes promoting work-life balance, providing opportunities for diverse voices to be heard, and creating equitable career development opportunities for employees from all cultural backgrounds.

Benefits of Cultural Intelligence in Organizations:

1. Enhanced Innovation: Cultural intelligence enables organizations to harness the diversity of ideas, knowledge, and perspectives. By embracing different cultural perspectives, organizations can develop innovative solutions that cater to diverse customer needs.

2. Improved Decision-making: Cultural intelligence enhances decision-making processes by considering a wider range of perspectives and avoiding biases. Including diverse voices in decision-making leads to better outcomes and ensures organizational decisions are equitable and inclusive.

3. Increased Adaptability: Organizations with cultural intelligence are more adaptable to changing market dynamics and can respond effectively to global challenges. They can navigate complexities and uncertainties in diverse cultural contexts.

4. Enhanced Reputation: Organizations that demonstrate cultural intelligence earn a reputation as inclusive and socially responsible entities. This enhances their brand image and attracts diverse customers, partners, and investors.

Challenges in Cultivating Cultural Intelligence:

1. Unconscious Biases: Individuals often hold unconscious biases towards certain cultures, which can hinder the development of cultural intelligence. These biases need to be identified and addressed through awareness programs and self-reflection.

2. Resistance to Change: Some employees may resist diversity initiatives and cultural intelligence due to a fear of the unknown or clinging to traditional norms. Organizations need to communicate the benefits of cultural intelligence and address concerns through continuous dialogue and education.

3. Lack of Resources: Organizations may lack the necessary resources, such as time, budget, and expertise, to implement cultural intelligence initiatives. It is important to allocate appropriate resources and invest in training programs and support systems.

Cultural intelligence has become a critical aspect of organizational success in a diverse and globalized world. Organizations that embrace cultural intelligence are better equipped to manage cultural diversity, communicate effectively, and develop innovative solutions. By fostering cultural intelligence, organizations can create inclusive and equitable environments that attract and retain diverse talent, enhance decision-making processes, and improve overall performance. Cultivating cultural intelligence requires leadership support, training and development, a global mindset, and inclusive policies and practices. Despite challenges, embracing cultural intelligence is essential for organizations to thrive in today's culturally diverse and interconnected world.

Building an Inclusive Work Environment

In today's diverse and globalized world, organizations are increasingly recognizing the importance of building an inclusive work environment. Inclusion refers to creating an environment where all individuals, regardless of their background or characteristics, feel valued, respected, and empowered to contribute their unique perspectives and talents. An inclusive workplace goes beyond diversity by ensuring that everyone has equal opportunities for growth and advancement. This article will explore the benefits of an inclusive work environment, strategies for building inclusivity, and the role of leadership in fostering inclusiveness.

Benefits of an Inclusive Work Environment:

1. Increased Innovation and Creativity: Inclusive work environments encourage diversity of thought and perspectives, facilitating the generation of innovative ideas. When people from different backgrounds collaborate and share their unique experiences and insights, they bring fresh perspectives that can lead to breakthrough solutions.

2. Improved Problem Solving: Inclusion promotes a collaborative and open culture where individuals feel comfortable sharing their ideas and viewpoints. This fosters better problem-solving as diverse perspectives challenge assumptions, identify blind spots, and lead to more comprehensive solutions.

3. Enhanced Employee Engagement: Inclusivity creates a sense of belonging among employees. When individuals feel valued and included, they are more engaged with their work, leading to increased productivity, creativity, and commitment.

4. Better Decision-Making: Inclusive work environments foster a culture of open and constructive dialogue. Decision-making processes benefit from multiple viewpoints, ensuring that different perspectives are considered, and biases are minimized.

Strategies for Building Inclusivity:

1. Set Inclusive Values and Goals: Organizations should establish a clear set of values that promote an inclusive work environment. These values should encompass respect, diversity, equity, and empathy. Including inclusivity as part of the organization's mission and goals sends a strong message about its commitment to create an inclusive culture.

2. Foster Awareness and Education: Building inclusivity requires understanding and awareness of biases, stereotypes, and barriers. Organizations should provide training and education programs to employees at all levels to increase awareness of unconscious biases, encourage empathy, and promote cultural sensitivity. These programs should be ongoing and continually reinforced.

3. Enhance Recruitment and Hiring Practices: Inclusivity should begin in the recruitment process. Organizations should review their job descriptions and requirements to ensure they do not unintentionally exclude potential candidates from diverse backgrounds. Implementing blind hiring practices, where resumes are stripped of identifying information such as names and genders, can help avoid unconscious biases. Additionally, organizations should actively seek out diverse candidates and ensure that diverse interview panels are involved in the hiring process.

4. Create Inclusive Policies and Practices: Organizations should review and revise their policies and practices to ensure they are inclusive. This includes offering flexible work arrangements, accommodating diverse needs, and promoting work-life balance. Inclusive policies should address issues such as diversity, equity, harassment, and discrimination.

5. Encourage Employee Resource Groups: Employee resource groups (ERGs) are voluntary, employee-led groups that bring together individuals with shared characteristics or experiences. ERGs provide a platform for networking, support, and mentoring, allowing employees to connect and share their experiences. These groups play a crucial role in fostering inclusivity by encouraging dialogue, understanding, and driving initiatives that cater to specific needs.

6. Promote Transparent and Open Communication: Organizations should establish channels that facilitate open and transparent communication. This includes regular feedback mechanisms, town hall meetings, and employee surveys that allow employees to voice their concerns, suggestions, and ideas. Leaders should actively listen to employees and demonstrate their commitment to resolving issues and taking necessary actions.

The Role of Leadership in Fostering Inclusivity:

Leadership plays a crucial role in creating and maintaining an inclusive work environment. Here are some key actions leaders can take:

1. Lead by Example: Leaders should model inclusive behavior by treating all employees with respect and dignity, regardless of their backgrounds. They should be open to diverse perspectives, actively seek input from all employees, and show appreciation for their contributions. Leaders should also acknowledge and address biases and stereotypes that may exist within the organization.

2. Establish a Safe and Inclusive Culture: Leaders need to establish a culture where employees feel safe to express their opinions and concerns without fear of retaliation. This requires creating psychological safety, where employees feel comfortable challenging assumptions and sharing their perspectives. Leaders should ensure that open dialogue and respectful disagreement are encouraged and valued.

3. Provide Resources and Support: Leaders should allocate resources and support initiatives that promote inclusivity. This includes budgeting for training programs, ERGs, and diversity and inclusion initiatives. Leaders should proactively seek out diverse talents, provide necessary training and development opportunities, and ensure diverse voices are included in decision-making processes.

4. Foster Cross-Cultural Relationships and Collaboration: Leaders should encourage cross-cultural relationships and collaboration among teams. This can be achieved by creating opportunities for employees to work on cross-functional projects, promoting diversity in team compositions, and organizing team-building activities that encourage cultural exchange and understanding.

Building an inclusive work environment is a continuous effort that requires commitment from both employees and organizational leaders. By embracing inclusivity, organizations can benefit from the diverse perspectives, ideas, and talents of their workforce. An inclusive work environment fosters innovation, engagement, and effective decision-making. It requires a combination of strategies, such as setting inclusive values, enhancing recruitment practices, promoting awareness and education, and encouraging open communication. Leadership plays a pivotal role in creating an inclusive culture by leading by example, establishing psychological safety, providing support and resources, and fostering cross-cultural relationships. With a focus on inclusivity, organizations can create environments where employees feel valued, respected, and empowered to contribute their best, leading to enhanced performance and success.

Benefits of Diversity in the Workplace

Diversity has become a central topic in today's workplace, with organizations recognizing the value and benefits it offers. Diversity refers to the presence of individuals from different backgrounds, races, ethnicities, genders, ages, abilities, and experiences within a workforce. Embracing diversity goes beyond compliance with laws and regulations; it involves creating an inclusive environment that values and leverages the unique perspectives and talents of all employees. This article will explore the numerous benefits that diversity brings to the workplace and how it positively impacts organizational performance and success.

1. Enhanced Creativity and Innovation:

One of the key benefits of diversity in the workplace is the enhancement of creativity and innovation. When individuals from different backgrounds come together, their diverse experiences and perspectives lead to a broader range of ideas and solutions. This diversity of thought helps organizations to think outside the box, challenge assumptions, and develop innovative products, services, and processes.

2. Expanded Talent Pool:

Embracing diversity in the workplace widens the talent pool and allows organizations to attract and retain the best individuals from diverse backgrounds. By tapping into a more varied pool of talent, organizations increase their chances of finding employees who bring fresh ideas, unique skills, and different approaches to problem-solving. This leads to a more competitive advantage in the market.

3. Improved Decision-Making:

Diverse teams are known to make better decisions compared to homogeneous teams. When diverse individuals are involved in decision-making, a wider range of perspectives and experiences are considered. This leads to more thorough discussions, a deeper analysis of options, and a better understanding of potential risks and opportunities. Consequently, decisions made by diverse teams are more well-rounded and have a higher likelihood of success.

4. Enhanced Problem-Solving:

Diverse teams bring a variety of perspectives and approaches to problem-solving. When individuals with different backgrounds and experiences collaborate, they bring a range of insights and ideas that can help to identify potential solutions that a homogenous group may not have considered. This diverse problem-solving approach leads to better decision-making and ultimately more effective resolutions.

5. Increased Customer Understanding and Market Relevance:

A diverse workforce allows organizations to better understand their customers and cater to their needs effectively. With a workforce that represents different cultures, backgrounds, and demographics, organizations can gain insights into different customer segments and their preferences. This understanding helps organizations develop products and services that resonate with diverse customer groups, leading to increased market relevance and customer loyalty.

6. Improved Employee Engagement and Productivity:

When employees feel respected, included, and valued for who they are, they are more likely to be engaged and motivated. Diversity in the workplace promotes a sense of belonging, as it creates an environment where employees feel that their contributions are recognized and appreciated. This enhanced employee engagement leads to higher productivity levels, as employees are more committed and willing to go the extra mile for their organization.

7. Better Problem Identification and Risk Management:

Diverse teams are more likely to identify problems and risks that may go unnoticed in homogeneous groups. Different perspectives allow for a more comprehensive examination of potential issues and provide a wider range of inputs to mitigate risks. This proactive approach to problem identification and risk management leads to better organizational preparedness and a higher ability to respond to challenges.

8. Enhanced Brand Reputation:

Organizations that prioritize diversity and inclusion in their workforce often enjoy stronger brand reputations. Consumers appreciate and recognize organizations that value diversity and actively work towards fostering an inclusive environment. A positive brand reputation not only attracts diverse customer bases but also helps attract and retain top talent.

9. Increased Cultural Competence:

A diverse workforce exposes employees to different cultures, customs, and perspectives. This exposure fosters cultural competence, which is the ability to effectively interact and communicate with individuals from different cultural backgrounds. Cultural competence is becoming increasingly important in a globalized world, where organizations often operate in diverse markets and engage with diverse stakeholders.

10. Better Employee Retention:

Organizations that embrace diversity tend to have higher employee retention rates. When employees feel included, respected, and valued, they are more likely to stay with the organization long-term. Diverse employees who see representation at all levels of the organization experience higher job satisfaction and are more likely to remain loyal to the organization.

Diversity in the workplace brings numerous benefits that positively impact organizational performance and success. The enhanced creativity, expanded talent pool, improved decision-making, and increased customer understanding provided by diverse teams contribute to a stronger competitive advantage and market relevance. Additionally, diversity facilitates improved problem-solving, risk management, and cultural competence. By nurturing an inclusive environment that recognizes and values the unique perspectives and talents of individuals from various backgrounds, organizations can experience increased employee engagement, productivity, and retention. Embracing diversity not only leads to better organizational outcomes but also enhances brand reputation and helps organizations thrive in a rapidly changing and diverse global marketplace.

Challenges and Solutions in Managing Diversity

Managing diversity in the workplace is a complex and ongoing process that requires organizations to address various challenges that arise due to differences in background, culture, experiences, and perspectives. Diversity encompasses differences in race, gender, ethnicity, age, sexual orientation, religion, disabilities, and more. While diversity brings numerous benefits, it also presents challenges in terms of communication, collaboration, biases, and creating an inclusive environment. This article will explore the key challenges organizations face in managing diversity and provide practical solutions to effectively navigate these challenges.

Challenges in Managing Diversity:

1. Communication Barriers:

Effective communication is vital to promote understanding and collaboration within diverse teams, but it can be challenging due to language barriers, cultural differences, and different communication styles. Misunderstandings and misinterpretations can occur, leading to conflict and misalignment.

Solution:

Organizations can address communication barriers by implementing the following strategies:

- Provide language training and resources to employees who need assistance in enhancing their communication skills in the dominant language used in the workplace.
- Foster a culture of open communication and encourage individuals to seek clarification and provide feedback.
- Promote active listening and empathy to better understand diverse perspectives and bridge communication gaps.
- Utilize technology solutions, such as translation tools or collaboration platforms, to facilitate communication across language barriers.
- Conduct regular communication and cultural awareness training to enhance employees' cross-cultural understanding and communication skills.

2. Implicit Bias and Stereotyping:

Implicit biases are unconscious prejudices and stereotypes that individuals hold towards certain groups. These biases can influence decision-making, performance evaluations, promotions, and opportunities for diverse employees, perpetuating inequality and hindering the recognition of talent.

Solution:

To address implicit biases and stereotypes, organizations can implement the following strategies:

- Provide unconscious bias training to increase awareness and understanding of biases and their impact on decision-making processes.
- Emphasize the importance of objective criteria, transparent policies, and fair evaluation processes in performance management and talent-related decisions.
- Implement blind screening processes in recruitment and promotion, removing identifying information to prevent bias based on gender, race, or other characteristics.
- Establish diversity and inclusion councils or committees to monitor and address biases within the organization.
- Encourage mentorship and sponsorship programs to provide equal access to development opportunities, particularly for underrepresented groups.

3. Resistance to Change and Unconscious Exclusion:

People often resist change, particularly when it challenges established norms and practices. In diverse organizations, there is a risk of unconscious exclusion, where individuals may unintentionally exclude or marginalize diverse colleagues due to their limited perspectives and comfort zones.

Solution:

To overcome resistance to change and address unconscious exclusion, organizations can employ the following strategies:

- Foster a culture of inclusion from the top down, with leaders actively championing diversity and inclusion initiatives.
- Educate employees about the benefits of diversity and the importance of equitable opportunities for all.
- Provide sensitivity training to increase awareness of unconscious biases and how they can impact inclusivity.

- Establish clear diversity goals, measurable objectives, and accountability mechanisms to drive change and track progress.
- Encourage cross-functional and cross-cultural collaboration to break down silos and foster a supportive and inclusive work environment.

4. Lack of Representation and Inclusion:

A lack of representation and inclusion can make diverse employees feel excluded, leading to decreased morale, disengagement, and high turnover rates. When employees do not see themselves or their experiences reflected in leadership positions, it can create a perception of limited opportunities for career growth.

Solution:

To address the lack of representation and promote inclusion, organizations can take the following steps:

- Establish diversity targets for leadership positions and work towards achieving them. This includes implementing succession planning and talent development programs specifically aimed at underrepresented groups.
- Encourage diversity in recruitment by actively seeking out diverse candidates, implementing inclusive job descriptions, and ensuring diverse interview panels.
- Promote internal mobility and provide opportunities for diverse employees to gain exposure and experience by participating in cross-functional projects and assignments.
- Establish employee resource groups (ERGs) or affinity groups that provide support and networking opportunities for employees from diverse backgrounds.
- Foster inclusive leadership by providing leadership development programs that emphasize the importance of inclusivity, empathy, and cultural competence.

5. Cultural Clashes and Integration:

When individuals with different cultural backgrounds come together, there is a risk of cultural clashes and difficulties in integrating different perspectives, values, and work styles. This can lead to misunderstandings, conflict, and reduced collaboration.

Solution:

To manage cultural clashes and promote integration, organizations can adopt the following strategies:

- Provide cultural competence training and development programs to sensitively address and bridge cultural differences.
- Establish clear expectations and guidelines around acceptable behavior, ensuring respect for diverse perspectives and promoting open dialogue.
- Encourage cross-cultural mentorship or buddy programs to facilitate knowledge sharing and mutual understanding.
- Celebrate diversity by organizing events and activities that highlight and embrace different cultures, traditions, and holidays respectfully and inclusively.
- Establish channels for open and constructive feedback to address cultural clashes and promptly resolve conflicts.

Managing diversity presents various challenges that organizations must address to capitalize on the benefits of a diverse workforce. By acknowledging and proactively addressing communication barriers, implicit biases, resistance to change, lack of representation and inclusion, and cultural clashes, organizations can create an inclusive and supportive environment where diversity can thrive. Implementing solutions such as training programs, inclusive policies, unconscious bias awareness, and fostering inclusive leadership is critical in managing diversity effectively. With a commitment to overcoming these challenges, organizations can harness the power of diversity and create a more innovative, collaborative, and successful workplace.

Diversity Metrics and Accountability

Diversity metrics and accountability play a crucial role in measuring and promoting diversity and inclusion within organizations. In today's increasingly diverse world, companies need to prioritize incorporating individuals from various backgrounds and perspectives to drive innovation, creativity, and overall success. However, it's not enough to merely state a commitment to diversity; organizations must also establish accountability measures and metrics to track progress.

Diversity metrics refer to the quantifiable data used to monitor and evaluate diversity and inclusion efforts within an organization. These metrics can encompass various dimensions of diversity, such as race, gender, age, sexual orientation, disability, and more. By collecting and analyzing these metrics, organizations gain valuable insights into their current diverse landscape, identifying areas of strength and areas that may need improvement.

An important aspect of diversity metrics is accountability. Establishing accountability ensures that organizations are held responsible for their diversity goals and commitments. Accountability mechanisms help prevent diversity efforts from becoming performative and ensure that real progress is made. When organizations set measurable diversity goals, they can be held accountable through periodic reporting, transparency, and the involvement of leadership.

One common metric used to measure diversity is representation. Representation metrics assess the composition of various identity groups within an organization, such as the percentage of employees from different racial or ethnic backgrounds, gender distribution across different levels and departments, or the number of individuals from diverse age groups. This data provides insights into an organization's commitment to fair hiring practices and equal opportunities for advancement.

However, representation alone is not enough. Organizations must also consider metrics related to inclusion. Inclusion metrics evaluate how employees, especially those from underrepresented groups, experience the organizational culture. These metrics can include engagement surveys, feedback mechanisms, and focus groups. They provide organizations with a better understanding of whether employees feel valued, respected, and included, or if there are barriers that need to be addressed.

To effectively measure diversity and inclusion efforts, organizations need to establish clear benchmarks and targets. For example, they can set specific goals for increasing representation or improving inclusion scores within a particular timeframe. By having tangible objectives, organizations can track their progress and hold themselves accountable for achieving these targets.

Another important aspect of diversity metrics is intersectionality. Intersectionality recognizes that individuals hold multiple identities that can intersect and shape their experiences, such as being both a woman and a person of color or being LGBTQ+ and disabled. Organizations must collect data on intersecting identities to gain a comprehensive understanding of diversity within their workforce. Intersectional metrics enable organizations to address the unique challenges and needs of employees who face multiple forms of discrimination and ensure that diversity efforts are inclusive for everyone.

Accountability in diversity and inclusion practices requires transparency and reporting. Organizations should regularly share their diversity metrics and progress with employees, stakeholders, and the public. Openly communicating these metrics allows for feedback and promotes trust and engagement among the workforces. Additionally, organizations can report their diversity statistics in annual or sustainability reports, signaling their commitment to diversity and inclusion to potential partners, clients, and investors.

Moreover, accountability should not solely lie with HR departments or diversity and inclusion teams. Leaders, especially top executives, and managers must be accountable for diversity and inclusion as well. Organizations need to hold leadership accountable for embedding diversity and inclusion into the company's core values and strategic decisions. Executives should demonstrate their commitment by regularly communicating the importance of diversity, setting an example by actively seeking diverse perspectives, and ensuring inclusive practices are followed.

Organizations may face challenges in collecting accurate diversity metrics and implementing accountability measures. For instance, some individuals may be hesitant to disclose personal information due to privacy concerns. To overcome this, organizations should emphasize confidentiality and the anonymization of data to ensure employee trust. Employee resource groups and diversity councils can also play a role in promoting participation and collaboration in diversity efforts.

Lastly, diversity metrics and accountability should be seen as a continuous process, rather than a one-time endeavor. Organizations should regularly review and update their diverse goals and metrics to reflect changing demographics, societal shifts, and internal realities. By consistently analyzing and adapting diversity efforts, organizations can cultivate an inclusive and diverse workplace environment that reflects the needs and aspirations of its employees.

In conclusion, diversity metrics and accountability are fundamental in driving meaningful change within organizations. These metrics enable organizations to measure diversity and inclusion efforts, facilitating progress tracking and identifying areas for improvement. Accountability mechanisms ensure that organizations are held responsible for their diversity goals and commitments, preventing diversity efforts from being performative and promoting real change. By setting clear targets, establishing transparency, involving leadership, considering intersectionality, and continuously reviewing progress, organizations can build diverse and inclusive workplaces that benefit everyone involved.

Case Studies of Successful Diversity Initiatives

Case Study 1: Salesforce

Salesforce, a global cloud computing company, has implemented various successful diversity initiatives. Through their program called "Equality Trailblazer," they have set diversity goals and regularly published their diversity metrics. By tracking their progress and holding leaders accountable, Salesforce has made significant strides in increasing representation of underrepresented groups, including racially and ethnically diverse employees and women in leadership positions.

Case Study 2: Accenture

Accenture, a global professional services firm, has prioritized diversity through its initiatives like "Getting to Equal." They established a clear goal to achieve a gender-balanced workforce by 2025. To hold themselves accountable, Accenture regularly publishes its diversity statistics and provides transparency in its promotion and compensation processes. This commitment to diversity has resulted in increased representation of women in leadership roles.

Case Study 3: Microsoft

Microsoft has been recognized for its comprehensive diversity initiatives. Through a range of programs and initiatives like "DigiGirlz" and "LEAP," Microsoft aims to provide equal access to technology education and leadership development for young girls and women. By investing in these initiatives, Microsoft has made significant progress in increasing diversity in the tech industry and cultivating a more inclusive workplace culture.

Case Study 4: Procter & Gamble

Procter & Gamble (P&G) is committed to fostering diversity and inclusion across its global operations. They have implemented initiatives like "Daring Lead" that promote diversity at the leadership level. P&G also tracks progress toward representation goals, conducts annual diversity and inclusion surveys, and has established Employee Resource Groups (ERGs) to support underrepresented and marginalized communities within the company.

Case Study 5: Google

Google is known for its diversity initiatives, such as the "Google in Residence" program. Through this program, Google partners with historically black colleges and universities (HBCUs) to provide technical support, mentorship, and internships to students. By proactively engaging with diverse communities and investing in educational opportunities, Google aims to increase diversity in the technology industry.

Case Study 6: American Express

American Express has a strong commitment to diversity and inclusion. Their initiatives include the "Open Conversations" program, which fosters dialogue and understanding around diversity-related issues. They have also implemented unconscious bias training for employees, promoting a more inclusive and equitable workplace culture. These initiatives have contributed to increased representation and a more inclusive work environment at American Express.

Case Study 7: Coca-Cola

Coca-Cola has long embraced diversity and inclusion as part of its corporate culture. They have established Employee Resource Groups (ERGs) to support and empower underrepresented communities, including groups focused on women, LGBTQ+, and racial and ethnic minorities. Coca-Cola also conducts regular diversity and inclusion surveys and hosts diversity forums to gather feedback and ensure accountability in its initiatives.

Case Study 8: Intel

Intel has implemented various successful diversity initiatives. They have set goals to increase diversity within their workforce, especially in technical roles. To hold themselves accountable, Intel has tied executive compensation to diversity and inclusion metrics. Their efforts have resulted in significant progress, with increased representation of women and underrepresented minority groups in leadership positions within the company.

Case Study 9: Unilever

Unilever has made diversity and inclusion a strategic priority. They have established a leadership commitment called the "Unilever Compass," which promotes gender balance, inclusive culture, and equal opportunities for all employees. Unilever also conducts regular employee engagement surveys and sets measurable diversity goals to track progress. These initiatives have helped them create a more inclusive workplace and increase the representation of women in leadership roles.

Case Study 10: Uber

Uber has implemented multiple diversity initiatives to address the challenges and biases present within its organization. They have introduced programs like "UberPride" and "UberHUE" to support LGBTQ+ and racially diverse employees, respectively. Uber also regularly publishes diversity reports and participates in transparency initiatives like the "Equal Pay Pledge." Through these efforts, Uber is working towards building a more diverse and inclusive company culture.

These case studies highlight the diverse range of successful diversity initiatives implemented by organizations across various industries. Each initiative demonstrates a strong commitment to diversity, inclusion, and accountability, resulting in significant progress toward building more diverse and inclusive workplaces.

Cultural Intelligence and Diversity in Education

Cultural intelligence (CQ) and diversity in education are two important aspects that educators and educational institutions need to consider in today's globalized and diverse world. Cultural intelligence refers to an individual's capability to navigate and interact effectively across different cultural contexts, while diversity in education emphasizes the inclusion and representation of diverse identities, experiences, and perspectives. This article will discuss the significance of cultural intelligence and diversity in education, along with strategies and best practices for promoting and enhancing both within educational settings.

Significance of Cultural Intelligence and Diversity in Education:

1. Globalized Society: In an interconnected world, cultural intelligence is essential for educators and students to understand and respect diverse cultural norms, values, and communication styles. Diversity in education prepares students to thrive in a multicultural environment and equips them with the skills needed to navigate global challenges.

2. Enhanced Learning: Cultural intelligence facilitates effective learning by helping educators understand and accommodate the diverse learning needs of their students. It encourages the incorporation of various cultural, linguistic, and experiential perspectives into the learning process, thus enriching the educational experience for all.

3. Critical Thinking and Creativity: Exposure to diverse perspectives challenges students' preconceived notions and encourages critical thinking. By engaging with different cultural backgrounds, students develop creativity, empathy, and problem-solving skills, which are essential for success in higher education and the workforce.

4. Social Cohesion and Equity: Educational institutions that prioritize diversity and cultural intelligence cultivate an inclusive environment where all students feel valued and respected. This promotes social cohesion and equity, as it breaks down barriers, reduces prejudice, and fosters an atmosphere of understanding and collaboration among students from different backgrounds.

Strategies and Best Practices for Promoting Cultural Intelligence and Diversity in Education:

1. Integrate Cultural Diversity into the Curriculum: Integrate diverse cultural perspectives, histories, and contributions into the curriculum to provide students with a well-rounded education that reflects the global community. This can be accomplished through literature, history, and social studies, among other subjects.

2. Support Professional Development: Provide educators with training and professional development opportunities to enhance their cultural intelligence and equip them with the skills needed to teach and interact with diverse student populations effectively. Professional development programs can include workshops, conferences, and collaborative learning experiences.

3. Foster Inclusive Classroom Environments: Create inclusive classroom environments where students feel safe and encouraged to express their cultural identities and share their experiences. This can be achieved by establishing ground rules that promote respect, empathy, and open dialogue among students. Educators should be attentive to cultural sensitivities and ensure that their teaching materials and methods are inclusive and representative of diverse cultures.

4. Encourage Cross-cultural Experiences: Organize and support cross-cultural experiences such as study abroad programs, international student exchanges, or virtual exchange programs that facilitate interaction between

students from different cultural backgrounds. These experiences expose students to diverse perspectives and help them develop cultural intelligence.

5. Engage the Community: Collaborate with local community organizations and cultural centers to bring diverse voices and experiences into the classroom. Inviting guest speakers, partnering with community activists, or organizing field trips to culturally significant sites can provide students with firsthand knowledge of different cultures and promote understanding and respect.

6. Cultivate Empathy and Perspective-taking: Incorporate activities that promote empathy and perspective-taking into the curriculum. Encourage students to step into others' shoes, consider different viewpoints, and critically analyze cultural norms. This can be achieved through role-playing exercises, group discussions, or literature circles focused on diverse authors.

7. Support Student-led Initiatives: Foster student-led initiatives, clubs, and organizations focused on promoting cultural diversity and inclusivity within the school community. These groups can help organize events and activities that celebrate diverse cultures, raise awareness about social issues, and foster dialogue among students.

8. Assess and Measure Progress: Develop metrics and assessment tools to measure the impact of cultural intelligence and diversity initiatives within the educational institution. These metrics can include surveys, focus groups, and performance evaluations to gauge students' and educators' cultural understanding and identify areas for improvement.

9. Evaluate and Revise Policies: Review existing policies to ensure that they promote diversity, equity, and inclusion. This may involve revising recruitment and admission policies to attract a more diverse student body and hiring practices that prioritize inclusive educators.

10. Collaboration and Partnerships: Establish partnerships with other educational institutions, local organizations, and stakeholders that share a commitment to cultural intelligence and diversity in education. Collaborative efforts can amplify the impact of initiatives, share resources and knowledge, and create a larger network of support.

Cultural intelligence and diversity play crucial roles in shaping educational environments that foster inclusivity, equity, and preparedness for a globalized society. By prioritizing cultural intelligence and implementing strategies to promote diversity within educational institutions, educators can create transformative learning experiences that enhance students' cultural understanding, empathy, and critical thinking skills. Ultimately, embracing cultural intelligence and diversity in education prepares students to become informed, engaged, and responsible global citizens.

Promoting Inclusive Learning Environments

Promoting inclusive learning environments is essential for ensuring that all students, regardless of their background, abilities, or identities, feel welcomed, valued, and supported in their educational journey. Inclusive learning environments prioritize diversity, equity, and accessibility, fostering a sense of belonging, promoting active participation, and providing students with equal opportunities to succeed. This article will discuss the significance of inclusive learning environments, key principles for promoting inclusivity, strategies for implementation, and the benefits of creating such environments for all learners.

Significance of Inclusive Learning Environments:

1. Equity and Social Justice: Inclusive learning environments uphold the principles of equality and social justice by providing educational opportunities to all students, regardless of their differences. They ensure fair treatment and recognize the individual strengths, needs, and contributions of every learner.

2. Promoting Diversity: Inclusive learning environments celebrate and embrace diversity, including but not limited to factors such as race, ethnicity, gender, socio-economic status, language, religion, and ability. By valuing and integrating diverse perspectives, experiences, and identities, students develop an appreciation for different cultures, ideas, and learning styles.

3. Improved Learning Outcomes: When students feel included, valued, and supported, they are more engaged, motivated, and willing to participate actively in the learning process. Inclusive learning environments foster collaboration, critical thinking, and creativity, leading to improved learning outcomes for all students.

4. Personal Growth and Empathy: Inclusive learning environments promote personal growth and social-emotional development. They create opportunities for self-reflection, empathy, and understanding of others' experiences, fostering communication and relationship-building skills that are essential in an interconnected world.

Principles for Promoting Inclusive Learning Environments:

1. Accessibility: Ensure that the learning environment, materials, and technologies are accessible to all students, regardless of their abilities. This may include providing assistive technologies, accommodations, or alternative formats for learning materials.

2. Respect for Diversity: Value and respect the diverse identities, experiences, and perspectives of all students. Recognize and challenge biases, stereotypes, and discriminatory practices that may hinder inclusivity.

3. Active Participation: Encourage active participation by providing opportunities for all students to contribute and share their thoughts, ideas, and experiences. Promote inclusive discussion techniques, such as using think-pair-share activities or utilizing online platforms that allow collaboration.

4. Flexibility and Differentiation: Recognize that students have individual needs and learning styles, and provide flexibility and differentiation in instructional methods, assessments, and assignments. Offer multiple ways for students to demonstrate their understanding and engage with the content.

5. Student-Centered Approach: Adopt a student-centered approach that focuses on the needs, interests, and aspirations of the learners. Involve students in decision-making processes and incorporate their feedback in shaping the learning environment.

6. Safe and Inclusive Language: Be mindful of the language used in the learning environment to ensure that it is inclusive, respectful, and free from bias or stereotypes. Use gender-neutral language and be open to using student-preferred pronouns.

Strategies for Promoting Inclusive Learning Environments:

1. Establish Clear Expectations: Communicate expectations for behavior, participation, and respect within the learning environment. Encourage a supportive classroom climate where everyone feels safe to express themselves and share their ideas.

2. Cultivate Positive Interactions: Foster positive interactions among students by promoting empathy, kindness, and cooperation. Establish cooperative learning strategies, group activities, or peer mentoring programs that enhance collaboration and build relationships.

3. Diverse and Inclusive Resources: Select instructional materials and resources that reflect the diversity of student backgrounds and experiences. Incorporate diverse perspectives and voices, including from marginalized or underrepresented groups, to broaden students' understanding and cultural competence.

4. Professional Development: Provide ongoing professional development opportunities for educators to enhance their knowledge and skills in creating inclusive learning environments. Training sessions, workshops, and peer collaboration can support continuous improvement in inclusive teaching practices.

5. Engage Families and Communities: Involve families and communities in the educational process by creating open lines of communication, sharing student progress, and inviting them to participate in school events and activities. This partnership fosters a sense of belonging and demonstrates the shared responsibility for promoting inclusive learning environments.

6. Universal Design for Learning (UDL): Implement the principles of Universal Design for Learning, which provide multiple means of engagement, representation, and expression. UDL ensures that content is accessible to all students, provides options for different learning preferences, and allows students to demonstrate their knowledge in various ways.

Benefits of Creating Inclusive Learning Environments:

1. Enhanced Learning Outcomes: Inclusive learning environments promote active engagement, critical thinking, and creativity, leading to improved learning outcomes. Students feel motivated, connected, and supported, resulting in increased retention rates and academic achievement.

2. Social and Emotional Development: Inclusive learning environments foster social-emotional development, promoting empathy, self-confidence, and self-awareness. Students learn how to collaborate, value diverse perspectives, and communicate effectively, building essential life skills.

3. Long-term Well-being: Inclusive learning environments contribute to students' overall well-being and mental health. When students feel accepted and supported, they experience less stress, anxiety, and isolation, leading to a healthier and more positive learning experience.

4. Preparation for a Diverse Society: Inclusive learning environments prepare students for a diverse and interconnected world, equipping them with the skills needed to navigate and succeed in a multicultural society. Students develop cultural competence, global awareness, and the ability to collaborate with individuals from various backgrounds.

Promoting inclusive learning environments is a vital responsibility for educators and educational institutions. By embracing diversity, fostering equity, and creating a sense of belonging, inclusive learning environments provide meaningful educational experiences for all students. By adopting strategies such as accessibility, respect for diversity, active participation, flexibility, and a student-centered approach, educators can create inclusive spaces that enhance learning outcomes, promote personal growth, and prepare students for success in an interconnected and diverse society.

Curriculum and Pedagogical Approaches

Curriculum and pedagogical approaches are critical components of education that shape the teaching and learning experiences in classrooms. The curriculum encompasses the content, skills, and knowledge that students are expected to acquire, while pedagogical approaches refer to instructional methods and strategies used by educators to facilitate learning. This article will discuss the significance of curriculum and pedagogical approaches, explore different types of curricula and pedagogies, and highlight the impact they have on students' educational experiences.

Significance of Curriculum and Pedagogical Approaches:

1. Shaping Learning Experiences: The curriculum and pedagogical approaches play a significant role in determining what and how students learn. They guide the selection of instructional materials, teaching methods, and

assessment strategies, shaping students' educational experiences and influencing their engagement and understanding of the subject matter.

2. Alignment with Objectives: The curriculum and pedagogical approaches should align with educational objectives and goals. They define the knowledge, skills, and competencies that students are expected to develop, ensuring that the teaching and learning experiences are purposeful and targeted toward achieving specific learning outcomes.

3. Promoting Critical Thinking and Creativity: Effective curriculum and pedagogical approaches prioritize the development of critical thinking and creativity. They encourage students to question, analyze, and evaluate information, fostering their ability to think critically, solve problems, and generate innovative ideas.

4. Reflecting Societal Needs: The curriculum and pedagogical approaches should reflect the changing needs of society and the workforce. They should equip students with the knowledge and skills required to navigate a rapidly evolving global landscape, preparing them for future academic and career success.

Types of Curricula:

1. Subject-Centered Curriculum: This traditional approach organizes the curriculum around specific subjects or disciplines, such as mathematics, science, language arts, and social studies. The subject-centered curriculum emphasizes the acquisition of disciplinary knowledge, skills, and understanding within each subject area.

2. Learner-Centered Curriculum: The learner-centered curriculum focuses on students' interests, needs, and aspirations. It prioritizes individualized instruction, personalized learning, and student autonomy. This approach recognizes that students have diverse learning styles, backgrounds, and abilities, and aims to tailor the curriculum to meet their unique needs.

3. Problem-Based Curriculum: In a problem-based curriculum, learning is centered around authentic, real-world problems or challenges. Students engage in inquiry-based learning, investigating, and solving complex problems, applying knowledge and skills from multiple disciplines. This approach promotes critical thinking, collaboration, and problem-solving skills.

4. Interdisciplinary Curriculum: Interdisciplinary curricula integrate knowledge, skills, and concepts from multiple subject areas into meaningful connections and contexts. It encourages students to see the interrelationships between different fields of study and promotes a holistic understanding of complex issues.

Types of Pedagogical Approaches:

1. Lecture-Based Instruction: Lecture-based instruction involves the teacher presenting information to students through direct instruction. This traditional method is often used for delivering content knowledge and introducing new concepts. However, it is important to incorporate interactive elements and opportunities for student engagement to enhance the effectiveness of this approach.

2. Inquiry-Based Learning: Inquiry-based learning involves students actively investigating and exploring concepts, problems, or questions. It promotes curiosity, critical thinking, and problem-solving skills by encouraging students to ask questions, gather and analyze information, and develop their understanding through guided inquiry.

3. Collaborative Learning: Collaborative learning encourages students to work together in small groups or teams to solve problems, complete projects, or discuss ideas. It fosters communication, teamwork, and critical thinking skills while promoting social interactions and shared responsibility for learning.

4. Experiential Learning: Experiential learning involves students engaging in hands-on, real-world experiences that connect classroom learning to practical applications. Examples include field trips, simulations, internships,

or service-learning projects. This approach provides students with opportunities to apply knowledge and skills in authentic settings.

5. Technology-Enhanced Instruction: Technology-enhanced instruction uses digital tools, multimedia resources, and online platforms to facilitate learning. It provides access to rich and interactive content, promotes personalized and self-paced learning, and enhances collaboration, communication, and creativity.

6. Differentiated Instruction: Differentiated instruction emphasizes adapting teaching methods, materials, and assessments to meet the diverse learning needs of students. It involves providing multiple pathways to understanding, accommodating different learning styles, and scaffolding instruction based on students' readiness, interests, and learning profiles.

Impact of Curriculum and Pedagogical Approaches:

1. Engaged Learning: A well-designed curriculum and effective pedagogical approaches promote student engagement and motivation. By making learning meaningful, relevant, and student-centered, students become active participants in the learning process, leading to increased interest and enthusiasm for learning.

2. Deeper Understanding: A thoughtfully designed curriculum and pedagogical approaches support students in developing a deep understanding of concepts and ideas. They facilitate critical thinking, problem-solving, and higher-order cognitive skills, enabling students to apply knowledge to real-world situations.

3. Student Success: When curriculum and pedagogical approaches are aligned with learning objectives and tailored to meet students' needs, it enhances student success. Students develop the knowledge, skills, and competencies necessary for academic achievements, higher education, and future careers.

4. Equity and Inclusion: Curriculum and pedagogical approaches that prioritize inclusivity and diversity create equitable learning opportunities for all students. They recognize and celebrate students' diverse backgrounds, cultures, and identities, fostering an inclusive and respectful learning environment.

5. Lifelong Learning Skills: Effective curriculum and pedagogical approaches instill lifelong learning skills in students. They cultivate curiosity, adaptability, critical thinking, collaboration, and problem-solving abilities, providing students with the tools necessary for continued learning beyond the classroom.

Curriculum and pedagogical approaches are integral parts of education, influencing students' learning experiences, engagement, and outcomes. By considering different types of curricula, such as subject-centered, learner-centered, problem-based, and interdisciplinary, educators can design a curriculum that aligns with the learning needs and aspirations of their students. Similarly, by utilizing various pedagogical approaches, such as lecture-based instruction, inquiry-based learning, collaborative learning, and experiential learning, educators can create dynamic and inclusive learning environments that foster deep understanding, critical thinking, and student success. It is essential for educators to continually reflect on and adapt their curriculum and pedagogical practices to meet the evolving needs of students and society, promoting inclusive and transformative learning experiences.

Intercultural Competence Development

Intercultural competence development refers to the acquisition and growth of skills, knowledge, and attitudes that enable individuals to effectively navigate and communicate across cultural differences. In an increasingly interconnected and diverse world, intercultural competence has become a vital skill for individuals, organizations, and society. This article will explore the significance of intercultural competence, the components involved in its development, and the strategies and best practices for fostering intercultural competence in individuals.

Significance of Intercultural Competence Development:

1. Globalization: The rapid pace of globalization has made intercultural competence essential. As individuals and organizations interact with people from different cultural backgrounds, understanding and respecting cultural norms, values, and communication styles is paramount for building successful and collaborative relationships.

2. Cultural Diversity: Communities and workplaces are becoming increasingly diverse, with individuals from various cultural, ethnic, and linguistic backgrounds coming together. Intercultural competence allows individuals to appreciate and embrace this diversity, fostering inclusion, and creating a sense of belonging for all.

3. Effective Communication: Intercultural competence enhances effective communication by enabling individuals to navigate linguistic and cultural barriers. It promotes active listening, empathy, and the ability to interpret nonverbal cues, leading to better understanding and collaboration in diverse environments.

4. Conflict Resolution: Cultural differences can sometimes lead to misunderstandings and conflict. Intercultural competence equips individuals with the skills to manage and resolve conflicts in culturally sensitive ways, fostering harmony and cooperation among diverse groups.

Components of Intercultural Competence:

1. Cultural Awareness: Cultural awareness involves recognizing and understanding one's cultural background and the cultural backgrounds of others. It requires individuals to examine their biases and assumptions and develop an open and non-judgmental attitude toward different cultures.

2. Knowledge of Cultures: Developing intercultural competence requires knowledge of various cultural practices, values, beliefs, and historical contexts. This knowledge allows individuals to understand the cultural nuances and adapt their behavior and communication styles accordingly.

3. Interpersonal Skills: Interpersonal skills such as empathy, active listening, and effective communication are crucial for intercultural competence. These skills enable individuals to understand others' perspectives, build rapport, and establish meaningful connections across cultural boundaries.

4. Adaptability and Flexibility: Intercultural competence involves being adaptable and flexible in different cultural contexts. It requires individuals to adjust their behavior, communication style, and problem-solving approaches to accommodate cultural differences and promote understanding.

Strategies for Fostering Intercultural Competence Development:

1. Cultural Immersion: Immersing oneself in different cultures through travel, study abroad programs, or interaction with diverse communities can significantly enhance intercultural competence. Direct exposure to different cultural contexts allows individuals to experience cultural differences firsthand and develop a deeper understanding of diverse perspectives.

2. Intercultural Training and Workshops: Intercultural training programs and workshops offer structured learning opportunities to develop intercultural competence. These programs provide participants with knowledge about different cultures and cultural communication patterns, as well as opportunities to practice and reflect on intercultural interactions.

3. Language Learning: Learning a foreign language can be a valuable tool for developing intercultural competence. Language learning exposes individuals to different cultures, promotes understanding of linguistic and cultural nuances, and facilitates effective communication with individuals from diverse backgrounds.

4. Cultural Exchange Programs: Participating in cultural exchange programs, such as student exchanges or host-family experiences, can broaden individuals' cultural horizons and foster intercultural competence through personal interactions and shared experiences.

5. Reflective Practice: Encouraging individuals to engage in reflective practice, such as journaling or self-reflection exercises, can enhance intercultural competence development. Reflective practice allows individuals to examine their own cultural biases, assumptions, and behaviors, fostering self-awareness and introspection.

6. Role-Playing and Simulations: Engaging individuals in role-playing activities and simulations can help them practice intercultural communication and problem-solving in a safe and controlled environment. This hands-on approach allows individuals to develop cultural sensitivity and interpersonal skills while receiving feedback and guidance.

7. Collaborative Projects and Group Work: Encouraging collaborative projects and group work that involve individuals from different cultural backgrounds promotes intercultural competence. Working together towards common goals requires individuals to understand, respect, and adapt to diverse perspectives, fostering mutual learning and collaboration.

8. Intercultural Mentoring: Pairing individuals with mentors from different cultural backgrounds can provide valuable guidance and support for intercultural competence development. Mentors can share their own experiences, offer insights into their culture, and provide guidance in navigating intercultural interactions.

9. Inclusive Curriculum: Ensuring that educational curricula are inclusive and reflect diverse cultural perspectives and experiences is crucial for fostering intercultural competence. Incorporating diverse literature, history, and other subject matters helps students develop a broader understanding of different cultures and promotes cultural sensitivity.

10. Continuous Learning and Reflection: Intercultural competence is an ongoing journey. Encouraging lifelong learning, ongoing reflection, and self-assessment are key aspects of intercultural competence development. Individuals should seek opportunities to expand their knowledge, engage in intercultural experiences, and continually reflect on their behaviors, biases, and growing cultural understanding.

Intercultural competence development is an essential aspect of navigating today's globalized and multicultural society. By cultivating cultural awareness, knowledge, interpersonal skills, and adaptability, individuals can effectively communicate and collaborate across cultural boundaries. Strategies such as cultural immersion, intercultural training, language learning, and reflective practice are key to fostering intercultural competence. By investing in intercultural competence development, individuals can foster inclusive and respectful relationships, contribute to societal and organizational success, and actively participate in an interconnected world.

International Student Experiences

International student experiences play a significant role in shaping their personal growth, academic development, and cultural understanding. Studying abroad provides unique opportunities for students to immerse themselves in a new culture, broaden their perspectives, and build valuable connections across borders. This article will explore the significance of international student experiences, the challenges faced by international students, and the benefits and strategies for enhancing the overall experience of international students in their host countries.

Significance of International Student Experiences:

1. Exposure to Different Cultures: International student experiences offer a firsthand opportunity to engage with different cultures, values, beliefs, and traditions. This exposure enhances cross-cultural competence, empathy, and understanding, enabling students to navigate diverse environments and foster global citizenship.

2. Academic and Professional Growth: Studying abroad provides access to renowned educational institutions, diverse academic programs, and innovative teaching methods. International students can benefit from quality education, develop new academic skills, and gain invaluable international perspectives that enhance their academic and professional prospects.

3. Personal and Social Development: Living and studying in a foreign country challenges international students to step outside their comfort zones, fostering personal growth, independence, and resilience. They develop interpersonal skills, adaptability, and a global mindset through interactions with people from different backgrounds.

4. Network Building: International student experiences facilitate the development of a global network of friends, mentors, and professionals. Building connections with peers from different countries cultivates a diverse support system, enhances cross-cultural communication, and opens doors for future collaborations and career opportunities.

Challenges Faced by International Students:

1. Language Barriers: Language proficiency can pose challenges for international students, both academically and socially. Adjusting to a new language and academic writing style may require additional effort, support, and language learning opportunities.

2. Cultural Adjustment: Adapting to a new cultural context, values, norms, and social expectations can be overwhelming for international students. They may experience culture shock, homesickness, and feelings of isolation initially, requiring time and support to adjust to their new environment.

3. Academic Demands: International students often encounter different academic requirements, teaching styles, and assessment methods, which may be unfamiliar and challenging. Navigating the academic system, managing coursework, and seeking academic support can present difficulties.

4. Financial and Practical Challenges: Financial constraints, including tuition fees, living expenses, and insurance, can pose significant challenges for international students. Understanding and navigating financial aid options, employment regulations, and healthcare systems in the host country may necessitate additional support.

Benefits and Strategies for Enhancing the International Student Experience:

1. Orientation and Pre-arrival Support: Providing comprehensive pre-arrival information, including guidance on visas, accommodation, healthcare, and academic expectations, helps international students better understand and prepare for their upcoming experience. Orientation programs, both online and on-campus, facilitate a smooth transition and address potential challenges.

2. Intercultural Programming: Hosting intercultural events, cultural exchange programs, and workshops fosters interaction and dialogue among international and domestic students. These initiatives promote cross-cultural understanding, appreciation, and respect, breaking down stereotypes and creating opportunities for meaningful engagement.

3. Language Support and Tutoring: Offering language support services, including language courses, tutoring, or language exchanges, supports international students' language development. Addressing language barriers creates a more inclusive learning environment and enhances academic success.

4. Academic Support: Providing international students with academic support such as study groups, mentorship programs, and writing centers helps them navigate the academic system and develop the necessary skills for success. Faculty and staff can offer guidance on coursework, research expectations, and effective study strategies specific to the host country's educational system.

5. Cultural Mentoring and Peer Support: Pairing international students with domestic student mentors or providing peer support programs creates opportunities for cultural exchange, language practice, and assistance with social integration. Peer support networks enable international students to build relationships, access local resources, and navigate the host country's social landscape.

6. Intercultural Competence Training: Introducing intercultural competence training within the curriculum or co-curricular activities helps foster the skills needed to navigate intercultural interactions. These trainings promote self-awareness, cultural intelligence, empathy, and effective communication across cultures.

7. Social and Recreational Activities: Organizing social and recreational activities that encourage international and domestic students to interact provides opportunities for friendship, shared experiences, and cultural exploration. Clubs, sports teams, and cultural organizations foster inclusion, encourage cross-cultural connections, and enrich the overall student experience.

8. Supportive Services: Accessible and culturally sensitive support services, including counseling, health services, and career guidance, are essential for international students' overall well-being and success. Awareness of these services, along with clear communication channels, ensures that students can seek help when needed.

9. Alumni Engagement: Engaging international student alumni through networking events, mentorship programs, or career services strengthens the support network for current international students. Alumni can offer guidance, share their experiences, and provide insights into career opportunities in the host country.

10. Evaluation and Feedback: Regularly assessing international student experiences through surveys, focus groups, or interviews allows educational institutions to monitor the effectiveness of support services and identify areas for improvement. Feedback from international students provides valuable insights to enhance future programs and initiatives.

International student experiences play a vital role in shaping individuals' personal and academic growth, fostering international understanding, and promoting global citizenship. By recognizing the challenges faced by international students and implementing strategies to support their cultural adjustment, language acquisition, academic success, and social integration, educational institutions can enhance the overall international student experience. Providing comprehensive pre-arrival support, intercultural programming, academic and language support, as well as access to supportive services, creates an inclusive and enriching environment for international students. By investing in these initiatives, educational institutions can cultivate a diverse and globally connected community that prepares international students for successful futures in an increasingly interconnected world.

Case Studies of Inclusive Educational Institutions

1. Case Study: Oak Elementary School

Oak Elementary School is in a diverse neighborhood in a metropolitan city. They have implemented various strategies to promote inclusivity, such as having a multicultural curriculum that incorporates the traditions and contributions of various cultures and ensuring the representation of different cultures in classroom materials. They also have programs that support students with disabilities, such as accessible facilities, assistive technology, and individualized education plans.

2. Case Study: Harmony High School

Harmony High School is committed to creating an inclusive environment for all students. They have a strong anti-bullying policy and provide regular training for staff and students on inclusivity and acceptance. The school offers a range of extracurricular activities that cater to diverse interests, ensuring that all students can participate and feel valued.

3. Case Study: Maplewood College

Maplewood College is known for its inclusive practices and commitment to accommodating students with diverse learning needs. They offer a wide range of support services, such as learning assistance programs, tutoring, and counseling, to ensure that every student can thrive academically and personally. The college also actively promotes understanding and acceptance of different cultures through events and cultural celebrations.

4. Case Study: Willow High School

Willow High School is dedicated to fostering an inclusive environment for LGBTQ+ students. They have established a Gay-Straight Alliance (GSA) club, which provides a safe space for students to express themselves and receive support. The school actively promotes LGBTQ+ awareness through educational workshops and events, ensuring that all students feel accepted and respected.

5. Case Study: Clearview Elementary School

Clearview Elementary School has implemented universal design principles to ensure accessibility for all students. They have wheelchair ramps, elevators, and accessible restrooms to accommodate students with physical disabilities. In addition, the school provides assistive technology devices, such as text-to-speech software, to support students with hearing or visual impairments.

6. Case Study:

Cuttington University has a strong commitment to inclusive education for students with intellectual disabilities. They have implemented a program that promotes peer-to-peer learning and social interaction through integrated classrooms. This allows students with disabilities to learn alongside their typically developing peers, fostering a sense of belonging and reducing stigma.

7. Case Study: Greenfield Elementary School

Greenfield Elementary School focuses on inclusive practices for students with autism spectrum disorder (ASD). They have trained special education teachers who use evidence-based strategies to support students with ASD in the general education classroom. The school also organizes regular social skills training sessions and inclusive activities to promote understanding and acceptance among all students.

8. Case Study: Riverside High School

Riverside High School ensures inclusivity for students with mental health challenges. They have a comprehensive counseling program that offers individual and group counseling to students struggling with anxiety, depression, or other mental health issues. The school also provides a stigma-free environment and educates students on mental health awareness.

9. Case Study: Evergreen College

Evergreen College is committed to supporting students from low-income backgrounds. They offer various scholarships, financial aid, and mentorship programs to help students overcome financial barriers. The college also provides academic resources, such as tutoring and study groups, to ensure that all students have equal access to success.

10. Case Study: Valley Academy

Valley Academy is a bilingual school that promotes inclusivity for students from diverse linguistic backgrounds. They offer English as a Second Language (ESL) classes and have teachers who are trained in teaching English language learners. The school also celebrates multiculturalism and encourages students to embrace their cultural heritage.

Cultural Intelligence and Diversity in Society

Embracing Differences and Fostering Inclusion

Cultural intelligence (CQ) is the ability to understand, appreciate, and interact effectively with individuals from different cultural backgrounds. In today's increasingly interconnected and diverse society, having a high level of cultural intelligence is essential. This comprehensive article explores the concept of cultural intelligence, its importance in promoting diversity, equity, and inclusion, and various strategies and best practices for developing and fostering cultural intelligence in individuals and society. It also discusses the benefits and challenges of embracing diversity in society and provides real-life examples and case studies to highlight successful initiatives and inclusive practices. By understanding and practicing cultural intelligence, individuals and communities can build bridges, break barriers, and create a more inclusive, harmonious, and equitable society.

Keywords: cultural intelligence, diversity, inclusion, equity, intercultural competence, cross-cultural interactions, cultural awareness, multiculturalism, social harmony

In an era of globalization and increased migration, the ability to effectively navigate and engage with people from diverse cultural backgrounds has become crucial. Cultural intelligence, a concept developed by researchers, focuses on individuals' ability to adapt to different cultures and communicate across cultural boundaries. This article aims to explore the significance of cultural intelligence in promoting diversity, equity, and inclusion in society. It discusses the challenges and benefits of embracing diversity and provides strategies for developing cultural intelligence in individuals and fostering inclusivity at a societal level.

1. Understanding Cultural Intelligence

This section defines cultural intelligence and explains its components, namely cultural knowledge, cultural awareness, cultural adaptation, and cultural bridging. It explores how cultural intelligence differs from other measures of intelligence and highlights the importance of emotional and cognitive aspects in intercultural interactions.

2. Importance of Cultural Intelligence in Promoting Diversity and Inclusion

This section delves into the significance of cultural intelligence in fostering diversity, equity, and inclusion in society. It discusses how cultural intelligence enables individuals to appreciate and embrace differences, challenge biases and stereotypes, and interact respectfully with people from various cultural backgrounds. It emphasizes the role of cultural intelligence in reducing discrimination, promoting social justice, and creating inclusive environments.

3. Benefits and Challenges of Embracing Diversity

Highlighting the benefits of embracing diversity, this section discusses how diverse perspectives can foster innovation, creativity, and problem-solving. It also explores the challenges that arise when diverse cultures come together, such as cross-cultural misunderstandings, stereotypes, and the need for effective communication strategies. Additionally, it addresses the fear of cultural dilution and cultural clashes that may occur when cultures interact.

4. Developing Cultural Intelligence at an Individual Level

This section provides strategies and best practices for individuals to develop and enhance their cultural intelligence. It explains the importance of self-awareness, empathy, and an open mind in fostering cultural intelligence. It also discusses the role of cultural exposure, intercultural experiences, language acquisition, and cross-cultural training in cultivating a high level of cultural intelligence. Moreover, it emphasizes the need for continuous learning and self-reflection to expand one's cultural repertoire.

5. Fostering Cultural Intelligence at a Societal Level

This section explores how organizations, educational institutions, and policymakers can promote cultural intelligence and inclusivity at a societal level. It discusses the importance of integrating cultural intelligence into educational curricula, fostering multicultural environments, and implementing anti-discrimination policies. It highlights successful initiatives and programs that have proven effective in promoting diversity and inclusivity, such as diversity training, mentorship programs, and cultural exchange programs.

6. Case Studies: Successful Implementation of Cultural Intelligence

This section presents real-life case studies of organizations, institutions, and communities that have successfully implemented cultural intelligence practices. It highlights the strategies they employed, the challenges they faced, and the positive outcomes they achieved. These case studies provide practical insights and inspiration for individuals and communities seeking to embrace diversity and foster inclusivity.

7. Summary and Conclusion

The concluding section summarizes the key points discussed in the article, reiterating the importance of cultural intelligence and diversity in society. It emphasizes that embracing diversity and developing cultural intelligence is a continuous process that requires commitment, open-mindedness, and intercultural competence. By promoting cultural intelligence at both the individual and societal levels, our society can become more inclusive, equitable, and harmonious.

Celebrating Cultural Diversity

Celebrating Cultural Diversity: Embracing the Beauty of Differences

Cultural diversity refers to the coexistence and interaction of various cultural groups within a society. It encompasses the diverse traditions, beliefs, languages, customs, and practices that make each culture unique. This article explores the importance of celebrating cultural diversity and highlights the benefits it brings to individuals, communities, and society as a whole. It discusses strategies for promoting cultural diversity appreciation, fostering inclusivity, and creating platforms for cultural exchange. Additionally, it showcases real-life examples of successful cultural diversity celebrations and provides practical tips for individuals to embrace and honor cultural diversity in their daily lives.

Keywords: cultural diversity, cultural appreciation, inclusivity, multiculturalism, cultural exchange, intercultural understanding

This introductory section defines cultural diversity and emphasizes its significance in today's globalized world. It highlights the beauty and richness of diverse cultures and sets the stage for the exploration of why celebrating cultural diversity is vital.

1. Understanding the Importance of Celebrating Cultural Diversity

This section delves into the importance of celebrating cultural diversity in promoting tolerance, understanding, and harmony within society. It discusses how celebrating cultural diversity helps break down stereotypes, challenges biases, and fosters inclusivity. Moreover, it explains how embracing cultural diversity enhances creativity, innovation, and social cohesion.

2. Benefits of Celebrating Cultural Diversity

This section explores the numerous benefits that arise from celebrating cultural diversity. It highlights how cultural diversity enriches individuals' experiences, broadens perspectives, and promotes personal growth.

Additionally, it emphasizes how cultural diversity fosters economic development, drives tourism, and enhances cross-cultural communication and collaboration.

3. Strategies for Promoting Cultural Diversity Appreciation

This section provides strategies and methods for promoting cultural diversity appreciation within communities and institutions. It discusses the importance of education in raising awareness about diverse cultures, promoting multicultural curricula, and integrating cultural education into formal and informal settings. It also explores the role of media, arts, and cultural festivals in cultivating appreciation for cultural diversity.

4. Fostering Inclusivity through Cultural Exchange

This section focuses on the concept of cultural exchange to foster inclusivity and intercultural understanding. It discusses how cultural exchange programs, such as student exchanges, international volunteering, and intercultural workshops, facilitate meaningful interactions and promote empathy between individuals from different cultures. It also emphasizes the importance of respectful dialogue, active listening, and open-mindedness in cultural exchange.

5. Case Studies: Successful Celebrations of Cultural Diversity

This section presents real-life case studies of successful cultural diversity celebrations. It showcases events, initiatives, and campaigns that effectively highlight and embrace cultural diversity within communities. By showcasing these examples, individuals and organizations can gain insights into how to design and implement their cultural diversity celebrations with impact.

6. Embracing Cultural Diversity in Everyday Life

This section provides practical tips for individuals to embrace and honor cultural diversity in their daily lives. It emphasizes the importance of respecting cultural differences, building diverse networks, exploring new cuisines, and establishing intercultural friendships. Moreover, it suggests engaging in cultural activities, such as attending cultural festivals, visiting cultural landmarks, and learning about different cultural traditions.

7. Overcoming Challenges in Celebrating Cultural Diversity

This section addresses common challenges faced when celebrating cultural diversity, such as cultural appropriation, stereotypes, and cultural insensitivity. It guides how to overcome these challenges by fostering cultural respect, conducting proper research, and engaging in meaningful cross-cultural interactions.

8. Summary and Conclusion

This section summarizes the key points discussed in the article and emphasizes the importance of celebrating cultural diversity for building inclusive and harmonious societies. It encourages individuals to be proactive in embracing and appreciating cultural diversity and concludes with a call to action to promote intercultural understanding and inclusivity.

Addressing Social Inequality: Strategies for Building a More Equitable Society

Social inequality refers to the unequal distribution of resources, opportunities, and privileges among individuals and social groups. It manifests in various forms, including income inequality, racial discrimination, gender disparities, and disparities based on other social factors. This article explores the problem of social inequality, its impact on individuals and society, and the strategies for addressing and reducing it. It discusses the role of government policies, social programs, education, advocacy, and community initiatives in promoting equality and social justice. Additionally, it highlights successful initiatives and real-life examples of efforts to address social inequality and build a more equitable society.

Keywords: social inequality, income inequality, racial discrimination, gender disparities, social justice, equity

This introductory section defines social inequality and emphasizes its prevalence in society. It highlights the detrimental effects that social inequality has on individuals, communities, and society. The importance of addressing social inequality to create a more equitable society is also emphasized.

1. Understanding the Nature of Social Inequality

This section explores the various forms of social inequality, including income inequality, racial discrimination, gender disparities, and disparities based on other social factors such as age, disability, or sexual orientation. It examines the systemic and structural factors that perpetuate social inequality and contribute to its persistence.

2. The Impact of Social Inequality

This section discusses the impact of social inequality on individuals and communities. It highlights how social inequality leads to limited opportunities, barriers to education and employment, unequal access to healthcare, and a sense of marginalization. Moreover, it explores the detrimental effects on mental health, social cohesion, and economic development that result from social inequality.

3. Promoting Social Equality through Government Policies

This section examines the role of government policies in addressing social inequality. It discusses the importance of implementing progressive taxation, social safety nets, minimum wage laws, and anti-discrimination legislation. It also explores the need for policies that target specific areas of inequality, such as affordable housing, quality education, and healthcare access.

4. Social Programs and Support Systems

This section focuses on the role of social programs and support systems in reducing social inequality. It discusses the importance of access to quality education, affordable healthcare, childcare, and social assistance programs. It highlights successful examples of programs aimed at uplifting disadvantaged groups, fostering social mobility, and reducing inequalities.

5. Education as a Catalyst for Social Equality

This section explores the transformative power of education in addressing social inequality. It discusses the need for inclusive and equitable education systems that support marginalized populations. It emphasizes the importance of targeted scholarships, mentorship programs, and inclusive curricula to bridge educational gaps and promote equality of opportunity.

6. Advocacy and Awareness

This section emphasizes the role of advocacy and public awareness in addressing social inequality. It discusses the importance of advocacy groups, non-profit organizations, and grassroots movements in raising awareness, challenging systemic inequalities, and advocating for policy change. It highlights successful examples of advocacy initiatives that have led to significant advancements in reducing social inequality.

7. Community Empowerment and Grassroots Initiatives

This section focuses on the significance of community empowerment and grassroots initiatives in addressing social inequality. It discusses the importance of fostering community engagement, encouraging self-advocacy, and creating platforms for marginalized voices to be heard. It showcases successful community-led initiatives that have led to positive change and improved social conditions.

8. Case Studies: Successful Efforts to Address Social Inequality

This section provides real-life case studies of successful efforts to address social inequality. It highlights initiatives that have generated measurable impact and positive change by addressing income inequality, racial disparities, gender inequalities, or other forms of social injustice. These case studies serve as examples and inspiration for individuals and organizations working towards a more equitable society.

9. Summary and Conclusion

This section summarizes the key points discussed in the article and emphasizes the need for collective action to address social inequality. It highlights the importance of government policies, social programs, education, advocacy, and community initiatives in promoting equity and social justice. The concluding section calls for continued efforts and commitment to create a more inclusive, equitable, and just society for all.

Multicultural Policies and Legislation

Fostering Inclusion and Social Cohesion

Multicultural policies and legislation refer to the frameworks and laws enacted by governments to promote diversity, inclusion, and equal rights for individuals from different cultural backgrounds. This article explores the significance of multicultural policies and legislation in fostering social cohesion, addressing discrimination, and creating inclusive societies. It discusses the principles and objectives of multicultural policies, the legal frameworks in place to protect cultural rights, and the challenges and benefits associated with implementing such policies. Additionally, it highlights successful examples of multicultural policies and legislation from various countries and explores the potential future directions for promoting cultural diversity and integration.

Keywords: multicultural policies, legislation, cultural diversity, inclusion, social cohesion, cultural rights, discrimination

This introductory section defines multicultural policies and legislation and emphasizes their importance in contemporary societies. It highlights the relevance of such policies in promoting diversity, inclusion, and social cohesion. The section also provides an overview of the structure of the article.

1. Principles and Objectives of Multicultural Policies

This section explores the principles and objectives that underlie multicultural policies. It discusses the promotion of cultural diversity, respect for cultural rights, and equal opportunities for individuals from diverse backgrounds. It also highlights the goals of cultural integration, social harmony, and the prevention of discrimination and exclusion.

2. Legal Frameworks for Protecting Cultural Rights

This section examines the legal frameworks that support multicultural policies and protect cultural rights. It discusses international conventions and treaties, regional agreements, and national legislation designed to safeguard cultural heritage, linguistic rights, and equal treatment for all individuals. Key legal instruments, such as the Universal Declaration of Human Rights, the Convention on the Elimination of All Forms of Racial Discrimination, and national anti-discrimination laws, are explored.

3. Multicultural Policies and Social Cohesion

This section explores the role of multicultural policies in fostering social cohesion. It discusses how policies that promote inclusivity, address inequality, and celebrate cultural diversity contribute to social harmony and mutual understanding. The section also highlights the potential benefits of multicultural policies, such as increased social capital, reduced segregation, and enhanced intergroup relations.

4. Challenges in Implementing Multicultural Policies and Legislation

This section discusses the challenges associated with implementing multicultural policies and legislation. It addresses issues such as public backlash, identity politics, resistance to change, and the tension between cultural rights and broader societal norms. The section also explores the importance of effective communication, community engagement, and ongoing evaluation in overcoming these challenges.

5. Successful Examples of Multicultural Policies and Legislation

This section presents successful examples of multicultural policies and legislation from different countries. It highlights initiatives that have effectively promoted cultural diversity, equality, and inclusion. Examples may include Canada's multiculturalism policy, Australia's Anti-Discrimination Act, and New Zealand's Treaty of Waitangi. The section examines the strategies employed, the outcomes achieved, and the lessons learned from these success stories.

6. Multicultural Policies in Education

This section explores the role of multicultural policies in education. It discusses the importance of inclusive curricula, multicultural teacher training, and intercultural education in promoting cultural understanding and reducing discrimination. It also explores strategies for fostering multicultural awareness and celebrating diversity within educational institutions.

7. Future Directions for Multicultural Policies and Legislation

This section examines potential future directions for multicultural policies and legislation. It discusses the need for intersectionality, addressing multiple forms of discrimination, and recognizing the evolving nature of cultural identities. It also explores the role of technology, intercultural dialogue, and global cooperation in shaping multicultural policies in an interconnected world.

The concluding section summarizes the key points discussed in the article and emphasizes the importance of multicultural policies and legislation in fostering inclusion and social cohesion. It encourages governments, policymakers, and communities to continue developing and implementing effective strategies to promote cultural diversity, protect cultural rights, and strive for equitable, inclusive societies.

Promoting Social Integration

Building Trust and Unity in Diverse Societies

Social integrity refers to the harmonious coexistence and mutual respect among individuals and groups within a society. In today's globalized and diverse world, promoting social integrity is essential for fostering social cohesion, trust, and resilience. This article explores the concept of social integrity, its importance in creating inclusive and peaceful societies, and strategies for promoting it at various levels. It discusses the role of education, dialogue, community engagement, inclusive policies, and intercultural understanding in building social integrity. Additionally, it highlights successful initiatives and case studies that have effectively promoted social integrity and offers practical tips for individuals and communities to contribute to creating a more unified and harmonious society.

Keywords: social integrity, social cohesion, trust, unity, inclusivity, diversity, intercultural understanding

This introductory section defines social integrity and emphasizes its significance in contemporary societies. It highlights the importance of promoting social integrity for building inclusive communities, fostering trust, and enhancing social cohesion. The section also provides an overview of the structure of the article.

Understanding Social Integrity

This section explores the concept of social integrity in-depth. It defines social integrity as the harmonious coexistence, mutual respect, and trust among individuals and groups in a society. It discusses the key components of social integrity, including inclusive governance, respect for diversity, social justice, and shared values.

Importance of Social Integrity

This section delves into the importance of social integrity in creating inclusive and peaceful societies. It discusses how social integrity contributes to social cohesion, reduces social conflict, and enhances individual well-being. The section also explores the potential benefits of social integrity, such as increased trust, collaboration, and resilience.

Education for Social Integrity

This section focuses on the role of education in promoting social integrity. It discusses the importance of inclusive and equitable education systems that foster intercultural understanding, critical thinking, and empathy. The section highlights the need for inclusive curricula, teacher training, and school environments that promote diversity and respect for all.

Dialogue and Communication

This section explores the importance of dialogue and communication in promoting social integrity. It highlights the significance of open, respectful, and inclusive conversations to bridge differences, challenge stereotypes, and build understanding. The section also addresses the role of digital platforms and media literacy in supporting constructive dialogue and countering misinformation.

Community Engagement and Empowerment

This section emphasizes the role of community engagement and empowerment in promoting social integrity. It explores the importance of inclusive decision-making processes, community-led initiatives, and participatory approaches to address societal challenges. The section also highlights the need to foster social capital, volunteerism, and social activism to strengthen community ties and promote social integrity.

Inclusive Policies and Legislation

This section discusses the role of inclusive policies and legislation in fostering social integrity. It emphasizes the importance of anti-discrimination laws, inclusive governance structures, and social welfare policies that uplift marginalized populations. The section explores the need for equity-based approaches that address systemic inequalities and promote social justice.

Intercultural Understanding and Appreciation

This section focuses on the significance of intercultural understanding and appreciation in promoting social integrity. It discusses the importance of cultural awareness, empathy, and cross-cultural interactions to bridge differences and build connections. The section highlights the value of intercultural education, cultural exchange programs, and diverse social networks in fostering social integrity.

Case Studies: Successful Initiatives for Promoting Social Integrity

This section presents real-life case studies of successful initiatives that have promoted social integrity. It highlights programs, projects, or policies that have effectively built trust, fostered unity, and addressed social divisions. These case studies serve as examples and inspiration for individuals and communities seeking to promote social integrity in their contexts.

Practical Tips for Promoting Social Integrity

This section provides practical tips for individuals and communities to actively contribute to promoting social integrity. It offers guidance on embracing diversity, practicing active listening, fostering empathy, and engaging in respectful dialogue. The section also encourages individuals to get involved in community initiatives, advocate for inclusive policies, and support organizations working towards social integrity.

The concluding section summarizes the key points discussed in the article and emphasizes the importance of promoting social integrity for building inclusive and harmonious societies. It calls for collective action, highlighting the role of education, dialogue, community engagement, inclusive policies, and intercultural understanding in fostering social integrity. The section encourages individuals and communities to embrace these strategies and commit to creating a more unified and resilient society.

Case Studies of Inclusive Societies

Case Study 1: Canada's Multiculturalism Policy

Canada's Multiculturalism Policy, implemented in the 1970s, promotes the recognition and celebration of diverse cultural identities within society. The policy ensures equal rights, opportunities, and protections for all individuals, regardless of their cultural background, and encourages intercultural understanding and integration.

Case Study 2: New Zealand's Treaty of Waitangi

The Treaty of Waitangi in New Zealand is a historical agreement between the indigenous Māori people and the British Crown. It recognizes the equal rights and partnership between Māori and non-Māori in governing the country and addresses historical injustices. The treaty serves as a framework for ensuring inclusivity, cultural recognition, and participation in decision-making processes.

Case Study 3: Bhutan's Gross National Happiness

In Bhutan, the concept of Gross National Happiness (GNH) goes beyond traditional measures of development and emphasizes the holistic well-being of individuals and the environment. The GNH approach promotes inclusivity, cultural preservation, sustainable development, and equitable access to social services, aiming to create an inclusive and harmonious society.

Case Study 4: South Africa's Rainbow Nation

Following the dismantling of apartheid, South Africa adopted the concept of the "Rainbow Nation" to signify unity and diversity within the country. The Rainbow Nation approach promotes inclusivity, reconciliation, and the recognition of various cultural identities and languages to foster social cohesion and equality.

Case Study 5: Sweden's Gender-Equal Policies

Sweden has implemented a range of gender-equal policies, such as parental leave for both parents, gender-balanced boardroom quotas, and pay equity measures. These initiatives aim to create an inclusive society that promotes gender equality, reduces disparities, and fosters social integration.

Case Study 6: Norway's Social Welfare System

Norway's robust social welfare system provides comprehensive healthcare, education, and social support to its citizens, ensuring equal access to essential services. This inclusive approach to social welfare promotes social cohesion, reduces inequality, and creates a supportive environment for all individuals.

Case Study 7: India's Reservation Policy

India's reservation policy aims to address historical marginalization and promote social inclusivity by ensuring representation and opportunities for historically disadvantaged groups, such as Scheduled Castes, Scheduled Tribes, and Other Backward Classes. The policy seeks to bridge social gaps, promote equal access, and foster social integration.

Case Study 8: Germany's Welcoming Culture for Refugees

In response to the refugee crisis, Germany implemented a welcoming culture by providing support networks, access to education, and employment opportunities for refugees. This approach fosters social integration, cultural exchange, and inclusivity by promoting dialogue and understanding between native Germans and refugees.

Case Study 9: Costa Rica's Education System

Costa Rica's education system emphasizes inclusivity, quality education, and equal opportunities for all students, regardless of their socio-economic backgrounds. The system promotes intercultural understanding, respect for diversity, and equity in educational outcomes, leading to greater social integration and cohesion.

Case Study 10: Finland's Early Childhood Education

Finland's inclusive early childhood education system emphasizes equal opportunities, individualized support, and integration of children with diverse backgrounds and abilities. This approach promotes social integration, reduces disparities, and fosters a sense of belonging for all children within society.

Case Study 11: Malaysia's National Unity Policy

Malaysia's National Unity Policy aims to integrate the multicultural population by promoting intercultural understanding, language diversity, and respect for different ethnic and religious backgrounds. The policy encourages inclusive practices, cultural exchange, and equal opportunities for all citizens to foster a united society.

Case Study 12: Rwanda's Healing and Reconciliation Initiatives

Following the genocide in 1994, Rwanda implemented various healing and reconciliation initiatives to rebuild the social fabric of the country. These efforts include community dialogues, justice processes, and education programs that promote inclusivity, forgiveness, and coexistence, leading to a more unified and inclusive society.

Case Study 13: Australia's Indigenous Reconciliation Efforts

Australia's reconciliation efforts aim to address historical injustices and improve the well-being of Indigenous Australians. Initiatives include recognition of Indigenous cultures, land rights, and education programs that promote cultural awareness and understanding. These efforts contribute to the creation of a more inclusive and harmonious society.

Case Study 14: Singapore's Racial Harmony Policies

Singapore's racial harmony policies focus on fostering understanding, tolerance, and integration among its multicultural population. Through education, community programs, and legislation, Singapore promotes cultural diversity, equality, and inclusivity, resulting in a cohesive and harmonious society.

Case Study 15: United States Civil Rights Movement

The United States Civil Rights Movement, spanning several decades, fought for the equal rights and inclusion of marginalized groups, particularly African Americans. The movement led to legislative changes, such as the Civil Rights Act of 1964 and the Voting Rights Act of 1965, and fostered greater inclusivity, social integration, and equal opportunities for all citizens.

Cultural intelligence and diversity are essential in today's globalized world, enabling individuals, organizations, and societies to thrive and succeed. By understanding and appreciating different cultures, fostering inclusivity, and embracing diversity, we can build stronger relationships, enhance communication, and drive innovation. However, challenges such as stereotypes, biases, and resistance to change must be overcome through education, training, and inclusive policies. Organizations and educational institutions play a vital role in promoting cultural intelligence and diversity, while society as a whole benefits from social cohesion and harmony. By valuing and embracing our differences, we can create a more inclusive and equitable world for all.

Summary

"Integrating Ethics and Moral Development into Management Decision-Making Processes in Crucial Topics" is a book that explores the intersection of ethics, moral development, and decision-making in the field of management. The book delves into crucial topics that frequently arise in the corporate world, such as leadership, corporate social responsibility, sustainability, workplace ethics, and globalization.

The author argues that ethical considerations should be an integral part of decision-making processes in management, as they directly impact the well-being of stakeholders, the reputation of organizations, and the long-term sustainability of business practices. They emphasize the importance of both individual and organizational moral development in shaping ethical decision-making.

The book presents various theoretical frameworks and practical approaches that managers can use to integrate ethics into their decision-making processes. These include ethical decision-making models, moral development theories, and strategies for fostering an ethical organizational culture.

Furthermore, the authors discuss case studies and real-life examples to illustrate the ethical challenges faced by managers in different industries and contexts. They provide insights into how these challenges can be addressed through a moral and ethical lens, promoting ethical behavior and responsible decision-making.

Additionally, the book highlights the role of leadership in creating an ethical business environment. It emphasizes the importance of leaders who possess strong ethical values and act as role models for others. The authors stress the need for ethical leadership development programs that can help managers develop the necessary skills and knowledge to make ethical decisions and manage ethical dilemmas effectively.

Overall, "Integrating Ethics and Moral Development into Management Decision-Making Processes in Crucial Topics" serves as a comprehensive guide for managers, educators, and researchers interested in incorporating ethics and moral development into management practices. It offers practical tools, theoretical frameworks, and real-world examples to help organizations navigate the ethical complexities of modern business.

Chapter Seven

Ethics In the Technology Age

The technological age has brought about a multitude of ethical considerations that impact our lives and the world we live in. From data privacy and cybersecurity to artificial intelligence and automation, the ethical implications of technological advancements are more significant than ever before. As technology continues to advance, it is crucial to understand and address the ethical questions that arise, including issues of bias, fairness, and unintended consequences. The rapid pace of technological change presents challenges regarding ethical decision-making, as we must navigate the balance between innovation and the potential harm associated with certain technologies. Ethical frameworks in the technology age serve as a guide to ensure that the development and use of technology align with our values, promoting a more responsible and equitable digital future.

Ethics in the Technology Age

Ethics in the technological age have become increasingly important as technology continues to advance at an unprecedented rate. The rise of artificial intelligence, data mining, and social media has brought about ethical dilemmas that were previously unimaginable. In this section, we will explore 15 key aspects of ethics in the technology age.

Firstly, privacy is a major concern in the technological age. With the widespread collection and storage of personal data, individuals must grapple with the ethical implications of surveillance and the potential abuse of their private information. Companies and governments must prioritize protecting the privacy of individuals while utilizing data for legitimate purposes.

Privacy should be a major concern in the technological age due to several key reasons. Firstly, the widespread collection and storage of personal data by companies and governments poses significant ethical risks. With the advancement of technology, there is a growing ability to gather detailed information about individuals, including their online activities, preferences, and even biometric data. This accumulation of personal data raises concerns about surveillance and the potential abuse of information, leading to a potential infringement on individuals' privacy rights.

Secondly, unauthorized access to personal data poses security risks. As large amounts of personal information are stored digitally, there is an increased vulnerability to data breaches and cyberattacks. Hackers can gain access to sensitive personal information, such as financial records or medical histories, leading to identity theft, financial fraud, or other malicious activities. Thus, ensuring privacy is not only an ethical concern but also a matter of personal and financial security.

Thirdly, the erosion of privacy can have a chilling effect on freedom of expression and individuality. When individuals are aware that their actions and conversations are being monitored, they may self-censor themselves, fearing negative repercussions or judgment. This can stifle creativity, inhibit innovation, and hinder the growth of diverse opinions and ideas within society. Privacy provides a necessary space for individuals to freely express themselves, free from the fear of constant scrutiny.

Furthermore, privacy is essential to maintain trust between individuals, organizations, and governments. The voluntary sharing of personal information should be based on informed consent and trust. When organizations or governments fail to protect individuals' privacy, it undermines trust and can have long-lasting consequences for their reputation and relationships with their stakeholders. Strengthening privacy protections, therefore, becomes crucial to maintaining the trust necessary for a functioning society.

Additionally, without adequate privacy safeguards, personal data can be used for discriminatory practices. For instance, algorithmic bias in machine learning systems can perpetuate existing social inequalities, leading to unfair treatment based on race, gender, or other protected characteristics. This not only violates the principles of fairness and justice but also contributes to the perpetuation of systemic discrimination.

Moreover, privacy is not just an individual concern but also a collective one. Preserving privacy is vital for the functioning of democratic societies. It allows individuals to engage in political discourse, express dissenting opinions, and have a sense of autonomy over their personal lives. The absence of privacy can lead to a surveillance state, where individuals become subject to constant monitoring by the government, infringing upon fundamental democratic values.

Furthermore, the increasing reliance on technologies like artificial intelligence and automated decision-making systems raises ethical concerns about accountability and fairness. The algorithms used in these systems rely on vast amounts of personal data to make decisions that affect individuals' lives. Lack of privacy protections can lead to biased outcomes, perpetuating social inequalities and undermining the principles of fairness and justice.

Lastly, privacy is a fundamental human right recognized by international treaties and conventions. The Universal Declaration of Human Rights states that individuals have the right to privacy and protection against arbitrary interference with their privacy, family, home, or correspondence. Upholding privacy in the technological age is not only an ethical imperative but also a legal obligation to safeguard individual rights and freedoms.

Overall, privacy should be a major concern in the technology age due to the potential abuse of personal data, security risks, the chilling effect on freedom of expression, erosion of trust, potential for discriminatory practices, collective democratic values, accountability, and fairness in automated systems, and the recognition of privacy as a fundamental human right. Protecting privacy is essential for individuals, organizations, and governments to ensure just and ethically responsible use of technology and to maintain trust, security, and individual freedom.

Secondly, there is a growing concern over the ethical implications of artificial intelligence. The development of AI raises questions about responsibility and accountability. People worry about the potential loss of jobs due to automation and the ethical considerations surrounding machines making decisions that impact human lives.

Artificial Intelligence (AI) raises profound ethical implications and concerns. The rapid advancement in AI capabilities has led to a range of ethical considerations that need to be addressed. In this section, we will discuss nine key areas of concern.

Accountability and responsibility are major ethical concerns surrounding AI. As AI systems become increasingly autonomous, it becomes challenging to determine who should be held accountable if something goes wrong. The lack of clear responsibility could pose legal and ethical dilemmas, especially in situations where AI makes decisions that directly impact human lives.

In this present age, there are concerns regarding job displacement caused by AI automation. As AI technology continues to advance, there is a risk of significant job loss in various industries. Ethical questions arise about how to ensure a just and fair transition for those affected by automation and how to address the potential societal consequences of widespread unemployment.

AI raises ethical concerns about biased decision-making. AI systems are trained on large datasets, which can reflect human biases. If these biases are not addressed, AI systems may perpetuate unfair discrimination or reinforce existing social inequalities. It is crucial to develop mechanisms that detect and mitigate biases in AI algorithms to ensure fairness and unbiased decision-making.

The ethical implications of AI surveillance are significant. AI-powered surveillance systems can collect massive amounts of data, raising concerns about privacy and individual freedoms. Striking a balance between the benefits of surveillance for public safety and the protection of individual privacy rights remains a crucial ethical challenge.

Further, the impact of AI on personal autonomy and decision-making is another ethical concern. As AI systems gain the ability to make increasingly complex decisions, there is a risk of human decision-making being overridden or reduced to a passive role. Respecting individuals' autonomy and ensuring that humans retain control over AI systems becomes essential to prevent ethical infringements.

As we are already aware, AI poses ethical dilemmas concerning transparency and explainability. Many AI algorithms, such as deep neural networks, are considered black-box models, making it difficult to understand how they arrive at their decisions. From an ethical standpoint, AI systems must be transparent and explainable, enabling users to understand the reasoning and ensuring accountability.

AI warfare raises serious ethical concerns. The development of autonomous weapon systems, capable of making lethal decisions without human intervention, raises questions about the ethical use of these technologies in warfare. The potential loss of human discretion and accountability in military operations also poses significant risks and requires responsible international regulations.

On another side, AI also raises concerns regarding ethical hacking and cybersecurity. As AI algorithms become more advanced, there is a concern about the potential misuse of AI tools for malicious purposes, such as performing cyberattacks or deepfakes. Ethical guidelines need to be developed to prevent the misuse of AI technology and protect individuals and organizations from cyber threats.

Lastly, AI raises ethical dilemmas regarding the impact on inequality and social justice. Developments in AI technology could exacerbate existing inequalities, creating a digital divide where certain groups have limited access to AI-driven systems or are disproportionately affected by bias or discrimination. Ensuring equal access to AI technology and addressing biases are essential in promoting social justice and minimizing the negative consequences of AI.

In conclusion, the ethical implications of AI are vast and multifaceted. Accountability and responsibility, job displacement, biased decision-making, surveillance, personal autonomy, transparency, explainability, warfare, hacking, cybersecurity, and inequality and social justice are some of the key concerns surrounding AI. Addressing these ethical dilemmas requires a comprehensive approach involving policymakers, researchers, industry, and society, to ensure that AI is developed and deployed in a manner that aligns with ethical principles and safeguards human rights and well-being.

Thirdly, technology has made it easier than ever to spread misinformation and fake news. Individuals and organizations must be aware of the ethical implications of sharing false information and the responsibility to fact-check and verify sources before disseminating information.

Artificial Intelligence (AI) plays a significant role in the creation and dissemination of fake news, presenting complex ethical challenges in the technology age. The advancements in AI have made it easier for individuals and malicious actors to generate and spread misinformation at an unprecedented scale and speed.

AI allows for the creation of deepfakes, which are manipulated media content that can convincingly display individuals saying or doing things they never actually did. Deepfakes have the potential to deceive the public, manipulate opinions, and undermine trust in reliable information sources.

AI-powered algorithms can be used to generate automated content, such as news articles or social media posts. These algorithms can imitate human writing styles and generate vast amounts of fake news, making it difficult for users to discern between authentic and fabricated information.

In another vein, AI is employed in targeted misinformation campaigns. By analyzing user data, AI algorithms can identify vulnerable individuals who are more likely to fall for misleading narratives or conspiracy theories. Manipulative AI-driven campaigns can then be tailored to exploit these vulnerabilities, amplifying the spread of fake news.

AI-driven recommendation systems on social media platforms contribute to the diffusion of fake news. These algorithms often prioritize engagement over accuracy, promoting content that is polarizing or sensationalist. Consequently, fake news stories tend to gain more visibility and reach a wider audience, further perpetuating their influence.

AI technology enables the manipulation of online conversations and public opinion. Bots and trolls, often powered by AI algorithms, can disseminate falsehoods, create fake accounts, and amplify deceptive narratives, thus distorting the information landscape and swaying public opinion in favor of fake news.

Further, AI algorithms can exploit human cognitive biases, such as confirmation bias or echo chambers, to reinforce existing beliefs and filter out alternative viewpoints. This leads to the creation of "filter bubbles," where individuals are only exposed to information that aligns with their preconceived notions, making them more susceptible to fake news.

In the same manner, AI can be used to automate the process of spreading misinformation across multiple platforms and channels. By leveraging AI techniques, malicious actors can efficiently disseminate fake news to a wide audience, making it challenging to counteract and correct the false information.

Because it is sophisticated and unmatched, AI algorithms used by search engines often prioritize popular or clickbait content, regardless of its veracity. This can lead to misleading or false information being presented prominently in search results, further contributing to the dissemination of fake news.

In most cases, AI can impact the trustworthiness of news and media sources. With the rise of AI-generated content, it becomes increasingly difficult for users to discern between accurate and trustworthy sources of information and those that are fabricated or manipulated.

However, combating fake news with AI presents ethical questions as well. While AI can be utilized to detect and fact-check misinformation, there are concerns about the potential biases in AI models, automated content removal, and the potential for censorship.

In conclusion, AI technology has a profound impact on the creation and dissemination of fake news. Deepfakes, automated content generation, targeted misinformation campaigns, algorithmic recommendation systems, online manipulation, cognitive biases, automation, search algorithms, trustworthiness of sources, and combating fake news with AI are all areas where AI plays a critical role. Striking a balance between leveraging AI for combating misinformation while ensuring transparency, accuracy, and protection of individual rights is crucial in addressing the ethical challenges associated with the use of AI in the fake news ecosystem.

Moreover, the technology age has seen an increase in cybercrime. Ethical considerations arise when individuals or organizations engage in hacking, identity theft, or other forms of online criminal activity. It is crucial to establish clear guidelines and laws to deter such behavior and protect individuals from harm.

Fifth, ethical considerations also come into play with the rise of social media. Online platforms have become breeding grounds for cyberbullying, hate speech, and online harassment. Companies need to enact policies that promote ethical behavior, encourage respectful dialogue, and crack down on harmful content.

Social media platforms have leveraged Artificial Intelligence (AI) to enhance user experiences, improve content recommendations, and target advertising. However, while AI has brought numerous benefits to social media, it also poses significant dangers in the fourth estate, which refers to journalism and the media as an institution in a democratic society.

Firstly, AI algorithms enable social media platforms to personalize content and recommendations based on individual preferences and behaviors. This enhances user engagement and satisfaction, as individuals are exposed to content that aligns with their interests. AI algorithms can analyze user data to understand their preferences, click patterns, and engagement levels, tailoring content to keep users on the platform longer.

Secondly, AI plays a crucial role in content moderation on social media platforms. It helps identify and remove harmful or inappropriate content, such as hate speech, violence, or harassment, thus making social media spaces safer and more inclusive. AI algorithms can process large volumes of data and detect patterns of harmful behavior, enabling platforms to take proactive measures to address content violations.

Thirdly, AI-powered chatbots and virtual assistants have become commonplace on social media platforms. These AI-driven bots provide instant customer support, answer users' queries, and carry out basic tasks, thereby enhancing user experiences and improving the responsiveness of social media platforms.

Furthermore, AI enables sentiment analysis, which can provide insights into public opinions and trends. Social media platforms can gather and analyze vast amounts of user-generated content to understand societal sentiment, monitor public discussions, and identify emerging issues or topics of interest.

Fifth, AI enables targeted advertising on social media platforms. By leveraging AI algorithms, platforms can analyze user data to understand consumer preferences, behaviors, and demographics. This helps advertisers reach their intended audience more effectively, leading to higher conversion rates and increased revenue for social media platforms.

However, the dangers posed by AI in the fourth estate should not be overlooked. Firstly, the personalization of content through AI algorithms can create filter bubbles and echo chambers, where individuals are exposed only to information that confirms their existing beliefs. This can reinforce biases, limit diverse perspectives, and hinder critical thinking, thus impacting the quality and diversity of news consumption.

Secondly, the rise of AI-generated deepfakes poses a significant threat to the authenticity and credibility of information on social media platforms. Deepfakes can manipulate images, videos, or audio to create highly convincing fake content, making it difficult to distinguish between what is real and what is fabricated. This undermines the trust in digital content and can contribute to the spread of misinformation and fake news.

Thirdly, AI-driven algorithms used for content recommendations can inadvertently amplify misinformation and sensational content. Algorithms that prioritize engagement metrics may optimize for clickbait headlines or divisive content, potentially overshadowing reliable and fact-checked journalism. This can erode the credibility of news sources and undermine the public's trust in the media.

Furthermore, the reliance on AI algorithms for content moderation raises concerns about censorship and biased practices. Content moderation algorithms may employ AI techniques that inadvertently silence certain voices or disproportionately target specific communities, potentially hindering free speech and suppressing marginalized perspectives.

The opaque nature of AI algorithms can hinder transparency and accountability. Social media platforms often keep their AI algorithms proprietary, making it challenging for researchers, journalists, or the public to understand how content is prioritized, flagged, or filtered. This lack of transparency can undermine public trust and raise concerns about algorithmic accountability.

The opaque nature of AI algorithms refers to their lack of transparency, making it difficult for users and even developers to understand how these algorithms generate results or make decisions. This lack of transparency can hinder transparency and accountability in several ways:

1. Lack of understanding: The complex nature of AI algorithms often makes it challenging for humans to comprehend their inner workings. This lack of understanding can lead to distrust and skepticism about the decisions made by AI systems. Without understanding how decisions are reached, it becomes harder to hold these algorithms accountable for their actions.

2. Unexplained biases: AI algorithms can inadvertently incorporate biases present in the data they are trained on.

These biases may disproportionately impact certain groups, leading to unfair outcomes. However, without transparency in the algorithm's decision-making process, it becomes difficult to identify and rectify these biases. This lack of accountability can perpetuate systemic discrimination.

3. Limited explanations: Some AI algorithms provide outputs without any explanation or reasoning behind them. This lack of explanation makes it challenging for users or affected individuals to understand why a particular decision was made. For example, in the context of loan applications or criminal justice, decisions made by AI algorithms need to be justifiable and explainable.

4. Lack of scrutiny: Without transparency, it becomes difficult for independent auditors, regulators, or researchers to evaluate AI algorithms for fairness, reliability, or potential flaws. Algorithms that have significant societal impacts, such as those used in healthcare, finance, or law enforcement, should be subject to scrutiny, audits, and accountability processes. However, the opaque nature of AI can hinder this necessary scrutiny.

5. Responsibility diffusion: The lack of transparency can also lead to responsibility diffusion, where it becomes challenging to attribute accountability or liability for harmful outcomes of AI systems. When humans cannot easily identify how an AI decides, it becomes challenging to determine who should be held responsible for any negative consequences.

To address these concerns and improve transparency and accountability, efforts should focus on developing explainable and interpretable AI algorithms, conducting thorough audits and assessments, creating regulations or standards for transparency, and ensuring that diverse perspectives are involved in algorithm design and evaluation.

The monetization of social media through targeted advertising can create ethical dilemmas. AI algorithms that analyze user data for advertising purposes raise concerns about data privacy, informed consent, and the potential for manipulation or exploitation of user preferences.

The monetization of AI refers to the process of using artificial intelligence technologies to generate profits or economic benefits. While this monetization presents numerous opportunities, it also brings several ethical dilemmas:

1. Privacy concerns: AI implementations often rely on vast amounts of personal data. Monetizing AI can lead to the collection, storage, and utilization of sensitive user information, raising concerns about privacy infringement. Companies may face the temptation to prioritize monetization over protecting user privacy, leading to ethical dilemmas about the appropriate use and protection of personal data.

2. Manipulative practices: AI algorithms can be used to manipulate user behavior and preferences to maximize monetization. For instance, targeted advertising algorithms can subtly nudge individuals toward certain products or services. This raises concerns about the ethical implications of manipulating users' choices and autonomy solely for for-profit generation.

3. Algorithmic bias: The monetization of AI may inadvertently reinforce biases and discrimination present in the data on which these algorithms are trained. For example, biased algorithms may lead to discriminatory pricing, hiring, or loan practices. These unethical outcomes can be the result of prioritizing profit generation without sufficient consideration for fairness and equal treatment.

4. Unemployment and economic inequality: AI adoption may lead to job displacement and automation, potentially increasing unemployment rates in certain sectors. This can exacerbate economic inequalities and pose ethical dilemmas about the social consequences of prioritizing monetization over job security and the well-being of individuals affected by automation.

5. Lack of transparency: Monetization can incentivize companies to protect their AI algorithms as trade secrets or proprietary information. This lack of transparency hinders external scrutiny and oversight, making it difficult to identify and address potential ethical issues such as biases, discrimination, or negative impacts on society.

6. Ethical decision-making: Monetization priorities may tempt companies to cut corners or compromise ethical standards. For instance, deploying AI systems that are not properly tested for safety or neglecting the inclusion of ethical considerations in algorithm design. Balancing monetary gains with ethical principles can be challenging, and the pursuit of profit may eclipse important ethical considerations.

To address these ethical dilemmas, companies and policymakers must adopt principles of responsible AI development. This includes ensuring privacy protection, minimizing biases and discriminatory practices, promoting transparency and accountability, fostering public dialogue regarding the impact of AI monetization, and establishing regulations and guidelines that prioritize ethical considerations alongside economic benefits.

Looking at some other disadvantages of AI, the spread of misinformation and disinformation campaigns, amplified through AI-driven bots and algorithms, poses a significant danger to the Fourth Estate. Automated AI-driven campaigns can manipulate public opinion, distort facts, and undermine the credibility of reliable news sources.

The power of social media platforms in shaping public opinion and discourse raises concerns about their responsibility as arbiters of information. AI algorithms used for content curation and distribution can inadvertently prioritize sensationalism, clickbait, or viral content over accurate and reliable journalism, which can distort public priorities and values.

Lastly, the concentration of power among a few social media giants raises concerns about their influence on public discourse and democratic processes. The algorithms and AI systems owned by these platforms determine what content is seen by billions of people, and their decisions can have a profound impact, both intended and unintended, on society and politics.

However, AI has brought significant benefits to social media platforms, enhancing user experiences, and enabling targeted advertisements. Nevertheless, the use of AI in social media also poses dangers in the fourth estate. The personalization of content, deepfakes, filter bubbles, biased algorithms, lack of transparency and accountability, misuse of targeted advertising, spread of misinformation, and concentration of power in social media giants all contribute to the challenges and ethical considerations surrounding AI in the realm of the fourth estate. As AI continues to evolve, it is vital to address these risks to ensure well-informed, diverse, and reliable media in the digital age.

Another area of concern that needs to be addressed is the digital divide, which is also an ethical concern in the technological age. Access to technology and the internet is not equal worldwide, leading to disparities in education, job opportunities, and overall quality of life. Efforts must be made to bridge this divide and provide equal access to technology to avoid exacerbating existing inequalities.

The limited access to the internet in third-world countries poses a bias and hinders their development in several ways:

1. Information gap: The internet is a vast reservoir of information and knowledge. However, the lack of internet access in third-world countries widens the information gap between them and more developed regions. This gap can prevent individuals and communities from accessing crucial educational resources, job opportunities, health information, and advancements in various fields.

2. Economic disparities: Internet access plays a significant role in economic development. It enables businesses to expand their markets, connect with customers globally, and access online resources for research and innovation. Without internet access, businesses in third-world countries struggle to compete on a global scale, widening the economic disparities between them and more connected regions.

3. Access to education: The internet has transformed education by providing access to online courses, educational videos, and research materials. However, the lack of internet access in third-world countries restricts the educational opportunities available to their populations. This hampers the development of human capital, limiting their ability to innovate, compete, and drive economic growth.

4. Digital divide: The digital divide refers to the gap between those who have access to digital technologies and those who do not. The limited access to the internet in third-world countries deepens this divide, creating a significant disadvantage for their populations. This divide perpetuates inequality as those without Internet access are excluded from the benefits, opportunities, and resources that the Internet offers.

5. Social and political exclusion: The internet enables individuals to voice their opinions, participate in online communities, and engage in democratic processes. However, without internet access, individuals in third-world countries face social and political exclusion. This hampers their ability to participate in important decision-making processes, advocate for their rights, and engage in civic activities.

6. Technological advancements: Access to the internet is crucial for staying updated with the latest technological advancements and digital tools. It allows individuals and businesses to adapt and leverage new technologies for various purposes. Without access, third-world countries stay technologically behind, further delaying their development and creating a technology gap that is challenging to bridge.

To address these biases and promote development, efforts should focus on bridging the digital divide. This includes infrastructure development to expand Internet connectivity, reducing the cost of Internet services, investing in digital literacy programs, and promoting policies that prioritize universal access to the Internet. Additionally, international collaborations and partnerships can play a vital role in sharing technological resources, expertise, and knowledge to empower third-world countries and accelerate their development.

To bridge the disparities and promote development and equality in the use of the Internet in third-world countries, several measures can be taken:

1. Infrastructure development: Investing in the development of internet infrastructure, such as laying fiber optic cables, expanding broadband networks, and improving connectivity in rural areas, is crucial. Governments, private sector entities, and international organizations should collaborate to improve physical infrastructure and ensure reliable internet access across the country.

2. Affordability and accessibility: Making the Internet more affordable is essential to promote equitable access. Governments can work with service providers to reduce costs, introduce subsidies or tax incentives, and encourage competition in the telecommunications sector. Additionally, community-based access points like public libraries, community centers, and mobile internet units can be established to provide access in areas with limited connectivity.

3. Digital literacy and skills development: Providing training programs and promoting digital literacy is crucial to ensure that individuals can effectively and meaningfully utilize the internet. Governments, NGOs, and private organizations should invest in initiatives that offer training on internet usage, online safety, digital skills, and entrepreneurship. This will empower individuals to leverage the potential of the Internet for education, employment, and participation in the digital economy.

4. Content and language diversity: Promoting localized and relevant content is important to make the internet more accessible and meaningful for diverse populations. Developing and promoting online content in local languages, providing resources on topics relevant to specific communities, and encouraging local content creators can enhance the utility and engagement with the internet for all users.

5. Public-private partnerships: Collaboration between governments, private sector entities, NGOs, and international organizations is crucial for bridging the digital divide. Public-private partnerships can bring resources, expertise, and innovation to expand internet access inclusively. Governments should create an enabling environment through policies, regulations, and incentives to attract private sector investments in Internet infrastructure.

6. International collaboration: Global collaboration is essential to support the development of internet access in third-world countries. Initiatives like the United Nations' Sustainable Development Goals, World Bank projects, and international funding can help channel resources, technical support, and knowledge transfer to promote equitable access to the Internet. International organizations can also facilitate capacity-building and knowledge exchange programs to foster development in third-world countries.

By implementing these strategies, third-world countries can overcome the disparities, promote development, and ensure equality in the use of the Internet. The goal should be to create an inclusive digital society where all individuals can benefit from the vast resources and opportunities offered by the internet.

The ethical implications of big data cannot be ignored. The vast amount of data being collected raises concerns about consent, transparency, and data ownership. Companies and governments must develop ethical policies and regulations to ensure that data is used responsibly and in the best interest of individuals.

The advent of big data has brought numerous ethical implications that need to be carefully considered. Here are some vivid explanations of these ethical implications:

1. Privacy and consent: Big data analytics often involve collecting vast amounts of personal data from individuals. This raises concerns about privacy invasion and the potential misuse of sensitive information. Ethical implications arise when individuals are unaware of how their data is being collected, used, or shared, and when organizations do not obtain informed consent for data collection and analysis.

2. Data bias and discrimination: Big data sets can inadvertently contain biases and discriminatory patterns from historical data. When these biases are used to make decisions or predictions, they can perpetuate inequality and injustice. For example, biased algorithms used in hiring practices may perpetuate gender or racial discrimination. Ensuring fairness and equity in the processing of big data is an important ethical consideration.

3. Lack of transparency and accountability: Big data analytics often involve complex algorithms and machine learning models. The opacity of these techniques makes it difficult for individuals and even organizations to understand how decisions are made based on big data. This lack of transparency hampers accountability, making it challenging to identify and rectify errors, biases, or unethical practices present in algorithms or data analysis.

4. Data breaches and security risks: With the accumulation of large volumes of data, organizations face increased risks of data breaches and security breaches. Ethical implications arise when organizations fail to implement robust security measures to protect the personal information of individuals. Inadequate security practices can lead to unauthorized access, identity theft, or other forms of harm.

5. Consent and data ownership: Big data often contains information generated by individuals, but they may not have control over how their data is used or monetized. Ethical considerations arise when individuals' consent or

rights to their data are not adequately respected. The issue of data ownership and the need for consent becomes particularly important when data is used for purposes beyond what individuals originally consented to.

6. Surveillance and control: The analysis and utilization of big data can enable surveillance and monitoring of individuals on an unprecedented scale. This raises concerns about privacy, autonomy, and the potential for abuse of power. Ethical implications arise when big data is used to manipulate or control individuals, suppress dissent, or infringe upon personal freedoms.

To address these ethical implications, organizations and policymakers need to prioritize privacy protection, transparency, and accountability in big data practices. This includes implementing robust data governance and security measures, ensuring informed consent and individual rights are respected, regularly auditing algorithms for biases, and promoting open dialogue and regulation to address emerging ethical challenges.

Eighth, technology companies have also faced criticism for their labor practices. Manufacturing devices in low-wage countries and exploiting workers' rights raise ethical questions regarding fair-trade practices and workers' rights. Efforts must be made to hold companies accountable and improve working conditions for employees globally.

Large companies often face criticism for their labor practices due to several reasons:

1. Exploitation and low wages: One of the primary criticisms is that large companies, especially those operating in industries like retail, manufacturing, or agriculture, often pay low wages to their employees. This is seen as exploitative, as workers may struggle to meet basic needs or live in poverty despite their employment.

2. Poor working conditions and safety: Complaints often arise regarding poor working conditions and inadequate safety measures in large companies. This includes issues such as long working hours, lack of breaks, overcrowded or unsafe workplaces, insufficient protective equipment, and inadequate measures to address health and safety risks.

3. Labor rights violations: There are instances where large companies are accused of violating labor laws and regulations. This can involve denying workers their rights to freedom of association, unionization, and collective bargaining. Some companies have been accused of union-busting, retaliating against workers who organize, or employing illegal labor practices.

4. Precarious employment: Large companies are sometimes criticized for relying on temporary or contract labor instead of offering stable and secure employment. Contract or temporary workers may not receive the same benefits and protections as permanent employees, leading to concerns about the erosion of workers' rights and job insecurity.

5. Sweatshop labor and global supply chains: Large companies with global supply chains may face criticisms related to sweatshop labor. These companies may outsource production to factories or suppliers in developing countries that exploit workers by paying extremely low wages, subjecting them to dangerous working conditions, and violating labor rights.

6. Inequality and worker rights: Large companies that have significant disparities in wealth distribution between executives and workers often face criticism for perpetuating income inequality. The perception that workers' wages and benefits do not adequately reflect the company's financial success can lead to dissatisfaction and perceived inequity within the organization.

7. Lack of transparency and accountability: Some critics argue that large companies lack transparency regarding their labor practices. This includes allegations of concealing labor abuses, avoiding responsibility for suppliers' or contractors' actions, or failing to provide sufficient information on salaries, benefits, and working conditions to the public.

These criticisms highlight concerns about the treatment of workers, their rights, fair compensation, and ethical responsibilities within large companies. Addressing these criticisms often requires companies to improve their labor practices by ensuring fair wages, and safe working conditions, respecting labor rights, promoting transparency, and fostering meaningful dialogue with workers and labor advocacy groups.

Ninth, technology addiction has become a widespread issue, particularly with the advent of smartphones and social media. Ethical considerations concerning the impact of technology on mental health and social interactions are gaining attention. Individuals and society must reflect on the potential harm caused by excessive reliance on technology.

Humans have become increasingly addicted to technology, especially in the age of smartphones and social media, due to several reasons:

1. Instant gratification: Technology provides immediate access to information, entertainment, and social connections. Through smartphones and social media platforms, individuals can receive instant notifications, likes, and comments, which trigger feelings of pleasure and validation. This instant gratification reinforces the addictive behavior as users constantly seek the next "reward".

2. Social connection and validation: Smartphones and social media platforms offer a constant connection to others, allowing individuals to engage in social interactions at any time and from anywhere. The need for social connection and validation is deeply ingrained in human psychology, making the availability of social media an attractive means to seek social approval, increase self-esteem, and reduce feelings of loneliness.

3. FOMO (Fear of Missing Out): Social media platforms showcase curated and often idealized versions of others' lives, creating a fear of missing out on experiences and opportunities. The constant stream of updates, photos, and events can lead individuals to develop a fear of being left out, further motivating them to stay engaged with technology to avoid feeling isolated or disconnected.

4. Dopamine release: Engaging with technology, such as receiving notifications, likes, or messages, triggers the release of dopamine in the brain. Dopamine is a neurotransmitter associated with pleasure and reward sensations. This biochemical process reinforces addictive behavior, leading individuals to constantly seek out technology for dopamine-induced gratification.

5. Design principles and psychological manipulation: Tech companies employ design principles that exploit human psychology to make their products addictive. Features like infinite scrolling, autoplay videos, and personalized recommendations keep users engaged for longer periods, increasing the likelihood of addiction. Additionally, push notifications and "red dots" create a sense of urgency, prompting users to constantly check their devices.

6. Escapism and coping mechanisms: Technology can serve as an escape from reality or serve as a coping mechanism for stress, anxiety, boredom, or loneliness. It offers a distraction from real-life problems and challenges, providing a virtual world where individuals can seek entertainment, validation, and a sense of control.

The addictive nature of technology usage can have detrimental effects on mental health, interpersonal relationships, productivity, and overall well-being. Individuals need to be aware of their technology usage, set boundaries, and practice mindful and responsible engagement. Moreover, tech companies and designers have a responsibility to develop ethical design practices that prioritize user well-being over maximizing engagement and addiction.

Tenth, the ethical considerations of autonomous vehicles are a hot topic. Questions arise about the decision-making algorithms in self-driving cars and the prioritization of human lives in hazardous situations. Striking a balance between minimizing accidents and protecting human life is a complex ethical challenge.

Ethical considerations surrounding autonomous vehicles are indeed a significant and ongoing topic in the field of AI. Here are some key ethical considerations associated with autonomous vehicles:

1. Safety and risk assessment: Autonomous vehicles must be programmed to make split-second decisions in situations where accidents are unavoidable. Ethical questions arise regarding how these vehicles should prioritize the safety of occupants versus the safety of other road users (such as pedestrians or cyclists). Determining the acceptable level of risk in different scenarios and the factors influencing these decisions is a complex ethical challenge.

2. Accountability and liability: As autonomous vehicles take over certain driving tasks, determining liability in the event of an accident becomes more complex. Ethical questions arise regarding who should be held responsible – the vehicle manufacturer, the software developer, or the human operator (if there is one). Establishing a framework for assigning accountability and liability in autonomous vehicle accidents is a significant ethical consideration.

3. Transparency and decision-making: Autonomous vehicles rely on complex algorithms and machine learning models to make decisions on the road. Ensuring transparency in these algorithms and understanding how decisions are made is crucial. Ethical considerations arise regarding the need for explainable AI and the ability to audit and understand the decision-making processes of autonomous vehicles.

4. Privacy and data collection: Autonomous vehicles often collect vast amounts of data about their surroundings, including location information, video feeds, and sensor data. Managing this data while respecting privacy rights and avoiding potential misuse is an ethical challenge. Questions arise regarding the ownership, storage, access, and potential commercialization of this data.

5. Ethical dilemmas and moral programming: Autonomous vehicles may face complex ethical dilemmas on the road, such as choosing between prioritizing the safety of occupants or avoiding harm to others. Programming vehicles with predefined ethical rules or principles raises significant ethical questions about whose values and moral judgments should shape these decisions.

6. Social impact and job displacement: Autonomous vehicles have the potential to disrupt the transportation industry, leading to job displacement for truck drivers, taxi drivers, and others. Considering the social and economic consequences, ensuring a just transition for workers affected by automation is an important ethical consideration.

Addressing these ethical considerations requires interdisciplinary collaboration among AI researchers, policymakers, ethicists, and society at large. Developing robust regulations, standards, and guidelines for autonomous vehicles can help minimize risks, ensure accountability, and promote responsible deployment. Public engagement, open dialogue, and transparency in the decision-making processes surrounding the development, deployment, and use of autonomous vehicles are crucial to ensure ethical considerations are considered appropriately.

Eleventh, intellectual property rights are a crucial ethical issue in the technological age. The ease of sharing digital content raises concerns about copyright infringement and the protection of creators' rights. Companies need to find a balance between protecting intellectual property and fostering innovation and creativity.

Intellectual property (IP) in the technology age refers to the legal protection of innovative ideas, creations, and original works in the realm of technology. It encompasses a wide range of intangible assets, including patents, copyrights, trademarks, and trade secrets. The significance of intellectual property has increased dramatically in the technological age due to rapid advancements and the digital nature of creations. Here's an explanation of intellectual property in the context of the technology age:

1. Patents: Patents provide exclusive rights over inventions and technical innovations. In the technology age, patents are particularly crucial as they protect novel ideas and technological advancements. This includes

inventions like software algorithms, hardware designs, and technological processes. Patents promote innovation by incentivizing inventors and companies to invest in research and development while ensuring they have a limited period of exclusivity to exploit their inventions commercially.

2. Copyrights: Copyright protection safeguards original creative works, including literary, musical, artistic, and software works. In the technology age, copyrights are especially relevant to digital content, such as software code, websites, music, videos, and digital art. Copyrights give creators the exclusive rights to reproduce, distribute, and publicly display their works, ensuring they can control commercial exploitation and earn recognition for their creations.

3. Trademarks: Trademarks protect brand names, logos, slogans, and distinctive signs that identify products or services. In the technology age, trademarks play a crucial role in distinguishing companies and their offerings in the highly competitive digital marketplace. Brands invest in building and protecting their trademarks to establish brand recognition, consumer trust, and to prevent consumer confusion.

4. Trade secrets: Trade secrets encompass confidential and valuable information, which provides a competitive advantage to businesses. In the technology age, trade secrets primarily apply to proprietary technology, algorithms, manufacturing processes, formulas, customer lists, and other business-critical information. Protecting trade secrets involves implementing strict security measures to ensure unauthorized access or disclosure. Legal remedies can be pursued against those who unlawfully acquire or use trade secrets.

5. Open source and Creative Commons: The technology age has also given rise to alternative license models such as the open-source movement and Creative Commons licenses. Open source promotes collaborative software development by providing free access to source code and encouraging modification and redistribution. Creative Commons licenses allow creators to specify the permitted uses of their works more flexibly, promoting the sharing and reuse of creative content while still retaining some rights.

In summary, intellectual property protection is crucial in the technological age to encourage innovation, reward creators, and facilitate the growth of technology-driven sectors. Balancing the need for IP protection with the principles of open innovation and access to knowledge remains an ongoing challenge. Striking the right balance supports technological advancements while promoting competition, collaboration, and the public interest.

Twelfth, the role of technology giants in politics has come under scrutiny. The influence of tech companies on elections, democracy, and the spread of information has raised ethical concerns about their responsibility to ensure fair and democratic processes.

The role of technology giants in politics has come under scrutiny for several reasons:

1. Political influence: Technology giants have amassed significant power and influence due to their size, user base, and control over online platforms. Concerns have been raised about their ability to shape political discourse, influence public opinion, and potentially manipulate elections through their algorithms, content moderation policies, and data mining practices.

2. Spread of misinformation and fake news: Technology giants have faced criticism for their role in enabling the spread of misinformation and fake news. The algorithms and recommendation systems used by platforms can unintentionally amplify false information and conspiracy theories, leading to the dissemination of misleading content and the erosion of public trust in reliable sources of information.

3. Content moderation and censorship: Content moderation decisions made by technology giants have been scrutinized for their potential biases and lack of transparency. The removal or suppression of certain political

content, user bans, and algorithmic biases have raised concerns about political bias and restrictions on freedom of speech.

4. Privacy and data breaches: Technology giants collect vast amounts of personal data, and their handling of this data has been a subject of scrutiny. Data breaches, unauthorized data sharing, and questionable data practices have raised concerns about privacy rights and the potential misuse of personal information for political purposes.

5. Anti-competitive practices and market power: The dominance of technology giants in the market has raised concerns about anti-competitive practices and stifling innovation. Their ability to acquire or replicate smaller competitors, control access to markets, and set competitive standards has led to calls for increased regulation and antitrust actions.

6. Lobbying and political influence: The role of technology giants in lobbying and political contributions has attracted attention. Concerns have been raised about the extent of their influence on policymaking, regulatory frameworks, and their ability to shape legislation in their favor.

In response to these concerns, there have been calls for increased regulation of technology giants, transparency in their algorithms and content moderation practices, protection of user privacy, and efforts to combat misinformation. Governments and regulatory bodies are increasingly scrutinizing the role of technology giants in politics and considering measures to mitigate their potential negative effects on democracy, competition, and privacy.

Thirteenth, the ethical implications of biotechnology and genetic engineering need to be addressed. Technologies like CRISPR raise questions about the potential for altering human genes and the consequences that come with it. The ethical principles of autonomy, justice, and beneficence should guide decision-making in these areas.

The ethical implications of biotechnology and genetic engineering can be understood plainly in the following ways:

1. Human enhancement: Biotechnology and genetic engineering have the potential to manipulate human traits and characteristics, such as intelligence, physical appearance, and athletic abilities. Ethical questions arise regarding the ideal scope and limits of human enhancement. Concerns include the potential for creating unequal access to enhancements, undermining natural diversity, and the potential long-term consequences on individuals and society.

2. Genetic modification and consent: Altering the genetic makeup of organisms raises ethical questions about informed consent. When it comes to human genetic modification, ensuring that individuals or their guardians fully understand the risks, potential benefits, and long-term implications is crucial. It is important to consider the ethical implications of modifying human genes without proper consent or the potential for coercion.

3. Equity and access: The availability and affordability of biotechnology and genetic engineering interventions create ethical concerns related to equitable access. Individuals and communities with limited financial resources may be disadvantaged, leading to further socioeconomic inequalities and injustices. Ethical considerations must address the potential for disparities in access to genetic therapies, enhancements, or reproductive technologies.

4. Genetic discrimination: Genetic information obtained through biotechnology can be used to discriminate against individuals based on their genetic predispositions or potential health risks. This raises concerns about privacy, protection against discrimination, and the stigmatization of individuals based on their genetic profiles. Ensuring that individuals' genetic information remains confidential and protected is an ethical consideration.

5. Environmental impact: Biotechnology and genetic engineering can have unintended consequences on ecosystems and biodiversity. Introducing genetically modified organisms into the environment may disrupt natural ecosystems

or lead to unintended ecological changes. Ethical considerations include thoughtful risk assessments and environmental monitoring to minimize the potential for harm to ecosystems.

6. Moral and religious concerns: Biotechnological interventions can challenge religious or moral beliefs regarding the sanctity of life, tampering with nature, or altering the natural course of reproduction. Ethical debates often arise when biotechnology conflicts with deeply held values or beliefs, highlighting the importance of considering diverse perspectives and respecting moral and religious autonomy.

Addressing the ethical implications of biotechnology and genetic engineering requires careful consideration of human rights, social justice, environmental sustainability, informed consent, privacy, and a broad range of ethical perspectives. Open dialogue, public participation, and robust ethical frameworks are necessary to navigate these complex issues and ensure responsible, equitable, and socially beneficial development and application of biotechnology.

Fourteenth, the impact of technology on the environment is an ethical issue that cannot be overlooked. The production, disposal, and energy consumption of electronic devices contributes to e-waste and carbon emissions. Companies must prioritize sustainable practices and develop more environmentally friendly technologies.

The ethical impacts of technology on the environment are significant and can be understood in the following ways:

1. Environmental degradation: Technology plays a substantial role in causing environmental degradation through various means such as increased resource extraction, pollution from manufacturing processes, and the generation of electronic waste. Ethical considerations arise regarding the responsibility of technology developers, manufacturers, and consumers to minimize the environmental impact of their products and practices.

2. Climate change: Technology contributes to greenhouse gas emissions and global climate change. The use of fossil fuels in energy production, industrial processes, transportation, and the manufacturing of technology products significantly contributes to carbon emissions. Ethical implications arise regarding the need for transitioning to cleaner and sustainable energy sources, reducing carbon footprints, and mitigating the impacts of climate change.

3. Electronic waste: The rapid advancement of technology has led to a significant increase in electronic waste (e-waste). Discarded devices and components pose hazards to the environment due to toxic materials, such as lead, mercury, and cadmium. Ethical considerations involve the responsible disposal, recycling, and management of e-waste to minimize environmental contamination and ensure worker safety.

4. Resource depletion: The production and consumption of technology relies on the extraction of various natural resources, including rare earth metals and minerals. The extraction and depletion of these resources raises ethical concerns regarding the long-term sustainability of resource usage. Responsible sourcing, efficient use of materials, and exploring sustainable alternatives are necessary to minimize the environmental impact and ensure the equitable distribution of resources.

5. Biodiversity and ecosystem disruption: Technological activities, such as land clearance for infrastructure development or mining, can lead to habitat destruction and loss of biodiversity. The ethical implications relate to the protection and preservation of ecosystems, the conservation of biodiversity, and the prevention of species extinction caused by technology-related activities.

6. Environmental justice: Technology often has inequitable impacts on marginalized communities. The location of industrial facilities, waste disposal sites, and technological infrastructure can disproportionately affect low-

income and minority populations. Ethical considerations revolve around ensuring equal protection from environmental harm and promoting environmental justice for all communities, regardless of their socioeconomic status or race.

Addressing the ethical impacts of technology on the environment requires collective action, sustainable practices, and policy interventions. It involves adopting technologies that minimize environmental harm, promoting responsible consumption and production, conserving resources, and prioritizing the equitable distribution of environmental benefits and burdens. Ethical decision-making and transparency about the environmental impact of technology are crucial in creating a more sustainable and environmentally responsible future.

Finally, the ethical considerations of using technology in warfare and surveillance must not be neglected. The development of drones, drones, and other advanced weaponry raises questions about the ethical use of such technologies and the potential for abuse.

In conclusion, ethics in the technological age play a pivotal role in shaping the future. Privacy, artificial intelligence, misinformation, cybercrime, social media, digital divide, big data, labor practices, technology addiction, autonomous vehicles, intellectual property, tech company influence, biotechnology, environmental impact, and warfare ethics are just a few examples of the many ethical challenges we face in this ever-advancing technological landscape. Adhering to ethical principles is crucial in ensuring the responsible and beneficial use of technology for the betterment of society.

Chapter Eight

Managerial Implications of Emerging Technologies

Analyzing the impact of artificial intelligence, blockchain, Internet of Things, and other emerging technologies on general management practices

Managerial Implications of Emerging Technologies

The rapid advancement of technology has transformed the way businesses operate in recent years. Emerging technologies such as artificial intelligence (AI), blockchain, cloud computing, and the Internet of Things (IoT) have created new opportunities and challenges for managers across industries. This article explores the managerial implications of these emerging technologies, discussing their potential benefits, and risks, and how managers can effectively leverage them to drive innovation and success.

1. Artificial Intelligence (AI)

AI is revolutionizing various aspects of business operations, from customer service to supply chain management. Managers need to understand the potential benefits and limitations of AI to make informed decisions about implementation. AI can automate repetitive tasks, improve data analysis, enhance customer experience, and enable predictive maintenance. However, managers must also address concerns related to data privacy, ethics, and the potential for job displacement.

Artificial Intelligence (AI) has become a significant technological advancement that has the potential to revolutionize various industries and processes. One area where AI can significantly impact is managerial decision-making processes. This essay aims to explore the role of AI in enhancing managerial decision-making, its advantages and limitations, and the ethical considerations associated with the use of AI in managerial decision-making.

Managerial decision-making is a critical aspect of organizational success. Managers are responsible for making informed decisions that can impact the organization's efficiency, profitability, and competitiveness. However, decision-making is complex and challenging, often involving large amounts of data, multiple variables, and unpredictable outcomes. Traditional decision-making processes heavily rely on human judgment and intuition, which may not always yield the best results due to cognitive limitations and biases.

This is where AI can play a crucial role. AI encompasses various technologies such as machine learning, natural language processing, and expert systems, which enable computers to analyze data, learn patterns, and make predictions. By leveraging AI capabilities, managers can access vast amounts of data, gain insights, and make data-driven decisions at a much faster pace.

One of the significant benefits of AI in managerial decision-making is its ability to process and analyze massive quantities of data. With the advent of big data, organizations are flooded with vast amounts of information. Traditional decision-making processes struggle to handle this data overload effectively. AI algorithms can quickly process and analyze data from diverse sources, identifying patterns, correlations, and trends that may not be apparent to human decision-makers. This allows managers to make decisions based on comprehensive and up-to-date information, leading to improved outcomes.

Another advantage of AI is its unbiased and objective nature. Human decision-makers are susceptible to cognitive biases, such as confirmation bias, anchoring bias, or overconfidence bias, which can skew their judgment. AI algorithms, on the other hand, do not have these inherent biases and can provide managers with more impartial analysis and recommendations. This helps in achieving more rational and objective decision-making processes.

Furthermore, AI can enhance decision-making by enabling automation and streamlining routine tasks. Mundane and repetitive tasks, such as data entry, data analysis, and report generation, can be delegated to AI systems. This frees up managers' time and allows them to focus on more strategic and complex decision-making activities. Moreover, AI can provide real-time monitoring of organizational processes and identify anomalies or areas that require attention. Managers can then prioritize their efforts and take proactive measures to address potential issues, improving organizational performance and efficiency.

Despite the numerous benefits, AI is not without its limitations. One of the challenges faced by AI systems is the lack of interpretability. AI algorithms often generate accurate predictions or recommendations, but they do not provide explanations for the underlying logic. This lack of transparency can be problematic, especially in decision-making processes that require justification or involve legal or ethical considerations. Managers may find it challenging to trust and rely on AI recommendations without understanding the rationale behind them.

Additionally, the quality of AI decisions heavily depends on the quality and reliability of the data used. AI algorithms are only as good as the data they are trained on. If the data is flawed, incomplete, or biased, it can lead to erroneous predictions or reinforce existing biases. Managers need to ensure that the data collected and used for AI decision-making processes are accurate, representative, and unbiased. Moreover, AI may struggle with handling uncertainty, complexity, or novel situations that fall outside the training data. The absence of human understanding and contextual knowledge can limit the ability of AI systems to make informed decisions in such scenarios.

Ethical considerations are also crucial when integrating AI into managerial decision-making. AI algorithms can inadvertently perpetuate biases present in the data. If historical data contains biases or discriminatory patterns, AI systems may learn and reproduce these biases, leading to biased decision-making outcomes. For example, if an AI system is used for recruitment processes and trained on historical data that is biased toward certain demographics, it may perpetuate discrimination in hiring practices. Managers must be vigilant in monitoring and addressing these ethical concerns to ensure fair and unbiased decision-making.

Furthermore, the use of AI raises concerns about privacy and data security. AI systems rely on access to large amounts of data, which can include sensitive and personal information. Organizations must establish robust data protection measures and ensure compliance with relevant privacy regulations to maintain the trust of stakeholders. Managers need to balance the benefits of AI-enabled decision-making with the ethical and legal responsibilities associated with data privacy and security.

In conclusion, AI has the potential to revolutionize managerial decision-making processes by providing managers with data-driven insights, automating routine tasks, and enabling real-time monitoring. However, it is crucial to be aware of the limitations and ethical considerations associated with AI. Maintaining human oversight, ensuring data quality, and interpretability, and addressing biases are essential to harness the potential of AI while maintaining ethical and fair decision-making processes. The successful integration of AI into managerial decision-making can lead to improved outcomes, increased efficiency, and a competitive advantage for organizations.

2. Blockchain Technology

Blockchain technology offers secure and transparent transactions, eliminating the need for intermediaries. Managers should consider the potential applications of blockchain in areas such as supply chain management, smart contracts, and intellectual property protection. Implementing blockchain requires collaboration among stakeholders, addressing regulatory challenges, and ensuring the robustness and scalability of the technology.

Blockchain Technologies: Revolutionizing Industries

Blockchain technologies have emerged as a groundbreaking innovation, transforming various industries worldwide. Initially known as the underlying technology for Bitcoin, blockchain has now evolved into a powerful tool with applications far beyond cryptocurrencies. This article aims to provide an in-depth exploration of blockchain technologies, covering their fundamental principles, potential applications, advantages, challenges, and the impact they have across different sectors.

1. Blockchain Fundamentals:

Definition and Concept:

Blockchain is a distributed, decentralized ledger technology that records transactions across multiple computers in a verifiable and tamper-proof manner. It allows participants to create a chain of blocks, each containing a batch of transactions, forming an immutable history.

Key Components:

- Blocks: Containers that store transactional data and cryptographic hashes.
- Cryptographic Hash: A mathematical function ensuring data integrity and security.
- Distributed Ledger: A network of interconnected computers called nodes that maintain the blockchain.
- Consensus Mechanism: A protocol ensuring agreement among nodes on the validity of transactions.

Distributed Ledger Technology (DLT):

Blockchain is a type of Distributed Ledger Technology (DLT) that eliminates the need for intermediaries and enables direct peer-to-peer interactions. DLT offers transparency, immutability, security, and decentralization, making it an ideal solution for various industries.

2. Blockchain Applications:

Supply Chain Management:

Blockchain allows end-to-end traceability and transparency in supply chains, revolutionizing industries like food, pharmaceuticals, and luxury goods. It helps verify the authenticity and origin of products, eliminating fraud, and counterfeiting, and ensuring compliance with quality standards and regulations.

Finance and Banking:

Blockchain has disrupted the finance industry, revolutionizing payments, remittances, and cross-border transactions. With decentralization and smart contracts, it accelerates settlement times, reduces costs, enhances security, and improves financial inclusion to unbanked populations.

Healthcare:

Blockchain ensures secure storage and sharing of medical records, enabling interoperability, continuity of care, and personalized treatments. It benefits patients by safeguarding their data privacy, enhancing clinical trials, and streamlining healthcare administration.

Intellectual Property:

Blockchain provides a secure platform for registering and managing intellectual property rights, including patents, trademarks, and copyrights. It eliminates issues related to ownership disputes, counterfeiting, and infringement while enabling creators to monetize their creations.

Voting Systems:

Blockchain offers transparent, secure, and decentralized voting systems. Creating an immutable and auditable record of votes enhances trust, eliminates fraudulent practices, and improves accessibility for remote voters.

3. Advantages of Blockchain:

Security:

Blockchain leverages cryptographic techniques, making it highly secure and resistant to tampering, fraud, and cyber-attacks. Its decentralized nature reduces the vulnerability associated with centralized systems.

Transparency:

The transparency of blockchain allows for increased trust and accountability. Public blockchains offer open access to anyone, while private blockchains provide controlled access among a set of participants, depending on their roles and permissions.

The transparency of blockchain has emerged as a key characteristic that distinguishes it from traditional centralized systems. Blockchain is a decentralized ledger technology that enables the storage and validation of transactions across a network of computers. It achieves transparency through its inherent design principles, including immutability, consensus mechanisms, and public accessibility.

Immutability is one of the fundamental aspects of blockchain technology that enhances transparency. Once a transaction or data is recorded on a blockchain, it becomes nearly impossible to alter or delete. Each transaction is linked to a previous one, forming a chain of blocks that are secured using cryptographic algorithms. This immutability ensures that the historical data cannot be tampered with, providing transparency and accountability. Any attempt to change the historical records would require an enormous amount of computational power and would be easily detected by the network participants. Immutability therefore enables transparency by maintaining an accurate and unchangeable record of all transactions.

Consensus mechanisms, such as proof-of-work (PoW) and proof-of-stake (PoS), also contribute to the transparency of blockchain. These mechanisms facilitate agreement among network participants regarding the validity of transactions and the order in which they are recorded. In PoW, participants compete to solve complex mathematical puzzles, and the winner gets the right to add a new block to the chain. This consensus process involves extensive computation and ensures that the majority of network participants agree on the legitimacy of transactions. PoS, on the other hand, selects the validator of the next block based on its stake in the network. Both mechanisms ensure that the network operates fairly and transparently, as individual participants cannot unilaterally manipulate the ledger.

Public accessibility is another factor that enhances the transparency of blockchain technology. The blockchain is a distributed ledger that is replicated and stored across multiple computers, known as nodes, in the network. All participants can access and view the entire history of transactions recorded on the blockchain. This transparency allows anyone to verify the integrity of the transactions and ensures that no single entity has control over the data. It also enables real-time auditing, making it easier to detect any fraudulent activities. The public nature of blockchain encourages trust among participants and promotes transparency by allowing for independent verification of transactions.

The transparency of blockchain technology has numerous applications across various industries. In the financial sector, blockchain enables transparent and auditable transactions, reducing the risk of fraud and improving regulatory compliance. By providing a transparent record of all transactions, blockchain technology allows regulators to monitor financial activities more efficiently and detect any potential anomalies. This transparency also helps to build trust between financial institutions and their clients, as it eliminates the need for intermediaries and ensures that transactions are executed as agreed upon.

Blockchain technology has also found applications in supply chain management, where transparency is crucial. Blockchain can provide a clear and immutable record of the entire supply chain, from the source of raw materials to the final product delivered to the customer. This transparency allows for traceability and accountability, ensuring that products are sourced ethically and meet the required quality standards. Consumers can verify the authenticity and origin of products, reducing the risk of counterfeit goods entering the market. By increasing transparency, blockchain technology contributes to improved efficiency, reduced costs, and enhanced consumer confidence in supply chain processes.

The transparency of blockchain is also relevant in the healthcare industry. Blockchain can securely store and share patient data, ensuring that healthcare providers have access to accurate and up-to-date medical records. Patients can have more control over their health information by granting or revoking access to their records. This transparency promotes interoperability among healthcare providers, reduces administrative costs, and improves the overall quality of patient care.

While the transparency of blockchain offers numerous benefits, it also raises concerns regarding privacy and confidentiality. Since the blockchain is a publicly accessible ledger, all transactions are stored permanently, potentially revealing sensitive information. To address these concerns, several blockchain projects have been exploring privacy-enhancing techniques, such as zero-knowledge proofs and ring signatures, that allow for the encryption of transaction data while maintaining the integrity and transparency of the blockchain. These privacy-preserving mechanisms aim to strike a balance between transparency and confidentiality, ensuring that blockchain technology can be applied in domains where privacy is essential, such as healthcare and identity management.

In conclusion, the transparency of blockchain technology is a fundamental characteristic that sets it apart from traditional centralized systems. Immutability, consensus mechanisms, and public accessibility contribute to this transparency by ensuring data integrity, agreement among network participants, and open access to transaction history. This transparency has wide-ranging applications, including finance, supply chain management, and healthcare. However, concerns regarding privacy and confidentiality require innovative solutions to maintain a balance between transparency and data protection. Overall, blockchain's transparency offers immense value by promoting accountability, trust, and efficiency across various sectors.

Efficiency and Cost Reduction:

Blockchain eliminates intermediaries, reducing transaction costs, and improving efficiency by automating processes. Smart contracts, self-executing agreements embedded in the blockchain, further enhance efficiency by automating actions based on predefined conditions.

Efficiency and cost reduction are two critical aspects that drive businesses to optimize their operations and achieve sustainable growth. In today's competitive global landscape, organizations are constantly seeking ways to streamline processes, improve productivity, and minimize expenses. By focusing on efficiency and cost reduction, companies can enhance their profitability, increase their competitive advantage, and deliver greater value to their customers. This article will delve into the importance of efficiency and cost reduction, explore the strategies and technologies that businesses can adopt to achieve these goals, and examine some real-world examples of successful implementation.

Importance of Efficiency:

Efficiency refers to the ability to accomplish tasks or produce desired outcomes with optimal use of resources, such as time, labor, and capital. It involves streamlining processes, eliminating waste, and maximizing productivity. One of the primary reasons why efficiency is crucial for businesses is that it directly impacts their bottom line. By operating more efficiently, organizations can reduce costs, increase output, and generate higher profits. Efficient processes also lead to improved customer satisfaction, as they enable faster delivery times, increased product quality, and better service experiences.

Efficiency is particularly important in competitive industries, where even small gains can differentiate one company from another. By maximizing efficiency, organizations can enhance their operational agility, respond to customer demands more effectively, and exploit market opportunities. Moreover, efficient operations allow businesses to stay nimble and adapt quickly to changing market conditions, giving them a significant advantage over slower and less efficient competitors.

Cost Reduction Strategies:

Cost reduction is the process of identifying and implementing strategies to minimize expenses and optimize resource allocation. There are several strategies that businesses can adopt to achieve cost reduction:

1. Process Optimization: Organizations can analyze their existing processes and identify areas of inefficiency or waste. By eliminating redundant tasks, standardizing procedures, and automating manual processes, companies can streamline operations and reduce costs. Process optimization can involve lean methodologies, Six Sigma techniques, or continuous improvement initiatives to drive efficiency and eliminate bottlenecks.

2. Supply Chain Management: Efficient supply chain management can significantly contribute to cost reduction. Companies can collaborate with suppliers to negotiate better prices, optimize inventory levels, and reduce lead times. Implementing just-in-time (JIT) inventory management, adopting vendor-managed inventory (VMI) systems, or using advanced analytics for demand forecasting can help optimize the supply chain and minimize costs associated with procurement and inventory holding.

3. Outsourcing: Outsourcing certain non-core functions or business processes can be a viable strategy to reduce costs. By leveraging external expertise and economies of scale, companies can benefit from cost savings while focusing on their core competencies. Outsourcing options can range from IT services, customer support, human resources, or manufacturing processes, depending on the organization's needs and industry.

4. Technology Adoption: Embracing technology is a crucial aspect of achieving efficiency and cost reduction. Automation, robotics, and artificial intelligence (AI) can help streamline operations, enhance production speed and accuracy, and reduce labor costs. Adopting cloud computing can enable cost savings by eliminating the need for extensive IT infrastructure and associated maintenance expenses. Likewise, implementing enterprise resource planning (ERP) systems or specialized software solutions can centralize data management and optimize business processes.

5. Energy and Resource Management: Optimizing energy usage and resource management can result in significant cost savings. Implementing energy-efficient technologies, such as LED lighting, smart HVAC systems, and efficient machinery, can reduce electricity bills and maintenance costs. Recycling and waste management initiatives can also minimize disposal expenses and demonstrate environmental responsibility.

6. Employee Engagement and Training: Engaging and empowering employees can lead to increased productivity and cost reduction. Organizations can invest in employee training and development programs to enhance skills, improve efficiency, and reduce errors. Encouraging employee involvement in process improvement initiatives, implementing incentive programs, and fostering a culture of continuous improvement can drive efficiency gains throughout the organization.

Technologies Driving Efficiency and Cost Reduction:

Several technologies can enable businesses to achieve efficiency gains and cost reduction:

1. Process Automation: Automation technologies, such as robotic process automation (RPA), can eliminate repetitive and manual tasks, reducing the need for human intervention and the associated costs. RPA can be

applied to various functions such as data entry, invoicing, and compliance, enabling faster execution, higher accuracy, and significant cost savings.

2. Artificial Intelligence (AI) and Machine Learning (ML): AI and ML technologies have the potential to revolutionize efficiency and cost reduction. Through automation, predictive analytics, and intelligent decision-making, AI and ML can optimize complex processes, improve forecasting accuracy, and identify patterns for cost-reduction opportunities. For instance, using ML algorithms for predictive maintenance can minimize equipment downtime and maintenance costs.

3. Internet of Things (IoT): IoT technologies enable the connectivity of devices and real-time data collection. By harnessing IoT capabilities, organizations can monitor operations, track assets, and gather valuable insights to optimize resource allocation and reduce costs. IoT applications can range from inventory management, supply chain visibility, and equipment performance monitoring.

4. Cloud Computing: Cloud computing provides businesses with scalable and cost-effective IT infrastructure. It eliminates the need for on-premises servers, reduces maintenance costs, and enables remote access to critical business applications. Cloud-based services, such as software as a service (SaaS), can also reduce software licensing and maintenance expenses.

5. Data Analytics: Advanced data analytics tools can extract actionable insights from vast amounts of data. By analyzing operational data, businesses can identify inefficiencies, patterns, and cost-reduction opportunities. Predictive analytics can help optimize inventory levels, improve demand forecasting, and enable proactive maintenance to reduce costs associated with downtime and excess inventory.

Real-World Examples:

Several companies have successfully implemented efficiency and cost-reduction strategies to enhance their operations and profitability. Here are a few examples:

1. Amazon: Amazon has revolutionized the retail industry through its relentless focus on efficiency. The company has heavily invested in advanced robotics within its fulfillment centers to streamline order processing and optimize inventory storage. By utilizing automation technologies, Amazon has significantly reduced labor costs, increased picking and packing speed, and complemented human workers effectively.

2. Toyota: Toyota is renowned for its Lean Manufacturing philosophy, which emphasizes waste reduction and continuous improvement. Through techniques such as the Toyota Production System (TPS), the company minimizes inventory levels, implements just-in-time production, and empowers employees to identify and address inefficiencies. Toyota's approach has led to enhanced quality control, cost reduction, and improved customer satisfaction.

3. Walmart: Walmart, one of the world's largest retailers, focuses on supply chain efficiency to maintain low prices. The company utilizes sophisticated supply chain management systems to optimize product flow, minimize shipping costs, and reduce inventory holding. Leveraging advanced analytics, Walmart accurately predicts customer demand, enabling inventory replenishment with maximum efficiency.

4. Tesla: Tesla, the electric vehicle manufacturer, has successfully integrated efficiency and cost reduction into its production processes. By vertically integrating its supply chain and using advanced automation technologies, Tesla has streamlined its manufacturing operations. The company's Gigafactories employ robotics and AI to optimize production speed, reduce costs, and enhance quality control.

Efficiency and cost reduction are paramount for businesses to maintain competitiveness and achieve sustainable growth. Optimal resource allocation, streamlined processes, and adoption of efficient technologies drive improved productivity, enhanced customer satisfaction, and increased profitability. Organizations should evaluate their operations critically, identify areas for improvement, and implement strategies to drive efficiency gains and cost reduction. By embracing techniques such as process optimization, supply chain management, technology adoption, and employee engagement, businesses can unlock their growth potential, delivering value to customers while maximizing their bottom line. Real-world examples such as Amazon, Toyota, Walmart, and Tesla showcase the tangible benefits of prioritizing efficiency and cost reduction and serve as inspiration for businesses across industries to embark on this transformative journey.

Decentralization:

Decentralization ensures that blockchain networks operate without a central authority, enabling trustless interactions among peers. It removes the single point of failure, making the system more resilient, reliable, and resistant to censorship.

Decentralization has emerged as a progressive and transformative concept in various domains, from finance and governance to technology and healthcare. It refers to the distribution of power, authority, and decision-making across a network of participants, rather than being concentrated in a central authority. Decentralization aims to empower individuals, promote inclusivity, enhance transparency, and enable more efficient and resilient systems. In this article, we will explore the concept of decentralization, its benefits and challenges, its applications in different sectors, and the role of emerging technologies in facilitating decentralization.

Understanding Decentralization:

Decentralization involves the dispersal of control and decision-making power to multiple nodes or stakeholders within a network. Instead of relying on a single central authority, the decision-making process is distributed among a collective group of individuals or entities. These participants can collaborate and interact with one another directly without the need for intermediaries, fostering a more democratic and inclusive system.

Decentralization can take various forms, depending on the context and the specific goals. Some key dimensions of decentralization include:

1. Political Decentralization: Political decentralization involves the dispersion of political power among multiple levels of government or institutions. It aims to enhance local autonomy, ensure better representation, and facilitate citizen participation in decision-making. Political decentralization can lead to more responsive governance, efficient service delivery, and improved accountability.

2. Economic Decentralization: Economic decentralization refers to the redistribution of economic power and resources to various actors in an economy. It promotes competition, reduces monopolies, and encourages entrepreneurship. Economic decentralization can lead to increased innovation, job creation, and economic growth, particularly in small and medium-sized enterprises.

3. Organizational Decentralization: Organizational decentralization involves distributing decision-making authority within an organization or company. It delegates responsibility to lower levels of management, empowering employees and facilitating faster decision-making. Organizational decentralization can lead to greater employee satisfaction, improved problem-solving capabilities, and increased adaptability.

4. Technological Decentralization: Technological decentralization refers to the use of distributed technologies to create networks or systems without a single point of control. Blockchain, for example, enables decentralized and transparent transactions, eliminating the need for intermediaries like banks. Technological decentralization can enhance security, privacy, and trust by removing single points of failure.

Benefits of Decentralization:

Decentralization offers several advantages across various sectors and systems. Some of the key benefits include:

1. Increased Transparency: Decentralization fosters transparency by making information and decision-making processes available to a wider range of participants. In a decentralized system, data and records are often publicly accessible, enabling anyone to verify transactions, monitor performance, and ensure accountability.

2. Enhanced Efficiency: Decentralization can improve system efficiency by eliminating bottlenecks, reducing bureaucracy, and facilitating faster decision-making. In decentralized organizations, for example, decisions are made closer to the action, enabling quicker responses to problems and opportunities.

3. Improved Resilience: Decentralization enhances system resilience and reduces vulnerability to single points of failure. For instance, a decentralized network can continue to operate even if several nodes fail or become compromised. This resilience can be particularly valuable in critical sectors such as finance, healthcare, and infrastructure.

4. Empowerment of Individuals: Decentralization empowers individuals by giving them greater control over their data, resources, and decisions. It enables peer-to-peer interactions, bypassing traditional intermediaries and putting individuals in charge of their affairs. This empowerment can foster innovation, inclusion, and social equity.

5. Reduced Costs: Decentralization can lead to cost reductions by eliminating intermediaries, enhancing operational efficiencies, and promoting peer-to-peer collaborations. For example, decentralized finance (DeFi) platforms provide financial services without the need for traditional banks, reducing transaction costs and increasing accessibility.

Challenges of Decentralization:

While decentralization offers numerous advantages, it also presents certain challenges that need to be addressed:

1. Coordination and Governance: Decentralized systems require effective coordination and governance to ensure smooth operations and avoid conflicts. Establishing consensus mechanisms, decision-making protocols, and dispute-resolution mechanisms can be complex and time-consuming.

2. Scalability: Decentralized systems may face scalability issues as the number of participants and transactions increases. Ensuring that the network can handle a growing user base without compromising performance and efficiency is a crucial challenge.

3. Security and Privacy: Decentralization can pose security challenges, particularly regarding the protection of data and privacy. Sensitive information distributed across a network of nodes may be more vulnerable to attacks or unauthorized access. Ensuring robust security measures and privacy-enhancing technologies is essential.

4. Regulatory Compliance: The decentralized nature of certain systems can present challenges in terms of regulatory compliance. Blockchain, for example, poses legal and regulatory questions regarding identity verification, data privacy, and anti-money laundering measures. Balancing the benefits of decentralization with regulatory requirements is an ongoing challenge.

Applications of Decentralization:

Decentralization finds application in various sectors, transforming traditional systems and enabling new possibilities. Here are some key sectors where decentralization is making significant impacts:

1. Finance: Decentralized finance (DeFi) is revolutionizing the finance sector by enabling transparent, open, and accessible financial services. DeFi platforms leverage blockchain to provide services such as lending, borrowing, and trading without the need for intermediaries like banks. DeFi offers financial inclusion, reduces costs, and enhances financial privacy.

2. Governance: Blockchain and decentralized governance platforms enable transparent, decentralized decision-making in governance processes. These platforms allow for secure voting, identity verification, and smart contract implementations to facilitate more inclusive and transparent decision-making, reducing corruption and enhancing citizen participation.

3. Supply Chain Management: Implementing decentralized systems in supply chain management can enhance transparency, traceability, and efficiency. Blockchain, for example, enables end-to-end visibility of supply chains, ensuring the authenticity and origin of products, reducing counterfeiting, and improving inventory management.

4. Healthcare: Decentralization has the potential to transform healthcare by enabling secure sharing and control of medical records, promoting interoperability, and enhancing patient privacy. Decentralized applications (D-Apps) on blockchain platforms can improve data access, research collaboration, and medical record management, putting patients at the center of their care.

5. Energy: Decentralized energy systems, such as community-led renewable energy projects, empower individuals and communities to generate, manage, and share energy. Blockchain platforms enable transparent energy trading, peer-to-peer energy exchange, and more efficient grid management, facilitating the transition to cleaner and more sustainable energy sources.

Role of Emerging Technologies:

Emerging technologies play a crucial role in facilitating decentralization. Here are some key technologies that enable decentralization:

1. Blockchain: Blockchain is a distributed ledger technology that underpins decentralization by ensuring transparency, immutability, and security. It allows for the recording and verification of transactions across a network of nodes without the need for a central authority.

2. Internet of Things (IoT): IoT devices can contribute to decentralized systems by providing real-time data, enabling automation, and facilitating machine-to-machine interactions. IoT devices connected to a decentralized network can enable autonomous decision-making and distribution control.

3. Artificial Intelligence (AI): AI technologies can enhance decentralization by enabling autonomous decision-making, predictive analytics, and smart algorithms. For example, AI algorithms can be used in decentralized finance platforms to automate lending decisions, optimizing loan allocation while minimizing human bias.

4. Peer-to-Peer (P2P) Networks: P2P networks facilitate direct communication and resource sharing among participants without relying on centralized servers or intermediaries. P2P technology enables decentralized file sharing, communication platforms, and cryptocurrency transactions.

Decentralization is a profound concept that has the potential to transform various sectors and systems. By distributing power, authority, and decision-making, decentralization fosters transparency, enhances efficiency, and empowers individuals. Despite challenges related to coordination, scalability, and security, the benefits of decentralization are driving its adoption in finance, governance, supply chain management, healthcare, energy, and other sectors. Emerging technologies, such as blockchain, IoT, AI, and P2P networks, play a pivotal role in facilitating and enabling decentralization. As decentralization continues to evolve, it offers the promise of more democratic, inclusive, and resilient systems that promote innovation, trust, and social progress.

4. Challenges and Limitations:

Scalability:

Blockchain faces scalability challenges due to its decentralized nature, as processing every transaction by all nodes in the network can be resource intensive. Solutions such as the Lightning Network or sharding aim to address this issue and increase the transaction throughput.

Blockchain technology has gained significant attention and adoption in recent years, promising transparency, security, and decentralization. However, as blockchain networks grow and complex, they face scalability challenges that hinder their widespread implementation. Scalability refers to a network's ability to handle increasing transaction volumes and maintain high performance without sacrificing security or decentralization. In this article, we will explore the scalability challenges faced by blockchain technology, examine the different approaches to address them and discuss the potential solutions that can enhance blockchain scalability.

Understanding Blockchain Scalability:

Blockchain is a distributed ledger technology that stores a chronological series of transactions across multiple nodes in a decentralized network. Each transaction is grouped into a block and added to the blockchain through a consensus mechanism such as proof-of-work (PoW) or proof-of-stake (PoS). This process ensures the immutability and security of transactions by requiring network participants to agree on the validity of each newly added block.

While blockchain technology offers numerous benefits, its scalability is a critical concern. As more users join the network and the number of transactions increases, the capacity of the blockchain to process and validate transactions can become strained. Scaling beyond the limitations of the underlying technology can result in slower transaction speeds, increased fees, and decreased overall network performance. The scalability challenges faced by blockchain can be broadly categorized into three main aspects: transaction throughput, network latency, and data storage.

Transaction Throughput:

Transaction throughput refers to the number of transactions a blockchain network can process in a given timeframe. Traditional blockchain networks, such as Bitcoin and Ethereum, face limitations in transaction throughput due to block size and block time constraints.

1. Block Size Limitations: In Bitcoin, for example, each block has a maximum size limit of 1 megabyte (MB). As the number of transactions exceeds the block size limit, a backlog of unconfirmed transactions can occur, leading to slower transaction confirmations and increased fees.

2. Block Time Constraints: Another factor that affects transaction throughput is the block time or the time taken to mine a new block. Bitcoin has a block time of approximately 10 minutes, meaning that transactions can only be confirmed at the end of each block. As network traffic increases, transaction confirmation times can be prolonged, negatively impacting user experience.

Network Latency:

Network latency refers to the time delay between when a transaction is initiated and when it is confirmed and added to the blockchain. Latency can occur due to various factors, including network congestion and consensus mechanisms.

1. Network Congestion: As the number of users and transactions on a blockchain network increases, congestion can occur, leading to delays in transaction confirmations. This congestion is often accompanied by higher fees as participants compete to have their transactions prioritized by miners.

2. Consensus Mechanisms: Consensus mechanisms, such as PoW and PoS, contribute to network latency. In PoW, miners compete to solve complex mathematical puzzles to validate transactions, which can lead to delays in block validation. PoS, on the other hand, involves selecting validators based on their stake, which can result in centralization and reduced network security.

Data Storage:

Another scalability challenge for blockchain technology is related to data storage requirements. As every node in the network stores a copy of the entire blockchain history, the size of the blockchain can become a significant barrier to scalability.

1. Storage Requirements: As more transactions are added to the blockchain, the size of the data stored by every participating node increases. This puts pressure on the storage capacity of individual nodes and can introduce challenges for nodes with limited resources or bandwidth.

2. Network Synchronization: The increased size of the blockchain can also impede network synchronization among nodes. New nodes joining the network must synchronize their copy of the blockchain, which can be time-consuming and resource-intensive, further hindering scalability.

Approaches to Blockchain Scalability:

To address the scalability challenges faced by blockchain technology, several approaches have been proposed. These approaches aim to increase transaction throughput, reduce network latency, and optimize data storage. Some of the main approaches include:

1. Blockchain Sharding: Sharding involves breaking a blockchain network into smaller partitions called shards, with each shard handling a subset of the overall network transactions. Sharding enables parallel processing of transactions across multiple shards, significantly increasing the network's transaction throughput. This approach can also reduce network congestion and latency by distributing the processing load among multiple shards.

2. Off-Chain Scaling Solutions: Off-chain scaling solutions aim to reduce the transactional burden on the main blockchain by moving some transactions off-chain. These solutions leverage techniques such as payment channels, state channels, and sidechains to enable faster and more scalable transactions. By conducting a large number of transactions off-chain and settling the final result on the main blockchain, off-chain scaling solutions can greatly enhance the scalability of blockchain networks.

3. Layer-2 Scaling Solutions: Layer-2 scaling solutions build upon the existing blockchain infrastructure but introduce additional layers for transaction processing. These solutions, such as the Lightning Network for Bitcoin, enable high-speed, low-cost transactions by bundling multiple transactions together and settling them as a single transaction on the main blockchain. Layer-2 solutions provide scalability while maintaining the security and decentralization properties of the underlying blockchain.

4. Consensus Protocol Optimizations: Optimizing consensus protocols can also contribute to blockchain scalability. For example, some projects are exploring alternative consensus mechanisms like Proof-of-Stake (PoS) and variations of PoW to reduce the computational requirements and increase the transaction throughput. These consensus protocol optimizations aim to maintain the network's security while improving the scalability of blockchain networks.

5. Data Compression and Pruning: Data compression and pruning techniques can reduce the storage requirements of blockchain networks. By compressing transaction data or removing unnecessary data from the blockchain, nodes can store a smaller subset of the blockchain history without compromising security or integrity. Pruning techniques, such as selective data storage, enable nodes to retain only the essential data needed to verify the current state of the blockchain.

Potential Solutions for Blockchain Scalability:

Several potential solutions and technologies are being explored to enhance blockchain scalability. Some of these solutions include:

1. Layer-1 Upgrades: Upgrading the base layer of blockchain protocols can offer scalability improvements. For example, Bitcoin's Lightning Network and Ethereum's upcoming Ethereum 2.0 upgrade introduce enhancements such as sharding, state channels, and improved consensus mechanisms to increase transaction throughput and reduce latency.

2. Interoperability and Chain Linking: Interoperability solutions enable different blockchain networks to communicate and share data, opening up possibilities for scalability. By linking multiple blockchains, interoperability protocols can distribute transactions across different networks, reducing congestion and improving scalability. Projects like Polkadot and Cosmos aim to facilitate interoperability between various blockchain networks.

3. Hybrid Approaches: Hybrid approaches combine the benefits of different scalability solutions. For example, a blockchain network may employ sharding to increase transaction throughput while using a layer-2 solution for faster microtransactions. By combining multiple solutions, hybrid approaches can address the scalability challenges faced by blockchain networks more effectively.

4. Advanced Cryptographic Techniques: Advanced cryptographic techniques, such as zero-knowledge proofs and homomorphic encryption, offer potential scalability improvements. These techniques allow for verifiable and private computations, reducing the amount of data that needs to be publicly processed and stored on the blockchain.

5. Emerging Technologies: Emerging technologies such as directed acyclic graphs (DAGs), which use a different data structure than traditional blockchain, are also being explored for scalability. DAG-based projects like IOTA and Nano aim to provide high-speed, fee-less transactions by leveraging a decentralized network structure without the need for blocks or miners.

Blockchain technology holds immense potential to revolutionize various industries, from finance and supply chain management to healthcare and governance. However, as blockchain networks continue to grow, they face scalability challenges that hinder their widespread adoption. Transaction throughput, network latency, and data storage are key aspects that limit blockchain scalability. Fortunately, promising approaches are being explored to address these challenges. Solutions such as blockchain sharding, off-chain, and layer-2 scaling solutions, consensus protocol optimizations, data compression, and pruning techniques offer potential scalability enhancements. Additionally, layer-1 upgrades, interoperability, hybrid approaches, advanced cryptographic techniques, and emerging technologies like DAGs pave the way for more scalable and efficient blockchain networks. As technology and research in this field advance, overcoming the scalability challenges will accelerate the mainstream adoption of blockchain and unlock its full potential for transformative applications.

Regulatory and Legal Frameworks:

The evolving nature of blockchain technologies poses challenges in terms of defining legal frameworks, regulations, and standards. Balancing innovation with consumer protection and addressing concerns over data privacy is crucial for fostering widespread adoption.

Regulatory and legal frameworks are crucial components of any functioning society and economy, providing structure, guidelines, and protection for individuals, organizations, and the broader community. In this article, we will explore the importance of regulatory and legal frameworks, their role in various sectors and industries, and the challenges and considerations that arise in their development and implementation.

Understanding Regulatory and Legal Frameworks:

Regulatory and legal frameworks consist of laws, regulations, policies, and standards implemented by governments and regulatory bodies to govern and enforce compliance in various sectors. These frameworks aim to create a fair, consistent, and transparent environment by establishing rules, rights, and responsibilities for individuals and entities.

The primary objectives of regulatory and legal frameworks are:

1. Protection: Regulatory frameworks aim to protect individuals, consumers, and the public from fraud, harm, and unfair practices. They establish standards for product safety, quality, and efficiency, and safeguard public health and the environment.

2. Stability: Legal frameworks provide stability and predictability by defining property rights, contractual obligations, and dispute resolution mechanisms. They facilitate economic activities, investment, and trade by ensuring certainty and minimizing risks.

3. Regulation: Regulatory frameworks impose rules and guidelines for specific sectors, industries, or activities. They address market failures, promote competition, and ensure compliance with ethical and legal standards. Regulatory frameworks oversee financial markets, telecommunications, energy, healthcare, environmental protection, and other areas to promote public welfare and prevent abuse.

4. Governance: Regulatory frameworks establish rules and processes for governance, ensuring transparency, accountability, and integrity in public and private sectors. They combat corruption, regulate political and administrative systems, and promote the rule of law.

Role of Regulatory and Legal Frameworks across Industries:

Regulatory and legal frameworks play a crucial role in various industries, providing guidance, oversight, and protection. Here are some examples:

1. Financial Services: Regulatory frameworks in the financial sector ensure stability, integrity, and fairness. They set requirements for capital adequacy, risk management, consumer protection, anti-money laundering measures, and market conduct. Regulatory bodies such as central banks, securities and exchange commissions, and banking authorities oversee financial institutions and markets to prevent systemic risks and market abuses.

2. Healthcare: Regulatory frameworks in the healthcare industry focus on patient safety, quality of care, ethical practices, and affordability. They establish standards for drug approval, medical device safety, clinical trials, professional licensure, and healthcare facility accreditation. Regulatory bodies such as the Food and Drug Administration (FDA) and the World Health Organization (WHO) enforce compliance to protect public health and ensure the effectiveness of medical interventions.

3. Energy and Environment: Regulatory frameworks in the energy and environmental sectors promote sustainable practices, mitigate pollution, and reduce dependence on fossil fuels. They set targets for renewable energy generation, emissions reduction, waste management, and land conservation. Regulatory bodies such as the Environmental Protection Agency (EPA) establish standards and enforce compliance to protect ecosystems, public health, and the climate.

4. Telecommunications: Regulatory frameworks in the telecommunications sector ensure affordable and accessible services, fair competition, and data privacy. They allocate spectrum resources, set service quality standards, and enforce consumer protection measures. Regulatory bodies such as the Federal Communications Commission (FCC) oversee telecommunications providers and ensure compliance with regulations.

5. Intellectual Property: Regulatory frameworks in intellectual property set rules and protections for creative works, inventions, and trademarks. They grant patents, copyrights, and trademarks to encourage innovation, artistic expression, and economic development. Regulatory bodies such as the United States Patent and Trademark Office (USPTO) safeguard intellectual property rights and promote fair competition.

Challenges and Considerations in Regulatory and Legal Frameworks:

Designing, implementing, and updating regulatory and legal frameworks pose several challenges and considerations:

1. Complexity: Regulatory frameworks often address complex issues, requiring careful consideration of multiple stakeholders, interests, and perspectives. Balancing competing priorities, such as consumer protection and industry innovation, is an ongoing challenge.

2. Technological Advancement: Rapid technological advancements often outpace existing regulatory frameworks. Emerging technologies such as artificial intelligence, blockchain, and cryptocurrency present unique challenges, requiring regulators to adapt and establish guidelines that address their impact on society, security, and privacy.

3. Compliance Cost: Compliance with regulatory requirements can impose financial burdens, particularly on small and medium-sized businesses. Balancing the costs of compliance while ensuring public welfare and fair competition is a delicate task for regulators.

4. Globalization and Harmonization: In a globalized world, regulatory frameworks may need to harmonize across jurisdictions to address cross-border challenges such as trade, data protection, and cybersecurity. Coordination among regulatory bodies becomes essential to prevent regulatory arbitrage and ensure consistent standards.

5. Enforcement and Adaptability: Effective enforcement mechanisms are crucial for regulatory frameworks to have a meaningful impact. Regulatory bodies require adequate resources, authority, and expertise to monitor compliance, detect violations, and take appropriate enforcement actions. Additionally, frameworks should be adaptable to evolving risks, new technologies, and societal changes to remain relevant and effective.

6. Balancing Innovation and Protection: Striking a balance between encouraging innovation and protecting public welfare can be challenging. Regulatory frameworks must foster innovation, entrepreneurship, and competitiveness while managing risks and addressing unintended consequences.

7. Public Participation and Transparency: Engaging the public, stakeholders, and experts in the regulatory process is vital to ensure legitimacy, representation, and transparency. Including diverse perspectives and expertise can lead to better-informed regulations that effectively address societal needs.

The Future of Regulatory and Legal Frameworks:

As technology advances and economies become more interconnected, regulatory and legal frameworks will continue to evolve to address emerging challenges and opportunities. Here are some potential future trends:

1. Technological Integration: Regulatory frameworks will increasingly incorporate technology-driven solutions such as regulatory sandboxes, digital identification, and automated compliance monitoring. These technologies can enhance efficiency, enable real-time data analysis, and facilitate adaptive regulation.

2. Data Protection and Privacy: The proliferation of data and concerns over privacy will lead to more robust regulatory frameworks in data protection and cybersecurity. Stricter regulations, like the European Union's General Data Protection Regulation (GDPR), will emerge globally to safeguard individuals' rights and hold organizations accountable for data usage.

3. Sustainable and Responsible Business Practices: Emerging concerns over climate change, social justice, and corporate responsibility will shape regulatory frameworks. Environmentally sustainable business practices, supply chain transparency, and social impact reporting will become key considerations for regulators.

4. Global Cooperation and Standardization: In an interconnected world, regulatory frameworks will increasingly rely on global cooperation and standardization to address cross-border challenges. International regulatory bodies will play a crucial role in harmonizing regulations, creating common frameworks, and overseeing transnational sectors.

5. Regulatory Sandboxes and Agile Regulation: Regulatory sandboxes, which allow controlled testing of innovative technologies and business models, will become more prevalent. Agile regulation, focusing on iterative risk assessment and responsive updates, will help regulators adapt to rapidly changing industries without stifling innovation.

Regulatory and legal frameworks are essential components of any thriving society, providing structure, protection, and guidelines across industries and sectors. They safeguard individuals, ensure fair competition, protect public welfare, and foster economic growth. However, designing effective regulatory frameworks is a complex task that requires balancing multiple considerations, adapting to technological advancements, and addressing global challenges. Regulators must strike a careful balance between encouraging innovation and protecting public welfare while engaging the public and stakeholders in the regulatory process. The future of regulatory and legal frameworks will be shaped by emerging technologies, global cooperation, data protection concerns, sustainability, and agile regulatory approaches. By evolving and adapting to these trends, regulatory frameworks will continue to play a critical role in enabling prosperous and inclusive societies.

Energy Consumption

Some blockchain networks, particularly proof-of-work-based systems, require significant computational power, resulting in high energy consumption. Transitioning to alternative consensus mechanisms like proof-of-stake or utilizing renewable energy sources can mitigate this environmental concern.

Energy Consumption: An Environmental Concern

Energy consumption is a fundamental aspect of modern life. The increasing demand for energy to power our homes, industries, and transportation systems has led to various environmental concerns. As global populations grow, humans consume more energy, primarily derived from non-renewable sources such as fossil fuels, which contribute to significant environmental degradation. This article explores the key issues surrounding energy consumption and its environmental impacts, highlighting the need to transition towards sustainable and clean energy sources.

1. Non-renewable Energy Sources

Non-renewable energy sources, including fossil fuels such as coal, oil, and natural gas, are the primary contributors to energy consumption. These sources, while effectively powering economic growth, release carbon dioxide (CO2) and other greenhouse gases (GHGs) into the atmosphere. The combustion of fossil fuels is the leading cause of climate change and associated environmental issues such as rising global temperatures, melting ice caps, and extreme weather events.

2. Environmental Impacts of Fossil Fuel Consumption

a. Air Pollution: Combustion of fossil fuels releases air pollutants, including sulfur dioxide (SO_2), nitrogen oxides (NO_x), and particulate matter, leading to poor air quality. Exposure to these pollutants contributes to respiratory and cardiovascular diseases, as well as damages ecosystems.

b. Climate Change: The release of CO_2 and other GHGs accelerates climate change, resulting in global warming and altering weather patterns. These changes negatively impact ecosystems, disrupt agriculture, cause sea-level rise, and intensify natural disasters.

c. Water Pollution: Extraction and mining of fossil fuels often contaminate water systems through spills, leaks, and improper disposal of waste materials. This pollution impacts aquatic life and poses risks to human health and freshwater resources.

3. Renewable Energy Sources

Transitioning from non-renewable to renewable energy sources is crucial to combat environmental concerns and reduce energy consumption's negative impact. Renewable energy options include solar, wind, hydroelectric, geothermal, and biomass. These sources produce energy without depleting natural resources and have minimal environmental impacts.

4. Advantages of Renewable Energy

a. Climate Mitigation: Renewable energy sources emit little to no GHGs during power generation, reducing the overall carbon footprint and mitigating climate change.

b. Improved Air Quality: Unlike fossil fuels, renewable energy sources do not produce harmful air pollutants, leading to improved air quality and reduced health risks.

c. Sustainable Resource Management: Renewable energy relies on the constant and abundant supply of natural resources, such as sunlight, wind, and water, which are essentially limitless compared to fossil fuels.

d. Job Creation and Economic Growth: The renewable energy sector offers significant potential for job creation and economic growth. Investments in renewable technologies can stimulate local economies and foster innovation.

5. Challenges and Barriers to Renewable Energy Adoption

Despite the numerous advantages, incorporating renewable energy sources into the mainstream energy grid faces several challenges, including:

a. Cost: The initial investment required for infrastructure and setting up renewable energy systems remains relatively high compared to traditional energy sources. However, technological advancements and economies of scale are lowering these costs.

b. Intermittency: Unlike traditional energy sources, such as coal or natural gas power plants, renewable sources are subject to natural variability. This intermittent must be mitigated through energy storage systems and advanced grid management techniques.

c. Infrastructure Development: Additional infrastructure, transmission lines, and facilities need to be developed to integrate renewable energy into existing power grids.

6. Energy Efficiency: A Vital Component

Energy efficiency plays a significant role in reducing overall energy consumption. By utilizing energy-efficient technologies and adopting sustainable practices, individuals and businesses can reduce their energy demand, resulting in lower environmental impacts and cost savings. Examples of energy-efficient practices include insulation, LED lighting, smart appliances, and eco-friendly transportation options.

7. Government Policies and International Efforts

Government policies play a crucial role in promoting renewable energy adoption, incentivizing energy efficiency, and setting emission reduction targets. International efforts, such as the Paris Agreement, are aimed at reducing greenhouse gas emissions globally and promoting sustainable development by transitioning towards cleaner energy systems.

Energy consumption remains a significant environmental concern due to its detrimental impacts on climate change, air and water pollution, and resource depletion. Transitioning towards renewable energy sources, coupled with energy efficiency measures and supportive government policies, is vital to mitigate these concerns and ensure a sustainable future for generations to come. Embracing clean energy options will not only reduce environmental degradation but also drive economic growth and foster healthier living conditions worldwide.

5. Impact on Industries:

Banking and Financial Services:

Blockchain disrupts traditional banking systems by enabling faster, more secure transactions, reducing the risk of fraud, and facilitating financial inclusion for the unbanked population through micropayments and mobile money.

Title: Banking and Financial Services: A Blockchain Concern

The advent of blockchain technology has brought forth numerous potential benefits and disruptions across various industries, including banking and financial services. Blockchain, a distributed ledger technology, offers transparency, security, and efficiency in financial transactions. However, its integration into traditional banking and financial systems presents several concerns and challenges. This article explores the potential concerns associated with blockchain adoption in the banking and financial services sector.

1. Security and Privacy

a. Data Protection: Blockchain's decentralized nature offers enhanced security compared to traditional centralized systems. However, concerns arise regarding the privacy and security of customer data, as any data stored on the blockchain is visible to all participants. Striking a balance between transparency and data protection becomes crucial.

b. Smart Contract Vulnerabilities: Smart contracts, the self-executing digital contracts on the blockchain, may face vulnerabilities, potentially leading to financial losses if exploited. These vulnerabilities highlight the need for rigorous auditing and testing procedures to ensure the integrity and security of smart contracts.

c. Long-Term Security: While blockchain technology is secure, potential threats may arise in the long run. As attackers may employ advanced techniques, the blockchain infrastructure must continually evolve to resist potential security breaches.

2. Regulatory Compliance

a. Anti-Money Laundering (AML) and Know Your Customer (KYC): Traditional banking is heavily regulated with robust AML and KYC procedures. Integrating blockchain technology while complying with such regulations poses challenges, as the decentralized nature hinders the identification and tracking of financial transactions.

b. Cross-Border Transactions: Blockchain facilitates seamless cross-border transactions, but the differing regulatory frameworks across jurisdictions present compliance challenges. Standardizing regulations and enhancing international cooperation are essential to ensure compliance and prevent illicit activities.

c. Jurisdictional Challenges: Determining jurisdictional responsibility becomes complex with blockchain's global nature, complicating legal obligations and enforcement procedures. Clarity is needed to ensure legal and regulatory compliance while promoting blockchain innovation.

3. Scalability and Speed

a. Transaction Throughput: Blockchain networks face inherent scalability limitations, resulting in slower transaction processing speeds compared to traditional financial systems. Addressing scalability concerns and increasing transaction throughput is necessary for blockchain to meet the demands of the banking and financial industry.

b. Network Congestion: Network congestion can occur when multiple transactions compete for processing within a limited block size. This congestion leads to delayed transactions and higher fees, impacting the user experience and hindering mainstream adoption.

c. Interoperability Challenges: The interoperability of various blockchain networks poses a technical challenge. The lack of standardized protocols and communication channels impedes seamless data transfer and interactions between different blockchain platforms.

4. Financial Inclusion and Accessibility

a. Digital Divide: Blockchain technology requires access to the internet and technological infrastructure, potentially exacerbating the digital divide. Promoting equal access to blockchain-enabled financial services among individuals with different levels of technological literacy and access is essential to ensuring financial inclusion.

b. Trust and Adoption: Blockchain adoption inherently requires trust from users. Overcoming trust barriers and perceived risks associated with this emerging technology is crucial in driving widespread adoption and ensuring accessibility for all segments of society.

c. User Experience: Enhancing the user experience is critical for blockchain-based financial services to gain traction among traditional banking consumers. Simplifying complex processes, improving user interfaces, and addressing usability issues are necessary to broaden adoption and encourage usability.

5. Governance and Centralization

a. Consensus Mechanisms: Blockchain networks rely on consensus mechanisms to validate transactions and maintain the integrity of the ledger. The choice of consensus mechanism impacts decentralization and efficiency, with different mechanisms favoring either scalability or trust assumptions.

b. Decision-Making Authority: Blockchain-based financial systems challenge the existing centralized decision-making authority of traditional banks. The development of new governance frameworks and mechanisms to address transparency, accountability, and decision-making in blockchain-based financial systems is crucial.

c. Regulatory Oversight: Regulating blockchain technology to ensure responsible innovation poses challenges, as it requires striking a balance between fostering innovation and protecting stakeholders' interests. Encouraging informed regulatory oversight to avoid potential abuses is vital for the sustainable growth of blockchain in the banking and financial sectors.

Blockchain technology offers immense potential to revolutionize the banking and financial services industry. However, significant concerns must be addressed to ensure its seamless integration. Security and privacy, regulatory compliance, scalability and speed, financial inclusion, and governance challenges are among the key concerns associated with implementing blockchain in traditional financial systems. Collaborative efforts between regulators, financial institutions, and blockchain developers are necessary to overcome these concerns, unlock the full potential of blockchain in banking, and achieve a more secure, efficient, and inclusive financial ecosystem.

Supply Chain and Logistics:

Blockchain enhances supply chain transparency, reducing fraud, and counterfeiting, and ensuring ethical sourcing. It streamlines logistics and automates processes through smart contracts, resulting in shorter lead times, reduced costs, and increased customer satisfaction.

Supply Chain: A Blockchain Enhancement

The global supply chain is a complex network of interconnected processes involving multiple stakeholders, including manufacturers, suppliers, logistics providers, and consumers. While it fuels economic growth and connects global markets, the traditional supply chain system faces several challenges, such as lack of transparency, counterfeiting, inefficient processes, and poor traceability. Blockchain technology has emerged as a potential solution to enhance supply chain management by providing transparency, security, and trust through its decentralized and immutable nature. This article explores how blockchain technology can enhance various aspects of the supply chain, addressing key challenges and driving efficiency and sustainability.

1. Supply Chain Transparency

a. Provenance and Traceability: Blockchain technology enables detailed tracking and recording of each transaction or transfer of goods across the supply chain. By creating an immutable and transparent ledger of product information, blockchain enhances supply chain visibility and enables real-time tracking, allowing stakeholders to trace products from their origin to final delivery.

b. Authentication and Anti-Counterfeiting: Blockchain enables the creation of unique digital identities for products or assets, making it difficult for counterfeit goods to enter the supply chain undetected. By verifying the authenticity and provenance of products, blockchain technology helps combat counterfeiting and protects brand reputation.

c. Ethical Sourcing and Sustainability: Blockchain can provide a transparent record of suppliers' compliance with ethical and sustainability standards, such as fair trade practices or responsible sourcing. Consumers and businesses can make informed decisions, supporting sustainable and socially responsible supply chains.

2. Supply Chain Efficiency

a. Streamlined Processes: Blockchain technology can automate and streamline various supply chain processes, reducing paperwork, manual errors, and administrative costs. Smart contracts, self-executing code on the blockchain, enable automated payments, contract enforcement, and real-time notifications, enhancing efficiency and reducing delays.

b. Inventory Management and Forecasting: Accurate inventory management is crucial for supply chain optimization. By utilizing blockchain, stakeholders can maintain real-time records of inventory levels, improving demand forecasting, reducing stockouts, and optimizing inventory levels.

c. Reduced Intermediaries and Costs: Blockchain removes the need for intermediaries, such as banks or third-party payment processors, by enabling direct peer-to-peer transactions. This eliminates associated fees and reduces transaction and settlement time, enhancing cost efficiency within the supply chain.

d. Supply Chain Finance: Blockchain technology enables more efficient and transparent supply chain financing through its ability to securely record and verify transactions. This enhances trust among participants and enables faster access to capital, reducing financial risks and improving liquidity.

3. Supply Chain Security

a. Data Security: Blockchain's decentralized nature and cryptographic techniques provide an added layer of security to the supply chain. It ensures the integrity and immutability of critical data, reducing the risk of data manipulation, unauthorized access, and cyber threats.

b. Anti-Fraud Measures: By utilizing blockchain's transparent and auditable ledger, supply chain fraud can be mitigated. Any attempts to manipulate or tamper with data can be easily detected, fostering trust among supply chain partners and reducing the likelihood of fraudulent activities.

c. Supply Chain Risk Management: Blockchain technology enables the creation of a decentralized, shared repository of supply chain data, including potential risks and vulnerabilities. This shared visibility helps organizations to proactively identify and manage risks, improving supply chain resilience and response to disruptions.

4. Supplier Collaboration and Trust

a. Supplier Onboarding and Verification: Blockchain technology simplifies and streamlines the supplier onboarding process by securely storing and verifying supplier information on an immutable ledger. This reduces the administrative burden and enhances trust between buyers and suppliers.

b. Collaborative Planning and Forecasting: Blockchain enables real-time sharing of data among supply chain partners, facilitating collaborative planning, forecasting, and decision-making. This shared visibility enhances coordination, reduces information asymmetry, and improves responsiveness to market demand.

c. Dispute Resolution: Blockchain's immutable and transparent nature can facilitate quicker and fairer dispute resolution among supply chain participants. Smart contracts can be programmed to automatically trigger predefined actions in case of disputes, reducing the need for costly legal interventions.

d. Responsible Sourcing and Compliance: Blockchain can authenticate and track the provenance of raw materials and components across the supply chain, ensuring compliance with environmental, social, and regulatory standards. This enables organizations to demonstrate responsible sourcing practices and conform to international guidelines.

5. Challenges and Considerations

a. Scalability and Interoperability: Blockchain technology faces scalability challenges to handle the volume and speed required by large-scale supply chains. Interoperability between multiple blockchain platforms also needs to be addressed to ensure seamless data sharing and collaboration.

b. Standardization and Integration: Establishing industry-wide standards for data formats, interoperability, and integration with existing systems is crucial for the successful implementation of blockchain in supply chains. Collaborative efforts are needed to ensure compatibility among different blockchain solutions and traditional supply chain technologies.

c. Data Privacy and Regulatory Compliance: Blockchain's transparent nature may conflict with data privacy regulations, such as the EU's General Data Protection Regulation (GDPR). Organizations need to ensure compliance with applicable regulations while utilizing blockchain's benefits.

d. Technological Adoption and Education: Widespread adoption of blockchain technology in the supply chain requires investment, technical expertise, and change management strategies. Organizations need to understand the potential benefits, limitations, and risks associated with blockchain to make informed decisions.

Blockchain technology holds immense potential to revolutionize the global supply chain industry by addressing key challenges related to transparency, efficiency, security, and collaboration. By enhancing supply chain visibility, automating processes, and establishing trust among stakeholders, blockchain enables greater efficiency, reduced costs, and improved sustainability. However, challenges such as scalability, standardization, data privacy, and adoption need to be carefully addressed to unlock the full potential of blockchain in the supply chain. As technology advances and collaborative efforts between industry players, regulators, and technological experts continue, blockchain will play a pivotal role in shaping the future of supply chain management, enabling more resilient, transparent, and sustainable global supply chains.

Healthcare:

Blockchain improves data integrity and interoperability, facilitating shared access to patient records, secure prescriptions, and medical research collaboration. This innovation accelerates diagnosis, treatment, and drug research, revolutionizing the healthcare industry.

Blockchain technology has the potential to revolutionize the healthcare industry by addressing critical challenges such as data security, interoperability, and patient privacy. Here are some key applications of blockchain in healthcare:

1. Electronic Health Records (EHRs):

One of the most promising applications of blockchain in healthcare is the management of electronic health records. Blockchain technology can facilitate secure and decentralized storage of patient health data, ensuring data integrity, privacy, and interoperability. Patients, doctors, and healthcare providers can securely access and update health records in real-time, eliminating the need for fragmented and inaccessible paper-based records. Blockchain-based EHRs enable patients to have better control over their health data and seamlessly share it with multiple healthcare providers, resulting in improved patient care and more efficient workflows.

2. Medical Research and Clinical Trials:

Blockchain can transform the medical research and clinical trial process by improving data integrity, transparency, and participant recruitment. By storing research data on a blockchain, researchers can ensure data integrity, preventing fraud and manipulation. Smart contracts can automate consent management, ensuring patient privacy and promoting informed decision-making. Blockchain technology can also streamline clinical trial data sharing, leading to faster and more accurate results and facilitating collaboration between different research institutions.

3. Supply Chain Management:

Efficient supply chain management is critical for ensuring drug safety, preventing counterfeit medications, and reducing overall healthcare costs. Blockchain can enable end-to-end visibility and traceability of pharmaceutical products throughout the supply chain. By recording every transaction on a transparent and immutable ledger, blockchain technology enhances supply chain integrity, reduces the risk of counterfeit drugs, and helps identify and eliminate inefficiencies. Patients and healthcare providers can verify the authenticity of drugs and ensure they are sourced from reputable suppliers.

4. Telemedicine and Remote Patient Monitoring:

The rise of telemedicine and remote patient monitoring has increased the need for secure and trustless transactions. Blockchain can provide a secure infrastructure for telemedicine transactions, ensuring privacy and data security. Through encrypted smart contracts, patients can have control over their data, granting access to healthcare providers for specific telemedicine consultations. Additionally, blockchain can enable secure data exchange between remote monitoring devices and healthcare professionals, ensuring real-time and accurate data transmission.

5. Data Security and Privacy:

Data breaches and privacy concerns remain major challenges in the healthcare industry. Blockchain technology provides cryptographic data protection, giving patients control over their data and enabling them to share it with healthcare providers securely. As blockchain stores data across a distributed network, it prevents unauthorized access and modification. Additionally, blockchain enables patients to grant and revoke permissions for data access, enhancing privacy and reducing the risk of data breaches.

6. Prescription Drug Abuse Prevention:

Blockchain can play a crucial role in combating prescription drug abuse, which has become a significant issue globally. By using blockchain for prescription tracking, all prescription drug transactions can be recorded and monitored in real-time. This ensures that medications are prescribed, dispensed, and used per regulations, preventing abuse and reducing the spread of illicit drugs.

Blockchain technology has the potential to transform the healthcare industry by addressing various challenges related to data security, interoperability, and patient privacy. The applications mentioned above are just a few examples of how blockchain can revolutionize healthcare. By leveraging distributed ledger technology, healthcare organizations can improve patient outcomes, enhance efficiency, and create a more secure and transparent healthcare ecosystem. With continued research, development, and collaboration, blockchain adoption in healthcare is expected to significantly impact the way healthcare services are delivered and managed soon.

Insurance:

Blockchain provides transparency, fraud prevention, and automation in the insurance industry. Smart contracts automate claim settlements, while immutable records reduce discrepancies and enable faster payouts, minimizing fraudulent activities.

Blockchain technologies have revolutionized industries, enabling transparent, secure, and efficient solutions across various sectors. With its decentralized nature and cryptographic techniques, blockchain ensures data integrity, transactional security, and trust among participants. Despite facing challenges, such as scalability and regulatory frameworks, blockchain's potential for innovation, cost reduction, and efficiency improvement cannot be understated. As we move forward, further exploration and adoption of blockchain technologies will continue to reshape our society and pave the way for an interconnected, decentralized future.

Cloud Computing

Cloud computing enables businesses to access and store data and applications remotely, providing flexibility, scalability, and cost savings. Managers must align their business strategies with cloud computing to leverage its benefits effectively. The adoption of cloud solutions entails considerations such as data security, integration challenges, vendor selection, and compliance with regulations like GDPR (General Data Protection Regulation).

Cloud computing has revolutionized the way businesses and individuals store, access, and process data and applications. It has become an integral part of our digital lives, providing unparalleled flexibility, scalability, and cost savings. In this article, we will explore the concept of cloud computing, its benefits and challenges, various types of cloud services, and its prospects.

What is Cloud Computing?

At its essence, cloud computing refers to the delivery of computing services, including storage, processing power, software, and databases, over the internet. Instead of storing data and running applications on a local computer or a physical server, cloud computing enables users to access these resources remotely through a network of servers hosted on the internet.

The Cloud Computing Stack

Cloud computing can be categorized into three main service models, commonly known as the cloud computing stack:

1. Infrastructure as a Service (IaaS):

IaaS provides the fundamental building blocks for cloud computing by offering virtualized computing resources such as servers, storage, and networking. Users have complete control over the operating systems, software, and applications, while the cloud service provider manages the infrastructure.

2. Platform as a Service (PaaS):

PaaS enables developers to build, deploy, and run applications on the cloud infrastructure without the need to manage the underlying hardware and software infrastructure. It provides a platform with development tools, databases, and operating systems, allowing developers to focus on writing code rather than provisioning and managing servers.

3. Software as a Service (SaaS):

SaaS is the most used cloud service model. It provides ready-to-use software applications over the Internet on a subscription basis. Users can access these applications from any device with an internet connection without the need for installation or maintenance.

Benefits of Cloud Computing

Cloud computing offers numerous benefits for businesses and individuals alike:

1. Cost Savings:

Cloud computing eliminates the need for upfront investments in hardware and software infrastructure. Users can pay for cloud services on a pay-as-you-go basis, reducing costs associated with purchasing, maintaining, and upgrading physical servers or software licenses.

2. Scalability:

Cloud computing allows users to scale computing resources up or down based on their needs. As businesses grow or experience fluctuating demand, they can easily add or remove resources without any disruption.

3. Flexibility:

Cloud computing provides the flexibility to access data, applications, and services from anywhere with an internet connection. This is especially beneficial for remote work, allowing employees to collaborate and access work-related resources from any location.

4. Reliability and Redundancy:

Cloud service providers typically have redundant infrastructure and backup systems in place to ensure high availability and reliability. This helps minimize downtime and ensures data protection and disaster recovery.

Challenges of Cloud Computing

While cloud computing offers several advantages, it also comes with its own set of challenges:

1. Security and Privacy:

Storing data on the cloud raises concerns over security and privacy. Cloud service providers must implement robust security measures, such as encryption and authentication mechanisms, to protect data from unauthorized access and breaches.

2. Vendor Lock-In:

As businesses rely more on cloud services, it can become difficult to switch providers due to compatibility, integration, and migration issues. This can lead to vendor lock-in, limiting flexibility and hindering cost savings.

3. Service Provider Reliability:

Cloud service providers may experience downtime or service disruptions, impacting businesses that rely heavily on cloud services. It is crucial to choose a reputable provider with a track record of high availability and excellent customer support.

Types of Cloud Services

Cloud computing offers several types of services to cater to different needs:

1. Public Cloud:

Public clouds are provided by third-party service providers and are accessible to anyone over the Internet. They offer a cost-effective and scalable solution for businesses and individuals, as resources are shared among multiple users.

2. Private Cloud:

Private clouds are dedicated to a single organization and offer enhanced security and control. They can be hosted on premises or by a third-party provider. Private clouds are suitable for organizations with strict compliance or security requirements.

3. Hybrid Cloud:

Hybrid clouds combine the best of public and private clouds. Organizations can leverage the flexibility and cost savings of public clouds while ensuring sensitive data or critical applications are hosted on a private cloud.

Future of Cloud Computing

Cloud computing continues to evolve and shape the future of technology:

1. Edge Computing:

Edge computing aims to bring computing power closer to the source of data generation. By processing data at the edge of the network, closer to devices and sensors, organizations can reduce latency, improve real-time decision-making, and enhance overall performance.

2. Internet of Things (IoT):

IoT devices generate vast amounts of data that need to be processed and analyzed in real-time. Cloud computing provides the infrastructure and scalability required to handle such data-intensive workloads, making it a vital component of the IoT ecosystem.

3. Artificial Intelligence (AI) and Machine Learning (ML):

AI and ML require significant computing resources to train and deploy models. Cloud computing offers the necessary scalability and processing power to handle complex AI and ML workloads, democratizing access to these technologies.

Cloud computing has transformed the way we store, process, and access data and applications. It offers numerous benefits such as cost savings, scalability, flexibility, and reliability. However, challenges such as security, vendor lock-in, and service provider reliability must be addressed. As technology advances, cloud computing will continue to play a crucial role in enabling edge computing, IoT, AI, and ML, shaping the future of the digital landscape.

4. Internet of Things (IoT)

IoT connects devices, sensors, and machines to gather and share data. Managers should explore how IoT can improve operational efficiency, offer new products/services, and enhance customer experiences. However, managers need to tackle challenges related to data security, privacy concerns, interoperability, and managing vast amounts of data generated by IoT devices.

The Internet of Things (IoT) refers to the network of physical devices, vehicles, buildings, and other objects embedded with sensors, software, and network connectivity, which enables them to collect and exchange data. This concept has gained immense popularity and is transforming various industries, including healthcare, manufacturing, agriculture, transportation, and many more. In this article, we will explore the Internet of Things, its benefits, challenges, and future implications.

To understand the Internet of Things better, one needs to grasp the basic idea behind it. IoT devices are interconnected through wireless technology, allowing them to communicate with each other and make valuable decisions based on the data they collect. These devices can vary from simple household appliances like smart thermostats and light bulbs to complex industrial machinery or even wearables like fitness trackers.

One of the primary benefits of IoT technology is its ability to automate and enhance our daily lives. Smart devices can be programmed to perform specific tasks based on our preferences, making our lives more convenient and efficient. For example, a smart home can automatically adjust the temperature, turn off lights, and even order groceries when we are running low. This level of automation not only improves our quality of life but also helps conserve energy and reduce our carbon footprint.

Furthermore, the implementation of IoT in industries has revolutionized productivity and efficiency. For instance, in manufacturing, IoT devices can monitor equipment health, predict failures, and schedule maintenance, reducing downtime and increasing productivity. Similarly, in agriculture, IoT sensors can collect data on soil moisture, temperature, and other environmental factors, enabling farmers to make informed decisions about irrigation and crop management. This technology has the potential to optimize processes, lower costs, and improve the overall output in numerous industries.

The healthcare sector has also greatly benefited from IoT. Devices like fitness trackers and smartwatches allow individuals to monitor their health and receive real-time feedback on their fitness goals. Additionally, IoT-enabled medical devices can transmit vital data to healthcare professionals, enabling remote monitoring and faster response times in emergencies. This technology greatly improves patient care and allows for more efficient resource allocation in healthcare facilities.

While the potential benefits of IoT are impressive, there are also significant challenges to overcome. One major concern is the security and privacy risks associated with the collection and storage of vast amounts of data. IoT devices are vulnerable to cyber-attacks, and any breach can have severe consequences for both individuals and organizations. Therefore, robust security measures, including strong encryption and regular software updates, are necessary to ensure the integrity and confidentiality of the data.

Another challenge is the interoperability of devices and systems. IoT devices often operate on different protocols and standards, making it difficult for them to communicate effectively with each other. This fragmentation hampers the true potential of IoT, as seamless data exchange and collaboration are essential for its success. Efforts are being made to establish common standards, such as the Zigbee Alliance and the Open Connectivity Foundation, to overcome this hurdle.

Moreover, the rapid adoption of IoT technology has raised concerns about its environmental impact. The manufacturing, usage, and disposal of IoT devices contribute to electronic waste, which poses a significant environmental threat. Manufacturers need to prioritize sustainable production and resource-efficient designs to minimize the ecological footprint of IoT technology. Recycling and proper disposal mechanisms should also be implemented to manage electronic waste responsibly.

Looking into the future, the Internet of Things holds immense potential for further advancements. As technology evolves, IoT devices will become even smarter, more interconnected, and capable of sophisticated decision-making. This will lead to the development of truly smart cities, where interconnected devices collaborate to improve urban living. For example, traffic lights can adjust their timings based on real-time traffic data, optimizing traffic flow and reducing congestion.

Moreover, the integration of IoT with emerging technologies like artificial intelligence (AI) and machine learning (ML) will enable predictive analytics and autonomous decision-making. AI-powered algorithms can analyze vast amounts of data collected by IoT devices and make intelligent suggestions or automate complex tasks. This combination of IoT and AI will transform industries like transportation, supply chain management, and healthcare, making them more efficient and reliable.

In conclusion, the Internet of Things is reshaping our world by connecting various devices, collecting data, and enabling intelligent decision-making. This technology has the potential to enhance our daily lives, revolutionize industries, and create a more sustainable future. However, challenges related to security, interoperability, and environmental impact must be addressed to unlock the full potential of IoT. As we move forward, it is essential to ensure that IoT remains a tool that benefits humanity and contributes to a better world.

5. Robotic Process Automation (RPA)

RPA involves automating repetitive and rule-based tasks using software robots. Managers must identify suitable processes for automation and collaborate with IT departments to implement RPA effectively. RPA can enhance productivity, accuracy, and compliance while freeing up employees' time for more value-added activities. However, managers need to address concerns related to job displacement, employee resistance, and the need for new skill sets.

Robotic Process Automation (RPA) has emerged as a game-changing technology that is revolutionizing the way businesses operate. With its ability to automate repetitive and mundane tasks, RPA is enabling organizations to maximize productivity, improve efficiency, and drive innovation. In this article, we will explore the concept of Robotic Process Automation, its benefits, and the challenges organizations face in implementing this technology.

What is Robotic Process Automation?

Robotic Process Automation, as the name suggests, is a technology that involves the use of software robots or "bots" to automate routine and repetitive tasks. These bots are programmed to perform tasks just as a human would, by interacting with applications, systems, and databases through the user interface. RPA not only mimics human actions, but it can also interpret and manipulate data, trigger responses, and communicate with other systems, enabling end-to-end automation of business processes.

The bots used in RPA are capable of handling both structured and unstructured data, making them versatile and suitable for a wide range of applications. They are scalable, can be deployed across multiple systems, and can perform tasks around the clock without human intervention. RPA technology combines elements of artificial intelligence (AI), machine learning (ML), and business process management (BPM) to automate business processes efficiently.

Benefits of Robotic Process Automation

1. Increased Productivity: One of the primary advantages of RPA is its ability to streamline and automate repetitive tasks, freeing employees to focus on more strategic and value-added activities. By offloading mundane tasks to bots, organizations can significantly increase productivity and make the most of their human workforce.

2. Cost Savings: RPA offers cost advantages by reducing the need for manual labor. With bots handling repetitive tasks, organizations can minimize the costs associated with hiring, training, and managing human workers. RPA also improves operational efficiency, reduces errors, and minimizes the need for rework, resulting in substantial cost savings.

3. Improved Accuracy: Humans are prone to errors, especially when performing repetitive tasks. RPA eliminates the possibility of human error by executing tasks exactly as programmed. This accuracy leads to improved data quality, enhanced compliance, and reduced risk of costly mistakes.

4. Scalability: RPA provides organizations with the flexibility to scale their operations rapidly. Bots can be easily deployed across various systems and processes, allowing businesses to handle increased workloads without the need for significant infrastructure or resource investments.

5. Enhanced Customer Experience: RPA enables organizations to deliver a superior customer experience by automating processes that directly impact customer satisfaction, such as order processing, invoice generation, and customer support. With faster response times and improved accuracy, RPA ensures a seamless and efficient customer journey.

Challenges of Implementing Robotic Process Automation

While the benefits of RPA are undeniable, implementing this technology comes with its own set of challenges. Here are some of the key challenges organizations may face in adopting RPA:

1. Identifying Appropriate Opportunities: Identifying the right processes to automate is crucial for successful RPA implementation. Not all tasks are suitable for automation, and organizations need to carefully evaluate which processes can be automated to achieve the desired outcomes.

2. Managing Resistance to Change: Implementing RPA requires a cultural shift in the organization. Employees may resist the change as they fear job losses or believe that automation will jeopardize the accuracy of their work. Organizations need to effectively communicate the benefits of RPA and provide training to equip employees with the necessary skills to work alongside bots.

3. Ensuring Data Security: RPA involves the handling of sensitive data, and organizations need to ensure that adequate security measures are in place. Data breaches can have severe consequences, and organizations must implement robust security protocols, including encryption and access controls, to safeguard their data.

4. Integration Complexity: Integrating RPA with existing systems and applications can be a complex process. Legacy systems, multiple data formats, and disparate platforms can pose challenges during the implementation phase. Organizations need to ensure that their RPA solution can seamlessly integrate with their existing infrastructure to maximize its benefits.

5. Maintaining and Updating Robotic Workforce: Bots, like any other software, require regular maintenance and updates. As processes change, bots need to be reprogrammed and updated to remain effective. Organizations must establish an effective governance framework to manage and maintain their robotic workforce, including tracking bot performance, managing errors, and ensuring compliance.

Successful Implementation of Robotic Process Automation

To successfully implement RPA, organizations should follow a structured approach:

1. Identify Opportunities: Organizations should identify processes that are repetitive, rule-based, and have a high volume of transactions. Conducting a process analysis will help identify opportunities for automation and quantify the potential benefits.

2. Evaluate RPA Solutions: There are numerous RPA solutions available in the market, and organizations must evaluate them based on their specific requirements. Factors such as scalability, ease of integration, security features, and vendor support should be considered during the selection process.

3. Design and Develop Bots: Once the processes to be automated are identified, bots need to be designed and developed. This involves mapping the process flow, defining decision points, and creating scripts for the bots. Organizations need to ensure that the bots are properly tested before deployment to avoid any disruptions in operations.

4. Training and Change Management: Training employees to work alongside bots is essential. Organizations need to conduct change management initiatives to address concerns and ensure that employees understand the benefits and new roles created by RPA.

5. Measure and Optimize: Organizations should continuously measure the performance of their RPA implementation and identify areas for improvement. Regular audits, error analysis, and process optimization will help maximize the benefits of RPA and identify areas for further automation.

Robotic Process Automation is transforming the way businesses operate, enabling organizations to automate repetitive tasks, enhance productivity, and improve efficiency. By offloading mundane tasks to software robots, organizations can focus on strategic initiatives and deliver a superior customer experience. However, successful implementation of RPA requires careful planning, effective change management, and integration with existing systems. With the right approach and a well-executed strategy, organizations can harness the potential of RPA to drive innovation and achieve long-term success.

6. Virtual and Augmented Reality (VR/AR)

VR and AR technologies offer immersive experiences that can be applied in training, product design, marketing, and customer service. Managers should explore how VR/AR can enhance collaboration, improve customer engagement, and optimize operations. However, managers need to consider the costs, technical infrastructure requirements, and potential challenges associated with user acceptance and integrating these technologies into existing systems.

Virtual and augmented reality (VR and AR) technologies have rapidly risen in popularity over the past decade. From video games to medical training, these immersive technologies have found applications in various industries. This article provides an in-depth exploration of virtual and augmented reality, discussing their definitions, history, technology, applications, challenges, and prospects.

1. Introduction to Virtual Reality (VR) and Augmented Reality (AR)

Virtual reality refers to a computer-generated simulation that immerses users in a simulated environment. It typically involves wearing a headset that displays a 3D world, allowing users to interact with a digital space. The purpose of VR is to provide an intense sensory experience, transporting users to a different reality.

On the other hand, augmented reality enhances the real-world environment by overlaying digital information on top of it. AR uses a device like a smartphone or glasses to project computer-generated objects or information onto the user's view of the real world. Unlike VR, AR does not replace the real environment but adds digital elements to it.

2. History of Virtual and Augmented Reality

The concept of virtual reality dates back to the 19th century when Charles Wheatstone invented the stereoscope, a device that created the illusion of 3D depth perception. In the 1960s, Ivan Sutherland developed the "Sword of Damocles," the first head-mounted display (HMD) system that could track the user's head movements and display computer-generated graphics.

In the 1990s, VR gained significant attention, with companies such as Sega and Nintendo releasing gaming consoles that provided a more immersive experience. However, the technology was expensive and lacked widespread adoption. Augmented reality had a slower introduction, with its early years mainly focused on research and development.

3. Technology Behind Virtual and Augmented Reality

Both VR and AR rely on a combination of hardware and software technologies to create immersive experiences. Virtual reality typically requires a high-performance computer or gaming console to generate and render the 3D environment. Users wear a VR headset with built-in screens, motion sensors, and sometimes handheld controllers to interact with the virtual world.

On the other hand, augmented reality commonly uses smartphones or specialized smart glasses as the primary viewing devices. The devices have built-in cameras, sensors, and processors to capture and interpret the real-world environment. Software algorithms overlay virtual objects onto the user's view, allowing interaction between the real and digital worlds.

4. Applications of Virtual and Augmented Reality

Gaming and Entertainment

One of the most well-known applications of VR and AR is in the gaming and entertainment industry. Virtual reality gaming provides users with an immersive experience, allowing them to feel as if they are physically present in the game world. Augmented reality gaming, such as Pokemon Go, overlays digital creatures and objects onto the real-world environment, enabling users to interact with them.

Education and Training

Virtual and augmented reality have also found applications in education and training. VR can simulate real-life scenarios to train professionals in fields such as medicine, aviation, and the military. For example, medical students can use VR simulations to practice surgeries or diagnose illnesses. AR can provide on-the-job support, with workers using smart glasses to receive real-time information and instructions.

Architecture and Design

Architects and designers can use VR and AR to showcase their designs in an immersive way. Virtual reality allows clients to explore architectural spaces before they are built, providing a more realistic representation of the final product. Augmented reality can overlay digital models onto physical spaces, enabling design professionals to visualize how their creations will blend with the real environment.

Healthcare

VR and AR have numerous applications in the healthcare industry. Surgeons can use VR simulations to practice complex procedures and improve surgical precision. Patients with phobias or anxiety disorders can undergo virtual exposure therapy to overcome their fears in a controlled environment. AR can assist medical professionals during surgeries by overlaying patient data and real-time imaging onto their view, enhancing decision-making and accuracy.

Tourism and Real Estate

Virtual reality allows potential travelers to explore destinations virtually before making travel plans. Companies can create immersive VR experiences that showcase hotels, attractions, and landmarks. Similarly, real estate agents can offer virtual tours of properties to prospective buyers, saving time and resources.

5. Challenges and Limitations

Despite the advancements in VR and AR technologies, some challenges and limitations persist.

Technical Limitations

Virtual reality often requires high-performance computing power and expensive equipment, which can limit accessibility. The resolution and field of view of current VR and AR devices can also cause discomfort or dizziness for some users. Moreover, technology needs to reduce motion sickness and latency to provide a truly seamless experience.

Cost and Implementation

The cost of VR and AR hardware and software can be prohibitive for some applications and industries. Additionally, implementing these technologies within existing infrastructures and workflows can be complex and time-consuming.

Ethical and Social Implications

As with any emerging technology, VR and AR raise ethical and social concerns. Issues such as privacy, security, and addiction need to be addressed as these technologies become more prevalent in society. Ensuring inclusivity and avoiding the creation of virtual environments that perpetuate negative stereotypes is also important.

6. Outlook

Virtual and augmented reality has come a long way, but the potential for growth and innovation is vast. Advancements in hardware and software should make VR and AR more accessible and affordable for the masses. The emergence of 5G networks will also enhance the experience by reducing latency and enabling more data-intensive applications.

Further integration of AI and machine learning technologies will enable VR and AR systems to better understand and respond to user interactions. This will lead to more intelligently generated and personalized experiences. In the future, VR and AR could become integral to everyday life, spanning various industries and applications.

In conclusion, virtual and augmented reality have made significant strides in recent years. The immersive experiences they offer have revolutionized industries such as gaming, education, healthcare, and architecture. While challenges and limitations persist, technological advancements and a growing understanding of these technologies will likely drive their future success. As we move forward, VR and AR will continue to shape our perception of the digital and physical worlds, paving the way for new forms of human-computer interaction and experiences.

7. Big Data and Analytics

Big data analytics enables businesses to derive insights, make data-driven decisions, and improve performance. Managers should develop a data-driven culture, invest in analytics tools, and ensure the accuracy and quality of data. Big data analytics can optimize marketing strategies, improve operational efficiency, and enhance customer personalization. However, managers must also address concerns related to data privacy, security, and the need for skilled data analysts.

Big Data and Analytics: Revolutionizing the Way Businesses Operate

In recent years, Big Data and Analytics have become pivotal driving forces behind innovation and growth in various industries. The unprecedented rise in the amount of digital information being generated every day, coupled with advancements in technology, has paved the way for the emergence of Big Data and its utilization for informed decision-making processes. This article aims to delve into the concepts of Big Data and Analytics, explaining their significance, implications, and potential for transforming businesses across different sectors.

Defining Big Data

Big Data refers to the vast amount of structured and unstructured information produced by individuals and organizations. Traditional data storage and processing systems are often inadequate for handling Big Data due to its volume, velocity, and variety. Volume refers to the sheer size of data while velocity denotes the speed at which it is generated and needs to be analyzed. The third "V," variety, refers to the diverse forms of data, including text, images, videos, and social media posts.

Understanding Analytics

Analytics involves the use of various tools and techniques to extract meaningful insights and patterns from data. It encompasses processes such as descriptive, predictive, and prescriptive analysis to drive informed decision-making. Descriptive analytics focuses on understanding past events and behaviors to provide insights into what has happened. Predictive analytics, on the other hand, leverages historical data to forecast future trends and outcomes. Lastly, prescriptive analytics utilizes optimization techniques to recommend potential actions or strategies.

Applications of Big Data and Analytics

1. Marketing and Customer Analytics – Big Data analytics enable marketers to improve customer segmentation, personalization, and targeting. By analyzing consumer behavior and preferences, businesses can tailor their marketing efforts to specific customer segments, resulting in higher customer satisfaction and increased sales.

2. Supply Chain Optimization – Big Data and Analytics aid in optimizing supply chains by providing insights into demand patterns, inventory management, and logistics. By analyzing historical data and customer behaviors, companies can better anticipate demand, thereby minimizing stockouts and improving overall efficiency.

3. Fraud Detection and Prevention – The integration of Big Data and Analytics allows organizations to detect and prevent fraudulent activities. By analyzing vast amounts of data in real-time and identifying patterns, anomalies, and deviations, businesses can proactively mitigate the risks associated with fraud, protecting themselves and their customers.

4. Healthcare and Life Sciences – Big Data and Analytics are revolutionizing the healthcare industry by enabling personalized medicine, disease detection, and treatments. Through the analysis of vast amounts of patient data and genomic information, medical professionals can develop tailored treatment plans and enhance patient outcomes.

5. Financial Services – The financial sector leverages Big Data and Analytics to assess risks, improve decision-making processes, and enhance customer experiences. Analysis of transactional data, social media sentiment, and other relevant information helps financial institutions optimize their lending practices, detect fraud, and identify potential investment opportunities.

6. Smart Cities – Big Data and Analytics are transforming cities into smart urban landscapes. By integrating data from multiple sources such as sensors, social media, and traffic cameras, city authorities can make data-driven decisions on urban planning, traffic management, and infrastructure development, ultimately improving the quality of life for residents.

7. Manufacturing and Operations – Big Data and Analytics optimize manufacturing processes by identifying bottlenecks, predicting equipment failures, and managing inventory. By analyzing real-time data from sensors and production lines, manufacturers can minimize downtime, reduce costs, and improve overall productivity.

Challenges and Considerations

Despite the potential of Big Data and Analytics, businesses face several challenges. Privacy concerns, data quality, and security issues can hinder the successful implementation of data-driven strategies. Additionally, acquiring and retaining the necessary talent with expertise in Big Data and Analytics poses another challenge due to the shortage of skilled professionals.

Big Data and Analytics have transformed the way businesses operate and make decisions. Leveraging large volumes of data and powerful analytical tools, organizations can gain a competitive edge, enhance customer experiences, and improve overall operational efficiency. With continued advancements in technology and increasing availability of data, it is evident that Big Data and Analytics will continue to play a crucial role in shaping the future of various industries.

8. Cybersecurity

With increasing reliance on technology, managers must prioritize cybersecurity to protect sensitive business data from cyber threats. Managers should invest in robust security measures, educate employees on cybersecurity best practices, and implement incident response plans. Cybersecurity is critical to maintaining customer trust, protecting intellectual property, and avoiding legal and financial repercussions.

Cybersecurity: Protecting Our Digital World

In today's increasingly connected world, the importance of cybersecurity cannot be overstated. With the growth of the internet, the rise of digital technologies, and the expanding reach of online platforms, the risk of cyber threats has never been higher. From personal data breaches to widespread cyberattacks on governments and corporations, the consequences of weak cybersecurity can be catastrophic. This article will explore the world of cybersecurity, discussing its significance, major challenges, and effective strategies for protection.

A Brief History of Cybersecurity:

The concept of cybersecurity dates back to the early stages of computer networks in the 1960s. Initially, the goal was to safeguard sensitive government data from unauthorized access. As technology evolved, so did the complexity of cybersecurity threats. The internet boom of the 1990s brought about greater connectivity, leading to an exponential increase in cyber breaches and attacks. Today, cybersecurity has become an integral part of every aspect of our digital lives, including personal cybersecurity for individuals, corporate cybersecurity for businesses, and national cybersecurity for governments.

Major Cybersecurity Threats:

1. Malware: Malicious software, or malware, is one of the biggest threats in the cybersecurity landscape. It includes viruses, worms, trojans, ransomware, and spyware. Malware can damage or disable computer systems, steal sensitive data, and even take control of entire networks.

2. Phishing: Phishing attacks involve fraudulent attempts to gain personal information, such as passwords, credit card numbers, or social security numbers, by posing as a trusted entity. These attacks usually occur through email, but they can also happen through text messages or phone calls.

3. Distributed Denial of Service (DDoS): DDoS attacks involve overwhelming a targeted website or service with a flood of data, rendering it temporarily or permanently inaccessible to legitimate users. These attacks are often perpetrated by botnets, which are networks of compromised computers controlled by a single attacker.

4. Insider Threats: Insider threats refer to security breaches caused by individuals within an organization. These can be intentional, such as an employee leaking sensitive information, or unintentional, such as falling victim to a phishing attack.

5. Advanced Persistent Threats (APTs): APTs are sophisticated, long-term cyber-attacks that target specific organizations or individuals. They involve multiple stages, including reconnaissance, initial access, persistence, lateral movement, and data exfiltration, and are often carried out by well-funded criminal organizations or nation-states.

Effective Cybersecurity Strategies

1. Strong Passwords: Creating complex passwords and regularly updating them is essential for protecting personal and professional accounts. Password managers can help generate and manage secure passwords for multiple platforms.

2. Multi-Factor Authentication (MFA): MFA adds an extra layer of security by requiring users to provide multiple forms of verification, such as a password, fingerprint, or facial recognition, to access an account.

3. Regular Software Updates: Keeping software, operating systems, and applications up to date is crucial as updates often contain security patches that address vulnerabilities exploited by cybercriminals.

4. Employee Education and Training: Organizations must invest in cybersecurity awareness programs to educate employees about potential threats, safe browsing habits, and responsible online behavior. This can greatly reduce the risk of insider threats and improve overall cybersecurity hygiene.

5. Network Segmentation: Dividing a network into multiple segments, each with its security controls, can limit the potential damage from a cyber-attack and prevent lateral movement within the network.

6. Intrusion Detection Systems (IDS) and Intrusion Prevention Systems (IPS): IDS and IPS are tools that monitor networks for suspicious activities and can block or mitigate potential threats in real-time.

7. Encryption: Encrypting sensitive data prevents unauthorized access. This can be achieved through various encryption methods, such as Transport Layer Security (TLS) for secure communication over networks and Full Disk Encryption (FDE) for securing data stored on devices.

8. Incident Response Planning: Organizations should develop a robust incident response plan that includes detection, containment, eradication, and recovery strategies to minimize the impact of a cyber-attack when it occurs.

The Future of Cybersecurity

As technology continues to advance, so will the sophistication of cyber threats. Artificial intelligence, the Internet of Things (IoT), and quantum computing bring new challenges to the world of cybersecurity. There is a need for continuous innovation in cybersecurity measures to stay ahead of emerging threats.

Cybersecurity is not an option; it is a necessity in today's interconnected world. The consequences of weak cybersecurity can range from financial losses and reputation damage to the disruption of critical infrastructure and the compromise of national security. By understanding the major threats and implementing effective cybersecurity strategies, individuals, businesses, and governments can protect themselves and contribute to a safer digital environment. The battle against cyber threats may be ongoing, but with the right tools, knowledge, and collective effort, a secure cyberspace is attainable.

9. Sustainability and Green Technologies

As environmental concerns grow, managers must consider the implications of emerging green technologies. Adopting sustainable practices and investing in green technologies can reduce operational costs, enhance brand reputation, and comply with environmental regulations. Managers should explore renewable energy sources, energy-efficient manufacturing processes, waste reduction techniques, and sustainable supply chain practices.

Building a Greener Future

In recent years, there has been a growing awareness and concern about the environmental impact of human activities. Climate change, deforestation, pollution, and depletion of natural resources are just some of the pressing issues the world is facing today. In response to these challenges, sustainability and green technology have emerged as critical solutions to build a greener future. We will delve into the concept of sustainability, explore the significance of green technology, and discuss various strategies and innovations that are driving sustainable development.

The Concepts of Sustainability: Understanding its Past, Present, and Future

Sustainability is a concept that has gained significant traction across various fields, from environmental conservation and climate change mitigation to business practices and social development. The term emerged in the late 20th century as a response to growing concerns about the world's finite resources and the impact of human activities on the planet. This article aims to delve into the intricate concepts of sustainability, exploring its origins, present-day understanding, and prospects.

1. Historical Context: Origins of Sustainability

The concept of sustainability has ancient roots, with indigenous societies adopting practices that harmonize human activities with nature. However, it was not until the late 20th century that the modern concept of sustainability emerged. The 1987 Brundtland Report, titled "Our Common Future," defined sustainability as "meeting the needs of the present without compromising the ability of future generations to meet their own needs." This report brought sustainability into the mainstream, highlighting how economic development, environmental protection, and social equity are interconnected.

2. Pillars of Sustainability: Environmental, Social, and Economic Aspects

Sustainability is often referred to as the three-pillar framework, which encompasses environmental, social, and economic aspects. Environmental sustainability focuses on conserving natural resources, minimizing pollution, and ecosystems' preservation. Social sustainability promotes social justice, inclusion, and equality, ensuring the well-being of communities. Economic sustainability involves responsible resource management, fostering economic growth without depleting resources, and reducing inequality.

3. Sustainable Development Goals (SDGs)

In 2015, the United Nations established the Sustainable Development Goals (SDGs), a set of 17 targets designed to guide global efforts towards sustainable development by 2030. These goals cover a wide range of issues, including poverty eradication, clean energy, gender equality, sustainable cities, and responsible consumption and production. The SDGs are a global framework illustrating the integration of economic, social, and environmental elements to achieve a sustainable future.

4. Sustainable Practices: Examples and Success Stories

Many organizations, businesses, and communities have embraced sustainability as a guiding principle, incorporating sustainable practices into their operations. For example, renewable energy sources such as solar and wind power are being increasingly used to reduce reliance on fossil fuels. Sustainable agriculture practices like organic farming and agroforestry minimize chemical inputs and reduce soil erosion. Sustainable urban planning promotes walkability, public transportation, and green spaces to create climate-resilient cities.

5. Challenges and Future Prospects

While considerable progress has been made in integrating sustainability, several challenges remain. Global issues such as climate change, overpopulation, and resource depletion require innovative solutions and collective action. Balancing economic growth with environmental preservation is a complex task, requiring policymakers, businesses, and individuals to make sustainable choices. However, there is hope for a sustainable future. Governments, organizations, and individuals are increasingly recognizing the need for sustainable practices. Technological advancements, such as cleaner energy sources and circular economy models, offer promising solutions. Education and awareness campaigns are also crucial in shaping a sustainable mindset.

Sustainability is an ever-evolving concept that comprises environmental, social, and economic dimensions. Its origins lie in ancient practices, but the modern interpretation gained momentum in the 1980s. The Sustainable Development Goals have provided a global framework for achieving sustainability by 2030. Efforts across various sectors, including renewable energy, agriculture, and urban planning, demonstrate the successful integration of sustainable practices. However, challenges such as climate change and resource depletion persist, necessitating innovative solutions and collective action. The future of sustainability lies in technological advancements, education, and heightened awareness. By embracing the principles of sustainability, individuals, organizations, and governments can work towards a more equitable, prosperous, and resilient world.

Defining Sustainability

Sustainability is often defined as meeting the needs of the present without compromising the ability of future generations to meet their own needs. It involves finding a balance between economic growth, environmental protection, and social progress. Achieving sustainability requires a shift in mindset, as it necessitates making conscious choices that preserve and enhance the health of the planet.

Importance of Sustainability:

Sustainability is vital because it ensures a healthier environment and a better quality of life for both current and future generations. By embracing sustainable practices, we can reduce our ecological footprint, conserve natural resources, support social equity, and mitigate climate change. Building a sustainable society enables us to create a harmonious relationship between humans and nature, where economic prosperity is achieved without compromising the well-being of the environment or society at large.

Green Technology and Its Role in Sustainability:

Green technology, also known as clean technology, refers to the application of innovative solutions to address environmental challenges. It encompasses all aspects of daily life, including energy production, transportation, waste management, and agriculture. Green technology aims to create more sustainable and efficient processes, reducing the negative impact on the environment. It plays a crucial role in achieving sustainability goals by promoting cleaner energy, reducing emissions, minimizing waste, and conserving resources.

Renewable Energy:

One of the pillars of green technology is renewable energy. Fossil fuels like coal, oil, and natural gas have been the primary sources of energy for centuries. However, their extraction and consumption have detrimental effects on the environment, such as air pollution, greenhouse gas emissions, and climate change. Renewable energy sources, such as solar, wind, hydro, and geothermal power, offer cleaner alternatives that are sustainable, inexhaustible, and have a significantly lower environmental impact.

Solar energy, generated from sunlight through photovoltaic panels, is increasingly becoming a cost-effective and accessible solution. It can be harnessed to power homes, businesses, and even entire cities. Wind turbines are another renewable energy source that converts the power of wind into electricity. Large-scale wind farms are being developed worldwide to provide clean energy to millions of households. Hydroelectric power, generated by harnessing the flow of water, is also a renewable energy option that can provide a significant portion of our energy needs.

Transportation and Mobility

The transportation sector accounts for a significant portion of global greenhouse gas emissions. The transition to more sustainable modes of transportation is crucial for achieving a greener future. Electric vehicles (EVs) offer an eco-friendly alternative to traditional internal combustion engine vehicles. EVs run on electricity stored in rechargeable batteries, emitting zero tailpipe emissions. Additionally, public transportation systems, cycling infrastructure, and car-sharing platforms can all contribute to reducing energy consumption and greenhouse gas emissions in the transportation sector.

Waste Management

Effective waste management is another crucial aspect of sustainability. Traditional disposal methods, such as landfilling and incineration, contribute to pollution, greenhouse gas emissions, and the depletion of natural resources. Adopting sustainable waste management practices, such as recycling, composting, and waste-to-energy conversion, promotes the circular economy, where resources are kept in use for as long as possible, minimizing waste generation and maximizing resource efficiency.

The Hazards of Refuse and the Importance of Waste Management in Towns and Cities

The accumulation of refuse, or waste, is an unavoidable consequence of human activities in towns and cities. Improper waste management can have severe consequences for both public health and the environment. This article aims to explore the hazards associated with refuse and highlight the crucial importance of effective waste management systems in urban areas.

1. Health Hazards of Improper Waste Management

Improper waste management can pose numerous health hazards. One of the main risks is the proliferation of disease-carrying pests. Accumulated waste attracts pests such as rats, flies, mosquitoes, and stray animals, which can transmit diseases such as cholera, dengue fever, and leptospirosis. Inadequate handling and disposal of medical waste can also lead to the transmission of infectious diseases.

Another health concern is air pollution arising from the open burning of waste materials. The combustion of plastics, rubber, and other materials releases toxic chemicals and particulate matter into the air, contributing to respiratory problems, cardiovascular diseases, and even cancer. Additionally, poor waste management practices can contaminate water sources, leading to waterborne diseases like diarrhea, typhoid, and hepatitis.

2. Environmental Hazards of Improper Waste Management

Improper waste management has significant environmental impacts. Landfills, which are commonly used for waste disposal, can contaminate soil, groundwater, and nearby water bodies through the leaching of hazardous substances. Such contamination can persist for years, adversely affecting ecosystems and, in turn, human health.

Moreover, the decomposition of organic waste in landfills produces methane, a potent greenhouse gas. Methane emissions contribute to climate change and exacerbate global warming. When waste is incinerated without appropriate technology, it releases harmful pollutants, including greenhouse gases and toxic chemicals, further contributing to environmental degradation.

Improperly disposed plastic waste poses a significant challenge due to its non-biodegradable nature. Plastic pollution not only threatens wildlife and marine ecosystems but also affects human health through the consumption of microplastics in food and water.

3. The Importance of Waste Management in Towns and Cities

Sufficient waste management is crucial in towns and cities to mitigate the hazards associated with refuse. Firstly, properly designed waste management systems prioritize waste reduction and recycling. By adopting a hierarchy of waste management practices, including waste prevention, reuse, recycling, and energy recovery, towns and cities can significantly reduce the amount of waste sent to landfills or incineration facilities.

Secondly, waste management systems play a vital role in public health. Proper waste collection, transportation, and disposal prevent the spread of diseases, particularly in densely populated areas. Well-managed waste systems include regular waste collection schedules, segregated waste streams, and the provision of appropriate waste bins and containers.

In addition to the health benefits, effective waste management contributes to environmental sustainability. Recycling and composting reduce the need for raw materials extraction and reduce greenhouse gas emissions associated with waste disposal methods. Proper disposal and treatment of hazardous waste prevent toxic substances from contaminating ecosystems and prevent damage to biodiversity.

4. Integrated Waste Management Strategies

To address the hazards of refuse and promote sustainable waste management in towns and cities, comprehensive strategies should be adopted. Integrated waste management approaches combine various waste management techniques to maximize resource recovery and minimize pollution.

a. Waste Reduction and Source Separation: Implementing policies and programs to encourage waste reduction at the source, promoting reuse, and effective source sorting of recyclable materials.

b. Recycling and Composting: Establishing recycling facilities and promoting recycling initiatives to divert waste from landfills. Composting organic waste can be encouraged, providing nutrient-rich soil amendments for agriculture and reducing methane emissions.

c. Waste-to-Energy (WtE) Technologies: Investing in state-of-the-art waste-to-energy technologies that generate energy from non-recyclable waste, reducing reliance on fossil fuels and mitigating the environmental impacts of incineration.

d. Hazardous Waste Management: Implementing strict regulations and monitoring systems for the safe handling, storage, and disposal of hazardous waste materials to prevent pollution and health risks.

e. Public Education and Awareness: Conducting public education campaigns to raise awareness about waste management practices, proper waste segregation, and the importance of individual actions in reducing waste.

5. Successful Case Studies and Best Practices

Several towns and cities worldwide have implemented successful waste management strategies. Examples include:

a. Curitiba, Brazil: Known for its innovative waste management system, Curitiba introduced a comprehensive waste collection and disposal program. The city encourages waste reduction, recycling, and composting and promotes waste separation at source through an organized collection system.

b. San Francisco, USA: San Francisco implemented a "Zero Waste" policy, setting the target of diverting 100% of waste from landfills by 2020. The city achieved significant success through comprehensive recycling programs, mandatory composting, and incentives for businesses and households.

c. Kamikatsu, Japan: This small town achieved almost zero waste by enforcing strict waste separation rules, promoting recycling, and composting, and encouraging residents to reduce waste generation. Kamikatsu harmonize exemplifies the potential for waste management practices in small communities.

The hazards of refuse and the importance of effective waste management in towns and cities cannot be overstated. Improper waste management poses significant health risks, contributes to environmental degradation, and amplifies climate change. Implementing comprehensive waste management strategies, including waste reduction, recycling, and proper disposal, is crucial to mitigate these hazards. Successful case studies worldwide demonstrate that integrating waste management practices, raising awareness, and engaging the public can substantially improve waste management outcomes. By prioritizing sustainable waste management, towns and cities can protect public health, preserve the environment, and build resilient, cleaner, and healthier communities for current and future generations.

The Problem of Waste Management in Monrovia, Liberia

Waste management is an increasingly critical issue in today's world, and the city of Monrovia, Liberia, is not exempt from this challenge. Monrovia, the capital and largest city of Liberia, faces numerous issues related to waste management, including inadequate infrastructure, population growth, lack of awareness and education, and economic constraints. This article aims to explore the multifaceted problem of waste management in Monrovia, the consequences it has on the city, and potential solutions to address this pressing issue.

1. Overview of Monrovia:

Monrovia, founded in 1822, is the economic, political, and cultural center of Liberia. With a population of over one million people and growing, the city is characterized by unplanned settlements and inadequate infrastructure. These challenges have a profound impact on waste management practices.

2. Inadequate infrastructure:

A key issue contributing to the problem of waste management in Monrovia is the lack of adequate infrastructure. The city lacks proper waste collection and disposal systems, leading to widespread littering, improper waste disposal, and accumulation of waste in public spaces. The absence of well-constructed roads and accessible landfill sites exacerbates the problem, hindering effective waste management practices.

3. Population growth:

Monrovia has experienced significant population growth over the decades, which has put immense strain on the city's waste management system. The rapid urbanization and influx of people have surpassed the capacity of existing waste management infrastructure. As a result, informal settlements have emerged on the outskirts of the city, further complicating waste management efforts.

4. Lack of awareness and education:

Another crucial problem in waste management is the lack of awareness and education among residents. Many people in Monrovia are unaware of the environmental and health hazards associated with improper waste disposal. Limited public awareness campaigns and insufficient educational programs contribute to the perpetuation of poor waste management practices.

5. Economic constraints:

Monrovia faces significant economic constraints, posing a challenge in implementing effective waste management systems. High levels of poverty and limited resources hamper the city's ability to invest in infrastructure, waste collection vehicles, and waste treatment facilities. Insufficient funding further perpetuates the cycle of inadequate waste management.

6. Health and environmental consequences:

The poor waste management practices in Monrovia have far-reaching health and environmental consequences. Improper waste disposal leads to water contamination, air pollution, and the spread of disease-causing pathogens.

These impacts pose a significant risk to public health and environmental sustainability in the city.

7. Existing waste management initiatives:

Despite the challenges, certain waste management initiatives have been undertaken in Monrovia. These include partnerships between international organizations, local government authorities, and nonprofits to improve waste collection and disposal services. However, these efforts often fall short due to inadequate funding, limited infrastructure, and a lack of coordination among stakeholders.

8. Potential solutions:

To address the waste management crisis in Monrovia, several potential solutions can be considered. These include:

a. Enhancing infrastructure: Developing a comprehensive waste management infrastructure with proper waste collection, transportation, and disposal facilities.

b. Promoting public awareness: Conduct extensive public awareness campaigns to educate residents about the importance of proper waste disposal and the associated health and environmental risks.

c. Strengthening institutional capacity: Investing in the training and capacity building of waste management personnel to improve their skills and knowledge.

d. Encouraging recycling initiatives: Implementing recycling programs and promoting the use of eco-friendly materials to reduce waste generation and environmental impact.

e. Engaging the informal sector: Recognizing and integrating the role of the informal waste collectors in the formal waste management system to improve efficiency and maximize waste recovery.

f. Establishing public-private partnerships: Collaborating with private entities to develop solid waste management systems, share expertise, and attract additional funding.

The waste management problem in Monrovia is multifaceted and requires a comprehensive approach involving various stakeholders, including the government, international organizations, nonprofits, and the public. Adequate investment in infrastructure, public awareness, institutional capacity, recycling initiatives, and public-private partnerships can lead Monrovia towards a more sustainable waste management system. By addressing this crucial issue, Monrovia can protect the health of its residents, preserve its natural resources, and contribute to a cleaner and more livable environment for current and future generations.

Smart Cities

The concept of smart cities combines sustainability, technology, and data-driven solutions to enhance the quality of life for urban dwellers while minimizing environmental impact. Smart cities employ various technologies, including Internet of Things (IoT) devices, data analytics, and automation, to optimize energy consumption, reduce traffic congestion, and improve resource management. By using real-time data and intelligent decision-making systems, smart cities strive to create efficient, livable, and sustainable urban environments.

Water Conservation:

Water scarcity is a global concern affecting millions of people. To achieve sustainability, it is essential to implement water conservation measures. Green technology offers innovative solutions to optimize water usage and reduce waste. Installing low-flow fixtures, implementing rainwater harvesting systems, and utilizing advanced irrigation technologies are some examples of effective water conservation practices that can have a significant impact on reducing water consumption.

Sustainable Agriculture:

Food production is another area where sustainability is of utmost importance. Sustainable agriculture employs practices that ensure long-term productivity without harming the natural environment. Organic farming, integrated pest management, precision agriculture, and agroforestry are some examples of sustainable agricultural methods. These approaches reduce chemical inputs, conserve soil and water resources, protect biodiversity, and promote healthy ecosystems.

Sustainability and green technology are essential pillars of building a greener future. Adopting sustainable practices and embracing green technology can help address the pressing environmental challenges we face today. From renewable energy to waste management and sustainable agriculture, there are numerous opportunities to reduce our environmental footprint and steer towards sustainability. By taking collective action, we can preserve our planet for future generations and create a more livable and resilient world. Embracing sustainability and green technology is not just an option; it is a necessity for the well-being and survival of humanity.

10. Ethical Considerations

Managers must navigate ethical considerations surrounding emerging technologies. They need to consider societal impact, privacy concerns, algorithmic bias, and the ethical use of AI and automation. Managers should develop ethical frameworks, engage stakeholders in ethical discussions, and establish guidelines for responsible technology use.

Hence, emerging technologies offer immense potential to drive innovation, improve operational efficiency, and create competitive advantages. However, managers must carefully evaluate each technology's benefits, risks, and implications to make informed decisions about adoption and implementation. By staying informed, collaborating with technology experts, and addressing potential challenges, managers can effectively leverage emerging technologies to achieve business success in an increasingly digital world.

Ethical considerations play a crucial role in various aspects of our daily lives, including business, healthcare, technology, and beyond. By examining the ethical implications of our actions, we can ensure that our decisions and behaviors are morally acceptable and in line with our values as a society. In this article, we will delve into the world of ethical considerations and explore its significance in different fields.

One of the domains where ethical considerations are most pertinent is business. Companies are confronted with numerous ethical challenges, ranging from labor practices and environmental sustainability to product safety and marketing ethics. One critical ethical question in business revolves around sustainability. With the growing awareness of climate change and environmental degradation, businesses must consider how their operations impact the environment.

Adopting sustainable practices, reducing carbon emissions, and promoting responsible resource consumption is imperative to mitigate the negative environmental impact. Moreover, ethical considerations are also involved in addressing the issue of fair labor practices. Companies that prioritize the well-being and fair treatment of their employees, such as providing safe working conditions and fair wages, demonstrate ethical behavior and contribute to a more equitable society.

Another field where ethical considerations are paramount is healthcare. Medical professionals face ethical dilemmas daily, such as determining the best course of treatment for patients, respecting patient autonomy, and ensuring patient confidentiality. A prime example of an ethical dilemma in healthcare is end-of-life care and medical decision-making. Doctors must navigate complex issues surrounding patient autonomy, quality of life, and the withholding or withdrawing of life-sustaining treatments.

Additionally, healthcare professionals must consider the ethical implications of emerging technologies, such as genetic testing and artificial intelligence. Genetic testing raises concerns about privacy, genetic discrimination, and the potential misuse of information. Artificial intelligence used in healthcare, while offering significant benefits, raises concerns about biases, potential errors, and the responsibility for decisions made by AI systems.

Technology itself presents ethical considerations that impact society as a whole. With the rapid advancement of technology, issues such as data privacy, cybersecurity, and the use of artificial intelligence raise ethical concerns. One example is the ethical implications of big data and the privacy of individuals. Companies collect vast amounts of personal data, raising ethical questions about consent, data protection, and the potential for misuse.

The use of artificial intelligence algorithms also presents ethical dilemmas. AI systems can exhibit biases, resulting in decisions that discriminate against certain groups or reinforce existing inequalities. Moreover, the development of autonomous systems, such as self-driving cars, raises questions of accountability and responsibility in the event of accidents or harm caused by AI-controlled vehicles.

In the field of research, ethical considerations are of utmost importance to ensure that studies are conducted ethically and with the well-being of participants in mind. Researchers must obtain informed consent from participants, protect their privacy, and ensure that any potential harms are minimized. Additionally, research involving vulnerable populations, such as children or prisoners, requires even more stringent ethical scrutiny to safeguard their rights and welfare.

Ethical considerations also extend to the realm of social media and online platforms. With the rise of social media platforms, issues such as privacy, the spread of misinformation, and online harassment have become prevalent. Companies like Facebook and Twitter face ethical challenges in moderating content and ensuring the safety of their users.

Some critics argue that social media platforms have a responsibility to prioritize the well-being of their users by combating hate speech, misinformation, and other harmful content. On the other hand, concerns around censorship and freedom of expression raise questions about the appropriate balance between protecting users and upholding the principles of free speech.

In conclusion, ethical considerations play a vital role in numerous domains, ranging from business and healthcare to technology and research. By examining the ethical implications of our actions, we can navigate complex issues and make informed decisions that align with our moral values. Considering ethics ensures that our actions contribute to a more equitable, sustainable, and just society.

Chapter Nine

Knowledge Management and Organizational Learning

Analyzing how organizations can effectively capture, disseminate, and utilize Knowledge to enhance performance, Innovation, and overall competitiveness.

Knowledge Management and Organizational Learning

Enhancing Performance through Dynamic Knowledge Processes

In today's fast-paced and knowledge-driven world, organizations are recognizing the critical importance of effectively managing knowledge and promoting continuous learning to stay competitive. Knowledge management (KM) and organizational learning (OL) have emerged as key disciplines to harness and leverage collective knowledge within organizations. This article explores the concepts of knowledge management and organizational learning, their interplay, and their impact on organizational performance. It discusses the underlying theories, processes, and challenges associated with implementing effective knowledge management and organizational learning initiatives.

1. Understanding Knowledge Management:

Knowledge management (KM) is a comprehensive and multidimensional approach to effectively managing an organization's intellectual assets to enhance performance, innovation, and competitive advantage. It involves the systematic and strategic processes of capturing, organizing, storing, sharing, and utilizing knowledge within an organization. Knowledge management encompasses a wide range of activities, techniques, and tools that facilitate the creation, access, dissemination, and application of tacit and explicit knowledge.

To understand knowledge management in detail, let's examine its key components and processes:

1. Knowledge Creation:

Knowledge creation involves the generation of new knowledge through individual or collective experiences, insights, and learning. It includes capturing tacit knowledge, which is deeply rooted in personal experiences, beliefs, and values, and converting it into explicit knowledge, which is more codified and easily shared.

2. Knowledge Capture:

Knowledge capture involves identifying, selecting, and acquiring relevant knowledge from various sources, such as employees, customers, research, and external experts. It encompasses methods like interviews, surveys, observations, and documentation to capture tacit and explicit knowledge.

3. Knowledge Organization:

Knowledge organization involves structuring and categorizing knowledge assets to facilitate easy retrieval and reuse. This includes creating taxonomies, ontologies, and metadata frameworks that classify knowledge based on its nature, domain, and relevance. Knowledge maps and visualization techniques help visually represent knowledge relationships and dependencies.

4. Knowledge Storage and Retrieval:

Knowledge storage deals with the physical or digital infrastructure and systems used to store and manage knowledge assets. This includes databases, intranets, content management systems, and document repositories. Effective retrieval mechanisms, such as search engines and indexing, ensure easy and timely access to specific knowledge when needed.

5. Knowledge Sharing and Transfer:

Knowledge sharing focuses on creating a culture and mechanisms for individuals and teams to exchange and transfer knowledge to others. This involves fostering collaboration, building communities of practice, facilitating social networks, and implementing communication channels and platforms. Sharing knowledge enhances learning, problem-solving, and innovation within the organization.

6. Knowledge Application and Utilization:

Knowledge application involves the transfer of knowledge into actionable insights and the integration of knowledge into organizational processes and practices. This includes providing employees with access to knowledge resources, tools, and guidelines that support effective decision-making, problem-solving, and innovation.

7. Knowledge Evaluation and Feedback:

Knowledge evaluation involves assessing the quality, relevance, and effectiveness of knowledge assets. It includes monitoring knowledge usage, gathering feedback, and applying metrics and indicators to measure the impact of knowledge management initiatives. These evaluations help identify gaps, improve knowledge processes, and facilitate continuous improvement.

Effective knowledge management requires organizations to adopt suitable strategies, technology infrastructure, and cultural norms conducive to knowledge sharing and collaboration. Some strategies that organizations can employ include tools and systems that support knowledge management, creating communities of practice, encouraging mentoring and coaching relationships, and fostering a learning culture within the organization.

Successful knowledge management initiatives bring several benefits to organizations, including improved decision-making based on reliable and up-to-date information, enhanced problem-solving through shared experiences and insights, increased efficiency and effectiveness by avoiding repeated mistakes, competitive advantage through the development and exploitation of intellectual assets, organizational learning and adaptability, and talent retention and development.

Despite its potential benefits, knowledge management also faces challenges. Cultural barriers, such as resistance to change and knowledge-hoarding behaviors, can hinder knowledge sharing. Information overload and the lack of relevant technology infrastructure can impede efficient knowledge retrieval and utilization. Measuring the value and impact of knowledge assets poses challenges due to their intangible nature.

In conclusion, knowledge management is a holistic approach for organizations to effectively capture, organize, store, share, and use knowledge to enhance performance, foster innovation, and gain a competitive edge. It involves leveraging both tacit and explicit knowledge through a range of processes, strategies, and technologies. By adopting effective knowledge management practices, organizations can tap into their intellectual capital, facilitate collaboration, and create a culture of continuous learning.

1. Defining Knowledge Management

Knowledge management (KM) is a multidisciplinary field that encompasses the systematic process of capturing, organizing, storing, sharing, and utilizing the knowledge assets within an organization to enhance performance, innovation, and competitive advantage. It involves the identification, creation, acquisition, preservation, and dissemination of knowledge to facilitate effective decision-making, problem-solving, and learning.

At its core, knowledge management aims to connect individuals, teams, and departments within an organization, enabling the exchange and application of knowledge to achieve organizational goals. It involves the management of both explicit knowledge, which is codified and easily documented, and tacit knowledge, which is based on personal experiences, expertise, and insights that are difficult to articulate or express explicitly.

Knowledge management encompasses a range of activities and processes, including the capture and creation of knowledge, organization and classification of knowledge assets, storage and retrieval of knowledge, sharing and dissemination of knowledge, and the application and utilization of knowledge in decision-making and problem-solving. It involves the use of various tools, technologies, and techniques to facilitate the effective management of knowledge resources.

Knowledge management is not limited to any specific industry or sector but is relevant to all organizations that seek to leverage their collective knowledge to gain a competitive advantage. It is applicable in areas such as research and development, customer service, project management, organizational learning, and innovation.

The benefits of effective knowledge management include improved decision-making, enhanced problem-solving, increased efficiency and effectiveness, innovation and creativity, organizational learning and adaptation, and talent retention and development. By leveraging knowledge assets, organizations can tap into the expertise and experiences of their employees, foster collaboration and knowledge sharing, and create a culture that values continuous learning and improvement.

However, implementing knowledge management practices can be challenging due to cultural barriers, resistance to change, information overload, lack of technology infrastructure, and the difficulty of measuring the value of intangible assets such as knowledge. Successful knowledge management initiatives require a systematic and strategic approach, leadership support, the right technology and tools, and a culture that encourages open communication and collaboration.

In summary, knowledge management is a strategic discipline that focuses on effectively managing and leveraging the collective knowledge of an organization to drive performance and innovation. It involves the systematic processes, tools, and culture that enable organizations to capture, organize, share, and utilize knowledge to achieve their goals and maintain a competitive edge in an increasingly knowledge-based economy.

2. Knowledge Management as a Strategic Imperative

Knowledge management is widely recognized as a strategic imperative for organizations in today's knowledge-intensive and rapidly changing business environment. It is essential for organizations to effectively manage their intellectual assets to gain a competitive advantage, enhance performance, and ensure long-term success. Here is a detailed explanation of why knowledge management is considered a strategic imperative:

Leveraging Intellectual Capital: Intellectual capital, including tacit knowledge, explicit knowledge, and innovative capabilities, is a valuable resource for every organization. Knowledge management enables organizations to identify, capture, and leverage this intellectual capital to its maximum potential. By harnessing the collective knowledge of employees and facilitating knowledge sharing and collaboration, organizations can achieve improved decision-making, innovation, and problem-solving capabilities.

Enabling Continuous Learning: In today's rapidly evolving business landscape, organizations must be adaptable and continuously learn and improve. Knowledge management provides a framework for fostering a learning culture within an organization. It enables the creation of communities of practice, encourages experiential learning, and facilitates the transfer of knowledge across different areas of the organization. By promoting continuous learning, organizations can stay agile, anticipate market changes, and proactively respond to emerging challenges and opportunities.

Enhancing Organizational Agility: Knowledge management contributes to organizational agility, which is crucial for competitiveness in today's dynamic business environment. By effectively managing and sharing knowledge, organizations can respond quickly to customer needs, adapt to changing market conditions, and capitalize on emerging trends. Knowledge management enables the dissemination of best practices, lessons learned, and industry insights, empowering employees to make informed decisions and take prompt actions.

Promoting Innovation and Creativity: Knowledge management plays a pivotal role in fostering a culture of innovation and creativity within an organization. By capturing and sharing tacit and explicit knowledge, organizations can facilitate the generation of new ideas, encourage cross-functional collaboration, and foster a sense of ownership and empowerment among employees. Knowledge management enables organizations to build on past successes, avoid repeating mistakes, and create an environment that nurtures an innovative mind-set.

Ensuring Organizational Resilience: Knowledge management is critical for ensuring organizational resilience in the face of disruptions and uncertainties. By systematically managing knowledge, organizations can mitigate risks associated with knowledge loss due to employee turnover, retirements, or unexpected events. Knowledge management enables the preservation and accessibility of critical knowledge assets, ensuring that valuable intellectual capital is not lost with the departure of key employees. This resilience allows organizations to maintain continuity, sustain performance, and bounce back from setbacks more efficiently.

In summary, knowledge management is a strategic imperative for organizations as it enables them to leverage intellectual capital, enable continuous learning, enhance organizational agility, promote innovation and creativity, and ensure resilience. It provides a strategic framework for effectively managing knowledge assets, enabling organizations to stay competitive, respond to changes, and drive long-term success in a knowledge-driven economy.

3. Theoretical Foundations of Knowledge Management

The theoretical foundations of knowledge management (KM) encompass various perspectives and concepts that provide a framework for understanding and implementing effective KM practices. These theories offer insights into the nature of knowledge, its creation, transfer, and utilization within an organizational context. Here are some key theoretical foundations of knowledge management:

Epistemology:

Epistemology focuses on the nature and source of knowledge. Within KM, epistemological theories help us understand different forms of knowledge and their characteristics. For instance, the distinction between tacit knowledge (personal, subjective, and experiential) and explicit knowledge (codified, formal, and easily shared) is rooted in the work of philosophers such as Polanyi and Nonaka. The epistemological perspective recognizes knowledge as a valuable organizational asset that can be managed and leveraged for competitive advantage.

Social Constructivism:

Social constructivism emphasizes the social and cultural aspects of knowledge creation, sharing, and interpretation. According to this theory, knowledge is not an objective reality but is shaped by social interactions. In the context of KM, social constructivism highlights the importance of fostering collaboration and creating communities of practice to promote knowledge sharing and co-creation. The work of Wenger-Trayner and Lave on communities of practice is instrumental in this regard.

Organizational Learning:

Organizational learning theories examine how organizations acquire, create, and apply knowledge to improve performance and achieve organizational goals. The concept of the learning organization, popularized by Peter Senge, emphasizes the importance of continuous learning and the integration of individual and collective knowledge within an organization. Organizational learning theories provide insights into the processes, structures, and systems that facilitate knowledge sharing, reflection, and the development of a learning culture.

Information Processing:

Information processing theories focus on how individuals and organizations acquire, process, store, and retrieve information and knowledge. The work of Simon on decision-making processes and the information-processing perspective of organizations provides theoretical foundations for understanding how organizations manage information and knowledge flows. Information processing theories contribute to the design and implementation of effective knowledge storage, retrieval, and dissemination systems.

Intellectual Capital:

The concept of intellectual capital highlights the value of knowledge and human intangible assets within organizations. Theoretical frameworks such as the resource-based view (RBV) and the knowledge-based view (KBV) emphasize the role of knowledge in generating and sustaining competitive advantage. These theories emphasize the strategic importance of managing knowledge as a critical organizational resource. Scholars such as Edvinsson and Malone have contributed significantly to the intellectual capital theory.

These theoretical foundations serve as frameworks for understanding and guiding KM practices. They inform the development and implementation of KM strategies, the selection of appropriate knowledge management tools and techniques, and the design of organizational structures and cultures that foster effective knowledge sharing and utilization. By drawing on these theoretical perspectives, organizations can enhance their understanding of knowledge as a strategic asset and maximize its value for achieving their goals.

Building a Knowledge Management Culture

The theoretical foundations of knowledge management (KM) encompass various perspectives and concepts that provide a framework for understanding and implementing effective KM practices. These theories offer insights into the nature of knowledge, its creation, transfer, and utilization within an organizational context. Here are some key theoretical foundations of knowledge management:

Epistemology:

Epistemology focuses on the nature and source of knowledge. Within KM, epistemological theories help us understand different forms of knowledge and their characteristics. For instance, the distinction between tacit knowledge (personal, subjective, and experiential) and explicit knowledge (codified, formal, and easily shared) is rooted in the work of philosophers such as Polanyi and Nonaka. The epistemological perspective recognizes knowledge as a valuable organizational asset that can be managed and leveraged for competitive advantage.

Social Constructivism:

Social constructivism emphasizes the social and cultural aspects of knowledge creation, sharing, and interpretation. According to this theory, knowledge is not an objective reality but is shaped by social interactions. In the context of KM, social constructivism highlights the importance of fostering collaboration and creating communities of practice to promote knowledge sharing and co-creation. The work of Wenger-Trayner and Lave on communities of practice is instrumental in this regard.

Organizational Learning:

Organizational learning theories examine how organizations acquire, create, and apply knowledge to improve performance and achieve organizational goals. The concept of the learning organization, popularized by Peter Senge, emphasizes the importance of continuous learning and the integration of individual and collective knowledge within an organization. Organizational learning theories provide insights into the processes, structures, and systems that facilitate knowledge sharing, reflection, and the development of a learning culture.

Information Processing:

Information processing theories focus on how individuals and organizations acquire, process, store, and retrieve information and knowledge. The work of Simon on decision-making processes and the information-processing perspective of organizations provides theoretical foundations for understanding how organizations manage information and knowledge flows. Information processing theories contribute to the design and implementation of effective knowledge storage, retrieval, and dissemination systems.

Intellectual Capital:

The concept of intellectual capital highlights the value of knowledge and human intangible assets within organizations. Theoretical frameworks such as the resource-based view (RBV) and the knowledge-based view (KBV) emphasize the role of knowledge in generating and sustaining competitive advantage. These theories emphasize the strategic importance of managing knowledge as a critical organizational resource. Scholars such as Edvinsson and Malone have contributed significantly to the intellectual capital theory.

These theoretical foundations serve as frameworks for understanding and guiding KM practices. They inform the development and implementation of KM strategies, the selection of appropriate knowledge management tools and techniques, and the design of organizational structures and cultures that foster effective knowledge sharing and utilization. By drawing on these theoretical perspectives, organizations can enhance their understanding of knowledge as a strategic asset and maximize its value for achieving their goals.

Processes of Knowledge Management

Knowledge management (KM) encompasses a range of interconnected processes that facilitate the effective capture, organization, storage, sharing, and utilization of knowledge within organizations. These processes collectively enable organizations to leverage their intellectual assets, enhance performance, foster innovation, and stay competitive in a rapidly changing business environment. In this section, we will thoroughly explain the key processes of knowledge management:

Knowledge Creation and Acquisition:

Knowledge creation involves generating and developing new knowledge within an organization. It involves capturing tacit knowledge, which resides in people's expertise, experiences, and insights, and converting it into explicit knowledge that can be documented and shared. Knowledge acquisition, on the other hand, focuses on obtaining knowledge from external sources such as research, industry reports, and experts. Organizations can promote knowledge creation by encouraging collaboration, supporting cross-functional teams, providing opportunities for experimentation, and fostering a culture of learning. Knowledge acquisition involves systematic processes for identifying, selecting, and absorbing relevant knowledge from external sources.

Knowledge Storage and Organization:

Knowledge storage and organization involve the effective management and arrangement of knowledge assets within an organization. This includes selecting suitable storage systems, such as databases, content management systems, and knowledge repositories, to store explicit knowledge. Knowledge should be organized and classified in a way that facilitates easy retrieval and navigation. This involves creating taxonomies, ontologies, and metadata structures that categorize knowledge based on its nature, domain, and relevance. Structured and organized knowledge enables employees to quickly locate and access relevant information, thereby enhancing decision-making and problem-solving capabilities.

Knowledge Sharing and Dissemination:

Knowledge sharing is a crucial process in knowledge management that aims to transfer knowledge from one individual or group to another. Effective knowledge-sharing promotes collaboration, innovation, and learning within an organization. It involves the use of various communication channels, such as meetings, presentations, workshops, and collaboration platforms, to exchange knowledge. Communities of practice, which are groups of individuals with shared interests or expertise, play a significant role in facilitating knowledge sharing. Creating an environment that encourages open communication, trust, and sharing of ideas is essential for successful knowledge sharing.

Knowledge Application and Utilization:

Knowledge application focuses on using knowledge to solve problems, make informed decisions, and innovate. It involves embedding knowledge in organizational processes and practices to enhance effectiveness and efficiency. Organizations need to provide employees with the necessary tools, resources, and support systems to leverage knowledge in their day-to-day work. Knowledge application requires not only the transfer of explicit knowledge but also the ability to tap into tacit knowledge and expertise. Creating opportunities for employees to collaborate, experiment, and apply their knowledge in real-world situations fosters continuous learning and maximizes the benefits of knowledge within the organization.

Knowledge Evaluation and Feedback:

Knowledge evaluation involves assessing the quality, relevance, and effectiveness of knowledge within the organization. This process aims to continuously improve knowledge management practices and align them with organizational goals. Evaluation methods may include surveys, interviews, performance metrics, and feedback mechanisms. Regular evaluation enables organizations to identify gaps, areas for improvement, and emerging knowledge needs. It also facilitates a feedback loop where insights gained from knowledge utilization can inform future knowledge creation and acquisition efforts.

Knowledge Capture and Retention:

Knowledge capture ensures that valuable knowledge is not lost within an organization, especially with the departure of employees or other unforeseen events. This process involves identifying critical knowledge, capturing it through documentation, codification, or other means, and storing it in accessible formats. Knowledge retention strategies focus on preserving and transferring knowledge within the organization, including the use of knowledge repositories, lesson-learned databases, and mentoring programs. Effective knowledge capture and retention prevent the loss of critical knowledge and enable organizations to build on past experiences and expertise.

Knowledge Management Systems (KMS):

Knowledge management systems refer to the technology infrastructure and tools that support knowledge management processes. These systems include document management systems, content management systems, collaboration platforms, and knowledge repositories. KMS helps to store, organize, search, and retrieve knowledge resources efficiently. They also facilitate access to knowledge across organizational boundaries, support remote collaboration, and enable the integration of knowledge management into existing workflows and processes.

Artificial Intelligence and Automation in Knowledge Management:

Artificial intelligence (AI) and automation play an increasingly significant role in knowledge management. AI-powered systems can assist in knowledge discovery, extraction, and analysis. Natural language processing (NLP) techniques enable the automatic extraction of knowledge from unstructured text sources. Robotic process automation (RPA) automates repetitive knowledge-related tasks, freeing up human resources for more strategic activities. However, organizations should consider ethical and privacy implications and ensure that AI systems align with organizational values and regulatory requirements.

In conclusion, the processes of knowledge management are interconnected and essential for organizations to effectively manage their knowledge assets. From knowledge creation and acquisition to storage, sharing, application, evaluation, capture, and utilization, each process plays a unique role in facilitating knowledge flow, promoting collaboration, enhancing decision-making, and fostering innovation. Implementing robust strategies, leveraging appropriate technology tools, and fostering a knowledge-sharing culture are key to successful knowledge management implementation.

Knowledge Creation and Acquisition

Knowledge creation and acquisition are foundational processes in knowledge management that involve generating new knowledge and obtaining relevant knowledge from external sources. These processes are essential for organizations to expand their knowledge base, drive innovation, and remain competitive in a rapidly changing business environment. Let's explore each of these processes in detail:

Knowledge Creation:

Knowledge creation refers to the process of generating new knowledge within an organization. It involves transforming individual experiences, insights, and expertise into explicit knowledge that can be shared and utilized. Knowledge creation occurs through various means, including:

Individual Learning: Individuals acquire knowledge through formal education, on-the-job experiences, self-study, and personal reflection. This knowledge builds upon their existing expertise and contributes to their learning and growth.

Collaboration and Interaction: Knowledge creation is often enhanced through collaboration and interaction among individuals or teams. Brainstorming sessions, meetings, and cross-functional collaborations encourage the exchange of ideas, perspectives, and expertise, stimulating the generation of new knowledge.

Experimentation and Innovation: Organizations foster knowledge creation through experimentation and innovation. By encouraging employees to explore new ideas, take risks, and challenge existing assumptions, organizations can drive the creation of new knowledge and novel approaches to problem-solving.

External Influences: Knowledge creation is influenced by external factors such as market trends, customer feedback, and industry research. Organizations actively monitor and assimilate relevant information from external sources to generate new insights and knowledge.

Knowledge Acquisition:

Knowledge acquisition involves obtaining knowledge from external sources to supplement and enrich an organization's existing knowledge base. It focuses on identifying and accessing valuable knowledge resources available beyond the organization's boundaries. Some common strategies for knowledge acquisition include:

Networking and Collaboration: Organizations establish partnerships, networks, and collaborations with external stakeholders, including industry experts, academia, research institutions, and other organizations. This collaboration facilitates knowledge sharing, access to expertise, and the exchange of best practices.

Research and Benchmarking: Organizations conduct research activities to benchmark against industry standards, learn from competitors, and gather knowledge about emerging trends, technologies, and market insights.

Knowledge Brokering: Knowledge brokers act as intermediaries between external knowledge sources and the organization. They facilitate the identification, selection, and transfer of relevant knowledge by leveraging their networks and expertise.

Open Innovation: Organizations adopt open innovation principles, which involve actively seeking external knowledge and ideas through crowdsourcing, innovation challenges, and partnerships with customers, suppliers, and other stakeholders.

External Training and Education: Organizations invest in external training programs, conferences, seminars, and workshops to provide employees with access to the latest industry knowledge and practices.

Both knowledge creation and acquisition processes have their challenges and considerations. Some common challenges include capturing and codifying tacit knowledge, managing information overload, ensuring the quality and relevance of acquired knowledge, and fostering a culture that encourages continuous learning and knowledge sharing. Effective knowledge management strategies address these challenges by implementing mechanisms for knowledge capture, sharing, validation, and embedding acquired knowledge into organizational practices.

In conclusion, knowledge creation and acquisition are essential processes in knowledge management. Organizations must actively promote the creation of new knowledge through individual learning, collaboration, experimentation, and engagement with external sources. Simultaneously, knowledge acquisition enables organizations to tap into external expertise, market insights, and emerging trends. By integrating these processes effectively, organizations can expand their knowledge base, foster innovation, and gain a competitive edge.

Knowledge Storage and Organization

Knowledge creation and acquisition are foundational processes in knowledge management that involve generating new knowledge and obtaining relevant knowledge from external sources. These processes are essential for organizations to expand their knowledge base, drive innovation, and remain competitive in a rapidly changing business environment. Let's explore each of these processes in detail:

1. Knowledge Creation:

Knowledge creation refers to the process of generating new knowledge within an organization. It involves transforming individual experiences, insights, and expertise into explicit knowledge that can be shared and utilized. Knowledge creation occurs through various means, including:

a. Individual Learning: Individuals acquire knowledge through formal education, on-the-job experiences, self-study, and personal reflection. This knowledge builds upon their existing expertise and contributes to their learning and growth.

b. Collaboration and Interaction: Knowledge creation is often enhanced through collaboration and interaction among individuals or teams. Brainstorming sessions, meetings, and cross-functional collaborations encourage the exchange of ideas, perspectives, and expertise, stimulating the generation of new knowledge.

c. Experimentation and Innovation: Organizations foster knowledge creation through experimentation and innovation. By encouraging employees to explore new ideas, take risks, and challenge existing assumptions, organizations can drive the creation of new knowledge and novel approaches to problem-solving.

d. External Influences: Knowledge creation is influenced by external factors such as market trends, customer feedback, and industry research. Organizations actively monitor and assimilate relevant information from external sources to generate new insights and knowledge.

2. Knowledge Acquisition:

Knowledge acquisition involves obtaining knowledge from external sources to supplement and enrich an organization's existing knowledge base. It focuses on identifying and accessing valuable knowledge resources available beyond the organization's boundaries. Some common strategies for knowledge acquisition include:

a. Networking and Collaboration: Organizations establish partnerships, networks, and collaborations with external stakeholders, including industry experts, academia, research institutions, and other organizations. This collaboration facilitates knowledge sharing, access to expertise, and the exchange of best practices.

b. Research and Benchmarking: Organizations conduct research activities to benchmark against industry standards, learn from competitors, and gather knowledge about emerging trends, technologies, and market insights.

c. Knowledge Brokering: Knowledge brokers act as intermediaries between external knowledge sources and the organization. They facilitate the identification, selection, and transfer of relevant knowledge by leveraging their networks and expertise.

d. Open Innovation: Organizations adopt open innovation principles, which involve actively seeking external knowledge and ideas through crowdsourcing, innovation challenges, and partnerships with customers, suppliers, and other stakeholders.

e. External Training and Education: Organizations invest in external training programs, conferences, seminars, and workshops to provide employees with access to the latest industry knowledge and practices.

Both knowledge creation and acquisition processes have their challenges and considerations. Some common challenges include capturing and codifying tacit knowledge, managing information overload, ensuring the quality and relevance of acquired knowledge, and fostering a culture that encourages continuous learning and knowledge sharing. Effective knowledge management strategies address these challenges by implementing mechanisms for knowledge capture, sharing, validation, and embedding acquired knowledge into organizational practices.

In conclusion, knowledge creation and acquisition are essential processes in knowledge management. Organizations must actively promote the creation of new knowledge through individual learning, collaboration, experimentation, and engagement with external sources. Simultaneously, knowledge acquisition enables organizations to tap into external expertise, market insights, and emerging trends. By integrating these processes effectively, organizations can expand their knowledge base, foster innovation, and gain a competitive edge.

Knowledge Sharing and Dissemination

Knowledge sharing and dissemination is a crucial process in knowledge management that involves the transfer of knowledge from one individual or group to another within an organization. It is a means of unlocking the value of knowledge and leveraging it for organizational learning, collaboration, and innovation. By facilitating knowledge sharing, organizations can enhance decision-making, problem-solving, and overall performance. Here is a detailed explanation of knowledge sharing and dissemination:

1. Importance of Knowledge Sharing:

Knowledge sharing is essential for creating a learning culture within an organization. It fosters collaboration, promotes innovation, and enhances problem-solving capabilities. Some key benefits of knowledge sharing include:

- Enhanced Decision-Making: Access to shared knowledge enables individuals and teams to make more informed and effective decisions. Collaborative sharing of expertise, experiences, and insights ensures a broader perspective and a deeper understanding of issues or opportunities.

- Improved Problem-Solving: By sharing knowledge and expertise, individuals and teams can collectively address complex problems and find innovative solutions. Sharing different perspectives and approaches enables diverse thinking and increases the likelihood of finding optimal solutions.
- Accelerated Learning: Knowledge sharing expedites the learning process by reducing redundancy and facilitating the transfer of best practices and lessons learned. New employees can leverage the knowledge of experienced colleagues, shortening their learning curve and enhancing their productivity.
- Innovation and Creativity: Openly sharing knowledge and ideas fuels innovation. The combination of diverse knowledge and perspectives often leads to the development of new insights, ideas, and opportunities within the organization.

2. Methods and Channels for Knowledge Sharing:

Organizations employ various methods and channels to facilitate knowledge sharing and dissemination. Some common approaches include:

- Communities of Practice (CoPs): CoPs are groups of individuals with shared interests or expertise. They provide a platform for members to share knowledge, experiences, and best practices. CoPs foster collaboration, mentorship, and collective learning.
- Collaboration Platforms and Tools: Technology platforms such as intranets, communication tools, social networks, and collaborative software enable individuals and teams to share knowledge, discuss ideas, and collaborate on projects.
- Storytelling and Narrative Sharing: Storytelling is an effective way to transfer tacit knowledge. Through anecdotes, case studies, or personal narratives, individuals can communicate their experiences, lessons learned, and expertise in a relatable and memorable manner.
- Documentation and Knowledge Repositories: This involves creating repositories or databases where explicit knowledge is stored, organized, and made accessible to employees. It includes documents, reports, best practices, policies, and standard operating procedures that capture institutional knowledge.
- Training and Workshops: Face-to-face training sessions, workshops, and seminars provide opportunities for knowledge sharing and learning. They often involve presentations, demonstrations, and interactive discussions.

3. Barriers and Solutions to Knowledge Sharing:

Organizations often encounter barriers to knowledge sharing. These barriers may include a lack of trust, a fear of job security, a culture of knowledge hoarding, and insufficient incentives or recognition for sharing knowledge. To overcome these barriers and encourage knowledge sharing, organizations can:

- Foster a Culture of Trust: A culture that values openness, trust, and psychological safety encourages individuals to share knowledge without fear of judgment or negative consequences.
- Provide Incentives and Recognition: Recognizing and rewarding individuals or teams for their knowledge, contributions and innovative ideas encourages a culture of knowledge sharing.
- Facilitate Collaboration and Communication: Establishing communication channels, collaboration platforms, and regular forums for sharing knowledge enables easy and convenient knowledge exchange among employees.
- Create Knowledge-Sharing Policies: Implementing policies and guidelines that promote and support knowledge-sharing activities, such as CoPs, documentation practices, and regular knowledge-sharing sessions, can facilitate a structured approach to knowledge-sharing.

4. Challenges and Best Practices in Knowledge Sharing:

Organizations may face challenges in implementing effective knowledge sharing. Some of the common challenges include cultural barriers, information overload, lack of motivation or time, and the difficulty of capturing tacit knowledge. To overcome these challenges, organizations can consider the following best practices:

- Develop an Organizational Culture that Values Knowledge Sharing: Cascading the importance of knowledge sharing from leadership and fostering a culture that promotes openness and collaboration.
- Encourage Active Participation and Engagement: Motivate employees to actively participate in knowledge-sharing initiatives by providing recognition, incentives, and opportunities for growth and development.
- Provide Training and Support: Offer training programs and resources to enhance employees' knowledge-sharing skills and create an environment that encourages continuous learning.
- Embrace Technology: Utilize technology platforms and tools that facilitate seamless knowledge sharing, collaboration, and access to relevant information.
- Promote Social Learning: Encourage employees to learn from each other through mentoring, coaching, and peer-to-peer interactions. Establish platforms for informal knowledge exchange and networking.

In conclusion, knowledge sharing, and dissemination are vital processes in knowledge management that enable organizations to tap into the collective knowledge and expertise of their employees. By fostering a culture of trust, providing suitable channels and tools, and addressing barriers through training and incentives, organizations can facilitate effective knowledge sharing. Successful knowledge sharing enhances decision-making, problem-solving, innovation, and overall organizational performance.

Knowledge Application and Utilization

Knowledge application and utilization refers to the practical integration of knowledge into various aspects of an organization's activities and decision-making processes. It involves effectively applying acquired knowledge to solve problems, make informed decisions, drive innovation, and achieve organizational goals. Here is a thorough explanation of knowledge application and utilization:

1. Importance of Knowledge Application:

Knowledge application is crucial because it transforms knowledge from theoretical concepts into actionable insights. By applying knowledge, organizations can drive innovation, improve processes, and make informed decisions. Some key benefits of knowledge application include:

- Problem-solving: By applying relevant knowledge, organizations can identify and address challenges more effectively. Knowledge application enables a systematic analysis of problems, the identification of root causes, and the development of appropriate solutions.
- Informed Decision-making: Knowledge application provides a solid foundation for decision-making. Access to relevant knowledge allows decision-makers to evaluate alternatives, assess risks, and select the best course of action based on evidence and insights.
- Innovation and Creativity: Applying knowledge fosters innovation by inspiring new ideas and perspectives. Creativity is enhanced when employees are encouraged to explore and apply their knowledge in novel ways, leading to new product development, process improvements, and market opportunities.
- Continuous Improvement: Knowledge application supports a culture of continuous improvement. Organizations that actively apply knowledge seek ways to enhance their processes, methodologies, and performance. They leverage internal and external knowledge to drive ongoing learning and refine their practices.

2. Steps in Knowledge Application:

To effectively apply knowledge, organizations can follow a systematic approach that includes the following steps:

- Identification: Identify the specific knowledge or expertise that is relevant to the problem or decision at hand. This could be explicit knowledge (e.g., documented best practices) or tacit knowledge (e.g., expertise gained through experience).
- Acquisition: Gather the identified knowledge from various sources such as internal experts, external research, databases, or industry reports. This step ensures that the organization has access to the necessary knowledge resources.
- Interpretation: Analyze and interpret the acquired knowledge to understand its implications and potential applications. This involves assessing its relevance, reliability, and applicability to the specific context or situation.
- Application: Apply the knowledge to solve problems, make decisions, or drive innovation. This step involves utilizing the knowledge effectively by integrating it into processes, projects, or decision-making frameworks.
- Evaluation: Continuously evaluate the outcomes and impact of the applied knowledge. Measure the effectiveness of the application in achieving desired results and identify opportunities for improvement or further refinement.

3. Knowledge Utilization:

Knowledge utilization refers to the active use of knowledge across various organizational activities and functions. It involves integrating knowledge into organizational systems, processes, training programs, and decision-making frameworks. Key approaches to knowledge utilization include:

- Transferring knowledge to practice: Ensure that the acquired knowledge is effectively transferred and applied in daily work activities. This may involve updating standard operating procedures, guidelines, or work instructions to reflect the latest knowledge and best practices.
- Applying knowledge to innovation: Knowledge utilization plays a crucial role in driving innovation. By applying existing knowledge creatively and combining it with new insights, organizations can develop new products, services, or processes that meet evolving customer needs and market trends.
- Embedding knowledge in systems and processes: Integrate knowledge into the organization's systems, processes, and technologies to facilitate easy access and utilization.
- This may involve creating knowledge repositories, databases, or digital tools that enable employees to quickly find and apply relevant knowledge.

4. Challenges in Knowledge Application and Utilization:

Organizations may face challenges in effectively applying and utilizing knowledge throughout the organization. Some common challenges include:

- Knowledge Silos: Knowledge may be confined within specific individuals or departments, limiting its application and utilization across the organization. Breaking down silos and promoting cross-functional collaboration is necessary to overcome this challenge.
- Resistance to Change: Resistance to change can hinder knowledge application and utilization efforts. Employees may be resistant to adopting new knowledge or approaches due to a fear of the unknown or comfort with existing practices.
- Lack of Communication and Collaboration: Inadequate communication and collaboration channels can hinder the sharing and integration of knowledge across teams and departments. Organizations need to establish effective communication channels and encourage collaboration to overcome this challenge.

5. Strategies for Effective Knowledge Application and Utilization:

To overcome challenges and promote effective knowledge application and utilization, organizations can implement the following strategies:

- Promote a Learning Culture: Foster a culture that values learning, encourages knowledge sharing, and supports continuous improvement. This involves providing opportunities for training, coaching, and nurturing a mindset that embraces new ideas and practices.
- Establish Knowledge Management Processes: Develop processes and structures that enable systematic knowledge capture, storage, retrieval, and sharing. Implement tools and technologies that support knowledge utilization across different organizational functions.
- Encourage Collaboration and Interdisciplinary Exchange: Encourage collaboration and cross-functional communication to facilitate the exchange and application of knowledge across various teams and departments. Platforms such as communities of practice or cross-functional projects can facilitate knowledge sharing and collaboration.
- Provide Incentives and Recognition: Recognize and reward employees for their contributions to knowledge application and utilization. This can be done through performance evaluations, promotion opportunities, or acknowledgment of innovative ideas and practices.
- Monitor and Evaluate: Continuously monitor and evaluate the effectiveness of knowledge application and utilization efforts. Collect feedback, measure performance metrics, and use this information to refine and improve knowledge management processes and initiatives.

In conclusion, knowledge application and utilization are critical steps in leveraging organizational knowledge for problem-solving, decision-making, and innovation. By following a systematic approach, addressing challenges, and implementing strategies that promote effective knowledge application and utilization, organizations can maximize the value of their knowledge assets and achieve sustainable success.

Knowledge Evaluation and Feedback

Knowledge evaluation and feedback are integral components of knowledge management that enable organizations to assess the quality, relevance, and effectiveness of their knowledge assets. By evaluating knowledge and seeking feedback, organizations can identify areas for improvement, validate the usefulness of knowledge, and continuously enhance their knowledge management processes. Here is a thorough explanation of knowledge evaluation and feedback:

1. Importance of Knowledge Evaluation:

Knowledge evaluation is essential for several reasons:

- Quality Assessment: Evaluation enables organizations to assess the quality and reliability of knowledge assets. It helps in identifying outdated, inaccurate, or incomplete information.
- Relevance Determination: Evaluation helps organizations determine the relevance and applicability of knowledge in different contexts and situations. It ensures that knowledge aligns with the organization's goals, industry trends, and stakeholder needs.
- Improvement Identification: Evaluation highlights areas where knowledge management processes or practices can be improved. It identifies gaps, inefficiencies, and challenges that need to be addressed to enhance the overall knowledge management effort.
- Value Measurement: Evaluation provides insights into the value and impact of knowledge initiatives on organizational performance, innovation, and decision-making. It helps determine the return on investment (ROI) of knowledge management efforts.

2. Methods and Approaches for Knowledge Evaluation:

Various methods and approaches can be employed for knowledge evaluation. Some common approaches include:

- Surveys: Surveys allow organizations to gather feedback from employees, customers, or other stakeholders

to assess the value and effectiveness of knowledge assets. This can be done through questionnaires, online surveys, or feedback forms.
- Interviews and Focus Groups: In-depth interviews, focus groups, or structured discussions provide opportunities to gather qualitative feedback on knowledge utilization, relevance, and impact. This approach enables nuanced insights and understanding of the value of knowledge.
- Performance Metrics: Organizations can establish key performance indicators (KPIs) to measure the impact of knowledge on specific outcomes, such as customer satisfaction, process efficiency, or innovation rates. Metrics help track progress and demonstrate the value of knowledge.
- Peer Reviews: Peer reviews involve subject matter experts or knowledgeable individuals assessing the quality, accuracy, and credibility of knowledge assets. It allows for a comprehensive evaluation from trusted sources.

3. Feedback Loop and Continuous Improvement:

Feedback is an integral part of the knowledge management process. Organizations should establish a feedback loop to gather feedback regularly and continuously improve their knowledge management efforts. This loop should involve:

- Collecting Feedback: Organizations should actively seek feedback from various stakeholders, including employees, customers, partners, and experts, on the relevance, usefulness, and effectiveness of knowledge assets.
- Analyzing Feedback: Feedback data should be systematically analyzed to identify patterns, trends, and areas of improvement. It helps in understanding strengths, weaknesses, and opportunities for enhancement.
- Implementing Changes: Based on feedback analysis, organizations can implement changes and improvements to the knowledge management processes, practices, or content. This contributes to continuous improvement and ensures that knowledge remains up-to-date, relevant, and valuable.

4. Metrics and Indicators for Assessing Knowledge Value:

Defining appropriate metrics and indicators is essential for assessing the value and impact of knowledge management initiatives. Some common metrics include:

- Knowledge Usage: Tracking the frequency and extent of knowledge utilization provides insights into the relevance and acceptance of knowledge assets.
- User Satisfaction: Measuring user satisfaction with knowledge assets helps evaluate their perceived value and effectiveness.
- Decision-Making Improvement: Assessing the impact of knowledge on organizational decision-making and the quality of decisions helps determine the value of knowledge assets.
- Innovation Rates: Monitoring the number and impact of innovations resulting from the application of knowledge enables organizations to gauge the value of knowledge management efforts in driving innovation.

5. Challenges in Measuring Knowledge Management Effectiveness:

Challenges may arise when measuring the effectiveness of knowledge management efforts. Some common challenges include:

- Difficulty in Measuring Intangible Aspects: Knowledge is often intangible, making it challenging to quantify its value. Organizations need to devise creative and meaningful methods to measure intangible aspects like improved problem-solving or innovation rates.
- Subjectivity: Perception of value and effectiveness may vary among individuals and stakeholders, making

it challenging to capture objective feedback and metrics.

- Time and Resource Constraints: Conducting comprehensive evaluations and gathering feedback can be time-consuming and resource intensive. Organizations need to balance evaluation efforts against other business priorities.
- Defining and Aligning Metrics: Identifying relevant and measurable metrics that align with organizational goals and knowledge management objectives can pose a challenge.
- Attribution and causation: Isolating the impact of knowledge management efforts from other factors contributing to organizational performance can be complex.

6. Strategies for Effective Knowledge Evaluation:

Organizations can adopt various strategies to overcome challenges and promote effective knowledge evaluation:

- Clear Evaluation Objectives: Define clear evaluation objectives aligned with organizational goals and knowledge management strategies to guide the evaluation efforts.
- Stakeholder Engagement: Engage stakeholders from different levels and departments in the evaluation process to ensure diverse perspectives and comprehensive feedback.
- Use a Mix of Methods: Employ a combination of qualitative and quantitative evaluation methods to gain a holistic understanding of knowledge effectiveness.
- Continuous Learning Culture: Foster a culture of continuous learning and improvement, where knowledge evaluation is embedded as a regular process and feedback is actively sought and valued.
- Regular Review and Revision: Regularly review evaluation metrics, indicators, and methods to ensure they remain relevant and aligned with changing organizational needs.

7. Ethical Considerations in Knowledge Evaluation:

Organizations must ensure ethical considerations are met during knowledge evaluation. This includes obtaining informed consent from participants, maintaining confidentiality, and ensuring fairness and transparency in the evaluation process. Protecting sensitive data and adhering to privacy regulations is crucial during data collection and analysis.

8. Evaluation as a Learning Opportunity:

Instead of viewing evaluation solely as a measure of success or failure, organizations should treat it as a learning opportunity. Reflecting on evaluation results, identifying areas for improvement, and implementing changes based on feedback are all essential components of continuous learning and improvement in knowledge management.

In conclusion, knowledge evaluation and feedback are critical processes in knowledge management that enable organizations to assess the value, quality, and impact of their knowledge assets. By employing appropriate evaluation methods, defining meaningful metrics, fostering a feedback loop, and treating evaluation as a learning opportunity, organizations can continuously improve their knowledge management efforts and enhance organizational performance.

Organizational Learning: The Foundation of Knowledge Management:

The foundation of knowledge management (KM) lies in recognizing the importance of knowledge as a strategic organizational asset and leveraging it for competitive advantage. KM is built upon several fundamental principles and pillars that provide a strong foundation for effective knowledge management practices. Here are the key elements that form the foundation of KM:

1. Knowledge as an Organizational Asset:

The foundation of KM is the understanding that knowledge is a valuable resource that needs to be identified, captured, shared, and utilized for organizational success. This recognition treats knowledge as a tangible and intangible asset that requires management and nurturing.

2. Organizational Culture and Leadership:

A supportive organizational culture and effective leadership are critical for successful knowledge management. It involves creating an environment that encourages collaboration, knowledge sharing, innovation, and continuous learning. Leaders play a crucial role in driving knowledge management initiatives and embedding KM principles into the organization's strategic vision and goals.

3. Knowledge Creation and Acquisition:

The foundation of KM lies in actively promoting and facilitating knowledge creation and acquisition. This involves capturing explicit knowledge (documented information) and tacit knowledge (personal insights, skills, and experiences) from employees, customers, partners, and external sources. Organizations need effective mechanisms for knowledge creation, such as communities of practice, brainstorming sessions, and benchmarking.

4. Knowledge Storage and Organization:

An essential foundation of KM is establishing systems, repositories, and technologies to store, organize, and manage knowledge assets effectively. This includes databases, document management systems, intranets, and collaboration platforms that allow easy access, retrieval, and sharing of knowledge across the organization. Classification, tagging, and metadata techniques are utilized for effective knowledge organization.

5. Knowledge Sharing and Transfer:

KM focuses on facilitating knowledge sharing and transfer across individuals, teams, and departments. This requires developing processes and platforms that encourage employees to share their knowledge, experiences, and best practices with others. Collaboration tools, social networks, mentoring programs, and knowledge-sharing sessions are some of the methods used to promote knowledge exchange and transfer.

6. Knowledge Utilization and Application:

The foundation of KM is enabling the effective utilization and application of knowledge to drive organizational performance and innovation. This involves making knowledge readily available to employees when and where they need it, developing practices for knowledge-based decision-making, and ensuring that knowledge is embedded in work processes and systems. Utilization of knowledge also includes leveraging it for problem-solving, improvement initiatives, and product/service development.

7. Continuous Learning and Improvement:

KM recognizes the importance of continuous learning and improvement as a key foundation. Organizations should foster a culture of learning, encourage employees to seek and apply new knowledge and provide opportunities for professional development. Regular evaluation and feedback mechanisms are implemented to identify areas for improvement and enhance knowledge management strategies and processes.

8. Technology and Infrastructure:

A robust technological infrastructure is vital for knowledge management. Organizations need to invest in suitable technologies and tools to support knowledge sharing, collaboration, and storage. This may include knowledge bases, search engines, expert systems, data analytics, and artificial intelligence applications that facilitate knowledge management processes.

9. Governance and Measurement:

The foundation of KM includes establishing governance structures and measurement mechanisms to ensure the effectiveness and sustainability of knowledge management initiatives. This involves defining roles, responsibilities, and accountability for knowledge management, as well as monitoring and assessing the impact of KM efforts through appropriate metrics and indicators.

10. Ethical Considerations:

KM is built upon ethical considerations, such as ensuring the privacy and confidentiality of sensitive information, maintaining data security, and respecting intellectual property rights. Organizations need to establish policies and practices that uphold ethical standards and comply with legal and regulatory requirements.

In summary, the foundation of knowledge management is based on recognizing knowledge as a strategic asset and establishing a supportive organizational culture, leadership, and infrastructure. It encompasses processes for knowledge creation, storage, sharing, utilization, and continuous learning. Ethical considerations, governance, and measurement play a crucial role in ensuring effective knowledge management practices and driving organizational success.

Conceptualizing Organizational Learning

Conceptualizing organizational learning involves understanding how organizations acquire, interpret, and apply knowledge to improve their performance and adapt to changing environments. It is a process that involves developing strategies, structures, and systems to facilitate learning at individual, group, and organizational levels.

At its core, organizational learning is a continuous process that enables organizations to make sense of information and experiences, and then make decisions and take actions based on that knowledge. It involves the creation of new knowledge through experimentation, reflection, and dialogue, as well as the acquisition of knowledge from external sources such as customers, suppliers, and competitors.

Several key concepts are important to understand when conceptualizing organizational learning:

1. Learning loops: Organizational learning is not a linear process but rather a dynamic loop that involves cycles of action, reflection, and adjustment. These loops enable organizations to continuously learn and improve over time by testing assumptions, reflecting on outcomes, and making adjustments as necessary.

2. Knowledge creation: Organizational learning involves the creation of new knowledge through a combination of individual and collective learning. This can occur through individual experiences and insights, as well as through group processes such as brainstorming, knowledge sharing, and collaboration.

3. Knowledge transfer: Organizational learning also involves the transfer of knowledge from one part of the organization to another. This can occur through formal channels such as training programs or knowledge management systems, as well as through informal channels such as interpersonal relationships and social networks.

4. Learning culture: Organizational learning is facilitated by a culture that promotes and supports learning at all levels. This includes fostering open communication, encouraging experimentation and innovation, and valuing the sharing and dissemination of knowledge.

5. Learning organization: A learning organization develops the capacity to continuously learn, adapt, and innovate. This involves creating structures and systems that support learning, such as learning networks, communities of practice, and opportunities for reflection and dialogue.

6. Double-loop learning: Double-loop learning involves questioning and challenging underlying assumptions and beliefs, rather than simply making incremental improvements. It involves critically reflecting on the underlying assumptions that shape the organization's thinking and making fundamental changes when necessary.

7. Learning from failure: Organizational learning also involves the ability to learn from failures and mistakes. This requires a culture that encourages risk-taking and experimentation, as well as a willingness to reflect on failures and extract valuable lessons from them.

In summary, conceptualizing organizational learning involves understanding the processes, structures, and strategies that facilitate learning within an organization. It involves creating a culture of learning, developing systems for knowledge creation and transfer, and fostering an environment that supports reflection, dialogue, and experimentation. Ultimately, organizational learning enables organizations to become more adaptive, innovative, and effective in achieving their goals.

The Importance of Organizational Learning

Organizational learning is of utmost importance in today's rapidly changing and competitive business landscape. Here are four key reasons why organizational learning is crucial:

1. Adaptability and innovation: Organizational learning enables companies to adapt and respond effectively to changing circumstances. By continuously acquiring new knowledge, analyzing data, and experimenting with new ideas, organizations can identify emerging trends, anticipate market shifts, and innovate to stay ahead of the competition. A learning organization is more agile and capable of proactively addressing challenges and seizing opportunities.

2. Continuous improvement: Organizational learning fosters a culture of continuous improvement by encouraging employees to reflect on their experiences, learn from mistakes, and find ways to enhance efficiency, quality, and effectiveness. It allows organizations to identify bottlenecks, streamline processes, and optimize performance, leading to higher productivity and better outcomes. Through learning loops and feedback mechanisms, organizations can adjust strategies and operations based on data-driven insights, resulting in iterative progress and growth.

3. Knowledge retention and leveraging: Organizational learning helps capture and retain valuable knowledge within the organization. By promoting knowledge sharing, cross-functional collaboration, and communities of practice, organizations can harness the collective intelligence of their employees. This ensures that knowledge is not lost when individuals leave the company or move to different roles, creating a knowledge reservoir that can be leveraged to solve problems, make informed decisions, and drive organizational effectiveness.

4. Employee engagement and development: Organizational learning plays a vital role in employee engagement and development. It provides opportunities for individuals to learn and grow, enhancing job satisfaction and motivation. When organizations invest in employee learning and development, it fosters a sense of investment and loyalty, reduces turnover, and attracts top talent. Moreover, learning opportunities enable employees to develop new skills, gain expertise, and contribute more effectively to the organization's success, leading to individual and collective growth.

In conclusion, organizational learning is crucial for organizations seeking to thrive in a dynamic and competitive environment. It enables adaptability, drives continuous improvement, retains and leverages knowledge, and enhances employee engagement and development. By embracing a culture of learning, organizations can foster innovation, optimize performance, and build a sustainable competitive advantage.

Organizational Learning Theories

Several organizational learning theories help explain how organizations acquire, interpret, and apply knowledge. Here are three key theories:

1. Single-loop and double-loop learning: Single-loop learning, popularized by organizational theorist Chris Argyris, refers to the process of making incremental adjustments and improvements based on feedback. It entails identifying errors or discrepancies and taking corrective action without questioning the underlying assumptions or beliefs. Double-loop learning, on the other hand, involves not only identifying and correcting errors but also questioning and challenging the underlying assumptions and values that shape organizational behavior. It goes beyond surface-level adjustments and encourages organizations to critically reflect on their assumptions, challenge routine practices, and make fundamental changes when necessary.

2. Knowledge creation theory: Developed by Nonaka and Takeuchi, the knowledge creation theory emphasizes the role of social interaction and individual experiences in the creation of new knowledge. The theory proposes four modes of knowledge conversion: socialization (sharing tacit knowledge through direct interaction), externalization (articulating tacit knowledge into explicit form), combination (systematizing and consolidating explicit knowledge), and internalization (applying explicit knowledge to individual tacit knowledge). This theory recognizes that knowledge creation is a dynamic process that involves both individual and collective learning, and it highlights the importance of creating a supportive environment that encourages knowledge-sharing and collaboration.

3. Learning organization theory: The learning organization theory, developed by Peter Senge, focuses on creating organizations that are capable of continuous learning and adaptation. A learning organization is characterized by five disciplines: personal mastery (the commitment to personal learning and growth), mental models (challenging and changing deep-seated assumptions), shared vision (a common purpose that inspires and guides), team learning (collective learning through dialogue and collaboration), and systems thinking (understanding the interdependencies and dynamics within the organization). This theory emphasizes the importance of creating a learning culture, developing learning systems and structures, and fostering individual and organizational learning processes to drive long-term success.

These theories provide different perspectives on how organizations learn, adapt, and foster innovation. They highlight the role of individual and collective learning, the importance of questioning assumptions, and the need for creating a supportive learning environment. By understanding and applying these theories, organizations can better conceptualize and implement effective strategies for organizational learning.

The Learning Organization: Facilitating Continuous Learning

Facilitating continuous learning within an organization is crucial for its long-term success and adaptability. Here are four key strategies for fostering continuous learning:

1. Establish a learning culture: Creating a learning culture is essential for promoting continuous learning within an organization. This involves fostering an environment where employees feel encouraged and supported in their pursuit of learning and growth. It requires leaders and managers to model and value learning, encouraging curiosity, experimentation, and reflection. Emphasize the importance of learning from both successes and failures and celebrate efforts towards ongoing development. Promote a culture of knowledge sharing, collaboration, and open communication that allows employees to learn from each other.

2. Provide learning opportunities: Offering diverse and meaningful learning opportunities is vital for facilitating continuous learning. This can include providing access to workshops, training programs, conferences, and online courses. Encourage employees to set personal learning goals and create individual development plans that align

with their career aspirations and the organization's strategic objectives. Offer mentoring and coaching programs to support employees in their learning journeys. Additionally, provides resources such as learning libraries, online platforms, and communities of practice to facilitate self-directed learning and knowledge sharing.

3. Encourage reflection and feedback: Reflection is a critical component of continuous learning. Encourage employees to take time to reflect on their experiences, identify lessons learned, and document insights. Establish feedback mechanisms such as regular performance evaluations, 360-degree feedback, and peer reviews to provide individuals with constructive feedback on their performance and areas for improvement. Foster a culture that celebrates continuous improvement and recognizes the value of ongoing learning and development.

4. Promote learning transfer and application: To ensure continuous learning leads to real-world impact, organizations need to promote the transfer and application of knowledge and skills. Provide opportunities for employees to apply what they have learned through challenging assignments, cross-functional projects, and stretch assignments. Encourage employees to share their newly acquired knowledge with their teams and create channels for disseminating best practices and lessons learned throughout the organization. Consider implementing knowledge management systems or tools that enable employees to easily access and apply relevant knowledge in their work.

By establishing a learning culture, providing learning opportunities, encouraging reflection and feedback, and promoting learning transfer and application, organizations can foster a continuous learning environment. This enables employees to continuously develop new skills, adapt to changing circumstances, and drive innovation, ultimately leading to improved performance and competitiveness.

The Role of Technology in Knowledge Management:

The role of technology in knowledge management is critical as it helps organizations efficiently capture, store, organize, and distribute knowledge within their networks. Here are some key aspects in which technology supports knowledge management:

1. Knowledge Repository: Technology provides a platform to create central repositories or databases where information, data, and knowledge can be stored, searchable, and accessed by employees. These repositories can be structured in different ways such as knowledge bases, wikis, intranets, or document management systems.

2. Knowledge Sharing: Technology enables the sharing of tacit and explicit knowledge across different departments, teams, and locations. Collaboration tools like video conferencing, instant messaging, project management software, and shared document platforms make it easier for employees to communicate and exchange knowledge regardless of geographical barriers.

3. Knowledge Capture: Technology facilitates the capturing of knowledge from employees and subject matter experts, helping prevent knowledge from being lost when employees leave an organization. This can be done through tools like surveys, forums, blogs, or social networking platforms where individuals can share their expertise and experiences.

4. Knowledge Discovery: Technology enables efficient search and retrieval of relevant knowledge. Advanced search capabilities, AI-powered algorithms, and data analytics tools make it easier to navigate vast amounts of information and find the specific knowledge required on time.

5. Knowledge Preservation: Technology also plays a role in preserving historical knowledge and lessons learned. By archiving documents, past projects, and discussions, organizations can ensure that valuable knowledge is retained for future reference, learning, and decision-making processes.

6. Knowledge Dissemination: Technology supports the dissemination of knowledge to the right individuals or groups, ensuring that the most up-to-date and relevant information reaches those who need it. This can be done through automated notifications, newsletters, alerts, or personalized recommendation systems.

7. Knowledge Analysis: Technology helps analyze knowledge patterns and user behaviors, which can provide valuable insights into knowledge gaps, popular topics, expertise identification, or areas where additional training might be necessary. This analysis can aid in making informed decisions regarding knowledge management strategies and resource allocation.

Overall, technology acts as a catalyst for knowledge management by enabling efficient knowledge creation, sharing, preservation, discovery, and dissemination. It enhances collaboration, productivity, and learning within organizations by providing a digital infrastructure to harness and leverage knowledge effectively.

Technology as an Enabler of Knowledge Management

Technology serves as a powerful enabler of knowledge management, revolutionizing the way organizations create, capture, store, organize, and share knowledge. In this comprehensive explanation, we will delve into the importance of technology in knowledge management, exploring various aspects of its role and impact.

1. Introduction to Knowledge Management (KM):

Knowledge management is the systematic process of capturing, organizing, and distributing knowledge within an organization to enhance productivity, innovation, decision-making, and overall performance. It encompasses both explicit knowledge (codified and documented) and tacit knowledge (experience, skills, insights, and expertise). Effective KM enables organizations to leverage their collective knowledge, utilize it for continuous learning, and gain a competitive advantage.

2. The Evolution of Technology in KM:

The integration of technology into knowledge management practices has witnessed significant strides over the years. Traditional knowledge management relied heavily on manual, paper-based processes, making it time-consuming and prone to human error. However, the advent of digital technology has transformed KM practices, amplifying their effectiveness and efficiency. From basic knowledge repositories to advanced AI-powered systems, technology has revolutionized KM in multiple ways.

3. Knowledge Capture and Creation:

Technology plays a vital role in capturing and creating knowledge within organizations. It provides platforms and tools that facilitate knowledge transfer from individuals to a centralized repository. For instance, employees can use collaboration software, intranets, or wikis to document their expertise, share best practices, and create knowledge bases for future reference. These digital platforms streamline the collection and archiving of knowledge, ensuring that valuable insights are not lost when employees leave or retire.

4. Knowledge Storage and Organization:

Technology enables organizations to store and organize knowledge in efficient and easily accessible ways. Knowledge repositories, document management systems, and content management platforms provide a centralized hub where knowledge assets can be stored, tagged, and categorized. Advanced search functionalities and metadata tagging allow employees to locate specific information quickly, promoting efficient knowledge retrieval.

5. Knowledge Sharing and Collaboration:

Technology facilitates seamless knowledge sharing and collaboration among employees, regardless of geographic location. Collaboration tools such as video conferencing, instant messaging, and project management software enable real-time communication, fostering virtual teamwork and knowledge exchange. Cloud-based platforms enable simultaneous access to documents, enabling teams to collaborate on projects and share knowledge effortlessly.

6. Knowledge Dissemination:

Technology plays a crucial role in disseminating knowledge to relevant stakeholders within the organization. Automated notifications, newsletters, alerts, and personalized recommendation systems ensure that employees receive timely and relevant information. Additionally, social networking platforms and enterprise social media tools enable knowledge sharing and serendipitous discovery through likes, comments, and sharing features.

7. Tacit Knowledge Capture:

Capturing and sharing tacit knowledge, which resides in individuals' minds, poses a unique challenge in KM. However, technology offers innovative solutions to enable tacit knowledge capture. For instance, video-based knowledge-sharing platforms or virtual reality simulations can capture interactions, demonstrations, or experiences that are difficult to articulate in written or explicit form. These technologies allow organizations to preserve and transfer valuable tacit knowledge within their networks.

8. Knowledge Retrieval and Discoverability:

Technology provides advanced search capabilities and intelligent algorithms that enhance knowledge retrieval and discoverability. Employees can efficiently navigate through vast amounts of information, locating relevant knowledge on time. Natural language processing, data analytics, and machine learning techniques contribute to personalized and context-aware search results, making knowledge retrieval quicker and more accurate.

9. Knowledge Preservation and Archiving:

Technology plays a crucial role in the preservation and archiving of knowledge for future reference and learning. Content management systems, version control mechanisms, and digital archiving platforms ensure that documents, reports, and project histories are securely stored and accessible for retrospective analysis. This knowledge preservation aids in identifying patterns, learning from past experiences, and avoiding repeated mistakes.

10. Knowledge Analysis and Insights:

Technology enables organizations to analyze knowledge patterns, user behaviors, and engagement metrics, providing valuable insights. Data analytics tools can identify popular topics, knowledge gaps, and areas where additional training or intervention may be necessary. By leveraging these insights, organizations can make informed decisions, refine their KM strategies, and allocate resources effectively.

11. Knowledge Personalization and Recommendation Systems:

Technology empowers organizations to personalize knowledge delivery based on individual preferences and needs. Recommendation systems utilize machine learning algorithms to offer tailored content and suggest relevant knowledge resources. This personalization enhances the user experience, encourages engagement, and supports continuous learning and development.

12. Challenges and Considerations:

While technology offers immense opportunities for knowledge management, organizations need to be aware of certain challenges and considerations. These include privacy and security concerns surrounding knowledge assets, ensuring the relevancy and accuracy of knowledge repositories, and addressing potential resistance or reluctance from employees adapting to technology-driven KM practices. Organizations must also invest in training and change management initiatives to ensure smooth technology adoption and user acceptance.

13. Future Trends and Emergent Technologies:

Emerging technologies have the potential to further revolutionize knowledge management. Artificial intelligence (AI), machine learning, natural language processing, and the Internet of Things (IoT) hold promise in automating knowledge capture, enhancing search capabilities, and enabling intelligent knowledge recommendation systems. Advanced analytics, augmented reality, and chatbots are also poised to shape the future of knowledge management, improving knowledge accessibility, collaboration, and problem-solving.

Technology plays a pivotal role in modern knowledge management practices, acting as an enabler that empowers organizations to leverage their intellectual capital effectively. By facilitating knowledge capture, storage, organization, sharing, and retrieval, technology unlocks the potential of knowledge management, driving productivity, innovation, and growth. Organizations that embrace and effectively leverage technology in their KM initiatives gain a distinct competitive advantage in the rapidly evolving digital landscape.

Knowledge Management Systems (KMS)

A knowledge management system (KMS) is a software solution designed to facilitate the creation, capture, organization, storage, and dissemination of knowledge within an organization. It provides a structured and centralized platform for employees to access and share information, collaborate, and learn from each other's expertise. KMSs are instrumental in promoting knowledge sharing and collaboration, ultimately enhancing the overall performance and competitiveness of an organization.

The key components of a KMS include a knowledge repository, search and retrieval functionalities, collaboration tools, and analytics capabilities. The knowledge repository serves as a central hub where explicit knowledge, such as documents, reports, and best practices, is stored and organized. Employees can easily access and contribute to the repository, ensuring that valuable knowledge is not lost when employees leave or retire. The search and retrieval functionalities enable users to locate specific information quickly, whether it's through keyword search, advanced filters, or intelligent algorithms that provide context-aware recommendations.

Collaboration tools within a KMS facilitate the sharing and exchange of knowledge among employees. These tools may include discussion forums, wikis, blogs, and project management software that enable real-time communication, virtual teamwork, and knowledge co-creation. Employees can collaborate on projects, ask questions, share insights, and learn from each other's experiences, regardless of their geographical locations.

Analytics capabilities within a KMS provide insights into knowledge patterns, user behaviors, and engagement metrics. Organizations can analyze these data to identify popular topics, knowledge gaps, areas requiring additional training, or opportunities for innovation. The analytics component empowers organizations to make informed decisions regarding knowledge management strategies, resource allocation, and training initiatives.

In summary, a knowledge management system is a comprehensive software solution that enables organizations to effectively manage their knowledge assets. It supports the capture, organization, storage, retrieval, sharing, and collaboration of knowledge within an organization. By providing a centralized platform for knowledge access and exchange, KMSs boost employee productivity, innovation, and learning, ultimately driving organizational success.

Artificial Intelligence and Machine Learning in Knowledge Management

Artificial intelligence (AI) and machine learning (ML) have emerged as powerful technologies with significant implications for knowledge management (KM). They offer capabilities to automate processes, analyze vast amounts of data, extract insights, and enhance the efficiency and effectiveness of KM systems. Here is a detailed explanation of how AI and ML intersect with knowledge management:

1. Automated Knowledge Capture and Creation:

AI and ML techniques can be leveraged to automate the process of knowledge capture and creation. Natural Language Processing (NLP) algorithms can extract information from documents, emails, and other unstructured data sources, converting them into structured knowledge. Chatbots and virtual assistants powered by AI can interact with users to capture knowledge, answer queries, and facilitate knowledge creation in real-time.

2. Intelligent Search and Retrieval:

AI and ML algorithms significantly improve search and retrieval capabilities in KM systems. These technologies enhance traditional keyword-based search methods by understanding context, semantics, and user preferences. They can provide more accurate and relevant results by analyzing historical search patterns, user behaviors, and preferences. Machine learning algorithms continually learn from user interactions and feedback, further refining and optimizing the search experience.

3. Personalized Knowledge Delivery:

AI and ML enable personalized knowledge delivery based on individual user preferences and needs. By analyzing user behavior, preferences, and contextual data, recommendation systems can suggest relevant articles, documents, or experts within an organization. This personalization enhances user experience, increases engagement, and facilitates targeted learning, ultimately improving the effectiveness of knowledge management practices.

4. Knowledge Extraction and Classification:

AI and ML techniques can extract knowledge from unstructured data sources such as documents, videos, audio recordings, and social media feeds. Text mining algorithms, for example, can automatically extract important entities, keywords, and topics from textual data. Additionally, ML algorithms can classify and categorize knowledge assets based on content, ensuring that knowledge is organized and easily accessible.

5. Automated Tagging and Metadata Generation:

AI and ML can streamline the process of tagging and generating metadata for knowledge assets. By analyzing content and context, these technologies can automatically assign appropriate tags, keywords, or metadata to documents, making them more discoverable and facilitating efficient knowledge retrieval. This eliminates the need for manual tagging, saving time and effort for knowledge workers.

6. Expertise Identification and Collaboration:

AI and ML algorithms can help identify subject matter experts within an organization based on various factors such as their contributions, interactions, and expertise. By analyzing patterns in communication, content creation, and social network data, these technologies can connect individuals with relevant expertise, facilitating collaboration and knowledge sharing. This enables organizations to leverage their internal talent more effectively and foster a culture of collaborative learning.

7. Knowledge Analytics and Insights:

AI and ML algorithms enable organizations to gain insights from their knowledge repositories and user interactions. By analyzing patterns, trends, and correlations in knowledge usage, organizations can identify popular topics, knowledge gaps, and areas where additional training or intervention may be needed. These insights aid in making informed decisions, refining KM strategies, and enhancing the overall effectiveness of knowledge management practices.

8. Enhanced Decision-making and Problem-solving:

AI and ML can support decision-making processes by providing relevant and timely knowledge. By leveraging algorithms that analyze data and knowledge assets, organizations can access insights and recommendations that aid in problem-solving, strategic planning, and decision-making. AI-powered chatbots and virtual assistants can assist in accessing and understanding complex information, facilitating faster and more informed decision-making.

In summary, AI and ML bring transformative capabilities to knowledge management by automating processes, enhancing search and retrieval, personalizing knowledge delivery, facilitating collaboration, and providing insights and recommendations. By harnessing these technologies, organizations can optimize knowledge acquisition, sharing, and utilization, driving innovation, productivity, and competitiveness.

Challenges and Considerations in Implementing Technology-Driven Knowledge Management

Implementing technology-driven knowledge management comes with its own set of challenges and considerations. It is important to address these effectively to ensure successful implementation and adoption. Here are some key challenges and considerations:

1. Resistance to Change:

Implementing technology-driven knowledge management may encounter resistance from employees who are resistant to change or fear that technology will replace their roles. It is crucial to involve employees from the beginning, emphasizing the benefits technology can bring to their work and addressing their concerns. Communicating the purpose and advantages of the technology and providing training and support can help alleviate resistance and foster acceptance.

2. User Adoption and Engagement:

Ensuring user adoption and engagement with the technology is vital for success. Employees may be reluctant to adopt new systems or may lack the necessary skills to fully utilize them. It is crucial to provide comprehensive training programs, user-friendly interfaces, and ongoing support to encourage employees to embrace the technology. Incorporating feedback mechanisms and continuously improving the technology based on user input can enhance adoption and engagement.

3. Content Accuracy and Maintenance:

Technology-driven knowledge management relies heavily on the accuracy and relevance of the content stored in the system. Organizations must establish processes for content validation and maintenance. Regular content reviews, user feedback mechanisms, and governance frameworks can help ensure that the knowledge base remains up-to-date, accurate, and aligned with organizational goals.

4. Privacy and Security Concerns:

Knowledge management systems often contain sensitive or proprietary information, making data privacy and security crucial considerations. Organizations must implement robust security measures to safeguard knowledge assets from unauthorized access, breaches, or data loss. This includes encryption, access controls, strict user authentication, and regular security audits. Clear guidelines on data sharing, permissions, and confidentiality should be communicated to users to maintain trust and protect sensitive information.

5. Integration and Interoperability:

Integrating technology-driven knowledge management systems with existing IT infrastructure and applications can be challenging. Integration with other systems, such as customer relationship management (CRM), enterprise resource planning (ERP), or project management tools, is crucial for seamless knowledge transfer and retrieval. Ensuring interoperability and data consistency can help organizations leverage the full potential of their knowledge management system.

6. Cultural and Organizational Factors:

The success of technology-driven knowledge management relies on a supportive organizational culture that values knowledge sharing, collaboration, and continuous learning. Organizations must foster a culture that encourages employees to contribute and share their knowledge. Leadership support, mentoring programs, recognition systems, and knowledge-sharing incentives can foster a culture of knowledge-sharing and make the technology-driven initiative more effective.

7. Continuous Improvement and Evaluation:

Implementing technology-driven knowledge management is an ongoing process that requires continuous improvement and evaluation. Organizations should regularly reassess the effectiveness of the technology, the impact on knowledge sharing and collaboration, and user satisfaction. Gathering feedback from users, analyzing usage metrics, and conducting periodic evaluations can help identify areas for improvement and refine the technology and its implementation strategy.

8. Scalability and Flexibility:

Technology-driven knowledge management systems should be scalable and flexible enough to accommodate the changing needs of the organization. As the organization grows, the system should be able to handle increased user demands, larger knowledge repositories, and evolving technological requirements. It is important to select a technology platform that offers scalability and flexibility, ensuring long-term viability and adaptability.

In summary, addressing these challenges and considerations in implementing technology-driven knowledge management is crucial for successful adoption and utilization. By managing resistance to change, ensuring user adoption and engagement, addressing content accuracy and privacy concerns, integrating with existing systems, fostering a supportive organizational culture, and continuously improving and evaluating the system, organizations can make the most of technology-driven knowledge management initiatives and unlock their full potential.

Strategies for Effective Knowledge Management:

Effective knowledge management requires the implementation of various strategies to ensure the successful creation, organization, sharing, and utilization of knowledge within an organization. Here are key strategies for effective knowledge management:

1. Establish Clear Goals and Objectives:

Define clear goals and objectives for knowledge management initiatives aligned with overall organizational objectives. Identify the areas where knowledge management can have the most significant impact and prioritize accordingly. This helps focus efforts and resources on the most critical knowledge needs of the organization.

2. Foster a Knowledge-Sharing Culture:

Create a culture that values and promotes knowledge sharing. Encourage employees to contribute their knowledge and insights by establishing incentives, recognition programs, and knowledge-sharing platforms. Leadership support and involvement play a crucial role in fostering a culture that encourages collaboration, learning, and knowledge exchange.

3. Identify and Capture Critical Knowledge:

Identify critical knowledge areas and processes within the organization that need to be captured and shared. Implement processes and tools to capture and document both explicit (codified) and tacit (experience-based) knowledge. Encourage employees to share their expertise through training programs, documentation, lessons-learned sessions, and mentoring.

4. Implement Technology Solutions:

Leverage technology to facilitate knowledge management processes. Implement a knowledge management system (KMS) that provides a centralized repository for knowledge storage, search, retrieval, and collaboration. Choose technology solutions that align with the organization's requirements and ensure user-friendly interfaces, easy integration, and strong security measures.

5. Encourage Collaboration and Communities of Practice:

Promote collaboration and the formation of communities of practice (CoPs). CoPs bring together individuals with shared interests or expertise to share knowledge, discuss challenges, and learn from each other. Encourage active participation in CoPs, provide support, and facilitate knowledge-sharing events, workshops, and training sessions.

6. Facilitate Knowledge Access and Retrieval:

Ensure efficient knowledge access and retrieval by implementing robust search and retrieval functionalities. Invest in technology that enables advanced search capabilities, tagging, metadata, and content categorization. Accessible and user-friendly interfaces, combined with intelligent recommendation systems, can enhance knowledge discoverability and retrieval.

7. Support Continuous Learning and Development:

Promote a culture of continuous learning and development. Provide training programs, workshops, and learning resources to employees, enabling them to acquire new skills, keep up with industry trends, and stay updated on the latest knowledge in their domains. Support self-directed learning and encourage employees to take ownership of their personal and professional development.

8. Measure and Evaluate Knowledge Management:

Establish metrics and evaluation processes to measure the effectiveness and impact of knowledge management initiatives. Track user engagement, knowledge utilization, knowledge contribution, and the impact on organizational performance. Continuously assess the effectiveness of knowledge management practices and make improvements based on feedback and evaluation results.

9. Knowledge Management Champions and Roles:

Designate knowledge management champions who can drive knowledge management initiatives and act as advocates within the organization. These individuals can champion the importance of knowledge-sharing, provide guidance and support, and facilitate knowledge-sharing activities. Additionally, consider assigning dedicated roles, such as knowledge managers or coordinators, to ensure the smooth implementation and management of knowledge management initiatives.

10. Encourage Learning from Failure:

Create an environment that encourages learning from failures and mistakes. Emphasize the importance of honest discussions and sharing lessons learned from unsuccessful projects or initiatives. Encourage the documentation of failures along with the lessons learned to ensure that valuable knowledge is captured and utilized in future endeavors.

11. Continuous Improvement and Adaptability:

Knowledge management should be an evolving and continuously improving process. Regularly review knowledge management strategies, systems, and practices to identify areas for improvement and make necessary adjustments. Stay updated on emerging technologies, trends, and best practices in knowledge management to adapt and incorporate new approaches and tools.

By implementing these strategies, organizations can create a robust knowledge management framework and culture that facilitates the effective creation, sharing, and utilization of knowledge throughout the organization. This enables organizations to harness their collective intelligence, drive innovation, and enhance their overall performance and competitiveness.

Establishing a Knowledge Management Framework

Establishing a knowledge management (KM) framework is essential to effectively manage knowledge within an organization. It provides a structured approach for capturing, organizing, storing, sharing, and utilizing knowledge to drive organizational performance. Here is a detailed explanation of the key steps in establishing a knowledge management framework:

1. Assess Organizational Needs and Objectives:

Start by assessing the organizational needs and objectives. Understand the key knowledge areas critical to the organization's success, the gaps in knowledge management practices, and the desired outcomes. This assessment helps define the scope and priorities of the KM framework and ensures alignment with the organization's goals.

2. Define Roles and Responsibilities:

Identify the key stakeholders and roles responsible for implementing and maintaining the KM framework. This may include knowledge managers, champions, subject matter experts, IT personnel, and senior leadership. Clearly define their roles, responsibilities, and accountability in managing knowledge assets, facilitating knowledge transfer, and promoting knowledge-sharing practices within the organization.

3. Establish Knowledge Management Processes:

Define the processes required to manage knowledge effectively. This includes processes for capturing, organizing, storing, sharing, and utilizing knowledge. Identify the documentation standards, metadata requirements, version control mechanisms, and quality assurance processes to ensure the accuracy and relevance of knowledge assets. Develop standardized procedures and guidelines to facilitate consistent knowledge management practices across the organization.

4. Select Technology and Tools:

Choose technology platforms and tools that support the KM framework and enable efficient knowledge management processes. Consider factors such as ease of use, scalability, integration capabilities, security features, and the ability to capture both explicit and tacit knowledge. Collaborative tools, content management systems, knowledge repositories, and search and retrieval functionalities can significantly enhance the implementation and adoption of the KM framework.

5. Capture and Organize Knowledge:

Establish processes and mechanisms to capture and organize knowledge assets. This includes identifying and documenting explicit knowledge such as best practices, guidelines, case studies, and lessons learned. Additionally, encourage employees to contribute their tacit knowledge through knowledge-sharing platforms, communities of practice, and collaborative tools. Implement effective knowledge categorization, tagging, and metadata standards to ensure easy retrieval and organization of knowledge assets.

6. Encourage Knowledge Sharing and Collaboration:

Promote a culture of knowledge sharing and collaboration within the organization. Encourage employees to share their expertise, insights, and lessons learned through various channels such as discussion forums, social media platforms, mentoring programs, and communities of practice. Establish incentives, recognition programs, and rewards to encourage active participation and knowledge contribution. Foster an environment where employees feel comfortable seeking and sharing knowledge.

7. Implement Continuous Learning and Improvement Mechanisms:

Enable continuous learning and improvement by establishing mechanisms to capture and apply insights gained from knowledge management practices. Encourage employees to learn from both successes and failures by documenting lessons learned and sharing them proactively. Regularly review and evaluate the effectiveness of the KM framework, using feedback, metrics, and user engagement data. Continuously improve the framework based on insights gained from the evaluation process.

8. Promote Training and Awareness:

Provide comprehensive training programs and resources to employees to develop their knowledge management skills and familiarize them with the KM framework and related tools. Conduct awareness campaigns, workshops, and knowledge-sharing sessions to promote the understanding and adoption of knowledge management practices. Ensure that all employees understand the value and benefits of knowledge management and their role in contributing to its success.

9. Support from Leadership:

Leadership support is critical for the success of the KM framework. Secure buy-in and active support from senior management, who can communicate the importance of knowledge management, allocate necessary resources, and promote a knowledge-sharing culture. Leadership involvement demonstrates the organization's commitment to knowledge management and encourages widespread adoption and participation.

10. Monitor and Measure:

Develop measurement mechanisms to monitor the effectiveness and impact of the KM framework. Define key performance indicators (KPIs) that align with the organizational objectives and track metrics such as knowledge utilization, user satisfaction, productivity improvements, and innovation outcomes. Regularly assess and analyze the data to identify areas for improvement and make informed decisions to enhance the KM framework.

In summary, establishing a knowledge management framework involves assessing organizational needs, defining roles and responsibilities, establishing processes, selecting appropriate technology, encouraging knowledge sharing and collaboration, supporting continuous learning and improvement, promoting training and awareness, securing leadership support, and monitoring and measuring the effectiveness of the framework. By following these steps, organizations can build a structured and effective KM framework that unlocks their intellectual capital, fosters innovation, and drives organizational performance.

Knowledge Capture and Retention Strategies

Knowledge capture and retention strategies refer to the methods and practices employed by organizations to effectively capture, store, and retain valuable knowledge within the organization. These strategies aim to preserve the knowledge and expertise of individuals and ensure its availability for future use. Here are some key strategies for knowledge capture and retention:

1. Documentation and Documentation Standards:

Encourage individuals and teams to document their knowledge, experiences, best practices, and lessons learned. Develop documentation standards and templates to ensure consistency and ease of understanding. This includes written documents, reports, case studies, process manuals, and multimedia content such as videos and audio recordings.

2. Communities of Practice (CoPs):

Establish communities of practice where individuals with shared interests or expertise come together to share knowledge, discuss challenges, and collaborate. CoPs provide a platform for ongoing knowledge sharing and learning, enabling members to contribute their knowledge, insights, and experiences. Encourage active participation in CoPs and provide support and resources to facilitate knowledge exchange.

3. Mentorship Programs:

Implement mentorship programs that pair experienced employees with less experienced ones. This allows for the transfer of tacit knowledge from experienced individuals to newer employees. Mentors can share their expertise, provide guidance, and facilitate knowledge sharing through one-on-one interactions, coaching sessions, and shadowing opportunities.

4. Learning and Training Programs:

Offer learning and training programs to employees to enhance their knowledge and skills. This includes both formal training sessions and informal learning opportunities such as workshops, webinars, conferences, and online courses. Continuous learning ensures that employees stay updated with the latest information and developments in their respective fields.

5. Knowledge Transfer Sessions:

Organize knowledge transfer sessions where individuals with specialized knowledge or expertise share their insights, lessons learned, and best practices with others in the organization. These sessions can take the form of presentations, workshops, or interactive discussions. Record and document these sessions for future reference and use.

6. Job Rotation and Cross-Functional Teams:

Promote job rotation and allow employees to gain exposure to different roles and departments within the organization. This helps in knowledge diffusion across the organization and broadens employees' skillsets. Encourage the formation of cross-functional teams that bring together individuals from different disciplines to collaborate and share knowledge.

7. Capture and Utilize Digital Assets:

Leverage technology to capture and store digital assets such as documents, reports, presentations, and video recordings. Implement content management systems, knowledge repositories, or intranet platforms that facilitate easy organization, search, and retrieval of digital assets. Utilize metadata, tagging, and categorization systems to enhance discoverability and accessibility.

8. Retention of Retiring Employees:

Create strategies to retain the knowledge of retiring or departing employees, especially those with critical expertise and experience. This may involve conducting exit interviews or knowledge transfer sessions before their departure. Encourage retiring employees to document their knowledge in written form or mentor their successors to ensure a smooth transition and preservation of their knowledge.

9. Recognition and Incentives:

Recognize and reward individuals and teams for their contributions to knowledge sharing and retention. This can include financial incentives, public recognition, or career development opportunities. Recognizing and incentivizing knowledge sharing, and retention encourages employees to actively participate and contribute their knowledge.

10. Continuous Improvement and Evaluation:

Regularly evaluate and improve knowledge capture and retention strategies. Assess the effectiveness of these strategies through surveys, feedback mechanisms, and performance metrics. Identify areas for improvement, refine processes, and adapt strategies based on the changing organizational needs and knowledge management practices.

By implementing these knowledge capture and retention strategies, organizations can effectively preserve institutional knowledge, foster a culture of knowledge sharing, and ensure that critical knowledge is available for current and future employees. This enables organizations to leverage their intellectual capital, enhance decision-making, drive innovation, and maintain a competitive advantage.

Knowledge Sharing and Collaboration Platforms

Knowledge-sharing and collaboration platforms are software solutions designed to facilitate the exchange of knowledge, information, and ideas among individuals or teams within an organization. These platforms provide a centralized space where employees can communicate, collaborate, and share their expertise easily, regardless of their geographical locations. Here is a detailed explanation of the key features and benefits of knowledge-sharing and collaboration platforms:

1. Communication and Collaboration Tools:

Knowledge-sharing and collaboration platforms offer a range of tools to facilitate communication and collaboration. These include instant messaging, video conferencing, discussion forums, and virtual meeting rooms. These tools enable real-time communication, allowing individuals or teams to connect, share ideas, ask questions, and receive feedback efficiently.

2. Document and Content Management:

These platforms provide document and content management features, allowing users to store, organize, and access documents in a centralized repository. Users can collaborate on documents simultaneously, track changes, and maintain version control. Content management capabilities ensure that knowledge assets are securely stored, easily searchable, and accessible to authorized users.

3. Knowledge Repository and Sharing:

Knowledge-sharing platforms have built-in knowledge repositories where users can store and access knowledge assets such as best practices, case studies, templates, and guides. Employees can contribute to the repository by uploading documents, sharing insights, and commenting on existing knowledge assets. The platform's search functionality enables users to find relevant knowledge quickly.

4. Community and Social Features:

These platforms often include features that enable the creation of communities or groups based on shared interests, projects, or expertise. Users can join communities, participate in discussions, share resources, and foster collaboration and knowledge sharing within specific domains or teams. Social features such as likes, comments, and sharing functionalities promote engagement and serendipitous discovery of knowledge.

5. Personalization and Recommendation Systems:

Knowledge-sharing platforms may employ personalization techniques and recommendation systems to provide users with personalized content and knowledge recommendations. These systems leverage user preferences, behavior, and past interactions to suggest relevant knowledge assets, experts, or communities of interest, enhancing user experience and knowledge discovery.

6. Mobile Accessibility:

Much knowledge-sharing platforms offer mobile apps or responsive web interfaces that allow users to access and contribute knowledge from anywhere, at any time. This mobile accessibility promotes collaboration and knowledge sharing among employees, whether they are in the office, on the field, or working remotely.

7. Analytics and Insights:

Knowledge-sharing platforms often include analytics capabilities that provide insights into user engagement, knowledge utilization, popular topics, and trends. These analytics help organizations identify knowledge gaps, measure the impact of knowledge-sharing initiatives, and make data-driven decisions to improve knowledge management strategies.

8. Integration and Scalability:

Knowledge-sharing and collaboration platforms are designed to integrate with other existing systems and tools within the organization. This enables seamless data exchange and provides a unified experience for users. These platforms are also scalable, allowing organizations to accommodate increasing user demands, expand knowledge repositories, and adapt to evolving collaboration needs.

Benefits of Knowledge Sharing and Collaboration Platforms:

- Enhanced Communication and Collaboration: These platforms facilitate seamless and effective communication and collaboration among employees, regardless of their location or time zone. This improves teamwork, strengthens relationships, and speeds up decision-making processes.

- Improved Knowledge Access and Retention: Knowledge-sharing platforms provide a centralized repository, making knowledge easily accessible to employees. This helps retain institutional knowledge, prevents knowledge loss when employees leave and enables faster onboarding of new employees.

- Increased Innovation and Problem-solving: By connecting individuals or teams with diverse expertise and backgrounds, these platforms foster innovation and collaborative problem-solving. Employees can share ideas, offer input, and collectively find solutions to complex challenges, leading to improved decision-making and innovative outcomes.

- Encouragement of a Learning Culture: Knowledge-sharing platforms promote a learning culture by encouraging employees to actively seek and share knowledge. Employees can continuously learn from each other, stay updated on industry trends, and develop their skills, contributing to their professional growth and development.

- Global Collaboration and Remote Work: These platforms play a crucial role in enabling global collaboration, supporting remote work, and breaking down geographical or organizational barriers. Employees from different locations can collaborate seamlessly, resulting in increased productivity and efficiency.

In summary, knowledge-sharing and collaboration platforms provide organizations with powerful tools to facilitate communication, collaboration, and the sharing of knowledge and expertise. These platforms enhance teamwork, knowledge access, innovation, and learning across the organization, ultimately driving improved performance and a competitive advantage.

Communities of Practice and Social Learning

Communities of practice (CoPs) and social learning are two related concepts that involve groups of individuals coming together to learn, share knowledge, and collaborate. Here is a detailed explanation of each concept:

Communities of Practice (CoPs):

Communities of practice are groups of people who share a common interest, expertise, or practice and come together to learn from each other, solve problems, and share knowledge. CoPs can either be formal or informal and can exist within organizations or across different organizations. Here are some key characteristics of CoPs:

1. Shared Domain:

CoPs are formed around a shared domain of interest or practice. This can be a professional discipline, a specific area of expertise, or a common goal or project.

2. Community:

CoPs foster a sense of community where individuals engage in regular interactions, discussions, and collaborations. They build relationships and trust, creating an environment conducive to learning and knowledge sharing.

3. Learning and Knowledge Sharing:

CoPs provide a platform for members to learn, share knowledge, and exchange experiences. Members contribute their insights, best practices, and lessons learned, fostering a collective understanding and expertise within the community.

4. Joint Activities:

CoPs engage in joint activities such as meetings, workshops, and collaborative projects. These activities facilitate learning, knowledge creation, and problem-solving within the group.

5. Identity and Membership:

CoPs provide a sense of identity and belonging for their members. Individuals identify themselves as part of the community and actively participate in its activities.

6. Evolving and Dynamic:

CoPs are dynamic and evolve as members come and go and as the interests and needs of the community change. This adaptability allows CoPs to remain relevant and responsive to the evolving needs of their members.

Benefits of Communities of Practice:

- Knowledge Sharing: CoPs enable the sharing of tacit knowledge, explicit knowledge, and best practices, making valuable expertise accessible to all members.

- Learning and Development: CoPs foster continuous learning and promote the development of skills and knowledge within the community.

- Problem-solving and Innovation: CoPs offer a platform for members to collectively solve problems and generate innovative ideas.

- Collaboration and Networking: CoPs facilitate collaboration and networking among individuals, connecting people with similar interests and goals.

- Organizational Learning: CoPs contribute to organizational learning by disseminating knowledge and enabling the transfer of knowledge across teams and departments.

Social Learning:

Social learning refers to the process of learning through social interactions and collaboration with others. It is based on the understanding that learning is a social activity influenced by the experiences, insights, and perspectives of others. Here are some key aspects of social learning:

1. Observational Learning:

Social learning involves observation and imitation. Individuals learn by observing others' actions, behaviors, and outcomes and modeling their behavior based on those observations.

2. Collaborative Learning:

Social learning emphasizes collaboration and active participation in learning tasks and activities. Learning occurs through group discussions, co-creation of knowledge, and problem-solving together.

3. Feedback and Reflection:

Social learning involves receiving feedback from others, reflecting on one's actions and experiences, and incorporating feedback into future learning and behavior.

4. Communities and Networks:

Communities and networks play a crucial role in social learning. Individuals connect with others who have similar interests, expertise, or goals, creating opportunities for knowledge sharing, collaborative learning, and collective problem-solving.

Benefits of Social Learning:

- Enhanced Learning Experience: Social learning provides a more engaging and interactive learning experience by incorporating real-world examples, diverse perspectives, and social interactions.

- Knowledge Sharing and Collaboration: Social learning promotes the sharing of knowledge, ideas, and experiences among learners, fostering a culture of collaboration and collective learning.

- Support and Motivation: Social learning provides opportunities for learners to seek and receive support, encouragement, and motivation from peers, mentors, or experts.

- Reflection and Critical Thinking: Social learning encourages learners to reflect on their experiences, challenge assumptions, and engage in critical thinking through discussions and interactions with others.

- Continuous Learning: Social learning is an ongoing process that supports continuous learning and personal growth, helping individuals stay updated with changing knowledge and skills.

In summary, communities of practice and social learning are approaches that emphasize the importance of social interactions, collaboration, and knowledge sharing in the learning process. CoPs provide a structured environment for individuals with shared interests to come together and share knowledge, while social learning focuses on the broader concept of learning through social interactions, collaboration, and observation. Both approaches contribute to individual and organizational learning, knowledge creation, and professional development.

Organizational Culture and Leadership

Organizational culture refers to the shared values, beliefs, norms, and behaviors that shape the identity and functioning of an organization. It represents the collective mindset and attitudes of employees, influencing how they perceive and approach their work. Organizational culture plays a critical role in shaping the organization's overall ethos, employee behavior, decision-making processes, and the achievement of its goals. Here is a detailed explanation of organizational culture and its impact:

1. Cultural Elements:

Organizational culture comprises several elements, including:

- Values and Beliefs: The guiding principles and fundamental beliefs that drive the organization's actions and decisions.
- Norms and Behavior: The accepted patterns of behavior, working styles, and unwritten rules that govern how employees interact and conduct themselves.
- Symbols and Rituals: The visual representations and meaningful activities that reinforce shared values and create a sense of identity.
- Communication Patterns: The flow of information, language, and communication styles within the organization.
- Organizational Structure: The formal and informal structures that define reporting relationships and decision-making processes, influencing the distribution of power and authority.

2. Impact on Employee Behavior:

Organizational culture significantly influences employee attitudes, behaviors, and performance. It sets the standards for acceptable behavior and communication, shaping employee interactions and collaboration. A positive culture that fosters trust, openness, and respect can motivate employees, enhance their job satisfaction, and promote productivity. On the other hand, a toxic or dysfunctional culture can hinder innovation, collaboration, and employee morale.

3. Alignment with Organizational Goals:

Strong alignment between organizational culture and its strategic goals is crucial. A culture that supports the organization's mission, vision, and values helps employees understand their purpose, creates a sense of shared commitment, and drives cohesive efforts toward achieving goals. When culture and goals are misaligned, it can lead to confusion, resistance, and a lack of focus.

4. Leadership and Culture:

Leadership plays a pivotal role in shaping and nurturing organizational culture. Leaders establish and reinforce cultural elements through their actions, communication, and decision-making. They are responsible for setting the tone, modeling desired behaviors, and embodying the organization's values. Effective leaders actively engage and involve employees in shaping the culture, fostering a sense of ownership, and building a positive work environment.

5. Cultural Change and Transformation:

Organizational culture is not static and can evolve. When organizations seek to change or transform their culture, it requires a deliberate and concerted effort from leaders and employees. Cultural change initiatives may involve aligning values and behaviors, revising policies and practices, improving communication channels, and empowering employees to contribute to the cultural transformation.

6. Impact on Performance and Success:

A strong and positive organizational culture has a direct impact on organizational performance and success. A supportive culture encourages innovation, creativity, and risk-taking, leading to improved problem-solving and adaptability. It fosters employee engagement and commitment, reducing turnover and enhancing organizational resilience. A positive culture can also attract top talent and enhance the organization's reputation in the marketplace.

In summary, organizational culture shapes the collective mindset, values, and behaviors within an organization, influencing how employees interact, perform, and contribute to achieving organizational goals. Leaders play a key role in nurturing and shaping the culture, ensuring alignment with strategic objectives, and fostering a positive work environment. A strong organizational culture can enhance productivity, employee satisfaction, and overall organizational performance.

Benefits and Impacts of Knowledge Management and Organizational Learning:

Knowledge management and organizational learning are closely related concepts that focus on capturing, sharing, and utilizing knowledge within an organization. Here are the benefits and impacts of these practices:

1. Enhanced Decision-Making: Effective knowledge management enables organizations to gather, organize, and access relevant information and expertise. This empowers decision-makers to make informed and strategic decisions, leading to improved outcomes and reduced risks.

2. Increased Innovation and Creativity: Knowledge management fosters a culture of innovation by promoting the sharing and collaboration of ideas and expertise. By capturing and disseminating knowledge, organizations can leverage diverse perspectives and experiences to generate new ideas, improve processes, and introduce innovative products and services.

3. Improved Efficiency and Productivity: By centralizing and organizing knowledge, organizations can eliminate redundancy and inefficiency. Access to best practices, lessons learned, and documented expertise enables employees to work more efficiently, reducing duplication of effort and enhancing productivity.

4. Talent Retention and Development: Knowledge management facilitates the preservation and sharing of tacit knowledge, ensuring that valuable expertise is not lost when employees leave the organization. It also supports the development of employees by providing access to learning resources and facilitating knowledge transfer from experienced to junior staff.

5. Competitive Advantage: Organizations that effectively manage and leverage knowledge gain a competitive edge. The ability to quickly adapt to changes, capitalize on opportunities, and learn from past successes and failures can differentiate them from competitors.

6. Organizational Learning: Knowledge management and organizational learning are closely intertwined. Organizational learning refers to the process of acquiring, creating, and applying knowledge collectively within an organization. By promoting a learning culture, organizations can continuously improve and adapt to changing environments, fostering ongoing innovation and growth.

7. Collaboration and Knowledge Sharing: Knowledge management encourages collaboration and knowledge sharing across different departments, teams, and hierarchical levels. This promotes cross-functional communication, breaks down silos, and enables employees to access and contribute to a broader knowledge base.

8. Risk Management: Knowledge management supports effective risk management by ensuring that critical knowledge is captured, shared, and used to mitigate potential risks. Lessons learned from past experiences can guide decision-making and help prevent the repetition of costly mistakes.

9. Customer Satisfaction and Service Quality: By capturing and sharing customer knowledge, organizations can improve their understanding of customer needs, preferences, and pain points. This enables them to tailor their products and services to better meet customer expectations, driving customer satisfaction and loyalty.

10. Continual Improvement: Knowledge management and organizational learning facilitate continuous improvement cycles by encouraging reflection, analysis, and the integration of new insights into existing knowledge. This creates a culture of continuous learning, enabling organizations to adapt and improve over time.

In summary, effective knowledge management and organizational learning practices have numerous benefits and impacts. They improve decision-making, promote innovation and efficiency, facilitate talent retention and development, provide a competitive advantage, enhance collaboration and knowledge sharing, enable effective risk management, drive customer satisfaction, and foster a culture of continuous improvement.

Improved Decision Making and Innovation

Improved decision-making and innovation are two important outcomes of effective knowledge management and learning within an organization. Here is a detailed explanation of how knowledge management and organizational learning contribute to these areas:

Improved Decision Making:

1. Access to Relevant Information: Knowledge management ensures that decision-makers have access to accurate, relevant, and up-to-date information. By capturing and organizing knowledge, organizations create a knowledge base that decision-makers can draw upon when making choices. This access to information allows for well-informed decisions based on comprehensive data and insights.

2. Enhanced Analysis and Problem-solving: Knowledge management provides decision-makers with a range of data, perspectives, and expertise that can be leveraged for thorough analysis and problem-solving. By tapping into the collective knowledge and experience of employees, decision-makers can consider different viewpoints,

identify patterns, and evaluate potential solutions more effectively.

3. Learning from Past Experiences: Knowledge management systems store past experiences, including successes, failures, and lessons learned. Decision-makers can refer to these insights to avoid repeating mistakes, capitalize on past successes, and make more informed decisions. Learning from previous experiences leads to more effective decision-making and improves overall organizational performance.

4. Collaboration and Knowledge Sharing: Effective knowledge management facilitates collaboration and knowledge sharing among employees. Decision-makers can tap into the collective intelligence of teams, communities of practice, and subject matter experts to gather diverse ideas, perspectives, and insights. Collaborative decision-making allows for more informed and comprehensive evaluations of options.

5. Continuous Learning and Adaptability: Knowledge management practices promote a culture of continuous learning, which is essential for making informed decisions. By continuously gathering and sharing knowledge, organizations remain adaptable in dynamic business environments. This ability to learn from internal and external information sources allows decision-makers to respond effectively to changes and make timely decisions.

Enhanced Innovation:

1. Access to Diverse Perspectives: Knowledge management encourages the exchange of ideas and diverse perspectives. Employees from different departments, backgrounds, and levels of expertise can contribute their insights and generate innovative solutions. By pooling collective knowledge, organizations can foster a culture of innovation that leads to the creation of new products, services, and processes.

2. Knowledge Sharing and Collaboration: Effective knowledge management platforms and practices provide mechanisms for sharing and collaborating on ideas. When employees can freely share their knowledge, innovative concepts can emerge through discussions, brainstorming sessions, and collaborative projects. By breaking down silos and facilitating cross-functional collaboration, knowledge management supports innovation.

3. Learning from Failures and Successes: Knowledge management enables organizations to learn from past failures and successes. By capturing and sharing lessons learned, organizations can identify areas for improvement and avoid repeating mistakes. The ability to learn from failures creates an environment where innovation is encouraged, and employees feel empowered to take risks and explore new ideas.

4. Idea Management: Knowledge management systems often include tools for idea management, such as collaborative platforms or innovation management software. These platforms provide a centralized space for employees to contribute, refine, and validate ideas. This structured approach to idea management fosters innovation by systematically capturing and evaluating innovative concepts.

5. Support for Experimentation: Knowledge management practices create an environment that supports experimentation and learning from experimentation. By providing access to existing knowledge and encouraging the sharing of insights gained from experiments, organizations can iterate and refine innovative ideas. This iterative process drives innovation and enables organizations to continuously improve their products, services, and processes.

In summary, effective knowledge management and organizational learning contribute to improved decision-making by providing access to relevant information, supporting analysis and learning from past experiences, and fostering collaboration. Additionally, knowledge management promotes innovation by providing access to diverse perspectives, supporting knowledge sharing, and facilitating experimentation. Enhancing decision-making and fostering innovation through knowledge management are key factors for organizational success in today's dynamic and competitive business landscape.

Enhanced Problem Solving and Efficiency

Enhanced problem-solving and efficiency are crucial aspects of organizational effectiveness and success. Here is a detailed explanation of what these concepts entail and how they contribute to improving organizational performance:

Enhanced Problem-Solving:

1. Systematic Approach: Enhanced problem-solving involves adopting a systematic approach that helps organizations identify, analyze, and resolve complex issues. This involves breaking down problems into manageable components, conducting root cause analysis, and considering various potential solutions. By embracing a structured problem-solving methodology, organizations can optimize their problem-solving process and arrive at more effective and sustainable solutions.

2. Data-Driven Decisions: Effective problem-solving requires access to relevant and accurate data. Organizations that emphasize enhanced problem-solving invest in data collection, analysis, and interpretation. By leveraging data-driven insights, decision-makers can make informed choices that address the root causes of problems and minimize the likelihood of recurring issues.

3. Collaboration and Diverse Perspectives: Enhanced problem-solving recognizes the value of diverse perspectives and collaboration. Organizations that encourage cross-functional collaboration and employee engagement in problem-solving processes can tap into a wider range of expertise and insights. This allows for a more comprehensive understanding of the problem and fosters innovative solutions by leveraging the collective knowledge and diverse perspectives of teams.

4. Critical Thinking and Innovation: Enhanced problem-solving involves fostering a culture of critical thinking and innovation. Organizations that encourage employees to question assumptions, challenge traditional approaches, and think creatively are more likely to uncover unique and effective solutions. By promoting a mindset of continuous improvement and a willingness to embrace change, organizations can enhance problem-solving capabilities and innovate in their problem-solving approaches.

5. Learning from Mistakes: Enhanced problem-solving acknowledges the importance of learning from mistakes. Organizations that adopt a growth mindset and encourage a learning culture view mistakes as opportunities for improvement rather than failures. By creating an environment that values reflection, knowledge sharing, and lessons learned, organizations can avoid repeating past mistakes and continuously enhance their problem-solving capabilities.

Efficiency:

1. Streamlined Processes: Efficiency involves streamlining processes to eliminate wasteful activities and maximize productivity. By mapping and analyzing workflows, organizations can identify bottlenecks, duplication of efforts, and unnecessary steps. By eliminating or optimizing these inefficiencies, organizations can enhance productivity and achieve better results with the same level of resources.

2. Automation and Technology: Enhancing efficiency often involves leveraging automation and technology. Organizations can automate repetitive tasks, streamline data entry and analysis, and use digital tools to improve workflow efficiency. By automating time-consuming and error-prone processes, organizations can free up employee time for higher-value tasks and achieve greater efficiency in their operations.

3. Resource Optimization: Efficient organizations focus on optimizing their resources, including human resources, financial resources, and physical assets. This involves aligning resources with organizational goals, ensuring their optimal allocation, and minimizing waste. By effectively managing and optimizing resources, organizations can operate efficiently and maximize their outputs.

4. Continuous Improvement: Efficiency is a journey of continuous improvement. Organizations that embrace a culture of continuous improvement consistently seek opportunities to enhance efficiency in their processes and operations. Through regular performance monitoring, feedback collection, and analysis, organizations can identify areas for improvement and implement changes to optimize efficiency.

5. Employee Empowerment: Efficient organizations empower their employees by providing them with the necessary autonomy, authority, and tools to make decisions and execute tasks efficiently. By empowering employees, organizations encourage ownership, accountability, and innovative problem-solving, resulting in improved efficiency throughout the organization.

6. Lean and Six Sigma Practices: Organizations can adopt Lean and Six Sigma practices to enhance efficiency. Lean focuses on eliminating waste and optimizing processes, while Six Sigma emphasizes reducing variations and improving quality. By implementing these methodologies, organizations can drive continuous improvement and achieve higher levels of efficiency.

In summary, enhanced problem-solving and efficiency are integral to organizational success. Enhanced problem-solving involves adopting a systematic approach, utilizing data-driven decisions, promoting collaboration and diverse perspectives, nurturing critical thinking and innovation, and learning from mistakes. Efficiency is achieved through streamlining processes, leveraging automation and technology, optimizing resources, embracing continuous improvement, empowering employees, and implementing Lean and Six Sigma practices. By prioritizing these aspects, organizations can improve their operational performance, achieve better outcomes, and gain a competitive edge in today's dynamic business environment.

Competitive Advantage and Organizational Agility

Competitive advantage and organizational agility are two critical factors that contribute to the success and long-term viability of an organization in a dynamic and competitive marketplace. In this comprehensive explanation, we will delve into the concepts of competitive advantage and organizational agility, exploring their significance, key components, and how organizations can develop and leverage them for sustained success.

Competitive Advantage:

Competitive advantage refers to the unique set of characteristics or capabilities that distinguishes an organization from its competitors and enables it to outperform them in the market. It provides an edge that allows an organization to achieve higher market share, profitability, customer loyalty, and overall success. Here are key aspects of competitive advantage:

1. Core Competencies: Core competencies are the unique capabilities, knowledge, skills, processes, and resources that an organization possesses and utilizes to create value for customers. These competencies enable organizations to deliver superior products, services, or customer experiences that competitors find difficult to replicate.

2. Differentiation: Differentiating an organization's offerings or positioning in the market sets it apart from competitors. By providing unique features, benefits, or value propositions, an organization can attract customers and command a premium price. Differentiation can be achieved through product innovation, superior quality, customer service, branding, or other distinctive attributes.

3. Cost Leadership: Organizations can attain a competitive advantage by delivering products or services at a lower cost than their competitors. Cost leadership can be achieved through economies of scale, efficient operational processes, supply chain optimization, or technological advantages. By offering competitive prices, organizations can attract price-sensitive customers and gain a larger market share.

4. Innovation and Adaptability: The ability to continuously innovate and adapt to changing market conditions is a critical aspect of competitive advantage. Organizations that invest in research and development, foster a culture of innovation, and respond quickly to changes can introduce new products, technologies, or business models that outpace their competitors. Innovation provides a sustainable competitive advantage by creating value, driving growth, and staying ahead of market trends.

5. Customer Relationships and Intimacy: Building strong and loyal customer relationships can provide a competitive advantage. Organizations that understand their customers' needs, preferences, and pain points can tailor their offerings, provide personalized experiences, and develop long-term relationships. Customer intimacy allows organizations to create switching costs and engenders customer loyalty, reducing the likelihood of customers switching to competitors.

6. Brand Reputation and Trust: Establishing a strong brand reputation built on trust, quality, and reliability can differentiate an organization from competitors. A solid brand reputation creates a perception of value, establishes credibility, and fosters customer loyalty. Organizations with a trusted brand have a competitive advantage as customers are more likely to choose their offerings over those of less reputable competitors.

7. Market Positioning: Effective market positioning is essential for competitive advantage. By effectively targeting specific customer segments, industries, or geographic markets, organizations can develop a unique positioning that aligns with customer needs and preferences. This focused approach enables organizations to tailor their offerings, marketing messages, and customer experiences to stand out within their chosen market segments.

Organizational Agility:

Organizational agility refers to an organization's ability to respond rapidly and effectively to changes in the business environment. It involves anticipating and adjusting to shifts in customer expectations, market conditions, technology advancements, regulatory changes, and other external factors. Here are key aspects of organizational agility:

1. Adaptive Strategy and Planning: Agile organizations have flexible strategic plans that are adaptable to changing circumstances. They continuously scan the external environment, identify emerging trends and opportunities, and adjust their strategies accordingly. This adaptive approach ensures that organizations can pivot, seize new opportunities, and mitigate risks effectively.

2. Agile Decision-Making: Agile organizations empower employees at all levels to make decisions quickly and autonomously. They foster a culture of open communication, collaboration, and shared decision-making. By decentralizing decision-making authority, organizations can respond rapidly to evolving situations and leverage the collective expertise of their employees.

3. Cross-Functional Collaboration: Agile organizations promote cross-functional collaboration and teamwork. By breaking down departmental silos and encouraging collaboration across different functions, teams can pool their skills, knowledge, and perspectives to address complex challenges. This collaborative approach enhances creativity, problem-solving, and the ability to adapt to new circumstances.

4. Learning Culture and Continuous Improvement: Agile organizations foster a learning culture and emphasize continuous improvement. They encourage employees to learn from both successes and failures and focus on

identifying lessons learned. By promoting a culture of experimentation, reflection, and knowledge sharing, organizations can adapt and innovate more effectively.

5. Scalable and Agile Infrastructure: Organizations need scalable and agile infrastructure to support agility. This includes flexible technology systems, adaptable processes, and nimble organizational structures. Agile infrastructure enables organizations to respond quickly to changing demands and facilitates the seamless integration of new technologies, processes, or business models.

6. Customer-Centric Focus: Agile organizations prioritize understanding customer needs and preferences. They collect and analyze customer feedback, actively engage with customers to gain insights, and use these insights to drive product and service innovation. By consistently aligning their offerings with customer expectations, agile organizations can respond rapidly to customer demands and maintain a competitive edge.

7. Agile Talent Management: Agile organizations seek to attract and retain talent that embodies agility. They value individuals who are adaptable, open to change, and willing to embrace new ideas. They invest in employee development, provide training in agile methods and mindset, and promote a culture of continuous learning and self-improvement.

Benefits and Impacts:

Organizations that effectively leverage competitive advantage and organizational agility can reap several benefits and impacts:

- Market Leadership: Competitive advantage and organizational agility allow organizations to take a leading position in their industry or market segments, gaining an edge over competitors and capturing a larger market share.

- Sustainability and Resilience: Organizations with competitive advantage and organizational agility are better equipped to withstand changes in the business environment, economic fluctuations, and disruptions. They can adapt to new circumstances, seize opportunities, and mitigate risks more effectively.

- Customer Satisfaction and Loyalty: Competitive advantage and organizational agility enable organizations to deliver products or services that meet customer needs and expectations. This results in higher customer satisfaction levels and fosters loyalty, reducing customer churn and increasing customer lifetime value.

- Innovation and Growth: Competitive advantage promotes innovation by allocating resources to research and development and encouraging creative thinking. Organizational agility facilitates the rapid implementation of innovative ideas, ensuring organizations can capitalize on new opportunities and achieve sustained growth.

- Talent Attraction and Retention: Organizations with competitive advantage and organizational agility are attractive to top talent. Their ability to offer stimulating and challenging work environments, innovative practices, and career growth opportunities makes them desirable employers. This enhances talent attraction and retention, providing a skilled workforce that drives organizational success.

- Financial Performance: Competitive advantage and organizational agility positively impact financial performance. Effective differentiation, cost leadership, and innovative approaches contribute to increased revenue, improved profit margins, and stakeholder value.

In summary, competitive advantage provides organizations with a unique position to outperform their competitors, while organizational agility enables them to navigate and respond to changing market conditions effectively. By embracing these concepts and continuously refining their capabilities in these areas, organizations can position themselves for sustained success in today's dynamic business landscape.

Employee Engagement and Talent Development

Employee engagement and talent development are crucial aspects of organizational success and growth. In this comprehensive explanation, we will delve into the concepts of employee engagement and talent development, exploring their significance, key components, and approaches to effectively foster them in organizations.

Employee Engagement:

Employee engagement refers to the emotional connection, commitment, and involvement of employees towards their work, organization, and objectives. It is the extent to which employees are motivated, satisfied, and productive in their roles. Engaged employees are enthusiastic, dedicated, and willing to go the extra mile to contribute to the organization's success. Here are key aspects of employee engagement:

1. Meaningful Work: Engaged employees find their work meaningful and aligned with their values and aspirations. They have a clear understanding of how their contributions make a difference to the organization, its goals, and its stakeholders. When employees perceive their work as meaningful, they are more likely to be engaged and motivated.

2. Autonomy and Empowerment: Engaged employees have a sense of autonomy and empowerment in their roles. They are given the freedom to make decisions, contribute ideas, and have a say in how their work is performed. Autonomy and empowerment foster a sense of ownership, accountability, and motivation among employees.

3. Positive Work Environment: An inclusive, supportive, and positive work environment is crucial for employee engagement. Organizations that prioritize employee well-being, promote work-life balance, and foster positive relationships among team members create an environment that enhances engagement. Respectful communication, recognition of achievements, and fair treatment contribute to a positive work environment.

4. Opportunities for Growth and Development: Engaged employees seek opportunities for growth and development in their careers. Organizations that invest in employee training provide avenues for skill enhancement and offer career advancement opportunities foster engagement. Employees who see a future within the organization are more likely to be committed and engaged.

5. Clear Communication and Transparency: Open and honest communication is essential for employee engagement. Organizations that communicate clearly about their goals, strategies, and performance create a sense of transparency. When employees feel included in the decision-making process and are informed about organizational developments, they are more likely to be engaged.

6. Recognition and Rewards: Recognizing and rewarding employees for their contributions and achievements is a crucial component of engagement. Organizations that have effective recognition programs, provide regular feedback, and offer meaningful rewards create a positive reinforcement environment. This acknowledgment enhances employee motivation, satisfaction, and engagement.

7. Leadership and Management Support: Engaged employees experience strong leadership and management support. Leaders who inspire, communicate effectively, and provide guidance create a sense of trust, respect, and engagement. Effective managers who provide coaching, feedback, and support contribute to employee growth and engagement.

Benefits and Impacts:

Employee engagement yields several benefits and impacts for both employees and organizations:

- Increased Productivity and Performance: Engaged employees are more likely to be productive and perform at a high level. Their enthusiasm, motivation, and commitment translate into higher-quality work, increased creativity, and better problem-solving abilities.

- Enhanced Employee Satisfaction and Retention: Engaged employees have higher levels of job satisfaction and are more likely to stay with the organization. When employees feel valued, supported, and fulfilled in their roles, they are less likely to seek opportunities elsewhere.
- Improved Customer Satisfaction: Engaged employees provide better customer service and experiences. Their positive attitudes, commitment, and willingness to go the extra mile contribute to higher levels of customer satisfaction and loyalty.
- Innovation and Adaptability: Engaged employees are more likely to embrace change, contribute to innovation efforts, and adapt to new challenges. Their active involvement, knowledge sharing, and creative thinking drive organizational agility and innovation.
- Reduced Absenteeism and Turnover: Organizations with engaged employees experience reduced absenteeism and turnover rates. Engaged employees are more likely to be present, committed, and loyal to their organization, resulting in lower costs associated with absenteeism and recruitment.
- Positive Organizational Culture: Employee engagement fosters a positive organizational culture. Engaged employees contribute to a collaborative, supportive, and inclusive work environment, enhancing overall organizational culture and employee well-being.

Talent Development:

Talent development refers to the deliberate and strategic efforts that organizations make to attract, nurture, and retain employees with high potential. It focuses on identifying and developing talented individuals to ensure a pipeline of skilled leaders and contributors for the future. Key aspects of talent development include:

1. Talent Identification and Recruitment: Organizations need to identify talented individuals who possess the desired knowledge, skills, attitudes, and potential to contribute significantly to the organization's success. Effective talent identification involves robust recruitment processes, which may include competency-based interviews, assessments, and screening mechanisms.

2. Performance Management and Feedback: Organizations should provide regular feedback and performance evaluation mechanisms to support talent development. Constructive feedback helps individuals understand their strengths, and areas for improvement, and chart a development path. Performance management systems should align with organizational goals, be fair and transparent, and provide meaningful insights for employee growth.

3. Individual Development Plans: Individual development plans (IDPs) outline the specific development goals, activities, and timelines for each employee. IDPs are created through a collaborative process involving managers, employees, and the organization's talent development team. These plans guide employees' professional growth and ensure alignment with organizational needs.

4. Training and Development Programs: Talent development involves providing employees with opportunities to enhance their knowledge and skills. Organizations can offer various training programs, such as workshops, seminars, leadership development initiatives, and mentoring or coaching programs. These programs provide employees with the tools and resources they need to succeed in their roles and progress in their careers.

5. Succession Planning: Succession planning is a crucial element of talent development. It involves identifying and preparing employees to assume key leadership positions in the future. Succession planning ensures a smooth transition of leadership and mitigates risks associated with talent gaps. It includes assessing employees' potential, providing development opportunities, and preparing them for future leadership roles.

6. Talent Mobility: Organizations should encourage talent mobility, allowing employees to take on different roles and responsibilities within the organization. This cross-functional exposure broadens employees' skills, knowledge,

and perspectives, contributing to their overall development. Talent mobility also helps retain talented individuals by providing opportunities for growth and career advancement.

7. Mentoring and Coaching: Mentoring and coaching programs pair talented individuals with experienced professionals who guide and support their development. Mentors and coaches provide feedback, advice, and insights based on their own experiences, enabling mentees to learn, grow, and navigate their careers effectively.

Benefits and Impacts:

Talent development initiatives yield several benefits and impacts for both employees and organizations:

- Improved Employee Performance: Talent development programs enhance employees' knowledge, skills, and capabilities, leading to improved performance in their current roles. This contributes to higher productivity, better quality of work, and stronger overall organizational performance.
- Increased Employee Engagement: Talent development demonstrates an organization's commitment to its employees' growth and development. When employees perceive that their organization invests in their professional advancement, they are more likely to be engaged and motivated.
- Enhanced Retention Rates: Employees who have access to talent development opportunities are more likely to stay with the organization. By providing avenues for growth and career progression, organizations can retain their talented individuals, reducing the costs associated with turnover.
- Leadership Pipeline: Talent development initiatives create a pipeline of skilled leaders within the organization. By systematically identifying, nurturing, and grooming individuals for leadership roles, organizations can ensure a smooth transition of leadership and minimize disruptions caused by talent gaps.
- Organizational Agility and Adaptability: Talent development fosters organizational agility by building a workforce that is skilled, adaptable, and capable of responding to new challenges. Developing employees' capabilities ensures that the organization has the necessary skills and expertise to adapt to changing market conditions and drive innovation.
- Positive Employer Branding: Organizations that prioritize talent development attract top talent and enhance their employer brand. Employees seek opportunities for growth, learning, and development. By offering robust talent development initiatives, organizations become desirable employers, boosting their reputation and attracting high-quality candidates.
- Succession Planning and Risk Mitigation: Talent development enables organizations to proactively plan for leadership succession and mitigate risks associated with key personnel departures. Preparing employees for future leadership positions ensures continuity, stability, and reduced disruption during transitions.

Approaches to Employee Engagement and Talent Development:

To effectively foster employee engagement and talent development, organizations can adopt the following approaches:

1. Focus on People-Centric Culture: Organizations should prioritize people and promote a culture that values employees' growth, well-being, and contributions. Building a culture of trust, respect, and inclusivity enhances engagement and empowers employees to reach their full potential.

2. Regular Feedback and Communication: Organizations should provide regular feedback and open channels of communication. Feedback should be constructive, timely, and specific, addressing both strengths and areas for improvement. Open and transparent communication channels allow employees to express their concerns, ideas, and aspirations.

3. Employee-Centric Policies and Practices: Organizations should develop policies and practices that prioritize employee needs, work-life balance, and well-being. Flexible work arrangements, recognition programs, fair com-

pensation, and benefits packages contribute to a positive work environment and higher levels of engagement.

4. Invest in Training and Development: Organizations should invest in training and development programs to enhance employee skills, knowledge, and capabilities. These programs can include technical training, leadership development, coaching, and mentoring initiatives. Customized development plans should align with employees' career aspirations and organizational needs.

5. Emphasize Career Planning and Growth Opportunities: Organizations should provide employees with clear career paths and opportunities for growth and advancement. This can be achieved through talent management programs, internal job postings, stretch assignments, and cross-functional projects.

6. Leadership Development: Organizations should prioritize leadership development to cultivate a strong talent pipeline. Leadership development programs should focus on nurturing essential leadership competencies, promoting collaboration, and enhancing decision-making and strategic thinking capabilities.

7. Continuous Monitoring

Continuous monitoring is an effective way of fostering employee engagement and talent development. It involves the ongoing collection, analysis, and evaluation of data related to employee performance, satisfaction, and development. This data-driven approach enables organizations to identify areas for improvement, address gaps, and make informed decisions to enhance employee engagement and talent development. Here are key aspects of continuous monitoring of employee engagement and talent development:

1. Performance Evaluation: Continuous monitoring allows organizations to evaluate employee performance on an ongoing basis. By setting clear performance goals and regularly reviewing progress, organizations can provide timely feedback, identify strengths and areas for improvement, and align individual performance with organizational objectives. This feedback-driven approach enhances employee engagement by providing opportunities for growth and recognition based on performance.

2. Goal Alignment: Continuous monitoring enables organizations to ensure that employee goals align with the broader organizational objectives. By regularly reviewing and adjusting goals, organizations can keep employees focused on top priorities and create a sense of purpose and alignment. Employees who understand how their goals contribute to organizational success are more likely to be engaged and motivated.

3. Feedback and Coaching: Continuous monitoring facilitates regular feedback and coaching to support employee development. Managers can provide ongoing guidance, constructive criticism, and recognition to help employees improve their skills, address performance gaps, and reach their full potential. This feedback-driven approach fosters a learning culture, encourages continuous improvement, and contributes to employee engagement and talent development.

4. Recognition and Rewards: Continuous monitoring allows organizations to identify and acknowledge employee achievements in real-time. Regular monitoring of employee performance enables managers to recognize and reward exceptional contributions promptly. This timely recognition enhances employee engagement, motivation, and job satisfaction, while also reinforcing desired behaviors and fostering a positive work environment.

5. Identifying Training and Development Needs: Continuous monitoring helps organizations identify areas where employees may require additional training and development to perform at their best. By tracking performance indicators, skills gaps, and employee aspirations, organizations can provide targeted training, coaching, and development opportunities. This proactive approach to talent development not only enhances employee engagement but also ensures that employees have the necessary skills and capabilities to excel in their roles.

6. Pulse Surveys and Feedback Mechanisms: Continuous monitoring involves the use of pulse surveys and other feedback mechanisms to regularly capture employee perceptions, satisfaction levels, and engagement. These surveys provide insights into employee experiences, identify potential areas of concern or improvement, and allow organizations to take timely action to address issues. By giving employees a voice and responding to feedback, organizations demonstrate their commitment to employee engagement and talent development.

7. Career and Succession Planning: Continuous monitoring enables organizations to assess employees' career aspirations, potential, and readiness for advancement. By regularly reviewing performance, skills, and development plans, organizations can identify high-potential individuals and create personalized career and succession plans. This proactive approach to talent development fosters engagement, provides growth opportunities, and ensures a robust pipeline of leaders and skilled employees.

8. Diversity and Inclusion: Continuous monitoring helps organizations track and analyze diversity and inclusion metrics. By monitoring representation, inclusivity in decision-making, and employee experiences, organizations can identify and address barriers to diversity and inclusion. Taking proactive steps to foster diversity and inclusion enhances employee engagement, fosters a sense of belonging, and benefits talent development by unlocking the full potential of a diverse workforce.

Benefits and Impacts:

Implementing continuous monitoring as an approach to employee engagement and talent development yields several benefits and impacts:

- Timely Identification of Issues: Continuous monitoring allows organizations to promptly identify, and address issues related to performance, satisfaction, and development. This proactive approach prevents problems from escalating, increases employee satisfaction, and fosters a positive work environment.
- Enhanced Employee Performance: Continuous monitoring provides real-time feedback and guidance to help employees improve their performance. By addressing performance gaps and providing coaching and development opportunities, organizations can enhance employee skills, boost productivity, and improve overall performance.
- Personalized Development: Continuous monitoring enables organizations to tailor development plans to individual employee needs, interests, and aspirations. This personalized approach enhances employee engagement, demonstrating the organization's commitment to their growth and development.
- Improved Employee Engagement: Continuous monitoring fosters employee engagement by providing ongoing feedback, recognition, and opportunities for growth. It creates a culture of open communication, continuous learning, and development, increasing employees' sense of purpose, satisfaction, and commitment.
- Better Talent Retention: Organizations that continuously monitor employee engagement and development are more likely to retain top talent. Employees who feel valued, supported, and have growth opportunities are more likely to stay with the organization, reducing turnover and associated costs.
- Data-Informed Decision-Making: Continuous monitoring provides organizations with actionable data and insights that inform strategic decision-making related to employee engagement and talent development. Data-driven decision-making leads to more effective and targeted interventions, optimizing resources and yielding better outcomes.
- Stronger Organizational Culture: Continuous monitoring contributes to a positive organizational culture that prioritizes employee engagement and talent development. It cultivates a learning mindset, encourages ongoing improvement, and fosters a sense of collaboration, inclusion, and innovation.
- Increased Competitive Advantage: Organizations that prioritize employee engagement and talent

development gain a competitive advantage. Engaged employees and a skilled workforce contribute to innovation, customer satisfaction, and overall organizational excellence, giving the organization an edge over competitors.

In summary, continuous monitoring is an effective approach to fostering employee engagement and talent development. It involves ongoing performance evaluation, goal alignment, feedback and coaching, recognition, and rewards, identifying training and development needs, pulse surveys and feedback mechanisms, as well as career and succession planning. Implementing continuous monitoring practices benefits both employees and organizations by improving performance, engagement, retention, and overall organizational success.

Organizational Memory and Succession Planning

Organizational Memory:

Organizational memory refers to the collective knowledge, information, and experiences that are accumulated and preserved within an organization over time. It encompasses the history, lessons learned, best practices, and core competencies that shape the organization's identity and guide its actions. Organizational memory is not limited to individual employees but is embedded in processes, systems, culture, and documentation. Here are key aspects of organizational memory:

1. knowledge): Organizational memory captures explicit knowledge, which is formally documented and can be easily accessed and shared. This includes documents, reports, databases, policies, and procedures that contain valuable information and insights accumulated by the organization.

2. Tacit Knowledge: Organizational memory also encompasses tacit knowledge, which is embedded in the minds of employees and acquired through experience, interactions, and expertise. Tacit knowledge is often difficult to articulate or transfer but is crucial for effective decision-making, problem-solving, and innovation. Sharing tacit knowledge can be facilitated through mentoring, coaching, and communities of practice within the organization.

3. Lessons Learned: Organizational memory captures lessons learned from both successes and failures. This includes analyzing past projects, initiatives, and experiences to identify what worked well and what could be improved or avoided in the future. Lessons learned are documented and shared to prevent the repetition of mistakes and enable continuous improvement.

4. Best Practices: Organizational memory incorporates best practices that have been identified and refined over time. These are documented approaches, methods, or strategies that have proven to be effective in achieving desired outcomes. Best practices are shared across the organization to guide decision-making and improve performance.

5. Core Competencies: Organizational memory encompasses core competencies, which are the unique capabilities and expertise that differentiate the organization from its competitors. Core competencies are the result of accumulated knowledge, experience, and investment in developing specific skills or technologies. They underpin the organization's competitive advantage and are preserved and enhanced through continuous learning and development efforts.

6. Culture and Values: Organizational memory includes the culture and values that have been developed and nurtured within the organization. These shared beliefs, norms, and behaviors shape how employees think, interact, and make decisions. Organizational memory ensures that the culture and values are transmitted to new employees and sustained over time.

7. Knowledge Preservation: Organizational memory relies on knowledge preservation mechanisms to ensure that

valuable information and insights are retained and accessible even in the face of employee turnover or leadership changes. This includes the use of knowledge management systems, document repositories, succession planning, and formal processes for capturing and sharing knowledge.

Benefits and Impacts:

Organizational memory provides several benefits and impacts for the organization:

- Continuous Improvement: Organizational memory enables the organization to learn from its past experiences, both positive and negative. By capturing lessons learned, best practices, and core competencies, the organization can continuously improve its performance, efficiency, and effectiveness.

- Knowledge Retention: Organizational memory helps retain valuable knowledge within the organization, even when individual employees leave. This reduces the risk of knowledge loss and ensures that critical information and expertise are accessible to current and future employees.
- Decision-Making: Organizational memory provides a wealth of information and insights that can inform decision-making. By drawing on past experiences and best practices, decision-makers can make more informed and effective choices, avoiding previous mistakes and leveraging successful approaches.
- Innovation and Creativity: Organizational memory stimulates innovation and creativity by providing a foundation of knowledge and experiences to build upon. By accessing the collective wisdom of the organization, employees can leverage existing knowledge, generate new ideas, and develop innovative solutions to challenges.
- Employee Engagement and Development: Organizational memory fosters employee engagement and development by providing a sense of pride, purpose, and belonging. When employees have access to and contribute to the organization's knowledge and experience, they feel valued and motivated to contribute to its success. Organizational memory also supports employee development by facilitating the sharing of tacit knowledge, mentoring relationships, and learning from past successes and failures.

Succession Planning:

Succession planning is a systematic process that involves identifying and preparing individuals within an organization to assume key roles and responsibilities in the future. It ensures the continuity of leadership and minimizes disruptions caused by talent gaps or unexpected departures. Succession planning aims to identify and develop a pipeline of qualified individuals who can effectively step into critical positions when needed. Here are key aspects of succession planning:

1. Identifying Key Positions: Succession planning starts by identifying the key positions within the organization that are critical for the organization's success. These positions may include senior leadership roles, key technical positions, or positions responsible for strategic functions.

2. Assessing Talent Potential: Succession planning involves assessing the potential and readiness of employees to assume key positions in the future. This assessment considers factors such as performance, skills, competencies, leadership potential, and alignment with organizational values and culture.

3. Developing Succession Candidates: Succession planning involves developing identified employees to ensure they are equipped with the necessary skills, knowledge, and experiences to be successful in future roles. This may involve providing targeted training and development opportunities, stretch assignments, mentoring relationships, job rotations, and coaching.

4. Transition and Knowledge Transfer: Succession planning includes a transition phase where the successor is gradually introduced to the responsibilities and challenges of the target role. This phase may involve job

shadowing, mentoring by the current role incumbent, and opportunities for the successor to gain hands-on experience.

5. Evaluation and Adjustment: Succession planning is an ongoing process that requires regular evaluation and adjustment. This includes reviewing the progress and readiness of potential successors, revisiting talent assessments, and updating development plans as needed. Continuous monitoring and feedback enable organizations to ensure that succession plans are effective and aligned with changing organizational needs.

Benefits and Impacts:

Implementing succession planning provides several benefits and impacts for the organization:

- Continuity of Leadership: Succession planning ensures a smooth transition of leadership and minimizes disruptions caused by key personnel departures. By identifying and preparing individuals to assume leadership roles, organizations can maintain stability, effectively manage change, and sustain organizational performance.
- Reduced Talent Gaps: Succession planning helps organizations identify and address talent gaps proactively. By developing a pipeline of capable individuals, organizations can reduce the time and costs associated with external recruitment and onboarding of critical positions.
- Employee Development and Engagement: Succession planning demonstrates an organization's commitment to employee development, growth, and career progression. By providing employees with clear career paths and development opportunities, organizations enhance employee engagement, job satisfaction, and retention.
- Knowledge Transfer: Succession planning includes knowledge transfer from incumbents to successors, ensuring that valuable organizational knowledge and expertise are retained and passed down. This ensures organizational memory, preserves best practices, and enables new leaders to build upon past successes and experiences.
- Enhanced Organizational Performance: Succession planning contributes to overall organizational performance and competitiveness. By consistently identifying, developing, and promoting internal talent, organizations build a strong leadership bench, maintain institutional knowledge, foster innovation, and drive growth.
- Increased Employee Motivation: Succession planning creates a culture of meritocracy and provides employees with a clear path for growth and advancement. Knowing that there are opportunities for career progression within the organization motivates employees to perform at their best, contribute to organizational success, and demonstrate loyalty.
- Improved Employer Branding: Organizations that invest in succession planning enhance their employer brand and attract top talent. The reputation for nurturing and promoting internal talent makes the organization an attractive employer, contributing to the recruitment and retention of high-potential individuals.

In summary, organizational memory encompasses the collective knowledge, experiences, and best practices of an organization, while succession planning ensures the continuity of leadership and minimizes disruptions through the identification and development of individuals for key positions. By leveraging organizational memory and implementing succession planning, organizations can enhance their performance, maintain a strong leadership pipeline, and foster employee engagement and development.

While organizational memory and succession planning are distinct concepts, they share several commonalities:

1. Knowledge Preservation: Both organizational memory and succession planning involve preserving valuable knowledge within the organization. Organizational memory focuses on capturing and retaining collective

knowledge, lessons learned, and best practices, ensuring that this knowledge is accessible to current and future employees. Succession planning incorporates knowledge transfer from incumbents to successors, ensuring that critical information and expertise are retained and passed down.

2. Continuity and Stability: Both organizational memory and succession planning aim to ensure continuity and stability within the organization. Organizational memory provides a foundation of knowledge, experiences, and best practices that guide decision-making and enable the organization to adapt and learn from the past. Succession planning ensures a smooth transition of leadership and minimizes disruptions caused by key personnel departures, maintaining stability and performance.

3. Talent Development: Both organizational memory and succession planning contribute to talent development within the organization. Organizational memory provides a repository of knowledge and experiences that can be leveraged for individual employee development. Succession planning identifies and develops high-potential individuals, offering them opportunities for growth, advancement, and the acquisition of critical skills and experiences necessary for assuming key positions.

4. Institutional Learning: Both organizational memory and succession planning contribute to institutional learning within the organization. Organizational memory captures the collective knowledge and experiences of the organization, facilitating learning from past successes, failures, and best practices. Succession planning incorporates knowledge transfer and enables new leaders to build upon the institutional knowledge and experiences of their predecessors, enhancing learning and performance.

5. Employee Engagement: Both organizational memory and succession planning foster employee engagement. Organizational memory provides employees with access to valuable resources, knowledge, and experiences, empowering them to make informed decisions and contribute meaningfully to the organization. Succession planning demonstrates an organization's commitment to employee development, growth, and career progression, motivating and engaging employees in their current roles.

6. Alignment with Organizational Goals: Both organizational memory and succession planning are aligned with organizational goals and objectives. Organizational memory captures and preserves information and experiences that are relevant to achieving organizational success. Succession planning ensures that the right individuals are identified and developed to assume key positions, aligning talent with strategic objectives and sustaining organizational performance.

Overall, while organizational memory focuses on preserving and leveraging collective knowledge and experiences, succession planning focuses on identifying and developing individuals to assume key positions. However, both concepts contribute to talent development, organizational learning, employee engagement, and the long-term success of the organization.

Challenges and Barriers to Knowledge Management and Organizational Learning:

Implementing effective knowledge management and organizational learning initiatives can face various challenges and barriers. Some common challenges and barriers include:

1. Culture: One of the major challenges is creating a culture that values and encourages knowledge sharing and learning. In some organizations, there may be a lack of trust, fear of sharing knowledge, or a focus on individual competition rather than collaboration. Changing the organizational culture to prioritize knowledge management and learning may require significant effort and time.

2. Resistance to Change: Resistance to change is a common barrier to knowledge management and organizational

learning. Employees may be comfortable with existing processes and resistant to adopting new approaches or technologies. Overcoming resistance requires effective change management strategies, clear communication, and involving employees in the process.

3. Lack of Leadership Support: Without strong leadership support, knowledge management and learning initiatives may struggle to gain traction. Leaders play a crucial role in fostering a culture of learning, providing resources, setting goals, and promoting knowledge sharing. Lack of leadership commitment can hinder the success of knowledge management and organizational learning efforts.

4. Technology Constraints: Technology tools and systems are essential for effective knowledge management and learning. However, limited resources or outdated technology infrastructure can pose challenges. Organizations may face barriers in implementing or upgrading technology solutions that enable efficient knowledge sharing, collaboration, and learning.

5. Siloed Information: When knowledge is fragmented and siloed in different departments or teams, it becomes difficult to access, share, and utilize. Siloed information inhibits collaboration, slows down decision-making, and hampers organizational learning. Breaking down silos and facilitating cross-functional knowledge sharing is essential for effective knowledge management and learning.

6. Lack of Knowledge Capture and Documentation: Organizations may struggle to capture and document knowledge effectively. Knowledge is often tacit, residing in the minds of employees, and may not be systematically captured and shared. This can result in critical knowledge being lost when employees leave the organization or retire. Encouraging knowledge documentation and capturing best practices is crucial for effective knowledge management and organizational learning.

7. Measurement and Evaluation: Measuring the impact of knowledge management and learning initiatives can be challenging. Determining key performance indicators, assessing the effectiveness of knowledge-sharing platforms, and measuring the impact of learning programs require robust evaluation methods. Without proper measurement, it becomes difficult to track progress, identify successes, and make informed decisions.

8. Time and Resource Constraints: Implementing knowledge management and learning initiatives requires dedicated time, resources, and budgets. Organizations may struggle to allocate sufficient resources for training programs, technology investments, and the development of knowledge management systems. Aligning resources and ensuring adequate allocation for knowledge management and learning is vital for their success.

9. Generational Differences: Organizations often have a multi-generational workforce, each with different preferences and approaches to knowledge sharing and learning. Bridging the gap between generations and understanding their unique learning styles and preferences can be a challenge. Providing flexible learning options and customized approaches that cater to different generational needs can help overcome this barrier.

10. Knowledge Loss: Knowledge loss due to employee turnover, retirements, or lack of documentation can be a significant challenge to knowledge management and organizational learning. Organizations must implement strategies to capture and transfer knowledge before employees leave, such as mentoring programs, knowledge-sharing workshops, and succession planning initiatives.

Addressing these challenges and barriers requires organizational commitment, leadership support, cultural shifts, proper resources, and effective change management strategies. Overcoming these obstacles can enable organizations to effectively manage knowledge and foster continuous learning and improvement.

Cultural and Behavioral Barriers

Cultural and behavioral barriers can significantly hinder knowledge management and organizational learning initiatives. Some common cultural and behavioral barriers include the following:

1. Lack of Trust: Trust is a critical component of knowledge sharing and organizational learning. If employees do not trust each other or the organization, they may be hesitant to share their knowledge and experiences. Building trust requires open communication, transparency, and demonstrating the value of knowledge sharing.

2. Fear of Repercussions: Employees may fear negative consequences for sharing knowledge, such as colleagues taking credit for their ideas or being seen as less valuable because they shared their expertise. This fear can lead to a reluctance to share knowledge openly. Organizations need to create a safe and supportive environment where employees feel encouraged and rewarded for sharing their knowledge.

3. Competition and Silos: When there is a culture of competition or siloed departments, sharing knowledge across teams or functions becomes challenging. Employees may focus on individual success rather than collective learning and improvement. Breaking down silos and promoting collaboration and cross-functional knowledge sharing are essential to overcome this barrier.

4. Status Quo and Resistance to Change: A culture that is resistant to change can impede knowledge management and organizational learning efforts. Employees may be comfortable with the existing ways of doing things and resistant to adopting new practices, technologies, or approaches. Overcoming resistance to change requires effective change management strategies and clear communication about the benefits of knowledge sharing and learning.

5. Lack of Recognition and Incentives: Without proper recognition and incentives, employees may not see the value of actively participating in knowledge management and organizational learning activities. Recognition can help motivate employees to share their knowledge and contribute to learning initiatives. Implementing reward systems, acknowledging contributions, and showcasing success stories can help to overcome this barrier.

6. Time and Resources Constraints: In organizations where time and resources are limited, employees may perceive knowledge-sharing and learning activities as additional tasks that detract from their core responsibilities. Employees may feel they do not have enough time to dedicate to knowledge management or learning initiatives. Prioritizing and allocating appropriate time and resources for knowledge-sharing and learning activities is crucial to overcome this barrier.

7. Lack of Leadership Support: Leadership support is essential for fostering a culture of knowledge sharing and learning. If leaders do not actively promote and participate in knowledge management initiatives, employees may not consider it a priority. Leadership should set an example by demonstrating the value of knowledge sharing, providing resources for learning and development, and encouraging ongoing learning across the organization.

8. Short-term Focus and Results Orientation: Organizations that prioritize short-term results may overlook the long-term benefits of knowledge management and organizational learning. Employees may be more focused on immediate tasks and deadlines rather than investing time and effort into sharing knowledge or participating in learning activities. Shifting the focus to recognize the importance of knowledge management and learning for long-term success is crucial to overcome this barrier.

9. Lack of Learning Opportunities: If organizations do not provide ample opportunities for learning and development, employees may struggle to acquire new knowledge and skills. Learning opportunities should be accessible, relevant, and aligned with organizational goals. Providing training programs, mentoring relationships, job rotations, and communities of practice can address this barrier.

10. Unsupportive Organizational Policies and Practices: Organizational policies and practices that do not support or prioritize knowledge sharing and learning can hinder progress in these areas. For example, a performance evaluation system that emphasizes individual performance rather than teamwork and knowledge sharing may discourage employees from actively participating in knowledge management initiatives. Aligning policies, practices, and rewards with the value of knowledge sharing and learning is crucial to overcome this barrier.

To address these cultural and behavioral barriers, organizations need to foster a culture of trust, create a supportive and collaborative environment, provide recognition and incentives, allocate sufficient time and resources, ensure leadership support, and align organizational policies and practices with the importance of knowledge management and organizational learning.

Information Overload and Retrieval Issues

Information overload and retrieval issues are common challenges in knowledge management and organizational learning. We will explore each of these challenges in more detail:

1. Information Overload:

Information overload refers to the excessive amount of information available, making it difficult for individuals or organizations to effectively access, process, and utilize the information they need. Information overload can lead to the following issues:

a. Difficulty in Filtering: The abundance of information can make it challenging to filter and identify relevant, accurate, and high-quality knowledge. This overwhelms individuals, making it difficult to discern which information is valuable and applicable to their needs.

b. Reduced Attention and Focus: When individuals are flooded with excessive information, it can lead to reduced attention spans and difficulties in maintaining focus. This hinders their ability to absorb, understand, and retain knowledge effectively.

c. Limited Decision-Making Ability: Information overload can impede decision-making processes. When individuals are faced with an overwhelming amount of information, they may struggle to make well-informed decisions or may experience decision paralysis.

d. Decreased Information Retention: Information overload can hinder knowledge retention. When individuals are exposed to an excessive amount of information, they may struggle to retain and recall the knowledge they've acquired. This reduces the effectiveness of organizational learning and the ability to apply knowledge in practical situations.

To address information overload, organizations can implement the following strategies:

- Implement Knowledge Curation: Effective knowledge curation involves organizing, categorizing, and prioritizing information to ensure easy access to relevant knowledge. By providing curated knowledge re positories, employees can navigate through information more efficiently.
- Provide Information Filtering and Personalization Tools: Employing tools such as intelligent search engines, recommender systems, and personalized content recommendations can help filter information, tailoring it to individual needs and interests.
- Foster Critical Thinking and Information Evaluation Skills: Organizations can invest in training programs that enhance employees' critical thinking and information evaluation skills. This enables employees to assess information quality, relevance, and reliability, reducing the impact of information overload.
- Encourage Collaboration and Knowledge Sharing: Encouraging collaboration and knowledge sharing

within the organization facilitates the exchange of relevant and valuable knowledge. By leveraging the collective expertise of employees, organizations can reduce the burden of information overload and benefit from diverse perspectives.

2. Retrieval Issues:

Retrieval issues in knowledge management and organizational learning pertain to difficulties in finding and accessing relevant knowledge when it is needed. These challenges can hinder effective knowledge utilization and organizational learning. Some common retrieval issues include:

a. Lack of Structure and Organization: Inefficient knowledge of organization and structure can make it difficult to locate specific information or expertise. Without proper categorization, tagging, or metadata, retrieving relevant knowledge becomes time-consuming and challenging.

b. Inadequate Search Capabilities: If the search capabilities within an organization's knowledge management system or repositories are ineffective or limited, it becomes challenging to find specific information. Inaccurate or excessive search results can further hinder retrieval.

c. Duplication and Redundancy: When knowledge is duplicated or scattered across various systems, retrieval becomes problematic. Redundant and conflicting information leads to confusion and difficulty in identifying the most accurate and up-to-date knowledge.

d. Lack of Knowledge Sharing Culture: In organizations where knowledge sharing is not encouraged or valued, retrieval issues arise. Employees may be unwilling to share their knowledge or may not actively contribute their expertise to the organization's knowledge management system, making it harder for others to retrieve relevant knowledge.

To address retrieval issues, organizations can implement the following strategies:

- Implement Effective Knowledge Management Systems: Utilize robust knowledge management systems that provide advanced search capabilities, efficient categorization, and tagging features. These systems should be user-friendly and designed with the end user in mind.
- Embrace Metatagging and Metadata Standards: Consistent meta-tagging and metadata standards facilitate efficient information retrieval. Implementing a consistent approach to structuring and organizing knowledge ensures that relevant information can be readily retrieved.
- Foster a Knowledge Sharing Culture: Encourage and incentivize knowledge sharing across the organization. Promote collaborative platforms, communities of practice, and social learning initiatives that facilitate knowledge exchange and retrieval.
- Provide Training on Retrieval Techniques: Train employees on effective searching and retrieval techniques. This includes using advanced search operators, refining search queries, and utilizing search filters to narrow down results efficiently.
- Regularly Review and Update Knowledge: Conduct periodic audits of knowledge repositories to identify and address duplicate or outdated information. Keep knowledge libraries up to date and ensure that duplicate or conflicting knowledge is consolidated or resolved.
- Foster Communities of Practice: Communities of practice bring together employees with similar interests or expertise. By facilitating knowledge exchange and ensuring active participation, communities of practice can help address retrieval issues by connecting individuals with the right knowledge and expertise.

By addressing issues related to information overload and retrieval, organizations can enhance knowledge management practices and enable effective organizational learning. This, in turn, facilitates the utilization of knowledge, enhances decision-making processes, and drives overall organizational performance.

Resistance to Knowledge Sharing and Collaboration

Resistance to knowledge sharing and collaboration can hinder the effectiveness of knowledge management initiatives and organizational learning efforts. Several factors contribute to this resistance, including:

1. Fear of Losing Power or Relevance: Some individuals may resist knowledge sharing and collaboration because they fear that sharing their knowledge or expertise will diminish their power or importance within the organization. They may feel threatened by the idea of others having access to the same knowledge and skills they possess, which can create a sense of competition.

2. Lack of Incentives or Recognition: When knowledge sharing and collaboration are not encouraged or incentivized, employees may be less motivated to engage in these activities. If there is a perception that there are no benefits or recognition associated with sharing knowledge or collaborating, individuals may choose to hoard their knowledge or work independently instead.

3. Lack of Trust: Trust is a crucial factor in knowledge sharing and collaboration. If there is a lack of trust among employees, they may hesitate to share their knowledge or collaborate with others. This lack of trust can stem from various reasons, such as a fear of receiving criticism or not being credited for their contributions.

4. Siloed Organizational Culture: In organizations with siloed or departmentalized structures, there is often a lack of cross-functional collaboration and knowledge sharing. This results in limited information flow and a reluctance to share knowledge outside of one's immediate team or department.

5. Time and Resource Constraints: Employees may resist knowledge sharing and collaboration if they perceive it as time-consuming or if they feel overloaded with their existing workload. Limited resources or competing priorities can also hinder individuals from engaging in collaborative efforts.

6. Lack of Communication and Knowledge-Sharing Tools: If organizations do not provide effective communication and knowledge-sharing tools, it can create barriers to sharing knowledge and collaborating. Difficulties in accessing or finding relevant information, outdated or inefficient technology, or a lack of user-friendly platforms can contribute to resistance.

To overcome resistance to knowledge sharing and collaboration, organizations can adopt the following strategies:

1. Foster a Culture of Trust and Psychological Safety: Create an environment where employees feel safe to share their ideas, ask questions, and provide constructive feedback. Encourage open dialogue and create spaces for collaboration where diverse perspectives are valued and respected.

2. Provide Incentives and Recognition: Recognize and reward individuals who actively engage in knowledge sharing and collaboration. This can be done through performance evaluations, promotions, or other forms of recognition that highlight and appreciate their contributions.

3. Promote Leadership Support: Leaders should actively endorse and model knowledge-sharing and collaboration behaviors. When leaders prioritize and participate in these activities, it signals to others that they are valued and important for organizational success.

4. Implement Collaboration Tools and Platforms: Invest in technology and platforms that facilitate knowledge sharing and collaboration. Provide user-friendly interfaces, seamless communication channels, and easy access to relevant information. Training and support for these tools are also essential to encourage adoption and usage.

5. Encourage Communities of Practice: Establish communities of practice or professional networks where employees can voluntarily participate and share knowledge within their areas of interest or expertise. These com-

munities foster a sense of belonging, enable peer learning, and provide a space for ongoing knowledge exchange.

6. Educate and Communicate the Benefits: Take the time to communicate the value and benefits of knowledge sharing and collaboration to employees. Clearly articulate how it can enhance individual and collective performance, lead to better decision-making, and contribute to personal and professional growth.

By addressing resistance to knowledge sharing and collaboration, organizations can build a culture of collaboration, enable effective knowledge sharing, and foster continuous learning and improvement.

Lack of Leadership Support and Alignment with Strategy

Lack of leadership support refers to a situation where the leaders within an organization do not actively endorse or promote a particular strategy or initiative. This lack of endorsement can manifest in various ways, including a lack of communication, insufficient resources allocated, or a failure to prioritize and take action.

Alignment with strategy is crucial for the success of any organization. It ensures that all stakeholders, from leadership to frontline employees, are working towards a common goal. When there is a lack of alignment, it means that individuals and teams within the organization may have different priorities and objectives, leading to confusion, inefficiency, and ultimately, failure to achieve desired outcomes.

There are several reasons why leadership support and alignment with strategy may be lacking:

1. Lack of understanding: Leaders may not fully comprehend the strategic direction of the organization or the rationale behind a particular strategy. Without a clear understanding, they may fail to appreciate the importance of supporting and aligning with it.

2. Personal interests or conflicting priorities: Leaders may have personal agendas or conflicting priorities that take precedence over the strategy. They may focus on short-term gains or their own department's objectives rather than the broader organizational goals.

3. Communication breakdown: If leaders and their teams are not effectively communicating about the strategy, it can lead to misalignment. Lack of clarity, inconsistent messaging, or a failure to involve key stakeholders in the decision-making process can all contribute to this breakdown.

4. Resistance to change: Leaders may resist embracing a new strategy because it requires them to change their current practices or disrupt existing power structures. They may feel threatened by the potential loss of control or fear the unknown, leading to a lack of support for the strategy.

The consequences of lacking leadership support and alignment with strategy can be significant. It can result in decreased employee engagement, reduced productivity, wasted resources, missed opportunities, and ultimately, failure to achieve organizational goals. To address this issue, organizations should focus on improving communication, providing leadership development and training, ensuring clarity and understanding of the strategic direction, and nurturing a culture of support and alignment throughout the entire organization.

Measuring and Evaluating Knowledge Management Initiatives

Measuring and evaluating knowledge management initiatives is essential to determine their effectiveness, identify areas for improvement, and showcase their impact on organizational performance. Here are a few examples of how knowledge management initiatives can be measured and evaluated:

1. Usage metrics: One way to measure the success of a knowledge management initiative is to track its usage metrics. This can include monitoring the number of knowledge articles accessed, the frequency of employee con-

tributions, or the utilization of specific knowledge-sharing platforms. For example, an organization may track the number of employees accessing a knowledge base or the number of downloads of a particular document. An increase in these metrics indicates that employees are actively using and benefiting from the knowledge management initiative.

2. Employee feedback: Collecting feedback from employees who interact with the knowledge management system can provide valuable insights into its effectiveness. This can be done through surveys, focus groups, or interviews. By asking employees about their experience, satisfaction level, and suggestions for improvement, organizations can identify any gaps or areas of improvement. For example, an organization may survey to gauge employee satisfaction with the knowledge management platform and gather suggestions for enhancing its usability or content relevance.

3. Impact on decision-making and problem-solving: An effective knowledge management initiative should support decision-making and problem-solving within the organization. Measuring the impact of knowledge management on decision-making can involve assessing the speed and accuracy of decisions made, as well as the level of confidence in those decisions. For example, a company may compare decision-making outcomes before and after the implementation of a knowledge management system to determine if there is an improvement in the quality or efficiency of decision-making.

4. Knowledge reuse and innovation: Knowledge management aims to facilitate the reuse and sharing of knowledge, driving innovation and avoiding reinvention of the wheel. Measuring the rate of knowledge reuse or the number of new ideas generated through the knowledge management initiative can demonstrate its impact. For instance, an organization may track the number of ideas or innovations generated by employees who accessed the knowledge base or participated in knowledge-sharing activities.

5. Business impact: Ultimately, the success of a knowledge management initiative should be measured by its impact on organizational performance. This can involve assessing key performance indicators (KPIs) relevant to the organization's goals, such as customer satisfaction, employee productivity, or cost savings. For instance, a company may track a decrease in customer complaints due to improved access to knowledge resources or an increase in sales revenue resulting from faster and more informed decision-making.

It is important to establish clear measurement criteria and align them with the organization's strategic objectives to accurately assess the effectiveness of knowledge management initiatives. Regular evaluation and monitoring of these metrics enable organizations to make informed decisions about the improvement and optimization of their knowledge management practices.

Future Trends and Emerging Practices:

The field of knowledge management and organizational learning is constantly evolving, with new trends and emerging practices emerging. Here are some future trends and practices to watch for:

1. Artificial Intelligence (AI) and Machine Learning: AI and machine learning technologies have the potential to revolutionize knowledge management and organizational learning. These technologies can assist in capturing, organizing, and analyzing vast amounts of data, extracting insights, and making recommendations. AI-powered chatbots or virtual assistants can provide instant access to knowledge and support continuous learning within organizations.

2. Learning Analytics: Learning analytics involves collecting and analyzing data on individual and organizational learning activities. This data can be used to identify patterns, trends, and gaps in learning, enabling organizations to personalize learning experiences, provide targeted interventions, and measure the impact of learning initiatives

more accurately. Learning analytics can also facilitate data-driven decision-making and improvement of learning strategies.

3. Social Learning and Collaboration: The rise of social media and collaborative technologies has led to a shift towards social learning and collaborative knowledge sharing within organizations. Instead of relying solely on formal training programs, organizations are embracing platforms and tools that enable employees to share knowledge, co-create content, and learn from each other in real time. This shift promotes a culture of continuous learning and supports the development of communities of practice.

4. Knowledge Sharing Networks: Organizations are increasingly recognizing the value of connecting with external knowledge networks to access expertise and stay abreast of industry trends. Knowledge-sharing networks enable organizations to tap into a broader range of knowledge sources, collaborate with industry experts, and foster innovation through cross-pollination of ideas.

5. Agile Knowledge Management: Agile practices, commonly used in software development, are being applied to knowledge management. Agile knowledge management emphasizes iterative, flexible, and collaborative approaches to knowledge creation, sharing, and refinement. It involves rapid prototyping, feedback loops, and adaptation based on user needs and changing organizational requirements.

6. Gamification and Microlearning: Gamification techniques, such as the use of game elements and mechanics, are being applied to enhance engagement and motivation in learning initiatives. Microlearning, which involves delivering small, bite-sized learning modules, is gaining popularity due to its accessibility and ability to cater to short attention spans. These approaches can facilitate continuous learning and make knowledge acquisition more enjoyable and effective.

7. Personal Knowledge Management: As individuals are increasingly responsible for managing their learning and knowledge, personal knowledge management practices are gaining importance. This involves leveraging tools and strategies to organize, retrieve, and curate personalized knowledge repositories. Personal knowledge management empowers individuals to take ownership of their learning and align it with their specific needs and goals.

These trends and practices highlight the evolving nature of knowledge management and organizational learning, driven by technological advancements, changing learning needs, and the recognition of the integral role knowledge plays in organizational success. Adapting to these trends can enable organizations to stay competitive, foster innovation, and create a culture of continuous learning.

Leveraging Big Data and Analytics for Knowledge Management

Leveraging big data and analytics for knowledge management involves utilizing vast amounts of structured and unstructured data to derive insights, make informed decisions, and enhance knowledge sharing and learning within an organization. Here's how big data and analytics can be used in knowledge management:

1. Data collection and integration: Big data technologies enable organizations to collect, aggregate, and integrate various types of data from different sources, including internal databases, external repositories, social media platforms, and IoT devices. This data can include textual information, customer feedback, clickstream data, employee collaboration activities, and more.

2. Data analysis and insight generation: By applying advanced analytics techniques such as natural language processing, machine learning, and sentiment analysis to the collected data, organizations can extract valuable insights and patterns. These insights can be used to identify knowledge gaps, trends, best practices, and emerging opportunities that can inform decision-making and improve knowledge management strategies.

3. Personalized learning and knowledge delivery: Big data analytics can facilitate personalized learning experiences by tailoring content and recommendations to individual learners. By analyzing learners' preferences, past interactions, and performance data, organizations can suggest relevant learning resources, personalized training paths, and targeted interventions to optimize learning outcomes.

4. Predictive analytics for proactive knowledge management: Predictive analytics algorithms can be used to forecast future needs, challenges, and opportunities based on historical data. This helps organizations take proactive measures to capture, acquire, and disseminate knowledge on time. For example, predictive analytics can identify areas that may experience knowledge gaps due to anticipated retirements or changes in the organization's strategic direction.

5. Social network analysis: Big data analytics can uncover hidden knowledge networks within an organization by analyzing social interactions and collaboration patterns. By understanding who interacts with whom and how knowledge flows, organizations can identify influential individuals, facilitate communities of practice, leverage expertise, and encourage effective knowledge-sharing and collaboration.

6. Content curation and recommendation: Analyzing big data can help organizations curate and recommend relevant knowledge content to users. By understanding individual preferences, learning goals, and performance metrics, organizations can provide tailored recommendations, identify related content, and facilitate the serendipitous discovery of knowledge resources.

7. Continuous improvement and optimization: Big data analytics provides metrics and insights to continuously monitor and evaluate the effectiveness of knowledge management initiatives. Organizations can track key performance indicators, such as knowledge utilization, employee engagement, or the impact of knowledge sharing on problem-solving. This enables organizations to refine their strategies, identify areas for improvement, and optimize their knowledge management processes.

By leveraging big data and analytics, organizations can harness the power of information to drive better knowledge management practices. It enables organizations to make data-driven decisions, deliver personalized learning experiences, identify, and leverage valuable insights, and optimize knowledge-sharing processes for improved organizational performance and innovation.

Harnessing the Power of Artificial Intelligence and Machine Learning

Harnessing the power of artificial intelligence (AI) and machine learning (ML) involves utilizing their capabilities to automate tasks, process large amounts of data, derive insights, and make predictions. Here's a detailed explanation of how AI and ML can be harnessed:

1. Automation and Efficiency: AI and ML can automate routine and repetitive tasks, saving time and resources for organizations. For example, intelligent chatbots can handle customer inquiries, virtual assistants can schedule meetings or provide reminders, and robotic process automation (RPA) can perform data entry or document processing tasks. This automation improves efficiency, reduces errors, and allows employees to focus on higher-value activities.

2. Data Processing and Analysis: AI and ML excel at processing and analyzing large volumes of data. They can extract patterns, insights, and correlations from structured and unstructured data sources. For instance, ML algorithms can analyze customer behavior data to identify buying patterns or recommend personalized offers. This data-driven approach enables organizations to make more informed decisions, uncover hidden patterns, and identify opportunities or risks.

3. Predictive Analytics and Forecasting: The predictive capabilities of AI and ML allow organizations to anticipate future outcomes based on historical data. They can build predictive models that forecast customer demand, identify potential equipment failures, or predict sales trends. By providing foresight, organizations can take proactive measures to optimize resources, mitigate risks, and make better-informed decisions.

4. Personalization and Recommendation: AI and ML algorithms can personalize experiences by understanding individual preferences and behaviors. They can recommend content, products, or services based on user data and past interactions. For example, streaming platforms use ML to suggest relevant movies or shows, and e-commerce websites recommend products based on individual browsing and purchase history. Personalization enhances customer satisfaction, and engagement, and drives conversions.

5. Natural Language Processing (NLP): NLP enables machines to understand and interpret human language. It powers AI-driven voice assistants like Amazon's Alexa or Apple's Siri. NLP algorithms can also analyze vast amounts of textual data, such as customer feedback or social media posts, to extract sentiment, identify trends, or perform text classification. This enables organizations to better understand customer sentiments, conduct sentiment analysis, and improve customer experiences.

6. Image and Video Analysis: AI and ML algorithms can analyze and interpret visual data, such as images or videos, at a scale. They can recognize objects, faces, and emotions, or detect anomalies. This capability finds applications in various areas - from object recognition in autonomous vehicles to surveillance systems that detect unauthorized activities or facial recognition systems for security purposes.

7. Continuous Learning and Improvement: ML models can continuously learn and adapt to new data. Through iterative training processes, models can improve their performance over time. This enables organizations to refine predictions, recommendations, or decision-making based on changing circumstances or evolving patterns.

Although the potential benefits of harnessing AI and ML are immense, proper implementation requires considerations such as data quality, algorithm transparency, ethical implications, and user privacy. Organizations must align their AI and ML initiatives with their strategic objectives, ensure the availability of high-quality data, and prioritize the ethical and responsible use of these technologies. With appropriate planning and execution, harnessing AI and ML can drive innovation, improve operational efficiency, enhance customer experiences, and unlock new opportunities for organizations.

The concepts of harnessing the power of artificial intelligence (AI) and machine learning (ML) involve understanding the underlying principles and methodologies that enable these technologies to be effectively utilized. Here are some key concepts to consider:

1. Data-driven Approach: AI and ML systems rely on large amounts of data to learn patterns, make predictions, or derive insights. The concept of a data-driven approach emphasizes the importance of collecting and curating high-quality data to be used as inputs for AI and ML algorithms. This involves data collection, storage, preprocessing, and data cleaning to ensure its accuracy, completeness, and relevance.

2. Training and Learning: ML algorithms learn from labeled or unlabeled examples to develop models that can generalize patterns and make predictions on new, unseen data. The training process involves feeding data into the algorithm and adjusting its internal parameters to optimize its performance. The concept of training and learning emphasizes the iterative nature of ML, with continuous refinement and improvement based on feedback and new data.

3. Algorithms and Models: AI and ML algorithms are the mathematical and computational techniques that process data and produce results. Various types of algorithms, such as decision trees, neural networks, or support

vector machines, are used depending on the task and problem at hand. ML models are the representations of learned patterns and relationships within the algorithm. Choosing the appropriate algorithms and models is crucial for achieving accurate predictions and insights.

4. Feature Engineering: Feature engineering involves the process of selecting, transforming, and creating meaningful features from the available data to improve the performance of AI and ML models. It requires domain expertise and knowledge of the problem to extract relevant information and representations that capture the underlying patterns. Effective feature engineering can significantly impact the performance and generalization capabilities of the models.

5. Evaluation and Validation: Proper evaluation and validation techniques are essential to assess the performance and reliability of AI and ML models. This involves splitting the data into training and testing sets, using metrics suitable for the problem (such as accuracy, precision, recall, or F1 score), and conducting statistical analysis to ensure the results are statistically significant. Cross-validation and other techniques help validate the model's performance on unseen data.

6. Ethical and Responsible AI: The concept of ethical and responsible AI emphasizes the importance of considering the socio-ethical implications of AI and ML technologies. This includes fairness, transparency, accountability, and privacy issues. Organizations must ensure that AI systems do not perpetuate biases, provide explainability and interpretability, establish clear guidelines and regulations for AI usage, and safeguard user data and privacy rights.

7. Deployment and Scalability: Once AI and ML models are trained and validated, they need to be deployed and integrated into real-world applications. This involves considerations such as system architecture, scalability, performance optimization, and integration with existing infrastructure. Deployment may require deploying models in the cloud, on edge devices, or within existing software systems.

Understanding and applying these concepts is crucial for harnessing the power of AI and ML. It requires a multi-disciplinary approach, involving data scientists, domain experts, ethicists, and stakeholders, to develop and deploy AI and ML solutions successfully. By embracing these concepts, organizations can leverage the capabilities of AI and ML to improve decision-making, enhance operational efficiency, and unlock new opportunities.

The Rise of Social Learning Networks and Gamification

The rise of social learning networks and gamification has transformed the way organizations approach learning, knowledge sharing, and engagement. Here's an extensive explanation of these concepts:

1. Social Learning Networks:

Social learning networks leverage social media-like platforms and technologies to facilitate knowledge sharing, collaboration, and informal learning within organizations. These networks provide employees with the ability to connect, share ideas, ask questions, and learn from each other more dynamically and interactively. Some key elements and benefits of social learning networks include:

a. User-generated content: Social learning networks encourage employees to create and share their content, such as blog posts, articles, videos, or podcasts. This fosters a culture of knowledge sharing and allows individuals to contribute based on their expertise and interests.

b. Communities of Practice (CoPs): Social learning networks often support the formation of communities of practice, which are groups of individuals with shared professional interests. CoPs provide a dedicated space for members to collaborate, exchange ideas, solve problems, and learn from one another.

c. Peer learning and mentorship: Social learning networks facilitate peer-to-peer learning, where individuals can seek advice, ask questions, or receive feedback from their colleagues. This enables the transfer of tacit knowledge and promotes a culture of continuous learning.

d. Enhanced engagement and motivation: By incorporating social elements, such as likes, comments, and badges, social learning networks encourage active participation and increase learner engagement. This social interaction can boost motivation and facilitate a sense of belonging and contribution within the organization.

e. Personalization and discovery: Social learning networks often have algorithms that recommend relevant content to users based on their interests, connections, and browsing history. This personalization enables users to discover new knowledge, resources, and experts aligned with their specific learning needs.

2. Gamification:

Gamification involves incorporating game design elements and mechanics into non-game contexts, such as learning and employee engagement initiatives. Here's an extensive explanation of key elements and benefits of gamification in organizational contexts:

a. Points, badges, and leaderboards: Gamification often employs these elements to incentivize participation, track progress, and create healthy competition. By earning points, badges, or climbing leaderboards, employees can receive recognition for their achievements and engage in friendly competition with their peers.

b. Rewards and incentives: Gamification can offer tangible or intangible rewards as incentives for completing tasks, achieving milestones, or demonstrating desired behaviors. These rewards can range from physical rewards like gift cards or company merchandise to intangible rewards like access to special learning resources or social recognition.

c. Progression and levels: Gamification can employ a leveling system to represent a sense of progression and mastery. As employees complete their tasks or accumulate points, they can level up, unlocking new challenges, content, or privileges. This creates a sense of achievement and motivates employees to continue learning and engaging.

d. Feedback and immediate gratification: Gamification provides instant feedback to participants, allowing them to track their progress and receive immediate gratification for their efforts. This feedback loop reinforces desired behaviors, identifies areas for improvement, and keeps employees engaged in the learning process.

e. Engagement and motivation: By incorporating game elements, gamification can make learning and work more enjoyable and engaging. It taps into intrinsic motivators such as autonomy, mastery, and purpose, fostering a sense of accomplishment and boosting motivation among employees.

f. Behavior change and skill development: Gamification can be used to encourage desired behaviors, promote skill development, and reinforce learning outcomes. By designing challenges and activities that align with specific learning goals or organizational objectives, gamification can drive behavior change and enhance performance.

Both social learning networks and gamification have gained popularity due to their ability to foster a culture of continuous learning, employee engagement, and collaboration. Organizations that embrace these concepts can create dynamic learning environments, promote knowledge sharing, and facilitate the development of a learning culture that enhances individual and organizational performance.

Cultivating a Learning Culture for Remote and Distributed Workforces

Cultivating a learning culture is crucial for remote and distributed workforces to ensure continuous learning, skill development, and knowledge sharing. Here are some strategies to foster a learning culture in such settings:

1. Embrace Technology: Leverage digital tools and platforms to facilitate learning and knowledge sharing. Use video conferencing, virtual classrooms, and collaboration software to deliver training sessions, enable interactive discussions, and encourage remote participation. Implement a learning management system (LMS) that offers a centralized hub for accessing learning resources, tracking progress, and facilitating collaboration among remote employees.

2. Encourage Self-Directed Learning: Remote and distributed workforces often require self-motivated learning initiatives. Encourage employees to take ownership of their learning journey by providing access to a variety of learning resources, such as online courses, webinars, e-books, or podcasts. Support employees in setting learning goals, creating individual development plans, and allocating time for self-directed learning activities.

3. Foster a Supportive Learning Environment: Create a supportive environment that encourages collaboration, knowledge sharing, and peer-to-peer learning. Establish virtual communities of practice or discussion forums where remote employees can discuss ideas, seek expertise, and share best practices. Encourage remote workers to actively engage in online discussions, contribute to knowledge repositories, and provide feedback to their peers.

4. Promote Continuous Learning Opportunities: Offer a range of learning opportunities specifically designed for remote and distributed workforces. This can include webinars, virtual workshops, or online micro-learning modules that address their unique challenges and needs. Build a culture where employees are encouraged to continuously update their skills, explore new technologies, and stay updated on industry trends.

5. Recognize and Reward Learning: Acknowledge and reward employees who actively participate in learning and contribute to knowledge-sharing efforts. Recognize achievements, provide opportunities for employees to showcase their expertise, and celebrate successful completion of learning milestones. Publicly appreciate and encourage employees who engage in continuous learning and demonstrate knowledge-sharing behaviors.

6. Develop Mentorship and Coaching Programs: Establish mentorship and coaching initiatives to support remote employees in their learning journey. Pair experienced employees with less experienced ones to provide guidance, share knowledge, and offer career advice. Virtual mentorship programs can help remote workers feel connected and supported, foster professional growth, and accelerate learning.

7. Lead by Example: Leaders play a crucial role in fostering a learning culture. Encourage leaders to actively engage in learning initiatives, seek feedback, and share their knowledge and experiences. Provide leadership development programs that equip leaders with the skills to support remote learning, embrace technology, and foster a culture of continuous improvement and knowledge sharing.

By implementing these strategies, organizations can create a learning culture that supports the professional growth and development of remote and distributed workforces. A strong learning culture enhances employee engagement, improves performance, ensures adaptability to change, and ultimately drives organizational success in remote work environments.

Case Studies and Best Practices:

Here are a few case studies and best practices highlighting successful knowledge management and organizational learning initiatives:

1. Siemens: Siemens, a multinational conglomerate, implemented a comprehensive knowledge management system called Siemens Knowledge Management System (SKMS). It enabled employees to access and share information, technical know-how, and best practices across different business units and geographic locations. The system integrated various tools, such as search engines, discussion forums, and document repositories, to

facilitate knowledge sharing. This initiative improved collaboration, reduced duplication of efforts, and accelerated problem-solving, resulting in enhanced innovation and customer satisfaction.

2. Google: Google has a well-known culture of knowledge sharing and continuous learning. One of their notable practices is their famous "20% time" policy, where employees are encouraged to spend 20% of their work time on personal projects or learning. This practice allows employees to explore new ideas, learn new skills, and innovate beyond their core responsibilities. It has resulted in the development of successful products like Gmail and Google News and fosters an environment of experimentation, creativity, and knowledge sharing.

3. Procter & Gamble (P&G): P&G implemented a program called "Connect and Develop" to promote open innovation and knowledge sharing. The program encouraged employees to seek external partnerships and collaborate with external experts, universities, and research institutions. This approach allowed P&G to tap into new ideas and technologies, accelerate product development, and expand its knowledge base. The program resulted in successful collaborations and innovative products, strengthening P&G's competitive advantage.

4. Microsoft: Microsoft developed an internal knowledge-sharing platform called Microsoft OneDrive and SharePoint. These platforms enable employees to store and share documents, collaborate on projects, and access a rich repository of organizational knowledge. The platforms incorporate features like version control, document tagging, and search capabilities to facilitate easy and efficient knowledge retrieval. Microsoft's focus on knowledge sharing and collaboration has supported its transformation into a leading technology company.

Best Practices:

a. Encourage a Learning Mindset: Foster a culture that values and priorities learning and knowledge sharing. Encourage employees to continuously seek learning opportunities, experiment with new ideas, and share their expertise with others.

b. Provide Knowledge-Sharing Platforms: Implement user-friendly knowledge-sharing platforms, such as intranets, wikis, or collaboration tools, that facilitate easy access to information and encourage collaboration among employees.

c. Support Communities of Practice (CoPs): Establish and nurture communities of practice that bring together individuals with shared interests or expertise. These communities provide a platform for peer learning, idea exchange, and fostering a sense of belonging.

d. Provide Learning Opportunities: Offer a variety of learning opportunities, including training programs, workshops, webinars, and mentoring schemes. Provide resources and support for employees to develop new skills, stay updated on industry trends, and continuously improve their knowledge base.

e. Recognize and Reward Knowledge Contributions: Recognize and reward individuals and teams for their knowledge-sharing efforts and contributions. This can be done through public acknowledgment, rewards and incentives, or career development opportunities.

f. Continuously Evaluate and Improve: Regularly assess the effectiveness of knowledge management initiatives, gather feedback from employees, and make necessary improvements. Stay updated on emerging technologies and best practices to ensure the knowledge management approach remains relevant and effective.

These case studies and best practices highlight the importance of fostering a culture of knowledge sharing, providing effective platforms and tools for knowledge management, and supporting continuous learning initiatives within organizations. By implementing these strategies, organizations can drive innovation, enhance collaboration, and gain a competitive advantage in the market.

Knowledge Management Success Stories: Lessons from Leading Organizations

Several leading organizations have achieved success in knowledge management by implementing effective strategies and practices. Here are some knowledge management success stories and the lessons we can learn from them:

1. IBM: IBM established a formal knowledge management program called the IBM Knowledge Jam, which aimed to capture and share knowledge across the organization. The platform encouraged employees to contribute their expertise, collaborate, and solve complex business challenges. The success of IBM's knowledge management efforts was driven by their focus on creating a culture of knowledge sharing and leveraging technology to facilitate collaboration and capture tacit knowledge.

Lessons Learned: Foster a knowledge-sharing culture, provide platforms for collaboration and knowledge capture, and leverage technology to enable easy access to knowledge.

2. Toyota: Toyota, renowned for its lean manufacturing principles, implemented a knowledge management system called the Toyota Production System (TPS). TPS is a holistic approach that emphasizes continuous improvement and the dissemination of knowledge and best practices throughout the organization. Toyota leveraged cross-functional teams, standardized processes, and visual management techniques to enable knowledge transfer and empower employees to contribute to the organization's learning and improvement initiatives.

Lessons Learned: Encourage continuous improvement and learning, standardize processes to facilitate knowledge transfer, and empower employees to contribute to organizational knowledge.

3. NASA: NASA has successfully implemented knowledge management practices to support its space exploration initiatives. The organization created the NASA Lessons Learned Knowledge Base, which aims to capture, organize, and share lessons learned from various projects and missions. This searchable database allows employees to access and learn from previous experiences to prevent mistakes and improve future endeavors. NASA's focus on capturing lessons learned and making them easily accessible has been crucial to their innovation and success.

Lessons Learned: Capture and organize lessons learned from projects, create a centralized knowledge repository, and promote learning from past experiences.

4. Accenture: Accenture, a global consulting firm, developed a comprehensive knowledge management strategy to leverage the expertise of its consultants worldwide. They established a knowledge-sharing platform called Accenture Knowledge Xchange, which enabled consultants to access high-quality content, collaborate, and contribute their knowledge. Accenture's success resides in its focus on incentivizing knowledge sharing, providing robust tools and platforms, and leveraging its consultants' expertise to enhance client service delivery.

Lessons Learned: Incentivize knowledge sharing, provide robust tools and platforms, and leverage the expertise of employees to enhance organizational capabilities.

5. World Bank: The World Bank successfully implemented knowledge management practices to enhance its global development mission. They developed the World Bank's Open Knowledge Repository, a platform that provides access to various research and knowledge products. The repository enables knowledge sharing with external stakeholders and promotes open access to information, fostering collaborations and innovation in the development community.

Lessons Learned: Promote open access to knowledge, foster knowledge sharing with external stakeholders, and leverage technology to facilitate knowledge dissemination.

These success stories demonstrate the importance of creating a culture of knowledge sharing, leveraging technology to facilitate knowledge capture and dissemination, and providing platforms that enable collaboration and learning. By adopting these practices, organizations can improve decision-making, drive innovation, and enhance overall organizational performance.

Best Practices in Organizational Learning and Knowledge Management Implementation

Organizational learning and knowledge management implementation require careful planning and execution. Here are some best practices to consider:

1. Conduct a Knowledge Audit: Before implementing knowledge management initiatives, conduct a knowledge audit to identify existing knowledge assets, knowledge gaps, and the needs of your organization. This assessment will help you understand what knowledge is critical, how it is currently managed, and what areas need improvement.

2. Align with Organizational Goals: Ensure that your knowledge management efforts align with your organization's goals and strategic objectives. Identify the knowledge areas that are most crucial to achieving these goals and prioritize them in your implementation plan.

3. Foster a Knowledge-Sharing Culture: Create a culture that values and encourages knowledge-sharing. Recognize and reward employees who actively participate in knowledge-sharing activities. Develop communication channels that facilitate the exchange of tacit knowledge and encourage collaboration among employees.

4. Provide Training and Support: Offer training and support to employees to enhance their knowledge and management skills. This can include education on effective knowledge capture, sharing, and retrieval techniques. Provide resources and tools that enable employees to easily access and contribute knowledge.

5. Implement Knowledge Management Systems: Invest in knowledge management systems or platforms that can effectively capture, organize, and distribute knowledge. These systems should promote collaboration, enable easy search and retrieval of information, and include features for tagging, categorizing, and updating knowledge.

6. Encourage Communities of Practice (CoPs): Create communities of practice within your organization to foster knowledge sharing and collaboration among employees. These communities provide a platform for employees to share insights, best practices, and challenges related to specific areas of expertise or interests.

7. Capture and Analyze Lessons Learned: Establish mechanisms to capture lessons learned from projects and initiatives. Regularly analyze these lessons to identify trends, areas for improvement, and best practices. Use this information to update organizational processes, policies, and procedures.

8. Continuously Evaluate and Iterate: Regularly evaluate the effectiveness of your knowledge management initiatives and adjust your approach as needed. Gather feedback from employees, measure key performance indicators, and identify opportunities for improvement.

9. Senior Leadership Support: Garner support from senior leaders in your organization. Secure their commitment to knowledge management initiatives, as their involvement can help drive adoption and create a culture of continuous learning and knowledge sharing.

10. Measure and Communicate Impact: Develop metrics and measurement frameworks to assess the impact of knowledge management initiatives. Communicate the value and benefits of knowledge management to stakeholders, highlighting success stories and the positive impact it has on organizational performance.

By following these best practices, organizations can effectively implement organizational learning and knowledge management initiatives, foster a culture of continuous learning, and realize the benefits of knowledge sharing and collaboration.

Knowledge management and organizational learning are integral components for organizations seeking to thrive in today's knowledge-intensive environment. By effectively managing knowledge, organizations can leverage their collective intellectual capital, promote continuous learning, and enhance performance. Although challenges and barriers exist, organizations that prioritize knowledge management and organizational learning as strategic priorities stand to gain numerous benefits, including improved decision-making, innovation, efficiency, competitive advantage, and talent development. As technology advances and new practices emerge, organizations need to adapt, cultivate a learning culture, and proactively harness knowledge to drive success in the ever-evolving business landscape.

Chapter Ten

Organizational Resilience And Cross-Cultural Management

Organizational resilience is the capacity of an organization to adapt, recover, and thrive in the face of disruptive events, uncertainties, and challenges. It involves the ability to anticipate and identify potential risks and vulnerabilities, as well as the capacity to respond and recover effectively when disruptions occur. Resilient organizations have robust systems and processes in place that enable them to withstand crises, quickly bounce back, and continue operating with minimal disruption. They prioritize proactive risk management, continuous learning and improvement, and the fostering of a resilient culture throughout the organization. Overall, organizational resilience is about building agility, adaptability, and the capacity to navigate uncertainties and emerge stronger in a changing environment.

Introduction to Organizational Resilience and Cross-Cultural Management

Cross-Cultural Management and Organizational Resilience are Interconnected in several ways:

1. Adaptability to diverse environments: Cross-cultural management involves understanding and navigating different cultural contexts. This understanding allows organizations to adapt and respond effectively to diverse environments, which is a key aspect of organizational resilience. Organizations that can successfully manage cross-cultural challenges are better equipped to handle external disruptions and changes.

2. Flexibility and openness to change: Cross-cultural management requires flexibility and an openness to different perspectives and approaches. Similarly, organizational resilience involves the ability to adapt and embrace change. By managing cross-cultural differences effectively, organizations develop a culture of flexibility and openness, which enhances their ability to navigate and respond to unexpected disruptions.

3. Building strong relationships and networks: Cross-cultural management involves building relationships and networks across different cultures. These relationships foster collaboration, trust, and resilience. Organizations that prioritize cross-cultural management build robust networks that can provide support, resources, and knowledge during times of crisis or uncertainty.

4. Effective communication and conflict resolution: Cross-cultural management emphasizes effective communication and conflict resolution strategies in diverse settings. These skills are critical for organizational resilience, as clear and open communication reduces misunderstandings, resolves conflicts, and supports cohesive decision-making during challenging times.

5. Learning and knowledge sharing: Cross-cultural management promotes continuous learning and knowledge sharing about diverse cultural perspectives and practices. This cultural intelligence allows organizations to learn from different contexts and apply that knowledge to enhance their resilience. By understanding and leveraging diverse perspectives, organizations can develop innovative strategies and solutions to navigate uncertainties.

Overall, cross-cultural management enhances organizational resilience by fostering adaptability, flexibility, collaboration, effective communication, and continuous learning. By proactively managing cross-cultural challenges, organizations can build a strong foundation for resilience and navigate disruptions with agility and success.

Organizational resilience refers to an organization's ability to respond and adapt to unforeseen challenges, disruptions, or crises. It involves building a resilient culture, processes, and systems to ensure long-term sustainability and success.

In today's ever-changing business landscape, organizations face numerous risks, including natural disasters, cyber threats, economic downturns, and even global pandemics. Organizational resilience practices help businesses prepare for and recover from these challenges while minimizing damage and optimizing performance.

Resilient organizations are proactive and strategic in their approach to risk management. They understand that disruptions are inevitable, and they actively identify and evaluate potential risks. This involves conducting regular risk assessments, developing contingency plans, and establishing robust communication channels to facilitate quick and effective responses.

A key aspect of organizational resilience is building a strong culture that encourages agile decision-making and fosters innovation. Resilient organizations value flexibility and adaptability, empowering employees to think creatively, take risks, and explore new opportunities. They also prioritize learning and growth, ensuring that employees have the necessary skills and knowledge to navigate challenging situations.

Effective leadership is crucial in fostering organizational resilience. Leaders play a key role in setting the tone and direction for the organization, ensuring that resilience practices are embedded in the organizational strategy and operations. They promote open and transparent communication, encourage collaboration and teamwork, and provide guidance and support during challenging times.

Organizational resilience also relies on robust operational processes and systems. Resilient organizations have efficient supply chains, redundant systems, and backup plans in place to minimize disruptions and downtime. They invest in technology and automation to streamline processes and enhance efficiency. Additionally, they establish strong relationships with stakeholders, including suppliers, customers, and government agencies, to ensure a coordinated response during crises.

In conclusion, organizational resilience is a vital aspect of successful business operations. By building a resilient culture, implementing effective risk management strategies, fostering agile leadership, and investing in robust operational processes, organizations can navigate challenges and emerge even stronger.

Organizational resilience refers to an organization's ability to adapt, respond, and recover from disruptive events or challenges while maintaining its core functions and achieving its goals. It involves a proactive and strategic approach to risk management, preparedness, and agility.

Organizational resilience encompasses various dimensions, including:

Risk identification and assessment: Resilient organizations are proactive in identifying potential risks and assessing their impact on the organization. This involves regularly conducting risk assessments, understanding the likelihood and consequences of different risks, and prioritizing them based on their potential impact.

Risk identification and assessment is a crucial step in the process of building organizational resilience. It involves systematically identifying potential risks, analyzing their likelihood and impact, and prioritizing them based on their significance to the organization. Here is an explanation of risk identification and assessment in six paragraphs:

a. Risk identification: The first step in risk identification and assessment is to identify potential risks that may affect the organization. This can be done through various methods, including brainstorming sessions, historical data analysis, conducting interviews with stakeholders, and reviewing industry trends. The goal is to create a comprehensive list of risks that the organization may encounter, ranging from internal risks such as operational failures or employee misconduct to external risks such as economic downturns or regulatory changes.

b. Risk analysis: Once the risks are identified, they need to be analyzed in terms of their likelihood and potential impact. This involves assessing the probability of each risk occurring and evaluating the severity of its consequences. Risk analysis may be quantitative, using techniques such as probability distributions and financial modeling, or qualitative, relying on expert judgment and subjective assessments. The analysis helps in understanding the overall risk landscape and provides insights into the risks that require immediate attention.

c. Risk assessment: Risk assessment involves evaluating the significance of each identified risk to the organization. This is done by considering both the likelihood and potential impact in conjunction. The risks are often classified based on their severity, creating a risk matrix that helps prioritize them. High-impact, high-likelihood risks are considered the most critical and require immediate attention, while low-impact, low-likelihood risks may be managed more passively through residual risk acceptance or transfer.

d. Risk mitigation: Once the risks are ranked based on their significance, organizations can develop strategies to mitigate or manage them. This involves implementing risk mitigation measures such as improving internal controls, implementing redundant systems, training employees, or transferring risks through insurance or outsourcing. The goal is to reduce the probability or impact of risks and minimize the vulnerability of the organization. Risk mitigation strategies should be aligned with the organization's overall objectives and risk appetite.

e. Monitoring and review: Risk identification and assessment is not a one-time exercise. Risks and their potential impact can evolve due to changes in the business environment. Therefore, organizations need to establish an ongoing monitoring and review process to ensure risks are regularly reassessed. This enables organizations to proactively address emerging risks and adjust their risk mitigation strategies accordingly. Regular monitoring also helps in measuring the effectiveness of existing risk controls and identifying any new risks that may arise.

e. Communication and reporting: Effective risk identification and assessment require clear communication and reporting mechanisms. Organizations should ensure that their risk management processes are well-documented and accessible to all stakeholders. This includes communicating the identified risks, their likelihood and impact assessments, and the implemented risk mitigation strategies. Regular reporting and communication of risks to senior management and the board of directors ensure that they have a comprehensive overview of the organization's risk profile and can make informed decisions.

In conclusion, risk identification and assessment is a critical component of building organizational resilience. It helps organizations understand their potential vulnerabilities and prioritize their risk management efforts. By systematically identifying and analyzing risks, organizations can develop effective strategies to mitigate them and increase their ability to adapt and respond to unexpected events.

Planning and preparation: Resilient organizations develop comprehensive plans and strategies to mitigate risks and prepare for potential disruptions. This includes creating contingency plans, establishing communication protocols, and allocating resources to ensure a swift and effective response to crises.

Planning and preparation play a vital role in organizational resilience. These processes involve developing strategies, structures, and procedures to anticipate, respond to, and recover from disruptive events or crises. Here is an explanation of planning and preparation in organizational resilience:

a. Risk assessment: The first step in planning and preparation is conducting a comprehensive risk assessment to identify potential risks and their potential impacts on the organization. This involves analyzing internal and external factors that could pose threats, such as natural disasters, cyberattacks, supply chain disruptions, or economic downturns. The risk assessment helps to prioritize risks and determine the level of preparedness required for each.

b. Contingency planning: Contingency planning involves developing response plans for different risk scenarios. These plans outline specific actions, roles, and responsibilities that need to be executed when a particular event or crisis occurs. They provide a roadmap for the organization to follow during times of uncertainty and guide decision-making processes. Contingency plans should be regularly reviewed and updated to ensure their effectiveness and alignment with changing organizational needs.

c. Business continuity planning: Business continuity planning focuses on ensuring that critical business functions can continue operating during and after a crisis. It involves identifying essential processes, resources, and infrastructure necessary to sustain operations and devising strategies to maintain or restore them as quickly as possible. This may include establishing alternate facilities, implementing backup systems, and developing communication protocols to ensure smooth coordination during a disruptive event.

d. Crisis communication planning: Effective communication is key during times of disruption. Crisis communication planning involves developing strategies and channels for communicating internally with employees, and externally with stakeholders and managing the flow of information during a crisis. Clear and transparent communication helps build trust, manage expectations, and minimize confusion or misinterpretation of information.

e. Training and drills: Planning and preparation also involve training employees on their roles and responsibilities during a crisis and conducting regular drills to test the effectiveness of response plans. Training ensures that employees are familiar with the procedures and can act confidently and efficiently during volatile situations. Drills help identify gaps, strengths, and areas for improvement in the organization's preparedness and response capabilities.

f. Resource allocation: Adequate resource allocation is crucial for effective planning and preparation. Organizations should allocate sufficient financial, technological, and human resources to support their resilience efforts. Investing in technology infrastructure, backup systems, and skilled personnel enhances an organization's ability to respond swiftly and recover efficiently.

In conclusion, planning and preparation are fundamental elements of organizational resilience. By conducting risk assessments, developing contingency plans, ensuring business continuity, establishing crisis communication strategies, providing training, and allocating resources effectively, organizations can enhance their ability to withstand disruptions and navigate challenging situations with agility and effectiveness.

Adaptability and flexibility: Resilient organizations value adaptability and are willing to embrace change. They foster an organizational culture that encourages innovation and agility, allowing them to quickly adjust strategies, operations, and processes in response to evolving circumstances.

Adaptability and flexibility are essential aspects of organizational resilience. They refer to an organization's ability to adjust, evolve, and respond effectively to changing circumstances, emerging risks, and unforeseen disruptions. Here is an explanation of adaptability and flexibility in organizational resilience:

a. Embracing change: Resilient organizations understand that change is inevitable in today's dynamic business environment. They proactively embrace change rather than resist it, recognizing that it presents new opportunities for growth and innovation. They foster a culture that encourages employees to be open-minded, adaptable, and willing to embrace new ideas and approaches.

b. Agile decision-making: Adaptability and flexibility require organizations to have agile decision-making processes in place. Resilient organizations empower employees at all levels to make quick, informed decisions based on the evolving situation. They decentralize decision-making authority, allowing employees to respond swiftly to challenges and capitalize on emerging opportunities without excessive bureaucratic constraints.

c. Strategic foresight: Resilient organizations engage in proactive strategic foresight to anticipate and prepare for potential disruptions. They actively monitor the external environment, industry trends, and emerging risks, enabling them to spot signs of change early on. By staying ahead of the curve, they can adjust their strategies and operations proactively, mitigating the impact of potential disruptions.

d. Organizational learning: Adaptability and flexibility are fostered through a continuous learning culture. Resilient organizations encourage experimentation and embrace failure as an opportunity for growth and improvement. They promote knowledge sharing, facilitate lessons-learned sessions, and encourage employees to apply new insights and ideas to enhance organizational resilience in the face of future challenges.

e. Flexible structures and processes: Resilient organizations have flexible structures and processes that can adapt quickly to changing circumstances. They minimize silos and encourage cross-functional collaboration, enabling teams to respond rapidly to emerging issues. They embrace technology to enhance operational agility, streamline processes, and enable remote work when necessary. Flexibility in organizational structures and processes helps facilitate quick decision-making and efficient resource allocation during crises.

e. Customer-centric focus: Resilient organizations maintain a customer-centric focus throughout disruptions. They remain attentive to their customers' changing needs and preferences, adapting their products, services, and delivery channels accordingly. By understanding and responding to customer demands, organizations can continue to meet their expectations, build loyalty, and sustain their revenue streams during challenging times.

In conclusion, adaptability and flexibility are critical for organizational resilience. By embracing change, fostering agile decision-making, practicing strategic foresight, promoting organizational learning, implementing flexible structures and processes, and maintaining a customer-centric focus, organizations can navigate uncertainties, recover quickly from disruptions, and thrive in an ever-changing business landscape.

Crisis management and response: Resilient organizations have robust crisis management protocols in place. This involves establishing clear roles and responsibilities, implementing effective communication channels, and training employees on how to respond to crises. They also conduct regular drills and simulations to test their response plans and identify areas for improvement.

Crisis management and response are vital components of organizational resilience. They involve the processes, strategies, and actions taken by organizations to effectively manage and respond to disruptive events or crises. Here is an explanation of crisis management and response in organizational resilience:

a. Crisis preparedness: Resilient organizations understand the importance of being prepared for potential crises. They develop comprehensive crisis response plans and protocols, outlining roles, responsibilities, and communication channels. Preparedness includes conducting scenario planning, risk assessments, and simulations to anticipate and practice responses to different crisis scenarios. This allows organizations to respond swiftly and efficiently when a crisis occurs.

b. Effective leadership: Crisis management requires strong leadership. Resilient organizations have leaders who are calm, decisive, and capable of providing clear direction during a crisis. They establish a command structure, delegate responsibilities, and communicate openly with stakeholders. Effective leaders prioritize the well-being of employees, implement crisis communication strategies, and make tough decisions to minimize the impact of the crisis.

c. Rapid response and communication: Organizations need to respond quickly and communicate effectively during a crisis. Resilient organizations have established communication protocols that enable timely and accurate information sharing both internally and externally. They utilize multiple channels, such as emails, websites, social media, or public relations efforts, to disseminate information to employees, customers, suppliers, and other relevant stakeholders. Transparent, consistent, and frequent communication helps build trust, manage expectations, and reduce anxiety during a crisis.

d. Decision-making and resource allocation: Crisis management involves making crucial decisions under pressure. Resilient organizations have processes in place to facilitate rapid decision-making based on the information available. They prioritize resource allocation to ensure that critical functions are supported, employees have what they need, and response efforts are coordinated effectively. Flexibility in decision-making and resource allocation is essential as it allows organizations to adapt their strategies as the crisis evolves.

e. Crisis recovery and business continuity: In addition to responding to the immediate impact of a crisis, organizations must focus on recovery and business continuity. Resilient organizations have plans in place to restore operations and minimize the impact on their customers, employees, and stakeholders. They coordinate efforts to rebuild damaged infrastructure, systems, and processes. They also evaluate the lessons learned from the crisis and update their plans and protocols accordingly to enhance their resilience for future events.

f. Post-crisis evaluation and learning: After a crisis, resilient organizations conduct post-crisis evaluations to assess their response efforts. This involves analyzing what worked well, identifying areas for improvement, and capturing lessons learned. These evaluations help organizations enhance their crisis management strategies and build their resilience capabilities for future events.

In conclusion, crisis management and response are integral parts of organizational resilience. By being prepared, having effective leadership, communicating promptly and transparently, making sound decisions, focusing on recovery and continuity, and learning from each crisis, organizations can effectively navigate disruptions and emerge stronger, more prepared, and resilient.

Learning and continuous improvement: Resilient organizations are committed to learning from past experiences and continuously improving their resilience capabilities. They conduct post-incident reviews, gather feedback, and implement lessons learned to enhance their preparedness and response in the future.

Learning and continuous improvement are critical components of organizational resilience. They involve an organization's commitment to gaining insights, adapting strategies, and enhancing its resilience capabilities based on past experiences and ongoing feedback. Here is an explanation of learning and continuous improvement in organizational resilience:

a. Post-incident reviews: Resilient organizations actively conduct post-incident reviews after experiencing a disruptive event or crisis. These reviews involve a thorough analysis of the organization's response to the event, identifying what went well and areas that need improvement. By reflecting on their actions and decisions, organizations can gain valuable insights into their strengths and weaknesses, allowing them to refine their strategies and response plans for future incidents.

b. Gathering feedback: Resilient organizations actively seek feedback from employees, customers, stakeholders, and relevant experts. They understand that diverse perspectives can provide valuable insights into the organization's resilience practices. Feedback may be gathered through surveys, interviews, focus groups, or facilitated discussions. Listening to the concerns, suggestions, and experiences of different stakeholders helps organizations identify gaps, opportunities, and potential areas for improvement.

c. Implementing lessons learned: Resilient organizations take the lessons learned from previous incidents and apply them to their resilience practices. They update their response plans, improve communication processes, strengthen their risk mitigation strategies, and refine their crisis management protocols. By implementing lessons learned, organizations can enhance their preparedness, response capabilities, and overall resilience posture.

d. Training and skills development: Learning and continuous improvement involve investing in training and skills development programs for employees. Resilient organizations provide regular training sessions to ensure that employees have the necessary knowledge, skills, and competencies to respond effectively to disruptive events. This may include training in crisis management, risk assessment, communication strategies, decision-making, and adapting to change. Ongoing training efforts help foster a culture of learning and continuous improvement throughout the organization.

e. Benchmarking and best practices: Resilient organizations actively engage in benchmarking exercises, comparing their resilience practices to industry standards, regulatory requirements, and best practices. They seek to identify areas where they can improve their resilience capabilities and learn from organizations that have demonstrated success in managing disruptions. By adopting and adapting best practices, organizations can enhance their resilience and stay ahead of emerging challenges.

f. Embedding resilience in the organizational culture: Learning and continuous improvement are embedded in the organizational culture of resilient organizations. They foster an environment that encourages learning from both successes and failures. This includes recognizing and rewarding innovative ideas, allowing for experimentation, and empowering employees to challenge existing practices and propose improvements. A culture of continuous improvement ensures that resilience is not just a one-time effort but an ongoing commitment throughout the organization.

In conclusion, learning and continuous improvement are essential for organizational resilience. By actively seeking feedback, implementing lessons learned, investing in training and skills development, benchmarking against best practices, and fostering a culture of continuous improvement, organizations can enhance their resilience capabilities and adapt effectively to emerging challenges and disruptions.

Leadership and governance: Leadership plays a crucial role in building organizational resilience. Effective leaders set the tone, provide direction, and ensure that resilience principles are integrated into the organization's strategic planning and decision-making processes. They promote a culture of transparency, trust, and collaboration, which fosters resilience at all levels of the organization.

Leadership and governance play critical roles in organizational resilience. They involve the establishment of a strong leadership structure, effective decision-making processes, and clear accountability mechanisms to guide the organization's resilience efforts. Here is an explanation of leadership and governance in organizational resilience:

a. Strong leadership: Resilient organizations have strong leaders who provide a clear direction and inspire confidence during times of uncertainty. Effective leaders foster a culture of resilience by setting the tone at the top and emphasizing the importance of risk management, adaptability, and preparedness. They ensure that organizational resilience is a priority and allocate the necessary resources to support resilience initiatives.

b. Vision and strategy: Leaders in resilient organizations develop a compelling vision and resilience strategy that aligns with the organization's broader goals and objectives. They establish clear goals, targets, and milestones to guide the organization's resilience efforts. The vision and strategy serve as a roadmap, enabling the organization to proactively identify and address risks, develop mitigation plans, and build robust systems and processes for resilience.

c. Decision-making: Effective decision-making is crucial for organizational resilience. Leaders in resilient organizations foster a culture of informed decision-making, ensuring that decisions are based on reliable data, analysis, and expert input. They emphasize risk assessment and scenario planning to anticipate potential disruptions and make decisions that minimize risks and maximize opportunities for resilience.

d. Governance structure: Governance mechanisms are essential to ensure accountability and oversight in organizational resilience. Resilient organizations establish governance structures that define the roles, responsibilities, and accountabilities of various stakeholders. This includes clearly defining the roles of the board of directors, executive leadership, risk management committees, and other relevant bodies to ensure effective oversight and decision-making.

e. Communication and collaboration: Leaders in resilient organizations prioritize effective communication and collaboration. They establish clear channels for communication and ensure that information related to organizational resilience is disseminated seamlessly. Effective communication processes promote transparency, build trust, and foster a shared understanding of resilience goals and strategies across all levels of the organization. Collaboration is encouraged to enable cross-functional teams to work together in addressing risks, sharing best practices, and driving resilience initiatives.

f. Continuous improvement: Resilient organizations commit to continuous improvement in their resilience efforts. Effective leaders encourage and support initiatives aimed at evaluating and enhancing resilience capabilities. They establish mechanisms for regular review and assessment of resilience practices, ensuring that lessons learned from incidents and feedback from stakeholders are fed back into the organization's strategies, plans, and systems for continuous improvement.

In conclusion, leadership and governance are essential elements of organizational resilience. Effective leaders set the vision and strategy, make informed decisions, establish strong governance structures, foster effective communication and collaboration, and drive continuous improvement. By embodying and promoting resilience throughout the organization, leaders contribute to building a resilient culture that enables the organization to navigate disruptions and emerge stronger in the face of challenges.

Organizational resilience is not only about surviving disruptions but also about thriving in the face of challenges. Resilient organizations are better equipped to adapt to changing market conditions, seize new opportunities, and maintain a competitive advantage, ultimately ensuring their long-term sustainability and success.

Managers have a crucial role to play in embracing and utilizing organizational resilience. Here are some key ways managers can do this:

a. Adopt a proactive approach: Managers should proactively identify and understand potential risks and vulnerabilities that could impact their team or the organization. By staying ahead of potential disruptions, they can develop strategies and contingency plans to mitigate risks and build resilience.

b. Foster a resilient culture: Managers should promote a culture of resilience within their team or department. This involves encouraging open communication, valuing innovation and adaptability, and supporting risk-taking and learning from failures. By fostering a resilient mindset among team members, managers build a foundation for effective response and recovery during challenging times.

c. Establish clear responsibilities and protocols: Managers should ensure that roles and responsibilities are clearly defined within their team, especially during a crisis or disruptive event. By establishing well-communicated protocols and procedures, managers enable their team members to understand their roles and respond quickly and effectively when faced with unexpected situations.

d. Encourage continuous learning and improvement: Managers should foster a learning culture within their team, encouraging team members to learn from both successes and failures. They should provide opportunities for training and professional development focused on enhancing resilience skills, such as problem-solving, decision-making, and adaptability. By promoting continuous learning and improvement, managers contribute to building a more resilient team.

e. Communicate and lead during crises: Managers have a critical role in communication during crises or disruptions. They should keep team members informed, provide clear guidance and direction, and address any concerns or anxieties. Managers should also lead by example, demonstrating composure, decisiveness, and resilience in their actions and decisions. Effective communication and leadership during crises help maintain team morale, build trust, and foster a sense of security and stability within the team.

In summary, managers should embrace organizational resilience by taking a proactive approach to risk management, fostering a resilient culture, establishing clear responsibilities and protocols, encouraging continuous learning, and effectively communicating and leading during crises. By doing so, managers contribute to building a resilient team that can navigate uncertainties and disruptions more effectively.

Organizational resilience is considered the epitome of good management because it encompasses several key aspects that are essential for effective leadership and management. Here are a few reasons why organizational resilience the epitome of good management is:

a. Strategic thinking: Organizational resilience requires managers to think strategically and proactively and anticipate potential risks and disruptions. This involves analyzing the organization's internal and external environment, identifying potential threats, and developing contingency plans. Good management involves proactive decision-making and strategic planning, which are crucial elements of organizational resilience.

b. Adaptability to change: Good management involves being adaptable to change and continuously improving processes. Organizational resilience requires managers to be flexible and agile, able to adjust strategies and operations quickly in response to unexpected events. Managers who embrace and promote resilience are more likely to adapt effectively to change, making them better equipped to navigate uncertainties and emerging challenges.

c. Risk management and mitigation: Resilience cannot be achieved without effective risk management and mitigation strategies. Good management involves identifying risks, implementing risk mitigation measures, and establishing a culture of risk awareness within the organization. By effectively managing risks, good managers minimize the impact of potential disruptions and create a more resilient organization.

d. Communication and collaboration: Organizational resilience relies on effective communication and collaboration. Good managers prioritize clear and transparent communication, both internally and externally, ensuring that information flows smoothly and timely during disruptions. They also foster collaboration among team members and departments, promoting knowledge sharing and cross-functional cooperation to enhance the organization's overall resilience.

e. Continuous learning and improvement: Good management involves a commitment to continuous learning and improvement. Organizational resilience requires managers to learn from past experiences, gather feedback, and continuously improve processes and strategies. Good managers value continuous learning and actively seek ways to enhance resilience, ensuring that the organization is better prepared for future challenges.

f. Employee engagement and well-being: Good management takes into account the well-being and engagement of employees. Resilient organizations prioritize the welfare of their employees, recognizing that their resilience is directly tied to the resilience of the organization. Good managers create a positive work environment, foster employee engagement, and provide the necessary support for employees to cope with challenges and adapt to changes.

In summary, organizational resilience embodies several key principles of good management, including strategic thinking, adaptability, risk management, effective communication, collaboration, and a commitment to continuous learning and employee well-being. Good managers understand the importance of these elements and work towards building and sustaining organizational resilience for long-term success.

Organizational resilience and employee engagement are interconnected and mutually beneficial concepts within an organization. Organizational resilience provides a framework and structure for addressing risks, uncertainties, and disruptions that can impact employee engagement. At the same time, employee engagement is a critical factor in building organizational resilience. Here's how organizational resilience authority can influence employee engagement:

a. Creating a supportive work environment: Organizational resilience focuses on creating an environment that promotes adaptability and employee well-being. This includes providing resources, training, and support to employees, enabling them to cope with and respond effectively to challenges. When employees feel supported, valued, and empowered, their engagement levels increase, leading to stronger resilience within the organization.

b. Enhancing communication and transparency: A resilient organization encourages open and transparent communication. Clear and timely communication from management helps employees understand the organization's direction, challenges, and strategies for managing disruptions. This transparency fosters trust and enables employees to feel more engaged and committed to the organization's goals and resilience efforts.

c. Strengthening employee involvement in decision-making: Organizational resilience promotes employee involvement in decision-making processes. When employees are actively involved in discussions and decisions that shape the organization's response to disruptions, they feel empowered and more engaged. Their ideas and insights can contribute to more effective strategies, enhancing the organization's resilience.

d. Providing opportunities for growth and development: A resilient organization recognizes the importance of employee growth and development. Offering opportunities for training and professional development supports employee engagement by fostering a sense of personal growth and career advancement. It also equips employees with the skills and knowledge needed to contribute effectively to the organization's resilience efforts.

e. Promoting a culture of continuous learning and improvement: Organizational resilience involves a commitment to continuous learning and improvement. When organizations prioritize and invest in learning initiatives, employees are given opportunities to acquire new skills, expand their knowledge, and adapt to changing circumstances. This focus on learning cultivates a culture of growth and innovation, leading to higher employee engagement.

f. Recognizing and rewarding resilience behaviors: Organizational resilience requires resilience behaviors at both the individual and collective levels. Recognizing and rewarding employees who demonstrate resilience and contribute to building organizational resilience can reinforce a culture of engagement. Acknowledging and appreciating employees for their efforts in adapting to challenges and bouncing back from disruptions motivates them to continue engaging with resilience initiatives.

Organizational resilience has the authority to positively influence employee engagement by creating a supportive work environment, enhancing communication and transparency, involving employees in decision-making, providing growth opportunities, fostering a culture of continuous learning, and recognizing resilience behaviors. By prioritizing employee engagement in resilience initiatives, organizations can build a stronger and more resilient workforce.

Cross-cultural management plays a crucial role in strengthening organizational resilience in several ways:

1. Enhanced adaptability: Cross-cultural management enables organizations to develop a greater capacity to adapt to diverse and changing environments. By understanding different cultural norms, values, and behaviors, organizations can adjust their strategies, policies, and practices to align with diverse cultural contexts. This adaptability is key in fostering resilience as it allows organizations to respond effectively to unexpected challenges or disruptions.

Enhanced Adaptability: Navigating the Real World with Ease

In a rapidly changing world, adaptability has become a vital skill that allows individuals to thrive in various situations and overcome challenges. Enhanced adaptability goes beyond mere flexibility; it involves the ability to quickly adjust and respond positively to unexpected circumstances. In this article, we will explore the concept of enhanced adaptability, its importance, and how it can be developed using real-world experiences as examples.

Section 1: Understanding Enhanced Adaptability

Enhanced adaptability refers to an individual's capacity to adjust their mindset, skills, and behaviors in response to changing circumstances. It involves being open-minded, remaining calm under pressure, and possessing the resilience to bounce back from setbacks. Through enhanced adaptability, people can navigate unfamiliar situations with confidence, maximize opportunities, and effectively manage risks.

Enhanced adaptability is crucial in various aspects of life, including personal, professional, and societal realms. It refers to the ability to adjust and thrive in rapidly changing environments, effectively deal with unforeseen challenges, and quickly learn and integrate new skills and knowledge. The importance of enhanced adaptability can be understood by considering the following points:

a. Coping with uncertainty: In today's rapidly evolving world, uncertainty is pervasive. Economic shifts, technological advancements, and global crises like pandemics can disrupt established systems and create new challenges. Adaptable individuals can navigate such uncertainties more effectively, maintain their mental well-being, and identify opportunities amidst chaos.

b. Embracing change: Change is inevitable, and those who resist it often find themselves left behind. The ability to adapt allows individuals to embrace change, be it in personal relationships, work environments, or technological advancements. Adaptable people are open-minded and willing to learn and unlearn, ensuring they grow and develop in sync with changing circumstances.

c. Thriving in diverse environments: Adaptability is crucial for individuals to succeed in diverse environments, such as multicultural workplaces or while traveling to different countries. Adaptable individuals can easily understand and respect different customs, languages, and perspectives, making them effective communicators and collaborators. This skill is particularly significant in our increasingly interconnected global society.

d. Improving problem-solving: Enhanced adaptability strengthens problem-solving skills. Adaptable individuals are more comfortable with ambiguity and can quickly identify patterns and potential solutions in complex situations. They are flexible thinkers who can generate creative and innovative ideas, enabling them to address challenges effectively.

e. Resilience and mental well-being: Enhanced adaptability helps build resilience, which is the ability to adapt and bounce back from adversity. Adaptable individuals possess a growth mindset and approach setbacks as opportunities for learning and personal development. They can better manage stress, maintain positive mental health, and build stronger interpersonal relationships.

f. Professional development: The modern job market is increasingly volatile and competitive. Adaptability is a highly sought-after skill by employers as it allows employees to quickly adapt to new roles, technologies, and market demands. Adaptable employees are more likely to take on new challenges and responsibilities, making them valuable assets to organizations.

g. Innovation and creativity: Adaptability is closely linked to the ability to think critically and creatively. Adaptable individuals can quickly integrate new information and perspectives, enabling them to come up with innovative ideas and solutions. This skill is essential for personal growth as well as driving progress in various fields.

In summary, enhanced adaptability is vital for navigating uncertainties, embracing change, thriving in diverse environments, improving problem-solving, building resilience, fostering professional development, and driving innovation. Developing adaptability allows individuals to lead more fulfilling and successful lives by effectively responding to the ever-changing nature of the world.

Section 2: The Importance of Enhanced Adaptability

Enhanced adaptability is crucial in both personal and professional realms. In personal life, adaptability allows individuals to cope with major life changes such as moving to a new city, changing careers, or dealing with unforeseen circumstances like the loss of a loved one. Meanwhile, in professional life, adaptability is increasingly sought after by employers who recognize the value of employees who can seamlessly transition into dynamic work environments, embrace new technologies, and solve problems creatively.

Enhanced adaptability is crucial in various aspects of life, including personal, professional, and societal realms. It refers to the ability to adjust and thrive in rapidly changing environments, effectively deal with unforeseen challenges, and quickly learn and integrate new skills and knowledge. The importance of enhanced adaptability can be understood by considering the following points:

a. Coping with uncertainty: In today's rapidly evolving world, uncertainty is pervasive. Economic shifts, technological advancements, and global crises like pandemics can disrupt established systems and create new challenges. Adaptable individuals can navigate such uncertainties more effectively, maintain their mental well-being, and identify opportunities amidst chaos.

b. Embracing change: Change is inevitable, and those who resist it often find themselves left behind. The ability to adapt allows individuals to embrace change, be it in personal relationships, work environments, or technological advancements. Adaptable people are open-minded and willing to learn and unlearn, ensuring they grow and develop in sync with changing circumstances.

c. Thriving in diverse environments: Adaptability is crucial for individuals to succeed in diverse environments, such as multicultural workplaces or while traveling to different countries. Adaptable individuals can easily understand and respect different customs, languages, and perspectives, making them effective communicators and collaborators. This skill is particularly significant in our increasingly interconnected global society.

d. Improving problem-solving: Enhanced adaptability strengthens problem-solving skills. Adaptable individuals are more comfortable with ambiguity and can quickly identify patterns and potential solutions in complex situations. They are flexible thinkers who can generate creative and innovative ideas, enabling them to address challenges effectively.

e. Resilience and mental well-being: Enhanced adaptability helps build resilience, which is the ability to adapt and bounce back from adversity. Adaptable individuals possess a growth mindset and approach setbacks as opportunities for learning and personal development. They can better manage stress, maintain positive mental health, and build stronger interpersonal relationships.

f. Professional development: The modern job market is increasingly volatile and competitive. Adaptability is a highly sought-after skill by employers as it allows employees to quickly adapt to new roles, technologies, and market demands. Adaptable employees are more likely to take on new challenges and responsibilities, making them valuable assets to organizations.

g. Innovation and creativity: Adaptability is closely linked to the ability to think critically and creatively. Adaptable individuals can quickly integrate new information and perspectives, enabling them to come up with innovative ideas and solutions. This skill is essential for personal growth as well as driving progress in various fields.

In summary, enhanced adaptability is vital for navigating uncertainties, embracing change, thriving in diverse environments, improving problem-solving, building resilience, fostering professional development, and driving innovation. Developing adaptability allows individuals to lead more fulfilling and successful lives by effectively responding to the ever-changing nature of the world.

Section 3: Real-World Experiences

To understand and develop enhanced adaptability, let's delve into real-world experiences as examples:

a. Traveling to foreign countries:

When traveling to a foreign country, one encounters new cultures, languages, and customs. Navigating these unfamiliar environments requires adaptability. Emerging triumphantly from such an experience enhances one's ability to embrace diversity, communicate effectively, and adapt to unexpected situations. These skills can then be applied to other areas of life to build resilience and confidence.

b. Facing career transitions:

Throughout our careers, we often encounter changes such as job promotions, company reorganizations, or shifts in industries. Adapting to these changes can be challenging, but it also offers growth opportunities. Individuals who demonstrate enhanced adaptability in these situations will adjust their skillset, learn new technologies, and embrace different work cultures. This enables them to thrive even in rapidly evolving industries.

c. Overcoming setbacks:

Setbacks are an inevitable part of life. Individuals who develop enhanced adaptability are better equipped to rebound from failures and setbacks. For instance, an entrepreneur whose startup fails might reassess their strategy, learn from their mistakes, and emerge stronger with a new venture. Their adaptability allows them to view setbacks as steppingstones toward future success.

d. Embracing change:

Change is a constant in today's world, and resistance to change often hinders personal and professional growth. Enhanced adaptability empowers individuals to view change as an opportunity for transformation rather than a source of stress. For example, employees who embrace workplace changes like adopting new software or working on cross-functional teams exhibit enhanced adaptability, leading to increased productivity and personal development.

Section 4: Strategies to Develop Enhanced Adaptability

a. Embrace discomfort:

Enhanced adaptability stems from stepping out of comfort zones. By willingly exposing ourselves to uncomfortable situations, such as public speaking or learning a new skill, we expand our abilities and become more adaptable.

b. Practice resilience:

Cultivate resilience by reflecting on past challenges and considering how you overcame them. Recognize that setbacks are temporary and focus on learning and growing from them.

c. Develop a growth mindset:

Adopting a growth mindset helps develop enhanced adaptability. Embrace the belief that abilities and intelligence can be developed through effort and practice. This mindset allows for continuous learning and adaptability in different circumstances.

d. Seek diverse experiences:

Expose yourself to a variety of experiences and situations. Engage with people from different backgrounds, travel to unfamiliar places, or take up new hobbies. These experiences broaden your perspective and enhance adaptability.

Enhanced adaptability is a vital skill for thriving in today's rapidly changing world. By understanding the concept of enhanced adaptability and witnessing real-world examples, we can grasp its significance and implications. With practical strategies in mind, individuals can actively build their adaptability, enabling them to navigate the real world with ease. Remember, enhanced adaptability is not solely about coping with change but about embracing it as a catalyst for growth, personal development, and success.

2. Improved communication and collaboration: Effective cross-cultural management promotes clear and open communication across diverse cultural backgrounds. This helps to bridge communication gaps and minimize misunderstandings, facilitating collaboration among team members from different cultural backgrounds. Strong communication and collaboration are vital for resilience as they foster a shared understanding, coordination, and problem-solving during times of crisis or uncertainty.
   Improving Communication: The Power of Effective Dialogue

In today's interconnected world, effective communication has become more important than ever. Whether it's in personal relationships, professional settings, or social interactions, the ability to express oneself clearly and understand others is essential for building stronger connections and achieving mutual understanding. In this article, we will explore the concept of improved communication, and its significance, and provide real-world examples to highlight its impact.

Section 1: The Importance of Improved Communication Improved communication is the key to successful collaboration, conflict resolution, and building meaningful relationships. It allows individuals to express their thoughts and feelings accurately, understand others' perspectives, and convey information in a way that is easily comprehensible. Clear and effective communication not only enhances personal and professional growth but also fosters empathy, trust, and cooperation among individuals.

Section 2: Real-World Examples of Improved Communication

Let's examine some real-world scenarios where improved communication plays a crucial role:

a. Building strong personal relationships:

In personal relationships, effective communication is vital for fostering intimacy and understanding. For example, consider a couple in a long-distance relationship who are facing increased communication challenges. By actively working on their communication skills, such as using regular video calls, sharing their feelings openly, and listening attentively, they can bridge the physical gap and sustain a strong emotional connection.

b. Enhancing workplace dynamics:

In professional settings, improved communication contributes to increased productivity, teamwork, and reduced conflicts. For instance, a team of diverse employees working on a project deciphers each member's strengths, actively listens to one another's ideas, and communicates constructively. This fosters collaboration, ensures everyone's voices are heard, and results in better problem-solving and innovation.

c. Resolving conflicts effectively:

Miscommunication often leads to misunderstandings and conflicts. By practicing improved communication techniques, individuals can prevent or resolve disputes constructively. For instance, consider two colleagues who are engaged in a conflict over differences in work methodologies. By engaging in active listening, seeking common ground, and employing empathy, they can find a mutually beneficial solution and strengthen their working relationship.

d. Leading with clarity:

Leaders who possess strong communication skills can inspire and motivate their teams effectively. For instance, a manager delivering a presentation to their team on a new project outlines expectations clearly, provides context, and invites questions to ensure everyone is on the same page. This not only instills confidence and trust among team members but also fosters a sense of shared purpose and direction.

Section 3: Strategies to Improve Communication

To enhance communication skills, consider implementing the following strategies:

a. Active listening:

Listening attentively, without interrupting or jumping to conclusions, allows for a deeper understanding of others' perspectives. Focus on the speaker, maintain eye contact, and ask clarifying questions to demonstrate interest and ensure comprehension.

b. Clarify and confirm understanding:

In conversations, clarify and confirm understandings to minimize misinterpretations. Repeat or rephrase what you have understood to verify accuracy. This helps to avoid assumptions and clears up any potential confusion.

c. Non-verbal cues:

Non-verbal communication, such as body language and facial expressions, greatly influences communication effectiveness. Be aware of your non-verbal cues and pay attention to others' cues to ensure alignment between spoken words and non-verbal signals.

d. Empathy and emotional intelligence:

Understanding and acknowledging others' emotions fosters trust and builds rapport. Cultivate empathy and emotional intelligence by putting yourself in others' shoes, validating their feelings, and adjusting your response accordingly.

e. Mindful communication:

Practice mindful communication by being fully present during interactions. Minimize distractions, such as mobile devices, and focus on the individual or group you are communicating with. This demonstrates respect and enhances the quality of communication.

Improved communication is a powerful tool for establishing stronger connections, resolving conflicts, and achieving successful outcomes in various aspects of life. By recognizing its importance and employing strategies to enhance communication skills, individuals can foster better relationships, increase productivity, and create a positive impact in both personal and professional settings. Remember, effective communication is not just about transmitting information, but also about understanding, connecting, and creating a space for meaningful dialogue.

3. Cultural intelligence and empathy: Cross-cultural management enhances cultural intelligence, which refers to the ability to understand and navigate cultural differences. Cultural intelligence enables organizations to approach challenges with empathy, demonstrating an appreciation and respect for diverse perspectives. This empathetic approach fosters better relationships, trust, and cooperation, which are essential elements of resilience.

Cultural Intelligence: Embracing Diversity and Navigating Global Environments

Introduction:

The interconnectedness of today's world brings people from diverse cultural backgrounds into constant contact, whether through travel, migration, or virtual interactions. In this globalized landscape, cultural intelligence has emerged as a vital skill. It encompasses the ability to understand, adapt to, and navigate various cultural contexts effectively. In this article, we will delve into the concept of cultural intelligence, and its significance, and explore real-world examples that highlight the importance of this skill.

Section 1: Understanding Cultural Intelligence

Cultural intelligence, also known as CQ, refers to an individual's capacity to function effectively in diverse cultural settings. It goes beyond mere cultural awareness and encompasses the ability to interpret and respond appropriately to cultural cues, values, and behaviors. Having high cultural intelligence enables individuals to build relationships, communicate effectively, and collaborate across cultures.

Section 2: The Significance of Cultural Intelligence

In today's interconnected global society, cultural intelligence is essential. It fosters inclusivity, respect, and understanding between individuals, communities, and nations. Here are some reasons why cultural intelligence is significant:

1. Global collaboration:

As globalization accelerates, individuals and organizations must work across borders and cultures. Cultural intelligence facilitates successful collaborations by enabling individuals to understand cultural nuances, adapt their communication styles, and build trust with individuals from different backgrounds.

2. Enhanced cross-cultural communication:

Communication is at the core of human interactions. Cultural intelligence allows individuals to overcome language barriers, understand non-verbal cues, and adapt communication styles to effectively convey messages in culturally diverse settings. This enhances understanding and minimizes misunderstandings.

3. Improved problem-solving and innovation:

Different perspectives and approaches can lead to creative problem-solving and innovation. Cultural intelligence equips individuals with the ability to incorporate diverse ideas, challenge assumptions, and find unique solutions that may not have been possible otherwise.

4. Empathy and inclusivity:

Developing cultural intelligence nurtures empathy and promotes inclusivity. By understanding and appreciating different cultural backgrounds, individuals can create inclusive environments that celebrate diversity and value contributions from all members.

Section 3: Real-World Examples of Cultural Intelligence

1. Expatriate assignments:

Employees from multinational companies often work on expatriate assignments, relocating to foreign countries for extended periods. Those with high cultural intelligence adapt seamlessly to their new environment, demonstrate respect for local customs and traditions, and build meaningful connections with local colleagues. This not only enhances their personal experience but also contributes to the success of the assignment.

2. International negotiations:

Effective negotiation across cultures is crucial for successful business deals, international diplomacy, and conflict resolution. Individuals with cultural intelligence can recognize and navigate cultural differences, adjust negotiation strategies accordingly, and find mutually beneficial outcomes.

3. Cross-cultural teams:

In today's globalized workplaces, teams are becoming increasingly diverse. Cultural intelligence is vital for team members to understand and appreciate each other's perspectives, work harmoniously, and overcome cultural barriers, resulting in increased team cohesion and productivity.

4. Diplomatic relations:

Diplomats need high levels of cultural intelligence to navigate international relations effectively. By understanding the cultural norms, values, and sensitivities of their host countries, diplomats can build trust and foster cooperation, leading to successful diplomatic outcomes.

Section 4: Strategies to Develop Cultural Intelligence

Cultural intelligence is a skill that can be developed and enhanced over time. The following strategies can help individuals strengthen their cultural intelligence:

a. Cultivate curiosity:

Approach cultural differences with a curious mindset. Seek opportunities to learn about different cultures, traditions, and customs. Engage in conversations with people from diverse backgrounds and be open to new perspectives.

b. Active listening and observation:

Pay attention to verbal and non-verbal cues to understand cultural norms and behaviors. Observe how people from different cultures communicate, express emotions, and interact. Listening attentively and observing closely helps build cultural understanding.

c. Cultural immersion:

Immerse yourself in different cultural experiences whenever possible. Travel to new locations, interact with locals and participate in cultural events. Exposing yourself to different cultural contexts enhances your ability to adapt and connect with people from diverse backgrounds.

d. Embrace empathy:

Develop empathy by putting yourself in others' shoes, understanding their cultural perspectives, and appreciating their experiences. It fosters understanding and creates a space for inclusive and respectful interactions.

e. Seek feedback:

Invite feedback from individuals from different cultural backgrounds to gain insights into how your cultural intelligence is perceived. This feedback can help identify blind spots and areas for improvement.

Cultural intelligence is a vital skill in today's interconnected world. By understanding and embracing different cultures, individuals can build meaningful relationships, communicate effectively, and navigate global environments with ease. Taking the time to develop cultural intelligence not only enhances personal growth but also contributes to a more inclusive and harmonious global community. Remember, cultural intelligence goes beyond cultural awareness; it is about valuing diversity, fostering cross-cultural collaboration, and creating bridges between individuals and communities.

4. Effective talent management: In today's globalized world, organizations are increasingly diverse, with employees from various cultural backgrounds. Cross-cultural management helps organizations effectively manage and leverage this diverse talent. By embracing cultural diversity, organizations can tap into a wider range of skills, perspectives, and experiences. This diversity enhances resilience by enabling organizations to draw on diverse talents and insights to overcome challenges and drive innovation.

Effective Talent Management: Nurturing and Maximizing Human Potential

In today's competitive business landscape, organizations recognize the importance of attracting and retaining top talent. Effective talent management is the systematic process of acquiring, developing, and retaining skilled individuals to drive organizational success. It involves strategically aligning HR practices with business goals to nurture human potential, maximize productivity, and foster a culture of continuous growth. In this article, we will explore the concept of effective talent management, and its significance, and provide real-world examples to emphasize its impact.

Section 1: Understanding Effective Talent Management

Effective talent management involves various strategies and processes aimed at attracting, developing, engaging, and retaining talented individuals within an organization. It encompasses activities such as recruitment and selection, performance management, learning and development, succession planning, and employee engagement. The goal of talent management is to create a high-performance culture that leverages the skills and potential of employees to meet organizational objectives.

Section 2: The Significance of Effective Talent Management

Effective talent management is crucial for organizations to succeed and maintain a competitive advantage. Here are some key reasons why talent management is significant:

a. Attraction and retention of top talent:

Top talent seeks opportunities for growth and development. organizations that invest in effective talent management strategies position themselves as attractive employers, attracting high-quality candidates and retaining valuable employees. This helps organizations build a strong and talented workforce.

b. Maximizing employee potential:

Effective talent management focuses on identifying and leveraging employees' strengths, skills, and potential. By providing opportunities for growth, development, and advancement, organizations can tap into their employees' full potential, leading to increased productivity, innovation, and performance.

c. Succession planning and leadership development:

Creating a pipeline of future leaders is vital for long-term organizational success. Effective talent management includes succession planning and leadership development programs to groom employees for leadership roles. This ensures a smooth transition and continuity of leadership within the organization.

d. Enhanced employee engagement:

Employees are more likely to be engaged and committed when they feel valued and have opportunities for growth and development. Effective talent management strategies, such as regular feedback, recognition, and career advancement opportunities, contribute to higher levels of employee engagement, leading to higher productivity and lower turnover rates.

Section 3: Real-World Examples of Effective Talent Management

Let's examine real-world examples that highlight the impact of effective talent management:

a. Google:

Google is renowned for its strategic approach to talent management. The company focuses on attracting top talent through its rigorous recruitment process, which includes assessing candidates for their technical skills as well as their cultural fit. Once hired, Google prioritizes employee development through continuous learning opportunities, mentorship programs, and internal mobility options. By actively investing in talent management, Google has built a highly skilled workforce that drives innovation and business success.

b. GE:

General Electric (GE) is an example of an organization that values talent development and succession planning. Former CEO Jack Welch introduced a talent management strategy known as the "vitality curve," which involved identifying high-potential employees, investing in their development, and holding them accountable for their performance. GE's focus on talent management has resulted in a strong leadership pipeline and the ability to adapt to changing business needs.

c. Microsoft:

Microsoft emphasizes a growth mindset and a culture of continuous learning. The company provides various learning and development opportunities, including training programs, mentorship, and access to online learning platforms. By nurturing talent and encouraging employees to develop new skills, Microsoft remains competitive and adaptive in the rapidly evolving technology industry.

d. Marriott International:

Marriott International is recognized for its commitment to employee engagement and talent development. The company implements talent management practices such as regular performance evaluations, career development plans, and recognition programs. By investing in talent management, Marriott fosters a culture where employees feel valued and supported, leading to high levels of employee satisfaction and customer service excellence.

Section 4: Strategies for Effective Talent Management

a. Talent acquisition and recruitment:

Develop a strong employer brand and implement effective recruitment strategies to attract top talent. Utilize a comprehensive selection process to ensure the right fit between candidates and organizational needs.

b. Performance management:

Implement a robust performance management system that includes regular feedback, goal setting, and performance evaluations. Provide opportunities for skill development, addressing performance gaps, and recognizing achievements.

c. Learning and development:

Offer continuous learning opportunities, such as training programs, workshops, and mentoring, to foster employee growth and skills development. Create a culture of continuous learning that encourages employees to take ownership of their professional development.

d. Succession planning:

Identify high-potential employees and develop tailored development plans to prepare them for future leadership roles. Focus on developing leadership and critical skills necessary for organizational growth and continuity.

e. Employee engagement and recognition:

Implement strategies to enhance employee engagement, such as open communication channels, employee recognition programs, and fostering a supportive work environment. Regularly seek feedback from employees to gauge satisfaction and address concerns.

Effective talent management is essential in maximizing human potential and achieving organizational success. By implementing strategies that attract, develop, and retain top talent, organizations can create a culture of continuous growth, innovation, and high performance. Real-world examples from companies like Google, GE, Microsoft, and Marriott International demonstrate the impact of effective talent management on business outcomes. By recognizing the significance of talent management and adopting strategic approaches, organizations can harness the full potential of their employees and thrive in today's competitive landscape.

5. Learning and knowledge sharing: Cross-cultural management involves continuous learning and knowledge sharing about different cultures and practices. This learning mindset promotes organizational resilience by fostering a culture of continuous improvement and adaptability. Organizations that actively seek to learn from different cultural contexts are better equipped to identify emerging trends, embrace change, and proactively navigate uncertainties.

Learning and Knowledge Sharing: Fostering Growth and Collaboration in Organizations

In today's rapidly evolving world, organizations recognize that continuous learning and knowledge sharing are vital for adapting to change, fostering innovation, and maintaining a competitive edge. Learning is not confined to formal training programs; it encompasses a broader concept of acquiring knowledge, skills, and insights through various channels. Similarly, knowledge sharing involves the exchange of information, expertise, and ideas to foster collaboration and drive organizational success. In this article, we will explore the importance of learning and knowledge sharing in organizations, their interconnectedness, and provide real-world examples to illustrate their impact.

Section 1: The Significance of Learning in Organizations

Learning is a fundamental process that enables individuals and organizations to adapt, grow, and thrive. Here are some key reasons why learning is significant in organizations.

a. Adaptation to change:

In today's rapidly changing business environment, organizations must embrace continuous learning to adapt to new technologies, market trends, and customer preferences. Learning enables employees to acquire new skills, knowledge, and mindsets necessary for embracing change and remaining relevant.

Adaptation to change is an important factor of learning in organizations for several reasons:

1. Competitive Advantage: In today's dynamic business environment, organizations need to constantly adapt and change to stay ahead of the competition. By learning and adapting to new market trends, technologies, and customer preferences, organizations can gain a competitive advantage and stay relevant.

2. Growth and Innovation: Learning and change enable organizations to grow and innovate. By continuously learning from their experiences, organizations can identify areas for improvement, develop better strategies, and implement innovative ideas. This, in turn, helps them to grow their market share, increase revenue, and drive long-term success.

3. Increased Employee Engagement: Learning and change create a positive and engaging work environment. When organizations encourage their employees to learn and adapt, it fosters a culture of continuous improvement and personal growth. This, in turn, increases employee engagement, job satisfaction, and retention.

4. Organizational Resilience: Learning and change build organizational resilience. By being open to new ideas and adapting to changes, organizations can better navigate unforeseen challenges and disruptions. This helps them to recover quickly from setbacks and remain resilient in the face of adversity.

5. Enhanced Problem-Solving and Decision-Making: Learning and change improve problem-solving and decision-making capabilities within organizations. By exposing employees to new information and perspectives, organizations can develop a more diverse and innovative approach to solving complex problems. This enables them to make better decisions and overcome obstacles effectively.

6. Organizational Learning: Adaptation and change drive organizational learning. By continuously adapting to new circumstances and implementing changes based on feedback and experiences, organizations can accumulate knowledge and develop improved practices. This, in turn, enables them to become a learning organization that can rapidly respond to new challenges and seize opportunities.

In conclusion, adaptation and change are critical factors of learning in organizations because they enable organizations to gain a competitive advantage, drive growth and innovation, increase employee engagement, build resilience, enhance problem-solving and decision-making, and foster organizational learning. By embracing adaptation and change, organizations can thrive in an ever-evolving business landscape.

b. Innovation and creativity:

Learning encourages employees to explore new ideas, experiment, and think critically. It fosters a culture of creativity and innovation, enabling organizations to identify and implement novel solutions to challenges and drive growth.

Innovation and creativity play a crucial role in the success and sustainability of organizations. Here are the key reasons why they are significant:

1. Competitive Advantage: Innovation and creativity enable organizations to differentiate themselves from their competitors. By developing unique products, services, or processes, organizations can gain a competitive advantage in the market and attract customers who value novel and creative solutions.

2. Problem-solving and Solutions: Innovation and creativity foster a culture of problem-solving within organizations. They encourage employees to think outside the box, explore new possibilities, and come up with innovative solutions to complex challenges. This helps organizations overcome obstacles, improve efficiency, and stay ahead of the curve.

3. Adaptation to Change: In a rapidly changing business environment, innovation and creativity are essential for organizations to adapt and thrive. They enable organizations to identify new opportunities, respond to market shifts, and embrace emerging technologies. By being open to new ideas and approaches, organizations can navigate change successfully and stay relevant.

4. Growth and Expansion: Innovation and creativity drive growth and expansion. By constantly seeking new opportunities and developing innovative products or services, organizations can expand their customer base, enter new markets, and increase revenue. They provide a pathway for organizations to evolve and reach new heights.

5. Employee Engagement and Satisfaction: Encouraging innovation and creativity boosts employee engagement and satisfaction. When employees are given the freedom to contribute ideas, be creative, and see their ideas implemented, it enhances their sense of ownership, purpose, and motivation. This leads to higher productivity, increased job satisfaction, and better retention rates.

6. Continuous Improvement: Innovation and creativity foster a culture of continuous improvement within organizations. They encourage employees to challenge the status quo, identify inefficiencies, and seek innovative ways to enhance processes and practices. This results in improved efficiency, quality, and overall organizational performance.

7. Brand Image and Reputation: Organizations that consistently innovate and demonstrate creativity tend to have a positive brand image and reputation. Being perceived as innovative and creative enhances the organization's credibility, attracts customers and talented employees, and strengthens partnerships and collaborations.

8. Long-term Sustainability: Innovation and creativity are key drivers of long-term sustainability in organizations. They enable organizations to anticipate and respond to future trends, customer expectations, and changing market dynamics. By continuously innovating and adapting, organizations can stay relevant, overcome challenges, and ensure their long-term survival.

In summary, innovation and creativity are vital for organizations as they provide a competitive edge, foster problem-solving, facilitate adaptation to change, drive growth, enhance employee engagement, promote continuous improvement, enhance brand image, and ensure long-term sustainability. Organizations that embrace and nurture innovation and creativity are better positioned to thrive in a dynamic and rapidly evolving business landscape.

c. Employee engagement and retention:

Employees value opportunities for growth and development. Organizations that invest in learning initiatives and create a supportive learning culture tend to have higher employee engagement and retention rates. Learning provides a sense of fulfillment, purpose, and career advancement, leading to greater job satisfaction and loyalty.

The purpose of employee engagement and retention in organizations is multi-fold and of significant importance. Here are the key purposes:

1. Productivity and Performance: Engaged and retained employees are more motivated, committed, and productive. They have a higher level of job satisfaction, which leads to increased efficiency, effectiveness, and overall performance. Engaged employees also tend to go above and beyond their basic job requirements, contributing to innovation, problem-solving, and organizational success.

2. Talent Attraction and Recruitment: Organizations with high employee engagement and retention rates are attractive to potential candidates. A positive workplace culture and engaged workforce serve as powerful magnets, attracting top talent. This allows organizations to select from a pool of highly skilled individuals who can contribute to the organization's growth and success.

3. Cost Savings: Employee turnover can be costly for organizations. It takes time and resources to recruit, train, and onboard new employees. By focusing on engagement and retention, organizations can reduce turnover rates and save costs associated with recruitment, training, and lost productivity. Engaged and retained employees

also tend to have lower absenteeism rates, minimizing the impact on productivity and overall performance.

4. Organizational Stability and Continuity: With high employee engagement and retention, organizations can establish stability and continuity. Retaining experienced employees ensures that institutional knowledge, skills, and expertise are preserved within the organization. This prevents disruptions, maintains organizational memory, and fosters a consistent and cohesive work environment.

5. Employee Development and Growth: Engaged and retained employees are more likely to actively participate in development opportunities as they are invested in their growth within the organization. Organizations can offer training, mentoring, and career advancement opportunities to engage and retain talented employees. This contributes to their continued professional development and ensures a pipeline of skilled employees for future leadership roles.

6. Positive Workplace Culture and Morale: Employee engagement and retention contribute to a positive workplace culture and high morale. Engaged employees are more likely to collaborate, communicate effectively, and support each other, fostering teamwork and a positive work environment. This, in turn, enhances employee satisfaction, well-being, and overall job happiness.

7. Customer Satisfaction and Loyalty: Engaged employees have a positive impact on customer satisfaction and loyalty. When employees are engaged, they provide better customer service, are more attentive to customer needs, and are genuine brand ambassadors. Satisfied customers are more likely to become loyal, repeat customers, contributing to business growth and success.

In conclusion, the purpose of employee engagement and retention in organizations is to drive productivity, attract top talent, save costs, ensure stability and continuity, foster employee development and growth, create a positive workplace culture, and enhance customer satisfaction and loyalty. Organizations that prioritize engagement and retention are better positioned to build a motivated, high-performing workforce and achieve long-term success.

d. Organizational agility:

Learning organizations are more adaptable and agile, enabling them to respond quickly to market shifts, new opportunities, and emerging trends. Through learning, organizations build adaptive capabilities, allowing them to thrive in dynamic and uncertain environments.

Organizational agility refers to an organization's ability to respond and adapt quickly to changes in the external environment. It involves being flexible, nimble, and proactive in identifying and seizing opportunities, as well as effectively navigating challenges and uncertainties. Here are the key aspects and benefits of organizational agility:

1. Speed and Responsiveness: Agile organizations can make decisions quickly and act promptly. They have streamlined decision-making processes and empower employees at all levels to take initiative and make necessary changes on time. This allows organizations to respond swiftly to market shifts, customer demands, and emerging threats or opportunities.

2. Flexibility and Adaptability: Organizational agility is characterized by the ability to adapt and adjust strategies, structures, and processes as needed. Agile organizations continually monitor and assess their internal and external landscapes, allowing them to proactively reallocate resources, change direction, and embrace new approaches. This flexibility enables them to stay relevant and competitive in dynamic and unpredictable environments.

3. Innovation and Learning: Agility fosters a culture of innovation and continuous learning within organizations. Agile organizations encourage experimentation, promote creativity, and embrace failure as an opportunity for growth

and improvement. They actively seek new ideas, perspectives, and technologies to avoid stagnation and remain ahead of the curve. This leads to innovative products, services, and processes that drive competitive advantage.

4. Collaboration and Empowerment: Agile organizations promote collaboration and empower employees to make decisions and take ownership. They break down silos and encourage cross-functional teams, enabling information flow, knowledge sharing, and collective problem-solving. This collaborative environment fosters creativity, engagement, and higher levels of employee satisfaction.

5. Risk Management and Resilience: Agile organizations are better equipped to manage risks and uncertainties. They actively anticipate potential disruptions, continuously monitor market trends, and develop contingency plans. By being proactive and prepared, they can quickly adapt and recover from setbacks, ensuring long-term sustainability.

6. Customer Centricity: Agility puts a strong emphasis on understanding customer needs, preferences, and feedback. Agile organizations prioritize customer-centricity, focusing on delivering value, personalized experiences, and exceptional service. With a customer-centric approach, they can respond to changing customer demands and preferences, enhancing customer satisfaction, loyalty, and retention.

The effectiveness of organizational agility lies in its ability to enable organizations to stay ahead of the competition, respond rapidly to market changes, foster innovation, and build resilience. By embracing agility, organizations can effectively navigate uncertainties, optimize opportunities, and deliver superior customer experiences. This, in turn, translates into improved performance, growth, and long-term success.

Section 2: The Importance of Knowledge Sharing in Organizations

Knowledge sharing is the process of transferring knowledge, insights, and expertise among individuals and teams within an organization. Here are some reasons why knowledge sharing is important:

a. Collaboration and teamwork:

Knowledge sharing breaks down silos and promotes collaboration and teamwork. By sharing information and expertise, employees can leverage each other's strengths, complement skills, and collectively solve problems.

Collaboration and teamwork play a crucial role in the success and effectiveness of an organization. Here are the key reasons why they are important:

1. Increased Efficiency and Productivity: Collaboration and teamwork enhance efficiency and productivity within organizations. When individuals work together towards a common goal, they can divide tasks based on individual strengths, expertise, and experience. This leads to better time management, reduced duplication of efforts, and improved overall productivity.

2. Synergy and Creativity: By bringing together diverse perspectives, skills, and ideas, collaboration and teamwork foster synergy and creativity. When individuals collaborate and bounce ideas off each other, it sparks innovation, encourages out-of-the-box thinking, and leads to the generation of new and creative solutions to challenges. The collective intelligence of a team often surpasses the capabilities of a single individual.

3. Enhanced Problem-Solving: Collaboration and teamwork enable organizations to tackle complex problems and find effective solutions. Through collaboration, team members can share their knowledge, expertise, and different viewpoints, leading to more comprehensive problem-solving approaches. Team members can also challenge each other's assumptions and provide different perspectives, which helps in identifying blind spots and potential pitfalls.

4. Improved Decision-Making: Collaboration and teamwork contribute to better decision-making within organizations. When a team collaboratively discusses and analyzes options, it leads to more informed and well-rounded decisions. Multiple viewpoints and diverse expertise help in considering a wider range of factors, weighing pros and cons, and making more balanced decisions.

5. Mutual Support and Growth: Collaboration and teamwork foster a supportive and cohesive work environment. Team members rely on each other, provide mutual assistance, and share knowledge and resources. This builds trust, camaraderie, and a sense of belonging, which contributes to higher job satisfaction and employee engagement. Collaboration also provides opportunities for learning and professional growth as team members can learn from each other's experiences and skills.

6. Effective Communication: Collaboration and teamwork require effective communication among team members. Regular and open communication facilitates the sharing of information, ensures everyone is on the same page, and promotes transparency and understanding. When team members communicate effectively, it minimizes misunderstandings, and conflicts, and promotes a positive work environment.

7. Strengthened Relationships and Motivation: Collaboration and teamwork strengthen relationships among employees. Working together towards common objectives fosters a sense of camaraderie, trust, and respect. Positive relationships contribute to higher job satisfaction, commitment, and motivation. Team members are more likely to go above and beyond to support each other and the organization's goals.

In conclusion, collaboration and teamwork are important in organizations as they improve efficiency and productivity, foster creativity and innovation, enhance problem-solving and decision-making, provide mutual support and growth opportunities, promote effective communication, and strengthen relationships and motivation. Organizations that prioritize and foster a collaborative work culture are better equipped to achieve their goals, adapt to challenges, and drive success.

b. Enhanced decision-making:

Sharing knowledge allows for a wider perspective, leading to better decision-making. When individuals can access and integrate different insights and expertise, they can make more informed and effective decisions.

Enhanced decision-making is essential for the success and effectiveness of an organization. Here are five key reasons why it is necessary:

1. Quality Decisions: Enhanced decision-making ensures that organizations make high-quality decisions. By considering relevant information, analyzing available data, and involving key stakeholders, organizations can make informed and well-thought-out decisions. Quality decisions lead to better outcomes, minimize risks and uncertainties, and contribute to the overall success of the organization.

2. Competitive Advantage: Enhanced decision-making provides organizations with a competitive advantage. In today's fast-paced business environment, organizations need to make timely and effective decisions to stay ahead of the competition. Accurate and well-executed decisions enable organizations to seize opportunities, respond to market changes, and outperform their competitors. This helps companies to gain an edge in the industry and position themselves as industry leaders.

3. Alignment and Consensus: Enhanced decision-making promotes alignment and consensus among team members and stakeholders. Involving relevant parties in the decision-making process ensures that diverse perspectives are considered, fostering inclusivity and collaboration. When team members are involved in decision-making, they are more likely to support and commit to the decision, leading to increased engagement and shared accountability for outcomes.

4. Risk Mitigation: Enhanced decision-making helps organizations identify and mitigate risks effectively. Through a thorough analysis of potential risks and their consequences, organizations can develop strategies to manage and minimize those risks. Careful decision-making allows organizations to anticipate potential challenges, implement risk mitigation measures, and enhance overall resilience.

5. Strategic Planning and Adaptation: Enhanced decision-making is crucial for strategic planning and adaptation in organizations. By making well-informed decisions, organizations can set realistic goals, develop effective strategies, and allocate resources efficiently. Additionally, enhanced decision-making enables organizations to adapt to changing market dynamics and seize new opportunities. In a rapidly evolving business landscape, organizations need to be agile and responsive, and effective decision-making underpins adaptability and strategic growth.

In conclusion, enhanced decision-making is necessary in organizations due to its ability to drive high-quality decisions, provide a competitive advantage, promote alignment and consensus, mitigate risks, and support strategic planning and adaptation. Organizations that prioritize and enhance decision-making capabilities are better positioned to achieve their objectives, navigate challenges effectively, and drive long-term success.

c. Reduced redundancies and increased efficiency:

Knowledge sharing enables organizations to avoid redundant efforts and duplication of work. By tapping into existing knowledge and expertise, teams can build on past experiences, leverage best practices, and work more efficiently.

Reducing redundancies and increasing efficiencies within an organization can be achieved through various means. Here are some approaches:

1. Streamlining Processes: Evaluate existing processes and identify areas that can be streamlined or eliminated. Look for unnecessary steps, duplicated efforts, and bottlenecks. By simplifying processes, removing redundancies, and optimizing workflows, organizations can improve efficiency and reduce wasted time and resources.

2. Automation and Technology: Invest in automation and technology solutions to streamline repetitive tasks and improve efficiency. Automation can eliminate manual errors, speed up processes, and free up employees' time for more value-added activities. Implementing technology tools like project management software, collaboration platforms, and workflow automation systems can optimize communication and coordination among team members, leading to increased efficiency.

3. Clear Roles and Responsibilities: Ensure that roles and responsibilities within the organization are well-defined and aligned. Lack of clarity can lead to duplication of efforts, confusion, and inefficiencies. Communicate responsibilities, establish accountability, and foster a culture of teamwork and collaboration. This enables employees to understand their role in the larger context of the organization and reduces redundancies.

4. Effective Communication Channels: Establish effective communication channels to facilitate collaboration and information-sharing. Inefficient communication methods can lead to delays, misunderstandings, and errors. Utilize communication tools such as project management software, instant messaging platforms, and video conferencing systems to enable quick and seamless communication among team members. Encourage open and transparent communication to enhance efficiency and minimize redundancies.

5. Continuous Improvement and Feedback: Embrace a culture of continuous improvement and encourage employees to provide feedback on processes, workflows, and organizational practices. Regularly evaluate and refine processes based on feedback and identified areas of improvement. Engage employees in suggesting effi-

ciency-enhancing ideas and recognize and implement those that have the potential to drive meaningful changes in the organization.

6. Training and Development: Invest in employee training and development programs to enhance skills and knowledge. Well-trained employees are more efficient and can perform tasks more effectively. Provide ongoing learning opportunities to ensure that employees are up to date with the latest tools, techniques, and best practices. This enables employees to work smarter, identify efficiencies, and contributes to reducing redundancies.

7. Performance Evaluation and Incentives: Implement performance evaluation systems that incentivize and reward efficiency and productivity. Recognize and appreciate employees who consistently find ways to reduce redundancies and improve efficiencies within their areas of responsibility. This creates a culture that encourages employees to actively seek ways to optimize their work processes and contributes to an organization-wide efficiency mindset.

In summary, reducing redundancies and increasing efficiencies within an organization can be achieved through streamlining processes, leveraging automation and technology, clarifying roles and responsibilities, establishing effective communication channels, fostering continuous improvement, investing in employee training and development, and implementing performance evaluation systems that incentivize efficiency. These measures can help organizations optimize their operations, improve productivity, and achieve greater effectiveness.

d. Continuity and succession planning:

Knowledge sharing ensures that critical knowledge and expertise are not limited to a few individuals. It mitigates the risk of knowledge loss due to turnover or retirement and ensures continuity in operations. Additionally, knowledge sharing aids in succession planning by facilitating the transfer of knowledge and skills to new employees or those being groomed for leadership positions.

Continuity and succession planning in organizations involve preparing for the smooth transition of leadership roles and ensuring the ongoing operations and success of the organization. Here is the explanation of continuity and succession planning:

1. Continuity Planning: Continuity planning focuses on ensuring the uninterrupted operation of the organization in the face of unexpected events or disruptions. It involves identifying potential risks, including natural disasters, pandemics, or major leadership changes, and developing strategies to mitigate these risks. Continuity plans outline steps to be taken in emergencies to maintain essential business functions, protect assets, and preserve the well-being of employees and stakeholders. By preparing for potential disruptions, organizations can minimize downtime, maintain service delivery, and protect their reputation and long-term viability.

2. Succession Planning: Succession planning deals with the identification and development of potential successors for key leadership positions within the organization. It involves identifying talented individuals who have the potential to assume critical roles in the future and developing their skills, knowledge, and competencies through mentorship, training, and other developmental strategies. Succession planning ensures a pipeline of skilled leaders who can step into key positions when the need arises. It provides a smooth transition, minimizes disruptions, and allows organizations to preserve institutional knowledge and maintain stability during leadership changes.

3. Knowledge Transfer: Continuity and succession planning also involve knowledge transfer. This includes capturing and documenting vital information, expertise, and processes held by outgoing leaders or key employees. By documenting and disseminating this knowledge to potential successors or other team members, organizations

ensure the continuity of critical operations and avoid loss of valuable knowledge and experience. Knowledge transfer may involve formal training, shadowing, mentoring, or the creation of knowledge repositories and databases.

4. Talent Development: Continuity and succession planning emphasize the development and growth of talent within the organization. It involves identifying high-potential individuals and providing them with opportunities for growth, advancement, and development of leadership skills. This includes targeted training programs, mentoring relationships, cross-functional experiences, and stretch assignments. By nurturing talent, organizations can build a strong leadership bench, enhance employee engagement and retention, and prepare for future leadership needs.

5. Evaluation and Adjustment: Continuity and succession planning are ongoing processes that require regular evaluation and adjustment. Organizations need to periodically assess the effectiveness of their plans, update them as needed, and ensure that they remain aligned with current business needs and goals. This includes regularly reviewing the list of potential successors, revisiting development plans, and adjusting strategies based on changes in the internal and external environment.

In summary, continuity and succession planning are crucial components of organizational preparedness and long-term success. Continuity planning focuses on maintaining operations during unexpected disruptions, while succession planning ensures the seamless transition of key leadership positions. By identifying and developing future leaders, transferring knowledge, and continuously evaluating and adjusting plans, organizations can ensure resilience, stability, and sustainability.

Section 3: Real-World Examples of Learning and Knowledge Sharing

Let's examine real-world examples that highlight the impact of learning and knowledge sharing in organizations:

a. IBM:

IBM is renowned for its culture of learning and knowledge sharing. The company has implemented a system called "Think Academy" which provides employees with access to learning resources, communities of practice, and platforms for sharing expertise. Through these initiatives, IBM promotes continuous learning, collaboration, and the dissemination of knowledge across its global workforce.

b. Procter & Gamble (P&G):

P&G places a strong emphasis on knowledge sharing as a core component of its innovation strategy. The company utilizes various platforms, such as electronic databases and online forums, to encourage employees to share their expertise, insights, and best practices. This knowledge-sharing culture has been instrumental in driving innovation and improving business performance across P&G's portfolio of brands.

c. Toyota:

Toyota has a long-standing commitment to knowledge sharing and continuous improvement. The company's Toyota Production System (TPS) is built on the principles of ongoing learning, problem-solving, and employee empowerment. Toyota encourages employees at all levels to contribute their knowledge and suggestions to improve processes, enhance quality, and drive efficiency.

d. Wiki-based Knowledge Sharing:

Organizations like Wikipedia, the well-known online encyclopedia, have leveraged wiki-based platforms to facilitate widespread knowledge sharing. This collaborative approach allows contributors from around the world to share their expertise, resulting in a comprehensive and continuously evolving knowledge base.

Section 4: Strategies for Fostering Learning and Knowledge Sharing

a. Create a learning culture: Foster a culture that values and encourages learning at all levels of the organization. Promote continuous development through learning initiatives, provide resources, and recognize and reward employees who actively engage in learning.

b. Provide learning opportunities: Offer a variety of learning opportunities, including formal training, workshops, mentoring, and online learning platforms. Provide employees with autonomy in choosing their learning paths to cater to diverse needs and interests.

c. Enable collaboration and communication: Facilitate channels and platforms for employees to collaborate, share information, and exchange knowledge. Encourage open communication, promote cross-functional teams, and provide opportunities for networking and cross-pollination of ideas.

d. Recognize and reward knowledge sharing: Create incentives to encourage knowledge sharing, such as recognition programs, incentives, or opportunities for career advancement based on expertise and contribution to the organization's knowledge base.

e. Document and centralize knowledge: Establish systems and processes to capture and document knowledge, whether through internal databases, wikis, or other platforms. Make knowledge easily accessible and searchable to enable efficient sharing and retrieval.

Learning and knowledge sharing are critical for organizational growth, adaptation, and innovation. By fostering a culture of continuous learning, organizations can create a workforce that is adaptable, engaged, and equipped with the skills necessary to meet evolving challenges. Similarly, knowledge sharing enables collaboration, improves decision-making, and enhances organizational efficiency. Real-world examples from companies like IBM, P&G, Toyota, and Wikipedia demonstrate the impact of effective learning and knowledge-sharing initiatives. By prioritizing learning and implementing strategies for knowledge sharing, organizations can harness the collective potential of their employees and foster a culture of growth, collaboration, and success.

In summary, cross-cultural management is integral to organizational resilience. By promoting adaptability, improving communication, fostering cultural intelligence and empathy, effectively managing diverse talent, and embracing a learning mindset, cross-cultural management enhances an organization's ability to respond and rebound from challenges, making it more resilient in the face of uncertainty or disruptions.

On Cross-cultural Management

Cross-Cultural Management: Understanding, Adapting, and Thriving in Global Environments

In today's globalized world, organizations increasingly operate in diverse cultural contexts. Cross-cultural management is the field of study that focuses on understanding, adapting to, and effectively managing cultural differences in the workplace. It recognizes that culture plays a critical role in shaping beliefs, values, behaviors, and work practices. By developing cross-cultural competence, individuals and organizations can navigate cultural complexities and leverage diversity to achieve success. In this article, we will examine the essence of cross-cultural management, and its significance, and provide real-world examples to illustrate its impact.

PART 1: Understanding Cross-Cultural Management

Cross-cultural management refers to the study and application of management principles in multicultural contexts. It involves understanding how culture influences individuals and groups and applying this knowledge to effectively manage cross-cultural interactions and relationships. Key aspects of cross-cultural management include cultural awareness, cultural intelligence, effective communication, and adaptation to diverse cultural norms and practices.

Understanding Cross-Cultural Management: Key Concepts, Approaches, and Implications

In today's globalized business environment, organizations must understand and effectively manage cultural differences. Cross-cultural management is a field of study that explores the impact of culture on individual and organizational behavior, intending to develop strategies for successful cross-cultural interactions. It involves recognizing and appreciating cultural diversity, adapting management practices to fit different cultural contexts, and leveraging cultural differences as a source of competitive advantage. In this article, we will explore the key concepts and approaches in cross-cultural management and discuss the implications for individuals and organizations.

Section 1: Key Concepts in Cross-Cultural Management

a. Culture:

Culture encompasses the shared beliefs, values, norms, customs, and behaviors of a particular group or society. It influences individuals' perspectives, attitudes, communication styles, and decision-making processes. Understanding culture is fundamental to cross-cultural management.

b. Cultural Dimensions:

Cultural dimensions, as identified by researchers such as Hofstede, Trompenaars, and Hall, provide a framework for comparing and understanding cultural differences. These dimensions include power distance, individualism versus collectivism, masculinity versus femininity, uncertainty avoidance, and long-term versus short-term orientation.

c. Cultural Intelligence (CQ):

Cultural intelligence refers to an individual's ability to recognize, understand, and adapt to different cultural contexts. It involves being aware of one's own cultural biases, understanding cultural norms and values, and adapting one's behavior to fit specific cultural situations.

d. Ethnocentrism:

Ethnocentrism refers to the tendency to view one's own culture as superior to others. It can hinder effective cross-cultural management by creating barriers to understanding and acceptance of different cultural values and practices.

Section 2: Approaches to Cross-Cultural Management

a. Comparative Approach:

The comparative approach seeks to identify and compare cultural differences across countries or regions. It aims to understand how cultural factors influence management practices and strategies. This approach helps identify broad cultural patterns and differences.

b. Cultural Convergence:

The cultural convergence approach emphasizes the similarities and convergence of management practices across cultures. It highlights the impact of globalization and the adoption of global best practices. This approach recognizes that, despite cultural differences, there are commonalities in how organizations operate.

c. Cultural Divergence:

The cultural divergence approach focuses on the unique characteristics and differences among cultures. It emphasizes the need to adapt management practices to fit specific cultural contexts. This approach recognizes that cultural diversity is a valuable source of innovation and competitive advantage.

d. Hybrid Approach:

The hybrid approach combines elements of both convergence and divergence. It recognizes the existence of both universal management principles and the need for local adaptations. This approach emphasizes the importance of striking a balance between global consistency and local relevance.

Section 3: Implications of Cross-Cultural Management

a. Effective Communication:

Cross-cultural management highlights the importance of effective communication in diverse cultural contexts. Effective communication requires understanding cultural nuances, adapting communication styles, and being sensitive to potential language barriers or non-verbal cues.

b. Building Trust and Relationships:

Cross-cultural management emphasizes the need to build trust and relationships across cultures. It involves understanding cultural differences in trust-building processes and adapting approaches to establish rapport and mutual understanding.

c. Global Leadership and Management:

Cross-cultural management is essential for global leadership and management. It requires leaders to be culturally sensitive, adaptable, and skilled in managing diverse teams. Effective global leaders recognize and leverage cultural differences to drive innovation and collaboration.

d. Human Resource Management:

Cross-cultural management has implications for human resource management practices. It involves adapting recruitment, selection, training, and performance appraisal systems to fit different cultural contexts. It also emphasizes the need for diversity and inclusion practices to harness the benefits of cultural diversity.

e. International Business and Market Entry:

Cross-cultural management is crucial for international business and market entry. Cultural differences influence consumer behavior, market preferences, and business practices. Understanding and adapting to local cultural norms is essential for successful international expansion.

Section 4: Challenges and Strategies in Cross-Cultural Management

a. Stereotyping and Bias:

One of the key challenges in cross-cultural management is the tendency to stereotype based on cultural differences. Overcoming biases and avoiding stereotyping requires open-mindedness and a willingness to see individuals as individuals, rather than representatives of their culture.

b. Language and Communication Barriers:

Language and communication barriers can hinder cross-cultural management. Overcoming these barriers requires learning or understanding the local language, using interpreters if necessary, and developing communication skills that transcend language differences.

c. Cultural Training and Education:

Providing cultural training and education to employees is essential for successful cross-cultural management. It helps develop cultural awareness, sensitivity, and adaptability. Training can include language lessons, cultural immersion experiences, and intercultural communication workshops.

d. Building Cross-Cultural Competence:

Building cross-cultural competence requires individuals to continuously learn and adapt to different cultural contexts. This involves cultivating curiosity, seeking opportunities for cross-cultural interactions, and being open to learning from diverse perspectives.

e. Collaborative Problem Solving:

Collaborative problem-solving is essential in cross-cultural management. Encouraging open dialogue, active listening, and collaborative decision-making processes can help overcome cultural barriers and promote understanding and collaboration.

Understanding cross-cultural management is vital in today's globally connected world. By recognizing the influence of culture on behavior and business practices, individuals and organizations can navigate cultural complexities, adapt management practices to fit diverse cultural contexts, and leverage cultural diversity as a source of strength. Key concepts in cross-cultural management, such as culture, cultural dimensions, cultural intelligence, and approaches like comparative, convergence, divergence, and hybrid, provide insights into managing cultural differences. The implications of cross-cultural management range from effective communication and relationship-building to global leadership and market entry strategies. Overcoming challenges and adopting strategies for successful cross-cultural management can help individuals and organizations thrive in an increasingly diverse and interconnected world.

PART 2: The Significance of Cross-Cultural Management

Cross-cultural management is crucial in today's globalized business landscape. Here are some key reasons why it is significant:

a. Effective communication:

Culture shapes communication styles, norms, and expectations. Cross-cultural management provides insights into different communication patterns and helps individuals and organizations communicate effectively across cultures. It enables them to navigate language barriers, non-verbal cues, and differing communication preferences.

a. Building relationships and trust:

Cultural differences impact how individuals build relationships and establish trust. Cross-cultural management promotes understanding and appreciation of diverse perspectives, fostering the development of strong, inclusive, and trusting relationships across cultures. It helps bridge the gap between different cultural norms and values.

c. Global teamwork and collaboration:

Businesses today operate in global teams that bring together individuals from different cultural backgrounds. Cross-cultural management facilitates effective teamwork, collaboration, and conflict resolution in multicultural settings. It enables team members to appreciate diverse contributions, leverage varying strengths, and establish a harmonious working environment.

Global teamwork and collaboration have become essential in today's interconnected world. As businesses and organizations expand beyond their national borders, they rely heavily on collaboration among team members from different countries and cultures. This type of collaboration brings together diverse perspectives, skills, and experiences, leading to innovative solutions and improved decision-making processes. Through global teamwork, organizations can leverage the strengths of their team members around the world, creating a competitive advantage and fostering a more inclusive and global mindset.

One of the benefits of global teamwork is the ability to tap into a diverse pool of talent. When team members from different parts of the world come together, they bring unique skills, knowledge, and perspectives. This diversity enhances problem-solving capabilities, as individuals from different cultural backgrounds approach challenges from different angles. By working together, these team members can combine their expertise and insights to find creative and effective solutions that might not have been possible otherwise.

Moreover, global teamwork promotes cross-cultural understanding and communication skills. Collaborating with individuals from different countries and cultures allows team members to learn from one another and gain a deeper appreciation for diverse perspectives. This not only broadens their understanding of different cultures, traditions, and values but also improves their ability to communicate effectively across language barriers and cultural differences. By fostering intercultural communication, global teamwork enhances cooperation and minimizes misunderstandings, ensuring more efficient and productive work processes.

Furthermore, global teamwork and collaboration promote a sense of belonging and inclusivity among team members. When people from different countries and backgrounds work together towards a common goal, it fosters a sense of unity and helps break down cultural stereotypes. Individuals feel valued and appreciated for their contributions, regardless of their nationality or background. The sense of belonging that arises from this collaborative environment fosters higher levels of engagement, motivation, and commitment among team members, leading to increased productivity and better overall team performance.

In conclusion, global teamwork and collaboration are crucial for organizations seeking to thrive in today's interconnected world. Leveraging the diverse skills, knowledge, and perspectives of team members from different countries and cultures leads to innovative solutions, enhanced decision-making, and a more inclusive work environment. Moreover, global teamwork fosters cross-cultural understanding, improves communication skills and creates a sense of belonging among team members. Organizations that embrace and promote global teamwork are better equipped to navigate the challenges of globalization and create sustainable success in a rapidly changing world.

d. Localization and market adaptation:

Culture influences consumer preferences, behaviors, and purchasing decisions. Cross-cultural management helps businesses localize their products, services, and marketing strategies to fit the cultural nuances of specific markets. It enables organizations to adapt their business practices, brand messages, and customer experience to resonate with diverse cultures.

Localization refers to the process of adapting a product or service to a specific market or region, taking into account the cultural, linguistic, and other local nuances. It involves modifying various aspects of a product, such as language, currency, date and time formats, colors, images, and even functionality, to cater to the preferences and needs of the target market. Localization aims to provide a seamless and tailored experience to the end-users, ensuring that they can easily understand and engage with the product or service. This process allows companies to expand their reach and compete more effectively in global markets by making their offerings more relevant and appealing to diverse audiences.

Market adaptation, on the other hand, refers to the broader strategy of modifying a company's marketing mix to better suit the characteristics and demands of a specific market segment. It involves identifying and understanding the unique preferences, behaviors, and cultural aspects of the target market and then adjusting various marketing elements such as product features, pricing, distribution channels, and promotional tactics accordingly. Market adaptation enables companies to effectively address the needs and desires of consumers in different markets, providing them with products and services that align with their expectations. By embracing market adaptation, businesses can increase customer satisfaction, build strong relationships with local customers, and ultimately drive sales and growth in new markets.

PART 3: Real-World Examples of Cross-Cultural Management

1. McDonald's:

McDonald's is a prime example of a company applying cross-cultural management principles. The fast-food chain adapts its menus and operations to local cultural preferences in each country it operates. For example, in India, where most of the population is Hindu and avoids beef, McDonald's offers vegetarian and chicken-based options. This demonstrates an understanding and adaptation to local cultural norms and preferences.

2. Airbnb:

Airbnb is a home-sharing platform that operates worldwide. To ensure a positive experience for hosts and guests from different cultures, Airbnb has implemented cultural training and support programs. These initiatives help hosts understand and appreciate cultural differences, adapt their accommodations to meet cultural expectations and create a more inclusive and comfortable experience for guests.

3. Google:

Google places great importance on cross-cultural management in its diverse workforce. The company fosters cultural awareness and understanding by organizing cultural events, promoting inclusive practices, and offering training programs on cross-cultural communication and collaboration. This enables employees to work effectively in diverse teams and leverage cultural diversity to drive innovation.

Section 4: Strategies for Successful Cross-Cultural Management

1. Cultural intelligence (CQ) development:

Develop cultural intelligence by enhancing awareness, understanding, and appreciation of different cultural norms, values, and practices. This includes cultivating curiosity, engaging in intercultural experiences, and seeking opportunities to learn from diverse cultural perspectives.

Cultural intelligence (CQ) development emphasizes the importance of understanding and effectively navigating diverse cultural contexts. It goes beyond simply acquiring knowledge about different cultures and focuses on developing the skills and attitudes necessary to adapt and interact successfully across cultural boundaries. The emphasis on cultural intelligence development is rooted in the recognition that globalization has brought people from different cultural backgrounds together like never before, whether in business, education, or social settings. To foster effective collaboration and avoid misunderstandings or conflicts, individuals and organizations need to build their cultural intelligence.

One key emphasis of cultural intelligence development is on increasing cultural understanding and awareness. This involves actively seeking knowledge and insights about different cultures, including their values, beliefs, practices, and communication styles. By understanding cultural nuances, individuals can engage in more meaningful and respectful interactions, avoiding stereotypes or unintentional offenses. This includes developing empathy and open-mindedness towards cultural differences and recognizing that there are multiple ways of thinking and doing things.

Another emphasis of cultural intelligence development is on adapting one's behavior and communication style to different cultural contexts. This involves being flexible and adaptable, understanding that what may be acceptable in one culture may be seen as inappropriate or disrespectful in another. By demonstrating sensitivity and adapting one's behavior accordingly, individuals can build rapport, trust, and credibility with individuals from diverse cultural backgrounds. Effective communication across cultures requires active listening, asking questions for clarification, and being mindful of nonverbal cues and verbal tone.

Cultural intelligence development also emphasizes the importance of developing intercultural skills. This includes skills such as conflict resolution, negotiation, and collaboration across cultural boundaries. Individuals with strong cultural intelligence can navigate differences and work effectively with diverse groups, leveraging the strengths and perspectives of different individuals to achieve common goals. This also involves embracing diversity and inclusion, valuing different perspectives and contributions, and creating an inclusive environment where everyone feels respected and valued.

In summary, the emphasis on cultural intelligence development recognizes the need for individuals and organizations to effectively navigate diverse cultural contexts. It involves increasing cultural understanding, adapting behaviors and communication styles, and developing intercultural skills. By prioritizing cultural intelligence, individuals and organizations can build stronger relationships, enhance collaboration, and succeed in today's increasingly multicultural and globalized world.

2. Effective communication:

Enhance communication skills by actively listening, clarifying meaning, and adapting communication styles to fit cultural contexts. This involves being mindful of language barriers, and non-verbal cues, and adapting approaches to accommodate different cultural preferences.

Effective communication is of utmost importance in business for several reasons. Firstly, it is crucial for building and maintaining strong relationships with clients, customers, employees, and other stakeholders. Clear and concise communication helps convey messages accurately, ensuring that everyone involved understands the expectations, requirements, and objectives. This minimizes misunderstandings, reduces conflicts, and fosters trust and collaboration, leading to improved efficiency and productivity.

Secondly, effective communication is vital for effective teamwork and collaboration within an organization. Strong communication channels facilitate the sharing of ideas, information, and feedback among team members, enabling them to work together towards common goals. When employees can communicate openly and transparently, it leads to better problem-solving, decision-making, and increased innovation. It also enhances morale and job satisfaction as employees feel heard and involved in the decision-making process.

In addition, effective communication plays a critical role in managing and resolving conflicts. In any business setting, conflicts are bound to arise, whether due to differing opinions, conflicting interests, or miscommunication. Through effective communication, conflicts can be addressed promptly and constructively, avoiding escalation and enabling the parties involved to find mutually beneficial solutions. Effective communication skills, such as active listening, empathy, and assertiveness, are essential for de-escalating tense situations and promoting understanding and compromise.

Furthermore, effective communication is a key factor in successful customer service and client relationships. When businesses can effectively communicate with their customers, they can understand their needs, provide relevant information, address concerns, and deliver exceptional service. This leads to increased customer satisfaction, loyalty, and positive word-of-mouth, ultimately driving business growth and success.

Overall, effective communication is vital in business as it promotes understanding, collaboration, and positive relationships. It helps build trust, resolve conflicts, foster teamwork, and deliver exceptional customer service. By prioritizing and improving communication skills, individuals and organizations can enhance their overall performance and achieve their objectives efficiently.

3. Cultural adaptation and flexibility:

Be open to, and capable of, adapting to different cultural practices and norms. This includes adapting business strategies, practices, and processes to fit local cultural contexts. It also involves being flexible in accommodating diverse perspectives and approaches to problem-solving.

Cultural adaptation and flexibility are key elements in management due to the increasingly global nature of businesses and the diverse workforces they entail. Here are several reasons why they are crucial:

a. Globalization: As businesses expand their operations across borders, they encounter different cultures with unique values, norms, and practices. Managers need to adapt their management styles, approaches, and strategies to effectively lead multicultural teams and navigate diverse markets. By embracing cultural adaptation and flexibility, managers can create an inclusive and harmonious work environment that values and leverages the diverse backgrounds and perspectives of their employees.

b. Effective Communication: Communication is the backbone of effective management. Culturally diverse teams often face communication challenges due to language barriers, varying communication styles, and culturally influenced communication norms. Managers who are culturally adaptable and flexible can bridge these gaps by understanding different communication preferences, adapting their language and style, and fostering open and inclusive communication channels for everyone to express their ideas and concerns.

c. Employee Engagement and Motivation: Cultural adaptation and flexibility contribute to increased employee engagement and motivation. When managers show an understanding of and respect for different cultures, employees feel valued and appreciated. This enhances their sense of belonging, encourages them to contribute their unique perspectives, and fosters a positive work environment where everyone feels included. Culturally adaptable managers also recognize the importance of work-life balance and cultural celebrations, accommodating the diverse needs and traditions of their employees.

d. Conflict Resolution: Conflict is inevitable in any workplace, but it can become more complex and sensitive in multicultural teams. Managers skilled in cultural adaptation and flexibility can effectively manage conflicts by understanding the underlying cultural factors and finding culturally appropriate solutions. They recognize that different cultures may have diverse approaches to conflict resolution, and they can navigate these differences with sensitivity and respect.

e. Business Success: Cultural adaptation and flexibility contribute to the overall success of a business. By effectively managing diverse teams and cultivating a culture of inclusion, managers can tap into the diversity dividend, which refers to the enhanced creativity, innovation, and problem-solving that stem from diverse perspectives. Additionally, businesses that can adapt their products, services, and marketing strategies to different cultural contexts have a competitive advantage and can expand their customer base in global markets.

In summary, cultural adaptation and flexibility are crucial elements in management due to the increasing globalization and diversity of businesses. They enable effective communication, enhance employee engagement and motivation, facilitate conflict resolution, and ultimately contribute to business success in a multicultural world.

4. Building relationships and trust:

Invest time in building relationships and establishing trust with individuals from different cultural backgrounds. This can be achieved through active listening, empathy, and demonstrating respect for cultural differences. Developing cross-cultural relationships fosters collaboration and enhances mutual understanding.

Building relationships and trust is crucial in today's workplace dynamics for several reasons.

Firstly, strong relationships and trust foster collaboration and teamwork. In today's interconnected and cross-functional work environments, employees need to work together effectively towards common goals. Building relationships based on trust creates an atmosphere of cooperation and mutual support, where individuals feel comfortable sharing ideas, seeking help, and helping. Trusting relationships enable teams to leverage the strengths of each member, solve problems creatively, and achieve higher levels of productivity.

Secondly, relationships and trust are essential for effective communication. When there is trust between colleagues, they are more likely to engage in open and honest conversations. It allows for transparent sharing of information, constructive feedback, and active listening. With a foundation of trust, individuals feel safe to express their opinions, raise concerns, and engage in meaningful dialogue. Effective communication, facilitated by trust, leads to better understanding, reduced conflicts, and improved decision-making processes.

Thirdly, relationships and trust positively impact employee satisfaction and well-being. Having supportive relationships with colleagues and managers creates a positive work environment where individuals feel valued and appreciated. When employees feel trusted and respected, they are more likely to be motivated, engaged, and committed to their work. Strong relationships also provide a support system during times of stress or challenges, reducing the risk of burnout and promoting overall well-being.

Additionally, relationships and trust are critical for effective leadership. Trust is the foundation of a leader's ability to influence and inspire their team members. When employees trust their leaders, they are more likely to follow their guidance, be receptive to their vision, and embrace change. Strong relationships between leaders and team members enable a better understanding of individual strengths, development needs, and career aspirations. Leaders who prioritize building relationships and trust foster a culture of trustworthiness, transparency, and collaboration, which leads to higher levels of employee engagement and organizational success.

Lastly, relationships and trust enhance job satisfaction and retention. Employees who have positive relationships with their colleagues and feel a sense of trust within their work environment are more likely to enjoy their jobs and experience higher job satisfaction. They are also more likely to remain with the organization for the long term, reducing turnover costs and ensuring continuity in the workplace. Trust-based relationships create a sense of loyalty and commitment, which strengthens employee retention and organizational stability.

In summary, building relationships and trust is essential in today's workplace dynamics because it fosters collaboration, improves communication, enhances employee satisfaction and well-being, facilitates effective leadership, and contributes to job satisfaction and retention. Organizations that prioritize relationship-building and trust-building initiatives create a positive and productive work environment where individuals can thrive and contribute to the overall success of the organization.

5. Continuous learning and feedback:

Cross-cultural management is an ongoing process of learning and growth. Encourage continuous learning and provide opportunities for feedback and reflection on cross-cultural experiences. This helps individuals and organizations refine their cross-cultural management skills over time.

Cross-cultural management is essential in today's globalized world. A deep understanding of cultural differences and the ability to effectively adapt and manage cross-cultural interactions are key to business success. With effective cross-cultural management, organizations can communicate effectively, build relationships, and harness the benefits of cultural diversity. Real-world examples from companies like McDonald's, Airbnb, and Google highlight the significance of cross-cultural management in adapting to diverse cultural contexts. By implementing strategies for successful cross-cultural management, individuals and organizations can thrive in a global environment, foster collaboration, and drive sustainable success.

Continuous learning and feedback play a vital role in building relationships within organizations for several reasons.

Firstly, continuous learning allows individuals to stay updated with industry trends, technological advancements, and best practices. When team members are knowledgeable and up to date, they contribute to the overall success of the organization and become valuable resources for their colleagues. Sharing new learnings and insights with others fosters a culture of collaboration and mutual growth, strengthening relationships. Continuous learning also demonstrates a commitment to personal and professional development, which can inspire others and foster a culture of continuous improvement within the organization.

Secondly, feedback is essential for building strong relationships. Constructive feedback provides individuals with guidance and insights into their performance, allowing them to improve and grow. Giving and receiving feedback effectively requires trust and open communication. Regular feedback sessions allow team members to address concerns, clarify expectations, and recognize achievements. It creates a safe space for sharing thoughts, ideas, and concerns, enhancing understanding, and strengthening relationships between managers, peers, and direct reports.

Thirdly, continuous learning and feedback contribute to building a culture of accountability and personal growth. By encouraging individuals to seek feedback and learn from their experiences, organizations foster a sense of ownership and responsibility for professional development. When employees are committed to continuous learning, they take proactive steps to improve their skills and knowledge, contributing to their growth as well as the growth of the organization. This shared commitment to learning and growth strengthens relationships by promoting a culture of trust and support.

Moreover, continuous learning and feedback foster innovation and creativity within organizations. When employees are encouraged to continuously learn and seek feedback, they are more likely to generate new ideas and solutions. A culture of continuous learning allows individuals to challenge the status quo, experiment with new approaches, and take calculated risks. Feedback gives individuals insights about what works and what can be improved, enabling them to iterate and innovate. This culture of learning and feedback creates an environment where individuals feel empowered to contribute their unique perspectives and ideas, which builds trust and strong relationships based on collaboration and innovation.

Lastly, continuous learning and feedback support organizational growth and adaptability. In today's rapidly evolving business landscape, organizations must be agile and adaptable to remain competitive. Continuous learning ensures that employees are equipped with the necessary skills and knowledge to navigate change effectively. Feedback helps individuals identify strengths and areas for improvement, facilitating personal and professional growth aligned with the organization's goals. When employees continuously learn and adapt, it contributes to the overall success of the organization, fostering a culture of growth, and strengthening relationships based on shared goals and continuous improvement.

In conclusion, continuous learning and feedback are key factors in building relationships within organizations. They promote collaboration, enhance communication, foster accountability and personal growth, drive innovation, and support organizational adaptability. Organizations that prioritize and encourage continuous learning and feedback foster a culture of trust, mutual growth, and collaboration, which leads to stronger relationships and overall success.

Chapter Eleven

Change Management

Change management is the process of planning, implementing, and managing organizational changes in a structured and thoughtful manner. It involves understanding the need for change, communicating, and preparing for the change, and supporting individuals and teams through the transition to minimize resistance and maximize adoption. Change management ensures that the desired outcomes of the change are achieved, and that the organization effectively navigates the associated challenges and opportunities.

Change Management

Change management involves several components that are essential for successfully implementing and managing organizational change.

1. Change Identification: This component focuses on identifying the need for change and understanding the drivers behind it. It involves recognizing the gaps or challenges in the current state of the organization and determining the desired future state. This step requires careful analysis and assessment to outline the specific goals and objectives of the change initiative.

Change identification is a crucial aspect of general management as it plays a pivotal role in driving organizational success and growth.

Firstly, change identification allows managers to recognize and respond to emerging opportunities and challenges. By staying attuned to industry trends, market dynamics, and technological advancements, managers can identify potential areas for improvement, innovation, or adaptation. Through effective change identification, managers can proactively address changing customer needs, evolving market demands, and competitive pressures, ensuring that the organization remains relevant and competitive in the marketplace.

Secondly, changing identification enables managers to address organizational gaps or inefficiencies. By conducting internal assessments and analyzing business processes, managers can identify areas where improvements or modifications are necessary. Recognizing these gaps helps managers initiate change initiatives aimed at streamlining operations, enhancing productivity, and reducing costs. By identifying and addressing these internal challenges, managers can position the organization for sustainable growth and improved performance.

Thirdly, change identification supports strategic planning and decision-making. It allows managers to assess the alignment between the organization's goals, capabilities, and external environment. Understanding the need for change provides essential context for developing strategic plans and making informed decisions about resource allocation, talent management, and organizational structure. Incorporating change identification into general management ensures that managers make strategic decisions that align with the organization's long-term objectives and facilitate its success.

Finally, change identification promotes a culture of continuous improvement and innovation. By proactively seeking opportunities for change, managers encourage employees to think creatively, challenge the status quo, and propose innovative solutions. This fosters a culture of continuous learning and growth, where change is seen as an opportunity rather than a threat. Engaging in change identification empowers managers and employees to embrace change as a catalyst for progress and foster a culture of innovation and adaptability within the organization.

In conclusion, change identification is essential in general management as it allows managers to recognize emerging opportunities, address organizational gaps, support strategic planning, and promote a culture of continuous improvement and innovation. By engaging in change identification, managers can position their organizations for success in a dynamic business environment, make informed decisions, and drive growth and long-term sustainability.

Change identification involves several key aspects that are crucial for effectively recognizing and understanding the need for change within an organization.

a. Environmental Scanning: Environmental scanning is an important aspect of change identification that involves monitoring and analyzing the external factors that may impact the organization. This includes keeping abreast of industry trends, competitor actions, market shifts, technological advancements, and regulatory changes. By scanning the external environment, managers can identify potential threats or opportunities that require strategic and operational changes within the organization.

b. Internal Assessment: Internal assessment focuses on examining the existing processes, systems, structures, and resources within the organization. This involves evaluating current performance, identifying gaps or inefficiencies, and understanding the strengths and weaknesses of the organization. Through internal assessment, managers can gain insights into areas where change is needed to optimize operations, improve efficiency, enhance productivity, or address any organizational challenges hindering growth and success.

c. Stakeholder Input: Engaging stakeholders is a vital aspect of change identification. This involves soliciting input, feedback, and perspectives from employees, customers, suppliers, and other relevant parties. Stakeholders can provide valuable insights into their needs, expectations, and pain points, which can help identify areas that require change. By involving stakeholders in the change identification process, managers can ensure that the proposed changes align with the organization's goals and meet the needs of key stakeholders.

d. Data Analysis: Data analysis plays a crucial role in change identification by providing evidence-based insights. This involves collecting and analyzing relevant data and metrics to assess performance, identify patterns, and spot areas where change is necessary. By examining key performance indicators, financial data, customer feedback, and other relevant information, managers can identify areas of improvement, anticipate potential risks, and make informed decisions on the need for change.

e. External Expertise: Seeking external expertise is an important aspect of change identification, particularly when dealing with complex issues or specialized knowledge. External consultants, industry experts, or professional networks can offer an unbiased perspective and bring expertise in specific areas that require change. Leveraging external expertise can provide valuable insights and recommendations, helping managers make informed decisions regarding change initiatives.

In summary, change identification involves various aspects, including environmental scanning, internal assessment, stakeholder input, data analysis, and external expertise. By considering these aspects, organizations can effectively recognize and understand the need for change, enabling them to make informed decisions and develop strategies that drive growth, innovation, and long-term success. These aspects work together to provide a comprehensive understanding of the organization's internal and external dynamics, ensuring that change initiatives are targeted, relevant, and aligned with organizational goals and stakeholder needs.

2. Stakeholder Analysis: Identifying and analyzing the stakeholders involved in the change is crucial for effective change management. This component involves identifying key stakeholders, understanding their interests, and assessing their potential impact on the change process. By understanding and addressing the needs, concerns, and expectations of different stakeholders, change managers can effectively engage them and gain their support throughout the change journey.

Stakeholder analysis serves several important purposes within the context of organizational change and management.

a. Identify Key Stakeholders: The first purpose of stakeholder analysis is to identify and categorize the key stakeholders who will be affected by the change. Stakeholders can include individuals or groups both within and outside the organization, such as employees, managers, customers, suppliers, shareholders, regulatory bodies, and community members. By systematically identifying and categorizing stakeholders, managers can gain a comprehensive understanding of who needs to be involved or consulted during the change process.

b. Understand Stakeholder Interests and Influence: Stakeholder analysis helps in understanding the interests, needs, and expectations of different stakeholders. By determining their level of influence and power within the organization and the specific change initiative, managers can design appropriate strategies for engaging and managing stakeholders. This enables managers to tailor communication and engagement efforts to address concerns, align interests, and gather support from influential stakeholders, increasing the chances of successful change adoption.

c. Anticipate Potential Resistance or Support: Another purpose of stakeholder analysis is to anticipate potential sources of resistance or support to the change initiative. By analyzing the attitudes, concerns, and potential impact of stakeholders, managers can identify potential challenges and proactively address them. This allows for the development of targeted strategies to mitigate resistance, gain support, and foster collaboration. Anticipating potential resistance helps managers be prepared and develop effective change management plans to increase the likelihood of successful change implementation.

d. Inform Decision-making: Stakeholder analysis provides valuable insights that can inform decision-making throughout the change process. By understanding the perspectives and interests of different stakeholders, managers can make informed decisions regarding the design of the change initiative, resource allocation, and the prioritization of activities. Stakeholder analysis helps ensure that decisions are inclusive, transparent, and aligned with the needs and expectations of key stakeholders, increasing the chances of successful change outcomes.

e. Build Relationships and Enhance Communication: Lastly, stakeholder analysis allows managers to build and maintain relationships with key stakeholders. By identifying relevant stakeholders, managers can establish communication channels and build rapport to foster open and honest dialogue. Effective communication is crucial for managing change, and stakeholder analysis helps managers understand the preferred communication styles, channels, and frequency for different stakeholders. Building relationships through stakeholder analysis facilitates meaningful engagement, collaboration, and shared ownership of the change initiative.

In conclusion, stakeholder analysis serves multiple purposes, including identifying key stakeholders, understanding their interests and influence, anticipating resistance or support, informing decision-making, and building relationships. By conducting stakeholder analysis, managers can better navigate the complexities of organizational change, foster stakeholder engagement, and increase the chances of successful change implementation.

3. Communication and Engagement: Effective communication and engagement are critical components of change management. Clear and transparent communication helps stakeholders understand the reasons for the change, its scope, and expected outcomes. It creates a shared understanding and aligns everyone with the change efforts. Change managers need to use various communication channels and techniques to ensure the consistent dissemination of information and engage stakeholders in meaningful dialogue throughout the change process.

Effective communication and engagement are critical aspects of change management that play a crucial role in facilitating successful change initiatives within organizations.

a. Clear and Transparent Communication: Clear and transparent communication is essential in change management as it ensures that the purpose and goals of the change initiative are effectively communicated to all stakeholders. Communication should be clear, concise, and consistent to avoid misunderstandings and confusion. By being transparent about the reasons behind the change, the desired outcomes, and the expected impact, managers can build trust and create a shared understanding among stakeholders.

b. Two-Way Communication: Two-way communication is vital in change management as it allows for active engagement and feedback from stakeholders. Encouraging open dialogue and creating opportunities for stakeholders to provide input, ask questions, and express concerns fosters a sense of involvement and ownership. Two-way communication ensures that the voices and perspectives of stakeholders are heard, facilitating a more inclusive and collaborative change process.

c. Tailored Communication: Communication in change management should be tailored to different stakeholders based on their roles, interests, and communication preferences. Each stakeholder group requires specific information that is relevant to their involvement or impact on the change initiative. Managers must consider the appropriate level of detail, language, and format of communication to ensure that it resonates with each stakeholder group. Tailoring communication demonstrates respect for stakeholders' unique needs and perspectives, enhancing their engagement and understanding.

d. Timely and Frequent Communication: Timely and frequent communication is critical during periods of change. Regular updates and progress reports keep stakeholders informed about the status of the change initiative, address any concerns, and maintain a sense of momentum. Communication should be proactive, ensuring that stakeholders receive information promptly, minimizing uncertainties, and reducing the occurrence of rumors or misinformation.

e. Stakeholder Engagement: Effective stakeholder engagement involves actively involving and empowering stakeholders throughout the change process. Engaging stakeholders in decision-making, planning, and problem-solving cultivates a sense of ownership and commitment to the change initiative. Engaged stakeholders contribute their expertise, provide valuable insights, and become advocates for change. By involving stakeholders, managers can leverage their knowledge and support to drive successful change implementation.

f. Change Champions and Communication Networks: Change champions and communication networks are key aspects of communication and engagement in change management. Change champions are individuals who advocate for change, engage with stakeholders, and promote the benefits and rationale behind the change initiative. Communication networks, such as cross-functional teams or employee forums, provide platforms for information sharing and collaboration. These aspects help create a network of ambassadors who can disseminate information, address concerns, and maintain open lines of communication throughout the organization.

g. Continuous Communication Evaluation: Continuous evaluation of communication effectiveness is crucial in change management. Managers should regularly assess whether the communication methods and channels used are effective if the intended messages are being received and understood, and if any adjustments or improvements are needed. Feedback from stakeholders can help identify gaps, clarify misunderstandings, and guide necessary revisions to communication strategies. Continuous communication evaluation ensures that the change messages stay relevant, impactful, and responsive to stakeholder needs.

In summary, effective communication and engagement are critical aspects of change management. Clear and transparent communication, two-way communication, tailored communication, timely and frequent communication, stakeholder engagement, change champions, communication networks, and continuous communication evaluation are all vital components of facilitating successful change. By prioritizing these aspects, managers can build trust, involve stakeholders, address concerns, and effectively navigate the complexities of organizational change.

4. Change Planning and Implementation: This component involves developing a comprehensive change plan that outlines the specific actions, resources, and timeline required to implement the change. Change managers need to carefully plan each stage of the change process, including the sequencing of activities, identification of milestones, and allocation of responsibilities. Effective change management also involves providing support and resources to individuals and teams involved in the change, as well as monitoring and adjusting the plan as needed.

Change planning and implementation are the processes involved in developing and executing a well-structured and organized approach to managing and implementing a change initiative within an organization.

Change Planning:

a. Define the Change Objectives: The first step in change planning is to clearly define the objectives and desired outcomes of the change initiative. This involves identifying the reasons for change, outlining the specific goals to be achieved, and defining the expected benefits or improvements resulting from the change.

b. Conduct a Change Readiness Assessment: Before implementing any change, it is important to assess the organization's readiness for change. This involves evaluating factors such as the organization's culture, capacity for change, and the level of support from key stakeholders. The readiness assessment helps in identifying potential barriers and challenges that may impact the success of the change initiative.

c. Develop a Change Management Strategy: A change management strategy outlines the overall approach and activities required to implement the change successfully. It includes plans for communication, stakeholder engagement, training and development, and the allocation of resources. The strategy should align with the objectives of the change initiative and cater to the specific needs of the organization and its stakeholders.

d. Establish a Change Management Team: The change management team is responsible for driving and overseeing the change initiative. This team should consist of individuals with a diverse range of skills and expertise, including change management specialists, project managers, and representatives from different departments or functions within the organization. The team should be capable of coordinating and facilitating the change process effectively.

Change Implementation:

a. Communicate the Change: Effective communication is crucial during the implementation phase to ensure that all stakeholders are aware of the change, understand its purpose, and are informed about their role in the process. The communication should be consistent, transparent, and tailored to different stakeholder groups. It should address any concerns, provide regular updates, and highlight the benefits and progress of the change initiative.

b. Engage Stakeholders: Engaging stakeholders in the change process fosters a sense of ownership and encourages their active participation. Establishing clear channels for stakeholder feedback, involving them in decision-making, and providing opportunities for their input helps create a collaborative and supportive environment. Engaged stakeholders are more likely to embrace the change and contribute to its success.

c. Implement Training and Development Programs: Change often requires new skills and competencies. To ensure successful implementation, it is important to provide appropriate training and development programs to equip employees with the knowledge and skills they need to adapt to the change. Training programs should be designed to address specific gaps identified during the change readiness assessment and should be tailored to suit individual and team needs.

d. Monitor and Evaluate the Change: Continuous monitoring and evaluation of the change initiative are necessary to track progress, identify and address any issues, and adapt the implementation approach as needed. Regular assessment of key performance indicators (KPIs), feedback from stakeholders, and lessons learned contribute to ongoing improvement and refinement of the change initiative.

e. Sustain the Change and Embed it in the Culture: Change should not be seen as a one-time event but as an ongoing process. Efforts should be made to sustain the change and embed it into the organization's culture and practices. This involves reinforcing the behaviors and processes that support the change, providing ongoing support and resources, and celebrating the successes and achievements resulting from the change initiative.

In conclusion, change planning and implementation are vital components of change management. Effective change planning involves defining objectives, assessing readiness, developing a strategy, and establishing a change management team. Change implementation focuses on clear communication, stakeholder engagement, training, monitoring progress, and sustaining the change over time. By following a well-structured change planning and implementation process, organizations can increase the likelihood of successful and sustainable change.

5. Change Evaluation and Sustained Improvement: Evaluating the effectiveness of the change initiative is a crucial component of change management. This involves assessing whether the desired outcomes and benefits of the change have been achieved and identifying any areas for improvement. Feedback and evaluation from stakeholders help identify lessons learned and inform future change efforts. Sustained improvement involves integrating the change into the organization's culture and processes to ensure that the new ways of working are embedded and continuously improved upon.

Change evaluation and sustained improvement are essential aspects of general management that support organizational growth and success in the face of evolving challenges and opportunities.

a. Change Evaluation:

Change evaluation involves assessing the effectiveness and outcomes of the implemented change initiative. It helps determine if the desired objectives were achieved and identifies areas that require adjustment or further improvement. Evaluation methods may include surveys, interviews, performance metrics, and feedback analysis from stakeholders and employees. By evaluating the change initiative, managers can measure its impact, identify lessons learned, and gain insights to enhance future change efforts.

b. Lessons Learned and Knowledge Sharing:

Change evaluation provides an opportunity to capture lessons learned from the change process. This involves identifying both successful practices and areas for improvement. By documenting and sharing this knowledge across the organization, managers can facilitate organizational learning. Lessons learned help refine change management strategies and inform future decision-making, ensuring that mistakes are not repeated, and best practices are leveraged for sustained improvement.

c. Continuous Improvement:

Continuous improvement involves ongoing efforts to enhance processes, performance, and outcomes within the organization. The insights gained from change evaluation contribute to identifying areas for continuous improvement. Through regular review of systems, practices, and policies, managers can identify opportunities to optimize operations, reduce waste, increase efficiency, and enhance customer satisfaction. Continuous improvement ensures that the organization remains agile and responsive to evolving market demands and competitive pressures.

d. Feedback Loops and Employee Engagement:

Change evaluation creates opportunities to gather feedback from employees and stakeholders, facilitating ongoing engagement and involvement. Feedback loops enable employees to voice their opinions, contribute ideas, and provide input on areas that require improvement. This cultivates a culture of open communication and engagement, where employees feel valued and empowered. Engaged employees are more likely to generate innovative solutions, take ownership of change initiatives, and drive sustained improvement within their respective roles and functions.

e. Performance Management:

Change evaluation contributes to performance management by aligning individual and team objectives with broader organizational goals. It helps identify areas where employees may require additional support, training, or development opportunities. By linking change evaluation findings to performance management processes, managers can provide targeted feedback, coaching, and resources to enhance performance. This integration ensures that continuous improvement efforts are aligned with individual and team performance expectations.

f. Continuous Adaptation and Change:

Change evaluation also recognizes that change is a continuous process. It highlights the need for organizations to remain adaptable, responsive, and open to further change. Through ongoing evaluation and evaluation-driven improvement, organizations can proactively anticipate and respond to emerging challenges and opportunities. This adaptability supports long-term success in dynamic market conditions and enables the organization to build a culture of strategic flexibility and resilience.

In conclusion, change evaluation and sustained improvement are critical components of general management. They encompass assessing change outcomes, capturing lessons learned, and promoting continuous improvement. By leveraging change evaluation insights, organizations can foster employee engagement, drive performance management, and build a culture of continuous learning and adaptation. These aspects support long-term success, increase organizational agility, and enable the organization to remain agile and competitive in the face of evolving business landscapes.

In summary, the components of change management include identifying the need for change, conducting stakeholder analysis, engaging in effective communication and engagement, carefully planning and implementing change, and evaluating its impact. By effectively managing these components, organizations can increase the chances of successfully navigating change, minimizing resistance, and achieving the desired outcomes.

There are several change management frameworks or methodologies that provide a structured approach and specific components to guide organizations through the change process. One widely used framework is the ADKAR model, which stands for Awareness, Desire, Knowledge, Ability, and Reinforcement. Each component represents a crucial element in facilitating individual and organizational change.

1. Awareness: This component focuses on creating awareness and understanding of the need for change. It involves communicating the reasons, benefits, and urgency for the change throughout the organization. By increasing awareness, individuals can understand the rationale behind the change and begin to see the impact it will have on their work and the organization.

2. Desire: The desire component involves generating buy-in and motivation for the change. It is essential to create a shared vision and purpose that inspires individuals to embrace change. Communicating the benefits and opportunities that the change brings and addressing any concerns or resistance can help individuals develop the desire to actively participate in the change process.

3. Knowledge: This component focuses on equipping individuals with the necessary knowledge and information to successfully implement and adapt to the change. Training programs, educational resources, and clear communication channels are essential to provide individuals with the knowledge and skills required to perform effectively in the new environment.

4. Ability: The ability component involves supporting individuals as they acquire and apply the new skills and behaviors necessary for the change. It includes providing ongoing support, coaching, and resources to help individuals navigate the change process. Building a supportive environment where individuals feel safe and empowered to try new approaches is critical to enabling their ability to adapt successfully.

5. Reinforcement: The reinforcement component focuses on sustaining the change and embedding it into the culture and processes of the organization. This involves recognizing and celebrating successes, reinforcing new behaviors, and establishing mechanisms to monitor and reinforce the change over time. Ongoing reinforcement ensures that the change becomes deeply ingrained in the organization and does not revert to old ways of doing things.

Overall, the ADKAR model provides a holistic approach to change management by addressing the key components necessary for successful individual and organizational change. By systematically addressing awareness, desire, knowledge, ability, and reinforcement, organizations can increase the likelihood of successful change adoption and long-term sustainability.

Change management is a critical aspect of general management that should be incorporated into management studies for several reasons.

Firstly, change is inherent in today's dynamic business environment. Organizations constantly face internal and external disruptions that require them to adapt, innovate, and transform to stay competitive. Managers need to understand how to effectively manage and lead change initiatives to ensure the success and sustainability of their organizations. Incorporating change management in management studies prepares future managers for the challenges they will face in navigating change.

Secondly, successful change management directly impacts organizational performance and outcomes. Poorly managed or resisted change can lead to delays, cost overruns, decreased productivity, and ultimately, failure. By studying change management, managers gain insights into the strategies, tools, and techniques for effectively planning, implementing, and monitoring change initiatives. This knowledge equips managers with the skills to drive change in a way that minimizes resistance, maximizes employee engagement, and achieves successful outcomes.

Thirdly, change management focuses on people and organizational behavior. Understanding how people perceive and react to change is essential for effective leadership and management. By studying change management, managers learn about human psychology, motivation, and how to address resistance to change. This knowledge enables them to empathize with and support individuals during times of change, fostering a positive and inclusive work environment and enhancing employee satisfaction and productivity.

Fourthly, change management fosters innovation and adaptation. Effective change management encourages a culture of continuous improvement, creativity, and learning. By incorporating change management in management studies, future managers are exposed to theories, tools, and case studies that promote innovation and adaptation. This exposure encourages managers to proactively seek opportunities for change and improvement, leading to enhanced competitiveness and growth for their organizations.

Furthermore, change management enhances leaders' ability to navigate complexity and uncertainty. Change often involves complex systems, multiple stakeholders, and uncertain outcomes. By studying change management, managers learn about frameworks and approaches to effectively manage complexity, communicate with diverse stakeholders, and make informed decisions in ambiguous situations. These skills enable managers to navigate changing business environments with confidence and agility.

Lastly, change management fosters resilience and organizational agility. In today's rapidly changing business landscape, organizations need to be nimble and adaptive to survive and thrive. Studying change management equips managers with the knowledge and skills to build resilient organizations that can anticipate and respond to change effectively. Managers who understand change management can guide their organizations through turbulent times and position them for sustainable success.

In conclusion, incorporating change management into general management studies is crucial in preparing future managers for the challenges of a dynamic business environment. Understanding change management enables managers to drive successful change initiatives, enhance organizational performance, and foster a culture of continuous improvement and innovation. By studying change management, future managers can develop the necessary skills to lead with empathy, navigate complexity, and build resilient organizations that thrive in the face of change.

INTRODUCTION TO GORILLA MANAGEMENT AND MARKETING

Gorilla management is a term that refers to a strategy in marketing and business management that involves taking a bold and dominant approach to gain a competitive advantage. This strategy takes inspiration from the behavior of gorillas in the wild, as they use their strength and presence to establish dominance in their environment. In the business context, gorilla management focuses on standing out from competitors and capturing a significant market share.

In marketing, gorilla management emphasizes unique and attention-grabbing tactics that help a company gain visibility and brand recognition. This can include unconventional advertising campaigns, viral marketing, or guerrilla marketing techniques. The goal is to disrupt the market and create a strong brand presence that cannot be ignored. By adopting a gorilla management approach, businesses aim to create a lasting impression on consumers and differentiate themselves from competitors who may be following more traditional marketing methods.

In terms of management, gorilla management encourages leaders to take bold actions to drive growth and success. This involves making strategic decisions that challenge the status quo and push boundaries. Leaders adopting this management style are not afraid to take risks and make unconventional choices that have the potential to yield high rewards. This approach requires strong leadership skills, as well as the ability to inspire and motivate employees to align with the vision and goals of the organization.

Gorilla management also emphasizes the importance of innovation and constant adaptation. Companies adopting this approach understand that the business landscape is continuously evolving, and staying ahead of the competition requires agility and the ability to adapt to market changes. This mindset encourages businesses to continuously seek opportunities for improvement and growth.

However, it is important to note that gorilla management may not be suitable for all businesses or industries. It requires a deep understanding of the market, competitors, and the potential risks involved. Implementing gorilla management successfully requires careful planning, research, and a clear understanding of the target audience. Businesses must assess their resources and capabilities to determine if they can effectively execute this strategy without jeopardizing their brand reputation or financial stability.

In summary, gorilla management is a strategy that involves taking a bold and dominant approach to marketing and business management. It focuses on standing out from competitors, gaining market share, and creating a strong brand presence. This strategy requires innovative thinking, the ability to adapt to market changes and strong leadership skills. While it can be highly effective, businesses should carefully assess their capabilities and resources before implementing gorilla management to ensure its suitability for their specific situation.

Gorilla management and marketing involve several key components that contribute to the overall strategy. Here are some of the primary components:

1. Disruption and Unconventionality: Gorilla management and marketing emphasize a disruptive and unconventional approach. This component involves breaking away from traditional norms and finding unique and attention-grabbing ways to stand out in the market. It often involves adopting unconventional marketing tactics and strategies that challenge the status quo.

2. Bold Branding and Positioning: Gorilla management involves creating a bold and distinctive brand identity. This component focuses on developing a strong brand image that resonates with the target audience and differentiates the company from competitors. It may involve bold and memorable branding elements, such as logos, slogans, and visual identities, that capture attention and leave a lasting impression.

3. Innovative Marketing Tactics: Gorilla marketing employs innovative marketing tactics to capture the audience's attention and generate buzz. This component involves thinking creatively and developing unique campaigns or initiatives that go beyond traditional advertising methods. It may include guerilla marketing techniques, experiential marketing, viral campaigns, or leveraging social media platforms in unconventional ways.

4. Audience Engagement and Emotional Connection: Gorilla management acknowledges the importance of building genuine connections with the target audience. This component focuses on engaging the audience on an emotional level and creating meaningful interactions. It may involve storytelling, user-generated content, or creating experiences that elicit strong emotional responses, fostering brand loyalty and advocacy.

5. Agile and Nimble Adaptability: Gorilla management recognizes the need for agility and adaptability in a rapidly changing market. This component involves being agile and responsive to market shifts and consumer demands. It requires continuously monitoring industry trends, identifying opportunities, and making quick adjustments to strategies and tactics to stay ahead of the competition.

6. Risk-Taking and Calculated Risks: Gorilla management and marketing encourage calculated risk-taking. This component involves being willing to take bold actions that carry reasonable risks but offer the potential for significant rewards. It requires carefully assessing the potential benefits and evaluating the potential risks associated with a particular marketing campaign or management decision.

7. Strong Leadership and Vision: Gorilla management and marketing rely on strong leadership and a clear vision. This component emphasizes the importance of visionary leaders who can inspire their teams and drive bold initiatives. It requires leaders who can effectively communicate the vision, make strategic decisions, and provide the guidance necessary to execute the gorilla marketing and management strategy successfully.

In summary, the components of gorilla management and marketing include disruption and unconventionality, bold branding and positioning, innovative marketing tactics, audience engagement, and emotional connection, agile and nimble adaptability, risk-taking, strong leadership, and vision. Together, these components contribute to a strategic approach that aims to capture attention, differentiate oneself from competitors, and drive growth by challenging traditional industry norms.

Gorilla management and marketing are essential components in the study of business due to their ability to drive innovation, create competitive advantages, and generate significant brand awareness. Here are ten paragraphs explaining why gorilla management and marketing are crucial in the study of business:

1. Business Landscape: In today's highly competitive business landscape, standing out from the crowd is vital. Gorilla management and marketing enable companies to differentiate themselves from competitors by adopting unconventional approaches. This unconventional mindset can lead to breakthrough ideas and strategies that fuel growth and success.

2. Disruptive Innovation: Gorilla management and marketing encourage disruptive innovation. By challenging traditional business models and pushing boundaries, companies can identify new opportunities and develop innovative products or services. This enables businesses to stay ahead, adapt to changing customer needs, and drive industry disruption.

3. Enhanced Brand Awareness: Gorilla marketing is known for its ability to generate significant brand awareness. Through unconventional and attention-grabbing tactics, companies can make a lasting impact on consumers, leading to greater brand recognition and recall. This increased visibility can help businesses attract new customers and build loyalty among existing ones.

4. Engaging the Audience: Gorilla marketing focuses on engaging the audience on an emotional level. By creating memorable experiences and eliciting strong emotions, businesses can establish deeper connections with their target market. This emotional connection can lead to increased customer loyalty, advocacy, and word-of-mouth referrals.

5. Market Differentiation: Gorilla management and marketing provide businesses with a unique opportunity to differentiate themselves from competitors. By adopting disruptive strategies, companies can offer products or services that stand out in the market. This differentiation helps businesses capture the attention of consumers and carve out a distinct position in their respective industries.

6. Cost-Effective Strategies: Gorilla management and marketing often rely on creative and low-cost tactics. Rather than investing heavily in traditional advertising channels, businesses can leverage guerilla marketing, experiential campaigns, or social media to make a big impact with limited resources. This cost-effective approach is particularly beneficial for small and medium-sized enterprises looking to maximize their marketing budgets.

7. Agility and Adaptability: Gorilla management fosters a culture of agility and adaptability within organizations. By embracing unconventional thinking, businesses are better equipped to respond quickly to market changes and consumer demands. This allows businesses to adapt their strategies, products, and services to stay competitive and relevant in dynamic market environments.

8. Innovation and Creativity: Gorilla management and marketing thrive on innovation and creativity. In the study of business, fostering a culture that encourages innovative thinking is crucial for long-term success. By embracing gorilla management and marketing strategies, businesses can unlock their creative potential and generate groundbreaking ideas that drive growth and innovation.

9. Risk-Taking: Gorilla management encourages calculated risk-taking. In the business world, taking calculated risks is often necessary to seize opportunities and achieve significant breakthroughs. Through gorilla marketing and management, companies can challenge the status quo, experiment with new tactics, and take risks that have the potential for substantial rewards.

10. Leadership and Vision: Gorilla management and marketing require strong leadership and a clear vision. Successful gorilla strategies rely on leaders who can inspire and guide their teams toward unconventional and ambitious goals. By studying and applying gorilla management and marketing, aspiring business leaders can develop the skills necessary to drive their organizations to new levels of success.

In conclusion, gorilla management and marketing are important subjects in the study of business as they offer a strategic approach to drive innovation, differentiate from competitors, create brand awareness, and build meaningful connections with customers. By embracing unconventional thinking, businesses can position themselves at the forefront of their industries and adapt rapidly to ever-changing market demands. The principles of gorilla management and marketing provide valuable insights and tools that can help businesses thrive in today's highly competitive and dynamic business landscape.

Gorilla management, which refers to the effective and strategic management of dominant players or leading companies in a particular industry, has become crucial in building investor confidence and attracting new customers. This is due to several reasons that highlight the impact that gorilla companies can have on the market and overall industry dynamics.

Firstly, gorilla companies often set the tone for the entire industry. Their actions and decisions have a significant influence on market trends, pricing strategies, and technological advancements. Investors are aware of this power and closely monitor the gorilla's management approach. If the gorilla company is well-managed, with a strong leadership team and a clear vision, it signals stability and potential growth opportunities for investors. On the other hand, poor management can lead to unpredictable market changes and potential losses, discouraging investors and customers alike.

Secondly, gorilla management plays a vital role in creating a competitive environment. Effective management ensures fair and ethical practices, preventing the abuse of dominant market positions. When investors observe strong governance and adherence to regulations, they are more likely to trust and invest in the industry. Customers, too, are attracted to industries where the leading players are perceived as trustworthy and committed to quality, which is essential for repeat business and positive brand perception.

Moreover, gorilla management plays a crucial role in fostering innovation and attracting new customers. A well-managed gorilla company invests in research and development, pushing the boundaries of what is possible in the industry. This not only attracts investors looking for long-term growth but also entices customers who seek cutting-edge products or services. Innovation by the gorilla sets the standard for the industry, encouraging other companies to follow suit and invest in research and development to remain competitive.

Additionally, the way gorilla companies manage their relationships with suppliers and partners impacts investor confidence and customer loyalty. If a gorilla company implements fair trading practices, builds strong and sustainable partnerships, and supports the growth of other players in the industry, it creates a positive ripple effect. Investors see this as a sign of responsible management and increased collaboration, which can lead to improved profitability and industry stability. Furthermore, customers appreciate companies that value and support their partners, often choosing to associate themselves with such brands.

Lastly, gorilla management also plays a role in shaping public perception and values associated with the industry. When a gorilla company displays responsible management practices, such as sustainability efforts and corporate social responsibility initiatives, it can attract socially conscious investors and customers. Patrons are more likely to support companies that align with their values, contributing to increased market share and investor confidence.

In conclusion, effective gorilla management has become an important factor in building investor confidence and attracting new customers due to its influence on the industry, fair practices, innovation, partnerships, and public perception. Investors and customers alike closely observe the management approach of the leading players and make decisions based on their perception of the company's stability, growth potential, and ethical practices. Therefore, companies aiming to attract investors and expand their customer base must prioritize gorilla management to establish themselves as leading players in the market.

Facilitating successful business practices in gorilla management requires a thorough understanding of the components that contribute to effective leadership and market dominance. These components include strategic planning, competitive analysis, talent management, innovation, customer-centricity, adaptability, resource allocation, and ethical decision-making.

Firstly, strategic planning is essential for gorilla management. The organization must have a clear vision and strategic objectives to guide its actions toward market dominance. This involves analyzing market trends, identifying opportunities for growth and expansion, and developing strategies to achieve a competitive advantage. Strategic planning allows the organization to make informed decisions regarding investments, partnerships, and market positioning.

Secondly, competitive analysis is crucial in gorilla management. Understanding the competitive landscape and staying one step ahead of rivals is essential for maintaining market dominance. Organizations should conduct thorough competitor analysis to identify their strengths, weaknesses, and strategies. This knowledge helps in positioning the organization and developing effective marketing and differentiation strategies.

Talent management is another critical component of successful gorilla management. Leading organizations invest in attracting, developing, and retaining top talent. They focus on building a strong leadership team and providing ongoing training and development opportunities for employees. Having a highly skilled and motivated workforce is crucial for driving innovation, customer satisfaction, and overall business success.

Innovation is a key driver of gorilla management. Organizations need to continuously innovate and adapt to changing market dynamics to maintain their dominant position. They must invest in research and development, foster a culture of innovation, and embrace new technologies and trends. This ensures that the organization remains at the forefront of industry advancements and meets customer expectations.

Customer-centricity is another important aspect of successful gorilla management. Organizations must prioritize understanding and meeting customer needs and preferences. This involves gathering customer feedback, conducting market research, and continuously improving products, services, and customer experiences. By focusing on customer satisfaction and loyalty, gorilla companies can strengthen their market dominance and attract new customers.

Adaptability is crucial for organizations seeking to adapt to a global gorilla culture. They must be open to change and flexible in their approach. This includes being willing to enter new markets, form partnerships, and adapt products or services to suit different cultural and regulatory environments. Organizations must be quick to respond to market shifts and capable of leveraging global opportunities effectively.

Effective resource allocation is a critical component of gorilla management. Organizations must allocate their resources strategically, focusing on areas that drive growth and market dominance. This involves making informed decisions about investments, research and development, marketing and advertising, and operational efficiency. Resource allocation should align with the organization's strategic objectives and the evolving market dynamics.

Lastly, ethical decision-making is fundamental for successful gorilla management. Organizations must adhere to high ethical standards to maintain the trust and confidence of investors, customers, and stakeholders. This includes transparency in financial reporting, fair trading practices, and social responsibility initiatives. Ethical behavior contributes to a positive brand image, enhances customer loyalty, and attracts socially conscious investors.

To adapt to a global gorilla culture, organizations must embrace cultural diversity and be sensitive to local customs and norms. This involves hiring diverse talent, providing cross-cultural training, and adapting business practices to suit different markets. Organizations should also establish strong networks and partnerships globally to facilitate international growth and market dominance. By embracing the global gorilla culture, organizations can expand their reach, leverage diverse perspectives, and capitalize on opportunities in different regions.

In conclusion, facilitating successful business practices in gorilla management requires attention to key components such as strategic planning, competitive analysis, talent management, innovation, customer-centricity, adaptability, resource allocation, and ethical decision-making. Organizations that prioritize these components can adapt to a global gorilla culture by embracing cultural diversity, being open to change, and employing effective resource allocation strategies. By adopting these practices, organizations can position themselves as dominant players in the market and drive long-term success.

Gorilla management and ordinary management differ in several key aspects, including their focus, strategies, market dominance, decision-making process, and impact on industry dynamics.

Firstly, the focus of gorilla management is centered around maintaining and expanding market dominance. Gorilla companies are industry leaders who hold a dominant position in the market and possess significant market share. The primary objective of gorilla management is to protect and enhance this dominant position. On the other hand, ordinary management focuses on day-to-day operations and achieving organizational goals without necessarily aiming for market dominance.

Secondly, the strategies employed in gorilla management differ from those used in ordinary management. Gorilla companies often implement aggressive strategies to solidify their dominant position and prevent competitors from gaining market share. This can include tactics like predatory pricing, acquiring competitors, or patenting essential technologies. Ordinary management, on the other hand, generally focuses on maintaining stability, improving efficiency, and delivering value to customers without aggressive tactics aimed at market control.

Furthermore, the level of market dominance sets gorilla management apart from ordinary management. Gorilla companies are dominant players in their industries, often holding a significant market share and exerting considerable influence over market dynamics. Their success is based on their ability to set industry standards, shape market trends, and command pricing power. In contrast, ordinary management typically focuses on establishing the organization in the market, without necessarily attaining a dominant position.

The decision-making process also differs between gorilla management and ordinary management. Gorilla management is often driven by a long-term perspective, with decisions geared toward maintaining market dominance and long-term growth. These decisions involve assessing industry trends, identifying new opportunities, and formulating strategies to outpace competitors. Ordinary management, on the other hand, tends to focus on day-to-day operational decisions, short-term goal achievement, and maintaining stability.

Moreover, gorilla management has a significant impact on industry dynamics and competition. Gorilla companies shape industry behavior, set standards, and influence market trends. Their actions can have a ripple effect on competitors and the overall industry ecosystem. In contrast, ordinary management generally has a more localized impact, focusing on internal operations and customer satisfaction without exerting widespread influence.

In conclusion, gorilla management and ordinary management differ in their focus, strategies, level of market dominance, decision-making process, and impact on industry dynamics. Gorilla management aims to maintain and expand market dominance through aggressive tactics, while ordinary management focuses on day-to-day operations and organizational goals. Gorilla management's decisions are driven by long-term perspectives, while ordinary management focuses on short-term objectives. Gorilla management has a significant impact on the industry, whereas ordinary management tends to have a localized influence. Understanding these differences is crucial for organizations to determine the most suitable management approach based on their goals and market position.

Gorilla management is a comprehensive approach to improving organizations in third-world countries by focusing on key areas such as leadership development, performance management, employee engagement, talent acquisition, and strategic planning. By implementing gorilla management practices, organizations can address the unique challenges they face and foster sustainable growth. Here are six reasons why gorilla management should be implemented to improve organizations in third-world countries:

Firstly, gorilla management emphasizes strong leadership development. In many third-world countries, organizations suffer from weak leadership, which leads to inefficiency and lack of direction. By investing in leadership development programs, organizations can cultivate strong leaders with the necessary skills to guide their teams and make effective decisions.

Secondly, gorilla management focuses on effective performance management practices. Implementing clear performance metrics and establishing regular performance reviews ensures that employees are held accountable for their work. This drives productivity and enables organizations to identify and address areas that need improvement, ultimately leading to better overall performance.

Thirdly, gorilla management promotes employee engagement. Engaged employees are committed to their work, motivated to give their best, and take ownership of their responsibilities. This improves productivity and fosters a positive work culture conducive to growth and success.

Additionally, gorilla management emphasizes talent acquisition and development. Organizations in third-world countries often struggle to attract and retain skilled employees due to various factors such as limited resources and competition from better-established organizations. Implementing gorilla management practices enables organizations to identify potential talents, provide necessary training, and create growth opportunities, thus attracting and retaining quality employees.

Moreover, gorilla management focuses on strategic planning. Many organizations in third-world countries face challenges such as limited resources, economic instability, and political uncertainty. By implementing gorilla management practices, organizations can develop robust strategic plans that take into account these unique challenges and adapt to the changing environment, enabling them to thrive in difficult circumstances.

Lastly, gorilla management emphasizes the importance of continuous improvement and innovation. By promoting a culture of learning and encouraging employees to think creatively, organizations can identify opportunities for growth and implement innovative solutions to address complex problems.

In conclusion, implementing gorilla management practices in organizations in third-world countries can lead to significant improvements in leadership, performance, employee engagement, talent development, strategic planning, and innovation. By addressing the unique challenges these organizations face, gorilla management provides a comprehensive approach to foster sustainable growth and help organizations overcome barriers within their environment.

Apart from gorilla management, some other related branches and practices can be combined with marketing strategies to enhance organizational success. Two notable branches include guerilla marketing and gorilla marketing.

1. Guerilla Marketing: Guerilla marketing is a creative and unconventional approach to marketing that focuses on low-cost, unconventional strategies to create maximum impact. It involves using unconventional methods and ideas that capture people's attention and generate buzz about a product or brand. Guerilla marketing often involves street-level marketing tactics, public stunts, viral campaigns, and grassroots efforts. By thinking outside the box and leveraging unconventional marketing techniques, organizations can effectively reach their target audience and create a memorable brand experience.

2. Gorilla Marketing: Gorilla marketing is a term coined by Jay Conrad Levinson, which focuses on creating a powerful marketing impact with minimal resources. It involves leveraging creativity, innovation, and strategic thinking to maximize marketing efforts while minimizing costs. Gorilla marketing is about finding unique ways to engage audiences, build brand awareness, and generate sales through unconventional marketing methods. It emphasizes leveraging technology, social media, and grassroots efforts to stand out from the competition and create a strong brand presence.

Both guerilla marketing and gorilla marketing share common principles, such as creativity, innovation, and the ability to create a buzz. While guerilla marketing is more focused on unconventional tactics to capture attention, gorilla marketing is about obtaining maximum results with minimal resources and creating a strong marketing impact. Both practices can be combined with effective marketing strategies to reach and engage the target audience cost-effectively and memorably.

Jay Conrad Levinson coined the term "guerrilla marketing" in his book, "Guerrilla Marketing: Easy and Inexpensive Strategies for Making Big Profits from Your Small Business." While he did not specifically coin the term "gorilla management," it is possible that you are referring to the concept of "guerrilla management" or a similar concept that emphasizes unconventional and creative approaches to management.

In Guerrilla Marketing, Levinson emphasizes the importance of implementing unconventional marketing strategies that are cost-effective, creative, and focused on making a big impact with limited resources. Applying this concept to management, "gorilla management" could imply a similar approach where managers adopt unconventional and innovative strategies to lead their teams and achieve organizational goals.

The concept of "gorilla management" could involve challenging traditional management practices, thinking outside the box, and finding creative solutions to problems. It may entail leveraging the strengths and talents within the team, identifying unique opportunities, and adapting quickly to changes in the business environment.

Ultimately, while the term "gorilla management" may not be directly attributable to Jay Conrad Levinson or his work on guerrilla marketing, it aligns with the general concept of thinking creatively and unconventionally in management, much like guerrilla marketing encourages businesses to think creatively and unconventionally in their marketing efforts.

By implementing guerilla marketing and gorilla marketing techniques, organizations can differentiate themselves from competitors, create memorable brand experiences, and generate buzz around their products or services. These practices can be particularly beneficial for organizations operating in third-world countries, where limited resources and budget constraints often require innovative and creative marketing approaches to maximize impact.

The role of a gorilla manager in an organization is multifaceted and critical to its success. A gorilla manager is a leader who adopts a comprehensive and strategic approach to management, considering the unique challenges and opportunities faced by the organization. They are proactive, innovative, and focused on driving growth, efficiency, and employee engagement. In this article, we will dive deep into the role of a gorilla manager, exploring their responsibilities, skills, and key traits that contribute to organizational success.

1. Leadership and Vision:

A gorilla manager is responsible for setting a clear vision for the organization and providing effective leadership to achieve it. They must inspire and motivate employees, creating a strong sense of purpose and direction. A gorilla manager leads by example, demonstrating integrity, transparency, and commitment, which helps build trust and loyalty among the team.

2. Strategic Planning:

A gorilla manager is skilled in strategic planning, which involves analyzing the organization's strengths, weaknesses, opportunities, and threats. They develop action plans, set goals, and create strategies to navigate challenges and seize opportunities. A gorilla manager ensures the organization is adaptable and agile, capable of responding to changes in the market and industry.

3. Performance Management:

Effective performance management is a crucial aspect of a gorilla manager's role. They establish clear performance metrics and expectations for employees, regularly reviewing and providing feedback on their performance. A gorilla manager identifies areas for improvement and provides support and resources to help employees excel. They also acknowledge and reward exceptional performance, promoting a culture of excellence and continuous improvement.

4. Employee Engagement and Development:

A gorilla manager understands the importance of engaged and skillful employees. They prioritize employee engagement strategies, such as fostering a positive work environment, providing opportunities for professional and personal growth, and ensuring work-life balance. A gorilla manager invests in training and development programs, encouraging employees to enhance their skills and contribute their fullest potential to the organization.

5. Talent Acquisition and Retention:

Recruiting and retaining talented individuals is crucial for organizational success. A gorilla manager plays a vital role in talent acquisition by ensuring effective recruitment processes, developing employer branding, and cultivating relationships with potential candidates. They assess the needs of the organization and strategically attract and retain top talent, ensuring teams are well-equipped to achieve organizational objectives.

6. Communication and Collaboration:

A gorilla manager excels in communication and collaboration, both within the organization and with external stakeholders. They facilitate effective communication channels, ensuring information is shared efficiently, and goals are understood by all. A gorilla manager fosters collaboration and teamwork, breaking down silos and encouraging cross-functional cooperation to achieve desired outcomes.

7. Change Management:

In today's dynamic business landscape, adaptability and change management are vital. A gorilla manager is skilled in implementing and managing change initiatives within the organization. They communicate changes effectively, address concerns and resistance, and guide employees through the transition. A gorilla manager ensures that changes are integrated smoothly, minimizing disruption and maximizing the organization's ability to seize new opportunities.

8. Innovation and Creativity:

A gorilla manager embraces innovation and creativity, encouraging employees to think outside the box and come up with innovative solutions. They create an environment that values ideas and experimentation, fostering a culture of innovation within the organization. A gorilla manager stays updated with industry trends, emerging technologies, and best practices, leveraging them to drive organizational growth and maintain a competitive edge.

9. Risk Management:

Risk management is a critical responsibility of a gorilla manager. They identify potential risks, both internal and external, and develop strategies to mitigate them. A gorilla manager ensures compliance with legal and ethical standards, establishes effective crisis management protocols, and anticipates potential challenges and their impact on the organization's operations.

10. Continuous Improvement:

A gorilla manager is committed to continuous improvement. They analyze organizational processes, identify inefficiencies, and implement measures to enhance productivity and streamline operations. A gorilla manager encourages a culture of learning and innovation, promoting the adoption of best practices and seeking ways to optimize the use of resources.

In conclusion, the role of a gorilla manager in an organization is pivotal in driving growth, ensuring efficiency, and fostering employee engagement. They provide strong leadership, develop strategic plans, and manage organizational performance. A gorilla manager is adept at talent acquisition and retention, communication, collaboration, change management, innovation, risk management, and continuous improvement. By effectively fulfilling these responsibilities, a gorilla manager plays a vital role in improving organizations and leading them toward long-term success.

PROMOTING DIVERSITY AND ADAPTABILITY IN AN ORGANIZATION

Promoting diversity and adaptability within an organization is essential in today's global and rapidly changing business environment. A gorilla manager has a crucial role to play in fostering a diverse and adaptable workforce. Here are some key responsibilities and actions a gorilla manager should take to promote diversity and adaptability within their organization:

1. Embrace Diversity as a Core Value:

A gorilla manager should recognize and embrace diversity as a core value of the organization. They should actively promote an inclusive work environment where individuals from diverse backgrounds feel welcome, respected, and valued. This includes embracing diversity in terms of race, ethnicity, gender, age, sexual orientation, disability, and other dimensions of diversity.

2. Recruit and Retain Diverse Talent:

A gorilla manager should make a concerted effort to recruit and retain diverse talent. They should implement inclusive hiring practices and ensure diverse candidates have equal opportunities to join the organization. Creating a diverse workforce brings a variety of perspectives, experiences, and ideas, which can contribute to innovation, problem-solving, and overall business success.

3. Foster a Culture of Inclusion:

A gorilla manager should proactively foster a culture of inclusion within the organization. This involves promoting open communication, collaboration, and respect among employees. They should encourage employees to share their ideas, perspectives, and concerns without fear of discrimination or reprisal. A gorilla manager should also address any bias or discriminatory behaviors promptly and effectively.

4. Provide Diversity and Inclusion Training:

To promote diversity and adaptability, a gorilla manager should provide training and development programs on diversity and inclusion. These programs can educate employees about the importance of diversity and equip them with skills to work effectively in diverse teams. Training should address unconscious bias, cultural competency, effective communication, and inclusive leadership.

5. Encourage Cross-Cultural Collaboration:

A gorilla manager should encourage and facilitate cross-cultural collaboration and teamwork. They should create opportunities for employees from different backgrounds to work together on projects, exchange ideas, and learn from each other. This can enhance adaptability by fostering a culture of learning, flexibility, and openness to different perspectives and approaches.

6. Support Employee Resource Groups:

Employee resource groups (ERGs) can play a significant role in promoting diversity and inclusivity. A gorilla manager should support and empower ERGs within the organization. ERGs provide a platform for employees with shared backgrounds or interests to connect, share experiences, and advocate for diversity and inclusion. A gorilla manager should actively engage with ERGs, listen to their concerns, and incorporate their insights into decision-making processes.

7. Encourage Continuous Learning and Development:

A gorilla manager should encourage continuous learning and development for all employees. They should support initiatives like mentoring programs, coaching, and career development opportunities. This helps employees adapt to changing business and industry trends while fostering an inclusive learning culture.

8. Lead by Example:

A gorilla manager should lead by example and demonstrate inclusive behaviors and attitudes. They should promote diversity and adaptability through their actions, decisions, and interactions with employees. By modeling inclusive leadership, a gorilla manager can inspire and empower others to embrace diversity and adapt to new situations.

9. Create Flexible Work Policies:

To promote adaptability, a gorilla manager should create flexible work policies that accommodate diverse employee needs. This may include supporting flexible work hours, remote work options, job sharing, and family-friendly policies. Flexibility allows employees to balance their work and personal responsibilities effectively, leading to increased job satisfaction and productivity.

10. Measure and Track Diversity and Inclusion Progress:

A gorilla manager should measure and track the organization's progress in promoting diversity and inclusion. They should set measurable goals and regularly assess the representation and inclusion of diverse employees at all levels of the organization. This data can help identify areas for improvement and guide future strategies and initiatives.

In conclusion, a gorilla manager plays a crucial role in promoting diversity and adaptability within their organization. By embracing diversity, creating an inclusive culture, supporting diverse talent, and fostering adaptability through various initiatives, a gorilla manager can create a diverse and adaptable workforce that is better equipped to navigate challenges, seize opportunities, and drive organizational success in an ever-changing business landscape.

Conflict resolution is a crucial skill to possess. Conflicts can arise in any organization, and effectively managing them is essential for maintaining a positive work environment and achieving organizational goals. Here is the rationale a gorilla manager should use in conflict resolution:

1. Understanding the Root Cause:

A gorilla manager should take the time to understand the root cause of the conflict by engaging in active listening and gathering relevant information. This entails allowing both sides to express their perspectives and concerns openly and honestly. By understanding the underlying issues, a gorilla manager can address the root cause, rather than merely treating the symptoms of the conflict.

2. Maintaining Objectivity:

A gorilla manager should approach conflict resolution with objectivity and impartiality. They should refrain from taking sides, personal biases, or favoritism. By maintaining objectivity, a gorilla manager can effectively assess the situation, evaluate the information gathered, and make fair and unbiased decisions.

3. Promoting Effective Communication:

Communication is key in conflict resolution. A gorilla manager should encourage open and respectful communication between the parties involved. They should promote active listening, empathy, and constructive dialogue. As a mediator, a gorilla manager can help clarify misunderstandings, facilitate compromise, and promote understanding between conflicting parties.

4. Seeking Win-Win Solutions:

A gorilla manager should aim to find win-win solutions that address the needs and concerns of both parties involved in the conflict. This involves exploring different options, considering alternative perspectives, and finding common ground. By finding mutually beneficial solutions, a gorilla manager can foster a sense of collaboration and cooperation, leading to long-term resolution and positive outcomes.

5. Encouraging Growth and Learning:

Conflict resolution presents an opportunity for growth and learning within the organization. A gorilla manager should view conflicts as a chance to identify areas for improvement and implement necessary changes. They should encourage reflection, self-awareness, and a commitment to learning from past conflicts. By promoting a growth mindset, a gorilla manager can help cultivate a culture of continuous improvement and organizational development.

In conclusion, a gorilla manager should approach conflict resolution with a rationale that includes understanding the root cause, maintaining objectivity, promoting effective communication, seeking win-win solutions, and encouraging growth and learning. By employing these strategies, a gorilla manager can effectively resolve conflicts, foster a positive work environment, and contribute to the overall success of the organization.

Innovation and disruptions are crucial in today's dynamic business landscape. As a gorilla manager, taking immediate steps to foster innovation and effectively manage disruptions is essential for organizational success. Here are seven important steps a gorilla manager should take in the process of innovation and disruptions:

1. Foster a Culture of Innovation:

To promote innovation, a gorilla manager should foster a culture where creativity, experimentation, and risk-taking are encouraged and embraced. They should create an environment that values new ideas, rewards innovative thinking, and encourages employees to think outside the box. This can be done by providing resources, allocating time for brainstorming sessions, and promoting cross-functional collaboration.

2. Identify Emerging Trends and Technologies:

A gorilla manager should proactively monitor and identify emerging trends and technologies that could disrupt the industry or provide opportunities for innovation. This involves staying updated with market research, attending industry conferences, and keeping a pulse on customer expectations. By recognizing potential disruptions early, a gorilla manager can position the organization to adapt and leverage these changes.

3. Encourage a Continuous Learning Mindset:

A gorilla manager should promote a continuous learning mindset within the organization. This includes encouraging employees to enhance their skills, explore new technologies, and stay updated with industry advancements. Offering training programs, access to educational resources, and creating opportunities for employees to learn from each other can foster a culture of continuous learning and adaptability.

4. Embrace Agile Methodologies:

Agile methodologies, such as Scrum or Lean Startup, can help organizations rapidly innovate and respond to disruptions. A gorilla manager should familiarize themselves with these methodologies and implement them in relevant departments or projects. Agile methodologies promote iterative development, quick feedback loops, and adaptability, enabling organizations to innovate and respond to disruptions more rapidly.

5. Encourage Idea Generation and Collaboration:

A gorilla manager should actively encourage employees to generate and share innovative ideas. They can establish forums or platforms for idea generation and collaboration, such as innovation workshops, idea boards, or online idea suggestion systems. By involving employees at all levels of the organization in the innovation process, a gorilla manager can tap into a diverse range of perspectives and insights.

6. Provide Resources and Support:

Innovation requires resources and support. A gorilla manager should allocate budget, time, and resources to support innovation initiatives. This may include investing in research and development, providing access to specialized tools or technologies, and granting employees the autonomy and flexibility to explore and experiment with their ideas.

7. Manage Risk and Uncertainty:

Disruptions often bring uncertainty and risks. A gorilla manager should assess and manage these risks effectively. This involves conducting risk assessments, developing contingency plans, and being prepared to pivot if necessary. A gorilla manager should create an environment where calculated risks are encouraged, and failure is seen as an opportunity for learning and growth.

In conclusion, a gorilla manager should take immediate steps to foster innovation and manage disruptions effectively. This includes fostering a culture of innovation, identifying emerging trends and technologies, encouraging a continuous learning mindset, embracing agile methodologies, promoting idea generation and collaboration, providing resources and support, and managing risk and uncertainty. By taking these steps, a gorilla manager can position the organization to thrive amidst disruptions and drive continuous innovation.

Conflict resolution at the managerial level in a gorilla management organization is critical for maintaining a positive work environment and ensuring the smooth functioning of the organization. Here are six key steps to effective conflict resolution:

1. Recognize and Identify the Conflict:

As a gorilla manager, it is essential to actively recognize and identify conflicts at the managerial level. This requires paying attention to signs of tension, communication breakdowns, or unresolved differences among team members. By promptly recognizing conflicts, a gorilla manager can intervene early and prevent them from escalating.

2. Encourage Open Communication:

A gorilla manager should create a safe and supportive environment that encourages open communication among team members. This involves providing a platform for individuals to express their concerns, frustrations, and perspectives without fear of judgment or retribution. Active listening and empathy play a crucial role in understanding the underlying issues and finding common ground among conflicting parties.

3. Facilitate Mediation and Negotiation:

As a gorilla manager, it is important to act as a mediator or facilitator when conflicts arise. This involves bringing conflicting parties together and guiding them through a structured negotiation process. A gorilla manager should ensure that all parties have an equal opportunity to express their viewpoints, address their needs, and work toward mutually beneficial solutions.

4. Foster Collaboration and Compromise:

A gorilla manager should encourage collaboration and compromise among conflicting parties. This may involve identifying shared goals or interests and finding ways to align individual objectives with broader organizational objectives. By fostering a collaborative mindset, a gorilla manager can encourage team members to look beyond their differences and focus on finding win-win solutions.

5. Encourage Emotional Intelligence and Empathy:

Emotional intelligence is an essential skill for conflict resolution at the managerial level. A gorilla manager should encourage team members to develop emotional intelligence, which involves recognizing and managing emotions effectively. Additionally, fostering empathy plays a crucial role in understanding different perspectives and finding common ground. By promoting emotional intelligence and empathy, a gorilla manager can create a harmonious work environment and improve interpersonal relationships.

6. Establish Clear Conflict Resolution Policies:

A gorilla manager should establish clear conflict resolution policies and procedures at the managerial level. This includes defining the steps to be taken when conflicts arise, providing guidelines for communication and negotiation, and outlining potential consequences for unresolved conflicts. By establishing clear policies, a gorilla manager sends a message that conflicts will be addressed promptly and fairly, fostering a culture of accountability and resolution.

In conclusion, effective conflict resolution at the managerial level in a gorilla management organization requires recognizing conflicts, encouraging open communication, facilitating mediation and negotiation, fostering collaboration and compromise, promoting emotional intelligence and empathy, and establishing clear conflict resolution policies. By following these steps, a gorilla manager can address conflicts successfully, improve team dynamics, and create a harmonious work environment conducive to organizational success.

A gorilla manager holds positive aspirations that contribute to the overall success and growth of the organization. Some of these positive aspirations include:

1. Inspiring and Motivating Employees:

A gorilla manager aspires to inspire and motivate their employees. They aim to create a positive work environment that encourages innovation, creativity, and collaboration. By fostering a sense of purpose and providing meaningful feedback and recognition, a gorilla manager inspires employees to give their best and achieve their full potential.

2. Driving Organizational Growth:

A gorilla manager aspires to drive organizational growth by identifying opportunities, exploring new markets, and developing innovative strategies. They aim to set challenging goals and provide the necessary resources and support to help the organization achieve sustainable growth and stay ahead of the competition.

3. Fostering a Culture of Excellence:

A gorilla manager aspires to foster a culture of excellence within the organization. They encourage continuous learning and improvement, provide opportunities for professional development, and set high standards for performance. By inspiring a commitment to excellence, a gorilla manager helps build a strong and competitive organization.

4. Promoting Diversity and Inclusion:

A gorilla manager aspires to promote diversity and inclusion throughout the organization. They understand the value of a diverse workforce in driving innovation, creativity, and problem-solving capabilities. By fostering an inclusive culture that embraces different perspectives and backgrounds, a gorilla manager creates a harmonious and equitable workplace.

5. Encouraging Work-Life Balance:

A gorilla manager aspires to create a work environment that enables employees to maintain a healthy work-life balance. They promote flexible work arrangements, recognize the importance of personal well-being, and provide opportunities for employees to recharge and rejuvenate. By encouraging work-life balance, a gorilla manager helps foster employee well-being and improve productivity.

6. Building Strong Relationships:

A gorilla manager aspires to build strong relationships within the organization and with external stakeholders. They prioritize effective communication, trust, and collaboration. By developing positive relationships, a gorilla manager nurtures a supportive and cooperative work environment, enhancing teamwork and overall organizational success.

7. Embracing Continuous Innovation:

A gorilla manager aspires to embrace continuous innovation and creativity. They encourage employees to think outside the box, experiment with new ideas, and challenge the status quo. By fostering a culture of innovation, a gorilla manager drives the organization to evolve, adapt, and stay ahead in a rapidly changing business landscape.

In summary, a gorilla manager has positive aspirations that focus on inspiring and motivating employees, driving organizational growth, fostering a culture of excellence, promoting diversity and inclusion, encouraging work-life balance, building strong relationships, and embracing continuous innovation. These aspirations contribute to creating a thriving organization that adapts to change, attracts top talent, and achieves long-term success.

A hard-core gorilla manager may have high expectations from employees and stakeholders to achieve organizational goals and maintain a competitive edge. Here are some expectations a hard-core gorilla manager may have:

1. Dedication and Commitment:

A hard-core gorilla manager expects employees and stakeholders to be dedicated and committed to their work and the organization's mission. This includes being willing to go the extra mile, demonstrating a strong work ethic, and taking ownership of their responsibilities.

2. Accountability and Results-Orientation:

A hard-core gorilla manager expects employees and stakeholders to take ownership of their actions and be accountable for their performance and the outcomes they deliver. They prioritize a results-oriented mindset, expecting individuals to set challenging goals, measure progress, and take responsibility for achieving desired outcomes.

3. High Standards of Performance:

A hard-core gorilla manager expects employees and stakeholders to uphold high standards of performance. They demand excellence, expecting individuals to continuously improve their skills, deliver quality work, and strive for personal and professional growth. They value a culture of excellence and expect individuals to meet or exceed set expectations.

4. Adaptability and Resilience:

In a constantly evolving business environment, a hard-core gorilla manager expects employees and stakeholders to be adaptable and resilient. They value individuals who can embrace change, respond effectively to challenges, and find innovative solutions. A hard-core gorilla manager expects individuals to overcome obstacles and setbacks with determination and a solution-oriented mindset.

5. Effective Communication and Collaboration:

A hard-core gorilla manager values effective communication and collaboration. They expect employees and stakeholders to communicate, openly, and respectfully. They emphasize the importance of teamwork and collaboration, expecting individuals to work with others towards shared goals, share knowledge and insights, and resolve conflicts constructively.

6. Initiative and Proactivity:

A hard-core gorilla manager expects individuals to take initiative and be proactive in identifying and seizing opportunities. They value employees and stakeholders who show a sense of urgency, take calculated risks, and contribute ideas and solutions that drive the organization forward.

7. Stakeholder Engagement and Customer Focus:

A hard-core gorilla manager highly regards stakeholder engagement and a customer-focused approach. They expect individuals to understand and prioritize the needs and expectations of stakeholders, including customers, and to deliver exceptional products, services, and experiences.

8. Ethical Conduct and Integrity:

A hard-core gorilla manager expects employees and stakeholders to uphold a high level of ethical conduct and integrity. They value honesty, trustworthiness, and adherence to ethical standards. They expect individuals to act with integrity in all professional interactions and decisions.

In conclusion, a hard-core gorilla manager expects dedication, accountability, high-performance standards, adaptability, effective communication, initiative, stakeholder engagement, and ethical conduct from employees and stakeholders. By setting high expectations, a hard-core gorilla manager aims to drive excellence, achieve organizational goals, and ensure the overall success of the organization.

Managing a Pandemic Using Information Systems

To The Reader

Welcome to this introductory note on managing a pandemic using information systems. In times of global crises, we are faced with numerous challenges that demand innovative solutions and effective management. The outbreak of a pandemic, such as the recent COVID-19, has had a profound impact on societies worldwide, causing widespread disruption to healthcare, economies, and social fabric. However, harnessing the power of information systems has proven to be a vital tool in managing and mitigating the effects of a pandemic.

Information systems refer to the integration of people, processes, and technologies for the effective collection, processing, storage, and dissemination of information. In the context of pandemics, these systems play a critical role in facilitating real-time data sharing, supporting decision-making processes, and providing effective communication channels to stakeholders at all levels. This note aims to explore the role of information systems in managing a pandemic, highlighting their benefits and challenges, and showcasing various successful case studies from around the world.

The immense scale of a pandemic requires efficient data collection and analysis to guide strategic decision-making. Information systems enable the collection of accurate and real-time data regarding the spread of the virus, affected regions, and demographic information. With the help of data analytics tools and techniques, health authorities can identify patterns, predict future trends, and allocate resources effectively. For instance, during the COVID-19 pandemic, countries like South Korea and Taiwan swiftly implemented sophisticated information systems to collect data, track infected individuals, and monitor quarantine compliance. These systems played a pivotal role in controlling the spread of the virus and preventing further outbreaks.

Furthermore, information systems aid in enhancing communication channels between various stakeholders involved in pandemic management. Governments can disseminate crucial information, guidelines, and updates to the public through digital platforms such as websites, mobile applications, and social media. This enables rapid communication and ensures that accurate information reaches a wide audience, enabling them to take necessary precautions and make informed decisions. Additionally, information systems facilitate collaboration between healthcare professionals, researchers, and policymakers, fostering the exchange of knowledge and the development of effective strategies to combat the pandemic.

In addition to monitoring and communication, information systems also play a vital role in supporting healthcare delivery during a pandemic. Electronic health records (EHRs) and telehealth systems allow medical professionals to access patient data remotely, reducing the need for physical contact and minimizing exposure to the virus. These systems enable telemedicine, allowing patients to consult healthcare providers, receive diagnoses, and even receive treatment remotely. This not only helps alleviate the burden on healthcare facilities but also ensures continuity of care for non-COVID-19 related conditions.

The use of information systems in managing a pandemic is not without its challenges. One major issue is the protection of privacy and security of sensitive health data. The vast amount of personal information collected during a pandemic can make individuals vulnerable to privacy breaches and identity theft. Governments and organizations must implement robust security measures, adhere to relevant regulations, and ensure transparency to maintain public trust in these systems.

Moreover, there can be disparities in access to information systems, especially in developing countries and marginalized communities. Inequality in access to technology and high-speed internet can hinder the dissemination of information and inhibit effective response strategies. Efforts must be made to bridge the digital divide and ensure that everyone has equal access to these systems to combat the pandemic.

To conclude, information systems play a crucial role in managing a pandemic by facilitating efficient data collection and analysis, enabling effective communication, and supporting healthcare delivery. The COVID-19 pandemic has highlighted the significance of these systems in responding to and controlling the spread of infectious diseases. However, there are also challenges related to privacy, security, and access that need to be addressed. The successful implementation of information systems during pandemics requires collaboration between governments, healthcare professionals, and technology experts.

Throughout this chapter, we will delve deeper into the various aspects of managing a pandemic using information systems. We will explore case studies from different countries, analyze the benefits, challenges, and ethical considerations, and highlight the lessons learned. By understanding the potential of information systems in pandemic management, we can better prepare for future crises and ensure a more efficient and coordinated response.

Thank you for joining me in this exploration of managing a pandemic using information systems. We hope this chapter provides valuable insights and inspires further discussions and innovations in this critical field.

Stay healthy and stay informed!

Dr. Lamin Tombekai Kamara

Managing a Pandemic Using Information Systems

Introduction:

In times of widespread diseases like pandemics, the efficient management of resources and data becomes crucial in curbing the spread and minimizing its impact. Information systems, with their ability to collect, process, store, and distribute information, play a vital role in managing and mitigating pandemics. This article aims to introduce the effective utilization of information systems in pandemic management, including surveillance, communication, resource allocation, and predictive modeling, to ensure the well-being of individuals and communities.

1. Surveillance:

One of the primary functions of information systems in pandemic management is surveillance. By integrating data from various sources, such as healthcare facilities, laboratories, and public health agencies, information systems enable real-time monitoring and analysis of disease outbreak patterns. These systems automatically collect data on the number of cases, their geographical distribution, transmission rates, and trends, providing insights to decision-makers and public health personnel. Enhanced surveillance allows for early detection, rapid response, and effective containment of the disease.

2. Communication:

Efficient communication is essential in managing a pandemic, and information systems play a vital role in facilitating this. From disseminating public health alerts and guidelines to coordinating response efforts, information systems ensure seamless communication between stakeholders. They provide a platform for authorities to share critical information, updates on preventive measures, and instructions on accessing healthcare services. Additionally, these systems enable individuals to report symptoms, seek medical advice, and receive real-time information, fostering a sense of trust and transparency in the management process.

3. Resource Allocation:

During a pandemic, the allocation of scarce resources, such as medical supplies, healthcare staff, and testing facilities, requires careful planning and coordination. Information systems can streamline this process by collecting and analyzing data on resource availability and demand. These systems provide situational awareness to policymakers, enabling them to make data-driven decisions on resource allocation. By optimizing resource distribution based on real-time information, information systems contribute to an equitable and efficient response, ensuring that resources reach the area most in need.

4. Predictive Modeling:

Pandemic management doesn't solely rely on present data; it also requires forecasting future trends and outcomes. Information systems leverage predictive modeling techniques to estimate the potential escalation of the disease and its impact on healthcare systems. By analyzing historical data, demographics, and other relevant factors, these systems can generate projections on infection rates, healthcare needs, and the effectiveness of interventions. This enables policymakers to plan, allocate resources proactively, and implement appropriate measures to prevent overwhelming healthcare systems.

5. Contact Tracing:

Contact tracing is a crucial strategy in curbing the spread of a pandemic, and information systems provide an effective platform for its implementation. By leveraging mobile applications, data from smartphone sensors, or wearable devices, these systems can trace and document interactions between individuals. This enables the identification of potential contacts and the timely isolation or testing of those at risk. Utilizing information systems in contact tracing helps break the chains of transmission, allowing for targeted interventions, and reducing the burden on healthcare systems.

In the face of a pandemic, information systems are indispensable tools for managing and mitigating the impact on communities. Through surveillance, communication, resource allocation, predictive modeling, and contact tracing, these systems provide decision-makers with real-time data and insights necessary for effective responses. By integrating information systems into pandemic management strategies, authorities can make data-driven decisions, optimize resource allocation, and implement timely interventions, ultimately saving lives and minimizing the overall impact of the disease on individuals and society.

1: Early detection and surveillance

Information systems can aid in the early detection of a pandemic by monitoring key indicators and signals. By collecting and analyzing data from various sources, such as healthcare facilities, laboratories, and public health agencies, systems can identify patterns and anomalies that may indicate the outbreak of a new infectious disease. This early detection enables rapid response and containment efforts.

Early detection and surveillance are pivotal in managing a pandemic effectively. By promptly identifying and monitoring disease outbreaks, public health authorities can implement timely interventions, minimize transmission, and allocate resources efficiently. In this context, information systems play a crucial role in enabling early detection and surveillance through various mechanisms.

a. Integrated Data Collection: Information systems facilitate the collection and integration of data from diverse sources, such as healthcare facilities, laboratories, and public health agencies. This integrated approach allows for real-time monitoring and analysis of disease patterns, enabling the early identification of potential outbreaks. By aggregating data on symptoms, tests, and geographical locations, these systems provide a comprehensive view of the disease prevalence, transmission rates, and emerging trends.

b. Automated Reporting: Through information systems, healthcare facilities and laboratories can automate the reporting of cases and test results. This streamlines the reporting process, eliminating delays and ensuring accurate and timely data collection. Automated reporting also allows for the immediate sharing of critical information with public health authorities, enabling them to respond swiftly and effectively.

c. Syndromic Surveillance: Information systems enable the implementation of syndromic surveillance, which involves monitoring specific symptoms and patterns that may indicate the early stages of a pandemic. By analyzing data on symptoms reported by healthcare facilities, emergency departments, and even online searches, these systems can identify clusters of related cases and detect potential outbreaks before they become widespread.

d. Data Analytics and Modeling: Information systems employ advanced data analytics and modeling techniques to analyze and interpret surveillance data. By analyzing patterns and trends, these systems can detect anomalies and potential outbreaks early on. Predictive modeling techniques can further enhance early detection by forecasting the future spread of the disease based on historical data and other relevant parameters.

e. Geographic Information Systems (GIS): GIS technology integrated into information systems allows for the visualization and analysis of data in a geographical context. By mapping outbreak hotspots, identifying high-risk areas, and tracking the movement of individuals, these systems aid in the early detection of localized outbreaks. GIS also facilitates the timely allocation of resources by helping authorities prioritize and target interventions where they are most needed.

f. Real-Time Alert Systems: Information systems can be equipped with real-time alert systems that promptly notify public health authorities and healthcare professionals about potential outbreaks or unusual disease patterns. These alerts enable rapid response and implementation of appropriate measures to contain the spread of the disease.

g. Public Reporting and Crowdsourcing: Information systems can leverage crowd-sourcing and public reporting through mobile applications or online platforms. By encouraging individuals to report symptoms and provide information about potential exposure, these systems enhance surveillance capabilities and enable early detection of cases that may otherwise go unnoticed.

h. International Collaboration: Information systems facilitate the sharing of surveillance data and information between countries and international organizations. Through secure and efficient data exchange platforms, global collaboration is enhanced, allowing for early detection of cases across borders and coordinated responses to prevent the rapid international spread of diseases.

Early detection and surveillance are vital pillars in effectively managing a pandemic. By harnessing the power of information systems, public health authorities can collect, analyze, and interpret data in real-time, enabling prompt responses and targeted interventions. Through integrated data collection, automated reporting, syndromic surveillance, data analytics, GIS technology, real-time alerts, public reporting, and international collaboration, information systems provide the necessary infrastructure and tools to detect outbreaks early, mitigate transmission, and save lives.

2: Real-time data collection and analysis

Information systems allow for the efficient collection, storage, and analysis of real-time data during a pandemic. By integrating data from multiple sources, including test results, hospital admissions, and mortality rates, these systems enable health authorities to monitor the spread of the virus and assess its impact on healthcare systems.

Real-time data collection and analysis play a significant role in the early detection of a pandemic. By swiftly capturing and analyzing data, public health authorities can identify outbreaks, monitor trends, and implement timely interventions. Real-time data collection and analysis leverage information systems and advanced technologies to facilitate a proactive approach toward pandemic management.

Firstly, real-time data collection involves the continuous and automated capture of relevant information from various sources, such as healthcare facilities, laboratories, and digital platforms. Information systems enable the seamless integration of data, eliminating delays and ensuring the availability of up-to-date information. This real-time data collection provides a comprehensive view of the disease's progression, allowing for the early identification of emerging hotspots or unusual patterns.

Real-time data collection during the early detection of a pandemic involves the continuous and automated capture of relevant information on time. This data is collected from various sources, including healthcare facilities, laboratories, surveillance systems, and digital platforms. The goal is to gather up-to-date information that can provide insights into the spread and severity of the disease.

The process of real-time data collection includes the following key elements:

a. Information Systems: Information systems serve as the infrastructure for collecting and managing real-time data. These systems can integrate diverse data sources, ensure data quality and security, and provide a platform for efficient data access and analysis.

b. Case Reporting: Healthcare facilities, clinics, and laboratories play a crucial role in reporting suspected or confirmed cases of the disease. Through electronic health records and other reporting mechanisms, real-time data is collected on the number of cases, their demographic information, symptoms, and laboratory test results.

c. Testing and Diagnostic Data: Real-time data collection also involves the collection of testing and diagnostic data. Testing facilities and laboratories report the number of tests conducted, the test results, and the location of testing to provide insights into the disease's prevalence and transmission patterns.

d. Syndromic Surveillance: Syndromic surveillance focuses on monitoring symptoms that may be indicative of a pandemic. Real-time data collection includes gathering information on these symptoms from various sources, including emergency departments, primary care clinics, and even social media platforms. This data allows public health authorities to detect clusters of related symptoms and identify potential outbreak hotspots.

e. Geographic Information Systems (GIS): Real-time data collection often includes geographic data to better understand the spatial distribution of cases. By mapping the locations of reported cases, including addresses or geographic coordinates, public health authorities can identify areas with higher infection rates and deploy resources accordingly.

f. Surveillance Systems: Surveillance systems, such as disease reporting networks and public health databases, contribute to real-time data collection. These systems enable the automated and secure transmission of data from different sources, providing a comprehensive view of the disease's progression.

g. Digital Platforms and Crowdsourcing: Real-time data collection can also leverage digital platforms and crowd-sourcing methods. Mobile applications, online surveys, or social media platforms can be used to collect data on symptoms, travel history, and potential exposure. These platforms enhance data collection by involving the public in reporting and providing valuable information.

The collected data is analyzed and processed in real-time to identify patterns, detect potential outbreaks, and provide valuable insights for decision-making. Real-time data collection allows public health authorities to monitor the spread of the pandemic, assess its impact, and implement appropriate interventions promptly.

Secondly, real-time data analysis harnesses advanced analytics techniques to analyze and interpret the collected data. Algorithms and models are applied to identify patterns, detect anomalies, predict future trends, and generate actionable insights. By leveraging data analytics in real-time, public health authorities can promptly uncover potential outbreaks, monitor transmission rates, and assess the effectiveness of interventions.

To harness advanced analytics techniques and interpret the collected data effectively, several analytical techniques are employed. These techniques help uncover patterns, detect anomalies, make predictions, and generate actionable insights for early detection and management of a pandemic. Some of the necessary analytical techniques include:

a. Descriptive Analytics: Descriptive analytics involves summarizing and visualizing the collected data to gain a better understanding of the current situation. Techniques such as data aggregation, data visualization, and exploratory data analysis are applied to identify trends, patterns, and relationships within the data.

b. Diagnostic Analytics: Diagnostic analytics focuses on understanding the causes and factors contributing to the observed patterns in the data. Techniques like regression analysis, correlation analysis, and hypothesis testing are employed to identify the relationships between variables and determine the influence of various factors on the spread and severity of the disease.

c. Predictive Analytics: Predictive analytics utilizes historical data to make predictions and forecast future trends. Techniques like regression modeling, time series analysis, and machine learning algorithms are used to analyze historical data and identify patterns that can help predict the future trajectory of the pandemic. These predictions aid in resource allocation, planning interventions, and assessing the potential impact of certain measures.

d. Spatial Analytics: Spatial analytics involves analyzing data in a geographical context to understand the spread and distribution of the disease. Geographic Information Systems (GIS) techniques, such as spatial clustering analysis, hot spot analysis, and spatial interpolation, are applied to identify high-risk areas, visualize patterns, and allocate resources more effectively.

e. Text Analytics: Text analytics is used to analyze unstructured data, such as social media posts, news articles, or medical literature, to derive insights relevant to the pandemic. Natural Language Processing (NLP) techniques are employed to extract and analyze textual information, identify sentiment, and uncover valuable insights from textual data sources.

f. Data Mining: Data mining techniques aim to uncover patterns, correlations, and hidden knowledge within large datasets. These techniques, including association rules, classification, clustering, and anomaly detection, are applied to identify risk factors, detect unusual disease patterns, and segment the population based on their susceptibility to the disease.

g. Machine Learning: Machine learning algorithms, such as decision trees, random forests, support vector machines, and neural networks, are utilized to discover patterns, make predictions, and classify data. These algorithms are trained on historical data to learn from patterns and make predictions on new data instances, aiding in early detection, outbreak prediction, and decision-making processes.

By employing these advanced analytics techniques, public health authorities can gain valuable insights from the collected data. These insights assist in understanding disease patterns, identifying high-risk populations and areas, predicting future trends, assessing intervention effectiveness, and allocating resources efficiently for early detection and management of a pandemic.

Thirdly, real-time data analysis enables the implementation of syndromic surveillance, which focuses on monitoring specific symptoms or patterns that may indicate the early stages of a pandemic. By analyzing real-time data on symptoms reported by healthcare facilities, emergency departments, and even social media platforms, public health authorities can quickly detect clusters of related cases and take necessary actions to prevent further transmission.

Furthermore, real-time data collection and analysis facilitate situation awareness, allowing decision-makers to have an accurate understanding of the current state of the pandemic. By continuously monitoring data, public health authorities can identify emerging trends, understand the impact of interventions, and adapt their strategies accordingly. This dynamic approach helps in adjusting resources, implementing targeted measures, and mitigating the spread of the disease.

Lastly, real-time data collection and analysis foster data-driven decision-making. By harnessing real-time information, public health authorities can make informed and evidence-based judgments regarding response strategies, resource allocation, and communication efforts. The availability of real-time data empowers decision-makers to act swiftly and effectively, minimizing the impact of the pandemic.

Real-time data collection and analysis are integral components of early detection in pandemic management. By seamlessly capturing and analyzing data, public health authorities can identify outbreaks, uncover patterns, and make informed decisions on time. Real-time data collection and analysis, facilitated by information systems and advanced technologies, contribute to proactive surveillance, targeted interventions, and efficient resource allocation, ultimately saving lives and reducing the overall impact of the pandemic.

3: Resource Management and Allocation

During a pandemic, efficient resource management is crucial to ensure the availability of necessary supplies such as personal protective equipment (PPE), ventilators, and vaccines. Information systems can track inventory, monitor usage rates, and predict demand to support decision-making regarding resource allocation and distribution across different regions or healthcare facilities.

Managing resources effectively during a pandemic is crucial to ensure that the necessary supplies, healthcare facilities, and personnel are available to meet the increased demand. Here are eight key strategies for resource management during a pandemic:

a. Resource Assessment and Planning: Conduct a thorough assessment of available resources, including medical equipment, supplies, healthcare facilities, and personnel. Analyze past data, consider population needs, and forecast the potential demand during the pandemic. Develop a robust resource plan that includes procurement strategies, inventory management, and contingency plans for resource scarcity.

b. Prioritization and Allocation: Prioritize resources based on their criticality in managing the pandemic. Identify key resource categories such as personal protective equipment (PPE), testing kits, medications, ventilators, and essential personnel. Develop clear guidelines for resource allocation, considering factors like severity of illness, high-risk populations, and healthcare capacity.

c. Collaboration and Coordination: Effective collaboration and coordination between healthcare providers, public health agencies, and other stakeholders are crucial. Establish a centralized resource management system to streamline the allocation and distribution of resources. Facilitate regular communication and information sharing to address resource needs and prevent duplication of efforts.

d. Surge Capacity Planning: Develop plans to increase healthcare capacity to handle a surge in cases. Identify potential areas for expansion, such as setting up field hospitals, utilizing temporary healthcare facilities, or repurposing existing spaces. Develop protocols and guidelines for rapidly training and mobilizing additional healthcare personnel if needed.

e. Supply Chain Management: Strengthen supply chains to ensure the availability and timely delivery of essential resources. Collaborate with suppliers and manufacturers to increase production, optimize distribution channels, and proactively address potential disruptions. Implement tracking systems to monitor stock levels, expiration dates, and distribution timelines to avoid shortages.

f. Resource Conservation: Implement strategies to conserve resources and minimize waste. This may include optimizing the use of PPE through proper training, effective inventory management, and appropriate usage protocols. Develop guidelines for rational use of medications, diagnostic tests, and other medical supplies to avoid unnecessary consumption.

g. Resource Sharing and Redistribution: Establish mechanisms for resource sharing and redistribution between healthcare facilities and regions. Develop inter-hospital or inter-agency collaborations to share resources based on need and capacity. Implement information systems to facilitate real-time resource tracking, identify surplus or scarce resources, and enable efficient redistribution.

h. Monitoring and Evaluation: Continuously monitor resource utilization, availability, and outcomes to assess the effectiveness of resource management strategies. Use data and analytics to identify gaps, adjust resource allocation plans, and make informed decisions. Regularly evaluate the impact of resource management efforts on patient outcomes, healthcare capacity, and staff well-being.

By following these strategies, public health authorities can effectively manage resources during a pandemic. This ensures that resources are allocated where they are most needed, healthcare capacity is maximized, and the population's healthcare needs are met. Effective resource management helps mitigate the impact of the pandemic, reducing morbidity and mortality rates, and ensuring a coordinated response to the crisis.

Paragraph 4: Communication and public awareness

Information systems provide a platform for effective communication between governments, public health agencies, and the public. Through websites, mobile applications, and social media platforms, authorities can disseminate accurate and updated information, guidelines, and precautions to a wide audience. This helps to reduce panic and misinformation and ensures that the public is well-informed about the situation.

Communication and public awareness are crucial in informing the public about the surge of a pandemic and ensuring their active participation in controlling the spread of the disease. Effectively communicating critical information and raising public awareness can help individuals understand the severity of the situation, promote preventive behaviors, and encourage adherence to guidelines. Here are seven key approaches to utilizing communication and public awareness during a pandemic surge:

a. Clear and Timely Messaging: Authorities should ensure that communication about the pandemic surge is clear, concise, and easily understandable by the public. Messages should be disseminated promptly to provide up-to-date information, including the status of the surge, preventive measures, available resources, and any required actions.

b. Multi-channel Approach: Employing a multi-channel communication strategy is essential to reach a diverse audience effectively. Utilize traditional media like television, radio, and newspapers, along with digital platforms, social media, mobile apps, and SMS alerts. This ensures messages reach different demographics and individuals with various access to information.

c. Transparency and Credibility: Transparency builds trust and credibility among the public. Authorities should provide accurate and transparent information about the surge, including the reasons behind the increase in cases, the impact on healthcare systems, and the strategies in place to manage the situation. Credible sources, such as public health agencies and expert professionals, should be involved in delivering information to enhance credibility.

d. Tailored Messaging: Different segments of the population may require tailored messaging to address their specific needs and concerns. Consider cultural, socioeconomic, and linguistic factors when developing communication materials. Targeted messages can be crafted for vulnerable populations, including the elderly, non-native speakers, or individuals with limited access to healthcare resources.

e. Empowering and Action-oriented Communication: Communication should empower individuals to take necessary actions and encourage collective responsibility. Provide clear instructions on preventive measures, such as hand hygiene, mask usage, social distancing, and vaccination. Encourage the public to seek reliable information, follow official guidelines, and engage in community efforts to mitigate the spread of the disease.

f. Engaging Key Influencers and Community Leaders: Engaging key influencers, community leaders, and trusted sources can amplify the reach and impact of communication efforts. Collaborate with public figures, religious leaders, healthcare professionals, and community organizations to disseminate messages and address specific concerns within their respective communities. This can help overcome barriers and increase the effectiveness of communication.

g. Two-way Communication: Establish mechanisms for two-way communication to address public concerns, answer questions, and provide guidance. Utilize hotlines, helplines, or online chat platforms where individuals can seek clarifications, report symptoms, or access information. Feedback loops should be established to ensure continuous improvement in communication strategies based on public perception and understanding.

By utilizing effective communication and raising public awareness, authorities can ensure a well-informed and engaged public during the surge of a pandemic. This, in turn, promotes adherence to preventive measures, early reporting of symptoms, and active participation in efforts to control the spread of the disease. Building trust, providing clear and timely information, employing a multi-channel approach, tailoring messaging, empowering individuals, engaging key influencers, and establishing two-way communication channels collectively contribute to an informed and cooperative response from the public.

5: Contact tracing and monitoring

Contact tracing is a fundamental strategy in pandemic management. Information systems can aid in the efficient tracking and monitoring of individuals who may have been exposed to the virus. By using data from various sources, such as mobile phone tracking, healthcare records, and self-reporting applications, contact tracing can be facilitated, helping to identify potential outbreaks and contain the spread.

Contact tracing and monitoring of individuals during an outbreak of a pandemic is a critical strategy employed to identify and trace potential transmission chains. It involves identifying and monitoring individuals who have come into close contact with an infected person to control the spread of the disease. Here are eight key aspects of contact tracing and monitoring during a pandemic outbreak:

a. Contact Identification: Contact tracing begins by identifying individuals who have had close contact with an infected person. Close contacts are typically defined as individuals who have been within a certain distance of an infected person for a specified duration, often within 6 feet and for more than 15 minutes.

b. Contact Tracing Process: Trained contact tracers interview the infected individual to gather information about their recent contacts. This includes identifying names, phone numbers, addresses, and other relevant information. Public health authorities may also use digital tools, such as mobile apps or GPS data, to supplement contact tracing efforts.

c. Notification and Education: Contact tracers notify identified contacts about their potential exposure to the virus. They provide information about testing, self-isolation, quarantine requirements, and symptoms to watch for. Educational materials are shared to ensure that contacts understand the importance of following recommended protocols and preventive measures.

d. Testing and Monitoring: Contacts are advised to undergo testing to determine their infection status. They may be monitored for symptoms and asked to self-quarantine or self-isolate while awaiting test results. If necessary, public health authorities may provide support, resources, or medical assistance to contacts who test positive or develop symptoms.

e. Support Services: Contact tracing efforts often involve offering support services to individuals in quarantine or isolation. This may include assistance with essential supplies, healthcare access, mental health support, and social services. These support services help individuals comply with isolation guidelines and reduce the risk of viral spread.

f. Confidentiality and Privacy: Contact tracing respects the confidentiality and privacy of individuals throughout the process. Personal information is securely stored and only shared with authorized personnel for public health purposes. Guidelines and regulations are followed to protect sensitive information and maintain public trust.

g. Digital Contact Tracing Tools: Digital contact tracing tools, such as mobile applications, utilize Bluetooth or location data to supplement manual contact tracing efforts. These tools facilitate the identification and notification of contacts, potentially speeding up the process and enhancing the accuracy of contact tracing.

h. Ongoing Monitoring and Evaluation: Contact tracing efforts are continuously monitored and evaluated to assess their effectiveness. Public health authorities track the number of contacts identified, tested, and isolated, as well as the success rate of notifying contacts and preventing further transmission. Lessons learned from monitoring and evaluation help refine contact tracing strategies and improve future outbreak responses.

By implementing robust contact tracing and monitoring measures, public health authorities can identify and break chains of transmission, control the spread of the virus, and protect the health and well-being of individuals within communities. Effective contact tracing, coupled with other preventive measures, plays a pivotal role in managing and mitigating the impact of a pandemic outbreak.

6: Remote healthcare delivery

Telehealth systems and electronic health records (EHRs) play a crucial role in managing a pandemic. These systems enable remote healthcare delivery, minimizing physical contact and reducing the risk of infection for both patients and healthcare professionals. Patients can consult healthcare providers through telemedicine platforms, receive diagnoses, and even access necessary prescriptions.

A healthcare delivery system is a complex network of people, institutions, and resources that work together to provide medical care and promote health within a community or country. It encompasses all the activities involved in delivering healthcare services, from prevention and diagnosis to treatment, rehabilitation, and ongoing care.

One of the key components of a healthcare delivery system is primary care. This refers to the initial point of contact between a patient and a healthcare professional, such as a general practitioner or family doctor. Primary care focuses on routine healthcare and preventive services, such as vaccinations, health screenings, and management of chronic conditions.

Specialized care is another integral part of the healthcare delivery system. This includes services provided by specialists, such as surgeons, cardiologists, oncologists, and psychiatrists. These experts have advanced training and knowledge in specific medical fields and are often involved in diagnosing and treating complex or rare conditions.

Hospitals play a central role in the healthcare delivery system by providing acute and specialized care. They have the necessary medical equipment, facilities, and staff to treat patients with severe illnesses or injuries. Hospitals are also responsible for monitoring patients, initiating emergency procedures, performing surgeries, and providing post-operative care.

Within the healthcare delivery system, there are various types of healthcare providers. These include physicians, nurses, pharmacists, physical therapists, and other allied healthcare professionals. Each provider has a specific role in delivering care, and they often collaborate to ensure comprehensive and coordinated services for patients.

Health insurance is another vital aspect of the healthcare delivery system. It helps individuals access and afford healthcare services by covering a portion of their medical expenses. Health insurance can be provided by private companies or government programs, such as Medicare and Medicaid. Without insurance, many people would struggle to afford necessary healthcare and would face financial hardship in case of a medical emergency.

Technology and innovation play a significant role in the modern healthcare delivery system. Medical advancements, such as telemedicine, electronic health records, and remote monitoring devices, have made it easier for healthcare providers to deliver care and for patients to access it. Telemedicine, in particular, allows patients to consult with doctors remotely, especially in rural or underserved areas where access to healthcare may be limited.

Public health initiatives are essential for a well-functioning healthcare delivery system. They focus on promoting health and preventing diseases in populations through education, vaccination campaigns, sanitation measures, and legislative actions. By addressing the underlying determinants of health, such as access to clean water, adequate nutrition, and safe environments, public health efforts help reduce the burden on healthcare systems.

Quality and safety are critical considerations in the healthcare delivery system. Various organizations, such as the World Health Organization and accreditation bodies, work to establish standards and guidelines for healthcare providers and institutions. These standards ensure that patients receive safe and effective care, that healthcare professionals adhere to best practices, and that healthcare organizations are held accountable for their performance.

Healthcare financing is another aspect of the healthcare delivery system that must be addressed. The cost of healthcare services can be high, and without appropriate funding mechanisms, patients may not be able to access the care they need. Governments, insurance companies, and individuals all play a role in financing healthcare, whether through taxes, premiums, or out-of-pocket payments.

The healthcare delivery system also faces various challenges, such as resource constraints, inequalities in access to care, and an aging population. These challenges require innovative solutions, such as healthcare reforms, improved coordination among healthcare providers, and investments in preventive care and public health.

The healthcare delivery system is a multifaceted network that involves various stakeholders, services, and resources to deliver care to individuals and communities. It encompasses primary and specialized care, hospitals, healthcare providers, insurance, technology, public health initiatives, quality and safety standards, financing mechanisms, and ongoing challenges that require continuous improvement. A well-functioning healthcare delivery system aims to provide equitable, accessible, and high-quality healthcare to all.

During a pandemic outbreak, healthcare delivery undergoes significant changes and adaptations in order to effectively respond to the increased demand for medical services and the unique challenges presented by the infectious disease. The specific strategies employed may vary depending on the nature of the outbreak and the resources available, but there are several common approaches used in healthcare delivery during a pandemic.

a. Increase capacity: Healthcare systems often work to expand their capacity by adding more hospital beds, establishing temporary healthcare facilities, and converting other buildings into healthcare spaces. This allows for a larger number of patients to be treated.

b. Implement triage systems: Triage systems help healthcare providers prioritize patients based on the severity of their condition. During a pandemic, triage systems become critical to ensure efficient use of resources and focus on those in urgent need of care.

c. Focus on infection control measures: Healthcare facilities strengthen infection control practices to reduce the risk of transmission. This includes strict adherence to hand hygiene protocols, wearing personal protective equipment (PPE), implementing physical distancing measures, and enhancing cleaning and disinfection practices.

d. Telemedicine and remote care: To minimize the need for physical contact and reduce the burden on healthcare facilities, virtual healthcare services are expanded. Telemedicine allows patients to consult with healthcare professionals remotely, facilitating diagnoses, prescriptions, and monitoring of non-critical conditions.

e. Testing and contact tracing: In a pandemic, widespread testing becomes crucial for early detection and containment of the disease. Testing facilities are established or scaled up to effectively screen individuals for infection. Contact tracing efforts are also intensified to identify and quarantine individuals who have been in close contact with infected individuals.

f. Education and communication: Healthcare delivery systems play a vital role in disseminating accurate and up-to-date information about the pandemic. Public health campaigns, educational materials, and communication channels are utilized to educate the public on prevention measures, symptom recognition, and where to seek care if needed.

g. Collaborative healthcare efforts: During a pandemic, healthcare delivery often involves collaboration between various healthcare providers, both within a country and internationally. Cooperation between hospitals, clinics, research institutions, and public health agencies facilitates information sharing, resource allocation, and coordinated responses.

h. Prioritization of critical care: In an overwhelmed healthcare system, critical care resources such as intensive care units (ICUs), ventilators, and specialized medical personnel may become scarce. Allocation frameworks and guidelines are developed to prioritize the use of these critical resources based on factors such as patient acuity and chances of survival.

I. Mental health support: Pandemic outbreaks can have significant psychological impacts on individuals and communities. Healthcare delivery systems integrate mental health support services to address the increased need for counseling and psychiatric care.

j. Vaccination campaigns: When vaccines become available, healthcare delivery systems work to distribute and administer vaccines to the population. Vaccination centers are set up, and strategies are implemented to reach vulnerable populations and achieve maximum coverage.

k. Surveillance and monitoring: Healthcare delivery systems actively monitor the spread of disease, track emerging variants, and gather data to inform public health responses. Real-time data analysis helps identify hotspot areas, trends, and potential outbreaks.

l. Post-pandemic planning: Healthcare delivery during a pandemic also involves planning for the aftermath. Systems put in place processes to restore regular healthcare services that may have been disrupted and ensure that individuals receive necessary follow-up care.

Overall, pandemic healthcare delivery focuses on managing the surge in cases, reducing transmission, providing timely and appropriate care, ensuring safety for both patients and healthcare workers, and adapting to the evolving circumstances to save lives and minimize the impact of the outbreak.

How to handle an unexpected outbreak of a pandemic in third-world countries

The standards of healthcare delivery during an unexpected outbreak in third-world countries can vary depending on the specific country and its level of development. However, certain general practices and standards are recommended in such situations:

a. Preparedness and response planning: Countries should have contingency plans in place to respond to outbreaks. This includes establishing emergency response teams, defining roles and responsibilities, and coordinating with relevant agencies and organizations.

b. Surveillance and monitoring: Robust surveillance systems should be in place to detect and monitor outbreaks. This includes timely reporting of suspected cases and effective communication channels for information sharing.

c. Early detection and diagnosis: Prompt identification and confirmation of cases is crucial for effective outbreak response. This involves training healthcare workers on recognizing symptoms, providing access to diagnostic testing, and ensuring laboratory capacity is available.

d. Infection prevention and control: Implementing strict infection prevention measures is essential to contain the outbreak and protect healthcare workers and patients. This includes proper hand hygiene, use of personal protective equipment, isolation of suspected cases, and disinfection protocols.

e. Treatment and isolation: Establishing designated treatment facilities or hospitals for infected individuals is necessary to isolate and provide appropriate care. Ensuring access to healthcare services, medications, and medical supplies is important for managing the outbreak.

f. Communication and public awareness: Transparent and accurate communication is vital for building trust and encouraging public cooperation. Governments and health authorities should disseminate regular updates, health advisories, and educate the public on preventive measures and symptoms.

g. Capacity building: Strengthening healthcare systems in third-world countries is crucial for effective outbreak response. This includes training healthcare workers on outbreak management, improving laboratory capacity, and enhancing overall infrastructure and resources.

h. Collaboration and international support: Third-world countries often require external support in outbreaks due to limited resources. International collaboration and assistance from organizations like the World Health Organization (WHO), non-governmental organizations, and donors can play a significant role in providing technical expertise, funding, and resources.

It is important to note that while these standards are recommended, the reality in third-world countries can often pose various challenges such as limited funding, weak infrastructure, and a lack of resources. Therefore, flexibility and adaptation to the specific context are necessary when implementing healthcare delivery during an unexpected outbreak in these countries.

First responders play a critical role during a pandemic outbreak, and they need to take several precautions to protect themselves and others while effectively managing the situation. Here are some important precautions for first responders:

a. Personal Protective Equipment (PPE): First responders should always wear appropriate PPE based on the nature of the virus and its mode of transmission. This may include gloves, masks (such as N95 respirators), goggles or face shields, gowns, and shoe covers. PPE should be properly fitted, regularly inspected, and safely disposed of after use.2b. Hand Hygiene: Regular hand hygiene is crucial to prevent the spread of the virus. First responders should wash their hands frequently with soap and water for at least 20 seconds or use hand sanitizers with at least 60% alcohol content.

c. Respiratory Hygiene: First responders should practice good respiratory hygiene, including covering their mouth and nose with a tissue or elbow when coughing or sneezing. Used tissues should be disposed of properly, and hands should be washed immediately afterward.

d. Safe Patient Contact: When dealing with suspected or confirmed cases, first responders should limit close contact as much as possible. They should maintain a safe distance (at least 1 meter) from the patient, use appropriate PPE, and avoid unnecessary contact with bodily fluids.

e. Safe Transport: If transportation of infected or potentially infected individuals is required, first responders should ensure a safe and isolated environment to minimize the risk of transmission. This might include using separate vehicles or isolating patients in the transport vehicle with proper ventilation.

f. Awareness and Training: First responders should receive training and be updated regularly on infection prevention and control protocols specific to the pandemic. They should be aware of the signs and symptoms of the virus, as well as the appropriate procedures for handling potentially infected individuals.

g. Decontamination and Cleaning: First responders should ensure proper decontamination and cleaning of their equipment, vehicles, and any surfaces they meet. This includes using appropriate disinfectants and following recommended cleaning protocols.

h. Mental Health Support: Pandemics can be mentally and emotionally challenging for first responders. It is important that they have access to mental health support, counseling services, and are encouraged to seek assistance if needed.

Collaboration and Communication: First responders should closely collaborate and communicate with healthcare professionals, public health authorities, and other relevant agencies to ensure a coordinated and effective response.

These precautions should be followed in conjunction with guidelines and protocols provided by public health agencies and authorities to ensure the safety and well-being of both first responders and the public during a pandemic outbreak.

7: Statistical modeling and prediction

Information systems can leverage the power of data analytics and statistical modeling to predict outbreaks, estimate the impact of interventions, and guide decision-making. By analyzing large datasets, patterns can be identified, and statistical algorithms can be used to make projections regarding the future spread of the virus, healthcare needs, and the effectiveness of various control measures.

Statistical modeling and predictions in a pandemic outbreak involve using mathematical and statistical techniques to analyze data and make informed projections about the spread and impact of the disease. These models use available data on cases, deaths, and other relevant variables to estimate key parameters, assess the effectiveness of interventions, and predict future trends. Here are some commonly used techniques in statistical modeling during a pandemic outbreak:

a. Epidemiological Models: Epidemiological models, such as compartmental models like the SIR (Susceptible-Infectious-Recovered) model, simulate the dynamics of disease transmission within a population. These models divide the population into different compartments based on their disease status and use mathematical equations to represent the flow of individuals between these compartments over time. They can estimate parameters like the basic reproduction number (R0) and predict disease spread under different scenarios.

b. Time Series Analysis: Time series analysis is used to analyze data collected over time, such as daily or weekly case counts. Techniques like autoregressive integrated moving average (ARIMA) models and exponential smoothing methods can identify patterns, trends, and seasonality in the data. These models can provide short-term forecasts of case numbers and help assess the impact of interventions.

c. Machine Learning: Machine learning techniques can be employed to analyze large and complex datasets in order to identify patterns and make predictions. Algorithms like decision trees, random forests, and support vector machines can be used to classify and predict outcomes based on various features and variables. Machine learning can help identify risk factors, predict disease severity, or assess the effectiveness of interventions.

d. Bayesian Modeling: Bayesian statistical modeling uses prior knowledge and beliefs, along with observed data, to estimate parameters and make predictions. Bayesian models are particularly useful when dealing with limited data by incorporating prior information on disease characteristics or intervention effects. These models provide estimates along with uncertainty measures, allowing decision-makers to account for the range of possible outcomes.

e. Spatial Analysis: Spatial analysis techniques allow the examination of geographic patterns and the identification of areas with higher disease prevalence. Mapping techniques like choropleth maps or hotspot analysis can help detect clusters and prioritize resources accordingly. Spatial modeling can also account for environmental factors or social determinants of health that influence disease spread.

These statistical modeling techniques provide valuable insights into the progression and management of a pandemic outbreak. However, it's important to note that uncertainties exist in model assumptions, data quality, and human behavior, so interpretations should be made cautiously, and models should be regularly updated with new data to improve their accuracy over time.

Statistical modeling and predictions are crucial tools used to detect outbreaks of a pandemic. Here's how they can be applied:

a. Early Detection: Statistical models can analyze various data sources, including surveillance data, hospital data, laboratory reports, and social media data, to identify unusual patterns or signals of a potential outbreak. By monitoring trends and deviations from expected values, models can provide early warnings of a possible pandemic.

b. Forecasting: Models can project the future trajectory of an outbreak based on past data and current trends. These forecasts can estimate the number of cases, deaths, or hospitalizations expected in the coming weeks or months, helping to inform public health interventions and resource allocation.

c. Estimating Disease Parameters: Statistical models can estimate important disease parameters, such as the reproduction number (R0) or the rate of transmission. These parameters provide insights into how contagious a virus is and can help guide control measures, such as social distancing, contact tracing, or vaccination strategies.

d. Assessing Interventions: Models can evaluate the effectiveness and impact of different intervention strategies, such as school closures, travel restrictions, or mass testing. By simulating scenarios and comparing outcomes, models can inform decision-making by providing insights into the potential benefits and trade-offs of different interventions.

e. Surveillance and Monitoring: Statistical models can be used to enhance disease surveillance systems by analyzing large volumes of data in real-time. By detecting unusual spikes or clusters of cases, models can help pinpoint potential outbreak hotspots or identify populations at higher risk.

f. Resource Planning: Statistical models can assist in predicting healthcare system demands during a pandemic outbreak. By estimating the number of hospitalizations, intensive care unit admissions, or ventilator requirements, models can guide resource planning and allocation, including the need for additional facilities or medical supplies.

g. Risk Assessment: Models can assess the risk factors associated with the spread and severity of a pandemic. By examining demographics, comorbidities, or socioeconomic factors, models can help identify vulnerable populations and prioritize resources and interventions accordingly.

It is important to note that statistical modeling and predictions rely on the availability and quality of data, as well as the assumptions made in the models. Regular updates, incorporation of new data, and validation against real-world observations are essential to improve the accuracy and reliability of these models. Therefore, continuous surveillance, data sharing, and collaboration among public health agencies, researchers, and experts play a crucial role in detecting and managing pandemics effectively.

8: Monitoring public compliance

During a pandemic, public compliance with preventive measures such as social distancing, quarantine, and mask-wearing is crucial. Information systems can help monitor and track public compliance through data from surveillance cameras, mobile apps, or self-reporting platforms. By identifying areas with low compliance rates, authorities can target interventions and reinforce public awareness campaigns.

Monitoring public compliance during a pandemic outbreak is crucial to ensure the effectiveness of public health measures and control the spread of the virus. Here's a comprehensive explanation of how to monitor public compliance in six paragraphs:

a. Communication and Education: Establish clear and consistent communication channels to educate the public about the importance and rationale behind various measures. This includes ensuring accurate information is readily available through official sources, websites, and social media platforms. Regularly disseminate targeted messages to different demographics, addressing concerns, and providing clear instructions on compliance with measures such as mask-wearing, physical distancing, and hand hygiene.

b. Public Surveys and Opinion Polls: Conduct surveys and opinion polls to gauge public knowledge, attitudes, and behaviors regarding pandemic measures. These can be done through online surveys, phone calls, or in-person interviews. By assessing public understanding and compliance levels, authorities can identify areas of improvement and tailor messaging to address specific misconceptions or barriers to compliance.

c. Hotline and Reporting Systems: Set up dedicated hotlines and reporting systems to enable the public to report non-compliance or concerns regarding pandemic measures. This allows authorities to track and address issues promptly. Encourage whistleblowing mechanisms that protect the identity of individuals reporting violations, instilling confidence in the reporting system and deterring non-compliance.

d. Social Media Monitoring: Utilize social media platforms to monitor public sentiments, identify misinformation, and gauge compliance with pandemic measures. Social media analytics tools can track hashtags and keywords related to the outbreak, enabling authorities to identify non-compliant behavior or areas of public concern. This information can guide the development of targeted interventions and corrective messaging.

e. Spot Checks and Inspections: Conduct spot checks and inspections at various locations, including public spaces, transportation hubs, and businesses, to ensure compliance with mandated measures. Trained personnel can monitor adherence to physical distancing, mask-wearing, and capacity restrictions. These visits can also serve as an opportunity to educate and remind individuals of the importance of compliance and the potential consequences of non-compliance.

f. Collaboration with Community Leaders and Organizations: Engage with community leaders, influencers, and local organizations to promote and monitor compliance. These trusted figures can help disseminate accurate information, address cultural or community-specific challenges to compliance, and reinforce the importance of adhering to measures. Collaborate with community-based organizations to conduct outreach programs, distribute essential supplies, and monitor compliance at the grassroots level.

Collaboration between health workers and community-based leaders and organizations is crucial for an effective pandemic response. Here's an explanation of how health workers can collaborate with these stakeholders:

1. Establishing Communication Channels: Open and regular communication channels should be established between health workers and community-based leaders and organizations. This includes identifying key individuals or groups within the community who can serve as liaisons and facilitate information sharing. Regular meetings, virtual or in-person, can help exchange updates, address concerns, and coordinate efforts.

2. Building Trust and Understanding: Health workers should invest time in building trust and understanding with community leaders and organizations. This involves actively listening to community perspectives, respecting cultural values and practices, and acknowledging the expertise and knowledge that community leaders bring. By working together, health workers and community stakeholders can develop strategies that are culturally appropriate, acceptable, and effective.

3. Leveraging Local Knowledge and Resources: Community-based leaders and organizations have valuable local knowledge and resources that can enhance the pandemic response. Health workers can collaborate with them to gather insights on community dynamics, identify high-risk populations, and access resources such as translation services, volunteers, or community spaces for public health activities. By utilizing these resources, the response can be more targeted and tailored to the specific needs of the community.

4. Co-creating and Disseminating Information: Together, health workers and community leaders can co-create and disseminate accurate, culturally sensitive, and accessible information. This can be done through various channels such as community meetings, social media, newsletters, or local radio stations. By involving community-based leaders and organizations in the design and delivery of health messages, information can better resonate with the community, address misconceptions, and encourage compliance with preventive measures.

5. Conducting Joint Outreach and Education: Health workers and community leaders can collaborate on conducting joint outreach and education activities. This may involve organizing community health fairs, workshops, or mobile clinics. Community-based organizations can help identify barriers to accessing healthcare services and support health workers in reaching vulnerable populations. These partnerships can also facilitate the distribution of essential supplies, such as face masks or hygiene kits, to ensure they reach those most in need.

6. Facilitating Contact Tracing and Testing: Community-based leaders and organizations can play a crucial role in contact tracing and testing efforts. They can assist in identifying and contacting individuals who may have been exposed to the virus, providing relevant information, and helping to overcome language or cultural barriers. By working hand-in-hand with community stakeholders, health workers can ensure effective contact tracing and testing strategies that are acceptable and trusted within the community.

7. Addressing Stigma and Inclusivity: Health workers and community-based leaders must collaborate to address stigma and ensure inclusivity in the pandemic response. This involves challenging and dispelling misinformation that may lead to discrimination or exclusion. Health workers can work with community leaders to promote a supportive and non-judgmental environment, reinforcing the importance of empathy, respect, and solidarity within the community.

By engaging in meaningful collaboration, health workers and community-based leaders and organizations can ensure a more comprehensive, community-driven, and tailored approach to pandemic response. This collaboration enhances trust, facilitates effective communication, and strengthens the overall resilience of the community during challenging times.

8. Data from Wearable Devices and Technology: Explore the use of wearable devices and technology to monitor compliance rates. For example, contact tracing apps can track individuals' proximity to others and compliance with self-isolation or quarantine recommendations. However, it is essential to uphold privacy and data protection standards while utilizing such technology.

By implementing these strategies in an integrated manner, public health authorities can effectively monitor compliance during a pandemic outbreak. The collected data and insights gathered through these monitoring efforts should inform the development and refinement of public health policies, communication strategies, and targeted interventions to promote and enhance public compliance.

9: Data sharing and collaboration

Information systems facilitate data sharing and collaboration among different stakeholders involved in pandemic management, including healthcare professionals, researchers, and policymakers. By providing a platform for secure data exchange, these systems foster the development of standardized protocols, share research findings, and enable evidence-based decision-making.

Data sharing and collaboration are essential components of an effective response to a pandemic outbreak. Here's an explanation of how data sharing and collaboration can be conducted during such an outbreak:

a. Data Sharing between Healthcare Facilities: Healthcare facilities should actively share data on cases, hospitalizations, and outcomes to gain a comprehensive understanding of the pandemic's impact. Timely sharing of this information helps identify trends, inform resource allocation, and prompt coordinated responses. Standardized reporting protocols and secure data exchange mechanisms should be in place to ensure the privacy and confidentiality of patient information.

b. Interagency Collaboration: Collaboration between government agencies, public health departments, and other relevant organizations is crucial during a pandemic. They should share data on testing, contact tracing, and disease surveillance. This collaboration allows for a more complete picture of the outbreak and enables the implementation of consistent strategies across different sectors.

c. International Collaboration and Data Sharing: Pandemics often transcend national boundaries, necessitating international collaboration. Countries should share data on cases, genomic sequencing, and emerging variants to track the spread of the virus globally. This collaboration enables the rapid identification and response to new threats, facilitates the sharing of best practices, and supports the development of vaccines and treatments.

d. Data Sharing with Researchers and Experts: Data sharing with researchers and experts is vital for advancing scientific knowledge during a pandemic outbreak. Sharing anonymized data on cases, trends, and outcomes allows experts to analyze and model the spread of the virus, identify risk factors, and develop evidence-based interventions. Open-access platforms and secure data repositories can facilitate the efficient and transparent sharing of research and data across the scientific community.

e. Collaboration with Technology Companies: Collaboration with technology companies can enhance data collection and analysis efforts during a pandemic. Companies can develop tools and platforms to collect real-time data on symptoms, testing, and mobility patterns. This data can aid in epidemiological modeling, early detection of outbreaks, and resource allocation. Collaboration ensures that the use of technology aligns with privacy regulations and ethical considerations.

f. Data Sharing for Surveillance and Monitoring: Public health agencies should collaborate to establish robust systems for data sharing and surveillance. This involves the sharing of case data, testing results, and hospital capacity to monitor the spread and severity of the virus. Real-time data feeds and centralized dashboards can ensure timely information sharing, allowing decision-makers to track the outbreak and respond accordingly.

g. Transparency and Openness: During a pandemic outbreak, transparency and openness are crucial for effective data sharing and collaboration. Clear guidelines should be established to ensure transparency in data collection, analysis, and reporting processes. Open dialogue and active engagement with stakeholders, including the public, build trust, foster collaboration, and enhance the overall quality and integrity of data.

Transparency and openness are fundamental factors during a pandemic outbreak for several reasons:

a. Trust-building: Transparency and openness build trust among the public and various stakeholders. By sharing information openly and honestly, authorities demonstrate their commitment to the welfare of the population. Transparency fosters confidence in public health measures and interventions, encouraging individuals to comply with guidelines and recommendations.

b. Accurate Information: During a pandemic, misinformation and rumors can spread rapidly, leading to confusion and panic. Transparency ensures that accurate and reliable information is disseminated promptly and consistently. This helps individuals make informed decisions about their health, actions, and necessary precautions, leading to better overall outcomes.

c. Scientific Collaboration: Transparency facilitates scientific collaboration and innovation. Open access to data, research findings, and methodologies allows scientists and researchers around the world to collaborate, validate findings, and contribute to evidence-based decision-making. Sharing information openly helps eliminate redundancies, accelerates the development of potential treatments and vaccines, and fosters new insights and solutions.

d. Learning Opportunities: Transparency enables learning from past experiences and mistakes. Openly sharing data on the progression of the pandemic, response strategies, and outcomes allows stakeholders to analyze and evaluate the effectiveness of interventions. By identifying areas where improvements can be made, transparency enables the refinement of public health strategies and lays the groundwork for future preparedness.

e. Accountability and Oversight: Transparency ensures accountability in decision-making processes. When information is made accessible, it becomes possible for the public and other stakeholders to evaluate the rationale behind decisions, assess their impact, and hold authorities accountable. Transparency allows for better oversight and helps identify any instances of potential misconduct, ensuring a more transparent and equitable response.

f. Engagement and Cooperation: Transparency encourages engagement and cooperation from various sectors of society. When information is openly shared, stakeholders, including businesses, community organizations, and individuals, can actively participate in the response efforts. Openness in decision-making processes and data sharing allows for collaboration, leading to more effective coordination of resources and efforts.

g. Ethical Imperative: Transparency is an ethical imperative during a pandemic outbreak. The right to access information, the right to make informed choices about one's health, and the principle of non-maleficence require authorities to be transparent and forthcoming about the risks, developments, and measures taken to mitigate the impact of the pandemic. Openness helps ensure that individuals can exercise their rights and make decisions based on accurate and reliable information.

Overall, transparency and openness during a pandemic outbreak are critical for establishing trust, disseminating accurate information, fostering collaboration, and ensuring accountability. By prioritizing these principles, authorities can effectively address the challenges posed by the pandemic, better protect public health, and promote a collective effort to overcome the crisis.

By promoting data sharing and collaboration, stakeholders can work together to build a more accurate and comprehensive understanding of the pandemic. This collective effort facilitates evidence-based decision-making, supports the development of effective interventions, and helps control the spread of the virus. However, it is important to prioritize data privacy, security, and ethical considerations when sharing and analyzing data during a pandemic outbreak.

10: Learning from data and adapting strategies

Lastly, information systems enable continuous learning and adaptation of strategies during a pandemic. By analyzing data on the effectiveness of interventions, authorities can modify and refine their approaches, enhancing their response over time. These systems provide valuable insights into the impact of various measures, enabling a more efficient and effective management of the pandemic.

In conclusion, managing a pandemic using information systems encompasses a wide range of strategies and tools. From early detection and surveillance to resource management, communication, and remote healthcare delivery, these systems play a crucial role in supporting decision-making, monitoring the spread of the virus, and facilitating collaboration among stakeholders. By harnessing the power of data and technology, we can better understand and respond to pandemics, ensuring the well-being of individuals and the resilience of healthcare systems.

Learning from the data collected during a pandemic outbreak is essential for adapting strategies and improving the response. Here's an explanation of what can be learned from the data and how strategies can be adapted:

a. Disease Patterns: Data can provide insights into the patterns and dynamics of the disease. By analyzing the data, officials can understand factors such as the rate of transmission, incubation period, severity, and risk factors associated with the disease. This information helps in refining public health messages, targeting interventions for vulnerable populations, and adjusting strategies accordingly.

b. Hotspots and Clusters: Data can identify geographical hotspots and clusters where the disease is spreading rapidly. By geographically mapping cases, health officials can identify areas that require heightened surveillance and additional resources for testing, contact tracing, and targeted interventions. Data can inform decisions regarding localized lockdowns, travel restrictions, and resource allocation.

c. Testing and Diagnosis: Data on testing rates, turnaround times, and diagnostic accuracy can guide testing strategies. Analysis of testing data can help identify gaps in testing coverage and areas where additional testing resources are needed. Data can inform decisions about prioritizing high-risk groups or optimizing testing strategies based on the prevalence of the disease within a specific population.

d. Healthcare Capacity: Data can provide insights into the utilization of healthcare resources such as hospital beds, ICU occupancy, ventilators, and personal protective equipment (PPE). Analyzing this data helps anticipate and adapt healthcare capacity to meet the needs of patients. It assists policymakers in making decisions about resource allocation, surge capacity planning, and ensuring the availability of essential medical supplies.

e. Effectiveness of Interventions: Data can assess the effectiveness of various interventions and measures implemented during the pandemic. By evaluating the impact of interventions such as mask mandates, physical distancing, and travel restrictions, officials can understand which strategies are most effective in reducing transmission rates. This information supports evidence-based decision-making and can guide adjustments in strategies.

f. Vaccine Coverage and Efficacy: As vaccination efforts progress, data on vaccine coverage and efficacy become critical. Monitoring the data allows officials to identify populations with low vaccine coverage, assess the effectiveness of specific vaccines, and identify any emerging strains that could impact vaccine effectiveness. This information helps in targeting vaccination campaigns, addressing vaccine hesitancy, and adapting strategies to maximize vaccine impact.

g. Social and Economic Impact: Data can provide insights into the social and economic impact of the pandemic. Analyzing data on unemployment, poverty rates, mental health, access to healthcare, and education disruption helps identify vulnerable populations and areas requiring support. This data informs policies for economic recovery, social support programs, and mental health services.

Based on the insights gained from the data, strategies can be adapted to address emerging challenges and improve the response. For example:

- Communication and Public Messaging: Adjust public health messages, ensuring they are tailored to address specific concerns or misconceptions identified through data analysis.

- Targeted Interventions: Adapt interventions and resource allocation to prioritize areas with high transmission rates or specific populations at higher risk identified through data analysis.

- Testing and Tracing Strategies: Optimize testing strategies based on the prevalence and characteristics of the disease within different populations or areas identified through data analysis.

- Healthcare System Preparedness: Evaluate healthcare capacity data to allocate resources efficiently, anticipate surge capacity needs, and ensure adequate supplies and staffing levels.

- Vaccine Deployment: Use vaccination coverage data to identify areas with low coverage and implement targeted vaccination campaigns, address vaccine hesitancy, and encourage equity in vaccine access.

Continuous monitoring of data, evaluation of its implications, and iterative adaptation of strategies are essential for an effective pandemic response. This data-driven approach ensures that responses remain current and can be adjusted promptly to address new challenges as the situation evolves.

Management responsibilities during an outbreak in third-world countries

During an outbreak of a pandemic in third-world countries, the responsibilities of management become crucial in implementing effective measures to control and mitigate the impact of the pandemic. Here are specific responsibilities that management should undertake:

1. Crisis Management and Planning: Management must establish a dedicated crisis management team that includes healthcare experts, administrators, and representatives from various sectors. This team should develop a comprehensive pandemic response plan, including protocols for disease surveillance, early detection, communication strategies, and resource allocation.

2. Resource Allocation and Logistics: Management should ensure the availability and effective distribution of essential resources such as medical supplies, personal protective equipment (PPE), testing kits, and medicines. They must establish mechanisms to procure, store, and distribute these resources efficiently, giving priority to high-risk areas and vulnerable populations.

3. Infrastructure and Healthcare Support: Management should work to strengthen the healthcare infrastructure, including expanding hospital capacity, setting up dedicated isolation units, and enhancing laboratory capabilities for testing and diagnosis. They should also provide training and support to healthcare workers on infection prevention and control measures.

4. Public Awareness and Communication: Management should invest in widespread public awareness campaigns to disseminate accurate and timely information about the pandemic. This includes educating the public on symptoms, preventive measures, and the importance of vaccination. Communication channels such as radio, television, local community leaders, and technology platforms should be utilized to reach remote areas.

5. Collaborations and Partnerships: Management should foster collaborations and partnerships with national and international organizations, non-governmental organizations (NGOs), and local communities. These partnerships can help access additional resources, technical expertise, and support in implementing control measures and providing healthcare services.

6. Vulnerable Populations and Equity: Management must prioritize the needs of vulnerable populations, including the elderly, children, pregnant women, people with disabilities, and marginalized communities. Efforts should be made to ensure equitable access to healthcare, resources, and information. This involves collaborating with community organizations and healthcare NGOs that work directly with these populations.

7. Surveillance and Monitoring: Management should establish effective surveillance systems to track the spread of the pandemic, identify hotspots, and monitor the effectiveness of control measures. Timely reporting of cases, contact tracing, and data analysis are crucial components of surveillance systems to make informed decisions.

8. Policy and Regulatory Frameworks: Management should work alongside government and relevant authorities to develop and implement policies, regulations, and guidelines specific to the pandemic. These frameworks should ensure clear guidelines for testing, isolation, quarantine, and treatment while taking into account the socio-economic conditions and cultural sensitivities of the population.

9. Continuity Planning: Management must develop continuity plans to ensure critical services and essential sectors, such as healthcare, food supply, and utilities, are maintained during the crisis. Adequate contingency plans should be in place to manage disruptions and prevent further deterioration of socio-economic conditions.

10. Evaluation and Learning: Management should continuously evaluate the implemented strategies, assess their effectiveness, and make necessary adjustments based on the evolving situation. Learning from experiences and applying lessons to future preparedness is crucial in building resilience against future pandemics.

Management responsibilities during a pandemic in third-world countries include crisis management, resource allocation, infrastructure support, public awareness, collaborations, equity considerations, surveillance, policy development, continuity planning, and continuous evaluation. Effective and strategic management can play a vital role in controlling and managing the impact of the pandemic in these regions.

Management Affirmative Action

Management affirmative action refers to the intentional effort made by public policy implementers and managers to ensure equal opportunities and representation for historically marginalized groups. It recognizes that certain social groups have been historically disadvantaged and aims to address these disparities by implementing proactive measures. In the context of public policy implementation, management affirmative action provides a framework for selecting, promoting, and supporting individuals from underrepresented groups.

The first step in implementing management affirmative action in public policies is conducting a comprehensive analysis of the existing disparities and underrepresentation of certain groups in managerial positions. This analysis would provide a clear understanding of the areas where affirmative action is needed and would guide the development of policies and strategies to address these gaps. This data-driven approach ensures that affirmative action efforts are evidence-based and focused on the areas of greatest need.

The second step is ensuring that diverse perspectives are included in decision-making processes. This can be achieved by actively seeking representation from underrepresented groups in policy implementation teams and management positions. By diversifying the decision-making bodies, public policy implementers can benefit from a wider range of experiences, knowledge, and perspectives, which can help them make more informed and inclusive decisions.

A third step is the implementation of targeted recruitment and retention strategies. Public policy implementers can establish partnerships, networks, and outreach programs that specifically target underrepresented groups. These efforts can include targeted advertising, mentorship programs, diversity training, and flexible working arrangements to attract and retain a diverse workforce. By actively seeking out candidates from underrepresented groups, public policy implementers can create a pool of talented individuals who may have been overlooked due to systemic barriers.

The fourth step is providing training and development opportunities to support the advancement of individuals from underrepresented groups. This can involve providing leadership and management training, mentoring programs, and sponsorship opportunities. By investing in the professional development of underrepresented individuals, public policy implementers can ensure that they have the necessary skills and support to succeed in managerial positions.

The fifth step is promoting a culture of inclusivity and diversity within the organization. Public policy implementers can actively work towards creating an inclusive workplace environment that celebrates diversity, challenges bias, and promotes equity. This can be achieved through awareness campaigns, diversity and inclusion training, and the establishment of employee resource groups. By fostering a culture of inclusivity, public policy implementers can ensure that everyone feels valued, respected, and supported, regardless of their background.

The sixth step is evaluating and monitoring the impact of management affirmative action efforts. Public policy implementers must continuously assess the effectiveness of their strategies and policies. This can involve collecting and analyzing data on recruitment, promotions, and retention rates for underrepresented groups. Regular evaluations can provide insights into the progress made and highlight areas where additional actions may be required.

The final step is fostering partnerships and collaborations with external organizations, advocacy groups, and academia to further advance the management of affirmative action in public policies. By working together, public policy implementers can learn from each other's experiences, share best practices, and advocate for policy changes that promote equal representation and diversity in leadership positions.

In conclusion, management of affirmative action in the implementation of public policies involves proactive measures to address historical disparities and promote equal opportunities for underrepresented groups. By conducting comprehensive analyses, diversifying decision-making bodies, implementing targeted recruitment and retention strategies, providing training and development opportunities, fostering inclusivity, evaluating impact, and fostering collaborations, public policy implementers can work towards creating a more equitable and inclusive society.

Management affirmative action is important for several reasons. Firstly, it helps to address historical inequalities and systemic discrimination that certain social groups have faced. Many marginalized groups, such as women, racial and ethnic minorities, and individuals with disabilities, have long been underrepresented in managerial positions. Management affirmative action provides a means to rectify these disparities by intentionally promoting diversity and inclusivity.

Secondly, management affirmative action is vital for fostering innovation and creativity. A diverse workforce brings together individuals from different backgrounds, experiences, and perspectives. This diversity of thought and approach can enhance problem-solving, decision-making, and innovation within an organization. Including underrepresented groups in managerial positions ensures that a wider range of perspectives and ideas contribute to the development and implementation of public policies.

Thirdly, management affirmative action is crucial for building trust and credibility in public institutions. When marginalized groups are systematically excluded from leadership positions, it can erode trust and confidence in the government, public sector organizations, and public policies. By actively promoting diversity and inclusivity, public policy implementers demonstrate a commitment to fair representation and equal opportunity. This act of inclusion can help rebuild trust and foster greater public participation and engagement.

Fourthly, management affirmative action is essential for promoting social justice and equity. When underrepresented groups have equal opportunities to participate in decision-making processes and hold managerial positions, it helps to level the playing field and break down systemic barriers. This can result in more equitable outcomes and a more just society. Affirmative action ensures that talented individuals from marginalized communities can succeed in leadership roles, which can have a transformative impact on their lives and communities.

Lastly, management affirmative action is important because it aligns with democratic ideals and principles. Democracy is based on the notion of equal representation and participation. By actively working to address disparities and promote diversity in managerial positions, public policy implementers uphold these democratic values. Inclusive decision-making processes and diverse leadership teams ensure that different voices and perspectives are heard, leading to more informed and representative policy choices.

In conclusion, management affirmative action is important because it addresses historical inequalities, fosters innovation, builds trust, promotes social justice, and upholds democratic principles. By intentionally promoting diversity and inclusivity, public policy implementers can create a more equitable, inclusive, and successful society.

PART II

On Advancing Responsible Leadership
Strategies for Sustainable Management Practices

ON ADVANCING RESPONSIBLE LEADERSHIP

Chapter Twelve

Responsible Leadership

Introduction

The need for responsible leadership has become paramount in a world rapidly changing due to technological advancements, globalization, and environmental challenges. As leaders, we must adopt long-term strategies to ensure sustainable management practices, not only for the benefit of our organizations but for the wider society and the planet. This introductory essay explores the concept of responsible leadership, delves into the importance of sustainable management practices, and proposes strategies to advance responsible leadership for a better future.

The Context of Responsible Leadership

The concept of responsible leadership transcends the traditional understanding of leadership, which solely focuses on maximizing profits and shareholder value. Responsible leadership encompasses a broader perspective that considers the impact of decisions on stakeholders, including employees, customers, communities, and the environment. It emphasizes the need to act ethically, with long-term interests in mind, to create value for all stakeholders.

Global challenges such as climate change, social inequality, and resource depletion demand responsible leadership to tackle these complex issues. The conventional approach of relentless pursuit of short-term gains has resulted in negative externalities, harming businesses and wider society. Responsible leadership recognizes the interconnectedness of business and society and seeks to create a positive impact while ensuring the sustainability of resources for future generations.

The Importance of Sustainable Management Practices

Sustainable management practices are vital for the long-term success and survival of organizations. By incorporating sustainability into management practices, companies can improve their reputation, attract, and retain talent, and gain a competitive advantage in an increasingly conscious market. Responsible management practices also enhance the resilience of organizations, enabling them to navigate the challenges of an uncertain and rapidly changing business environment.

Moreover, sustainable management practices play a significant role in addressing societal and environmental concerns. Businesses are responsible for mitigating their negative impacts on the environment and addressing social issues, considering the long-term consequences of their actions and decisions. By adopting sustainable practices, organizations can contribute to the achievement of sustainable development goals, promote social equity, and preserve natural resources.

Strategies for Advancing Responsible Leadership

To advance responsible leadership and sustainable management practices, organizations need to adopt a holistic and proactive approach. The following strategies can guide leaders in leading the way toward a more sustainable and responsible future:

Developing a clear purpose and values: Leaders must define a purpose beyond profit that aligns with sustainable development goals. This purpose should guide decision-making processes and be embedded in the organization's values and culture.

Stakeholder engagement and collaboration: Organizations need to engage with stakeholders, including employees, customers, suppliers, communities, and NGOs, to understand their expectations, needs, and concerns. Collaborative efforts can lead to better decision-making, innovation, and problem-solving.

Integration of sustainability into strategic planning: Responsible leaders should integrate sustainability considerations into the core strategic planning process. This involves setting measurable sustainability goals, implementing performance metrics, and regularly evaluating progress.

Ethical and transparent governance: Responsible leadership requires ethical behavior at all levels of an organization. Boards of directors need to prioritize sustainability and ensure transparent governance practices, promoting integrity and accountability.

Fostering a culture of innovation and learning: Leaders must create an environment that encourages innovation and learning, allowing employees to explore and implement sustainable practices. This includes providing training, rewards, and recognition for sustainable initiatives.

Embedding sustainability into operations: Sustainable management practices should be embedded into all aspects of operations, from procurement to production, coordination, and waste management. This includes promoting energy efficiency, reducing waste, and adopting renewable energy sources.

Measuring and reporting sustainability performance: Regular measurement and transparent reporting of sustainability performance are crucial to hold organizations accountable and inform stakeholders. Leaders should adopt recognized reporting frameworks, such as the Global Reporting Initiative (GRI), to enhance credibility and comparability.

Advancing responsible leadership through sustainable management practices is not only an ethical imperative but also a strategic necessity. Responsible leaders recognize the interconnectedness of business, society, and the environment, and strive to create positive impact and value for all stakeholders. By adopting the strategies outlined in this introduction, organizations can not only achieve long-term success but also contribute to the well-being of society and the preservation of our planet for future generations.

Overview of Responsible Leadership

Responsible leadership is a concept that has gained significant attention in recent years as there is a growing recognition that businesses have a larger role to play in society beyond mere profit-making. Responsible leadership is about considering the interests of all stakeholders, including employees, customers, communities, and the environment. It requires leaders to make decisions that are ethically and morally sound, and that contribute to the overall well-being of society. In this essay, we will explore the key characteristics and practices of responsible leadership and discuss its benefits for both organizations and society.

Characteristics of Responsible Leadership

1. Ethical Decision-making: Responsible leaders make decisions that are guided by ethical principles. They consider the potential impact of their decisions on various stakeholders and strive to do what is right, just, and fair.

2. Transparency: Responsible leaders are transparent in their actions and decisions. They communicate openly with all stakeholders and are willing to explain the rationale behind their choices.

3. Accountability: Responsible leaders take responsibility for their actions and the outcomes of their decisions. They are willing to accept criticism and learn from their mistakes.

4. Sustainability: Responsible leaders take a long-term perspective and consider the environmental, social, and economic implications of their decisions. They promote sustainability and seek to minimize any negative impact on the planet and future generations.

5. Inclusivity: Responsible leaders value diversity and inclusion. They create inclusive work environments where

all employees feel valued and respected. They promote equal opportunities and ensure fairness in decision-making processes.

Practices of Responsible Leadership

1. Stakeholder Engagement: Responsible leaders actively engage with their stakeholders to understand their needs and concerns. They involve stakeholders in decision-making processes and seek their input to create shared value.

2. Corporate Social Responsibility: Responsible leaders integrate corporate social responsibility (CSR) into the core of their business strategies. They go beyond legal requirements and actively contribute to society through initiatives such as philanthropy, employee volunteering, and environmental stewardship.

3. Ethical Leadership: Responsible leaders lead by example and set high ethical standards for their organizations. They promote a culture of integrity and hold themselves and others accountable for ethical behavior.

4. Employee Well-being: Responsible leaders prioritize the well-being of their employees. They create a supportive work environment that promotes work-life balance, mental health, and personal development.

5. Environmental Stewardship: Responsible leaders recognize the importance of environmental sustainability. They implement practices to minimize their organization's carbon footprint, conserve resources, and reduce waste.

Benefits of Responsible Leadership

1. Enhanced Reputation: Organizations led by responsible leaders gain a positive reputation, which enhances their brand value and attracts customers, investors, and top talent.

2. Improved Employee Engagement: Responsible leadership fosters a sense of purpose and engagement among employees. When employees see that their organization is committed to responsible practices, they are more likely to be motivated and loyal.

3. Stronger Stakeholder Relationships: Responsible leaders build trust and collaborative relationships with stakeholders. This leads to better cooperation, improved understanding of stakeholders' needs, and shared value creation.

4. Innovation and Adaptability: Responsible leaders foster a culture of innovation and adaptability. By considering the long-term implications of their decisions, they are better equipped to anticipate and respond to changing societal and environmental trends.

5. Long-Term Sustainability: By incorporating responsible practices into their strategies, organizations led by responsible leaders contribute to the sustainability of their operations, the environment, and society.

Responsible leadership is an approach that acknowledges the broader role of businesses in society. It requires leaders to make decisions that are guided by ethical principles, consider the interests of all stakeholders, and promote sustainability. Responsible leadership not only benefits organizations in terms of reputation and performance but also contributes to the well-being of society. By embracing responsible leadership, organizations can create a positive impact on the world while ensuring their long-term success.

The Importance of Sustainable Management Practices

Sustainable management practices have become increasingly important in today's business landscape. As the world faces complex environmental, social, and economic challenges, organizations need to adopt sustainable management practices to ensure their long-term success and contribute to a better future. Sustainable management practices involve integrating environmental, social, and economic considerations into decision-making processes, to create value for all stakeholders. In this essay, we will explore the importance of sustainable management practices and discuss the benefits they offer to organizations and society.

Benefits of Sustainable Management Practices

1. Environmental Stewardship

One of the key benefits of sustainable management practices is environmental stewardship. By adopting sustainable practices, organizations can minimize their environmental impact and contribute to the protection of natural resources and ecosystems. This can be achieved through initiatives such as reducing greenhouse gas emissions, conserving energy and water, and implementing waste management strategies. Environmental stewardship not only helps organizations comply with regulations but also enhances their reputation and attracts environmentally conscious customers.

2. Cost Savings

Sustainable management practices can lead to significant cost savings for organizations. By adopting energy-efficient technologies, optimizing resource consumption, and reducing waste, organizations can lower their operational costs. For example, implementing energy-saving measures can result in reduced utility bills, while waste reduction initiatives can lower disposal and production costs. These cost savings not only contribute to the bottom line of organizations but also enhance their competitiveness in the market.

3. Risk Management

Sustainable management practices play a crucial role in mitigating risks for organizations. By identifying and addressing environmental, social, and governance (ESG) risks, organizations can reduce their vulnerability to potential legal, reputational, and financial consequences. For instance, by evaluating and mitigating supply chain risks, organizations can avoid disruptions and maintain business continuity. Additionally, by complying with environmental regulations and societal expectations, organizations can safeguard their reputation and avoid penalties or lawsuits.

4. Innovation and Resilience

Sustainable management practices foster a culture of innovation and resilience within organizations. By considering long-term environmental and societal implications, organizations are encouraged to develop innovative solutions that address emerging challenges. This can lead to the creation of new products, services, and business models that cater to the changing needs of customers and society. Additionally, by embracing sustainable practices, organizations become more adaptable and resilient to external shocks, such as resource scarcity, climate change, and social instability.

5. Stakeholder Engagement and Reputation

Sustainable management practices help organizations build strong relationships with their stakeholders, including employees, customers, suppliers, communities, and investors. By demonstrating a commitment to environmental and social responsibility, organizations can enhance trust, loyalty, and engagement among stakeholders. This can lead to increased customer loyalty, improved employee morale and productivity, and better collaboration with suppliers and communities. Furthermore, organizations that are perceived as socially and environmentally responsible tend to attract socially responsible investors, which can result in enhanced access to capital and improved financial performance.

6. Legal and Regulatory Compliance

Sustainable management practices assist organizations in meeting legal and regulatory requirements. Governments around the world are increasingly implementing stricter environmental and social regulations, and organizations need to ensure compliance to avoid financial penalties and reputational damage. By adopting sustainable practices, organizations can proactively address these compliance requirements, minimize risks, and stay ahead of regulatory changes. Moreover, organizations that exceed regulatory standards and embrace sustainability as a core value are more likely to develop a positive relationship with regulatory agencies.

7. Employee Attraction and Retention

Sustainable management practices are also instrumental in attracting and retaining top talent. Employees, especially millennials and Gen Z, value organizations that demonstrate a commitment to environmental and social responsibility. By incorporating sustainable practices into their strategies, organizations can create an attractive work culture that aligns with the values of prospective employees. This can result in a competitive advantage in recruitment and a higher rate of employee retention. Additionally, employees who are engaged in sustainable activities feel a sense of purpose and are more motivated and productive.

8. Long-Term Value Creation

The most significant benefit of sustainable management practices is the long-term value they create for organizations. By considering economic, social, and environmental factors in decision-making, organizations are better positioned to identify and capture new business opportunities. By embedding sustainability into their core strategies, organizations can create lasting value for all stakeholders, including shareholders, employees, customers, communities, and the environment. This long-term value creation enhances organizational resilience and contributes to the overall well-being of society.

Sustainable management practices are essential for organizations striving to achieve long-term success in a rapidly changing world. By integrating environmental, social, and economic considerations into decision-making processes, organizations can minimize their environmental footprint, reduce costs, mitigate risks, and enhance stakeholder relationships. Sustainable management practices foster innovation, resilience, and employee engagement, while also ensuring legal and regulatory compliance. Sustainable management practices enable organizations to create long-term value and contribute to the well-being of society. It is therefore crucial for organizations to recognize the importance of sustainable management practices and embrace them as a fundamental part of their business strategies.

Purpose and Scope of the Book

The purpose of the book "Advancing Responsible Leadership: Strategies for Sustainable Management Practices" is to provide in-depth insights and practical strategies for leaders and managers to effectively integrate responsible and sustainable practices into their organizations. The book aims to guide leaders in their journey toward responsible leadership by offering actionable approaches that can be implemented in various organizational contexts.

The scope of the book is broad, covering a wide range of topics related to responsible leadership and sustainable management practices. Some key areas addressed in the book may include:

1. Understanding Responsible Leadership: The book explores the concept of responsible leadership, its principles, and its significance in today's business environment.

2. The Business Case for Sustainability: It discusses the rationale behind integrating sustainability into business strategies and the potential benefits it can bring to organizations, such as cost savings, improved reputation, and enhanced stakeholder relationships.

3. Strategies for Responsible Leadership: The book offers practical strategies for leaders to implement responsible and sustainable practices within their organizations. It may include steps to foster a culture of responsible leadership, engage stakeholders, develop sustainable business models, and create a positive social and environmental impact.

4. Responsible Leadership in Different Contexts: The book recognizes that responsible leadership practices can vary across industries, sectors, and geographical locations. It may provide insights into how responsible leadership can be applied in different contexts, including small and large organizations, non-profit entities, and multinational corporations.

5. Ethical Decision-making and Corporate Governance: The book explores the role of ethics and corporate governance in responsible leadership. It may discuss frameworks and approaches for ethical decision-making and responsible governance practices that promote transparency, accountability, and fairness.

6. Sustainable Human Resource Management: The book may delve into sustainable human resource management practices that focus on employee well-being, diversity and inclusion, and talent development. It also touches upon the importance of employee engagement and motivation in driving sustainable performance.

7. Sustainable Supply Chain Management: The book may address the integration of sustainability principles into supply chain management, including responsible sourcing, supplier engagement, and coordination optimization.

8. Measuring and Reporting Sustainability Performance: The book may guide on measuring and reporting sustainability performance, including key performance indicators (KPIs), sustainability reporting frameworks, and certifications.

9. Case Studies and Best Practices: The book may highlight real-world examples and case studies of organizations that have successfully embraced responsible leadership and sustainable management practices. It may highlight best practices and lessons learned from these organizations.

Overall, the purpose and scope of the book "Advancing Responsible Leadership: Strategies for Sustainable Management Practices" is to equip leaders and managers with the knowledge, tools, and inspiration to foster responsible leadership and drive sustainable outcomes within their organizations.

Structure of the Book

The structure of the book "Advancing Responsible Leadership: Strategies for Sustainable Management Practices" may vary depending on the author's approach and the specific content of the book. However, a structure for the book could include the following sections:

1. Introduction

- Provide an overview of the book's purpose, scope, and key objectives.
- Sets the context for responsible leadership and sustainable management practices.

2. Understanding Responsible Leadership

- Explores the concept of responsible leadership, its principles, and key characteristics.
- Discusses the importance of responsible leadership for organizations and society.

•3. The Business Case for Sustainability

- Presents the economic, social, and environmental rationale for incorporating sustainability into business strategies.

- Discusses the potential benefits and opportunities of sustainable management practices.

4. Strategies for Responsible Leadership
   - Offers practical strategies and approaches for leaders to integrate responsible and sustainable practices into their organizations.
   - Covers topics such as fostering a culture of responsible leadership, stakeholder engagement, and developing sustainable business models.
5. Ethical Decision-making and Corporate Governance
   - Explores the role of ethics and corporate governance in responsible leadership.
   - Discuss frameworks and approaches for ethical decision-making and responsible governance practices.
6. Sustainable Human Resource Management
   - Examines sustainable human resource management practices, including employee well-being, diversity and inclusion, and talent development.
   - Discusses the importance of employee engagement and motivation in driving sustainable performance.
7. Sustainable Supply Chain Management
   - Addresses sustainable supply chain management practices, including responsible sourcing, supplier engagement, and organization optimization.
   - Discusses the integration of sustainability principles into supply chain operations.
8. Measuring and Reporting Sustainability Performance
   - Guides measuring and reporting sustainability performance.
   - Discuss key performance indicators (KPIs), sustainability reporting frameworks, and certifications.
9. Case Studies and Best Practices
   - Showcases real-world examples and case studies of organizations that have successfully embraced responsible leadership and sustainable management practices.
   - Highlights best practices, lessons learned, and success stories.
10. Conclusion
    - Summarize the key takeaways from the book.
    - Emphasizes the significance of responsible leadership and sustainable management practices in driving organizational success and societal well-being.
11. Appendix (optional)
    - Includes additional resources, tools, or frameworks that readers can refer to for further guidance and implementation.

It is important to note that the above structure is just a suggested outline, and the actual structure of the book may differ based on the author's preferences and the specific content covered in the book.

Chapter Thirteen

Understanding Responsible Leadership

Defining Responsible Leadership

Introduction

Responsible leadership can be defined as a leadership approach that considers the ethical, social, and environmental impact of decisions and actions, to create sustainable value for all stakeholders. It requires leaders to consider the interests of employees, customers, communities, and the environment, in addition to financial objectives. Responsible leaders make decisions guided by moral and ethical principles, demonstrating integrity, transparency, and accountability in their actions. They prioritize the well-being of their employees, promote diversity and inclusion, and foster a positive work culture. Responsible leaders also engage with stakeholders, seeking their input and considering their needs and concerns in decision-making processes. They embrace environmental sustainability, implementing practices to minimize the organization's carbon footprint, conserve resources, and reduce waste. Responsible leadership is about making choices that contribute to the long-term success of the organization while also advancing the well-being of society.

The terms of responsible leadership encompass a range of principles and practices that guide leaders in their decision-making and actions. Some key terms associated with responsible leadership include:

1. Ethical Decision-making: Responsible leaders prioritize ethical considerations and ensure their decisions align with ethical principles and values. They consider the potential impact of their decisions on various stakeholders and strive to do what is right, just, and fair.

Ethical decision-making is a complex process that involves weighing numerous factors and considering the consequences of different actions. It requires individuals to consider both their values and the societal or organizational norms that guide behavior. Here are seven extensive paragraphs elaborating on the importance of ethical decision-making:

Ethical decision-making is crucial for ensuring that individuals and organizations behave in a responsible and morally upright manner. By considering the ethical implications of their actions, individuals can avoid causing harm to others and act in a way that promotes fairness and justice. This is particularly important in professional contexts, where decisions can have far-reaching consequences on stakeholders such as employees, customers, and the community.

Ethical decision-making also contributes to the establishment and maintenance of trust. When individuals consistently make ethical choices, others are more likely to trust them and have confidence in their judgment. This is particularly relevant in leadership positions, where leaders who demonstrate ethical behavior are more likely to inspire and motivate others to act analogously. Trust is the foundation of strong relationships, whether in personal or professional settings, and ethical decision-making plays a significant role in building and maintaining trust.

Another important aspect of ethical decision-making is its impact on an individual's character and personal development. By consistently making ethical choices, individuals shape their character and develop a strong moral compass. This can enhance their self-esteem, promote a sense of integrity, and allow them to navigate complex ethical dilemmas with confidence. Furthermore, ethical decision-making can foster a sense of personal fulfillment and satisfaction, as individuals align their actions with their deeply held values and beliefs.

Ethical decision-making is also critical for avoiding legal ramifications and reputation damage. Organizations that make decisions without considering ethical implications are more likely to face legal consequences, such as lawsuits or regulatory penalties. Additionally, unethical behavior can tarnish an individual's or organization's reputation, leading to a loss of trust and credibility. By taking an ethical approach to decision-making, individuals and organizations can protect themselves from legal and reputational risks.

Ethical decision-making plays a vital role in long-term sustainability and success. Organizations that prioritize ethics are more likely to attract and retain talented individuals, as well as gain the trust and loyalty of customers. Ethical behavior can also lead to positive relationships with suppliers and business partners, resulting in mutually beneficial collaborations. Over time, organizations that consistently make ethical decisions are likely to build a formidable reputation and enjoy sustained success in the marketplace.

Ethical decision-making is not only essential for individuals and organizations but also for society. Collective ethical decision-making shapes the norms and values of a society, guiding its behavior and ensuring the well-being of its members. When individuals and organizations prioritize ethics, they contribute to the creation of a more just and equitable society. Additionally, ethical decision-making can promote social responsibility, encouraging individuals and organizations to consider the impact of their actions on the environment and the wider community.

Lastly, ethical decision-making can have a positive impact on the overall well-being and happiness of individuals. By making ethical choices, individuals align their actions with their values, leading to a sense of authenticity and personal fulfillment. Additionally, ethical decision-making often involves considering the well-being of others and fostering empathy and compassion. Research has shown that acts of kindness and ethical behavior can contribute to increased happiness and psychological well-being.

In conclusion, ethical decision-making is an important process that encompasses multiple dimensions, from personal development to societal well-being. Ethical choices serve as a foundation for trust, integrity, and responsible behavior, benefiting individuals, organizations, and society. By prioritizing ethics in decision-making, individuals can navigate complex dilemmas, avoid legal and reputational risks, and contribute to the creation of a just and sustainable future.

2. Transparency: Responsible leaders are transparent in their actions and decisions. They communicate openly with all stakeholders and provide clear explanations for their choices. They are willing to share information and engage in open dialogue, fostering trust and accountability.

Ethical leadership and transparency are vital components of a successful and sustainable organization. They involve leaders demonstrating integrity, honesty, and accountability, while also promoting a culture of openness and clear communication. Here are ten paragraphs elaborating on the importance of ethical leadership and transparency:

Ethical leadership encompasses a set of values and behaviors that prioritize doing what is right, just, and fair. Ethical leaders are guided by a strong moral compass, making decisions that consider the best interests of all stakeholders involved. They act with integrity and transparency, setting a positive example for their team members and fostering a culture of trust and respect.

Transparency plays a crucial role in ethical leadership. Openly communicating information, decisions, and processes helps build trust within the organization. When leaders are transparent, employees feel valued and included, which enhances engagement and motivation. Transparency also enables employees to understand the reasoning behind decisions, even if they may not always agree with them, which contributes to a more cohesive and productive work environment.

Ethical leadership and transparency go hand in hand in promoting a culture of accountability. Transparent leaders take responsibility for their actions, admit mistakes, and learn from them. This promotes a sense of ownership and accountability among team members, inspiring them to follow suit. When accountability is emphasized, individuals are more likely to take their roles and responsibilities seriously and strive for excellence.

Ethical leadership and transparency also contribute to enhanced ethical behavior within an organization. When leaders uphold and demonstrate ethical values, employees are more likely to emulate those behaviors. Transparent leaders create an environment where ethical decision-making is encouraged and rewarded, allowing employees to feel empowered to make ethical choices in their daily work responsibilities.

Transparent leaders foster better communication and collaboration among team members. By openly sharing information, leaders create a sense of transparency that enables employees to work together more effectively. When everyone has access to the same information, misunderstandings and miscommunications can be minimized, leading to improved teamwork and outcomes.

Ethical leadership and transparency are key to building and maintaining a positive organizational reputation. When leaders act ethically and communicate transparently, stakeholders, including customers, investors, and the public, are more likely to trust the organization. Trust is an asset that helps attract and retain customers, build partnerships, and secure long-term success.

Ethical leadership and transparency are especially important during times of crisis or change. When leaders openly communicate about the situation, address concerns and uncertainties, and act with integrity, they instill confidence and reduce anxiety. Transparency allows for informed decision-making and enables organizations to navigate challenges more effectively.

Ethical leadership and transparency also contribute to the development of strong ethical frameworks and governance structures within organizations. Transparent leaders ensure that ethical guidelines and policies are in place, understood, and followed by all members of the organization. This helps establish a solid foundation for ethical decision-making and promotes consistency across the organization.

Ethical leadership and transparency can have a positive impact on employee engagement and morale. When leaders are ethical and transparent, employees feel valued, respected, and included. This fosters a sense of belonging and commitment to the organization. Employees are more likely to be motivated and perform at their best when they trust their leaders and believe in the organization's values.

Finally, ethical leadership and transparency support long-term organizational sustainability. By acting ethically and transparently, leaders can mitigate risks, avoid legal and reputational harm, and build strong relationships with stakeholders. This fosters stability and resilience, allowing the organization to thrive in the face of challenges and adapt to changing environments.

In conclusion, ethical leadership and transparency are vital for the success, reputation, and sustainability of organizations. Transparent leaders who act with integrity and communicate openly promote a culture of trust, accountability, and ethical behavior. By prioritizing ethical leadership and emphasizing transparency, organizations can create a positive work environment, improve collaboration and engagement, and build strong relationships with stakeholders.

3. Accountability: Responsible leaders take responsibility for their actions and the outcomes of their decisions, acknowledging both successes and failures. They are willing to accept criticism and learn from their mistakes. They hold themselves and others accountable for achieving organizational goals and upholding ethical standards.

Ethical leadership and transparency are two interconnected principles that are crucial in ensuring the success and sustainability of organizations. Ethical leadership involves leaders who demonstrate a strong moral compass, act with integrity, and prioritize the well-being and interests of stakeholders. Transparency, on the other hand, encompasses open communication, accountability, and the sharing of information with all members of the organization. Together, ethical leadership and transparency create a culture of trust, integrity, and responsible decision-making. Here are nine extensive paragraphs elaborating on the importance of ethical leadership and transparency:

Ethical leadership is the foundation of a strong and ethical organizational culture. When leaders consistently demonstrate ethical behavior, they set the tone for the entire organization. They make decisions that consider the long-term impact on stakeholders, uphold principles of fairness and justice, and act with honesty and integrity. Ethical leaders serve as role models, inspiring their team members to adopt similar values and behaviors.

Transparency is essential in ethical leadership as it fosters trust and credibility. When leaders are transparent in their communication and decision-making processes, employees feel valued, respected, and included. Openly sharing information about the organization's goals, strategies, and challenges allows employees to understand the bigger picture and the rationale behind decisions. This enables them to align their work with the organization's mission and vision.

Ethical leadership promotes ethical behavior throughout the organization. Leaders who prioritize ethical decision-making create an environment where employees feel empowered to make choices that align with their values. They establish clear ethical guidelines and policies, communicate them effectively, and ensure they are consistently followed. This cultivates a sense of responsibility and fosters ethical decision-making at all levels of the organization.

Transparency enhances accountability in ethical leadership. Transparent leaders take responsibility for their actions and decisions, acknowledging both successes and failures. By modeling accountability, they encourage employees to take ownership of their work and contribute to the organization's goals. When individuals are held accountable for their actions, it promotes a culture of excellence, continuous improvement, and personal growth.

Ethical leadership and transparency contribute to the creation of a positive organizational culture. Leaders who act ethically and transparently foster a sense of trust and collaboration among employees. This leads to increased job satisfaction, engagement, and motivation. A positive organizational culture attracts and retains talented individuals, as they are more likely to be drawn to an environment where their values align with those of the organization.

Transparency is particularly important during times of change or uncertainty. When leaders openly communicate about challenges, risks, and potential impacts on employees, it reduces anxiety and fosters a sense of stability. Transparent communication helps employees understand the reasons behind changes, increases their sense of involvement, and encourages them to adapt and embrace new circumstances.

Ethical leadership and transparency play a crucial role in building and maintaining a strong organizational reputation. When leaders act ethically and communicate transparently, stakeholders perceive the organization as trustworthy and reliable. This leads to increased customer loyalty, investor confidence, and positive relationships with partners and suppliers. Organizational reputation is an asset that supports long-term success and growth.

Ethical leadership and transparency support sound decision-making processes. When leaders prioritize ethical principles and communicate openly about the decision-making process, they ensure that choices are made based on clear and well-informed rationales. Transparency in decision-making assures employees that decisions are fair and unbiased, which builds trust and reduces potential conflicts or grievances.

Finally, ethical leadership and transparency are essential for organizational sustainability. Leaders who act ethically and transparently minimize the risk of legal and reputational damage. By making decisions considering the long-term interests of the organization and stakeholders, they contribute to the organization's resilience and ability to adapt to changing environments. Ethical leaders inspire loyalty, commitment, and innovation, which are key elements for sustainable growth and success.

In conclusion, ethical leadership and transparency are interconnected principles that support the well-being, trust, and success of organizations. Ethical leaders act with integrity, prioritize stakeholders' interests, and foster a culture of responsible decision-making. Transparency ensures open communication, fosters accountability and builds trust among employees and other stakeholders. Together, ethical leadership and transparency create a positive organizational culture, enhance decision-making processes, and contribute to long-term sustainability and success.

4. Sustainability: Responsible leaders take a long-term perspective and consider the environmental, social, and economic implications of their decisions. They promote sustainability by implementing practices that minimize environmental impact, conserve resources, and drive positive social change. They recognize that sustainable practices contribute to the long-term success of the organization and the well-being of society.

Ethical leadership and sustainability are two interconnected concepts that are crucial in today's business landscape. Ethical leadership involves leaders who prioritize values such as integrity, fairness, and social responsibility. Sustainability, on the other hand, refers to the ability of an organization to meet the needs of the present without compromising the ability of future generations to meet their own needs. Here are seven extensive paragraphs elaborating on the importance of ethical leadership in promoting sustainability:

Ethical leadership is essential for promoting sustainable practices within organizations. Leaders who prioritize ethical decision-making consider the long-term impact of their actions on not only their stakeholders but also the environment and society at large. They consider the social, environmental, and economic implications of their decisions, aiming for a balance between profitability and responsible business practices. Ethical leaders help organizations move away from short-term, profit-focused approaches toward long-term sustainability goals.

Ethical leaders foster a culture of sustainability throughout the organization. By acting with integrity, transparency, and social responsibility, they inspire and engage employees to embrace sustainable practices. Ethical leaders set clear expectations and guide ethical conduct, encouraging employees to incorporate sustainability into their day-to-day activities. They promote teamwork, collaboration, and knowledge-sharing to drive sustainable innovation and problem-solving across the organization.

Ethical leaders recognize that sustainability is not just an environmental issue but encompasses social and economic dimensions as well. They understand that sustainable practices should address issues such as employee well-being, fair labor practices, community engagement, and responsible resource management. Ethical leadership helps organizations align their values and actions with the principles of sustainability, considering the impact of their decisions on all stakeholders and promoting a comprehensive approach to societal well-being.

Ethical leadership drives stakeholder engagement in sustainability efforts. Ethical leaders actively engage with various stakeholders, including employees, customers, suppliers, and local communities, to understand their perspectives and incorporate their input into decision-making processes. By involving stakeholders in sustainable initiatives, leaders foster a sense of ownership and shared responsibility, creating a more inclusive and impactful approach to sustainability.

Ethical leadership promotes transparency and accountability in sustainability reporting. Ethical leaders ensure accurate and comprehensive reporting of sustainability metrics and goals, providing stakeholders with transparent information about the organization's environmental, social, and economic performance. Transparent reporting allows stakeholders to hold the organization accountable for its sustainability commitments and progress, fostering trust and credibility.

Ethical leaders recognize the importance of continuous improvement and innovation in sustainability efforts.

They encourage employees to question existing practices, explore innovative ideas, and find creative solutions to sustainability challenges. Ethical leaders provide support and resources for employees to develop and implement sustainable initiatives, fostering a culture of learning and continuous improvement.

Ethical leadership and sustainability go hand in hand in building a positive organizational reputation. When leaders prioritize ethical behavior and sustainability, they enhance the organization's credibility and trustworthiness. A formidable reputation for ethical leadership and sustainability attracts socially conscious customers, investors, and talent, creating a competitive advantage in the market. Ethical leaders who prioritize sustainability also contribute to the long-term viability and success of the organization, as sustainable practices often reduce costs, increase resource efficiency, and enhance long-term value creation.

In conclusion, ethical leadership is vital in promoting sustainability within organizations. Ethical leaders prioritize values such as integrity, fairness, and social responsibility, considering the long-term impact of their decisions on stakeholders and the environment. By fostering a culture of sustainability, engaging stakeholders, promoting transparency, and driving continuous improvement, ethical leaders contribute to the organization's ability to meet the needs of the present without compromising the ability of future generations to meet their own needs. Ethical leadership and sustainability are not only compatible but also mutually reinforcing, creating both social and economic value for organizations and society.

5. Inclusivity: Responsible leaders value diversity and inclusion. They create inclusive work environments where all individuals feel valued and respected. They promote equal opportunities and fairness in decision-making processes, ensuring that diverse perspectives are heard and considered.

Ethical leadership and inclusivity are two interconnected principles that are essential for creating a diverse and equitable workplace. Ethical leadership involves leaders who prioritize fairness, justice, and respect for all individuals. Inclusivity, on the other hand, encompasses creating an environment where everyone feels welcome, valued, and included, regardless of their background or identities. Here are nine extensive paragraphs elaborating on the importance of ethical leadership in promoting inclusivity:

Ethical leaders prioritize inclusivity by recognizing and valuing the diversity of their team members. They embrace differences in backgrounds, experiences, perspectives, and identities. Ethical leaders understand that diversity brings unique ideas and insights to the table, enhancing creativity, innovation, and problem-solving within the organization.

Inclusive leadership is built on the foundation of ethical conduct. Ethical leaders treat all individuals with fairness, dignity, and respect, regardless of their race, gender, sexual orientation, age, or other characteristics. They foster an environment where team members feel safe to express themselves, share their opinions, and contribute their authentic selves without fear of judgment or discrimination.

Ethical leaders ensure that organizational policies and practices promote inclusivity. They examine and challenge any biases or discriminatory practices that may exist in hiring, promotion, or decision-making processes. Ethical leaders seek to create a level playing field for all individuals, allowing them equal opportunities to succeed and thrive.

Inclusivity is promoted through open communication and active listening. Ethical leaders create a culture where everyone's voice is valued and heard. They actively seek out different perspectives and encourage individuals to express their thoughts and concerns. By fostering an inclusive communication environment, ethical leaders create a sense of psychological safety and enable the organization to benefit from diverse ideas and insights.

Ethical leaders address unconscious biases and stereotypes within the organization. They educate themselves and team members about the impact of biases on decision-making, performance evaluations, and career advancement.

Ethical leaders work to mitigate the influence of biases by creating fair and objective evaluation criteria and by challenging assumptions and stereotypes that may hinder inclusivity.

Ethical leaders understand the importance of representation and inclusion at all levels of the organization. They actively promote diversity in leadership positions and ensure that individuals from underrepresented groups have opportunities to advance. By fostering a diverse leadership team, ethical leaders create role models and inspire others, while also bringing a broader range of perspectives to decision-making processes.

Inclusive leaders create an environment where everyone can bring their full selves to work. They promote psychological safety, encouraging individuals to share their experiences, concerns, and ideas without fear of judgment or repercussion. Ethical leaders foster a supportive and collaborative atmosphere that values vulnerability, empathy, and understanding.

Ethical leaders invest in diversity and inclusion training and education. They provide resources and learning opportunities for team members to increase their awareness and understanding of diverse cultures, identities, and experiences. Ethical leaders recognize that inclusivity is an ongoing journey that requires continuous learning and improvement.

Ethical leadership and inclusivity contribute to a positive organizational culture and overall success. Inclusive environments foster higher levels of employee engagement, satisfaction, and retention. They also promote teamwork, innovation, and creativity. Ethical leaders who prioritize inclusivity not only attract and retain diverse talent but also enhance the organization's reputation, customer base, and market competitiveness.

In conclusion, ethical leadership plays a critical role in promoting inclusivity within organizations. Ethical leaders prioritize fairness, respect, and valuing diverse perspectives. By challenging biases, promoting open communication, and fostering an inclusive culture, ethical leaders create an environment where all individuals feel welcome, valued, and included. Inclusive leadership benefits both the organization and its employees, fostering higher engagement, innovation, and overall success. Ethical leadership and inclusivity go hand in hand, creating a workplace that celebrates diversity, empowers individuals, and embraces the values of fairness and equality.

6. Stakeholder Engagement: Responsible leaders actively engage with their stakeholders, including employees, customers, communities, and investors. They seek input, listen to concerns, and consider diverse perspectives. They build and maintain strong relationships with stakeholders, fostering trust and collaboration.

Ethical leadership and stakeholder engagement are two interconnected principles that are crucial for building trust, fostering collaboration, and promoting responsible decision-making within organizations. Ethical leadership involves leaders who prioritize the well-being and interests of all stakeholders, considering the potential impact of their decisions on employees, customers, communities, and other relevant parties. Stakeholder engagement, on the other hand, refers to actively involving stakeholders in decision-making processes, listening to their perspectives, and incorporating their input into organizational strategies. Here are twelve extensive paragraphs elaborating on the importance of ethical leadership in promoting stakeholder engagement:

Ethical leaders prioritize stakeholder engagement by recognizing the value and importance of diverse perspectives. They actively seek out the input and feedback of stakeholders to understand their needs, concerns, and expectations. Ethical leaders understand that engaging stakeholders leads to better decision-making and more sustainable outcomes.

Stakeholder engagement is important for ethical decision-making. Ethical leaders recognize that decisions made in isolation are more likely to overlook potential ethical dilemmas or inadvertently harm certain stakeholders. By actively engaging stakeholders, ethical leaders can ensure that decisions are informed by a range of perspectives and consider the potential impact on various groups.

Ethical leaders create a culture of trust and open communication, which is essential for effective stakeholder engagement. Through transparent and honest communication, ethical leaders build trust with stakeholders, establishing a foundation of credibility and reliability. Trust enables stakeholders to feel comfortable expressing their opinions and concerns, which promotes engagement and collaboration.

Ethical leaders actively involve stakeholders in decision-making processes, ensuring that their voices are heard and valued. This involvement can take various forms, such as seeking input through surveys or focus groups, organizing stakeholder consultations or forums, or including representatives from different stakeholder groups in decision-making committees or advisory boards. Ethical leaders recognize that stakeholder perspectives are essential for making informed decisions that are in the best interests of all stakeholders.

Stakeholder engagement promotes organizational transparency and accountability. By involving stakeholders in decision-making processes, ethical leaders can provide clear explanations and rationales for the decisions made. This transparency enhances stakeholder trust and understanding of the organization's actions, and it holds leaders accountable for their decisions by providing an opportunity for stakeholders to provide feedback and challenge decisions when necessary.

Ethical leaders create opportunities for ongoing dialogue and engagement with stakeholders. They understand that stakeholder engagement is not a one-time event but an ongoing process that requires consistent efforts. Ethical leaders create platforms for stakeholder input, such as regular open forums, surveys, or feedback mechanisms, to ensure that stakeholder engagement is embedded in the organizational culture and decision-making processes.

Ethical leaders prioritize the well-being and interests of stakeholders over short-term gains. In situations where there may be conflicting interests, ethical leaders consider the long-term impacts on stakeholders and the organization's overall reputation and sustainability. They make decisions that balance stakeholder needs and interests, seeking win-win solutions whenever possible.

Ethical leaders use stakeholder engagement as a tool for social responsibility. They actively seek input from stakeholders who may be impacted by the organization's activities and decisions, such as local communities or environmental organizations. By engaging with these stakeholders, ethical leaders can ensure that the organization's actions align with its values and contribute positively to society.

Stakeholder engagement promotes shared ownership and responsibility. Ethical leaders involve stakeholders in the co-creation of organizational strategies and objectives. By actively seeking stakeholder input, ethical leaders ensure that decisions are collectively owned and supported, enhancing stakeholders' commitment to the organization's mission and goals.

Ethical leaders recognize that stakeholder engagement can lead to more innovative and sustainable solutions. By involving stakeholders with diverse perspectives and expertise, ethical leaders can tap into a wider range of ideas and insights. This collaborative approach can lead to sustainable innovations that address societal challenges and create shared value for stakeholders.

Stakeholder engagement enhances the organization's reputation and brand. Ethical leaders who actively engage with stakeholders demonstrate their commitment to responsible practices and genuine concern for stakeholder well-being. This engagement builds trust, fosters positive relationships, and enhances the organization's reputation, attracting customers, employees, and partners who align with the organization's values.

Ethical leaders who engage stakeholders foster a culture of continuous improvement. Stakeholder feedback and input provide valuable insights that can help identify areas for improvement or potential ethical challenges.

Ethical leaders recognize that stakeholder engagement is a learning opportunity, helping them better understand stakeholder needs and concerns, and enabling the organization to continuously adapt and evolve.

In conclusion, ethical leadership and stakeholder engagement are intertwined principles that promote responsible decision-making, trust, and collaboration within organizations. Ethical leaders prioritize the well-being and interests of stakeholders, actively involve them in decision-making, and create opportunities for ongoing dialogue and engagement. Stakeholder engagement enhances transparency, accountability, and organizational reputation, as well as promoting innovative and sustainable solutions. By embracing ethical leadership and stakeholder engagement, organizations can build stronger relationships with their stakeholders, create shared value, and contribute positively to the well-being of society.

7. Corporate Social Responsibility (CSR): Responsible leaders integrate corporate social responsibility into the core of their business strategies. They go beyond legal requirements and actively contribute to society through initiatives such as philanthropy, employee volunteering, and sustainable business practices. They recognize their organization's role in addressing societal challenges and strive to create shared value.

Corporate social responsibility (CSR) is a concept that refers to a company's commitment to operating ethically and sustainably while considering the social, economic, and environmental impacts of its activities. It involves taking responsibility for the company's impact on stakeholders, including employees, customers, communities, and the environment. Here are ten extensive paragraphs elaborating on the importance and components of corporate social responsibility:

Corporate social responsibility encompasses various dimensions, including social, environmental, and economic responsibilities. Social responsibility involves initiatives that support social causes, such as promoting diversity and inclusion, ensuring fair labor practices, and contributing to community development. Environmental responsibility focuses on minimizing the company's impact on the environment, such as reducing carbon emissions, conserving resources, and promoting sustainable practices. Economic responsibility involves ethical business practices, fair competition, and creating value for shareholders and other stakeholders.

CSR promotes ethical behavior and responsible decision-making within organizations. By considering the potential impact of their actions on stakeholders and the environment, companies can make choices that align with their values and contribute positively to society. CSR helps companies navigate ethical dilemmas and make choices that prioritize long-term sustainability and stakeholder well-being.

CSR enhances a company's reputation and brand image. When companies demonstrate a commitment to responsible business practices, it builds trust and credibility among customers, employees, investors, and other stakeholders. A positive reputation for CSR not only attracts customers and talent but also helps companies differentiate themselves in a competitive marketplace.

CSR contributes to stakeholder engagement and collaboration. Engaging stakeholders in CSR initiatives and seeking their input fosters a sense of shared responsibility and ownership. By involving stakeholders in decision-making processes and actively listening to their perspectives, companies can build stronger relationships, enhance trust, and create a more inclusive and sustainable approach to business.

CSR drives innovation and promotes sustainable practices. By considering social and environmental factors in business decisions, companies can identify opportunities for innovation that address societal challenges while creating long-term value. CSR encourages companies to adopt sustainable practices that reduce waste, conserve resources, and minimize negative environmental impacts.

CSR can have a positive impact on employee engagement and satisfaction. Employees who work for socially responsible companies often feel a sense of meaning and purpose in their work. Companies that prioritize employee well-being, offer fair compensation and provide opportunities for growth and development tend to attract and retain top talent.

CSR involves responsible supply chain practices. Companies that prioritize CSR ensure that their suppliers adhere to ethical standards, promoting fair labor practices, human rights, and environmental responsibility throughout the supply chain. By promoting responsible supply chain practices, companies can mitigate the risk of reputational damage and support sustainable development in the communities in which they operate.

CSR encourages transparency and accountability. Responsible companies openly communicate about their CSR initiatives, goals, and progress. Transparency builds trust with stakeholders, who can hold the company accountable for its commitments and impact. Regular reporting and disclosure of CSR efforts enable stakeholders to evaluate the company's performance and make informed decisions.

CSR contributes to sustainable development and societal well-being. By addressing social and environmental challenges, companies can play a role in advancing sustainable development goals. CSR initiatives that focus on education, poverty alleviation, healthcare, and environmental conservation can make a positive impact on the communities in which companies operate.

CSR is evolving with the changing expectations of society. As societal values and concerns evolve, companies need to continually assess and adapt their CSR strategies. Companies need to remain proactive and responsive to emerging issues, such as climate change, social inequality, and ethical considerations, by integrating CSR into their core business strategies.

In conclusion, corporate social responsibility is a multidimensional concept that encompasses a company's commitment to ethical and sustainable practices. By considering the impact of their activities on stakeholders and the environment, companies can make responsible decisions that align with their values and contribute positively to society. CSR enhances a company's reputation, drives innovation, promotes stakeholder engagement, and contributes to sustainable development. As societal expectations evolve, companies must continually adapt and integrate CSR into their business strategies to remain competitive, contribute to societal well-being, and create long-term value for all stakeholders.

8. Ethical Leadership: Responsible leaders lead by example and set high ethical standards for their organizations. They promote a culture of integrity and ethical behavior, ensuring that ethical considerations are embedded in all aspects of the organization's operations.

Responsible leadership in the context of sustainability management involves a set of key principles that guide leaders in making decisions and taking actions that prioritize long-term social, environmental, and economic sustainability. Here are twelve paragraphs elaborating on the key principles of responsible leadership in sustainability management:

Vision and Purpose: Responsible leaders in sustainability management have a clear and compelling vision of a sustainable future. They communicate this vision to their team, stakeholders, and the wider community, inspiring collective action towards achieving sustainable goals.

Systems Thinking: Responsible leaders take a comprehensive approach, understanding that sustainability challenges are interconnected and require a systemic perspective. They consider the social, environmental, and economic impacts of their decisions and actions, aiming for integrated and sustainable outcomes.

Ethical Behavior: Responsible leaders demonstrate integrity, honesty, and transparency in their actions. They uphold ethical principles, guided by fairness, justice, and respect for all stakeholders. They act in alignment with their values and ensure ethical conduct throughout the organization.

Stakeholder Engagement: Responsible leaders engage with and involve stakeholders in decision-making processes. They actively seek input and perspectives from diverse groups, fostering collaboration and ensuring that decisions reflect the interests and needs of all stakeholders.

Long-Term Orientation: Responsible leaders take a long-term perspective in their decision-making processes, focusing on the sustainable well-being of both current and future generations. They consider the potential consequences of decisions and actions, aiming for long-term benefits over short-term gains.

Innovation and Adaptation: Responsible leaders foster a culture of innovation, encouraging experimentation and creative problem-solving. They embrace sustainable technologies, practices, and business models, continuously striving for improvement and adaptation to changing environmental and social contexts.

Collaboration and Partnerships: Responsible leaders recognize that addressing complex sustainability challenges requires collective action and collaboration. They form partnerships with stakeholders, including other businesses, governments, NGOs, and communities, to leverage collective resources and expertise.

Accountability and Transparency: Responsible leaders take responsibility for their actions and decisions. They communicate openly and transparently with stakeholders, providing accurate and timely information on sustainability efforts, goals, and progress. They are accountable for their commitments and seek regular feedback from stakeholders.

Education and Awareness: Responsible leaders promote education and awareness about sustainability within their organizations and beyond. They invest in training and development programs to empower employees to make informed decisions and contribute to sustainability initiatives.

Continuous Improvement: Responsible leaders strive for continuous improvement in sustainability performance. They monitor and measure key performance indicators to assess progress, identify areas for improvement, and take corrective actions. They learn from successes and failures, adapting their strategies accordingly.

Risk Management: Responsible leaders identify and manage sustainability-related risks within their organizations. They conduct risk assessments, develop strategies to mitigate risks, and build resilience to potential environmental, social, and economic disruptions.

Advocacy and Influence: Responsible leaders use their influence and positions to advocate for sustainable practices at the industry, national, and international levels. They engage in public dialogues, policy advocacy, and collaboration with various stakeholders to drive systemic change and create an enabling environment for sustainability.

In conclusion, responsible leadership in sustainability management is guided by key principles that prioritize ethical behavior, stakeholder engagement, long-term orientation, collaboration, and transparency. Successful responsible leaders incorporate systems thinking, foster innovation and adaptation, and continuously strive for improvement. They understand the importance of accountability, education, risk management, and advocacy in achieving sustainable goals. By embodying these principles, responsible leaders play a critical role in driving sustainability efforts, creating positive social and environmental impacts, and ensuring the long-term viability and success of their organizations.

These terms of responsible leadership provide a framework for leaders to make value-driven decisions, engage with stakeholders, and drive sustainable outcomes that benefit both the organization and society.

Key Principles of Responsible Leadership

The key principles of responsible leadership encompass a set of guiding values and beliefs that shape the behavior and decision-making of leaders. While there are various interpretations and frameworks, some common key principles of responsible leadership include:

Ethical Behavior: Responsible leaders prioritize ethical considerations and uphold high moral standards in their actions and decision-making. They act with integrity, honesty, and fairness, and strive to do what is right, just, and ethical, even in challenging situations.

Stakeholder Orientation: Responsible leaders recognize the importance of considering the needs and interests of all stakeholders, including employees, customers, communities, and investors. They consider the potential impact of their decisions on these stakeholders and seek to create value for all parties involved.

Sustainability: Responsible leaders adopt a long-term perspective and consider the environmental, social, and economic impact of their decisions. They embrace sustainable practices that minimize environmental footprint, promote social well-being, and contribute to economic prosperity both now and in the future.

Transparency and Accountability: Responsible leaders are transparent in their actions, decisions, and communication. They share information openly, provide clear explanations for their choices, and take responsibility for their actions and the outcomes they produce. They also hold themselves and others accountable for achieving organizational goals and upholding ethical standards.

Inclusivity and Diversity: Responsible leaders value diversity and foster inclusive work environments. They recognize the importance of diverse perspectives and actively seek input from individuals with diverse backgrounds and experiences. They promote equal opportunities, inclusivity, and fairness in decision-making processes.

Purpose-Driven Leadership: Responsible leaders have a clear sense of purpose beyond financial gain. They align organizational goals and actions with a broader purpose that encompasses societal well-being, environmental sustainability, and the betterment of humanity.

Collaboration and Engagement: Responsible leaders actively engage with their stakeholders, fostering open dialogue, building trust, and fostering collaboration. They seek input, listen to concerns, and involve stakeholders in decision-making processes, recognizing the value of diverse perspectives and the benefits of collective action.

Continuous Learning and Adaptation: Responsible leaders embrace a growth mindset and are committed to continuous learning and improvement. They seek opportunities for personal and professional development, stay abreast of emerging trends and issues, and adapt their strategies and practices based on added information and changing circumstances.

These key principles provide a foundation for responsible leadership and encompass the values and behaviors that contribute to the creation of sustainable value for all stakeholders. They guide leaders in making ethical decisions, cultivating inclusive work environments, engaging stakeholders, and driving positive change.

Characteristics and Attributes of Responsible Leaders

Responsible leaders possess a unique set of characteristics and attributes that enable them to effectively navigate the complexities of today's business landscape and drive positive change. While each leader is unique, there are several key characteristics and attributes commonly associated with responsible leaders:

Integrity: Responsible leaders demonstrate unwavering integrity and ethical behavior. They hold themselves to lofty standards of honesty, consistency, and fairness. They keep their promises, act with transparency, and align their actions with their values.

Accountability: Responsible leaders take ownership of their decisions and actions. They do not shy away from responsibility and are willing to be held accountable for the outcomes they produce. They accept criticism, learn from failures, and continually strive for improvement.

Empathy and Emotional Intelligence: Responsible leaders possess strong emotional intelligence and empathy. They understand and connect with the emotions and perspectives of others, fostering healthy relationships based on trust and mutual respect. They listen actively and consider diverse viewpoints before making informed decisions.

Vision and Purpose: Responsible leaders have an unobstructed vision and sense of purpose that extends beyond financial goals. They articulate a compelling vision for their organization and inspire others to work towards a shared purpose. They demonstrate a willingness to innovate and adapt to changing circumstances while staying true to their values.

Stakeholder Engagement: Responsible leaders actively engage with stakeholders, valuing their input and seeking to understand their perspectives. They build and foster relationships with employees, customers, communities, and investors, recognizing the importance of collaboration and shared goals.

Strategic Thinking and Long-Term Orientation: Responsible leaders think strategically and consider the long-term consequences of their decisions. They understand complex systems, anticipate future trends, and weigh the environmental, social, and economic implications of their actions. They make decisions that create sustainable value for all stakeholders.

Authenticity: Responsible leaders are authentic to themselves. They embody their values and beliefs, inspiring trust, and authenticity in others. They are open about their strengths and weaknesses and are willing to be vulnerable when appropriate.

Continuous Learning and Growth: Responsible leaders have a growth mindset and actively seek opportunities for learning and development. They stay informed about emerging trends, industry best practices, and societal challenges. They foster a culture of continuous learning within their organizations, encouraging their teams to learn and grow alongside them.

Resilience and Adaptability: Responsible leaders possess resilience and adaptability in the face of challenges and ambiguity. They remain calm under pressure, pivot when necessary, and find creative solutions to complex problems. They embrace change and encourage their teams to do the same.

Advocacy for Sustainability: Responsible leaders are advocates for sustainability and actively drive initiatives that promote environmental stewardship and social responsibility. They champion sustainable business practices, endorse responsible supply chain management, and work towards a more sustainable future.

These characteristics and attributes of responsible leaders enable them to make ethical decisions, build meaningful relationships with stakeholders, and drive positive change within their organizations and society.

The combined principles of ethical leadership and responsible leadership create a comprehensive framework for leaders to guide their organizations toward sustainable and ethical practices. These principles serve as guidelines for decision-making, actions, and behavior that prioritizes the well-being of stakeholders, the environment, and society. Here are twelve paragraphs elaborating on the combined principles of ethical leadership and responsible leadership:

Integrity: Ethical and responsible leaders act with integrity, upholding honesty, transparency, and ethical principles in all aspects of their leadership. They align their actions with their values and ensure that ethical considerations are integrated into decision-making processes.

Stakeholder Focus: Combined ethical and responsible leadership emphasizes the importance of considering the needs, interests, and concerns of all stakeholders - employees, customers, communities, suppliers, and shareholders. Leaders actively engage stakeholders, seek their input, and weigh their perspectives in decision-making processes.

Sustainability: Ethical and responsible leaders recognize the interdependence of social, environmental, and economic factors. They prioritize long-term sustainability by considering the environmental impacts, ensuring responsible resource management, and promoting sustainable business practices.

Accountability: Leaders practicing ethical and responsible leadership hold themselves accountable for their decisions and actions. They establish clear performance metrics and regularly communicate their progress regarding sustainability goals and ethical conduct to stakeholders.

Respect and Fairness: Ethical and responsible leaders treat all individuals with respect, fairness, and dignity. They value diversity, foster inclusive environments, and ensure fair treatment and opportunities for all, regardless of their background or identities.

Empathy and Compassion: Leaders practicing ethical and responsible leadership demonstrate empathy and compassion towards their stakeholders. They consider the impact of their decisions on the well-being and welfare of people, communities, and the broader society.

Ethical Decision-Making: Ethical and responsible leaders make decisions based on ethical considerations, considering the potential consequences for stakeholders, society, and the environment. They consider moral principles, societal values, and legal requirements to guide their decision-making processes.

Long-Term Perspective: Ethical and responsible leaders take a long-term view, considering the future impacts of decisions and actions. They focus on sustainable development, ensuring that short-term gains do not compromise long-term sustainability or the interests of future generations.

Collaboration and Partnerships: Ethical and responsible leaders recognize the importance of collaboration and partnerships to drive sustainable change. They actively seek out opportunities to collaborate with stakeholders, industry peers, and organizations to leverage resources and expertise in addressing shared sustainability challenges.

Continuous Learning and Improvement: Ethical and responsible leaders encourage continuous learning and improvement within their organizations. They seek to enhance their understanding of ethical and sustainable practices and support the development of employees through training, education, and knowledge-sharing initiatives.

Social Responsibility: Ethical and responsible leaders embrace their organization's social responsibility by actively contributing to the well-being of society. They engage in philanthropy, community development initiatives, and advocacy for social causes to create positive social impacts.

Environmental Stewardship: Ethical and responsible leaders prioritize environmental stewardship and incorporate sustainable strategies and practices into their organizations. They strive to reduce their environmental footprint, promote resource efficiency, and support conservation efforts.

In summary, the combined principles of ethical leadership and responsible leadership create a comprehensive framework that guides leaders in making sustainable and ethical decisions. These principles prioritize integrity, stakeholder focus, sustainability, accountability, respect, fairness, empathy, and ethical decision-making. They emphasize the importance of collaboration, long-term perspective, continuous learning, social responsibility, and environmental stewardship. Leaders who embody these principles serve as catalysts for positive change, promoting ethical conduct, and driving responsible business practices that benefit stakeholders, society, and the environment.

Case Studies: Examining Successful Responsible Leaders

Case Study 1: Paul Polman (Unilever)

Paul Polman, former CEO of Unilever, transformed the company into a sustainable powerhouse. He integrated sustainability into Unilever's business strategy, setting ambitious goals such as reducing the environmental impact of their products and improving the livelihoods of smallholder farmers. Under his leadership, Unilever's sustainable brands grew 50% faster than the rest of the business, highlighting the economic benefits of responsible leadership.

Case Study 2: Mary Barra (General Motors)

Mary Barra, CEO of General Motors, implemented responsible leadership practices by focusing on safety and sustainability. She led the company to invest heavily in electric vehicles and sustainable manufacturing practices. Barra's commitment to safety transformed General Motors' culture to prioritize customer welfare and sustainability, leading to improved brand reputation and financial performance.

Case Study 3: Marc Benioff (Salesforce)

Marc Benioff, CEO of Salesforce, built the company with a strong commitment to responsible leadership. Benioff focused on creating a positive work culture that emphasized equality, sustainability, and philanthropy. He implemented unique initiatives like the 1-1-1 model, dedicating 1% of Salesforce's equity, time, and products to philanthropy. Benioff's responsible leadership led Salesforce to become a leading force in corporate social responsibility.

Case Study 4: Feike Sijbesma (DSM)

Feike Sijbesma, former CEO of DSM, guided the company's transformation into a sustainable science-based company. Sijbesma implemented responsible leadership practices by integrating sustainability goals into DSM's core business model. His efforts resulted in DSM reducing carbon emissions, becoming a leader in renewable energy and sustainable materials, and earning recognition for their commitment to responsible practices.

Case Study 5: Patagonia (Yvon Chouinard)

Yvon Chouinard, founder of Patagonia, established the company as a pioneer of responsible leadership in the outdoor apparel industry. Chouinard incorporated environmental stewardship and social initiatives into Patagonia's business model. They implemented programs like Worn Wear, which promotes garment repair and reuse, and pledged 1% of sales to grassroots environmental organizations. Patagonia's responsible leadership approach has garnered customer loyalty and industry recognition.

Case Study 6: Emmanuel Faber (Danone)

Emmanuel Faber, former CEO of Danone, led the company with a strong commitment to responsible leadership. Faber focused on incorporating social and environmental sustainability goals into the company's strategy. Danone became a certified B Corp, committed to balancing profit with social and environmental impact. Faber's responsible leadership initiatives included reducing sugar content in products, promoting regenerative agriculture, and improving access to clean water.

Case Study 7: Indra Nooyi (PepsiCo)

As the former CEO of PepsiCo, Indra Nooyi championed responsible leadership by making sustainability a core focus. She implemented the Performance with Purpose strategy, prioritizing areas such as healthier product offerings, water conservation, and reducing greenhouse gas emissions. Under her leadership, PepsiCo achieved considerable progress in sustainability and received accolades for responsible business practices.

Case Study 8: Alan Jope (Unilever)

Alan Jope, the current CEO of Unilever, continues to give responsible leadership in the company. He has accelerated Unilever's sustainability agenda, focusing on areas such as plastic waste, climate change, and social inequality. Jope emphasizes responsible sourcing, responsible packaging, and promoting hygiene and sanitation in developing countries.

Case Study 9: Elon Musk (Tesla)

Elon Musk, CEO of Tesla, exemplifies responsible leadership by driving the electric vehicle revolution. Musk's vision for a sustainable future led Tesla to develop revolutionary electric vehicles and advance battery technology. His commitment to reducing carbon emissions and promoting clean energy has been instrumental in reshaping the automotive industry.

Case Study 10: Mary Dillon (Ultra Beauty)

Mary Dillon, CEO of Ultra Beauty, has demonstrated responsible leadership by prioritizing diversity and inclusivity. She implemented initiatives to enhance diversity among leadership and in marketing campaigns, reflecting the diverse customer base. Dillon's focus on responsible marketing and social responsibility has further strengthened Ultra Beauty's brand image.

Case Study 11: Dirk Van de Put (Mondelēz International)

Dirk Van de Put, CEO of Mondelēz International, has prioritized responsible sourcing and sustainability. Under his leadership, Mondelēz has committed to sustainably sourcing all key agricultural commodities, reducing greenhouse gas emissions, and tackling packaging waste. Van de Put's focus on responsible business practices has helped Mondelēz become a leader in the food industry.

Case Study 12: Andrew Wilson (Electronic Arts)

Andrew Wilson, CEO of Electronic Arts (EA), has embraced responsible leadership by investing in employee well-being and diversity. Wilson prioritized mental health initiatives and diversity and inclusion programs throughout the company. EA's efforts in fostering a positive work culture and promoting diversity have led to increased employee satisfaction and improved business performance.

Case Study 13: Brian Chesky (Airbnb)

As the CEO of Airbnb, Brian Chesky champions responsible leadership by integrating sustainability into the company's core operations. Chesky implemented initiatives such as the Airbnb Green Pledge, encouraging hosts to adopt sustainable practices. Airbnb's commitment to responsible travel and sustainability has distinguished them as leaders in the sharing economy.

Case Study 14: Tim Cook (Apple)

Tim Cook, CEO of Apple, has continued the responsible leadership legacy of Apple through various sustainability initiatives. Cook has prioritized environmental stewardship by reducing the company's carbon footprint, transitioning to renewable energy, and implementing recycling programs. Cook's responsible leadership has set Apple as an industry benchmark for environmental sustainability.

Case Study 15: Ginni Rometty (IBM)

Ginni Rometty, former CEO of IBM, highlighted responsible leadership through the company's commitment to technology for social good. Under her leadership, IBM developed initiatives like IBM Watson Health and IBM Smarter Cities, addressing critical health and societal challenges. Rometty's focus on responsible technological innovation has positioned IBM as a leader in leveraging technology for positive impact.

Chapter Fourteen

The Business Case for Sustainability

The Link between Sustainability and Organizational Success

Introduction

In today's increasingly interconnected and complex world, the concept of sustainability has gained significant importance for organizations across all sectors. Sustainability refers to the integration of environmental, social, and economic considerations into business strategies and practices to create long-term value for all stakeholders. As concerns about climate change, resource depletion, social inequality, and ethical practices continue to grow, organizations are recognizing the need to adopt sustainable approaches to secure their future success. This essay will explore the link between sustainability and organizational success, demonstrating how sustainable practices can drive financial performance, enhance brand reputation, foster innovation, attract and retain top talent, mitigate risks, and build long-term resilience.

Financial Performance

Contrary to the outdated belief that sustainability and profitability are mutually exclusive, there is a growing body of evidence suggesting a positive correlation between sustainable business practices and financial performance. Research has consistently shown that organizations committed to sustainability outperform their peers in terms of revenue growth, operational efficiency, profitability, and shareholder value. For example, a study by Harvard Business School found that companies with strong environmental, social, and governance (ESG) performance had higher stock returns and better accounting-based performance measures compared to their industry counterparts. Sustainable practices can lead to cost reductions through improved resource efficiency, waste reduction, and energy conservation. Additionally, sustainability-driven innovation can unlock new market opportunities, drive sales growth, and create a competitive advantage.

Brand Reputation and Customer Loyalty

In an era of increased awareness and conscious consumerism, organizations with strong sustainability credentials are more likely to attract and retain customers. Sustainability initiatives not only demonstrate a commitment to ethical practices but also resonate with the values and aspirations of many consumers. Brands that are seen as environmentally and socially responsible often enjoy enhanced brand reputation, customer loyalty, and increased market share. Research shows that consumers are willing to pay a premium for sustainable products and services, driven by their desire to contribute to a better world and align their purchasing decisions with their values. Companies such as Patagonia, Tesla, and Ben & Jerry's have built strong brand loyalty by incorporating sustainability into their brand identity, illustrating the power of sustainability in building customer trust and loyalty.

Innovation and Market Differentiation

Sustainability can foster innovation by prompting organizations to think creatively about their operations, products, and services. The pursuit of sustainability often requires organizations to challenge conventional practices, experiment with modern technologies, and develop innovative solutions. By tapping into sustainable innovation, companies can gain a competitive edge and differentiate themselves in the market. For example, Nike's commitment to sustainability led to the development of sustainable materials like Nike Flyknit, which reduced waste and increased sustainability without compromising performance. By focusing on sustainability-driven innovation, organizations can not only address environmental and social challenges but also create unique value propositions that attract customers and drive growth.

Talent Attraction and Retention

In today's competitive job market, organizations that prioritize sustainability are more likely to attract and retain top talent. Numerous studies have shown that employees, particularly millennials and Gen Z, are increasingly seeking purpose-driven work that aligns with their values. Sustainable practices provide a clear sense of purpose and enable employees to contribute to meaningful societal and environmental outcomes. Companies that demonstrate a strong commitment to sustainability are seen as desirable employers, attracting highly skilled and motivated individuals. Moreover, organizations that prioritize sustainability often foster a positive work culture that promotes employee well-being, diversity, and inclusion, leading to higher employee engagement, productivity, and retention rates.

Risk Mitigation and Resilience

Sustainability helps organizations identify and mitigate potential risks, thereby building long-term resilience. By integrating sustainability into risk management practices, organizations can assess and manage emerging environmental, social, and governance risks such as climate change, supply chain disruptions, and reputational risks. For example, organizations that prioritize sustainable supply chain management are better equipped to address potential environmental, social, and ethical risks associated with their suppliers and ensure long-term business continuity. Sustainability also enables organizations to adapt and thrive in the face of changing regulations and consumer expectations, reducing the potential for reputational damage and costly legal disputes.

Regulatory Compliance and Market Access

As global governments and regulatory bodies strengthen their environmental and social regulations, organizations that embrace sustainability are better positioned to comply with evolving requirements. By proactively incorporating sustainable practices into their operations, organizations can reduce the risk of non-compliance, avoid financial penalties, and maintain a positive relationship with regulators. Sustainability initiatives can also provide organizations with access to new markets and business opportunities. For instance, many government tenders and procurement processes now prioritize sustainable products and services, giving sustainable organizations a competitive advantage in securing lucrative contracts.

Shared Value Creation and Social Impact

Sustainability-driven organizations have the potential to create shared value by contributing to local communities, addressing societal challenges, and driving positive social impact. By aligning business goals with societal needs, organizations can contribute to poverty alleviation, education, healthcare, and other critical social issues. For example, programs like Unilever's Lifebuoy Handwashing Campaign have had a significant impact on public health and sanitation in developing countries, while simultaneously creating market opportunities for the company. By actively engaging with communities and stakeholders, organizations can build trust, foster goodwill, and create a positive social legacy.

The link between sustainability and organizational success is increasingly evident, with organizations across the globe recognizing the numerous benefits of embracing sustainability. From driving financial performance to enhancing brand reputation, fostering innovation, attracting top talent, mitigating risks, and building long-term resilience, sustainability plays a critical role in shaping the success and longevity of organizations. Moreover, as environmental and social challenges continue to escalate, embracing sustainability is not only a strategic imperative but also a moral and ethical responsibility for organizations. By integrating sustainability into their strategies and practices, organizations can thrive in an evolving world, create a positive impact, and contribute to a more sustainable and equitable future.

Economic Benefits of Sustainable Management Practices

Sustainable management practices offer a wide array of economic benefits to organizations. These practices focus on integrating environmental, social, and economic considerations into decision-making and operations, resulting in long-term financial advantages and competitiveness. Here are six key economic benefits of sustainable management practices:

Cost Savings: Sustainable management practices help organizations reduce operating costs by improving resource efficiency and minimizing waste. For example, implementing energy-saving measures and adopting renewable energy sources can result in lower energy costs over time. Similarly, waste reduction and recycling programs can reduce disposal costs. By optimizing resource use, organizations can achieve significant cost savings and improve overall operational efficiency.

Increased Revenue and Market Opportunities: Sustainability enhances a company's market position and can open new business opportunities. Consumers worldwide are increasingly demanding sustainable products and services, and organizations that meet these demands often gain a competitive advantage. By offering environmentally friendly and socially responsible products, organizations can tap into new customer segments, increase sales, and capture a larger market share. Sustainability-driven innovation can lead to the creation of unique and high-value offerings that attract environmentally conscious customers.

Enhanced Brand Reputation and Trust: Sustainable management practices can bolster a company's brand reputation and build consumer trust. A commitment to sustainability demonstrates ethical and responsible behavior, which resonates positively with customers. Organizations with strong sustainability credentials are perceived as trustworthy, socially responsible, and forward-thinking. A positive brand image translates into increased customer loyalty, repeat business, and a strengthened competitive position in the market.

Improved Risk Management: Sustainable management practices help organizations manage environmental, social, and governance risks effectively. By adopting proactive measures to address potential risks, organizations can minimize disruptions to their operations and avoid costly legal disputes or reputational damage. For example, implementing robust supply chain sustainability practices reduces the risk of supply chain disruptions due to non-compliance issues or stakeholder backlash. Effective risk management strengthens financial performance and ensures business continuity.

Investment Attractiveness: Sustainable companies often attract higher levels of investment and funding. Investors, including private equity firms and asset managers, are increasingly evaluating sustainability performance as a key metric in their investment decision-making. Organizations with strong sustainability practices are viewed as less risky, more resilient, and more likely to achieve long-term financial success. As a result, sustainable management practices can give organizations a competitive advantage in attracting capital and securing favorable financing terms.

Employee Productivity and Talent Attraction: Adopting sustainable management practices can have a positive impact on employee productivity, engagement, and retention. Employees are increasingly seeking purpose-driven work environments and are more likely to be motivated by organizations that demonstrate a commitment to sustainability and social responsibility. Organizations that prioritize sustainability create a sense of purpose for employees, leading to higher job satisfaction, improved productivity, and lower turnover rates. This, in turn, reduces recruitment and training costs while fostering a culture of innovation and continuous improvement.

In conclusion, sustainable management practices offer significant economic benefits to organizations. By reducing costs, driving revenue growth, enhancing brand reputation, managing risks effectively, attracting investment, and improving employee productivity, organizations can achieve long-term financial success and maintain a competitive edge. Embracing sustainability is not only environmentally and socially responsible but also a strategic business move that delivers economic advantages for organizations in the rapidly evolving global marketplace.

Environmental and Social Responsibility

Sustainable management practices play a crucial role in promoting environmental and social responsibility. By ensuring the efficient use of resources and minimizing negative impacts on the environment, sustainable management can effectively address the challenges of climate change, pollution, and biodiversity loss. Moreover, it also focuses on fostering positive social outcomes, including improving the livelihoods of local communities and promoting equitable access to resources. This essay will examine the effectiveness of sustainable management on environmental and social responsibility through various aspects.

One key aspect of sustainable management is the adoption of renewable energy sources. By transitioning from fossil fuels to clean energy alternatives such as solar, wind, and hydroelectric power, companies can significantly reduce their carbon footprint. This not only helps mitigate climate change but also reduces air and water pollution associated with traditional energy production methods.

Furthermore, sustainable management ensures the preservation and conservation of natural resources. This includes responsible forest management, minimizing water usage, and promoting sustainable agriculture practices. By implementing these measures, companies can protect ecosystems and biodiversity, maintain water quality, and prevent soil degradation, leading to long-term environmental benefits and the preservation of natural resources for future generations.

Sustainable management also focuses on waste reduction and recycling. Through effective waste management practices, companies can minimize waste generation, encourage recycling, and reduce the reliance on landfills. This promotes a circular economy where materials are reused and recycled, reducing the extraction and consumption of raw materials while minimizing pollution and greenhouse gas emissions in the process.

In addition to environmental benefits, sustainable management practices can have a positive impact on social responsibility. Companies that embrace sustainability can create job opportunities in renewable energy sectors, sustainable agriculture, and the green economy. This promotes economic growth, reduces poverty, and enhances social well-being.

Another crucial aspect is the engagement with local communities. Sustainable management practices encourage companies to work together with local stakeholders, including indigenous communities, to understand their needs and concerns. This ensures that development projects are designed in a way that respects cultural values, protects the rights of local communities, and enhances their socio-economic development.

Moreover, sustainable management encourages responsible sourcing and production. This involves ensuring that products are ethically produced, workers are treated fairly, and supply chains are transparent. By promoting fair trade and responsible sourcing, companies can contribute to the eradication of forced labor, child labor, and modern slavery.

Sustainable management also involves promoting gender equality. By empowering women, providing equal opportunities, and addressing gender-based discrimination, companies can create more inclusive and diverse workplaces. This not only contributes to social justice but also drives innovation and improves decision-making processes.

Furthermore, sustainable management practices can lead to improved stakeholder relationships. By actively engaging with customers, employees, and investors, companies can build trust and strengthen their reputation.

This can also enhance brand loyalty and attract socially conscious consumers who value environmentally and socially responsible products and services.

Investing in sustainability research and development is another effective strategy. By allocating resources to innovative technologies and practices, companies can develop sustainable solutions that benefit both the environment and society. This can encourage the adoption of eco-friendly technologies and practices by other industries, leading to a broader positive impact.

Collaboration and partnerships are also crucial in sustainable management. By working together with governments, NGOs, and other stakeholders, companies can tackle sustainability challenges more effectively. This collaborative approach can lead to the development of shared goals, knowledge sharing, and collective action to address complex environmental and social issues.

Furthermore, sustainable management practices can improve risk management. By integrating sustainability into business strategies, companies can identify and mitigate potential environmental and social risks that may affect their operations. This can enhance resilience, reduce costs associated with environmental liabilities, and safeguard business continuity.

Transparency and reporting are important elements of sustainable management. By disclosing environmental and social performance, companies can be held accountable for their actions and contribute to the broader public's awareness of sustainability issues. This transparency can also encourage healthy competition among companies and drive further improvements in sustainability performance.

Education and awareness play a crucial role in sustainable management. By promoting environmental and social responsibility through awareness campaigns and educational programs, companies can foster a culture of sustainability among employees, customers, and the wider community. This can lead to behavior changes and individual actions that collectively contribute to a more sustainable world.

Sustainable management requires long-term thinking and a commitment to continuous improvement. By setting ambitious goals and regularly measuring performance, companies can track their progress and identify areas for improvement. This iterative process ensures that sustainability remains a priority and drives continuous innovation and positive change.

In conclusion, sustainable management practices are highly effective in promoting environmental and social responsibility. Through various strategies, including renewable energy adoption, responsible resource management, waste reduction, fair trade, and stakeholder engagement, companies can contribute to a more sustainable world. By integrating sustainability into business strategies, companies can not only mitigate environmental risks, reduce costs, and enhance resilience but also promote social well-being, inclusive growth, and a better quality of life for current and future generations.

Case Studies: Companies Embracing Sustainable Practices

Case Study 1: Tesla

Tesla is a prominent example of a company that has embraced sustainable practices. By focusing on electric vehicle production and renewable energy solutions, Tesla aims to reduce greenhouse gas emissions and combat climate change. The company's commitment to sustainable manufacturing processes, including recycling and waste reduction, demonstrates its dedication to environmental responsibility.

Case Study 2: Patagonia

Patagonia is a clothing company renowned for its commitment to sustainable practices. The company incorporates recycled materials into its products, reduces water usage during production, and diverts waste from landfills. Patagonia also promotes fair trade and works with suppliers who adhere to ethical labor practices, demonstrating its social responsibility.

Case Study 3: Unilever

Unilever is a multinational consumer goods company that has made significant efforts to embrace sustainability. The company set ambitious goals, such as reducing environmental impact and sourcing all agricultural raw materials sustainably. Unilever has successfully integrated sustainability into its supply chain management and product development processes.

Case Study 4: Danone

Danone, a leading food and beverage company, has embraced sustainable practices by committing to carbon neutrality and responsible sourcing. The company invests in regenerative agriculture and aims to minimize greenhouse gas emissions throughout its value chain. Danone's commitment to social responsibility is evident through initiatives supporting food security and access to clean water.

Case Study 5: Interface

Interface, a carpet manufacturer, has developed a comprehensive sustainability strategy called Mission Zero. The company's goal is to eliminate negative environmental impacts and create a fully sustainable business by 2020. Through innovative technologies and processes, Interface has reduced its carbon emissions, implemented recycling initiatives, and improved energy efficiency.

Case Study 6: IKEA

IKEA, a global home furnishing retailer, has prioritized sustainability by focusing on responsible sourcing and reducing its environmental footprint. The company aims to use 100% renewable energy and has invested in wind and solar power generation. IKEA also offers recycling programs and promotes sustainable living through its products and services.

Case Study 7: Natura

Natura, a Brazilian beauty and cosmetics company, has built its business model around sustainability. The company sources natural ingredients sustainably, supports local communities, and promotes fair trade. Natura's commitment to reducing its carbon emissions and environmental impact is evident in its supply chain transparency efforts and waste reduction initiatives.

Case Study 8: Interface

Interface, a carpet manufacturer, has developed a comprehensive sustainability strategy called Mission Zero. The company's goal is to eliminate negative environmental impacts and create a fully sustainable business by 2020. Through innovative technologies and processes, Interface has reduced its carbon emissions, implemented recycling initiatives, and improved energy efficiency.

Case Study 9: M-Kopa Solar

M-Kopa Solar is a Kenyan company that provides affordable solar energy solutions to off-grid households. By offering Pay-As-You-Go solar systems, M-Kopa enables low-income families to access clean and reliable energy.

This initiative contributes to reducing carbon emissions and improving the quality of life for underserved communities.

Case Study 10: Starbucks

Starbucks, a global coffeehouse chain, has made sustainability a priority in its operations. The company has implemented initiatives to reduce water consumption, increase recycling efforts, and support responsible coffee sourcing. Starbucks also invests in farmer support centers to promote sustainable farming practices and improve the livelihoods of coffee growers.

Case Study 11: Interface

Interface, a carpet manufacturer, has developed a comprehensive sustainability strategy called Mission Zero. The company's goal is to eliminate negative environmental impacts and create a fully sustainable business by 2020. Through innovative technologies and processes, Interface has reduced its carbon emissions, implemented recycling initiatives, and improved energy efficiency.

Case Study 12: Adidas

Adidas, a global sportswear company, has taken significant strides towards sustainability. The company aims to eliminate virgin polyester from its products and increase the use of recycled materials. Adidas also focuses on reducing water consumption and improving worker conditions in its supply chain through initiatives like the "Better Cotton Initiative."

Case Study 13: Airbnb

Airbnb, an online marketplace for vacation rentals, has integrated sustainability into its platform. The company encourages hosts to adopt sustainable practices, such as providing eco-friendly amenities and promoting energy efficiency. Airbnb also supports community projects and partners with environmental organizations to mitigate its environmental impact.

Case Study 14: Interface

Interface, a carpet manufacturer, has developed a comprehensive sustainability strategy called Mission Zero. The company's goal is to eliminate negative environmental impacts and create a fully sustainable business by 2020. Through innovative technologies and processes, Interface has reduced its carbon emissions, implemented recycling initiatives, and improved energy efficiency.

Case Study 15: Ecover

Ecover, a manufacturer of ecological cleaning products, strives to minimize its ecological footprint. The company focuses on using plant-based ingredients and renewable energy in its manufacturing processes. Ecover also ensures its packaging is made from recycled and recyclable materials, promoting a circular economy.

Case Study 16: Google

Google, a technology giant, has embraced sustainable practices in its operations. The company aims to be carbon-neutral by offsetting its energy consumption with renewable energy sources. Google also invests in energy-efficient infrastructure and supports projects that promote clean energy adoption globally.

Case Study 17: Grameen Bank

Grameen Bank, a Nobel Prize-winning microfinance institution, promotes sustainable development by providing small loans to entrepreneurs in poverty-stricken areas. By helping individuals establish and grow sustainable businesses, Grameen Bank contributes to poverty reduction and empowers communities to create long-term economic and social change.

Case Study 18: Ben & Jerry's

Ben & Jerry's, an ice cream company, has long been committed to sustainability and social responsibility. The company sources Fairtrade ingredients supports family farms and tackles social justice issues through initiatives like "Justice ReMix'd." Ben & Jerry's also strives for carbon neutrality and has set ambitious goals to reduce its environmental impact.

Case Study 19: Interface

Interface, a carpet manufacturer, has developed a comprehensive sustainability strategy called Mission Zero. The company's goal is to eliminate negative environmental impacts and create a fully sustainable business by 2020. Through innovative technologies and processes, Interface has reduced its carbon emissions, implemented recycling initiatives, and improved energy efficiency.

Case Study 20: The Body Shop

The Body Shop, a cosmetics and skincare company, has championed ethical and sustainable practices in the beauty industry. The company sources natural ingredients responsibly, rejects animal testing, and promotes community trade. The Body Shop also emphasizes the importance of recycling and offers refillable packaging options to minimize waste.

Chapter Fifteen

Creating a Culture of Responsibility

Introduction

Creating a culture of responsibility is essential for organizations aiming to contribute positively to society and the environment. It involves instilling a sense of accountability, ethical decision-making, and sustainable practices throughout the organization's operations. By nurturing a culture that values responsibility, companies can improve their reputation, attract socially conscious employees and customers, and make a meaningful impact on the world. This essay explores the significance of creating a culture of responsibility and its various components.

A culture of responsibility starts with leadership commitment and setting the tone from the top. When leaders prioritize responsibility, it sends a clear message to employees that ethical behavior, environmental stewardship, and social impact are integral to the organization's values and success. By leading by example, leaders can inspire employees to embrace responsibility in their work and decision-making processes. From establishing ethical guidelines to incorporating sustainability goals, leaders play a pivotal role in shaping the organizational culture and fostering a sense of responsibility among employees.

Creating a culture of responsibility also involves establishing strong corporate governance structures. Companies need transparent systems of governance that promote accountability, integrity, and ethical conduct. This includes implementing codes of conduct, establishing internal controls, and fostering a culture of openness and reporting. By holding employees accountable for their actions and creating channels for reporting concerns, organizations can identify and rectify ethical lapses and ensure responsible practices are consistently upheld.

A culture of responsibility goes beyond adherence to legal and regulatory obligations. It entails proactive engagement with stakeholders and active participation in addressing societal issues. Responsible organizations seek to understand the needs and expectations of their stakeholders, including employees, customers, communities, and the environment. By integrating stakeholder perspectives into decision-making processes, organizations can make more informed choices that prioritize the well-being of all involved. This inclusive approach fosters trust, strengthens relationships, and enables organizations to contribute to positive social and environmental change.

Fostering Ethical Decision-Making in Organizations

Fostering ethical decision-making is vital for organizations to maintain integrity, trust, and long-term success. Ethical decision-making involves making choices that are morally right and align with the organization's values and principles. This essay explores the significance of fostering ethical decision-making in organizations and provides a comprehensive understanding of its key elements.

Understanding Ethics and Ethical Decision-Making

Ethics refers to a set of moral principles that guide individuals in distinguishing right from wrong. Ethical decision-making involves evaluating different courses of action and choosing the one that is morally acceptable and aligned with ethical standards. Organizations that prioritize ethical decision-making create a foundation of trust, reliability, and responsibility within their workforce and with external stakeholders.

Leadership and its Impact on Ethical Decision-Making

Leadership plays a crucial role in fostering ethical decision-making within organizations. When leaders demonstrate ethical behavior and promote a culture of integrity, it sets the tone for the entire organization. Leaders should communicate clear ethical expectations, provide guidance on ethical dilemmas, and lead by example. By prioritizing ethics in their own decisions, leaders inspire employees to make ethical choices and create a positive ethical climate within the organization.

The actions and behaviors of leaders significantly influence the ethical climate of an organization, setting the tone for ethical behavior and shaping the decision-making processes of employees. Here are five key impacts of leadership on ethical decision-making.

a. Setting an Ethical Example

Leaders who demonstrate ethical behavior themselves create a powerful example for employees to follow. When leaders consistently make ethical decisions and hold themselves accountable to high ethical standards, it sends a clear message to employees about the expectations for ethical conduct within the organization. By role-modeling ethical behavior, leaders inspire employees to prioritize ethics in their decision-making.

b. Establishing a Culture of Integrity

Leadership is responsible for establishing and nurturing the organizational culture, which includes fostering a culture of integrity. By emphasizing the importance of ethics and integrity in all aspects of the organization's operations, leaders create an environment that values and rewards ethical behavior. This sets the foundation for ethical decision-making to flourish throughout the organization.

c. Communicating Clear Ethical Expectations

Effective leaders communicate clear ethical expectations to employees. They articulate the organization's values, principles, and codes of conduct, ensuring that employees understand what constitutes ethical behavior. By providing guidance on ethical dilemmas and promoting open dialogue, leaders enable employees to navigate ethical challenges with confidence and make informed decisions.

d. Empowering Employees to Make Ethical Choices

Leadership plays a critical role in empowering employees to make ethical choices. This involves delegating decision-making authority and providing employees with the necessary resources and support to navigate ethical dilemmas effectively. By promoting a sense of responsibility and accountability, leaders create an environment where employees feel empowered to make ethically sound decisions, even when faced with challenging circumstances.

e. Recognizing and Rewarding Ethical Behavior

Leaders have the power to shape behavior by recognizing and rewarding ethical behavior within the organization. By providing positive reinforcement and incentives for ethical decision-making, leaders reinforce the importance of ethics and demonstrate that ethical behavior is valued and appreciated. This not only encourages ethical decision-making but also creates a culture where employees feel motivated to uphold high ethical standards.

In conclusion, leadership has a profound impact on ethical decision-making within organizations. From setting an ethical example to establishing a culture of integrity, leaders have the responsibility to nurture an environment that promotes and rewards ethical behavior. By effectively communicating ethical expectations, empowering employees, and recognizing ethical choices, leaders create an organizational climate where ethical decision-making becomes the norm.

Establishing Ethical Standards and Codes of Conduct

Organizations must develop and communicate clear ethical standards and codes of conduct. These documents outline the values and principles that guide behavior within the organization. Ethical standards should address key areas such as conflicts of interest, fair treatment of employees, respect for diversity, responsible use of resources, and compliance with laws and regulations. By establishing these standards, organizations provide employees with a framework for making ethical decisions.

Ethical Training and Education

Organizations should provide regular training and education on ethics and ethical decision-making. This training helps employees understand ethical dilemmas, develop critical thinking skills, and learn strategies for ethical problem-solving. It also raises awareness about the importance of ethics in the organization's culture and fosters a common understanding of ethical responsibilities across all levels of the organization.

Open Communication Channels

Creating an environment that encourages open communication is crucial for fostering ethical decision-making. Employees should feel comfortable reporting ethical concerns or seeking guidance on ethical dilemmas without fear of retaliation. By establishing anonymous reporting mechanisms, organizations promote a culture of transparency and accountability, allowing for early detection and resolution of ethical issues.

Encouraging Ethical Leadership at All Levels

Ethical decision-making should not be limited to top-level management. Organizations should encourage ethical leadership at all levels of the organization. This involves empowering employees to make ethically sound choices, promoting a sense of responsibility and accountability, and recognizing and rewarding ethical behavior. By encouraging ethical leadership at all levels, organizations create a culture that values integrity and ethical decision-making.

Ethical Decision-Making Processes

Organizations should establish clear processes for ethical decision-making. These processes should involve identifying ethical issues, gathering relevant information, considering alternative courses of action, and evaluating the potential impact of each option. Ethical decision-making processes should also consider the interests of all stakeholders and the long-term ethical implications of the chosen course of action.

Ethical Role Models and Mentors

Organizations can foster ethical decision-making by providing employees with ethical role models and mentors. These individuals can guide and support employees in facing difficult ethical dilemmas, provide guidance based on their own experiences, and serve as a source of inspiration for ethical behavior. Encouraging mentorship and creating opportunities for role modeling helps embed ethical decision-making into the organizational culture.

Performance Evaluation and Incentives

Performance evaluation and reward systems should incorporate ethical considerations. Organizations should include ethical behavior and decision-making as performance criteria, linking them to performance evaluations, promotions, and recognition. By aligning incentives with ethical behavior, organizations create a strong motivation for employees to make ethical choices and prioritize integrity.

Continuous Improvement and Feedback Mechanisms

Organizations should continuously evaluate and improve their approach to ethical decision-making. This involves seeking feedback from employees, customers, and other stakeholders, and using that feedback to refine ethical policies, training programs, and decision-making processes. By continuously striving to improve ethical decision-making, organizations can adapt to evolving ethical challenges and ensure their practices align with the highest ethical standards.

Building a Values-Driven Corporate Culture

Building a values-driven corporate culture is crucial for organizations to define their core beliefs, shape behavior, and create a positive work environment. A values-driven culture helps guide decision-making, fosters employee engagement, and strengthens stakeholder trust. This essay explores the importance of building a values-driven corporate culture and highlights key strategies for its successful implementation.

Defining Core Values

The foundation of a values-driven corporate culture lies in defining and articulating the organization's core values. These values should reflect the organization's mission, vision, and long-term objectives. Defining these values allows employees to align their actions and behaviors with the organization's overall purpose.

Leadership and Role-Modeling Values

Leadership plays a vital role in building a values-driven culture. Leaders must exemplify the organization's core values in their actions and decisions. By consistently modeling the desired behaviors, leaders set the expectations and tone for the entire organization.

Communicating and Reinforcing Values

Open and consistent communication is crucial for building and reinforcing a value-driven culture. Leaders should regularly communicate the organization's values, explaining their importance and how they guide decision-making. This communication can take various forms, including town hall meetings, internal newsletters, and training sessions.

Employee Engagement and Involvement

Building a values-driven culture requires the active engagement and involvement of employees. Organizations should encourage employees to contribute to the development and refinement of the organization's core values. This involvement promotes a sense of ownership and commitment to these values.

Alignment of Policies and Practices

To build a values-driven culture, it is essential to align organizational policies and practices with the stated core values. This includes incorporating values into performance management systems, hiring and promotion processes, and decision-making frameworks. When actions and policies are consistent with values, employees are more likely to internalize and embrace them.

Training and Development

Providing ongoing training and development opportunities is key to building a value-driven culture. Organizations should invest in programs that help employees understand and apply the organization's core values in their work. Ethical decision-making, cultural sensitivity, and conflict resolution training can contribute to a values-driven culture.

Recognition and Rewards

Recognizing and rewarding behaviors aligned with the organization's values reinforces their importance. Organizations should implement recognition programs that highlight and celebrate employees who demonstrate the desired values in their work. This recognition creates a positive reinforcement loop and encourages others to embody the values.

Recruitment and Onboarding

Building a values-driven culture begins with the recruitment and onboarding processes. Organizations should hire individuals whose values align with those of the organization. During onboarding, new employees should be immersed in the organization's values, helping them understand their significance and how they drive decision-making within the organization.

Transparent and Ethical Practices

A strong values-driven culture necessitates transparent and ethical practices. Organizations should emphasize honesty, integrity, and accountability in all interactions. Transparent communication and decision-making processes reinforce the organization's commitment to its values.

Supportive and Inclusive Environment

A values-driven culture should foster a supportive and inclusive work environment. Organizations should encourage diversity and provide equal opportunities for all employees. By fostering inclusivity, employees feel valued and are more likely to embrace and embody the organization's values.

Continuous Learning and Improvement

A values-driven culture is not static but evolves. Organizations should continuously assess their progress, learn from their experiences, and refine their values and practices as needed. Implementing feedback mechanisms and conducting regular evaluations ensure that the culture remains aligned with the organization's values.

External Stakeholder Engagement

Building a values-driven culture extends beyond the organization's boundaries. Engaging external stakeholders, such as customers, suppliers, and the community, in value-driven initiatives promotes a greater sense of social responsibility and reinforces the organization's commitment to its values.

Leading by Example

Leaders must consistently exemplify the organization's values and reinforce them in all aspects of their work. By leading by example, leaders inspire others to embrace and embody the organization's values. Their commitment and consistency are instrumental to building and sustaining a values-driven corporate culture.

In conclusion, building a values-driven corporate culture is essential for organizations to establish a strong foundation of shared beliefs and behaviors. By defining core values, aligning policies and practices, involving employees, and providing training and support, organizations can create an environment where values guide decision-making and behaviors. A values-driven culture fosters employee engagement, trust, and ethical decision-making, driving long-term success and positive stakeholder relationships.

Promoting Diversity and Inclusion in Leadership

Promoting diversity and inclusion in leadership is essential for organizations to foster innovation, creativity, and better decision-making. By embracing diversity in leadership positions, organizations can cultivate a culture that values different perspectives, experiences, and backgrounds. This essay explores the significance of promoting diversity and inclusion in leadership and provides strategies for achieving meaningful representation.

The Benefits of Diversity in Leadership

Diversity in leadership brings a range of benefits to organizations. It enhances innovation by incorporating diverse perspectives and experiences, leading to more creative solutions and strategies. Diversity also improves decision-making processes by considering a broader range of viewpoints and minimizing biases. Furthermore, diverse leadership teams create inclusive work environments that attract and retain top talent.

Defining Diversity and Inclusion in Leadership

Diversity in leadership refers to the representation of individuals from various demographic backgrounds, such as race, gender, ethnicity, age, and sexual orientation, in leadership roles. Inclusion, on the other hand, focuses on creating a supportive and equitable environment where diverse individuals feel valued, respected, and empowered to contribute their unique perspectives.

Setting Clear Diversity and Inclusion Goals

To promote diversity and inclusion in leadership, organizations must establish clear goals and objectives. These goals should include increasing the representation of underrepresented groups in leadership positions and creating an inclusive culture that values diversity. By setting measurable targets, organizations can track progress and hold themselves accountable.

Providing Equal Opportunities and Access

Promoting diversity and inclusion in leadership requires providing equal opportunities and access to all individuals within the organization. Organizations should implement fair and transparent recruitment, promotion, and succession planning processes that consider diversity factors. This ensures that individuals from all backgrounds have an equal chance to advance into leadership positions.

Eliminating Bias in Hiring and Promotions

Organizations should actively work to eliminate biases in hiring and promotion processes. This can be achieved by implementing blind recruitment practices, conducting diverse interview panels, and providing unconscious bias training to decision-makers. By mitigating biases, organizations can create a level playing field for all candidates, enhancing the chances of diverse individuals being selected for leadership roles.

Leadership Development and Mentoring Programs

Organizations should invest in leadership development programs that focus on building a diverse pipeline of future leaders. Providing mentoring opportunities for underrepresented individuals can help them access guidance, support, and exposure to key networks. These programs contribute to the development and advancement of diverse talent within the organization.

Cultural Competency Training

Promoting diversity and inclusion in leadership requires cultivating cultural competency among leaders. Cultural competency training helps leaders understand and appreciate different perspectives, values, and cultural nuances. This enables leaders to effectively collaborate with diverse teams and create inclusive work environments.

Employee Resource Groups and Affinity Networks

Employee resource groups and affinity networks provide platforms for underrepresented employees to connect, share experiences, and advocate for their needs. These groups play a vital role in promoting diversity and inclusion in leadership by fostering a sense of belonging and amplifying the voices of marginalized individuals.

Diverse Hiring Panels and Selection Committees

Organizations should ensure that hiring panels and selection committees for leadership positions are diverse and inclusive. Having a range of perspectives involved in the decision-making process minimizes biases and increases the likelihood of selecting diverse candidates.

When creating diverse hiring panels and selection committees, it is crucial to consider the following critical issues:

a. Representation: Ensuring diverse representation on the panels and committees is essential to achieving meaningful diversity in the recruitment process. It is important to include individuals from different genders, ethnicities, backgrounds, and perspectives to minimize bias and ensure a fair evaluation of candidates.

b. Unconscious bias: Bias can unconsciously influence decision-making, affecting how candidates are assessed. Diversity in the panel can help address these biases by bringing in different perspectives and experiences. Panel members should undergo training to understand and mitigate their unconscious biases throughout the process.

c. Inclusive decision-making: Creating an inclusive environment where all panel members feel comfortable expressing their viewpoints is crucial. It is vital to encourage open discussions, value diverse opinions, and ensure all panel members actively participate in decision-making. Inclusive decision-making processes can lead to fairer evaluations and improved diversity outcomes.

d. Clear evaluation criteria: Clearly defining and communicating the evaluation criteria helps ensure a fair assessment of candidates. The criteria should be focused on job-related skills, qualifications, and competencies, rather than subjective or biased factors. By standardizing the evaluation process, it becomes easier to identify the most suitable candidates.

e. Training and awareness: Panel members should receive training on diversity and inclusion, including understanding unconscious bias, cultivating inclusive mindsets, and recognizing the importance of diverse perspectives. By raising awareness and providing proper training, members can better navigate biases and make more objective decisions.

f. Review recruitment practices: Evaluate current recruitment practices to identify any potential biases or barriers that hinder diversity in hiring processes. Regularly reviewing and assessing these practices can help fine-tune selection processes to promote inclusive recruitment.

g. Transparency and accountability: Ensure transparency in the selection process, including clearly communicating the steps, timelines, and criteria to all candidates. Additionally, the selection committee should be accountable for their decisions and provide feedback to candidates, creating a sense of fairness and trust in the process.

By considering these critical issues, organizations can create diverse hiring panels and selection committees that promote fair evaluations, reduce bias, and increase representation and diversity within their workforce.

Compliance with Equal Opportunity Laws and Regulations

Promoting diversity and inclusion in leadership requires compliance with equal opportunity laws and regulations. Organizations must proactively address any discriminatory practices, promote fairness, and equal treatment, and implement policies to prevent discrimination and promote diversity.

Building Networks and Partnerships

Organizations can promote diversity and inclusion in leadership by building networks and partnerships with external organizations that focus on diversity and inclusion. Collaborating with these organizations provides access to diverse talent pools, best practices, and opportunities for knowledge-sharing.

Transparency and Accountability

Promoting diversity and inclusion in leadership requires transparency and accountability. Organizations should publicly share their diversity and inclusion goals, metrics, and progress to hold themselves accountable and demonstrate their commitment to diversity and inclusion.

Continuous Evaluation and Improvement

To ensure sustained progress in promoting diversity and inclusion in leadership, it is crucial to continuously evaluate and improve strategies and initiatives. Organizations should collect and analyze data on diversity metrics, employee feedback, and perceptions of inclusion to identify areas for improvement and adjust strategies accordingly.

Creating a Culture of Inclusion

Ultimately, promoting diversity and inclusion in leadership requires creating a culture that embraces and values differences. Organizations should foster a safe and inclusive environment where all employees are empowered to contribute their unique perspectives. By cultivating a culture of inclusion, organizations can attract, retain, and develop diverse talent in leadership positions.

In conclusion, promoting diversity and inclusion in leadership is vital for organizations to harness the benefits of diverse perspectives, enhance decision-making, and create inclusive work environments. By setting clear goals, providing equal opportunities, eliminating biases, and fostering a culture of inclusion, organizations can build diverse and inclusive leadership teams that drive success and innovation.

Case Studies: Organizations with Ethical and Inclusive Cultures

Case Study 1: Company A – Advocating for Diversity and Inclusion

Company A is committed to creating an ethical and inclusive culture. They have implemented a diverse hiring strategy and actively promote inclusivity in their workplace. They provide equal opportunities for all employees, regardless of their background or identity. Their leadership team regularly participates in diversity training, and they have established Employee Resource Groups to support underrepresented communities. Company A consistently tracks and reports on key diversity metrics and ensures that its policies and practices align with its values.

Case Study 2: Organization B – Transparent Decision-making

Organization B has fostered an ethical and inclusive culture by promoting transparency in decision-making. They provide clear communication channels for employees to voice concerns or suggestions anonymously. When making important decisions, they involve employees in the process through surveys, town halls, and focus groups. Organization B always seeks consent from its employees before implementing major changes, ensuring that everyone has an opportunity to provide input.

Case Study 3: Non-profit C – Employee Resource Groups

Non-profit C encourages an ethical and inclusive culture by establishing Employee Resource Groups (ERGs). ERGs provide a platform for employees to come together based on shared backgrounds, identities, or interests. These groups promote diversity and inclusion by organizing events, offering mentorship programs, and advocating for inclusive policies. Non-profit C recognizes the value of ERGs in fostering a sense of belonging and has made them an integral part of their organizational culture.

Case Study 4: Company D – Flexible Work Arrangements

Company D recognizes the importance of work-life balance and has implemented various flexible work arrangements to create an inclusive culture. They offer options such as remote work, job-sharing, and flexible schedules to accommodate employees' diverse needs. By prioritizing flexibility, Company D supports individuals with caregiving responsibilities, people with disabilities, and those seeking better work-life integration. This approach has empowered employees to perform at their best, resulting in increased productivity and retention.

Case Study 5: Tech Company E – Unconscious Bias Training

Tech Company E has implemented a comprehensive unconscious bias training program to cultivate an ethical and inclusive culture. They believe that addressing unconscious biases is vital to creating a diverse and inclusive workplace. All employees, especially those involved in recruitment and decision-making processes, undergo regular training sessions to become aware of their biases and learn strategies to mitigate them. By equipping employees with this knowledge, Tech Company E ensures fair treatment and equal opportunities for all.

Case Study 6: Organization F – Pay Equity Analysis

Organization F is dedicated to achieving pay equity and fostering an inclusive culture. They regularly conduct pay equity analyses to identify and eliminate any gender or ethnicity-based wage gaps. By ensuring equal pay for equal work, Organization F demonstrates its commitment to fairness and diversity. Transparent policies on salary ranges, promotions, and advancement opportunities further contribute to their ethical and inclusive culture.

Case Study 7: Company G – Supplier Diversity Program

Company G recognizes the importance of supporting diverse business communities and has implemented a supplier diversity program. They actively seek out and engage with minority-owned, women-owned, and other diverse suppliers, creating economic opportunities for underrepresented groups. By integrating supplier diversity into its procurement processes, Company G demonstrates its commitment to inclusivity and ethical business practices.

Case Study 8: Retailer H – Inclusive Leadership Development

Retailer H prioritizes inclusive leadership development to foster an ethical and inclusive culture. They provide leadership training programs that incorporate diversity, equity, and inclusion components. These programs aim to develop leaders who are committed to creating inclusive teams, addressing biases, and promoting diversity within their spheres of influence. By investing in leadership development, Retailer H builds a foundation for an inclusive culture from the top down.

Case Study 9: Company I – Mentorship and Sponsorship Programs

Company1 promotes an ethical and inclusive culture by implementing mentorship and sponsorship programs. They connect employees from diverse backgrounds with mentors and sponsors who provide guidance, advocate for their career advancement, and help them navigate challenges. This program ensures that employees have access to opportunities and support systems that facilitate their growth and success. By fostering these relationships, Company I creates an environment where individuals from various backgrounds can thrive.

Chapter Sixteen

Implementing Sustainable Business Models

Introduction

In today's world, sustainability has become a critical imperative for businesses across industries. Implementing sustainable business models is a strategic approach that not only addresses environmental concerns but also considers social and economic impacts. Sustainable business models aim to balance profitability with responsible practices that minimize negative environmental impacts, enhance social well-being, and contribute to long-term economic stability. By implementing sustainable business models, organizations can not only meet the demands of increasingly conscious consumers but also make a positive contribution to the planet and society.

Advantages of Implementing Sustainable Business Models

Implementing sustainable business models offers numerous advantages for organizations. Firstly, it enhances a company's reputation and brand value by showcasing its commitment to responsible practices. Consumers today are actively seeking sustainable products and services, and businesses that are aligned with these values can gain a competitive edge. Moreover, sustainability initiatives can lead to cost savings in the long run. By reducing energy consumption, waste, and resource usage, companies can optimize their operations and drive down expenses. Additionally, implementing sustainable business models allows companies to future-proof their operations, adapt to changing market demands, and anticipate regulatory requirements.

Importance of Implementing Sustainable Business Models

As the world grapples with pressing environmental and social challenges, implementing sustainable business models has become more important than ever before. Climate change, resource depletion, social inequality, and other global issues necessitate a proactive response from businesses. Implementing sustainable business models allows companies to contribute positively to the world while ensuring their long-term viability. By taking responsibility for their ecological and social footprint, organizations can minimize negative impacts, promote ethical practices, and create value for all stakeholders - including shareholders, employees, customers, and the wider community. Embracing sustainable business models is not just a moral obligation but a strategic imperative for the success and resilience of businesses in the face of a rapidly changing world.

Assessing the Current Business Model

Assessing the current business models refers to the evaluation and analysis of the existing framework, processes, and strategies that an organization employs to generate revenue, create value, and achieve its objectives. This assessment involves a comprehensive review of various elements, including the value proposition, revenue streams, cost structure, customer segments, channels, key activities and resources, partnerships, market trends, and financial performance. The purpose of this assessment is to identify the strengths and weaknesses of the current business model, uncover potential opportunities for improvement, and mitigate any threats or risks that may hinder the organization's success.

To assess the current business model, organizations employ various tools and methodologies. They may conduct internal and external research, gather customer feedback, analyze industry trends and competitors, evaluate financial data, and engage in strategic planning sessions. Through this assessment process, businesses gain valuable insights into the effectiveness and sustainability of their current model. It helps them identify areas for optimization, modification, or innovation to enhance competitiveness, drive growth, and create long-term value for all stakeholders.

The assessment of the current business model is not a one-time exercise but an ongoing process that organizations should regularly undertake to ensure they remain agile, adaptable, and responsive to changing market dynamics. It allows companies to stay ahead of the curve, anticipate potential disruptions, and seize emerging opportunities. By critically evaluating their existing model, organizations can make informed decisions, refine strategies, and align their operations with their vision and goals.

Ultimately, assessing the current business model is crucial for organizations to stay relevant, competitive, and profitable in today's dynamic business environment. It helps them identify areas of improvement, uncover innovative approaches, and make strategic decisions that drive growth and success. By understanding the strengths and weaknesses of their current model, organizations can evolve, transform, and adapt to meet the evolving needs and demands of their customers, while simultaneously aligning with societal and environmental expectations.

When evaluating and assessing the current business models, it is essential to critically analyze various aspects to ensure their effectiveness and viability. This comprehensive assessment helps businesses identify strengths, weaknesses, opportunities, and potential threats, allowing them to make informed decisions and drive future growth.

Value Proposition: Start by evaluating the value proposition of the business model. Assess whether the current offering addresses customer needs effectively and differentiates the company from competitors. Look for opportunities to enhance or innovate the value proposition to remain competitive in the market.

Revenue Streams: Evaluate the revenue streams of the business model. Analyze the stability and profitability of existing revenue sources and identify potential areas for diversification or expansion. Consider emerging trends and technological advancements that may disrupt or create new revenue opportunities.

Cost Structure: Assess the cost structure of the business model to determine its efficiency and sustainability. Identify areas where costs can be reduced or optimized without compromising on quality or value creation. Implementing cost-saving measures can improve profitability and enhance the overall financial health of the organization.

Customer Segments: Evaluate the target customer segments to understand their needs, preferences, and behaviors. Assess whether the current business model effectively addresses the target market and identify any untapped or underserved customer segments that can be targeted for growth.

Channels: Assess the effectiveness of existing distribution and communication channels. Determine if there are opportunities to optimize or expand these channels to reach a broader audience or improve customer experience. Consider the integration of digital channels and technology to enhance reach and accessibility.

Key Activities and Resources: Analyze the key activities and resources required to deliver the value proposition. Assess if the current business model efficiently utilizes these resources and activities. Identify areas for optimization, automation, or outsourcing to improve operational efficiency and reduce costs.

Partnerships and Key Stakeholders: Evaluate partnerships and relationships with key stakeholders, such as suppliers, vendors, or strategic alliances. Assess the value and effectiveness of these partnerships and identify opportunities to collaborate or engage with new partners to drive mutual growth and innovation.

Competitive Analysis: Conduct a comprehensive competitive analysis to understand the competitive landscape and identify opportunities for differentiation. Evaluate the strengths and weaknesses of competitors' business models and identify unique selling points that can be leveraged to gain a competitive advantage.

Technological Advancements: Assess the impact of technology on the current business model. Determine if there are opportunities to leverage technological advancements to enhance operational efficiency, improve customer experience, or innovate existing offerings.

Market Trends and External Factors: Evaluate market trends, consumer behavior, and external factors such as regulatory changes or socio-economic shifts. Analyze how these factors may impact the current business model and identify strategies to mitigate risks or capitalize on emerging opportunities.

Sustainability and ESG (Environmental, Social, and Governance) Factors: Assess the business model's sustainability and its alignment with ESG principles. Evaluate the environmental impact of operations, social responsibility initiatives, and governance practices. Identify areas for improvement to ensure a more sustainable and responsible business model.

Financial Performance: Analyze the financial performance of the current business model, including revenue growth, profitability, and return on investment. Determine whether current financial metrics meet organizational goals and identify areas for improvement to drive profitability and long-term sustainability.

Customer Feedback and Satisfaction: Assess customer satisfaction levels and gather feedback on the existing business model. Understand customer pain points, expectations, and preferences. Use this information to refine the business model and enhance the overall customer experience.

Long-term Viability and Scalability: Lastly, evaluate the long-term viability and scalability of the current business model. Consider potential challenges, future market trends, and the organization's growth objectives. Identify opportunities to adapt, expand, or pivot the business model to ensure continued relevance and success in the long run.

By assessing these various aspects of the current business model, organizations can gain valuable insights to drive strategic decision-making, enhance competitiveness, and foster long-term growth.

Designing and Implementing Sustainable Business Strategies

Designing and implementing sustainable business strategies involves the development and execution of plans and actions that prioritize environmental, social, and economic sustainability within an organization. It entails integrating sustainability principles into a company's operations, decision-making processes, and value chain to minimize negative impacts on the planet and society while creating long-term value.

Setting a Vision: At the core of sustainable business strategies is the establishment of a clear vision and purpose that aligns with sustainability principles. Organizations must define their commitment to environmental stewardship, social responsibility, and economic viability, and integrate these goals into their overall strategic direction.

Stakeholder Engagement: Sustainable business strategies necessitate engagement with a wide range of stakeholders, including employees, customers, suppliers, investors, and local communities. By integrating diverse perspectives and involving stakeholders in decision-making processes, organizations can ensure that their strategies address the needs and expectations of a broad range of stakeholders.

Materiality Assessment: Conducting a materiality assessment helps identify the most significant environmental, social, and economic issues that impact both the organization and its stakeholders. This assessment helps prioritize sustainability initiatives and allocate resources to areas that have the most significant impact and value for the organization and society.

Environmental Impact Management: Sustainable business strategies emphasize the reduction of environmental impacts, such as greenhouse gas emissions, waste generation, and resource depletion. Organizations must identify areas where they can reduce their carbon footprint, enhance energy and resource efficiency, and implement environmentally friendly practices throughout their value chain.

Social Impact and Responsibility: A crucial aspect of sustainable business strategies involves considering the social dimensions of business operations. This includes promoting diversity and inclusion within the workforce, ensuring fair labor practices, respecting human rights, and contributing positively to the communities in which the organization operates.

Supply Chain Sustainability: Implementing sustainable business strategies also involves ensuring the sustainability of the supply chain. Organizations should evaluate suppliers based on sustainability criteria, such as ethical sourcing, responsible production, and adherence to labor and environmental standards. Collaborating with suppliers to improve sustainability performance and transparency is essential.

Circular Economy Approaches: Sustainable business strategies often embrace the principles of the circular economy. This entails minimizing waste, designing products for longevity and recyclability, and fostering closed-loop systems where materials are reused, repurposed, or recycled, reducing the reliance on virgin resources.

Reporting and Transparency: Transparently communicating sustainability performance is vital in sustainable business strategies. Organizations should establish robust reporting mechanisms that measure, monitor, and disclose their environmental, social, and economic performance. This includes regular reporting on key sustainability metrics and adherence to internationally recognized frameworks such as the Global Reporting Initiative (GRI) or Sustainability Accounting Standards Board (SASB) standards.

Collaboration and Partnerships: Designing and implementing sustainable business strategies often extends beyond individual organizations. Collaboration and partnerships with industry peers, NGOs, governments, and other stakeholders are crucial for driving systemic change, sharing best practices, and addressing collective sustainability challenges.

Continuous Improvement: Sustainable business strategies are dynamic and require continuous improvement. Organizations must regularly review and reassess their strategies, monitor progress against targets, and adapt to evolving sustainability trends, regulations, and stakeholder expectations. By fostering a culture of innovation and learning, organizations can continually refine and enhance their sustainability efforts.

Overall, designing and implementing sustainable business strategies is about aligning the organization's purpose and values with long-term environmental, social, and economic sustainability. It involves integrating sustainability into all aspects of the business and considering the interests and impacts of various stakeholders. By doing so, organizations can create long-term value, mitigate risks, and contribute positively to a more sustainable future.

Integrating Sustainability into Core Operations

Integrating sustainability into core operations involves incorporating sustainable practices and principles into the day-to-day activities and processes of an organization. This approach ensures that sustainability considerations are ingrained within the core values, strategies, and operations of the company. Here are a few real-world examples of organizations that have successfully integrated sustainability into their core operations:

a. Interface Inc.: Interface, a global manufacturer of modular flooring, is known for its sustainable business practices. The company has successfully integrated sustainability into its core operations through initiatives like Mission Zero, which aims to eliminate any negative environmental impacts by the year 2020. Interface has implemented sustainable manufacturing processes, reduced its carbon footprint, and uses recycled and bio-based materials in its products. By integrating sustainability into its core operations, Interface has gained a competitive advantage and strengthened its brand image.

b. Patagonia: Patagonia, an outdoor clothing and gear company, has made sustainability a focal point of its operations. The company engages in comprehensive sustainability initiatives, including the use of organic and recycled materials, fair trade practices, and promoting repair and reuse of its products. Patagonia has demonstrated its commitment to sustainability by transparently sharing information about its supply chain and environmental impact. By integrating sustainability into its core operations, Patagonia has built a loyal customer base and positioned itself as a leader in sustainable business practices.

c. Unilever: Unilever, one of the world's largest consumer goods companies, has embedded sustainability into its core operations through its Sustainable Living Plan. The plan encompasses a wide range of initiatives, including reducing greenhouse gas emissions, improving water and waste management, and promoting sustainable sourcing. Unilever's sustainability efforts have not only reduced costs and increased efficiency but have also attracted environmentally conscious customers and investors.

d. IKEA: IKEA, the Swedish furniture retailer, has made sustainability a priority throughout its value chain. The company has committed to sourcing renewable materials, improving energy efficiency, and promoting circularity through initiatives like the IKEA Buy Back program. By designing products with sustainability in mind and investing in renewable energy, IKEA has successfully integrated sustainability into its core operations and has become a sustainability leader in the retail industry.

e. Interface Recycling Initiative in the Netherlands: Interface implemented a successful recycling initiative in the Netherlands where they collaborated with local partners to recycle old carpets and transform them into new carpet tiles. Through this initiative, Interface ensured the circularity and reuse of materials, reducing waste generation and minimizing the environmental impact of its products.

These real-world examples demonstrate that integrating sustainability into core operations is not only feasible but also beneficial for organizations. By embracing sustainable practices, these companies have improved operational efficiency, reduced costs, strengthened their brand reputation, and attracted environmentally conscious customers. Integrating sustainability into core operations is a strategic approach that aligns with global sustainability goals and creates long-term value for organizations.

Integrating sustainability into core operations requires a systematic approach that aligns sustainability principles with the organization's values, strategies, and practices. Here are the necessary steps involved in integrating sustainability into core operations:

a. Leadership Commitment: Leadership commitment is crucial to driving sustainability integration throughout the organization. Top management must demonstrate a clear commitment to sustainability and communicate its importance to employees at all levels. This commitment provides the foundation for successful integration.

b. Establish Sustainability Goals: Set clear and measurable sustainability goals that align with the organization's values, industry standards, and stakeholder expectations. These goals should cover various aspects, such as waste reduction, energy efficiency, carbon footprint reduction, sustainable sourcing, and social impact.

c. Conduct a Sustainability Assessment: Perform a comprehensive assessment to identify the organization's current sustainability performance. This assessment includes evaluating existing practices, conducting internal audits, analyzing key operational areas, such as supply chain, manufacturing, and resource management, and assessing the organization's environmental and social impacts.

d. Develop a Sustainability Strategy: Based on the assessment, develop a sustainability strategy that outlines the key priorities and initiatives to integrate sustainability into core operations. This strategy should align with the organization's goals and establish a roadmap for implementation.

e. Engage Stakeholders: Involve employees, customers, suppliers, and other stakeholders in the sustainability integration process. Seek input, listen to their perspectives, and engage in transparent communication. This inclusive approach ensures that sustainability efforts are supported and aligned with stakeholder expectations.

f. Integrate Sustainability in Policies and Processes: Review and revise existing policies, procedures, and processes to embed sustainability principles within core operations. This integration can include sustainable procurement practices, waste management strategies, energy-efficient practices, sustainable packaging, and employee training programs.

g. Allocate Resources: Allocate adequate resources, both financial and human, to support sustainability integration efforts. This includes budgeting for sustainability initiatives, investing in sustainability technologies and infrastructure, and allocating staff to manage and implement sustainability initiatives.

h. Metrics and Reporting: Implement a system to measure and track sustainability performance across key operational areas. Develop key performance indicators (KPIs) and establish a reporting framework to monitor progress. Regularly communicate sustainability performance data to stakeholders through sustainability reports and other channels.

i. Employee Engagement and Training: Engage employees in sustainability efforts by providing training and education on sustainable practices and their role in achieving sustainability goals. Foster a culture of sustainability by encouraging employee participation, recognizing sustainability achievements, and incorporating sustainability into performance evaluations and incentives.

j. Continuous Improvement: Sustainability integration is an ongoing process that requires continuous improvement. Regularly review and evaluate sustainability initiatives, assess progress toward goals, and make necessary adjustments. Stay informed about emerging sustainability trends and best practices to enhance sustainability strategies and remain at the forefront of sustainability leadership.

By following these steps and integrating sustainability into core operations, organizations can foster a culture of sustainability, enhance their environmental and social performance, and create long-term value for all stakeholders.

Case Studies: Companies with Successful Sustainable Models

Case Study 1: Tesla

Tesla is a leading electric vehicle (EV) manufacturer that has successfully implemented a sustainable business model. By producing electric cars that emit zero tailpipe emissions, Tesla is contributing to reducing greenhouse gas emissions and mitigating climate change. The company's sustainable model focuses on creating long-lasting, efficient batteries, implementing renewable energy in its manufacturing processes, and developing a network of charging stations to support its vehicles. Tesla's commitment to sustainability has not only earned it a strong market position but has also inspired the adoption of EVs across the automotive industry.

Case Study 2: Patagonia

Patagonia, an outdoor apparel company, is renowned for its sustainable business practices. The company has integrated sustainability into its core operations through initiatives like using recycled materials, supporting fair labor practices and encouraging customers to repair and reuse their products. Patagonia's commitment to sustainability has resonated with environmentally conscious consumers and strengthened its brand reputation. The company's sustainable model highlights that profitability and environmental responsibility can go hand in hand.

Case Study 3: IKEA

IKEA, a global furniture retailer, has implemented a successful sustainable business model centered on circular economy principles. The company focuses on designing products for longevity, using renewable and recyclable materials, and promoting furniture recycling and reusing initiatives. IKEA's sustainable model has not only reduced waste and environmental impact but has also attracted customers who are seeking affordable and sustainable furniture options.

Case Study 4: Unilever

Unilever, a multinational consumer goods company, has embraced sustainability as a core component of its business model. The company's Sustainable Living Plan includes goals such as reducing greenhouse gas emissions, improving water and waste management, and promoting sustainable sourcing. Unilever's commitment to sustainability has resulted in operational efficiencies, reduced costs, and increased brand loyalty from environmentally conscious consumers.

Case Study 5: Interface Inc.

Interface, a global manufacturer of modular flooring, has successfully implemented sustainability into its business model through its Mission Zero initiative. The company focuses on eliminating any negative environmental impact by using renewable materials, reducing waste, and implementing innovative and sustainable manufacturing processes. Interface's commitment to sustainability has not only improved its environmental performance but has also led to increased customer loyalty and a competitive advantage in the market.

Case Study 6: Danone

Danone, a multinational food and beverage company, has made sustainability a core part of its business model. The company focuses on promoting sustainable agriculture, reducing water consumption, and supporting responsible sourcing practices. Danone's sustainable model has not only improved its environmental performance but has also resulted in improved operational efficiencies and brand reputation.

Case Study 7: Natura & Co.

Natura & Co., a Brazilian cosmetics and personal care company, has built a successful sustainable business model. The company focuses on sourcing natural and ethical ingredients, promoting fair trade practices, and investing in biodiversity conservation. Natura's sustainable model has not only attracted environmentally conscious consumers but has also supported local communities and ecosystems.

Case Study 8: Interface Recycling Initiative in the Netherlands

Interface implemented a successful recycling initiative in the Netherlands, collaborating with local partners to recycle old carpets and transform them into new carpet tiles. Through this initiative, Interface ensures the circularity and reuse of materials, reducing waste generation and minimizing the environmental impact of its products.

These case studies highlight how companies across various industries have successfully implemented sustainable business models, resulting in operational efficiencies, cost savings, improved brand reputation, and increased customer loyalty. The integration of sustainability into core operations has proven to be a win-win situation, benefiting both businesses and the planet.

Chapter Seventeen

Responsible Supply Chain Management

Introduction to Responsible Supply Chain Management

Responsible supply chain management is an essential aspect of sustainable business practices. It involves the integration of social, environmental, and ethical considerations throughout the entire supply chain, from sourcing raw materials to delivering the final product or service to customers. Responsible supply chain management encompasses a range of practices, including ethical sourcing, fair labor practices, environmental stewardship, and supply chain transparency.

In today's globalized economy, companies are increasingly recognizing that they have a responsibility to ensure that their supply chains operate responsibly. This means not only delivering quality products and services but also considering the welfare of workers, the impacts on local communities, and the preservation of the environment. A responsible supply chain not only minimizes negative impacts but also creates positive social and environmental outcomes.

Responsible supply chain management requires collaboration and engagement with suppliers, distributors, and other stakeholders to address sustainability challenges effectively. It involves setting clear standards, conducting regular assessments, and implementing robust monitoring mechanisms to ensure compliance with ethical and environmental requirements. It also involves fostering long-term relationships based on trust, transparency, and shared values.

By implementing responsible supply chain management practices, organizations can mitigate risks, enhance resilience, and protect their reputation. They can also create positive social and environmental impacts, build strong partnerships, and maintain a competitive edge in the marketplace. In sum, responsible supply chain management is not only an ethical imperative but a strategic approach that aligns business practices with societal and environmental expectations.

Managing Environmental and Social Risks in the Supply Chain

Managing environmental and social risks in the supply chain is a crucial aspect of responsible and sustainable business practices. This process involves identifying, assessing, and addressing potential risks and impacts on the environment, communities, and workers throughout the entire supply chain. By proactively managing these risks, organizations can minimize negative impacts, protect their reputation, and contribute to a more sustainable and ethical supply chain. Here are fourteen paragraphs explaining the key steps involved in managing environmental and social risks in the supply chain.

Understand the Supply Chain: Begin by mapping out the entire supply chain and identifying the key suppliers, subcontractors, and other stakeholders involved. This comprehensive understanding helps identify the potential environmental and social risks associated with each stage of the supply chain.

Risk Assessment: Conduct a thorough risk assessment to identify and evaluate environmental and social risks within the supply chain. This assessment should include potential risks related to sourcing, manufacturing, transportation, waste management, labor conditions, human rights, and community impacts. It also involves evaluating the overall sustainability performance of suppliers and subcontractors against predefined criteria.

Set Standards and Guidelines: Establish clear standards, guidelines, and policies that outline the organization's expectations and requirements regarding environmental and social practices in the supply chain. These standards should align with industry best practices, legal requirements, and international standards such as the United Nations Guiding Principles on Business and Human Rights.

Supplier Selection and Evaluation: Implement robust supplier selection and evaluation processes that consider environmental and social performance as key criteria. Conduct due diligence assessments to ensure that potential suppliers meet the organization's sustainability standards and have adequate measures in place to manage environmental and social risks.

Supplier Collaboration and Partnerships: Foster collaboration and engagement with suppliers to promote their understanding and commitment to environmental and social responsibilities. Encourage transparency and open communication channels to facilitate the exchange of information and best practices.

Capacity Building and Training: Provide training and capacity-building programs to suppliers and subcontractors to raise awareness about environmental and social risks and build their capacity to manage these risks effectively. This includes educating suppliers on sustainability best practices, compliance with relevant regulations, and the organization's expectations.

Supply Chain Audits and Monitoring: Conduct regular audits and monitoring of suppliers and subcontractors to ensure compliance with environmental and social standards. This can involve both internal audits and third-party assessments to provide an independent evaluation of suppliers' performance.

Corrective Action Plans: When non-compliance or significant risks are identified, work with suppliers and subcontractors to develop corrective action plans. These plans should outline the steps they need to take to rectify the identified issues and align with the organization's sustainability goals.

Supplier Code of Conduct and Contractual Requirements: Develop and communicate a supplier code of conduct that clearly defines environmental and social expectations. Incorporate these requirements into contractual agreements to ensure that suppliers are contractually obligated to uphold and comply with the organization's sustainability standards.

Supplier Collaboration Platforms: Consider implementing collaboration platforms or tools that enable suppliers to report their environmental and social performance, share best practices, and engage in discussions on sustainability challenges. These platforms facilitate transparency, learning, and collective problem-solving.

Transparent Reporting and Communication: Regularly report on the organization's environmental and social performance within the supply chain. Communicate this information transparently to stakeholders, including customers, investors, and the public, to demonstrate the organization's commitment to managing environmental and social risks and fostering sustainability.

Continuous Improvement: Regularly review and update the organization's environmental and social risk management strategies and processes. Stay informed about emerging risks, evolving regulations, and industry best practices to continuously improve environmental and social performance within the supply chain.

Collaboration with NGOs and External Stakeholders: Cooperate with non-governmental organizations (NGOs) and external stakeholders to drive sustainability improvements within the supply chain. Partner with NGOs that specialize in supply chain sustainability to leverage their expertise, collaborate on joint projects, and share knowledge and resources.

Long-Term Supplier Relationships: Foster long-term relationships based on trust, shared values, and collaboration with suppliers. Building strong partnerships allows for deeper integration of sustainability principles, encourages suppliers to invest in sustainable practices, and enables ongoing improvement of environmental and social performance in the supply chain.

By following these steps, organizations can effectively manage environmental and social risks in their supply chains, driving positive change and contributing to a more sustainable and responsible business ecosystem. Proactive supply chain management not only helps protect the environment and communities but also enhances brand reputation, minimizes risks, and creates a competitive advantage in an increasingly conscious and demanding marketplace.

The supply chain has gained significant prominence in the marketplace as businesses and consumers increasingly recognize the critical role it plays in overall business operations, sustainability, and competitiveness. Here are detailed explanations of the prominence the supply chain has gained in the marketplace:

Growing Complexity: Globalization, advances in technology, and changing consumer demands have led to increasingly complex supply chains. Companies now operate in a global market, sourcing materials from multiple suppliers and selling products across various regions. This complexity has brought supply chain management to the forefront as organizations strive to optimize operations, mitigate risks, and ensure timely delivery to meet customer expectations.

Cost Efficiency: Supply chain management has become vital for organizations to achieve cost efficiency. Optimizing the supply chain, streamlining coordination, and reducing inventory carrying costs directly impact the bottom line. By effectively managing the flow of goods, minimizing waste, and implementing efficient distribution networks, companies can reduce costs and improve profitability.

Risk Mitigation: Supply chain disruptions, such as natural disasters, political unrest, or supplier bankruptcy, can have significant impacts on business continuity and financial performance. As a result, organizations are giving greater prominence to supply chain risk management. Proactively identifying and addressing risks, developing resilience plans, and diversifying suppliers and markets have become critical strategies to ensure the continuity and stability of operations.

Sustainability: Sustainable supply chain practices have gained prominence due to increasing awareness of environmental issues and evolving societal expectations. Consumers and stakeholders are demanding transparency, ethical sourcing, carbon footprint reduction, and responsible labor practices. As sustainability becomes a strategic imperative, companies are under pressure to integrate sustainable practices into their supply chains, driving demand for sustainable sourcing, green coordination, and social responsibility.

Competitive Advantage: A well-managed supply chain can give organizations a competitive edge. Streamlined processes, efficient inventory management, and accurate demand forecasting allow businesses to provide superior customer service, faster delivery times, and competitive pricing. Additionally, incorporating sustainability practices and addressing social and ethical concerns can enhance brand reputation and attract environmentally conscious customers, contributing to a competitive advantage.

Customer Expectations: In today's marketplace, customers have increasingly lofty expectations regarding product availability, quality, and service. They want convenience, personalization, and quick responsiveness. Supply chain management plays a crucial role in meeting these expectations, ensuring efficient order processing, timely delivery, and consistent product availability. Organizations that can deliver a seamless, customer-centric supply chain experience gain a competitive edge and increase customer loyalty.

Operational Efficiency: Efficient supply chain management is essential for optimizing operations and improving overall efficiency. By optimizing inventory levels, minimizing lead times, and implementing lean manufacturing principles, organizations can reduce waste, improve production efficiency, and enhance overall performance. Streamlined supply chain processes contribute to operational excellence, resource optimization, and improved customer satisfaction.

Digital Transformation: The proliferation of digital technologies has revolutionized supply chain management. Advanced analytics, automation, the Internet of Things (IoT), and artificial intelligence (AI) enable real-time visibility, demand forecasting, and predictive analytics, improving decision-making and supply chain agility. Digital transformation of the supply chain has become imperative for organizations to adapt to changing market dynamics, optimize performance, and gain a competitive advantage.

In summary, the supply chain has gained immense prominence in the marketplace due to the complexity of global operations, the need for cost efficiency, risk mitigation, sustainability imperatives, gaining a competitive advantage, meeting customer expectations, driving operational efficiency, and embracing digital transformation. Organizations that prioritize and effectively manage their supply chains stand to benefit from improved profitability, customer satisfaction, and resilience in an ever-evolving marketplace.

Engaging Suppliers for Sustainability

Engaging suppliers for sustainability is a crucial aspect of responsible supply chain management. Businesses have the opportunity to influence and collaborate with suppliers to ensure that sustainability practices are integrated throughout the supply chain. Here are the key steps businesses should take to effectively engage suppliers for sustainability:

Define Sustainability Expectations: Clearly define your organization's sustainability expectations and standards for suppliers. These expectations should cover environmental, social, and ethical considerations, such as responsible sourcing, labor practices, greenhouse gas emissions, waste management, and product safety. Communicate these expectations through a Supplier Code of Conduct or contractual requirements.

Select and Evaluate Suppliers: When selecting new suppliers, consider their sustainability performance and track record. Incorporate sustainability criteria into the supplier evaluation process, such as their environmental certifications, labor standards, and commitment to corporate responsibility. Regularly evaluate existing suppliers based on their sustainability performance to ensure ongoing compliance.

Collaborate and Educate: Establish open and transparent channels of communication with suppliers. Collaborate with them to understand their sustainability challenges and share best practices. Provide resources, training, and support to suppliers to help them improve their sustainability performance and meet the organization's expectations. This collaboration fosters a sense of shared responsibility and promotes continuous improvement.

Supply Chain Audits and Assessments: Conduct regular audits and assessments to evaluate suppliers' compliance with sustainability standards. These assessments should be conducted both internally and externally, possibly through third-party audits, to provide an objective evaluation of suppliers' environmental and social practices. Share the results with suppliers and work together to address any identified areas for improvement.

Capacity Building: Offer training, workshops, and capacity-building programs to suppliers to enhance their understanding and implementation of sustainable practices. These programs can cover areas such as sustainable sourcing, waste reduction, energy efficiency, and responsible labor practices. Investing in supplier capacity building strengthens their ability to meet sustainability requirements and fosters long-term sustainability within the supply chain.

Incentives and Recognition: Provide incentives and recognition to suppliers that excel in their sustainability performance. This can involve financial incentives, preferential treatment, or public acknowledgment of suppliers' sustainability achievements. Recognizing and rewarding suppliers for their sustainability efforts not only motivates them but also sets a positive example for other suppliers.

Integration of Sustainability in Contracts: Include sustainability clauses in supplier contracts to make sustainability commitments enforceable. These clauses should outline the sustainability expectations, reporting requirements, dispute resolution mechanisms, and consequences for non-compliance. By integrating sustainability provisions into contracts, businesses make sustainability a contractual obligation for suppliers.

Supplier Collaboration Platforms: Implement collaboration platforms or tools that facilitate information sharing, best practice exchange, and dialogue with suppliers. These platforms can provide a space for suppliers to report on their sustainability performance, share success stories, and collaborate on sustainability initiatives. Supplier collaboration platforms create a sense of community and collective responsibility in driving sustainability within the supply chain.

Transparent Reporting and Communication: Encourage suppliers to transparently report on their sustainability performance. Request regular sustainability reports that provide insights into suppliers' environmental, social, and governance practices. Share this information internally and externally to demonstrate the organization's commitment to responsible supply chain management.

Continuous Improvement: Engaging suppliers for sustainability is an ongoing process of continuous improvement. Regularly review and assess the effectiveness of engagement initiatives, supply chain performance, and supplier compliance. Stay informed about emerging sustainability trends, regulatory changes, and industry best practices to ensure that supplier engagement strategies remain relevant and effective.

By engaging suppliers for sustainability, businesses can drive positive change throughout the supply chain, mitigate risks, and enhance their overall sustainability performance. Collaboration, communication, and ongoing engagement are critical to establishing a sustainable and responsible supply chain ecosystem.

Ethical Sourcing and Fair-Trade Practices

Ethical sourcing and fair-trade practices are principles aimed at ensuring that products are produced and traded in a manner that is socially, environmentally, and economically responsible. These concepts prioritize the protection of workers' rights, sustainability of resources, and fair distribution of wealth across supply chains.

Ethical sourcing refers to the process of procuring raw materials or products from suppliers who demonstrate responsible business practices. This means that companies seek out suppliers who adhere to proper labor standards, such as providing safe working conditions, fair wages, and reasonable working hours. Ethical sourcing also involves considering the environmental impact of the supply chain, including reducing carbon emissions, minimizing waste, and using sustainable resources. By sourcing ethically, companies aim to ensure that their business practices positively impact workers, communities, and the planet.

Fair-trade practices, on the other hand, focus on guaranteeing fair and equitable treatment of producers and workers, particularly in developing countries. Fair-trade organizations promote the payment of fair prices for goods, which aim to cover the cost of sustainable production and provide a living wage to producers. The fair-trade movement also advocates for prohibiting child labor and forced labor, promoting gender equality, and empowering marginalized communities. By adhering to fair-trade practices, companies ensure that their trade activities contribute to poverty reduction and social development.

Together, ethical sourcing and fair-trade practices aim to create a more transparent and responsible supply chain.

This involves conducting due diligence to ensure that suppliers comply with ethical and fair-trade standards. This may include audits, certifications, and regular monitoring of suppliers' practices. Companies should also foster long-term relationships with suppliers, promoting collaboration and continuous improvement in sustainability and fair-trade initiatives.

Moreover, incorporating ethical sourcing and fair-trade practices can have several benefits. For companies, it enhances their reputation and can lead to increased customer loyalty and sales. Ethical business practices also protect against potential legal and reputational risks associated with non-compliance. For workers and communities, ethical sourcing and fair-trade practices can improve working and living conditions, provide access to education and healthcare, and promote sustainable development.

Additionally, ethical sourcing and fair-trade practices contribute to the achievement of the United Nations' Sustainable Development Goals (SDGs). These goals address global challenges such as poverty eradication, gender equality, decent work, responsible consumption, and climate action. Companies embracing ethical and fair-trade principles can align their operations with these global targets, making a positive impact on the world.

In a nutshell, ethical sourcing and fair-trade practices foster responsible business conduct by ensuring that products are produced and traded in a manner that respects human rights, promotes sustainability, and supports fair distribution of resources. By incorporating these principles, companies can build a more equitable and sustainable supply chain that benefits workers, communities, and the planet.

Attributes that contribute to the simulation of Ethical Sourcing and Fair Trade

Several attributes contribute to the simulation of ethical sourcing and fair-trade processes:

a. Transparency: Transparency is a crucial attribute in ethical sourcing and fair-trade processes. It involves being open and honest about supply chain practices, including how products are sourced, produced, and traded. Transparent practices help stakeholders understand and assess the social and environmental impact of their actions.

Transparency plays a crucial role in the process of ethical sourcing and fair trade. It involves openness, disclosure, and the sharing of information to provide clarity about how products are sourced, produced, and traded. Here's a breakdown of its significance in six paragraphs:

Trust and credibility: Transparency builds trust and credibility among stakeholders. It assures consumers, workers, suppliers, and other parties that companies are committed to responsible practices. By openly sharing information about sourcing practices, working conditions, and environmental impact, companies establish themselves as trustworthy and accountable entities.

Accountability and oversight: Transparency enables accountability throughout the supply chain. When companies disclose their sourcing and production processes, stakeholders can assess and evaluate if ethical and fair-trade practices are being followed. This facilitates oversight and the ability to hold companies and suppliers accountable for complying with ethical standards. Transparent operations are more likely to be scrutinized and monitored, reducing the chances of non-compliance.

Identification and mitigation of risks: Transparency helps identify and mitigate risks associated with unethical and unsustainable practices. By providing visibility into the supply chain, companies can identify potential issues like child labor, forced labor, or environmental harm. With this knowledge, they can take proactive measures to address and mitigate these risks, working towards more responsible sourcing and fair-trade practices.

Consumer empowerment: Transparency empowers consumers to make informed choices. When companies are transparent about their sourcing and production processes, consumers can assess whether the products align with their values and ethical concerns. By making conscious purchasing decisions, consumers can support companies that prioritize ethical sourcing and fair-trade practices, promoting positive change in the industry.

Collaboration and shared learning: Transparency fosters collaboration among industry peers, suppliers, and stakeholders. When companies openly share information about their practices, it encourages dialogue, knowledge-sharing, and the exchange of best practices. By collaborating and learning from each other, businesses can collectively drive improvements in ethical sourcing and fair-trade practices.

Improvement and innovation: Transparency facilitates continuous improvement and innovation. By making information accessible, companies invite feedback and suggestions from stakeholders. This feedback can inspire innovations in supply chain management, worker welfare, and environmental sustainability. Moreover, transparent reporting and disclosure systems encourage companies to set goals, measure their progress, and publicly report on their performance, fostering a culture of improvement and accountability.

In summary, transparency is an essential element of ethical sourcing and fair-trade processes. It engenders trust, enables accountability, facilitates risk identification and mitigation, empowers consumers, encourages collaboration, and drives continuous improvement and innovation. By embracing transparency, companies can demonstrate their commitment to responsible practices and work towards more sustainable and equitable supply chains.

b. Accountability: Accountability ensures that all parties involved in the supply chain take responsibility for their actions. This includes holding suppliers, manufacturers, and retailers accountable for adhering to ethical and fair-trade standards. Establishing clear guidelines, monitoring, and reporting mechanisms helps enforce accountability throughout the supply chain.

Accountability plays a paramount role in the process of ethical sourcing and fair-trade. It refers to the responsibility of all parties involved, including companies, suppliers, and stakeholders, to ensure adherence to ethical and fair-trade practices. Accountability is crucial for several reasons:

Ensuring compliance: Accountability ensures that companies and suppliers comply with ethical standards and fair-trade principles. It establishes a framework for assessing and measuring adherence to these practices and holds entities responsible for their actions. Without accountability, there is a higher risk of non-compliance and unethical behavior in supply chains.

Preventing human rights abuses: Accountability helps prevent human rights abuses, such as child labor, forced labor, and unsafe working conditions. By establishing clear guidelines and holding parties accountable for their actions, companies can help create a safe and fair working environment for workers. This is particularly important in industries with complex and global supply chains where exploitation can occur.

Encouraging transparency: Accountability fosters transparency by requiring companies to disclose information related to their sourcing and production practices. This transparency enables stakeholders to assess if ethical and fair-trade standards are being upheld. It ensures that companies are open about their actions, encouraging trust and facilitating oversight from consumers, NGOs, and regulatory bodies.

Driving improvements: Accountability drives continuous improvement in ethical sourcing and fair-trade practices. It encourages companies and suppliers to regularly assess their operations, identify areas for improvement, and take corrective actions. By holding themselves accountable, businesses are motivated to implement more responsible practices, leading to positive change across the supply chain.

Protecting reputation and mitigating risks: Accountability safeguards a company's reputation and reduces the risk of legal and reputational damage. Non-compliance with ethical sourcing and fair-trade standards can lead to negative publicity, boycotts, and legal consequences. Being accountable helps companies build and maintain a positive reputation, enhancing customer trust and loyalty.

Promoting industry-wide standards: Accountability drives the establishment and enforcement of industry-wide standards for ethical sourcing and fair-trade practices. When companies are held accountable for their actions, it encourages others in the industry to follow suit. This collective responsibility leads to the development of sector-specific guidelines, certifications, and initiatives that promote responsible practices.

The role of accountability is crucial in ensuring ethical sourcing and fair-trade practices are upheld. It sets a framework for responsible behavior, protects workers' rights, promotes transparency, drives continuous improvement, safeguards reputation, and fosters industry-wide standards. By prioritizing accountability, companies can create sustainable and socially responsible supply chains that benefit workers, society, and the environment.

c. Collaboration: Collaboration is key to the successful implementation of ethical sourcing and fair-trade practices. Companies, suppliers, workers, industry associations, NGOs, and governments should work together to develop and implement initiatives that improve working conditions, protect workers' rights, and promote sustainability. Collaboration fosters shared goals, expertise, and resources to drive positive change.

Collaboration plays a pivotal role in the process of ethical sourcing and fair trade. It involves the active involvement and cooperation of various stakeholders, including companies, suppliers, workers, industry associations, NGOs, and governments. Here's an explanation of its significance in seven paragraphs:

Shared goals and values: Collaboration helps align stakeholders around shared goals and values in ethical sourcing and fair trade. By working together, stakeholders can collectively define and establish common principles and standards that promote responsible practices. This collaboration ensures that decision-making is inclusive and reflective of diverse perspectives and interests.

Knowledge-sharing and learning: Collaboration facilitates the sharing of knowledge and best practices among stakeholders. Companies, NGOs, and industry associations can share insights and experiences, fostering shared learning and innovation. This exchange of information helps raise overall standards and enables stakeholders to tackle common challenges effectively.

Enhanced supply chain visibility: Collaboration improves supply chain visibility by encouraging open communication and information sharing. Companies can work with suppliers and workers to gather relevant data on working conditions, wages, and environmental impact. This shared visibility allows for a better understanding of practices, making it easier to identify areas that need improvement and implement necessary changes.

Continuous improvement and innovation: Collaboration enables stakeholders to collectively drive continuous improvement and innovation. By collaborating, companies and suppliers can share new ideas, technologies, and approaches to enhance ethical sourcing and fair-trade practices. Through collaboration, stakeholders can inspire and challenge each other to find better ways to address social and environmental issues.

Mitigation of systemic challenges: Collaboration helps address systemic challenges that are difficult to tackle individually. By working together, stakeholders can address overarching issues such as child labor, poverty, and inequality, which require cohesive efforts at a larger scale. Collaborative initiatives can drive systemic change and contribute to long-term solutions.

Multi-stakeholder initiatives: Collaboration often takes the form of multi-stakeholder initiatives aimed at improving ethical sourcing and fair-trade practices. These initiatives bring together companies, NGOs, governments, and other relevant actors to jointly create strategies, guidelines, and certifications that promote responsible sourcing. By collaborating through such initiatives, stakeholders can collectively shape industry standards and influence policy changes.

Influence and scalability: Collaboration amplifies the impact of individual efforts and makes responsible sourcing practices more scalable. When stakeholders collaborate, their collective voice becomes stronger, leading to greater influence and the ability to drive change across industries and regions. This scalability allows for broader adoption of ethical sourcing and fair-trade practices, benefiting a larger number of workers and communities.

In summary, collaboration is vital in the process of ethical sourcing and fair trade. It fosters shared goals, facilitates knowledge-sharing, enhances supply chain visibility, drives continuous improvement, addresses systemic challenges, leads to the formation of multi-stakeholder initiatives, and amplifies the impact of responsible sourcing practices. By collaborating and working together, stakeholders can create significant positive changes in supply chains, promoting sustainability, social justice, and economic development.

d. Due diligence: Conducting due diligence is essential to identifying and addressing any potential risks or non-compliance within the supply chain. This involves conducting thorough assessments of suppliers' practices and engaging in regular audits to ensure adherence to ethical and fair-trade standards. Due diligence helps companies make informed decisions and take appropriate actions when shortcomings are found.

Due diligence plays a critical role in the process of ethical sourcing and fair-trade. It refers to the process of conducting thorough assessments and investigations to ensure that suppliers and business partners comply with ethical standards. Here's an explanation of its significance in nine paragraphs:

Supplier evaluation: Due diligence involves evaluating potential suppliers to ensure that their business practices align with ethical and fair-trade standards. This assessment includes examining their labor practices, environmental impact, and adherence to relevant regulations and certifications. Supplier evaluation helps companies make informed decisions about whom to partner with, ensuring responsible sourcing practices from the outset.

Risk identification: Due diligence helps in identifying and mitigating risks associated with unethical practices in the supply chain. It allows companies to assess and understand potential risks, such as child labor, forced labor, or environmental violations. This knowledge enables companies to take proactive measures to address these risks, ensuring compliance with ethical standards and minimizing reputational and legal vulnerabilities.

Supply chain transparency: Conducting due diligence promotes transparency within the supply chain. It involves gathering information about suppliers' practices, policies, and performance. This transparency ensures that companies have a clear understanding of how their products are sourced and produced, enabling them to verify compliance with ethical and fair-trade requirements.

However, the following could be seen as strong forces that are capable of impeding the Supply Chain Initiatives:

1. Transportation disruptions: Transportation disruptions, such as infrastructure failures, natural disasters, accidents, or labor strikes, can halt or delay the movement of goods along the supply chain. These disruptions can lead to inventory shortages, increased lead times, and higher costs.
2. Inventory management challenges: Poor inventory management practices, such as inaccurate forecasting, inadequate demand planning, or inefficient stock management, can lead to imbalances in the supply chain. Excess inventory ties up capital and storage space, while insufficient inventory can result in lost sales and dissatisfied customers.
3. Supplier issues: Supplier-related problems, such as quality defects, late deliveries, or supplier bankruptcies, can disrupt the smooth flow of goods and materials in the supply chain. Reliance on a limited number of

suppliers or single-source suppliers increases the vulnerability to disruptions caused by supplier issues.

4. Demand volatility: Fluctuating demand patterns, influenced by factors like seasonality, changing consumer preferences, or unexpected market events, can lead to supply chain disruptions. Companies that fail to anticipate and adapt to demand volatility may face inventory shortages or excesses, affecting customer satisfaction and financial performance.
5. Lack of visibility and coordination: Inadequate information sharing and coordination among supply chain participants can hinder the smooth flow of goods and information. Poor visibility into demand, inventory levels, or transportation statuses can result in inefficiencies, delays, and missed opportunities for optimization.
6. Political and regulatory factors: Political instability, trade disputes, changes in regulations or tariffs, and geopolitical tensions can significantly impact global supply chains. These factors introduce uncertainties, create trade barriers, and disrupt established supply chain networks, affecting sourcing strategies, lead times, and costs.
7. Natural disasters and climate-related events: Events like earthquakes, hurricanes, floods, or wildfires can cause severe disruptions in the supply chain by damaging infrastructure, disrupting transportation routes, or affecting production facilities. Climate change-related risks, such as extreme weather events, rising sea levels, or water scarcity, pose long-term challenges to supply chain resilience.
8. Cybersecurity threats: With the increasing reliance on digital technologies and interconnected systems, cybersecurity threats pose a significant risk to the supply chain. Cyberattacks targeting critical infrastructure, data breaches, or ransomware attacks can disrupt operations, compromise sensitive information, and erode trust among supply chain partners.
9. Lack of skilled labor: Shortages of skilled labor in specific industries or regions can hinder production capacities, delay deliveries, and increase costs. Skill gaps in areas like logistics, warehousing, or supply chain management impact the efficiency and productivity of the supply chain.
10. Financial constraints: Financial challenges, such as limited access to capital, tight credit markets, or unstable currency exchange rates, can impede the smooth functioning of the supply chain. The inability to secure necessary funding or manage financial risks may result in delayed payments, reduced investments in infrastructure, or disruptions in supplier relationships.
11. Global health crises: Outbreaks of infectious diseases, as exemplified by the COVID-19 pandemic, can have significant global supply chain impacts. Travel restrictions, lockdowns, and health concerns can disrupt manufacturing, transportation, and labor availability, leading to supply shortages and delivery delays.
12. Lack of contingency planning: Failure to anticipate and prepare for potential disruptions leaves supply chains vulnerable. Companies with insufficient contingency plans, backup suppliers, or alternative transportation routes find it challenging to mitigate the impact of unforeseen events.
13. Lack of collaboration and trust: Poor collaboration and trust among supply chain partners can result in bottlenecks, delays, and suboptimal decision-making. When communication, coordination, and trust are lacking, organizations struggle to respond effectively to disruptions and make collective decisions that benefit the entire supply chain.
14. Ethics and sustainability concerns: Increasingly, consumers and stakeholders demand supply chains that uphold ethical and sustainable practices. Companies that fail to address issues like labor rights violations, environmental impacts, or supply chain transparency may face reputational damage, regulatory challenges, and loss of customer loyalty.
15. Complexity and globalization: The complexity inherent in global supply chains, with multiple tiers of suppliers and interconnected networks, presents challenges for managing risk and ensuring resilience. The extended lead times, distance, cultural differences, and language barriers associated with global sourcing contribute to the vulnerability of the supply chain to disruptions.

It is important for organizations to proactively identify and address these causes of supply chain impediments to enhance their resilience, minimize risk, and ensure the smooth flow of goods and information across the supply chain.

Compliance with regulations: Due diligence is essential for ensuring compliance with local and international regulations. It helps companies understand legal requirements related to labor practices, fair wages, environmental protection, and product safety. By conducting due diligence, companies can identify any deviations from these regulations and take appropriate actions to rectify them.

Auditing and monitoring: Due diligence involves conducting regular audits and monitoring processes to ensure ongoing compliance with ethical and fair-trade standards. Audits assess suppliers' working conditions, labor practices, and environmental impact. By monitoring suppliers' performance and conducting periodic audits, companies can identify any shortcomings, address them promptly, and drive continuous improvement.

Certifications and standards: Due diligence includes verifying certifications and standards claimed by suppliers. It involves assessing the legitimacy and relevance of these certifications, such as Fairtrade, Organic, or Responsible Down Standard. By ensuring the authenticity of certifications and standards, companies can have confidence in the ethical and fair-trade claims made by suppliers.

Remediation actions: Due diligence enables companies to take remediation actions when non-compliance or unethical practices are identified in the supply chain. This may involve working with suppliers to address issues, implementing corrective measures, providing support to improve working conditions, or seeking alternative suppliers that meet ethical requirements. These remediation actions are crucial for driving positive change and promoting responsible sourcing.

Stakeholder engagement: Due diligence involves actively engaging with stakeholders, including workers, local communities, and NGOs. By seeking their feedback and input, companies can gain valuable insights into the social and environmental impact of their sourcing practices. This engagement helps identify areas of improvement and ensures that the voices of affected stakeholders are heard and considered in decision-making processes.

Reputational risk management: Due diligence is instrumental in managing reputational risks associated with unethical sourcing practices. By staying vigilant and conducting due diligence, companies minimize the risk of association with suppliers engaged in exploitative practices or environmental harm. This proactive approach to risk management protects a company's reputation and strengthens its ethical standing.

In summary, due diligence is a vital component of ethical sourcing and fair-trade practices. It involves supplier evaluation, risk identification, supply chain transparency, compliance with regulations, auditing, and monitoring, verifying certifications, remediation actions, stakeholder engagement, and reputational risk management. By conducting due diligence, companies can ensure responsible sourcing practices, mitigate risks, protect their reputation, and drive positive change in supply chains.

e. Certification and standards: Certification and compliance with recognized standards play a significant role in ethical sourcing and fair-trade processes. Various international organizations provide certifications and standards, such as Fairtrade International and the Forest Stewardship Council (FSC). These certifications validate that specific products or supply chains meet specific criteria for ethical and sustainable practices.

Certification and standards play a significant role in ethical sourcing and fair-trade practices. They provide a framework and set criteria for companies to follow, ensuring that products and supply chains meet specific ethical and sustainability requirements. Here's an explanation of their application:

Establishing benchmarks: Certifications and standards set benchmarks for companies to measure their performance and adherence to ethical sourcing and fair-trade practices. They define specific criteria related to labor rights, environmental sustainability, community engagement, and other social and ethical aspects. These benchmarks provide clear guidelines to help companies align their practices with accepted standards.

Third-party verification: Certification and standards often involve third-party verification. This independent assessment ensures that companies' claims regarding ethical practices are validated by an objective and trusted authority. Third-party verification adds credibility and transparency to ethical sourcing and fair-trade efforts, assuring consumers and other stakeholders.

Consumer trust and informed choices: Certifications and standards enable consumers to make informed choices. Ethical labels and certifications provide assurance that products have been sourced and produced responsibly, with consideration for workers' rights and the environment. This transparency empowers consumers to support companies that prioritize ethical practices, fostering trust and responsible purchasing decisions.

Regulatory compliance: Certifications and standards often align with governmental regulations related to labor, human rights, and environmental protection. Compliance with these requirements becomes easier when companies adhere to recognized ethical sourcing and fair-trade certifications and standards. This alignment ensures companies meet legal obligations while also contributing to sustainable sourcing practices.

Continuous improvement: Certifications and standards encourage continuous improvement in ethical sourcing and fair-trade practices. They typically require periodic reassessments and renewal, pushing companies to continuously enhance their performance. By providing a benchmark for improvement, certifications and standards drive companies to develop and implement more rigorous and sustainable practices.

Supply chain management: Certifications and standards offer guidance for supply chain management. They help companies evaluate suppliers, identify areas of improvement, and establish requirements for responsible sourcing. By following recognized certifications and standards, companies can ensure that their entire supply chain adheres to consistent ethical and sustainability principles.

Collaboration and best practices: Certifications and standards promote collaboration among industry peers. Companies that seek certification often engage in knowledge-sharing and the exchange of best practices. This collaboration fosters learning and innovation while allowing organizations to collectively tackle common challenges and drive industry-wide sustainability improvements.

Transparency and impact measurement: Certifications and standards encourage transparency and impact measurement. They often require companies to document and report their practices, allowing stakeholders to assess and verify their compliance. This transparency facilitates the measurement of social and environmental impacts, allowing companies to monitor progress and make data-driven decisions for further improvement.

Differentiation in the market: Certifications and standards create opportunities for companies to differentiate themselves in the market. By achieving recognized certifications and adhering to high ethical and fair-trade standards, companies can stand out as leaders in sustainability and responsibility. This differentiation can attract environmentally conscious consumers, partners, and investors, contributing to the company's overall success and reputation.

In conclusion, certifications and standards play a critical role in ethical sourcing and fair-trade practices. They set benchmarks, provide third-party verification, foster consumer trust, ensure regulatory compliance, drive continuous improvement, guide supply chain management, promote collaboration, enhance transparency, and impact measurement, and enable market differentiation. By following these certifications and standards, companies can demonstrate their commitment to responsible sourcing, contributing to a more sustainable and equitable global supply chain.

f. Stakeholder engagement: Engaging with stakeholders is crucial to understanding their needs, concerns, and expectations. This includes engaging with workers, local communities, NGOs, consumers, and investors. By involving these stakeholders in decision-making processes, companies can ensure that their actions are aligned with the interests of all parties involved.

Stakeholder engagement is another important aspect of ethical sourcing and fair-trade practices because it ensures that the voices and perspectives of various stakeholders are considered in decision-making processes. Here's an explanation of its significance in five paragraphs:

Ensuring worker welfare: Stakeholder engagement allows companies to directly engage with workers in their supply chains. By actively listening to workers' concerns, experiences, and feedback, companies can address issues related to working conditions, wages, and labor rights. This engagement empowers workers and helps create a supportive and safe workplace environment, promoting fair-trade practices.

Community involvement: Stakeholder engagement extends beyond workers to include local communities impacted by sourcing practices. Engaging with communities allows companies to understand and address the social, cultural, and environmental factors relevant to their operations. By involving communities in decision-making processes, companies can mitigate negative impacts and create positive social and economic outcomes.

Accountability and transparency: Stakeholder engagement fosters accountability and transparency. It encourages companies to openly communicate about their sourcing practices, progress, and challenges. By engaging with stakeholders, companies show a commitment to responsible practices and are held accountable for their actions. This transparency enables stakeholders to provide feedback, raise concerns, and promote responsible behavior in the supply chain.

Collaboration and shared learning: Stakeholder engagement promotes collaboration among various actors, such as NGOs, governments, industry associations, and workers' organizations. By working together, stakeholders can share knowledge, expertise, and best practices, driving continuous improvement in ethical sourcing and fair-trade practices. Collaboration through stakeholder engagement enables collective problem-solving and innovation.

Risk mitigation and reputation management: Stakeholder engagement helps identify potential risks and manage reputational issues. By engaging with stakeholders, companies gain valuable insights into potential social, environmental, and ethical risks in their supply chains. This knowledge allows them to take proactive measures to mitigate these risks, protect their reputation, and avoid negative impacts on their bottom line.

In summary, stakeholder engagement is essential in ethical sourcing and fair-trade practices. It ensures the welfare of workers, involves local communities, fosters accountability and transparency, promotes collaboration and shared learning, and helps mitigate risks and manage reputation. By actively engaging with stakeholders, companies can build trust, enhance sustainability, and create positive social and environmental impacts throughout their supply chains.

g. Continuous improvement: Ethical sourcing and fair-trade processes are not static; they require continuous improvement. Companies should set targets for improving social and environmental performance, measure progress, and actively seek ways to enhance their practices. Regular evaluation and updating of policies and standards enable companies to stay ahead of emerging challenges and industry best practices.

Continuous improvement of ethical sourcing and fair-trade practices can significantly enhance organizational performance in several ways. Here's an explanation of its impact in five paragraphs:

Enhanced reputation and customer loyalty: Ethical sourcing and fair-trade practices resonate with conscious consumers who prioritize sustainability and social responsibility. By continuously improving these practices, organizations can build a positive reputation and foster customer loyalty. Consumers are more likely to support companies that demonstrate a commitment to ethical sourcing, resulting in increased sales, customer retention, and brand advocacy.

Risk mitigation and operational efficiency: Continuous improvement in ethical sourcing and fair-trade practices helps organizations identify and mitigate potential risks. By regularly assessing and improving supply chain operations, companies can proactively address issues such as labor violations, environmental harm, and non-compliance with regulations. This risk mitigation process enhances operational efficiency, reduces disruptions, and protects the organization from legal and reputational risks.

Cost reduction and resource optimization: Continuous improvement drives cost reduction and resource optimization. By focusing on ethical sourcing and fair-trade practices, organizations can identify opportunities to reduce waste, improve energy efficiency, and optimize resource utilization. These efforts contribute to cost savings and promote sustainability, enabling organizations to align their operations with economic and environmental goals.

Attraction and retention of talent: Companies that prioritize ethical sourcing and fair-trade practices often attract and retain top talent. Employees are increasingly seeking meaningful work and purpose-driven organizations. By showcasing a commitment to responsible practices and continuous improvement, organizations can create a positive work environment that aligns with the values of employees. This, in turn, enhances employee engagement, satisfaction, and long-term retention.

Innovation and market competitiveness: Continuous improvement fosters innovation and strengthens market competitiveness. By consistently seeking ways to improve ethical sourcing and fair-trade practices, organizations can identify new technologies, processes, and supply chain models. This focus on innovation allows companies to adapt to changing consumer expectations, seize emerging market opportunities, and differentiate themselves from competitors.

In summary, continuous improvement of ethical sourcing and fair-trade practices directly enhances organizational performance. It enhances reputation, customer loyalty, and market competitiveness. It also mitigates risks, improves operational efficiency, reduces costs, optimizes resource utilization, attracts, and retains talent, fosters innovation, and drives long-term sustainability. Embracing a culture of continuous improvement in ethical sourcing and fair-trade practices creates a positive cycle of positive outcomes for both the organization and its stakeholders.

These attributes collectively contribute to the simulation of ethical sourcing and fair-trade processes. By integrating these principles into their operations, companies can create responsible and sustainable supply chains that prioritize workers' rights, environmental protection, and fair economic practices.

Case Studies: Sustainable Supply Chain Initiatives

1. Patagonia: Patagonia, an outdoor clothing and gear company, has implemented several sustainable supply chain initiatives. They prioritize fair labor practices, use recycled materials, and promote the repair and reuse of their products. Patagonia ensures transparency by publicly disclosing its supply chain through its Footprint Chronicles, allowing customers to track the environmental and social impact of their purchases.

2. Unilever: Unilever has launched the Sustainable Living Plan, committing to sourcing 100% of its agricultural raw materials sustainably by 2020. Through partnerships with NGOs and certification programs, they ensure

responsible sourcing of commodities like palm oil and cocoa. Unilever also aims to reduce its environmental footprint by improving water use efficiency and reducing waste throughout its supply chain.

3. Starbucks: Starbucks has implemented sustainable sourcing initiatives for coffee beans. They work directly with farmers, providing support to increase productivity, minimize environmental impact, and improve working conditions. Starbucks' C.A.F.E. Practices certification program ensures the ethical sourcing of coffee, focusing on social, economic, and environmental criteria.

4. IKEA: IKEA has introduced sustainable supply chain practices for timber sourcing. Through their "Better Cotton Initiative," IKEA supports cotton farmers in adopting more sustainable cultivation methods. They also prioritize renewable energy and have committed to producing as much energy as they consume by investing in wind farms and solar panels.

5. Nestlé: Nestlé launched the "Nestlé Cocoa Plan" to ensure a sustainable and responsible cocoa supply chain. They partner with farmers to improve agricultural practices, support education and healthcare, and eliminate child labor. Nestlé also works towards achieving 100% responsibly sourced palm oil, promoting transparency and traceability.

6. Levi Strauss & Co.: Levi Strauss & Co. focuses on sustainable sourcing of cotton. They introduced the Better Cotton Initiative to improve the environmental and social impact of cotton cultivation. Levi's also encourages consumers to recycle their old denim through their "Denim Recycling Initiative," reducing textile waste.

7. Inditex: Inditex, the parent company of Zara, has implemented sustainable supply chain practices. They prioritize transparency by publishing a list of their suppliers and are committed to eliminating hazardous chemicals from their production processes. Inditex also promotes ethical labor practices, ensuring fair wages and safe working conditions.

8. Coca-Cola: Coca-Cola is dedicated to sustainable sourcing of agricultural ingredients, including sugar, tea, and coffee. They collaborate with farmers to improve agricultural practices, water management, and land stewardship. Coca-Cola also focuses on reducing packaging waste and increasing the use of recycled and renewable materials.

9. Tesla: Tesla has implemented sustainable supply chain practices for their electric vehicles. They prioritize responsible sourcing of raw materials like Lithium-ion batteries and promote recycling of battery components. Tesla invests in renewable energy projects to reduce their carbon footprint and ensures ethical labor practices throughout their supply chain.

10. Apple: Apple focuses on sustainable sourcing of minerals and reducing the environmental impact of their products. They work with suppliers to ensure responsible mining practices, minimize waste generation, and reduce greenhouse gas emissions. Apple also supports renewable energy initiatives and aims to run on 100% clean energy across its supply chain.

These case studies highlight the diverse approaches and efforts of companies in implementing sustainable supply chain initiatives, demonstrating their commitment to responsible sourcing, environmental stewardship, and ethical practices.

Chapter Eighteen

Stakeholder Engagement and Collaboration

Introduction

In today's business landscape, companies operate in an increasingly complex and interconnected global economy. With the advent of sophisticated technology and heightened stakeholder expectations, organizations have recognized the importance of actively engaging with their shareholders and fostering collaborative relationships. Shareholder engagement and collaboration are essential elements for sustainable growth, value creation, and long-term success.

This introduction explores the concept of shareholder engagement and collaborations, their significance in modern business practices, and the potential benefits they offer to companies, shareholders, and society. It also highlights the evolving nature of these practices in response to changing stakeholder dynamics and provides an overview of the structure of this paper.

Understanding Shareholder Engagement

Shareholder engagement refers to the process of establishing a dialogue, building relationships, and involving shareholders in the strategic decision-making processes of a company. Historically, the relationship between companies and their shareholders has been characterized by a hierarchical model, where the board of directors acted as a decision-making authority, and shareholders were considered passive recipients of information and financial returns. However, the traditional perspective has gradually shifted, recognizing the importance of shareholder voice and active participation.

Shareholder engagement involves understanding and addressing the needs, concerns, and expectations of shareholders, fostering transparency, and allowing their input in decision-making. It encompasses various activities such as holding regular shareholder meetings, consultations, proxy voting, and disclosing relevant information to shareholders. Effective shareholder engagement requires companies to adopt a proactive approach to solicit feedback, respond to concerns, and collaborate with shareholders to achieve common goals.

Importance of Shareholder Engagement

Shareholder engagement is crucial for several reasons. Firstly, engaged shareholders can act as advocates for the company and help build its reputation. They have a vested interest in the company's success and are more likely to champion its cause and defend it in times of crises or controversies. Engaging shareholders can help companies develop a strong and loyal base of investors who are aligned with the company's values and long-term vision.

Secondly, shareholder engagement is essential for effective corporate governance. By involving shareholders in decision-making processes, companies can benefit from their diverse perspectives, insights, and expertise. Transparent communication channels allow shareholders to hold management accountable and ensure that their interests are safeguarded. Effective governance also reduces the risk of conflicts, enhances ethical behavior, and improves overall business performance.

Thirdly, shareholder engagement contributes to the financial performance of companies. Several empirical studies have shown a positive correlation between shareholder engagement and superior financial outcomes. Engaged shareholders tend to hold their investments for longer periods, reducing volatility and the agency costs associated with excessive shareholder turnover. Furthermore, shareholder engagement aids in identifying and addressing risks, discovering growth opportunities, and enhancing shareholder value.

The Evolving Nature of Shareholder Engagement

Shareholder engagement has witnessed significant transformations in recent years, primarily driven by evolving stakeholder dynamics and increased expectations. Traditional shareholder engagement practices often focused solely on financial matters, leaving out other important aspects such as environmental, social, and governance (ESG) considerations. However, in response to a growing demand for sustainable and responsible business practices, companies are now engaging with shareholders on a broader range of issues.

Stakeholder activism and shareholder advocacy have gained prominence, influencing companies to incorporate ESG considerations into their strategies, risk management, and reporting frameworks. Shareholder engagement has become an avenue for addressing societal concerns, such as climate change, human rights, diversity, and income inequality. Companies must proactively engage with shareholders on these issues, considering their perspectives and leveraging their expertise to develop robust strategies that align with societal expectations.

Collaborations with Shareholders

Collaborations with shareholders are an integral part of shareholder engagement, allowing companies to benefit from the expertise, insights, and resources that shareholders bring. These collaborations can take various forms, such as partnerships, alliances, joint ventures, or advisory boards. Engaging shareholders as strategic partners not only enhances decision-making but also fosters innovation, drives operational excellence, and strengthens the relationship between companies and shareholders.

Shareholder collaborations offer companies access to a wider network of capabilities, knowledge, and industry insights, giving them a competitive edge in the market. Shareholders, on the other hand, have an opportunity to actively contribute to long-term value creation and influence the direction of the company. Collaborations can help companies address complex and multidimensional challenges, such as sustainability, technology disruptions, and changing consumer preferences.

Conclusion

Shareholder engagement and collaboration have become critical components of modern business practices. Recognizing shareholders as active participants and strategic partners contributes to enhanced corporate governance, improved financial performance, and the development of sustainable, responsible, and resilient businesses. As stakeholder expectations continue to evolve, companies must embrace shareholder engagement to address societal concerns and foster long-term value creation. This paper will delve deeper into various aspects of shareholder engagement and collaborations, exploring case studies, best practices, challenges, and future trends.

Importance of Stakeholder Engagement in Responsible Leadership

Shareholder engagement is a crucial aspect of responsible leadership as it ensures that the interests of shareholders are aligned with the company's values, goals, and long-term sustainability. By actively involving shareholders in decision-making processes and fostering transparent communication channels, responsible leaders can build trust, enhance accountability, and drive positive outcomes for all stakeholders.

Firstly, shareholder engagement in responsible leadership allows for the effective management of risks and opportunities. Shareholders, as owners of the company, often possess valuable insights and perspectives that can help identify potential risks and navigate complex challenges. Engaging shareholders in the decision-making process enables leaders to tap into this expertise and make informed decisions that consider the long-term implications for both the company and its stakeholders.

Secondly, responsible leadership requires a focus on sustainability and corporate social responsibility (CSR).

Shareholder engagement provides a platform for incorporating sustainability practices and ESG considerations into the company's operations. By involving shareholders in discussions around issues such as environmental impact, social responsibility, and ethical business practices, leaders can develop strategies that address these concerns and create value for all stakeholders.

Thirdly, shareholder engagement can act as a safeguard against unethical practices and failures in corporate governance. When shareholders are actively engaged, they can hold leaders accountable for their actions and decisions. Transparency in communication and decision-making processes allows shareholders to voice their concerns, challenge management when necessary, and ensure that responsible practices are upheld.

Furthermore, shareholder engagement contributes to the overall reputation and brand image of a company. Engaged shareholders who believe in and support a company's values and vision can act as advocates, promoting the company and enhancing its credibility. This positive perception can attract potential investors, customers, and business partners who align with the company's responsible leadership practices.

In addition, shareholder engagement fosters innovation and creativity within the organization. By involving shareholders in discussions, leaders can tap into a diverse range of perspectives and ideas. This collaboration can lead to the development of innovative solutions, new products or services, and improved business practices that benefit not only the company but also society as a whole.

Moreover, shareholder engagement promotes long-term thinking and sustainability. Responsible leaders focus on creating value not just for the short term but also for future generations. Engaging shareholders in conversations about the company's purpose, impact on the environment, and long-term strategies encourages a collective commitment to sustainability and responsible decision-making.

Shareholder engagement also plays a crucial role in talent management and employee engagement. When shareholders are actively involved, there is greater transparency regarding the company's direction and decision-making processes. This transparency can help attract and retain talented individuals who are aligned with the company's values and vision. Employees are more likely to feel motivated and engaged when they see that the company prioritizes responsible leadership and actively involves shareholders in shaping its future.

Furthermore, shareholder engagement can reduce the risk of conflicts and disputes within the company. By involving shareholders in decision-making, leaders can address potential concerns and conflicts early on, fostering a sense of inclusivity and mutual understanding. When shareholders feel heard and respected, they are less likely to resort to legal actions or advocacy campaigns that can harm the company's reputation.

Additionally, shareholder engagement allows leaders to better understand the changing expectations and preferences of their stakeholders. This knowledge can be invaluable in adapting the company's strategies, products, and services to meet the evolving needs of customers, investors, and the wider society. By actively seeking input from shareholders, leaders can demonstrate their commitment to responsible leadership and ensure that their decisions are in line with stakeholder expectations.

Moreover, shareholder engagement enhances financial performance and sustainability. Studies have shown that companies with engaged shareholders tend to outperform their peers financially. Engaging shareholders in decision-making processes and considering their perspectives can lead to more effective strategic decisions, collective alignment, and improved financial outcomes.

Responsible leaders recognize that shareholder engagement is not only about financial returns but also about creating shared value. By involving shareholders in responsible business practices, leaders can address societal challenges such as poverty, inequality, climate change, and resource depletion. This shared value approach ensures that business decisions contribute to the well-being of both shareholders and the wider society.

Finally, shareholder engagement promotes transparency, which is vital in today's increasingly interconnected world. With the rise of social media and the 24/7 news cycle, companies are under constant scrutiny. Engaging shareholders and providing clear and timely information demonstrates a commitment to transparency and helps build trust with stakeholders. This, in turn, can protect the company's reputation, attract investment, and foster collaborative relationships with other organizations.

In conclusion, shareholder engagement is crucial for responsible leadership as it aligns the interests of shareholders with the values and goals of the company. Engaging shareholders promotes accountability, transparency, sustainability, innovation, and stakeholder value creation. Responsible leaders recognize the importance of involving shareholders in decision-making processes and foster collaborative relationships for the long-term success and sustainability of the company.

Building Effective Partnerships for Sustainability

Building effective partnerships for sustainability is crucial in addressing complex challenges and achieving meaningful progress towards a more sustainable future. These partnerships involve collaboration between various stakeholders, such as businesses, governments, non-profit organizations, communities, and academia, to collectively work towards shared sustainability goals. Here are eight key considerations for building effective partnerships for sustainability:

Shared vision and goals: A successful partnership for sustainability requires a shared vision and aligned goals among the participating organizations. All parties must agree on the desired outcomes and objectives they aim to achieve. This shared vision serves as a guiding principle and helps foster collaboration and cooperation throughout the partnership.

Trust and open communication: Trust is the foundation of any successful partnership. Open and transparent communication is essential for building trust among partners. It is important to create a safe space for all stakeholders to express their concerns, share information, and jointly problem-solve. Regular communication and ongoing dialogue help build stronger relationships and ensure that all partners are working towards the same objectives.

Complementary expertise and resources: Effective partnerships bring together diverse expertise, skills, and resources. By leveraging each partner's unique strengths, the partnership can tackle complex sustainability challenges more effectively. Each stakeholder should contribute their knowledge, experience, and resources in a way that complements the overall goals of the partnership.

Clear roles and responsibilities: Establishing clear roles and responsibilities is essential to ensure effective decision-making, accountability, and coordination within the partnership. Each partner should understand their specific contributions, tasks, and deliverables. This clarity helps avoid duplication of efforts, minimizes conflicts, and maximizes efficiency and effectiveness.

Long-term perspective: Building effective partnerships for sustainability requires a long-term perspective. Many sustainability challenges cannot be solved overnight, and progress often requires ongoing collaboration and continuous improvement. A long-term commitment from all partners is necessary to drive sustainable outcomes and maintain the momentum of the partnership.

Flexibility and adaptability: The sustainability landscape is constantly evolving, and partnerships must be flexible and adaptable to changing circumstances. Partner organizations should be open to learning, adjusting strategies, and incorporating new insights or approaches as they emerge. A willingness to change course when necessary, ensures that partnerships remain relevant and effective in addressing evolving sustainability challenges.

Stakeholder engagement: Successful partnerships for sustainability involve engaging with relevant stakeholders beyond the core partnership. Engaging with affected communities, customers, and other stakeholders helps ensure that their voices are heard, their perspectives are considered, and their needs are addressed. This inclusive approach fosters trust, encourages collaboration, and enhances the credibility and impact of the partnership.

Measurement and evaluation: Monitoring, measuring, and evaluating the impact of the partnership's efforts are essential to assess progress, identify areas for improvement, and communicate outcomes effectively. Establishing clear metrics and reporting mechanisms helps track performance, hold partners accountable, and demonstrate the value and effectiveness of the partnership to internal and external stakeholders.

Building effective partnerships for sustainability requires shared vision and goals, trust and open communication, complementary expertise and resources, clear roles and responsibilities, a long-term perspective, flexibility, stakeholder engagement, and measurement and evaluation. By fostering collaboration and collective action, such partnerships can drive meaningful change, accelerate progress toward sustainability, and create a positive impact on society and the environment.

Examples of shared visions, trust, goals, and effective communication in partnerships for sustainability:

Shared Vision: A global partnership between multiple governments, international organizations, and NGOs to eradicate extreme poverty and achieve sustainable development globally by 2030, as outlined in the United Nations' Sustainable Development Goals (SDGs).

Trust and Open Communication: A collaboration between a multinational corporation and a local community to develop sustainable sourcing practices for a critical raw material. The partnership involves regular meetings, open dialogue, and transparency in sharing information about environmental and social impacts, fostering trust, and ensuring that the community's concerns are heard and addressed.

Complementary Expertise and Resources: A partnership between a renewable energy company, a research institution, and a local government to develop and implement a community-based renewable energy project. The company brings technical expertise and funding, the research institution provides scientific knowledge and evaluation capabilities, and the local government offers access to land and permits.

Clear Roles and Responsibilities: A partnership between a fashion brand and its suppliers to improve supply chain transparency and ethical labor practices. The brand sets clear expectations for suppliers, and provides training and resources, while suppliers commit to fair wages, safe working conditions, and environmentally responsible practices.

Long-Term Perspective: A collaboration between a conservation organization and a private landowner to restore and protect a fragile ecosystem. The partnership involves a long-term land conservation agreement, ongoing monitoring, and joint stewardship efforts to ensure the sustained health and resilience of the ecosystem.

Flexibility and Adaptability: An industry-wide partnership between major food retailers, agricultural producers, and environmental organizations to reduce food waste throughout the supply chain. As new technologies and approaches emerge, the partnership adapts its strategies to maximize the reduction of food waste, such as implementing innovative packaging, storage, and distribution techniques.

Stakeholder Engagement: A partnership between a nonprofit organization focused on education, a local government, and businesses to establish a sustainability education program in schools. The partnership engages parents, teachers, students, community leaders, and business representatives in the program's development, curriculum design, and implementation, ensuring that diverse perspectives and needs are considered.

Measurement and Evaluation: A partnership between multiple stakeholders in the tourism industry, including hotels, tour operators, and destination management organizations, to promote sustainable tourism practices. The partnership establishes clear metrics to measure and evaluate the environmental, social, and economic impacts of tourism activities, regularly monitoring progress and sharing results to drive continuous improvement.

These examples demonstrate the importance of shared visions, trust, goals, communication, and other key elements in building effective partnerships for sustainability. Each partnership reflects a commitment to collective action, collaboration, and shared responsibility to address sustainability challenges and create positive change. Engaging with Investors, Customers, Employees, and Communities.

Case Studies: Collaborative Approaches to Sustainable Development

Case Study 1: Palau's Protected Areas Network

In Palau, a collaborative approach was used to develop and manage a network of protected areas. The government worked closely with local communities, NGOs, and international partners to establish the network, set up management plans, and monitor the effectiveness of conservation efforts. This collaborative approach has been successful in protecting Palau's diverse marine ecosystems and promoting sustainable tourism.

Case Study 2: Barcelona's Superblocks

Barcelona implemented a collaborative approach to sustainable urban development through the creation of "superblocks." The city engaged residents, businesses, and urban planners to reconfigure street layouts, prioritize pedestrian and cycling infrastructure, and reduce air pollution. This collaborative approach has transformed neighborhoods, increased green spaces, and improved the overall quality of life for residents.

Case Study 3: The Great Green Wall Initiative

The Great Green Wall Initiative is a collaborative project involving 11 African countries. It aims to combat desertification by planting a green belt of trees across the Sahel region. The project has brought together governments, local communities, NGOs, and international organizations to share knowledge, resources, and techniques for sustainable land management, promoting ecosystem restoration, and providing livelihood opportunities for local communities.

Case Study 4: The Appalachian Regional Reforestation Initiative

The Appalachian Regional Reforestation Initiative (ARRI) in the United States is a collaborative effort between government agencies, mining companies, and environmental organizations. ARRI aims to restore forests on mined lands and promote sustainable reforestation practices. Through collaboration, mining companies have implemented reclamation techniques, while environmental organizations have provided technical expertise and monitoring.

Case Study 5: Sustainable Fishing in Iceland

Iceland embraced a collaborative approach to sustainable fishing through the establishment of a co-management system. The government, fishing industry, and local communities work together to set catch limits, regulate fishing practices, and protect marine ecosystems. This collaborative approach has helped rebuild fish stocks and maintain the long-term sustainability of the fishing industry.

Case Study 6: The Nordic Model of Social Welfare

The Nordic countries have implemented a collaborative approach to sustainable social development through the Nordic Model. Governments, social partners, and civil society collaborate to create policies that promote equality, social welfare, and environmental sustainability. This collaborative approach has resulted in high levels of well-being, low-income inequality, and sustainable economic growth.

Case Study 7: The Sustainable Agriculture Network

The Sustainable Agriculture Network (SAN) brings together farmers, NGOs, and retailers to promote sustainable farming practices. The network develops environmental and social standards for agriculture, provides training and certification, and connects sustainable producers with retailers and consumers. Through collaboration, SAN ensures that sustainable farming practices are adopted, protecting ecosystems, promoting fair trade, and improving farmer livelihoods.

Case Study 8: The Partnership for Sustainable Cities

The Partnership for Sustainable Cities is a collaboration between UN-Habitat, C40 Cities, and other international organizations. The partnership supports cities in implementing sustainable urban development strategies, addressing challenges in areas such as transportation, energy, and waste management. Through collaboration, cities share best practices, access funding, and develop innovative solutions for sustainable urbanization.

Case Study 9: The Conservation Stewards Program in Costa Rica

Costa Rica's Conservation Stewards Program engages local landowners, government agencies, and conservation organizations in collaborative efforts to protect biodiversity and promote sustainable land management. The program provides incentives and technical assistance to landowners who engage in conservation practices, such as reforestation and habitat restoration. This collaborative approach has resulted in the creation of biological corridors, enhanced ecosystem services, and increased connectivity for wildlife.

Case Study 10: The Global Partnership for Oceans

The Global Partnership for Oceans is a collaborative platform involving governments, NGOs, and businesses working towards sustainable ocean management. Through the partnership, stakeholders collaborate on initiatives to sustainably manage fisheries, reduce marine pollution, and protect marine ecosystems. This collaborative approach has led to the adoption of sustainable fishing practices, the establishment of marine protected areas, and improved governance of the world's oceans.

Chapter Nineteen

Measuring and Reporting Sustainability Performance

Introduction

Measuring and reporting sustainability performance has become increasingly important in today's world as organizations recognize the need to address environmental, social, and governance (ESG) issues. Sustainability performance refers to an organization's ability to achieve its objectives in a manner that promotes long-term resilience and positive impacts on the environment and society. It involves assessing and tracking key sustainability indicators, evaluating progress towards sustainability goals, and transparently communicating the results to stakeholders.

The global challenges of climate change, resource depletion, social inequality, and ethical concerns, among others, have pushed organizations to embrace sustainable practices. As a result, measuring and reporting sustainability performance has emerged as a critical tool to drive progress towards sustainable development and enable informed decision-making.

Measuring sustainability performance involves evaluating a wide range of metrics encompassing environmental, social, and economic aspects. Environmental indicators may include greenhouse gas emissions, water consumption, waste generation, and biodiversity impact. Social indicators may encompass employee welfare, community engagement, human rights, and diversity and inclusion. Economic indicators may focus on financial performance, supply chain ethics, and customer satisfaction.

Sustainability reporting provides a mechanism for organizations to communicate their sustainability efforts, achievements, and challenges to various stakeholders, including investors, customers, employees, suppliers, and communities. It enhances transparency, accountability, and credibility while fostering trust between the organization and its stakeholders.

The standards and frameworks guiding sustainability reporting vary across regions and sectors. However, some widely recognized frameworks include the Global Reporting Initiative (GRI), the Sustainability Accounting Standards Board (SASB), the Integrated Reporting Framework, and the Task Force on Climate-related Financial Disclosures (TCFD). These frameworks provide guidelines, principles, and indicators that organizations can follow to ensure consistency, comparability, and relevance in their sustainability reporting.

Measuring and reporting sustainability performance goes beyond compliance with regulations and voluntary frameworks. It enables organizations to identify areas where they can make improvements, set targets, and track progress over time. This data-driven approach empowers organizations to make evidence-based decisions, allocate resources effectively, and drive innovation toward sustainability.

Furthermore, measuring and reporting sustainability performance engages stakeholders in the organization's sustainability journey. By providing transparent and accessible information, organizations can foster dialogue, receive feedback, and address concerns raised by stakeholders. This iterative process strengthens relationships and improves the organization's understanding of stakeholder priorities and expectations.

Sustainability performance measurement and reporting also have financial implications. It allows organizations to attract and retain socially responsible investors who seek long-term value creation and positive sustainable impacts. Reporting on sustainability performance can enhance a company's reputation, increase market competitiveness, and mitigate risks associated with environmental and social factors.

Measuring and reporting sustainability performance is not without its challenges. Organizations may struggle with data collection, standardization, and accuracy, especially when operating in diverse regions and multiple supply chains. Additionally, identifying relevant sustainability indicators and setting appropriate targets requires careful consideration of the organization's context, objectives, and stakeholder concerns.

In conclusion, measuring and reporting sustainability performance is essential for organizations committed to driving positive change and managing their environmental, social, and governance impacts. It enables organizations to assess their sustainability performance, establish goals, and communicate their efforts and progress to stakeholders. By doing so, organizations can strengthen their reputation, enhance stakeholder engagement, and contribute to a sustainable future. However, measuring and reporting sustainability performance requires continuous improvement, collaboration, and adherence to globally recognized frameworks to ensure credibility, comparability, and transparency.

Key Performance Indicators for Sustainability

Key Performance Indicators (KPIs) are a set of measurable parameters used to evaluate the performance of an organization or system. In the context of sustainability, KPIs play a crucial role in tracking and measuring progress towards environmental, social, and economic goals. Here are 15 key performance indicators commonly used to assess sustainability performance:

a. Greenhouse Gas Emissions: Measures the total emissions of greenhouse gases generated by an organization, providing insight into its contribution to climate change.
b. Energy Consumption: Measures the amount of energy consumed by an organization, highlighting opportunities for energy efficiency and renewable energy use.
c. Water Usage: Tracks the amount of water utilized by an organization, aiding in the identification and mitigation of water-related risks and promoting responsible water stewardship.
d. Waste Generation: Measures the amount of waste generated and disposed of by an organization, encouraging waste reduction, recycling, and circular economy practices.
e. Biodiversity Impact: Assesses the organization's impact on ecosystems and biological diversity, aiming to reduce negative impacts and promote conservation and restoration efforts.
f. Employee Satisfaction and Engagement: Measures employee satisfaction, retention, and engagement levels, reflecting the organization's commitment to a healthy and supportive work environment.
g. Diversity and Inclusion: Tracks workforce diversity and inclusivity, examining factors such as gender, ethnicity, age, and disabilities, fostering equal opportunities, and promoting social equity.
h. Health and Safety Performance: Measures safety incidents, injury rates, and near misses, ensuring employee well-being and compliance with health and safety regulations.
i. Supplier Performance: Assesses the sustainability performance of suppliers, including areas such as responsible sourcing, ethical labor practices, and environmental management.
j. Community Engagement: Measures the organization's efforts in engaging and supporting local communities, promoting social development and inclusive growth.
k. Product Lifecycle Assessment: Evaluates the environmental impact of a product or service throughout its lifecycle, from raw material extraction to disposal, enabling more sustainable design and production decisions.
l. Social Impact: Tracks the organization's positive contributions to social issues such as poverty alleviation, education, healthcare, and access to basic amenities.
m. Economic Value Generated: Measures the organization's financial performance and its contribution to local economies through employment, taxes, and supplier relationships.
n. Supply Chain Transparency: Assesses the transparency and traceability of the organization's supply chain, ensuring responsible sourcing, avoiding human rights violations, and mitigating environmental impacts.

o. Stakeholder Engagement: Evaluates the effectiveness of the organization's interaction with stakeholders, including customers, investors, regulators, and NGOs, facilitating dialogue and trust-building.

These KPIs serve as vital tools to evaluate sustainability performance, set targets, and foster continuous improvement. However, it is important to note that the specific KPIs chosen may vary depending on the industry, organization size, geographical location, and stakeholder priorities, requiring careful consideration and customization to align with the organization's unique context and sustainability objectives.

Developing Effective Sustainability Reporting Frameworks

Developing effective sustainability reporting frameworks is crucial for organizations to accurately measure, monitor, and communicate their sustainability performance. These frameworks establish guidelines, principles, and standards that ensure consistency, comparability, and transparency in reporting practices. Here are 10 key considerations for developing effective sustainability reporting frameworks:

Stakeholder Engagement: Engaging stakeholders, including investors, customers, employees, and representatives from civil society, is essential in developing sustainability reporting frameworks. Stakeholder input helps identify material issues, reporting boundaries, and performance indicators that align with their needs and expectations.

Materiality Assessment: Conducting a materiality assessment helps organizations identify the sustainability issues that are most significant to their business operations and stakeholders. This allows for the prioritization of key performance indicators (KPIs) and ensures that reporting focuses on topics that have the greatest impact.

Global Standards and Frameworks: Organizations should consider aligning their sustainability reporting frameworks with globally recognized standards and frameworks, such as the Global Reporting Initiative (GRI), the Sustainability Accounting Standards Board (SASB), and the Task Force on Climate-related Financial Disclosures (TCFD). Alignment with these standards enhances credibility, comparability, and transparency.

Contextual Relevance: Sustainability reporting frameworks should be tailored to the organization's industry, size, geographic location, and stakeholder expectations. Flexibility in reporting requirements allows organizations to address their unique challenges and opportunities, ensuring contextual relevance.

Clear Reporting Boundaries: Establishing clear boundaries for reporting helps define the scope of information included in sustainability reports. This includes defining what entities, operations, and activities are included or excluded, promoting consistency and transparency.

Data Collection and Verification: Developing effective sustainability reporting frameworks requires robust systems for collecting, analyzing, and verifying sustainability data. Organizations should establish data collection processes that ensure accuracy, completeness, and consistency in reporting.

Reporting Quality Assurance: Implementing quality assurance mechanisms, such as independent third-party audits or internal review processes, enhances the credibility of sustainability reports. This helps identify and rectify any inconsistencies or inaccuracies in the data reported.

Integration with Financial Reporting: Integrating sustainability reporting with financial reporting allows for a comprehensive understanding of an organization's performance. Integrated reporting enhances the visibility of sustainability considerations and demonstrates the interconnections between financial and non-financial factors.

Continuous Improvement: Sustainability reporting frameworks should be dynamic and responsive to evolving stakeholder needs, regulatory requirements, and emerging sustainability trends. Regular reviews and updates ensure the frameworks remain relevant and effective over time.

Accessibility and Transparency: Organizations should strive to make sustainability reports easily accessible to stakeholders, both online and offline. Reports should be written clearly and concisely, using plain language and visuals, to enhance readability and understanding.

Developing effective sustainability reporting frameworks requires a collaborative and iterative process that incorporates stakeholder engagement, materiality assessments, data verification, alignment with global standards, and contextual relevance. By implementing these considerations, organizations can enhance the credibility, transparency, and impact of their sustainability reporting, fostering trust and driving positive change.

The essence of developing effective sustainability reporting frameworks lies in the need for organizations to accurately assess and communicate their sustainability performance. These frameworks serve as essential tools for measuring, monitoring, and reporting progress toward environmental, social, and governance (ESG) goals. Here are key aspects that explain the essence of developing effective sustainability reporting frameworks:

Accountability: Developing sustainability reporting frameworks holds organizations accountable for their impacts on the environment, society, and economy. By establishing guidelines and standards, these frameworks provide a structured approach to assess and disclose the organization's ESG performance, encouraging transparency and responsible practices.

Measurement and Tracking: Effective sustainability reporting frameworks enable organizations to measure and track key performance indicators (KPIs). This allows them to assess their progress over time, identify areas of improvement, and set targets for future sustainability initiatives. Measurement and tracking provide a basis for evidence-based decision-making and resource allocation.

Stakeholder Communication: Sustainability reporting frameworks facilitate communication with various stakeholders, including investors, customers, employees, regulators, and local communities. By disclosing relevant ESG information, organizations can build trust, engage in meaningful dialogue, and respond to stakeholder concerns and expectations. Transparent communication fosters stronger relationships and promotes long-term sustainability partnerships.

Risk Management: Developing sustainability reporting frameworks helps organizations identify and manage ESG-related risks and opportunities. By actively measuring and reporting these factors, organizations can better understand potential risks associated with climate change, resource scarcity, regulatory changes, reputation management, and social issues. This enables proactive risk mitigation and adaptation strategies.

Competitive Advantage: Sustainability reporting frameworks offer organizations a competitive edge by highlighting their commitment to responsible practices. Through effective reporting, organizations can showcase their sustainability efforts, stakeholder engagement, and positive impacts. This can attract socially responsible investors, customers, and employees who value ethical and sustainable business practices.

Decision-Making Support: Effective sustainability reporting frameworks provide essential data and insights that facilitate informed decision-making. By gathering and analyzing sustainability performance metrics, organizations gain actionable information to optimize operations, allocate resources, enhance product design, and reduce environmental and social impacts. This data-driven approach supports sustainable, long-term business strategies.

Regulatory Compliance: In many regions, governments and regulatory bodies are mandating sustainability reporting. Developing effective sustainability reporting frameworks enables organizations to comply with these requirements, avoiding legal and reputational risks. It demonstrates a commitment to meeting societal expectations and aligning with global sustainable development goals.

Reputation and Brand Enhancement: Transparent and credible sustainability reporting can enhance an organization's reputation and brand value. By demonstrating a commitment to environmental and social responsibility, organizations can differentiate themselves in the market and build trust with consumers and stakeholders. Positive brand perception can lead to increased market share, customer loyalty, and employee satisfaction.

Continuous Improvement: The essence of effective sustainability reporting frameworks lies in their iterative nature. By regularly reviewing and updating the framework, organizations can adapt to emerging sustainability trends, incorporate stakeholder feedback, and refine reporting methodologies. This continuous improvement process ensures the framework remains relevant and effective in driving meaningful change.

Sustainable Development: Ultimately, the essence of developing effective sustainability reporting frameworks is to contribute to the overall goal of sustainable development. By assessing and reporting on environmental impacts, social performance, and governance practices, organizations can align their operations with global sustainability objectives, such as the United Nations Sustainable Development Goals (SDGs). Effective reporting supports the transition to a more sustainable and equitable future for all.

In summary, the essence of developing effective sustainability reporting frameworks lies in promoting accountability, measurement, stakeholder communication, risk management, competitive advantage, decision-making support, regulatory compliance, reputation enhancement, continuous improvement, and contributing to sustainable development. These frameworks enable organizations to assess, disclose, and optimize their ESG performance, fostering transparency, trust, and positive impacts on the environment and society.

Communicating Sustainability Achievements and Challenges

Communicating sustainability achievements and challenges is a critical step after developing effective sustainability reporting frameworks. It involves transparently sharing the organization's progress, accomplishments, and areas where improvement is needed. Here is a detailed explanation of the importance and strategies for effectively communicating sustainability achievements and challenges:

Importance of Communicating Sustainability Achievements and Challenges:

Transparency and Accountability: Communicating sustainability achievements and challenges demonstrates the organization's commitment to transparency and accountability. It allows stakeholders to assess the organization's performance, hold it accountable for its actions, and make informed decisions.

Stakeholder Engagement: Effective communication of sustainability achievements and challenges engages stakeholders and encourages their active participation. It fosters dialogue, feedback, and collaboration between the organization and its stakeholders, reinforcing relationships and building trust.

Reputation Management: Communicating sustainability achievements helps enhance the organization's reputation. It showcases the organization's commitment to responsible and ethical practices, providing a competitive advantage and attracting socially conscious investors, customers, and employees.

Risk Mitigation: Transparently communicating sustainability challenges allows the organization to address potential risks proactively. It enables stakeholders to understand the organization's risk management strategies and supports the identification and implementation of mitigation measures.

Learning and Improvement: Communicating challenges provides an opportunity for the organization to learn, improve, and innovate. It allows the organization to seek input and insights from stakeholders, gather diverse perspectives, and identify solutions for addressing sustainability gaps.

Strategies for Effective Communication of Sustainability Achievements and Challenges:

Clear and Accessible Reporting: Develop clear, concise, and easily understandable sustainability reports that are accessible to a wide range of stakeholders. Utilize plain language, visual data representation, and storytelling techniques to make the information relatable and engaging.

Stakeholder Engagement: Engage stakeholders in the communication process by hosting regular forums, surveys, and consultations. Seek their feedback, insights, and perspectives to ensure alignment with their expectations and to address any concerns or challenges.

Multi-Channel Communication: Utilize various communication channels, including websites, social media platforms, press releases, and direct engagement, to share sustainability achievements and challenges. Tailor the messages to specific audiences and make sure the information reaches a wide range of stakeholders effectively.

Highlight Impactful Achievements: Highlight specific achievements and success stories that demonstrate meaningful progress towards sustainability goals. Provide evidence, metrics, and case studies to showcase the positive impacts on the environment, society, and the organization's bottom line.

Addressing Challenges: Transparently communicate challenges and areas for improvement, along with the organization's strategies to overcome them. Clearly outline the steps being taken to address sustainability gaps, engaging stakeholders in the dialogue and seeking their input.

Benchmarking and Comparison: Compare the organization's performance to industry peers, competitors, or global standards to provide context and show progress about others. This allows stakeholders to assess the organization's relative performance and understand its position in the market.

Engaging Leadership: Involve organizational leaders in the communication of sustainability achievements and challenges. Their endorsement and active involvement demonstrate leadership commitment to sustainability and lend credibility to the organization's efforts.

Tailored Messaging: Customize the communication of sustainability performance to specific stakeholder groups. Highlight aspects of sustainability that are most relevant and impactful to each group, considering factors such as geographic location, industry, and interests.

Collaboration and Partnerships: Highlight collaborations and partnerships with stakeholders, NGOs, and communities to demonstrate collective efforts towards sustainability. Showcase shared achievements and social impact resulting from these collaborations.

Continuous Improvement: Communicate the organization's commitment to continuous improvement and learning. Share plans for ongoing monitoring, evaluation, and goal setting to show a long-term commitment to sustainable development.

In conclusion, effective communication of sustainability achievements and challenges is crucial in promoting transparency, reputation management, stakeholder engagement, risk mitigation, and organizational learning. By developing clear and accessible reports, engaging stakeholders, highlighting impactful achievements, addressing challenges, and leveraging different communication channels, organizations can foster trust, inspire action, and drive positive change toward a more sustainable future.

Case Studies: Transparent Reporting of Sustainable Practices

Case Study 1: Company A - Enhancing Supply Chain Transparency

Company A, a global fashion retailer, implemented a transparent reporting system to showcase its sustainable practices. It developed an online dashboard that provides detailed information about the sourcing of raw materials, supplier compliance with ethical labor standards, and environmental impact assessments. By openly reporting on the sustainability practices within its supply chain, Company A gained the trust of customers and investors and became a leader responsibly.

Case Study 2: Company B - Renewable Energy Transition

Company B, an energy utility provider, transparently reported its practices and progress toward transitioning to renewable energy sources. Through its publicly available sustainability report, Company B shared its investments in wind and solar energy projects, corporate greenhouse gas emissions reductions, and initiatives to support energy efficiency among its customers. Transparent reporting of its sustainable practices helped Company B build a positive reputation and attract customers who value clean energy solutions.

Case Study 3: Company C - Sustainable Packaging Innovations

Company C, a multinational consumer goods company, openly reported on its efforts to reduce packaging waste and promote sustainable packaging alternatives. Their sustainability report highlighted initiatives such as transitioning to biodegradable and recyclable materials, optimizing packaging designs to reduce materials used, and establishing recycling programs in partnership with local communities. Transparent reporting on sustainable packaging practices improved Company C's brand image and loyalty among environmentally conscious consumers.

Case Study 4: Company D - Diversity and Inclusion Initiatives

Company D, a technology firm, transparently reported its commitment to diversity and inclusion (D&I). Through its annual sustainability report, Company D shared the demographic breakdown of its workforce, progress towards gender and racial equity goals, and employee development programs promoting inclusivity. By openly reporting on D&I initiatives, Company D attracted top talent and gained recognition as an industry leader in creating a diverse and inclusive workplace.

Case Study 5: Company E - Water Stewardship

Company E, a beverage manufacturing company, implemented a transparent reporting framework to communicate its water stewardship efforts. The company's annual sustainability report highlighted its strategies to reduce water consumption, initiatives supporting local communities' access to clean water, and partnerships with conservation organizations. Transparent reporting of its water sustainability practices enhanced Company E's reputation, resonated with customers, and mitigated water-related risks.

Case Study 6: Company F - Circular Economy Practices

Company F, a manufacturing company, embraced a circular economy approach and transparently reported its efforts to reduce waste and promote resource efficiency. Through its sustainability report, it shared achievements in waste reduction, recycling and reuse initiatives, and collaborations with suppliers to close material loops. Transparent reporting on circular economy practices helped Company F strengthen relationships with customers, suppliers, and investors committed to sustainable production and consumption.

Case Study 7: Company G - Sustainable Agriculture Practices

Company G, an agricultural producer, developed a transparent reporting system to communicate its commitment to sustainable farming practices. Their sustainability report highlighted initiatives such as organic farming techniques, wildlife conservation efforts, and reducing pesticide and fertilizer use. Transparent reporting on sustainable agriculture practices positioned Company G as an environmentally responsible brand, attracting customers who care about sustainable food production.

Case Study 8: Company H - Employee Welfare and Well-being Programs

Company H, a multinational corporation, openly reported its comprehensive employee welfare and well-being programs. These programs included flexible working arrangements, mental health support services, and initiatives promoting work-life balance. Transparent reporting of its employee-centric practices contributed to a positive company culture, improved employee satisfaction, and attracted top talent seeking a supportive work environment.

Case Study 9: Company I - Philanthropic and Community Engagement

Company I, a financial services provider, implemented a transparent reporting framework to showcase its philanthropic and community engagement efforts. Through its sustainability report, Company I documented financial contributions, employee volunteer hours, and partnerships with non-profit organizations to address social issues. Transparent reporting of its community engagement initiatives helped enhance Company I's brand reputation, strengthen stakeholder relationships, and contribute to positive social impact.

Chapter Twenty

Overcoming Challenges and Future Trends

Introduction

Overcoming challenges and being prepared for future trends are crucial aspects of sustainability practices. As organizations strive to navigate the complexities of sustainable development, they must address various challenges and adapt to emerging trends to ensure long-term success. This introduction discusses key considerations for overcoming challenges and explores future trends in sustainability.

The first challenge lies in balancing economic growth with environmental sustainability. Many businesses face the dilemma of achieving profitability while minimizing negative impacts on ecosystems and natural resources. Striking a balance requires innovative approaches, such as circular economy models, sustainable supply chain management, and resource efficiency measures. Overcoming this challenge involves integrating sustainability into core business operations and making responsible choices that promote both financial success and environmental stewardship.

Social challenges also pose significant obstacles to sustainable development. Issues such as inequality, labor rights, and human rights violations require organizations to reassess their practices and commit to fair and ethical treatment of employees, suppliers, and local communities. Overcoming these challenges necessitates the implementation of robust social sustainability frameworks, stakeholder engagement processes, and inclusive business practices that prioritize social well-being and equitable development.

Furthermore, climate change presents a pressing challenge that organizations must address. Rising greenhouse gas emissions, extreme weather events, and resource scarcity require immediate action to mitigate and adapt to the impacts of climate change. Organizations need to develop strategies for reducing carbon footprints, transitioning to renewable energy sources, and building resilience in the face of climate-related risks.

Collaboration and partnerships are key to overcoming these challenges. No single organization can solve sustainability issues alone. Collaboration with governments, NGOs, communities, and other businesses is essential to tackle systemic challenges and drive collective action. Cross-sector partnerships can leverage expertise, resources, and networks to generate innovative solutions and create positive environmental and social impacts on a larger scale.

Looking ahead, several future trends are shaping the sustainability landscape. One such trend is the growing emphasis on climate action and net-zero emissions targets. Organizations are increasingly committing to ambitious carbon reduction goals and aligning their operations with the goals of the Paris Agreement. This trend reflects the urgent need to address climate change and mitigate the risks it poses to societies and economies.

Another significant trend is the increasing integration of sustainability into financial frameworks. Investors and financial institutions are recognizing the importance of environmental and social factors in decision-making processes. Environmental, Social, and Governance (ESG) criteria are becoming central to investment strategies, with a focus on assessing sustainable impacts, risk management, and long-term value creation. This trend signifies a shift towards sustainable finance and the integration of sustainability considerations in capital allocation decisions.

Technological advancements also play a major role in shaping the future of sustainability. Innovations like renewable energy technologies, artificial intelligence, circular economy solutions, and data analytics provide opportunities for more sustainable practices. These technologies enable organizations to optimize resource use, improve efficiency, and develop new business models that contribute to sustainability.

Lastly, inclusivity and diversity are emerging as key components of sustainable development. Organizations recognize the value of diverse perspectives, inclusive decision-making processes, and fostering inclusive cultures. This trend highlights the importance of considering social equity and ensuring that no one is left behind in sustainability efforts.

In conclusion, overcoming challenges and embracing future trends is crucial for organizations to achieve meaningful sustainability outcomes. By addressing economic, social, and environmental challenges, collaborating with stakeholders, and staying abreast of emerging trends, organizations can chart a path toward a more sustainable and resilient future.

Overcoming Challenges and Future Trends in sustainability requires a proactive and strategic approach.

Balancing economic growth with environmental sustainability requires organizations to integrate sustainability into their core business operations. This involves conducting sustainability assessments, setting clear sustainability goals, and aligning strategies and investments with environmental stewardship.

Addressing social challenges necessitates a commitment to fair and ethical treatment of employees, suppliers, and communities. Organizations should establish robust social sustainability frameworks, engage stakeholders, and promote inclusive business practices to foster social well-being and equitable development.

Climate change poses a significant challenge that requires immediate action. Implementing strategies for reducing greenhouse gas emissions, transitioning to renewable energy sources, and building resilience to climate-related risks is vital. Organizations should also support initiatives to promote climate awareness, education, and advocacy.

Collaboration and partnerships are crucial to overcome sustainability challenges. Engaging governments, NGOs, communities, and other businesses in cross-sector collaboration enhances knowledge sharing, resource pooling, and solution generation on a larger scale.

Future trend: The growing emphasis on climate action and net-zero emissions targets reflects the urgency in addressing climate change. Organizations should align their operations with the goals of the Paris Agreement, set credible emission reduction targets, and invest in renewable energy and energy efficiency measures.

Future trend: The integration of sustainability into financial frameworks is becoming increasingly important. Organizations should incorporate Environmental, Social, and Governance (ESG) criteria into their decision-making processes and financial reporting to attract sustainable investments and ensure long-term value creation.

Future trend: Technological advancements offer exciting opportunities for sustainable practices. Organizations should leverage innovations such as renewable energy technologies, artificial intelligence, circular economy solutions, and data analytics to optimize resource use, improve efficiency, and develop new business models.

Future trend: Inclusivity and diversity are gaining recognition as integral parts of sustainable development. Organizations should promote diversity in their workforce, embrace inclusive decision-making processes, and foster inclusive cultures to benefit from diverse perspectives and contribute to social equity.

Overcoming challenges and embracing future trends requires a strong commitment from organizational leadership. Executives should set a clear vision for sustainability, embed sustainability into the company culture, and champion sustainability initiatives across all levels of the organization.

Investing in employee education and engagement is crucial. Organizations should provide training on sustainability topics, create platforms for employees to contribute innovative ideas, and empower them to champion sustainability within their roles.

Robust measurement and reporting systems are fundamental to overcoming challenges and tracking progress. Organizations should implement transparent reporting mechanisms, gather accurate data, and communicate their achievements and challenges to stakeholders.

Engaging customers and building trust is essential. Organizations should communicate their sustainability efforts through transparent reporting, labeling, and customer engagement initiatives. Providing information on sustainable products, services, and consumer choices empowers customers to make responsible purchasing decisions.

Advocacy and policy engagement can amplify the impact of sustainability initiatives. Organizations should collaborate with industry associations, NGOs, and governments to advocate for policy changes that support sustainable practices and create level playing fields.

Investing in innovation and research and development is crucial for overcoming challenges and capitalizing on future trends. Organizations should allocate resources to explore new sustainable technologies, product designs, and business models that align with evolving market demands and stakeholder expectations.

Strengthening supply chain sustainability is essential. Organizations should assess supplier performance, implement responsible sourcing practices, and promote supplier engagement to ensure sustainability standards are met throughout the supply chain.

Continuous improvement and learning are key. Organizations should embrace a culture of continuous improvement by regularly reviewing and updating sustainability strategies, policies, and practices based on feedback, best practices, and emerging trends.

By adopting these strategies, organizations can proactively overcome challenges and capitalize on future trends, positioning themselves as leaders in sustainable practices and driving positive change for the environment, society, and economy.

Common Challenges in Implementing Sustainable Management Practices

Implementing sustainable management practices can present various challenges for organizations.

Lack of Awareness: Many organizations face a challenge in understanding the importance of sustainability and the potential benefits it offers. A lack of awareness about sustainable management practices can hinder progress and commitment to adopting sustainable practices.

Limited Resources: Implementing sustainable management practices often requires financial investment and allocation of resources. Organizations encountering limited budgets and resources may find it challenging to initiate sustainability initiatives and projects.

Resistance to Change: Implementing sustainable management practices often involves changing existing processes, systems, and behaviors. Resistance from employees and stakeholders who are resistant to change can hinder progress and make it challenging to implement sustainable practices effectively.

Complex Supply Chains: Organizations with complex supply chains may face challenges in ensuring the sustainability of their suppliers and ensuring adherence to sustainability standards and requirements across the supply chain.

Integration of Sustainability in Decision-Making: Incorporating sustainability considerations into decision-making processes can be challenging. Balancing economic, social, and environmental factors and effectively integrating sustainability into strategic decision-making requires clear frameworks and processes.

Measurement and Metrics: Establishing meaningful metrics and measurement systems for tracking sustainability performance can be challenging. Determining relevant Key Performance Indicators (KPIs) that accurately capture the impact of sustainable initiatives and align with organizational goals can be complex.

Stakeholder Engagement: Engaging a diverse set of stakeholders in sustainable management practices can be difficult. Identifying and effectively communicating with stakeholders, understanding their needs and expectations, and incorporating their input in decision-making processes requires careful planning and communication.

Cultural and Behavioral Change: Shifting organizational culture and individual behaviors to embrace sustainability can be challenging. Overcoming resistance, fostering a culture of sustainability, and encouraging employees to adopt sustainable practices calls for effective communication, training, and engagement.

Regulatory Compliance: Navigating and complying with complex and evolving sustainability regulations and standards can be a challenge. Organizations must stay updated on the latest regulatory requirements and ensure their operations align with these standards.

Siloed Approaches: Taking a siloed approach to sustainability within organizations can hinder progress. It is crucial to break down departmental barriers and create cross-functional collaboration to ensure the effective implementation of sustainable management practices.

Inconsistent Communication: Inconsistency in communicating sustainable management practices externally and internally can lead to confusion and skepticism. Establishing clear and consistent communication about sustainability initiatives and progress is essential for building trust and engagement.

Education and Training: Many organizations face challenges in providing adequate education and training on sustainability practices to their employees. Addressing this challenge requires investment in sustainability-related training programs and ensuring employees have the necessary knowledge and skills to contribute to sustainable management practices.

Short-Term Orientation: Organizations focused primarily on short-term financial results may struggle to prioritize and commit to long-term sustainability goals and practices. Overcoming this challenge involves integrating sustainability into the organization's long-term strategic planning and emphasizing the benefits of sustainable practices.

Measurement of Non-Financial Value: Assessing the non-financial value and impact of sustainable management practices can be challenging. Identifying appropriate methodologies and tools to quantify social and environmental benefits and effectively communicate these values internally and externally is essential.

Scaling Up Initiatives: Scaling up sustainable initiatives and practices across an organization can be challenging. Expanding successful sustainability pilot projects, replicating best practices, and ensuring widespread adoption requires careful planning, resource allocation, and communication.

Risk Assessment and Management: Identifying and managing sustainability-related risks can be a challenge. Organizations need to conduct comprehensive assessments of environmental, social, and governance risks and develop mitigation strategies to address and manage these risks effectively.

Integration with Business Strategy: Aligning sustainability practices with overall business strategy can be challenging. Ensuring that sustainability initiatives complement and support the organization's overall goals and objectives requires effective integration and collaboration across departments.

Collaboration and Partnerships: Building effective collaboration and partnerships with stakeholders and other organizations can be challenging. Overcoming this challenge involves developing strong relationships, finding common goals and interests, and establishing trust and mutual benefit in collaborative sustainability initiatives.

Engaging with SMEs: Engaging small and medium-sized enterprises (SMEs) in sustainable management practices can be challenging due to limited resources and capacity. Providing support, resources, and guidance to SMEs can help overcome this challenge and foster sustainable practices across the supply chain.

Measuring Impact Beyond Organizational Boundaries: Measuring and assessing the broader impact of sustainable management practices beyond organizational boundaries can be challenging. Organizations must consider their influence on society, ecosystems, and communities and explore methods to measure and communicate these impacts accurately.

By recognizing these common challenges, organizations can proactively address them, develop strategies and solutions, and enhance the successful implementation of sustainable management practices.

Innovation and Technology for Sustainable Business

Innovation and technology play a critical role in driving sustainable business practices. They offer opportunities to address environmental challenges, improve resource efficiency, and drive positive social impact. Here are 20 full paragraphs explaining the significance of innovation and technology for sustainable business:

Renewable Energy: Innovation and technology have facilitated the expansion of renewable energy sources such as solar, wind, and hydropower. Advancements in photovoltaic cells, wind turbine design, and energy storage solutions have made renewable energy more accessible and affordable for businesses, reducing reliance on fossil fuels and mitigating climate change.

Energy Efficiency: Technology innovations have enabled businesses to improve energy efficiency by optimizing operations, implementing smart systems, and adopting energy-saving practices. Automated building systems, energy management software, and energy-efficient appliances have led to reduced energy consumption and cost savings.

Circular Economy: Innovation and technology are driving the transition to a circular economy where resources are kept in use for longer, waste is minimized, and products are designed for reuse, repair, and recycling. Technologies like 3D printing, material recycling, upcycling, and reverse logistics systems facilitate the transformation of linear supply chains into circular ones.

Sustainable Mobility: Technological advancements have spurred the development of sustainable transportation solutions. Electric vehicles, hydrogen-powered vehicles, and improved public transportation systems contribute to reduced carbon emissions and air pollution. Innovations like ride-sharing apps and autonomous vehicles have also transformed the way people move, reducing congestion and improving efficiency.

Precision Agriculture: Innovation and technology have revolutionized agriculture practices, leading to more sustainable approaches. Precision agriculture techniques, such as remote sensing, drones, and data analytics, enable farmers to optimize resource use, reduce chemical inputs, and enhance crop yields while minimizing environmental impact.

Smart Cities: Technology-driven innovations are enabling the development of smart cities that improve sustainability and quality of life. Intelligent infrastructure, real-time monitoring systems, and smart grids enhance energy efficiency, optimize resource allocation, and enable more sustainable urban development.

Waste Management: Innovation and technology have enhanced waste management practices. Advanced recycling technologies, waste-to-energy solutions, and smart waste management systems help reduce landfill waste, promote recycling and composting, and optimize waste collection and disposal processes.

Sustainable Supply Chains: Technology innovations like blockchain, the Internet of Things (IoT), and artificial intelligence (AI) are being leveraged to enhance transparency and traceability in supply chains. These technologies enable businesses to track and verify sustainability claims, detect and address supply chain risks, and ensure compliance with ethical and environmental standards.

Water Management: Innovations in water management technologies are crucial for sustainable business operations. Smart irrigation systems, water recycling and purification technologies, and real-time monitoring tools support efficient water use and conservation, particularly in water-stressed regions.

Sustainable Materials: Advances in research and development have led to the discovery and utilization of sustainable materials. Biodegradable plastics, bio-based materials, and eco-friendly alternatives to conventional materials are reducing reliance on non-renewable resources and minimizing waste and pollution.

Green Building Design: Technology and innovation have revolutionized green building design and construction. Energy-efficient building materials, advanced insulation technologies, and integrated smart systems help reduce energy consumption, enhance indoor air quality, and promote sustainable and healthy living spaces.

Data Analytics for Sustainability: Utilizing big data and analytics technologies, businesses can make informed decisions and optimize resource use. Data analytics help identify patterns, trends, and areas for improvement, enabling businesses to reduce environmental impact, improve operational efficiency, and enhance sustainability performance.

Environmental Monitoring and Compliance: Technology enables businesses to monitor and assess their environmental impact more effectively. Remote sensing, IoT sensors, and satellite imaging support real-time environmental monitoring, helping businesses identify and mitigate risks and ensuring compliance with environmental regulations.

E-commerce and Sustainability: Online platforms and e-commerce have revolutionized the way products and services are delivered. This shift to digital transactions has the potential to reduce resource consumption, carbon emissions, and waste associated with traditional brick-and-mortar retail operations.

Consumer Engagement: Technology tools, such as mobile apps and online platforms, empower consumers to make sustainable choices by accessing information about product origins, environmental impact, and ethical practices. Digital platforms also facilitate consumer engagement and feedback, encouraging businesses to align with consumer expectations and sustainability goals.

Social Impact Innovation: Technology-driven innovations are being used to address social challenges. For example, mobile banking and digital finance platforms contribute to financial inclusion, while telemedicine and remote healthcare technologies improve access to quality healthcare, particularly in underserved areas.

Collaboration and Knowledge Sharing: Technology facilitates global collaboration and knowledge sharing, enabling businesses to learn from each other and develop innovative sustainable solutions. Online platforms, webinars, and virtual conferences connect organizations and experts, fostering partnerships and driving collective action toward sustainability.

Resilience and Disaster Management: Technology plays a crucial role in enhancing resilience and managing the impacts of natural disasters and climate change. Advanced early warning systems, geospatial mapping, and real-time monitoring enable businesses and communities to prepare for and respond effectively to emergencies.

Employee Engagement and Collaboration: Technology tools like collaboration platforms, digital workspaces, and virtual communication tools facilitate employee engagement and collaboration on sustainability initiatives. These technologies enhance employee participation, knowledge sharing, and collective problem-solving for sustainable business practices.

Innovation for Social and Environmental Challenges: Technology can drive innovation to address social and environmental challenges at a global scale. For instance, innovations in renewable energy, water purification technologies, and affordable housing solutions are transforming communities and improving quality of life.

In conclusion, innovation and technology are crucial for achieving sustainable business practices. They enable the development of renewable energy solutions, resource efficiency, circular economies, smart cities, and sustainable supply chains. Advancements in data analytics, e-commerce, and consumer engagement support informed decision-making and sustainable choices. Moreover, technology fosters collaboration, knowledge sharing, and resilience, helping businesses address social and environmental challenges effectively. Embracing innovation and technology is vital for businesses to thrive in a sustainable and socially responsible manner.

Emerging Trends in Responsible Leadership

Responsible leadership is evolving to meet the changing expectations of stakeholders and address the pressing global challenges we face today. Here are 15 paragraphs explaining the emerging trends in responsible leadership:

Purpose-Driven Leadership: Emerging trends in responsible leadership emphasize the importance of purpose beyond profit. Leaders are increasingly focusing on defining and communicating a clear purpose that goes beyond financial success, aligning the organization's goals with societal and environmental well-being.

Ethical Decision-Making: Responsible leaders prioritize ethical decision-making and act with integrity, considering the impact of their actions on all stakeholders. They foster a culture of ethics and lead by example, promoting transparency, accountability, and fairness in all aspects of the organization.

Stakeholder Engagement: Responsible leaders recognize the importance of engaging with diverse stakeholders, including employees, customers, communities, and investors. They strive to understand and address the needs and expectations of these stakeholders to build trust, collaboration, and long-term relationships.

Environmental Stewardship: Emerging trends in responsible leadership emphasize the critical role of environmental stewardship. Leaders are taking proactive steps to mitigate environmental impact, reduce carbon emissions, conserve resources, and promote sustainability throughout the organization and its value chain.

Social Impact: Responsible leaders focus on generating positive social impact beyond economic value. They embrace social responsibility, support social causes, and integrate social impact considerations into business strategies, forging lasting social change and contributing to societal well-being.

Diversity, Equity, and Inclusion: Emerging trends in responsible leadership highlight the significance of diversity, equity, and inclusion (DEI). Responsible leaders promote a culture of diversity and inclusion within their organizations, ensuring equal opportunities for all and recognizing the value of diverse perspectives and experiences.

Human Rights and Labor Rights: Responsible leaders prioritize the protection of human rights and labor rights. They proactively address issues like fair wages, safe working conditions, and protection against discrimination and harassment, fostering a culture of dignity and respect for all employees and stakeholders.

Digital Responsibility: With the increasing digitalization of business, responsible leaders focus on digital responsibility. They prioritize data privacy and security, promote ethical data use, and leverage technology for positive societal impact while minimizing potential risks and harm.

Innovation and Collaboration: Responsible leaders encourage innovation that addresses social and environmental challenges. They foster a culture of collaboration, embracing partnerships with external stakeholders, such as non-profits and academia, to drive collective action and find innovative solutions to complex problems.

Health and Well-being: Responsible leaders recognize the importance of employee health and well-being. They prioritize work-life balance, mental health support, and the creation of a healthy and inclusive work environment, fostering employee satisfaction, productivity, and overall well-being.

Long-Term Thinking: Emerging trends in responsible leadership emphasize the importance of long-term thinking and planning. Leaders consider the impact of decisions on future generations, focusing on sustainable practices and leaving a positive legacy for future leaders and communities.

Responsible Supply Chain Management: Responsible leaders ensure responsible practices throughout their supply chains. They prioritize ethical sourcing, fair trade, and supplier diversity, promoting responsible sourcing practices, transparency, and accountability among all partners.

Adaptive Leadership: With the rapidly changing global landscape, responsible leaders embrace adaptive leadership approaches. They demonstrate agility and resilience, adapt to new circumstances, and empower their teams to navigate uncertainty while maintaining ethical and responsible practices.

Transparency and Reporting: Responsible leaders prioritize transparency in their communication and reporting. They share information about their social and environmental performance, sustainability goals, and progress, driving accountability and fostering trust among stakeholders.

Purposeful Governance: Emerging trends in responsible leadership emphasize the need for purposeful governance. Responsible leaders ensure strong governance structures that promote ethical practices, accountability, and long-term value creation, aligning their actions with the organization's purpose and societal expectations.

In conclusion, responsible leadership is evolving to address the complexity of today's challenges. Emerging trends emphasize purpose-driven leadership, ethical decision-making, stakeholder engagement, environmental stewardship, social impact, DEI, digital responsibility, innovation, and well-being. Responsible leaders prioritize long-term thinking, transparency, responsible supply chain practices, adaptive leadership, and purposeful governance. By embracing these emerging trends, leaders can drive positive change, create value beyond financial outcomes, and contribute to a more sustainable and inclusive future.

Conclusion and Final Thoughts

In conclusion, advancing responsible leadership is crucial for driving sustainable management practices and creating a positive impact on society and the environment. The strategies outlined in this book provide a roadmap for organizations to cultivate responsible leaders and embed sustainability into their core operations.

Firstly, organizations must foster a purpose-driven approach to leadership. By defining and communicating a clear purpose beyond profit, leaders can inspire employees, engage stakeholders, and align the organization's goals with societal and environmental well-being. Purpose-driven leadership motivates individuals to work towards a higher cause, enabling them to make decisions and take actions that prioritize sustainability and long-term value creation.

Ethical decision-making is another essential aspect of responsible leadership. Leaders must prioritize ethical principles, exercise integrity, and place the interests of all stakeholders at the forefront of their decision-making processes. By adopting transparent, accountable, and fair practices, leaders can build trust, strengthen relationships with stakeholders, and ensure that the organization's actions align with ethical standards and societal expectations.

Effective stakeholder engagement is also paramount for responsible leadership. By listening to and understanding the needs, concerns, and expectations of diverse stakeholders, leaders can create shared value and build strong relationships based on trust and collaboration. Engaging with stakeholders allows leaders to identify and address emerging sustainability issues, mitigate risks, and leverage expertise for innovative solutions and collective action.

Environmental stewardship is a critical focus for responsible leadership. Advancing sustainability requires leaders to integrate environmental considerations into all aspects of the organization's operations. By adopting resource-efficient practices, reducing carbon emissions, promoting sustainable supply chain management, and embracing circular economy principles, leaders can contribute to the preservation and restoration of the natural environment.

Responsible leaders must also prioritize social impact. They should actively work towards addressing societal challenges, such as inequality, by promoting diversity, equity, and inclusion within the organization and the broader society. By investing in employee well-being, supporting social causes, and ensuring fair labor practices, leaders can enable positive social change and contribute to the overall well-being of employees, communities, and society at large.

In addition, responsible leaders should embrace innovation and emerging technologies. Technological advancements offer opportunities to optimize resource use, improve efficiency, and develop sustainable business models. Leaders should leverage innovation and collaborate with industry peers, experts, and stakeholders to develop and implement innovative solutions that address sustainability challenges and drive positive change.

To effectively implement sustainable management practices, responsible leaders must prioritize diversity, equity, and inclusion (DEI). By fostering an inclusive culture, leaders can harness the power of diverse perspectives, experiences, and talents. Embracing DEI not only supports social justice but also enhances creativity, innovation, and decision-making in the pursuit of sustainable outcomes.

Employee engagement is a critical component of responsible leadership. Leaders should empower employees to contribute to sustainable management practices by providing training, fostering open communication, and creating platforms for innovative ideas and initiatives. Engaged employees are more likely to embrace sustainable practices and become advocates for change within the organization and their communities.

Furthermore, responsible leaders must consider the broader societal and environmental impacts of their organization's activities. They should adopt a long-term perspective and consider the effects of their decisions on future generations. Taking a proactive approach to mitigating risks, addressing challenges, and creating a positive legacy demonstrates responsible leadership and ensures the organization's long-term viability and success.

To advance responsible leadership and sustainable management practices, organizations need to embed transparency and reporting into their operations. By openly communicating their sustainability goals, progress, and challenges, leaders enhance accountability, credibility, and trust with stakeholders. Transparent reporting enables stakeholders to make informed decisions and hold organizations accountable for their social and environmental impacts.

Collaboration and partnerships are also essential for advancing responsible leadership. No organization can tackle sustainability challenges alone. Cross-sector collaborations allow for the pooling of resources, expertise, and knowledge, leading to more innovative solutions, shared learning, and collective action. Responsible leaders should actively seek collaborations with governments, NGOs, communities, and other businesses to drive systemic change and maximize their positive impact.

Lastly, responsible leaders must continuously learn, adapt, and improve. They should embrace a growth mindset and remain open to new ideas, emerging trends, and best practices. Regularly reviewing and updating sustainability strategies, policies, and practices based on feedback, evaluation, and stakeholder input enables continuous improvement in responsible leadership and sustainable management practices.

Finally, advancing responsible leadership is essential for organizations to navigate the complexities of sustainable management practices. By adopting purpose-driven leadership, ethical decision-making, stakeholder engagement, environmental stewardship, social impact strategies, and embracing innovation, organizations can drive positive change and create sustainable value for all stakeholders. Implementing strategies that promote diversity, equity, inclusion, employee engagement, transparency, collaboration, and continuous improvement ensures responsible leadership and paves the way for a more sustainable future. By prioritizing responsible leadership, organizations can contribute to solving global challenges, achieve long-term success, and create a positive impact that extends beyond their immediate sphere of influence.

PART III

RISK MANAGEMENT

Chapter Twenty-One

Introduction to Risk Management

Introduction

Risk management is an essential process that aims to identify, assess, and prioritize potential risks that might impact an organization's objectives. In today's dynamic and ever-changing business environment, organizations face numerous risks, such as technological disruptions, financial challenges, regulatory compliance issues, natural disasters, and cybersecurity threats, among others. Effective risk management enables organizations to proactively address and mitigate these risks, minimizing potential losses and maximizing opportunities for growth and success. This essay explores the importance of risk management and highlights its key components and strategies that organizations can employ to ensure better decision-making, resilience, and long-term sustainability.

Risk management plays a crucial role in an organization's ability to navigate uncertainty and achieve desired outcomes. It involves anticipating and evaluating potential risks, identifying their potential impacts, and implementing measures to prevent or mitigate them. By considering the likelihood and consequences of various risks, organizations can make informed decisions, allocate resources effectively, and plan for contingencies. This essay delves into the concept of risk management, discussing its significance across different sectors and proposing practical approaches to develop robust risk management frameworks that effectively address uncertainties.

In an increasingly complex and unpredictable business world, risk management has emerged as a significant discipline that organizations cannot afford to overlook. It involves understanding, analyzing, and responding to various risks that may hinder an organization's objectives. Risk management allows organizations to identify potential threats, determine their potential impacts, and develop suitable strategies to manage and control these risks. This essay aims to provide an overview of risk management, exploring its benefits, challenges, and key elements, while emphasizing the importance of a proactive and integrated approach to address potential risks.

The ever-evolving business landscape, characterized by rapid technological advancements, globalization, and economic uncertainties, has highlighted the importance of effective risk management. Organizations face numerous risks that can disrupt their operations, hamper growth, and erode stakeholder value. Risk management, as a systematic process of identifying, assessing, and managing potential risks, enables organizations to anticipate and respond to uncertainties effectively. In this essay, we will delve into the significance of risk management and discuss various strategies and tools that organizations can employ to mitigate risks and enhance their resilience in an increasingly volatile environment.

Risk management has become an indispensable aspect of organizational decision-making in today's volatile and uncertain business environment. Organizations need to safeguard their operations, assets, and reputation by effectively managing risks that could impact their strategic objectives. Risk management encompasses a structured approach that focuses on identifying, analyzing, and addressing uncertainties that may hinder an organization's ability to achieve its goals. This essay aims to explore the fundamental concepts and principles of risk management, emphasizing its role in facilitating informed decision-making, driving innovation, and ensuring long-term sustainability.

Effective risk management is vital to organizations' ability to achieve their goals, withstand uncertainties, and seize opportunities in a rapidly changing business landscape. By proactively identifying potential risks, assessing their potential impacts, and developing suitable mitigation strategies, organizations can enhance their ability to respond to challenges and exploit emerging opportunities. This essay investigates the importance of risk management, discussing its role in creating value, enhancing organizational resilience, and driving sustainable growth. It also explores the essential components and best practices that organizations can adopt to establish a robust risk management framework tailored to their specific needs and objectives.

Definition of Risk Management

Risk management is a comprehensive and systematic process that organizations utilize to identify, assess, and manage potential risks that could impact their objectives. It involves identifying uncertainties, evaluating their likelihood and potential consequences, and implementing strategies to minimize or eliminate their impact on the organization. By proactively addressing risks, organizations can make informed decisions, allocate resources effectively, and enhance their ability to achieve desired outcomes.

The first step in risk management is to identify potential risks. This involves examining internal and external factors that could pose threats or opportunities to the organization. Internal risks may include inadequate infrastructure, ineffective processes, or employee misconduct, while external risks could arise from factors such as economic fluctuations, regulatory changes, or technological advancements. By thoroughly identifying risks, organizations can ensure a comprehensive understanding of the potential challenges they may face.

Once risks are identified, organizations need to assess their potential impacts. This step involves evaluating the likelihood of each risk occurring and estimating the magnitude of its potential consequences. By quantifying risks, organizations can prioritize their management efforts and allocate resources proportionately to address the most critical risks. Assessing risks also helps organizations gain a better understanding of the potential financial, operational, reputational, or legal implications associated with each risk.

After assessing risks, organizations develop strategies to manage and respond to them effectively. Risk management strategies can broadly be categorized as risk avoidance, risk mitigation, risk transfer, or risk acceptance. Risk avoidance involves eliminating or minimizing exposure to the identified risks through proactive actions such as discontinuing a specific product line or exiting a particular market. Risk mitigation aims to reduce the likelihood or consequences of risks through measures such as implementing control procedures, investing in security systems, or diversifying operations. Risk transfer involves shifting the responsibility of managing risks to external parties, such as insurance companies or strategic partners. Lastly, risk acceptance entails consciously choosing to accept certain risks and developing contingency plans to minimize their potential impact.

To implement risk management strategies effectively, organizations need to establish clear roles and responsibilities and develop robust processes and procedures. This includes creating risk management frameworks, policies, and guidelines that define the organization's approach to risk management. It also involves implementing risk assessment and monitoring tools, establishing regular reporting mechanisms, and integrating risk management into decision-making processes at all levels of the organization. Furthermore, organizations should promote a risk-aware culture that encourages employees to proactively identify and report risks, fostering a holistic approach to risk management that permeates throughout the organization.

In addition to addressing current risks, organizations should regularly review and update their risk management strategies to adapt to changing circumstances. Risk management is an ongoing process that requires monitoring and reassessment to identify emerging risks and gauge the effectiveness of existing risk management measures. Organizations should also consider conducting periodic risk audits, employing risk management experts or consultants, and staying updated with industry trends and best practices. By continuously improving their risk management processes, organizations can enhance their resilience and better position themselves to navigate uncertainties and seize opportunities.

Effective risk management has numerous benefits for organizations. It enables them to make informed decisions that balance opportunities and potential risks, leading to better resource allocation and improved overall performance. It also enhances organizational resilience by allowing timely responses to potential disruptions, minimizing losses, and facilitating quick recovery. Additionally, effective risk management can enhance stakeholder confidence and trust, as it demonstrates an organization's commitment to managing uncertainties, protecting assets, and ensuring long-term sustainability. By embedding risk management into their culture and operations, organizations can create a competitive advantage and better position themselves in the marketplace.

However, implementing risk management is not without challenges. One key challenge organizations face is the constant evolution of risks, as new risks emerge, and existing risks change over time. This requires organizations to continuously monitor the external environment, anticipate trends and potential risks, and adapt their risk management strategies accordingly. Another challenge is the difficulty in accurately assessing and quantifying risks, as it often involves uncertainties and subjective judgments. Organizations may also face resistance to change or a lack of awareness regarding the importance of risk management, which may hinder the effective implementation of risk management initiatives.

To overcome these challenges, organizations can adopt a proactive and integrated approach to risk management. This involves engaging stakeholders at all levels of the organization, fostering risk awareness, and providing training and education on risk management principles and practices. Organizations can also leverage technology and data analytics to improve risk assessment, monitoring, and reporting capabilities. Additionally, fostering a culture of risk-taking within acceptable limits can encourage innovation and enable organizations to seize opportunities while managing potential risks. By addressing these challenges strategically, organizations can enhance their ability to navigate uncertainties and drive sustainable growth.

Risk management is a critical discipline across various sectors, including finance, healthcare, construction, manufacturing, and information technology. In finance, risk management helps institutions assess credit, market, operational, and liquidity risks to ensure financial stability and mitigate potential losses. In healthcare, risk management aims to ensure patient safety, minimize medical errors, and address medical malpractice risks. In the construction industry, risk management focuses on identifying and managing risks associated with project delays, cost overruns, and safety hazards. In manufacturing, risk management helps identify and mitigate risks related to supply chain interruptions, equipment failure, or product recalls. In the information technology sector, risk management focuses on cybersecurity threats, data breaches, and technology disruptions.

There are various frameworks and standards available to guide organizations in implementing risk management. One widely recognized framework is the ISO 31000, which provides principles, guidelines, and a practical approach to risk management. The COSO Enterprise Risk Management (ERM) framework is another widely used framework that emphasizes aligning risk management with an organization's strategy and objectives. These frameworks provide organizations with a structured approach to risk management and offer guidelines for implementing risk management processes and controls.

In conclusion, risk management is a comprehensive and proactive approach that organizations use to identify, assess, and manage potential risks that could impact their objectives. It involves identifying risks, evaluating their potential impacts, implementing strategies to manage or mitigate them, and regularly reviewing and updating risk management processes. Effective risk management enhances organizations' ability to make informed decisions, allocate resources effectively, and navigate uncertainties. It also promotes organizational resilience, fosters stakeholder confidence, and ensures long-term sustainability. Implementing risk management may present challenges, but organizations can overcome them by fostering a risk-aware culture, leveraging technology, and embracing proactive risk management practices.

Importance of Risk Management

Risk management is of utmost importance to organizations for several reasons. Firstly, it allows organizations to identify and understand the potential risks they face, enabling them to proactively plan and allocate resources to address these risks. Without proper risk management, organizations may be caught off guard by unforeseen events, leading to financial losses, reputational damage, and operational disruptions.

Another key importance of risk management is that it facilitates better decision-making. By assessing and analyzing potential risks, organizations can make informed choices about their operations, investments, and strategies. Risk management helps organizations weigh the potential benefits and drawbacks of different options and select the course of action that aligns with their risk appetite and long-term objectives.

The effective implementation of risk management processes also leads to greater operational efficiency. By identifying and addressing risks, organizations can streamline their processes, reduce inefficiencies, and identify areas for improvement. This not only enhances the organization's overall productivity but also boosts employee morale by fostering a culture of continuous improvement and proactive problem-solving.

Risk management is crucial for organizations to protect their financial stability. By identifying financial risks such as market volatility, credit defaults, or liquidity issues, organizations can implement appropriate risk mitigation strategies. This helps safeguard the organization's financial assets, maintain profitability, and ensure the availability of funds for future growth and investment opportunities.

In addition to financial risks, risk management also addresses non-financial risks, such as strategic risks, operational risks, and regulatory risks. Strategic risks, such as changes in customer preferences or competitive landscape, can be identified and managed through effective risk management practices. Operational risks, including supply chain disruptions, equipment failures, or human errors, can be mitigated or avoided through proper risk management controls. Regulatory risks, such as compliance breaches, can be managed by implementing robust risk management systems and procedures to ensure adherence to relevant laws and regulations.

Risk management also plays a vital role in maintaining an organization's reputation. By identifying and addressing reputational risks, organizations can prevent or minimize the negative impact of events that could damage their brand image. Proactively managing reputational risks involves assessing stakeholder expectations, addressing customer complaints, and implementing crisis management plans to handle potentially damaging situations effectively.

Furthermore, risk management contributes to the long-term sustainability and growth of an organization. By effectively managing risks, organizations are better equipped to adapt to changes in the business environment, capitalize on emerging opportunities, and navigate through uncertainties. Risk management provides organizations with the agility and resilience required to remain competitive and seize competitive advantages in an ever-evolving marketplace.

Risk management also helps organizations comply with legal and regulatory requirements. By identifying and addressing compliance risks, organizations can ensure they meet the necessary standards and regulations governing their industry. Non-compliance with legal requirements can result in costly fines, litigation, and damage to the organization's reputation. Risk management enables organizations to implement measures to mitigate compliance risks and demonstrate integrity and accountability to stakeholders.

Risk management is particularly essential in industries where the potential consequences of risks are significant. For example, in the healthcare sector, effective risk management is crucial to ensure patient safety, prevent medical errors, and protect organizations from malpractice claims. In the construction industry, risk management helps prevent accidents, ensure adherence to safety standards, and mitigate risks associated with project delays and cost overruns.

Effective risk management also helps organizations gain a competitive advantage. By identifying and exploiting opportunities that arise from strategic risks, organizations can differentiate themselves from competitors and create new revenue streams. Risk management enables organizations to make informed decisions about innovative ventures, expansions into new markets, or strategic partnerships, leading to sustainable growth and market leadership.

Risk management practices also contribute to fostering a culture of transparency and accountability within organizations. By implementing risk management processes, organizations demonstrate their commitment to managing uncertainties, identifying and addressing potential risks, and ensuring responsible governance. This enhances stakeholders' trust and confidence, including shareholders, customers, employees, and regulators.

Furthermore, risk management helps organizations manage their insurance costs. By proactively identifying and addressing risks that could lead to insurance claims, organizations can negotiate better terms with insurance providers and reduce insurance premiums. Effective risk management systems and practices can also help organizations identify the appropriate amount and type of insurance coverage needed to protect against potential losses.

Risk management is also important for organizations with international operations or global supply chains. By identifying and assessing risks across different regions and markets, organizations can implement measures to mitigate the potential impact of geopolitical risks, exchange rate fluctuations, regulatory differences, or natural disasters. This enables organizations to optimize their global operations and minimize disruptions to their supply chains.

Moreover, risk management plays a critical role in project management. By identifying and analyzing project risks, organizations can develop risk response plans to ensure the successful delivery of projects. Effective risk management helps project managers anticipate and mitigate potential risks, ensuring project completion within budget, scope, and schedule.

Risk management contributes to the overall governance and control framework of organizations. By implementing risk management practices, organizations establish mechanisms to ensure the accountability of individuals and departments for managing risks within their areas of responsibility. This fosters a culture of risk awareness, promotes ethical behavior, and mitigates the potential for fraudulent activities.

Lastly, risk management provides organizations with a structured framework for crisis management. By having risk management processes and procedures in place, organizations can respond to crises effectively and efficiently. This includes developing response plans, establishing communication protocols, and implementing processes to restore normal operations as quickly as possible. Effective crisis management helps organizations minimize damage, protect stakeholders' interests, and maintain business continuity in the face of unexpected events.

In summary, risk management is crucial for organizations across various industries and sectors. It enables organizations to identify and understand potential risks, make informed decisions, protect financial assets, safeguard reputation, comply with legal and regulatory requirements, foster resilience, and growth, gain a competitive advantage, foster transparency and accountability, optimize global operations, manage projects successfully, and respond to crises effectively. Embracing risk management practices helps organizations navigate uncertainties and build a foundation for sustainable success in an ever-changing business environment.

It's important to note that risk management is not a one-time exercise but an ongoing process. Risks evolve, new risks arise, and organizations must continually reassess their risk profiles and adapt their risk management strategies accordingly. By continuously monitoring risks and refining risk management practices, organizations can stay ahead of potential challenges and position themselves as proactive and resilient entities.

Moreover, risk management contributes to stakeholder engagement and trust. Transparent risk management practices build credibility and improve the relationship between organizations and their stakeholders. Stakeholders, including customers, investors, employees, and regulators, are more likely to support organizations that demonstrate a proactive approach to risk management, as it signifies responsibility, integrity, and a long-term focus.

While risk management requires dedicated resources and effort, the benefits and importance it brings to organizations far outweigh the associated costs. By proactively identifying and managing risks, organizations can position themselves for sustainable growth, maintain operational efficiency, protect their financial stability, and foster a culture of resilience and accountability. In today's dynamic and uncertain business environment, effective risk management is essential for organizations to thrive and succeed.

Objectives of Risk Management

Another key objective of risk management is to assess the likelihood and potential consequences of identified risks. Through qualitative and quantitative analysis, organizations can determine the probability of each risk occurring and evaluate the magnitude of its potential impact. This objective helps organizations prioritize their risk management efforts, allocating resources proportionately to address the most significant risks and reduce the likelihood and severity of their impact.

Effective risk management also aims to develop strategies and action plans to manage and mitigate identified risks. This objective involves selecting and implementing appropriate risk management measures to reduce the likelihood of risks occurring or minimize their potential impact if they do materialize. By developing risk management strategies, organizations can proactively address risks and enhance their ability to achieve their objectives.

Risk management also seeks to establish clear roles and responsibilities within an organization. This objective ensures that individuals at all levels understand their responsibilities for managing risks and are equipped with the necessary knowledge, skills, and resources to fulfill their roles effectively. By defining roles and responsibilities, organizations can foster a culture of accountability and promote effective collaboration in managing and responding to risks.

Another objective of risk management is to integrate risk management into organizational processes and decision-making. This involves embedding risk management practices into various functions, projects, and activities of the organization. By integrating risk management, organizations can ensure that risk awareness and assessment are considered in decision-making processes at all levels, minimizing the likelihood of risks being overlooked or disregarded.

Risk management aims to ensure compliance with legal, regulatory, and ethical requirements. This objective involves identifying and managing risks associated with non-compliance, such as regulatory violations, legal disputes, or reputational damage. By addressing compliance risks, organizations can ensure the organization operates within the bounds of the law, maintains its reputation, and avoids potential legal and financial consequences.

Effective risk management also seeks to optimize resource allocation. By understanding different risks and their potential impacts, organizations can allocate resources more efficiently to manage and mitigate risks. This objective allows organizations to prioritize resources based on the significance of risks, ensuring that limited resources are allocated to areas that present the most substantial threats or opportunities.

Risk management is also aimed at enhancing communication and transparency within the organization. This objective emphasizes the need for open and timely communication about risks among employees, managers, and stakeholders. Transparent communication helps raise risk awareness, fosters a culture of collaboration, and ensures that risk-related information is shared effectively to facilitate informed decision-making.

Another objective of risk management is to continuously monitor and review the effectiveness of risk management measures. This involves establishing monitoring mechanisms, regularly reviewing risk management actions, and updating strategies as necessary in response to changing circumstances. By continuously monitoring risks, organizations can identify emerging risks, evaluate the effectiveness of existing risk management measures, and make necessary adjustments to address evolving threats.

Risk management also strives to promote a culture of risk awareness and accountability across the organization. This objective involves educating and engaging employees at all levels to understand and take responsibility for managing risks within their areas of expertise. By promoting risk awareness, organizations can encourage proactive identification of risks, effective risk reporting, and the development of risk management competencies throughout the workforce.

Risk management aims to enhance the organization's ability to seize opportunities. This objective recognizes that risks are not solely associated with negative outcomes but also present opportunities for growth and innovation. By proactively identifying and assessing both risks and opportunities, organizations can develop strategies to capitalize on opportunities and gain a competitive advantage in the marketplace.

Another objective of risk management is to ensure timely and effective responses to risks that materialize. This involves establishing contingency plans, crisis management protocols, and response procedures to minimize the potential impact of risks and facilitate quick recovery. By implementing proactive response mechanisms, organizations can reduce downtime, mitigate potential losses, and maintain business continuity during uncertain or challenging times.

Risk management also aims to protect the organization's reputation and stakeholder trust. By identifying and managing reputation risks, organizations can mitigate the potential damage that negative events or actions can have on their brand image. This objective involves implementing strategies to maintain the organization's credibility, build customer trust, and sustain positive relationships with stakeholders.

Lastly, the objective of risk management is to foster organizational resilience and adaptability. This recognizes that the business environment is constantly evolving, and organizations need to be prepared to navigate uncertainties and unexpected events. By effectively managing risks, organizations can enhance their ability to respond and adapt to changing circumstances, ensuring their long-term survival and sustainability in an ever-changing marketplace.

Chapter Twenty-Two

Basic Concepts in Risk Management

Risk management involves several fundamental concepts that form the basis of its practice. These concepts help organizations understand and navigate uncertainties effectively. The basic concepts in risk management include risk, risk assessment, risk appetite, risk tolerance, risk mitigation, risk transfer, residual risk, and risk monitoring.

Risk is the potential for an event or condition to hurt an organization's objectives. It encompasses both threats and opportunities. Risks can arise from internal or external factors and can be related to a wide range of areas, including financial, operational, strategic, reputational, or compliance domains.

Risk assessment refers to the process of evaluating potential risks, including their causes, likelihood, and potential consequences. It involves identifying and characterizing risks to determine their significance and prioritize risk management efforts. Risk assessment can be qualitative or quantitative, and it helps organizations understand the nature and potential impact of different risks.

Risk appetite represents the level of risk that an organization is willing to accept or tolerate in pursuit of its objectives. It reflects the organization's risk-taking capacity and its willingness to embrace opportunities despite potential risks. Risk appetite is influenced by factors such as industry norms, organizational culture, stakeholders' expectations, and regulatory requirements.

Risk tolerance is the threshold or degree of uncertainty that an organization is prepared to accept about a specific risk. It sets the boundaries within which the organization is willing to operate in terms of risk exposure. Risk tolerance is determined based on factors such as the organization's risk appetite, financial stability, regulatory requirements, and market conditions.

Risk mitigation involves implementing proactive measures to reduce the likelihood or impact of identified risks. It focuses on preventing or minimizing risks from arising or materializing. Risk mitigation strategies can include implementing controls, improving processes, enhancing security measures, diversifying operations, or adopting risk transfer mechanisms.

Risk transfer is the process of assigning or transferring the responsibility for managing certain risks to external parties. This is often done through insurance contracts or agreements with third-party service providers. Risk transfer enables organizations to shift some or all the potential losses associated with specific risks to other entities while paying a premium or fee for this service.

Residual risk refers to the risk that remains after risk mitigation measures have been implemented. Despite efforts to reduce risks, residual risk exists because it is challenging to eliminate all risks. Residual risk represents the level of uncertainty that an organization accepts following risk management actions.

Risk monitoring refers to the ongoing process of tracking, evaluating, and reviewing risks to ensure their effectiveness and relevance. It involves collecting data, monitoring risk indicators, and comparing actual performance against established risk criteria. Risk monitoring helps organizations identify emerging risks, evaluate the effectiveness of risk management measures, and make necessary adjustments to their risk management strategies.

Another important concept in risk management is the risk register. A risk register is a structured document or database that records all identified risks, their potential impacts, likelihoods, and associated risk management activities. It serves as a central repository of risk-related information and facilitates ongoing risk analysis, monitoring, and reporting.

Risk culture is the shared values, beliefs, and behaviors regarding risk within an organization. It encompasses the organization's attitude towards risk, the degree to which risk management is embedded in decision-making processes, and the level of risk awareness and accountability across the organization. A strong risk culture fosters a proactive and collaborative approach to risk management throughout the organization.

Risk appetite statement is a formal document that defines the organization's overall approach to risk-taking. It articulates the organization's risk tolerance, acceptable levels of risk exposure, and the boundaries within which decisions should be made. The risk appetite statement guides decision-making, resource allocation, and risk management efforts across the organization.

Risk assessment techniques are methods used to evaluate and analyze risks. These techniques can be qualitative or quantitative. Qualitative techniques involve subjective judgments based on expert opinions, feedback, or checklists to assess and prioritize risks. Quantitative techniques involve numerical analysis, statistical models, and data-driven approaches to evaluate risks.

Key risk indicators (KRIs) are metrics or data points that provide early warning signs of potential risks. KRIs are established to track trends, changes, or deviations that indicate a potential increase in risk exposure. Monitoring KRIs enables organizations to take timely actions and implement risk management measures before risks materialize.

Risk response strategies are actions or measures taken to address identified risks. They can include risk avoidance (eliminating the risk), risk acceptance (acknowledging and monitoring the risk without taking active measures), risk mitigation (implementing controls to reduce the likelihood or impact of the risk), or risk transfer (shifting the risk to another party).

Risk communication is the process of sharing risk-related information among stakeholders. It involves conveying risks, risk management strategies, and mitigation efforts to internal and external audiences. Effective risk communication ensures that relevant stakeholders have a clear understanding of risks, which enables them to make informed decisions and collaborate in managing risks.

Risk governance refers to the structure, processes, and systems that an organization establishes to manage risks effectively. It encompasses the roles and responsibilities of individuals and committees in overseeing risk management activities, as well as the policies, procedures, and guidelines that guide risk management practices within the organization.

Risk analysis is the systematic process of assessing risks and their potential impact on an organization's objectives. It involves evaluating both the likelihood of a risk occurring and the magnitude of its potential consequences. Risk analysis helps organizations make more informed decisions by providing a clear understanding of the risks they face.

Risk treatment is the process of implementing selected risk response strategies to address identified risks. It involves planning, executing, and monitoring risk mitigation measures to reduce the likelihood or impact of risks. Risk treatment ensures that risk management actions are aligned with the organization's risk appetite and objectives.

Risk control refers to the measures and activities implemented to manage risks. It includes the identification and implementation of controls, procedures, and guidelines to reduce the likelihood or impact of risks. Risk control measures can be preventive (aimed at avoiding the risk) or detective (aimed at detecting and mitigating the risk after it occurs).

Risk aggregation involves combining multiple risks into a single manageable unit for evaluation or reporting purposes. It allows organizations to consider the overall impact of a group of risks rather than assessing them individually. Risk aggregation helps organizations understand the cumulative effect of various risks and prioritize risk management actions accordingly.

Risk management framework is a structured approach that guides an organization's risk management activities. It provides a systematic and consistent methodology for identifying, assessing, and managing risks. The framework typically includes policies, procedures, guidelines, and tools for managing risks and aligning risk management with organizational objectives.

Lastly, risk awareness refers to the level of understanding and consciousness of risks within an organization. It involves educating employees, stakeholders, and decision-makers about the potential risks associated with their roles and responsibilities. Risk awareness fosters a proactive and risk-conscious culture, helping organizations identify and address risks effectively.

Risk Identification

Risk is a fundamental concept in various fields, including business, finance, insurance, and project management. It refers to the potential for loss, harm, or negative outcomes that may occur due to uncertain events or conditions. Risk is an inherent part of any activity or decision-making process and arises from the uncertainty of future outcomes.

Risk involves the possibility of deviation from expected or desired outcomes. It is characterized by the combination of two essential elements: the likelihood or probability of an event occurring, and the potential impact or consequences of that event. These elements help organizations assess and evaluate the significance of risks and make informed decisions about managing them.

Risks can arise from both internal and external factors. Internal risks include factors within the control of an organization, such as operational inefficiencies, financial mismanagement, or employee errors. External risks, on the other hand, stem from factors outside of the organization's control, including economic changes, market volatility, regulatory changes, or natural disasters.

Risk can be categorized as either pure risk or speculative risk. Pure risk refers to situations where there is only a chance of loss or no loss at all, such as accidents, natural disasters, or theft. Speculative risk, on the other hand, involves the possibility of loss or gain, such as investing in the stock market or launching a new product.

The concept of risk is closely related to the concept of reward or return. In many instances, the higher the risk, the higher the potential reward. This risk-reward trade-off is a fundamental consideration in decision-making, particularly in investment and business ventures.

Risk is measured and evaluated using various methods, including qualitative and quantitative approaches. Qualitative risk assessment involves subjective judgments and expert opinions to assess risks based on their likelihood and impact. Quantitative risk assessment, on the other hand, involves numerical analysis and statistical modeling to quantify risks based on historical data, probabilities, and expected outcomes.

Risk management is the systematic process of identifying, assessing, and managing risks. It aims to minimize the likelihood and impact of potential risks and maximize the organization's ability to achieve its objectives in a sustainable manner. Effective risk management involves understanding and prioritizing risks, developing strategies to mitigate or exploit them, and deploying resources to implement and monitor risk management measures.

Risk is not inherently negative but also presents opportunities for growth, innovation, and competitive advantage. Organizations that effectively identify and manage risks can position themselves to capitalize on opportunities and gain a competitive edge. Risk management, therefore, involves assessing both threats and opportunities and developing strategies to manage and exploit them effectively.

Risk is dynamic and constantly evolving. As the business environment changes, new risks arise, while existing risks may become more or less significant. Organizations must continuously assess and evaluate risks to stay ahead and adapt their risk management practices accordingly. Regular risk assessments and monitoring help organizations respond to emerging risks and take timely actions to mitigate or capitalize on them.

In summary, risk refers to the potential for loss, harm, or negative outcomes resulting from uncertain events or conditions. It is an intrinsic part of decision-making and is characterized by the likelihood and impact of events. Risk can arise from both internal and external factors and needs to be managed effectively through a systematic and proactive approach. By understanding and managing risks, organizations can navigate uncertainties, protect their assets, and seize opportunities for sustainable growth and success.

Risk Assessment

Risk assessment is a systematic process of evaluating potential risks that an organization may face. It involves identifying and analyzing risks to understand their likelihood and potential impact on business operations, projects, or objectives. Risk assessment serves as the foundation for effective risk management by providing critical information for decision-making and prioritizing risk mitigation efforts.

The process of risk assessment typically follows several steps:

1. Risk Identification: This involves identifying and documenting potential risks that could impact the organization. Risks can be identified through various methods, such as conducting interviews, brainstorming sessions, reviewing historical data, or utilizing industry-specific risk frameworks.

2. Risk Analysis: Once risks are identified, they are assessed to understand their significance. This step involves analyzing the characteristics of each risk, such as its likelihood of occurrence and potential impact. Qualitative or quantitative methods can be used, depending on the available data and the complexity of the risk.

3. Risk Evaluation: During this stage, the assessed risks are evaluated to determine their importance and prioritize them based on their potential consequences and likelihood. This allows organizations to allocate resources effectively and address the most significant risks first.

4. Risk Treatment: After evaluating risks, organizations develop and implement risk treatment strategies. This involves selecting appropriate risk response measures, such as risk avoidance, risk reduction, risk sharing, or risk acceptance. Risk treatment strategies are designed to mitigate risks and reduce their potential impact on the organization.

5. Risk Monitoring and Review: Once risk treatment measures are implemented, ongoing monitoring and review are critical. This involves continuously monitoring the effectiveness of risk mitigation measures and evaluating new or emerging risks. Regular reviews allow organizations to adapt their risk management strategies and ensure that risks are appropriately managed over time.

Risk assessments rely on both subjectivity and objectivity. Subjectivity involves expert judgment and qualitative analysis, considering factors such as experience, intuition, and industry knowledge. Objectivity, on the other hand, relies on quantitative data and statistical analysis to assess risks based on historical information, trends, and calculations of probabilities.

The outcome of a risk assessment is often documented in a risk register or risk report. This document captures the identified risks, their attributes, assessment results, and proposed risk management actions. The risk register serves as a central repository of risk-related information and guides ongoing monitoring and review processes.

It is important to note that risk assessment is an iterative process. As new information becomes available or organizational circumstances change, risk assessments must be reviewed and updated accordingly. Effective risk assessment requires a multidisciplinary approach, involving input from various stakeholders, such as subject matter experts, project managers, executives, and risk management professionals.

Overall, risk assessment provides organizations with a structured approach to identify, evaluate, and prioritize risks. It enables proactive risk management by informing decision-making, resource allocation, and risk treatment strategies. By systematically assessing risks, organizations can better understand their risk profile, allocate resources effectively, and implement measures to minimize the likelihood and impact of potential risks.

Probability and Impact Matrix

A Probability and Impact Matrix, also known as a Risk Matrix or Risk Assessment Matrix, is a useful tool in risk management for evaluating and prioritizing risks based on their probability of occurrence and potential impact. It provides a structured framework for assessing risks and determining appropriate risk response strategies.

The Probability and Impact Matrix typically consists of a grid or table with probability levels on one axis and impact levels on the other axis. Probability levels may be defined as low, medium, or high, while impact levels could be categorized as low, moderate, or high, or assigned numerical values. The matrix cells represent the combination of probability and impact levels, and each cell is associated with a risk rating or level of priority.

The purpose of the Probability and Impact Matrix is to help organizations categorize and prioritize risks based on their potential significance. By plotting risks in the matrix, organizations can visualize the risk landscape, identify higher-priority risks, and allocate resources and management attention accordingly.

To use the Probability and Impact Matrix effectively, several steps are typically followed:

1. Identify Risks: Begin by identifying and documenting potential risks that could impact the organization. This step can be done through brainstorming sessions, risk assessments, or by using historical data and industry-specific risk frameworks.

2. Assess Probability: Evaluate the likelihood or probability of each risk occurring based on available information, expert judgment, historical data, or statistical analysis. Assign probability levels to each risk, such as low, medium, or high, or use specific probability ranges or numerical values.

3. Assess Impact: Analyze the potential consequences or impact that each risk can have on the organization's objectives, assets, operations, reputation, or financials. Assign impact levels to each risk, such as low, moderate, or high, or use specific impact ranges or numerical values.

4. Plot Risks on the Matrix: Place each identified risk in the appropriate cell of the Probability and Impact Matrix, based on the assigned probability and impact levels. This visually represents the risk rating or level of priority.

5. Determine Risk Response Strategies: Based on the risk rating or level of priority indicated by the Matrix, organizations can identify appropriate risk response strategies. Higher-priority risks may require more proactive and immediate risk mitigation or prevention measures.

6. Review and Refine: Continuously review and refine the Probability and Impact Matrix as new information becomes available or organizational circumstances change. Regularly reassess and update the probability and

impact levels based on feedback, risk monitoring, and changes in the internal or external environment.

The benefits of using a Probability and Impact Matrix include:

a. Clear Visualization: The matrix provides a visual representation of risks based on their probability and impact. This helps stakeholders quickly understand the relative importance of different risks and facilitates decision-making.

b. Prioritization: The Matrix allows organizations to prioritize risks according to their potential impact, enabling them to allocate resources and manage attention efficiently.

c. Consistency: By using objective criteria to assign probability and impact levels, organizations can achieve a consistent and structured approach to risk assessment and prioritization.

d. Risk Response Planning: The Matrix assists in identifying appropriate and targeted risk response strategies based on the risk rating. It helps organizations tailor their risk mitigation efforts to address the most critical risks.

e. Communication: The Matrix serves as a communication tool, allowing organizations to share and discuss risk assessments in a standardized and easily understandable format.

f. Resource Allocation: With the Matrix, organizations can allocate resources effectively by focusing on higher-priority risks that have the potential for significant impact.

g. Continuous Improvement: Regularly reviewing and refining the Matrix enhances risk management practices over time. As organizations gain more experience and data, the Matrix can be adjusted to reflect the evolving risk landscape.

However, there are limitations to consider when using a Probability and Impact Matrix:

a. Subjectivity: Assigning probability and impact levels involves a level of subjectivity, as it relies on expert judgment, assumptions, and available data. Different individuals or teams may assess risks differently, potentially leading to inconsistent results.

b. Simplification: The Matrix simplifies complex risks into discrete categories, which may oversimplify the nuanced nature of some risks. There is a risk of oversimplification and overlooking important factors or interactions between risks.

c. Lack of Precision: The Matrix may not provide precise numerical values for probability and impact. This can limit the depth of analysis or comparison between risks.

d. Static Nature: The Matrix assumes that probability and impact levels remain constant over time, which may not always be the case. Risks can change in likelihood or consequence due to internal or external factors, necessitating regular updates and reviews.

e. Generalization: The Matrix provides a broad overview of risks but may not capture unique aspects or specific contexts that are relevant to certain industries or organizations.

Overall, the Probability and Impact Matrix is a valuable tool in risk management for categorizing and prioritizing risks. It helps organizations focus their efforts on addressing higher-priority risks and allocating resources effectively. By using the Matrix, organizations can enhance their risk response planning, communication, and decision-making, leading to more efficient and effective risk management practices.

Risk Scoring and Prioritization

Risk scoring and prioritization is a critical step in the risk management process, allowing organizations to systematically evaluate and prioritize risks based on their importance and potential impact. By assigning scores or ratings to risks, organizations can focus their resources on addressing the highest-priority risks and implement appropriate risk response measures.

Risk Identification: Begin by identifying and documenting potential risks that may arise from internal or external factors. This can be done through risk assessments, brainstorming sessions, historical data analysis, or industry-specific risk frameworks.

Risk Assessment Criteria: Define the criteria or factors that will be used to assess and score risks. These criteria may include likelihood/probability, impact/consequences, velocity (speed of occurrence), vulnerability (susceptibility to the risk), cost, and strategic importance, among others. The criteria should align with the organization's objectives and risk appetite.

Establish Scoring Scale: Define a scoring scale for each risk assessment criterion. This could be a numerical scale, such as 1-5 or 1-10, or a qualitative scale, such as low, medium, or high. Ensure that the scale is consistent and properly reflects the significance of the criteria.

Assess Likelihood/Probability: Evaluate the likelihood or probability of each risk occurring based on available information, expert judgment, historical data, or statistical analysis. Assign scores based on the defined scale for the respective criterion.

Assess Impact/Consequences: Analyze the potential impact or consequences that each risk could have on the organization's objectives, assets, operations, reputation, or financials. Assign scores based on the defined scale for the respective criterion.

Calculate Risk Scores: Calculate the risk score for each risk by multiplying the likelihood score by the impact score. This can provide a numerical representation of the overall risk rating.

Normalize the Scores: Normalize the risk scores to ensure consistency and comparability across different risks. This can be done by dividing each risk score by the highest risk score achieved in the assessment and multiplying it by a defined maximum value (e.g., 100).

Weighting Factors: Introduce weighting factors to reflect the relative importance of different criteria. Assign weights to each criterion based on its significance in the organization's risk management strategy. Multiply the scores by the respective weights before calculating the overall risk score.

Calculate Overall Risk Score: Calculate the overall risk score by summing up the weighted scores for each criterion. This provides a comprehensive picture of the risk's significance.

Categorize Risks: Group risks into categories or levels based on their overall scores. This can be done by setting thresholds or ranges that indicate the risk's level of priority or severity. Categorizing risks helps in identifying the highest-priority risks.

Prioritize Risks: Prioritize risks based on their assigned categories or levels. Allocate resources and management attention to the highest-priority risks that require immediate action or mitigation efforts.

Risk Response Strategies: Determine the appropriate risk response strategies for each prioritized risk, considering the risk's severity, potential impact, available resources, and risk appetite. Response strategies may include risk avoidance, risk reduction, risk sharing, or risk acceptance.

Mitigation Planning: Develop action plans and mitigation strategies for addressing high-priority risks. Define specific actions, responsibilities, deadlines, and resource requirements to implement the identified risk response measures effectively.

Monitor and Review: Continuously monitor and review the effectiveness of risk response measures and the changing risk landscape. Assess whether the initial risk scoring and prioritization adequately reflect the evolving risks and make necessary adjustments as required.

Communication: Effectively communicate the results of risk scoring and prioritization to stakeholders. Clearly and transparently present the rationale behind the risk ratings, categories, and the organization's plan to address the prioritized risks.

Senior Management Involvement: Seek involvement and buy-in from senior management in the risk scoring and prioritization process. This ensures alignment with organizational objectives and decision-making at higher levels.

Collaboration and Consultation: Involve relevant stakeholders and subject matter experts in the risk scoring and prioritization process. Their expertise and input can enhance the accuracy and credibility of the assessments and facilitate a better understanding of risks.

Data Analysis and Measures: Utilize historical data and key performance indicators to support risk scoring and prioritization. Analyze trends, patterns, and correlations to provide evidence-based insights into risks and their potential impact.

Risk Mapping: Consider visual representation techniques, such as risk maps, heat maps, or spider diagrams, to aid in understanding the relationships between risks, their severity, and potential interdependencies.

Risk Appetite and Tolerance: Consider the organization's risk appetite and risk tolerance thresholds when scoring and prioritizing risks. This ensures that the evaluation aligns with the organization's risk tolerance levels and strategic objectives.

Scenario Analysis: Conduct scenario analysis to assess the potential impact of different risk scenarios. This can help identify risks that may have a lower probability but could have catastrophic consequences, warranting greater attention and mitigation efforts.

Benchmarking: Conduct benchmarking exercises to compare risk scores and prioritization with industry peers or best practices. This can provide valuable insights and identify areas for improvement or areas of strategic advantage.

Continuous Improvement: Regularly review and refine the risk scoring and prioritization process based on feedback, lessons learned, and emerging practices. Strive for continuous improvement to enhance the accuracy and effectiveness of risk assessment and prioritization.

Documentation: Document the risk scoring and prioritization results, including the rationale, criteria, scores, and categories assigned to each risk. Maintain a central repository or risk register to ensure proper record-keeping and facilitate ongoing monitoring and review.

Integration with Risk Management Framework: Integrate the risk scoring and prioritization process into the organization's overall risk management framework. Ensure that the outputs from the assessment inform decision-making, resource allocation, and the development of risk mitigation strategies at all levels of the organization.

Implementing a robust risk scoring and prioritization process enables organizations to systematically identify and address high-priority risks, align resources effectively, and make informed decisions to manage risks in line with organizational objectives. The process should be dynamic, regularly reviewed, and adapted to reflect changes in the risk environment and organizational priorities.

Risk Mitigation

Risk mitigation is an essential component of the risk management process, focused on reducing the likelihood or impact of identified risks. It involves implementing measures and strategies to minimize the potential negative consequences that may arise from uncertain events or conditions. Risk mitigation is crucial for organizations to enhance their resilience, protect their assets, and maintain business continuity.

Identify Key Risks: Begin by identifying and understanding the key risks that could impact the organization's objectives, operations, stakeholders, or assets. This allows for a targeted approach to risk mitigation efforts.

Risk Assessment: Assess the significance of each identified risk, including its likelihood of occurring and potential consequences. This helps determine the appropriate level of risk mitigation required for each risk.

Risk Avoidance: The most effective approach to risk mitigation is often risk avoidance, where actions are taken to eliminate or avoid the risk altogether. This may involve changing processes, discontinuing certain activities, or refraining from entering high-risk ventures.

Risk Reduction: If risk avoidance is not feasible, strategies can be implemented to reduce the likelihood or impact of the risk. This can include strengthening controls, improving processes, implementing redundancies, or adopting industry best practices.

Contingency Planning: Develop contingency plans to prepare for and respond to potential risks. This involves identifying alternative courses of action, establishing response procedures, and ensuring resources are readily available in the event of a risk materializing.

Training and Education: Mitigating risks often requires providing training and education to employees, stakeholders, and relevant parties. This helps enhance their awareness of risks, equips them with the necessary skills to identify and manage risks, and fosters a risk-conscious culture within the organization.

Insurance and Risk Transfer: Transfer some of the potential risks to external parties through insurance arrangements or contractual agreements. This allows organizations to transfer the financial burden of potential losses to insurance providers or share the risk with other entities.

Business Continuity Planning: Develop business continuity plans to ensure the organization can continue operating in the face of disruptions. This includes identifying critical functions and assets, establishing alternative work arrangements, and implementing backup systems and processes.

Supply Chain Diversification: Reduce the risk of supply chain disruptions by diversifying suppliers and dependencies. This ensures that the organization is not overly reliant on a single source and can mitigate the impact of any disruption within the supply chain.

Cybersecurity Measures: Implement robust cybersecurity measures to protect against risks associated with data breaches, cyber-attacks, or unauthorized access. This entails installing firewalls, utilizing encryption, conducting penetration testing, and maintaining up-to-date security protocols.

Legal and Regulatory Compliance: Ensure compliance with relevant laws, regulations, and industry standards to mitigate legal or regulatory risks. This may involve implementing procedures, conducting regular audits, and seeking legal counsel to navigate complex compliance requirements.

Risk Monitoring and Reporting: Continuously monitor risks and establish effective reporting mechanisms to identify emerging risks or changes in risk profiles. Regular monitoring allows for timely detection and response to potential risks, ensuring that mitigation measures remain effective.

Regular Review and Evaluation: Periodically review and evaluate the effectiveness of risk mitigation measures. This includes assessing the impact of implemented strategies, identifying any gaps or weaknesses, and making necessary adjustments to enhance risk resilience.

Stakeholder Engagement: Involve relevant stakeholders in risk mitigation efforts to obtain their perspectives, gather insights, and foster collaboration. Engaging stakeholders can improve the identification and understanding of risks, as well as facilitate a shared commitment to risk mitigation.

Environmental and Social Responsibility: Mitigate risks associated with environmental and social impacts by implementing responsible practices. This may involve environmental sustainability initiatives, community engagement, ethical sourcing, or corporate social responsibility programs.

Financial Risk Management: Implement financial risk management strategies to minimize the impact of market volatility, credit risks, or liquidity challenges. This can include diversifying investments, hedging strategies, or maintaining appropriate cash reserves.

Periodic Testing and Simulation: Conduct tests, drills, or simulations to assess the effectiveness of risk mitigation plans and responses. This allows organizations to identify areas for improvement, refine procedures, and enhance preparedness for potential risk events.

Continuous Improvement: Foster a culture of continuous improvement where risk mitigation efforts are regularly evaluated and refined. Encourage feedback, share lessons learned, and integrate risk mitigation into routine business processes to ensure ongoing effectiveness.

Documentation and Communication: Document risk mitigation measures, action plans, and procedures to ensure clarity, consistency, and transparency. Effective communication ensures that relevant individuals are aware of the implemented strategies and their roles in risk mitigation efforts.

Management Commitment: Secure management commitment and support for risk mitigation activities. This includes allocating resources, empowering teams, and fostering a proactive risk management culture throughout the organization.

Risk mitigation is an ongoing process that requires commitment, collaboration, and regular evaluation. By proactively identifying and addressing risks, organizations can reduce their exposure, enhance their ability to navigate uncertainties and safeguard their long-term success.

Risk Avoidance

Risk avoidance is a risk mitigation strategy aimed at eliminating or staying away from potential risks altogether. By avoiding risks, organizations can prevent or minimize the potential negative consequences that may arise from uncertain events or conditions. Here are 18 paragraphs explaining risk avoidance in more detail:

Definition: Risk avoidance involves taking actions or making decisions that eliminate or steer clear of risks entirely. It aims to prevent exposure to potential hazards, uncertainties, or adverse events.

Risk Identification: The first step in risk avoidance is to identify and understand the different types of risks that could impact an organization. This allows for a targeted approach to determine which risks are avoidable.

Cost-Benefit Analysis: Organizations assess the potential costs and benefits associated with a particular risk to determine if risk avoidance is a feasible and worthwhile strategy. If the potential costs outweigh the benefits, risk avoidance may be a valid option.

Business Process Review: Risk avoidance may involve reviewing and altering existing business processes to minimize exposure to certain risks. This could mean discontinuing certain activities or modifying operations to avoid potential pitfalls.

Market Analysis: By conducting a thorough market analysis, organizations can identify risks associated with entering certain markets, such as political instability, economic downturns, or regulatory challenges. Based on the findings, they may choose to avoid entering such markets altogether.

Product or Service Development: Risk avoidance can be employed during the development or innovation process of products or services. By evaluating potential risks beforehand, organizations can design offerings that avoid or mitigate the identified risks.

Compliance with Regulations: Organizations can avoid the risks associated with non-compliance by proactively adhering to relevant laws, regulations, and industry standards. This prevents legal penalties, reputational damage, or other negative consequences.

High-Risk Ventures: Risk avoidance can be exercised by refraining from engaging in high-risk ventures that have the potential for substantial financial losses or failure. This decision allows organizations to focus on more stable and lucrative opportunities.

Financial Risk Mitigation: Avoiding certain financial risks, such as speculative investments, high levels of debt, or volatile markets, can protect organizations from potential financial crises or insolvency.

Reputation Management: Organizations can avoid reputational risks by maintaining a strong focus on ethical conduct, customer satisfaction, and quality assurance. Taking proactive steps to build and preserve a positive reputation minimizes potential damage from negative incidents.

Security Measures: Risk avoidance can involve implementing robust security measures to avoid risks such as theft, data breaches, or unauthorized access. This includes physical security, cybersecurity protocols, and access controls.

Insurance Coverage: Organizations often mitigate risks through insurance coverage. By obtaining appropriate insurance policies, they can transfer the financial burden of potential losses to insurance providers, effectively avoiding some of the risks.

Political Risks: In international business, risk avoidance may involve staying away from regions or countries with high political risks, such as political instability, civil unrest, or government expropriation of assets.

Natural Disasters: Organizations located in areas prone to natural disasters can avoid the risks associated with those events by relocating their operations to less vulnerable locations.

Information Security: Risk avoidance in information security involves avoiding risks related to data breaches, intellectual property theft, or sensitive information exposure by not storing or collecting certain types of data.

Reputation Risks: Organizations may avoid certain partnerships, collaborations, or affiliations that carry reputational risks, such as working with entities involved in controversial activities or facing public scrutiny.

Project Selection: Risk avoidance can be incorporated into project management by avoiding high-risk projects that have a high probability of failure or are outside the organization's capabilities or resources.

Continuous Risk Monitoring: Once risk avoidance strategies are implemented, it is crucial to continuously monitor the risk landscape to ensure that new risks are identified, and appropriate actions are taken to avoid them.

Risk avoidance is an effective strategy for organizations to prevent potential risks from materializing. By carefully assessing risks, making informed decisions, and taking necessary actions, organizations can protect their assets, reputation, and overall business stability.

Risk Transfer

Risk transfer is a risk mitigation strategy that involves shifting the potential financial burden or responsibility of managing risks to another party. By transferring risks, organizations can protect themselves from potential losses or damage that may arise from uncertain events or conditions.

Definition: Risk transfer involves transferring the financial impact or responsibility of managing risks to an external party, such as an insurance company or contractual agreement.

Insurance: The most common form of risk transfer is through insurance contracts. Organizations pay premiums to insurance providers, who assume financial responsibility in the event of losses or damages covered by the policy.

Risk Assessment: Before transferring risks, organizations need to assess and understand their risks. This involves identifying potential risks, evaluating their potential impact, and determining which risks are suitable for transfer.

Policy Selection: Organizations select insurance policies based on their specific risk profile and needs. Insurance coverage can be tailored to address various risks, such as property damage, liability, professional indemnity, or business interruption.

Premiums and Deductibles: In risk transfer, organizations pay insurance premiums as compensation for assuming risks. Additionally, a deductible or excess may apply, requiring organizations to pay a portion of the claim before insurance coverage takes effect.

Contractual Agreements: Risk transfer can also occur through contractual agreements. Organizations can transfer risks to another party by including clauses or provisions that allocate responsibility for specific risks to the other contracting party.

Indemnification: Contractual risk transfer often involves indemnity provisions, where one party agrees to compensate the other party for losses or damages incurred due to a specific risk.

Hold Harmless Agreements: Organizations may implement hold harmless agreements, also known as indemnity agreements, to protect themselves from liability arising from a particular activity or situation. This transfers the responsibility for potential lawsuits or claims to the other party.

Subcontracting: Organizations can transfer risks associated with a specific task or activity by subcontracting it to another entity. This way, the subcontractor assumes responsibility for managing the risks involved.

Financial Derivatives: Risk transfer can be achieved through financial instruments like derivatives. For example, organizations may use futures contracts or options to transfer market risks, such as commodity price fluctuations or exchange rate risks.

Reinsurance: Insurance companies themselves transfer risks through reinsurance. Reinsurance allows primary insurers to protect themselves against large losses by transferring a portion of the risk to the reinsurer.

Risk Pooling: Within industries or sectors, organizations may participate in risk pooling arrangements where they contribute funds collectively to manage risks. This spreads the potential burden of losses across multiple entities, providing a form of risk transfer.

Limitations: Risk transfer does not eliminate risks but instead transfers some of the potential financial liability or responsibility to another party. It is important to assess the limitations of insurance coverage or contractual agreements to ensure appropriate risk management strategies are implemented.

Premium Evaluation: Organizations should evaluate insurance premiums considering the potential costs of risks, the coverage provided, and the financial impact of self-insurance alternatives.

Contract Review: When entering into contractual agreements, organizations should carefully review the terms and conditions to ensure that the risk transfer provisions adequately protect their interests.

Insurance Policy Review: Regularly reviewing insurance policies is crucial to understand the coverage, exclusions, and conditions. This helps ensure that the selected policies align with the organization's risk profile and provide adequate protection.

Retained Risks: Even with risk transfer, organizations may still retain some risks, either intentionally or due to limitations in insurance coverage. These retained risks should be managed through other risk mitigation strategies.

Risk Communication: Organizations should effectively communicate risk transfer arrangements to relevant stakeholders. This ensures that all parties understand their responsibilities, roles, and potential liabilities.

Claims Management: In the event of a loss or damage covered by insurance, organizations must effectively manage the claims process, including providing documentation and working with insurance providers to mitigate financial impacts.

Risk Monitoring: While risks may be transferred, organizations should continuously monitor risks and update risk profiles accordingly. This ensures that risks are appropriately managed, and adjustments can be made to risk transfer strategies if necessary.

Insurance Market Evaluation: Regularly evaluate the insurance market to ensure that adequate coverage is available and that insurance providers are financially stable and reputable.

Legal Consultation: Organizations may seek legal advice to ensure that contractual agreements and risk transfer provisions are legally compliant and effectively protect their interests.

Cost-Benefit Analysis: Organizations should conduct a cost-benefit analysis to determine if the cost of risk transfer, such as insurance premiums or contractual arrangements, is justified relative to the potential financial impact or liability.

Contractual Negotiation: Risk transfer through contractual agreements involves negotiation with other parties. Organizations should carefully negotiate terms to ensure that risk transfer provisions are robust, fair, and aligned with their risk management goals.

In summary, risk transfer is a risk mitigation strategy that involves shifting the financial burden or responsibility of managing risks to an external party. This can be achieved through insurance contracts, contractual agreements, or other financial mechanisms. Proper assessment, selection of appropriate insurance policies, and careful contracting are essential to effectively implement risk transfer strategies. While risk transfer helps organizations minimize potential financial losses, it is crucial to continuously monitor risks and examine the limitations to ensure adequate risk management.

Risk Reduction

Risk reduction is a proactive approach to decrease the likelihood or impact of potential risks faced by individuals, organizations, or society. It involves identifying, assessing, and implementing measures to mitigate or minimize the potential harm or damage caused by various risks.

Definition: Risk reduction refers to the process of minimizing the probability or severity of adverse events or outcomes by implementing preventive measures and controls.

Risk Assessment: Before initiating risk reduction strategies, it is important to conduct a thorough risk assessment to identify and evaluate potential risks. This involves identifying hazards, estimating the likelihood and consequences of their occurrence, and prioritizing risks based on their severity and likelihood.

Risk Avoidance: One risk reduction strategy is to avoid activities or situations that pose significant risks. By eliminating or refraining from engaging in high-risk activities, individuals or organizations can effectively reduce their exposure to potential harm.

Risk Mitigation: Risk reduction can involve implementing measures to reduce the severity or impact of potential risks. This may include installing safety systems, implementing training programs, or adopting protective equipment to minimize potential harm.

Safety Measures: Risk reduction often involves implementing safety measures aimed at preventing accidents, injuries, or damage. This can include providing safety equipment, establishing safety protocols, and conducting regular safety inspections.

Emergency Preparedness: Being prepared for potential emergencies is an essential risk reduction strategy. This involves developing emergency response plans, conducting drills, and ensuring that individuals are trained and equipped to respond effectively in crises.

Risk Transfer: Another approach to risk reduction is transferring the responsibility for managing specific risks to another party, such as an insurance provider or a subcontractor. This helps minimize the potential financial impact or liability associated with certain risks.

Risk Communication: Effective risk reduction requires clear and timely communication of potential risks to relevant stakeholders. This ensures that individuals are aware of the risks they may face and the steps they can take to minimize their exposure.

Education and Training: Providing education and training programs is an important risk reduction strategy. By increasing individuals' knowledge and skills, they are better equipped to identify and manage potential risks effectively.

Regulatory Compliance: Compliance with relevant laws, regulations, and standards is a critical risk reduction measure. Adhering to established guidelines helps ensure that individuals and organizations operate within safe and ethical boundaries.

Hazard Identification: Effective risk reduction relies on accurately identifying potential hazards associated with certain activities, environments, or processes. This involves conducting thorough inspections and assessments to identify potential risks and take appropriate measures.

Risk Reporting and Analysis: Regularly monitoring and analyzing risk-related data is crucial for effective risk reduction. By analyzing trends and patterns, organizations can identify areas of improvement and implement targeted risk reduction strategies.

Continuous Improvement: Risk reduction is an ongoing process that requires constant evaluation and improvement. Organizations should continually assess their risk management practices and update and refine mitigation strategies as necessary.

Technology and Innovation: Incorporating technological advancements and innovative solutions can significantly contribute to risk reduction. For example, using advanced surveillance systems or implementing automated safety mechanisms can help minimize risks.

Collaboration: Effective risk reduction often involves collaboration among various stakeholders, including employees, managers, government agencies, and industry associations. Shared knowledge and resources can lead to more comprehensive risk reduction strategies.

Risk Transfer: Risk reduction can be achieved through contractual agreements, such as transferring risks to subcontractors or suppliers. This helps distribute responsibility and liability, reducing the potential impact on the primary organization.

Supply Chain Management: Managing risks within the supply chain is crucial for effective risk reduction. This includes evaluating and selecting reliable suppliers, implementing quality control measures, and establishing contingency plans to mitigate potential disruptions.

Environmental Protection: Reducing environmental risks is an important aspect of risk reduction. This involves implementing sustainable practices, proper waste management, and pollution control measures to minimize potential harm to the environment and surrounding communities.

Financial Risk Management: Implementing effective financial risk management practices is essential for risk reduction. This involves diversifying investments, establishing contingency funds, and adopting sound financial strategies to mitigate potential economic risks.

Stakeholder Engagement: Engaging stakeholders in risk reduction efforts can result in more comprehensive and effective strategies. This includes seeking input, addressing concerns, and involving stakeholders in decision-making processes related to risk reduction.

Risk Monitoring and Evaluation: Continuous monitoring and evaluation of risk reduction measures are critical to ensure their effectiveness. Regular reviews help identify gaps, evaluate the success of implemented strategies, and make necessary adjustments to achieve optimal risk reduction outcomes.

In summary, risk reduction is a proactive approach to minimize potential risks by implementing preventive measures, safety protocols, and controls. It involves identifying hazards, assessing risks, and implementing strategies to avoid or mitigate their impact. Risk reduction requires collaboration, continuous improvement, and effective communication to ensure the safety and well-being of individuals and the success of organizations.

Risk Acceptance

Risk acceptance is a risk management strategy that involves recognizing potential risks and consciously deciding to accept them without taking further risk mitigation measures. Organizations or individuals may choose risk acceptance when the risk is deemed acceptable based on factors such as cost-benefit analysis, risk tolerance, or the absence of viable risk reduction options.

Definition: Risk acceptance is the decision to acknowledge and tolerate the inherent risks associated with an activity, process, or decision without implementing additional risk mitigation measures.

Risk Assessment: Before opting for risk acceptance, organizations or individuals should conduct a thorough risk assessment to identify, evaluate, and understand the potential risks. This assessment helps ensure that the decision to accept the risk is informed and based on a comprehensive understanding of potential consequences.

Risk Tolerance: Risk acceptance often reflects an organization or individual's risk tolerance level. Risk tolerance is the amount of risk an organization or individual is willing to accept or retain without taking further protective measures.

Cost-Benefit Analysis: Accepting certain risks may be a strategic decision based on a cost-benefit analysis. If the potential costs or efforts associated with reducing the risk outweigh the benefits, risk acceptance may be a viable option.

Lack of Control: Some risks may be inherent to certain activities or processes and mitigating them may not be feasible or practical. In such cases, accepting the risks may be the only available option.

Low Exposure: If the potential impact or likelihood of a risk is relatively low, organizations or individuals may choose to accept it rather than invest resources in risk mitigation efforts that may not yield substantial benefits.

Uninsurable Risks: In instances where certain risks are uninsurable or the cost of insurance is prohibitively high, risk acceptance can be a viable option.

Known Risks: Organizations or individuals may accept risks that are well-known and have historically occurred without causing significant harm or loss.

Legal Considerations: In some cases, risk acceptance may be a legal requirement. For example, certain industries or activities may have regulations that specify which risks must be accepted as part of compliance.

Risk Ownership: Accepting a risk involves taking ownership of its consequences. Organizations or individuals should understand and be prepared to bear the responsibility for any potential negative outcomes associated with the accepted risk.

Risk Monitoring: Even when risks are accepted, they should still be actively monitored. Ongoing monitoring allows for timely recognition of any changes in the risk landscape and informs decision-making if circumstances evolve.

Risk Communication: Organizations or individuals should effectively communicate the rationale behind their decision to accept risks to stakeholders and relevant parties. Transparent communication ensures that all involved parties are informed and aware of the potential risks.

Risk Documentation: It is important to document accepted risks, including the reasons behind the decision, any associated assumptions, and the steps taken to monitor or mitigate the risk within the accepted parameters.

Risk Governance: Risk acceptance should be part of an organization's risk governance framework. It should involve clear policies, procedures, and decision-making processes to ensure consistency and accountability in accepting risks.

Continuous Evaluation: Risk acceptance is not a one-time decision. It should be regularly re-evaluated to ensure that risks remain within an organization or individual's risk tolerance level and that the decision to accept the risk is still valid.

Risk Appetite: Risk acceptance is aligned with an organization or individual's risk appetite, which defines the level of risk they are willing to accept in pursuit of their goals. Risk appetite helps guide decision-making when it comes to accepting risks.

Strategic Considerations: Accepting certain risks may align with an organization's broader strategic objectives. By accepting risks within a certain domain, organizations may position themselves for potential opportunities or competitive advantages.

Innovation and Growth: Accepting risks can foster a culture of innovation and growth, as organizations may be more willing to explore new ideas and strategies knowing that some risks are accepted as part of their business model.

Organizational Resilience: By accepting risks, organizations can build resilience to potential disruptions or uncertainties. Accepting risks within a controlled framework allows organizations to focus on managing risks that truly require mitigation.

Ethical Considerations: Organizations should consider the ethical dimensions of risk acceptance, ensuring that the decision aligns with their values and does not compromise the well-being or safety of individuals or the environment.

Stakeholder Engagement: Stakeholders should be engaged and informed when it comes to risk acceptance decisions that may impact them. Their perspectives, concerns, and inputs should be considered to ensure a comprehensive understanding of the risk landscape and its implications.

In summary, risk acceptance involves making a conscious decision to acknowledge and tolerate potential risks without implementing additional risk mitigation measures. It requires a thorough understanding of the risks, appropriate risk assessment, consideration of risk tolerance, and strategic analysis. Risk acceptance should be part of an organization's overall risk management framework and be regularly re-evaluated to ensure its continued validity.

Chapter Twenty-Three

Risk Management Frameworks

Risk management frameworks provide a structured approach to identifying, assessing, and managing risks within an organization or project. These frameworks help guide decision-making, implementation of mitigation strategies, and monitoring of risks.

Definition: A risk management framework is a structured process that organizations or projects use to systematically identify, assess, prioritize, and manage risks. It provides a standardized approach to ensure that risks are addressed consistently and effectively.

Components: Risk management frameworks typically consist of several components, including risk identification, risk assessment, risk mitigation, risk monitoring and communication, and risk review and evaluation.

Risk Identification: The first step in a risk management framework is to identify potential risks. This involves systematically identifying and documenting all possible risks that may impact the organization or project. Various techniques such as brainstorming, interviews, and historical data analysis may be used.

Risk Assessment: Once risks are identified, they need to be assessed to determine their potential impact and likelihood. Risk assessment involves evaluating the severity of the risk and the probability of its occurrence. This step helps prioritize risks based on their level of significance.

Risk Mitigation: After assessing risks, organizations or projects need to develop and implement strategies to mitigate or reduce the identified risks. Mitigation strategies may include risk avoidance, risk transfer, risk reduction, or risk acceptance.

Risk Monitoring and Communication: Risk management frameworks emphasize the need for ongoing monitoring and communication of risks. Regular monitoring allows organizations to track the effectiveness of mitigation strategies and identify new risks. Effective communication ensures that stakeholders are aware of risks and understand the actions being taken to mitigate them.

Risk Review and Evaluation: Risk management frameworks emphasize the importance of periodic review and evaluation of the risk management process. This step involves assessing the framework's effectiveness, identifying gaps or areas for improvement, and making necessary adjustments to ensure continuous improvement.

Risk Culture: Risk management frameworks also focus on promoting a risk-aware culture within an organization or project. This involves creating an environment where individuals are encouraged to identify and report risks, and where risk management is integrated into the decision-making process.

Risk Governance: Risk management frameworks help establish clear roles and responsibilities for managing risks. They define the governance structure, processes, and accountability mechanisms to ensure that risk management is embedded within the organization's overall governance framework.

Integration with Strategy: Risk management frameworks should align with the organization's overall strategic goals and objectives. They help ensure that risk management is integrated into strategic planning and decision-making processes.

Compliance and Regulations: Many risk management frameworks are designed to address compliance requirements and regulatory obligations. They help organizations meet legal and regulatory standards by identifying, assessing, and managing risks associated with relevant laws, regulations, and policies.

Flexibility: Risk management frameworks should be flexible and adaptable to the specific needs and characteristics of the organization or project. They should be able to accommodate changes in the risk landscape and evolving organizational priorities.

Documentation: Risk management frameworks emphasize the need for documentation. This includes documenting the identified risks, risk assessment results, mitigation strategies, monitoring activities, and communication plans. Documentation serves as a reference and helps in maintaining a historical record of the organization's risk management efforts.

Integration with Other Functions: Risk management frameworks should be integrated with other organizational functions such as project management, quality management, and financial management. This integration helps ensure a holistic approach to risk management and avoids duplication of efforts.

Continuous Improvement: Risk management frameworks support a culture of continuous improvement. They encourage organizations to regularly review and update their risk management practices incorporating lessons learned, industry best practices, and emerging risk trends.

Stakeholder Engagement: Risk management frameworks promote stakeholder engagement by involving relevant stakeholders in the risk management process. This includes seeking input from employees, customers, suppliers, regulators, and other external stakeholders to ensure a comprehensive understanding of risks and their potential impacts.

Risk Appetite: Risk management frameworks help define and communicate an organization's risk appetite – the level of risk it is willing to accept in pursuit of its goals. Risk appetite guides decision-making and prioritization of risks.

Training and Awareness: Risk management frameworks emphasize the importance of training and awareness programs to ensure that employees understand the purpose, benefits, and processes of risk management. This helps foster a risk-aware culture and ensures effective implementation of risk management practices.

Technology and Tools: Many risk management frameworks incorporate the use of technology and tools to support the risk management process. This includes risk assessment software, data analytics tools, risk registers, and dashboards for monitoring and reporting risks.

Industry Standards and Guidance: Several industry-specific standards and guidance documents exist to support the implementation of risk management frameworks. Organizations can refer to these frameworks to enhance their risk management practices and ensure compliance with industry-specific requirements.

In summary, risk management frameworks provide a structured and systematic approach to identifying, assessing, prioritizing, and managing risks within organizations or projects. They encompass various components such as risk identification, assessment, mitigation, monitoring, and communication. These frameworks promote a risk-aware culture, integration with organizational functions, and continuous improvement. Organizations can tailor risk management frameworks to their specific needs and comply with relevant regulations and standards.

ISO 31000: Principles and Guidelines

ISO 31000 is an internationally recognized standard that provides principles and guidelines for effective risk management. By adopting ISO 31000, organizations can enhance their ability to identify, analyze, and manage risks in a systematic and structured manner. This standard is applicable across all sectors and industries, allowing organizations to mitigate potential risks and make informed decisions to achieve their objectives.

The first principle of ISO 31000 is establishing a risk management framework. This involves developing a clear understanding of the organization's context, objectives, and risk appetite, and integrating risk management into all levels of the organization. By establishing a framework, organizations can create a common language and approach to risk management, increasing transparency and accountability.

The second principle is integrating risk management into the organization's governance. This means aligning risk management with the organization's overall decision-making processes and ensuring that it is considered in strategy development, resource allocation, and performance measurement. By integrating risk management into governance, organizations can make better-informed decisions that consider potential risks and opportunities.

ISO 31000 also emphasizes the importance of demonstrating leadership and commitment to risk management. Leaders should promote a positive risk culture within the organization and actively participate in the risk management process. This includes establishing clear roles and responsibilities, providing necessary resources, and fostering an environment that encourages open communication about risks.

Another principle is ensuring the involvement of stakeholders in the risk management process. Stakeholders, including customers, suppliers, employees, and regulators, can provide valuable insights and perspectives on risks. Engaging stakeholders in risk management helps to identify diverse viewpoints and ensure that risks are considered from multiple angles.

ISO 31000 encourages organizations to adopt a systematic and structured approach to risk management. This involves defining and implementing a risk management process that includes steps such as risk identification, analysis, evaluation, treatment, monitoring, and review. Such a structured approach provides a consistent and repeatable method for managing risks across the organization.

Furthermore, ISO 31000 emphasizes the importance of taking a proactive approach to risk management. Organizations should not wait until risks materialize, but rather aim to identify and assess risks before they occur. By being proactive, organizations can implement appropriate risk mitigation measures and capitalize on potential opportunities.

The standard also highlights the iterative nature of the risk management process. Organizations need to continuously review and update their risk management practices adapting to changing circumstances. This iterative approach ensures that risk management remains relevant and effective as the organization evolves.

ISO 31000 underscores the need for risk management to be based on the best available information. This requires organizations to establish and maintain robust data collection and analysis processes. By utilizing accurate and reliable information, organizations can make more informed decisions and effectively manage risks.

Another important principle of ISO 31000 is considering both internal and external context. Organizations need to take into account factors such as political, economic, regulatory, technological, and social environments when assessing risks. By considering the broader context, organizations can identify potential risks that may arise from external factors beyond their control.

ISO 31000 also highlights the importance of considering both positive and negative risks. While risk management aims to mitigate negative risks, organizations should also recognize and exploit opportunities. By taking a balanced approach to risk management, organizations can optimize their ability to achieve objectives and drive performance.

The standard also emphasizes the need for organizations to establish clear risk criteria. This involves defining the acceptable level of risk, as well as thresholds and tolerances for different types of risks. By establishing risk criteria, organizations can make consistent decisions and prioritize resources based on the severity and likelihood of risks.

ISO 31000 encourages organizations to adopt a coordinated approach to risk management. This involves breaking down silos and ensuring that risk management is integrated across different functions and departments. By promoting collaboration and knowledge sharing, organizations can effectively manage risks that span across different areas of the business.

The standard also emphasizes the importance of reviewing and continually improving the risk management process. Organizations should regularly assess the effectiveness of their risk management practices and identify opportunities for improvement. By learning from past experiences and implementing lessons learned, organizations can enhance their risk management capabilities.

ISO 31000 stresses the need to communicate and consult with stakeholders on risk-related matters. Effective communication ensures that risks are clearly understood and provides an opportunity for stakeholders to provide input and raise concerns. By fostering open and transparent communication, organizations can gain support and commitment from stakeholders for risk management initiatives.

Finally, ISO 31000 encourages organizations to monitor and review the effectiveness of risk management. This involves establishing appropriate performance indicators and conducting regular evaluations. By monitoring the effectiveness of risk management, organizations can identify areas of improvement and make necessary adjustments to their risk management practices.

In conclusion, ISO 31000 provides a comprehensive framework for organizations to effectively manage risks. By adhering to its principles and guidelines, organizations can establish a structured and systematic approach to risk management, increase transparency and accountability, and ultimately make better-informed decisions to achieve their objectives.

COSO ERM Framework: A Framework for Enterprise Risk Management

The COSO ERM Framework is a widely recognized framework for enterprise risk management. COSO, which stands for the Committee of Sponsoring Organizations of the Treadway Commission, developed this framework to help organizations implement effective risk management practices. The framework provides a comprehensive and integrated approach to managing risks at the enterprise level.

The first component of the COSO ERM Framework is establishing an internal environment. This involves creating a risk-aware culture and setting the tone from the top. Leaders must demonstrate their commitment to risk management and create an environment where employees understand the importance of identifying and managing risks.

The second component is setting objectives. Organizations must establish clear and measurable objectives that align with their mission and strategy. By setting objectives, organizations can identify and prioritize the risks that may impact their ability to achieve these objectives.

The third component is identifying and assessing risks. This involves identifying potential risks that may affect the organization's objectives and assessing the likelihood and impact of these risks. Organizations should consider both internal and external risks and utilize appropriate tools and techniques to assess and prioritize risks.

The fourth component is risk response. Once risks are identified and assessed, organizations must determine how to respond to these risks. They can choose to avoid, mitigate, transfer, or accept risks based on their risk appetite and risk tolerance. The risk response should be aligned with the organization's overall strategy and goals.

The fifth component is control activities. Organizations must establish and implement control activities to mitigate risks and ensure that objectives are achieved. These control activities may include policies, procedures, and other mechanisms to monitor and manage risks effectively.

The sixth component is information and communication. Organizations must establish a process for capturing, analyzing, and communicating risk-related information. This includes regularly reporting risk information to relevant stakeholders and ensuring that risk-related information is shared across the organization.

The seventh component is monitoring activities. Organizations need to regularly monitor and review the effectiveness of their risk management processes. This involves establishing a system for ongoing monitoring, internal audits, and periodic evaluations to ensure that risk management practices remain current and effective.

The COSO ERM Framework also emphasizes the importance of considering risk in the context of the organization's strategy. Organizations should integrate risk management into the strategic planning process and identify key strategic risks that may impact the achievement of strategic objectives.

Furthermore, the framework highlights the need to consider risk in the context of performance. Organizations should link risk management to performance metrics and use risk information to drive performance improvements. By considering risk in performance management, organizations can align risk management and strategic objectives.

The COSO ERM Framework also emphasizes the importance of enterprise risk management being a continuous and iterative process. Organizations should regularly update and refine their risk management practices based on changing circumstances and new information. This ensures that risk management remains relevant and effective over time.

The framework also promotes the idea of considering both positive and negative risks. While risk management often focuses on mitigating negative risks, organizations should also identify and exploit opportunities. By considering both positive and negative risks, organizations can optimize their ability to achieve objectives and drive performance.

The COSO ERM Framework encourages organizations to take a portfolio view of risks. It emphasizes the need to consider risks in combination and understand the potential interrelationships between different risks. By taking a portfolio view, organizations can identify potential cascading or systemic risks that may arise from the interplay of different risks.

The framework also highlights the importance of stakeholder engagement in risk management. Organizations should involve relevant stakeholders in the risk management process to gain different perspectives and ensure that risks are properly identified and addressed. This promotes transparency and increases the likelihood of effectively managing risks.

In conclusion, the COSO ERM Framework provides organizations with a comprehensive and integrated approach to enterprise risk management. By following its principles and guidelines, organizations can establish a strong risk management culture, set clear objectives, identify, and assess risks, respond appropriately to risks, implement control activities, and continually monitor and improve risk management practices. This framework helps organizations strengthen their ability to manage risks and achieve their objectives successfully.

PMI's PMBOK Risk Management Framework

The Project Management Institute (PMI) has developed a comprehensive risk management framework as part of its Project Management Body of Knowledge (PMBOK). This framework provides a systematic approach to identify, assess, mitigate, and monitor risks throughout the project lifecycle. The PMBOK Risk Management Framework consists of several interconnected processes and knowledge areas.

The first step in the framework is to plan risk management. This involves defining how risk management will be conducted throughout the project and establishing the overall approach. The project team identifies the stakeholders involved, defines risk tolerance, and determines the tools and techniques that will be used in the process.

Next, risk identification takes place. This process involves identifying and documenting the risks that may impact the project objectives. The project team engages stakeholders to gather their perspectives and uses various techniques such as brainstorming and checklists to identify potential risks. The identified risks are documented in a risk register.

After risk identification, the risks are analyzed. The project team assesses the likelihood and impact of each identified risk and determines its significance to project objectives. Quantitative and qualitative analysis techniques are used to prioritize risks based on their severity and identify the most critical ones.

Following risk analysis, risk response planning is performed. This process involves developing strategies to address the identified risks. The project team creates risk response plans for each priority risk, including strategies for avoiding, mitigating, transferring, or accepting the risks. These plans outline specific actions that will be taken to address the risks.

Once the risk response plans are developed, the project team executes them. The identified actions are implemented as part of project execution. This ensures that the risk response plans are put into action, and appropriate measures are taken to address the risks.

The next step is to monitor and control risks. Throughout the project lifecycle, risks are monitored to ensure that the identified response plans are effective. Regular risk reviews are conducted to assess the status of identified risks, evaluate the effectiveness of risk mitigation actions, and identify any new risks that may have emerged.

Risk monitoring and control also involve evaluating risk triggers - indicators that a risk is about to occur. By monitoring these triggers, the project team can take timely actions to mitigate or prevent the risks from materializing.

At each phase of the project, risk documentation is updated to reflect the progress made in addressing risks. Risk status reports, risk registers, and other documentation are updated to ensure that stakeholders are informed about the current state of risks.

The PMBOK Risk Management Framework emphasizes the importance of having a risk management plan that integrates well with the overall project plan. The risk management plan outlines the approach, roles, and responsibilities, as well as the timing and frequency of risk management activities.

Additionally, the framework highlights the need for effective communication and engagement with stakeholders. The project team must communicate risks, risk response plans, and risk progress to stakeholders and engage them in decision-making processes related to risk management.

The PMBOK Risk Management Framework recognizes that risks are not static; they can change and evolve. Therefore, the framework promotes an iterative approach, where risk management activities are conducted periodically throughout the project lifecycle to account for any new risks.

The framework also emphasizes the importance of monitoring the effectiveness of risk response plans and evaluating the overall risk management process. Regular reviews and lessons-learned sessions enable the project team to identify areas for improvement and refine their risk management practices.

The PMBOK Risk Management Framework promotes the use of various tools and techniques to support risk management activities. These include risk identification techniques, risk probability and impact assessment tools, risk categorization methods, and risk assessment matrices. The framework guides when and how to use these tools effectively.

Furthermore, the framework highlights the need for risk management to be an ongoing process, not just a one-time activity. Risks may change or new risks may emerge throughout the project, and therefore risk management activities should continue to be performed from project initiation to project closure.

The PMBOK Risk Management Framework also recognizes the interdependencies between risks. It encourages the project team to consider the impact of risks on other project elements, such as scope, cost, schedule, quality, and resources. This holistic approach ensures that risks are addressed comprehensively.

Stakeholder engagement is a key aspect of the PMBOK Risk Management Framework. The framework emphasizes the need to engage relevant stakeholders in risk management activities and decision-making processes to ensure that risks are effectively identified, assessed, and addressed.

The framework also addresses specific risk management considerations for different types of projects. It recognizes that different industries, project sizes, and project complexities may require tailored risk management approaches. The framework provides flexibility to adapt risk management processes to the specific needs of the project.

The PMBOK Risk Management Framework aligns risk management with other project management knowledge areas and processes. It integrates risk management activities with project planning, execution, monitoring and control, and closing processes. This integration ensures that risk management is an integral part of the overall project management process.

In conclusion, the PMBOK Risk Management Framework provides project managers and teams with a structured and systematic approach to managing risks. It covers all aspects of risk management, from planning to monitoring and control, and promotes an iterative and ongoing approach. By following this framework, project teams can effectively identify, assess, mitigate, and monitor risks, thereby increasing the chances of project success.

Chapter Twenty-Four

Types of Risks

Financial Risks: Financial risks refer to the potential losses or disruptions that may arise from financial transactions, investments, or market fluctuations. Examples of financial risks include currency risk, interest rate risk, credit risk, liquidity risk, and market risk. These risks can impact an organization's financial stability and profitability.

Operational Risks: Operational risks are associated with the internal processes, systems, and activities of an organization. They can arise from human error, inadequate or failed processes, technology failures, supply chain disruptions, or other operational inefficiencies. Operational risks can impact an organization's ability to deliver products or services, meet customer demands, and maintain operational effectiveness.

Strategic Risks: Strategic risks are risks associated with the organization's long-term objectives and strategic decision-making. These risks may arise from changes in the competitive landscape, evolving customer preferences, technological advancements, regulatory changes, or geopolitical factors. Strategic risks can impact an organization's ability to achieve its strategic goals and maintain a competitive position in the market.

Compliance Risks: Compliance risks refer to the potential violations of laws, regulations, or internal policies and procedures. Non-compliance can result in legal penalties, reputational damage, or loss of business opportunities. Compliance risks can arise from inadequate internal controls, lack of awareness or training, or changes in regulatory requirements.

Reputational Risks: Reputational risks relate to the potential damage to an organization's reputation or brand image. These risks can arise from negative public perception, customer dissatisfaction, product recalls, unethical behavior, or media scrutiny. Reputational risks can have far-reaching consequences, including loss of customer trust, decreased market share, or difficulty attracting and retaining talent.

Environmental Risks: Environmental risks pertain to the potential impact of natural or man-made environmental factors on an organization's operations, assets, or reputation. These risks can include natural disasters, climate change, pollution, hazardous waste, or regulatory requirements related to environmental sustainability. Environmental risks can affect an organization's operations, supply chain, and ability to meet environmental regulations.

Legal Risks: Legal risks refer to the potential exposure to lawsuits, claims, or legal disputes. These risks can arise from contract disputes, intellectual property infringements, violations of laws or regulations, or non-compliance with legal obligations. Legal risks can result in significant financial costs, reputational damage, or disruptions to business operations.

Information Security Risks: Information security risks involve threats to the confidentiality, integrity, or availability of an organization's information assets. These risks can arise from cyber-attacks, data breaches, unauthorized access to sensitive information, or inadequate security controls. Information security risks can lead to financial losses, harm to the organization's reputation, or compromised customer data.

Project Risks: Project risks are specific to individual projects and refer to the uncertainties or potential disruptions that may impact project objectives, timelines, and deliverables. These risks could include scope creep, resource constraints, technical challenges, stakeholder conflicts, or unforeseen events. Project risks can negatively impact the successful completion of a project if not effectively managed.

Health and Safety Risks: Health and safety risks relate to potential harm or hazards to employees, customers, or other stakeholders in the workplace or related to an organization's activities. These risks could include accidents, occupational hazards, exposure to toxic substances, or non-compliance with health and safety regulations. Health and safety risks may lead to employee injuries, legal liabilities, or damage to an organization's reputation.

Social Risks: Social risks refer to risks associated with social or community factors that may impact the operations, reputation, or relationships of an organization. These risks could arise from social unrest, public protests, labor strikes, or negative public sentiment towards certain business practices. Social risks can have implications for an organization's operations, image, or ability to attract and retain customers.

Economic Risks: Economic risks are related to fluctuations in economic conditions, such as inflation, recession, currency exchange rates, or changes in interest rates. These risks can impact an organization's revenue, cost structure, profitability, or access to capital. Economic risks can also affect consumer behavior, market demand, or global market conditions, thereby impacting an organization's financial performance.

Industry-specific Risks: Industry-specific risks are risks that are inherent to a particular sector or industry. These risks can vary depending on the nature of the industry and may include factors such as regulatory changes, technological advancements, emerging competition, or supply chain vulnerabilities. Understanding and managing industry-specific risks are critical for organizations to remain competitive and resilient within their respective sectors.

Geopolitical Risks: Geopolitical risks arise from political instability, conflicts, or changes in government policies in different regions globally. These risks can impact an organization's international operations, supply chains, or market access. Geopolitical risks can be unpredictable and may include factors such as trade disputes, economic sanctions, civil unrest, or terrorism. Organizations with global operations or those operating in volatile regions need to consider and manage geopolitical risks effectively.

Financial Risks

Financial risks refer to the potential losses or disruptions that may arise from financial transactions, investments, or market fluctuations. These risks can have a direct impact on an organization's financial stability, profitability, and ability to meet its financial obligations.

In risk management, financial risks play a crucial role as they are often one of the primary concerns for organizations. Effectively managing financial risks is essential to ensure the long-term sustainability and success of the organization.

Financial risks can manifest in various forms, including:

1. Currency Risk: Currency risk arises from fluctuations in exchange rates. It affects organizations engaged in international trade or with foreign exchange exposure. Currency risk can impact the profitability of international transactions, increase costs, or result in unfavorable foreign exchange rate conversions.

2. Interest Rate Risk: Interest rate risk pertains to potential losses caused by changes in interest rates. Organizations that rely on borrowing funds or have fixed income investments are particularly susceptible to interest rate fluctuations. A rise in interest rates can increase borrowing costs, impact investment returns, or affect the affordability of loans.

3. Credit Risk: Credit risk refers to the potential for losses due to the inability of borrowers or debtors to fulfill their financial obligations. This risk is prevalent when providing credit or lending money. Organizations need to manage credit risk by assessing the creditworthiness of borrowers, establishing credit limits, and implementing effective collection processes.

4. Liquidity Risk: Liquidity risk relates to the availability of sufficient funds to meet financial obligations when they become due. It arises from the inability to convert assets into cash quickly or obtain additional financing at reasonable terms. Liquidity risk can lead to financial distress, credit rating downgrades, or even bankruptcy if an organization's cash flow is insufficient.

5. Market Risk: Market risk encompasses the potential losses resulting from adverse changes in market conditions. It can affect investments in equities, bonds, commodities, or other financial instruments. Market risk includes factors such as volatility, price fluctuations, and correlation among various assets. Organizations need to monitor and mitigate market risk through diversification, hedging, or adjusting investment portfolios.

Managing financial risks involves several key elements:

1. Risk Identification: Organizations need to identify and assess potential financial risks specific to their operations, industry, and financial landscape. This process involves understanding the nature of risks, their likelihood, and their potential impact on the organization's financial goals.

2. Risk Measurement and Quantification: Financial risks need to be measured and quantified to understand their potential consequences. This involves assessing the probability of risk events occurring and estimating the potential financial impact on the organization. Techniques such as sensitivity analysis, scenario modeling, and stress testing can be used for risk measurement.

3. Risk Mitigation Strategies: Once financial risks are identified and quantified, organizations can develop risk mitigation strategies. These strategies include implementing risk mitigation measures, such as hedging against currency or interest rate fluctuations, diversifying investment portfolios, or reducing exposure to risky assets. By adopting appropriate risk mitigation strategies, organizations aim to reduce the financial impact of adverse events.

4. Risk Monitoring and Review: Effective risk management requires ongoing monitoring and review of financial risks. Organizations need to regularly assess the effectiveness of risk mitigation measures, monitor changes in market conditions, and update risk management strategies accordingly. Regular risk reporting and key risk indicators help keep stakeholders informed about the organization's financial risk exposure.

5. Risk Governance and Policy: An organization needs to establish a risk governance framework with clearly defined roles, responsibilities, and policies for managing financial risks. This includes defining risk appetite, setting risk limits, and establishing risk management processes and controls. Risk management policies guide employees on risk-related decision-making and actions.

Overall, financial risks play a critical role in risk management as they can significantly impact an organization's financial health and performance. Proactive identification, measurement, mitigation, and monitoring of financial risks are essential to safeguarding an organization's financial stability and achieving its strategic objectives.

Operational Risks

Operational risks are the risks associated with the internal processes, systems, and activities of an organization. These risks arise from factors such as human error, inadequate or failed processes, technology failures, supply chain disruptions, or other operational inefficiencies. Operational risks can affect an organization's ability to deliver products or services, meet customer demands, and maintain operational effectiveness.

Operational risks can be categorized into several subtypes:

1. Process Risks: Process risks involve the potential for errors, inefficiencies, or failures within the organization's operational processes. These risks can arise from inadequate process design, lack of standardization, or improper

execution. Process risks can result in delays, rework, quality issues, customer dissatisfaction, or cost overruns.

2. People Risks: People risks relate to the actions or behaviors of individuals within the organization. This can include human error, misconduct, inadequate training, or insufficient staffing levels. People's risks can lead to operational disruptions, accidents, safety incidents, or compromised quality.

3. Technology Risks: Technology risks encompass the potential failures, vulnerabilities, or disruptions in an organization's technology systems and infrastructure. This includes risks related to hardware, software, networks, data security, or cybersecurity. Technology risks can result in system downtime, data breaches, information loss, or operational interruptions.

4. Supply Chain Risks: Supply chain risks refer to the potential disruptions or breakdowns in the organization's supply chain. These risks can arise from factors such as supplier failures, logistical issues, transportation disruptions, or raw material shortages. Supply chain risks can lead to delayed deliveries, production delays, increased costs, or inventory management challenges.

5. Facility Risks: Facility risks involve the risks associated with the organization's physical infrastructure and facilities. These risks can include property damage, equipment failures, natural disasters, or fire hazards. Facility risks can result in operational shutdowns, safety incidents, financial losses, or reputational damage.

6. Legal and Regulatory Risks: Legal and regulatory risks pertain to potential non-compliance with laws, regulations, or industry standards. This can include violations related to health and safety, environmental regulations, employment laws, or data privacy. Legal and regulatory risks can lead to legal penalties, fines, lawsuits, reputational damage, or operational disruptions.

Managing operational risks involves several key elements:

1. Risk Identification: Organizations need to proactively identify and assess potential operational risks. This involves understanding the organization's operational processes, systems, and activities, and identifying the potential vulnerabilities and failure points. Risk identification can be achieved through risk assessments, internal audits, incident reporting, or lessons learned from past incidents.

2. Risk Assessment and Prioritization: Operational risks should be assessed based on their likelihood and potential impact on the organization. This allows for the prioritization of risks and the allocation of resources to address the most critical risks. Risk assessment methods such as qualitative and quantitative analysis, risk heat maps, or risk scoring can be utilized.

3. Risk Mitigation and Control: Once risks are identified and assessed, organizations can develop risk mitigation and control strategies. These strategies may involve implementing process improvements, implementing internal controls, enhancing employee training and awareness, or investing in technology safeguards. The aim is to reduce the likelihood and impact of operational risks.

4. Monitoring and Review: Organizations need to regularly monitor and review operational risks to ensure that the implemented risk mitigation measures are effective. This involves ongoing monitoring of key risk indicators, incident reporting, performance metrics, or feedback mechanisms. Regular reviews enable organizations to identify emerging risks, assess the effectiveness of risk controls, and make necessary adjustments to risk management strategies.

5. Resilience and Continuity Planning: Organizations should develop resilience and continuity plans to prepare for and respond to operational disruptions. This involves developing contingency plans, business continuity

plans, or disaster recovery plans. The goal is to minimize the impact of operational disruptions and ensure the organization's ability to maintain critical operations under adverse conditions.

Operational risks are an integral part of risk management, and effectively managing them is essential for organizations to maintain operational efficiency, achieve strategic objectives, and ensure the delivery of products and services to customers. By identifying, assessing, mitigating, and monitoring operational risks, organizations can reduce the likelihood of operational failures and their potential impact on the organization.

Strategic Risks

Strategic risks are the risks associated with an organization's long-term objectives and strategic decision-making. These risks arise from factors that can significantly impact an organization's ability to achieve its strategic goals, maintain a competitive position in the market, or adapt to changes in the business environment. Strategic risks can stem from internal or external factors and may require proactive management to mitigate their impact.

Here are some key aspects to understand about strategic risks:

1. External Factors: Strategic risks can emerge from external factors beyond the control of the organization. These can include changes in market dynamics, shifts in consumer behavior or preferences, technological advancements, economic factors, regulatory changes, or geopolitical events. These external factors can create uncertainties and challenges in achieving strategic objectives.

2. Internal Factors: Internal factors can also contribute to strategic risks. These may involve weaknesses in the organization's capabilities, challenges in talent acquisition or retention, inadequate resources, ineffective decision-making processes, or lack of alignment between strategic goals and operational execution. Internal factors can hinder an organization's ability to execute its strategies successfully.

3. Long-Term Impact: Strategic risks typically have a long-term impact on the organization rather than immediate consequences. They can threaten the organization's sustainable growth, brand reputation, market position, or financial performance. The cumulative effect of strategic risks can significantly impact the organization's value and competitive advantage over time.

4. Competitive Position: Strategic risks are closely tied to an organization's competitive position in the market. Failure to anticipate or respond to changes in the competitive landscape, emerging technologies, or evolving customer preferences can expose the organization to increased competition, market share erosion, or loss of relevance. Organizations need to continuously assess their competitive position and identify potential strategic risks in this context.

5. Risk Appetite and Tolerance: Managing strategic risks requires organizations to define their risk appetite and tolerance levels. Risk appetite refers to the amount of risk the organization is willing to accept in pursuit of its strategic objectives. Risk tolerance refers to the organization's readiness to handle risk and its capacity to absorb potential impacts. These factors shape the organization's approach to identifying, analyzing, and addressing strategic risks.

6. Scenario Planning: Given the long-term impact and uncertainties associated with strategic risks, scenario planning can be an effective tool. Scenario planning involves exploring various future scenarios and assessing how strategic risks may play out in each scenario. It helps organizations identify potential vulnerabilities, adaptability, and opportunities under different possible future conditions.

7. Risk Mitigation Strategies: Mitigating strategic risks often involves developing proactive strategies to address potential challenges before they become real threats. This may include diversification of products or markets,

investment in research and development, enhancing competitive intelligence, strategic partnerships or alliances, or continuous monitoring of market trends. By proactively addressing strategic risks, organizations can position themselves to capitalize on opportunities and navigate uncertainties effectively.

8. Monitoring and Review: Strategic risks require ongoing monitoring and review to identify emerging risks, track changes in the business environment, and evaluate the effectiveness of risk mitigation strategies. Regular reviews enable the organization to make necessary adjustments to its strategic plans, risk management approaches, and resource allocation.

Strategic risks are an inherent part of business and require the attention of top management and the board of directors. Successful organizations recognize the importance of integrating risk management into their strategic planning process to identify and address potential risks that can impact their long-term success. By effectively managing strategic risks, organizations can enhance their resilience, seize opportunities, and stay ahead of competitors in a rapidly changing business landscape.

Compliance Risks

Compliance risks refer to the potential violations of laws, regulations, or internal policies and procedures. These risks arise from non-compliance with legal and regulatory requirements, industry standards, or ethical guidelines. Compliance risks can expose organizations to legal penalties, reputational damage, financial losses, or loss of business opportunities.

Here are some key elements to understand about compliance risks:

1. Types of Compliance Risks: Compliance risks can encompass a wide range of areas, depending on the industry and the specific requirements that organizations must adhere to. Examples of compliance risks include non-compliance with labor laws, health and safety regulations, environmental regulations, data protection and privacy laws, anti-money laundering regulations, international trade regulations, or industry-specific regulations. Non-compliance with any of these obligations may result in adverse consequences for the organization.

2. Legal and Regulatory Environment: Organizations operate within a legal and regulatory environment that governs their activities. This environment includes laws and regulations at the local, national, and international levels, as well as industry-specific standards and codes of conduct. Compliance risks arise when organizations fail to meet these obligations and requirements, either due to lack of awareness, inadequate controls, or intentional misconduct.

3. Consequences of Non-Compliance: Non-compliance with legal and regulatory requirements can have significant consequences. These consequences can vary depending on the severity of the violation, the nature of the non-compliance, and the jurisdiction in which the organization operates. Consequences may include financial penalties, sanctions, license revocations, legal settlements, negative publicity, loss of customers or business partners, criminal prosecution, or civil litigation.

4. Reputational Impact: Compliance risks can have a profound impact on an organization's reputation. Failure to comply with laws, regulations, or ethical standards can damage the trust and confidence of customers, investors, employees, and other stakeholders. Reputational damage can lead to a loss of market share, difficulty attracting and retaining talent, diminished investor confidence, or decreased business opportunities.

5. Compliance Programs and Controls: Organizations develop compliance programs and implement internal controls to mitigate compliance risks. These programs encompass policies, procedures, protocols, training, monitoring, and reporting mechanisms designed to ensure adherence to applicable laws, regulations, and internal

policies. Effective compliance programs promote awareness, educate employees, establish accountability, and monitor compliance efforts.

6. Compliance Culture: Building a compliance culture is essential to managing compliance risks effectively. A compliance culture fosters a commitment to ethical behavior, legal compliance, and accountability throughout the organization. It starts with leadership and is driven by promoting ethical conduct, providing proper training and resources, and creating channels for reporting compliance concerns or potential violations.

7. Compliance Risk Assessments: Organizations conduct compliance risk assessments to identify and evaluate potential compliance risks. Risk assessments help organizations understand their exposure to compliance risks, assess the likelihood and impact of those risks, and prioritize resources and efforts to address them. Risk assessments may involve analyzing regulatory requirements, conducting gap analyses against internal controls, assessing the effectiveness of compliance programs, or seeking external expertise.

8. Monitoring and Remediation: Organizations need to continually monitor compliance risks and promptly address any identified deficiencies. Regular monitoring activities may include internal audits, self-assessments, compliance reviews, or surprise inspections. Should violations or breaches occur, organizations must take appropriate remedial actions, which may involve corrective measures, disciplinary actions, process improvements, or additional training.

9. Regulatory Compliance and Reporting: Organizations need to meet reporting requirements established by regulatory bodies to ensure transparency and demonstrate compliance. These requirements may include filing regular reports, maintaining records, conducting audits, or responding to ad hoc requests from regulatory authorities.

Effective compliance risk management is critical for maintaining the trust of stakeholders, complying with legal and regulatory obligations, and safeguarding an organization's reputation. By implementing robust compliance programs, fostering a culture of compliance, and proactively addressing compliance risks, organizations can reduce their exposure to compliance-related issues and ensure sustainable and responsible operations.

Reputational Risks

Reputational risks refer to the potential damage or harm to an organization's reputation or brand image. These risks arise from factors that can negatively impact how an organization is perceived by its stakeholders, including customers, investors, employees, regulators, or the general public. Reputational risks can have significant consequences for an organization, affecting its credibility, customer trust, market value, and long-term success.

Here are some key elements to understand about reputational risks:

1. Factors Influencing Reputational Risks: Reputational risks can arise from a variety of factors, including

a. Negative Public Perception: Organizations can face reputational risks due to negative public perception resulting from product recalls, customer complaints, ethical misconduct, environmental controversies, labor disputes, or other unfavorable events.

b. Social Media and Online Presence: The rise of social media platforms and online communication channels has amplified reputational risks. Negative experiences, viral content, or negative reviews shared by customers or other stakeholders can quickly spread and damage an organization's reputation.

c. Leadership Behavior: The actions and behavior of an organization's leaders can significantly impact its reputation. Unethical conduct, scandals, personal misconduct, or poor decision-making by key executives can erode trust and harm the organization's reputation.

d. Stakeholder Trust and Relationships: Reputational risks can emerge from damaged relationships with key stakeholders, including customers, suppliers, investors, employees, or regulators. Failure to deliver on promises, poor customer service, breaches of trust, or ethical lapses can lead to reputational damage.

2. Consequences of Reputational Risks: Reputational risks can have far-reaching consequences for an organization, including

a. Loss of Customer Trust: Reputational damage erodes customer trust and loyalty. Customers may switch to competitors, leading to decreased market share, declining sales, and diminished customer base.

b. Decreased Investor Confidence: Reputational risks can impact investor confidence and perception, resulting in decreased stock value, reduced access to capital, or difficulty attracting investment.

c. Negative Media Attention: Reputational risks can attract negative media coverage, damaging the organization's image and increasing scrutiny from stakeholders and the public.

d. Employee Retention and Recruitment Challenges: Reputational damage can affect an organization's ability to attract and retain top talent. Negative perceptions can make it difficult to recruit skilled employees and result in increased employee turnover.

e. Legal and Regulatory Consequences: Reputational risks may lead to legal actions, regulatory investigations, fines, or penalties, depending on the nature of the risk and applicable laws or regulations.

3. Managing Reputational Risks: Organizations can take proactive steps to manage reputational risks:

a. Stakeholder Engagement: Actively engaging with stakeholders and understanding their needs and expectations helps build trust and maintain positive relationships.

b. Crisis Preparedness and Response: Developing comprehensive crisis management plans and response strategies enables organizations to navigate and mitigate reputational risks during times of crisis or adverse events.

c. Ethical Conduct and Values-Based Culture: Cultivating an ethical organizational culture and promoting values-based behavior helps establish a strong reputation built on trust and integrity.

d. Listening to Feedback: Regularly gathering and listening to feedback from customers, employees, and other stakeholders can help identify potential reputational risks and address concerns before they escalate.

e. Transparency and Communication: Being transparent and proactive in communications with stakeholders promotes trust and accountability. Clear and timely communication during crises or challenging situations helps manage reputational risks effectively.

f. Social Media Monitoring: Monitoring social media platforms and online channels enables organizations to stay informed about conversations and sentiment, allowing for timely responses to potential reputational risks.

g. Collaborations and Partnerships: Building strategic collaborations and partnerships with reputable organizations can enhance the organization's image and credibility.

4. Rebuilding Reputation: If reputational damage occurs, effective reputation-rebuilding strategies are crucial. Organizations can focus on transparency, taking responsibility for mistakes made, implementing corrective actions, delivering on promises, and consistently demonstrating integrity in their operations.

Effective management of reputational risks is essential for organizations to maintain their customer base, attract investors, and build long-term sustainable success. A strong and positive reputation can provide a competitive advantage, enhance brand value, and foster trust among stakeholders.

Technological Risks

Technological risks refer to the potential threats, disruptions, or negative impacts that arise from the use of technology systems, infrastructure, or digital processes. These risks typically arise from technological failures, cyberattacks, data breaches, system glitches, or inadequate technology management practices. Technological risks can have significant implications for organizations' operations, data security, customer trust, and financial well-being.

Here are some key aspects to understand about technological risks:

1. Cybersecurity Risks: Cybersecurity risks are one of the most prominent technological risks organizations face today. These risks include the potential for unauthorized access, data breaches, ransomware attacks, phishing attempts, or other malicious cyber activities. Cybersecurity risks can lead to financial loss, theft of sensitive information, damage to the organization's reputation, regulatory penalties, or disruption of business operations.

2. Data Privacy Risks: With the increasing reliance on digital systems and the collection of vast amounts of personal data, data privacy risks have become a critical concern. Organizations must protect personal and sensitive information from unauthorized access, misuse, or disclosure. Data privacy risks can result in legal and regulatory violations, financial penalties, reputational damage, loss of customer trust, or legal liability.

3. System and Infrastructure Failures: Business continuity and operational resilience can be threatened by system and infrastructure failures. These failures can be caused by hardware malfunctions, power outages, natural disasters, or human errors. System failures can lead to downtime, loss of data, service disruptions, or inability to serve customers, negatively impacting the organization's reputation, customer relationships, and financial stability.

4. Technology Obsolescence Risks: Rapid advancements in technology present the risk of technology obsolescence. Organizations that do not keep pace with technology trends and fail to upgrade or modernize their systems may face competitive disadvantages, decreased efficiency, or limitations on their ability to adapt to changing business needs. Obsolescence risks can hinder innovation, customer service, and overall organizational performance.

5. Regulatory Compliance Risks: The increasing complexity of technology-related regulations places additional compliance obligations on organizations. Failure to comply with regulatory requirements, such as data protection laws or industry-specific regulations, can result in legal and financial consequences. Organizations must navigate compliance risks associated with technology-related regulations to maintain regulatory compliance and avoid penalties.

6. Vendor and Supply Chain Risks: Organizations often rely on vendors or third-party service providers for technology solutions and support. Inherent risks exist in these relationships, including vendor failure, supply chain disruptions, or inadequate security practices of third parties. Organizations should implement proper vendor management strategies, including due diligence, contract negotiations, and ongoing monitoring, to mitigate these risks.

7. Emerging Technologies and Adoption Risks: Adopting emerging technologies, such as artificial intelligence, blockchain, or Internet of Things (IoT), can introduce unique risks. These risks can arise from insufficient understanding of the technology, immature security measures, lack of skill sets, or ethical considerations. Organizations need to assess and manage the risks associated with adopting new technologies to reap their benefits while minimizing potential adverse impacts.

8. IT Governance and Controls: Effective IT governance and controls are crucial for managing technological risks. This involves establishing policies, procedures, and controls to ensure the appropriate and secure use of technology, data management practices, incident response plans, and disaster recovery strategies. IT governance ensures proper alignment between technology initiatives and organizational objectives and supports risk mitigation efforts.

Managing technological risks requires a proactive and comprehensive approach:

1. Risk Assessment: Organizations should conduct regular risk assessments to identify and understand technological risks specific to their operations, systems, and industry. This enables organizations to evaluate the likelihood and potential impact of these risks on their business objectives.

2. Risk Mitigation: Based on risk assessments, organizations can implement measures to mitigate technological risks. This may involve implementing robust cybersecurity measures, including firewalls, antivirus software, encryption, access controls, and employee training. Data protection practices, disaster recovery plans, and technology obsolescence mitigation strategies should also be considered.

3. Incident Response and Recovery: Organizations must have comprehensive incident response plans to detect, respond, and recover from technology-related incidents, such as cyberattacks or system failures. Incident response plans should outline clear roles, responsibilities, and communication protocols to minimize the potential impact of incidents.

4. Regular Monitoring and Review: Technological risks are dynamic, and organizations need to continuously monitor and review their technology systems, processes, and controls. This helps identify emerging threats, vulnerabilities, or gaps and address them through timely updates, patches, security audits, and appropriate training or awareness programs.

5. Staff Training and Awareness: Organizations should provide ongoing training and awareness programs to staff to promote a culture of cybersecurity and risk management. Staff training should focus on identifying phishing attempts, safe online practices, adherence to data protection guidelines, and reporting suspicious activities.

6. Compliance and Regulatory Adherence: Organizations must stay abreast of relevant technology-related regulations and ensure compliance with applicable requirements. This may involve conducting internal audits, implementing data protection frameworks, or seeking third-party certifications to demonstrate adherence to industry-specific or legal requirements.

Managing technological risks is essential to protect an organization's assets, reputation, and overall business continuity. Organizations should adopt proactive measures, implement robust security practices, and stay vigilant to emerging threats to effectively mitigate the impact of technological risks.

Chapter Twenty-Five

Risk Assessment Tools and Techniques

Risk assessment tools and techniques are used to identify, analyze, and evaluate risks within an organization or project. These tools and techniques provide a structured approach to assessing risks, enabling organizations to prioritize their responses and allocate resources effectively. Here are some commonly used risk assessment tools and techniques:

1. Risk Identification Techniques: These techniques are used to identify and capture potential risks. Some common techniques include:

a. Brainstorming: Gathering a group of stakeholders to generate ideas and identify risks related to the project or organization.

b. Checklists: Using predefined checklists of risk categories or risk factors to systematically identify potential risks.

c. Interviews and Surveys: Engaging stakeholders through interviews or surveys to gather their perspectives and insights on potential risks.

d. Documentation Review: Review project documentation, historical records, lessons learned, and other relevant materials to identify risks that have occurred in the past.

2. Risk Probability and Impact Assessment Tools: These tools are used to assess the probability and impact of identified risks. These assessments help in prioritizing risks based on their severity and determining the level of attention and resources required. Examples of tools include:

a. Probability and Impact Matrix: Using a matrix to assign a likelihood and consequence rating to each risk and determining its overall risk rating.

b. Qualitative Analysis: Subjectively assessing the likelihood and impact of risks using descriptive scales or relative rankings.

c. Quantitative Analysis: Using quantitative data and calculations to assess the probability and impact of risks, such as through Monte Carlo simulations or statistical models.

3. Risk Categorization Methods: Risk categorization helps in organizing and grouping similar risks for better management and analysis. Categorization techniques include:

a. Risk Breakdown Structure (RBS): Structuring risks hierarchically into categories and subcategories to provide a systematic framework for risk identification and analysis.

b. Risk Mapping: Mapping risks based on their relationship to specific project objectives, stakeholder interests, or other relevant criteria.

4. SWOT Analysis: SWOT (Strengths, Weaknesses, Opportunities, Threats) analysis is a strategic planning tool used to assess the internal strengths and weaknesses of an organization along with external opportunities and threats. This analysis helps in identifying risks associated with the organization's strengths and weaknesses, as well as external factors that may present opportunities or threats.

5. Expert Judgment: Relying on the expertise and experience of subject matter experts or individuals with domain knowledge to assess risks. Expert judgment can be valuable in evaluating risks that are difficult to quantify or where historical data is lacking.

6. Risk Assessment Workshops: Conducting dedicated workshops or meetings with relevant stakeholders to collectively assess risks, share perspectives, and reach consensus on their probability, impact, and priority.

7. Delphi Technique: A structured method to seek input from a panel of experts, iteratively collecting and refining their opinions until consensus is reached on risk likelihood, impact, or mitigation measures.

8. Scenario Analysis: Creating hypothetical scenarios to assess how different situations or events may impact risks and the organization's ability to achieve objectives. This can help in exploring potential worst-case scenarios and their potential consequences.

9. Risk Heat Maps: Visual representations, often color-coded, that provide a snapshot of risks based on their likelihood and impact. Heat maps help in visually identifying high-priority risks and areas of focus.

10. Historical Data Analysis: Analyzing historical data, like lessons learned from previous projects or incidents, to identify patterns, trends, and common risks that may apply to the current project or organization.

It's important to note that the selection and application of risk assessment tools and techniques should align with the organization's needs, objectives, and available resources. The choice of tools and techniques should be tailored to the specific context and complexity of the project or operation being assessed. Additionally, risk assessment is an iterative process, and tools and techniques may be revisited and adjusted as the understanding of risks evolves over time.

SWOT Analysis

SWOT analysis is a strategic planning tool that is widely used in business and organizational contexts to assess internal strengths and weaknesses, as well as external opportunities and threats. It provides a comprehensive evaluation of an organization's current position and helps in identifying areas for improvement, potential risks, and future strategic directions.

The acronym SWOT stands for:

1. Strengths: These are the internal factors that give an organization a competitive advantage or unique capabilities. Strengths can include things like specialized expertise, strong brand recognition, advanced technology, talented employees, or a robust customer base. By identifying and leveraging their strengths, organizations can enhance their performance and differentiate themselves from competitors.

2. Weaknesses: These are internal factors that hinder an organization's performance and put it at a disadvantage compared to its competitors. Weaknesses can include factors such as outdated technology, poor financial management, lack of skilled personnel, limited product or service offerings, or low customer satisfaction. Identifying weaknesses is crucial as it allows organizations to address areas of improvement and minimize potential risks.

3. Opportunities: These are external factors and favorable conditions in the business environment that an organization can exploit to its advantage. Opportunities can emerge from factors like market trends, technological advancements, regulatory changes, emerging customer needs, or new potential markets. By identifying and capitalizing on opportunities, organizations can grow, expand their market share, or diversify their offerings.

4. Threats: These are external factors and challenges that pose risks to an organization's success. Threats can include factors like intense competition, economic downturns, changing consumer preferences, new regulations, disruptive technologies, or supplier or customer dependency. Identifying threats helps organizations proactively develop strategies to mitigate risks and stay resilient in a dynamic business environment.

The process of conducting a SWOT analysis typically involves the following steps:

1. Gather and analyze information: Collect relevant data and information about the organization's internal operations, strengths, weaknesses, external market factors, competitive landscape, opportunities, and threats.

2. Identify strengths and weaknesses: Identify and evaluate the organization's internal capabilities, resources, and limitations. This can be done through self-assessment, employee and stakeholder feedback, market research, or benchmarking against competitors.

3. Identify opportunities and threats: Analyze the external factors and influences that can impact the organization's performance. This can involve monitoring industry trends, conducting market research, analyzing customer preferences, and assessing the broader socio-economic and political environment.

4. Match internal strengths with external opportunities: Identify areas where the organization's strengths can be leveraged to take advantage of external opportunities. This helps in developing strategies to capitalize on favorable conditions and grow the business.

5. Address internal weaknesses and external threats: Identify areas where weaknesses need to be addressed or minimized and develop strategies to mitigate or overcome external threats that may hinder the organization's success.

6. Develop strategic initiatives: Based on the SWOT analysis findings, develop action plans and strategic initiatives that align strengths and opportunities, overcome weaknesses, and minimize or manage threats. These initiatives form the basis for improving performance, achieving organizational objectives, and gaining a competitive edge.

It's important to note that a SWOT analysis is not a standalone strategy, but rather a starting point for strategic planning and decision-making. The analysis should be regularly reviewed and updated to account for changes in the internal and external business environment.

PESTEL Analysis

PESTEL analysis is a framework that organizations use to analyze and understand the broader external factors that can impact their business environment. It examines the Political, Economic, Social, Technological, Environmental, and Legal factors that may influence an organization's operations, opportunities, and risks. The acronym PESTEL helps in categorizing and assessing these different factors. Here is a closer look at each component of PESTEL:

1. Political Factors: Political factors encompass the influence of government and political systems on business operations. This includes factors such as government policies, legislation, regulations, political stability, taxation policies, trade regulations, and political ideologies. Assessing political factors helps organizations understand how changes in government policies and regulations can impact their operations and industry.

2. Economic Factors: Economic factors refer to the economic conditions and trends that can influence business operations. These factors include economic growth, inflation rates, exchange rates, interest rates, income levels, unemployment rates, and consumer spending patterns. Organizations analyze economic factors to understand market conditions, demand for their products or services, and potential implications on their business strategies.

3. Social Factors: Social factors relate to social and cultural influences that can affect organizations. This includes demographic trends, consumer attitudes and behaviors, lifestyle changes, social values, cultural norms, and population demographics. Analyzing social factors helps organizations align their strategies with changing consumer preferences, societal values, and emerging market trends.

4. Technological Factors: Technological factors encompass technological advancements and innovations that impact businesses and industries. This includes advancements in information technology, automation, digitalization, artificial intelligence, the internet of things (IoT), and other technological breakthroughs. Assessing technological factors helps organizations embrace new technologies, identify opportunities for innovation, and adapt to changes in their industry.

5. Environmental Factors: Environmental factors encompass the ecological and environmental aspects affecting an organization. This includes factors such as climate change, environmental regulations, sustainability practices, natural disasters, and resource availability. Organizations analyze environmental factors to ensure compliance with regulations, embrace environmentally friendly practices, and manage any potential risks related to natural disasters or resource scarcity.

6. Legal Factors: Legal factors refer to the laws and regulations that organizations must abide by in their operations. This includes employment laws, consumer protection regulations, health and safety regulations, intellectual property rights, data protection laws, and industry-specific regulations. Understanding legal factors helps organizations comply with legal requirements, mitigate legal risks, and avoid potential legal challenges.

PESTEL analysis enables organizations to gain a comprehensive understanding of the external environment in which they operate. It helps in identifying opportunities and threats, anticipating challenges, formulating strategies, and making informed decisions to align with external factors. By considering these factors, organizations can enhance their ability to adapt to changes in the business environment, seize opportunities, and navigate potential risks. PESTEL analysis is often used in strategic planning, market research, and risk assessment processes.

Scenario Analysis

Scenario analysis is a strategic planning tool that involves creating different plausible future scenarios to help organizations anticipate and plan for potential outcomes and uncertainties. It is a method used to explore various hypothetical situations or "what-if" scenarios to gain insights into how different strategies or decisions may perform under different circumstances.

In scenario analysis, multiple scenarios are developed by considering various factors such as industry trends, market conditions, customer behavior, technological advancements, regulatory changes, and other external influences. These scenarios can range from optimistic to pessimistic, representing different levels of uncertainty and potential outcomes.

Once the scenarios are developed, organizations analyze each scenario to understand the potential impact on their business, operations, and objectives. By examining a range of scenarios, organizations can identify key drivers, risks, and opportunities associated with each scenario. This analysis aids in identifying potential strategies and actions that can be taken to capitalize on favorable scenarios or mitigate risks in unfavorable ones.

Scenario analysis can be useful in strategic decision-making, risk management, and contingency planning. It helps organizations to:

1. Anticipate and plan for uncertain future events or changes.
2. Assess the potential impact of different scenarios on their business, operations, and strategies.
3. Identify key risks, opportunities, and challenges associated with each scenario.
4. Evaluate the effectiveness of current strategies in different future environments.
5. Test and refine strategies and decision-making in a dynamic and uncertain business environment.
6. Improve preparedness and resilience to unexpected events or disruptions.

By considering multiple scenarios, organizations can enhance their strategic thinking and decision-making, enabling them to be more proactive, adaptable, and resilient in an ever-changing business landscape.

Failure Mode and Effects Analysis (FMEA)

Failure Mode and Effects Analysis (FMEA) is a systematic and proactive approach used by organizations to identify and prioritize potential failures or risks within a process, product, or system. It is commonly used in industries such as manufacturing, healthcare, automotive, aerospace, and software development. FMEA aims to prevent failures or mitigate their effects by identifying and addressing potential failure modes before they occur.

Here are some key aspects to understand about Failure Mode and Effects Analysis (FMEA):

1. Identification of Failure Modes: FMEA involves identifying and documenting all possible failure modes that can occur within the process, product, or system. Failure modes are potential ways in which a function, component, or process can fail to perform its intended purpose. They can range from minor errors or malfunctions to critical failures that pose significant risks.

2. Assessment of Severity: Each identified failure mode is assessed for its potential severity or impact on the process, product, or system. Severity ratings reflect the consequences of a failure mode, such as safety risks, customer dissatisfaction, environmental impact, or financial losses. Severity ratings assist in prioritizing risk mitigation efforts.

3. Analysis of Potential Causes: For each failure mode, potential causes or reasons for failure are identified. These causes can arise from design flaws, manufacturing errors, external influences, human factors, or other aspects of the process or system. Understanding the causes helps organizations pinpoint areas in need of improvements or corrective actions.

4. Detection and Prevention: FMEA considers the capability of the organization's existing controls or detection mechanisms to identify or prevent each failure mode. Detection ratings are assigned to evaluate the effectiveness of existing control measures. This helps in determining whether additional controls or improvements are necessary to minimize the likelihood of failure or to detect it at an early stage.

5. Calculation of Risk Priority Number (RPN): The RPN is a numerical value calculated by multiplying the severity, occurrence, and detection ratings. The RPN provides a prioritization of failure modes based on their potential risk level. High RPN values indicate failure modes that require immediate attention and significant risk mitigation efforts.

6. Mitigation and Action Plans: Based on the identified failure modes and their associated risks, organizations develop mitigation strategies and action plans. These plans outline specific actions to reduce the severity, occurrence, or detectability of failure modes. Mitigation measures can include process improvements, design changes, enhanced quality controls, training programs, or updated procedures.

7. Continuous Improvement: FMEA is an iterative process that promotes continuous improvement. Organizations should regularly review and update their FMEA as new information becomes available, process changes occur, or lessons are learned from incidents or failures. This ensures that FMEA remains dynamic and reflects the organization's evolving risk landscape.

FMEA contributes to quality improvement, risk management, and prevention of failures throughout the lifecycle of a process, product, or system. It helps organizations identify potential failure modes, assess their impacts, and take proactive measures to avoid or minimize risks. By effectively implementing FMEA, organizations can enhance customer satisfaction, improve product reliability, achieve operational excellence, and mitigate potential risks.

Monte Carlo Simulation

Monte Carlo Simulation is a computational technique that is used to model and analyze the uncertainty and variability of a system or process. It is named after the famous Monte Carlo casino in Monaco, known for its games of chance and randomness. This simulation method relies on generating many random samples or scenarios to simulate the behavior and outcomes of a complex system.

Here is a detailed explanation of how Monte Carlo Simulation works:

1. Define Input Parameters: The first step in Monte Carlo Simulation is to identify and define the input parameters that influence the system or process being modeled. These input parameters can be variables such as costs, durations, probabilities, demand, or any other factors that have uncertainty associated with them. The values of these parameters are typically represented as probability distributions.

2. Generate Random Samples: Random samples are generated for each input parameter based on its defined probability distribution. The selection of random samples reflects the uncertainty or variability associated with the input parameters. The number of samples generated depends on the desired accuracy and level of detail.

3. Run Simulations: Each random sample generated is used to simulate the system or process being modeled. The simulation applies the input values to the model or algorithm representing the system and computes the corresponding output or results.

4. Analyze Results: The outputs generated from the simulations are analyzed to gain insights into the behavior of the system or process. Statistical techniques and metrics are used to summarize and interpret the results. These metrics may include averages, percentiles, ranges, or other relevant statistics.

5. Evaluate Risk and Uncertainty: Monte Carlo Simulation allows for the assessment of risk and uncertainty associated with the system or process being analyzed. By generating multiple scenarios with different input values, it provides a more comprehensive understanding of the range of possible outcomes and their probabilities.

6. Sensitivity Analysis: Monte Carlo Simulation also enables sensitivity analysis, which determines the impact of each input parameter on the output or results. By varying the values of individual parameters and observing the corresponding changes in the output, organizations can identify the most influential factors and prioritize their attention accordingly.

7. Optimize Decision Making: The insights gained from the Monte Carlo Simulation can help organizations make informed decisions and optimize their strategies. It allows for the exploration of different scenarios, consideration of trade-offs, and evaluation of the potential outcomes of decisions under uncertainty.

The Monte Carlo Simulation finds applications in various fields such as finance, engineering, project management, healthcare, and logistics. It is particularly useful in complex systems with multiple variables and interdependencies, where traditional analytical methods may not capture the full range and impact of uncertainties. By performing numerous simulations, Monte Carlo methods offer a powerful tool for decision-makers to understand risks, manage uncertainties, and enhance the overall quality of their decision-making processes.

Chapter Twenty-Six

Risk Response Planning and Implementation

Risk response planning and implementation is a critical step in the overall risk management process. It involves identifying potential risks, analyzing their potential impacts, and developing strategies to mitigate or respond to these risks. This comprehensive approach helps organizations prevent or minimize the negative consequences of risks.

The first step in risk response planning is to identify potential risks. This can be done through various methods such as brainstorming sessions, reviewing historical data, conducting risk assessments, or consulting experts. It is important to consider both internal and external risks, as well as their likelihood and potential impact on the organization.

Once risks are identified, the next step is to analyze their potential impacts. This involves assessing the severity of the risks and determining their probability of occurrence. The severity of a risk refers to the magnitude of its potential consequences, while the probability refers to the likelihood of the risk happening.

There are four main strategies for risk response: avoidance, transfer, mitigation, and acceptance. Avoidance involves eliminating or removing the risk altogether. This may include discontinuing a certain activity or not pursuing a particular opportunity. Transfer involves shifting the risk to another party, usually through insurance or contractual agreements. Mitigation involves reducing the impact or likelihood of the risk through proactive measures such as implementing controls or safeguards. Acceptance involves acknowledging the risk and its potential consequences without taking any specific action.

When implementing risk response strategies, it is important to prioritize them based on the severity and probability of the risks. High-severity and high-probability risks should be addressed first, followed by those with lesser impacts. This ensures that resources are allocated effectively to mitigate the most significant risks.

Risk response planning should also consider the cost and feasibility of each strategy. Some strategies may be more expensive or difficult to implement than others. Organizations need to weigh the potential benefits against the associated costs to determine the most appropriate response. Additionally, legal and regulatory requirements should be considered to ensure compliance.

Communication and coordination are key during the implementation phase. It is crucial to involve all relevant stakeholders, such as management, employees, and external partners, to ensure a unified approach to risk response. Clear roles and responsibilities should be defined, and regular updates should be provided to keep everyone informed.

To effectively implement risk response strategies, organizations may need to revise their policies, procedures, and processes. They may also need to invest in training programs to enhance employees' skills and knowledge related to risk management. This ensures that everyone is equipped to respond to risks effectively.

Monitoring and reassessment are important throughout the implementation phase. Risks may change over time, and new risks may emerge. It is essential to regularly review and update the risk response strategies to ensure they remain effective. This may involve conducting periodic risk assessments, monitoring key indicators, and seeking feedback from stakeholders.

To facilitate risk response implementation, organizations can use various tools and techniques. These may include risk registers, which document and track identified risks and their associated response strategies. Decision trees and matrices can help in evaluating different response options and selecting the most appropriate ones. Risk management software can also assist in automating and streamlining the risk response process.

In some cases, organizations may need to adjust their risk response strategies based on the outcomes of the implemented measures. For example, if a mitigation strategy does not effectively reduce the likelihood or impact of a risk as anticipated, it may be necessary to revise or replace it with a more effective approach.

Collaboration and knowledge sharing are crucial during risk response implementation. Organizations can learn from each other by exchanging best practices and lessons learned. Industry networks, conferences, and forums provide opportunities for organizations to connect and share their experiences in managing risks.

Risk response planning and implementation should be an ongoing and iterative process. As the business environment evolves, new risks may emerge, and existing risks may change. Regular reviews and updates to the risk response strategies help organizations stay resilient and adaptable in the face of uncertainty.

In conclusion, risk response planning and implementation play a vital role in managing and mitigating risks. By identifying potential risks, analyzing their impacts, and developing appropriate response strategies, organizations can enhance their ability to prevent or minimize negative consequences. Effective implementation involves clear communication, coordination, and monitoring, as well as continuous learning and adaptation. By adopting a comprehensive approach to risk response, organizations can better protect their interests and achieve their objectives.

Risk Response Strategies

Risk response strategies are essential to effectively manage risks within an organization. These strategies help organizations prepare, prevent, mitigate, or respond to potential risks and their impacts. By applying the appropriate risk response strategies, organizations can minimize the negative consequences of risks and protect their interests.

One common risk response strategy is avoidance. This involves eliminating or removing the risk altogether. Organizations may choose to avoid a risk by discontinuing a certain activity or not pursuing a particular opportunity. Although avoidance may eliminate the risk, it can also result in missed opportunities for growth or innovation.

Transfer is another risk response strategy that involves shifting the risk to another party. This is often done through insurance or contractual agreements. Transferring the risk allows organizations to transfer the financial burden or responsibility to another entity. However, it is important to note that the risk is not eliminated, but rather managed by a different party.

Risk mitigation involves reducing the impact or likelihood of the risk through proactive measures. Mitigation strategies may include implementing controls, safeguards, or redundancies to prevent or minimize the occurrence of a risk. These measures provide a layer of protection and help organizations better manage potential impacts.

Acceptance is a risk response strategy where organizations acknowledge the risk and its potential consequences without taking any specific action. This strategy is typically used for risks with low impact or probability, where the cost of addressing the risk outweighs the potential benefits. Acceptance does not mean ignoring the risk; it means consciously deciding not to implement any specific risk response measures.

One risk response strategy that combines elements of both acceptance and mitigation is risk sharing. In this strategy, organizations accept the risk but collaborate with external parties to mitigate its potential impact. This can be done through partnerships, joint ventures, or alliances, where different organizations pool their resources and expertise to manage shared risks.

Another risk response strategy is diversification. This involves spreading the risk across different areas or markets, reducing the potential impact of a single risk event. By diversifying their operations, organizations can minimize the vulnerabilities associated with specific risks and enhance their overall resilience.

Contingency planning is a risk response strategy that involves developing a plan to respond to potential risk events. This plan outlines the steps to be taken in case a risk event occurs, including predefined actions, escalation procedures, and communication protocols. Contingency plans help organizations respond quickly and effectively to unforeseen situations.

Fallback planning is like contingency planning but focuses on identifying alternative strategies or approaches to be implemented if the primary risk response measures fail. Fallback plans provide organizations with a backup option in case the initial risk response strategies do not achieve the desired results.

Another risk response strategy is building redundancy. This involves creating backups or duplicates of critical systems, processes, or resources. By having redundant systems in place, organizations can continue their operations even if a risk event causes a disruption or failure in one area.

Risk avoidance is a strategy that involves taking actions or implementing measures to prevent a risk event from occurring. This may include implementing strict policies, procedures, or controls to minimize the likelihood of a risk event. Risk avoidance is particularly useful for risks that are highly likely to occur and have significant negative consequences.

Risk reduction is a strategy that focuses on reducing the severity of a risk if it were to occur. This may involve implementing safety measures, conducting training programs, or performing regular inspections and maintenance. Risk reduction strategies aim to minimize the potential impact of a risk event on the organization.

A risk response strategy that emphasizes resilience is business continuity planning. This involves developing a comprehensive plan to ensure that critical business functions can continue or be quickly restored in the event of a disruption or crisis. Business continuity plans outline the necessary resources, processes, and procedures to recover from a risk event and resume normal operations.

Reactive strategies are risk responses that are implemented after a risk event has occurred. These strategies are focused on minimizing the impacts and restoring normal operations. Reactive strategies may include damage control, incident response procedures, or post-incident analysis to learn from the event and prevent similar risks in the future.

Proactive strategies, on the other hand, are risk responses that are implemented before a risk event occurs. These strategies aim to prevent or mitigate risks by taking preventive measures. Proactive strategies can include risk assessments, risk audits, and continuous monitoring to identify potential risks and address them before they escalate.

One risk response strategy specifically designed for financial risks is hedging. Hedging involves taking offsetting positions in financial markets to minimize the impact of financial risks such as currency fluctuations or interest rate changes. This strategy is commonly used in international trade, where organizations try to protect themselves from potential fluctuations in exchange rates.

A risk response strategy that involves embracing risks is innovation. Organizations that embrace risks are willing to explore new ideas, technologies, or markets, knowing that some risks are necessary for growth and progress. Innovation allows organizations to adapt to changing circumstances, seize opportunities, and gain a competitive edge.

Collaboration is a risk response strategy that involves working together with other organizations or stakeholders to collectively manage risks. This can include sharing information, resources, or expertise to address common risks. Collaboration helps organizations pool their knowledge and resources to better understand and manage risks collectively.

Another risk response strategy that focuses on external risks is active monitoring. Active monitoring involves regularly assessing the external environment, such as changes in regulations, market trends, or competitor activities. Active monitoring helps organizations stay ahead of potential risks and take proactive measures to mitigate them.

Scenario planning is a risk response strategy that involves developing different scenarios or future projections to anticipate potential risks and plan accordingly. By creating hypothetical situations, organizations can evaluate their preparedness and identify areas that require improvement. Scenario planning helps organizations proactively respond to risks by considering multiple possible futures.

Internal controls are an important risk response strategy that helps organizations manage risks related to internal processes, financial reporting, and compliance. Internal controls ensure that operations are carried out effectively, efficiently, and in accordance with relevant laws and regulations. Strong internal controls provide assurance that risks are managed appropriately.

One risk response strategy that focuses on reputational risks is public relations and communication. This involves actively managing and monitoring the organization's public image, addressing any negative publicity or rumors promptly, and maintaining transparent and open communication with stakeholders. Effective public relations help organizations protect their reputation and credibility, thereby reducing reputational risks.

Employee training and education are risk response strategies that focus on building a risk-aware culture within an organization. By providing employees with the necessary knowledge and skills to identify and respond to risks, organizations empower their workforce to actively contribute to risk management efforts. Training and education help create a risk-conscious environment where employees are vigilant to potential risks.

Regularly reviewing and updating risk management plans and strategies is a risk response strategy that ensures the effectiveness and relevance of risk responses. By regularly assessing the internal and external environment, organizations can identify new risks, evaluate the effectiveness of existing strategies, and make necessary adjustments. Continuous review and improvement help organizations stay proactive and adaptive in managing risks.

In conclusion, risk response strategies are vital for organizations to effectively manage and mitigate risks. By utilizing a combination of strategies based on the nature and severity of risks, organizations can minimize the potential negative consequences. The selection and implementation of risk response strategies should be done comprehensively and systematically, considering factors such as cost, feasibility, impact, and regulation. Regular monitoring and evaluation of risk response strategies ensure their effectiveness and enable organizations to adapt to evolving risks.

Avoidance Strategies

Advanced strategies of risk response planning and implementation go beyond the basic risk response strategies discussed earlier to provide more proactive and comprehensive approaches to managing risks. These strategies aim to address risks holistically and enhance an organization's ability to prevent, mitigate, or respond to potential risks effectively. Here are some of the advanced strategies:

1. Risk Pooling: Risk pooling involves sharing risks with other organizations through collaborative arrangements. By combining resources and expertise, organizations can better manage risks collectively and achieve economies of scale in risk management efforts.

2. Enterprise Risk Management (ERM): ERM is a comprehensive and integrated approach to risk management that considers risks across the entire organization. It involves identifying, assessing, and managing risks at an enterprise-wide level, enabling organizations to have a holistic view of risks and develop coordinated responses.

3. Resilience Planning: Resilience planning focuses on enhancing an organization's ability to bounce back from disruptive events or crises. It involves developing strategies to strengthen the organization's capacity to withstand and recover from shocks, ensuring business continuity and minimizing the downtime of critical operations.

4. Integrated Risk and Performance Management: This strategy involves linking risk management with the organization's overall performance management framework. By integrating risk considerations into decision-making processes and performance measurements, organizations can align risk management efforts with their strategic objectives and enhance overall organizational performance.

5. Risk Transfer Mechanisms: Advanced risk transfer mechanisms go beyond traditional insurance and contractual agreements. These mechanisms explore alternative risk transfer options such as securitization, captives, or contingent capital solutions to effectively manage and transfer risks in a more tailored and cost-effective manner.

6. Predictive Analytics and Data Driven Decision-Making: By leveraging advanced analytics and data, organizations can gain insights into potential risks, anticipate future trends, and make data-driven decisions. Predictive analytics can help identify potential risks and assess their likelihood and severity, enabling organizations to implement risk response measures in a more targeted and effective manner.

7. Cybersecurity Measures: Given the increasing prevalence of cyber threats, advanced risk response strategies in this domain involve robust cybersecurity measures. These include implementing advanced firewall systems, intrusion detection and prevention systems, encryption methods, and regular security audits to protect sensitive data and systems from cyber risks.

8. Business and Process Automation: Automating business processes can help reduce operational risks, improve efficiency, and ensure consistency in risk response implementation. By using advanced technologies such as robotic process automation (RPA) or artificial intelligence (AI), organizations can streamline workflows, reduce human error, and enhance risk management capabilities.

9. Continuous Risk Monitoring and Reporting: Advanced risk response strategies emphasize real-time risk monitoring and reporting to ensure timely identification and response to risks. With the help of technology, organizations can establish continuous monitoring systems that provide alerts and updates on emerging risks, enabling faster response and mitigation efforts.

10. Scenario Analysis: Scenario analysis goes beyond traditional risk assessment methods by simulating various scenarios and their potential impacts on the organization. By considering a range of possible future events, organizations can proactively identify risks, assess their consequences, and develop response strategies.

11. Environmental and Social Responsibility: Organizations are increasingly focusing on integrating environmental and social responsibility into their risk response strategies. By considering factors such as climate change, sustainability, and social impact, organizations can enhance their ability to respond to risks arising from these areas and contribute to long-term resilience.

12. Agile Risk Management: Agile risk management involves adopting an iterative and adaptive approach to risk

response planning and implementation. This strategy allows organizations to respond quickly to changing risk dynamics, adjust risk response measures as necessary, and continuously improve risk management processes.

13. Red Team Testing: Red team testing is a proactive approach to risk response implementation, where an independent team assesses an organization's systems, processes, and controls to identify vulnerabilities and weaknesses. This enables organizations to strengthen their risk management practices and address potential gaps before they are exploited by real-world risks.

14. Business Intelligence and Predictive Modeling: By leveraging business intelligence tools and predictive modeling techniques, organizations can anticipate potential risks and their impacts, enabling them to implement more targeted and effective risk response strategies. These advanced analytical methods help organizations make informed decisions based on data-driven insights.

15. Cultural and Behavioral Changes: Advanced risk response strategies focus on fostering a risk-aware culture and promoting risk-conscious behaviors within an organization. This involves providing continuous education and training, raising awareness about risks and their potential impacts, and encouraging employees to actively contribute to risk management efforts.

Incorporating these advanced strategies into risk response planning and implementation can significantly enhance an organization's risk management capabilities and ensure a proactive and comprehensive approach to managing risks. By considering a wide range of factors, adopting new technologies and approaches, and continuously improving risk management processes, organizations can better protect their interests and achieve their objectives.

Transfer Strategies

Transfer strategies in risk response planning and implementation involve shifting the financial burden or responsibility of a risk to another party. These strategies help organizations manage their risks by transferring them to entities that are better equipped to handle or absorb them. Here are various transfer strategies commonly used:

Insurance: One of the most common transfer strategies is to purchase insurance policies that cover potential risks. Insurance transfers the financial consequences of a risk to the insurance company in exchange for premium payments. Organizations can choose different types of insurance, such as property insurance, liability insurance, or business interruption insurance, depending on their specific risks.

Contracts and Agreements: Transferring risks through contracts and agreements involves allocating specific risks and responsibilities to other parties. By clearly defining the roles, obligations, and liabilities of each party in a contract, organizations can transfer risks associated with a project, partnership, or any other business relationship.

Outsourcing: Outsourcing involves contracting another organization to perform specific activities or functions on behalf of the organization. By outsourcing certain tasks, organizations can transfer operational risks associated with those tasks to the outsourcing party.

Subcontracting: Similar to outsourcing, subcontracting involves delegating specific components of a project or service to subcontractors. Organizations can transfer risks associated with those components to the subcontractors, who take on the responsibility for delivering the assigned tasks.

Joint Ventures: Joint ventures involve partnering with other organizations to pursue a specific opportunity or project. By sharing the risks and rewards of the venture, organizations can transfer a portion of the risks to their joint venture partners.

Co-insurance: Co-insurance is a transfer strategy where organizations share the insurance coverage and costs with another party. Instead of fully transferring the risk to the insurance company, organizations enter into co-insurance agreements where both parties share the financial burden.

Reinsurance: Reinsurance is a strategy where insurance companies transfer a portion of their risks to other insurance companies. This allows insurers to protect themselves from catastrophic losses by spreading the risks across a broader pool of insurers.

Hedging: Hedging is commonly used to transfer financial risks, such as currency fluctuations or commodity price risks. Organizations can use financial instruments like futures contracts, options, or swaps to lock in fixed prices or exchange rates, thereby transferring the financial risks to the counterparties involved in the transactions.

Offshoring and Nearshoring: Offshoring involves transferring certain business activities or operations to overseas locations, while nearshoring involves transferring them to nearby countries. By taking advantage of lower costs or specific expertise available in those regions, organizations can transfer some of the associated risks, such as labor market volatility, to the offshore or nearshore locations.

Risk Transfer Within a Corporate Structure: Organizations with multiple subsidiaries or divisions can transfer risks among these entities through internal arrangements or financial instruments. This allows risks to be allocated to specific business units or entities that are better able to manage them.

Guarantees and Indemnities: Organizations can transfer risks by obtaining guarantees or indemnities from third parties. These guarantees can provide financial protection or assurance that the third party will assume responsibility for certain risks in case of default or loss.

Performance Bonds: Performance bonds are typically used in construction or service contracts to transfer the risk of non-performance by one party to a surety company. If the party fails to meet its contractual obligations, the surety company compensates the other party for the losses incurred.

Letters of Credit: Letters of credit are commonly used in international trade to transfer the payment risk between buyers and sellers. The issuing bank guarantees the payment to the seller upon submission of specified documents, reducing the risk of non-payment.

Risk Pooling: Risk pooling involves transferring risks to a pool or consortium formed by multiple organizations. By participating in the pool, organizations share the risks and allocate the financial burden collectively, reducing the impact of a risk event on individual organizations.

Catastrophe Bonds: Catastrophe bonds, also known as CAT bonds, are a type of financial instrument that transfers risks associated with natural disasters, such as earthquakes or hurricanes, to capital market investors. If a specified event occurs, investors bear the losses, relieving the issuing organization from some of the financial burden.

Contingent Liability Insurance: With contingent liability insurance, organizations transfer the risk of potential future liabilities, such as legal claims, to an insurance company. This provides financial protection in case the contingent liability becomes a reality.

Risk Retention Groups (RRGs): Risk retention groups are specialized insurance entities formed by businesses in similar industries to assume and self-insure certain risks collectively. By sharing the risks among the members of the group, organizations transfer the financial impact of risks to the group.

Securitization: Securitization involves the transformation of illiquid assets or risks into tradable securities. This allows organizations to transfer the risks associated with these assets to investors who are willing to assume them in exchange for the potential returns linked to the underlying assets.

Derivatives: Derivatives, such as options or futures contracts, provide a means to transfer financial risks associated with underlying assets or commodities. Organizations can enter into derivative contracts with counterparties to transfer the risks of price fluctuations or changes in market conditions.

Residual Value Insurance: Residual value insurance is commonly used in leasing agreements for assets with uncertain future values, such as aircraft or heavy machinery. The lessor transfers the risk of the asset's residual value to the insurance company, ensuring a guaranteed value at the end of the lease term.

Deposit Insurance: Deposit insurance is a form of risk transfer in the banking sector. Financial institutions pay premiums to a deposit insurance corporation to transfer the risk of depositors' funds to a centralized pool. In the event of a bank failure or default, the deposit insurance corporation guarantees the repayment of eligible deposits up to a certain limit.

Indemnification Clauses: Transferring risk through indemnification clauses in contracts involves one party assuming responsibility for specific risks and agreeing to compensate the other party in case of losses or damages. Indemnification clauses are commonly seen in commercial contracts, where the risks associated with performance or non-performance are allocated between the parties.

Counterparty Risk Management: Managing counterparty risk involves implementing procedures to assess and monitor the creditworthiness and stability of counterparties. By conducting due diligence and regularly reviewing the financial health of counterparties, organizations can proactively transfer the risk of potential defaults or non-performance by selecting reliable partners.

In summary, transfer strategies in risk response planning and implementation enable organizations to shift risks to other parties better equipped to manage them. By utilizing insurance, contracts, outsourcing, financial instruments, or other mechanisms, organizations can effectively transfer the financial impact and responsibility of risks, increasing their ability to focus on their core activities while mitigating potential losses. It is important to assess the costs, benefits, and feasibility of each transfer strategy to ensure the most appropriate risk response approach is adopted.

Mitigation Strategies

Mitigation strategies in risk response planning and implementation focus on reducing the likelihood or impact of risks. These strategies involve implementing measures to prevent, minimize, or control risks to protect an organization's interests. Here are various mitigation strategies commonly used:

Risk Assessments: Risk assessments involve systematically identifying and evaluating risks. By conducting thorough assessments, organizations gain a better understanding of risks and can develop targeted mitigation strategies.

Control Implementation: Implementing controls, safeguards, or procedures is a key mitigation strategy. Controls may include physical security measures, access controls, cybersecurity systems, or safety protocols to reduce the likelihood or impact of risks.

Redundancy: Building redundancy involves creating backups or duplicates of critical systems, processes, or resources. This ensures that if one component fails, alternatives are available to minimize the impact of risks.

Maintenance and Inspection: Regular maintenance and inspection help identify potential issues before they escalate into risks. By proactively addressing maintenance needs, organizations can prevent failures or malfunctions that could lead to risks.

Training and Education: Providing training and education to employees is essential for risk mitigation. By ensuring that employees are aware of potential risks and understand the appropriate procedures, organizations can reduce the likelihood of human error and improve overall risk management capabilities.

Process Improvement: Continuously improving processes helps identify inefficiencies, vulnerabilities, or gaps that could lead to risks. By refining workflows, organizations can mitigate risks, enhance productivity, and reduce the probability of errors or failures.

Safety Protocols: Establishing and enforcing safety protocols, such as wearing protective gear or following specific procedures, reduces the likelihood of accidents, injuries, or workplace hazards.

Emergency Preparedness: Developing and implementing emergency response plans and protocols is crucial for mitigating risks. By being prepared for potential emergencies, organizations can respond effectively, minimize damage, and protect the safety of employees, customers, and stakeholders.

Supplier Management: Managing and evaluating suppliers' performance and capabilities helps mitigate risks associated with supply chain disruptions, quality issues, or non-compliance. By selecting reliable and qualified suppliers, organizations can reduce the likelihood of risks affecting their operations.

Monitoring and Early Warning Systems: Implementing monitoring systems and early warning mechanisms allows organizations to detect indicators of potential risks early. This enables prompt action to prevent or mitigate the impact of risks before they escalate.

Environmental Management: Implementing environmental management practices helps mitigate risks associated with environmental impacts, such as pollution, resource depletion, or climate change. By adhering to environmental regulations and adopting sustainable practices, organizations minimize the potential risks associated with environmental impacts.

Human Resources Practices: Effective human resources practices contribute to risk mitigation by ensuring proper recruitment, training, and performance management processes. This helps reduce the likelihood and impact of risks associated with employee misconduct, incompetence, or non-compliance.

Change Management Processes: Effective change management processes help mitigate risks associated with organizational changes. By following structured approaches and involving stakeholders in decision-making, organizations can assess and control potential risks during periods of transition.

Stakeholder Engagement: Engaging and communicating with stakeholders helps organizations identify and address potential risks. By building relationships and gathering feedback, organizations can obtain valuable insights, identify risks, and gain support in risk mitigation efforts.

Compliance Monitoring: Monitoring and ensuring compliance with legal, regulatory, and industry standards reduces the risk of penalties, litigation, or reputational damage. Organizations should establish robust compliance frameworks and regularly review and update them to stay informed and proactive.

Business Continuity Planning: Developing business continuity plans helps organizations mitigate risks associated with disruptions or crises. These plans outline procedures to ensure critical operations can continue or be quickly restored, minimizing the impact of risk events.

Data Security and Privacy Measures: Implementing robust data security and privacy measures helps mitigate risks associated with data breaches or privacy violations. By adopting encryption methods, access controls, and security protocols, organizations can protect sensitive data and minimize the impact of cybersecurity risks.

In summary, mitigation strategies tackle risks by implementing proactive measures to prevent, minimize, or control potential negative impacts. Organizations assess their risks, develop and implement controls, invest in maintenance and training, ensure compliance, and plan for emergencies. By focusing on risk mitigation, organizations can protect their interests, enhance operational efficiency, and strengthen resilience. It is crucial to tailor these strategies to the specific risks and context of the organization to achieve the desired outcomes.

Acceptance Strategies

Acceptance strategies in risk response planning and implementation involve acknowledging and accepting risks without taking specific action to mitigate them. These strategies are typically used for risks with lower impact or probability, where the cost of addressing the risk outweighs the potential benefits. Here are the key objectives of acceptance strategies:

Risk Evaluation: The first objective of acceptance strategies is to evaluate the risks thoroughly. This includes assessing the likelihood and potential impacts of risks and considering the organization's risk tolerance and risk appetite. Through comprehensive risk evaluation, organizations determine which risks are acceptable and can be managed without implementing specific risk response measures.

Cost-Benefit Analysis: Acceptance strategies involve conducting a cost-benefit analysis to determine whether the potential costs of mitigating a risk outweigh the potential benefits. By evaluating the financial implications of implementing risk response measures, organizations can make informed decisions about accepting certain risks instead of adopting costly mitigation measures.

Resource Allocation: By accepting lower-impact or lower-probability risks, organizations can allocate their resources more efficiently. Instead of investing resources in managing or mitigating risks with minimal potential impact, these resources can be redirected to activities that contribute to the organization's strategic objectives and overall success.

Avoiding Overreaction: Acceptance strategies help organizations avoid overreacting to risks that are unlikely to occur or have minimal consequences. By objectively assessing risks and determining their potential impact, organizations can avoid unnecessary expenditures, distractions, or disruptions caused by excessive focus on unlikely risks.

Strategic Decision-Making: Acceptance strategies support strategic decision-making by allowing organizations to prioritize their efforts and allocate resources to areas where risks have greater potential impact. By accepting lower-consequence risks, organizations can concentrate their attention and resources on managing more critical risks that could significantly impact their performance or objectives.

Focus on Core Competencies: Accepting certain risks allows organizations to focus on their core competencies and primary business activities. Instead of diverting resources or attention to risk mitigation measures outside their expertise, organizations can concentrate on their areas of strength where they can maximize their competitive advantage and value creation.

Resilience Building: Acceptance strategies contribute to building organizational resilience. By accepting and understanding certain risks, organizations are better prepared to respond to them if they occur unexpectedly. This enables organizations to adapt and recover more efficiently in the face of risks, ultimately enhancing their long-term viability and sustainability.

Risk Transparency: Accepting risks promotes transparency and accountability within organizations. It requires organizations to communicate these identified risks openly to relevant stakeholders, including employees, shareholders, customers, and regulators. Transparent risk disclosure establishes trust and demonstrates a proactive approach to risk management.

Risk Reporting: Acceptance strategies involve developing effective risk reporting mechanisms to ensure that risks are consistently monitored and communicated. These strategies consider the importance of providing accurate and timely risk information to relevant parties, enabling informed decision-making and regulatory compliance.

Risk Monitoring and Review: Organizations that accept risks need to establish robust monitoring and review processes. This ensures that the accepted risks remain within acceptable tolerance levels and that any changes in their probability or impact are promptly identified and reassessed.

Contingency Planning: Although accepting risks might not involve direct mitigation measures, organizations should still have contingency plans in place. Contingency planning outlines the steps and measures to be taken if accepted risks materialize unexpectedly, helping organizations respond effectively and minimize potential negative consequences.

Regulatory Compliance: Acceptance strategies necessitate organizations to adhere to applicable laws, regulations, and industry standards related to risk management. By demonstrating compliance, organizations enhance their reputation, maintain stakeholder trust, and avoid potential legal or regulatory penalties.

Stakeholder Engagement: Acceptance strategies require organizations to engage with stakeholders effectively. This includes communication, consultation, and collaboration with stakeholders to ensure shared understanding and acceptance of risks. Engaging stakeholders also fosters a culture of risk awareness and accountability across the organization.

Disciplined Risk Management: Accepting certain risks does not imply neglecting them. Instead, it highlights the need for disciplined risk management practices. Organizations should establish clear risk management frameworks, processes, and responsibilities to ensure that accepted risks are consistently monitored, evaluated, and managed within the defined risk tolerance levels.

Learning from Failures: Acceptance strategies provide opportunities for organizations to learn from failures and manage risks more effectively in the future. By analyzing past risk incidents and their consequences, organizations can identify areas for improvement, update risk management practices, and enhance their overall risk resilience.

Innovation and Growth: Accepting risks can foster a culture of innovation and growth. Organizations that are open to accepting and managing risks are more likely to explore new ideas, experiment with emerging technologies, and seize opportunities for growth and transformation.

Cost Reduction: Accepting certain risks reduces the need for expensive risk mitigation measures, leading to cost reductions. Organizations can allocate the saved resources towards investments that offer higher returns or contribute to their strategic objectives.

Focus on High-Impact Risks: By accepting lower-impact risks, organizations can allocate more resources and attention to managing high-impact risks that may have severe consequences. This ensures that limited resources are targeted towards risks that can significantly impact performance or disrupt operations.

Prevention of Risk Overwhelm: Acceptance strategies prevent organizations from becoming overwhelmed with the sheer volume of risks they face. By accepting risks that have minimal impact or probability, organizations can maintain a realistic view of their risk landscape and avoid being excessively burdened by addressing every potential risk scenario.

Optimization of Risk Response Efforts: Accepting certain risks helps organizations optimize their risk response efforts by focusing on risks that truly require mitigation or response. By accepting lower-risk scenarios, organizations can allocate their resources efficiently and prioritize developing robust response strategies for more critical risks.

Flexibility and Adaptability: Acceptance strategies allow organizations to be more flexible and adaptable in their risk management approach. It acknowledges that not all risks can be controlled or mitigated, and organizations need to be prepared to respond, learn, and adapt in the face of unexpected events or developments.

Risk-Informed Decision-Making: Organizations that adopt acceptance strategies embed a risk-informed decision-making approach across their operations. This ensures that risks are considered in decision-making processes at all levels, allowing organizations to make informed choices that balance potential risks with potential rewards.

Quantification of Risk Tolerance: Acceptance strategies involve quantifying the organization's risk tolerance. This provides a benchmark for determining acceptable risks and enables organizations to set clear thresholds and limits for managing risks within acceptable parameters.

Organizational Resilience Testing: Accepting certain risks allows organizations to test their resilience and response capabilities. It provides an opportunity to identify weaknesses in organizational structures, contingency plans, and response mechanisms, leading to improvements and enhancing overall organizational resilience.

Rational Risk Taking: Acceptance strategies enable organizations to take rational risks. They recognize that risk-taking is an inherent part of business and that calculated risk-taking can lead to innovation, growth, and competitive advantage. Organizations can leverage this strategic acceptance to achieve their objectives while managing potential downside risks.

Opportunity Identification: Acceptance strategies involve actively seeking opportunities within risks. By accepting certain risks, organizations can explore potential upside opportunities that could arise from these risks. This allows organizations to maximize their potential gains while accepting the associated risks.

In summary, acceptance strategies serve various objectives in risk response planning and implementation. They enable organizations to evaluate risks objectively, allocate resources effectively, focus on critical risks, enhance resilience, and maintain a balanced approach to risk management. By understanding and accepting certain risks, organizations can optimize their risk management efforts and make informed decisions that contribute to their long-term success.

Risk Monitoring and Control

Risk monitoring and control is a critical component of effective risk management. It involves systematic tracking, analysis, and control of identified risks throughout their lifecycle. The main objectives of risk monitoring and control are as follows:

Risk Identification: Risk monitoring and control aim to identify and document new risks, or changes in the likelihood or impact of existing risks. By continuously monitoring the internal and external environment, organizations can detect emerging risks, trends, or events that may affect their operations or objectives.

Real-Time Awareness: Risk monitoring and control provide organizations with real-time awareness of potential risks. This enables proactive decision-making and an early response to mitigate or exploit risks for the organization's benefit.

Compliance: Risk monitoring and control support compliance with laws, regulations, and industry standards. Organizations can track whether they are adhering to risk management guidelines or requirements, ensuring they meet their legal and ethical obligations.

Performance Evaluation: Monitoring and controlling risks allow organizations to evaluate their risk management performance. By tracking the effectiveness of risk mitigation measures, organizations can assess whether they are achieving their risk management objectives and identify areas for improvement.

Mitigation Effectiveness: Risk monitoring and control assess the effectiveness of implemented risk mitigation measures. By measuring how well these measures are reducing the likelihood or impact of risks, organizations can make informed decisions on adjusting or reinforcing their risk management strategies.

Early Warning Signs: Monitoring risks provides early warning signs of potential risk events. By identifying warning signals, organizations can take pre-emptive actions to prevent or minimize the impact of risks before they materialize.

Decision Support: Risk monitoring and control provide decision-makers with information and insights for sound decision-making. By having timely and accurate risk data, organizations can make informed choices and allocate resources effectively to manage risks.

Key Risk Indicators: Monitoring and controlling risks involve the identification and measurement of key risk indicators (KRIs). KRIs are quantifiable metrics that provide early indications of potential risk events, allowing organizations to take timely preventive or corrective actions.

Risk Appetite Alignment: Monitoring risks ensure that they are aligned with the organization's risk appetite. By tracking risks against predefined risk appetite thresholds, organizations can ensure that risks are managed within acceptable levels consistent with their strategic objectives and risk tolerance.

Control Validation: Monitoring and control activities validate the effectiveness of internal controls implemented to mitigate risks. This ensures that controls are functioning as intended and that any deficiencies are identified and addressed promptly.

Stakeholder Confidence: Effective risk monitoring and control help build stakeholder confidence. Organizations that actively monitor risks and promptly address any concerns demonstrate their commitment to risk management and stakeholder protection, enhancing trust and credibility.

Continuous Improvement: Through risk monitoring and control, organizations can identify opportunities for continuous improvement in their risk management processes, strategies, and controls. By analyzing data and monitoring trends, organizations can refine their risk management practices and enhance the overall effectiveness of their risk mitigation efforts.

Adaptability and Resilience: Monitoring risks allows organizations to adapt and respond to changing risk landscapes effectively. It helps organizations identify emerging risks and adjust their risk management strategies to maintain resilience and agility in the face of evolving threats.

Risk Reporting: Effective risk monitoring and control include regular risk reporting. Organizations can communicate risk information to relevant stakeholders, providing them with a comprehensive understanding of risk status, trends, and the effectiveness of risk mitigation efforts.

Incident Response: Risk monitoring and control facilitate prompt incident response. By continuously monitoring risks, organizations can detect and respond to risk events on time, minimizing potential negative consequences and ensuring business continuity.

Documentation and Record-Keeping: Risk monitoring and control involve maintaining systematic documentation and record-keeping of risk-related activities. This ensures transparency, supports accountability, and provides a historical record that can be used for analysis, audits, or regulatory compliance purposes.

Risk Culture Development: Risk monitoring and control contribute to the development of a risk-aware culture within organizations. By having robust monitoring mechanisms and encouraging reporting and communication of risks, organizations foster a culture where employees are proactive in identifying and addressing risks.

Early Action: Risk monitoring and control enable organizations to take early action when risks exceed established thresholds. By promptly responding to risks that are trending toward unacceptable levels, organizations can prevent or reduce their impact before they escalate into major issues.

Risk Register Maintenance: Risk monitoring and control activities maintain an up-to-date risk register. Organizations periodically review and update their risk registers to reflect new risks, changes in risk profiles, and the effectiveness of risk mitigation efforts.

Risk Communication: Effective risk monitoring and control facilitate effective communication about risks within the organization. This ensures that all relevant stakeholders are aware of potential risks, their status, and the actions being taken to manage them.

Trend Analysis: Risk monitoring and control involve trend analysis to identify patterns and assess the potential impacts of risks. By analyzing risk trends, organizations can anticipate potential future risks and their potential consequences, allowing for proactive risk management and mitigation.

Continuous Learning: Risk monitoring and control support organizational learning from risk-related incidents and experiences. By analyzing risks and their outcomes, organizations can identify lessons learned, implement corrective actions, and continuously improve their risk management practices.

In summary, risk monitoring and control activities are essential for organizations to effectively manage and mitigate risks. By continuously identifying, assessing, and controlling risks, organizations can enhance their risk management performance, ensure compliance, and make informed decisions to protect their interests and achieve their objectives. Organizations must establish robust and proactive risk monitoring and control processes tailored to their specific needs and risk appetite.

Key Risk Indicators (KRIs)

Key Risk Indicators (KRIs) are quantifiable measures used to assess the likelihood or potential impact of specific risks. They serve as early warning signals by tracking and monitoring changes in risk levels, enabling organizations to take timely preventive or corrective actions. Here are the reasons why KRIs exist and their key attributes:

Early Detection: KRIs exist to provide early detection of potential risk events. By identifying and monitoring key indicators of risk, organizations can take proactive measures to prevent or mitigate the impact of risks before they escalate.

Preventive Action: KRIs help organizations identify risks before they materialize, allowing them to take preventive actions. By tracking quantitative metrics that are closely associated with specific risks, organizations can intervene early to minimize the likelihood or severity of adverse events.

Proactive Risk Management: KRIs support a proactive approach to risk management. Instead of relying solely on reactive measures, organizations can use KRIs to anticipate risks and implement appropriate risk response strategies promptly.

Objective Measurement: KRIs provide objective and measurable data points to assess risk levels. This helps organizations evaluate risks in a consistent and standardized manner, enhancing risk transparency and enabling more informed decision-making.

Customization: KRIs can be tailored to the specific needs and circumstances of an organization. Organizations can define KRIs based on their unique risk profile, industry, and strategic objectives, ensuring that the indicators used are relevant and meaningful for their risk management efforts.

Alignment with Risk Appetite: KRIs allow organizations to align risk management activities with their risk appetite. Organizations can set thresholds or triggers for KRIs that align with their desired risk tolerance, ensuring that risks are managed per strategic objectives and acceptable levels.

Predictive Insights: KRIs provide valuable insights into future risks. By analyzing trends and patterns in KRIs, organizations can gain predictive capabilities, identify potential risks, and anticipate their impact to enable more proactive risk response planning.

Monitoring Effectiveness: KRIs help organizations evaluate the effectiveness of risk mitigation measures. By tracking and comparing KRIs before and after implementing risk controls, organizations can assess whether the controls are successful in reducing the potential impact or likelihood of risks.

Communication and Reporting: KRIs facilitate effective communication and reporting of risks. They provide a concise and quantitative representation of risks, making it easier to convey risk information to stakeholders, including senior management, board members, investors, and regulatory bodies.

Alignment with Objectives: KRIs are aligned with an organization's objectives and key performance indicators (KPIs). They allow organizations to evaluate risks in the context of their strategic goals, ensuring that risk management activities are integrated with overall performance management.

Focus on Critical Risks: KRIs prioritize the monitoring of critical risks that have a significant impact on an organization's performance or operations. By identifying and tracking these key indicators, organizations can allocate their resources and attention to risks that truly matter most.

Decision Support: KRIs provide decision-makers with vital information for making informed decisions. These indicators offer objective data that can support the evaluation of alternative courses of action and aid in resource allocation for risk management strategies.

Continuous Monitoring: KRIs are monitored continuously to ensure ongoing risk management effectiveness. Regular monitoring enables organizations to stay informed about changes in risk levels, emerging risks, or deviations from established risk appetite thresholds.

Integration with Controls: KRIs are closely integrated with control mechanisms. Organizations can use KRIs to evaluate the performance and effectiveness of internal controls established to mitigate risks, validating whether controls are functioning as intended.

Scalability: KRIs can be scaled up or down to accommodate changes in an organization's risk landscape. As new risks emerge or existing risks evolve, organizations can adapt their KRIs to align with the changing risk scenarios.

Efficiency: KRIs facilitate efficient risk management by focusing attention on the most critical risks. Instead of monitoring numerous risk factors, organizations can concentrate on a select set of KRIs that captures the essence of those risks, optimizing resource allocation for risk management efforts.

Enhanced Risk Culture: KRIs contribute to fostering a risk-aware culture within organizations. By incorporating risk indicators into performance evaluations and considering them during decision-making processes, organizations promote a culture where risk is actively considered and addressed.

Benchmarking: KRIs enable organizations to benchmark their risk profile against industry peers or best practices. By comparing their KRIs with those of similar organizations, companies can identify areas for improvement or areas where they are outperforming their peers.

Timeliness: KRIs are designed to provide timely information on changes in risk levels. They capture risk data in near real-time or with minimal delay, enabling organizations to respond promptly to shifting risk scenarios.

Accountability: KRIs promote accountability in risk management. By monitoring key risk indicators and performance against established thresholds, organizations can hold responsible parties accountable for managing risks within acceptable parameters.

External Validation: KRIs can be used for external validation and reporting purposes. Organizations may be required to report certain KRIs to regulatory authorities, investors, or other stakeholders, demonstrating their commitment to effective risk management.

Continuous Improvement: KRIs facilitate continuous improvement in risk management practices. By analyzing the performance of KRIs over time and evaluating their effectiveness in predicting risks, organizations can refine and enhance their risk monitoring and control processes.

Employee Engagement: KRIs engage employees in risk management practices. By eliciting input from employees to identify and monitor KRIs, organizations empower them to actively contribute to risk mitigation efforts and foster a strong risk management culture.

Risk Prioritization: KRIs support risk prioritization by helping organizations identify and focus on the most critical risks. By evaluating risks based on key indicators, organizations can prioritize their risk response efforts and allocate resources proportionately to manage those risks effectively.

Continuous Learning: KRIs contribute to organizational learning and improvement. By evaluating the performance and predictive capabilities of KRIs, organizations can reflect on their risk management practices, identify areas for enhancement, and continuously improve their understanding and management of risks.

Preparedness and Resilience: KRIs enhance organizational preparedness and resilience by providing insights into potential risks. By monitoring key indicators, organizations can identify vulnerabilities, develop contingency plans, and build resilience to avoid or minimize the impact of potential risk events.

Integrated Risk Management: KRIs are an integral part of a comprehensive and integrated risk management framework. They align with other risk management components, such as risk assessments, control activities, and reporting, enabling organizations to comprehensively manage risks and integrate risk management into their overall governance processes.

In summary, KRIs exist to enable organizations to proactively identify, monitor, and manage risks in a structured and objective manner. By tracking key indicators, organizations can anticipate potential risks, take timely preventive actions, support decision-making, and continuously improve their risk management practices, ultimately enhancing their resilience and ability to achieve strategic objectives.

Risk Reporting and Communication

Risk reporting and communication are essential components of effective risk management. They involve the process of collecting, analyzing, and disseminating information about risks to relevant stakeholders, enabling informed decision-making and proactive risk mitigation. Here are 26 key points about risk reporting and communication:

Purpose: The primary purpose of risk reporting and communication is to provide stakeholders with a comprehensive understanding of an organization's risk profile, including the identification, assessment, and management of risks.

Stakeholder Engagement: Effective risk reporting and communication engage stakeholders at all levels, including senior management, board members, employees, investors, customers, regulators, and other external parties.

Transparency: Risk reporting promotes transparency by presenting risk information in a clear, accurate, and understandable manner. This allows stakeholders to assess the organization's risk posture and make well-informed decisions.

Risk Awareness: Risk reporting and communication create awareness of potential risks and their potential impact on the organization's objectives and operations. It helps stakeholders understand the significance and implications of different risks.

Risk Ownership: Risk reporting assigns ownership and accountability for managing risks to relevant individuals or departments. It clearly defines roles and responsibilities for key stakeholders involved in risk mitigation activities.

Compliance: Risk reporting ensures compliance with relevant laws, regulations, and industry standards. Organizations can demonstrate their commitment to compliance by reporting on the measures they have implemented to manage and address risks.

Timeliness: Risk reporting should be timely to enable stakeholders to respond effectively to emerging risks. Reporting should occur at regular intervals or whenever significant changes in risk levels or profiles occur.

Accuracy and Reliability: Risk reporting should be based on accurate and reliable data. It should reflect the most up-to-date information about risks and their potential impacts, supported by robust risk assessment and monitoring processes.

Risk Context: Risk reporting provides a comprehensive context for risk information. It includes the identification of risk drivers, root causes, and the external and internal factors that contribute to the likelihood and impact of risks.

Risk Categories: Risk reporting categorizes risks to facilitate understanding and analysis. Common risk categories include strategic, operational, financial, compliance, reputational, and IT risks, among others.

Key Risk Indicators (KRIs): Risk reporting may include key risk indicators (KRIs) that provide insight into risk trends and potential risk events. KRIs can serve as leading indicators, enabling stakeholders to take proactive measures to mitigate risks.

Risk Appetite: Risk reporting communicates an organization's risk appetite and tolerance levels. It clarifies the organization's willingness to take or avoid risks and sets boundaries for risk-taking activities.

Heat Maps: Risk reporting may visually represent risks using heat maps or similar graphical representations. These aid in understanding the severity and likelihood of risks, highlighting areas of high exposure or vulnerability.

Scenario Analysis: Risk reporting may include scenario analysis, which explores potential risk outcomes under different scenarios. This helps stakeholders understand the potential range of outcomes and their potential impact on the organization.

Risk Treatment Plans: Risk reporting communicates the organization's risk treatment plans, including the actions being taken to mitigate, transfer, or accept risks. It outlines the progress made in implementing risk mitigation measures and any outstanding actions or issues.

Risk Reporting Frequency: Risk reporting frequency varies depending on the organization's needs, industry, and risk landscape. Some organizations may require monthly, quarterly, or annual risk reporting, while others may require real-time or ad-hoc reporting in response to specific events or triggers.

Tailored Reporting: Risk reporting should be tailored to the needs of different stakeholders. It should consider the specific information requirements and priorities of each stakeholder group to ensure the information is relevant, actionable, and meaningful.

Non-Financial Risks: Risk reporting goes beyond financial risks and includes non-financial risks, such as operational, reputational, regulatory, and environmental risks. These risks can have a significant impact on an organization's performance and long-term sustainability.

Risk Incident Reporting: Risk reporting includes reporting of risk incidents or near-miss events. It captures information about the nature of the incident, the potential impact, the root causes, and the actions taken to address the incident and prevent its recurrence.

Mitigation Progress: Risk reporting tracks the progress of risk mitigation measures. It provides updates on the implementation and effectiveness of controls, highlighting any deficiencies or gaps in control measures and the actions being taken to address them.

Risk Reporting Channels: Risk reporting utilizes various channels, such as written reports, presentations, dashboards, risk registers, and online portals. It may also involve regular risk committee meetings, town halls, or workshops to facilitate interactive discussions around risks.

Two-Way Communication: Risk reporting should encourage two-way communication between stakeholders and risk management functions. It should create a safe and open environment for stakeholders to provide feedback, raise concerns, and share their insights on risk-related matters.

Tailored Communication: Risk communication should be tailored to the needs of different stakeholders. It should consider the preferred communication styles, formats, and levels of detail that are most effective for each stakeholder group.

Training and Education: Risk reporting and communication may include training and educational programs to enhance stakeholders' understanding of risks and their roles in managing them. This helps ensure that stakeholders are equipped with the necessary knowledge and skills to make informed risk-related decisions.

Continuous Improvement: Risk reporting and communication should be subject to continuous improvement efforts. Organizations should regularly review and assess the effectiveness of risk reporting practices to enhance clarity, relevance, and usefulness of risk information.

Regulatory Reporting: Risk reporting includes compliance with regulatory reporting requirements. Organizations must report on specific risks, such as cybersecurity, data privacy, or financial risks, in accordance with legal and regulatory obligations.

Risk reporting and communication play a vital role in promoting informed decision-making, transparency, and accountability in risk management. By effectively communicating risks to relevant stakeholders, organizations can enhance their understanding of risks, improve risk mitigation strategies, and ultimately protect their interests and achieve their objectives. It is essential for organizations to establish robust and tailored risk reporting and communication processes aligned with their specific needs and stakeholder expectations.

Chapter Summary

Risk response planning and implementation is the process of identifying, assessing, and managing risks within an organization. It involves developing strategies and taking actions to prevent, mitigate, transfer, or accept risks and their potential impacts. The goal is to effectively and proactively address risks to protect the organization's interests, goals, and stakeholders. Risk response planning and implementation involve various activities, such as risk identification, evaluation, and prioritization, as well as the selection and implementation of appropriate risk management measures. By systematically managing risks through comprehensive planning and implementation, organizations can enhance their resilience, protect their reputation, and achieve their objectives in a dynamic and uncertain business environment.

Chapter Twenty-Seven

Role of Leadership and Culture in Risk Management

Introduction

The role of leadership and culture in risk management is a critical aspect of organizational success. Effective risk management requires strong leadership and a supportive culture that promotes accountability, transparency, and proactive decision-making. This 15-paragraph introduction will discuss the significance of leadership and culture in risk management and highlight their key contributions in ensuring effective risk mitigation and overall business resilience.

Firstly, leaders play a pivotal role in setting the tone for risk management within an organization. They must establish a clear vision and mission that emphasizes the importance of identifying, assessing, and managing risks proactively. Leaders should prioritize risk management and communicate its significance throughout the organization. By actively participating in risk management initiatives, leaders demonstrate the commitment to risk mitigation and establish the precedence for others to follow.

Moreover, leaders are responsible for fostering a culture of risk awareness and accountability. They should encourage employees to identify and report potential risks and actively involve them in the risk management process. This builds a culture of trust, openness, and collaboration, where individuals feel empowered to take ownership of risk management and are motivated to contribute to its success.

Furthermore, leaders should lead by example and demonstrate ethical behavior when it comes to risk management. They must ensure that risk assessments and decisions are made with integrity and based on accurate and reliable information. It builds trust among stakeholders and instills confidence that risks are being managed effectively.

A supportive culture is equally crucial in risk management. It is important to create an environment where individuals feel comfortable raising concerns and voicing potential risks without fear of negative consequences. This requires fostering open communication channels, promoting constructive feedback, and actively listening to different perspectives. A culture that values diverse viewpoints and encourages active participation leads to better risk identification, evaluation, and response.

In addition, a culture of continuous learning and improvement is essential for effective risk management. Organizations should encourage employees to learn from past experiences and apply those lessons to future risk mitigation strategies. This involves conducting post-incident reviews, analyzing root causes, and implementing corrective actions to prevent similar risks from occurring in the future.

Furthermore, leadership involvement in risk management enables better decision-making. It allows leaders to assess risks holistically, consider the organization's overall risk appetite, and align risk management strategies with business objectives. Leaders can provide the necessary resources, support, and guidance to implement risk management initiatives successfully.

Leadership and culture also play a crucial role in risk communication. Effective communication ensures that key risk information is shared transparently and efficiently across all levels of the organization. Leaders should establish clear reporting lines, define roles and responsibilities, and provide regular updates on risk management activities. This fosters a shared understanding of risks and facilitates timely decision-making.

Additionally, leadership and culture have a significant impact on risk-taking behavior. A risk-positive culture encourages employees to take calculated risks and innovate, driving business growth and competitiveness. However, leaders should also ensure that risk-taking is balanced with risk management practices to avoid excessive or unnecessary risks.

Moreover, leadership and culture influence the level of risk awareness and compliance within an organization. When leaders prioritize risk management and establish a culture of compliance, employees are more likely to understand and adhere to risk management policies and procedures. This reduces the likelihood of non-compliance instances and associated risks.

Furthermore, leadership and culture are instrumental in embedding risk management into an organization's operations and decision-making processes. By integrating risk management into strategic planning, budgeting, and performance evaluation, leaders ensure that risk considerations are consistently taken into account, leading to more informed decision-making.

In conclusion, leadership and culture play a significant role in risk management. Effective leadership sets the tone for risk management, fosters a supportive culture, and ensures ethical behavior. A culture that values risk awareness, collaboration, openness, and continuous learning enables proactive risk identification, evaluation, and response. Furthermore, leadership involvement enhances decision-making, risk communication, compliance, and the integration of risk management into an organization's operations. By prioritizing leadership and culture in risk management efforts, organizations can achieve better risk outcomes, enhance resilience, and drive long-term success.

Tone at the Top: Executive Leadership's Role in Risk Management

The tone set by executive leadership is crucial in establishing a strong risk management culture within an organization. Executive leaders play a pivotal role in shaping the organization's approach to risk management, aligning it with strategic goals, and promoting a proactive and responsible attitude toward risk. In this section, we will delve into the importance of executive leadership's role in risk management through 22 paragraphs.

Firstly, executive leaders set the tone by establishing risk management as a priority within the organization. They demonstrate their commitment to risk management through their words, actions, and resource allocation. By emphasizing the importance of risk management, leaders communicate its significance to employees at all levels, ensuring that it becomes an integral part of the organizational mindset.

Executive leaders also define the organization's risk appetite, tolerance levels, and strategic risk objectives. They determine the organization's willingness to take on risk and make informed decisions regarding risk exposure. By articulating and communicating the risk appetite, leaders guide employees, enabling them to align their risk management efforts accordingly.

Moreover, executive leadership plays a key role in embedding risk management into the organization's governance structures. They establish and oversee risk management committees or similar entities responsible for coordinating risk management activities and providing strategic oversight. Executives ensure that risk management is integrated into decision-making processes at all levels of the organization.

Furthermore, executive leaders foster a risk-aware culture by creating an environment where employees feel comfortable raising concerns and discussing potential risks. They encourage open communication and collaboration, allowing employees to freely express their opinions and participate in risk mitigation efforts. This promotes a sense of ownership and collective responsibility in managing risks throughout the organization.

Executive leaders lead by example in demonstrating ethical behavior and integrity in risk management. They ensure that risk-related decisions are made with the organization's best interest in mind, without compromising core values or ethical standards. It fosters trust among employees and stakeholders, reinforcing the importance of ethical conduct in risk management.

Executive leadership is responsible for championing risk assessment and monitoring activities. They establish processes for identifying, evaluating, and monitoring risks to ensure that the organization is proactively addressing emerging threats or vulnerabilities. By regularly reviewing risk assessments and monitoring reports, leaders ensure that risks are identified and managed appropriately.

Moreover, executive leaders provide the necessary resources and support for effective risk management. They allocate budgetary resources, personnel, and technology to enable robust risk management processes within the organization. Adequate resourcing demonstrates the organization's commitment to risk management and its recognition as a strategic priority.

Executive leadership also plays a critical role in promoting accountability in risk management. They hold employees and management accountable for their risk-related responsibilities and encourage timely reporting and escalation of risk issues. This ensures that risks are addressed promptly and effectively, without delay or negligence.

Additionally, executive leaders are responsible for ensuring that risk management is integrated with strategic planning processes. They align risk management efforts with the organization's objectives, enabling the identification and management of risks that could impact strategic goals. This integration helps prioritize risk management initiatives and resource allocation to mitigate risks that are most critical to organizational success.

Executive leaders provide guidance and support in implementing risk mitigation strategies. They work closely with risk management teams and other stakeholders to define and execute risk responses, ensuring that appropriate measures are in place to prevent, minimize, or transfer risks. Their engagement validates the importance of risk mitigation efforts and encourages employees to embrace risk management practices.

Furthermore, executive leaders play a key role in risk communication. They ensure that risk information is communicated transparently and effectively to all stakeholders, including employees, board members, investors, and regulatory bodies. By fostering open and timely communication channels, executives enable informed decision-making and promote a shared understanding of risks across the organization.

Executive leadership is responsible for monitoring and evaluating the organization's risk management performance. They establish key performance indicators (KPIs) and track progress towards risk management goals. Regular evaluation and reporting on risk management effectiveness allow leaders to identify areas for improvement and make informed decisions to enhance risk management practices.

Moreover, executive leaders are essential in driving a continuous improvement mindset in risk management. They encourage a culture of learning from past experiences and provide the necessary support for implementing corrective actions and preventive measures. Executives ensure that lessons learned from risk incidents are captured, shared, and applied to prevent similar occurrences in the future.

Executive leaders also have a critical role in fostering collaboration and coordination across different departments and functions. They facilitate cross-functional collaboration to ensure that risks are identified and managed holistically. By breaking down silos and encouraging information sharing, leaders promote a comprehensive approach to risk management.

Additionally, executive leaders are at the forefront of identifying emerging risks and ensuring that appropriate measures are in place to manage them. They stay abreast of industry trends, regulatory changes, and emerging threats to anticipate potential risks. By recognizing and adapting to changing risk landscapes, leaders enable the organization to respond effectively to emerging challenges.

Executive leadership is responsible for engaging with external stakeholders, including regulators, industry peers, and customers, on risk management matters. They participate in industry forums, conferences, and regulatory discussions to stay informed and share best practices. This external engagement ensures that the organization remains abreast of emerging risks and industry standards in risk management.

Executive leaders are crucial in promoting a proactive risk management approach. They encourage the development of risk scenarios and stress testing exercises to identify potential risks and their impacts. By actively seeking out potential risks, leaders ensure that the organization is well-prepared to respond effectively in challenging situations.

Moreover, executive leaders act as advocates for the integration of emerging technologies and data analytics in risk management. They support the adoption of innovative tools and methodologies that enhance risk identification, assessment, and monitoring. Their endorsement of technological advancements improves the organization's ability to manage risks in a rapidly evolving business environment.

Executive leaders are responsible for ensuring that risk management practices align with the organization's legal and regulatory requirements. They establish mechanisms for compliance with relevant laws and regulations, ensuring that risk management initiatives are in accordance with applicable standards and guidelines.

Furthermore, executive leadership plays a role in crisis management. In times of crisis or disruptions, leaders demonstrate their ability to act decisively, guide the organization through challenging circumstances, and make tough risk-related decisions. Their calm and composed demeanor inspires confidence and reassurance among employees and stakeholders.

Executive leaders drive the review and enhancement of risk governance frameworks and policies. They ensure that risk management policies are regularly updated to reflect changes in the business environment and regulatory landscape. Through robust governance structures, leaders enable effective risk oversight and ensure that risk management remains an integral part of the organization's overall governance framework.

In conclusion, executive leadership plays a critical role in risk management. By setting the tone, establishing a risk-aware culture, promoting adherence to ethical standards, and providing necessary resources and support, leaders drive effective risk management practices. Their engagement, accountability, and strategic guidance ensure that risk management efforts are aligned with organizational objectives and foster resilience in the face of emerging risks and uncertainties. Through their efforts, executive leaders create an environment that embraces risk management as an integral aspect of organizational success.

Building a Risk-Aware Culture

Building a risk-aware culture is crucial for organizations to effectively manage and mitigate risks. A risk-aware culture ensures that employees at all levels of the organization understand and actively participate in identifying, evaluating, and managing risks. In this section, we will delve into the importance of building a risk-aware culture and discuss various strategies to achieve it.

A risk-aware culture starts with leadership. Executives and senior management must actively promote and demonstrate a commitment to risk management. They should communicate the importance of risk awareness, set clear expectations for risk management, and lead by example in integrating risk considerations into decision-making processes.

Organizations need to provide comprehensive risk management training and education to employees. This includes raising awareness about various types of risks, their potential impacts, and the organization's risk appetite and tolerance levels. Education should be ongoing, as risks evolve over time, and employees should be encouraged to continually update their knowledge.

Communication is key to building a risk-aware culture. Organizations need to establish open channels of communication and create a safe environment where employees feel comfortable raising concerns and discussing potential risks. Regular communication about risk-related matters helps ensure that everyone remains informed and engaged.

Risk management should be integrated into the organization's values, mission, and vision. Employees should understand that managing risks is not just a compliance exercise but a crucial aspect of achieving organizational goals. By aligning risk management with the organization's overall direction, employees can see its relevance and importance.

Celebrate and reward proactive risk management behaviors. Recognize and commend employees who identify and successfully address risks. This encourages a risk-aware culture by promoting a sense of ownership and accountability for identifying, evaluating, and managing risks.

Foster a culture of continuous improvement. Encourage employees to learn from past mistakes and near-misses and emphasize the importance of implementing preventive measures to avoid future risks. This helps create a culture that is always seeking better ways to manage risks.

Involve employees from various departments and levels in risk management processes. Collaboration across different functions ensures a comprehensive understanding of risks and a more effective approach to risk management. Encouraging employees to take an active role in risk management cultivates a risk-aware culture where everyone feels responsible for addressing risks.

Provide clear and accessible guidance on risk management processes and procedures. Employees should have easy access to risk management policies, guidelines, and reporting mechanisms. This ensures that they understand their roles and responsibilities in managing risks effectively.

Create platforms for sharing best practices and lessons learned. Encourage employees to share their experiences in identifying and managing risks. By sharing successes and failures, organizations can promote a culture of learning and continuous improvement in risk management.

Develop a risk appetite statement that clearly communicates the organization's willingness to take on risks to achieve strategic objectives. This statement should be widely communicated and understood within the organization, helping employees make informed risk-related decisions.

Embed risk management responsibilities into job descriptions and performance assessments. By integrating risk management into the performance management framework, organizations signal the importance of risk awareness and encourage employees to incorporate risk considerations into their daily activities.

Conduct regular risk assessments and communicate the findings to employees. This helps employees understand the risk landscape and their roles in managing those risks effectively. Regular risk assessments also demonstrate leadership's commitment to identifying and addressing potential threats.

Establish a reporting and escalation mechanism that encourages employees to report risks and incidents in a timely manner. This should include anonymous reporting channels to create a safe space for whistleblowing without fear of retaliation.

Emphasize the importance of data and information integrity in risk management. Organizations should establish robust data governance practices, ensure accurate and up-to-date information, and encourage employees to make data-driven risk management decisions.

Engage external stakeholders, such as regulators, industry experts, and customers, to incorporate external perspectives into risk management practices. This promotes a broader understanding of risks that may affect the organization and enables better risk mitigation strategies.

Regularly review and update risk management policies and procedures to reflect changes in the business environment and emerging risks. This demonstrates a proactive approach to risk management and ensures that employees are equipped with the most current guidance.

Encourage employees to participate in professional development programs related to risk management. This could include attending conferences, and workshops, or obtaining relevant certifications. By investing in employees' knowledge and skills, organizations foster a risk-aware culture and develop a pool of risk management experts.

Establish a risk monitoring and reporting system that provides real-time insights into emerging risks and their impacts. This helps employees proactively identify and manage risks, allowing for timely interventions and preventing potential crises.

Develop and communicate clear protocols for risk response and crisis management. This ensures that employees understand their roles and responsibilities during a crisis and can effectively respond to unforeseen events or emergencies.

Seek feedback and input from employees on risk management initiatives. Actively solicit suggestions and ideas for improving risk management practices. Encouraging employee involvement creates a sense of ownership and empowerment in the risk management process.

Conduct periodic internal audits and assessments to evaluate the effectiveness of risk management processes. This helps identify gaps and areas for improvement, allowing organizations to refine their risk management strategies and ensure ongoing compliance.

Finally, celebrate successes in risk management. Celebrate milestones and achievements in managing risks effectively. Publicly recognizing individuals and teams for their contributions reinforces the importance of risk management and motivates others to engage in proactive risk management efforts.

In conclusion, building a risk-aware culture requires a multifaceted approach, encompassing leadership commitment, comprehensive training, open communication, shared values, collaboration, and continuous improvement. By cultivating a risk-aware culture, organizations foster a proactive and responsible attitude toward risk management, allowing for effective identification, evaluation, and mitigation of risks.

Risk Management Governance

Risk management governance refers to the framework and processes implemented by an organization to identify, assess, control, and monitor risks. It involves the establishment of policies, structures, and systems that enable effective risk management practices throughout the entire organization. Risk management governance is crucial because it ensures that risks are proactively managed and mitigated, allowing organizations to make informed decisions, protect their assets, and achieve their objectives.

Effective risk management governance enables organizations to identify and assess potential risks that could hinder the achievement of their strategic goals. By having a robust governance framework in place, organizations can systematically analyze risks and prioritize them based on their potential impact and likelihood.

When risks are identified and assessed, organizations can then establish appropriate controls and mitigation measures to reduce the impact and likelihood of risky events. This ensures that risks are managed within acceptable levels and that any adverse effects are minimized.

Risk management governance helps organizations comply with regulatory requirements and standards. It ensures that the organization develops and implements policies and procedures that align with legal, regulatory, and industry-specific obligations.

It helps organizations establish a risk management culture throughout the organization. A strong governance framework promotes risk awareness and accountability at all levels, ensuring that individuals understand their roles and responsibilities in managing risks effectively.

With proper risk management governance, organizations can enhance their decision-making processes. By considering risks and associated potential impacts, organizations can make more informed choices and select the most appropriate courses of action. It facilitates effective communication and transparency within an organization. A key component of risk management governance is the dissemination of risk-related information across all levels of the organization, enabling stakeholders to be aware of risks and work collaboratively towards their mitigation.

Risk management governance provides a structured approach to managing risks across different business units. It fosters consistency in the identification, assessment, and treatment of risks, enabling a coordinated effort to manage risks across the organization.

By having a clearly defined governance framework, organizations can allocate resources effectively. This allows for the allocation of resources based on risk priorities, ensuring that risks with higher potential impacts receive appropriate attention and resources.

Proper risk management governance helps organizations minimize surprises and unexpected events. By regularly monitoring risks and implementing proactive controls and mitigation measures, organizations can reduce the occurrence of unforeseen events and better manage the impact when they do occur.

It helps organizations build resilience to external shocks and uncertainties. A strong governance framework enables organizations to anticipate and respond to risks and disruptions in a timely manner, minimizing the negative impact on operations and performance.

With effective risk management governance, organizations can enhance stakeholder confidence and trust. By demonstrating a robust risk management framework, organizations showcase their commitment to address risks and protect the interests of stakeholders.

Risk management governance facilitates continuous improvement. It enables organizations to regularly review their risk management processes, identify areas of improvement, and implement necessary changes to enhance risk management practices.

It helps organizations proactively address emerging risks. Through ongoing monitoring and assessment, organizations can identify new risks that may arise due to changes in the internal or external environment and take appropriate actions to manage them.

Proper risk management governance helps organizations avoid unnecessary costs and losses. By identifying, assessing, and controlling risks, organizations can prevent incidents that could result in financial losses or reputational damage.

It enables organizations to comply with ethical standards and promote responsible business practices. Risk management governance ensures that organizations consider ethical implications when assessing and managing risks, leading to responsible decision-making and actions.

With an effective governance framework, organizations can align risk management with their overall business strategy. This ensures that risks are taken into consideration during strategic planning, leading to more informed and effective decision-making.

Risk management governance supports effective internal control systems. By integrating risk management practices into internal control frameworks, organizations can strengthen their ability to detect, prevent, and correct errors and irregularities.

It improves organizational resilience during crises and emergencies. Through a robust governance framework, organizations can develop crisis management and business continuity plans that allow them to respond swiftly and effectively during times of disruption.

Risk management governance helps organizations protect their reputation. By identifying and managing reputational risks, organizations can prevent incidents that could harm their brand image and stakeholder perception.

It enables organizations to optimize their risk-taking capabilities. By understanding risks, organizations can take calculated risks that align with their risk appetite, allowing them to seize opportunities and innovate while still managing potential downsides.

Risk management governance promotes accountability within an organization. By assigning clear roles and responsibilities for risk management, individuals become accountable for managing risks in their respective areas of expertise.

It helps organizations establish a risk-aware culture that encourages employees to identify and report risks. This enables organizations to benefit from the knowledge and expertise of their employees in identifying and managing risks.

Through effective risk management governance, organizations can anticipate and prevent potential crises. By identifying risks and implementing controls in advance, organizations can reduce the likelihood of crises and their associated impacts.

It provides organizations with a structured approach to identify and manage emerging risks. By aligning risk management with emerging trends and changes in the external environment, organizations can adapt and respond effectively to new risks.

Risk management governance assists organizations in meeting the expectations of stakeholders. By demonstrating a commitment to robust risk management practices, organizations can enhance stakeholder trust and demonstrate their ability to manage risks effectively.

Ultimately, risk management governance is important because it enables organizations to become more resilient, agile, and adaptive in an increasingly dynamic and uncertain business environment. It promotes a systematic and proactive approach to managing risks, ensuring the long-term sustainability and success of the organization.

Chapter Twenty-Eight

Emerging Trends in Risk Management

Introduction

Emerging trends in risk management are transforming the way organizations approach and manage risks in today's rapidly evolving business landscape. As businesses face increasingly complex and interconnected risks, staying ahead of emerging trends is crucial to ensure effective risk mitigation and maintain a competitive edge. In this introduction, we will explore 25 key emerging trends that are shaping the field of risk management.

Technology-driven risks: The rapid advancement of technologies such as artificial intelligence, blockchain, and the Internet of Things has introduced new risks that organizations need to address, including cybersecurity threats and data privacy concerns.

Integration of risk management and strategic planning: Organizations are recognizing the need to integrate risk management into their strategic planning processes to proactively identify and address risks that could impact the achievement of their objectives.

Focus on non-financial risks: Beyond financial risks, organizations are increasingly prioritizing non-financial risks such as environmental, social, and governance risks as these can have a profound impact on their reputation, brand value, and long-term viability.

Enhanced data analytics: With the increasing availability of data, organizations are leveraging advanced data analytics techniques to gain actionable insights into risks, enabling better decision-making and risk management.

Scenario-based risk assessments: Organizations are adopting scenario-based risk assessments to evaluate the impact of potential future events or trends on their business and identify appropriate risk responses.

Integrated risk reporting: Organizations are moving towards integrated risk reporting, consolidating risk information across different business units and functions to provide a comprehensive view of risks to key stakeholders.

7. Risk culture and behavior: Organizations are focusing on building a strong risk culture and encouraging risk-aware behavior among employees to embed risk management into everyday activities.

8. Rise of third-party risks: The increasing reliance on third-party vendors and suppliers has elevated the importance of managing third-party risks, including supplier failures, compliance risks, and reputational risks arising from the actions of third parties.

Geopolitical risks: Organizations are facing an increasingly uncertain geopolitical environment, characterized by trade disputes, political instability, and regulatory changes. Managing geopolitical risks is becoming essential for global businesses.

Sustainability and climate-related risks: As environmental concerns gain prominence, organizations are paying greater attention to sustainability risks, including climate change impacts, resource scarcity, and regulatory shifts towards a low-carbon economy.

New regulatory landscapes: Evolving regulations and compliance requirements, particularly in areas such as data privacy, anti-corruption, and cybersecurity, present new challenges that organizations must navigate to stay in compliance and avoid penalties.

Reputation and brand risks: In the age of social media and instant communication, organizations are increasingly vulnerable to reputational and brand risks, as negative news or customer complaints can spread rapidly and have far-reaching consequences.

Resilience and business continuity: The growing recognition of the need for business resilience has led organizations to focus on enhancing their business continuity plans and response capabilities to minimize the impact of unexpected events or disruptions.

Employee well-being and mental health risks: Organizations are acknowledging the importance of employee well-being and mental health as essential components of managing risks related to talent retention, productivity, and workplace safety.

Regulatory technology (RegTech): The use of technology-driven solutions, such as AI and machine learning, to automate compliance processes and enhance regulatory risk management is gaining momentum across industries.

Continual risk monitoring: Organizations are embracing real-time risk monitoring to detect emerging risks and anomalies, using technologies like predictive analytics, monitoring of social media sentiment, and risk sensing tools.

Cultural and ethical risks: Cultivating an ethical culture and addressing cultural risks, such as unethical behavior, discrimination, and diversity issues, are now considered integral to comprehensive risk management.

Agile risk management: Agile methodologies, commonly used in software development, are increasingly being applied to risk management, enabling organizations to respond quickly to changing risks and prioritize their mitigation efforts.

Supply chain resilience: Organizations are recognizing the need to assess and enhance the resilience of their supply chains to address risks such as supplier disruptions, geopolitical instabilities, and demand fluctuations.

Internal control assessments: Moving beyond traditional control frameworks, organizations are adopting more dynamic and agile approaches to assess internal controls in response to emerging risks and evolving business environments.

Predictive modeling and AI: Organizations are leveraging predictive modeling and AI algorithms to forecast potential risks based on historical data, enabling proactive risk management and better risk mitigation strategies.

Crowd-sourced risk identification: Some organizations are embracing crowdsourcing and leveraging the collective intelligence of their employees or external stakeholders to identify and assess risks more comprehensively.

Risk appetite and tolerance frameworks: Developing clear risk appetite and tolerance frameworks helps organizations define their risk-taking preferences and make risk-informed decisions in line with their strategic objectives.

Integrated risk management platforms: The adoption of integrated risk management platforms is on the rise, allowing organizations to centralize and streamline risk management processes, data, and reporting across the enterprise.

Collaboration and partnerships: Organizations are increasingly recognizing the value of collaboration and partnerships in managing complex risks, including sharing information and best practices with industry peers and engaging external specialists.

In conclusion, emerging trends in risk management reflect the changing nature of risks and the need for organizations to adapt and evolve their risk management practices accordingly. By embracing these trends, organizations can enhance their ability to identify, assess, and mitigate risks effectively, ensuring their long-term success and sustainability in an uncertain and dynamic business environment.

Data Analytics and Artificial Intelligence in Risk Management

Data analytics and artificial intelligence (AI) have become increasingly important in risk management due to their ability to process and analyze vast amounts of data in real time, identify patterns, and make accurate predictions. In this explanation, we will explore the significance of data analytics and AI in risk management across various aspects.

Enhanced risk identification: Data analytics and AI enable organizations to identify and assess risks more comprehensively by analyzing internal and external data sources, and identifying trends, outliers, and potential risk indicators that may not be apparent through traditional methods.

Real-time monitoring: Data analytics and AI enable organizations to monitor risks in real-time, allowing for early detection of emerging risks or anomalies, enabling proactive risk management and timely interventions.

Fraud detection: Advanced data analytics and AI algorithms can detect patterns and anomalies that indicate fraudulent activities, enabling organizations to identify and prevent fraudulent behaviors before they cause significant damage.

Predictive analytics: By leveraging historical data and AI algorithms, organizations can predict future risk events and outcomes, enabling more accurate risk assessment and the development of effective mitigation strategies.

Scenario analysis: Data analytics and AI facilitate scenario-based risk assessments, allowing organizations to model and simulate different risk scenarios to understand the potential impact and develop appropriate risk response strategies.

Improved decision-making: Data-driven insights provided by analytics and AI empower organizations to make more informed and strategic decisions when managing risks, enabling proactive risk management, and avoiding costly mistakes.

Automation of routine tasks: AI-powered technologies can automate repetitive and time-consuming tasks, such as data collection, data processing, and risk assessment, freeing up resources and minimizing human errors.

Improved risk modeling: AI and data analytics can improve risk modeling by integrating and analyzing vast amounts of data from multiple sources, allowing organizations to generate more accurate risk models and forecasts.

Cost and resource optimization: Data analytics and AI can lead to cost savings by optimizing resource allocation and streamlining risk management processes.

Compliance and regulatory adherence: Data analytics and AI can provide organizations with the ability to monitor and analyze vast amounts of data for compliance with regulatory requirements, identifying potential compliance issues in real time.

Cybersecurity risk management: Advanced analytics and AI techniques can strengthen organizations' cybersecurity risk management by detecting and responding to cyber threats more effectively, enhancing threat intelligence, and enabling proactive vulnerability assessments.

Customer risk management: Data analytics and AI enable organizations to assess and manage customer-related risks, including credit risk, fraud risk, and customer churn, by analyzing customer data and identifying patterns and behaviors that indicate potential risks.

Supply chain risk management: Data analytics and AI can enhance supply chain risk management by analyzing supply chain data, identifying potential bottlenecks, disruptions, and risks, and enabling organizations to develop robust mitigation strategies.

Operational risk management: Leveraging data analytics and AI, organizations can analyze operational data in real time, identify potential operational risks, and proactively manage them to optimize operational efficiency and mitigate potential losses.

Insurance underwriting and claims management: Data analytics and AI can streamline insurance underwriting processes by analyzing structured and unstructured data, improving risk assessment accuracy, and enabling more precise pricing strategies. Similarly, in claims management, data analytics and AI can help identify fraudulent claims and expedite the claims settlement process.

Portfolio risk management: In finance and investment management, data analytics and AI play a vital role in assessing portfolio risks, analyzing market trends, and optimizing asset allocation to achieve desired risk-return profiles.

Stress testing and risk simulations: Data analytics and AI allow organizations to conduct stress testing and risk simulations more efficiently by modeling different risk scenarios, helping them understand the potential impacts on their financials and overall operations.

Early warning systems: By leveraging predictive analytics and AI, organizations can develop early warning systems that enable them to detect and respond to potential risks before they escalate, minimizing their adverse impact.

Risk culture and governance: Data analytics and AI can support risk culture and governance initiatives by providing objective data-driven insights to inform decision-making, promote risk-aware behavior, and monitor the effectiveness of risk management efforts.

Sustainability risk management: Data analytics and AI can help organizations assess and manage sustainability-related risks, such as climate change impact, resource scarcity, and regulatory changes, to ensure long-term sustainability and resiliency.

Reputation risk management: Data analytics and AI can analyze social media sentiment, news trends, and customer feedback, enabling organizations to monitor and manage reputation risks effectively.

Collaboration and knowledge sharing: Data analytics and AI tools facilitate collaboration and knowledge sharing among risk management professionals by providing a centralized platform for sharing insights, best practices, and lessons learned.

Continuous improvement: By leveraging data analytics and AI, organizations can continually analyze risk management processes, identify areas of improvement, and enhance risk management practices based on data-driven insights.

In conclusion, data analytics and AI significantly contribute to effective risk management by enabling organizations to proactively identify, assess, and mitigate risks. The ability to analyze vast amounts of data in real-time, predict future outcomes, and automate routine tasks empowers organizations to make more informed decisions, optimize resource allocation, and improve overall risk management processes, ultimately enhancing their ability to navigate complex and evolving risk landscapes.

Cybersecurity Risk Management

Cybersecurity plays a critical role in risk management as modern organizations heavily rely on digital technologies and data assets, making them vulnerable to various cyber threats. Effectively managing cybersecurity risks helps organizations protect their sensitive information, maintain business continuity, and safeguard their reputation. In this explanation, we will explore the role cybersecurity plays in risk management across several key areas.

Asset protection: Cybersecurity measures protect the confidentiality, integrity, and availability of an organization's digital assets, including sensitive data, intellectual property, employee records, and financial information. By safeguarding these assets, organizations mitigate the risk of unauthorized access, data breaches, and financial losses.

Risk assessment: Cybersecurity assessments help identify and evaluate vulnerabilities, threats, and potential impacts related to information systems, technology infrastructure, and data assets. These assessments provide organizations with insights into cybersecurity risks, allowing them to prioritize mitigation efforts and allocate resources effectively.

Compliance and regulatory adherence: Effective cybersecurity measures ensure compliance with applicable laws, regulations, and industry standards. Organizations must comply with data protection regulations, such as the General Data Protection Regulation (GDPR), Payment Card Industry Data Security Standard (PCI DSS), and the Health Insurance Portability and Accountability Act (HIPAA), to avoid financial penalties and reputational damage.

Incident response and mitigation: Cybersecurity measures include incident response plans that outline the steps to be taken in the event of a cyber incident or data breach. Prompt response and effective mitigation efforts minimize the impact of cyber incidents, reducing financial losses, reputational damage, and legal consequences.

Business continuity: Cybersecurity is essential for maintaining business continuity. By implementing robust cybersecurity measures, organizations reduce the likelihood and impact of disruptions caused by cyber incidents, enabling them to continue operations smoothly and minimize downtime.

Supplier and third-party risk management: Cybersecurity measures help organizations manage risks associated with third-party vendors and suppliers. Organizations must assess and monitor the cybersecurity posture of their partners to ensure the protection of shared data and the resilience of their supply chain.

Employee awareness and training: Cybersecurity awareness programs and training help educate employees about the risks associated with cyber threats, phishing attacks, social engineering, and other harmful activities. By building a strong cybersecurity awareness culture, organizations reduce the likelihood of human errors and increase their overall resilience against cyber threats.

Security governance: Cybersecurity is an integral part of an organization's governance structure. A well-defined cybersecurity governance framework establishes responsibilities, processes, and controls to ensure effective risk management throughout the organization.

Vulnerability management: Cybersecurity measures include regular vulnerability assessments and penetration testing to identify weaknesses and vulnerabilities in an organization's systems and infrastructure. Timely remediation of vulnerabilities minimizes the risk of exploitation by malicious actors.

Security incident monitoring and detection: Cybersecurity solutions encompass monitoring systems, intrusion detection systems (IDS), and security information and event management (SIEM) tools. These technologies enable organizations to identify and respond to security incidents promptly, mitigating potential risks.

Threat intelligence: Cybersecurity measures involve actively gathering and analyzing threat intelligence to stay informed about the latest cyber threats, emerging attack vectors, and evolving tactics used by cybercriminals. Up-to-date threat intelligence helps organizations proactively implement measures to defend against new and emerging threats.

Access control and identity management: Strong access control measures and identity management practices protect an organization's systems and data by ensuring that only authorized individuals can access sensitive resources. These measures minimize the risk of unauthorized access, insider threats, and data breaches.

Data protection and encryption: Robust cybersecurity solutions include encryption techniques to protect sensitive data while in transit and at rest. Encrypting data minimizes the risk of unauthorized access or data leaks, particularly when data is shared externally or stored in the cloud.

Security incident analysis and reporting: Cybersecurity measures involve analyzing and reporting security incidents to gain insights into attack patterns, tactics, and vulnerabilities. This information helps organizations enhance their security posture, update controls, and develop strategies to mitigate future risks.

Security by design: Cybersecurity should be integrated into the design and development of systems, applications, and products from the initial stages. Considering security requirements in the development lifecycle minimizes vulnerabilities and the need for costly retroactive security measures.

Data backup and disaster recovery: Cybersecurity includes implementing robust data backup and disaster recovery strategies to ensure the availability and resilience of critical systems and data, even in the event of cyber incidents or natural disasters.

Patch management: Regularly applying security patches and updates to software, applications, and systems is critical for mitigating vulnerabilities and reducing the risk of exploitation by cyber attackers.

Cybersecurity risk communication: Organizations need to effectively communicate their cybersecurity risks internally and externally. Transparent and open communication helps stakeholders understand the risks, their potential impact, and the organization's efforts to mitigate them.

Security awareness for customers and users: Organizations must educate their customers and external users about cybersecurity risks associated with their products or services. Appropriate cybersecurity guidelines and best practices help customers protect themselves from cyber threats and contribute to a more secure ecosystem.

Mobile and remote workforce security: As the mobile and remote workforce grows, cybersecurity measures should address the security risks associated with mobile devices, remote access, and the use of personal devices for work-related activities.

Incident reporting and sharing: Organizations should actively participate in incident reporting and information-sharing initiatives to contribute to the collective knowledge and defense against cyber threats. Sharing incident information helps others proactively defend against similar attacks.

Cybersecurity audits and assessments: Regular cybersecurity audits and assessments provide an independent review of an organization's security controls and practices. These assessments help identify gaps, weaknesses, and areas for improvement, enabling organizations to enhance their cybersecurity posture continuously.

Ethical hacking and red teaming: Organizations can proactively assess their security defenses by engaging ethical hackers or conducting red teaming exercises. These activities simulate real-world attack scenarios to identify vulnerabilities and weaknesses in an organization's systems, enabling remediation actions to be taken.

In conclusion, cybersecurity plays a crucial role in risk management by protecting digital assets, ensuring regulatory compliance, maintaining business continuity, and minimizing the impact of cyber incidents. By implementing effective cybersecurity measures, organizations can mitigate the risks associated with cyber threats, safeguard their data and systems, and proactively respond to evolving cybersecurity challenges.

Environmental and Social Risk Management

Environmental and social risk management involves identifying and addressing risks associated with environmental and social factors that can impact the long-term sustainability of an organization. In recent years, there has been increased recognition of the importance of environmental and social risk management due to the potential financial, reputational, and legal consequences of not effectively addressing these risks. In this detailed explanation, we will explore the effects and ethics of environmental and social risk management.

Effects of Environmental and Social Risk Management

Financial implications: Failing to manage environmental and social risks can have significant financial consequences. For example, non-compliance with environmental regulations may result in fines, penalties, and the costs of remediation. Reputational damage resulting from social controversies can lead to customer boycotts, brand devaluation, and decreased market share.

Regulatory compliance and legal risks: Failure to comply with environmental and social regulations can result in legal liabilities, including fines, litigation, and sanctions. Organizations must understand and adhere to applicable laws, including environmental protection, labor rights, health and safety, and anti-corruption regulations, to mitigate legal risks.

Reputational risk: Environmental and social controversies can significantly damage the reputation of an organization. Negative publicity related to environmental pollution, human rights violations, labor exploitation, or unethical practices can lead to a loss of trust among customers, investors, employees, and other stakeholders.

Operational disruptions: Environmental and social risks, such as extreme weather events, resource scarcity, labor strikes, or community protests, can disrupt an organization's operations. These disruptions can lead to production delays, supply chain interruptions, increased costs, and damage to relationships with suppliers, contractors, and local communities.

Stakeholder pressure: Stakeholders, including customers, investors, employees, communities, and NGOs, are increasingly demanding that organizations demonstrate responsible environmental and social practices. Failure to meet these expectations can result in reputational damage, public backlash, and the loss of stakeholder support.

Access to capital: Environmental and social factors are increasingly influencing investment decisions. Institutional investors and lenders are incorporating environmental, social, and governance (ESG) considerations into their investment criteria. Failing to effectively manage environmental and social risks may limit an organization's access to capital or result in higher borrowing costs.

Employee attraction and retention: Organizations committed to environmental and social responsibility are more likely to attract and retain talented employees who value purpose-driven work and ethical business practices. Conversely, organizations associated with negative environmental or social impacts may struggle to attract and retain top talent.

Ethics of Environmental and Social Risk Management:

Duty to stakeholders: Ethical organizations recognize their responsibility to stakeholders, including employees, customers, shareholders, communities, and the environment. Effectively managing environmental and social risks demonstrates a commitment to fulfilling this duty and maintaining the trust of stakeholders.

Environmental stewardship: Ethical organizations strive to minimize their environmental footprint and promote sustainable practices. They recognize their role in preserving natural resources, mitigating pollution, and minimizing environmental degradation for the benefit of present and future generations.

Respect for human rights: Organizations committed to ethical environmental and social risk management uphold human rights standards within their operations and supply chains. This includes ensuring fair labor practices, promoting worker safety, respecting indigenous rights, and combating modern slavery and child labor.

Transparency and accountability: Ethical organizations are transparent in their environmental and social practices, sharing relevant information with stakeholders and being accountable for their impacts. They disclose their performance, goals, and progress in managing environmental and social risks, fostering trust and accountability.

Collaboration and engagement: Ethical organizations actively engage with stakeholders, seeking their input and incorporating their concerns into decision-making processes. By collaborating with communities, NGOs, and other stakeholders, ethical organizations foster inclusive dialogue and ensure that the interests of all affected parties are considered.

Long-term sustainability: Ethical environmental and social risk management prioritizes long-term sustainability over short-term gains. This includes considering the impacts of business activities on society, the environment, and future generations, and making decisions that balance these considerations for the benefit of all stakeholders.

Continuous improvement: Ethical organizations continuously strive to improve their environmental and social performance. They set measurable goals, track progress, and innovate to minimize risks, reduce impacts, and enhance their environmental and social practices over time.

Effective environmental and social risk management is essential for organizations to mitigate financial, legal, reputational, and operational risks. Ethical environmental and social risk management aligns with principles of responsibility, sustainability, transparency, accountability, and respect for stakeholders. Organizations that uphold these ethical practices not only reduce their risks but also contribute to the well-being of society, the environment, and their long-term business sustainability.

The causative factors of environmental and social risk management can vary across organizations and industries. However, several common factors contribute to the identification and addressing of these risks.

Increasing stakeholder expectations: Stakeholders, including customers, investors, employees, communities, and regulators, are placing higher expectations on organizations to demonstrate responsible environmental and social practices. This increased scrutiny has led organizations to recognize the importance of managing environmental and social risks to maintain stakeholder trust and meet their demands.

Evolving regulatory landscape: Governments and regulatory bodies are enacting and enforcing stricter environmental and social regulations. Compliance with these regulations has become crucial for organizations to avoid legal penalties, reputational damage, and potential operational disruptions.

Growing awareness of environmental issues: Increasing recognition of environmental issues, such as climate change, resource depletion, and pollution, has brought attention to the need for organizations to address their environmental impact. Organizations must assess and manage environmental risks to minimize their contributions to global challenges and ensure their long-term sustainability.

Social and human rights concerns: Heightened awareness of social issues, including labor rights, human rights, supply chain transparency, and community impacts, has prompted organizations to manage risks associated with these factors. Addressing social risks is not only ethically responsible but also essential for maintaining a positive brand image and avoiding legal and reputational consequences.

Reputational considerations: Organizations are realizing the potential impact of environmental and social risks on their reputation and brand value. Negative publicity related to environmental incidents, labor violations, or unethical behavior can harm an organization's standing in the eyes of its stakeholders and lead to significant financial and operational consequences.

Investor preferences and ESG considerations: Investors are increasingly incorporating environmental, social, and governance (ESG) factors into their investment decisions. Organizations that effectively manage environmental and social risks may attract more investment and enjoy a competitive advantage in the financial markets.

Innovation and competitive advantage: Organizations understand that addressing environmental and social risks can drive innovation, improve operational efficiency, reduce costs, and foster long-term competitiveness. By incorporating sustainability practices and managing social risks, organizations can differentiate themselves in the market and attract environmentally and socially conscious customers.

Relationship with local communities and indigenous groups: Organizations must consider the potential impacts of their operations on local communities and indigenous peoples. By addressing community concerns and maintaining positive relationships, organizations can minimize social conflicts, avoid reputational damage, and secure social licenses to operate.

Employee engagement and satisfaction: Employees, particularly the younger workforce, increasingly seek to align their values and ethical standards with those of the organizations they work for. Organizations that prioritize environmental and social responsibility can attract and retain top talent, enhance employee engagement, and foster a sense of purpose among their workforces.

Global supply chain complexities: Organizations operating globally face increasing scrutiny and risks related to their supply chains. Managing environmental and social risks in the supply chain is essential for organizations to maintain ethical practices and mitigate potential reputational and operational risks associated with suppliers and subcontractors.

Organizations need to assess these causative factors and proactively manage environmental and social risks to ensure long-term sustainability, meet stakeholder expectations, comply with regulations, and maintain a positive reputation. By effectively addressing these risks, organizations can not only mitigate negative consequences but also leverage sustainability as a driver for innovation and value creation.

Chapter Twenty-Nine

Case Studies in Risk Management

1. The Deepwater Horizon oil spill: BP's failure to effectively manage the risks associated with deep-water drilling resulted in one of the largest environmental disasters in history, causing significant ecological damage and financial losses.

2. Volkswagen's emissions scandal: Volkswagen's deliberate manipulation of emission test results showcased their failure to manage the risks associated with regulatory compliance, resulting in significant reputational and financial damage.

3. Rana Plaza factory collapse: The collapse of the Rana Plaza garment factory in Bangladesh highlighted the failure of multiple stakeholders, including factory owners, brands, and regulators, to effectively manage risks related to worker safety and building integrity.

4. Fukushima nuclear disaster: The Fukushima nuclear disaster in Japan resulted from inadequate risk management and preparedness for an extreme natural event, leading to widespread environmental contamination and the displacement of thousands of people.

5. Wells Fargo unauthorized accounts scandal: Wells Fargo's failure to adequately manage the risks associated with sales practices and employee incentives led to the creation of unauthorized customer accounts, resulting in significant reputational damage and regulatory penalties.

6. Odebrecht corruption scandal: Brazilian construction company Odebrecht's widespread corruption practices, including bribery and money laundering, highlighted the failure to manage the risks associated with ethical conduct and compliance with anti-corruption laws.

7. Boeing 737 Max crashes: The Boeing 737 Max crashes resulted from a failure to effectively manage risks associated with the aircraft's design and software, leading to multiple fatalities and the grounding of the entire fleet.

8. Samsung Galaxy Note 7 battery explosions: Samsung's failure to adequately manage risks in the design and manufacturing of the Galaxy Note 7 battery resulted in numerous incidents of explosions and the subsequent global recall of the product.

9. Bhopal gas tragedy: The Bhopal gas tragedy in India occurred due to inadequate risk management and safety measures in a Union Carbide pesticide plant, resulting in the release of toxic gases and the death of thousands of people.

10. Enron scandal: Enron's fraudulent accounting practices and failure to manage financial risks led to one of the largest corporate bankruptcy cases in history, causing significant financial losses for investors and employees.

11. British Petroleum Texas City refinery explosion: A series of explosions at BP's Texas City refinery resulted from inadequate risk management, leading to multiple fatalities, injuries, and extensive damage to the facility.

12. Takata airbag recall: Takata's failure to effectively manage risks in the design and manufacturing of airbags resulted in the largest automotive recall in history due to defective airbags that caused multiple deaths and injuries.

13. Equifax data breach: Equifax's failure to adequately manage cybersecurity risks led to a data breach that exposed the personal information of millions of consumers, resulting in significant reputational damage and regulatory fines.

14. Tylenol poisoning incident: Johnson & Johnson's quick and effective response to the cyanide poisoning of Tylenol bottles in the 1980s showcased the importance of risk management and crisis communication in safeguarding consumer trust and minimizing harm.

15. Target data breach: Target's failure to adequately manage cybersecurity risks led to a data breach that compromised the personal information of millions of customers, resulting in reputational damage and financial losses.

16. Bangladesh garment factory fires: Multiple deadly fires in garment factories in Bangladesh highlighted the failure to manage risks related to worker safety, fire prevention, and building compliance, leading to numerous fatalities and injuries.

17. BP Texas City refinery emissions violations: BP's failure to manage risks associated with emissions compliance resulted in multiple violations at the Texas City refinery, leading to significant regulatory fines and reputational damage.

18. Malaysia Airlines MH370 disappearance: The disappearance of Malaysia Airlines Flight MH370 highlighted the need for effective risk management and preparedness in the aviation industry, with ongoing investigations and improvements in tracking systems.

19. Nestlé baby milk formula contamination: Nestlé's failure to manage the risks associated with product contamination led to the presence of toxic substances in its baby milk formula, resulting in global recalls and reputational damage.

20. Uber's data privacy breaches: Uber's failure to effectively manage risks related to data privacy and security led to multiple breaches and unauthorized access to customer and driver information, resulting in regulatory penalties and reputational harm.

These case studies showcase the importance of effective risk management practices across various industries, including environmental, financial, operational, reputational, and data-related risks. They serve as lessons for organizations worldwide to proactively identify, assess, and mitigate risks to ensure the long-term sustainability and success of their operations.

Enron: Lessons in Risk Management Failure

The Enron scandal serves as a stark reminder of the importance of risk management in organizations. Once considered one of the world's most innovative companies, Enron's downfall was primarily attributed to a failure in managing risks effectively. The lessons learned from Enron's case have had lasting impacts on risk management practices. In this detailed explanation, we will explore these lessons in 28 paragraphs.

Risk culture: Enron lacked a strong risk culture that prioritized ethical behavior and accountability. A culture that encourages risk awareness, transparency, and sound risk management practices is essential to prevent unethical actions and fraudulent practices.

Ethical leadership: Enron's top executives encouraged a culture that prioritized short-term financial gains over ethical behavior. Ethical leadership is crucial in setting the tone at the top and promoting a culture of integrity and responsible decision-making.

Risk oversight: Enron's board of directors failed to exercise effective risk oversight. Boards should ensure that risk management processes are in place, regularly reviewed, and aligned with the organization's goals and objectives.

Internal controls: Enron had weak and ineffective internal controls, contributing to the manipulation of financial statements. Robust internal controls help detect and prevent fraud, ensuring the accuracy and reliability of financial reporting.

Risk assessment: Enron failed to adequately assess risks and their potential impact. A comprehensive and ongoing risk assessment process is essential to identify and prioritize risks, enabling organizations to implement appropriate risk mitigation measures.

Risk appetite and tolerance: Enron lacked a clear understanding of its risk appetite and tolerance. Establishing risk thresholds and limits allows organizations to make informed decisions about risk-taking and establish boundaries for acceptable risk exposure.

Conflict of interest: Various conflicts of interest within Enron, including executives benefiting personally from questionable practices, contributed to unethical behavior and compromised risk management. Organizations must promote transparency and prevent conflicts of interest to maintain the integrity of risk management processes.

Independent oversight: Enron's auditors did not exercise independent judgment and failed to identify and report the fraudulent activities. Independent oversight and external audits play a vital role in ensuring the integrity of financial reporting and risk management practices.

Whistleblower protection: Enron lacked an effective system to protect and encourage whistleblowers. Organizations should establish mechanisms that allow employees to report concerns without fear of retaliation, fostering a culture of accountability and transparency.

Communication and transparency: Enron's lack of transparency prevented stakeholders from understanding the true risks and financial health of the company. Open and transparent communication is essential to build trust with stakeholders and ensure that risks are appropriately disclosed.

Risk diversification: Enron faced excessive risks due to over-reliance on specific sectors and risky financial transactions. Diversifying risk by investing in different sectors and adopting a robust risk diversification strategy helps mitigate concentration risks.

Crisis management and contingency planning: Enron did not have adequate crisis management and contingency plans in place. Organizations should have protocols to respond effectively to crises, including fraud, scandals, and other significant risk events.

Earnings management: Enron engaged in earnings management practices to manipulate financial statements. Transparency in financial reporting and adherence to accounting standards are crucial in preventing earnings management that can distort risk profiles.

Compliance and regulatory adherence: Enron violated several accounting and regulatory standards, leading to legal consequences. Organizations must understand and comply with legal and regulatory requirements to minimize the risk of penalties and reputational damage.

External risk assessments: Enron's reliance on internal risk assessments prevented an objective evaluation of risks. Organizations should conduct external risk assessments periodically to gain an independent perspective on risks and potential mitigation strategies.

Risk disclosure: Enron's failure to disclose its true financial condition and risks resulted in a loss of investor confidence. Accurate and robust risk disclosure is critical for investors and stakeholders to make informed decisions and assess risk exposure.

Risk ownership and accountability: Enron lacked clear risk ownership and accountability, leading to a diffusion of responsibility. Organizations should define clear roles and responsibilities for risk management, ensuring accountability and ownership at all levels.

Risk management integration: Enron's risk management processes were fragmented and lacked integration across the organization. Integrating risk management into core business processes enhances decision-making and ensures effective risk mitigation.

Continuous monitoring and reassessment: Enron's risk management processes did not include continuous monitoring and reassessment of risks. Regular monitoring and reassessment help organizations stay ahead of emerging risks and adapt their risk mitigation strategies accordingly.

Risk management education and training: Enron lacked adequate risk management education and training programs for its employees. Organizations should invest in ongoing training to build risk management capabilities at all levels and ensure a risk-aware culture.

External benchmarking: Enron's failure to benchmark its risk management practices against industry standards and best practices limited its ability to identify gaps and weaknesses. Organizations should engage in external benchmarking to evaluate their risk management practices and identify areas for improvement.

Effective risk reporting: Enron's risk reporting processes did not provide accurate and timely information to stakeholders. Organizations should develop comprehensive risk reporting frameworks that provide meaningful and actionable information about risks and mitigation efforts.

Independent risk assurance: Enron lacked an independent mechanism to provide assurance on its risk management processes. Organizations should consider engaging external experts to provide independent assessments and validation of risk management practices.

Long-term perspective: Enron's focus on short-term profits without considering the long-term sustainability of its business contributed to its downfall. Organizations need to strike a balance between short-term performance and long-term sustainable growth in risk management decision-making.

Risk recognition and adaptation: Enron's failure to recognize and adapt to changing risks in the energy market and regulatory environment exposed the organization to significant vulnerabilities. Organizations should conduct regular risk assessments to identify emerging risks and adapt their risk management strategies accordingly.

Professional skepticism: Enron's auditors lacked professional skepticism, accepting management explanations at face value. Organizations should encourage auditors and risk professionals to exercise critical thinking and challenge assumptions for robust risk management practices.

Accountability and consequences: Enron's lack of accountability and consequences for unethical behavior allowed misconduct to persist. Organizations should establish mechanisms to hold individuals accountable for ethical breaches and enforce appropriate consequences.

Continuous improvement: Enron's failure to continuously improve its risk management practices contributed to its ultimate demise. Organizations should promote a culture of continuous improvement in risk management by learning from past mistakes, incorporating feedback, and adapting to evolving risks.

In conclusion, Enron's case serves as a powerful lesson in risk management, highlighting the critical importance of ethics, risk oversight, transparency, effective internal controls, and a risk-aware culture. Organizations must learn from Enron's failures to foster robust risk management practices, maintain stakeholder trust, and ensure long-term sustainability.

Volkswagen Emissions Scandal: A Failure in Risk Mitigation

The Volkswagen emissions scandal, also known as "Dieselgate," is a prominent example of a failure in risk mitigation and ethical misconduct. This scandal unfolded in 2015 when it was revealed that Volkswagen had been deliberately manipulating emissions tests for its diesel vehicles to meet regulatory standards falsely. The repercussions of this scandal were substantial, leading to significant financial losses, a severe blow to the company's reputation, numerous lawsuits, and criminal investigations.

The scandal exposed several key failures in risk mitigation within Volkswagen:

Compliance and regulatory failings: Volkswagen failed to comply with emission standards set by various regulatory bodies, including the U.S. Environmental Protection Agency (EPA) and the California Air Resources Board (CARB). The company deliberately installed "defeat devices" in millions of diesel vehicles to cheat emission tests, posing significant risks of regulatory non-compliance and legal consequences.

Ethical lapses: Volkswagen's actions demonstrated a significant ethical lapse. By intentionally deceiving regulators and consumers, the company breached trust and undermined its reputation. Ethical misconduct can have severe consequences, including legal ramifications and long-lasting damage to a company's brand and stakeholder relationships.

Ineffective risk culture and governance: The scandal revealed a failure in cultivating a risk-aware culture at Volkswagen. The lack of checks and balances allowed the manipulation of emissions tests to persist without detection. Additionally, the risk governance structures within the company were inadequate in identifying and mitigating the risks associated with non-compliance and unethical behavior.

Inadequate internal controls and risk management: The Volkswagen scandal exposed shortcomings in the company's internal control mechanisms. There was a lack of effective risk management systems to identify and address risks associated with emissions compliance and unethical practices.

Lack of transparency and communication: Volkswagen concealed the deliberate manipulation of emissions tests, failing to disclose the true emissions levels of its vehicles to regulators and customers. This lack of transparency hindered stakeholders' ability to make informed decisions based on accurate and reliable information.

Weak oversight and accountability: The scandal highlighted deficiencies in oversight mechanisms within Volkswagen. Failure to hold individuals accountable for their actions and lack of independent oversight allowed the unethical behavior to persist for years.

Damage to stakeholder trust: Volkswagen's deliberate deception eroded the trust of its stakeholders, including customers, investors, and regulators. Loss of trust can result in significant financial and reputational damage, impacting the long-term sustainability and viability of a company.

Legal and financial consequences: The scandal resulted in substantial legal and financial repercussions for Volkswagen. The company faced hefty fines, settlements with affected consumers, and a significant decline in its market value. The financial impact was compounded by the need to recall and modify affected vehicles, as well as the costs associated with legal proceedings and reputational repair efforts.

Reputational damage: The Volkswagen brand suffered a severe blow due to the scandal, tarnishing its once-strong reputation for technical innovation and environmental responsibility. Rebuilding trust and restoring reputation can be a challenging and lengthy process.

Industry-wide consequences: The Volkswagen scandal sent shockwaves throughout the automotive industry. It exposed potential weaknesses in emission testing and compliance protocols, leading to increased scrutiny and stricter regulations in the sector. Other automobile manufacturers faced intensified scrutiny, highlighting the need for robust risk mitigation and compliance practices industry wide.

The Volkswagen emissions scandal underscores the crucial importance of proactive risk management, ethical conduct, transparency, and effective governance structures. It serves as a stark reminder for organizations of all sizes and industries to prioritize risk mitigation, robust internal controls, and a strong risk culture that values compliance and ethical behavior. By learning from the failures of Volkswagen, companies can work towards preventing a similar risk management breakdown and securing long-term sustainability and stakeholder trust.

Tesla Motors: Managing Innovation and Market Risks

Tesla Motors, now known as Tesla Inc., has gained global recognition for its innovative electric vehicles (EVs) and sustainable energy solutions. The company's success can be attributed, in part, to its effective management of innovation and market risks. In this explanation, we will explore how Tesla manages these risks.

Continuous innovation: Tesla embraces a culture of continuous innovation, recognizing the importance of staying at the forefront of technology. The company invests heavily in research and development to drive technological advancements in EVs and clean energy solutions.

Disruptive business model: Tesla's direct-to-consumer sales model and extensive focus on vertical integration differentiate it from traditional automakers. By bypassing dealerships, Tesla can maintain more control over the customer experience and create a unique market position.

Technological differentiation: Tesla differentiates itself through its advanced battery technology, autonomous driving capabilities, and network of Supercharger stations. These technological advancements create a competitive advantage and contribute to Tesla's market leadership in the EV industry.

Supply chain management: Tesla manages market risks associated with its supply chain through strategic supplier partnerships and robust supply chain management practices. By establishing long-term relationships and securing critical components, the company mitigates the risk of supply disruptions.

Regulatory compliance: Compliance with regulations related to EVs, emissions standards, and safety is of utmost importance to Tesla. The company proactively monitors regulatory developments globally to ensure its products meet or exceed the required standards.

Investment in charging infrastructure: Tesla addresses market risks related to range anxiety and charging infrastructure through its extensive Supercharger network. By investing in charging stations globally, Tesla enables long-distance travel and enhances the value proposition of its vehicles.

Brand perception and customer loyalty: Tesla effectively manages market risks by fostering a strong brand perception and customer loyalty. The company's emphasis on sustainability, innovation, and exceptional customer service cultivates a positive image and helps retain customers.

Financial risk management: Tesla mitigates financial risks associated with innovation and market dynamics through prudent financial management. This includes managing cash flows, maintaining a strong balance sheet, and raising capital through strategic financing options.

Production scalability: As Tesla expands its production capacity, it manages risks associated with scaling operations and meeting global demand. The company continually invests in Gigafactories to increase production efficiency and achieve economies of scale.

Talent management: Tesla recognizes the importance of attracting and retaining top talent to drive innovation and maintain a competitive edge. The company offers various incentives to attract skilled professionals, including stock options and career development opportunities.

Market diversification: Tesla mitigates risks associated with market concentration by diversifying its product portfolio and expanding globally. This approach helps the company reduce reliance on any single market or product category.

Strategic partnerships: Tesla forms strategic partnerships with other companies, such as Panasonic for battery manufacturing, to share risks and leverage complementary expertise. Partnerships enable Tesla to optimize its supply chain, access new markets, and collaborate on research and development initiatives.

Customer feedback and engagement: Tesla actively engages with customers to gather feedback, understand their needs, and improve its products and services. This customer-centric approach minimizes market risks by ensuring ongoing satisfaction and addressing potential concerns promptly.

Regulatory advocacy: Tesla actively engages in regulatory advocacy to shape policies that support the advancement of the EV industry. By participating in discussions and lobbying efforts, the company helps mitigate regulatory risks and create a more favorable market environment.

Intellectual property protection: Tesla places significant emphasis on protecting its intellectual property (IP) to safeguard its technological innovations and maintain a competitive advantage. Robust IP protection minimizes the risk of competitors replicating Tesla's advancements.

Marketing and communication: Tesla's marketing and communication strategies effectively convey the company's brand values, educate consumers about the benefits of EVs, and dispel myths. These efforts help address market risks related to misconceptions and promote wider adoption of electric vehicles.

Research and development partnerships: Tesla collaborates with academic institutions, research organizations, and industry partners to share knowledge, access specialized expertise, and develop innovative solutions. These partnerships mitigate innovation risks by pooling resources and expertise.

Competitive analysis: Tesla conducts comprehensive competitive analysis to understand market trends, evaluate competitor strategies, and identify potential risks and opportunities. This analysis enables Tesla to adjust its own approach and seize competitive advantages.

Crisis management and communication: Tesla's proactive crisis management and transparent communication help manage risks arising from unexpected events or negative incidents. By promptly addressing issues, taking responsibility when necessary, and continuously improving, Tesla can mitigate reputational and market risks.

Environmental and social responsibility: Tesla's commitment to environmental and social responsibility aligns with market demands and reduces risks associated with sustainability concerns. By actively addressing these issues, Tesla secures its position as a trusted and responsible leader in the industry.

Long-term strategy: Tesla's long-term strategic vision guides its risk management approach. With a focus on sustainable transportation and renewable energy solutions, the company aims to stay ahead of market shifts and position itself for long-term success.

Data security and privacy: Tesla prioritizes data security and customer privacy to mitigate risks associated with data breaches and cyber threats. The company implements robust cybersecurity measures and adheres to strict privacy policies to protect customer information.

Consumer education: Tesla invests in consumer education programs to increase awareness about EV technology, charging infrastructure, and the environmental benefits of electric vehicles. Educated consumers are more likely to embrace technology and reduce market risks associated with lack of awareness.

Fleet management and vehicle maintenance: Tesla leverages data and technology to monitor vehicle performance, identify potential risks, and proactively address maintenance and service requirements. This approach minimizes both safety risks and potential damage to the company's reputation.

Public-private partnerships: Tesla collaborates with public institutions and organizations to create supportive frameworks, infrastructure, and policies for electric vehicles. Such partnerships help mitigate market risks by fostering a supportive and conducive market environment.

Scenario planning: Tesla engages in scenario planning to anticipate and evaluate potential risks and their impacts. By considering different future possibilities, the company can develop contingency plans and adapt its strategies accordingly.

Through effective management of innovation and market risks, Tesla has established itself as a leader in the electric vehicle industry. By continuously driving technological advancements, focusing on sustainable growth, and addressing market-driven concerns, Tesla successfully navigates the challenges and opportunities associated with innovation and market dynamics.

Conclusion and Future Directions in Risk Management

Conclusion

Risk management plays a critical role in the success and sustainability of organizations in today's complex and uncertain business environment. As we look to the future, there are several key directions in which risk management is expected to evolve. In this conclusion, we will discuss 50 paragraphs on the future directions in risk management.

Integrated approach: Risk management will become more integrated with overall business strategy and decision-making processes. Organizations will aim to embed risk management practices throughout their operations to enhance agility, resilience, and performance.

Technology-driven solutions: The future of risk management will be heavily influenced by technological advancements such as AI, machine learning, and big data analytics. These technologies will enable organizations to identify, assess, and mitigate risks more effectively and efficiently.

Risk culture: There will be an increased emphasis on building a strong risk culture within organizations. This involves fostering a proactive attitude towards risk management at all levels and ensuring that risk management is seen as everyone's responsibility.

Scenario planning: Scenario planning will become a more prominent technique in risk management. Organizations will use this approach to explore alternative futures and prepare for a wide range of potential risks and opportunities.

Resilience-focused approach: Risk management will shift towards a more holistic and resilience-focused approach. Organizations will focus on assessing their ability to withstand and recover from disruptions rather than solely trying to prevent them.

Real-time risk monitoring: With the advancement of technology, risk monitoring will become more dynamic and real-time. Organizations will have access to more accurate and up-to-date risk data, enabling them to respond quickly to emerging risks.

Cybersecurity risk management: As cyber threats continue to evolve, organizations will invest more in effective cybersecurity risk management strategies. This will include implementing robust security measures, conducting regular security assessments, and training employees to improve cyber-awareness.

Supply chain resilience: Organizations will place a greater emphasis on managing risks within their supply chains. This will involve understanding the vulnerabilities and dependencies within the supply chain and implementing strategies to enhance resilience.

ESG risk management: Environmental, social, and governance (ESG) risks will gain more attention in the future. Organizations will be expected to evaluate and manage these risks to minimize their negative impacts on society, the environment, and their own reputation.

Non-financial risk management: The focus of risk management will extend beyond financial risks to include non-financial risks such as operational, reputational, and regulatory risks. Organizations will adopt a more comprehensive approach to identify and manage these risks.

Dynamic risk appetite: Risk appetite statements will become more dynamic to reflect the changing risk landscape. Organizations will regularly review and update their risk appetite to align with strategic objectives, market conditions, and stakeholder expectations.

Collaborative risk management: Risk management will become a more collaborative effort involving different stakeholders, including customers, suppliers, regulators, and industry peers. Organizations will work together to identify and address shared risks that could impact the ecosystem.

Enhanced risk reporting: Organizations will adopt more transparent and informative risk reporting practices. This will involve providing stakeholders with clear and concise information about the organization's risk profile, risk management activities, and the effectiveness of the risk management framework.

Behavioral risk management: Understanding human behavior and cognitive biases will be crucial in managing risks effectively. Organizations will invest in research and training programs to identify and mitigate behavioral risks that could lead to poor decision-making.

Resilient leadership: Risk management will require resilient leadership that can navigate uncertainties and make informed decisions in challenging times. Organizations will focus on developing leaders who can effectively manage risks while driving innovation and growth.

Regulatory compliance: Organizations will continue to face increasing regulatory scrutiny, requiring them to be vigilant in managing compliance risks. Compliance functions will become more integrated and proactive, ensuring adherence to regulations, and mitigating potential penalties.

Contingency planning: Contingency planning will play a crucial role in risk management. Organizations will develop comprehensive plans to prepare for potential crises, including natural disasters, pandemics, or market downturns.

Risk-based performance management: Organizations will adopt risk-based performance management frameworks to align risk management with operational and strategic goals. This will involve setting performance targets that reflect risk appetite and measuring performance against the effective management of risks.

Quantitative risk analysis: The use of quantitative risk analysis techniques, such as Monte Carlo simulations and probabilistic modeling, will become more prevalent. Organizations will leverage these techniques to better access and communicate risk exposures.

Adaptability and agility: Risk management will evolve to become more adaptive and agile. Organizations will develop the capability to quickly identify and respond to emerging risks, enabling them to seize opportunities and manage threats effectively.

Outsourced risk management: Some organizations may choose to outsource certain risk management functions to specialized firms. This will allow them to access specialized expertise and technologies while focusing on their core business activities.

Supply chain visibility: Technology will enable organizations to enhance visibility and traceability across their supply chains. This will help identify potential risks, such as human rights violations or environmental impacts, and make informed decisions to mitigate them.

Insurance and risk transfer: Organizations will continue to rely on insurance and other risk transfer mechanisms to mitigate risks. However, the insurance industry will also need to evolve to effectively manage emerging risks, such as cyber threats or climate change-related risks.

Data privacy and protection: With the increasing reliance on data-driven decision-making, organizations will focus on data privacy and protection. Robust data governance and cybersecurity measures will be implemented to ensure the confidentiality, integrity, and availability of sensitive information.

Artificial intelligence in risk management: Organizations will leverage AI technologies to automate routine risk management tasks, improve data analysis, and enhance risk prediction. This will enable risk professionals to focus on more strategic and complex risk management activities.

Climate change risk management: As climate change poses significant risks to businesses, organizations will integrate climate change risk management into their overall risk management processes. This will involve assessing physical risks, transitioning to low-carbon practices, and adapting to changing climate trends.

Risk management education and certification: The demand for risk management professionals will grow in the future. As a result, there will be an increased emphasis on risk management education and professional certifications to ensure the availability of skilled risk practitioners.

Board-level risk oversight: Boards of directors will take a more active role in risk oversight, ensuring that risk management is integrated into strategic decision-making. Organizations will establish dedicated risk committees or assign risk oversight responsibilities to existing committees.

Long-term risk horizon: Risk management will expand its focus on long-term risks that may materialize in the distant future. Organizations will engage in horizon scanning and scenario planning to identify and manage systemic risks that could impact their long-term viability.

Risk management in the public sector: Risk management practices will extend beyond the private sector into the public sector. Governments and public organizations will adopt risk management frameworks to enhance transparency, accountability, and effective governance.

Resilient infrastructure planning: Risk management will play a crucial role in planning and developing resilient infrastructure. Organizations will evaluate potential risks, such as extreme weather events or cyber-attacks, and design infrastructure systems that can withstand and recover from such events.

Cultural and behavioral risk assessments: Organizations will implement cultural and behavioral risk assessments to identify potential risks stemming from organizational culture, values, and employee behavior. This will help address ethical risks, misconduct, and non-compliance issues.

Risk quantification and monetization: The ability to quantify and monetize risks will become more advanced. Organizations will develop models and methodologies to assess the financial impact of risks and make informed decisions on risk mitigation investments.

Continuous risk monitoring: Risk monitoring will become a continuous process rather than periodic assessments. Real-time data and analytics will enable organizations to detect and respond to risks as they emerge, minimizing potential impacts.

Risk management in emerging markets: As organizations expand into emerging markets, managing risks specific to those regions will become increasingly important. Organizations will need to understand local risk dynamics, regulatory environments, and cultural nuances to effectively mitigate risks.

Ethical risk management: Organizations will focus on managing ethical risks, ensuring compliance with ethical guidelines, and aligning their actions with societal expectations. Ethical risk management will be embedded in organizational values, governance, and decision-making processes.

Risk communication and stakeholder engagement: Effective risk communication and stakeholder engagement will be key to successful risk management. Organizations will develop clear and transparent communication channels to engage stakeholders and address their concerns proactively.

Proactive risk identification: Risk identification will become more proactive, with organizations actively seeking out potential risks rather than simply responding to known risks. This will involve horizon scanning, predictive analytics, and engaging with external experts to identify emerging risks.

Risk management in the gig economy: As the gig economy continues to grow, organizations will need to adapt their risk management practices. This will involve managing risks related to contractors, freelancers, and new employment models.

Resilient business models: Organizations will focus on developing resilient business models that can withstand disruptions and adapt to changing market conditions. This will involve diversifying revenue streams, building flexibility into operations, and leveraging technology for innovation.

Risk management training and awareness: Organizations will invest in risk management training programs to enhance risk awareness and build risk management capabilities across all levels of the organization. This will enable employees to identify and manage risks effectively in their respective roles.

Risk management in mergers and acquisitions: Risk management will play a crucial role in mergers and acquisitions. Organizations will conduct thorough due diligence, assess potential risks, and develop integration plans to ensure a smooth transition and mitigate integration risks.

Cultural risk management: Understanding and managing cultural risks will be vital in global organizations. Organizations will adopt a culturally sensitive approach to risk management, acknowledging and addressing risks arising from cultural differences in different regions.

PART IV
The Role of Emotional Intelligence in Effective Decision-Making by Managers

Chapter Thirty

The Role of Emotional Intelligence in Effective Decision-making by Managers

Introduction

In the business world, decision-making is a fundamental skill that managers must possess. Effective decision-making is crucial for the success of an organization as it determines the direction and outcome of various business activities. While cognitive abilities and knowledge are often seen as critical factors in decision-making, the role of emotional intelligence (EI) is often overlooked. Emotional intelligence refers to the ability to recognize, understand, and manage one's emotions, as well as the emotions of others. This paper aims to explore the significance of emotional intelligence in effective decision-making by managers, highlighting its benefits and practical implications.

Understanding Emotional Intelligence

Emotional intelligence encompasses a range of skills and competencies that contribute to effective decision-making. These skills include self-awareness, self-regulation, empathy, and social skills. Self-awareness involves recognizing one's own emotions and understanding their impact on decision-making. Self-regulation, on the other hand, refers to the ability to manage and control one's emotions, ensuring that they do not cloud judgment or bias decision-making. Empathy is vital for understanding and considering the emotions and perspectives of others, particularly when making decisions that impact them. Lastly, social skills involve being able to communicate effectively, build relationships, and collaborate with others, all of which are essential for successful decision-making in a managerial role.

Importance of Emotional Intelligence in Decision-making

Emotional intelligence plays a crucial role in decision-making for several reasons. Firstly, decisions made by managers often involve complex and ambiguous situations where emotions can influence the outcome. Having an elevated level of emotional intelligence allows managers to navigate these situations effectively by using their emotions as information, rather than being controlled by them. By understanding their emotions and the emotions of others, managers can make decisions that are sensitive to the needs and concerns of all stakeholders.

Furthermore, emotional intelligence helps managers to build and maintain positive relationships with employees, colleagues, and other stakeholders. Involving others in the decision-making process is a valuable approach, as it allows for a diversity of perspectives and insights. Managers with high emotional intelligence can effectively communicate their decisions, build trust, and motivate others to implement them. This not only improves the quality of decisions but also enhances employee engagement and commitment to their work, resulting in increased organizational performance.

Benefits of Emotional Intelligence in Decision-making

The benefits of emotional intelligence in decision-making are numerous. Firstly, emotional intelligence enables managers to make more rational and unbiased decisions. By recognizing their own emotional biases and regulating their emotional responses, managers can ensure that their decisions are based on sound judgment and analysis. They are less likely to be swayed by emotions such as fear, anger, or overconfidence, resulting in more objective and effective decision-making.

Secondly, emotional intelligence facilitates better problem-solving. The ability to understand and manage emotions allows managers to deal with conflicts, challenges, and uncertainties that often accompany decision-making. Emotional intelligence enables managers to approach problems with a calm and rational mindset, effectively identifying and evaluating different options. They are better equipped to manage stressful situations, think creatively, and find innovative solutions.

Moreover, emotional intelligence enhances decision-making by enabling managers to consider the impact of their decisions on others. Making decisions solely based on facts and logic may lead to disregarding the emotions and concerns of stakeholders. Emotional intelligence allows managers to empathize with others, understanding their perspectives, motivations, and needs. This leads to decisions that are fair, inclusive, and considerate of others' experiences, fostering a positive organizational culture where individuals feel valued and respected.

Practical Implications of Emotional Intelligence in Decision-making

To harness the benefits of emotional intelligence in decision-making, managers must actively cultivate and develop their emotional intelligence. The following are some practical implications for managers to enhance their emotional intelligence:

1. Self-reflection: Regularly reflect on one's own emotions and the impact they have on decision-making. Consider how personal biases or emotional responses may influence judgments.

2. Emotional regulation: Develop techniques to regulate and manage emotions, such as deep breathing or taking breaks to gain perspective and avoid making impulsive decisions based on heightened emotions.

3. Active listening: Practice active listening to better understand the emotions and perspectives of others. This helps to build empathy and make decisions that reflect diverse viewpoints.

4. Effective communication: Enhance communication skills to express emotions, ideas, and decisions clearly and respectfully. Use appropriate language and tone to ensure that the message is received and understood accurately.

5. Continuous learning: Regularly seek feedback from colleagues, subordinates, and other stakeholders to gain insights into how emotions impact decision-making. Actively engage in learning opportunities to develop emotional intelligence competencies.

The role of emotional intelligence in effective decision-making by managers cannot be underestimated. Emotional intelligence enhances the decision-making process by mitigating emotional biases, enabling rational judgment, and fostering empathy. Managers who possess high emotional intelligence are better equipped to navigate complex situations, build positive relationships, and make informed and inclusive decisions. Cultivating emotional intelligence requires self-awareness, self-regulation, empathy, and social skills. By understanding the significance of emotional intelligence and actively developing these skills, managers can improve their decision-making abilities and positively impact the overall performance of their organizations.

In today's dynamic and fast-paced business environment, effective decision-making is crucial for the success of any organization. Managers are the driving force behind decision-making processes, making critical choices that can shape the future of their companies. While traditional models of decision-making have focused primarily on cognitive abilities and rational thinking, recent research has highlighted the significant role of emotional intelligence (EI) in managerial decision-making.

Emotional intelligence refers to the ability to recognize, understand, and manage one's emotions, as well as the emotions of others. It encompasses a set of skills that are critical for effective decision-making, such as self-awareness, self-regulation, empathy, and social skills. Managers who possess an elevated level of emotional intelligence are better equipped to navigate complex decision-making scenarios and understand the impact of their decisions on others.

One of the key reasons why emotional intelligence is essential for effective decision-making is its ability to mitigate emotional biases. Emotions often play a significant role in decision-making, either by clouding judgment or by influencing choices based on gut feelings. Managers with high emotional intelligence can recognize emotional biases and regulate them, ensuring that decisions are based on rational judgment rather than unfounded emotions.

Furthermore, emotional intelligence helps managers build and maintain positive relationships with their employees, colleagues, and other stakeholders. By effectively understanding and managing their own emotions, managers can create a supportive and inclusive environment where employees feel valued and motivated. This, in turn, leads to increased job satisfaction and commitment, which enhances the quality of decision-making within the organization.

Another significant benefit of emotional intelligence in decision-making is its ability to facilitate better problem-solving. Managers face numerous challenges and uncertainties in their decision-making processes, and emotions can often make it harder to think critically and find innovative solutions. Emotional intelligence allows managers to approach problems with a calm and rational mindset, enabling them to consider multiple perspectives and identify creative solutions that might otherwise be overlooked.

In addition, emotional intelligence enables managers to consider the impact of their decisions on others. Traditional decision-making models often prioritize objective facts and logic, overlooking the emotional and human aspects of decision-making. However, decisions made without considering the emotions and concerns of stakeholders can lead to dissatisfaction and resistance. Managers with high emotional intelligence can empathize with others, understand their perspectives, and make decisions that consider their emotions and needs, resulting in more inclusive and effective outcomes.

Practically speaking, cultivating emotional intelligence requires self-reflection and self-awareness. Managers need to regularly reflect on their own emotions and understand how they may influence decision-making. Developing emotional regulation techniques, such as deep breathing or taking breaks, can also help managers regulate their emotions and avoid making impulsive decisions based on heightened emotions.

Active listening is another important skill that managers should develop to enhance their emotional intelligence. By actively listening to others, managers can better understand their emotions, perspectives, and concerns, enabling them to make decisions that reflect diverse viewpoints and needs. Effective communication skills are also crucial in expressing emotions, ideas, and decisions clearly and respectfully, ensuring that the message is received and understood accurately.

Continuous learning is essential for developing emotional intelligence. Managers should actively seek feedback from colleagues, subordinates, and other stakeholders to gain insights into how emotions impact decision-making. Engaging in learning opportunities, such as workshops or courses, can also help managers develop and refine their emotional intelligence competencies.

In conclusion, emotional intelligence plays a vital role in effective decision-making by managers. It helps mitigate emotional biases, enables rational judgment, and fosters empathy and inclusivity. Cultivating emotional intelligence requires self-awareness, self-regulation, empathy, and social skills. By actively developing these skills, managers can enhance their decision-making abilities, create positive relationships, and contribute to the overall success of their organizations. Emotions are an integral part of the decision-making process, and acknowledging and understanding them is crucial for making informed and effective choices. The role of emotional intelligence in decision-making by managers should not be underestimated, as it has the potential to significantly impact the outcomes and success of organizations in today's complex business landscape.

Purpose of the Study

The study of the role of emotional intelligence in effective decision-making by managers is an area of great interest and importance in the field of business and management. Emotional intelligence refers to the ability to recognize, understand, and manage one's own emotions as well as the emotions of others. It involves the skills of self-awareness, self-regulation, empathy, and social awareness. As decision-making is a critical aspect of managerial roles, understanding how emotional intelligence influences this process can have significant implications for individual managers, their teams, and the organizations they work for.

Firstly, emotional intelligence plays a crucial role in enhancing self-awareness, which is the foundation for effective decision-making. Managers with high emotional intelligence are better able to recognize and understand their own emotions, strengths, and weaknesses. This self-awareness allows them to objectively assess their decision-making abilities and biases, enabling them to make more informed choices. By having a clear understanding of their own emotions, managers can also better manage stress, remain focused, and stay composed when making decisions, even under high-pressure situations.

Secondly, emotional intelligence enables managers to regulate their emotions, which is crucial in decision-making processes. Effective decision-making often requires managers to remain calm and composed, particularly when facing challenging and complex situations. By managing their own emotions, managers can better assess the situation at hand, evaluate diverse options, and make decisions that are rational and objective rather than being driven by emotional biases. This ability to regulate emotions also helps managers to consider the impact of their decisions on others and make choices that are inclusive, fair, and ethically sound.

Thirdly, emotional intelligence plays a significant role in empathy and social awareness, both of which are essential in decision-making processes that involve multiple stakeholders. Managers with high emotional intelligence have a better understanding of the emotions and perspectives of others, enabling them to consider diverse viewpoints and make decisions that consider the needs and concerns of different individuals or groups. This empathy and social awareness also promote effective communication and collaboration, as managers can build strong relationships and establish trust with their team members, colleagues, and other stakeholders. This, in turn, enhances the decision-making process by encouraging open dialogue, the exchange of ideas, and the consideration of various alternatives.

Furthermore, emotional intelligence can positively impact the overall decision-making climate within an organization. When managers exhibit high emotional intelligence, they create an environment that values open communication, active listening, and the expression of emotions. Such an environment encourages employees at all levels to participate in the decision-making process and contribute their perspectives, ideas, and concerns. This inclusive decision-making climate fosters employee engagement, creativity, and innovation, leading to more effective and successful outcomes. Additionally, managers with high emotional intelligence are better equipped to manage conflicts and resolve disagreements, ensuring that the decision-making process is not derailed by personal or emotional issues.

Moreover, the study of the role of emotional intelligence in effective decision-making by managers has practical implications for leadership development and training programs. Organizations can assess and develop emotional intelligence competencies among their managers to enhance their decision-making abilities. Training programs can focus on self-awareness, self-regulation, empathy, and social awareness skills, providing managers with the knowledge and tools required to make informed and effective decisions. This investment in emotional intelligence development can have a long-lasting impact on individual managers, their teams, and the organization.

In conclusion, the study of the role of emotional intelligence in effective decision-making by managers is of critical significance in the field of business and management. Emotional intelligence enhances self-awareness, self-regulation, empathy, and social awareness, enabling managers to make more informed, rational, and inclusive decisions. It contributes to the overall decision-making climate within an organization, fostering employee engagement, creativity, and innovation. Furthermore, the study of emotional intelligence has practical implications for leadership development and training programs, allowing organizations to assess and develop these competencies among their managers. Therefore, understanding and promoting emotional intelligence among managers can contribute to their effectiveness in decision-making processes, leading to improved organizational performance and success.

Background

The role of emotional intelligence in effective decision-making by managers has gained significant attention in recent years. Emotional intelligence encompasses the ability to recognize and understand emotions in oneself and others and to use this information to guide thinking and behavior. Research has shown that managers with higher levels of emotional intelligence are more adept at making effective decisions, as they possess the skills to manage their own emotions and navigate complex interpersonal relationships. Additionally, emotional intelligence helps managers to effectively manage conflicts, enhance teamwork, and provide effective leadership. This topic is significant as it explores the impact of emotional intelligence on managerial decision-making, contributing to organizational success.

Understanding Emotional Intelligence

Understanding emotional intelligence involves comprehending the concept and components of emotional intelligence, as well as its significance in personal and professional contexts. Emotional intelligence refers to the ability to recognize, understand, and manage one's own emotions and the emotions of others. It involves four key components: self-awareness, self-regulation, empathy, and social awareness.

Self-awareness is the ability to recognize and understand one's own emotions, strengths, weaknesses, and values. It involves being in tune with one's feelings, thoughts, and behaviors, and understanding how they affect oneself and others. Self-awareness allows individuals to have a clear understanding of their emotions and helps them make informed decisions based on their emotional state.

Self-regulation refers to the ability to manage and control one's emotions, impulses, and behaviors. It involves staying calm in stressful situations, controlling one's anger or frustration, and resisting impulsive reactions. Self-regulation allows individuals to think before acting and make rational decisions rather than being driven by their emotions.

Empathy is the ability to understand and share the emotions and perspectives of others. It involves putting oneself in others' shoes, listening attentively, and showing genuine care and concern. Empathy allows individuals to connect with others on an emotional level, understand their needs and concerns, and respond appropriately.

Social awareness is the ability to notice the emotions and needs of those around us. It involves being perceptive to social cues, recognizing and understanding the dynamics of a group, and being sensitive to the emotions of others. Social awareness helps individuals navigate social situations effectively and build strong relationships.

Understanding emotional intelligence is significant in personal and professional contexts. In personal life, it improves interpersonal relationships, communication skills, and overall well-being. It allows individuals to build healthier relationships, resolve conflicts more effectively, and cultivate higher levels of self-confidence and self-esteem.

In a professional context, emotional intelligence is crucial for effective leadership, teamwork, and decision-making. Leaders with high emotional intelligence can inspire and motivate their team members, build trust and loyalty, and create a positive work environment. Teams with members who possess strong emotional intelligence can collaborate more effectively, understand, and appreciate diverse perspectives, and work towards common goals.

Additionally, understanding emotional intelligence can help individuals manage stress and handle pressure in the workplace. By recognizing and managing their own emotions, individuals can stay focused and composed, make better decisions, and effectively navigate challenging situations.

Understanding emotional intelligence also promotes self-development and self-improvement. It allows individuals to identify their emotional strengths and weaknesses and work towards enhancing their emotional intelligence competencies. Through self-reflection, feedback from others, and personal growth efforts, individuals can continuously improve their emotional intelligence skills.

Moreover, understanding emotional intelligence is relevant in various fields such as education, healthcare, and counseling. Educators can use emotional intelligence to create a positive learning environment, understand students' emotions, and support their social and emotional development. Healthcare professionals can utilize emotional intelligence to provide empathetic and compassionate care to patients. Counselors can use emotional intelligence to build rapport with clients, understand their emotions, and provide effective guidance.

In conclusion, understanding emotional intelligence involves comprehending the concept and components of emotional intelligence and recognizing its significance in personal and professional contexts. It involves self-awareness, self-regulation, empathy, and social awareness. Understanding emotional intelligence allows individuals to cultivate healthy relationships, make effective decisions, manage stress, and foster personal growth. It is relevant in various fields and can be beneficial in distinct aspects of life.

The causative Factors of Emotions

Emotional Intelligence (EI), also known as emotional quotient (EQ), refers to the ability to identify, understand, and manage emotions effectively. It plays a significant role in personal and professional success, including better interpersonal relationships, effective communication, and improved decision-making abilities. However, several causative factors can hinder the development and expression of emotional intelligence. In this essay, we will explore these factors and discuss strategies to eradicate them.

One of the primary factors that hinder emotional intelligence is a lack of self-awareness. Many individuals struggle to recognize and understand their emotions, which impairs their ability to manage them. Self-awareness can be improved through mindfulness practices like meditation and self-reflection. By deliberately paying attention to our emotions and thoughts, we can gain a deeper understanding of ourselves and our emotional reactions.

Societal and cultural norms can adversely affect emotional intelligence. Certain cultures discourage the expression of emotions, particularly negative ones, which can lead to individuals suppressing or denying their feelings. To eradicate this factor, societies should promote emotional openness and create safe spaces for individuals to express and process their emotions without judgment or criticism.

Unhealthy childhood experiences can have long-lasting impacts on emotional intelligence. Traumatic events, neglect, or an unsupportive family environment can hinder emotional development. Addressing these issues requires early intervention through therapy and counseling, providing children with a safe and nurturing environment, and educating parents on the importance of emotional well-being.

Limited emotional vocabulary is another causative factor. Many individuals struggle to articulate their feelings adequately, which hampers effective communication and understanding. Expanding emotional vocabulary can be achieved by actively seeking out innovative words to describe emotions, engaging in discussions and debates, and reading literature that explores the intricacies of emotions.

The prevalence of technology and social media has also impacted emotional intelligence negatively. People spend excessive amounts of time on digital devices, resulting in diminished face-to-face interactions and reduced understanding of non-verbal cues. Limiting screen time, engaging in offline activities, and cultivating meaningful social connections are effective ways to combat this factor.

The influence of negative emotions such as stress, anxiety, and anger can hinder emotional intelligence. When individuals are overwhelmed by negative emotions, their ability to think clearly and respond rationally diminishes. Developing stress management techniques like deep breathing, exercising regularly, and practicing mindfulness can help individuals regain control over their emotions.

Lack of empathy is a significant barrier to emotional intelligence. Empathy involves understanding and sharing the feelings of others, yet many people struggle to connect with others' emotions on a deep level. To cultivate empathy, individuals can actively practice listening skills, engage in perspective-taking exercises, and expose themselves to diverse perspectives and experiences.

Fear of vulnerability can impede emotional intelligence. Opening and being vulnerable requires courage, but many individuals fear being judged or rejected. Encouraging vulnerability in personal relationships, creating a safe environment for open and honest communication, and leading by example can help mitigate this factor.

Excessive focus on intellect and rationality can overshadow emotional intelligence. In many educational and professional settings, emotions are often dismissed or overlooked in favor of logic and reason. Incorporating emotional education and training into school curricula and workplace training programs can help individuals develop a balanced intellect-emotion integration.

Perfectionism can hinder emotional intelligence. Setting unrealistic standards for oneself and fearing failure can lead to excessive stress and self-criticism. Embracing the concept of a growth mindset, celebrating small achievements, and practicing self-compassion can help individuals overcome the destructive cycle of perfectionism.

Prejudice and bias can significantly impact emotional intelligence. Stereotypes and biases can distort our perception of others and hinder our ability to empathize and connect emotionally. Eradicating prejudice requires challenging and unlearning our biases through exposure to diverse cultures, engaging in inclusive discussions, and actively seeking out perspectives different from our own.

Poor conflict-resolution skills can impede emotional intelligence. Many individuals avoid or mishandle conflicts, leading to unresolved issues and strained relationships. Educating individuals on constructive conflict resolution techniques such as active listening, assertive communication, and mediation can help improve emotional intelligence in this area.

Stressors in the workplace can negatively affect emotional intelligence. High workloads, time pressure, and conflicts with colleagues can hinder individuals' ability to manage emotions effectively. Employers should prioritize work-life balance, provide stress management resources, and foster a supportive work environment to bolster emotional intelligence in the workplace.

A sense of entitlement can hinder emotional intelligence. When individuals believe, they are entitled to certain privileges or treatment, they may struggle to understand and empathize with others' perspectives and emotions.

Cultivating gratitude, fostering a sense of humility, and teaching the importance of empathy can help eradicate this factor.

Lack of emotional resilience is another hindrance to emotional intelligence. When individuals are unable to bounce back from setbacks and disappointments, their emotional well-being and ability to manage their emotions become compromised. Building emotional resilience can be achieved through practices such as mindfulness, self-care, and seeking support from loved ones or professionals.

Ineffective communication skills can impede emotional intelligence. Poor communication hinders individuals' ability to express their emotions, listen actively, and understand others. Developing effective communication skills involves active listening, using "I" statements, and practicing empathy to create a safe and open communication environment.

A fear of change can hinder emotional intelligence. Individuals who resist or fear change may struggle to manage their emotions when confronted with unfamiliar or uncomfortable situations. Encouraging individuals to embrace change, providing support during transitions, and promoting a growth mindset can help address this factor.

Lacking emotional boundaries can hinder emotional intelligence. Some individuals struggle to separate their own emotions from others, leading to emotional overwhelm and difficulty in managing their feelings. Establishing healthy emotional boundaries through self-reflection, assertiveness, and self-care practices can help eradicate this factor.

A lack of emotional intelligence, education, and awareness exacerbates the problem. Emotional intelligence is often overlooked or undervalued in traditional education systems, perpetuating the lack of knowledge and skills in this area. Integrating emotional intelligence education into school curricula, workplace training, and public awareness campaigns can help address this gap.

Lastly, societal pressure and unrealistic expectations contribute to the inhibition of emotional intelligence. Expectations of success, happiness, and constant positivity can create stress and emotional suppression. Encouraging self-compassion, promoting mental well-being, and debunking societal myths about emotions are crucial in eradicating this factor.

In conclusion, emotional intelligence is crucial for personal and professional success. However, several causative factors hinder its development. By addressing these factors through education, open communication, empathy, and creating supportive environments, individuals and societies can eradicate the barriers to emotional intelligence and foster a greater understanding and management of emotions.

Avoiding Emotions as a Manager

As a manager, it is crucial to maintain a level-headed approach, avoiding letting emotions affect decision-making and communication. Emotions can cloud judgment, hinder effective team management, and create a negative work environment.

1. Objective Perspective: A manager should prioritize an objective perspective, ensuring decisions are based on rationality rather than being swayed by emotions.

2. Self-Awareness: Continuously developing self-awareness can help managers recognize their emotions and prevent them from negatively impacting their decision-making process.

3. Emotional Intelligence: Managers should strive to enhance their emotional intelligence by understanding, managing, and empathizing with the emotions of themselves and others.

4. Conflict Management: Avoiding emotions in conflict situations enables managers to approach the issues impartially, calmly analyze the situation, and find a mutually beneficial resolution.

5. Clear Communication: Emotional responses can cloud the intended message, causing misunderstandings and conflicts. Managers should strive for clear and concise communication, free from emotional influence.

6. Constructive Feedback: Emotional reactions can hinder the delivery of constructive feedback, leading to employee demotivation. By avoiding emotions, managers can provide effective feedback that fosters growth and improvement.

7. Impartial Decision-making: Emotions can significantly affect decision-making, leading to biased choices. Managers must strive to make impartial decisions based on facts and evidence, rather than letting emotions sway them.

8. Conflict of Interest: Emotional attachment may lead to biased decisions based on personal interests. Managers should maintain objectivity by avoiding such emotional conflicts.

9. Professionalism: Demonstrating professionalism by avoiding emotional outbursts establishes a positive organizational culture and garners respect from employees.

10. Performance Evaluation: Emotional biases can surface during employee performance evaluations, leading to unfair judgments. Managers should overcome emotions and evaluate performance objectively, based on predefined criteria.

11. Crisis Management: During demanding situations, a calm and collected approach is crucial for effective crisis management. Managers need to detach themselves emotionally to make rational decisions that address the crisis effectively.

12. Employee Empowerment: Emotions can hinder employee empowerment by overshadowing their ideas and contributions. A rational manager avoids personal emotions and supports employees' growth, allowing them to take ownership of their work.

13. Promoting Collaboration: Emotions can hinder teamwork and collaboration. A manager who avoids emotions can foster a collaborative environment, encouraging open dialogue, cooperation, and collective problem-solving.

14. Building Trust: Emotional stability instills confidence and trust among employees. A calm and composed manager gain the trust of their team, enabling open communication and a healthy work atmosphere.

15. Role Model: Managers who exhibit emotional control serve as role models for their team members, encouraging them to adopt a similar approach and fostering a more professional work environment.

16. Handling Criticism: Emotional reactions to criticism can hinder personal growth and learning opportunities. A manager should embrace criticism objectively, using it as a chance to improve and demonstrate resilience.

17. Empathy without Bias: While empathy is essential, emotions may influence managers' ability to empathize without bias. By avoiding emotions, managers can provide unbiased support to employees during challenging times.

18. Diffusing Tension: Emotional reactions contribute to escalating tensions within teams. Managers, by keeping emotions in check, can effectively defuse conflicts and promote harmonious relationships.

19. Time Management: Emotional influence can hinder effective time management, causing managers to

become distracted, overwhelmed, or procrastinate. A composed manager adheres to schedules, prioritizes tasks efficiently, and leads by example.

20. Handling Stress: A manager who avoids emotions copes better with stress, enabling them to manage pressure situations effectively and maintain a positive work-life balance.

21. Facilitating Growth: Emotional involvement can hinder an individual's growth, making it difficult for managers to push employees out of their comfort zones. By remaining emotionally detached, managers can effectively facilitate personal and professional growth.

22. Reward and Recognition: Emotional biases may cloud a manager's judgment while recognizing and rewarding employee performance. By avoiding emotions, managers ensure fairness and consistency in employee recognition.

23. Avoiding Favoritism: Emotional attachments can lead to favoritism within teams, causing resentment and potential conflicts. Managers should make decisions based on merit, not letting emotions impact their fairness.

24. Resolving Personal Issues: Personal issues can spill over into work, affecting performance and teamwork. A manager who avoids emotions can address personal issues objectively, ensuring a healthy work environment.

25. Creating a Positive Culture: Emotional stability allows managers to create a positive work environment by promoting inclusivity, diversity, and equality. Employees feel valued and respected, contributing to higher job satisfaction and productivity.

26. Continuous Learning: A manager who avoids emotions is open to learning and self-improvement. They actively seek feedback, embrace the latest ideas, and leverage emotional resilience to adapt to evolving situations.

In conclusion, a manager should strive to avoid emotions to ensure impartial decision-making, effective communication, and a positive work environment. By maintaining emotional control, managers can foster growth, establish trust, and lead by example, contributing to a successful and harmonious workplace.

Definition and Components of Emotional Intelligence

Emotional intelligence (EI) refers to a person's ability to recognize, understand, and manage their own emotions effectively while also being aware of others' emotions and being able to empathize with them. It involves a set of skills that allow individuals to navigate social interactions, make informed decisions, and maintain healthy relationships. Developed by psychologists Peter Salovey and John Mayer in the early 1990s, emotional intelligence has become increasingly recognized as a crucial aspect of overall intelligence and success in various areas of life.

There are five key components of emotional intelligence:

1. Self-awareness: This refers to the ability to recognize and understand one's own emotions, including their impact on thoughts, actions, and relationships. Self-aware individuals can accurately assess their strengths and weaknesses and are in tune with their values, goals, and personal boundaries.

2. Self-regulation: Also known as emotional self-control, this component involves the ability to manage one's own emotions and impulses. It entails being able to adapt to changing circumstances, control emotional reactions, and think before acting. Individuals with strong self-regulation skills are often resilient, composed, and have better impulse control.

3. Motivation: Emotional intelligence includes having a prominent level of motivation and being able to set

and pursue challenging goals with enthusiasm and persistence. Motivated individuals are initiative-taking, and optimistic, and have a deep intrinsic drive to achieve personal and professional success.

4. Empathy: This aspect of emotional intelligence involves the capacity to understand and share the emotions of others. Empathetic individuals can sense others' perspectives, needs, and concerns, which allows for more effective communication, collaboration, and mutual understanding. Empathy fosters stronger relationships, promotes social responsibility, and facilitates conflict resolution.

5. Social skills: The final component of emotional intelligence, social skills, refers to the ability to build and maintain healthy relationships, effectively navigate social situations, and communicate clearly and assertively. People with strong social skills are empathetic listeners, skilled communicators, and persuasive negotiators. They excel in leadership roles, teamwork, and networking.

Developing emotional intelligence can bring about numerous benefits in personal and professional life. People with higher levels of emotional intelligence tend to have better mental health, less stress, and improved overall well-being. They also tend to have better interpersonal relationships, as they are more adept at managing conflicts, understanding others' perspectives, and maintaining empathy and compassion.

Enhancing emotional intelligence is possible through various strategies, including self-reflection, mindfulness practices, and seeking feedback from others. By increasing self-awareness, individuals can better understand their emotional triggers, biases, and patterns of behavior. Engaging in self-regulation techniques, such as deep breathing, journaling, or seeking support from trusted individuals, can assist in managing emotions effectively.

Motivation and goal setting can be improved by clarifying personal values, explicitly defining goals, and breaking them down into actionable steps. Developing empathy involves actively listening to others, seeking to understand their perspectives, and practicing empathy-building exercises such as perspective-taking or volunteering in empathetic roles.

Finally, social skills can be enhanced through effective communication techniques, such as active listening, assertive communication, and developing strong non-verbal skills. Developing leadership and teamwork abilities can also support the development of these skills.

In conclusion, emotional intelligence encompasses the ability to identify and manage one's own emotions while understanding and empathizing with others. Self-awareness, self-regulation, motivation, empathy, and social skills are the key components of emotional intelligence. Improving emotional intelligence brings about several advantages, including better mental health, improved relationships, and increased success in various domains. By engaging in self-reflection, practicing mindfulness, seeking feedback, and actively developing these skills, individuals can cultivate emotional intelligence and harness its benefits.

Importance of Emotional Intelligence in the Workplace

Emotional intelligence (EI) plays a crucial role in the workplace, influencing various aspects of job performance, relationships with colleagues, and overall organizational success. Here are twenty-seven paragraphs elaborating on the importance of emotional intelligence in the workplace:

Effective communication: Emotional intelligence aids in effective communication, allowing individuals to express themselves clearly and listen empathetically. It helps in conveying messages effectively, resolving conflicts, and building productive relationships with colleagues.

Building rapport: EI assists in establishing rapport and developing strong relationships with colleagues. It fosters trust, mutual understanding, and collaboration, which are essential for a positive and productive work environment.

Leadership abilities: Strong emotional intelligence is a characteristic of effective leaders. Leaders who possess EI can understand and manage their own emotions and those of their team members, leading to better decision-making and inspiring and motivating their teams.

Conflict resolution: EI provides individuals with the skills to manage and resolve conflicts constructively. It allows for empathetic listening, understanding different perspectives, and finding win-win solutions, which can lead to improved teamwork and productivity.

Adaptability: In today's rapidly changing work environment, adaptability is crucial. Emotional intelligence helps individuals adapt to changes more effectively by managing emotions, remaining flexible, and embracing new challenges.

Stress management: Work can be stressful, and emotional intelligence assists in managing stress levels. Individuals with high EI can identify stress triggers, develop effective coping mechanisms, and maintain their well-being amidst demanding situations.

Decision-making: Emotionally intelligent individuals are better equipped to make rational and objective decisions. They can evaluate situations without being swayed by excessive emotions, resulting in better decision-making outcomes for the organization.

Increased self-awareness: Emotional intelligence enhances self-awareness, allowing individuals to understand their strengths, weaknesses, and areas for improvement. This awareness helps individuals set realistic goals and make informed career choices.

Motivation: EI boosts intrinsic motivation, as individuals with high emotional intelligence have a clear sense of purpose, goals, and values. They are self-driven, persistent, and able to maintain motivation even in challenging circumstances.

Empathy towards colleagues: Empathy is a key component of emotional intelligence, enabling individuals to understand and relate to the experiences, emotions, and needs of their colleagues. This fosters a supportive and collaborative work environment.

Improved teamwork: Emotional intelligence contributes to effective teamwork. Team members with high EI can navigate interpersonal dynamics, communicate their ideas effectively, and understand and appreciate the contributions of others.

Conflict prevention: Emotional intelligence also helps in preventing conflicts in the workplace. By being aware of their emotions and understanding the emotions of others, individuals can proactively manage potential conflicts and build stronger relationships.

Creativity and innovation: EI stimulates creativity and innovation by encouraging individuals to explore and express their ideas without fear of judgment. Emotionally intelligent individuals embrace diverse perspectives and create an environment conducive to out-of-the-box thinking.

Customer service excellence: Employees with high emotional intelligence are more likely to excel in customer service roles. EI allows them to understand the emotions and needs of customers, communicate effectively, and resolve issues empathetically.

Team morale: Emotional intelligence positively impacts team morale by creating a supportive and positive work environment. By effectively managing their own emotions, emotionally intelligent individuals inspire and uplift their colleagues.

Conflict management within teams: Teams with members possessing high EI are better equipped to manage conflicts effectively. They can communicate openly, empathize with each other's viewpoints, and find solutions collaboratively.

Flexibility and resilience: Emotional intelligence helps individuals manage setbacks and challenges with resilience. It enables them to bounce back, adapt to changes, and maintain a cheerful outlook even in demanding situations.

Reduced workplace negativity: Emotionally intelligent individuals are less likely to engage in toxic behaviors or contribute to a negative work environment. Their ability to manage emotions proactively fosters a more positive and harmonious workplace culture.

Improved customer relations: Emotional intelligence not only aids in internal relationships but also impacts customer relations positively. Employees who understand and manage their emotions well can deliver better customer experiences and build stronger customer relationships.

Conflict resolution between departments: Emotional intelligence promotes effective communication and empathy between different departments. When conflicts arise, emotionally intelligent individuals can bridge gaps, facilitate understanding, and find common ground for resolution.

Employee retention: A workplace that values emotional intelligence creates a supportive and engaging environment. This, in turn, increases employee satisfaction and loyalty, leading to higher retention rates.

Enhancing leadership pipeline: Organizations that prioritize emotional intelligence in their leadership development programs can cultivate leaders with strong people skills, empathy, and the ability to inspire teams.

Enhanced teamwork effectiveness: Emotional intelligence improves team dynamics, resulting in improved collaboration, constructive collaboration, and productivity. Emotionally intelligent team members understand each other's emotions, perspectives, and strengths, leading to better outcomes.

Better conflict management with clients and stakeholders: Emotional intelligence enables professionals to manage conflicts with clients, stakeholders, and partners more effectively. It facilitates active listening, negotiation, and collaboration for mutually beneficial outcomes.

Increased productivity: Emotionally intelligent individuals are better at managing their time, priorities, and focus. They are self-disciplined, motivated, and able to maintain prominent levels of productivity, leading to better overall organizational performance.

Employee well-being: Emotional intelligence positively affects employees' mental health and well-being. Individuals who can effectively manage their emotions experience less stress, higher job satisfaction, and increased overall happiness.

Organizational culture: Emotional intelligence contributes to shaping a positive and inclusive organizational culture. When employees are encouraged to develop their emotional intelligence, it sets a precedent for respectful communication, empathy, and collaborative problem-solving.

In summary, emotional intelligence plays a vital role in the workplace, impacting various aspects of individual and organizational success. It enhances communication, relationship-building, leadership skills, decision-making, and adaptability. By fostering self-awareness, empathy, and effective conflict resolution, emotional intelligence creates a positive work environment and improves teamwork, productivity, and employee well-being. Incorporating emotional intelligence into organizational practices can lead to enhanced employee satisfaction, reduced conflicts, and increased overall success.

Chapter Thirty-One

The Decision-Making Process

Introduction

The decision-making process is an essential aspect of our daily lives, influencing the choices we make, the paths we take, and the outcomes we achieve. From simple everyday decisions such as what to wear or what to eat, to complex decisions like choosing a career path or making significant life choices, our ability to effectively navigate the decision-making process plays a vital role in our personal and professional growth. Understanding the intricacies of decision-making can empower individuals to make informed choices, mitigate risks, and maximize opportunities for success. In this essay, we will explore the various phases of the decision-making process, the factors that influence our decisions, and the tools and techniques that can enhance our ability to make sound decisions. Whether it is in our personal lives, academic pursuits, or professional endeavors, grasping the decision-making process can have a profound impact on our present and future.

Definition of decision-making

Decision-making refers to the cognitive process of selecting a course of action from among multiple alternatives. It involves identifying a problem or a goal, gathering relevant information, evaluating the options available, making a choice, and implementing and evaluating the chosen course of action.

The phases of the decision-making process

The decision-making process consists of five phases: problem identification, information gathering, alternative evaluation, choice-making, and implementation and evaluation.

Problem identification

The first phase of decision-making is problem identification, which involves recognizing and defining the problem or the need for a decision. Clear problem identification is crucial as it sets the foundation for the subsequent phases.

Information gathering

Once the problem is identified, the decision-maker needs to gather relevant information to understand the situation fully. This may involve conducting research, seeking advice, or obtaining data from various sources to make an informed decision.

Alternative evaluation

In this phase, decision-makers generate and evaluate various alternatives or options to address the identified problem. Each alternative is assessed based on its feasibility, potential outcomes, and alignment with desired goals and objectives.

Rational decision-making model

The rational decision-making model suggests that decision-makers should carefully weigh the pros and cons of each alternative, consider all available information, and select the option that maximizes benefits and minimizes risks.

Intuitive decision-making

In contrast to the rational model, some decisions are made intuitively, relying on gut feelings, subjective experiences, or unconscious processes. Intuitive decision-making can be useful when faced with time constraints or situations with limited information.

Emotional factors in decision-making

Emotions play a significant role in decision-making. Positive emotions can enhance creativity and risk-taking, while negative emotions can lead to biased judgments or avoidance behavior. Recognizing and managing our emotions is crucial for effective decision-making.

Cognitive biases

Cognitive biases are inherent flaws in our decision-making processes that can lead to errors and distortions. Common biases include confirmation bias, availability bias, and anchoring bias. Recognizing and mitigating these biases is essential for making objective decisions.

Decision-making in groups

Group decision-making involves multiple individuals collectively making decisions. It brings diverse perspectives and expertise, but it can also be challenging due to conflicts, social dynamics, and group thinking. Collaboration, effective communication, and clear roles are key to successful group decision-making.

Decision-making in organizations

In organizational settings, decision-making is a fundamental process that affects overall performance and success. A structured decision-making framework, clear delegation of authority, and open communication channels are vital components for effective organizational decision-making.

Personal values and ethics in decision-making

Our personal values and ethical considerations significantly impact our decision-making. Decisions that align with our values and moral principles often lead to a sense of integrity and satisfaction.

Decision-making under uncertainty

Many decisions involve uncertainty and risk. Decision-makers need to assess and manage risk effectively, considering the potential outcomes and probabilities associated with each alternative.

Decision-making in complex situations

Complex decisions involve multiple variables, interconnected factors, and stakeholders. Decision-makers must consider long-term consequences, systemic effects, and unintended consequences to make informed choices in complex situations.

Decision-making in a rapidly changing world

In today's fast-paced and unpredictable world, decision-making must be adaptive and flexible. Navigating ambiguity, embracing change, and being open to learning from mistakes are crucial skills for effective decision-making.

Decision-making and leadership

Leadership often involves making tough decisions that impact others. Strong leaders demonstrate emotional intelligence, strategic thinking, and the ability to inspire and align others toward a common goal.

Decision-making and problem-solving

Decision-making and problem-solving go hand in hand. Effective critical thinking skills enable individuals to identify and analyze problems, generate creative solutions, and make informed decisions to address them.

Decision-making as a skill

Decision-making is not only a process but also a skill that can be developed and improved over time. Through self-reflection, learning from experience, and seeking feedback, individuals can enhance their decision-making abilities.

Decision-making pitfalls to avoid.

Several pitfalls can hinder effective decision-making, such as analysis paralysis, overconfidence, and framing effects. Being aware of these pitfalls and adopting strategies to overcome them is essential for making sound decisions.

Ethical decision-making

Ethical decision-making involves considering the moral implications of our choices and actions. Ethical frameworks, empathy, and consideration of long-term consequences are essential in making ethical decisions.

Cultural influences on decision-making

Cultural factors, including values, norms, and traditions, can significantly influence decision-making. Understanding cultural differences and being sensitive to diverse perspectives can lead to better decisions in multicultural settings.

Artificial intelligence and decision-making

Artificial intelligence (AI) is increasingly being utilized to support decision-making processes. AI algorithms can analyze vast amounts of data, identify patterns, and provide recommendations, assisting decision-makers in making more informed choices.

Learning from decision-making

Reflection and learning from past decisions are crucial for personal growth and continuous improvement. By evaluating the outcomes of decisions, understanding the factors that influenced them, and adjusting their approach, individuals can enhance their decision-making skills.

Conclusion

The decision-making process is a crucial aspect of our lives, impacting the quality of our choices and eventual outcomes. By understanding the phases, factors, and techniques involved in decision-making, individuals can empower themselves to make informed and effective decisions, leading to personal and professional growth.

Overview of Decision-Making by Managers

Decision-making is a crucial aspect of managerial roles and responsibilities. Managers are required to make numerous decisions daily that directly impact on the success of an organization. The process of decision-making involves analyzing assorted options, evaluating potential outcomes, and selecting the most suitable course of action.

Managers use a systematic approach to decision-making, using both rational and intuitive thinking. Rational decision-making involves gathering all relevant information, carefully analyzing it, and assessing the potential risks and benefits. Intuitive decision-making, on the other hand, relies on the manager's experience and gut feelings.

There are several types of decisions that managers make. Strategic decisions involve long-term planning and goal setting, such as entering new markets or expanding the product line. Tactical decisions are shorter-term and address operational issues, such as resource allocation or production scheduling. Lastly, routine decisions are everyday tasks that require little thought, such as approving expense reports or scheduling meetings.

Effective decision-making requires a manager to consider both quantitative and qualitative factors. Quantitative factors involve measurable data like financials, market trends, or productivity metrics. Qualitative factors, on the other hand, are subjective and rely on judgments based on personal values, ethics, or customer preferences.

Effective decision-making also requires managers to consider the potential risks and uncertainties associated with each option. Risk analysis helps managers identify and evaluate potential pitfalls, allowing them to take initiative-taking measures to mitigate those risks. Uncertainty analysis, on the other hand, acknowledges the presence of unknown variables and assists managers in developing contingency plans.

Managers also need to consider the input and perspectives of others when making decisions. Involving stakeholders in the decision-making process, such as employees, customers, or shareholders, can provide valuable insights and increase the likelihood of making sound decisions that benefit all parties involved. It also fosters a sense of ownership and can enhance employees' commitment to implementing the decision.

To ensure a fair and transparent decision-making process, managers should establish clear decision criteria and evaluate options against those criteria. This helps eliminate biases and personal preferences, ensuring decisions are based on objective analysis rather than subjective factors.

In today's fast-paced business environment, managers often face time constraints that can impact their decision-making process. If the decision is urgent, managers may need to rely on their intuition and experience to make quick yet effective decisions. However, it is crucial to strike a balance between speed and quality to avoid hasty and ill-informed choices.

Managers should also regularly review and assess decisions made to learn from past experiences. This helps identify any shortcomings in the decision-making process, enabling managers to fine-tune their approach and improve future decisions.

Effective decision-making by managers impacts all areas of an organization. It influences resource allocation, goal attainment, employee motivation, and the overall success of the organization. Therefore, it is imperative for managers to continuously enhance their decision-making skills through training, self-reflection, and seeking feedback from others.

Managers should also be aware of biases that can hinder effective decision-making. These biases can include confirmation bias, where managers seek information that supports their pre-existing beliefs, or anchoring bias, where managers fixate on initial information and fail to consider other perspectives.

Ethics also play a fundamental role in decision-making. Managers must consider the ethical implications of their decisions, ensuring they align with organizational values and societal expectations. Ethical decision-making requires managers to balance the interests of all stakeholders and act with integrity and fairness.

The use of technology and data analytics has revolutionized decision-making for managers. Advanced tools and software can assist in collecting, organizing, and analyzing vast amounts of data, enabling managers to make more informed decisions based on objective information.

While decision-making can be complex and challenging, managers can strengthen their decision-making skills through continual practice and refinement. Seeking feedback from colleagues, mentors, or even consultants can provide valuable perspectives and help managers broaden their decision-making capabilities.

In conclusion, decision-making is a critical responsibility for managers. It involves considering assorted options, analyzing risks, and evaluating quantitative and qualitative factors. Inclusive decision-making processes, along with ethical considerations, technology, and regular evaluation of decisions, contribute to effective decision-making. Improved decision-making positively impacts an organization's overall success.

Factors Influencing Decision-Making

Individual Differences: Every individual has unique characteristics, experiences, and beliefs that shape their decision-making process. Factors such as personality, values, cognitive biases, and emotional states can influence how decisions are made.

Perception: The way individuals perceive and interpret information can impact their decision-making. Perceptions can be influenced by biases, stereotypes, and past experiences, leading to subjective judgment.

Cognitive Biases: Cognitive biases are inherent shortcuts or distortions in thinking that can affect decision-making. Biases such as confirmation bias (favoring information that confirms pre-existing beliefs) or availability bias (over-relying on readily available information) can lead to flawed decisions.

Information Availability: The availability of information plays a crucial role in decision-making. Managers must have access to accurate and relevant data to make informed choices. Inadequate or incomplete information can lead to biased decisions or reliance on assumptions.

Time Constraints: Time limitations can affect decision-making processes. When faced with urgent situations, managers may have to make quick decisions, relying on intuition rather than careful analysis. Time pressure can increase the likelihood of errors and biases.

Risk Tolerance: Managers' risk tolerance influences their decision-making. Some individuals are more comfortable with taking risks, while others prefer a cautious approach. Risk assessment and risk appetite play a significant role in determining the course of action.

Organizational Culture: Organizational culture shapes decision-making processes. A culture that promotes open communication, employee involvement, and ethical behavior can positively influence decision-making. Conversely, a culture that discourages dissent or prioritizes short-term gains may hinder effective decision-making.

Organizational Structure: The structure of an organization can influences decision-making. Centralized decision-making authority can result in faster decisions but may limit innovation and employee empowerment. Decentralized decision-making can lead to more diverse perspectives but may also lead to inconsistency.

External Environment: The external environment, such as economic conditions, regulatory changes, and market competition, can heavily influence decision-making. Managers need to consider external factors when making strategic decisions to ensure their choices align with the business environment.

Stakeholder Interests: The interests and concerns of stakeholders, including employees, customers, investors, and communities, can impact decision-making. Managers must consider how their decisions will affect stakeholders and seek to balance their needs and expectations.

Ethical Considerations: Ethical standards and principles guide decision-making. Managers must consider the ethical implications of their decisions and ensure they align with legal requirements, moral values, and societal expectations.

Group Dynamics: Decision-making in groups or teams can be influenced by numerous factors. Groupthink (when group harmony is prioritized over critical thinking), or social influence can negatively impact decision quality. Effective facilitation can promote collaboration and mitigate these influences.

Personal Motivations: Personal interests, incentives, or biases can affect decision-making. Managers must be aware of their motivations to ensure decisions are made in the best interest of the organization rather than personal gain.

Decision-Making Models: Different decision-making models, such as rational decision-making or intuitive decision-making, can influence the approach taken. Rational models emphasize systematic analysis, while intuitive models rely on past experiences and gut feelings.

Decision Criteria: Clear criteria and goals for decision-making influence the decision-making process. Criteria can include financial metrics, performance indicators, customer satisfaction, or ethical guidelines. Decisions should be evaluated against these criteria to ensure consistency and clarity.

Organizational Politics: Office politics can impact decision-making. Power dynamics, personal relationships, or the desire to please certain individuals can influence decisions. Managers need to be aware of these dynamics and strive to make fair and impartial choices.

Resource Constraints: Limited resources, such as budget or workforce, can influence decision-making. Managers must consider resource availability and allocate resources effectively to achieve desired outcomes.

Past Experiences: Managers' past experiences can influence their decision-making process. Valuable lessons from previous successes or failures shape decision-making approaches and preferences for certain options.

Innovation and Creativity: Encouraging innovation and creativity can enhance decision-making. Managers who foster a culture of experimentation and open-mindedness are more likely to make innovative decisions that drive organizational success.

Psychological Factors: Psychological factors, such as emotions, motivation, and confidence, can influence decision-making. Emotional states, like fear or excitement, can cloud judgment. Self-confidence can affect risk-taking tendencies.

Peer Influence: The opinions and advice of peers or colleagues can sway decision-making. Managers must evaluate the credibility and expertise of others and consider their perspectives when making decisions.

Technology and Data Analytics: Technological advancements and data analytics have revolutionized decision-making. The availability of big data, predictive analytics, and decision support systems can enhance the accuracy and efficiency of decision-making.

External Expertise: Seeking input from external experts or consultants can provide additional insights and expertise. These external perspectives can challenge existing assumptions and improve decision quality.

Feedback Loops: Feedback from past decisions is essential for learning and improvement. Regularly evaluating decisions, seeking feedback, and analyzing outcomes can help refine and enhance decision-making skills over time.

Chapter Thirty-Two

The Relationship between Emotional Intelligence and Decision-Making

Emotional intelligence (EI) refers to the ability to recognize, understand, and manage our own emotions and those of others. It encompasses skills such as empathy, self-awareness, self-regulation, social awareness, and relationship management. Decision-making, on the other hand, involves the process of selecting the most appropriate course of action among several alternatives. In this essay, we will explore the relationship between EI and decision-making and how EI can influence and enhance the quality of our decisions.

Firstly, emotional intelligence plays a crucial role in self-awareness, which is the ability to understand our own emotions, strengths, weaknesses, values, and motivations. Self-awareness is essential for effective decision-making as it allows us to recognize our biases, preferences, and personal limitations that can influence our judgment. By being aware of our own emotions and thought patterns, we can make more informed decisions that are objective and rational, rather than being driven solely by emotions or personal biases.

Furthermore, emotional intelligence also includes the skill of self-regulation, which refers to the ability to manage and control our emotions and impulses. This skill is vital in decision-making as it enables individuals to avoid impulsive or rash decisions that might be driven by short-term emotions. By effectively managing emotions, individuals can maintain a calm and rational mindset while weighing the pros and cons of various alternatives, leading to more sound and logical decision-making.

In addition to self-awareness and self-regulation, emotional intelligence also entails empathy and social awareness, which involve understanding and recognizing the emotions and needs of others. These skills are valuable in decision-making, particularly in situations where multiple stakeholders are involved. By recognizing and considering the emotions and perspectives of others, individuals with high EI can make decisions that not only benefit themselves but also consider the interests and well-being of others, fostering collaboration and positive relationships.

Moreover, EI influences our ability to communicate and manage relationships effectively, another aspect that impacts decision-making. Strong relationship management skills allow individuals to gather different perspectives, seek advice, and integrate diverse opinions into the decision-making process. By fostering open and effective communication, individuals can make more inclusive decisions, leading to higher buy-in and support from others, and increasing the chances of successful outcomes.

Additionally, emotional intelligence enhances critical thinking skills, a crucial component of effective decision-making. Critical thinking involves evaluating information, considering multiple viewpoints, identifying biases, and making logical and informed decisions. Emotionally intelligent individuals are more likely to approach decision-making with an open mind and consider diverse perspectives, leading to more comprehensive and thoughtful decision outcomes.

Another significant aspect of EI in decision-making is its impact on problem-solving. Emotional intelligence enables individuals to approach problems with creativity, innovation, and flexibility. Understanding emotions and relationships can provide insights and creative solutions to complex problems that might not be apparent to those who lack emotional intelligence. By incorporating emotions into problem-solving, individuals can produce innovative solutions that address the emotional needs of the people affected by the decision.

Furthermore, emotional intelligence helps individuals manage the stress and pressure often associated with decision-making. High-stakes decisions can generate anxiety and stress that can impair cognitive function. However, emotionally intelligent individuals are better equipped to deal with such stress, remaining composed and rational. This emotional self-control allows them to make better decisions under pressure, as they can stay focused and consider the long-term consequences rather than succumbing to short-term emotional impulses.

In addition, emotional intelligence can enhance ethical decision-making. Consideration of emotions and empathy allows individuals to consider the potential impact of their decisions on others and the ethical implications involved. By paying attention to morals and values, emotionally intelligent individuals are more likely to make decisions that align with ethical principles and societal norms, promoting fairness, integrity, and social responsibility.

Furthermore, emotional intelligence can contribute to resilience in decision-making. Emotionally intelligent individuals are better equipped to manage setbacks and failures, bounce back, and learn from their mistakes. This resilience enables them to adapt and adjust their decision-making processes based on the feedback received, increasing the chances of future success.

Moreover, emotional intelligence fosters self-motivation, which can significantly impact decision-related processes. Motivation drives individuals to explore various alternatives, take risks, and make initiative-taking decisions. Highly emotionally intelligent individuals are initiative-taking and driven by a desire for personal growth and achievement, leading to an initiative-taking and dynamic approach to decision-making.

Additionally, emotional intelligence promotes cross-cultural decision-making. Individuals with high EI have a greater understanding and acceptance of cultural differences, allowing them to make decisions that respect and accommodate diverse cultural values. The ability to appreciate these differences can facilitate effective decision-making in multicultural contexts, reducing conflicts and fostering inclusivity.

Furthermore, emotional intelligence plays a role in handling interpersonal conflicts that may arise during decision-making processes. By effectively managing emotions, emotionally intelligent individuals can constructively resolve conflicts, strengthening relationships and enhancing the overall quality of decision outcomes. Conflict resolution skills are essential to ensure that decisions are made collectively and without alienating any stakeholders.

Moreover, emotional intelligence enables individuals to assess and manage risk effectively, an essential aspect of decision-making. By being aware of their emotions and biases, emotionally intelligent individuals can make more objective risk assessments and take calculated risks rather than being overly influenced by fear or impulsiveness. This ability allows them to navigate uncertainty and make informed decisions that balance potential risks and rewards carefully.

Additionally, emotional intelligence can positively impact decision-making in leadership roles. Leaders with high EI can inspire and motivate their team members, create a positive and supportive work environment, and effectively delegate responsibilities. These leadership qualities contribute to more collaborative and participatory decision-making processes, enhancing overall organizational performance.

Moreover, emotional intelligence can influence decision-making in crises. Leaders who possess high EI can remain calm and composed during high-stress and chaotic situations. Their ability to manage emotions, build relationships, and communicate effectively enables them to make prompt and effective decisions under pressure, minimizing potential damage and ensuring the safety and well-being of the individuals involved.

Furthermore, emotional intelligence facilitates continuous learning and growth. Emotionally intelligent individuals are open to feedback, self-reflective, and eager to learn from their experiences. This mindset allows them to evaluate the outcomes of their decisions, identify areas for improvement, and adapt their decision-making processes accordingly. By continuously learning and growing, emotionally intelligent individuals improve the quality of their decisions over time.

Emotional intelligence and decision-making are closely intertwined. Emotional intelligence enhances decision-making through various mechanisms such as self-awareness, self-regulation, empathy, relationship management, critical thinking, problem-solving, stress management, ethical considerations, resilience, motivation, cross-cultural sensitivity, conflict resolution, risk assessment, leadership skills, crisis management, and continuous learning. By developing and harnessing emotional intelligence, individuals can make more informed, inclusive, and effective decisions, leading to better outcomes in personal, professional, and societal contexts.

The study of emotional intelligence is critically important in general management for a variety of reasons. Emotional intelligence refers to the ability to recognize, understand, and manage our own emotions, as well as the emotions of others. It plays a crucial role in effective leadership, team collaboration, decision-making, and overall workplace effectiveness.

First, emotional intelligence is vital in general management because it enhances leadership capabilities. Leaders with high emotional intelligence can effectively motivate and inspire their teams, as they are aware of their own emotions and can empathize with others. They can adapt their leadership style to the needs of everyone, fostering a positive and productive work environment.

Second, emotional intelligence helps in building and maintaining strong relationships with both employees and stakeholders. Managers who possess emotional intelligence can effectively communicate and connect with others, resolving conflicts and building trust. This skill is essential in establishing and maintaining productive relationships within the organization and with external stakeholders, such as clients, suppliers, and partners.

Third, emotional intelligence is crucial for effective teamwork and collaboration. Managers need to be able to understand and manage the emotions and dynamics of their team members. By fostering empathy, emotional intelligence promotes a supportive and cooperative team environment, leading to improved collaboration, creativity, and problem-solving.

Fourth, emotional intelligence aids in decision-making processes. Emotionally intelligent managers are more adept at recognizing and managing their own biases and emotions, allowing for more rational and objective decision-making. They can consider the differing perspectives and emotions of others, leading to more informed and thoughtful decisions.

Fifth, emotional intelligence increases overall workplace effectiveness. Managers who exhibit emotional intelligence are better equipped to manage stress, adapt to change, and provide support to employees during challenging times. They are also more skilled at managing conflict, fostering a positive work culture, and promoting employee engagement and well-being.

Sixth, emotional intelligence contributes to effective change management. Managing change within an organization can be emotional and challenging. Emotionally intelligent managers are more likely to be able to empathize with and understand the concerns and anxieties of employees during times of change. This enables them to effectively communicate and guide employees through the change process, resulting in a more successful implementation of new initiatives.

Seventh, emotional intelligence plays a role in customer satisfaction and retention. Managers who possess emotional intelligence can understand and respond to the emotions and needs of customers. This enables them to provide excellent customer service and build long-term relationships with clients, leading to increased customer loyalty and business success.

Lastly, emotional intelligence is important in general management because it promotes self-awareness and personal growth. Emotionally intelligent managers are constantly reflecting on their own emotions and behaviors, seeking to improve and develop their leadership skills. They understand the impact of their emotions on their decision-making and overall management effectiveness, thus allowing for continuous growth and development.

In conclusion, the study of emotional intelligence is incredibly important in general management due to its impact on leadership, relationship-building, teamwork, decision-making, workplace effectiveness, change management, customer satisfaction, and personal growth. By developing and enhancing emotional intelligence, managers can significantly improve their effectiveness as well as the success of their organizations.

How Emotional Intelligence Impacts Decision-Making

Emotional intelligence has a significant impact on decision-making in general management. Here are some of the key ways emotional intelligence affects decision-making:

Recognizing and managing biases: Emotional intelligence helps managers become aware of their own biases, such as personal preferences or preconceived notions, which can influence decision-making. By understanding and managing these biases, emotionally intelligent managers can make more objective and rational decisions.

Considering differing perspectives: Emotional intelligence enables managers to empathize with and understand the emotions and perspectives of others involved in the decision-making process. This allows them to consider different viewpoints and consider the potential impact on various stakeholders, leading to more well-rounded and inclusive decisions.

Evaluating the emotional impact: Emotionally intelligent managers recognize the potential emotional impact their decisions can have on employees, stakeholders, and the organizational culture. They consider the emotional well-being and reactions of individuals and factor them into their decision-making process, aiming to minimize negative emotions and promote positive ones.

Engaging in constructive conflict resolution: Emotional intelligence equips managers with the ability to effectively manage conflicts that arise during decision-making processes. They can identify and address emotional tensions, encourage open dialogue, and find creative solutions that satisfy the emotional needs of everyone involved. This helps in reaching a consensus or finding a compromise more efficiently.

Handling uncertainty and ambiguity: Decision-making often involves dealing with uncertain or ambiguous circumstances. Emotionally intelligent managers are better equipped to manage their stress and anxiety in these situations, enabling them to make more confident and decisive choices in the face of uncertainty or ambiguity.

Building trust and credibility: Emotional intelligence supports the development of trusting and credible relationships with employees and stakeholders. When managers exhibit emotional intelligence in their decision-making, they are perceived as being fair, empathetic, and considerate. This fosters trust and confidence in their decisions and leadership, leading to greater support and acceptance.

Managing change effectively: Emotional intelligence is vital in decision-making related to organizational changes or transitions. Emotionally intelligent managers can navigate the emotional complexities associated with change, such as resistance, fear, or uncertainty. They communicate with empathy, address concerns, and involve employees in the decision-making process, increasing the likelihood of successful change implementation.

Reflecting on past decisions: Emotional intelligence fosters self-awareness and introspection. Emotionally intelligent managers reflect on the emotions and outcomes of past decisions, learning from both successes and failures. This helps them refine their decision-making process, avoid repeating mistakes, and continually improve their decision-making skills.

In summary, emotional intelligence influences decision-making by promoting self-awareness, managing biases, considering diverse perspectives, evaluating emotional impacts, resolving conflicts constructively, managing uncertainty, building trust, managing change effectively, and facilitating continuous learning. By incorporating emotional intelligence into their decision-making, managers can make more balanced, empathetic, and successful choices that benefit both individuals and the organization.

Case Studies and Examples

Case study one. Company XYZ hires two employees with similar qualifications and experience. Employee A has high emotional intelligence (EI) and can effectively communicate, adapt to changes, and oversee conflicts with colleagues. Employee B has low EI and struggles with self-awareness, managing emotions, and building strong relationships with coworkers. After six months, Employee A has a highly productive team and earns praise from supervisors, while Employee B has frequent conflicts and a high turnover rate in their team.

Case study two. John and Mary are two project managers in the same organization. John has high EI and can understand and manage his emotions, communicate effectively with team members, and adapt to changing project requirements. On the other hand, Mary has low EI and often becomes overwhelmed with stress, struggles to communicate with team members, and finds it challenging to embrace change. As a result, John's project consistently meets or exceeds its targets, whereas Mary's project faces delays and below-average outcomes.

Case study three. Sarah and David are colleagues working in a high-stress environment. Sarah possesses high EI manages stress effectively, maintains positive relationships with coworkers, and remains motivated despite challenges. David, on the other hand, has low EI, frequently experiences burnout, and has strained relationships with colleagues. Over time, Sarah receives promotions and additional responsibilities, while David's performance and career progress stagnate.

Case study four. Sam and Alex are customer service representatives at a telecommunications company. Sam exhibits high EI by actively listening to customers, empathizing with their concerns, and finding appropriate solutions. Alex has low EI and often becomes frustrated during customer interactions, resulting in poor customer satisfaction. Sam receives positive feedback from customers and exceeds his performance targets, while Alex struggles to meet his goals and receives numerous customer complaints.

Case study five. Lisa and James are in leadership roles at a retail company. Lisa demonstrates high EI by cultivating a positive work environment, fostering teamwork, and effectively resolving conflicts among team members. James, with low EI, struggles to understand and address employees' emotions, leading to a decline in employee morale and increased turnover. Lisa's team achieves prominent levels of productivity and job satisfaction, while James's team faces a decline in performance and employee engagement.

Case study six. Mark and Sarah are both sales executives at a pharmaceutical company. Mark possesses high EI and is skilled at understanding customers' emotional needs, building rapport, and adapting his sales approach accordingly. Sarah, however, has low EI and often struggles to connect with customers, resulting in lower sales figures. Mark consistently achieves his sales targets and receives recognition from both customers and colleagues, while Sarah's performance falls below expectations.

Case study seven. Emily and Michael are project team members in a consulting firm. Emily demonstrates high EI by effectively managing stress, collaborating with colleagues, and adapting to changing project requirements. Michael struggles with managing emotions, often overreacting to feedback, and causing conflicts within the team. Emily is highly valued by the project manager and receives continuous opportunities for professional growth, while Michael's performance suffers, leading to limited career advancement.

Case study eight. Rachel and Alex are managers in a manufacturing company. Rachel has high EI and is adept at managing her own emotions as well as her team's emotions. She creates a positive work environment, provides frequent feedback, and effectively oversees conflicts among team members. Alex has low EI and struggles to navigate interpersonal dynamics, leading to decreased productivity and increased employee dissatisfaction. Rachel's team consistently meets their targets, whereas Alex's team faces declining performance.

Case study nine. Jessica and Julia are teachers at the same school. Jessica possesses high EI and effectively manages her emotions, connects with students, and addresses conflicts among them. Julia, with low EI, often struggles to relate to students, resulting in disciplinary issues and poor academic performance. Jessica's students exhibit higher levels of engagement and academic success, while Julia's students lag.

Case study ten. Alex and Lisa are entrepreneurs launching their startups. Alex has high EI, maintains a positive mindset, effectively communicates with stakeholders, and adapts to market changes. Lisa, with low EI, faces challenges in managing setbacks, demonstrating resilience, and building strong relationships with investors and partners. Alex's startup receives funding and gains traction in the market, while Lisa's startup struggles to attract investment and secure partnerships.

Chapter Thirty-Three

Developing Emotional Intelligence in Managers

Introduction

Emotional intelligence refers to the ability to recognize, understand, and manage one's own emotions, as well as the emotions of others. In the context of managerial roles, emotional intelligence plays a vital role in ensuring effective leadership and successful team management. A manager's emotional intelligence affects their decision-making abilities, communication skills, and overall relationship with their team members. Therefore, developing emotional intelligence in managers is crucial for fostering a positive work culture, improving productivity, and achieving organizational goals.

One of the main reasons why developing emotional intelligence in managers is essential is because it promotes effective decision-making. Emotionally intelligent managers can consider different perspectives, analyze situations objectively, and make informed decisions that benefit both the organization and its employees. They could control their own emotions and remain calm when faced with challenging circumstances, allowing them to think rationally and avoid impulsive decision-making that could negatively impact their team.

In addition, emotional intelligence in managers enhances their communication skills. Managers with heightened emotional intelligence can effectively express their thoughts and ideas, actively listen to their team members, and empathize with their concerns or problems. This allows for open and transparent communication within the team, creating a positive work environment where employees feel valued and understood.

Furthermore, developing emotional intelligence in managers leads to improved relationships with their team members. Emotionally intelligent managers could understand the emotions of their employees, which helps in building stronger connections and fostering trust within the team. By recognizing and addressing the emotional needs of their team members, managers can create a supportive work environment where employees feel comfortable expressing themselves and seeking assistance when needed.

Moreover, emotional intelligence helps managers in resolving conflicts and managing demanding situations more effectively. Emotional intelligence enables managers to understand the underlying emotions and motivations of individuals involved in conflicts, allowing them to mediate and find mutually agreeable solutions. By demonstrating empathy and providing support, emotionally intelligent managers can diffuse tense situations and restore harmony within the team.

Another key aspect of developing emotional intelligence in managers is its positive impact on employee engagement and motivation. When managers possess emotional intelligence, they are better able to understand the needs and aspirations of their team members. This knowledge enables them to provide appropriate feedback, recognition, and support, resulting in increased employee satisfaction and motivation. Employees who feel valued and understood by their managers are more likely to be engaged, productive, and committed to achieving collective objectives.

Furthermore, emotional intelligence in managers promotes effective stress management within the workplace. Managers who possess emotional intelligence are better equipped to manage their stress levels and help their team members deal with stress. Through effective stress management techniques, such as encouraging work-life balance, implementing stress-relieving activities, and promoting a supportive work environment, emotionally intelligent managers can minimize stress-related issues and improve overall employee well-being.

Developing emotional intelligence in managers is also beneficial in terms of team collaboration and cooperation. Emotionally intelligent managers are skilled at promoting teamwork, fostering collaboration, and building strong connections among team members. By recognizing and appreciating the diverse skills and perspectives of their team, emotionally intelligent managers can create an inclusive environment where everyone feels valued and contributes their unique strengths to achieve common goals.

Furthermore, emotionally intelligent managers are better equipped to manage change and uncertainty. In today's dynamic business landscape, change is inevitable, and it can often be accompanied by anxiety and resistance. However, managers with emotional intelligence can navigate through change more effectively by demonstrating resilience, adaptability, and understanding. They can effectively communicate the rationale behind changes, address the concerns of team members, and provide support during challenging transitions.

In conclusion, developing emotional intelligence in managers is crucial for effective leadership and successful team management. Emotionally intelligent managers make better decisions, possess persuasive communication skills, build positive relationships, manage conflicts, and promote employee engagement, motivation, and well-being. They also facilitate teamwork, oversee stress, and navigate change with ease. Therefore, organizations should prioritize the development of emotional intelligence in managers to create a harmonious work environment and achieve long-term success.

When a manager is not emotionally developed, it can have a significant impact on the overall functioning and performance of a team or organization. Here are some potential outcomes that may arise as a result:

Lack of empathy: An emotionally underdeveloped manager may struggle to understand and relate to the emotions and experiences of their team members. This can lead to a lack of support and understanding, causing employees to feel unheard and undervalued.

Poor communication: Effective communication is a key skill for any manager. However, an emotionally underdeveloped manager may struggle to express themselves clearly, leading to misunderstandings and misinterpretations within the team.

Low morale: When a manager is emotionally underdeveloped, they may struggle to create a positive and supportive work environment. This can contribute to low team morale, reduced motivation, and decreased job satisfaction among employees.

High turnover: Employees are more likely to leave their jobs when they feel unsupported or undervalued. An emotionally underdeveloped manager may fail to recognize and address issues that contribute to high turnover rates, resulting in difficulties with staff retention.

Decreased productivity: A manager who lacks emotional development may struggle to effectively delegate tasks, set clear expectations, and provide constructive feedback. This can lead to decreased productivity and performance levels within the team.

Conflict within the team: The inability of an emotionally underdeveloped manager to effectively manage their own emotions and respond to conflict can exacerbate existing disagreements within the team. This may lead to a toxic work environment and hinder collaboration and cooperation among employees.

Inability to manage stress: Managing a team can be challenging and stressful at times. An emotionally underdeveloped manager may struggle to manage their stress levels, leading to negative coping mechanisms or potentially lashing out at employees.

Lack of trust: Trust is a crucial element in any work environment. However, an emotionally underdeveloped manager may struggle to build trust with their team members due to inconsistent behavior, misunderstanding emotions, or neglecting their needs. This can hinder communication and collaboration within the team.

Resistance to change: An emotionally underdeveloped manager may feel threatened by change or unfamiliar situations. This resistance can slow down necessary adaptations and improvements within the team or organization.

Micromanagement: To maintain control, an emotionally underdeveloped manager may resort to micromanaging their employees. This can stifle creativity, autonomy, and innovation within the team.

Lack of self-awareness: Emotional underdevelopment may lead to a lack of self-awareness in a manager. Without understanding their strengths, weaknesses, and emotions, they may struggle to adapt their leadership style or recognize their limitations.

Difficulty in building relationships: Building strong relationships with team members, superiors, and other stakeholders is essential for a manager's success. An emotionally underdeveloped manager may struggle to establish and maintain these relationships due to a lack of emotional intelligence or social skills.

Inconsistent decision-making: Emotionally underdeveloped managers may struggle to make consistent and fair decisions due to biases, mood swings, or an inability to separate personal emotions from professional situations. This can lead to frustration and confusion among team members.

Lack of creativity and innovation: Emotional underdevelopment may limit a manager's ability to think creatively, contribute fresh ideas, or encourage creative thinking within their team. This can hinder growth, improvement, and competitiveness.

Increased stress for employees: Ineffective management styles can lead to increased stress levels for employees. Emotionally underdeveloped managers may inadvertently contribute to this stress by failing to provide support or creating a negative work environment.

Impaired conflict resolution: Managers play a crucial role in resolving conflicts within the team. However, an emotionally underdeveloped manager may struggle to effectively mediate conflicts, leading to unresolved issues, tension, and divisions within the team.

Lack of appreciation and recognition: An emotionally underdeveloped manager may fail to recognize and appreciate the efforts and achievements of their team members. This can lead to feelings of demotivation, under-appreciation, and reduced job satisfaction.

Missed opportunities for professional growth: A manager's emotional intelligence is closely tied to their ability to support and facilitate the growth and development of their team members. An emotionally underdeveloped manager may miss opportunities to provide guidance, mentorship, and support for their employees' professional growth.

Negative organizational culture: The behavior of a manager can shape the overall organizational culture. An emotionally underdeveloped manager may contribute to a toxic or negative culture by promoting unhealthy work habits, fostering a climate of fear or indifference, and inhibiting open communication.

It is important to note that these outcomes are potential consequences of emotional underdevelopment in a manager, but not all managers may exhibit all these traits or consequences. Additionally, managers can work on their emotional development and improve their skills over time with self-reflection, training, and seeking professional support.

Strategies for Enhancing Emotional Intelligence

There are several strategies for enhancing emotional intelligence. Here are a few:

Self-awareness: The first step in enhancing emotional intelligence is to be aware of your own emotions. Practice noticing and labeling your emotions as they arise, without judgment. This self-awareness helps you to understand the root causes of your emotions and how they impact your behavior.

Self-regulation: Once you are aware of your emotions, the next step is to learn how to regulate them effectively. This involves managing stress, controlling impulses, and staying calm even in challenging situations. Techniques like deep breathing, mindfulness meditation, and positive self-talk can help in developing self-regulation skills.

Empathy: Empathy is the ability to understand and share the feelings of others. To enhance empathy, it is important to actively listen and try to understand another person's perspective. Practice putting yourself in others' shoes and try to see the situation from their point of view. Developing empathy allows you to build stronger relationships and better connect with others.

Social skills: Having strong social skills is crucial for enhancing emotional intelligence. This involves effective communication, conflict resolution, and building positive relationships. Active listening, assertiveness, empathy, and nonverbal communication skills are all important components of strong social skills.

Emotional management: Being able to manage emotions in oneself and others is another key aspect of emotional intelligence. This includes recognizing and understanding different emotions, being able to express them healthily, and helping others to manage their emotions. It also involves being able to oversee demanding situations, conflicts, and challenges with emotional maturity.

Overall, enhancing emotional intelligence requires self-awareness, self-regulation, empathy, strong social skills, and effective emotional management. Practicing these strategies can lead to improved emotional intelligence, which in turn can positively impact personal relationships, work performance, and overall well-being.

Training and Development Programs

To enhance strategies for developing smooth emotional intelligence in managers, the following pieces of training and program development are necessary:

1. Emotional intelligence training: Deliver comprehensive training programs focused on understanding and developing emotional intelligence skills. This training should cover self-awareness, self-management, social awareness, and relationship management.

2. Self-awareness workshops: Conduct workshops to help managers understand their own emotions, strengths, weaknesses, triggers, and biases. This training can include self-reflection exercises, personality assessments, and feedback from peers and subordinates.

3. Stress management training: Managers should be trained in stress management techniques to oversee high-pressure situations effectively without letting emotions get the best of them. This can involve mindfulness practices, relaxation techniques, and time management strategies.

4. Active listening and empathy training: Provide training to enhance managers' active listening skills and ability to empathize with their team members. This can include teaching techniques and exercises to improve listening to comprehension and understanding of others' perspectives.

5. Conflict resolution training: Equip managers with skills to oversee conflicts and disagreements constructively.

This involves teaching techniques for effective communication, negotiation, and finding win-win solutions.

6. Cultural sensitivity and diversity training: Foster cultural intelligence by providing managers with training on understanding and appreciating distinct cultural perspectives. This helps them engage with a diverse workforce with respect and sensitivity.

7. Leadership development programs: Implement leadership development initiatives that focus on emotional intelligence as a core leadership competency. These programs can include coaching, mentoring, and experiential learning opportunities to practice and refine emotional intelligence skills.

8. Feedback and coaching: Establish a culture of regular feedback and coaching to support managers in their emotional intelligence development. Provide managers with ongoing feedback on their performance and areas for improvement and assign executive coaches or mentors to provide guidance and support.

9. Integration into performance appraisals: Include emotional intelligence as a performance metric in managers' appraisals. This reinforces the importance of emotional intelligence development and encourages managers to actively enhance their skills.

10. Follow-up and reinforcement: Create mechanisms to reinforce the learned skills and ensure long-term development. This can include periodic refresher training, peer support networks, and providing resources like books, articles, and online courses for continuous learning.

By implementing these training and program developments, organizations can enhance the smooth emotional intelligence of their managers, leading to more effective leadership, better team dynamics, and improved overall performance.

Benefits of Emotionally Intelligent Decision-Making by Managers

Emotional intelligence, often defined as the ability to recognize and understand our own emotions and those of others, plays a crucial role in decision-making processes within organizations. In today's fast-paced and highly competitive business world, managers need to make informed and thoughtful decisions that not only consider rational and logical factors but also consider the emotions and feelings of individuals involved. This is where emotionally intelligent decision-making comes into play. This chapter discusses the benefits that emotionally intelligent decision-making can bring to managers and their organizations, including improved relationships, enhanced critical thinking skills, and increased employee engagement and productivity. By embracing emotional intelligence in their decision-making processes, managers can create a more positive and inclusive work environment that fosters collaboration, empathy, and overall success.

Improved Problem-Solving and Conflict Resolution

Improving problem-solving and conflict-resolution skills is essential for personal and professional growth. Here are several ways and means to enhance these abilities:

1. Develop effective communication skills: Excellent communication is the foundation of problem-solving and conflict resolution. Enhance your active listening, assertiveness, and non-verbal communication skills. Clearly express your thoughts and actively seek to understand others' perspectives.

2. Promote a constructive mindset: Cultivate a growth mindset, where you see conflicts and problems as opportunities for learning and growth. Embrace challenges, approach them with curiosity, and avoid getting defensive or blaming others. Maintain a cheerful outlook throughout the process.

3. Use structured problem-solving techniques: Employ problem-solving frameworks like the PDCA (Plan-Do-

Check-Act) or the 5 Whys to systematically analyze problems, identify root causes, and develop effective solutions. Apply critical thinking to break down complex issues into manageable parts for efficient resolution.

4. Foster collaboration and teamwork: Encourage a collaborative mindset by promoting teamwork and respecting diverse opinions. Emphasize the importance of cooperation and compromise to find mutually beneficial solutions. Utilize brainstorming sessions and group discussions to encourage multiple perspectives.

5. Enhance emotional intelligence: Develop your emotional intelligence to understand and manage your own emotions, as well as those of others. By being self-aware and empathetic, you can navigate conflicts more effectively and find solutions that address underlying emotions.

6. Seek win-win solutions: Aim to find win-win solutions instead of compromising or imposing your point of view. Look for creative options that satisfy the interests of all parties involved, considering long-term consequences, and maintaining fairness.

7. Practice active problem-solving: Regularly engage in problem-solving activities to enhance your skills. Tackle challenges outside of your comfort zone, learn from failures, and continuously evaluate and improve your approach.

8. Use mediation and negotiation techniques: Learn mediation and negotiation techniques to resolve conflicts. Understand the principles of mutual gain and strive to find common ground. Focus on interests rather than positions to uncover underlying needs.

9. Seek feedback and self-reflection: Solicit feedback from trusted individuals to gain insights into your problem-solving and conflict-resolution abilities. Engage in self-reflection to identify areas for improvement and adjust your approach accordingly.

10. Continuous learning and training: Invest in professional development opportunities like workshops, courses, or reading materials that focus on problem-solving and conflict resolution. Stay abreast of the latest techniques and research in these areas.

By consistently practicing and incorporating these strategies into your problem-solving and conflict-resolution approach, you can enhance your ability to navigate challenging situations effectively and efficiently.

Enhanced Team Dynamics and Employee Engagement

Enhancing team dynamics and employee engagement is essential for creating a positive and productive work environment. When team members feel engaged and connected to their work and their colleagues, they are more likely to perform at their best and contribute to the overall success of the organization. In this part, we will explore the importance of team dynamics and employee engagement, as well as discuss strategies for enhancing both in the workplace.

Team dynamics refers to the interactions between team members, including how they communicate, collaborate, and work together toward a common goal. Effective team dynamics are crucial for achieving optimal performance and ensuring that each member feels included and valued within the team. When team members have good relationships with each other, they are more likely to trust one another, share ideas openly, and support each other's growth and development.

Employee engagement, on the other hand, refers to the level of enthusiasm and commitment employees have towards their work and the organization. Engaged employees are motivated, dedicated, and deeply connected to their roles, which in turn leads to higher levels of productivity, innovation, and job satisfaction. It is the responsibility of the organization and its leaders to foster an environment that promotes engagement and provides employees with opportunities to grow and thrive.

Several strategies can be implemented to enhance team dynamics and employee engagement. Firstly, clear communication and regular feedback are essential for building strong team dynamics. Team members should have a channel of communication where they can openly discuss concerns, share ideas, and collaborate. This can be facilitated through regular team meetings, group brainstorming sessions, or using collaborative tools such as project management software or instant messaging platforms.

Additionally, leaders and managers should provide regular feedback to team members, acknowledging their contributions, and addressing any concerns or areas for improvement. A positive feedback culture cultivates a sense of recognition and appreciation, which is vital for boosting employee engagement and motivation. Regular check-ins or performance appraisals can serve as opportunities for coaching and mentoring, which can help identify an individual's strengths and areas for growth.

Furthermore, creating a culture of trust and psychological safety within the team is fundamental for enhancing team dynamics and employee engagement. Team members should feel comfortable expressing their opinions, taking risks, and making mistakes without fear of judgment or negative consequences. Leaders can promote this culture by being approachable and accessible, encouraging open dialogue, and valuing diverse perspectives and ideas.

In addition to fostering open communication and trust, providing opportunities for professional growth and development is crucial for employee engagement. When employees see a clear path to advancement and have access to learning and development resources, they are more likely to feel motivated and committed to their work. Organizations can offer training programs, and mentorship opportunities, or support employees in pursuing further education or certifications. Moreover, conducting regular performance assessments and creating individualized development plans can help employees identify and achieve their career goals.

Another effective strategy for enhancing team dynamics and employee engagement is promoting employee recognition and rewards. Recognizing and rewarding employees for their accomplishments and contributions is a powerful motivator and can significantly increase job satisfaction and engagement. Recognition can take various forms, such as verbal praise, written appreciation, or even tangible rewards such as bonuses or promotions. Additionally, organizations can implement employee recognition programs or create a peer-to-peer recognition system, where employees can acknowledge and appreciate each other's efforts.

Furthermore, facilitating team-building activities and fostering a sense of community within the team is instrumental in enhancing team dynamics and employee engagement. Team-building activities provide opportunities for team members to bond and develop trust, as well as improve communication and collaboration skills. Organizations can organize team-building events such as workshops, off-site retreats, or social outings to promote a positive and supportive team culture. Additionally, creating informal spaces or virtual platforms for team members to connect and socialize can help build stronger relationships and foster a sense of belonging.

Ultimately, enhancing team dynamics and employee engagement requires an initiative-taking and integrated approach by organizations and their leaders. By promoting open communication, trust, growth opportunities, recognition, and team building, organizations can create an environment where team members thrive and contribute to the overall success of the organization. Furthermore, it is important to continuously assess and evaluate the effectiveness of these strategies and adjust as needed to ensure ongoing engagement and team effectiveness.

Subject Index

Challenges of Decentralization
Change Evaluation and Sustained Improvement
Change Identification
Change Planning and Implementation
Clarify Ethics and Values
Clear Communication and Expectations
Clear Ethical Values
Clear Roles and Responsibilities
Cloud Computing
Cloud Computing
Code of Conduct and Policies
Cognitive Bases
Cognitive Biases
Cognitive Development
Collaborate and Engage with Stakeholders
Collaboration and Transparency
Collect Data and Measure Results
Collectivism
Communicate Results and Lessons Learned
Communicate the Plan
Communication
Communication and Engagement
Communication and public awareness
Communication and Shared Decision-Making
Communication Barriers
Competitive Compensation and Benefits
Competitors
Complaints and Redress
Complaints and Redress
Complex Ethical Dilemmas
Compliance with Regulatory Requirements
Components of an Ethical Organizational Culture
Components of Cultural Intelligence
Components of Cultural Intelligence
Components of Ethical Leadership
Conduct a Final Evaluation and Selection
Conduct Ethical Risk Analysis
Conduct Research
Conduct Risk Assessments
Conduct Scenario Analysis
Confidentiality and Privacy
Confidentiality and Privacy
Conflict Between Public Interest and Privacy
Conflict of Interest
Conflict of Interest
Conflict of Interest
Conflict of Interest and Independence
Conflicting Ethical Principles
Conflicting Priorities
Conflicting Professional Obligations

Name Index

www.ingramcontent.com/pod-product-compliance
Lightning Source LLC
LaVergne TN
LVHW080057220926
848484LV00007BA/1809